INTERNET & WORLD WIDE WEB

HOW TO PROGRAM
THIRD EDITION

Deitel® Books, Cyber Classrooms, Complete Tra
published by

How To Program Series

Advanced Java™ 2 Platform How to Program
C How to Program, 4/E
C++ How to Program, 4/E
C#® How to Program
e-Business and e-Commerce How to Program
Internet and World Wide Web How to Program, 3/E
Java™ How to Program, 5/E
Perl How to Program
Python How to Program
Visual Basic® 6 How to Program
Visual Basic® .NET How to Program, 2/E
Visual C++® .NET How to Program
Wireless Internet & Mobile Business How to Program
XML How to Program

.NET How to Program Series
C# How to Program
Visual Basic® .NET How to Program, 2/E
Visual C++® .NET How to Program

Visual Studio® Series
C# How to Program
*Getting Started with Microsoft® Visual
    C++® 6 with an Introduction to MFC*
*Simply C#: An Application-Driven Tutorial
    Approach*
*Simply Visual Basic® .NET: An Application-
    Driven Tutorial Approach
    (Visual Studio .NET 2002 Edition)*
*Simply Visual Basic® .NET: An Application-
    Driven Tutorial Approach
    (Visual Studio .NET 2003 Edition)*
Visual Basic® 6 How to Program
Visual Basic® .NET How to Program, 2/E
Visual C++® .NET How to Program

CS1 Programming Series
Java™ Software Design

Simply Series
*Simply C#: An Application-Driven Tutorial
    Approach*
*Simply Java™ Programming: An
    Application-Driven Tutorial Approach*
*Simply Visual Basic® .NET: An Application
    Driven Tutorial Approach
    (Visual Studio .NET 2002 Edition)*
*Simply Visual Basic® .NET: An Application
    Driven Tutorial Approach
    (Visual Studio .NET 2003 Edition)*

Deitel® Developer Series
*Java™ Web Services for Experienced
    Programmers*
Web Services A Technical Introduction

Computer Science Series
Operating Systems, 3/E

For Managers Series
e-Business and e-Commerce for Managers

ining Courses and Web-Based Training Courses
Prentice Hall

The Complete Training Course Series

The Complete C++
    Training Course, 4/E
The Complete C#
    Training Course
The Complete e-Business and
    e-Commerce Programming
    Training Course
The Complete Internet and World Wide Web
    Programming Training Course, 2/E
The Complete Java™ 2
    Training Course, 5/E
The Complete Perl
    Training Course
The Complete Python
    Training Course
The Complete Visual Basic® 6
    Training Course
The Complete Visual Basic® .NET
    Training Course, 2/E
The Complete Wireless Internet &
    Mobile Business Programming
    Training Course
The Complete XML Programming
    Training Course

Interactive *Multimedia Cyber Classroom* Series

C++ Multimedia Cyber Classroom, 4/E
C# Multimedia Cyber Classroom
e-Business and e-Commerce Multimedia
    Cyber Classroom
Internet and World Wide Web Multimedia
    Cyber Classroom, 2/E
Java™ 2 Multimedia Cyber Classroom, 5/E
Perl Multimedia Cyber Classroom
Python Multimedia Cyber Classroom
Visual Basic® 6 Multimedia Cyber
    Classroom
Visual Basic® .NET Multimedia Cyber
    Classroom, 2/E
Wireless Internet & Mobile Business
    Programming Multimedia Cyber
    Classroom
XML Multimedia Cyber Classroom

Interactive *Web-Based Training* Series

Premium CourseCompass Version of Visual
    Basic® .NET Multimedia Cyber
    Classroom, 2/E
Premium CourseCompass Version of Java 2
    Multimedia Cyber Classroom, 5/E
Premium CourseCompass Version of C++
    Multimedia Cyber Classroom, 4/E

To follow the Deitel publishing program, please register at:

    www.deitel.com/newsletter/subscribe.html

for the free *DEITEL® BUZZ ONLINE* e-mail newsletter.

To communicate with the authors, send e-mail to:

    deitel@deitel.com

For information on Deitel instructor-led, corporate training seminars offered worldwide visit:

    www.deitel.com

For continuing updates on Prentice Hall and Deitel publications visit:

    www.deitel.com,
    www.prenhall.com/deitel or
    www.InformIT.com/deitel

Library of Congress Cataloging-in-Publication Data

On file

Vice President and Editorial Director, ECS: *Marcia J. Horton*
Senior Acquisitions Editor: *Kate Hargett*
Assistant Editor: *Sarah Parker*
Associate Editor: *Jennifer Cappello*
Editorial Assistant: *Michael Giacobbe*
Vice President and Director of Production and Manufacturing, ESM: *David W. Riccardi*
Executive Managing Editor: *Vince O'Brien*
Managing Editor: *Tom Manshreck*
Production Editor: *John F. Lovell*
Production Editor, Media: *Bob Engelhardt*
Director of Creative Services: *Paul Belfanti*
Creative Director: *Carole Anson*
Art Director: *Geoffrey Cassar*
Cover Art and Chapter Opener Art: *David Merrell*
Cover Designer: *Geoffrey Cassar, Dr. Harvey Deitel*
Manufacturing Manager: *Trudy Pisciotti*
Manufacturing Buyer: *Lisa McDowell*
Marketing Manager: *Pamela Hersperger*
Marketing Assistant: *Barrie Reinhold*

 © 2004 by Pearson Education, Inc.
Upper Saddle River, New Jersey 07458

10 9 8 7 6 5 4 3 2 1

ISBN 0-13-145091-3

Pearson Education Ltd., *London*
Pearson Education Australia Pty. Ltd., *Sydney*
Pearson Education Singapore, Pte. Ltd.
Pearson Education North Asia Ltd., *Hong Kong*
Pearson Education Canada, Inc., *Toronto*
Pearson Educacion de Mexico, S.A. de C.V.
Pearson Education–Japan, *Tokyo*
Pearson Education Malaysia, Pte. Ltd.
Pearson Education, Inc., *Upper Saddle River, New Jersey*

INTERNET & WORLD WIDE WEB

HOW TO PROGRAM

THIRD EDITION

H. M. Deitel
Deitel & Associates, Inc.

P. J. Deitel
Deitel & Associates, Inc.

A. B. Goldberg
Deitel & Associates, Inc.

PEARSON EDUCATION, INC., Upper Saddle River, New Jersey 07458

Trademarks

In loving memory of Lena and Morris Deitel.

Harvey and Paul Deitel

In loving memory of my mother, Susan Goldberg, whose inspiration and encouragement will continue to guide me always.

Andrew

Contents

30　Dynamic HTML: Structured Graphics ActiveX Control (On CD)　1080

31　Dynamic HTML: Path, Sequencer and Sprite ActiveX Controls (On CD)　1098

32　VBScript (On CD)　1118

Preface

Live in fragments no longer. Only connect.
Edward Morgan Forster

Welcome to the Internet & World Wide Web! At Deitel & Associates, we write college-level programming-language textbooks and professional books. We work hard to keep our published books up-to-date with a steady flow of new editions. Writing *Internet & World Wide Web How to Program, Third Edition* was a joy. The Web increases the prominence of the Internet in information systems, strategic planning and implementation. Organizations want to integrate the Internet "seamlessly" into their information systems and the Web offers endless opportunity to do so.

This book and its support materials have everything instructors and students need for an informative, interesting, challenging and entertaining educational experience. We have tuned the writing, the pedagogy, our coding style and the book's ancillary package. Also, we have included a Tour of the Book in this Preface to help instructors, students and professionals get a sense of the rich coverage of Web technologies this book provides. We also provide a dependency chart to indicate prerequisites for each chapter in the book.

In this Preface, we overview the teaching conventions used in this book, such as syntax coloring the code examples, "code washing" and highlighting important code segments to help focus students' attention on key concepts introduced in each chapter. We also overview the new features of this edition.

We discuss the software Prentice Hall has bundled with the book as well as the comprehensive suite of educational materials that help instructors maximize their students' learning experience. These include an Instructor's Resource CD with solutions to the book's chapter exercises and a Test-Item File with hundreds of multiple-choice examination questions and answers. Additional instructor resources are available at the book's Companion Web Site (`www.prenhall.com/deitel`), which includes a Syllabus Manager and customizable PowerPoint® Lecture Notes. PowerPoint slides and additional support materials are available for students at the Companion Web Site, as well.

Internet & World Wide Web How to Program, Third Edition, was reviewed by a team of distinguished academics and industry professionals. We list their names and affiliations so you can get a sense of how carefully this book was scrutinized. The Preface concludes with information about the authors and about Deitel & Associates, Inc. As you read this book, if you have any questions, please send an e-mail to deitel@deitel.com; we will respond promptly. Please visit our Web site, www.deitel.com, regularly and be sure to sign up for the *DEITEL*® *Buzz Online* e-mail newsletter at www.deitel.com/newsletter/subscribe.html. We use the Web site and the newsletter to keep our readers current on all Deitel publications and services.

Features of Internet & World Wide Web How to Program, Third Edition

This edition contains many new features and enhancements including:

Full-Color Presentation
The book enhances live-code examples by using full color. Readers see sample outputs as they would appear on their computer screens.

Syntax Coloring
We syntax color all the program code, as do many integrated development environments and code editors. This greatly improves code readability—an especially important goal, given that this book contains over 17,229 lines of code. Our syntax-coloring conventions are as follows:

```
comments appear in green
keywords appear in dark blue
ASP.NET, ASP, PHP, ColdFusion and JSP delimiters appear in red
constants and literal values appear in light blue
all other code appears in black
```

Code Highlighting
We have added extensive code highlighting to make it easier for readers to spot the featured segments of each program. This feature also helps students review the material rapidly when preparing for exams or labs.

"Code Washing"
"Code washing" is our term for commenting, using meaningful identifiers, applying indentation and using vertical spacing to separate meaningful program units. This process results in programs that are much more readable and self-documenting. We have added extensive and descriptive comments to all of the code, including a comment before and after every major control statement, to help the student clearly understand the flow of the program. We have done extensive code washing of all the source code programs in the text and the ancillaries.

XHTML (Chapters 4 & 5)
This edition uses XHTML as the primary means of describing Web content. The World Wide Web Consortium deprecated HTML 4 and replaced it first with XHTML 1.0 (Extensible Hypertext Markup Language) and now with XHTML 1.1. XHTML is derived from XML (Extensible Markup Language), which allows Web developers to create their own tags and languages. XHTML is replacing HTML as the standard for marking up Web content.

Macromedia Flash™ MX 2004 (Chapters 17 & 18)

Flash is a cutting-edge multimedia application that enables Web developers to create interactive, animated content. Through hands-on examples, we show how to add interactivity, sound and animation to Web sites while teaching the fundamentals of Flash and **ActionScript**—Flash's scripting language. The examples in Chapter 17 show readers how to create interactive buttons, animated banners and animated splash screens (called **animation pre-loaders**). Chapter 18 presents a case study that demonstrates how to build an interactive game in Flash MX 2004 using intermediate to advanced ActionScript.

Macromedia® Dreamweaver® MX 2004 (Chapter 19)

This edition features a new chapter that demonstrates Macromedia Dreamweaver MX 2004, the leading WYSIWYG (What You See Is What You Get) editor used by Web programmers today. While our book advocates a thorough knowledge of XHTML and its accompanying scripting languages, Dreamweaver is a useful tool for creating and maintaining Web pages. By displaying XHTML elements exactly as a browser would, Dreamweaver allows users to apply text formatting and insert images, lists, tables and forms into Web pages with relative ease.

XML (Chapter 20)

Throughout the book we emphasize XHTML, which derived from XML and HTML. XML derives from SGML (Standardized General Markup Language), whose sheer size and complexity limits its use beyond heavy-duty, industrial-strength applications. XML is a technology created by the World Wide Web Consortium for describing data in a portable format. Document authors use XML's extensibility to create entirely new markup languages for describing specific types of data, including mathematical formulas, chemical molecular structures and music. We also introduce Web services and XML-based applications that promote a flow of information between business organizations and individuals.

Server-Side Technology

We present condensed treatments of seven popular Internet/Web programming languages for building the server side of Internet- and Web-based client/server applications. In Chapters 23 and 24, we discuss ASP.NET—Microsoft's technology for server-side scripting. In Chapters 25 and 26, we introduce Perl and PHP—two open-source scripting languages used extensively for programming Web-based applications. Chapter 27 is a new chapter for this edition and introduces Macromedia's server-side technology, ColdFusion®. Chapters 33–34 (both on CD) present Active Server Pages, the predecessor to ASP.NET. Chapter 35 (on CD) presents Python, an interpreted, interactive, object-oriented programming language responsible for the server-side of many Web applications. Finally, in Chapters 36 and 37 (both on CD), we provide two bonus chapters for Java programmers on Java™ servlets and JavaServer Pages™ (JSP).

Macromedia ColdFusion MX (Chapter 27)

This edition features a new server-side technology: Macromedia ColdFusion MX. ColdFusion is a popular Web application server that enables quick and easy dynamic Web-site development. The popularity of ColdFusion lies in its server-side, tag-based **ColdFusion Markup Language** (CFML). CFML is based around a set of tags that work like XHTML tags, making it easy to learn for most Web-site developers. In addition, CFML offers many advanced features that make it as rich as a full-scale programming language.

Teaching Approach

Why We Wrote *Internet & World Wide Web How to Program, Third Edition*
Our goal in creating this book was clear: Produce a textbook for introductory university-level courses in computer programming for students with little or no programming experience, yet offer the depth and rigorous treatment of theory and practice demanded by traditional, upper-level programming courses and professionals. We also wanted the book to expose all readers—beginners and experienced traditional programmers alike—to the great opportunities the Web offers the field of Computer Science. To meet these goals, we produced a comprehensive book that teaches the principles of control statements, object-based programming, various markup languages (e.g., XHTML, XML) and scripting languages. Throughout the book, we develop practical Web-based applications from which even the most experienced programmers can benefit. After mastering the material in this book, students entering upper-level programming courses and industry will be well prepared to take advantage of the Internet and the Web.

Dr. Harvey M. Deitel taught introductory programming courses in universities for 20 years with an emphasis on developing clearly written, well-designed programs. Much of what is taught in these courses are the basic principles of programming with an emphasis on the effective use of control statements and functionalization. We present these topics in *Internet & World Wide Web How to Program, Third Edition,* the way HMD has done in his university courses. Students are highly motivated by the fact that they are learning eight leading-edge scripting technologies (JavaScript, JScript .NET, Flash ActionScript, Perl, PHP, ColdFusion, VBScript and Python) and a leading-edge programming paradigm (object-based programming). We also teach Dynamic HTML, a means of adding "dynamic content" to Web pages. Instead of Web pages with only text and static graphics, Web pages "come alive" with audio, video, animation, interactivity and three-dimensional moving images. These programming languages will be useful to students immediately as they leave the university environment and head into a world in which the Internet and Web have massive prominence.

This book is intended for several academic markets, namely, the introductory course sequences in which C++, Java and Visual Basic are traditionally taught; upper-level elective courses for students who already know programming and as a supplement in introductory courses, where students are first becoming familiar with computers, the Internet and the Web. The book offers a solid one- or two-semester introductory programming experience or an extensive one-semester upper-level elective. The book is also intended for professional programmers in corporate training programs or for self study.

Many books about the Web concentrate on developing attractive Web pages. We discuss Web-page design intensely. But more importantly, the key focus of this book is on Web-based applications development. Our audiences want to build real-world, industrial-strength, Web-based applications. These audiences care about good-looking Web pages, but they also care about client/server systems, databases, distributed computing, etc. Many books about the Web are reference manuals with exhaustive listings of features. That is not our style. We concentrate on creating real applications. We provide the live-code examples on the CD accompanying this book (and at `www.deitel.com`) so that you can run the applications and see and hear the multimedia outputs. You can interact with our game and art programs. The Web is an artist's paradise. Your creativity is your only limitation. However, the Web contains so many tools and mechanisms to leverage your abilities that even if you are not artistically inclined, you can create stunning output. Our goal is to help you master these tools so that you can maximize your creativity and development abilities.

People want to communicate. Sure, they have been communicating since the dawn of civilization, but computer communications have been limited mostly to digits, alphabetic characters and special characters. The next major wave of communication technology is multimedia. People transmit color pictures and they transmit voices, sounds and audio clips as well. They transmit full-motion color video. At some point, they will insist on three-dimensional, moving-image transmission. Our current flat, two-dimensional televisions eventually will be replaced with three-dimensional versions that turn our living rooms into "theaters-in-the-round." Actors will perform their roles as if we were watching live theater. Our living rooms will be turned into miniature sports stadiums. Our business offices will enable video conferencing among colleagues half a world apart, as if they were sitting around one conference table. The possibilities are intriguing, and the Internet will play a key role in making many of these possibilities become reality. There have been predictions that the Internet will eventually replace the telephone system. Why stop there? It could also replace radio and television as we know them today. It is not hard to imagine the Internet and the Web replacing newspapers with electronic news media. Many newspapers and magazines already offer Web-based versions, some fee based and some free. Increased bandwidth makes it possible to stream audio and video over the Web. Both companies and individuals run their own Web-based radio and television stations. Just a few decades ago, there were only a few television stations. Today, standard cable boxes accommodate about 100 stations. In a few more years, we will have access to thousands of stations broadcasting over the Web worldwide. This textbook may someday appear in a museum alongside radios, TVs and newspapers in an "early media of ancient civilization" exhibit.

Internet & World Wide Web How to Program, Third Edition contains a rich collection of examples, exercises and projects drawn from many fields to provide the student with a chance to solve interesting real-world problems.

The book concentrates on the principles of software engineering and stresses program clarity. We are educators who teach edge-of-the-practice topics in industry classrooms worldwide. This text emphasizes good pedagogy.

Font Conventions
We use fonts to distinguish on-screen components (such as menu names and menu items) from other elements that appear on screen. Our convention is to emphasize on-screen components in a sans-serif bold **Helvetica** font (for example, **Properties**), and to emphasize program text in a serif Lucida font (for example, int x = 5).

Live-Code Approach
Internet & World Wide Web How to Program, Third Edition, is loaded with numerous live-code examples—each new concept is presented in the context of a complete, working program that is immediately followed by one or more sample executions showing the program's input/output dialog. This style exemplifies the way we teach and write about programming. We call this method of teaching and writing the live-code approach. *We use programming languages to teach programming languages.* Reading the examples in the text is much like typing and running them on a computer.

This textbook "jumps right in" with XHTML in Chapter 4, then rapidly proceeds with programming in JavaScript, Microsoft's Dynamic HTML, Flash ActionScript, XML,

ASP.NET, Perl, PHP, ColdFusion, VBScript (on CD), Python (on CD), Java Servlets (on CD) and JavaServer Pages (on CD). Many students wish to "cut to the chase;" there is great stuff to be done in these languages so let's get to it! Web programming is not trivial by any means, but it is fun, and students can see immediate results. Students can get graphical, animated, multimedia-based, audio-intensive, database-intensive, network-based programs running quickly through "reusable components." They can implement impressive projects. They can be more creative and productive in a one- or two-semester course than is possible in introductory courses taught in conventional programming languages, such as C, C++, Visual Basic and Java. [*Note*: This book includes Java Servlets and JavaServer Pages as "bonus chapters;" it does not teach the fundamentals of Java programming. Readers who want to learn Java may want to consider reading our book *Java How to Program, Fifth Edition*. Readers who desire a deeper, more developer-oriented treatment of Java may want to consider reading our book, *Advanced Java 2 Platform How to Program*.]

Web Access

All of the source-code examples for *Internet & World Wide Web How to Program, Third Edition,* (and our other publications) are available on the Internet as downloads from the following Web sites:

```
www.deitel.com
www.prenhall.com/deitel
```

Registration is quick and easy and the downloads are free. We suggest downloading all the examples, then running each program as you read the corresponding text. Making changes to the examples and immediately seeing the effects of those changes is a great way to enhance your learning experience. [*Note*: The examples are also on the CD that accompanies the book.]

Objectives

Each chapter begins with a statement of objectives. This tells students what to expect and gives students an opportunity, after reading the chapter, to determine if they have met these objectives. This is a confidence builder and a source of positive reinforcement.

Quotations

The learning objectives are followed by quotations. Some are humorous, some are philosophical and some offer interesting insights. Our students enjoy relating the quotations to the chapter material. Many of the quotations are worth a "second look" *after* reading the chapter.

Outline

The chapter outline helps the student approach the material in top-down fashion. This, too, helps students anticipate what is to come and set a comfortable and effective learning pace.

17,229 Lines of Code in 282 Example LIVE-CODE Programs (with Program Outputs)

We present Internet & Web technologies in the context of complete, working programs, that range from just a few lines of code to substantial examples with several hundred lines of code. The examples are available on the accompanying CD and as downloads from our Web site (www.deitel.com) and Prentice Hall's Web site (www.prenhall.com\deitel).

701 Illustrations/Figures
An abundance of charts, line drawings and program outputs is included.

457 Programming Tips
We have included programming tips to help students focus on important aspects of program development. We highlight hundreds of these tips in the form of *Good Programming Practices*, *Common Programming Errors*, *Error-Prevention Tips*, *Performance Tips*, *Portability Tips*, *Software Engineering Observations* and *Look-and-Feel Observations*. These tips and practices represent the best we have gleaned from decades of programming and teaching experience. One of our students—a mathematics major—told us that she feels this approach is like the highlighting of axioms, theorems and corollaries in mathematics books; it provides a foundation on which to build good software programs.

82 Good Programming Practices

Good Programming Practices *are tips for writing clear programs. These techniques help students produce programs that are more readable, self-documenting and easier to maintain.*

137 Common Programming Errors

Students learning a language—especially in their first programming course—tend to make certain kinds of errors frequently. Focusing on these Common Programming Errors *helps students avoid making the same errors. It also helps reduce long lines outside instructors' offices during office hours!*

45 Performance Tips

In our experience, teaching students to write clear and understandable programs is by far the most important goal for a first programming course. But students want to write the programs that run the fastest, use the least memory, require the smallest number of keystrokes, or dazzle in other nifty ways. Students really care about performance. They want to know what they can do to "turbo charge" their programs. So we highlight opportunities for improving program performance—making programs run faster or minimizing the amount of memory that they occupy.

30 Portability Tips

Software development is a complex and expensive activity. Organizations that develop software often produce versions customized to a variety of computers and operating systems. So there is a strong emphasis today on portability, i.e., on producing software that will run on a variety of computer systems with few, if any, changes. Some people assume that if they implement an application in a programming language, the application will automatically be portable. This is simply not the case. Achieving portability requires careful and cautious design. There are many pitfalls. We include numerous Portability Tips *to help students write portable code.*

106 Software Engineering Observations

The Software Engineering Observations *highlight techniques, architectural issues and design issues, etc. that affect the architecture and construction of software systems, especially large-scale systems. Much of what the student learns here will be useful in upper-level courses and in industry as the student begins to work with large, complex real-world systems.*

43 Error-Prevention Tips

When we first designed this "tip type," we thought we would use them strictly to tell people how to test and debug programs and in previous editions we labelled these as "Testing and Debugging Tips." In fact, many of the tips describe aspects of programming that reduce the likelihood of "bugs" and thus simplify the testing and debugging processes.

14 Look-and-Feel Observations

We provide Look-and-Feel Observations *to highlight graphical user interface conventions. These observations help students design their own graphical user interfaces to conform with industry norms.*

Summary (1413 Summary bullets)

Each chapter includes additional pedagogical devices. We present a thorough, bullet-list-style summary of the chapter. On average, each chapter contains 37 summary bullets that help students review and reinforce important concepts.

Terminology (3096 Terms)

We include an alphabetized list of the important terms defined in each chapter—again, for further reinforcement. There is an average of 81 terms per chapter. Each term also appears in the index, so the student can locate terms and definitions quickly.

605 Self-Review Exercises and Answers (Count Includes Separate Parts)

Extensive self-review exercises and answers are included for self-study. This gives the student a chance to build confidence with the material and to prepare for the regular exercises.

657 Exercises (Solutions in Instructor's Manual; Count Includes Separate Parts)

Each chapter concludes with a substantial set of exercises, including simple recall of important terminology and concepts; writing individual statements; writing small portions of functions; writing complete functions and scripts; and writing major term projects. The large number of exercises across a wide variety of topics enables instructors to tailor their courses to the unique needs of their audiences and to vary course assignments each semester. Instructors can use these exercises to form homework assignments, short quizzes and major examinations. The solutions for the vast majority of the exercises are included in the *Instructor's Manual* and on the disks *available only to instructors* through their Prentice-Hall representatives. [*NOTE*: **Please do not write to us requesting the instructor's manual. Distribution of this publication is strictly limited to college professors teaching from the book. Instructors may obtain the solutions manual only from their regular Prentice Hall representatives. We regret that we cannot provide the solutions to professionals.**] The student should have two key projects in mind while reading through this book as well—developing a personal Web site using XHTML markup and JavaScript coding, and developing a complete client/server, database-intensive Web-based application by using techniques taught throughout this book.

Approximately 6800 Index Entries (with approximately 9500 Page References)

We have included an extensive index at the back of the book. This helps students find any term or concept by keyword. The *Index* is useful to people reading the book for the first time and is especially useful to practicing programmers who use the book as a reference. Most of the terms in the *Terminology* sections appear in the *Index* (along with many more index items from each chapter). Thus, students can use the *Index* in conjunction with the *Terminology* sections to be sure they have covered the key material of each chapter.

"Double Indexing" of All Live-Code Examples and Exercises

Internet & World Wide Web How to Program, Third Edition has 282 live-code examples and 657 exercises (including parts). We have double indexed each of the live-code examples and most of the more challenging projects. For every source-code program in the book, we took the file name and indexed it both alphabetically and as a subindex item under "Examples." This makes it easier to find examples using particular features. The more substantial exercises are indexed both alphabetically and as subindex items under "Exercises."

Bibliography

An extensive bibliography of books, articles and online documentation is included to encourage further reading.

Software Included with Internet & World Wide Web How to Program, Third Edition

[*Note:* We assume readers have Microsoft's Internet Explorer 6 installed on their machines. If you do not have IE 6, you can download for free at `www.microsoft.com/windows/ie/downloads/critical/ie6sp1/default.asp`.] The CD that accompanies this book contains Microsoft Agent 2.0, Adobe® Reader 6.0, MySQL 4.0, PHP 4.3.3, Apache HTTP Server 2.0.47, Microsoft .NET Framework Redist version 1.1, .NET Framework Software Development Kit (SDK) 1.1, Macromedia Flash MX 2004 (30-day full-trial version), Dreamweaver MX 2004 (30-day full-trial version) and ColdFusion MX 6.1 (30-day full-trial version that turns into a free developer edition). The CD also contains the book's examples and a Web page with links to the Deitel & Associates, Inc. Web site, to the Prentice Hall Web site and to a Web page containing links to the Web resources mentioned in the chapters. If you have access to the Internet, this Web page can be loaded into your World Wide Web browser to give you quick access to all the resources.

For the Perl and Python chapters, you will need to download and install appropriate versions of these languages. We developed these chapters using ActiveState ActivePerl 5.8.0 (`www.activestate.com/Products/ActivePerl`) and ActiveState ActivePython 2.2.2 (`www.activestate.com/Products/ActivePython`). Also, a 30-day evaluation copy of Adobe Photoshop Elements 2.0, used in Chapter 3 to illustrate how to create Web graphics, can be downloaded at `www.adobe.com/products/photoshopel`. [*Note:* All of the software included on the CD that accompanies this text and the links to download software were current and active at the time of publication. However, please be aware that Web links have a tendency to change or break, and companies upgrade software to newer versions on a regular basis.]

If you have any questions about the software or Web links on the CD, please read the introductory documentation on the CD. We will post additional information and additional software installation instructions on the book's Web site, `www.deitel.com/books/iw3HTP3/index.html`. If you have any technical questions about CD installation or about any of the software supplied with Deitel/Prentice Hall products, please e-mail `media.support@pearsoned.com`. They will respond promptly.

Ancillary Package for Internet & World Wide Web How to Program, Third Edition

Internet & World Wide Web How to Program, Third Edition, has extensive ancillary materials for instructors. The *Instructor's Resource CD (IRCD)* contains solutions to most of the end-of-chapter exercises. This CD is available only to instructors through their Prentice

Hall representatives. [*Note*: **Please do not write to us requesting the instructor's CD. Distribution of this CD is limited strictly to college professors teaching from the book. Instructors may obtain the solutions manual only from their Prentice Hall representatives.**] The ancillaries for this book also include a *Test Item File* of multiple-choice questions. In addition, we provide PowerPoint slides containing all the code and figures in the text and bulleted items that summarize the key points in the text. Instructors can customize the slides. The PowerPoint slides are downloadable from www.deitel.com and are available as part of Prentice Hall's Companion Web Site (www.prenhall.com/deitel) for *Internet & World Wide Web How to Program, Third Edition*, which offers resources for both instructors and students. For instructors, the Companion Web Site offers a Syllabus Manager, which helps instructors plan courses interactively and create online syllabi.

Students also benefit from the functionality of the *Companion Web Site*. Book-specific resources for students include:

- Customizable PowerPoint slides
- Source code for all example programs
- Reference materials from the book appendices (such as operator-precedence chart, character set and Web resources)

Chapter-specific resources available for students include:

- Chapter objectives
- Highlights (e.g., chapter summary)
- Outline
- Tips (e.g., *Common Programming Errors*, *Good Programming Practices*, *Portability Tips*, *Performance Tips*, *Look-and-Feel Observations*, *Software Engineering Observations* and *Error-Prevention Tips*)
- Online Study Guide—contains additional short-answer self-review exercises (e.g., true/false questions) with answers and provides immediate feedback to the student

Students can track their results and course performance on quizzes using the *Student Profile* feature, which records and manages all feedback and results from tests taken on the *Companion Web Site*. To access DEITEL® Companion Web Sites, visit www.prenhall.com/deitel.

DEITEL® Buzz Online E-mail Newsletter

Our free e-mail newsletter, the DEITEL® *Buzz Online*, includes commentary on industry trends and developments, links to free articles and resources from our published books and upcoming publications, product-release schedules, errata, challenges, anecdotes, information on our corporate instructor-led training courses and more. To subscribe, visit

    www.deitel.com/newsletter/subscribe.html

DEITEL® e-Learning Initiatives

Wireless devices will have an enormous role in the future of the Internet. Given recent bandwidth enhancements and the emergence of 2.5 and 3G technologies, it is projected that, within a few years, more people will access the Internet through wireless devices than through desktop computers. Deitel & Associates is committed to wireless accessibility and has published *Wireless Internet & Mobile Business How to Program*. We are investigating new electronic formats, such as wireless e-books so that students and professors can access content virtually anytime, anywhere. For periodic updates on these initiatives subscribe to the *DEITEL® Buzz Online* e-mail newsletter, `www.deitel.com/newsletter/subscribe.html` or visit `www.deitel.com`.

DEITEL® Developer Series

Deitel & Associates, Inc., is making a major commitment to covering leading-edge technologies for industry software professionals through the launch of our *DEITEL® Developer Series*. The first books in the series are *Web Services A Technical Introduction* and *Java Web Services for Experienced Programmers*. We are working on *ASP .NET with Visual Basic .NET for Experienced Programmers*, *ASP .NET with C# for Experienced Programmers* and many more. Please visit `www.deitel.com` or subscribe to our e-mail newsletter at `www.deitel.com/newsletter/subscribe.html` for continuous updates on all published and forthcoming *DEITEL Developer Series* titles.

The *DEITEL Developer Series* is divided into three subseries. The *A Technical Introduction* subseries provides IT managers and developers with detailed overviews of emerging technologies. The *A Programmer's Introduction* subseries is designed to teach the fundamentals of new languages and software technologies to programmers and novices from the ground up; these books discuss programming fundamentals, followed by brief introductions to more sophisticated topics. The *For Experienced Programmers* subseries is designed for seasoned developers seeking a deeper treatment of new programming languages and technologies, without the encumbrance of introductory material; the books in this subseries move quickly to in-depth coverage of the features of the programming languages and software technologies being covered.

Tour of the Book

In this section, we take a tour of the subjects you will study in *Internet and World Wide Web How to Program, Third Edition*. Many of the chapters end with a Web Resources section that provides a listing of resources through which you can enhance your knowledge and use of the Web. In addition, you may want to visit the book's Web site `www.deitel.com/books/iw3HTP3/index.html` for additional resources. Due to the volume of information presented in this book, Chapters 30 and higher and Appendix G can be found on the accompanying CD as Adobe PDF documents. [*Note*: The table of contents and index indicate material located on the CD with red text.]

Chapter 1—Introduction to Computers and the Internet
In Chapter 1, we present historical information about computers and computer programming and introductory information on the Internet and the Web. We also overview the technologies and concepts discussed in the remaining chapters of the book.

Chapter 2—Microsoft Internet Explorer 6
Prior to the explosion of interest in the Internet and the Web, if you heard the term **browser**, you probably thought about browsing at a bookstore. Today "browser" has a whole new meaning—an important piece of software that enables you to view Web pages. The two

most popular browsers are Microsoft's Internet Explorer and Netscape. Throughout this book, we use Internet Explorer 6, but we provide a solid introduction to Netscape 7.1 at www.deitel.com. Using tools included with Internet Explorer, we demonstrate how to use the Web. This chapter shows readers unfamiliar with the Web how to browse the Web with Internet Explorer. We demonstrate several commonly used features for searching the Web, keeping track of the sites you visit and transferring files between computers. The chapter also covers e-mail and instant messaging technologies, which allow users to communicate over the Internet in real time. The chapter concludes with a discussion of alternative browsers and their features and functionality.

Chapter 3—Adobe Photoshop Elements: Creating Web Graphics

The Internet and Web are rich in multimedia content. Web pages contain colorful graphics, sounds and text. Graphics are an essential element of Web-page design that convey visual information about a site's contents. In this chapter, we introduce **Adobe Photoshop Elements**—a graphics software package that contains an extensive set of tools and features for creating high-quality graphics and animations. These tools include filters for applying special effects and screen capturing for taking "snap shots" of the screen. Chapter examples demonstrate creating title images for a Web page, creating a navigation bar that contains a series of buttons used to connect a Web site's pages and manipulating images by using advanced photographic effects. We focus on creating and manipulating the two most popular image formats used in Web documents: **Graphics Interchange Format (GIF)** and **Joint Photographic Expert Group (JPEG)** files. We also discuss the **Portable Network Graphic (PNG)** format, an increasingly popular image format. [*Note*: Readers can download a 30-day evaluation copy of Photoshop Elements from www.adobe.com/products/photoshopel. The chapter examples were developed using that version of Photoshop Elements.]

Chapter 4—Introduction to XHTML: Part 1

In this chapter, we unlock the power of Web-based application development by introducing **XHTML**—the **Extensible HyperText Markup Language**. XHTML is a **markup language** for identifying the elements of an XHTML document (or Web page) so that a browser can render (i.e., display) that document on a computer screen. We introduce basic XHTML Web-page creation using a technique we call the live-code approach. Every concept is presented in the context of a complete, working XHTML document. We render each working example in Internet Explorer and show the screen outputs. We present many short Web pages that demonstrate XHTML features. Later chapters introduce more sophisticated XHTML techniques, such as **tables**, which are useful for formatting information retrieved from a database. We introduce XHTML **tags** and **attributes**, which describe the document's information. A key issue when using XHTML is the separation of the **presentation** of a document (i.e., how the document is rendered on the screen by a browser) from the **structure** of the information in that document (i.e., the information the document contains). This chapter begins our in-depth discussion of this issue. As the book proceeds, you will be able to create appealing and powerful Web pages and Web-based applications. Other topics in this chapter include incorporating text, images and special characters (such as copyright and trademark symbols) into an XHTML document, validating an XHTML document to ensure that it is written correctly, placing information inside **lists**, separating parts of an XHTML document with horizontal lines (called **horizontal rules**) and linking to other XHTML documents on the Web.

Chapter 5—Introduction to XHTML: Part 2

In this chapter, we discuss more substantial XHTML elements and features. We demonstrate how to present information in tables and how to gather user input. We explain and demonstrate **internal linking** and **image maps** to make Web pages more navigable and how to use **frames** to display multiple XHTML documents in a browser. **XHTML forms** are one of the most important features introduced in this chapter—forms display information to the user and accept user input. By the end of this chapter, readers should be familiar with the most popular XHTML tags and features used to create Web sites.

Chapter 6—Cascading Style Sheets (CSS™)

Web browsers control the appearance (i.e., the rendering) of every Web page. For instance, one browser may render an h1 (i.e., a large heading) element in an XHTML document differently than another browser. With the advent of **Cascading Style Sheets (CSS)**, Web developers can control the appearance of their Web pages more accurately. CSS allows Web developers to specify the style of their Web page's elements (spacing, margins etc.) separately from the structure of their pages (section headers, body text, links etc.). This **separation of structure from content** allows greater manageability and makes changing document styles easier and faster. We introduce **inline**, **embedded** and **external** style sheets. Inline style sheets are applied to individual XHTML elements, embedded style sheets are entire style sheets placed directly inside an XHTML document and external style sheets are style sheets located outside an XHTML document.

Chapter 7—JavaScript:[1] Introduction to Scripting

Chapter 7 presents our first JavaScript **programs**[2] (also called **scripts**). Scripting helps Web pages "come alive." Web developers dynamically manipulate Web-page elements through scripting as clients browse Web pages. Chapters 7–12 present JavaScript, which is then used in Chapters 13–16 and in Chapters 30–31 (which are on the CD) to manipulate Web-page content. We present the key fundamental computer-science concepts of JavaScript at the same depth as we do in our other books on conventional programming languages (such as C, C++, C#, Java and Visual Basic), but in the exciting context of the Web. Using our live-code approach, we present every concept in the context of a working JavaScript program that is immediately followed by the screen output. The chapter introduces nonprogrammers to basic programming concepts and constructs. The scripts in this chapter illustrate how to output text to a browser and how to obtain user input through the browser. Some of the input and output is performed using the browser's capability to display predefined **graphical user interface (GUI)** windows (called **dialogs**). This allows nonprogrammers to concentrate on fundamental programming concepts and constructs rather than

---

1. JavaScript was originally created by Netscape; Microsoft's version is called JScript. The two scripting languages have a common subset between them known as ECMA-262. ECMA-262 defines a universal, client-side scripting language that ECMA International (originally the European Computer Manufacturers Association) developed in conjunction with Netscape, Microsoft and other companies. JavaScript and JScript each conform to the ECMA-262 standard. We typically refer to ECMA-262 as JavaScript.

2. The book's JavaScript examples execute in Microsoft Internet Explorer 6. We have tested these examples on Internet Explorer 6 and Netscape 7.1. For those few examples that do not execute in Netscape 7.1, we have (when possible) created Netscape 7.1 equivalent examples. These examples and the test results are available at www.deitel.com.

on GUI components and on GUI **event handling**. Chapter 7 also provides detailed treatments of **decision making** and **arithmetic operations**.

Chapter 8—JavaScript: Control Statements I

Chapter 8 focuses on the program-development process. The chapter discusses how to develop a working JavaScript program from a **problem statement** (i.e., a **requirements document**). We show the intermediate steps using, a program development tool called **pseudocode**. The chapter introduces some simple control statements used for decision making (`if` and `if...else`) and repetition (`while`). We examine counter-controlled repetition and sentinel-controlled repetition and introduce the increment, decrement and assignment operators. Simple flowcharts illustrate graphically the flow of control through each of the control statements. This chapter helps the student develop good programming habits in preparation for the more substantial programming tasks in the remainder of the book.

Chapter 9—JavaScript: Control Statements II

Chapter 9 discusses much of the material JavaScript has in common with the Java programming language, especially the **sequence**, **selection** and **repetition** control statements. Here, we introduce one additional control statement for decision making (`switch`) and two additional control statements for repetition (`for` and `do...while`). This chapter also introduces several operators that allow programmers to define complex conditions in their decision-making and repetition statements. The chapter uses flowcharts to illustrate the flow of control through each of the control statements, and concludes with a summary that enumerates each of the statements. The techniques discussed in this chapter and in Chapter 10 constitute a large part of what has been traditionally taught in universities under the topic of structured programming.

Chapter 10—JavaScript: Functions

Chapter 10 takes a deeper look inside scripts. Scripts contain data called **global** (or **script-level**) **variables** and executable units called **functions**. We discuss JavaScript functions, programmer-defined functions and **recursive** functions (i.e., functions that call themselves). The techniques presented in Chapter 10 are essential to produce properly structured programs, especially large programs that Web developers are likely to build in real-world, Web-based applications. The **divide-and-conquer** strategy is presented as an effective means for solving complex problems by dividing them into simpler, interacting components. The chapter offers an introduction to recursion and includes a table summarizing the recursion examples and exercises found in Chapters 10–13. We introduce **events** and event handling—elements required for programming graphical user interfaces (GUIs) in XHTML forms. Events are notifications of state changes, such as button clicks, mouse clicks, pressing keyboard keys, etc. JavaScript allows programmers to respond to various events by coding functions called **event handlers**. This begins our discussion of **event-driven programming**—the user drives the program by interacting with GUI components (causing **events such as mouse clicks**), and the scripts respond to the events by performing appropriate tasks (**event handling**). The event-driven programming techniques introduced here are used in scripts throughout the book. Dynamic HTML event handling is introduced in Chapter 14. Chapter 10 contains a rich set of exercises that include the Towers of Hanoi, computer-aided instruction and a guess-the-number game.

Chapter 11—JavaScript: Arrays

Chapter 11 explores the processing of data in lists and tables of values. We discuss the structuring of data into **arrays**, or groups, of related data items. The chapter presents numerous examples of both single-subscripted arrays and double-subscripted arrays. It is widely recognized that structuring data properly is as important as using control statements effectively in the development of properly structured programs. Examples in the chapter investigate various common array manipulations, searching arrays, sorting data and passing arrays to functions. This chapter introduces JavaScript's for...in control statement, which interacts with collections of data stored in arrays. The end-of-chapter exercises include a variety of interesting and challenging problems, such as the **Sieve of Eratosthenes** and the design of an airline reservations system. The chapter exercises also include a delightful simulation of the classic race between the tortoise and the hare.

Chapter 12—JavaScript: Objects

This chapter discusses **object-based programming** with JavaScript's built-in objects. The chapter introduces the terminology of objects. We overview the methods (functions associated with particular objects) of the JavaScript Math object and provide several examples of JavaScript's string-, date- and time-processing capabilities with the String and Date objects. An interesting feature of the String object is a set of methods that help a programmer output XHTML from a script by enclosing strings in XHTML elements. The chapter also discusses JavaScript's Number and Boolean objects, useful for performing mathematical and logical operations, and JavaScript's document, window, history and location objects specifically designed for the Web. In addition, we demonstrate how to personalize Web sites using cookies (small pieces of data) stored on client computers. At the end of the chapter, we build an interesting example that combines many of the JavaScript concepts presented in Chapters 7–12. Many challenging, yet entertaining, string-manipulation exercises are included.

Chapter 13—Dynamic HTML:[3] DHTML Object Model and Collections

A massive switch is occurring in the computer industry. The procedural programming style used since the inception of the industry is being replaced by the object-oriented style of programming. The vast majority of new software efforts use object technology in one form or another. The scripting languages we discuss in this book usually manipulate existing objects by sending messages that either inquire about the objects' attributes or ask the objects to perform certain actions. In this chapter, we continue the discussion of object technology by presenting Microsoft's Dynamic HTML object model. As Internet Explorer downloads a Web page from a server, it converts each element to an object. Objects store data (their attributes) and perform functions (their methods). Through scripting languages such as JavaScript, you can write commands that *get* or *set* (i.e., read or write) an object's attributes. You can also write commands that invoke an object's methods. The chapter exercises provide the opportunity to program the classic "15-puzzle" game.

---

3. Microsoft Dynamic HTML and Netscape Dynamic HTML are incompatible. In this book, we focus on Microsoft Dynamic HTML. We have tested all of the Dynamic HTML examples in Internet Explorer 6 and Netscape 7.1. All of these examples execute in Internet Explorer, but do not execute in Netscape 7.1. We have posted the testing results at www.deitel.com/books/iw3HTP3/index.html. In this book, we also present Macromedia Flash content which executes in Internet Explorer and Netscape.

Chapter 14—Dynamic HTML: Event Model

We have discussed how scripting can control XHTML pages. Dynamic HTML includes an **event model** that enables scripts to respond to user actions. This allows Web applications to be more responsive and user friendly. With the event model, scripts can respond to a user moving or clicking the mouse, scrolling up or down the screen or entering keystrokes. Content becomes more dynamic, while interfaces become more intuitive. We discuss how to use the event model to respond to user actions. We provide examples of event handling, which range from mouse capture to error handling to form processing. For example, we call the `onreset` event to confirm that a user wants to reset the form (i.e., the GUI in which the user inputs data). For one of the chapter exercises, the reader creates an interactive script that displays an image alongside the mouse pointer. When the mouse pointer is moved, the image moves with it.

Chapter 15—Dynamic HTML: Filters and Transitions

Internet Explorer includes a set of **filters** that allow developers to perform complex image transformations entirely in the Web browser without the need for additional downloads from a Web server. Filters are scriptable, so the developer can create stunning, customized animations with a few lines of client-side JavaScript. We introduce the `fliph` and `flipv` filters, which mirror text and images horizontally and vertically. We explain the `gray`, `xray` and `invert` filters, which all apply simple transformations to images. We introduce many of the filters that apply effects such as shadows, transparency gradients and distortions. Internet Explorer enables **transitions** that are similar to transitions between slides in PowerPoint-like presentations. The `revealTrans` filter applies visual effects such as box in, circle out, wipe left, vertical blinds, checkerboard across, random dissolve, split horizontal in, strips right up and random bars horizontal. This chapter also introduces the `blendTrans` filter, which allows you to fade in or fade out of an XHTML element over a set interval.

Chapter 16—Dynamic HTML: Data Binding with Tabular Data Control

This is one of the most important chapters in the book for people who want to build substantial, real-world Web-based applications. Businesses thrive on data, and Dynamic HTML helps Web developers build data-intensive applications. With **data binding**, data does not reside exclusively on the server. Data are sent from the server to the client, and all subsequent manipulations of the data occur on the client. Data can be maintained on the client in a manner that distinguishes the data from the XHTML markup. Manipulating data on the client improves performance by eliminating server activity and network delays. Once data is available on the client, the data can be **sorted** (i.e., arranged into ascending or descending order) and **filtered** (i.e., selected according to some criterion) in various ways. We present examples of each of these operations. To bind external data to XHTML elements, Internet Explorer employs software capable of connecting the browser to live data sources, known as **Data Source Objects (DSOs)**. Several DSOs are available in Internet Explorer—in this chapter, we discuss the most popular DSO, **Tabular Data Control (TDC)**.

Chapter 17—Macromedia Flash MX 2004: Building Interactive Animations

Macromedia Flash is a cutting-edge multimedia application that creates interactive content for the World Wide Web. Through hands-on examples, this chapter shows how to add interactivity, sound and animation to Web sites, while teaching the fundamentals of Macromedia Flash and **ActionScript**, Flash's scripting language. The chapter examples include creating interactive buttons, animated banners and animated splash screens (called **animation pre-loaders**). The exercises ask the reader to create a navigation bar, a spotlight effect and a morphing effect. The morphing effect exercise in particular is a wonderful illustration of the power of Flash. From this chapter, the reader will gain a thorough knowledge of Flash's graphic and animation capabilities, as well as an introductory understanding of ActionScript.

Chapter 18— Macromedia Flash MX 2004: Building an Interactive Game

While Chapter 17 provides a comprehensive introduction to Flash animation, it just begins to introduce the student to ActionScript's vast capabilities. Chapter 18 leads the student, step-by-step, through creating an interactive game. The skills learned in this case study include, but are not limited to, creating global variables, accessing objects on different layers, creating ActionScript functions, handling various events with event handlers, detecting object collisions with collision detectors and creating a time counter. Ultimately, the student is rewarded with a game in which the user has a limited amount of time to knock out pieces of a moving target. The exercises include adding a final score display and creating multiple levels of play.

Chapter 19— Macromedia Dreamweaver MX 2004

Macromedia Dreamweaver is the leading WYSIWYG (What You See Is What You Get) editor used by Web programmers today. While our book advocates a thorough knowledge of XHTML and its accompanying scripting languages, we acknowledge Dreamweaver as a useful tool for creating and maintaining Web pages and complete Web sites. This chapter walks the reader through using Dreamweaver to add elements, such as images, lists, line breaks, special characters and text formatting to a Web page. We provide comprehensive hands-on examples, including table and form creation. We also discuss Dreamweaver's powerful site creation and management capabilities. Finally, we discuss incorporating JavaScript into Dreamweaver pages. Since server-side scripting languages are discussed in later chapters of the book, we do not cover them in detail in this chapter. Still, Dreamweaver's integration with ASP.NET, ColdFusion, JSP and PHP is explained briefly. The exercises include creating complex tables and forms.

Chapter 20—Extensible Markup Language (XML)

Throughout the book, we have been emphasizing XHTML. This language derives from SGML (Standardized General Markup Language), which became an industry standard in 1986. SGML is employed in publishing applications worldwide, but it has not been incorporated into mainstream computing and information technology curricula. Its sheer size and complexity limit its use beyond heavy-duty, industrial-strength applications. The Extensible Markup Language (XML) is an effort to make SGML-like technology available to a much broader community. XML, a condensed subset of SGML, contains additional features for usability. XML differs in concept from XHTML. XHTML is a markup language, and XML is a language for *creating* markup languages. XML enables document authors to create their own markup for virtually any type of information. As a result, document authors use this extensibility to create entirely new markup languages to describe specific types of data, including mathematical formulas, chemical molecular structures, music and recipes. Markup languages created with XML include XHTML (Chapters 4 and 5), MathML (for mathematics), VoiceXML (for speech), SMIL™ (the Synchronized Multimedia Integration Language, for multimedia presentations), SVG (Scalable Vector Graphics, for vector and raster graphics), CML (Chemical Markup Language, for chemistry) and XBRL (Extensible Business Reporting Language, for financial data exchange). XML is a technology created by the World Wide Web Consortium for describing data in a portable format. XML is one of most important technologies in industry today and is being integrated into almost every field. Every day, companies and individuals are finding new and exciting uses for XML. In this chapter, we present examples that illustrate the basics of marking up data using XML. We demonstrate several XML-derived markup languages, such as MathML, CML, MusicXML, RSS, **XML Schema** (for checking an XML document's grammar) and **XSLT (Extensible Stylesheet Language Transformations**, for transforming an XML document's data into XML or XHTML documents). We also introduce Web services and Water (an XML-native programming language that simplifies Web service programming). The reader interested in a deeper treatment of XML may want to consider our book, *XML How to Program.*

Chapter 21—Web Servers (IIS and Apache)

Through Chapter 20, we focus on the client side of Web-based applications. Chapters 21–27 and Chapters 33–37 (on the CD) focus on the server side, discussing many technologies crucial to implementing successful Web-based systems. A Web server is part of a **multitiered application**—sometimes referred to as an *n*-tier application. A three-tier application contains a **data tier (bottom tier)**, **middle tier** and **client tier (top tier)**. The bottom tier is an organization's database. The middle tier receives client requests from the top tier, references the data stored in the bottom tier and sends the requested information to the client. The client tier renders a Web page and executes any scripting commands contained in the Web page. A crucial decision in building Web-based systems is which Web server to use. The *Apache Web Server* and Microsoft *Internet Information Services (IIS)* are the two most popular Web servers used in industry. Each of these is an "industrial-strength" server designed to handle the high volumes of transactions that occur in real-world systems. They require considerable system resources and administrative support. In this chapter, we provide a brief introduction to IIS and Apache. We discuss how to request XHTML, ASP.NET, Perl, Python and PHP documents from these Web servers when using Internet Explorer. The chapter concludes by listing some additional Web servers that are available on the Internet. [*Note*: Server software is complex and evolving quickly. Our goal in this chapter is to give you a "handle" on setting up and using server-side software. Deitel & Associates, Inc., does not provide software support for these servers. We suggest that you browse the Web sites we list at the end of this chapter for organizations that may provide such support.]

Chapter 22—Database: SQL, MySQL, DBI and ADO.NET

The vast majority of an organizations' data is stored in databases. In this chapter, we introduce databases as well as **Structured Query Language (SQL)** for making database queries. The chapter also introduces *MySQL*, an open source, enterprise-level database server, and highlights several key features of this database server. We provide a list of data objects that access MySQL through various programmatic libraries called **database interfaces (DBIs)**. We specifically discuss DBIs for Perl, Python and PHP. In addition, a brief discussion of Microsoft's version of data storage, called **universal database access (UDA)**, is provided. A key UDA component is ActiveX Data Objects .NET (ADO.NET), which we introduce in this chapter and use in Chapter 23, ASP.NET. We list additional resources related to MySQL and Microsoft Access at www.deitel.com/books/iw3HTP3/index.html.

Chapter 23—ASP.NET

This chapter introduces Microsoft's ASP.NET (Active Server Pages .NET), the first of the seven server-side software development paradigms we discuss. ASP.NET applications can be programmed in a variety of languages including JScript .NET, C# and VBScript (VBScript is Chapter 32 on the CD). We use JScript .NET as our programming language. ASP.NET implements middle-tier business logic while taking advantage of Microsoft's .NET framework, which provides useful Web service components. In this chapter, we introduce the reader to **dynamic content generation** (i.e., the process by which a scripting language generates an XHTML document, an XML document etc.). Chapter examples include several server-side programming topics, such as writing text files, querying an Access database, Web security and Web services. Key examples include an ASP.NET document that allows users to create Web pages, a guestbook application, an ASP.NET document that displays information about the client's browser and a simple Web service. This is a crucial chapter for those readers who want to implement Web-based applications by using Microsoft technologies.

Chapter 24—Case Study: ASP.NET and XML

In this chapter, we build on the material presented in Chapter 23 by creating an online message forum using ASP.NET. Message forums are "virtual" bulletin boards in which users discuss a variety of topics. The case study presented allows users to post messages to an existing forum and to create new forums. Each forum's data are stored in XML documents that are dynamically manipulated using ASP.NET. This chapter integrates many of the technologies presented earlier in the book, including XHTML, CSS, ASP.NET, XML and XSLT. Chapter exercises ask the reader to modify the case study to delete individual messages from a forum and to delete individual forums.

Chapter 25—Perl and CGI[4] (Common Gateway Interface)

Historically, the most widely used server-side technology for developing Web-based applications has been Perl/CGI. Despite the emergence of newer technologies such as ASP.NET (Chapters 23 and 24), PHP (Chapter 26), ColdFusion (Chapter 27), Python (Chapter 35 on the CD), Java servlets (Chapter 36 on the CD) and JavaServer Pages (Chapter 37 on the CD), the Perl community is well entrenched, and Perl will remain popular for the foreseeable future. Chapter 25 presents an introduction to Perl/CGI, including many real-world, live-code examples and discussions, and demonstrations of some of the most recent features of each of these technologies. Key examples demonstrate how to interact with a MySQL database and how to use **regular expressions** (i.e., expressions that efficiently search strings for patterns of characters).

Chapter 26—PHP

In this chapter, we introduce PHP, another popular server-side scripting language for Web-based application development. Similar to Perl (Chapter 25) and Python (Chapter 35 on the CD), PHP has a large community of users and developers. We begin the chapter by introducing basic syntax, data types, operators and arrays, string processing and regular expressions. Chapter coverage includes form processing and business logic, connecting to a

---

4. The reader interested in a deeper treatment of Perl and CGI may want to consider our book, *Perl How to Program.*

database and writing cookies. The chapter examples include a three-tier Web-based application that queries a MySQL database and a dynamically generated form that allows users to submit information to a mailing list database.

Chapter 27— Macromedia ColdFusion MX

This chapter describes the ColdFusion Markup Language (CFML), a popular server-side markup language for building dynamic Web sites. Macromedia's ColdFusion MX implements the CFML language and is used in this chapter to demonstrate basic and intermediate CFML capabilities. The language provides many markup tags, as well as support for functions, variables and expressions. Similar to ASP.NET and PHP, CFML enables developers to create database-driven Web sites, but with a quicker learning curve and shorter development time. The chapter includes a two-section case study on building an online bookstore with a shopping cart that tracks users' book selections.

Chapter 28—Multimedia: Audio, Video, Speech Synthesis and Recognition

This chapter focuses on the explosion of audio, video and speech technology appearing on the Web. We discuss adding sound, video and animated characters to Web pages (primarily using existing audio and video clips). Your first reaction may be a sense of caution, because these are complex technologies about which most readers have had little education. You quickly will see how easy it is to incorporate multimedia into Web pages and control multimedia components with Dynamic HTML. Multimedia files can be large. Some multimedia technologies require that an entire multimedia file be downloaded to the client before the audio or video begins playing. With **streaming audio** and **streaming video** technologies, audio and video can begin playing while the files are downloading, thus reducing delays. Streaming technologies are popular on the Web. This chapter demonstrates how to incorporate the **RealNetworks RealOne Player** into a Web page to receive streaming media. The chapter also includes an extensive set of Internet and Web resources that discuss interesting ways in which designers use multimedia-enhanced Web pages. This chapter introduces an exciting technology called **Microsoft Agent** for adding **interactive animated characters** to an XHTML document. **Agent characters** include *Peedy the Parrot*, *Genie*, *Merlin* and *Robby the Robot,* as well as those created by third-party developers. Each character allows users to interact with the application, using more natural human communication techniques such as speech. The agent characters accept mouse and keyboard interaction, speak and hear (i.e., they support speech synthesis and speech recognition). With these capabilities, your Web pages can speak to users and can actually respond to their voice commands! Microsoft Agent is included on the CD-ROM that accompanies this book. The chapter exercises ask the reader to create a karaoke machine and to incorporate an agent character into a Web page.

Chapter 29—Accessibility

Currently, the Web presents a challenge to individuals with disabilities. Multimedia-rich Web sites are difficult for text readers and other programs to interpret, especially for deaf users and users with visual impairments. To rectify this situation, the World Wide Web Consortium (W3C) launched the **Web Accessibility Initiative (WAI)**, which provides guidelines for making Web sites accessible to people with disabilities. This chapter provides a description of these guidelines, such as using the `alt` attribute of the `img` element to describe images and XHTML and using CSS to ensure that a page can be viewed on any type of display or reader. We discuss accessibility options available in Macromedia Flash, a predominantly visual and aural medium. We also introduce **VoiceXML** and **CallXML**, two technologies for increasing the accessibility of Web-based content. VoiceXML helps people with visual impairments to access Web content via speech synthesis and speech recognition. CallXML allows users with visual impairments to access Web-based content through a telephone. In the chapter exercises, readers create their own voicemail applications using CallXML.

Chapter 30 (on CD)—Dynamic HTML: Structured Graphics ActiveX Control

Although high-quality content is important to a Web site, it does not attract or maintain visitors' attention like eye-catching, animated graphics. This chapter explores the **Structured Graphics ActiveX Control** included with Internet Explorer. The Structured Graphics Control is a Web interface for the **DirectAnimation** subset of Microsoft's DirectX software. DirectAnimation is used in many popular video games and graphical applications. This control allows you to create complex graphics containing lines, shapes, textures and fills. In addition, scripting allows the graphics to be manipulated dynamically. The exercises at the end of the chapter ask the reader to create three-dimensional shapes and rotate them.

Chapter 31 (on CD)—Dynamic HTML: Path, Sequencer and Sprite ActiveX Controls

In this chapter, we discuss three additional DirectAnimation ActiveX controls available for Internet Explorer: the **Path Control**, the **Sequencer Control** and the **Sprite Control**. Each of these controls allows Web developers to add animated multimedia effects to Web pages. The Path Control allows the user to determine the positioning of elements on the screen. This is more elaborate than CSS absolute positioning, because the user can define lines, ovals and other shapes as paths along which objects move. Every aspect of motion is controllable through scripting. The Sequencer Control performs tasks at specified time intervals. This is useful for presentation-like effects, especially when used with the transitions discussed in Chapter 15. The Sprite Control creates Web animations. We also discuss, for comparison purposes, animated GIFs—another technique for producing Web-based animations.

Chapter 32 (on CD)—VBScript

Visual Basic Scripting Edition (VBScript) is a scripting language developed by Microsoft. Although it is not supported by many leading browsers, **plug-ins** help some of those browsers understand and process VBScript. Before the development of the Microsoft .NET Framework, however, VBScript was the most widely used language for writing Active Server Pages (ASP) prior to ASP.NET. This chapter prepares you to use VBScript on the client side in Microsoft communities and in Microsoft-based **intranets** (i.e., internal networks that use the same communications protocols as the Internet). This chapter will prepare readers to develop ASP pages in Chapters 33 and 34, as well as maintain existing ASP pages previously written in VBScript.

Chapter 33 (on CD)—Active Server Pages (ASP)

This chapter presents the original Active Server Pages technology, Microsoft's server-side technology before the advent of .NET. The chapter covers the same topics as Chapter 23 but uses ASP and VBScript instead of ASP.NET and JScript .NET.

Chapter 34 (on CD)—Case Study: Active Server Pages and XML

Chapter 34 presents the same message forum case study as Chapter 24 but uses ASP and VBScript instead of ASP.NET and JScript .NET. This chapter integrates many of the technologies presented earlier in the book, including XHTML, CSS, ASP, XML and XSLT.

Chapter 35 (on CD)—Python[5]

In this chapter, we introduce Python, an interpreted, cross-platform, object-oriented, general-purpose programming language. We begin by presenting basic syntax, data types, control statements and functions. We then introduce **lists** (i.e., data structures similar to a JavaScript array), **tuples** (i.e., immutable lists) and **dictionaries**, which are high-level data structures that store pairs of related data items. String processing and regular expressions are discussed, as is **exception handling**, which provides a structured mechanism for recovering from run-time errors. Chapter examples include implementing an XHTML registration form and showing how to use **cookies** (i.e., small text files written to the client machine). In addition, a three-tier Web-based example queries a MySQL database for author information.

Chapter 36 (on CD)—Servlets: Bonus for Java™ Developers

Java servlets represent a fifth popular way of building server-side Web-based applications. Servlets are written in Java (not JavaScript), which requires a substantial book-length treatment to learn. We do not teach Java in *Internet and World Wide Web How to Program, Third Edition*. This chapter (from our book *Java How to Program, 5/e*) is provided as a "bonus chapter" for readers familiar with Java. Readers who want to learn Java may want to consider reading this textbook.

Chapter 37 (on CD)—JavaServer Pages (JSP): Bonus for Java™ Developers

In this chapter (from our book *Java How to Program, 5/e*), we introduce **JavaServer Pages (JSP)**—an extension of Java servlet technology. JavaServer Pages enable Web-application programmers to create dynamic Web content, using familiar XML syntax and scripting with Java. Using JavaServer Pages, Web-application programmers can create **custom tag libraries** that encapsulate complex and dynamic functionality in XML tags. Web-page designers who are not familiar with Java can use these custom tag libraries to integrate information from databases, business-logic components and other resources into dynamically generated Web pages. This chapter is provided as a "bonus" chapter for readers familiar with Java. Readers who want to learn Java may want to consider reading our book *Java How to Program, Fifth Edition*.

Chapter 38 (on CD)—E-Business and E-Commerce

Chapter 38 explores the world of e-business and e-commerce. It begins by discussing the various business models associated with e-businesses. These include storefronts, auctions, portals, dynamic pricing, comparison shopping and demand-sensitive and name-your-price models. We also discuss the management and maintenance of an e-business, which includes advertising and marketing, accepting online payments, securing online transactions and understanding legal issues. We address such topics as branding, e-advertising, customer relationship management, e-wallets, micropayments, privacy and copyright. We also discuss security topics, including public-key cryptography, **Secure Socket Layer (SSL)** and wireless security. This chapter also discusses the emergence of XML and how it enables the standardization of business transactions worldwide. The final section of this chapter introduces wireless technology and mobile business concepts including wireless security, marketing, location-based services, privacy and more.

---

5. The reader interested in a deeper treatment of Python may want to consider our book, *Python How to Program*.

Appendix A—XHTML Special Characters

This appendix shows many commonly used XHTML special characters, called **character entity references** by the World Wide Web Consortium (W3C).

Appendix B—XHTML Colors

This appendix explains how to create colors by using either color names or hexadecimal RGB values. Included is a table that matches colors to values.

Appendix C—Operator Precedence Chart

This appendix contains a JavaScript operator precedence chart.

Appendix D—ASCII Character Set

This appendix contains a table of the 128 ASCII alphanumeric symbols.

Appendix E—Number Systems

This appendix explains the binary, octal, decimal and hexadecimal number systems. It shows how to convert between bases and perform mathematical operations in each base.

Appendix F—Unicode®

This appendix introduces the **Unicode Standard**, an encoding scheme that assigns unique numeric values to the world's characters. It includes an XML-based example that uses Unicode encoding to print a welcome message in 10 different languages.

Appendix G (on CD)—Career Opportunities

The Internet presents valuable resources and services for job seekers and employers. Automatic search features allow employees to scan the Web for open positions. Employers also can find job candidates by using the Internet. This greatly reduces the amount of time spent preparing and reviewing resumes, as well as travel expenses for distance recruiting and interviewing. In this appendix, we explore career services on the Web from the perspectives of job seekers and employers. We introduce comprehensive job sites, industry-specific sites (including sites geared specifically for Java and wireless programmers) and contracting opportunities, as well as additional resources and career services designed to meet the needs of a variety of individuals.

Dependency Chart

Figure 1 illustrates the dependencies that exist between chapters in the book. We recommend studying the topics of the book in the order indicated by the arrows, though other orders are certainly possible. Some of the dependencies apply only to sections of chapters, so we advise readers to browse the material before designing a course of study. This book is widely used in courses that teach pure client side Web programming, courses that teach pure server side Web programming, and courses that mix and match some client side and some server side Web programming. Curricula for courses in Web programming are still evolving, and many syllabi exist to organize the material in this book. You can search the Web for "syllabus," "Internet," "Web" and "Deitel" to find syllabi currently used with this book. Readers only interested in studying server side technologies should begin with an understanding of how to build basic Web pages (using XHTML and CSS) and have a firm grasp of introductory object-based programming concepts (presented in the JavaScript

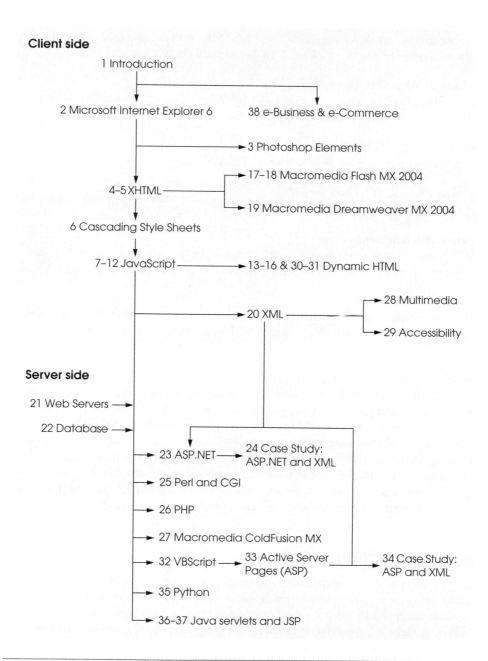

Fig. 1 Flowchart illustrating the dependencies between chapters in the book.

chapters of this book). Note the positioning of XML in the dependency chart. XML could be taught in several places: part of a client side unit, beginning of a server side unit or split between the two. Also note that the book is designed to cover both non-Microsoft and Microsoft technologies (e.g., Dynamic HTML, ASP.NET) in a way that makes it convenient for instructors to include or omit the Microsoft material.

Acknowledgments

One of the great pleasures of writing a textbook is acknowledging the efforts of many people whose names may not appear on the cover, but whose hard work, cooperation, friendship and understanding were crucial to the production of the book. Many people at Deitel & Associates, Inc. devoted long hours to this project.

- Abbey Deitel, President
- Barbara Deitel, Chief Financial Officer
- Christi Kelsey, Director of Business Development

We would also like to thank the participants in our Deitel & Associates, Inc. College Internship Program[6] who have contributed to this project. Jonathan Emanuele is a graduate of Cornell University and holds a BS in Operations Research. He is currently a Masters Student in Computer Science at Cornell. He co-authored Chapter 27 and revised Chapters 4, 5, 6 and 22. David Zolotusky is a Computer Science major at Cornell University. He revised Chapters 7–12 and contributed to Chapters 21, 29 and 35. Eric Hsu is a Computer Science major with minors in Operations Research and Management Science at Cornell University. He revised Chapters 2, 3 and 32–34, and co-authored Chapters 20, 23 and 24. Andrew McNay is a Computer Science and Visual Arts major at Stanford University. He revised Chapters 13–17, 26, 28 and 30–31, and co-authored Chapters 18 and 19. Bei Zhou is a Computer Science major at Northeastern University. He assisted with the ancillary materials and tested all XHTML and Dynamic HTML examples in Internet Explorer 6 and Netscape 7.1. Jonathan Henry is a Computer Science major at Northeastern University. He assisted with the ancillary materials.

We are fortunate to have worked on this project with the talented and dedicated team of publishing professionals at Prentice Hall. We especially appreciate the extraordinary efforts of our Computer Science Editor, Kate Hargett and her boss and our mentor in publishing—Marcia Horton, Editorial Director of Prentice Hall's Engineering and Computer Science Division. Vince O'Brien, Tom Manshreck and John Lovell did a marvelous job managing the production of the book. Carole Anson and Geoffrey Cassar did a wonderful job on the design of the book, and Sarah Parker managed the publication of the book's extensive ancillary package.

We wish to acknowledge the efforts of our *Third Edition* reviewers and to give a special note of thanks to Carole Snyder and Jennifer Cappello of Prentice Hall who managed the extraordinary review effort for this book.

---

6. The Deitel & Associates, Inc. College Internship Program is a highly competitive program that offers a limited number of salaried positions to Boston-area college students majoring in Computer Science, Information Technology, Marketing, Management and English. Students work at our corporate headquarters in Maynard, Massachusetts full-time in the summers and (for those attending college in the Boston area) part-time during the academic year. We also offer full-time internship positions for students interested in taking a semester off from school to gain industry experience. Regular full-time positions are available from time to time to college graduates. For more information, please contact our president, Abbey Deitel—`abbey.deitel@deitel.com`—and visit our Web site, `www.deitel.com`.

Internet & World Wide Web How to Program, Third Edition Reviewers
Americ Azevedo (University of California at Berkeley)
Tim Buntel (Macromedia, Inc.)
Sylvia Candelaria de Ram (Cognizor, LLC; HumanMarkup.org)
Wesley J. Chun (CyberWeb Consulting)
Marita Ellixson (Eglin AFB)
Jay Glynn (American General AIG)
James Greenwood (Poulternet)
Timothy Greer (Middle Tennessee State University)
James Huddleston (Independent Consultant)
Lynn Kyle (Yahoo!, Inc.)
Dan Livingston (Independent Consultant)
Oge Marques (Florida Atlantic University)
Mark Merkow (American Express Technologies)
Dan Moore (Independent Consultant)
George Semeczko (Royal & Sun Alliance Insurance Canada)
Deborah Shapiro (Cittone Institutes)
Matt Smith (Institute of Technology at Blanchardstown)
Narayana Rao Surapaneni (Patni Computer Systems Limited)
Stephanie Tauber (Tufts University)
Yateen Thakkar (Syntel India, Ltd.)
Cynthia Waddell (International Center for Disability Resources on the Internet)
Loran Walker (Lawrence Technological University)
Alnisa White (ILL Designs)

We wish to acknowledge again the efforts of our previous edition reviewers (some first edition and some second edition; the affiliations were current at the time of the review):

Richard Albright (University of Delaware)
Joan Aliprand (Unicode Consortium)
Race Bannon (Information Architects)
Kamaljit Bath (Microsoft)
Sunand Bhattacharya (ITT Technical Schools)
Paul Bohman (WebAIM)
Jason Bronfeld (Bristol-Myers Squibb Company)
Steve Burnett (RSA)
Carl Burnham (Southpoint.com)
Sylvia Candelaria de Ram (Editor, Python Journal)
Shane Carareo (Active State)
Kelly Carey (West Valley College)
Chris Constentino (Cisco Systems Inc., PTR Author)
Kevin Dorff (Honeywell)
Fred Drake (PythonLabs)
Bob DuCharme (XML Author)
Jonathan Earl (Technical Training and Consulting)
Amanda Farr (Virtual-FX.net)
Avi Finkel (WhizBang! Labs)

Seth Fogie (Donecker's, PTR Author)
Steven Franklin (UC Irvine)
Charles Fry (thesundancekid.org)
Jim Gips (Boston College)
Jesse Glick (NetBeans)
Phillip Gordon (Berkeley)
Christopher Haupt (Adobe)
Jesse Heines (UMass Lowell)
Shelly Heller (George Washington University)
Auda Hesham (CUNY)
Damon Houghland (Prentice Hall PTR Author "Essential WAP for Web Professionals")
Bryan Hughes (Adobe)
Jeff Isom (WebAIM)
John Jenkins (Unicode Consortium)
Simon Johnson (Shake Communications Pty Ltd)
Peter Jones (SUN Microsystems)
Alwyn Joy (Whiz Networks Pvt. Ltd.)
Ankur Kapoor (MIND UR Web)
David Kershaw (Art Technology)
Ryan Kuykendall (Amazon)
Hunt LaCascia (Engenius, Inc.)
Yves Lafon (W3C)
Daniel LaLiberte (W3C/Mosaic/NASA)
Elizabeth Lane Lawley (RIT)
Mike Leavy (Adobe)
Ze-Nian Li (Simon Frasier University)
Luby Liao (University of San Diego)
Wen Liu (ITT)
Maxim Loukianov (SoloMio Corp.)
Marc Loy (Consultant)
Dan Lynch (CyberCash)
Massimo Marchiori (W3C)
Rick McGowan (Unicode Consortium)
Julie McVicar (Oakland Community College)
Jasmine Merced (PerlArchive.com)
Mark Michael (Kings College)
Scott Mitchell (Consultant)
Dan Moore (XOR, Inc.)
Charles McCathie Neville (W3C)
Simon North (Synopsys)
Dr. Cyrus Peikari (VirusMD Corp., PTR Author)
Steven Pemberton (CWI, Amsterdam)
Shep Perkins (Fidelity Select Wireless Portfolio)
Corrin Pitcher (DePaul University)
Ashish Prakash (IBM)
Paul Prescod (Active State)

Keith Roberts (Prentice Hall PTR Author "Core CSS")
Rama Roberts (SUN Microsystems)
Chad Rolfs (Adobe)
Robert Rybaric (PRO-INFO Systems)
Arie Schlessinger (Columbia University)
Deb Shapiro (Computer Learning Centers)
Devan Shepherd (Shepherd Consulting Services)
Steve Smith (ASP Alliance)
M.G. Sriram (HelloBrian Corp.)
Dan Steinman (Consultant)
Sumanth Sukumar (IBM Transarc Labs [HTTP / AFS & DCE DFS])
Scott Tilley (University of California, Riverside)
Vadim Tkachenko (Sera Nova)
Guido Van Rossum (python.org)
Nic Van't Schip (vanschip.com)
William Vaughn (Microsoft)
Michael Wallent (Microsoft)
Susan Warren (Microsoft)
Ken Whistler (Sybase; Unicode Consortium)
Monty Widenius (MySQL)
Jesse Wilkins (Metalinear Media)
Michael Willett (wavesys.com)
Bernard Wong (Microsoft)
Ed Wright (Jet Propulsion Laboratory)
Stephen Wynne (IBM Transarc Labs/Carnegie Mellon University)

These reviewers scrutinized every aspect of the text and made countless suggestions for improving the accuracy and completeness of the presentation.

Contacting Deitel & Associates

We would sincerely appreciate your comments, criticisms, corrections and suggestions for improving the text. Please address all correspondence to:

deitel@deitel.com

We will respond promptly.

Errata

We will post all errata for the *Third Edition* at www.deitel.com.

Customer Support

Please direct all software and installation questions to Pearson Education Technical Support:

- By phone: 1-800-677-6337
- By email: media.support@pearsoned.com
- On the Web: 247.prenhall.com

Please direct all Internet & World Wide Web questions to deitel@deitel.com. We will respond promptly.

Welcome to the exciting world of the Internet & World Wide Web programming. We sincerely hope you enjoy learning with this book.

Dr. Harvey M. Deitel
Paul J. Deitel
Andrew B. Goldberg

About the Authors

Dr. Harvey M. Deitel, Chairman and Chief Strategy Officer of Deitel & Associates, Inc., has 42 years experience in the computing field, including extensive industry and academic experience. Dr. Deitel earned B.S. and M.S. degrees from the Massachusetts Institute of Technology and a Ph.D. from Boston University. He worked on the pioneering virtual-memory operating-systems projects at IBM and MIT that developed techniques now widely implemented in systems such as UNIX, Linux and Windows XP. He has 20 years of college teaching experience, including earning tenure and serving as the Chairman of the Computer Science Department at Boston College before founding Deitel & Associates, Inc., with his son, Paul J. Deitel. He and Paul are the co-authors of several dozen books and multimedia packages and they are writing many more. With translations published in Japanese, German, Russian, Spanish, Traditional Chinese, Simplified Chinese, Korean, French, Polish, Italian, Portuguese, Greek, Urdu and Turkish, the Deitels' texts have earned international recognition. Dr. Deitel has delivered professional seminars to major corporations, government organizations and the military.

Paul J. Deitel, CEO and Chief Technical Officer of Deitel & Associates, Inc., is a graduate of the MIT's Sloan School of Management, where he studied Information Technology. Through Deitel & Associates, Inc., he has delivered C, C++, Java, Internet and World Wide Web courses to industry clients, including IBM, Sun Microsystems, Dell, Lucent Technologies, Fidelity, NASA at the Kennedy Space Center, the National Severe Storm Laboratory, Compaq, White Sands Missile Range, Rogue Wave Software, Boeing, Stratus, Cambridge Technology Partners, Open Environment Corporation, One Wave, Hyperion Software, Adra Systems, Entergy, CableData Systems and many other organizations. He has lectured on C++ and Java for the Boston Chapter of the Association for Computing Machinery and has taught satellite-based Java courses through a cooperative venture of Deitel & Associates, Prentice Hall and the Technology Education Network. He and his father, Dr. Harvey M. Deitel, are the world's best-selling Computer Science textbook authors.

Andrew B. Goldberg is a recent graduate of Amherst College, where he earned a degree in Computer Science. His senior honors thesis, entitled *"Highly Constrained Sports Scheduling With Genetic Algorithms,"* brought together several of Andrew's research interests, including artificial intelligence, artificial life and genetic algorithms (i.e., algorithms that mimic evolution and the process of natural selection to solve problems). Andrew enjoys database-driven, dynamic Web programming and has developed applications for Amherst College and several independent Web sites. Andrew has contributed to other Deitel publications including *Operating Systems, Third Edition.*

About Deitel & Associates, Inc.

Deitel & Associates, Inc., is an internationally recognized corporate training and content-creation organization specializing in Internet/World Wide Web software technology, e-business/e-commerce software technology, object technology and computer programming languages education. The company provides instructor-led courses on Internet and World Wide Web programming, wireless Internet programming, object technology, and major programming languages and platforms, such as C, C++, Visual C++ .NET, Visual Basic .NET, C#, Java, Advanced Java, XML, Perl, Python and more. The founders of Deitel & Associates, Inc., are Dr. Harvey M. Deitel and Paul J. Deitel. The company's clients include many of the world's largest computer companies, government agencies, branches of the military and business organizations. Through its 27-year publishing partnership with Prentice Hall, Deitel & Associates, Inc. publishes leading-edge programming textbooks, professional books, interactive CD-based multimedia *Cyber Classrooms*, *Complete Training Courses*, Web-based training courses and course management systems e-content for popular CMSs such as WebCT™, Blackboard™ and CourseCompass^{SM}. Deitel & Associates, Inc., and the authors can be reached via e-mail at:

deitel@deitel.com

To learn more about Deitel & Associates, Inc., its publications and its worldwide corporate on-site training curriculum, see the last few pages of this book or visit:

www.deitel.com

Individuals wishing to purchase Deitel books, *Cyber Classrooms*, *Complete Training Courses* and Web-based training courses can do so through bookstores, online booksellers and:

www.deitel.com
www.prenhall.com/deitel
www.InformIT.com/deitel
www.InformIT.com/cyberclassrooms

Bulk orders by corporations and academic institutions should be placed directly with Prentice Hall. See the last few pages of this book for worldwide ordering instructions.

1

Introduction to Computers and the Internet

Objectives

- To understand basic computing concepts.
- To become familiar with different types of programming languages.
- To understand the evolution of the Internet and the World Wide Web.
- To understand the roles of XHTML, JavaScript, JScript .NET, Dynamic HTML, ASP.NET, Perl, PHP, ColdFusion, Python, Java servlets and JavaServer Pages in developing distributed client/server applications for the Internet and the World Wide Web.

Our life is frittered away by detail . . . Simplify, simplify.
Henry David Thoreau

What networks of railroads, highways and canals were in another age, networks of telecommunications, information and computerization . . . are today.
Bruno Kreisky

My object all sublime
I shall achieve in time.
W. S. Gilbert

He had a wonderful talent for packing thought close, and rendering it portable.
Thomas Babington Macaulay

Outline

1.1 Introduction

Welcome to Internet and World Wide Web programming! We have worked hard to create what we hope will be an informative, entertaining and challenging learning experience for you. As you read this book, you may want to refer to our Web site

```
www.deitel.com
```

for updates and additional information.

The technologies you will learn in this book are fun for novices, and simultaneously are appropriate for experienced professionals who build substantial information systems. *Internet and World Wide Web How to Program, Third Edition* is designed to be an effective learning tool for each of these audiences. How can one book appeal to both groups? The answer is that the core of this book emphasizes achieving program *clarity* through the proven techniques of **structured programming**, **object-based programming** and—in the optional Java sections—**object-oriented programming**. Beginners will learn programming the right way from the beginning. We have attempted to write in a clear and straightforward manner.

Perhaps most important, the book presents hundreds of working examples and shows the outputs produced when these examples are rendered in browsers or run on computers. We present all concepts in the context of complete working programs. We call this the **LIVE-CODE approach**. These examples are available on the CD-ROM inside the back cover of this book and by download from our Web site, www.deitel.com.

The early chapters introduce computer fundamentals, the Internet and the World Wide Web. We show how to use software for browsing the Web and for creating images for the Web. We present a carefully paced introduction to Web programming, using the popular JavaScript programming language. In this book, we will often refer to "programming" as **scripting** for reasons that will soon become clear. Novices will find that the material in the JavaScript chapters presents a solid foundation for the deeper treatment of scripting in Perl, PHP, ASP.NET, ColdFusion, Python, VBScript and JSP in the later chapters. Experienced programmers will read the early chapters quickly and find the treatment of scripting in the later chapters to be rigorous and challenging.

Most people are familiar with the exciting things computers do. Using this textbook, you will learn how to command computers to perform specific tasks. **Software** (i.e., the instructions you write to command the computer to perform **actions** and make **decisions**) controls computers (often referred to as **hardware**). JavaScript is among today's most popular software development languages for Web-based applications.

Computer use is increasing in almost every field of endeavor. In an era of steadily rising costs, computing costs have been decreasing dramatically because of rapid developments in both hardware and software technologies. Computers that filled large rooms and cost millions of dollars just two decades ago can now be inscribed on the surfaces of silicon chips smaller than fingernails, costing perhaps a few dollars each. Silicon is one of the most abundant materials on earth—it is an ingredient in common sand. Silicon chip technology has made computing so economical that hundreds of millions of general-purpose computers worldwide are helping people in business, industry, government, education and in their personal lives.

Until recently, students in introductory programming courses learned only the methodology called **structured programming**. As you study the various scripting languages in this book, you will learn *both* structured programming and the newer methodology called **object-based programming**. After this, you will be well prepared to study today's popular full-scale programming languages such as C++, Java, C# and Visual Basic .NET and to learn the even more powerful programming methodology of **object-oriented programming**. We believe that object-oriented programming will be the key programming methodology at least for the next decade.

Today's users are accustomed to applications with graphical user interfaces (GUIs). Users want applications that employ the multimedia capabilities of graphics, images, animation, audio and video. They want applications that can run on the Internet and the World Wide Web and communicate with other applications. Users want to apply both file-processing techniques and database technologies. They want applications that are not limited to the desktop or even to some local computer network, but that can integrate Internet and World Wide Web components, and remote databases as well. Programmers want to use all these capabilities in a truly portable manner so that applications will run without modification on a variety of **platforms** (i.e., different types of computers running different operating systems).

In this book, we present a number of powerful software technologies that will enable you to build these kinds of systems. The first part of the book (through Chapter 20) concentrates on using technologies such as Extensible HyperText Markup Language (XHTML), JavaScript, Dynamic HTML, Flash, Dreamweaver and Extensible Markup Language (XML) to build the portions of Web-based applications that reside on the **client side** (i.e., the portions of applications that typically run on Web browsers such as Netscape or Microsoft's Internet Explorer). The second part of the book concentrates on using technologies such as Web servers, databases, ASP.NET, Perl/CGI, PHP and ColdFusion. Programmers use these technologies to build the **server side** of Web-based applications. These portions of applications typically run on "heavy-duty" computer systems on which organizations' business-critical Web sites reside. Readers who master the technologies in this book will be able to build substantial Web-based, client/server, database-intensive, "multi-tier" applications. We begin with a discussion of computer hardware and software fundamentals. If you are generally familiar with computers, you may want to skip portions of Chapter 1.

1.2 What Is a Computer?

A **computer** is a device capable of performing computations and making logical decisions at speeds millions, even billions, of times faster than human beings can. For example, a person operating a desk calculator might require a lifetime to complete the hundreds of millions of calculations a powerful personal computer can perform in one second. (Points to ponder: How would you know whether the person had added the numbers correctly? How would you know whether the computer had added the numbers correctly?) Today, the world's fastest **supercomputers** can perform hundreds of billions of additions per second, and computers that perform several trillion instructions per second are already functioning in research laboratories!

Computers process **data** under the direction of sets of instructions called **computer programs**. Computer programs guide the computer through orderly sets of actions specified by people called **computer programmers**.

The various devices, such as the keyboard, screen, disks, memory and processing units, that comprise a computer system are referred to as **hardware**. Regardless of differences in physical appearance, virtually every computer may be envisioned as being divided into six **logical units** or sections. These are as follows:

1. **Input unit**. This is the "receiving" section of the computer. It obtains information (data and computer programs) from various **input devices** and makes the information available to the other units so that it can be processed. Most information is entered into computers today through keyboards, "mouse" or pointing devices, disks and network connections. Information also is entered by speaking to computers, by electronically scanning images and by video recording.

2. **Output unit**. This is the "shipping" section of the computer. It takes information processed by the computer and sends it to various **output devices** to make the information available for use outside the computer. Information output from computers is displayed on screens, printed on paper, played through audio speakers and video devices, sent to other computers and magnetically recorded on disks and tapes. This processed information can be used to control other devices.

3. **Memory unit**. This is the rapid-access, relatively low-capacity "warehouse" section of the computer. It temporarily retains information entered through the input unit so that the information may be made available for processing. The memory

unit also retains information which has already been processed until it can be placed on output devices by the output unit. The main memory unit often is called either **memory**, **primary memory** or **random access memory (RAM)**.

4. **Arithmetic and logic unit (ALU)**. This is the "manufacturing" section of the computer. It is responsible for performing calculations, such as addition, subtraction, multiplication and division. It contains the decision mechanisms that allow the computer, for example, to compare two items from the memory unit to determine whether they are equal.

5. **Central processing unit (CPU)**. This is the "administrative" section of the computer. The CPU acts as the computer's coordinator and is responsible for supervising the operation of the other sections. The CPU tells the input unit when information should be read into the memory unit, tells the ALU when information from the memory unit should be used in calculations and tells the output unit when to send information from the memory unit to certain output devices.

6. **Secondary storage unit**. This is the long-term, high-capacity "warehousing" section of the computer. Programs or data not being used by the other units are normally placed on secondary storage devices (e.g., hard disk drives) until they are needed, possibly hours, days, months or even years later. Information in secondary storage takes longer to access than information in primary memory. The cost per unit of secondary storage is much less than the cost per unit of primary memory.

1.3 Programming Language Types

The computer programs that run on a computer are referred to as **software**. Programmers write the instructions that comprise software in various programming languages, some that the computer can understand and others that require intermediate translation steps. The hundreds of computer languages in use today may be divided into three types:

1. Machine languages

2. Assembly languages

3. High-level languages

Any computer can directly understand only its own **machine language**. Machine language is the "natural language" of any given computer and is defined by its hardware design. Machine languages generally consist of strings of numbers (ultimately reduced to 1s and 0s) that instruct computers to perform their most elementary operations one at a time. Machine languages are **machine dependent** (i.e., a particular machine language can be used on only one platform, or type, of computer). Machine languages are cumbersome for humans, as illustrated by the following machine language that adds overtime pay to base pay and stores the result in gross pay:

```
+1300042774
+1400593419
+1200274027
```

As computers became more popular, it became apparent that machine-language programming was too slow and tedious for most programmers. Instead of using strings of numbers that computers could directly understand, programmers began using **natural language** (e.g., English-like) abbreviations to represent the elementary operations of the computer. These abbreviations formed the basis of **assembly languages**. **Translator programs**, called **assemblers**, were developed to convert assembly-language programs to machine language at computer speeds. The following section of an assembly-language program also adds overtime pay to base pay and stores the result in gross pay, but reads more clearly than its machine-language equivalent.

```
LOAD    BASEPAY
ADD     OVERPAY
STORE   GROSSPAY
```

Although such code is understandable to humans, it is incomprehensible to computers until translated to machine language.

Computer use increased rapidly with the advent of assembly languages, but programming in these still required many instructions to accomplish even the simplest tasks. To speed the programming process, **high-level languages** were developed, in which single statements could be written to accomplish substantial tasks. The translator programs that convert high-level language programs into machine language are called **compilers**. High-level languages allow programmers to write instructions that are similar to everyday English and contain commonly used mathematical notations. A payroll program written in a high-level language might contain the statement:

```
grossPay = basePay + overTimePay
```

From this, it is easy to see why programmers find high-level languages more desirable than either machine languages or assembly languages. C++, Java, C# and Visual Basic .NET are among the most powerful and most widely used high-level programming languages.

The process of compiling a high-level language program into machine language can take a considerable amount of computer time. **Interpreter** programs were developed to execute high-level language programs directly, without the need for compiling them into machine language. Although compiled programs execute faster than interpreted programs, interpreters are popular in program-development environments, in which programs are recompiled frequently as new features are added and errors are corrected. In this book, we study eight key programming languages: JavaScript, JScript, ActionScript, Perl, PHP, ColdFusion, Python and VBScript (along with many other languages, including XHTML and XML). Each of these **scripting languages** is processed by interpreters. You will see that interpreters have played an especially important role in helping scripting languages achieve their goal of portability across a variety of platforms.

Performance Tip 1.1

Interpreters have an advantage over compilers in the scripting world. An interpreted program can begin executing as soon as it is downloaded to the client's machine, without the need to be compiled before it can execute.

1.4 Other High-Level Languages

Only a few high-level languages have achieved broad acceptance, out of the hundreds developed. IBM Corporation developed **Fortran** (FORmula TRANslator) from 1954 to 1957 for scientific and engineering applications that required complex mathematical computations. Fortran is still widely used.

A group of computer manufacturers and government and industrial computer users developed **Cobol** (Common Business Oriented Language) in 1959. Commercial applications that manipulate large amounts of data are programmed in Cobol. Today, about half of all business software is still programmed in Cobol.

Basic was developed in 1965 at Dartmouth College as a simple language to help novices learn programming. Bill Gates implemented Basic on several early personal computers. Today, **Microsoft**—the company Bill Gates created—is the world's leading software development organization. Gates has become one of the world's most recognized people, and Microsoft is included in the list of prestigious stocks that form the Dow Jones Industrials—from which the Dow Jones Industrial Average is calculated as a measure of stock market performance.

1.5 Structured Programming

During the 1960s, many large software development efforts encountered severe difficulties. Software schedules were typically late, costs greatly exceeded budgets and the finished products were unreliable. People began to realize that software development was a far more complex activity than they had imagined. Research activity in the 1960s resulted in the evolution of **structured programming**—a disciplined approach to writing programs that are clearer than unstructured programs, easier to test and debug and easier to modify. Chapters 7–9 discuss the principles of structured programming.

One of the more tangible results of this research was the development of the **Pascal** programming language by Professor Nicklaus Wirth in 1971. Pascal, named after the 17th-century mathematician and philosopher Blaise Pascal, was designed for teaching structured programming in academic environments and rapidly became the preferred programming language in most universities.

The **Ada** programming language was developed under the sponsorship of the United States Department of Defense (DoD) during the 1970s and early 1980s. Hundreds of separate languages had been used to produce DoD's massive command-and-control software systems. DoD wanted a single language that would fulfill most of the department's needs. Pascal was chosen as a base, but the final Ada language is quite different from Pascal. The language was named after Augusta Ada Byron King, Lady Lovelace, daughter of the poet Lord Byron. Lady Lovelace is generally credited with writing the world's first computer program, in the early 1800s (for the Analytical Engine mechanical computing device designed by Charles Babbage).

One important capability of Ada is called **multitasking**, which allows programmers to have many activities running simultaneously. Java, through a technique called **multithreading**, also enables programmers to write programs with actions that can be processed in parallel. Other widely used high-level languages, such as C and C++, generally allow programs to perform only one activity at a time (although they can support multithreading through special-purpose libraries).

1.6 History of the Internet

In the late 1960s, one of the authors (HMD) was a graduate student at MIT. His research at MIT's Project Mac (now the Laboratory for Computer Science—the home of the World Wide Web Consortium) was funded by ARPA—the Advanced Research Projects Agency of the

Department of Defense. ARPA sponsored a conference at which several dozen ARPA-funded graduate students were brought together at the University of Illinois at Urbana-Champaign to meet and share ideas. During this conference, ARPA rolled out the blueprints for networking the main computer systems of about a dozen ARPA-funded universities and research institutions. They were to be connected with communications lines operating at a then-stunning 56Kbps (i.e., 56,000 bits per second)—this at a time when most people (of the few who could) were connecting over telephone lines to computers at a rate of 110 bits per second. HMD vividly recalls the excitement at the conference. Researchers at Harvard talked about communicating with the Univac 1108 "supercomputer" at the University of Utah to handle calculations related to their computer graphics research. Many other intriguing possibilities were raised. Academic research was on the verge of taking a giant leap forward. Shortly after this conference, ARPA proceeded to implement the **ARPANET**, the grandparent of today's **Internet**.

Things worked out differently from what was originally planned. Rather than the primary benefit of researchers sharing one other's computers, it rapidly became clear that enabling researchers to communicate quickly and easily via what became known as **electronic mail** (**e-mail**, for short) was the key benefit of the ARPANET. This is true even today on the Internet, as e-mail facilitates communications of all kinds among hundreds of millions of people worldwide.

One of the primary goals for ARPANET was to allow multiple users to send and receive information simultaneously over the same communications paths (e.g., phone lines). The network operated with a technique called **packet switching**, in which digital data was sent in small bundles called **packets**. The packets contained address, error control and sequencing information. The address information allowed packets to be routed to their destinations. The sequencing information helped reassemble the packets (which, because of complex routing mechanisms, could actually arrive out of order) into their original order for presentation to the recipient. Packets from different senders were intermixed on the same lines. This packet-switching technique greatly reduced transmission costs, as compared with the cost of dedicated communications lines.

The network was designed to operate without centralized control. If a portion of the network failed, the remaining working portions would still route packets from senders to receivers over alternative paths.

The protocols for communicating over the ARPANET became known as **TCP**—the **Transmission Control Protocol**. TCP ensured that messages were properly routed from sender to receiver and that they arrived intact.

As the Internet evolved, organizations worldwide were implementing their own networks for both intraorganization (i.e., within the organization) and interorganization (i.e., between organizations) communications. A wide variety of networking hardware and software appeared. One challenge was to get these different networks to communicate. ARPA accomplished this with the development of **IP**—the **Internet Protocol**, truly creating a "network of networks," the current architecture of the Internet. The combined set of protocols is now commonly called **TCP/IP**.

Initially, Internet use was limited to universities and research institutions; then the military began using the Internet. Eventually, the government decided to allow access to the Internet for commercial purposes. Initially, there was resentment in the research and military communities—these groups were concerned that response times would become poor as "the Net" became saturated with users.

In fact, the exact opposite has occurred. Businesses rapidly realized that they could tune their operations and offer new and better services to their clients, so they started spending vast amounts of money to develop and enhance the Internet. This generated fierce competition among communications carriers and hardware and software suppliers to meet this demand. The result is that **bandwidth** (i.e., the information carrying capacity) on the Internet has increased tremendously and costs have decreased significantly.

1.7 Personal Computing

In 1977, Apple Computer popularized the phenomenon of **personal computing**. Initially, it was a hobbyist's dream, but computers quickly became economical enough for people to buy for personal use. In 1981, IBM, the world's largest computer vendor, introduced the **IBM Personal Computer**, making computing legitimate in business, industry and government organizations.

However, these computers were "stand-alone" units—people did their work on their own machines and then transported disks back and forth to share information (this was called "sneakernet"). Although early personal computers were not powerful enough to time-share several users, these machines could be linked together in computer networks, sometimes over telephone lines and sometimes in **local area networks** (**LANs**) within an organization. This led to the phenomenon of **distributed computing**, in which an organization's computing, instead of being performed strictly at a central computer installation, is distributed over networks to the sites at which the bulk of the organization's work is performed. Personal computers were powerful enough to handle the computing requirements of individual users and to enable the basic communications tasks of passing information back and forth electronically.

Today's most powerful personal computers are as powerful as the million-dollar machines of two decades ago. Desktop computers—called **workstations**—and portable computers—called **laptops**—provide individual users with enormous capabilities. Information is easily shared across computer networks such as the Internet in which some computers, called **servers**, offer common stores of programs and data that may be used by **client** computers distributed throughout the network—hence the term **client/server computing**. Today's popular operating systems, such as UNIX, Linux, Mac OS X, Windows 2000 and Windows XP, provide the kinds of capabilities discussed in this section.

1.8 History of the World Wide Web

The **World Wide Web** allows computer users to locate and view multimedia-based documents (i.e., documents with text, graphics, animations, audios or videos) on almost any subject. Even though the Internet was developed decades ago, the introduction of the World Wide Web is a relatively recent event. In 1990, **Tim Berners-Lee** of CERN (the European Organization for Nuclear Research) developed the World Wide Web and several communication protocols that form the backbone of the Web. The use of the Web "exploded" with the availability in 1993 of the Mosaic browser, which featured a user-friendly graphical interface. Marc Andreessen, whose team at the National Center for Supercomputing Applications (NCSA) developed Mosaic, went on to found Netscape, the company that many people credit with initiating the explosive Internet economy of the late 1990s.

The Internet and the World Wide Web surely will be listed among the most important and profound creations of humankind. In the past, most computer applications ran on "stand-alone" computers (i.e., computers that were not connected to one another). Today's applications can be written to communicate with hundreds of millions of computers. The Internet mixes computing and communications technologies. It makes information instantly and conveniently accessible worldwide. It makes our work easier. Individuals and small businesses can receive worldwide exposure on the Internet. It is changing the nature of the way business is done. People can search for the best prices on virtually any product or service. Special-interest communities can stay in touch with one another, and researchers can learn of scientific and academic breakthroughs worldwide.

1.9 World Wide Web Consortium (W3C)

In October 1994, Tim Berners-Lee founded an organization—called the **World Wide Web Consortium** (**W3C**)—devoted to developing nonproprietary, interoperable technologies for the World Wide Web. One of the W3C's primary goals is to make the Web universally accessible—regardless of ability, language or culture.

The W3C is also a standardization organization. Web technologies standardized by the W3C are called **Recommendations**. W3C Recommendations include the Extensible HyperText Markup Language (XHTML), Cascading Style Sheets (CSS), HyperText Markup Language (HTML; now considered a "legacy" technology) and the Extensible Markup Language (XML). A recommendation is not an actual software product, but a document that specifies a technology's role, syntax rules and so forth. For detailed information about the W3C Recommendation process, see "6.2 The W3C Recommendation track" at

www.w3.org/Consortium/Process/Process-19991111/process.html#Recs

The W3C comprises three primary hosts—the Massachusetts Institute of Technology (MIT), the European Research Consortium for Informatics and Mathematics (ERCIM) and Keio University in Japan—and hundreds of members. Members provide the primary financing for the W3C and help provide the strategic direction of the Consortium.

The W3C home page (www.w3.org) provides extensive resources on Internet and Web technologies. For each Internet technology with which the W3C is involved, the site provides a description of the technology and its benefits to Web designers, the history of the technology and the future goals of the W3C in developing the technology. The site organizes W3C Activities (i.e., technology areas under development) into the following domains: Architecture, Interaction, Technology and Society and Web Accessibility Initiative.

1.10 Hardware Trends

The Internet community thrives on the continuing stream of dramatic improvements in hardware, software and communications technologies. In general, people expect to pay at least a little more for most products and services every year. The opposite generally has been the case in the computer and communications fields, especially with regard to the hardware costs of supporting these technologies. For many decades, and with no change expected in the foreseeable future, hardware costs have fallen rapidly. This is a phenomenon of technology. Every year or two, the capacities of computers tend to double, especially the amount of **memory** they have in which to execute programs, the amount of **secondary**

storage (e.g., disk storage) they have to hold programs and data over the longer term, and the processor speeds—the speed at which computers execute their programs (i.e., do their work). The same has been true in the communications field, especially in recent years, with the enormous demand for communications bandwidth attracting tremendous competition. We know of no other fields in which technology moves so quickly and costs fall so rapidly.

When computer use exploded in the 1960s and 1970s, there was talk of the huge improvements in human productivity that computing and communications would bring about. However, these productivity improvements did not materialize. Organizations were spending vast sums on computers and distributing them to their workforces, but without immediate productivity gains. On the hardware side, it was the invention of microprocessor chip technology and its wide deployment in the late 1970s and 1980s which laid the groundwork for significant productivity improvements in the 1990s. On the software side, productivity improvements are now coming from object technology, which we use extensively in this book.

Recently, hardware has been moving more and more toward mobile, wireless technology. Small hand-held devices are now more powerful than the super computers of the early 1970s. Portability has become a major focus for the computer industry. Wireless data transfer speeds have become so fast that many Internet users' primary access to the Web is through local wireless networks. The speed of global roaming connections (via satellite) still lags behind LAN connections, though. The next few years will undoubtedly hold significant advances in wireless capabilities for personal users and businesses.

1.11 Key Software Trend: Object Technology

One of the authors, HMD, remembers the frustration that was felt in the 1960s by software development organizations, especially those developing large-scale projects. During his undergraduate years, HMD had the privilege of working summers at a leading computer vendor on the teams developing time-sharing, virtual-memory operating systems. In the summer of 1967, however, reality set in when the company "decommitted" from commercially producing the system that hundreds of people had been working on for many years. It was difficult to get this software right. Software is "complex stuff."

Hardware costs have been declining rapidly in recent years, to the point that personal computers have become a commodity. Unfortunately, software development costs have been rising steadily as programmers develop ever more powerful and complex applications without significantly improving the underlying technologies of software development.

Objects are essentially reusable software **components** that model real-world items. Software developers are discovering that using a modular, object-oriented design and implementation approach can make software development groups much more productive than was possible with previous popular programming techniques, such as structured programming. Object-oriented programs are often easier to understand, correct and modify.

Improvements to software technology began to appear as the benefits of structured programming (and the related discipline of **structured systems analysis and design**) were realized in the 1970s. It was not until the technology of object-oriented programming became widely used in the 1980s, and especially in the 1990s, that software developers finally felt they had the tools to make major strides in the software development process.

Actually, object technology dates back at least to the mid-1960s. The C++ programming language, developed at AT&T by Bjarne Stroustrup in the early 1980s, is based on two languages: C, which was initially developed at AT&T to implement the UNIX operating system in the early 1970s, and Simula 67, a simulation programming language developed in Europe and released in 1967. C++ absorbed the capabilities of C and added Simula's capabilities for creating and manipulating objects.

Before object-oriented languages appeared, programming languages (e.g., Fortran, Pascal, Basic and C) focused on actions (verbs), rather than things or objects (nouns). This style of programming is called **procedural programming**. One of the key problems with procedural programming is that the program units programmers create do not mirror real-world entities effectively, so they are not particularly reusable. We live in a world of objects. Just look around you. Cars, planes, people, businesses, animals, buildings, traffic lights and elevators are all examples of objects. It is not unusual for programmers to "start fresh" on each new project and wind up writing similar software from scratch. This wastes resources as people repeatedly "reinvent the wheel."

With object technology, properly designed software tends to be more reusable in future projects. Libraries of reusable components, such as **Microsoft Foundation Classes (MFC)**, Sun Microsystems's **Java Foundation Classes**, Microsoft's .NET **Framework Class Library (FCL)** and those produced by other software development organizations, can greatly reduce the effort it takes to implement certain kinds of systems (compared with the effort required to reinvent these capabilities on new projects).

Some organizations report that software reuse is not, in fact, the key benefit they derive from object-oriented programming. Rather, companies indicate that object-oriented programming tends to produce software that is more understandable, better organized and easier to maintain. These improvements are significant, because it has been estimated that as much as 80% of software costs are not associated with the original effort to develop the software, but are, in fact, attributed to the evolution and maintenance of the software throughout its lifetime. Whatever perceived benefits object orientation offers, it is clear that object-oriented programming will be the primary programming methodology for at least the next decade or two.

Software Engineering Observation 1.1

Use a building-block approach to creating programs. Avoid reinventing the wheel. Use existing pieces—this is called software reuse, *and it is central to object-oriented programming.*

[*Note*: We will include many **Software Engineering Observations** throughout the text to explain concepts that affect and improve the overall architecture and quality of a software system, and particularly of large software systems. We also highlight **Good Programming Practices** (practices that can help you write programs that are clearer, more understandable, more maintainable and easier to test and debug), **Common Programming Errors** (problems to watch out for so you do not make these same errors in your programs), **Performance Tips** (techniques that will help you write programs that run faster and use less memory), **Portability Tips** (techniques that will help you write programs that can run, with little or no modification, on a variety of computers), **Error-Prevention Tips** (techniques that will help you remove bugs from your programs and, more important, techniques that will help you write bug-free programs in the first place) and **Look-and-Feel Observations** (techniques that will help you design the "look" and "feel" of your graphical user interfaces for appearance and ease of use). Many of these techniques and practices are only guidelines; you will, no doubt, develop your own preferred programming style.]

Performance Tip 1.2

Reusing proven code components instead of writing your own versions can improve program performance, because these components normally are written to perform efficiently.

Software Engineering Observation 1.2

Extensive class libraries of reusable software components are available over the Internet and the World Wide Web. Many of these libraries are available at no charge.

1.12 JavaScript: Object-Based Scripting for the Web

JavaScript is an object-based scripting language with strong support for proper software engineering techniques. Students learn to create and manipulate objects from the start in JavaScript. JavaScript processing is available free in today's most popular Web browsers.

Does JavaScript provide the solid foundation of programming principles typically taught in first programming courses—the intended audience for this book? We think so.

The JavaScript chapters of this book are much more than just an introduction to the language. The chapters also present an introduction to computer programming fundamentals, including control structures, functions, arrays, recursion, strings and objects. Experienced programmers will read Chapters 7–12 quickly and master JavaScript by reading our live-code examples and by examining the corresponding input/output screens. Beginners will learn computer programming in these carefully paced chapters by reading the code explanations and completing a large number of exercises. We provide answers to only some of the exercises, because this is a textbook—college professors use the other exercises for homework assignments, labs, short quizzes, major examinations and even term projects.

JavaScript is a powerful scripting language. Experienced programmers sometimes take pride in creating strange, contorted, convoluted JavaScript expressions. This kind of coding makes programs more difficult to read, test and debug. This book is also geared for novice programmers; for them we stress program *clarity*.

Good Programming Practice 1.1

Write your programs in a simple and straightforward manner. This is sometimes referred to as KIS ("keep it simple"). Do not "stretch" the language by trying bizarre uses.

You will read that JavaScript is a portable scripting language and that programs written in JavaScript can run in many different Web browsers. Actually, *portability is an elusive goal*.

Portability Tip 1.1

Although it is easier to write portable programs in JavaScript than in many other programming languages, differences among interpreters and browsers make portability difficult to achieve. Simply writing programs in JavaScript does not guarantee portability. Programmers occasionally need to research platform variations and write their code accordingly.

Error-Prevention Tip 1.1

Always test your JavaScript programs on all systems and in all Web browsers for which they are intended.

Good Programming Practice 1.2

Read the documentation for the JavaScript version you are using to access JavaScript's rich collection of features.

Error-Prevention Tip 1.2

Your computer and JavaScript interpreter are good teachers. If you are not sure how a feature works even after studying the documentation, experiment and see what happens. Study each error or warning message and adjust the code accordingly.

JavaScript was created by Netscape. Microsoft's version of JavaScript is called JScript. Both Netscape and Microsoft have been instrumental in the standardization of JavaScript/ JScript by ECMA International as ECMAScript. ECMA International (formerly the European Computer Manufacturers Association) encourages Netscape and Microsoft to add new capabilities that build upon the ECMAScript standard. JScript, for example, provides access to several specialized objects that interact with other Microsoft technologies. Throughout most of this book, we refer to JavaScript and JScript generically as JavaScript. However, in Chapters 23–24, which focus on Microsoft's ASP.NET technology, we must specifically use Microsoft's JScript. We program ASP.NET pages using the next generation of JScript, JScript .NET, which has many characteristics of a fully object-oriented, high-level programming language, but retains all the features of a scripting language. After learning JavaScript in Chapters 7–12, the transition to JScript .NET should be straightforward.

1.13 Browser Portability

Ensuring a consistent look and feel on client-side browsers is one of the great challenges of developing Web-based applications. Currently, a standard does not exist to which software developers must adhere when creating Web browsers. Although browsers share a common set of features, each browser might render pages differently. Browsers are available in many versions (1.0, 2.0, etc.) and on many different platforms (UNIX, Microsoft Windows, Apple Macintosh, IBM OS/2, Linux, etc.). Vendors add features to each new version that result in increased cross-platform incompatibility issues. Clearly it is difficult, if not impossible, to develop Web pages that render correctly on all versions of each browser. This book attempts to minimize these problems by teaching XHTML, which is widely supported by browsers.

This book focuses on platform-independent topics, such as XHTML, JavaScript, Cascading Style Sheets, XML, Apache Web server, database/SQL/MySQL, Perl/CGI, PHP, ColdFusion and Python. However, it also features many topics that are Microsoft Windows–specific, including the Internet Explorer 6 browser, the Adobe Photoshop Elements graphics package for Windows, Dynamic HTML, VBScript, Internet Information Services (IIS), database access via ActiveX Data Objects .NET (ADO.NET) and ASP.NET.

Portability Tip 1.2

The Web is populated with many different browsers, which makes it difficult for authors and Web developers to create universal solutions. The W3C is working toward the goal of a universal client-side platform.

1.14 C and C++

For many years, the Pascal programming language was preferred for introductory and intermediate programming courses. The C language evolved from a language called B, developed by Dennis Ritchie at Bell Laboratories. C was implemented in 1972, making C a contemporary of Pascal. C initially became known as the development language of the UNIX operating system. Today, virtually all new major operating systems are written in C and/or C++.

Bjarne Stroustrup developed C++, an extension of C, in the early 1980s. C++ provides a number of features that "spruce up" the C language, but more importantly, it provides capabilities for object-oriented programming. C++ is a hybrid language: It is possible to program in either a C-like style (procedural programming) in which the focus is on actions, or an object-oriented style (in which the focus is on objects) or both. C and C++ have influenced many subsequent programming languages, such as Java, C#, JavaScript and JScript, each of which have a syntax similar to C and C++.

1.15 Java

Intelligent consumer electronic devices may be the next major area in which microprocessors will have a profound impact. Recognizing this, Sun Microsystems funded an internal corporate research project that was code-named Green in 1991. The project resulted in the development of an object-oriented language (based on C and C++), which its creator, James Gosling, called Oak, after an oak tree outside his office window. It was later discovered that a computer language already in use was named Oak. When a group of Sun employees visited a local coffee shop, the name **Java** was suggested, and it stuck.

The Green project ran into some difficulties, because the marketplace for intelligent consumer electronic devices was not developing as quickly as Sun had anticipated. Worse yet, a major contract for which Sun had competed was awarded to another company. The Green project was in jeopardy of being cancelled. By sheer good fortune, the World Wide Web exploded in popularity in 1993, and the people on the Green project saw the immediate potential to use Java as a Web programming language. This breathed new life into the project.

Java allows programmers to create Web pages that contain dynamic and interactive content. Developers can also use Java to create large-scale enterprise applications, to enhance the functionality of **Web servers** (software that provides the content we see in our Web browsers), to provide applications for consumer devices (e.g., wireless phones and personal digital assistants) and much more.

In 1995, we were carefully following Sun's development of Java. In November 1995, we attended an Internet conference in Boston in which a representative from Sun gave a rousing presentation on Java. As the talk proceeded, it became clear to us that Java would play an important part in developing Internet-based applications. Since its release, Java has become one of the most widely used programming languages in the world.

In addition to its prominence in developing Internet- and intranet-based applications, Java has become a language of choice for implementing software for devices that communicate over a network. Do not be surprised when your new stereo and other devices in your home are networked together using Java technology! Although we do not teach Java in this book, we have included, as a bonus for Java programmers, Chapter 36, Java Servlets, and Chapter 37, JavaServer Pages (both on the CD). Readers interested in learning Java may wish to read our texts, *Java How to Program, Fifth Edition* and *Advanced Java 2 Platform How to Program.*

1.16 Microsoft .NET

In June 2000, Microsoft announced its **.NET initiative**, a broad new vision for integrating the Internet and the Web in the development, engineering, distribution and use of software. Rather than forcing developers to use a single programming language, the .NET initiative permits them to create .NET applications in any .NET-compatible language (e.g., JScript .NET, C#, Visual Basic .NET, Visual C++ .NET and many others). Part of the initiative includes Microsoft's ASP.NET technology, which allows programmers to create Web-based, database-intensive, client/server applications. Using JScript .NET as the scripting language, we provide a thorough introduction to ASP.NET in Chapter 23 and a case study using ASP.NET and XML to build an online discussion forum in Chapter 24.

The .NET strategy extends the idea of software reuse to the Internet by allowing programmers to concentrate on their specialties without having to implement every component of every application. Instead, companies can buy **Web services**, which are Web-based programs that organizations can incorporate into their systems to speed the Web-application-development process. [*Note*: Microsoft's .NET strategy is not the only approach to Web services. Several Java-based systems for developing Web services also exist. We provide a more significant discussion of Web services, including examples and information about developing Web services, in Chapter 20, XML, and Chapter 23, ASP.NET.]

The Microsoft **.NET Framework** is at the heart of the .NET strategy. This framework executes applications and Web services, contains a class library (called the Framework Class Library, or FCL) and provides many other programming capabilities used to build .NET applications. In Chapters 23–24 of this book, you will learn how to develop .NET software with ASP.NET. Steve Ballmer, Microsoft's CEO, stated in May 2001 that Microsoft was "betting the company" on .NET. Such a dramatic commitment surely indicates a bright future for ASP.NET programmers.

1.17 Dynamic HTML

Dynamic HTML is geared to developing high-performance Web-based applications in which much of an application is executed directly on the client rather than on the server. Dynamic HTML makes Web pages "come alive" by providing stunning multimedia effects that include animation, audio and video. What exactly is Dynamic HTML? This is an interesting question, because if you walk into a computer store or scan online software stores, you will not find a product by this name offered for sale. Rather, Dynamic HTML, which has at least two versions—Microsoft's and Netscape's—consists of a number of technologies that are freely available and are known by other names. Microsoft *Dynamic HTML*, for example, includes XHTML, JavaScript, Cascading Style Sheets, the Dynamic HTML object model and event model, and ActiveX controls—each of which we discuss in this book—and other related technologies. Netscape *Dynamic HTML* provides similar capabilities.[1] Microsoft *Dynamic HTML* is introduced in Chapters 13–16, and additional Dynamic HTML features are presented as bonus material in Chapters 30–31 (on the CD).

1.18 Internet and World Wide Web How to Program

In 1998, we saw an explosion of interest in the Internet and the World Wide Web. We immersed ourselves in these technologies, and a clear picture started to emerge in our minds of the next direction to take in writing textbooks for introductory programming courses. **Electronic commerce**, or **e-commerce**, as it is typically called, began to dominate the business, financial and computer industry news. This was a total reconceptualization of the way business was conducted. We still wanted to teach programming principles, but we felt compelled to do it in the context of the technologies that businesses and organizations needed to create Internet-based and Web-based applications. With this realization, the first edition of *Internet and World Wide Web How to Program* was born and published in December of 1999.

Internet and World Wide Web How to Program, Third Edition teaches programming languages and programming-language principles. In addition, we focus on the broad range of technologies that will help you build real-world Internet-based and Web-based applications that interact with other applications and with databases. These capabilities allow programmers to develop the kinds of enterprise-level, distributed applications popular in industry today. If you have been hearing a great deal about the Internet and the World Wide Web lately, and if you are interested in developing applications to run over the Internet and the Web, then learning the software-development techniques discussed in this book could be the key to challenging and rewarding career opportunities for you. Please be sure to check out Appendix G, Career Opportunities (on the CD).

In this book, you will learn computer programming and basic principles of computer science and information technology. You also will learn proven software-development methods—top-down stepwise-refinement, functionalization and object-based programming. JavaScript is our primary programming language, a condensed programming language that is especially designed for developing Internet- and Web-based applications. Chapters 7–12 present a rich discussion of JavaScript and its capabilities, including dozens of complete examples followed by screen images that illustrate typical program inputs and outputs.

After you learn programming principles from the detailed JavaScript discussions, we present condensed treatments of seven other popular Internet/Web programming languages for building the server side of Internet- and Web-based client/server applications. In Chapters 23–24, we discuss ASP.NET—Microsoft's technology for server-side scripting. ASP.NET pages can be written in several full-scale programming languages, including Visual Basic .NET and C#; however, since this book focuses on scripting languages, we code ASP.NET pages using Microsoft's JScript .NET. Chapter 25 introduces Perl—throughout the 1990s, Perl was the most widely used scripting language for programming Web-based applications, and it is certain to remain popular for many years. Chapter 26 introduces PHP, another popular scripting language. Chapter 27 presents ColdFusion, a tag-based, server-side technology from Macromedia designed to build powerful database-intensive Web applications. Chapter 32 introduces the VBScript scripting language that is used in Chapters 33 and 34 to code Active Server Pages (ASP), the predecessor to ASP.NET. Chapter 35 familiarizes the reader

---

1. Microsoft Dynamic HTML and Netscape Dynamic HTML are incompatible. In this book, we focus on Microsoft Dynamic HTML. We have tested all of the Dynamic HTML examples in Microsoft Internet Explorer 6 and Netscape 7.1. All of these examples execute in Microsoft Internet Explorer; most do not execute in Netscape 7.1. We have posted the testing results at www.deitel.com. The Macromedia® Flash™ material we present in Chapters 17–18 executes properly in the latest Microsoft and Netscape browsers.

with Python, a cross-platform, object-oriented scripting language comparable to Perl and PHP. Finally, Chapters 36–37 are bonus chapters for Java programmers on Java servlets and JavaServer Pages (JSP). [*Note*: Due to the volume of information presented in this book, Chapters 30 and higher can be found on accompanying CD-ROM as Adobe PDF documents. You can download the Adobe® Reader® (formerly Adobe Acrobat® Reader) program from www.adobe.com/products/acrobat/readstep2.html.]

Well, there you have it! We have worked hard to create this book, which is loaded with hundreds of working, live-code examples, programming tips, self-review exercises and answers, challenging exercises and projects and numerous study aids to help you master the material. The technologies we introduce will help you write Web-based applications quickly and effectively. As you read the book, if something is not clear or if you find an error, please write to us at deitel@deitel.com. We will respond promptly, and we will post corrections, clarifications and additional materials on our Web site

> www.deitel.com

Prentice Hall maintains www.prenhall.com/deitel—a Web site dedicated to our Prentice Hall textbooks, multimedia packages and Web-based e-learning training products. For each of our books, the site contains "Companion Web Sites" that include frequently asked questions (FAQs), sample downloads, errata, updates, additional self-test questions, Microsoft® PowerPoint® slides and other resources.

You are about to start on a challenging and rewarding path. We hope you will enjoy learning with *Internet and World Wide Web How to Program, Third Edition*!

1.19 Web Resources

www.deitel.com
Please check this site for updates, corrections and additional resources for all Deitel & Associates, Inc., publications.

netforbeginners.about.com
The About.com *Internet for Beginners* guide provides valuable resources for further exploration of the history and workings of the Internet and the World Wide Web.

www.learnthenet.com/english/index.html
Learn the Net is a Web site containing a complete overview of the Internet, the World Wide Web and the underlying technologies. The site contains much information appropriate for novices.

www.w3.org
The World Wide Web Consortium (W3C) Web site offers a comprehensive description of Web technologies. For each Internet technology with which the W3C is involved, the site provides a description of the technology, its benefits to Web designers, the history of the technology and the future goals of the W3C in developing the technology.

www.ukans.edu/cwis/units/coms2/class/intro/index.htm
This University of Kansas Web site gives a comprehensive overview of the Internet and the World Wide Web, with an interactive slide presentation of each topic covered.

members.tripod.com/~teachers/index.html
This site introduces novices to the Internet and the World Wide Web, targeting users who will be surfing the Web in a classroom setting.

www.ed.gov/pubs/OR/ConsumerGuides/internet.html
The U.S. Department of Education's Consumer Guide provides a clear, concise tutorial on the structure, content and compatibilities of the Internet and the Web.

SUMMARY

- In an era of steadily rising costs, computing costs have been decreasing dramatically because of rapid developments in both hardware and software technologies.

- Technologies such as Extensible HyperText Markup Language (XHTML), JavaScript, Dynamic HTML, Flash, Dreamweaver and Extensible Markup Language (XML) are used to build the portions of Web-based applications that reside on the client side (i.e., the portions of applications that typically run on Web browsers such as Netscape or Microsoft's Internet Explorer).

- Technologies such as Web servers, databases, ASP.NET, CGI, Perl, PHP and ColdFusion are used to build the server side of Web-based applications. These portions of applications typically run on "heavy-duty" computer systems on which organizations' business-critical Web sites reside.

- A computer is a device capable of performing computations and making logical decisions at speeds billions of times faster than human beings can.

- Computers process data under the direction of sets of instructions called computer programs.

- Computer programs guide the computer through orderly sets of actions specified by people called computer programmers.

- The various devices, such as the keyboard, screen, disks, memory and processing units, that comprise a computer system are referred to as hardware.

- The computer programs that run on a computer are referred to as software. Programmers write the instructions that comprise software in various programming languages, some that the computer can apply directly and others that require intermediate translation steps.

- Research activity in the 1960s resulted in the evolution of structured programming—a disciplined approach to writing programs that are clearer and easier to test, debug and modify.

- In the late 1960s, ARPA, the USA Advanced Research Projects Agency of the Department of Defense rolled out the blueprints for networking the main computer systems of about a dozen ARPA-funded universities and research institutions. ARPA then proceeded to implement the ARPANET, the predecessor to today's Internet.

- In 1977, Apple Computer popularized personal computing. Initially, it was a hobbyist's dream, but computers quickly became economical enough for people to buy for personal use.

- In 1981, IBM, the world's largest computer vendor, introduced the IBM Personal Computer, legitimizing computing in business, industry and government organizations.

- Information is easily shared across computer networks such as the Internet in which some computers, called servers, offer common stores of programs and data that may be used by client computers distributed throughout the network—hence the term client/server computing.

- The World Wide Web allows computer users to locate and view multimedia-based documents (i.e., documents with text, graphics, animations, audios or videos) on almost any subject.

- In 1990, Tim Berners-Lee of CERN (the European Organization for Nuclear Research) developed the World Wide Web and several communication protocols that form the backbone of the Web.

- The use of the Web exploded with the availability in 1993 of the Mosaic browser, which featured a user-friendly graphical interface. Marc Andreessen, whose team at the National Center for Supercomputing Applications (NCSA) developed Mosaic, went on to found Netscape, the company that many people credit with initiating the explosive Internet economy of the late 1990s.

- In October 1994, Tim Berners-Lee founded the World Wide Web Consortium (W3C)—an organization devoted to developing nonproprietary, interoperable technologies for the World Wide Web.

- Every year or two, the capacities of computers tend to double, especially the amount of memory they have in which to execute programs, the amount of secondary storage (e.g., hard disk drives) they have to hold programs and data over the longer term, and the processor speeds—the speed at which computers execute their programs (i.e., do their work).

- Objects are essentially reusable software components that model real-world items.

- Using a modular, object-oriented design and implementation approach can make software development groups much more productive than was possible with previous popular programming techniques, such as structured programming.

- Object-oriented programs are often easier to understand, correct and modify.

- Before object-oriented languages appeared, programming languages (e.g., Fortran, Pascal, Basic and C) focused on actions (verbs), rather than things or objects (nouns). This style of programming is called procedural programming.

- Libraries of reusable components, such as MFC (Microsoft Foundation Classes), Sun Microsystems's Java Foundation Classes, Microsoft's .NET Framework Class Library and those produced by other software development organizations, can greatly reduce the effort it takes to implement certain kinds of systems.

- Object-oriented programming tends to produce software that is more understandable, better organized and easier to maintain.

- JavaScript is an object-based scripting language with strong support for proper software engineering techniques.

- JavaScript was created by Netscape. Microsoft's version of JavaScript is called JScript. Both Netscape and Microsoft have been instrumental in the standardization of JavaScript/JScript by ECMA International as ECMAScript.

- The latest generation of JScript, JScript .NET, has many characteristics of a fully object-oriented, high-level programming language, but retains all the features of a scripting language.

- Ensuring a consistent look-and-feel on client-side browsers is one of the great challenges of developing Web-based applications.

- Java allows programmers to create Web pages with dynamic and interactive content. Developers can use it to create large-scale enterprise applications, to enhance the functionality of Web servers (software that provides the content we see in our Web browsers), to provide applications for consumer devices (e.g., wireless phones and personal digital assistants) and much more.

- The .NET strategy extends the idea of software reuse to the Internet by allowing programmers to concentrate on their specialties without having to implement every component of every application.

- Web services are Web-based programs that organizations can incorporate into their systems to speed the Web-application-development process.

- The Microsoft .NET Framework executes applications and Web services, contains a class library (called the Framework Class Library or FCL) and provides many other programming capabilities used to build .NET applications.

- Dynamic HTML is geared to developing high-performance Web-based applications in which much of an application is executed directly on the client rather than on the server.

- Dynamic HTML makes Web pages "come alive" by providing stunning multimedia effects that include animation, audio and video.

TERMINOLOGY

ASP.NET	bandwidth
action	Basic
ActionScript	browser

ActiveX Data Objects .NET (ADO.NET)
Ada
Apache Web Server
arithmetic and logic unit (ALU)
ARPA
ARPANET
assembly language
client-side scripting
Cobol
ColdFusion
compiler
computer
computer program
computer programmer
database
decision
disk
Dynamic HTML
e-commerce
e-mail
Extensible HyperText Markup
    Language (XHTML)
Extensible Markup Language (XML)
Fortran
Graphical User Interface (GUI)
hardware
high-level language
input device
input unit
input/output (I/O)
Internet
Internet Explorer 6
Internet Information Services (IIS)
interpreter
intranet
IP (Internet Protocol)
Java
Java servlet
JavaScript
JavaServer Pages (JSP)
JScript
JScript .NET
KIS (keep it simple)
machine language
memory unit
Microsoft
multimedia
multitasking

C
C#
C++
Cascading Style Sheets (CSS)
central processing unit (CPU)
client
client/server computing
multithreading
multi-tier application
MySQL database
.NET Framework
Netscape
object
object-based programming (OBP)
object-oriented programming (OOP)
output device
output unit
packet switching
Pascal
Perl
personal computing
Photoshop Elements
PHP
platform
primary memory (RAM)
procedural programming
programming language
Python
reusable component
scripting language
secondary storage unit
server-side scripting
Simula 67
software
software reuse
structured programming
Sun Microsystems
supercomputer
TCP (Transmission Control Protocol)
TCP/IP
translator program
UNIX
VBScript
Visual Basic .NET
W3C Recommendation
Web server
Web services
World Wide Web Consortium (W3C)

SELF-REVIEW EXERCISES

1.1   Fill in the blanks in each of the following statements:
a) The company that popularized personal computing was _____.
b) The computer that made personal computing legitimate in business and industry was the _____.
c) Computers process data under the control of sets of instructions called _____.
d) The six key logical units of the computer are the _____, _____, _____, _____, _____ and _____.
e) The three classes of languages discussed in the chapter are _____, _____ and _____.
f) The programs that translate high-level language programs into machine language are called _____ or interpreters.

1.2   Fill in the blanks in each of the following statements:
a) The _____ programming language was created by Professor Nicklaus Wirth and was intended for academic use.
b) One important capability of Ada is called _____; this allows programmers to specify that many activities are to occur in parallel.
c) The _____ was the predecessor to the Internet.
d) The information-carrying capacity of a communications medium like the Internet is called _____.
e) The acronym TCP/IP stands for _____.

1.3   Fill in the blanks in each of the following statements.
a) The _____ allows computer users to locate and view multimedia-based documents on almost any subject over the Internet.
b) _____ developed the World Wide Web and several of the communications protocols that form the backbone of the Web.
c) _____ are essentially reusable software components that model items in the real world.
d) C initially became widely known as the development language of the _____ operating system.
e) In a typical client/server relationship, the _____ requests that some action be performed and the _____ performs the action and responds.

ANSWERS TO SELF-REVIEW EXERCISES

1.1   a) Apple. b) IBM Personal Computer. c) programs (or scripts). d) input unit, output unit, memory unit, arithmetic and logic unit, central processing unit, secondary storage unit. e) machine languages, assembly languages, high-level languages. f) compilers.

1.2   a) Pascal. b) multitasking. c) ARPANET. d) bandwidth. e) Transmission Control Protocol/Internet Protocol.

1.3   a) World Wide Web. b) Tim Berners-Lee. c) Objects. d) UNIX. e) client, server.

EXERCISES

1.4   Categorize each of the following items as either hardware or software:
a) CPU
b) compiler
c) ALU
d) interpreter

    e) input unit

    f) an editor program

1.5   Fill in the blanks in each of the following statements:

    a) Which logical unit of the computer receives information from outside the computer for use by the computer? _____.

    b) The process of instructing the computer to solve specific problems is called _____.

    c) What type of computer language uses English-like abbreviations for machine-language instructions? _____.

    d) Which logical unit of the computer sends information that has already been processed by the computer to various devices so that the information may be used outside the computer? _____.

    e) Which logical unit of the computer retains information? _____.

    f) Which logical unit of the computer performs calculations? _____.

    g) Which logical unit of the computer makes logical decisions? _____.

    h) The level of computer language most convenient to the programmer for writing programs quickly and easily is _____.

    i) The only language that a computer can directly apply is called that computer's _____.

    j) Which logical unit of the computer coordinates the activities of all the other logical units? _____.

1.6   What is the relationship between JavaScript, JScript and ECMAScript?

1.7   Fill in the blanks in each of the following statements:

    a) Microsoft's .NET initiative permits developers to create .NET applications in any .NET-compatible language (e.g., _____, _____, _____ and _____).

    b) The Microsoft .NET Framework contains a class library called the _____ that provides many programming capabilities used to build .NET applications.

    c) _____ are Web-based programs that organizations can incorporate into their systems to speed the Web-application-development process.

2

Microsoft Internet Explorer 6

Objectives

- To become familiar with the Microsoft Internet Explorer 6 (IE6) Web browser's capabilities.
- To be able to use IE6 to search the "world of information" available on the World Wide Web.
- To be able to use the Internet as an information tool.
- To become familiar with e-mail.
- To learn about instant messaging.
- To become aware of the differences between various browsers.

Give us the tools, and we will finish the job.
Sir Winston Churchill

We must learn to explore all the options and possibilities that confront us in a complex and rapidly changing world.
J. William Fulbright

2.1 Introduction to the Internet Explorer 6 Web Browser

The Internet is an essential medium for communicating and interacting with people world-wide. The need to publish and share information has fueled the rapid growth of the Web. **Web browsers** are software programs that allow users to access the Web's rich multimedia content. Whether for business or for personal use, millions of people use Web browsers to access the tremendous amount of information available on the Web.

The two most popular Web browsers are Microsoft's *Internet Explorer* and *Netscape*. This chapter focuses on the features of Internet Explorer (IE6) to view, exchange and transfer information, such as images, messages and documents, over the Internet. We provide an equivalent chapter-length treatment on Netscape 7.1 at our Web site, www.deitel.com. This chapter also introduces e-mail, instant messaging and alternative Web browsers.

2.2 Connecting to the Internet

A computer alone is not enough to access the Internet. In addition to Web browser software, the computer needs specific hardware and a connection to an Internet Service Provider to view Web pages. This section describes the necessary components that enable Internet access.

First, a computer must have a **modem** or **network card**. A modem is hardware that enables a computer to connect to a **network**. A modem converts data to audio tones and transmits the data over phone lines. A network card, also called a **network interface card** (**NIC**), is hardware that allows a computer to connect to the Internet through a network or a high-speed Internet connection, such as a **local area network** (**LAN**), **cable modem** or a **Digital Subscriber Line** (**DSL**).

After ensuring that a computer has a modem or a network card (most computers come with one or both of these), the next step is to register with an **Internet Service Provider** (**ISP**). Computers connect to an ISP using a modem and phone line, or via a NIC using a LAN, DSL or cable modem. The ISP connects computers to the Internet. Many college campuses have free network connections available. If a network connection is not available, then popular commercial ISPs, such as America Online (`www.aol.com`), Microsoft Network (`www.msn.com`) and NetZero (`www.netzero.net`), are alternatives.

Bandwidth and cost are two considerations when deciding which commercial ISP service to use. Bandwidth refers to the amount of data that can be transferred through a communications medium in a fixed amount of time. Different ISPs offer different types of high-speed connections, called **broadband connections**, which include DSL, cable modem, **Integrated Services Digital Network (ISDN)** and slower **dial-up connections**, each of which has a different bandwidth and cost to users.

Broadband is a category of high-bandwidth Internet service that is most often provided to home users by cable television and telephone companies. DSL is a broadband service that allows computers to be connected at all times to the Internet over existing phone lines, without interfering with telephone services. However, DSL requires a special modem provided by the ISP. Like DSL, cable modems enable the computer to be connected to the Internet at all times. Cable modems transmit data over the cables that bring television to homes and businesses. Unlike DSL, the bandwidth is shared by many users. This sharing can reduce the bandwidth available to each person when many use the system simultaneously. ISDN provides Internet service over either digital or standard telephone lines. ISDN requires specialized hardware, called a **terminal adaptor (TA)**, which is usually obtained from the ISP.

Dial-up service uses an existing telephone line. If a computer is connected to the Internet, the user usually cannot receive voice calls during this time. If the voice calls do connect, the Internet connection is interrupted. To prevent this, users often install an extra phone line dedicated to Internet service.

Once a network connection is established, the **Internet Connection Wizard** (ICW) in Windows 98 and 2000, or the **New Connection Wizard** in Windows XP, can be used to configure the computer to connect to the Internet. You can access either wizard through the **Start** menu. Select the **Accessories** option in the **Programs** menu (**All Programs** in Windows XP), then **Communications** and **Internet Connection Wizard** (**New Connection Wizard** in Windows XP). Input the connection information provided by the ISP, following the instructions in the **Internet Connection Wizard** dialog (Fig. 2.1).[1] Click **Tutorial** (in Windows 2000 only) to learn more about the Internet and its features. Once the **Internet Connection Wizard** finishes, the computer can connect to the Internet.

2.3 Internet Explorer 6 Features

A Web browser is software that allows the user to view certain types of Internet files in an interactive environment. Figure 2.2 shows the Deitel Home Page using Internet Explorer 6 Web browser. The **URL (Uniform Resource Locator)** `http://www.deitel.com/` is found in the **Address** bar. The URL specifies the address (i.e., location) of the Web page displayed in the browser window. Each Web page on the Internet is associated with a unique URL. URLs usually begin with `http://`, which stands for **Hypertext Transfer Protocol (HTTP)**, the industry standard protocol (or set of communication rules) for transferring Web documents over the Internet. URLs of Web sites that handle private information, such as credit card numbers, often begin with `https://`, the abbreviation for **Secure Hypertext Transfer Protocol (HTTPS)**, the standard for transferring encrypted data over the Internet.

---

1.   All screen shots in this chapter were taken on a computer running Windows 2000. Screen shots may differ slightly for Windows XP users.

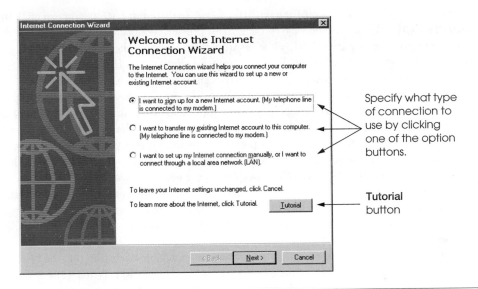

Specify what type
of connection to
use by clicking
one of the option
buttons.

Tutorial
button

Fig. 2.1   **Internet Connection Wizard** helps configure Internet access.

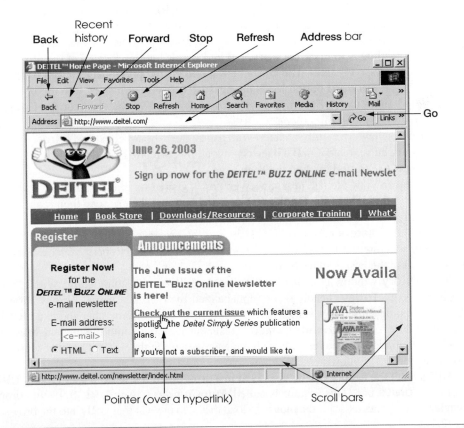

Fig. 2.2   Deitel® Web site.

There are several techniques for navigating between different URLs. You can click the **Address** field and type a Web page's URL, then press *Enter* or click **Go** to request the Web page located at that URL. For example, to visit Yahoo!'s Web site, type `www.yahoo.com` in the **Address** bar and press the *Enter* key. IE6 adds the `http://` prefix to the Web site name because HTTP is the default protocol used for the Web.

Another way to navigate the Web is via visual elements on Web pages called **hyperlinks** that, when clicked, load a specified Web document. Both images and text may be hyperlinked. When the mouse pointer hovers over a hyperlink, the default arrow pointer changes into a hand with the index finger pointing upward. Often hyperlinked text appears underlined or as a different color than the text that is not hyperlinked. Originally used as a publishing tool for scientific research, hyperlinking creates the effect of the "Web."

Hyperlinks can reference other Web pages, e-mail addresses and files. If a hyperlink is an e-mail address, clicking the link loads the browser's default e-mail program and opens a **message window** addressed to the specified recipient's e-mail address. E-mail is discussed later in this chapter.

If a hyperlink references a file that the browser is incapable of displaying, the browser prepares to **download** the file by prompting the user for information. When a file is downloaded, it is copied onto the user's computer. Programs, documents, images and sound files are all examples of downloadable files.

IE6 maintains a **history** list of previously visited URLs in chronological order. This feature allows users to return to recently visited Web sites easily.

The history feature can be accessed several different ways. The simplest and most frequently used method is to click the **Forward** and **Back** buttons located at the top of the browser window (see Fig. 2.2). The **Back** button reloads the previously viewed page into the browser. The **Forward** button loads the next URL from the history into the browser. The keyboard shortcut for **Forward** is *Alt+Right Arrow*, and the shortcut for **Back** is *Alt+Left Arrow* or simply *Backspace*.

When users view frequently updated Web pages, they should click the **Refresh** button to load the most current version. If a page is not loading correctly or is slow, click the **Stop** button or press *Esc* to stop loading the Web page.

The user can view the last/next nine Web pages visited by clicking the down-arrows immediately to the right of the **Back** and **Forward** buttons; the user can then request one of the recently viewed pages by clicking the title of the page in the drop-down list.

Clicking the **History** button (Fig. 2.3) divides the browser window into two sections: the **History** window (on the left) and the content window. The **History** window lists the URLs visited in the past 20 days by default.

The **History** window contains heading levels ordered chronologically. Within each time frame (e.g., **Today**) headings are alphabetized by Web site name. This window is useful for finding previously visited URLs without having to remember the exact URL. Selecting a URL from the **History** window loads the Web page into the content window. The **History** window can be resized by clicking and dragging the vertical bar that separates it from the content window.

URLs from the history can be displayed in a drop-down list when a user types a URL into the **Address** bar. This feature is called **AutoComplete**. Any URL from this drop-down list can be selected with the mouse to load the Web page at that URL into the browser (Fig. 2.4).\

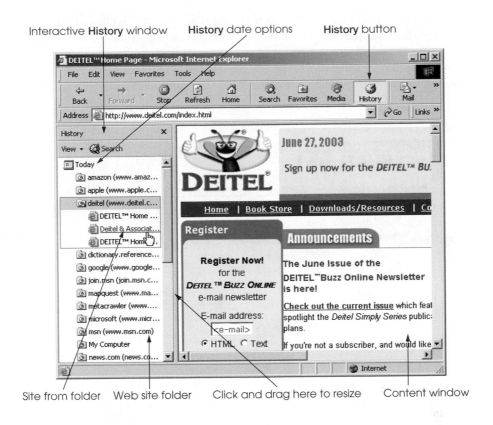

Fig. 2.3　The **History** menu lists previously visited Web sites.

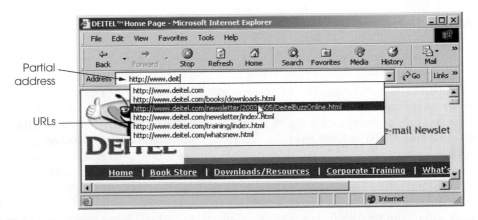

Fig. 2.4　AutoComplete suggests possible URLs when given a partial address.

For some users, such as those with dial-up connections, maintaining a connection for long periods of time may not be practical. For this reason, Web pages can be saved directly to the computer's hard drive for **off-line** browsing (i.e., browsing while not connected to the Internet). Select **Save As...** from the **File** menu at the top of the browser window to save a Web page and all its components (e.g., images).

Individual images from a Web site can also be saved by clicking the image with the right mouse button and selecting **Save Picture As...** from the displayed **context menu** (Fig. 2.5).

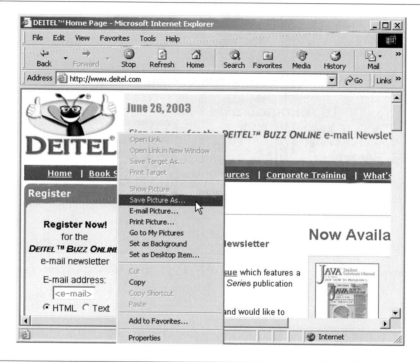

Fig. 2.5   Saving a picture from a Web site.

2.4 Searching the Internet

The Internet provides a wealth of information on virtually any topic. You might think that the volume of information would make it difficult for users to find specific information. To help users locate information, many Web sites provide **search engines** that explore the Internet and maintain searchable records containing information about Web site content. This section explains how search engines work and discusses two types of search engines.

Search engines such as Google (`www.google.com`), Yahoo! (`www.yahoo.com`), AlltheWeb (`www.alltheweb.com`), AltaVista (`www.altavista.com`) and Lycos (`www.lycos.com`) store information in data repositories called **databases** that facilitate quick information retrieval. When the user enters a word or phrase, the search engine returns a list of hyperlinks to sites that satisfy the search criteria. Each search-engine site has different criteria for narrowing searches, such as publishing date, language and relevance. Using multiple search engines may provide the best results in finding the desired content quickly.

Sites such as MSN (www.msn.com) and MetaCrawler (www.metacrawler.com) use **metasearch engines**, which do not maintain databases. Instead, they send the search criteria to other search engines and aggregate the results. IE6 has a built-in metasearch engine that is accessed by clicking the **Search** button in the toolbar (Fig. 2.6). As with the history feature, the browser window divides into two sections, with the **Search** window on the left and the content window on the right. Several predefined searching categories are provided. Type the keyword for which you are searching and click the **Search** button. The search results appear as hyperlinks in the **Search** window. Clicking a hyperlink loads the Web page at that URL into the content window.

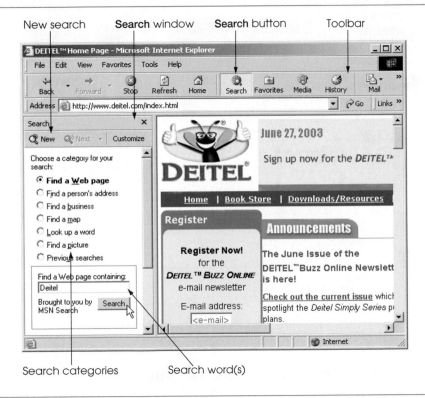

Fig. 2.6   Searching the Internet with IE6.

2.5 Online Help and Tutorials

Web browsers are complex pieces of software with rich functionality. Although browser designers make every effort to produce user-friendly software, users still need time to familiarize themselves with each Web browser and its particular features. Answers to frequently asked questions about using the Web browser are included with IE6. This information is accessible through the built-in help feature available in the **Help** menu (Fig. 2.7).

A good source for locating help about a specific feature is the **Contents and Index** menu item accessible through the **Help** menu. When **Contents and Index** is selected, the Microsoft Internet Explorer help dialog is displayed. The **Contents** tab organizes the help topics by category, the **Index** tab contains an alphabetical list of **Help** topics and the

Help menu

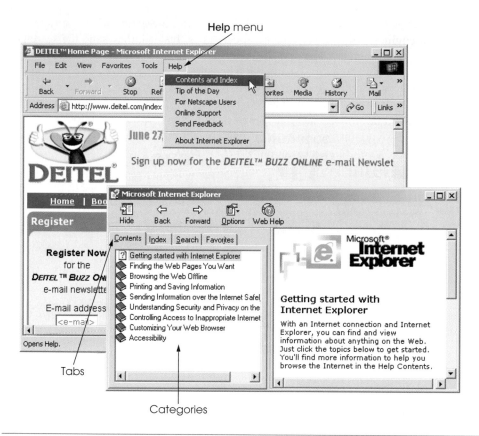

Fig. 2.7   IE6 **Help** dialog.

Search tab provides capabilities for searching the help documents. The **Favorites** tab allows users to maintain a list of frequently used help topics.

2.6 Keeping Track of Your Favorite Sites

As users browse the Web, they often visit certain sites repeatedly, and may want to record their URL and title. Internet Explorer provides a feature called **favorites** for bookmarking (keeping track of) such sites (Fig. 2.8). Any page's URL can be added to the list of favorites using the **Favorites** menu's **Add to Favorites...** command. A **Favorites** window can also be accessed by clicking the **Favorites** icon on the toolbar.

Favorites can be accessed at any time by selecting them with the mouse from the **Favorites** menu. Favorites can be categorized and grouped into folders in the **Organize Favorites** dialog (displayed when **Organize Favorites...** is selected from the **Favorites** menu). These folders appear as sub-menus in the **Favorites** menu. The **Organize Favorites** dialog also allows users to rename, delete and move favorites between folders. For each favorite, the **Organize Favorites** dialog displays information about how frequently that page is visited. Favorites may also be saved for off-line browsing by selecting the **Make available offline** checkbox in the **Organize Favorites** dialog.

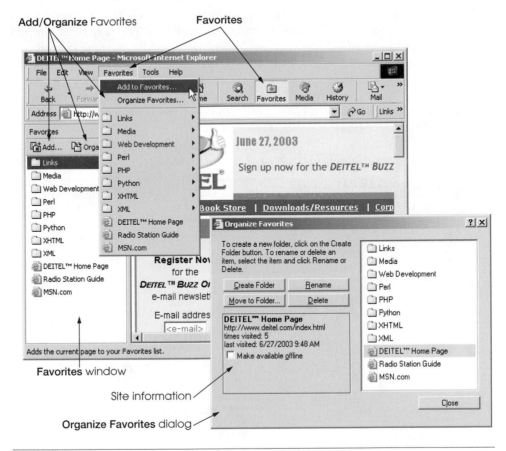

Fig. 2.8   **Favorites** menu helps organize frequently visited Web sites.

2.7 File Transfer Protocol (FTP)

As mentioned earlier, files from the Internet may be copied to a computer's hard drive by a process called **downloading.** This section discusses the types of documents commonly downloaded from the Internet and techniques for downloading them.

The most common Internet downloads are **applications** (i.e., software that performs specific functions, such as word processing) and **plug-ins**. Plug-ins are specialized pieces of software that extend other applications, such as IE6, by providing additional functionality. An example of an IE6 plug-in is the **Acrobat Reader** from **Adobe, Inc.** (www.adobe.com), which allows users to view **PDF** (**Portable Document Format**) documents that otherwise cannot be rendered by the browser. Another popular plug-in allows the browser to render **Macromedia Shockwave** content, which adds audio, video and animation effects to a Web site. To view sites enabled with Shockwave, download the Shockwave Player plug-in at sdc.shockwave.com/shockwave/download/download.cgi. Normally the browser prompts the user to download a plug-in when one is needed. Plugins may also be downloaded from CNET (www.download.com). This site has a large, searchable index and database of many plug-in programs available for download.

When browsing the Web, downloading often is initiated by clicking a hyperlink that references a document at an **FTP (File Transfer Protocol)** site. FTP is an older, but still popular, protocol for transferring information, especially large files, over the Internet.

An FTP site's URL begins with `ftp://` rather than `http://`. FTP sites are typically accessed via hyperlinks, but can also be accessed by any software that supports FTP. Such software may or may not use a Web browser. **Ipswitch WS_FTP™ LE** is a popular stand-alone FTP client that functions outside of a Web browser. It is free for noncommercial users and can be downloaded from `www.ftpplanet.com`.

When IE6 is pointed to an FTP site's URL, the contents of the specified site directory appear in the right side of the window, with FTP information on the left (Fig. 2.9). Two types of icons may appear in a directory: files and directories. Files are downloaded by right clicking their icons, selecting **Copy to Folder...** and specifying the location where the files are to be saved.

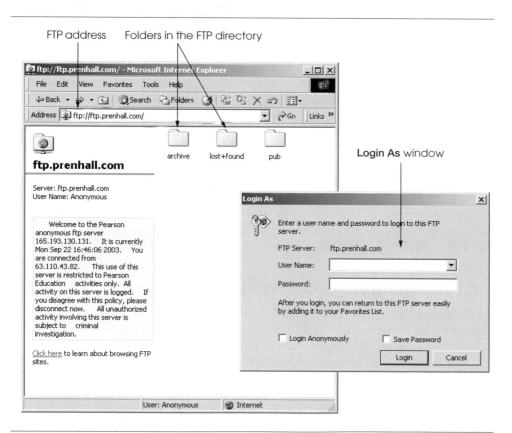

Fig. 2.9 FTP site access in IE6.

When a user visits an FTP site, IE6 sends the user's e-mail address and name (which is set by default to *anonymous*) to the site. This procedure occurs on FTP sites that allow **anonymous FTP access**, where any user is permitted access. Many FTP sites on the Internet contain directories with **restricted access**; only users with authorized user names and passwords are permitted to access such directories. When a user is trying to enter a restricted-access FTP directory, a **Login As** dialog like the one in Fig. 2.9 is displayed, prompting the user for log-in information.

Transferring a file from the local machine to another location on the Internet is called **uploading** and can be accomplished using the FTP protocol. To place information on a Web site, the files must be uploaded to a specific restricted-access FTP server (this is dependent on the ISP). The process involves uploading the file to a directory on the FTP site that is accessible through the Web.

2.8 Customizing Browser Settings

Internet Explorer 6 has many settings that determine how sites are displayed, how security measures are applied and how outputs are rendered. Most of these settings are located in the **Internet Options** dialog (Fig. 2.10). The default settings are usually adequate for normal browsing, but these settings can be customized to suit each user's preferences.

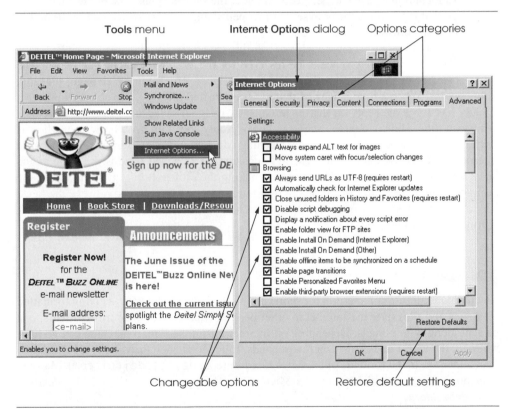

Fig. 2.10   Internet Options in IE6.

Consider some of the more significant options that affect your browsing experience. If you are browsing the Web with a slow connection, the page download time can be decreased by deselecting the **Show Pictures** setting, located in the **Multimedia** category under the **Advanced** tab. Toggling this setting off (i.e., unchecking it) prevents the browser from loading Web-page images. Images can require considerable time to download, so this toggle could save time during browsing sessions. [*Note*: Many Web pages rely on images to display properly. Deselecting the **Show Pictures** setting may affect these pages' functionality.]

Default programs used for common Internet procedures such as sending e-mail are set in the **Programs** tab. These settings allow the user to specify which programs IE6 should execute when there is a need for their respective technologies while browsing. For example, if Microsoft Outlook Express is designated as the default e-mail program, every time an e-mail hyperlink is clicked, Outlook Express opens an e-mail message dialog addressed to the designated recipient.

The security level for IE6 can be set under the **Privacy** tab. There are four levels of security. The most lenient level permits the downloading of **cookies** (text files that are placed on the computer by Web sites to retain or gather information about the user); the most strict level renders a constant flow of alerts and alarms about browsing security and might prevent certain Web sites from working correctly.

A personal home page can be specified under the **General** tab. The home page is the Web page that loads when the browser is first opened and appears when the **Home** button at the top of the browser window is clicked.

History options also may be adjusted in this category. By clicking the **Settings...** button, the amount of disk space to be reserved for the Web page **cache** can be set. The cache is an area on the hard drive that a browser designates for saving Web pages for rapid future access. When a page is viewed that has been visited recently, IE6 checks whether it already has some elements on that page (such as images) saved in the cache, to reduce download time. Having a large cache can considerably speed up Web browsing, whereas having a small cache saves disk space. Caching can sometimes cause problems, because Internet Explorer does not always check to ensure that a cached page is the same as the latest version residing on the Web server. Clicking the **Refresh** button at the top of the browser window remedies this problem by forcing Internet Explorer to retrieve the latest version of the Web page from the Web site. Once the **Internet Options** are set, click **Apply** and click **OK**.

2.9 Electronic Mail

Electronic mail (**e-mail** or **email** for short) is a method of sending and receiving formatted messages and files over the Internet to other people. Other files, called **attachments**, can be sent along with e-mails. Depending on Internet traffic, an e-mail message can go anywhere in the world in as little as a few seconds. Internet Service Providers (ISPs) issue e-mail addresses in the form *username@domainname* (e.g., `deitel@deitel.com`). Many e-mail programs are available, such as Microsoft's *Outlook Express* (Fig. 2.11), *Pegasus Mail* and *Eudora*.

E-mail programs must be configured to access an e-mail account. Client e-mail programs require users to input incoming and outgoing e-mail server names. These names are the addresses of servers located at the ISP that administers incoming and outgoing e-mail. The server addresses can be obtained from the network administrator or ISP. E-mail programs also allow users to set up newsgroup accounts. Newsgroups allow users to post and respond to messages in discussion groups on a wide variety of topics. There are tens of thousands of newsgroups where users can find people who have similar interests or knowledge in a specific field.

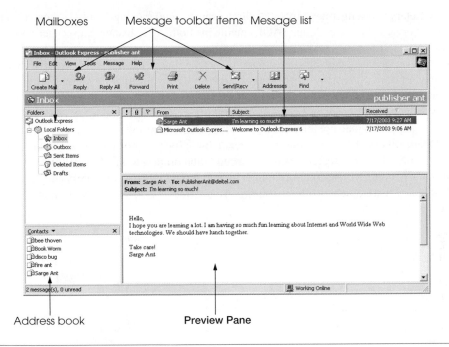

Mailboxes   Message toolbar items   Message list

Address book   **Preview Pane**

Fig. 2.11   Outlook Express e-mail main screen.

Post Office Protocol (POP) and **Internet Message Access Protocol (IMAP)** are two major protocols for accessing e-mail from servers. POP services store e-mail messages on a remote server until a user chooses to view the messages and download them onto a local machine. IMAP mail services also store e-mails on a remote server, but allow users to manipulate e-mail messages directly on the server without downloading the messages. Because POP servers require users to download e-mails before viewing, accessing e-mails from different machines scatters the messages among them. IMAP allows users to leave messages on the server, so that users can access e-mails from multiple machines without distributing the messages over them. To send messages from server to server, most e-mail systems use **Simple Mail Transfer Protocol (SMTP)**.

Many free Web-based e-mail services are also available. Hotmail (`www.hotmail.com`) and Yahoo! Mail (`mail.yahoo.com`) are two such services. These services configure accounts for users. Web-based e-mail allows users to access their e-mail from any Web browser.

2.10 Instant Messaging

Instant messaging (IM) allows two or more users to exchange text, image and audio messages in real time, provided that the users have compatible messaging services. Communicating by IM is also called **chatting**.

The available instant messaging programs include *AOL Instant Messenger* (`www.aim.com`), *Yahoo! Messenger* (`messenger.yahoo.com`), *ICQ* (`web.icq.com`), *MSN Messenger* (`messenger.msn.com`) and *Trillian* (`www.trillian.cc`). AOL Instant Messenger (AIM), Yahoo! Messenger, ICQ (short for "I seek you") and MSN Messenger use proprietary messenger networks that allow users to send messages only to those who use the same service. America Online (AOL) maintains both AOL Instant Messenger and ICQ, however, so AOL Instant Messenger and ICQ users can communicate with one other. Trillian users can communicate with any of the previously mentioned services. Trillian is a client program, not a messaging service, that connects to each of the different messaging networks. If you have accounts on multiple services, you can use Trillian to access all your accounts.

AOL Instant Messenger (Fig. 2.12), Yahoo! Messenger, ICQ and MSN Messenger also allow users to hold video conferences and send messages to mobile devices (e.g., cell phones and PDAs). Other communications and instant messaging programs, such as *Windows Messenger* and *NetMeeting*, feature more advanced collaboration tools. They allow a group of users to share control of a program running on a group member's computer. They also have a **whiteboard** feature, which allows sharing visual effects (e.g., drawings) with others.

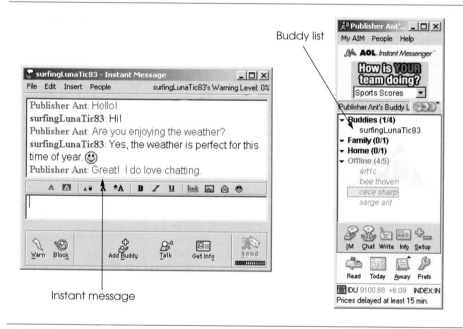

Fig. 2.12   Buddy list and an instant message. (AOL screenshots © 2003 America Online, Inc. Used with permission.)

To start instant messaging, users must download and install the messaging program of their choice, and each user must create a **screen name** (or use an existing screen name). A screen name is a unique name that a user assumes when communicating on a messaging network. Users can then sign-on to a messaging network. Instant messaging allows users to communicate quickly and conveniently and is used by many companies to increase productivity.

Each messaging program allows users to maintain a personalized list of screen names called a **buddy list** or **friend list**. The buddy list in AOL Instant Messenger allows users to organize screen names into folders and show which members are available for chatting (Fig. 2.12). IM services also allow users to transfer files and set up **chat rooms** where a group of IM users can type messages that are seen by everyone in the group. **File transfer** allows one user to download and save an application or file from another user's computer.

2.11 Other Web Browsers

Besides Internet Explorer and Netscape, many other Web browsers are available, such as *Mozilla* (www.mozilla.org), *Opera* (www.opera.com) and *Amaya* (www.w3.org/Amaya). All these browsers differ in functionality, speed and features. Also, they employ different HTML layout engines. Layout engines determine how a Web page displays in a browser. Netscape and Mozilla (Fig. 2.13) use Gecko as their layout engine. Opera and IE have their own engines.

Fig. 2.13   Mozilla Web browser. (Courtesy of The Mozilla Organization.)

Opera is a fast and lightweight browser, while Internet Explorer and Mozilla offer many features for programmers. Amaya is a combined **Web editor/browser** designed to create and update Web documents and demonstrate W3C standards. Because browsers use different HTML layout engines, they may display the same Web page differently. Additionally, some capabilities supported in one browser may not be supported in another. The existence of different browser functionality and features makes cross-browser compatibility difficult to achieve.

In this chapter we introduced the features of Internet Explorer 6, showed how to search the Internet and introduced some of the exciting Internet technologies available. In the next chapter we introduce Adobe Photoshop Elements and show how to create graphics for the Web.

SUMMARY

- Web browsers are software programs that allow users to access the Web's rich multimedia content.
- The two most popular Web browsers are Microsoft's *Internet Explorer* and *Netscape*.
- A computer alone is not enough to access the Internet. In addition to Web browser software, the computer needs specific hardware and a connection to an Internet Service Provider to view Web pages.

- A modem is hardware that enables a computer to connect to the Internet. A modem converts data to audio tones and transmits the data over phone lines. A network card, also called a network interface card (NIC), is hardware that allows a computer to connect to the Internet through a network or a high-speed Internet connection, such as a LAN, cable modem or a Digital Subscriber Line (DSL).

- Bandwidth and cost are two considerations when deciding which commercial ISP service to use. Bandwidth refers to the amount of data that can be transferred through a communications medium in a fixed amount of time. Different ISPs offer different types of high-speed connections, called broadband connections, that include DSL, cable modem, Integrated Services Digital Network (ISDN) and slower dial-up connections, each of which has different bandwidths and costs to users.

- Broadband is a category of high-bandwidth Internet service that is most often provided by cable television and telephone companies to home users.

- DSL is a broadband service that allows computers to be connected at all times to the Internet over existing phone lines, without interfering with voice services. However, DSL requires a special modem that is obtained from the ISP.

- Cable modems enable the computer to be connected to the Internet at all times. Cable modems transmit data over the cables that bring television to homes and businesses. The bandwidth is shared by many users.

- ISDN provides Internet service over either digital or standard telephone lines. ISDN requires specialized hardware, called a terminal adaptor (TA), which is usually obtained from the ISP.

- The **Internet Connection Wizard** (**New Connection Wizard** in Windows XP) can be used to configure the computer to connect to the Internet.

- The URL is the address of the Web page displayed in the browser window. Each Web page is associated with a unique URL. URLs usually begin with `http://`, which stands for Hypertext Transfer Protocol (HTTP), the industry standard protocol (or set of communication rules) for transferring Web documents over the Internet.

- URLs of Web sites that handle private information, such as credit card numbers, often begin with `https://`, the abbreviation for Secure Hypertext Transfer Protocol (HTTPS), the standard for transferring encrypted data over the Internet.

- Several techniques are available for navigating between different URLs. A user can click the **Address** field and type a Web page's URL. The user can then press *Enter* or click **Go** to request the Web page located at that URL.

- Another way to navigate the Web is via visual elements on Web pages called hyperlinks that, when clicked, load a specified Web document. Both images and text server as hyperlinks.

- Hyperlinks can reference other Web pages, e-mail addresses and files. If a hyperlink is an e-mail address, clicking the link loads the computer's default e-mail program and opens a message window addressed to the specified recipient's e-mail address.

- When a file is downloaded, it is copied onto the user's computer. Programs, documents, images and sound files are all downloadable files.

- IE6 maintains a list of previously visited URLs. This list is called the history and stores URLs in chronological order.

- The **History** window contains heading levels ordered chronologically. Within each time frame headings are alphabetized by site directory name. This window is useful for finding previously visited URLs without having to remember the exact URL.

- URLs from the history are displayed in a drop-down list when a user types a URL into the **Address** bar. This feature is called AutoComplete. Any URL from this drop-down list can be selected with the mouse to load the Web page at that URL into the browser.

- Web pages can be saved directly to the computer's hard drive for off-line browsing (i.e., browsing while not connected to the Internet). Select **Save As...** from the **File** menu at the top of the browser window to save a Web page and all its components (e.g., images).

- Individual images from a Web site can also be saved by clicking the image with the right mouse button and selecting **Save Picture As...** from the displayed context menu (i.e., pop-up menu).

- Search engines explore the Internet and maintain searchable records containing information about Web sites.

- Metasearch engines do not maintain databases. Instead, they send the search criteria to other search engines and aggregate the results. IE6 has a built-in metasearch engine that is accessed by clicking the **Search** button on the toolbar.

- As users browse the Web, they often visit certain sites repeatedly. Internet Explorer provides a feature called favorites for bookmarking such sites.

- Plug-ins are specialized pieces of software that extend (or upgrade) other applications, such as IE6, by providing additional functionality. Normally the browser prompts the user to download a plug-in when a plug-in is needed.

- FTP (file transfer protocol) is an older protocol for transferring information, especially large files, over the Internet. An FTP site's URL begins with `ftp://` rather than `http://`. FTP sites are typically accessed via hyperlinks, but can also be accessed by any software that supports FTP.

- FTP sites with anonymous access allow any user access. Many FTP sites on the Internet have restricted access; only users with authorized user names and passwords are permitted to access such sites.

- Transferring a file from the local machine to another location on the Internet is called uploading and can be accomplished using the FTP protocol.

- Internet Explorer has many settings that determine how sites are displayed, how security measures are applied and how outputs are rendered.

- Default programs used for common Internet procedures, such as sending e-mail, are set in the **Programs** tab of the **Internet Options** dialog. Specifying these settings causes the designated programs to execute when there is a need for their respective technologies while browsing.

- The security level for IE6 can be set under the **Privacy** tab of the **Internet Options** dialog. There are four levels of security. The most lenient level permits downloading and cookies (files that are placed on the computer by Web sites to retain or gather information about the user); the strictest level renders a constant flow of alerts and alarms about browsing security and might prevent certain Web sites from working correctly.

- A personal home page can be specified under the **General** tab of the **Internet Options** dialog. The home page is the Web page that loads when the browser is first opened and appears when the **Home** button at the top of the browser window is clicked.

- History and cache options also may be adjusted in the **General** tab of the **Internet Options** dialog. By clicking the **Settings...** button, the amount of disk space to be reserved for Web page cache can be set. The cache is an area on the hard drive that a browser designates for saving Web pages and their elements for rapid future access.

- Electronic mail (e-mail or email for short) is a method of sending and receiving formatted messages and files over the Internet to other people. Internet Service Providers issue e-mail addresses in the form *username@domainname*. Many e-mail programs, such as Pegasus Mail, Eudora and Microsoft's Outlook Express, are available.

- Post Office Protocol (POP) services store e-mail on a remote server until a user chooses to view the message and download the e-mail onto a local machine. Internet Message Access Protocol

(IMAP) mail services also store e-mails on a remote server but allow users to manipulate e-mail without downloading the messages.

- Most e-mail systems use Simple Mail Transfer Protocol (SMTP) to send messages from server to server.

- Instant messaging (IM) allows two or more users to exchange text, image and audio messages in real time, provided that the users have compatible messaging services.

- A buddy list or friend list shows which contacts are available for chatting.

- The existence of different browser functionality and features makes cross-browser compatibility difficult to achieve.

TERMINOLOGY

Address bar
Address Book
Adobe Acrobat Reader
Amaya
anonymous
AOL Instant Messenger
applications
AutoComplete
Back button
bandwidth
broadband connection
buddy list
cable modem
cache
chat
context menu
cookie
database
dial-up connection
Digital Subscriber Line (DSL)
download
electronic mail (e-mail)
e-mail server
Favorites
file transfer
File Transfer Protocol (FTP)
Forward button
Help menu
History
home page
Hotmail
HTML layout engine
hyperlink
Hypertext Transfer Protocol (HTTP)
ICQ
Inbox
Integrated Services Digital Network (ISDN)

Internet Connection Wizard (ICW)
Internet Explorer 6 (IE6)
Internet Message Access Protocol (IMAP)
Internet Options
Internet Service Provider (ISP)
Macromedia Shockwave
metasearch engine
Microsoft Internet Explorer
Microsoft Outlook Express
modem
Mozilla
MSN Messenger
Netscape
network
New Connection Wizard
off-line browsing
Opera
Portable Document Format (PDF)
Post Office Protocol (POP)
priority
Privacy
public access
restricted access
Search
search engine
security level
sharing
Simple Mail Transfer Protocol (SMTP)
terminal adaptor (TA)
Trillian
Uniform Resource Locator (URL)
uploading
Web browser
Web editor
whiteboard
Windows Messenger
Yahoo! Messenger

SELF-REVIEW EXERCISES

2.1   Fill in the blanks in each of the following statements:
   a) The two most popular Web browsers are _____ and _____.
   b) A browser is used to view files on the _____.
   c) The location of a file on the Internet is called its _____.
   d) The element in a Web page that, when clicked, causes a new Web page to load is called a(n) _____; when your mouse passes over this element, the mouse pointer changes into a _____ in IE6.
   e) The list IE6 keeps of visited URLs is called the _____.
   f) You can save an image from a Web page by right clicking the image and selecting _____.
   g) The feature of IE6 that provides options for completing URLs is called _____.
   h) The feature of IE6 that enables the user to save URLs of frequently visited sites is called _____.

2.2   State whether each of the following is *true* or *false*. If the statement is *false*, explain why.
   a) A whiteboard is a drawing application that makes it possible to share visual effects with others in Windows Messenger or NetMeeting.
   b) There are approximately 1,000 newsgroups on the Internet.
   c) Plug-ins must be downloaded and installed in order to use them.
   d) MSN Messenger users can chat with ICQ users.
   e) FTP is a popular Internet mechanism by which files are uploaded and downloaded.
   f) You can access any FTP site by logging in with the user name anonymous.

ANSWERS TO SELF-REVIEW EXERCISES

2.1   a) Internet Explorer, Netscape Navigator. b) Internet and the Web. c) URL. d) hyperlink, hand. e) history. f) **Save Picture As…**. g) AutoComplete. h) **Favorites**.

2.2   a) True. b) False. There are tens of thousands of newsgroups, and more are added every day. c) True. d) False. Only AOL and Trillian users can chat with ICQ users. MSN users are on a different messaging network. e) True. f) False. Many FTP sites are restricted and do not admit the general public.

EXERCISES

2.3   Spell out the following acronyms, and include a brief description of each:
   a) HTTP
   b) FTP
   c) URL
   d) DSL
   e) PDF
   f) ISP
   g) SMTP
   h) IMAP

2.4   Use Internet Explorer's FTP capability to access ftp.cdrom.com and sunsite.unc.edu. List the directory output for both sites.

2.5   Create an ICQ screen name. Then log onto ICQ Messenger Service and initiate a conversation with a friend.

2.6   Start a chat room using AOL Instant Messenger and initiate a conversation with multiple friends.

2.7   Go to `www.shockwave.com/software/shockwaveplayer` and download the Shockwave Player to your computer. Use the Shockwave plug-in to view shockwave content from `www.shockwave.com`.

2.8   Download and install the Opera (`www.opera.com`) and Mozilla (`www.mozilla.org`) Web browsers. Go to your favorite Web sites and try to observe any differences in speed, appearance and functionality.

3

Adobe Photoshop Elements: Creating Web Graphics

Objectives

- To explore the basic features of Photoshop Elements.
- To be able to design images for Web pages.
- To learn how colors are represented in image files and to understand "color mode" and "transparency."
- To understand the techniques of layering, selection, image slicing and other image-preparation processes.
- To understand the differences between graphic file formats.
- To be able to take screen shots using screen-capture technology.

Now follow in this direction, now turn a different hue.
Theognis of Megara

Beware lest you lose the substance by grasping at the shadow.
Aesop

Before a diamond shows its brilliancy and prismatic colors it has to stand a good deal of cutting and smoothing.
Anonymous

Outline

3.1 Introduction

The most successful Web pages use both text and graphics to enhance the user's experience. The graphic design of a Web page can greatly influence the amount of time a user spends at a site. For instance, if a company's Web site contains only text, it may not produce as many online sales. Web site graphics, such as buttons, banners or product images, define the user experience and distinguish a company's site from its competition. Many images are available free for download on the Internet, but creating original images helps make a Web site unique. This chapter teaches basic image-creation techniques for producing attractive, user-friendly Web pages.

This chapter introduces Adobe® Inc.'s *Photoshop® Elements*[1]—an easy-to-use graphics package that offers the functionality of more expensive packages at an economical price. Graphics such as title images, banners, buttons and advanced photographic effects all can be created using this program. A free 30-day trial version of Photoshop Elements is available at `www.adobe.com/products/photoshopel`.[2] The full version also can be purchased at this site. Please download and install Photoshop Elements before continuing with this chapter.

The graphics editing skills learned in this chapter can be applied to other commercial and free graphics editors. Commercial graphics editors include Adobe *Photoshop*® (`www.adobe.com/products/photoshop/main.html`), Macromedia® *Fireworks*® (`www.macromedia.com/software/fireworks`) and Jasc® *Paint Shop*™ *Pro*® (`www.jasc.com/products/paintshoppro`). The *GIMP* (GNU Image Manipulation Program), available at `www.gimp.org/download.html`, is one of the leading free graphics editors.

---

1. All screen shots and descriptive text are based on Adobe Photoshop Elements 2.0, the latest version at the time of publication. Screen shots and steps may differ for readers using other versions.
2. *Caution*: Do not change the system clock settings of a computer after installing Photoshop Elements. Doing so causes the 30-day trial to expire, immediately disabling the program. Photoshop Elements cannot be re-enabled, even after reinstalling it.

3.2 Image Basics

Photoshop Elements is best taught by example. This chapter provides several examples that illustrate how to use the Photoshop Elements tools and functions. This section examines the basic steps for creating original images.

Begin by opening Photoshop Elements. When the program first opens, the **Welcome** screen appears in the center of the screen and presents several options (Fig. 3.1). The options include creating a new file, opening an existing file and acquiring an image from an outside source such as a scanner or a digital camera. This window appears when the program is started, but also may be accessed at any time by selecting **Welcome** from the **Window** menu. The **File** menu also opens new or existing files.

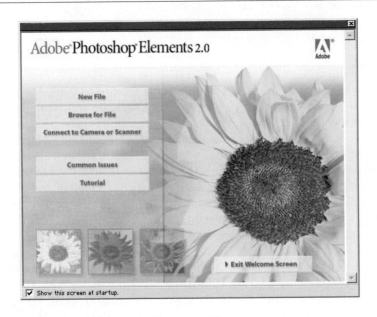

Fig. 3.1   **Welcome** screen. (Adobe product screen shot(s) reprinted with permission from Adobe Systems Incorporated.)

Click **New File** on the **Welcome** screen to open the **New** dialog (Fig. 3.2), to begin creating an image.

The **New** dialog specifies initial image settings and appears each time a new image file is created. The initial image settings include **Height** and **Width** and the units in which these are measured. The dialog sets the image **resolution**. Resolution is a measurement of image clarity and is measured in **pixels** per unit—every image in Photoshop Elements is composed of a grid of dots called pixels, which store color information. Photoshop Elements has preset height, width and resolution values for a variety of formats.

Performance Tip 3.1

Higher image resolutions result in better image clarity. However, higher resolutions produce larger file sizes. The standard resolution for the Web is 72 pixels per inch.

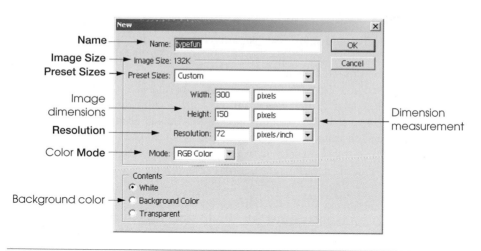

Fig. 3.2   New-image creation in Photoshop Elements.

The **New** dialog sets an image's **Background Color** and color **Mode**. The three color modes available are **red-green-blue (RGB)**, **grayscale** and **bitmap**. Color mode determines the number of colors that Photoshop Elements uses to compose an image. RGB and grayscale are the most commonly used color modes for creating Web graphics. Color images use the RGB mode, and black-and-white images use the grayscale mode.

In RGB mode, each pixel in the image is assigned an **intensity value** for the **primary colors in light** (i.e., red, green and blue) that create a color range of 16.7 million colors when combined in different intensity values from 0 (minimum intensity) to 255 (maximum intensity). This spectrum is comparable to that of human vision and is adequate for developing screen images. For instance, a bright-blue pixel might have a red value of 16, a green value of 20 and a blue value of 200. Grayscale mode uses only **neutral grays** which have identical red, green and blue values. The bitmap mode uses only black and white.

Create a new image by entering `typefun` in the **New** dialog's **Name** field. Select **Custom** in the **Preset Sizes** field. Set the image width to **300** pixels, the height to **150** pixels and the resolution to **72** pixels per inch (the default value for Web graphics) by typing the numbers into the **Width**, **Height** and **Resolution** fields. Choose the measurement units from the drop-down lists.

Select the **RGB Color** mode from the color **Mode** drop-down list. Set the **Background Color** to white by clicking the **White** radio button in the **Contents** frame. These settings can be changed at any point during the image-editing process. The background color is the image's initial color. Click **OK** to create the new file `typefun`. A new **image window** should open in the development environment with the name **typefun** in the title bar (Fig. 3.3).

The development environment is the gray area that contains the toolbox, palettes and image window. The toolbox is the vertical window to the left of the image window that contains different tools to create images. Palettes are windows that contain different image-editing options. The **Hints** and **How To** palettes are open by default.

The development environment can be customized to suit the user's preferences. For instance, the image window may be resized by clicking and dragging any of the sides or corners. A window can also be minimized, maximized or closed by clicking the appropriate button at the top right of the window. Also, the palettes, toolbox and image window can be

Active tool options bar   Title bar   Main menu bar   Palette well   **Hints** palette

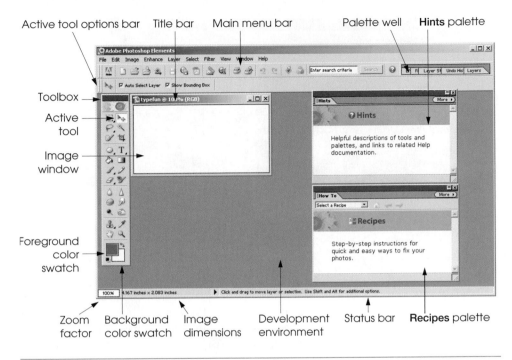

Toolbox

Active tool

Image window

Foreground color swatch

Zoom factor   Background color swatch   Image dimensions   Development environment   Status bar   **Recipes** palette

Fig. 3.3   Photoshop Elements development environment.

dragged to different locations. Selecting **Reset Palette Locations** from the **Window** menu restores the default development-environment settings.

Palettes, located inside the **palette well**, are windows that contain image editing and effects options. A palette is opened by clicking its tab in the palette well, and it is closed by clicking outside the palette. Palettes may be organized in different ways to make image editing easier. Several palettes can be open at one time by clicking and dragging their tabs out of the palette well and into the development environment. Palettes outside the palette well remain open until they are closed by clicking the **x** button in the upper-right corner of the palette. Different palette options will be discussed shortly.

The **toolbox** contains **selection**, **editing**, **painting** and **type tools** that add or remove graphic elements from images. The **active tool** (i.e., the currently selected tool) applies changes to an image and is highlighted in the toolbox. Only one tool can be active at a time. Tips for using the active tool are found in the **status bar** at the bottom of the screen or in the **Hints** palette.

The two squares at the bottom of the toolbox represent the two **active colors**—the foreground color and the background color. These squares are called **swatches**. Click one of them to display the **Color Picker** dialog (Fig. 3.4), which allows the user to select the foreground or background color. Colors are selected based on the **HSB (Hue, Saturation, Brightness)** model or the **RGB (Red, Green, Blue)** model. These color models form the 16.7 million colors available in the RGB model based on combinations of their three primary values. Both color models produce the same colors but measure color differently.

Hue is selected for the HSB mode from the vertical color slider in the **Color Picker** dialog (Fig. 3.4). **Hue** is measured in degrees from 0 to 360 representing the colors of the

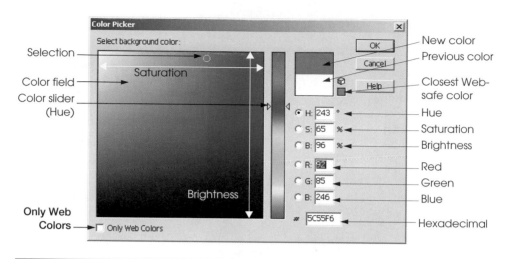

Fig. 3.4   Color Picker dialog.

color wheel. The color wheel is a theoretical model that shows how colors are created from combinations of the three primary colors in light—red, green and blue. **Saturation** is a color's intensity measured in the percentage of gray that the color contains. Saturated colors appear more vivid; less saturated colors appear dull. **Brightness** is a color's relative lightness or darkness and is measured in the amount of black or white a color contains.

RGB color selection is based on the same principle as the RGB color mode, in which each pixel has a red, green and blue value between 0 and 255 assigned to it. When RGB values are entered into the **Color Picker**, the HSB values change to reflect the selection.

The **Color Picker** allows the user to choose colors from a **Web-safe palette**, restricting color selection to the 216 colors that are cross-platform (e.g., Windows, Macintosh and UNIX) and cross-browser (e.g., Internet Explorer and Netscape) compatible. To enforce Web-safe colors, select the **Only Web Colors** checkbox in the lower-left corner of the window.

 Portability Tip 3.1

Web-safe colors should display identically in any browser on any platform. However, some color inconsistencies do occur on different platforms and browsers. It is a good idea to choose only Web-safe colors when designing original images for the Web.

 **Look-and-Feel Observation 3.1**

Too many colors make a site look confusing and erratic. Pick three or four main colors to use as the prominent colors for images and text.

When selecting a foreground or background color, either click inside the color field on the desired color or enter the color's numerical values. The **Color Picker** dialog also allows the user to choose colors based on **hexadecimal** notation. Hexadecimal notation is equivalent to RGB notation except that it uses a 6-digit combination of the numbers 0–9 and the letters A–F to represent the 256-color range for each red, green and blue specification. The first two digits are the red value, the second two are the green value and the last two are the blue value—00 signifies the least intensity and FF the greatest intensity. For more information on hexadecimal notation, see Appendix E, Number Systems.

Portability Tip 3.2

It is easy to tell whether a color is part of the Web-safe palette by examining its hexadecimal notation. The hexadecimal notation for any Web-safe color contains only the digits 00, 33, 66 and 99 and the letters CC and FF for each red, green and blue value.

Select a foreground color by adjusting the color slider to the desired hue, then pick the color from the color field and click **OK**. This color displays in the foreground color swatch of the toolbox.

Adding Text to an Image

The following example shows how to place text into an image and how to apply special effects to the text. Select the **type tool** from the toolbox by clicking the tool containing the capital letter **T**. Note that the active tool options bar changes to reflect the new active tool (Fig. 3.5).

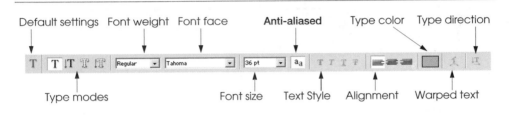

Fig. 3.5   Type options bar.

As in a word-processing program, the **Type** options bar allows the user to alter text properties such as **font face**, **font weight** and **alignment**. For this example, choose **Helvetica 30 point bold** and click the image with the type tool. A cursor appears indicating the point where the text begins. Type in two lines of text and select it with the cursor. Type properties may be changed when text is selected. For instance, double clicking the type color swatch in the **Type** options bar changes the type color.

Be sure to have the **Anti-aliased** checkbox selected in the **Type** options bar. **Anti-aliasing** is a process that smooths edges on scalable fonts and other graphics by blending the color of the edge pixels with the color of the background on which the text is placed. Fonts can look jagged without anti-aliasing (Fig. 3.6).

Fig. 3.6   Anti-aliasing.

Once the text is typed, it can be moved with either the type tool or the **move tool**. The move tool is indicated by an arrow with cross-hairs (Fig. 3.7). As soon as the move tool is selected, a **bounding box** with side and corner **anchors** appears around the text. Anchors are the small boxes that appear on the edges of a bounding box. Clicking and dragging the anchors resizes the contents of the bounding box.

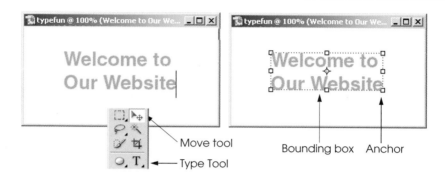

Fig. 3.7   Type tool creates text that can be moved by the move tool.

Applying Text Effects

Select the move tool and click and hold the mouse button anywhere within the bounding box. Drag the text to the center of the image window. Click and drag any anchor to resize the text. Dragging a corner anchor while pressing the *Shift* key resizes the bounding box contents proportionately.

Photoshop Elements has several image processing options for applying special effects to text and images. Click and drag the **Layer Styles** tab out of the **palettes well** to open the **Layer Styles** palette. If this palette tab is not visible in the palettes well, it can be opened by selecting **Layer Styles** from the **Window** menu. The **Layer Styles** palette offers several effects that can be applied to text or shapes. Select **Drop Shadows** as the style type from the drop-down list inside this palette (Fig. 3.8).

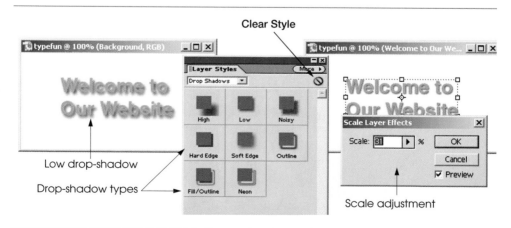

Fig. 3.8   Adding a drop shadow with the **Layer Styles** palette.

Next select **Low** as the type of drop shadow from the style selection. A drop-shadow effect is applied to the text. Any layer style can be removed by clicking the **Clear Style** button in the **Layer Styles** palette.

A user can edit an effect, such as a drop shadow, in two ways. The first is by selecting **Scale Effects...** from the **Layer Style** submenu of the **Layer** menu. The scale adjustment in the **Scale Effects** dialog increases or decreases the intensity of any layer effect. Scale the low drop shadow to **31** percent (Fig. 3.8).

The second way to adjust a layer style is through the **Layers** palette. Drag the **Layers** palette out of the palette well. This palette controls the use of **layers** in Photoshop Elements. Layers organize the different components that compose an image. The **active layer** is highlighted in blue in the **Layers** palette. When using tools or applying special effects, only the active layer is affected. Note that the text occupies its own **type layer**, indicated by a **T** on its layer in the **Layers** palette (Fig. 3.9). Having the type on its own layer enables it to be edited independently of any other part of the image. Click the type layer in the **Layers** palette to activate it. The **f** symbol in the blue area of the type layer indicates that the layer has a style applied to it. Double click the **f** to open the **Style Settings** dialog (Fig. 3.9).

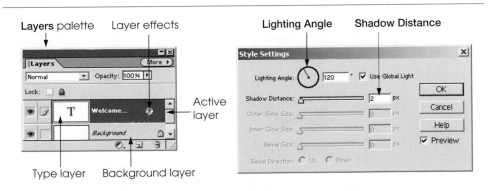

Fig. 3.9   Layer-effect style settings.

Different options are available depending on the type of style applied to the layer. Set the drop shadow **Lighting Angle** to **120** degrees and the **Shadow Distance** to **3** pixels. The **Lighting Angle** controls the direction of the light source creating the shadow. The **Shadow Distance** determines the size of the drop shadow. Press **OK** to apply these changes.

Text also can be warped to conform to a shape. Select the type tool from the toolbox to reveal the **Type** options bar. Click the warp text button in the **Type** options bar, indicated by a **T** with an arc beneath it, to open the **Warp Text** dialog (Fig. 3.10).

The **Warp Text** dialog allows the user to select different shapes. For this example, select **Flag** from the **Styles** drop-down list and set the **Bend** slider to **+50%**. The three sliders, respectively, modify the bend, horizontal distortion and vertical distortion of the text shape. The text changes to reflect the selection in real time in the original image window; however, the change is not applied until **OK** is clicked in the dialog.

The next step is to create the effect of **transparency**. Transparency allows the background of the Web page to show through in the white portions of the image. Recall that when this file was created, the background color was set to white. A transparent background could have been specified. Creating a transparent background at this stage requires using the **Layers** palette (Fig. 3.11).

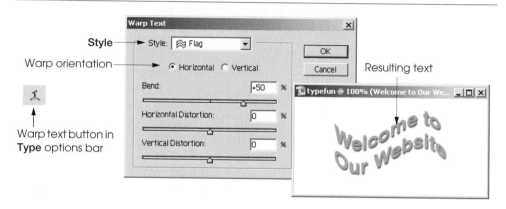

Fig. 3.10   Warp Text dialog.

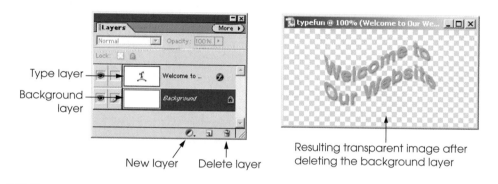

Fig. 3.11   Deleting a layer using the **Layers** palette.

New layers are transparent by default. The type layer is transparent, with the exception of the type and its effects. Deleting the white background layer makes the image background transparent. Select the background layer in the **Layers** palette to make it the active layer. Click the trash can button to delete this layer (deleting a layer is permanent). The new image should have a gray-and-white checkerboard background, representing transparency. When the image is placed in a Web document, the background color of the Web page appears in the transparent parts.

Options for Saving Web Images

Photoshop Elements provides an option for saving images for the Web. Choosing the **Save for Web...** option, located under the **File** menu, opens the **Save for Web** dialog. This dialog allows the user to determine the file format and color settings for saving an image. The original image appears on the left side of the dialog and the **optimized** version appears on the right (Fig. 3.12). Information about the graphic file, including file type, file size, estimated download time and the **number of colors**, appears for each image.

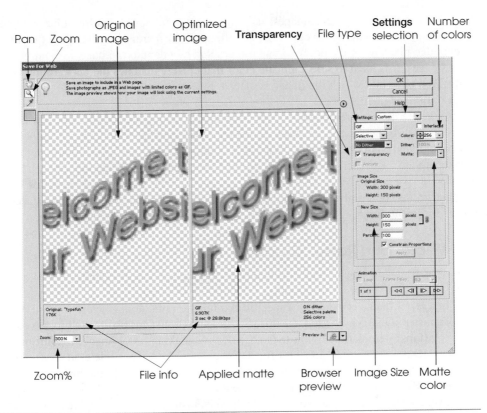

Fig. 3.12 Matte color added to a transparent GIF in the **Save for Web** dialog.

The optimized version is a preview of what the image will look like after it is saved. The different optimization settings, such as file type, **compression quality** and number of colors the image utilizes, are all set in the **Save for Web** dialog. The file type determines the **compression** Photoshop Elements uses to save an image. Compression is defined by an algorithm that Photoshop Elements uses to save file data. The compression quality is the accuracy of the compression algorithm and determines the quality of the saved image.

The number of colors an image contains also affects the image quality. The more colors an image uses, the higher the image clarity. The number of colors may only be selected with certain file types.

Reducing the number of colors or the compression quality may decrease file size, thus lessening the image's download time. Optimization is the process of finding the correct balance between the number of colors, edging, the compression quality and the file size such that the download time is ideal for the target audience.

Different file formats are appropriate for different types of graphics. The **GIF** (Compuserve Graphics Interchange Format) format preserves transparency (saving pixels that do not have color information), making GIF ideal for transparent Web graphics such as typefun. Other file formats are discussed later in this chapter. Select **GIF** from the file type drop-down list. Make sure that the **Transparency** box is checked in the **Save for Web** dialog; otherwise, the image will not be saved as a transparent image.

When saving transparent images, it is important to choose a **matte color** with the **Matte** selector. A matte color optimizes the effect of transparency by blending the transparent edge pixels with the color so that the graphic blends into the page without having jagged edges. It is ideal to select a matte color that closely matches the background color of the Web page into which the image is placed. Select a matte color and note the change to the optimized image.

An image may be previewed in a Web browser by clicking the **browser preview** button before it is saved. This option creates a temporary Web document with the image embedded. The background color of the preview is the **Matte** color. This preview also provides information about the image, such as file format, image dimensions, file size and file settings. Close the browser window to return to Photoshop Elements and click **OK** in the **Save for Web** dialog. Choose a descriptive name for the file so that it is easily identified when it is placed in a Web document. Inserting images into Web pages is introduced in Chapters 4 and 5.

3.3 Vector and Raster Graphics

Photoshop Elements creates and edits two types of graphics that are standard for Web design—**raster** and **vector**. A raster image is composed of pixels organized on a grid. Each pixel in a raster image is stored as a specific combination of colors when it is saved. If the size of a raster image is increased, the image-editing program adds pixels in a process called **interpolation**. Interpolation lowers the image quality, making raster images **resolution dependent**. Raster graphics are ideal for fixed-size images that have subtle gradations of colors, such as photographs and original artwork, or images created with the raster tool set in Photoshop Elements. Raster tools are discussed in the next section.

A vector graphic is not stored as a grid of pixels. Instead, a vector graphic is created by a set of user-determined mathematical properties called **vectors**. These properties include a graphic's dimensions, attributes and position. Examples of vector graphics in Photoshop Elements are text created with the type tool and shapes created with the **shape tool**. The shape tool can create rectangles, ellipses, polygons, lines and custom shapes. Vector images exist as individual objects that can be edited separately from one another. They can also be resized without losing clarity because vector information is stored as sets of instructions instead of groups of pixels. It is this characteristic which makes vector graphics **resolution independent.** Vector graphics are ideal for creating solid areas of color and text; however, they cannot handle the image quality of photographs or other color-complex images. Figure 3.13 demonstrates the difference between scaling raster and vector graphics. The raster image becomes **pixelated**, whereas the vector does not lose any clarity.

Fig. 3.13   Raster and vector graphics.

3.4 Toolbox

Photoshop Elements offers tools that simplify the image-composition process. The toolbox, which appears by default on the left side of the editing area, groups these tools by editing function. The tool names are highlighted in Fig. 3.14.

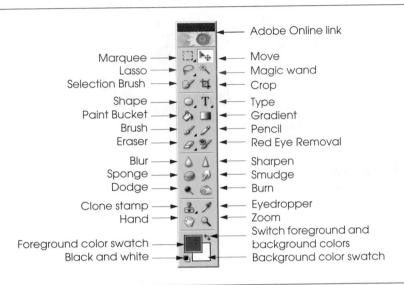

Fig. 3.14   Photoshop Elements toolbox.

Photoshop Elements provides **navigation tools** that aid the user in the editing process. The **magnifying glass** is a navigation tool that **zooms in** on an image. Click and drag with the magnifying glass tool to zoom into a particular area. Click a spot to zoom into, with that spot centered in the image window. Hold down the *Alt* key while clicking to zoom out.

Clicking and dragging with the **hand tool** pans from one side of an image to the other. This tool is useful when an image is large or when an image is magnified. The hand tool is accessible at any time by holding down the *Spacebar* key.

Some tools have **hidden tools** beneath them in the toolbox. A small triangle in the lower-right corner of the tool button indicates hidden tools. For instance, the **marquee tool,** the **type tool** and the **lasso tool** have hidden tools beneath them. Click and hold the tool button to reveal hidden options.

3.4.1 Selection Tools

The **selection tools**—marquee, lasso and magic wand—create a border called a **marquee.** A marquee bounds a selected area of pixels that can be modified by **filters,** moved or have their colors adjusted. Filters are special effects that perform uniform changes to an area of pixels. A selection marquee is moved by dragging it with a selection tool. Moving a selection marquee with the move tool moves the pixels bounded inside the marquee, leaving the area the selection previously occupied transparent and revealing any layers beneath (Fig. 3.15).

The **rectangular marquee** and the **elliptical marquee** tools select areas of pixels. The default marquee is the rectangular marquee tool, and the elliptical marquee is hidden beneath it. These tools may be constrained to either a perfect circle or a square by pressing the *Shift* key while clicking and dragging.

Fig. 3.15 Moving a selection.

The lasso tools (regular, polygonal and magnetic) allow the user to customize a selection area. The **regular lasso**, the default, draws a freehand marquee around an area of pixels, following every move of the mouse. Clicking and dragging the **magnetic lasso** tool, hidden behind the regular lasso, traces a selection area by adhering to the edges of an object in an image. The magnetic lasso finds the edges by the difference in pixel color. The **polygonal lasso** draws straight-edged selections by clicking at the selection corner points. Figure 3.16 illustrates the selections using the regular and magnetic lasso tools.

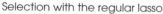

Selection with the regular lasso   Selection with the magnetic lasso

Fig. 3.16 Lasso tools draw selection areas.

The **magic wand** tool selects areas of similarly colored adjacent pixels. The **tolerance** setting increases or decreases the pixel color range that the magic wand selects (Fig. 3.17). The **Magic Wand** options bar provides the tolerance settings.

The selection tool option bars help customize selection areas (Fig. 3.18). A selection can be added to, subtracted from or intersected with another selection with these options. These options also may be used while toggling between different selection tools.

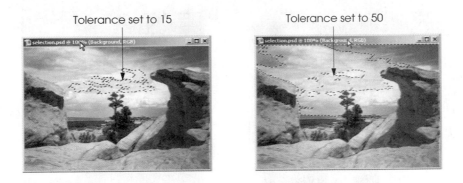

Fig. 3.17   Magic wand tolerance affects the size of a selection.

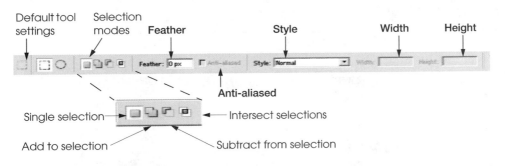

Fig. 3.18   Multiple selections using the selection tool options bar.

Using the Selection Tools

The next example shows how to use the selection tools to create a blurred frame for an image so that it gradually blends into the background color of a Web page. Open the file `eiffel.jpg` located in the Chapter 3 examples directory on the CD-ROM that accompanies this book. Choose the rectangular marquee tool from the toolbox, and set the **feathering** to 8 pixels in the **Marquee tool** options bar. Feathering blurs the edges of a selection so that the pixels inside the selection blend with the pixels outside the selection. The number of pixels, in this case, determines the amount of blur around the selection's edge. The effects of feathering a selection are shown in Fig. 3.19.

Click and drag the rectangular marquee tool from the upper left to the lower right of the photograph, leaving some space between the edge of the picture and the selection. Any selection may be removed or modified. Clicking the image with any of the selection tools while a marquee is active removes the marquee. Note that the corners of the selection are rounded, indicating that it is feathered. The image on the left in Fig. 3.19 has selection feathering set to 0.

Select **Inverse** from the **Select** menu or use the shortcut *Ctrl+Shift+I* to invert the selection. Inverting selects all the pixels outside the current selection marquee. Click the foreground color and choose RGB **204, 0, 1** or **#CC0033** in the **Color Picker** dialog. Choose **Fill...** from the **Edit** menu. The **Fill** dialog (Fig. 3.20) presents several options for filling a selection or layer. For this example, set the fill to **Foreground Color**, leave the

Feathering set to 0 pixels   Feathering set to 8 pixels

Fig. 3.19   Feathering a selection.

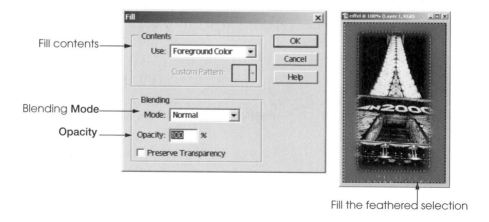

Fill contents

Blending **Mode**

Opacity

Fill the feathered selection

Fig. 3.20   Filling a selection with color.

blending mode set to **Normal** and click **OK**. The shortcut to fill any selection with the foreground color is *Alt+Backspace*. Alternatively, pressing *Ctrl+Backspace* fills a selection with the background color. These shortcuts only work with the **normal blending mode**. The blending mode determines how color interacts with the image color to which it is applied. Blending modes are explored in a later example.

Look-and-Feel Observation 3.2

Changing the blending mode in the **Fill** *dialog produces different blending effects between the border and the image. Test the different blending modes to view the differences.*

Choose **Deselect** from the **Select** menu or use the shortcut *Ctrl+D* to remove a selection marquee. As in the first example in which we created the file typefun, save this image for the Web. This time save the file in **JPEG** (Joint Photographic Experts Group) format, by selecting **JPEG** as the file type in the **Save for Web** dialog. JPEG is a format commonly used on the Web for saving photographic-quality images.

The JPEG format allows the user to specify the quality of the image being saved. For this image, set the quality to 50, which is medium quality. Most JPEG images intended for the Web are saved as medium or low quality to reduce their file size. JPEG images are previewed in a Web browser in the same way as GIF files. Choose RGB **204, 0, 1** or **#CC0033** as the matte color so that the background color of the preview Web page will be the same as the blurred frame around the photograph (Fig. 3.21).

Fig. 3.21   Previewing the feathered image in a Web browser.

3.4.2 Painting Tools

The second group of toolbox tools comprises the **painting tools,** which apply color to an image in simulated brush strokes or in constrained shapes. **Paintbrush** and **airbrush** are raster tools that draw with virtual paintbrush or airbrush strokes when they are clicked or dragged on the image area. Different brush size and stroke options are selected in the options bar.

The **paint bucket** tool adds the foreground color to selections or areas of similar-colored pixels. The pixel selection process for this tool is the same as the selection process for the magic wand tool. The paint bucket tool fills large areas with color.

Another interesting way to fill an area with color is with the **gradient** tool, which fills an area with a progression of colors (Fig. 3.22). The area to be filled must be selected with one of the selection tools before a gradient is applied to it; otherwise the gradient will fill the entire canvas. Click and drag with the gradient tool in the direction of the gradient movement to create patterns of color. Gradients can be created in many shapes and colors depending on which options are selected in the **Gradients** options bar.

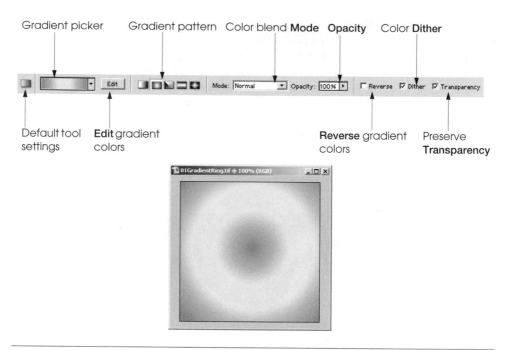

Fig. 3.22   Gradient pattern created using gradient tools.

Using Painting Tools

The following example uses the painting tools, filters and type tools to create a title image for a Web page. Create a new image that is 200 pixels high, 600 pixels wide with a white background in RGB mode. Select RGB **153**, **204**, **255** or **#99CCFF** (a light blue) as the foreground color and RGB **0**, **0**, **153** or **#000099** (a darker blue) as the background color. Fill the background layer with the foreground color by using the shortcut *Alt+Backspace*. This shortcut works on an entire layer if no selection is made. Next choose the paintbrush tool and select a **brush size** of **15** from the **Paintbrush** options bar. Several brush types and sizes are available in this options bar, including some that are hidden. The hidden brushes are found in different categories under the **Brushes** drop-down list (Fig. 3.23). This brush menu may also be accessed by right clicking in the image area with any of the paint brush tools.

Feel free to experiment with these different brushes. For this example, it does not matter which brushes are used because the painting will be distorted. Painting tools always paint with the foreground color. For this example, we want to paint with the dark-blue background color. Make the background color become the foreground color by clicking the **switch foreground and background** arrow found directly above the background color swatch in the toolbox. Once the colors are switched, paint randomly on the canvas with the dark-blue color (Fig. 3.24).

This "painting" will eventually become a design that fills the title text. Designs can be created by using one of the many **filters** provided by Photoshop Elements. Begin to create the pattern by choosing **Liquify...** from the **Distort** submenu of the **Filters** menu. The **liquify** filter distorts an image by modifying color placement. When the **Liquify** dialog opens

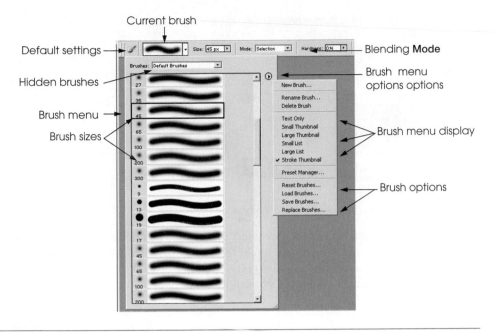

Fig. 3.23   Brush options.

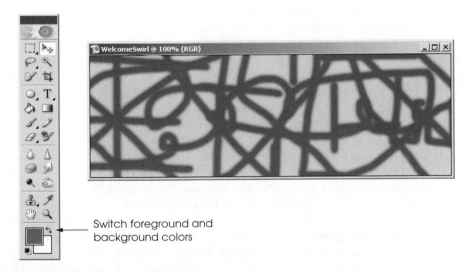

Fig. 3.24   Painting with the paintbrush tool.

(Fig. 3.25), choose a brush size of **50** with a brush pressure of **50**. The brush size determines the area affected by the filter. The brush pressure determines the filter's intensity. Click and drag in the painted area to apply the liquify filter. Eight different modes for the liquify filter can be selected with buttons along the left side of the dialog. The default mode for this tool is **warp,** but feel free to experiment with the other modes. If you make a mistake, click **Revert** to change the image back to its original appearance.

Fig. 3.25   **Liquify** filter morphing an image.

The liquify filter is one of the few filters that creates its effects based on the artistic input of the user, making it more like a tool than an actual filter. Most of the other filter effects are performed uniformly on image pixels. Continue to click and drag with the liquify brush until a design is created. Press **OK** to apply the filter to the original image.

Performance Tip 3.2

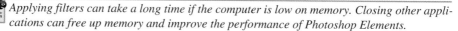

Applying filters can take a long time if the computer is low on memory. Closing other applications can free up memory and improve the performance of Photoshop Elements.

The next step is to define the text area to which the design is applied. Instead of creating regular text, we want to create a selection marquee in the shape of text. Select the type tool and choose the **type selection** option from the **Type** options bar. The type selection tool is indicated by a dashed line **T** (Fig. 3.26). Choose a font face of **Brush Script** (or another font if Brush Script is not available on your system) with font size **100** point (type the font size). The purpose of using the type selection tool instead of the regular type tool is to capture the pattern inside the selection boundaries of the type. Then the selection can be separated from the rest of the pattern and placed onto a new layer. Set the alignment for the type selection tool to **center** and click the middle of the image. The image turns red, indicating that a text selection is being made. Type the word "Welcome." The background remains red and the type shows through in the original blue color (Fig. 3.26).

The selection is not applied until another tool is chosen. For this example, select the move tool to apply the selection. The move tool creates a bounding box around the selection.

Separate the text from the background by copying its contents to a new layer. Select the **New** submenu of the **Layer** menu, and use the **Layer via Copy** function to create a new layer with the selected contents. Even though the text exists in its own layer, it is still not visible because it is hidden by the background layer. Turn off the background layer **visibility** by opening the **Layers** palette and clicking the layer's visibility button (Fig. 3.27). A layer is not deleted when the visibility is turned off; it is only deactivated so that the contents of other layers can be better identified. The copied text in the new layer should be the only visible element.

The next step is to crop out the background area using the **crop** tool located in the toolbox next to the type tool. Click and drag with the crop tool to make a **crop box** that eliminates the extra background area. The area being cropped turns gray and a bounding box with anchors surrounds the remaining area (Fig. 3.28). Adjust the bounding box that

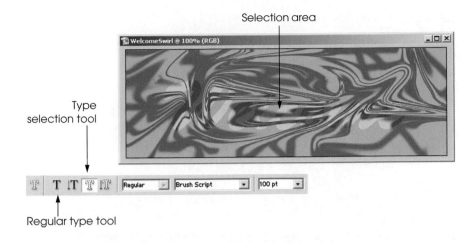

Fig. 3.26   Using the type selection tool to create a title image.

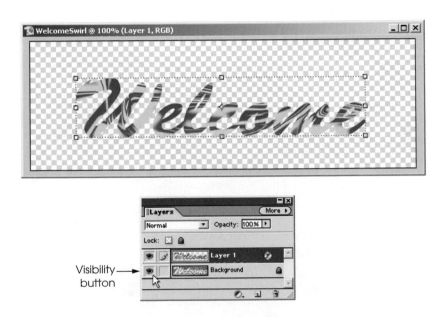

Fig. 3.27   **Layers** palette allows users to view specific layers.

eliminates the background area around the word. Once the crop selection is set, press the *Enter* key to permanently crop the image.

The next step in creating the title image is to give the word a layer effect to raise it off the page. Select the background layer in the **Layers** palette if it has not already been selected. As in the first example, open the **Layer Styles** palette. Instead of applying a **Drop Shadow**, this time choose **Bevels** from the style-selection drop-down list. Apply the **Simple Sharp Inner** bevel to the "Welcome" layer (Fig. 3.29).

Fig. 3.28   Crop tool eliminates excess image area.

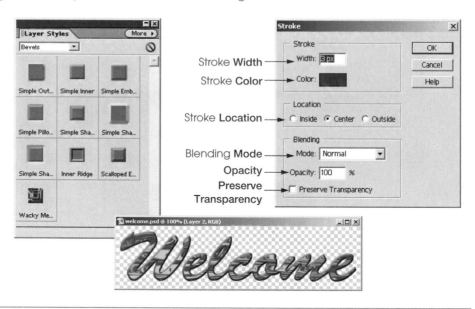

Fig. 3.29   Simple inner bevel and stroke adjustment applied to an image.

The last step is to create a color border to outline the text. Choose the magic wand tool and click outside the word, selecting the transparent area. Add spaces inside the **o, e** and **l** by either clicking the **Add to selection** button in the **Magic Wand** options bar (Fig. 3.18) or holding down *Shift* while clicking the letter spaces with the magic wand tool. Next, invert the selection so that the word is selected instead of the transparent background (*Ctrl+Shift+I*). Create a line with an even pixel weight along the selection by choosing **Stroke** from the **Edit** menu. The **Stroke** dialog has options for stroke width, stroke color, stroke location, blending mode and opacity (Fig. 3.29).

Set the **line weight** to 3 pixels and **Location** to center in the **Stroke** dialog. The stroke **Color** defaults to the current foreground color, and can be changed by double clicking the stroke swatch. Make sure that the **Preserve Transparency** box is unchecked, otherwise the stroke will not appear in the transparent area around the word. Click **OK**. Finally, save the file.

3.4.3 Shape Tools

The **shape** tool draws vector shapes filled with color. Unlike raster graphics in the same layer, vector graphics can be edited independently from one another. Every time a shape tool is used, a new vector **shape layer** is created. Shape layers contain only shapes created with the shape tool and cannot contain raster graphics. The shape tool's default setting is a rectangle; however, the shape can be changed to an ellipse, polygon, line or custom shape with the **Shape** options bar. The options change depending on the selected tool (Fig. 3.30).

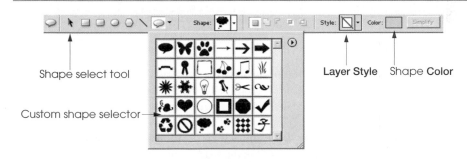

Fig. 3.30   **Shape** options bar.

To demonstrate the shape tool, we will create a four-button navigation bar. Each button on the bar is created as a vector shape with the shape tool and converted into a raster graphic to create the navigation bar.

Create a new file that is 625 pixels wide and 100 pixels high. For guidance when creating the navigation bar, turn on the grid by choosing **Show Grid** from the **View** menu. This option helps to space the buttons evenly. The settings for the grid are changed in the **Grid Preferences** dialog by choosing **Grid...** from the **Preferences** submenu of the **Edit** menu. Set the grid lines to appear for every pixel and set the grid line color to light blue. Also select **Snap To Grid** in the **View** menu. The snap option makes selections adhere to grid lines.

Choose a new foreground color to become the color of the buttons. The navigation buttons are created as a series of duplicate rectangles. Select the shape tool from the toolbox, and select the rectangle tool from the **Shape** options bar. Create a rectangle that fills a little less than 1/4 of the image width, approximately 10 grid squares, as shown in Fig. 3.31.

Duplicate this rectangle three times (once for each link in the navigation bar). Select the **shape select** tool, indicated by an arrow, from the **Shape** options bar. Copy the rectangle to the **clipboard** by using the shortcut *Ctrl+C*. The clipboard is an area of temporary memory in the computer in which text and graphics can be stored for immediate reuse. The **paste** command places the information from the clipboard into a document. Use the paste shortcut *Ctrl+V* to paste the rectangle from the clipboard back into the main image. This

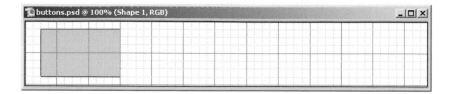

Fig. 3.31   Shape tool can create rectangles.

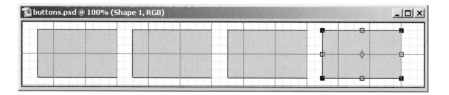

Fig. 3.32   Multiple rectangles and the move shape tool.

new rectangle is placed directly on top of the existing rectangle in the same vector layer. Use the shape select tool to drag the new rectangle to the right of the original. Space the rectangles two grid lines apart. Repeat the copy-and-paste step two more times to create the four navigation bar buttons (Fig. 3.32).

    If the rectangles were placed unevenly, adjust their position using the shape select tool. It is also possible to use the **Undo** command in the **Edit** menu, or the *Ctrl+Z* command, to correct mistakes. Actions can be undone as far back as the last time the image was saved by using the **History** palette. The **History** palette (Fig. 3.33) displays every action performed since the last save. Selecting an action in the palette creates a preview of the image if the action was undone. Click the trash can button in the **History** palette to undo an action permanently.

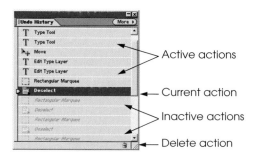

Fig. 3.33   **History** palette has reverse action tools.

    The rectangles should now be in a straight line and evenly spaced. The next step is to change the shape of the rectangles uniformly, turning them into parallelograms by **skewing** them with the **transformation** option to tilt them along the horizontal or vertical axis. To achieve this, select all the rectangles by clicking each with the shape select tool while holding down the *Shift* key. All the rectangles are selected simultaneously when each has a shape selection box around it. Apply a skew transformation by selecting **Skew** from the **Transform Shape** submenu of the **Image** menu. During the skew transformation a bounding box encloses all four rectangles. Hover near the top center anchor until a two-way arrow appears. Click and drag the bounding box two grid lines to the right, transforming the rectangles (Fig. 3.34).

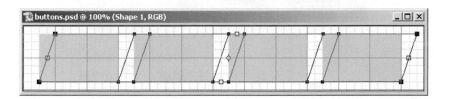

Fig. 3.34   Skew transformation.

All four rectangles slant to the right when the mouse is released. Transformations are not applied until the *Enter* key is pressed, so if the shapes do not look correct, the transformation still can be changed.

A **navigation bar** effect is created by connecting the buttons. For this example, the buttons will be connected by a heavy-weight line created with the **line shape** tool. The line shape tool is located in the **Shape** options bar between the **polygon** tool and the **custom shape** tool. Set the line weight for the line tool to **20** pixels in the tool options bar. Click and drag from left to right with the line shape tool, creating a line in a new vector layer (Fig. 3.35).

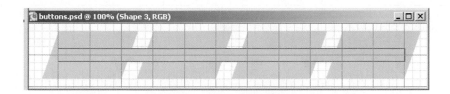

Fig. 3.35   Line added to link the skewed rectangles together.

The four parallelograms and their connecting line outline the navigation bar. We apply a bevel to these shapes to make them appear as buttons. The steps to do this are more complicated than applying layer styles to text or create lone shapes. First the rectangles and line layers must be converted from vector shape layers into regular raster layers. Then they must be merged together so that the buttons and line are treated as one area of pixels.

Open the **Layers** palette and select the line layer. Change both the line layer and buttons layer into regular raster layers separately by choosing **Simplify Layer** from the layer options menu (Fig. 3.36). Both the line and the parallelograms are no longer individual vector objects. Instead they are raster areas of pixels.

The next step is to merge the line layer with the rectangles layer so that when the bevel is applied, it is applied uniformly around the perimeter of the navigation bar. Merge the layers by selecting the line layer in the **Layers** palette and choose **Merge Down** from the

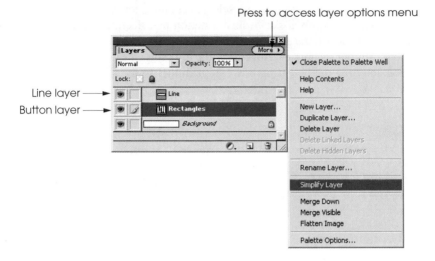

Fig. 3.36   Simplifying a shape layer using the **Layers** palette.

Layer options menu. Merging two raster layers unifies their contents into a combined area of pixels. Next, layer styles may be applied to the navigation bar. Create the button effect by applying a simple sharp inner bevel with the **Layer Styles** palette.

The navigation bar is completed by adding titles to the buttons. Select a large font face and type the following button labels: **Links**, **News**, **Files** and **E-mail**. Center the type over the buttons with the move tool (Fig. 3.37). This example uses font face Tahoma, italic at 35 point.

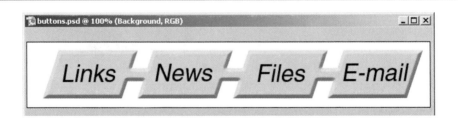

Fig. 3.37   Navigation bar.

There are several ways to implement a navigation bar on a Web page. One way is to create **hot spots** which are sensitive to the mouse and link to different locations. Another way is to break apart the navigation bar into separate buttons through a process called **image slicing**. Image slicing creates smaller individual images from an original larger image. First turn the grid back on and turn off the visibility of the background layer. Reduce the file size by eliminating the unnecessary background area with the crop tool.

Select each button with the rectangular marquee tool and then copy the selection contents into a new document. First check to make sure that **snap** is on by checking **Snap To Grid** in the **View** menu. Click and drag the rectangular marquee tool using the grid as a guide to select only the links button (Fig. 3.38).

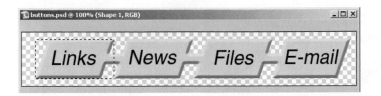

Fig. 3.38　Slicing an image with the rectangular marquee tool.

Copy the contents of the selection to the clipboard by choosing **Copy Merged** from the **Edit** menu. This command copies pixels within the selection from all visible layers. Open a new file with a transparent background. The default height and width should automatically match the contents of the clipboard, so do not change them. Now paste the links button into the new file to be saved as a transparent GIF. Repeat these steps for each of the buttons (Fig. 3.39). These files are ready to be inserted into a Web document by rebuilding the navigation bar. Each section of the image can be linked to the appropriate page or action. We show how to implement links in Chapters 4 and 5.

Fig. 3.39　Sliced image as individual buttons.

3.5 Layers

One of the most important features of Photoshop Elements is the ability to edit images in **layers**. Any image can be composed of many layers, each with its own attributes and effects. Each element of an image can be moved and edited independently if kept in its own layer. Layers are sometimes complicated; however, they ultimately save time in the overall process. The concept of layers is somewhat like **animation cells**. An animator uses separate layers of transparencies to create a scene so that each item can be edited individually.

Photoshop Elements has three categories of layers: **vector**, **raster** and **adjustment**. Each object on a vector layer is an independent element that is stored as a set of properties. Raster layers exist as a grid of colored pixels. Editing the elements in a raster layer affects all the other parts of the layer. Open the file `arches.psd` located in the Chapter 3 examples directory on the CD-ROM that accompanies this book. This file shows the different types of layers.

Portability Tip 3.3

The psd extension, which stands for Photoshop Document, is a file format that is specific to Adobe image-editing programs. This file format supports layers, making it ideal for images that are in the middle of the editing process and for archiving. Web documents do not support this file format.

This file has several different layers which can be seen individually in the **Layers** palette. The layers are arranged hierarchically, with the uppermost layer at the top of the list. The active layer is highlighted in blue (Fig. 3.40).

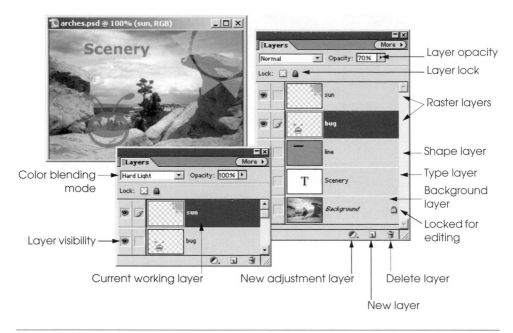

Fig. 3.40   Layers in the **Layers** palette.

Click the **New Layer** button in the **Layers** palette to create a new raster layer. Only raster layers are created with the **New Layer** button. Vector layers are created when a vector tool such as the type or shape tool is used. The different ways vector information and raster information are stored prevents these two types of graphics from existing on the same layer.

Each layer occupies one row in the palette. A row displays the layer's name, its position relative to other layers and several properties that modify the function of the layer. It is a good idea to name each layer for the objects it contains to make it easier to remember what layers affect what images. Select the **Arrange** submenu from the **Layers** menu to move a layer up or down in the hierarchy. Layers also can be dragged up or down in the hierarchy inside the **Layers** palette.

The **background layer** is always a raster layer anchored to the bottom of the image. The layer order, color blending mode and opacity cannot be changed on the background layer. Convert the background layer into a regular raster layer by double clicking **Background** in the **Layers** palette. The displayed dialog provides the option of renaming the layer. Renaming a background layer converts it to an independent raster layer. Files with transparent backgrounds do not have background layers. Instead the bottommost layer is an independent raster layer named **Layer 1**.

The **layer opacity** is the measure of a layer's transparency, given as a percentage. The **Bug** layer in arches.psd (Fig. 3.40) has an opacity of 70%, making the layer beneath it visible through the bug. An opacity of 0% makes the layer completely transparent.

The **color blending mode** determines how a layer is affected by painting or editing tools. The blending mode for the **Sun** layer in arches.psd is set to **Hard Light**, affecting the image in the **Sun** layer as if a spotlight were pointed at it. There are several blending modes from which to choose. Select the **Sun** layer from the **Layers** palette. Try applying different blending modes by changing the selection in the blending modes drop-down list in the **Layers** palette, and note the varying effects.

An **adjustment layer** allows color adjustments to be made to the layer beneath it without affecting color in the other layers. An adjustment layer acts as a preview of what a particular adjustment would look like if directly applied to a layer, without making any permanent changes. Select the background layer in the **Layers** palette for the arches.psd file. Create an adjustment layer by clicking the **New Adjustment Layer** button (Fig. 3.41). The new adjustment layer is placed directly above the selected layer.

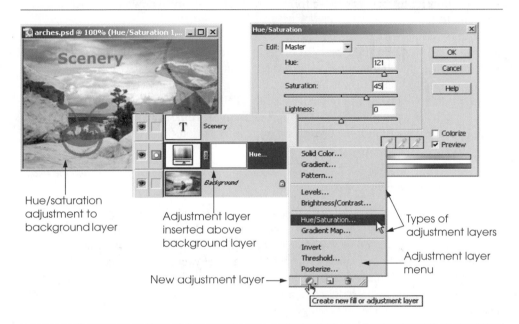

Fig. 3.41   Adjustment layer altering hue and saturation.

When the **New Adjustment Layer** button is pressed, a menu opens allowing the user to choose the type of adjustment. Choose **Hue/Saturation** from this menu to open the **Hue/Saturation** dialog. Change the hue to **+121** and the saturation to **+45**, then click **OK** to apply the adjustment to the background layer. Note that the adjustment only affects the background layer. If the visibility of an adjustment layer is turned off, the layers beneath appear as if no changes were made.

3.6 Screen Capture

Screen capturing is a widely used technique to create images from a screen display. The process takes the content of a screen and "captures" it so that the capture can be used as an image. For instance, the diagrams in this chapter that show actual windows and tools from Photoshop Elements were all created using screen capture. Screen capturing in Photoshop Elements works like the copy and paste functions—when performing a screen capture, the image is copied to the clipboard until it is pasted into a document.

Press the *Print Screen* key on the keyboard, found above the *Delete* and *Insert* keys, to capture the entire screen area. Pressing this button copies the screen contents to the clipboard. Open a new image in Photoshop Elements. The default dimensions for the new image are the same as the screen capture on the clipboard. Then paste the screen capture into the new image. Pressing *Alt+Print Screen* captures only the active window.

3.7 File Formats: GIF, JPEG and PNG

The three major file formats for images on the Web are **GIF**, **JPEG** and **PNG**. Each format has a specific use when saving images for the Web. Web developers and designers need to know the differences between these formats in order to optimize download times and user compatibility.

The **Graphics Interchange Format (GIF)**, developed by CompuServe, is based on a 256-color palette. GIF is best used for screen captures, line drawings, graphics with sharp edges and images with transparency. When reducing colors to the 256 available in the GIF file format, Photoshop Elements performs **dithering** on the image. Dithering simulates the desired color with a color from the GIF palette. GIF is a **lossless** format, meaning that the picture quality is not reduced by the **compression algorithm**. The compression algorithm is the formula that a file format uses to store file information.

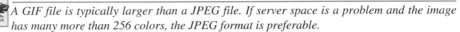

Performance Tip 3.3

A GIF file is typically larger than a JPEG file. If server space is a problem and the image has many more than 256 colors, the JPEG format is preferable.

Dithering may be effective, but often it destroys the quality of an image that has color complexity. Such richness is characteristic of real-world images such as photographs, scanned images and computer art created with 3-D rendering programs. Images that are "color complex" are better suited to the JPEG format. However, this format is not without limitations. JPEG is a **lossy** format (i.e., saving an image in this format gradually reduces the quality of the image due to loss of color information). The JPEG compression algorithm handles sharp edges and abrupt changes poorly.

Performance Tip 3.4

*The JPEG format has scalable compression. When saving a JPEG image in the **Save Options** dialog, sliding the compression slider to the right causes the image to retain high quality, but the file size also remains large. Sliding the compression slider to the left causes the file size to decrease, but image quality suffers. This graduated scale helps in finding a good balance between file size and image quality.*

One feature that GIF and JPEG share is **interlacing** (in GIF terminology) or **progressive encoding** (in JPEG terminology). Interlacing or progressive encoding creates a rough image preview at the beginning of the download process. The image clarity then gradually increases as the image loads. This behavior often holds the user's attention while a page loads. Interlacing is specified in the **Save for Web** dialog. Non-interlaced images download at the highest quality and are ideal for images that have small file sizes.

Performance Tip 3.5

Do not place too many interlaced images on any one Web page; doing so slows page rendering.

A newer image standard is making its mark on the Web. The **Portable Network Graphics (PNG**, pronounced **ping**) format was developed in response to a decision by the

UniSys corporation to start charging royalties on the GIF format, on which UniSys holds a patent. PNG is a suitable replacement for GIF and JPEG because it has the better qualities of both formats. For example, PNG can encode in **RGBA**—the A stands for **alpha transparency**, which makes images transparent against any background, similar to opacity. The PNG file format solves many problems that previously existed with transparency. An image with both color complexity and transparency could not be saved as a transparent GIF or a JPEG. The PNG file format supports millions of colors as well as transparency. This makes it a great alternative for both GIF and JPEG. Photoshop Elements supports the PNG format, as do the latest versions of both Netscape and Internet Explorer. Web developers increasingly are using the PNG file format. For more information on the PNG format, visit `www.w3.org/Graphics/PNG`.

3.8 Web Resources

Many resources are available on the topic of using Photoshop Elements to create images for Web pages. A good resource is the **interactive help file** packaged with Photoshop Elements. This help file covers almost every function Photoshop Elements has to offer. The interactive help file is accessed by clicking the question mark button on the main menu bar. Also check out `www.adobe.com` (Adobe Inc.'s home page) to stay up-to-date on general information about Photoshop Elements. Most of the information on the Web, however, is available at user-run sites offering general information, examples and tutorials. For example, `www.photoshopcafe.com` has excellent in-depth tutorials, for both Photoshop beginners and experts who want to explore new techniques. Another site for tutorials is located at `www.planetphotoshop.com`. Many Photoshop tutorials were written for versions of Photoshop other than Elements, but many of the main concepts carry over to the Elements version. If looking for effects more diverse than those included in Photoshop Elements, new filters can be downloaded for free from sites such as `www.plugins.com/plugins/photoshop`. Plug-in filters, brushes and fonts are installed to the hard drive of the computer under the Photoshop Elements directory.

SUMMARY

- The most successful Web pages use both text and graphics to enhance the user experience.
- Adobe Inc.'s Photoshop Elements is an easy-to-use graphics package that offers the functionality of more expensive packages at an economical price.
- The graphics editing skills learned through Photoshop Elements can be applied to other graphics editors such as Adobe Photoshop, Jasc Paint Shop Pro, Macromedia Fireworks and the GIMP (GNU Image Manipulation Program).
- The **File** menu is used to open new or existing files.
- Initial image settings, such as image height and width, image resolution and background color, are specified in the **New** dialog that appears every time a new image file is created.
- Every image in Photoshop Elements is composed of a series of dots called pixels organized in a grid.
- The number of pixels per unit measure is called the image resolution. The resolution is set in the **New** dialog.
- The three color modes available are RGB, Grayscale and Bitmap, of which RGB and Grayscale are the most commonly used for creating Web graphics.

- Red, green and blue are the primary colors in light; when combined in different intensity values from 0 to 255, they create a color range of 16.7 million colors.
- Palettes are opened by clicking their tabs in the palette well. Each palette contains options for image editing and effects.
- The toolbox contains selection, editing, painting and type tools that are all used to modify existing images or to create new ones.
- The two squares at the bottom of the toolbox are the two active colors—the foreground color and the background color.
- The **Color Picker** dialog is where the foreground or background color is selected.
- A Web-safe palette refers to the 216 colors that are cross-platform and cross-browser compatible.
- Hexadecimal notation is the color code used in most Web documents to define font and background colors.
- Anti-aliasing is a process that smooths image edges by blending the color of the edge pixels with the color of the background on which the text is being placed.
- The move tool moves an object or resizes a selected object.
- The **Layer Styles** palette offers a variety of special effects that can be applied to text or shapes.
- Photoshop Elements uses layers so that items can be edited independently.
- Type (text) layers are indicated by a **T** in the **Layers** palette.
- Clicking the trash can button in the **Layers** palette deletes the active layer.
- The **Save for Web...** option sets the file format and color strategy for saving an image based on certain Internet standards.
- GIF (Compuserve Graphics Interchange Format) is a file format that preserves transparency (saving pixels void of color information), making GIF appropriate for transparent Web graphics.
- Photoshop Elements creates and edits two different types of graphics that are standard for Web design—raster and vector.
- Raster images are composed of pixels organized on a grid.
- Vector images exist as individual objects that can be edited separately from one another.
- The selection tools—the lasso, magic wand, and marquee tools—create a border called a marquee which bounds a selected area of pixels that can be modified by filters, moved or have color adjustments made.
- Feathering blurs the edges of a selection such that the pixels inside the selection will blend with the pixels outside the selection.
- Inverting a selection selects all the pixels outside the current selection marquee.
- A selection is filled with a color by choosing **Fill...** from the **Edit** menu.
- Patterns can be created from scratch by using one of many filters.
- The type (text) selection tool, indicated by a dashed line **T** in the **Type** options bar, creates a marquee selection in the shape of text.
- The crop tool eliminates unnecessary image area.
- The shape tool is a vector tool that draws precise shapes filled with a particular color.
- Paste a clipboard item into an image by using the shortcut *Ctrl+V*.
- Image slicing creates smaller images from an original larger image by separating it into pieces.
- Layers organize the different parts of an image.
- Photoshop Elements has three categories of layers: vector, raster and adjustment.

- The active layer is highlighted in blue in the **Layers** palette.
- Each layer occupies one row in the palette which displays the layer's name, its position relative to other layers and several properties that modify the function of the layer.
- Adjustment layers allow adjustments to be made to the layers beneath them without affecting any of the pixels in the lower layers.
- Photoshop Elements performs screen captures and adds the convenience of being able to edit them.
- The two major file formats used for images are GIF and JPEG.
- GIF is best used for screen captures, line drawings and other graphics with sharp edges.
- JPEG is ideal for images with "color complexity," such as photographs and original art.
- The PNG file format supports millions of colors as well as transparency, making it an effective alternative to both GIF and JPEG.

TERMINOLOGY

active layer	fill selection
active tool options bar	filter
adjustment layer	font
alignment	font face
alpha transparency	font weight
anchor	foreground color
animation cell	GIF (Graphics Interchange Format)
anti-alias	gradient tool
background color	grayscale color mode
background layer	grid
blending mode	hexadecimal
bounding box	hidden tool
brightness	**History** palette
browser preview	hot spot
brush pressure	HSB color model
brush size	hue
clipboard	image slicing
color blending mode	image window
color mode	interlacing
Color Picker	interpolation
color wheel	invert selection
compression algorithm	JPEG (Joint Photographic Experts Group)
compression quality	lasso tool
constrain proportions	layer
Copy	layer opacity
Copy Merged	layer order
crop tool	layer styles
custom shape tool	**Layers** palette
Deselect	line tool
development environment	line weight
dithering	**Liquify** filter
drop shadow	lossless format
elliptical marquee	lossy format
feathering	magic wand tool
file size	magnetic lasso

magnifying glass tool
marquee tool
matte
matte color
move tool
multiple selections
New Layer
New Layer via Copy
normal blending mode
opacity
optimize
paintbrush tool
palette
palette well
paste
Photoshop Document (`psd`) extension
pixel
PNG (Portable Network Graphics)
polygon tool
polygonal lasso
primary colors in light
progressive encoding
`.psd` extension
raster layer
rectangular marquee
regular raster layer
Reset Palette Locations

resize
resolution dependent
resolution independent
Revert
RGB color mode
RGB color model
saturation
Save for Web
screen capture
selection tool
shape layer
shape tool
skew
status bar
stroke selection
swatches
tolerance
toolbox
transform
transparency
transparent GIF
type layer
type selection tool
type tool
vector layer
warped text
Web-safe palette

SELF-REVIEW EXERCISES

3.1   Fill in the blanks in each of the following statements:
   a) The _____ palette is used to organize different image components.
   b) A(n) _____ is the dashed line that indicates a selected part of an image.
   c) A full screen capture is performed by hitting the _____ button.
   d) Selection _____ causes the pixels inside a selection to be blended with the pixels outside a selection.
   e) The **Fill** command is found under the _____ menu.

3.2   State whether each of the following is *true* or *false*. If the answer is *false*, explain why.
   a) The best file formats to save transparent images are GIF or PNG.
   b) Raster images do not lose image quality when they are enlarged.
   c) The three main types of layers are transparent, color and drawing.
   d) The type selection tool creates a marquee selection in the shape of text.
   e) Hexadecimal color notation produces different colors than the RGB color notation.

ANSWERS TO SELF-REVIEW EXERCISES

3.1   a) **Layers**. b) marquee. c) *Print Screen*. d) feathering. e) **Edit**.

3.2   a) True. b) False. Raster images lose image quality as they are enlarged because of pixels being added in the interpolation process. c) False. The three main types of layers are vector, raster and adjustment. d) True. e) False. Hexadecimal produces the same colors as the RGB color notation.

EXERCISES

3.3   Create a vertical navigation bar (145 × 350 px) with six different-colored, identical-shaped, elliptical navigation buttons. Name these buttons **About Us**, **News**, **Portfolio**, **Programs**, **Events** and **Contact**. Give the buttons a simple inner bevel. Slice the image into six different files and save each button as a transparent GIF.

3.4   This exercise uses several of the filters which Photoshop Elements has to offer, all of which can be found in the **Filters** palette in the palette well. Create a title image (500 × 150 px) with a transparent background. Choose white as the foreground color and a medium green as the background color. Using the type selection tool, type in the title of a Web page and center the selection on the page. Expand the borders of the selection by 1 pixel by choosing **Expand** from the **Modify** submenu of the **Select** menu. Apply the **Clouds** filter. To create a texture, apply the **Grain** filter, with grain intensity set to **40**, the contrast set to **50**, and the grain type to regular. Now apply the **Watercolor** filter with the brush detail set to **14**, the shadow intensity set to **0** and the texture set to **1**. Finally, apply the **Glowing Edges** filter with the edge brightness set to **4** and the smoothness set to **1**. Stroke the text selection with yellow, a pixel weight of **2**, inside the selection. Save the image as a transparent GIF.

3.5   Create a new image (250 × 250 px) with a white background. Create five separate ellipses with the ellipse shape tool on five separate shape layers. Make each ellipse a different color. Make the ellipses overlap one another in several places, but not completely. For each layer, change the blending mode to **Multiply** (from the drop-down list of the **Layers** palette). Save the image for the Web.

3.6   Create a new image (500 × 150 px) with a white background. Apply the render clouds filter. Apply the chrome filter with detail set to **4** and smoothness set to **7**. Using the text selection tool, type "Chrome" with a large, heavy font. With this selection, make a new layer via copy. On the new layer, apply a simple outer bevel. Select the background layer and add a contrast adjustment layer to it. Increase the brightness to **+50**. Now select the type layer. Change the color balance by choosing **Hue/Saturation** from the **Color** submenu of the **Enhance** menu. With the **Colorize** checkbox selected, adjust the hue to **245**, the saturation to **50** and the lightness to **17**. Save the image for Web as a JPEG.

3.7   Discuss the differences between the GIF, JPEG and PNG file formats and when each should be used.

3.8   Define each of the following terms:
   a) Interlacing.
   b) Tolerance.
   c) Matte.
   d) Feathering.
   e) Web-safe palette.
   f) Filter.
   g) Image slicing.

Introduction to XHTML: Part 1

Objectives

- To understand important components of XHTML documents.
- To use XHTML to create Web pages.
- To be able to add images to Web pages.
- To understand how to create and use hyperlinks to navigate Web pages.
- To be able to mark up lists of information.

To read between the lines was easier than to follow the text.
Henry James

High thoughts must have high language.
Aristophanes

Outline

4.1 Introduction

Welcome to the world of opportunity created by the World Wide Web. The Internet is now three decades old, but it was not until the Web became popular in the 1990s that the explosion of opportunity that we are still experiencing began. Exciting new developments occur almost daily—the pace of innovation is unprecedented by any other technology. In this chapter, you will develop your own Web pages. As the book proceeds, you will create increasingly appealing and powerful Web pages. In the later portion of the book, you will learn how to create complete Web-based applications.

This chapter begins unlocking the power of Web-based application development with **XHTML**—the **Extensible HyperText Markup Language**. In later chapters, we introduce more sophisticated XHTML techniques, such as **tables**, which are particularly useful for structuring information from **databases** (i.e., software that stores structured sets of data), and **Cascading Style Sheets** (**CSS**), which make Web pages more visually appealing.

Unlike procedural programming languages such as C, Fortran, Cobol and Pascal, XHTML is a **markup language** that specifies the format of the text that is displayed in a Web browser such as Microsoft's *Internet Explorer* or *Netscape*.

One key issue when using XHTML is the separation of the **presentation** of a document (i.e., the document's appearance when rendered by a browser) from the **structure** of the document's information. XHTML is based on HTML (HyperText Markup Language)—a legacy technology of the World Wide Web Consortium (W3C). In HTML, it was common to specify the document's content, structure and formatting. Formatting might specify where the browser placed an element in a Web page or the fonts and colors used to display an element. XHTML 1.1 (W3C's latest version of W3C XHTML Recommendation at the time of publication) allows only a document's content and structure to appear in a valid XHTML document, and not its formatting. Normally, such formatting is specified with Cascading Style Sheets (Chapter 6). All our examples in this chapter are based upon the XHTML 1.1 Recommendation.

4.2 Editing XHTML

In this chapter, we write XHTML in its **source-code form**. We create **XHTML documents** by typing them in a text editor (e.g., *Notepad*, *Wordpad*, *vi*, *emacs*) and saving them with either an `.html` or an `.htm` file-name extension.

Good Programming Practice 4.1

Assign documents file names that describe their functionality. This practice can help you identify documents faster. It also helps people who want to link to a page, by giving them an easy-to-remember name. For example, if you are writing an XHTML document that contains product information, you might want to call it `products.html`*.*

Machines running specialized software called **Web servers** store XHTML documents. Clients (e.g., Web browsers) request specific **resources** such as the XHTML documents from the Web server. For example, typing `www.deitel.com/books/downloads.html` into a Web browser's address field requests `downloads.html` from the Web server running at `www.deitel.com`. This document is located on the server in a directory named `books`. We discuss Web servers in detail in Chapter 21. For now, we simply place the XHTML documents on our machine and open them using Internet Explorer.

4.3 First XHTML Example

In this chapter and the next, we present XHTML markup and provide screen captures that show how Internet Explorer renders (i.e., displays) the XHTML.[1] Every XHTML document we show has line numbers for the reader's convenience. These line numbers are not part of the XHTML documents.

Our first example (Fig. 4.1) is an XHTML document named `main.html` that displays the message "Welcome to XHTML!" in the browser.

```
1   <?xml version = "1.0"?>
2   <!DOCTYPE html PUBLIC "-//W3C//DTD XHTML 1.1//EN"
3      "http://www.w3.org/TR/xhtml11/DTD/xhtml11.dtd">
4
5   <!-- Fig. 4.1: main.html -->
6   <!-- Our first Web page   -->
7
8   <html xmlns = "http://www.w3.org/1999/xhtml">
9      <head>
10        <title>Internet and WWW How to Program - Welcome</title>
11     </head>
12
13     <body>
14        <p>Welcome to XHTML!</p>
15     </body>
16  </html>
```

Fig. 4.1   First XHTML example. (Part 1 of 2.)

---

1. All the examples presented in this book are available at `www.deitel.com` and on the CD-ROM that accompanies the book.

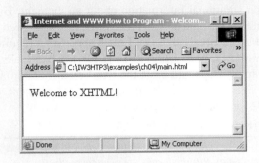

Fig. 4.1   First XHTML example. (Part 2 of 2.)

The key line in the program is line 14, which tells the browser to display "Welcome to XHTML!" Now let us consider each line of the program.

Lines 1–3 are required in XHTML documents to conform with proper XHTML syntax. For now, copy and paste these lines into each XHTML document you create. The meaning of these lines is discussed in detail in Chapter 20, Extensible Markup Language (XML).

Lines 5–6 are **XHTML comments**. XHTML document creators insert comments to improve markup readability and describe the content of a document. Comments also help other people read and understand an XHTML document's markup and content. Comments do not cause the browser to perform any action when the user loads the XHTML document into the Web browser to view the document. XHTML comments always start with `<!--` and end with `-->`. Each of our XHTML examples includes comments that specify the figure number and file name, and provide a brief description of the example's purpose. Subsequent examples include comments in the markup, especially to highlight new features.

> **Good Programming Practice 4.2**
>
> *Place comments throughout your markup. Comments help other programmers understand the markup, assist in debugging and list useful information that you do not want the browser to render. Comments also help you understand your own markup when you revisit a document to modify or update it in the future.*

XHTML markup contains text that represents the content of a document and **elements** that specify a document's structure. Some important elements of an XHTML document are the **html** element, the **head** element and the **body** element. The html element encloses the **head section** (represented by the head element) and the **body section** (represented by the body element). The head section contains information about the XHTML document, such as its **title**. The head section also can contain special document formatting instructions called **style sheets** and client-side programs called **scripts** for creating dynamic Web pages. (We introduce style sheets in Chapter 6 and scripting with JavaScript in Chapter 7.) The body section contains the page's content that the browser displays when the user visits the Web page.

XHTML documents delimit an element with **start** and **end** tags. A start tag consists of the element name in angle brackets (e.g., <html>). An end tag consists of the element name preceded by a / in angle brackets (e.g., </html>). In this example, lines 8 and 16 define the start and end of the html element. Note that the end tag in line 16 has the same name as the start tag, but is preceded by a / inside the angle brackets. Many start tags have **attributes** that provide additional information about an element. Browsers can use this additional information to determine how to process the element. Each attribute has a **name** and a **value** separated by an equals sign (=). Line 8 specifies a required attribute (xmlns) and value (http://www.w3.org/1999/xhtml) for the html element in an XHTML document. For now, simply copy and paste the html element start tag in line 8 into your XHTML documents. We discuss the details of the html element's xmlns attribute in Chapter 20, Extensible Markup Language (XML).

Common Programming Error 4.1

Not enclosing attribute values in either single or double quotes is a syntax error. However, some Web browsers may still render the element correctly.

Common Programming Error 4.2

Using uppercase letters in an XHTML element or attribute name is a syntax error. However, some Web browsers may still render the element correctly.

An XHTML document divides the html element into two sections—head and body. Lines 9–11 define the Web page's head section with a head element. Line 10 specifies a title element. This is called a **nested element** because it is enclosed in the head element's start and end tags. The head element is also a nested element because it is enclosed in the html element's start and end tags. The title element describes the Web page. Titles usually appear in the **title bar** at the top of the browser window and also as the text identifying a page when users add the page to their list of **Favorites** or **Bookmarks** that enables them to return to their favorite sites. Search engines (i.e., sites that allow users to search the Web) also use the title for cataloging purposes.

Good Programming Practice 4.3

Indenting nested elements emphasizes a document's structure and promotes readability.

Common Programming Error 4.3

XHTML does not permit tags to overlap—a nested element's end tag must appear in the document before the enclosing element's end tag. For example, the nested XHTML tags <head><title>hello</head></title> cause a syntax error, because the enclosing head element's ending </head> tag appears before the nested title element's ending </title> tag.

Good Programming Practice 4.4

Use a consistent title-naming convention for all pages on a site. For example, if a site is named "Bailey's Web Site," then the title of the links page might be "Bailey's Web Site—Links." This practice can help users better understand the Web site's structure.

Line 13 opens the document's body element. The body section of an XHTML document specifies the document's content, which may include text and tags.

Some tags, such as the **paragraph tags** (**<p>** and **</p>**) in line 14, mark up text for display in a browser. All the text placed between the <p> and </p> tags forms one paragraph. When the browser renders a paragraph, a blank line usually precedes and follows paragraph text.

This document ends with two end tags (lines 15–16). These tags close the body and html elements, respectively. The </html> tag in an XHTML document informs the browser that the XHTML markup is complete.

To view this example in Internet Explorer, perform the following steps:

1. Copy the Chapter 4 examples onto your machine from the CD that accompanies this book (or download the examples from www.deitel.com).

2. Launch Internet Explorer and select **Open...** from the **File** Menu. This displays the **Open** dialog.

3. Click the **Open** dialog's **Browse...** button to display the **Microsoft Internet Explorer** file dialog.

4. Navigate to the directory containing the Chapter 4 examples and select the file main.html, then click **Open**.

5. Click **OK** to have Internet Explorer render the document. Other examples are opened in a similar manner.

At this point your browser window should appear similar to the sample screen capture shown in Fig. 4.1. (Note that we resized the browser window to save space in the book.)

4.4 W3C XHTML Validation Service

Programming Web-based applications can be complex, and XHTML documents must be written correctly to ensure that browsers process them properly. To promote correctly written documents, the World Wide Web Consortium (W3C) provides a **validation service** (validator.w3.org) for checking a document's syntax. Documents can be validated either from a URL that specifies the location of the file or by uploading a file to the site validator.w3.org/file-upload.html. Uploading a file copies the file from the user's computer to another computer on the Internet. Figure 4.2 shows main.html (Fig. 4.1) being uploaded for validation. The W3C's Web page indicates that the service name is **MarkUp Validation Service**, and the validation service is able to validate the syntax of XHTML documents. All the XHTML examples in this book have been validated successfully using validator.w3.org.

By clicking **Browse...**, users can select files on their own computers for upload. After selecting a file, clicking the **Validate this file** button uploads and validates the file. Figure 4.3 shows the results of validating main.html. This document does not contain any syntax errors. If a document does contain syntax errors, the validation service displays error messages describing the errors. In Exercise 4.13, we ask the reader to create an invalid XHTML document (i.e., one that contains syntax errors) and check its syntax using the W3C validation service. This will enable the reader to see the types of error messages generated by the validator.

Error-Prevention Tip 4.1

Most current browsers attempt to render XHTML documents even if they are invalid. This often leads to unexpected and possibly undesirable results. Use a validation service, such as the W3C MarkUp Validation Service, to confirm that an XHTML document is syntactically correct.

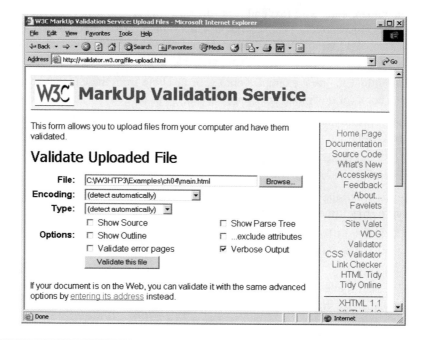

Fig. 4.2   Validating an XHTML document. (Courtesy of World Wide Web
Consortium (W3C).)

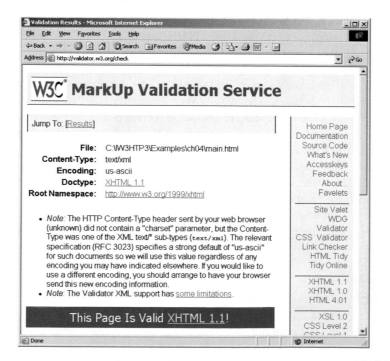

Fig. 4.3   XHTML validation results. (Courtesy of World Wide Web Consortium (W3C).)

4.5 Headers

Some text in an XHTML document may be more important than other text. For example, the text in this section is considered more important than a footnote. XHTML provides six **headers**, called **header elements**, for specifying the relative importance of information. Figure 4.4 demonstrates these elements (h1 through h6). Header element h1 (line 15) is considered the most significant header and is typically rendered in a larger font than the other five headers (lines 16–20). Each successive header element (i.e., h2, h3, etc.) is typically rendered in a progressively smaller font.

```
1   <?xml version = "1.0"?>
2   <!DOCTYPE html PUBLIC "-//W3C//DTD XHTML 1.1//EN"
3       "http://www.w3.org/TR/xhtml11/DTD/xhtml11.dtd">
4
5   <!-- Fig. 4.4: header.html -->
6   <!-- XHTML headers           -->
7
8   <html xmlns = "http://www.w3.org/1999/xhtml">
9       <head>
10          <title>Internet and WWW How to Program - Headers</title>
11      </head>
12
13      <body>
14
15          <h1>Level 1 Header</h1>
16          <h2>Level 2 header</h2>
17          <h3>Level 3 header</h3>
18          <h4>Level 4 header</h4>
19          <h5>Level 5 header</h5>
20          <h6>Level 6 header</h6>
21
22      </body>
23  </html>
```

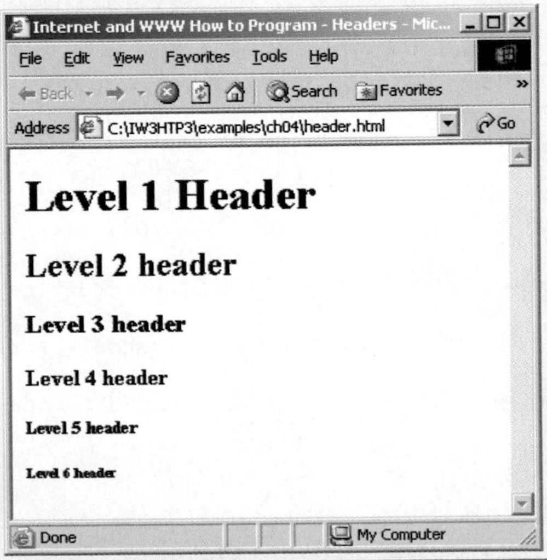

Fig. 4.4   Header elements h1 through h6.

Portability Tip 4.1

The text size used to display each header element can vary significantly between browsers. In Chapter 6, we discuss how to control the text size and other text properties.

Look-and-Feel Observation 4.1

Placing a header at the top of every XHTML page helps viewers understand the purpose of each page.

Look-and-Feel Observation 4.2

Use larger headers to emphasize more important sections of a Web page.

4.6 Linking

One of the most important XHTML features is the **hyperlink,** which references (or **links to**) other resources, such as XHTML documents and images. In XHTML, both text and images can act as hyperlinks. Web browsers typically underline text hyperlinks and color their text blue by default, so that users can distinguish hyperlinks from plain text. In Fig. 4.5, we create text hyperlinks to four different Web sites.

```
1   <?xml version = "1.0"?>
2   <!DOCTYPE html PUBLIC "-//W3C//DTD XHTML 1.1//EN"
3      "http://www.w3.org/TR/xhtml11/DTD/xhtml11.dtd">
4
5   <!-- Fig. 4.5: links.html        -->
6   <!-- Introduction to hyperlinks -->
7
8   <html xmlns = "http://www.w3.org/1999/xhtml">
9      <head>
10        <title>Internet and WWW How to Program - Links</title>
11     </head>
12
13     <body>
14
15        <h1>Here are my favorite sites</h1>
16
17        <p><strong>Click a name to go to that page.</strong></p>
18
19        <!-- Create four text hyperlinks -->
20        <p><a href = "http://www.deitel.com">Deitel</a></p>
21
22        <p><a href = "http://www.prenhall.com">Prentice Hall</a></p>
23
24        <p><a href = "http://www.yahoo.com">Yahoo!</a></p>
25
26        <p><a href = "http://www.usatoday.com">USA Today</a></p>
27
28     </body>
29  </html>
```

Fig. 4.5   Linking to other Web pages. (Part 1 of 2.)

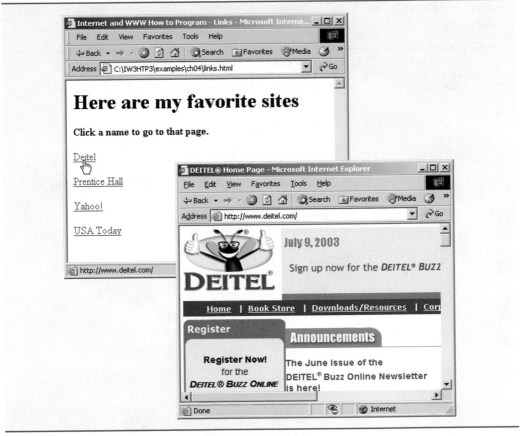

Fig. 4.5   Linking to other Web pages. (Part 2 of 2.)

Line 17 introduces the **strong** element. Browsers typically display such text in a bold font.

Links are created using the **a (anchor) element**. Line 20 defines a hyperlink that links the text Deitel to the URL assigned to attribute **href**, which specifies the location of a linked resource, such as a Web page, a file or an e-mail address. This particular anchor element links to a Web page located at http://www.deitel.com. When a URL does not indicate a specific document on the Web site, the Web server returns a default Web page. This page is often called index.html; however, most Web servers can be configured to use any file as the default Web page for the site. (Open http://www.deitel.com in one browser window and http://www.deitel.com/index.html in a second browser window to confirm that they are identical.) If the Web server cannot locate a requested document, it returns an error indication to the Web browser, and the browser displays a Web page containing an error message to the user.

Anchors can link to e-mail addresses using a **mailto:** URL. When someone clicks this type of anchored link, most browsers launch the default e-mail program (e.g., Outlook Express) to enable the user to write an e-mail message to the linked address. Figure 4.6 demonstrates this type of anchor. Lines 17–19 contain an e-mail link. The form of an e-mail

anchor is <a href = "mailto:*emailaddress*">...</a>. In this case, we link to the e-mail
address deitel@deitel.com.

```
1   <?xml version = "1.0"?>
2   <!DOCTYPE html PUBLIC "-//W3C//DTD XHTML 1.1//EN"
3      "http://www.w3.org/TR/xhtml11/DTD/xhtml11.dtd">
4
5   <!-- Fig. 4.6: contact.html  -->
6   <!-- Adding email hyperlinks -->
7
8   <html xmlns = "http://www.w3.org/1999/xhtml">
9      <head>
10        <title>Internet and WWW How to Program - Contact Page</title>
11     </head>
12
13     <body>
14
15        <p>
16           My e-mail address is
17           <a href = "mailto:deitel@deitel.com">
18              deitel@deitel.com
19           </a>
20           . Click the address and your browser will
21           open an e-mail message and address it to me.
22        </p>
23     </body>
24   </html>
```

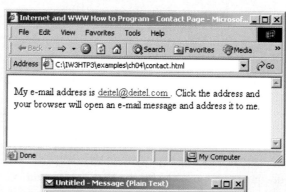

Fig. 4.6   Linking to an e-mail address.

4.7 Images

The examples discussed so far demonstrate how to mark up documents that contain only text. However, most Web pages contain both text and images. In fact, images are an equal, if not essential, part of Web-page design. The three most popular image formats used by Web developers are Graphics Interchange Format (GIF), Joint Photographic Experts Group (JPEG) and Portable Network Graphics (PNG) images. Users can create images using specialized pieces of software, such as Adobe Photoshop Elements 2.0 (discussed in Chapter 3), Macromedia Fireworks (www.macromedia.com) and Jasc Paint Shop Pro (www.jasc.com). Images may also be acquired from various Web sites, such as the Yahoo! Picture Gallery (gallery.yahoo.com). Figure 4.7 demonstrates how to incorporate images into Web pages.

Lines 16–17 use an **img** element to insert an image in the document. The image file's location is specified with the img element's **src** attribute. In this case, the image is located in the same directory as this XHTML document, so only the image's file name is required. Optional attributes **width** and **height** specify the image's width and height, respectively. The document author can scale an image by increasing or decreasing the values of the image width and height attributes. If these attributes are omitted, the browser uses the image's actual width and height. Images are measured in **pixels** ("picture elements"), which represent dots of color on the screen. The image in Fig. 4.7 is 183 pixels wide and 238 pixels high.

 Good Programming Practice 4.5

Always include the width and the height of an image inside the <img> tag. When the browser loads the XHTML file, it will know immediately from these attributes how much screen space to provide for the image and will lay out the page properly, even before it downloads the image.

```
1   <?xml version = "1.0"?>
2   <!DOCTYPE html PUBLIC "-//W3C//DTD XHTML 1.1//EN"
3       "http://www.w3.org/TR/xhtml11/DTD/xhtml11.dtd">
4
5   <!-- Fig. 4.7: picture.html    -->
6   <!-- Adding images with XHTML -->
7
8   <html xmlns = "http://www.w3.org/1999/xhtml">
9       <head>
10          <title>Internet and WWW How to Program - Welcome</title>
11      </head>
12
13      <body>
14
15          <p>
16              <img src = "xmlhtp.jpg" height = "238" width = "183"
17                  alt = "XML How to Program book cover" />
18              <img src = "jhtp.jpg" height = "238" width = "183"
19                  alt = "Java How to Program book cover" />
20          </p>
21      </body>
22  </html>
```

Fig. 4.7   Images in XHTML files. (Part 1 of 2.)

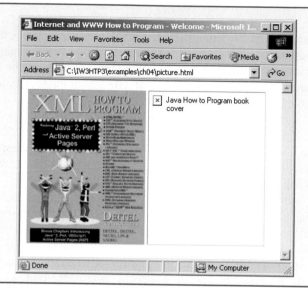

Fig. 4.7   Images in XHTML files. (Part 2 of 2.)

Performance Tip 4.1

Including the `width` and `height` attributes in an `<img>` tag can result in the browser loading and rendering pages faster.

Common Programming Error 4.4

Entering new dimensions for an image that change its inherent width-to-height ratio distorts the appearance of the image. For example, if your image is 200 pixels wide and 100 pixels high, you should ensure that any new dimensions have a 2:1 width-to-height ratio.

Every `img` element in an XHTML document has an **alt** attribute. If a browser cannot render an image, the browser displays the `alt` attribute's value. A browser may not be able to render an image for several reasons. It may not support images—as is the case with a **text-based browser** (i.e., a browser that can display only text)—or the client may have disabled image viewing to reduce download time. Figure 4.7 shows Internet Explorer 6 rendering the `alt` attribute's value when a document references a nonexistent image file (`jhtp.jpg`).

The `alt` attribute is important for creating **accessible** Web pages for users with disabilities, especially those with vision impairments who use text-based browsers. Specialized software called a **speech synthesizer** often is used by people with disabilities. This software application "speaks" the `alt` attribute's value so that the user knows what the browser is displaying. We discuss accessibility issues in detail in Chapter 29.

Some XHTML elements (called **empty elements**) contain only attributes and do not mark up text (i.e., text is not placed between the start and end tags). Empty elements (e.g., `img`) must be terminated, either by using the **forward slash character** (/) inside the closing right angle bracket (>) of the start tag or by explicitly including the end tag. When using the forward slash character, we add a space before the forward slash to improve readability (as shown at the ends of lines 17 and 19). Rather than using the forward slash character, lines 18–19 could be written with a closing `</img>` tag as follows:

```
<img src = "jhtp.jpg" height = "238" width = "183"
   alt = "Java How to Program book cover"></img>
```

By using images as hyperlinks, Web developers can create graphical Web pages that link to other resources. In Fig. 4.8, we create six different image hyperlinks.

```
1   <?xml version = "1.0"?>
2   <!DOCTYPE html PUBLIC "-//W3C//DTD XHTML 1.1//EN"
3       "http://www.w3.org/TR/xhtml11/DTD/xhtml11.dtd">
4
5   <!-- Fig. 4.8: nav.html            -->
6   <!-- Using images as link anchors -->
7
8   <html xmlns = "http://www.w3.org/1999/xhtml">
9      <head>
10        <title>Internet and WWW How to Program - Navigation Bar
11        </title>
12     </head>
13
14     <body>
15
16        <p>
17           <a href = "links.html">
18              <img src = "buttons/links.jpg" width = "65"
19                 height = "50" alt = "Links Page" />
20           </a><br />
21
22           <a href = "list.html">
23              <img src = "buttons/list.jpg" width = "65"
24                 height = "50" alt = "List Example Page" />
25           </a><br />
26
27           <a href = "contact.html">
28              <img src = "buttons/contact.jpg" width = "65"
29                 height = "50" alt = "Contact Page" />
30           </a><br />
31
32           <a href = "header.html">
33              <img src = "buttons/header.jpg" width = "65"
34                 height = "50" alt = "Header Page" />
35           </a><br />
36
37           <a href = "table1.html">
38              <img src = "buttons/table.jpg" width = "65"
39                 height = "50" alt = "Table Page" />
40           </a><br />
41
42           <a href = "form.html">
43              <img src = "buttons/form.jpg" width = "65"
44                 height = "50" alt = "Feedback Form" />
45           </a><br />
46        </p>
```

Fig. 4.8   Images as link anchors. (Part 1 of 2.)

```
47
48        </body>
49    </html>
```

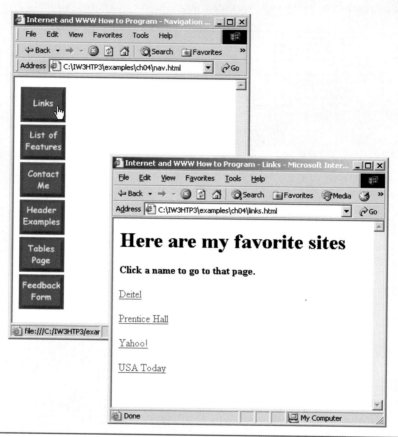

Fig. 4.8   Images as link anchors. (Part 2 of 2.)

Lines 17–20 create an **image hyperlink** by nesting an `img` element in an anchor (`a`) element. The value of the `img` element's `src` attribute value specifies that this image (`links.jpg`) resides in a directory named `buttons`. The `buttons` directory and the XHTML document are in the same directory. Images from other Web documents also can be referenced (after obtaining permission from the document's owner) by setting the `src` attribute to the name and location of the image. Clicking an image hyperlink takes a user to the Web page specified by the surrounding anchor element's `href` attribute.

In line 20, we introduce the **br element**, which most browsers render as a **line break**. Any markup or text following a `br` element is rendered on the next line. Like the `img` element, `br` is an example of an empty element terminated with a forward slash. We add a space before the forward slash to enhance readability. [*Note:* The last two image hyperlinks in Fig. 4.8 link to XHTML documents (i.e., `table1.html` and `form.html`) presented as examples in Chapter 5 and included in the Chapter 5 examples directory. Clicking these links now will result in errors.]

4.8 Special Characters and More Line Breaks

When marking up text, certain characters or symbols (e.g., <) may be difficult to embed directly into an XHTML document. Some keyboards do not provide these symbols, or the presence of these symbols may cause syntax errors. For example, the markup

```
<p>if x < 10 then increment x by 1</p>
```

results in a syntax error because it uses the less-than character (<), which is reserved for start tags and end tags such as <p> and </p>. XHTML provides **character entity references** (in the form &*code*;) for representing special characters. We could correct the previous line by writing

```
<p>if x &lt; 10 then increment x by 1</p>
```

which uses the character entity reference **<** for the less-than symbol.

Figure 4.9 demonstrates how to use special characters in an XHTML document. For a list of special characters, see Appendix A, XHTML Special Characters.

```
1   <?xml version = "1.0"?>
2   <!DOCTYPE html PUBLIC "-//W3C//DTD XHTML 1.1//EN"
3       "http://www.w3.org/TR/xhtml11/DTD/xhtml11.dtd">
4
5   <!-- Fig. 4.9: contact2.html      -->
6   <!-- Inserting special characters -->
7
8   <html xmlns = "http://www.w3.org/1999/xhtml">
9      <head>
10        <title>Internet and WWW How to Program - Contact Page
11        </title>
12     </head>
13
14     <body>
15
16        <!-- special characters are entered -->
17        <!-- using the form &code;           -->
18        <p>
19           Click
20           <a href = "mailto:deitel@deitel.com">here</a>
21           to open an e-mail message addressed to
22           deitel@deitel.com.
23        </p>
24
25        <hr /> <!-- inserts a horizontal rule -->
26
27        <p>All information on this site is <strong>&copy;</strong>
28           Deitel <strong>&amp;</strong> Associates, Inc. 2004.</p>
29
30        <!-- to strike through text use <del> tags    -->
31        <!-- to subscript text use <sub> tags         -->
32        <!-- to superscript text use <sup> tags       -->
33        <!-- these tags are nested inside other tags  -->
```

Fig. 4.9   Special characters in XHTML. (Part 1 of 2.)

```
34        <p><del>You may download 3.14 x 10<sup>2</sup>
35            characters worth of information from this site.</del>
36            Only <sub>one</sub> download per hour is permitted.</p>
37
38        <p>Note: <strong>&lt; &frac14;</strong> of the information
39            presented here is updated daily.</p>
40
41      </body>
42    </html>
```

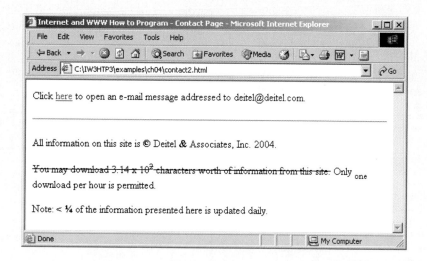

Fig. 4.9   Special characters in XHTML. (Part 2 of 2.)

Lines 27–28 contain other special characters, which can be expressed as either character entity references (i.e., word abbreviations such as amp for ampersand and copy for copyright) or **numeric character references**—decimal or **hexadecimal (hex)** values representing special characters. For example, the & character is represented in decimal and hexadecimal notation as & and &, respectively. Hexadecimal numbers are base 16 numbers—digits in a hexadecimal number have values from 0 to 15 (a total of 16 different values). The letters A–F represent the hexadecimal digits corresponding to decimal values 10–15. Thus in hexadecimal notation we can have numbers like 876 consisting solely of decimal-like digits, numbers like DA19F consisting of digits and letters and numbers like DCB consisting solely of letters. We discuss hexadecimal numbers in detail in Appendix E, Number Systems.

In lines 34–36, we introduce three new elements. Most browsers render the **del** element as strike-through text. With this format users can easily indicate document revisions. To **superscript** text (i.e., raise text on a line with a decreased font size) or **subscript** text (i.e., lower text on a line with a decreased font size), use the **sup** or **sub** element, respectively. We also use character entity reference < for a less-than sign and **¼** for the fraction 1/4 (line 38).

In addition to special characters, this document introduces a **horizontal rule**, indicated by the **<hr />** tag in line 25. Most browsers render a horizontal rule as a horizontal line. The <hr /> tag also inserts a line break above and below the horizontal line.

4.9 Unordered Lists

Up to this point, we have presented basic XHTML elements and attributes for linking to resources, creating headers, using special characters and incorporating images. In this section, we discuss how to organize information on a Web page using lists. In Chapter 5, we introduce another feature for organizing information, called a table. Figure 4.10 displays text in an **unordered list** (i.e., a list that does not order its items by letter or number). The unordered list element **ul** creates a list in which each item begins with a bullet symbol (called a **disc**). Each entry in an unordered list (element ul in line 20) is an **li** (**list item**) element (lines 23, 25, 27 and 29). Most Web browsers render these elements with a line break and a bullet symbol indented from the beginning of the new line.

```
1   <?xml version = "1.0"?>
2   <!DOCTYPE html PUBLIC "-//W3C//DTD XHTML 1.1//EN"
3       "http://www.w3.org/TR/xhtml11/DTD/xhtml11.dtd">
4
5   <!-- Fig. 4.10: links2.html              -->
6   <!-- Unordered list containing hyperlinks -->
7
8   <html xmlns = "http://www.w3.org/1999/xhtml">
9      <head>
10         <title>Internet and WWW How to Program - Links</title>
11     </head>
12
13     <body>
14
15        <h1>Here are my favorite sites</h1>
16
17        <p><strong>Click on a name to go to that page.</strong></p>
18
19        <!-- create an unordered list -->
20        <ul>
21
22           <!-- add four list items -->
23           <li><a href = "http://www.deitel.com">Deitel</a></li>
24
25           <li><a href = "http://www.w3.org">W3C</a></li>
26
27           <li><a href = "http://www.yahoo.com">Yahoo!</a></li>
28
29           <li><a href = "http://www.cnn.com">CNN</a></li>
30        </ul>
31     </body>
32  </html>
```

Fig. 4.10   Unordered lists in XHTML. (Part 1 of 2.)

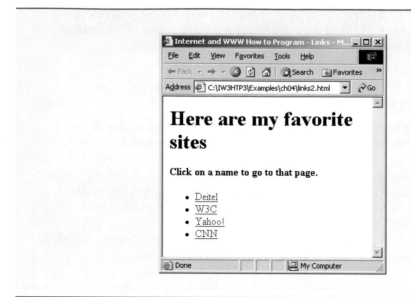

Fig. 4.10   Unordered lists in XHTML. (Part 2 of 2.)

4.10 Nested and Ordered Lists

Lists may be nested to represent hierarchical relationships, as in an outline format. Figure 4.11 demonstrates nested lists and **ordered lists**. The ordered list element **ol** creates a list in which each item begins with a number.

A Web browser indents each nested list to indicate a hierarchical relationship. The first ordered list begins at line 33. Items in an ordered list are enumerated one, two, three and so on. Nested ordered lists are enumerated in the same manner. The items in the outermost unordered list (line 18) are preceded by discs. List items nested inside the unordered list of line 18 are preceded by **circles**. Although not demonstrated in this example, subsequent nested list items are preceded by **squares**.

```
1   <?xml version = "1.0"?>
2   <!DOCTYPE html PUBLIC "-//W3C//DTD XHTML 1.1//EN"
3       "http://www.w3.org/TR/xhtml11/DTD/xhtml11.dtd">
4
5   <!-- Fig. 4.11: list.html              -->
6   <!-- Advanced Lists: nested and ordered -->
7
8   <html xmlns = "http://www.w3.org/1999/xhtml">
9      <head>
10         <title>Internet and WWW How to Program - Lists</title>
11      </head>
12
13      <body>
```

Fig. 4.11   Nested and ordered lists in XHTML. (Part 1 of 3.)

```
14
15          <h1>The Best Features of the Internet</h1>
16
17          <!-- create an unordered list -->
18          <ul>
19             <li>You can meet new people from countries around
20                 the world.</li>
21             <li>
22                 You have access to new media as it becomes public:
23
24                 <!-- this starts a nested list, which uses a -->
25                 <!-- modified bullet. The list ends when you -->
26                 <!-- close the <ul> tag.                      -->
27                 <ul>
28                     <li>New games</li>
29                     <li>
30                         New applications
31
32                         <!-- nested ordered list -->
33                         <ol>
34                             <li>For business</li>
35                             <li>For pleasure</li>
36                         </ol>
37                     </li>
38
39                     <li>Around the clock news</li>
40                     <li>Search engines</li>
41                     <li>Shopping</li>
42                     <li>
43                         Programming
44
45                         <!-- another nested ordered list -->
46                         <ol>
47                             <li>XML</li>
48                             <li>Java</li>
49                             <li>XHTML</li>
50                             <li>Scripts</li>
51                             <li>New languages</li>
52                         </ol>
53
54                     </li>
55
56                 </ul> <!-- ends the nested list of line 27 -->
57             </li>
58
59             <li>Links</li>
60             <li>Keeping in touch with old friends</li>
61             <li>It is the technology of the future!</li>
62
63          </ul>    <!-- ends the unordered list of line 18 -->
64
65      </body>
66  </html>
```

Fig. 4.11 Nested and ordered lists in XHTML. (Part 2 of 3.)

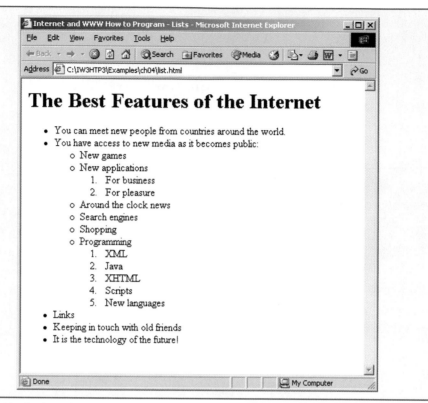

Fig. 4.11   Nested and ordered lists in XHTML. (Part 3 of 3.)

4.11 Web Resources

`www.w3.org/TR/xhtml11`
The *XHTML 1.1 Recommendation* contains XHTML 1.1 general information, compatibility issues, document type definition information, definitions, terminology and much more.

`www.xhtml.org`
XHTML.org provides XHTML development news and links to other XHTML resources, including books and articles.

`www.w3schools.com/xhtml/default.asp`
The *XHTML School* provides XHTML quizzes and references. This page also contains links to XHTML syntax, validation and document type definitions.

`validator.w3.org`
This is the W3C XHTML validation service site.

`hotwired.lycos.com/webmonkey/00/50/index2a.html`
This site provides an article about XHTML. Key sections of the article overview XHTML and discuss tags, attributes and anchors.

`wdvl.com/Authoring/Languages/XML/XHTML`
The *Web Developers Virtual Library* provides an introduction to XHTML. This site also contains articles, examples and links to other technologies.

`www.w3.org/TR/2001/REC-xhtml11-20010531`
The XHTML 1.1 DTD documentation site provides technical specifications of XHTML 1.1 syntax.

SUMMARY

- XHTML (Extensible HyperText Markup Language) is a markup language for creating Web pages.

- A key issue when using XHTML is the separation of the presentation of a document (i.e., the document's appearance when rendered by a browser) from the structure of the information in the document.

- In XHTML, text is marked up with elements delimited by tags that are names contained in pairs of angle brackets. Some elements may contain attributes that provide additional information about the element.

- A machine that runs a specialized piece of software called a Web server stores XHTML documents.

- XHTML documents that are syntactically correct are guaranteed to render properly. XHTML documents that contain syntax errors may not display properly.

- Validation services (e.g., validator.w3.org) ensure that an XHTML document is syntactically correct.

- Every XHTML document contains a start `<html>` tag and an end `</html>` tag.

- Comments in XHTML always begin with `<!--` and end with `-->`. The browser ignores all text inside a comment.

- Every XHTML document contains a `head` element, which generally contains information, such as a title, and a `body` element, which contains the page content. Information in the `head` element generally is not rendered in the display window but may be made available to the user through other means.

- The `title` element names a Web page. The title usually appears in the colored bar (called the title bar) at the top of the browser window and also appears as the text identifying a page when users add your page to their list of **Favorites** or **Bookmarks**.

- The `body` of an XHTML document is the area in which the document's content is placed. The content may include text and tags.

- All text placed between the `<p>` and `</p>` tags forms one paragraph.

- XHTML provides six headers (`h1` through `h6`) for specifying the relative importance of information. Header element `h1` is considered the most significant header and is rendered in a larger font than the other five headers. Each successive header element (i.e., `h2`, `h3`, etc.) is rendered in a progressively smaller font.

- Web browsers typically underline text hyperlinks and color them blue by default.

- The `strong` element typically causes the browser to render text in a bold font.

- Users can insert links with the `a` (anchor) element. The most important attribute for the `a` element is `href`, which specifies the resource (e.g., page, file, e-mail address) being linked.

- Anchors can link to an e-mail address using a `mailto:` URL. When someone clicks this type of anchored link, most browsers launch the default e-mail program (e.g., Outlook Express) to initiate an e-mail message addressed to the linked address.

- The `img` element's `src` attribute specifies an image's location. Optional attributes `width` and `height` specify the image width and height, respectively. Images are measured in pixels, which represent dots of color on the screen. Every `img` element in a valid XHTML document must have an `alt` attribute, which contains text that is displayed if the client cannot render the image.

- The `alt` attribute makes Web pages more accessible to users with disabilities, especially those with vision impairments.

- Some XHTML elements are empty elements that contain only attributes and do not mark up text. Empty elements (e.g., `img`) must be terminated, either by using the forward slash character (/) or by explicitly writing an end tag.

- The br element causes most browsers to render a line break. Any markup or text following a br element is rendered on the next line.
- XHTML provides special characters or entity references (in the form &*code*;) for representing characters that cannot be rendered otherwise.
- Most browsers render a horizontal rule, indicated by the <hr /> tag, as a horizontal line. The hr element also inserts a line break above and below the horizontal line.
- The unordered list element ul creates a list in which each item in the list begins with a bullet symbol (called a disc). Each entry in an unordered list is a li (list item) element. Most Web browsers render these elements with a line break and a bullet symbol at the beginning of the line.
- The ordered list element ol creates a list in which each item begins with a number.
- Lists may be nested to represent hierarchical data relationships.

TERMINOLOGY

<!--...--> (XHTML comment)
a element (<a>...</a>)
alt attribute (img)
& (& special character)
anchor
angle brackets (< >)
attribute
body element
br element (line break)
character entity reference
comment in XHTML
© (© special character)
disc
element
e-mail anchor
empty tag
Extensible HyperText Markup Language
    (XHTML)
head element
header
h1 through h6 (header elements)
height attribute (img)
hexadecimal code
hr element (horizontal rule)
href attribute (a)
.htm (XHTML file-name extension)
<html> tag
.html (XHTML file-name extension)
hyperlink
img element
level of nesting

li element (list item)
linked document
mailto: URL
markup language
nested list
numeric character reference
ol element (ordered list)
p element (paragraph)
special character
src attribute (img)
strong element
sub element
subscript
superscript
syntax
tag
text editor
text-based browser
title element
ul element (unordered list)
valid document
Web page
width attribute (img)
World Wide Web (WWW)
XHTML (Extensible HyperText
    Markup Language)
XHTML comment
XHTML markup
XHTML tag
XML declaration
xmlns attribute

SELF-REVIEW EXERCISES

4.1   State whether each of the following is *true* or *false*. If *false*, explain why.
   a) An ordered list cannot be nested inside an unordered list.

b) XHTML is an acronym for XML HTML.

c) Element br represents a line break.

d) Hyperlinks are denoted by link elements.

4.2 Fill in the blanks in each of the following:

a) The _____ element inserts a horizontal rule.

b) A superscript is marked up using element _____ and a subscript is marked up using element _____.

c) The least important header element is _____ and the most important header element is _____.

d) Element _____ marks up an unordered list.

e) Element _____ marks up a paragraph.

ANSWERS TO SELF-REVIEW EXERCISES

4.1 a) False. An ordered list can be nested inside an unordered list and vice versa. b) False. XHTML is an acronym for Extensible HyperText Markup Language. c) True. d) False. Hyperlinks are denoted by a elements.

4.2 a) hr. b) sup, sub. c) h6, h1. d) ul. e) p.

EXERCISES

4.3 Use XHTML to create a document that contains the following text:

Internet and World Wide Web How to Program: Third Edition
Welcome to the world of Internet programming. We have provided topical coverage for many Internet-related topics.

Use h1 for the title (the first line of text), p for text (the second and third lines of text) and sub for each word that begins with a capital letter. Insert a horizontal rule between the h1 element and the p element. Open your new document in a Web browser to view the marked up document.

4.4 Why is the following markup invalid?

```
<p>Here is some text...
<hr />
<p>And some more text...</p>
```

4.5 Why is the following markup invalid?

```
<p>Here is some text...<br>
And some more text...</p>
```

4.6 An image named deitel.gif is 200 pixels wide and 150 pixels high. Write a separate XHTML statement using the width and height attributes of the img element to perform each of the following transformations:

a) Increase the size of the image by 100%.

b) Increase the size of the image by 50%.

c) Change the width-to-height ratio to 2:1, keeping the width attained in part (a).

4.7 Create a link to each of the following:

a) The file index.html, located in the files directory.

b) The file index.html, located in the text subdirectory of the files directory.

c) The file index.html, located in the other directory in your parent directory. [*Hint*: .. signifies parent directory.]

     d) The President's e-mail address (`president@whitehouse.gov`).

     e) The file named README in the pub directory of `ftp.cdrom.com`. [*Hint*: Use `ftp://`.]

4.8   Create an XHTML document that marks up your resume.

4.9   Create an XHTML document containing three ordered lists: ice cream, soft serve and frozen yogurt. Each ordered list should contain a nested, unordered list of your favorite flavors. Provide a minimum of three flavors in each unordered list.

4.10   Create an XHTML document that uses an image as an e-mail link. Use attribute `alt` to provide a description of the image and link.

4.11   Create an XHTML document that contains links to your favorite Web sites. Your page should contain the header "My Favorite Web Sites."

4.12   Create an XHTML document that contains an unordered list with links to all the examples presented in this chapter. [*Hint*: Place all the chapter examples in one directory.]

4.13   Modify the XHTML document (`picture.html`) in Fig. 4.7 by removing all end tags from inside the document's body. Attempt to validate this document using the W3C validation service. What happens? Next remove the `alt` attributes from the `<img>` tags and revalidate your document. What happens?

4.14   Identify each of the following as either an element or an attribute:
     a) `html`
     b) `width`
     c) `href`
     d) `br`
     e) `h3`
     f) `a`
     g) `src`

4.15   State which of the following statements are *true* and which are *false*. If *false*, explain why.
     a) A valid XHTML document can contain uppercase letters in element names.
     b) Tags need not be closed in a valid XHTML document.
     c) XHTML documents can have the file extension `.htm`.
     d) Valid XHTML documents can contain tags that overlap.
     e) `&less;` is the character entity reference for the less-than (<) character.
     f) In a valid XHTML document, `<li>` can be nested inside either `<ol>` or `<ul>` tags.

4.16   Fill in the blanks in each of the following:
     a) XHTML comments begin with `<!--` and end with _____.
     b) In XHTML, attribute values must be enclosed in _____.
     c) _____ is the character entity reference for an ampersand.
     d) Element _____ can be used to bold text.

Introduction to XHTML: Part 2

Objectives

- To be able to create tables with rows and columns of data.
- To be able to control table formatting.
- To be able to create and use forms.
- To be able to create and use image maps to aid in Web-page navigation.
- To be able to make Web pages accessible to search engines using `<meta>` tags.
- To be able to use the `frameset` element to display multiple Web pages in a single browser window.

Yea, from the table of my memory
I'll wipe away all trivial fond records.
William Shakespeare

Outline

5.1 Introduction

In the preceding chapter, we introduced XHTML. We built several complete Web pages featuring text, hyperlinks, images, horizontal rules and line breaks. In this chapter, we discuss more substantial XHTML features, including presentation of information in **tables** and incorporating **forms** for collecting information from a Web-page visitor. We also introduce **internal linking** and **image maps** for enhancing Web-page navigation, and **frames** for displaying multiple documents in the browser.

By the end of this chapter, you will be familiar with the most commonly used XHTML features and will be able to create more complex Web documents. In Chapter 6, we discuss how to make Web pages more visually appealing by manipulating fonts, colors and text.

5.2 Basic XHTML Tables

Tables are frequently used to organize data into rows and columns. Our first example (Fig. 5.1) creates a table with six rows and two columns to display price information for fruit.

```
1   <?xml version = "1.0"?>
2   <!DOCTYPE html PUBLIC "-//W3C//DTD XHTML 1.1//EN"
3      "http://www.w3.org/TR/xhtml11/DTD/xhtml11.dtd">
4
5   <!-- Fig. 5.1: table1.html    -->
6   <!-- Creating a basic table   -->
7
8   <html xmlns = "http://www.w3.org/1999/xhtml">
9      <head>
10        <title>A simple XHTML table</title>
11     </head>
12
```

Fig. 5.1   XHTML table. (Part 1 of 3.)

```
13      <body>
14
15          <!-- the <table> tag opens a table -->
16          <table border = "1" width = "40%"
17              summary = "This table provides information about
18                  the price of fruit">
19
20              <!-- the <caption> tag summarizes the table's      -->
21              <!-- contents (this helps the visually impaired) -->
22              <caption><strong>Price of Fruit</strong></caption>
23
24              <!-- the <thead> is the first section of a table -->
25              <!-- it formats the table header area              -->
26              <thead>
27                  <tr>                    <!-- <tr> inserts a table row -->
28                      <th>Fruit</th> <!-- insert a heading cell -->
29                      <th>Price</th>
30                  </tr>
31              </thead>
32
33              <!-- the <tfoot> is the last section of a table -->
34              <!-- it formats the table footer                  -->
35              <tfoot>
36                  <tr>
37                      <th>Total</th>
38                      <th>$3.75</th>
39                  </tr>
40              </tfoot>
41
42              <!-- all table content is enclosed   -->
43              <!-- within the <tbody>               -->
44              <tbody>
45                  <tr>
46                      <td>Apple</td> <!-- insert a data cell -->
47                      <td>$0.25</td>
48                  </tr>
49
50                  <tr>
51                      <td>Orange</td>
52                      <td>$0.50</td>
53                  </tr>
54
55                  <tr>
56                      <td>Banana</td>
57                      <td>$1.00</td>
58                  </tr>
59
60                  <tr>
61                      <td>Pineapple</td>
62                      <td>$2.00</td>
63                  </tr>
64              </tbody>
65
```

Fig. 5.1   XHTML table. (Part 2 of 3.)

```
66              </table>
67
68       </body>
69   </html>
```

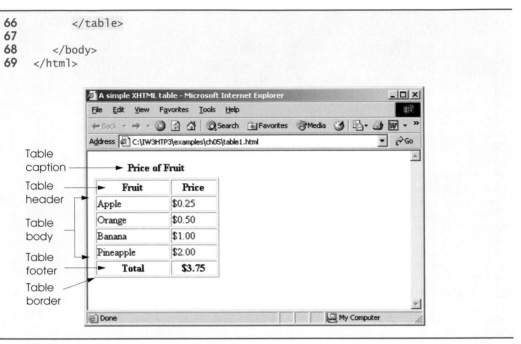

Table
caption

Table
header

Table
body

Table
footer

Table
border

Fig. 5.1   XHTML table. (Part 3 of 3.)

Tables are defined with the **table** element (lines 16–66). Lines 16–18 specify the start tag for a table element that has several attributes. The **border** attribute specifies the table's border width in pixels. To create a table without a border, set border to "0". This example assigns attribute width the value "40%" to set the table's width to 40 percent of the browser's width. A developer can also set attribute width to a specified number of pixels. Try resizing the browser window to see how the width of the window affects the width of the table.

As its name implies, attribute **summary** (lines 17–18) describes the table's contents. Speech devices use this attribute to make the table more accessible to users with visual impairments. The **caption** element (line 22) describes the table's content and helps text-based browsers interpret the table data. Text inside the <caption> tag is rendered above the table by most browsers. Attribute summary and element caption are two of the many XHTML features that make Web pages more accessible to users with disabilities. We discuss accessibility programming in detail in Chapter 29, Accessibility.

A table has three distinct sections—**head**, **body** and **foot**. The head section (or header cell) is defined with a **thead** element (lines 26–31), which contains header information such as column names. Each **tr** element (lines 27–30) defines an individual **table row**. The columns in the head section are defined with **th** elements. Most browsers center text formatted by th (table header column) elements and display them in bold. Table header elements are nested inside table row elements.

The foot section (lines 35–40) is defined with a **tfoot** (table foot) element. The text placed in the footer commonly includes calculation results and footnotes. Like other sections, the foot section can contain table rows, and each row can contain columns.

The body section, or **table body**, contains the table's primary data. The table body (lines 44–64) is defined in a **tbody** element. In the body, each **tr** element specifies one row. **Data cells** contain individual pieces of data and are defined with **td** (**table data**) elements within each row.

5.3 Intermediate XHTML Tables and Formatting

In the preceding section, we explored the structure of a basic table. In Fig. 5.2, we enhance our discussion of tables by introducing elements and attributes that allow the document author to build more complex tables.

The table begins in line 17. Element **colgroup** (lines 22–27) groups and formats columns. The **col** element (line 26) specifies two attributes in this example. The **align** attribute determines the alignment of text in the column. The **span** attribute determines how many columns the col element formats. In this case, we set align's value to "right" and span's value to "1" to right align text in the first column (the column containing the picture of the camel in the sample screen capture).

Table cells are sized to fit the data they contain. Document authors can create larger data cells by using the attributes **rowspan** and **colspan**. The values assigned to these attributes specify the number of rows or columns occupied by a cell. The th element at lines 36–39 uses the attribute rowspan = "2" to allow the cell containing the picture of the camel to use two vertically adjacent cells (thus the cell *spans* two rows). The th element in lines 42–45 uses the attribute colspan = "4" to widen the header cell (containing Camelid comparison and Approximate as of 9/2002) to span four cells.

```
1   <?xml version = "1.0"?>
2   <!DOCTYPE html PUBLIC "-//W3C//DTD XHTML 1.1//EN"
3      "http://www.w3.org/TR/xhtml11/DTD/xhtml11.dtd">
4
5   <!-- Fig. 5.2: table2.html      -->
6   <!-- Intermediate table design -->
7
8   <html xmlns = "http://www.w3.org/1999/xhtml">
9      <head>
10         <title>Internet and WWW How to Program - Tables</title>
11      </head>
12
13      <body>
14
15         <h1>Table Example Page</h1>
16
17         <table border = "1">
18            <caption>Here is a more complex sample table.</caption>
19
20            <!-- <colgroup> and <col> tags are used to -->
21            <!-- format entire columns                 -->
22            <colgroup>
23
24               <!-- span attribute determines how many columns -->
25               <!-- the <col> tag affects                      -->
26               <col align = "right" span = "1" />
27            </colgroup>
```

Fig. 5.2   Complex XHTML table. (Part 1 of 3.)

```
28
29          <thead>
30
31              <!-- rowspans and colspans merge the specified    -->
32              <!-- number of cells vertically or horizontally    -->
33              <tr>
34
35                  <!-- merge two rows -->
36                  <th rowspan = "2">
37                      <img src = "camel.gif" width = "205"
38                          height = "167" alt = "Picture of a camel" />
39                  </th>
40
41                  <!-- merge four columns -->
42                  <th colspan = "4" valign = "top">
43                      <h1>Camelid comparison</h1><br />
44                      <p>Approximate as of 9/2002</p>
45                  </th>
46              </tr>
47
48              <tr valign = "bottom">
49                  <th># of Humps</th>
50                  <th>Indigenous region</th>
51                  <th>Spits?</th>
52                  <th>Produces Wool?</th>
53              </tr>
54
55          </thead>
56
57          <tbody>
58
59              <tr>
60                  <th>Camels (bactrian)</th>
61                  <td>2</td>
62                  <td>Africa/Asia</td>
63                  <td>Yes</td>
64                  <td>Yes</td>
65              </tr>
66
67              <tr>
68                  <th>Llamas</th>
69                  <td>1</td>
70                  <td>Andes Mountains</td>
71                  <td>Yes</td>
72                  <td>Yes</td>
73              </tr>
74
75          </tbody>
76
77      </table>
78
79   </body>
80 </html>
```

Fig. 5.2   Complex XHTML table. (Part 2 of 3.)

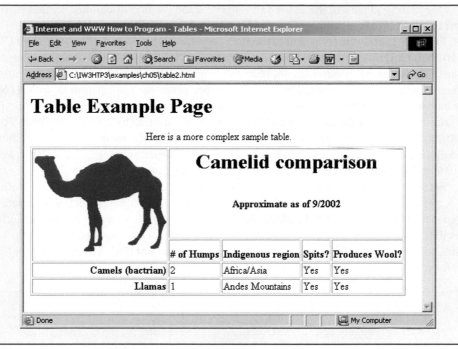

Fig. 5.2   Complex XHTML table. (Part 3 of 3.)

 Common Programming Error 5.1

When using colspan and rowspan to adjust the size of table data cells, keep in mind that the modified cells will occupy more than one column or row. Other rows or columns of the table must compensate for the extra rows or columns spanned by individual cells. If they do not, the formatting of your table will be distorted and you may inadvertently create more columns and rows than you originally intended.

Line 42 introduces the attribute **valign**, which aligns data vertically and may be assigned one of four values—**"top"** aligns data with the top of the cell, **"middle"** vertically centers data (the default for all data and header cells), **"bottom"** aligns data with the bottom of the cell and **"baseline"** ignores the fonts used for the row data and sets the bottom of all text in the row on a common **baseline** (i.e., the horizontal line at which each character in a word is aligned).

5.4 Basic XHTML Forms

When browsing Web sites, users often need to provide such information as search keywords, e-mail addresses and zip codes. XHTML provides a mechanism, called a **form**, for collecting such data from a user.

Data that users enter on a Web page normally is sent to a Web server that provides access to a site's resources (e.g., XHTML documents, images). These resources are located either on the same machine as the Web server or on a machine that the Web server can access through the network. When a browser requests a Web page or file that is located on a server, the server processes the request and returns the requested resource. A request contains the name and path of the desired resource and the method of communication (called a **protocol**). XHTML documents use the Hypertext Transfer Protocol (HTTP).

Figure 5.3 sends the form data to the Web server, which passes the form data to a **CGI** (**Common Gateway Interface**) script (i.e., a program) written in Perl, C or some other language. The script processes the data received from the Web server and typically returns information to the Web server. The Web server then sends the information as an XHTML document to the Web browser. We discuss Web servers in Chapter 21. [*Note*: This example demonstrates client-side functionality. If the form is submitted (by clicking **Submit Your Entries**) an error occurs because we have not yet configured the required server-side functionality. In later chapters, we present the server-side programming (e.g., ASP.NET, Perl, PHP and ColdFusion) necessary to process information entered into a form.]

Forms can contain visual and nonvisual components. Visual components include clickable buttons and other graphical user interface components with which users interact. Nonvisual components, called **hidden inputs**, store any data that the document author specifies, such as e-mail addresses and XHTML document file names that act as links. The form is defined in lines 23–52 by a **form** element. Attribute **method** (line 23) specifies how the form's data is sent to the Web server.

```
1   <?xml version = "1.0"?>
2   <!DOCTYPE html PUBLIC "-//W3C//DTD XHTML 1.1//EN"
3      "http://www.w3.org/TR/xhtml11/DTD/xhtml11.dtd">
4
5   <!-- Fig. 5.3: form.html    -->
6   <!-- Form Design Example 1 -->
7
8   <html xmlns = "http://www.w3.org/1999/xhtml">
9      <head>
10         <title>Internet and WWW How to Program - Forms</title>
11      </head>
12
13      <body>
14
15         <h1>Feedback Form</h1>
16
17         <p>Please fill out this form to help
18            us improve our site.</p>
19
20         <!-- this tag starts the form, gives the    -->
21         <!-- method of sending information and the -->
22         <!-- location of form scripts              -->
23         <form method = "post" action = "/cgi-bin/formmail">
24
25            <p>
26               <!-- hidden inputs contain non-visual -->
27               <!-- information                      -->
28               <input type = "hidden" name = "recipient"
29                  value = "deitel@deitel.com" />
30               <input type = "hidden" name = "subject"
31                  value = "Feedback Form" />
```

Fig. 5.3   Form with hidden fields and a text box. (Part 1 of 2.)

```
32              <input type = "hidden" name = "redirect"
33                 value = "main.html" />
34          </p>
35
36          <!-- <input type = "text"> inserts a text box -->
37          <p><label>Name:
38              <input name = "name" type = "text" size = "25"
39                 maxlength = "30" />
40          </label></p>
41
42          <p>
43              <!-- input types "submit" and "reset" insert  -->
44              <!-- buttons for submitting and clearing the  -->
45              <!-- form's contents                          -->
46              <input type = "submit" value =
47                 "Submit Your Entries" />
48              <input type = "reset" value =
49                 "Clear Your Entries" />
50          </p>
51
52      </form>
53
54   </body>
55 </html>
```

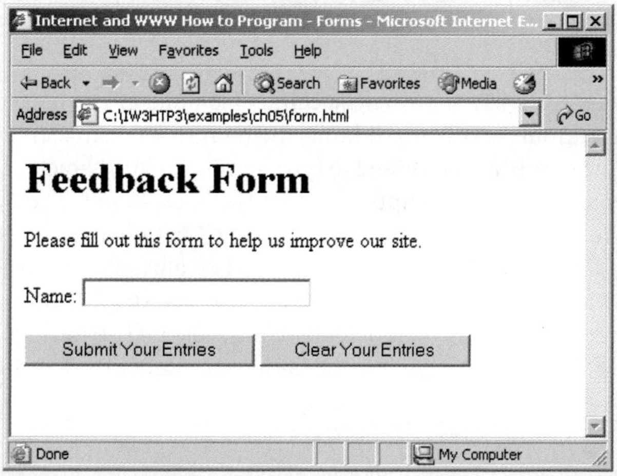

Fig. 5.3   Form with hidden fields and a text box. (Part 2 of 2.)

Using **method = "post"** appends form data to the browser request, which contains the protocol (i.e., HTTP) and the requested resource's URL. Scripts located on the Web server's computer (or on a computer accessible through the network) can access the form data sent as part of the request. For example, a script may take the form information and update an electronic mailing list. The other possible value, **method = "get"**, appends the form data directly to the end of the URL. For example, the URL /cgi-bin/formmail might have the form information name = bob appended to it. The *post* and *get* methods for sending form data are discussed in detail in Chapter 21, Web Servers.

The **action** attribute in the <form> tag specifies the URL of a script on the Web server; in this case, it specifies a script that e-mails form data to an address. Most Internet Service Providers (ISPs) have a script like this on their site; ask the Web site system administrator how to set up an XHTML document to use the script correctly.

Lines 28–33 define three **input** elements that specify data to provide to the script that processes the form (also called the **form handler**). These three input elements have the **type** attribute **"hidden"**, which allows the document author to send form data that is not input by a user.

The three hidden inputs are: an e-mail address to which the data will be sent, the e-mail's subject line and a URL where the browser will be redirected after submitting the form. Two other input attributes are **name**, which identifies the input element, and **value**, which provides the value that will be sent (or posted) to the Web server.

Good Programming Practice 5.1

Place hidden input elements at the beginning of a form, immediately after the opening <form> tag. This placement allows document authors to locate hidden input elements quickly.

We introduce another type of input in lines 38–39. The **"text"** input inserts a **text box** into the form. Users can type data in text boxes. The **label** element (lines 37–40) provides users with information about the input element's purpose.

Look-and-Feel Observation 5.1

Include a label element for each form element to help users determine the purpose of each form element.

The input element's **size** attribute specifies the number of characters visible in the text box. Optional attribute **maxlength** limits the number of characters input into the text box. In this case, the user is not permitted to type more than 30 characters into the text box.

There are two other types of input elements in lines 46–49. The **"submit"** input element is a button. When the user presses a **"submit"** button, the browser sends the data in the form to the Web server for processing. The **value** attribute sets the text displayed on the button (the default value is **Submit Query**). The **"reset"** input element allows a user to reset all form elements to their default values. The **value** attribute of the **"reset"** input element sets the text displayed on the button (the default value is **Reset**).

5.5 More Complex XHTML Forms

In the preceding section, we introduced basic forms. In this section, we introduce elements and attributes for creating more complex forms. Figure 5.4 contains a form that solicits user feedback about a Web site.

```
1   <?xml version = "1.0"?>
2   <!DOCTYPE html PUBLIC "-//W3C//DTD XHTML 1.1//EN"
3      "http://www.w3.org/TR/xhtml11/DTD/xhtml11.dtd">
4
5   <!-- Fig. 5.4: form2.html  -->
6   <!-- Form Design Example 2 -->
```

Fig. 5.4   Form with text areas, a password box and checkboxes. (Part 1 of 4.)

```
 7
 8  <html xmlns = "http://www.w3.org/1999/xhtml">
 9     <head>
10        <title>Internet and WWW How to Program - Forms</title>
11     </head>
12
13     <body>
14
15        <h1>Feedback Form</h1>
16
17        <p>Please fill out this form to help
18           us improve our site.</p>
19
20        <form method = "post" action = "/cgi-bin/formmail">
21
22           <p>
23              <input type = "hidden" name = "recipient"
24                 value = "deitel@deitel.com" />
25              <input type = "hidden" name = "subject"
26                 value = "Feedback Form" />
27              <input type = "hidden" name = "redirect"
28                 value = "main.html" />
29           </p>
30
31           <p><label>Name:
32              <input name = "name" type = "text" size = "25" />
33           </label></p>
34
35           <!-- <textarea> creates a multiline textbox -->
36           <p><label>Comments:<br />
37              <textarea name = "comments" rows = "4" cols = "36">
38  Enter your comments here.
39              </textarea>
40           </label></p>
41
42           <!-- <input type = "password"> inserts a    -->
43           <!-- textbox whose display is masked with   -->
44           <!-- asterisk characters                    -->
45           <p><label>E-mail Address:
46              <input name = "email" type = "password"
47                 size = "25" />
48           </label></p>
49
50           <p>
51              <strong>Things you liked:</strong><br />
52
53              <label>Site design
54              <input name = "thingsliked" type = "checkbox"
55                 value = "Design" /></label>
56
57              <label>Links
58              <input name = "thingsliked" type = "checkbox"
59                 value = "Links" /></label>
```

Fig. 5.4　Form with text areas, a password box and checkboxes. (Part 2 of 4.)

```
60
61              <label>Ease of use
62              <input name = "thingsliked" type = "checkbox"
63                 value = "Ease" /></label>
64
65              <label>Images
66              <input name = "thingsliked" type = "checkbox"
67                 value = "Images" /></label>
68
69              <label>Source code
70              <input name = "thingsliked" type = "checkbox"
71                 value = "Code" /></label>
72          </p>
73
74          <p>
75             <input type = "submit" value =
76                "Submit Your Entries" />
77             <input type = "reset" value =
78                "Clear Your Entries" />
79          </p>
80
81       </form>
82
83    </body>
84  </html>
```

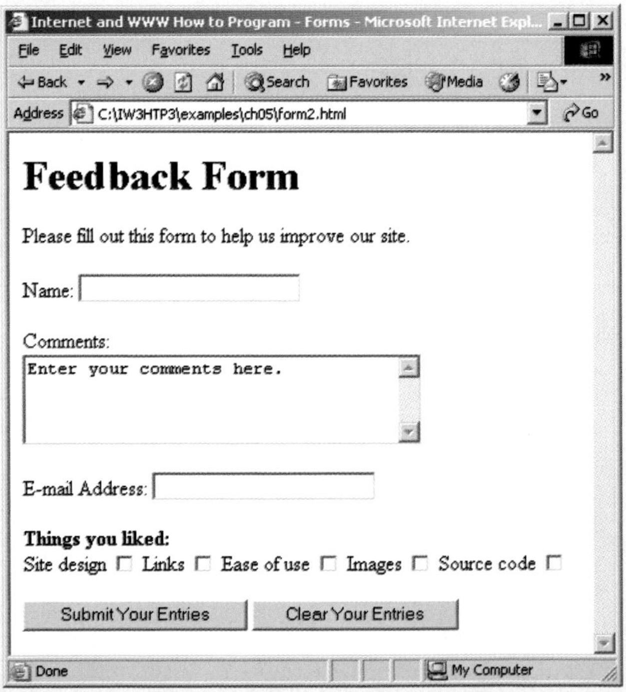

Fig. 5.4   Form with text areas, a password box and checkboxes. (Part 3 of 4.)

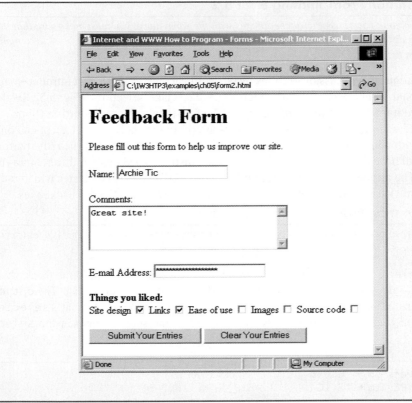

Fig. 5.4   Form with text areas, a password box and checkboxes. (Part 4 of 4.)

The **textarea** element (lines 37–39) inserts a multiline text box, called a **text area**, into the form. The number of rows is specified with the **rows** attribute, and the number of columns (i.e., characters) is specified with the **cols** attribute. In this example, the textarea is four rows high and 36 characters wide. To display default text in the text area, place the text between the **<textarea>** and **</textarea>** tags. Default text can be specified in other **input** types, such as text boxes, by using the **value** attribute

The **"password"** input in lines 46–47 inserts a password box with the specified **size**. A password box allows users to enter sensitive information, such as credit card numbers and passwords, by "masking" the information input with asterisks (*). The actual value input is sent to the Web server, not the characters that mask the input.

Lines 54–71 introduce the **checkbox** **form** element. Checkboxes enable users to select from a set of options. When a user selects a checkbox, a check mark appears in the check box. Otherwise, the checkbox remains empty. Each **"checkbox"** **input** creates a new checkbox. Checkboxes can be used individually or in groups. Checkboxes that belong to a group are assigned the same **name** (in this case, **"thingsliked"**).

Common Programming Error 5.2

When your form *has several checkboxes with the same* name, *you must make sure that they have different* values, *or the scripts running on the Web server will not be able to distinguish them.*

We continue our discussion of forms by presenting a third example that introduces several additional form elements from which users can make selections (Fig. 5.5). In this example, we introduce two new input types. The first type is the **radio button** (lines 76–94) specified with type **"radio"**. Radio buttons are similar to checkboxes, except that only one radio button in a group of radio buttons may be selected at any time. The radio buttons in a group all have the same name attributes and are distinguished by their different value attributes. The attribute-value pair **checked = "checked"** (line 77) indicates which radio button, if any, is selected initially. The checked attribute also applies to checkboxes.

Common Programming Error 5.3

Not setting the name *attributes of the radio buttons in a form to the same name is a logic error because it lets the user select all of them at the same time.*

The **select** element (lines 104–117) provides a drop-down list of items from which the user can select an item. The name attribute identifies the drop-down list. The **option** element (lines 105–116) adds items to the drop-down list. The option element's **selected attribute** specifies which item initially is displayed as the selected item in the select element.

```
1   <?xml version = "1.0"?>
2   <!DOCTYPE html PUBLIC "-//W3C//DTD XHTML 1.1//EN"
3      "http://www.w3.org/TR/xhtml11/DTD/xhtml11.dtd">
4
5   <!-- Fig. 5.5: form3.html  -->
6   <!-- Form Design Example 3 -->
7
8   <html xmlns = "http://www.w3.org/1999/xhtml">
9      <head>
10         <title>Internet and WWW How to Program - Forms</title>
11      </head>
12
13      <body>
14
15         <h1>Feedback Form</h1>
16
17         <p>Please fill out this form to help
18            us improve our site.</p>
19
20         <form method = "post" action = "/cgi-bin/formmail">
21
22            <p>
23               <input type = "hidden" name = "recipient"
24                  value = "deitel@deitel.com" />
25               <input type = "hidden" name = "subject"
26                  value = "Feedback Form" />
```

Fig. 5.5   Form including radio buttons and a drop-down list. (Part 1 of 4.)

```
27                  <input type = "hidden" name = "redirect"
28                      value = "main.html" />
29          </p>
30
31          <p><label>Name:
32                  <input name = "name" type = "text" size = "25" />
33          </label></p>
34
35          <p><label>Comments:<br />
36                  <textarea name = "comments" rows = "4"
37                      cols = "36"></textarea>
38          </label></p>
39
40          <p><label>E-mail Address:
41                  <input name = "email" type = "password"
42                      size = "25" /></label></p>
43
44          <p>
45              <strong>Things you liked:</strong><br />
46
47              <label>Site design
48                  <input name = "thingsliked" type = "checkbox"
49                      value = "Design" /></label>
50
51              <label>Links
52                  <input name = "thingsliked" type = "checkbox"
53                      value = "Links" /></label>
54
55              <label>Ease of use
56                  <input name = "thingsliked" type = "checkbox"
57                      value = "Ease" /></label>
58
59              <label>Images
60                  <input name = "thingsliked" type = "checkbox"
61                      value = "Images" /></label>
62
63              <label>Source code
64                  <input name = "thingsliked" type = "checkbox"
65                      value = "Code" /></label>
66          </p>
67
68          <!-- <input type = "radio" /> creates a radio      -->
69          <!-- button. The difference between radio buttons -->
70          <!-- and checkboxes is that only one radio button -->
71          <!-- in a group can be selected.                   -->
72          <p>
73              <strong>How did you get to our site?:</strong><br />
74
75              <label>Search engine
76                  <input name = "howtosite" type = "radio"
77                      value = "search engine" checked = "checked" />
78              </label>
79
```

Fig. 5.5   Form including radio buttons and a drop-down list. (Part 2 of 4.)

```
80            <label>Links from another site
81                <input name = "howtosite" type = "radio"
82                   value = "link" /></label>
83
84            <label>Deitel.com Web site
85                <input name = "howtosite" type = "radio"
86                   value = "deitel.com" /></label>
87
88            <label>Reference in a book
89                <input name = "howtosite" type = "radio"
90                   value = "book" /></label>
91
92            <label>Other
93                <input name = "howtosite" type = "radio"
94                   value = "other" /></label>
95
96         </p>
97
98         <p>
99            <label>Rate our site:
100
101               <!-- the <select> tag presents a drop-down -->
102               <!-- list with choices indicated by the     -->
103               <!-- <option> tags                            -->
104            <select name = "rating">
105               <option selected = "selected">Amazing</option>
106               <option>10</option>
107               <option>9</option>
108               <option>8</option>
109               <option>7</option>
110               <option>6</option>
111               <option>5</option>
112               <option>4</option>
113               <option>3</option>
114               <option>2</option>
115               <option>1</option>
116               <option>Awful</option>
117            </select>
118
119            </label>
120         </p>
121
122         <p>
123            <input type = "submit" value =
124               "Submit Your Entries" />
125            <input type = "reset" value = "Clear Your Entries" />
126         </p>
127
128      </form>
129
130   </body>
131 </html>
```

Fig. 5.5   Form including radio buttons and a drop-down list. (Part 3 of 4.)

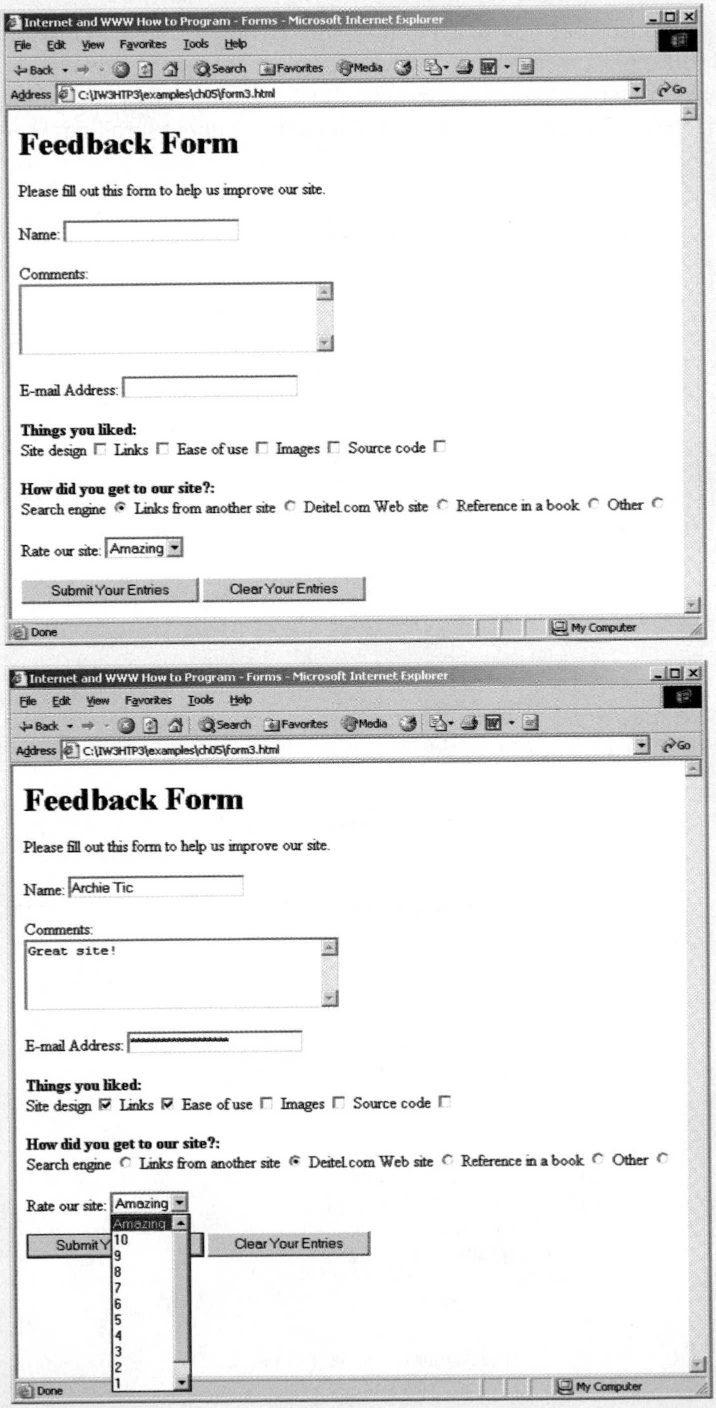

Fig. 5.5   Form including radio buttons and a drop-down list. (Part 4 of 4.)

5.6 Internal Linking

In Chapter 4, we discussed how to hyperlink one Web page to another. Figure 5.6 introduces **internal linking**—a mechanism that enables the user to jump between locations in the same document. Internal linking is useful for long documents that contain many sections. Clicking an internal link enables users to find a section without scrolling through the entire document.

```
1   <?xml version = "1.0"?>
2   <!DOCTYPE html PUBLIC "-//W3C//DTD XHTML 1.1//EN"
3      "http://www.w3.org/TR/xhtml11/DTD/xhtml11.dtd">
4
5   <!-- Fig. 5.6: links.html -->
6   <!-- Internal Linking       -->
7
8   <html xmlns = "http://www.w3.org/1999/xhtml">
9      <head>
10        <title>Internet and WWW How to Program - List</title>
11     </head>
12
13     <body>
14
15        <!-- id attribute creates an internal hyperlink destination -->
16        <h1 id = "features">The Best Features of the Internet</h1>
17
18        <!-- an internal link's address is "#id" -->
19        <p><a href = "#bugs">Go to <em>Favorite Bugs</em></a></p>
20
21        <ul>
22           <li>You can meet people from countries
23              around the world.</li>
24
25           <li>You have access to new media as it becomes public:
26              <ul>
27                 <li>New games</li>
28                 <li>New applications
29                    <ul>
30                       <li>For Business</li>
31                       <li>For Pleasure</li>
32                    </ul>
33                 </li>
34
35                 <li>Around the clock news</li>
36                 <li>Search Engines</li>
37                 <li>Shopping</li>
38                 <li>Programming
39                    <ul>
40                       <li>XHTML</li>
41                       <li>Java</li>
42                       <li>Dynamic HTML</li>
43                       <li>Scripts</li>
```

Fig. 5.6   Internal hyperlinks to make pages more navigable. (Part 1 of 3.)

```
44                    <li>New languages</li>
45                 </ul>
46              </li>
47           </ul>
48        </li>
49
50        <li>Links</li>
51        <li>Keeping in touch with old friends</li>
52        <li>It is the technology of the future!</li>
53     </ul>
54
55     <!-- id attribute creates an internal hyperlink destination -->
56     <h1 id = "bugs">My 3 Favorite Bugs</h1>
57
58     <p>
59
60        <!-- internal hyperlink to features -->
61        <a href = "#features">Go to <em>Favorite Features</em>
62        </a></p>
63
64     <ol>
65        <li>Fire Fly</li>
66        <li>Gal Ant</li>
67        <li>Roman Tic</li>
68     </ol>
69
70     </body>
71  </html>
```

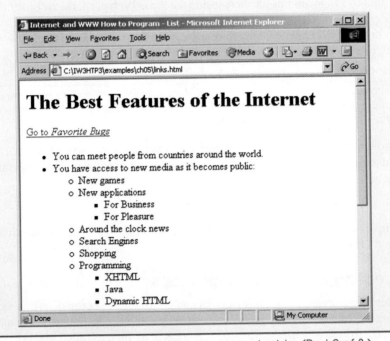

Fig. 5.6   Internal hyperlinks to make pages more navigable. (Part 2 of 3.)

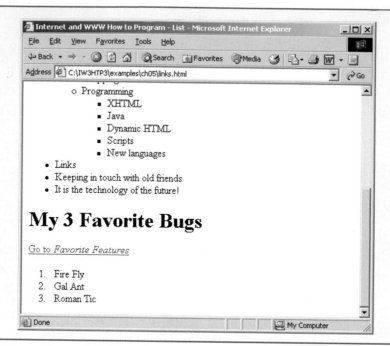

Fig. 5.6   Internal hyperlinks to make pages more navigable. (Part 3 of 3.)

Line 16 contains a tag with the **id** attribute (called `"features"`) for an internal hyperlink. To link to a tag with this attribute inside the same Web page, the `href` attribute of an anchor element includes the `id` attribute value preceded by a pound sign (as in `#features`). Lines 61–62 contain a hyperlink with the id `features` as its target. Selecting this hyperlink in a Web browser scrolls the browser window to the `h1` tag in line 16.

Look-and-Feel Observation 5.2

Internal hyperlinks are useful in XHTML documents that contain large amounts of information. Internal links to different parts of the page makes it easier for users to navigate the page. They do not have to scroll to find the section they want.

Although not demonstrated in this example, a hyperlink can specify an internal link in another document by specifying the document name followed by a pound sign and the `id` value, as in:

>   href = "*filename*.html#*id*"

For example, to link to a tag with the `id` attribute called `booklist` in `books.html`, `href` is assigned `"books.html#booklist"`.

5.7 Creating and Using Image Maps

In Chapter 4, we demonstrated how images can be used as hyperlinks to link to other resources on the Internet. In this section, we introduce another technique for image linking called **image maps**, which designates certain areas of an image (called **hotspots**) as links.[1] Figure 5.7 introduces image maps and hotspots.

```
1   <?xml version = "1.0" ?>
2   <!DOCTYPE html PUBLIC "-//W3C//DTD XHTML 1.0 Transitional//EN"
3       "http://www.w3.org/TR/xhtml1/DTD/xhtml1-transitional.dtd">
4
5   <!-- Fig. 5.7: picture.html          -->
6   <!-- Creating and Using Image Maps -->
7
8   <html xmlns = "http://www.w3.org/1999/xhtml">
9      <head>
10        <title>
11           Internet and WWW How to Program - Image Map
12        </title>
13     </head>
14
15     <body>
16
17        <p>
18
19        <!-- the <map> tag defines an image map -->
20        <map id = "picture">
21
22           <!-- shape = "rect" indicates a rectangular    -->
23           <!-- area, with coordinates for the upper-left -->
24           <!-- and lower-right corners                   -->
25           <area href = "form.html" shape = "rect"
26              coords = "2,123,54,143"
27              alt = "Go to the feedback form" />
28           <area href = "contact.html" shape = "rect"
29              coords = "126,122,198,143"
30              alt = "Go to the contact page" />
31           <area href = "main.html" shape = "rect"
32              coords = "3,7,61,25" alt = "Go to the homepage" />
33           <area href = "links.html" shape = "rect"
34              coords = "168,5,197,25"
35              alt = "Go to the links page" />
36
37           <!-- value "poly" creates a hotspot in the shape -->
38           <!-- of a polygon, defined by coords             -->
39           <area shape = "poly" alt = "E-mail the Deitels"
40              coords = "162,25,154,39,158,54,169,51,183,39,161,26"
41              href = "mailto:deitel@deitel.com" />
42
43           <!-- shape = "circle" indicates a circular -->
44           <!-- area with the given center and radius  -->
45           <area href = "mailto:deitel@deitel.com"
46              shape = "circle" coords = "100,36,33"
47              alt = "E-mail the Deitels" />
48        </map>
```

Fig. 5.7   Image with links anchored to an image map. (Part 1 of 2.)

1. Current Web browsers do not support XHTML 1.1 image maps. For this reason we are using XHTML 1.0 Transitional, an earlier W3C version of XHTML. In order to validate the code in Figure 5.7 as XHTML 1.1, remove the # from the usemap attribute of the img tag (line 53).

```
49
50              <!-- <img src =... usemap = "#id"> indicates that the -->
51              <!-- specified image map is used with this image       -->
52              <img src = "deitel.gif" width = "200" height = "144"
53                 alt = "Deitel logo" usemap = "#picture" />
54           </p>
55        </body>
56     </html>
```

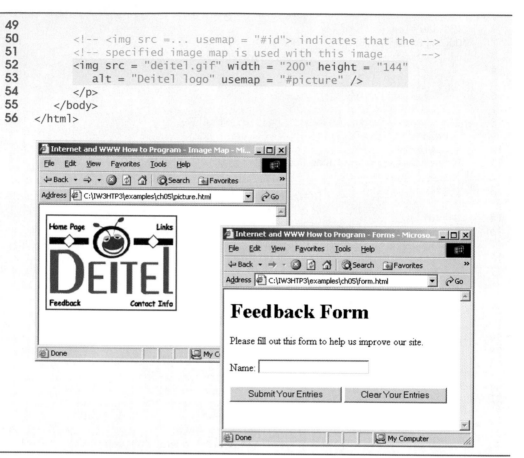

Fig. 5.7   Image with links anchored to an image map. (Part 2 of 2.)

Lines 20–48 define an image map by using a **map** element. Attribute **id** (line 20) identifies the image map. If id is omitted, the map cannot be referenced by an image (which we will see momentarily). Hotspots are defined with **area** elements (as shown in lines 25–27). Attribute href (line 25) specifies the link's target (i.e., the resource to which to link). Attributes **shape** (line 25) and **coords** (line 26) specify the hotspot's shape and coordinates, respectively. Attribute alt (line 27) provides alternative text for the link.

 Common Programming Error 5.4

Not specifying an id attribute for a map element prevents an img element from using the map's area elements to define hotspots.

The markup in lines 25–27 creates a **rectangular hotspot** (shape = **"rect"**) for the **coordinates** specified in the coords attribute. A coordinate pair consists of two numbers representing the locations of a point on the x-axis and the y-axis, respectively. The x-axis extends horizontally and the y-axis extends vertically from the upper-left corner of the image. Every point on an image has a unique x-y-coordinate. For rectangular hotspots, the required coordinates are those of the upper-left and lower-right corners of the rectangle. In this case, the upper-left corner of the rectangle is located at 2 on the x-axis and 123 on the y-axis, annotated as *(2, 123)*. The lower-right corner of the rectangle is at *(54, 143)*. Coordinates are measured in pixels.

Common Programming Error 5.5

Overlapping coordinates of an image map cause the browser to render the first hotspot it encounters for the area.

The map `area` at lines 39–41 assigns the `shape` attribute **"poly"** to create a hotspot in the shape of a polygon using the coordinates in attribute `coords`. These coordinates represent each **vertex**, or corner, of the polygon. The browser connects these points with lines to form the hotspot's area.

The map `area` at lines 45–47 assigns the `shape` attribute **"circle"** to create a **circular hotspot**. In this case, the `coords` attribute specifies the circle's center coordinates and the circle's radius, in pixels.

To use an image map with an `img` element, you must assign the `img` element's **usemap** attribute to the `id` of a `map`. Lines 52–53 reference the image map **"#picture"**. The image map is located within the same document, so internal linking is used.

5.8 meta Elements

Search engines are used to find Web sites. They usually catalog sites by following links from page to page (often known as spidering or crawling) and saving identification and classification information for each page. One way that search engines catalog pages is by reading the content in each page's **meta** elements, which specify information about a document.

Two important attributes of the `meta` element are **name**, which identifies the type of `meta` element, and **content**, which provides the information search engines use to catalog pages. Figure 5.8 introduces the `meta` element.

```
1   <?xml version = "1.0"?>
2   <!DOCTYPE html PUBLIC "-//W3C//DTD XHTML 1.1//EN"
3      "http://www.w3.org/TR/xhtml11/DTD/xhtml11.dtd">
4
5   <!-- Fig. 5.8: main.html -->
6   <!-- <meta> tag          -->
7
8   <html xmlns = "http://www.w3.org/1999/xhtml">
9      <head>
10        <title>Internet and WWW How to Program - Welcome</title>
11
12        <!-- <meta> tags provide search engines with -->
13        <!-- information used to catalog a site      -->
14        <meta name = "keywords" content = "Web page, design,
15           XHTML, tutorial, personal, help, index, form,
16           contact, feedback, list, links, frame, deitel" />
17
18        <meta name = "description" content = "This Web site will
19           help you learn the basics of XHTML and Web page design
20           through the use of interactive examples and
21           instruction." />
```

Fig. 5.8   meta tags provide keywords and a description of a page. (Part 1 of 2.)

```
22
23      </head>
24
25      <body>
26
27          <h1>Welcome to Our Web Site!</h1>
28
29          <p>We have designed this site to teach about the wonders
30          of <strong><em>XHTML</em></strong>. <em>XHTML</em> is
31          better equipped than <em>HTML</em> to represent complex
32          data on the Internet. <em>XHTML</em> takes advantage of
33          XML's strict syntax to ensure well-formedness. Soon you
34          will know about many of the great new features of
35          <em>XHTML.</em></p>
36
37          <p>Have Fun With the Site!</p>
38
39      </body>
40  </html>
```

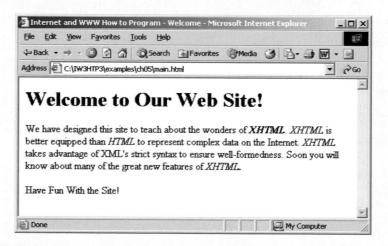

Fig. 5.8   meta tags provide keywords and a description of a page. (Part 2 of 2.)

Lines 14–16 demonstrate a **"keywords"** meta element. The content attribute of such a meta element provides search engines with a list of words that describe a page. These words are compared with words in search requests. Thus, including meta elements and their content information can draw more viewers to your site.

Lines 18–21 demonstrate a **"description"** meta element. The content attribute of such a meta element provides a three- to four-line description of a site, written in sentence form. Search engines also use this description to catalog your site and sometimes display this information as part of the search results.

Software Engineering Observation 5.1

meta elements are not visible to users and must be placed inside the head section of your XHTML document. If meta elements are not placed in this section, they will not be read by search engines.

5.9 frameset Element

All of the Web pages we present in this book have the ability to link to other pages, but can display only one page at a time. **Frames** allow a Web developer to display more than one XHTML document in the browser simultaneously. Figure 5.9 uses frames to display the documents in Fig. 5.8 and Fig. 5.10.

Most of our earlier examples adhere to the XHTML 1.1 document type, whereas these use the XHTML 1.0 document types.[2] These document types are specified in lines 2–3 and are required for documents that define framesets or use the `target` attribute to work with framesets.

A document that defines a frameset normally consists of an `html` element that contains a `head` element and a **frameset** element (lines 23–40). In Fig. 5.9, the **<frameset>** tag (line 23) informs the browser that the page contains frames. Attribute **cols** specifies the frameset's column layout. The value of `cols` gives the width of each frame, either in pixels or as a percentage of the browser width. In this case, the attribute `cols` = "110,*" informs the browser that there are two vertical frames. The first frame extends 110 pixels from the left edge of the browser window, and the second frame fills the remainder of the browser width (as indicated by the asterisk). Similarly, `frameset` attribute **rows** can be used to specify the number of rows and the size of each row in a frameset.

```
1   <?xml version = "1.0"?>
2   <!DOCTYPE html PUBLIC "-//W3C//DTD XHTML 1.0 Frameset//EN"
3      "http://www.w3.org/TR/xhtml1/DTD/xhtml1-frameset.dtd">
4
5   <!-- Fig. 5.9: index.html -->
6   <!-- XHTML Frames I        -->
7
8   <html xmlns = "http://www.w3.org/1999/xhtml">
9      <head>
10        <title>Internet and WWW How to Program - Main</title>
11        <meta name = "keywords" content = "Webpage, design,
12           XHTML, tutorial, personal, help, index, form,
13           contact, feedback, list, links, frame, deitel" />
14
15        <meta name = "description" content = "This Web site will
16           help you learn the basics of XHTML and Web page design
17           through the use of interactive examples
18           and instruction." />
19
20     </head>
21
22     <!-- the <frameset> tag sets the frame dimensions     -->
23     <frameset cols = "110,*">
```

Fig. 5.9   XHTML frames document with navigation and content. (Part 1 of 3.)

2. XHTML 1.1 no longer supports the use of frames. The W3C recommends using Cascading Style Sheets to achieve the same effect. Frames are still widely used on the Internet and supported by most browsers, however. The `frameset` element and the `target` attribute are still supported in the XHTML 1.0 Frameset and the XHTML 1.0 Transitional document type definitions, respectively. Please refer to www.w3.org/TR/xhtml1/#dtds for more information.

```
24
25          <!-- frame elements specify which pages -->
26          <!-- are loaded into a given frame       -->
27          <frame name = "leftframe" src = "nav.html" />
28          <frame name = "main" src = "main.html" />
29
30          <noframes>
31             <body>
32                <p>This page uses frames, but your browser does not
33                support them.</p>
34
35                <p>Please, <a href = "nav.html">follow this link to
36                browse our site without frames</a>.</p>
37             </body>
38          </noframes>
39
40       </frameset>
41    </html>
```

Fig. 5.9   XHTML frames document with navigation and content. (Part 2 of 3.)

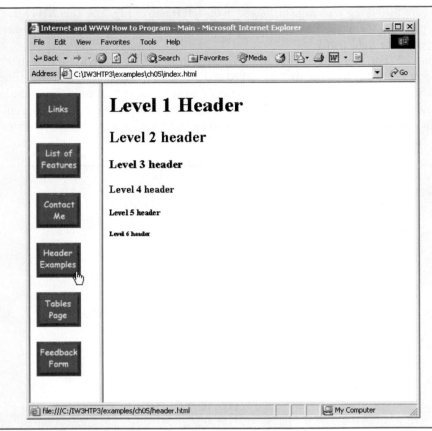

Fig. 5.9   XHTML frames document with navigation and content. (Part 3 of 3.)

The documents that will be loaded into the frameset are specified with **frame** elements (lines 27–28 in this example). Attribute src specifies the URL of the page to display in the frame. Each frame has name and src attributes. The first frame (which covers 110 pixels on the left side of the frameset) is named leftframe and displays the page nav.html (Fig. 5.10). The second frame is named main and displays the page main.html (Fig. 5.8).

Attribute name identifies a frame, enabling hyperlinks in a frameset to specify the **target** frame in which a linked document should display when the user clicks the link. For example

```
<a href = "links.html" target = "main">
```

loads links.html in the frame whose name is "main".

Not all browsers support frames. XHTML provides the **noframes** element (lines 30–38) to enable XHTML document designers to specify alternative content for browsers that do not support frames.

 Portability Tip 5.1

Some browsers do not support frames. Use the noframes element inside a frameset to direct users to a nonframed version of your site.

Figure 5.10 is the Web page displayed in the left frame of Fig. 5.9. This XHTML document provides the navigation buttons that, when clicked, determine which document is displayed in the right frame.

Line 27 (Fig. 5.9) displays the XHTML page in Fig. 5.10. Anchor attribute `target` (line 18 in Fig. 5.10) specifies that the linked documents are loaded in frame `main` (line 28 in Fig. 5.9). A `target` can be set to a number of preset values: `"_blank"` loads the page into a new browser window, `"_self"` loads the page into the frame in which the anchor element appears and `"_top"` loads the page into the full browser window (i.e., removes the `frameset`).

```
1   <?xml version = "1.0"?>
2   <!DOCTYPE html PUBLIC "-//W3C//DTD XHTML 1.0 Transitional//EN"
3       "http://www.w3.org/TR/xhtml1/DTD/xhtml1-transitional.dtd">
4
5   <!-- Fig. 5.10: nav.html            -->
6   <!-- Using images as link anchors -->
7
8   <html xmlns = "http://www.w3.org/1999/xhtml">
9
10     <head>
11        <title>Internet and WWW How to Program - Navigation Bar
12        </title>
13     </head>
14
15     <body>
16
17        <p>
18           <a href = "links.html" target = "main">
19              <img src = "buttons/links.jpg" width = "65"
20                 height = "50" alt = "Links Page" />
21           </a><br />
22
23           <a href = "list.html" target = "main">
24              <img src = "buttons/list.jpg" width = "65"
25                 height = "50" alt = "List Example Page" />
26           </a><br />
27
28           <a href = "contact.html" target = "main">
29              <img src = "buttons/contact.jpg" width = "65"
30                 height = "50" alt = "Contact Page" />
31           </a><br />
32
33           <a href = "header.html" target = "main">
34              <img src = "buttons/header.jpg" width = "65"
35                 height = "50" alt = "Header Page" />
36           </a><br />
37
38           <a href = "table1.html" target = "main">
39              <img src = "buttons/table.jpg" width = "65"
40                 height = "50" alt = "Table Page" />
41           </a><br />
```

Fig. 5.10   XHTML document displayed in the left frame of Fig. 5.9. (Part 1 of 2.)

```
42
43              <a href = "form.html" target = "main">
44                  <img src = "buttons/form.jpg" width = "65"
45                      height = "50" alt = "Feedback Form" />
46          </a><br />
47      </p>
48
49    </body>
50  </html>
```

Fig. 5.10   XHTML document displayed in the left frame of Fig. 5.9. (Part 2 of 2.)

5.10 Nested framesets

You can use the `frameset` element to create more complex layouts in a Web page by nesting `frameset`s, as in Fig. 5.11. The nested `frameset` in this example displays the XHTML documents in Fig. 5.7, Fig. 5.8 and Fig. 5.10.

```
1   <?xml version = "1.0"?>
2   <!DOCTYPE html PUBLIC "-//W3C//DTD XHTML 1.0 Frameset//EN"
3       "http://www.w3.org/TR/xhtml1/DTD/xhtml1-frameset.dtd">
4
5   <!-- Fig. 5.11: index2.html -->
6   <!-- XHTML Frames II          -->
7
8   <html xmlns = "http://www.w3.org/1999/xhtml">
9     <head>
10        <title>Internet and WWW How to Program - Main</title>
11
12        <meta name = "keywords" content = "Webpage, design,
13            XHTML, tutorial, personal, help, index, form,
14            contact, feedback, list, links, frame, deitel" />
15
16        <meta name = "description" content = "This Web site will
17            help you learn the basics of XHTML and Web page design
18            through the use of interactive examples
19            and instruction." />
20
21    </head>
22
23    <frameset cols = "110,*">
24        <frame name = "leftframe" src = "nav.html" />
25
26        <!-- nested framesets are used to change the -->
27        <!-- formatting and layout of the frameset   -->
28        <frameset rows = "175,*">
29            <frame name = "picture" src = "picture.html" />
30            <frame name = "main" src = "main.html" />
31        </frameset>
32
33        <noframes>
```

Fig. 5.11   Framed Web site with a nested frameset. (Part 1 of 2.)

```
34              <body>
35                  <p>This page uses frames, but your browser does not
36                  support them.</p>
37
38                  <p>Please, <a href = "nav.html">follow this link to
39                  browse our site without frames</a>.</p>
40              </body>
41          </noframes>
42
43      </frameset>
44  </html>
```

Fig. 5.11   Framed Web site with a nested frameset. (Part 2 of 2.)

The outer **frameset** element (lines 23–43) defines two columns. The left frame extends over the first 110 pixels from the left edge of the browser, and the right frame occupies the rest of the window's width. The **frame** element on line 24 specifies that the document **nav.html** (Fig. 5.10) will be displayed in the left column.

Lines 28–31 define a nested **frameset** element for the second column of the outer frameset. This **frameset** defines two rows. The first row extends 175 pixels from the top of the browser window, as indicated by **rows = "175,*"**. The second row occupies the remainder of the browser window's height. The **frame** element at line 29 specifies that the first row of the nested `frameset` will display `picture.html` (Fig. 5.7). The `frame` element in line 30 specifies that the second row of the nested `frameset` will display `main.html` (Fig. 5.8).

Error-Prevention Tip 5.1

When using nested `frameset` elements, indent every level of `<frame>` tag. This practice makes the page clearer and easier to debug.

This chapter presented XHTML for marking up information in tables, creating forms for gathering user input, linking to sections within the same document, using `<meta>` tags and creating frames. In Chapter 6, we build upon the XHTML introduced in this chapter by discussing how to make Web pages more visually appealing with Cascading Style Sheets.

5.11 Web Resources

`www.vbxml.com/xhtml/articles/xhtml_tables`
The *VBXML.com* Web site contains a tutorial on creating XHTML tables.

`www.webreference.com/xml/reference/xhtml.html`
This Web page contains a list of frequently used XHTML tags, such as header tags, table tags, frame tags and form tags. It also provides a description of each tag.

SUMMARY

- XHTML tables mark up tabular data and are one of the most frequently used features of XHTML.

- The `table` element defines an XHTML table. Attribute `border` specifies the table's border width, in pixels. Tables without borders set this attribute to `"0"`.

- Element `summary` summarizes the table's contents and is used by speech devices to make the table more accessible to users with visual impairments.

- Element `caption` describe's the table's content. The text inside the `<caption>` tag is rendered above the table in most browsers.

- A table can be split into three distinct sections: head (`thead`), body (`tbody`) and foot (`tfoot`). The head section contains such information as table titles and column headers. The table body contains the primary table data. The table foot contains such information as footnotes.

- Element `tr`, or table row, defines individual table rows. Element `th` defines a header cell. Text in `th` elements is centered and displayed in bold by most browsers. This element can be present in any section of the table.

- Data within a row is defined with `td`, or table data, elements.

- Element `colgroup` groups and formats columns. Each `col` element can format any number of columns (specified with the `span` attribute).

- The document author has the ability to merge data cells with the `rowspan` and `colspan` attributes. The values assigned to these attributes specify the number of rows or columns occupied by the cell. These attributes can be placed inside any data cell tag.

- XHTML provides forms for collecting information from users. Forms contain visual components, such as buttons, that users click. Forms may also contain nonvisual components, called hidden inputs, which are used to store any data, such as e-mail addresses and XHTML document file names, used for linking.

- A form begins with the `form` element. Attribute `method` specifies how the form's data is sent to the Web server.

- The `action` attribute of the `form` element specifies the script to which the `form` data will be sent.

- The `"text"` input inserts a text box into the form. Text boxes allow the user to input data.

- The `input` element's `size` attribute specifies the number of characters visible in the `input` element. Optional attribute `maxlength` limits the number of characters input into a text box.

- The `"submit"` input submits the data entered in the form to the Web server for processing. Most Web browsers create a button that submits the form data when clicked. The `"reset"` input allows a user to reset all `form` elements to their default values.

- The `textarea` element inserts a multiline text box, called a text area, into a form. The number of rows in the text area is specified with the `rows` attribute, and the number of columns (i.e., characters) is specified with the `cols` attribute.

- The `"password"` input inserts a password box into a form. A password box allows users to enter sensitive information, such as credit card numbers and passwords, by "masking" the information input with another character. Asterisks are the masking character used for password boxes. The actual value input is sent to the Web server, not the asterisks that mask the input.

- The checkbox input allows the user to make a selection. When the checkbox is selected, a check mark appears in the checkbox. Otherwise, the checkbox is empty. Checkboxes can be used individually and in groups. Checkboxes that are part of the same group have the same `name`.

- A radio button is similar in function and use to a checkbox, except that only one radio button in a group can be selected at any time. All radio buttons in a group have the same `name` attribute value but different attribute `value`s.

- The `select` input provides a drop-down list of items. The `name` attribute identifies the drop-down list. The `option` element adds items to the drop-down list. The `selected` attribute, like the `checked` attribute for radio buttons and checkboxes, specifies which list item is displayed initially.

- Image maps designate certain sections of an image as links. These links are more properly called hotspots.

- Image maps are defined with `map` elements. Attribute `id` identifies the image map. Hotspots are defined with the `area` element. Attribute `href` specifies the link's target. Attributes `shape` and `coords` specify the hotspot's shape and coordinates, respectively, and `alt` provides alternative text.

- One way that search engines catalog pages is by reading the `meta` elements's contents. Two important attributes of the `meta` element are `name`, which identifies the type of `meta` element, and `content`, which provides information a search engine uses to catalog a page.

- Frames allow the browser to display more than one XHTML document simultaneously. The `frameset` element informs the browser that the page contains frames. Not all browsers support frames. XHTML provides the `noframes` element to specify alternative content for browsers that do not support frames.

- You can use the `frameset` element to create more complex layouts in a Web page by nesting `frameset`s.

TERMINOLOGY

`action` attribute (`form`)	`col` element
`area` element	`colgroup` element
`border` attribute (`table`)	`cols` attribute (`textarea`)
browser request	`colspan` attribute (`th`, `td`)
`caption` element	`coords` element
checkbox	form
`checked` attribute (`input`)	`form` element

frame element
frameset element
header cell
hidden input element
hotspot
href attribute (a)
image map
img element
input element
internal hyperlink
internal linking
map element
maxlength attribute (input)
meta element
method attribute (form)
name attribute
navigational frame
nested frameset element
nested tag
noframes element
password box
radio button

rows attribute (textarea)
rowspan attribute (th, tr)
selected attribute (option)
size attribute (input)
table element
target = "_blank"
target = "_self"
target = "_top"
tbody element
td element
textarea
textarea element
tfoot element (table foot)
thead element (table head)
tr element (table row)
type attribute (input)
usemap attribute (img)
valign attribute (th)
value attribute (input)
Web server
XHTML form
x-y coordinate

SELF-REVIEW EXERCISES

5.1   State whether the following statements are *true* or *false*. If *false*, explain why.
   a) The width of all data cells in a table must be the same.
   b) Framesets can be nested.
   c) You are limited to a maximum of 100 internal links per page.
   d) All browsers can render framesets.

5.2   Fill in the blanks in each of the following statements:
   a) The _____ attribute in an input element inserts a button that, when clicked, clears the contents of the form.
   b) The spacing of a frameset is set by including the _____ attribute or the _____ attribute inside the <frameset> tag.
   c) The _____ element marks up a table row.
   d) _____ are used as masking characters in a password box.
   e) The common shapes used in image maps are _____, _____ and _____.

5.3   Write XHTML markup to accomplish each of the following:
   a) Insert a framed Web page, with the first frame extending 300 pixels across the page from the left side.
   b) Insert a table with a border of 8.
   c) Indicate alternative content to a frameset.
   d) Insert an image map in a page using deitel.gif as an image and map with name = "hello" as the image map, and set the alt text to "hello".

ANSWERS TO SELF-REVIEW EXERCISES

5.1   a) False. You can specify the width of any column, either in pixels or as a percentage of the table width. b) True. c) False. You can have an unlimited number of internal links. d) False. Some browsers are unable to render a frameset and must therefore rely on the information that you include inside the <noframes>...</noframes> tags.

5.2   a) type = "reset". b) cols, rows. c) tr. d) asterisks. e) poly (polygons), circles, rect (rectangles).

5.3   a) <frameset cols = "300,*">...</frameset>
        b) <table border = "8">...</table>
        c) <noframes>...</noframes>
        d) <img src = "deitel.gif" alt = "hello" usemap = "#hello" />

EXERCISES

5.4   Categorize each of the following as an element or an attribute:
        a) width
        b) td
        c) th
        d) frame
        e) name
        f) select
        g) type

5.5   What will the frameset produced by the following code look like? Assume that the pages referenced are blank with white backgrounds and that the dimensions of the screen are 800 by 600. Sketch the layout, approximating the dimensions.

```
<frameset rows = "20%,*">
    <frame src = "hello.html" name = "hello" />
        <frameset cols = "150,*">
            <frame src = "nav.html" name = "nav" />
            <frame src = "deitel.html" name = "deitel" />
        </frameset>
</frameset>
```

5.6   Write the XHTML markup to create a frame with a table of contents on the left side of the window, and have each entry in the table of contents use internal linking to scroll down the document frame to the appropriate subsection.

5.7   Create the XHTML markup that produces the table shown in Fig. 5.12. Use <em> and <strong> tags as necessary. The image (camel.gif) is included in the Chapter 5 examples directory on the CD-ROM that accompanies this book.

5.8   Write an XHTML document that produces the table shown in Fig. 5.13.

5.9   A local university has asked you to create an XHTML document that allows prospective students to provide feedback about their campus visit. Your XHTML document should contain a form with text boxes for a name, address and e-mail. Provide checkboxes that allow prospective students to indicate what they liked most about the campus. The checkboxes should include: students, location, campus, atmosphere, dorm rooms and sports. Also, provide radio buttons that ask the prospective students how they became interested in the university. Options should include: friends, television, Internet and other. In addition, provide a text area for additional comments, a submit button and a reset button.

5.10   Create an XHTML document titled "How to Get Good Grades." Use <meta> tags to include a series of keywords that describe your document.

5.11   Create an XHTML document that displays a tic-tac-toe table with player X winning. Use <h2> to mark up both Xs and Os. Center the letters in each cell horizontally. Title the game using an <h1> tag. The title should span all three columns. Set the table border to 1.

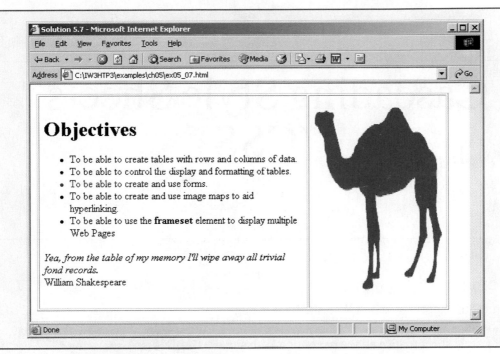

Fig. 5.12 XHTML table for Exercise 5.7.

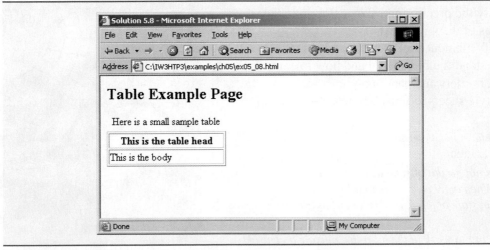

Fig. 5.13 XHTML table for Exercise 5.8.

6

Cascading Style Sheets™ (CSS)

Objectives

- To control the appearance of a Web site by creating style sheets.
- To use a style sheet to give all the pages of a Web site the same look and feel.
- To use the `class` attribute to apply styles.
- To specify the precise font, size, color and other properties of displayed text.
- To specify element backgrounds and colors.
- To understand the box model and how to control the margins, borders and padding.
- To use style sheets to separate presentation from content.

Fashions fade, style is eternal.
Yves Saint Laurent

A style does not go out of style as long as it adapts itself to its period. When there is an incompatibility between the style and a certain state of mind, it is never the style that triumphs.
Coco Chanel

How liberating to work in the margins, outside a central perception.
Don DeLillo

I've gradually risen from lower-class background to lower-class foreground.
Marvin Cohen

6.1 Introduction

In Chapters 4 and 5, we introduced the Extensible HyperText Markup Language (XHTML) for marking up information. In this chapter, we shift our focus to formatting and presenting information. To do this, we use a W3C technology called **Cascading Style Sheets** (CSS) that allows document authors to specify the presentation of elements on a Web page (e.g., fonts, spacing, margins, etc.) separately from the structure of the document (section headers, body text, links, etc.). This **separation of structure from presentation** simplifies maintaining and modifying a document's layout.

6.2 Inline Styles

A Web developer can declare document styles in many ways. This section presents **inline styles** that declare an individual element's format using the XHTML attribute **style**. Inline styles override any other styles applied using the techniques we discuss later in the chapter. Figure 6.1 applies inline styles to p elements to alter their font size and color.

```
1    <?xml version = "1.0"?>
2    <!DOCTYPE html PUBLIC "-//W3C//DTD XHTML 1.1//EN"
3       "http://www.w3.org/TR/xhtml11/DTD/xhtml11.dtd">
4
5    <!-- Fig. 6.1: inline.html -->
6    <!-- Using inline styles   -->
7
8    <html xmlns = "http://www.w3.org/1999/xhtml">
9       <head>
10          <title>Inline Styles</title>
```

Fig. 6.1   Inline styles. (Part 1 of 2.)

```
11    </head>
12
13    <body>
14
15       <p>This text does not have any style applied to it.</p>
16
17       <!-- The style attribute allows you to declare -->
18       <!-- inline styles. Separate multiple styles    -->
19       <!-- with a semicolon.                          -->
20       <p style = "font-size: 20pt">This text has the
21       <em>font-size</em> style applied to it, making it 20pt.
22       </p>
23
24       <p style = "font-size: 20pt; color: #0000ff">
25       This text has the <em>font-size</em> and
26       <em>color</em> styles applied to it, making it
27       20pt. and blue.</p>
28
29    </body>
30    </html>
```

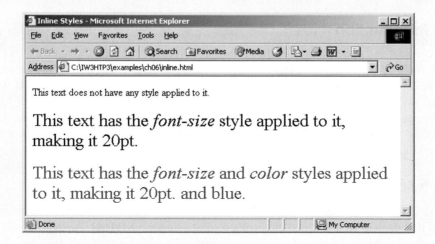

Fig. 6.1   Inline styles. (Part 2 of 2.)

The first inline style declaration appears in line 20. Attribute `style` specifies the style for an element. Each **CSS property** (the **font-size** property in this case) is followed by a colon and a value. In line 20, we declare this particular p element to use 20-point font size. Line 21 uses element **em** to "emphasize" text, which most browsers do by making the font italic.

Line 24 specifies the two properties, `font-size` and **color**, separated by a semicolon. In this line, we set the given paragraph's `color` to blue, using the hexadecimal code `#0000ff`. Color names may be used in place of hexadecimal codes, as we demonstrate in the next example. We provide a list of hexadecimal color codes and color names in Appendix B.

6.3 Embedded Style Sheets

A second technique for using style sheets is **embedded style sheets**. Embedded style sheets enable a Web-page author to embed an entire CSS document in an XHTML document's head section. Figure 6.2 creates an embedded style sheet containing four styles.

```
1   <?xml version = "1.0"?>
2   <!DOCTYPE html PUBLIC "-//W3C//DTD XHTML 1.1//EN"
3      "http://www.w3.org/TR/xhtml11/DTD/xhtml11.dtd">
4
5   <!-- Fig. 6.2: declared.html                          -->
6   <!-- Declaring a style sheet in the header section. -->
7
8   <html xmlns = "http://www.w3.org/1999/xhtml">
9      <head>
10        <title>Style Sheets</title>
11
12        <!-- this begins the style sheet section -->
13        <style type = "text/css">
14
15           em        { background-color: #8000ff;
16                        color: white }
17
18           h1        { font-family: arial, sans-serif }
19
20           p         { font-size: 14pt }
21
22           .special { color: blue }
23
24        </style>
25     </head>
26
27     <body>
28
29        <!-- this class attribute applies the .special style -->
30        <h1 class = "special">Deitel & Associates, Inc.</h1>
31
32        <p>Deitel &amp; Associates, Inc. is an internationally
33        recognized corporate training and publishing organization
34        specializing in programming languages, Internet/World
35        Wide Web technology and object technology education.
36        Deitel &amp; Associates, Inc. is a member of the World Wide
37        Web Consortium. The company provides courses on Java,
38        C++, Visual Basic, C, Internet and World Wide Web
39        programming, and Object Technology.</p>
40
41        <h1>Clients</h1>
42        <p class = "special"> The company's clients include many
43        <em>Fortune 1000 companies</em>, government agencies,
44        branches of the military and business organizations.
45        Through its publishing partnership with Prentice Hall,
46        Deitel &amp; Associates, Inc. publishes leading-edge
47        programming textbooks, professional books, interactive
```

Fig. 6.2   Embedded style sheets. (Part 1 of 2.)

```
48           CD-ROM-based multimedia Cyber Classrooms, satellite
49           courses and World Wide Web courses.</p>
50
51      </body>
52   </html>
```

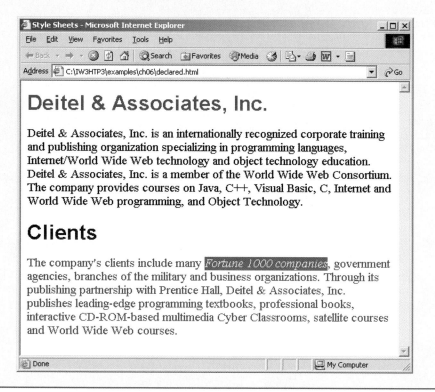

Fig. 6.2   Embedded style sheets. (Part 2 of 2.)

The `style` element (lines 13–24) defines the embedded style sheet. Styles placed in the `head` apply to matching elements wherever they appear in the entire document. The `style` element's `type` attribute specifies the **Multipurpose Internet Mail Extensions (MIME) type** that describes a file's content. CSS documents use the MIME type `text/css`. Other MIME types include `image/gif` (for GIF images) and `text/javascript` (for the JavaScript scripting language, which we discuss in Chapters 7–12).

The body of the style sheet (lines 15–22) declares the **CSS rules** for the style sheet. We declare rules for `em` (lines 15–16), `h1` (line 18) and `p` (line 20) elements. When the browser renders this document, it applies the properties defined in these rules to every element to which the rule applies. For example, the rule in lines 15–16 will be applied to all `em` elements (in this example, there is one in line 43). The body of each rule is enclosed in curly braces (`{` and `}`).

Line 22 declares a **style class** named `special`. Style classes define styles that can be applied to any type of element. In this example, we declare class `special`, which sets `color` to `blue`. We can apply this style to elements of any type, whereas the other rules in this style sheet apply only to specific element types (i.e., em, h1 or p). Style class declarations are preceded by a period. We will discuss how to apply a style class momentarily.

CSS rules in embedded style sheets use the same syntax as inline styles; the property name is followed by a colon (:) and the value of the property. Multiple properties are separated by semicolons (;). In the rule for em elements, the color property specifies the color of the text, and property **background-color** specifies the background color of the element.

The **font-family** property (line 18) specifies the name of the font to use. In this case, we use the arial font. The second value, sans-serif, is a **generic font family**. Not all users have the same fonts installed on their computers, so Web-page authors often specify a comma-separated list of fonts to use for a particular style. The browser attempts to use the fonts in the order they appear in the list. Many Web-page authors end a font list with a generic font family name in case the other fonts are not installed on the user's computer. In this example, if the arial font is not found on the system, the browser instead will display a generic sans-serif font, such as helvetica or verdana. Other generic font families include serif (e.g., times new roman, Georgia), cursive (e.g., script), fantasy (e.g., critter) and monospace (e.g., courier, fixedsys).

The **font-size** property (line 20) specifies a 14-point font. Other possible measurements in addition to **pt** (point) are introduced later in the chapter. Relative values— **xx-small**, **x-small**, **small**, **smaller**, **medium**, **large**, **larger**, **x-large** and **xx-large**— also can be used. Generally, relative values for font-size are preferred over point sizes because an author does not know the specific measurements of the display for each client. Relative font-size values permit more flexible viewing of Web pages. For example, a user may wish to view a Web page on a handheld device with a small screen. Specifying an 18-point font size in a style sheet will prevent such a user from seeing more than one or two characters at a time. However, if a relative font size is specified, such as large or larger, the actual size is determined by the browser that displays the font. Using relative sizes also makes pages more accessible to users with disabilities. Users with impaired vision, for example, may configure their browser to use a larger default font, upon which all relative sizes are based. Text that the author specifies to be smaller than the main text still displays in a smaller size font, yet it is clearly visible to each user.

Line 30 uses attribute **class** in an h1 element to apply a style class—in this case class special (declared as .special in the style sheet). When the browser renders the h1 element, note that the text appears on screen with the properties of both an h1 element (arial or sans-serif font defined in line 18) and the .special style class applied (the color blue defined in line 22).

The formatting for the p element and the .special class are applied to the text in lines 42–49. All the styles applied to an element (the **parent** or **ancestor element**) also apply to the element's nested elements (**child** or **descendant elements**). The em element nested in the p element in line 43 **inherits** the style from the p element (namely, the 14-point font size in line 20), but retains its italic style. The em element has its own color property, so it overrides the color property of the special class. We discuss the rules for resolving these conflicts in the next section.

6.4 Conflicting Styles

Cascading style sheets are "cascading" because styles may be defined by a user, an author or a **user agent** (e.g., a Web browser). Styles "cascade," or flow together, such that the ultimate appearance of elements on a page results from combining styles defined in several ways. Styles defined by the user take precedence over styles defined by the user agent, and styles defined by authors take precedence over styles defined by the user. Styles defined for parent elements are also inherited by child (nested) elements. In this section, we discuss the rules for resolving conflicts between styles defined for elements and styles inherited from parent and ancestor elements.

Figure 6.2 presented an example of **inheritance** in which a child em element inherited the font-size property from its parent p element. However, in Fig. 6.2, the child em element had a color property that conflicted with (i.e., had a different value than) the color property of its parent p element. Properties defined for child and descendant elements have a greater **specificity** than properties defined for parent and ancestor elements. According to the W3C CSS Recommendation, conflicts are resolved in favor of properties with a higher specificity. In other words, the styles explicitly defined for a child element are more specific than the styles defined for the child's parent element; therefore, the child's styles take precedence. Figure 6.3 illustrates examples of inheritance and specificity.

```
1    <?xml version = "1.0"?>
2    <!DOCTYPE html PUBLIC "-//W3C//DTD XHTML 1.1//EN"
3       "http://www.w3.org/TR/xhtml11/DTD/xhtml11.dtd">
4
5    <!-- Fig 6.3: advanced.html       -->
6    <!-- More advanced style sheets -->
7
8    <html xmlns = "http://www.w3.org/1999/xhtml">
9       <head>
10         <title>More Styles</title>
11
12         <style type = "text/css">
13
14            a.nodec   { text-decoration: none }
15
16            a:hover   { text-decoration: underline;
17                        color: red;
18                        background-color: #ccffcc }
19
20            li em     { color: red;
21                        font-weight: bold }
22
23            ul        { margin-left: 75px }
24
25            ul ul     { text-decoration: underline;
26                        margin-left: 15px }
27
28         </style>
29      </head>
30
31      <body>
32
33         <h1>Shopping list for <em>Monday</em>:</h1>
34
```

Fig. 6.3   Inheritance in style sheets. (Part 1 of 2.)

```
35      <ul>
36          <li>Milk</li>
37          <li>Bread
38              <ul>
39                  <li>White bread</li>
40                  <li>Rye bread</li>
41                  <li>Whole wheat bread</li>
42              </ul>
43          </li>
44          <li>Rice</li>
45          <li>Potatoes</li>
46          <li>Pizza <em>with mushrooms</em></li>
47      </ul>
48
49      <p><a class = "nodec" href = "http://www.food.com">
50      Go to the Grocery store</a></p>
51
52   </body>
53 </html>
```

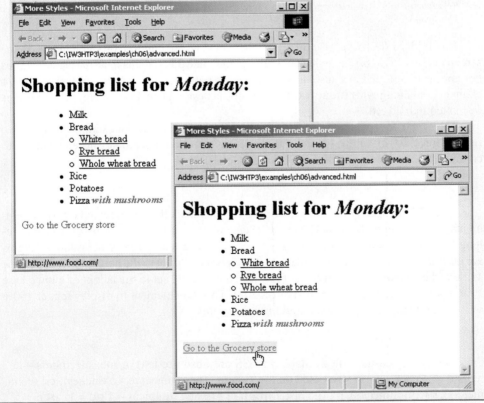

Fig. 6.3   Inheritance in style sheets. (Part 2 of 2.)

Line 14 applies property text-decoration to all a elements whose class attribute is set to nodec. The text-decoration property applies **decorations** to text within an element. By default, browsers underline the text of an a (anchor) element. Here, we set the text-decoration property to none to indicate that the browser should not underline hyperlinks. Other possible values for text-decoration include **overline**, **line-through**, **underline** and **blink**. [*Note*: blink is not supported by Internet Explorer.] The .nodec appended to a is an extension of class styles; this style will apply only to a elements that specify nodec in their class attribute.

Portability Tip 6.1

To ensure that your style sheets work in various Web browsers, test them on all the client Web browsers that will render documents using your styles.

Lines 16–18 specify a style for hover, which is a **pseudoclass**. Pseudoclasses give the author access to content not specifically declared in the document. The hover pseudoclass is activated dynamically when the user moves the mouse cursor over an element. Note that pseudoclasses are separated by a colon (with no surrounding spaces) from the name of the element to which they are applied.

Common Programming Error 6.1

Including a space before or after the colon separating a pseudoclass from the name of the element to which it is applied is an error that prevents the pseudoclass from being applied properly.

Lines 20–21 declare a style for all em elements that are children of li elements. In the screen output of Fig. 6.3, note that **Monday** (which line 33 contains in an em element) does not appear in bold red, because the em element is not in an li element. However, the em element containing **with mushrooms** (line 46) is nested in an li element; therefore, it is formatted in bold red.

The syntax for applying rules to multiple elements is similar. For example, to apply the rule in lines 20–21 to all li and em elements, you would separate the elements with commas, as follows:

```
li, em  { color: red; font-weight: bold }
```

Lines 25–26 specify that all nested lists (ul elements that are descendants of ul elements) are to be underlined and have a left-hand margin of 15 pixels. A pixel is a **relative-length measurement**—it varies in size, based on screen resolution. Other relative lengths are **em** (the so-called *M*-height of the font, which is usually set to the height of an uppercase *M*), **ex** (the so-called *x*-height of the font, which is usually set to the height of a lowercase *x*) and percentages (e.g., margin-left: 10%). To set an element to display text at 150% of its default text size, the author could use the syntax

```
font-size: 1.5em
```

Other units of measurement available in CSS are **absolute-length measurements**—i.e., units that do not vary in size based on the system. These units are **in** (inches), **cm** (centimeters), **mm** (millimeters), pt (points; 1 pt=1/72 in) and **pc** (picas—1 pc = 12 pt).

Good Programming Practice 6.1

Whenever possible, use relative-length measurements. If you use absolute-length measurements, your document may not be readable on some client browsers (e.g., wireless phones).

In Fig. 6.3, the entire list is indented because of the 75-pixel left-hand margin for top-level `ul` elements. However, the nested list is indented only 15 pixels more (not another 75 pixels) because the child `ul` element's `margin-left` property (in the `ul ul` rule in line 25) overrides the parent `ul` element's `margin-left` property.

6.5 Linking External Style Sheets

Style sheets are a convenient way to create a document with a uniform theme. With **external style sheets** (i.e., separate documents that contain only CSS rules), Web-page authors can provide a uniform look and feel to an entire Web site. Different pages on a site can all use the same style sheet. When changes to the styles are required, the Web-page author needs to modify only a single CSS file to make style changes across the entire Web site. Figure 6.4 presents an external style sheet. Lines 1–2 are **CSS comments**. Like XHTML comments, CSS comments describe the content of a CSS document. Comments may be placed in any type of CSS code (i.e., inline styles, embedded style sheets and external style sheets) and always start with /* and end with */. Text between these delimiters is ignored by the browser.

```
1   /* Fig. 6.4: styles.css   */
2   /* An external stylesheet */
3
4   a           { text-decoration: none }
5
6   a:hover { text-decoration: underline;
7               color: red;
8               background-color: #ccffcc }
9
10  li em    { color: red;
11               font-weight: bold;
12               background-color: #ffffff }
13
14  ul        { margin-left: 2cm }
15
16  ul ul    { text-decoration: underline;
17               margin-left: .5cm }
```

Fig. 6.4   External style sheet (`styles.css`).

Figure 6.5 contains an XHTML document that references the external style sheet in Fig. 6.4. Lines 11–12 (Fig. 6.5) show a **link** element that uses the **rel** attribute to specify a **relationship** between the current document and another document. In this case, we declare

```
1   <?xml version = "1.0"?>
2   <!DOCTYPE html PUBLIC "-//W3C//DTD XHTML 1.1//EN"
3       "http://www.w3.org/TR/xhtml11/DTD/xhtml11.dtd">
4
5   <!-- Fig. 6.5: external.html        -->
6   <!-- Linking external style sheets  -->
```

Fig. 6.5   Linking an external style sheet. (Part 1 of 3.)

```
 7
 8   <html xmlns = "http://www.w3.org/1999/xhtml">
 9      <head>
10         <title>Linking External Style Sheets</title>
11         <link rel = "stylesheet" type = "text/css"
12            href = "styles.css" />
13      </head>
14
15      <body>
16
17         <h1>Shopping list for <em>Monday</em>:</h1>
18         <ul>
19            <li>Milk</li>
20            <li>Bread
21               <ul>
22                  <li>White bread</li>
23                  <li>Rye bread</li>
24                  <li>Whole wheat bread</li>
25               </ul>
26            </li>
27            <li>Rice</li>
28            <li>Potatoes</li>
29            <li>Pizza <em>with mushrooms</em></li>
30         </ul>
31
32         <p>
33         <a href = "http://www.food.com">Go to the Grocery store</a>
34         </p>
35
36      </body>
37   </html>
```

Fig. 6.5   Linking an external style sheet. (Part 2 of 3.)

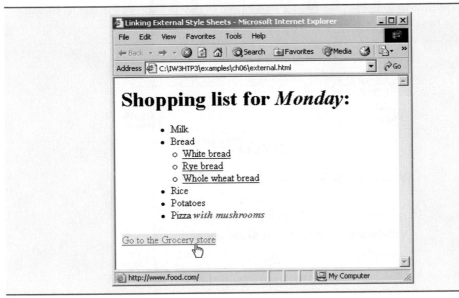

Fig. 6.5   Linking an external style sheet. (Part 3 of 3.)

the linked document to be a **stylesheet** for this document. The `type` attribute specifies the MIME type as `text/css`. The `href` attribute provides the URL for the document containing the style sheet. In this case, `styles.css` is in the same directory as `external.html`.

Software Engineering Observation 6.1

External style sheets are reusable. Creating them once and reusing them reduces programming effort.

Software Engineering Observation 6.2

*The `link` element can be placed only in the `head` element. The user can specify `next` and `previous` as values of the `rel` attribute, which allow the user to link a whole series of documents. This feature allows browsers to print a large collection of related documents at once. (In Internet Explorer, select **Print all linked documents** in the **Print...** submenu of the **File** menu.)*

6.6 W3C CSS Validation Service

The W3C provides a validation service (`jigsaw.w3.org/css-validator`) that validates external CSS documents to ensure that they conform to the W3C CSS Recommendation. Like XHTML validation, CSS validation ensures that style sheets are syntactically correct. The validator provides the option of either entering the CSS document's URL, pasting the CSS document's contents into a text area or uploading a CSS document.

Figure 6.6 illustrates uploading a CSS document, using the file upload feature available at `jigsaw.w3.org/css-validator/validator-upload.html`.

To validate the document, click the **Browse...** button to locate the file on your computer. Like many W3C Recommendations, the CSS Recommendation is being developed in stages (or **versions**). The current version under development is Version 3, so select **CSS version 3** in the **Profile** drop-down list. This field indicates to the validator the CSS Recommendation against which the uploaded file should be validated. Click **Submit this CSS**

file for validation to upload the file for validation. Figure 6.7 shows the results of validating `styles.css` (Fig. 6.4).

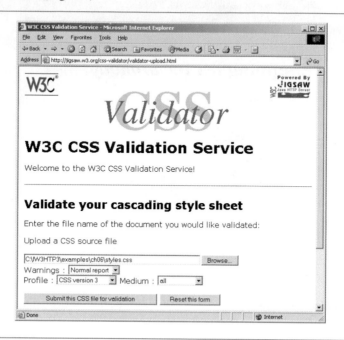

Fig. 6.6   Validating a CSS document. (Courtesy of World Wide Web Consortium (W3C).)

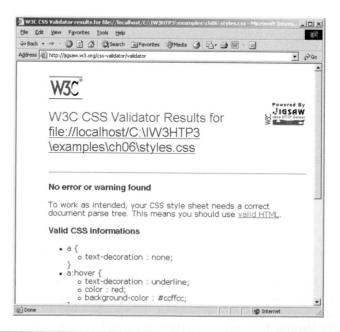

Fig. 6.7   CSS validation results. (Courtesy of World Wide Web Consortium (W3C).)

6.7 Positioning Elements

Before CSS, controlling the positioning of elements in an XHTML document was difficult—the browser determined positioning. CSS introduced the **position** property and a capability called **absolute positioning**, which gives authors greater control over how document elements are displayed. Figure 6.8 demonstrates absolute positioning.

```
1   <?xml version = "1.0"?>
2   <!DOCTYPE html PUBLIC "-//W3C//DTD XHTML 1.1//EN"
3       "http://www.w3.org/TR/xhtml11/DTD/xhtml11.dtd">
4
5   <!-- Fig 6.8: positioning.html         -->
6   <!-- Absolute positioning of elements -->
7
8   <html xmlns = "http://www.w3.org/1999/xhtml">
9      <head>
10         <title>Absolute Positioning</title>
11     </head>
12
13     <body>
14
15        <p><img src = "i.gif" style = "position: absolute;
16           top: 0px; left: 0px; z-index: 1"
17           alt = "First positioned image" /></p>
18        <p style = "position: absolute; top: 50px; left: 50px;
19           z-index: 3; font-size: 20pt">Positioned Text</p>
20        <p><img src = "circle.gif" style = "position: absolute;
21           top: 25px; left: 100px; z-index: 2" alt =
22           "Second positioned image" /></p>
23
24     </body>
25  </html>
```

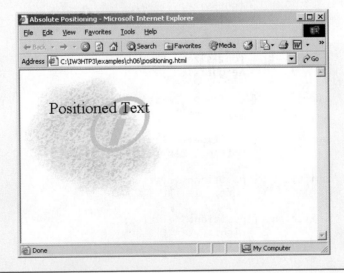

Fig. 6.8   Absolute positioning of elements with CSS.

Lines 15–17 position the first img element (i.gif) on the page. Specifying an element's position as **absolute** removes the element from the normal flow of elements on the page, instead positioning it according to the distance from the top, left, right or bottom margins of its **containing block-level element** (i.e., an element such as body or p). Here, we position the element to be 0 pixels away from both the top and left margins of the p element (lines 15–17).

The **z-index** attribute allows you to layer overlapping elements properly. Elements that have higher z-index values are displayed in front of elements with lower z-index values. In this example, i.gif has the lowest z-index (1), so it displays in the background. The img element in lines 20–22 (circle.gif) has a z-index of 2, so it displays in front of i.gif. The p element in lines 18–19 (Positioned Text) has a z-index of 3, so it displays in front of the other two. If you do not specify a z-index or if elements have the same z-index value, the elements are placed from background to foreground in the order they are encountered in the document.

Absolute positioning is not the only way to specify page layout. Figure 6.9 demonstrates **relative positioning**, in which elements are positioned relative to other elements.

```
1   <?xml version = "1.0"?>
2   <!DOCTYPE html PUBLIC "-//W3C//DTD XHTML 1.1//EN"
3      "http://www.w3.org/TR/xhtml11/DTD/xhtml11.dtd">
4
5   <!-- Fig. 6.9: positioning2.html       -->
6   <!-- Relative positioning of elements  -->
7
8   <html xmlns = "http://www.w3.org/1999/xhtml">
9      <head>
10        <title>Relative Positioning</title>
11
12        <style type = "text/css">
13
14           p            { font-size: 1.3em;
15                          font-family: verdana, arial, sans-serif }
16
17           span         { color: red;
18                          font-size: .6em;
19                          height: 1em }
20
21           .super       { position: relative;
22                          top: -1ex }
23
24           .sub         { position: relative;
25                          bottom: -1ex }
26
27           .shiftleft   { position: relative;
28                          left: -1ex }
29
30           .shiftright  { position: relative;
31                          right: -1ex }
32
33        </style>
```

Fig. 6.9   Relative positioning of elements with CSS. (Part 1 of 2.)

```
34        </head>
35
36        <body>
37
38            <p>The text at the end of this sentence
39            <span class = "super">is in superscript</span>.</p>
40
41            <p>The text at the end of this sentence
42            <span class = "sub">is in subscript</span>.</p>
43
44            <p>The text at the end of this sentence
45            <span class = "shiftleft">is shifted left</span>.</p>
46
47            <p>The text at the end of this sentence
48            <span class = "shiftright">is shifted right</span>.</p>
49
50        </body>
51    </html>
```

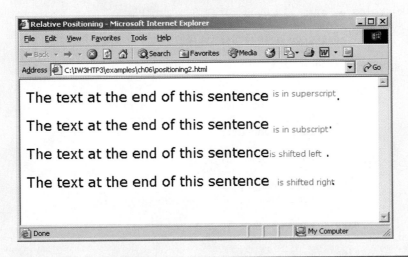

Fig. 6.9   Relative positioning of elements with CSS. (Part 2 of 2.)

Setting the `position` property to `relative`, as in class `super` (lines 21–22), lays out the element on the page and offsets it by the specified `top`, `bottom`, `left` or `right` value. Unlike absolute positioning, relative positioning keeps elements in the general flow of elements on the page, so positioning is relative to other elements in the flow. Recall that `ex` (line 22) is the *x*-height of a font, a relative length measurement typically equal to the height of a lowercase *x*.

We introduce the **span** element in line 39. Element `span` is a **grouping element**—it does not apply any inherent formatting to its contents. Its primary purpose is to apply CSS rules or `id` attributes to a block of text. Element `span` is an **inline-level element**—it is displayed inline with other text and with no line breaks. Lines 17–19 define the CSS rule for `span`. A similar element is the **div** element, which also applies no inherent styles but is displayed on its own line, with margins above and below (a block-level element).

Common Programming Error 6.2

Because relative positioning keeps elements in the flow of text in your documents, be careful to avoid unintentionally overlapping text.

6.8 Backgrounds

CSS provides control over the element backgrounds. In previous examples, we introduced the `background-color` property. CSS also can add background images to documents. Figure 6.10 adds a corporate logo to the bottom-right corner of the document. This logo stays fixed in the corner even when the user scrolls up or down the screen.

```
1   <?xml version = "1.0"?>
2   <!DOCTYPE html PUBLIC "-//W3C//DTD XHTML 1.1//EN"
3       "http://www.w3.org/TR/xhtml11/DTD/xhtml11.dtd">
4
5   <!-- Fig. 6.10: background.html                    -->
6   <!-- Adding background images and indentation -->
7
8   <html xmlns = "http://www.w3 .org/1999/xhtml">
9       <head>
10          <title>Background Images</title>
11
12          <style type = "text/css">
13
14              body   { background-image: url(logo.gif);
15                       background-position: bottom right;
16                       background-repeat: no-repeat;
17                       background-attachment: fixed; }
18
19              p      { font-size: 18pt;
20                       color: #aa5588;
21                       text-indent: 1em;
22                       font-family: arial, sans-serif; }
23
24              .dark { font-weight: bold }
25
26          </style>
27      </head>
28
29      <body>
30
31          <p>
32          This example uses the background-image,
33          background-position and background-attachment
34          styles to place the <span class = "dark">Deitel
35          &amp; Associates, Inc.</span> logo in the bottom,
36          right corner of the page. Notice how the logo
37          stays in the proper position when you resize the
38          browser window.
39          </p>
40
```

Fig. 6.10   Background image added with CSS. (Part 1 of 2.)

```
41        </body>
42    </html>
```

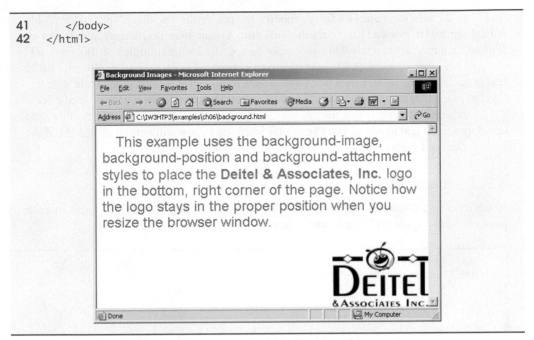

Fig. 6.10   Background image added with CSS. (Part 2 of 2.)

The **background-image** property (line 14) specifies the image URL for the image `logo.gif` in the format `url( fileLocation )`. The Web-page author also can set the `background-color` property in case the image is not found.

The **background-position** property (line 15) places the image on the page. The keywords **top**, **bottom**, **center**, **left** and **right** are used individually or in combination for vertical and horizontal positioning. An image can be positioned using lengths by specifying the horizontal length followed by the vertical length. For example, to position the image as horizontally centered (positioned at 50% of the distance across the screen) and 30 pixels from the top, use

```
background-position: 50% 30px;
```

The **background-repeat** property (line 16) controls the **tiling** of the background image. Tiling places multiple copies of the image next to each other to fill the background. Here, we set the tiling to **no-repeat** to display only one copy of the background image. The `background-repeat` property can be set to **repeat** (the default) to tile the image vertically and horizontally, **repeat-x** to tile the image only horizontally or **repeat-y** to tile the image only vertically.

The final property setting, **background-attachment: fixed** (line 17), fixes the image in the position specified by `background-position`. Scrolling the browser window will not move the image from its position. The default value, **scroll**, moves the image as the user scrolls through the document.

Line 21 indents the first line of text in the element by the specified amount, in this case `1em`. An author might use this property to create a Web page that reads more like a novel, in which the first line of every paragraph is indented.

Line 24 uses the **font-weight** property to specify the "boldness" of text. Possible valucs are **bold**, **normal** (the default), **bolder** (bolder than bold text) and **lighter** (lighter than normal text). Boldness also can be specified with multiples of 100, from 100 to 900 (e.g., 100, 200, ..., 900). Text specified as normal is equivalent to 400, and bold text is equivalent to 700. However, many systems do not have fonts that can scale with this level of precision, so using the values from 100 to 900 might not display the desired effect.

Another CSS property that formats text is the **font-style** property, which allows the developer to set text to **none**, **italic** or **oblique** (oblique will default to italic if the system does not support oblique text).

6.9 Element Dimensions

In addition to positioning elements, CSS rules can specify the actual dimensions of each page element. Figure 6.11 demonstrates how to set the dimensions of elements.

```
1   <?xml version = "1.0"?>
2   <!DOCTYPE html PUBLIC "-//W3C//DTD XHTML 1.1//EN"
3       "http://www.w3.org/TR/xhtml11/DTD/xhtml11.dtd">
4
5   <!-- Fig. 6.11: width.html                      -->
6   <!-- Setting box dimensions and aligning text   -->
7
8   <html xmlns = "http://www.w3.org/1999/xhtml">
9      <head>
10         <title>Box Dimensions</title>
11
12         <style type = "text/css">
13
14            div { background-color: #ffccff;
15                  margin-bottom: .5em }
16         </style>
17
18      </head>
19
20      <body>
21
22         <div style = "width: 20%">Here is some
23         text that goes in a box which is
24         set to stretch across twenty percent
25         of the width of the screen.</div>
26
27         <div style = "width: 80%; text-align: center">
28         Here is some CENTERED text that goes in a box
29         which is set to stretch across eighty percent of
30         the width of the screen.</div>
31
32         <div style = "width: 20%; height: 30%; overflow: scroll">
33         This box is only twenty percent of
34         the width and thirty percent of the height.
35         What do we do if it overflows? Set the
```

Fig. 6.11   Element dimensions and text alignment. (Part 1 of 2.)

```
36              overflow property to scroll!</div>
37
38      </body>
39  </html>
```

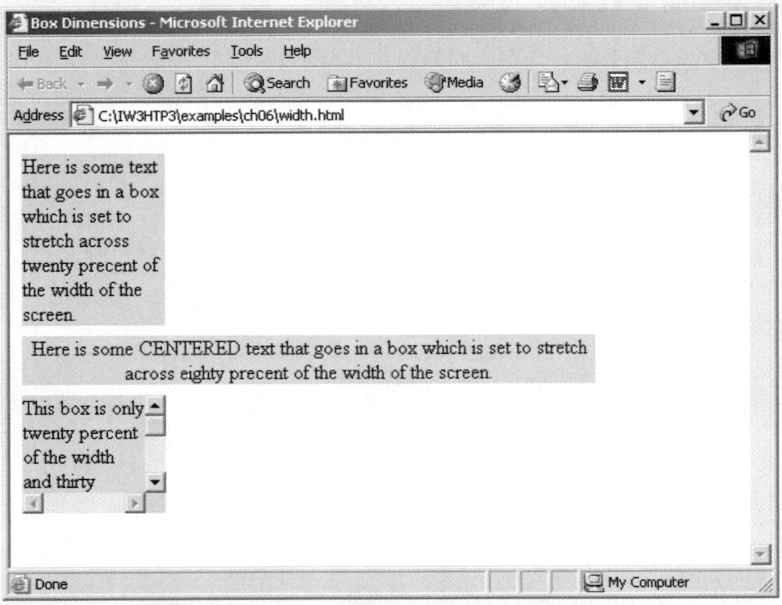

Fig. 6.11   Element dimensions and text alignment. (Part 2 of 2.)

The inline style in line 22 illustrates how to set the **width** of an element on screen; here, we indicate that the div element should occupy 20% of the screen width. Most elements are left-aligned by default; however, this alignment can be altered to position the element elsewhere. The height of an element can be set similarly, using the **height** property. The height and width values also can be specified as relative or absolute lengths. For example

width: 10em

sets the element's width to be equal to 10 times the font size. Line 27 sets text in the element to be **center** aligned; other values for the text-align property include **left** and **right**.

One problem with setting both dimensions of an element is that the content inside the element can exceed the set boundaries, in which case the element is simply made large enough for all the content to fit. However, in line 32, we set the **overflow** property to **scroll**, a setting that adds scrollbars if the text overflows the boundaries.

6.10 Text Flow and the Box Model

A browser normally places text and elements on screen in the order in which they appear in the XHTML document. However, as we have seen with absolute positioning, it is possible to remove elements from the normal flow of text. **Floating** allows you to move an element to one side of the screen; other content in the document then flows around the floated element. In addition, each block-level element has a virtual box drawn around it, based on what is known as the **box model**. The properties of this box can be adjusted to control the amount of padding inside the element and the margins outside the element (Fig. 6.12).

```
1   <?xml version = "1.0"?>
2   <!DOCTYPE html PUBLIC "-//W3C//DTD XHTML 1.1//EN"
3      "http://www.w3.org/TR/xhtml11/DTD/xhtml11.dtd">
4
5   <!-- Fig. 6.12: floating.html            -->
6   <!-- Floating elements and element boxes -->
7
8   <html xmlns = "http://www.w3.org/1999/xhtml">
9      <head>
10        <title>Flowing Text Around Floating Elements</title>
11
12        <style type = "text/css">
13
14           div { background-color: #ffccff;
15                 margin-bottom: .5em;
16                 font-size: 1.5em;
17                 width: 50% }
18
19           p   { text-align: justify }
20
21        </style>
22
23     </head>
24
25     <body>
26
27        <div style = "text-align: center">
28           Deitel &amp; Associates, Inc.</div>
29
30        <div style = "float: right; margin: .5em;
31           text-align: right">
32           Corporate Training and Publishing</div>
33
34        <p>Deitel &amp; Associates, Inc. is an internationally
35        recognized corporate training and publishing organization
36        specializing in programming languages, Internet/World
37        Wide Web technology and object technology education.
38        The company provides courses on Java, C++, Visual Basic, C,
39        Internet and World Wide Web programming, and Object Technology.</p>
40
41        <div style = "float: right; padding: .5em;
42           text-align: right">
43           Leading-Edge Programming Textbooks</div>
44
45        <p>The company's clients include many Fortune 1000
46        companies, government agencies, branches of the military
47        and business organizations.</p>
48
```

Fig. 6.12   Floating elements, aligning text and setting box dimensions. (Part 1 of 2.)

```
49        <p style = "clear: right">Through its publishing
50        partnership with Prentice Hall, Deitel &amp; Associates,
51        Inc. publishes leading-edge programming textbooks,
52        professional books, interactive CD-ROM-based multimedia
53        Cyber Classrooms, satellite courses and World Wide Web
54        courses.</p>
55
56     </body>
57  </html>
```

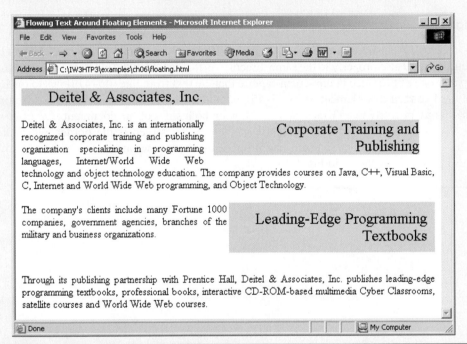

Fig. 6.12   Floating elements, aligning text and setting box dimensions. (Part 2 of 2.)

In addition to text, whole elements can be **floated** to the left or right of content. This means that any nearby text will wrap around the floated element. For example, in lines 30–32 we float a `div` element to the `right` side of the screen. As you can see from the sample screen capture, the text from lines 34–39 flows cleanly to the left and underneath the `div` element.

The second property in line 30, `margin`, specifies the distance between the edge of the element and any other element on the page. When the browser renders elements using the box model, the content of each element is surrounded by **padding**, a **border** and a **margin** (Fig. 6.13).

Margins for individual sides of an element can be specified by using the properties **margin-top**, **margin-right**, **margin-left** and **margin-bottom**.

Lines 41–43 specify a `div` element that floats at the right side of the content. Property **padding** for the `div` element is set to `.5em` (half a line's height). **Padding** is the distance between the content inside an element and the element's border. Like the `margin`, the padding can be set for each side of the box, with p**adding-top**, **padding-right**, **padding-left** and **padding-bottom**.

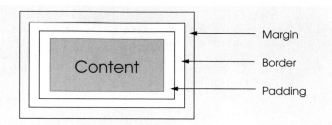

Fig. 6.13   Box model for block-level elements.

Lines 49–54 show that you can interrupt the flow of text around a floated element by setting the clear property to the same direction as that in which the element is floated— right or left. Notice in the screen capture that the text from lines 45–47 flows to the left of the floated div element (lines 43–45), but the text from lines 49–54 does not. Setting the **clear** property to **all** interrupts the flow on both sides of the document.

Another property of every block-level element on screen is the border, which lies between the padding space and the margin space, and has numerous properties for adjusting its appearance, as shown in Fig. 6.14.

```
 1   <?xml version = "1.0"?>
 2   <!DOCTYPE html PUBLIC "-//W3C//DTD XHTML 1.1//EN"
 3      "http://www.w3.org/TR/xhtml11/DTD/xhtml11.dtd">
 4
 5   <!-- Fig. 6.14: borders.html        -->
 6   <!-- Setting borders of an element -->
 7
 8   <html xmlns = "http://www.w3.org/1999/xhtml">
 9      <head>
10         <title>Borders</title>
11
12         <style type = "text/css">
13
14            body    { background-color: #ccffcc }
15
16            div     { text-align: center;
17                      margin-bottom: 1em;
18                      padding: .5em }
19
20            .thick  { border-width: thick }
21
22            .medium { border-width: medium }
23
24            .thin   { border-width: thin }
25
26            .groove { border-style: groove }
27
28            .inset  { border-style: inset }
29
```

Fig. 6.14   Borders of block-level elements. (Part 1 of 2.)

```
30              .outset { border-style: outset }
31
32              .red    { border-color: red }
33
34              .blue   { border-color: blue }
35
36          </style>
37      </head>
38
39      <body>
40
41          <div class = "thick groove">This text has a border</div>
42          <div class = "medium groove">This text has a border</div>
43          <div class = "thin groove">This text has a border</div>
44
45          <p class = "thin red inset">A thin red line...</p>
46          <p class = "medium blue outset">
47              And a thicker blue line</p>
48
49      </body>
50  </html>
```

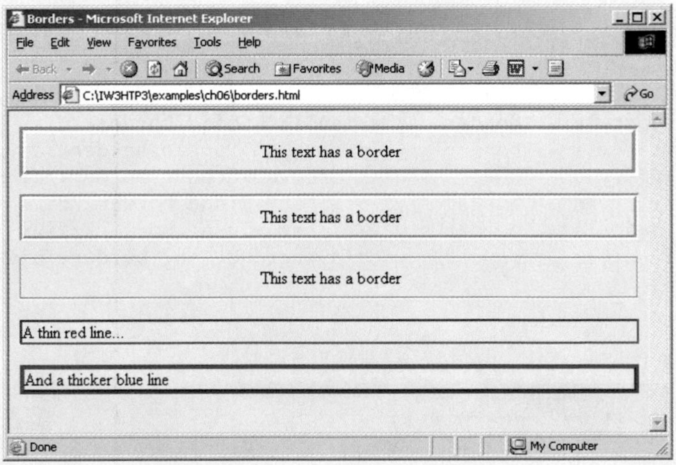

Fig. 6.14   Borders of block-level elements. (Part 2 of 2.)

In this example, we set three properties—**border-width**, **border-color** and **border-style**. The border-width property may be set to any valid CSS length or to the predefined value of **thin**, **medium** or **thick**. The border-color property sets the color. [*Note*: This property has different meanings for different style borders.]

As with padding and margins, each of the border properties may be set for an individual side of the box (e.g., border-top-style or border-left-color). A developer can assign more than one class to an XHTML element by using the class attribute, as shown in line 41.

The border-styles are **none**, **hidden**, **dotted**, **dashed**, **solid**, **double**, **groove**, **ridge**, **inset** and **outset**. Borders groove and ridge have opposite effects, as do inset and outset. Figure 6.15 illustrates these border styles.

```
1    <?xml version = "1.0"?>
2    <!DOCTYPE html PUBLIC "-//W3C//DTD XHTML 1.1//EN"
3        "http://www.w3.org/TR/xhtml11/DTD/xhtml11.dtd">
4
5    <!-- Fig. 6.15: borders2.html   -->
6    <!-- Various border-styles      -->
7
8    <html xmlns = "http://www.w3.org/1999/xhtml">
9       <head>
10         <title>Borders</title>
11
12         <style type = "text/css">
13
14            body    { background-color: #ccffcc }
15
16            div     { text-align: center;
17                      margin-bottom: .3em;
18                      width: 50%;
19                      position: relative;
20                      left: 25%;
21                      padding: .3em }
22         </style>
23      </head>
24
25      <body>
26
27         <div style = "border-style: solid">Solid border</div>
28         <div style = "border-style: double">Double border</div>
29         <div style = "border-style: groove">Groove border</div>
30         <div style = "border-style: ridge">Ridge border</div>
31         <div style = "border-style: inset">Inset border</div>
32         <div style = "border-style: outset">Outset border</div>
33
34      </body>
35   </html>
```

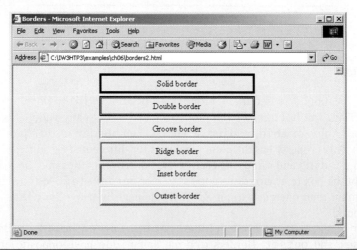

Fig. 6.15   border-style property of the box model.

6.11 User Style Sheets

Users can define their own **user style sheets** to format pages based on their preferences. For example, people with visual impairments may want to increase the page's text size. Web-page authors need to be careful not to inadvertently override user preferences with defined styles. This section discusses possible conflicts between **author styles** and **user styles**.

Figure 6.16 contains an author style. The font-size is set to 9pt for all <p> tags that have class note applied to them.

```
1   <?xml version = "1.0"?>
2   <!DOCTYPE html PUBLIC "-//W3C//DTD XHTML 1.1//EN"
3      "http://www.w3.org/TR/xhtml11/DTD/xhtml11.dtd">
4
5   <!-- Fig. 6.16: user_absolute.html   -->
6   <!-- User styles                     -->
7
8   <html xmlns = "http://www.w3.org/1999/xhtml">
9      <head>
10         <title>User Styles</title>
11
12         <style type = "text/css">
13
14            .note { font-size: 9pt }
15
16         </style>
17      </head>
18
19      <body>
20
21         <p>Thanks for visiting my Web site. I hope you enjoy it.
22         </p><p class = "note">Please Note: This site will be
23         moving soon. Please check periodically for updates.</p>
24
25      </body>
26   </html>
```

Fig. 6.16   pt measurement for text size.

User style sheets are external style sheets. Figure 6.17 shows a user style sheet that sets the body's font-size to 20pt, color to yellow and background-color to #000080.

```
1   /* Fig. 6.17: userstyles.css */
2   /* A user stylesheet          */
3
4   body     { font-size: 20pt;
5              color: yellow;
6              background-color: #000080 }
```

Fig. 6.17   User style sheet.

   User style sheets are not linked to a document; rather, they are set in the browser's options. To add a user style sheet in Internet Explorer 6, select **Internet Options...**, located in the **Tools** menu. In the **Internet Options** dialog (Fig. 6.18) that appears, click **Accessibility...**, check the **Format documents using my style sheet** checkbox, and type the location of the user style sheet. Internet Explorer 6 applies the user style sheet to any document it loads.

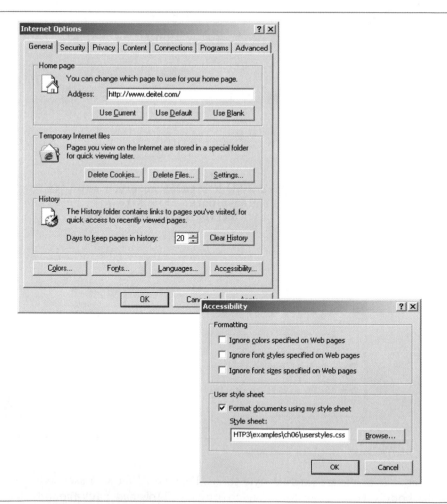

Fig. 6.18   User style sheet in Internet Explorer 6.

The Web page from Fig. 6.16 is displayed in Fig. 6.19, with the user style sheet from Fig. 6.17 applied.

Fig. 6.19   User style sheet applied with **pt** measurement.

In this example, if users define their own **font-size** in a user style sheet, the author style has a higher precedence and overrides the user style. The **9pt** font specified in the author style sheet overrides the **20pt** font specified in the user style sheet. This small font may make pages difficult to read, especially for individuals with visual impairments. A developer can avoid this problem by using relative measurements (e.g., **em** or **ex**) instead of absolute measurements, such as **pt**. Figure 6.20 changes the **font-size** property to use a relative measurement (line 14) that does not override the user style set in Fig. 6.17. Instead, the font size displayed is relative to the one specified in the user style sheet. In this case, text enclosed in the **<p>** tag displays as **20pt** ,and **<p>** tags that have class **note** applied to them are displayed in **15pt** (**.75** times **20pt**).

```
1   <?xml version = "1.0"?>
2   <!DOCTYPE html PUBLIC "-//W3C//DTD XHTML 1.1//EN"
3      "http://www.w3.org/TR/xhtml11/DTD/xhtml11.dtd">
4
5   <!-- Fig. 6.20: user_relative.html    -->
6   <!-- User styles                      -->
7
8   <html xmlns = "http://www.w3.org/1999/xhtml">
9      <head>
10         <title>User Styles</title>
11
12         <style type = "text/css">
13
14            .note { font-size: .75em }
15
16         </style>
17      </head>
18
19      <body>
20
```

Fig. 6.20   **em** measurement for text size. (Part 1 of 2.)

```
21          <p>Thanks for visiting my Web site. I hope you enjoy it.
22          </p><p class = "note">Please Note: This site will be
23          moving soon. Please check periodically for updates.</p>
24
25      </body>
26  </html>
```

Fig. 6.20   em measurement for text size. (Part 2 of 2.)

Figure 6.21 displays the Web page from Fig. 6.20 with the user style sheet from Fig. 6.16 applied. Note that the second line of text displayed is larger than the same line of text in Fig. 6.19.

Fig. 6.21   User style sheet applied with em measurement.

6.12 Web Resources

www.w3.org/TR/css3-roadmap
The W3C *Cascading Style Sheets, Level 3* specification contains a list of all the CSS properties. The specification also provides helpful examples detailing the use of many of the properties.

www.ddj.com/webreview/style
This site has several charts of CSS properties, including a list stating which browsers support what attributes and to what extent.

`tech.irt.org/articles/css.htm`
This site contains articles dealing with CSS.

SUMMARY

- The inline style allows a developer to declare a style for an individual element by using the `style` attribute in the element's start tag.
- Each CSS property is followed by a colon and the value of the attribute.
- The `color` property sets text color. Color names and hexadecimal codes may be used as the value.
- Styles that are placed in a `style` element apply to the entire document.
- `style` element attribute `type` specifies the MIME type (the specific encoding format) of the style sheet. Style sheets use `text/css`.
- Each rule body in a style sheet begins and ends with a curly brace ({ and }).
- Style class declarations are preceded by a period and are applied to elements of the specific class.
- The CSS rules in a style sheet use the same format as inline styles: The property is followed by a colon (`:`) and the value of that property. Multiple properties are separated by semicolons (`;`).
- The `background-color` attribute specifies the background color of the element.
- The `font-family` attribute names a specific font that should be displayed. Generic font families allow authors to specify a type of font instead of a specific font, in case a browser does not support a specific font. The `font-size` property specifies the size used to render the font.
- The `class` attribute applies a style class to an element.
- Pseudoclasses give the author access to content not specifically declared in the document. The `hover` pseudoclass is activated when the user moves the mouse cursor over an element.
- The `text-decoration` property applies decorations to text within an element, such as `underline`, `overline`, `line-through` and `blink`.
- To apply rules to multiple elements, separate the elements with commas in the style sheet.
- A pixel is a relative-length measurement: It varies in size based on screen resolution. Other relative lengths are `em`, `ex` and percentages.
- The other units of measurement available in CSS are absolute-length measurements—that is, units that do not vary in size. These units can be `in` (inches), `cm` (centimeters), `mm` (millimeters), `pt` (points; 1 `pt`=1/72 `in`) or `pc` (picas; 1 `pc` = 12 `pt`).
- External linking of style sheets can create a uniform look for a Web site; separate pages can all use the same styles. Modifying a single style sheet file makes changes to styles across an entire Web site.
- `link`'s `rel` attribute specifies a relationship between two documents.
- The CSS `position` property allows absolute positioning, which provides greater control over where on a page elements reside. Specifying an element's `position` as `absolute` removes it from the normal flow of elements on the page and positions it according to distance from the `top`, `left`, `right` or `bottom` margin of its parent element.
- The `z-index` property allows a developer to layer overlapping elements. Elements that have higher `z-index` values are displayed in front of elements with lower `z-index` values.
- Unlike absolute positioning, relative positioning keeps elements in the general flow on the page and offsets them by the specified `top`, `left`, `right` or `bottom` value.
- Property `background-image` specifies the URL of the image, in the format `url`(*fileLocation*). The property `background-position` places the image on the page using the values `top`, `bottom`,

center, left and right individually or in combination for vertical and horizontal positioning. You can also position by using lengths.

- The background-repeat property controls the tiling of the background image. Setting the tiling to no-repeat displays one copy of the background image on screen. The background-repeat property can be set to repeat (the default) to tile the image vertically and horizontally, to re-peat-x to tile the image only horizontally or to repeat-y to tile the image only vertically.

- The property setting background-attachment: fixed fixes the image in the position specified by background-position. Scrolling the browser window will not move the image from its set position. The default value, scroll, moves the image as the user scrolls the window.

- The text-indent property indents the first line of text in the element by the specified amount.

- The font-weight property specifies the "boldness" of text. Values besides bold and normal (the default) are bolder (bolder than bold text) and lighter (lighter than normal text). The val-ue also may be justified using multiples of 100, from 100 to 900 (i.e., 100, 200, ..., 900). Text specified as normal is equivalent to 400, and bold text is equivalent to 700.

- The font-style property allows the developer to set text to none, italic or oblique (ob-lique will default to italic if the system does not have a separate font file for oblique text, which is normally the case).

- span is a generic grouping element; it does not apply any inherent formatting to its contents. Its main use is to apply styles or id attributes to a block of text. Element span is displayed inline (an inline element) with other text and with no line breaks. A similar element is the div element, which also applies no inherent styles, but is displayed on a separate line, with margins above and below (a block-level element).

- The dimensions of elements on a page can be set with CSS by using properties height and width.

- Text within an element can be centered using text-align; other values for the text-align property are left and right.

- One problem with setting both vertical and horizontal dimensions of an element is that the content inside the element might sometimes exceed the set boundaries, in which case the element must be made large enough for all the content to fit. However, a developer can set the overflow property to scroll; this setting adds scroll bars if the text overflows the boundaries set for it.

- Browsers normally place text and elements on screen in the order in which they appear in the XHTML file. Elements can be removed from the normal flow of text. Floating allows you to move an element to one side of the screen; other content in the document will then flow around the float-ed element.

- CSS uses a box model to render elements on screen. The content of each element is surrounded by padding, a border and margins. The properties of this box are easily adjusted.

- The margin property determines the distance between the element's edge and any outside text.

- Margins for individual sides of an element can be specified by using margin-top, margin-right, margin-left and margin-bottom.

- The padding property determines the distance between the content inside an element and the edge of the element. Padding also can be set for each side of the box by using padding-top, padding-right, padding-left and padding-bottom.

- A developer can interrupt the flow of text around a floated element by setting the clear prop-erty to the same direction in which the element is floated—right or left. Setting the clear property to all interrupts the flow on both sides of the document.

- The border of a block-level element lies between the padding space and the margin space and has numerous properties with which to adjust its appearance.

- The `border-width` property may be set to any of the CSS lengths or to the predefined value of `thin`, `medium` or `thick`.
- The `border-styles` available are `none`, `hidden`, `dotted`, `dashed`, `solid`, `double`, `groove`, `ridge`, `inset` and `outset`.
- The `border-color` property sets the color used for the border.
- The `class` attribute allows more than one class to be assigned to an XHTML element by separating each class name from the next with a space.

TERMINOLOGY

absolute positioning
absolute-length measurement
`arial` font
`background` property
`background-attachment` property
`background-color` property
`background-image` property
`background-position` property
`background-repeat` property
`blink` text decoration
block-level element
border
`border-color` property
`border-style` property
`border-width` property
box model
Cascading Style Sheets (CSS)
`class` attribute
`clear` property value
cm (centimeter)
colon (:)
`color` property
CSS rule
`cursive` generic font family
`dashed` border-style
`dotted` border-style
`double` border-style
em (size of font)
embedded style sheet
ex (*x*-height of font)
floated element
`font-style` property
generic font family
`groove` border style
`hidden` border style
`href` attribute
`in` (inch)
inline style
inline-level element
`inset` border-style

`large` relative font size
`larger` relative font size
`left` property value
`line-through` text decoration
`link` element
linking to an external style sheet
`margin` property
`margin-bottom` property
`margin-left` property
`margin-right` property
`margin-top` property
`medium` relative border width
`medium` relative font size
MIME (Multipurpose Internet Mail
     Extensions) type
mm (millimeter)
`monospace` font
`none` border-style
`outset` border-style
`overflow` property
`overline` text decoration
`padding` property
parent element
pc (pica)
pseudoclass
pt (point)
`rel` attribute (`link`)
relative positioning
relative-length measurement
`repeat` property value
`ridge` border-style
`right` property value
`sans-serif` generic font family
`scroll` property value
separation of structure from content
`serif` generic font family
`small` relative font size
`smaller` relative font size
`solid` border-style
`span` element

style	`thick` border width
`style` attribute	`thin` border width
style class	user style sheet
style in header section of document	`x-large` relative font size
text flow	`x-small` relative font size
`text/css` MIME type	`xx-large` relative font size
`text-align` property	`xx-small` relative font size
`text-decoration` property	`z-index` property-
`text-indent` property	

SELF-REVIEW EXERCISES

6.1   Assume that the size of the base font on a system is 12 points.
  a) How big is a 36-point font in ems?
  b) How big is a 9-point font in ems?
  c) How big is a 24-point font in picas?
  d) How big is a 12-point font in inches?
  e) How big is a 1-inch font in picas?

6.2   Fill in the blanks in the following statements:
  a) Using the _____ element allows authors to use external style sheets in their pages.
  b) To apply a CSS rule to more than one element at a time, separate the element names with a(n) _____.
  c) Pixels are a(n) _____ -length measurement unit.
  d) The _____ pseudoclass is activated when the user moves the mouse cursor over the specified element.
  e) Setting the `overflow` property to _____ provides a mechanism for containing inner content without compromising specified box dimensions.
  f) While _____ is a generic inline element that applies no inherent formatting and _____ is a generic block-level element that applies no inherent formatting.
  g) Setting property `background-repeat` to _____ tiles the specified `background-image` vertically.
  h) If you `float` an element, you can stop the flowing of text by using property _____.
  i) The _____ property allows you to indent the first line of text in an element.
  j) Three components of the box model are the _____, _____ and _____.

ANSWERS TO SELF-REVIEW EXERCISES

6.1   a) 3 ems. b) 0.75 ems. c) 2 picas. d) 1/6 inch. e) 6 picas.

6.2   a) `link`. b) comma. c) relative. d) `hover`. e) `scroll`. f) `span`, `div`. g) `y-repeat`. h) `clear`. i) `text-indent`. j) padding, border, margin.

EXERCISES

6.3   Write a CSS rule that makes all text 1.5 times larger than the base font of the system and colors the text red.

6.4   Write a CSS rule that removes the underlines from all links inside list items (`li`) and shifts all list items left by 3 ems.

6.5   Write a CSS rule that places a background image halfway down the page, tiling it horizontally. The image should remain in place when the user scrolls up or down.

6.6 Write a CSS rule that gives all h1 and h2 elements a padding of 0.5 ems, a grooved border style and a margin of 0.5 ems.

6.7 Write a CSS rule that changes the color of all elements containing attribute class = "greenMove" to green and shifts them down 25 pixels and right 15 pixels.

6.8 Write an XHTML document that shows the results of a color survey. The document should contain a form with radio buttons that allows users to vote for their favorite color. One of the colors should be selected as a default. The document should also contain a table showing various colors and the corresponding percentage of votes for each color. (Each row should be displayed in the color to which it is referring.) Use attributes to format width, border and cell spacing for the table.

6.9 Add an embedded style sheet to the XHTML document in Fig. 4.5. The style sheet should contain a rule that displays h1 elements in blue. In addition, create a rule that displays all links in blue without underlining them. When the mouse hovers over a link, change the link's background color to yellow.

6.10 Modify the style sheet in Fig. 6.4 by changing a:hover to a:hver and margin-left to margin left. Validate the style sheet using the CSS Validator. What happens?

7

JavaScript: Introduction to Scripting

Objectives

- To be able to write simple JavaScript programs.
- To be able to use input and output statements.
- To understand basic memory concepts.
- To be able to use arithmetic operators.
- To understand the precedence of arithmetic operators.
- To be able to write decision-making statements.
- To be able to use relational and equality operators.

Comment is free, but facts are sacred.
C. P. Scott

The creditor hath a better memory than the debtor.
James Howell

When faced with a decision, I always ask, "What would be the most fun?"
Peggy Walker

Equality, in a social sense, may be divided into that of condition and that of rights.
James Fenimore Cooper

7.1 Introduction

In the first six chapters, we introduced the Internet and World Wide Web, Internet Explorer 6, Adobe Photoshop Elements, XHTML and Cascading Style Sheets (CSS). In this chapter, we begin our introduction to the **JavaScript scripting language**, which facilitates a disciplined approach to designing computer programs that enhance the functionality and appearance of Web pages.[1]

In Chapters 7–12, we present a detailed discussion of JavaScript—the *de facto* standard client-side scripting language for Web-based applications due to its highly portable nature. Our treatment of JavaScript serves two purposes—it introduces client-side scripting (used in Chapters 7–20), which makes Web pages more dynamic and interactive, and it provides the programming foundation for the more complex server-side scripting presented in Chapters 23–27 and Chapters 33–37.

We now introduce JavaScript programming and present examples that illustrate several important features of JavaScript. Each example is carefully analyzed one line at a time. In Chapters 8–9, we present a detailed treatment of **program development** and **program control** in JavaScript.

7.2 Simple Program: Printing a Line of Text in a Web Page

JavaScript uses notations that may appear strange to nonprogrammers. We begin by considering a simple **script** (or **program**) that displays the text "Welcome to JavaScript Programming!" in the body of an XHTML document. The Internet Explorer Web browser contains a **JavaScript interpreter**, which processes the commands written in JavaScript. The JavaScript code and its output are shown in Fig. 7.1.

---

1. Microsoft's version of JavaScript is called JScript. JavaScript was originally created by Netscape. Both Netscape and Microsoft have been instrumental in the standardization of JavaScript/JScript by ECMA International as ECMAScript. Detailed information about the current ECMAScript standard can be found at www.ecma-international.org/publications/standards/ECMA-262.htm. Throughout this book, we frequently refer to JavaScript and JScript generically as JavaScript.

```
1    <?xml version = "1.0"?>
2    <!DOCTYPE html PUBLIC "-//W3C//DTD XHTML 1.0 Strict//EN"
3       "http://www.w3.org/TR/xhtml1/DTD/xhtml1-strict.dtd">
4
5    <!-- Fig. 7.1: welcome.html     -->
6    <!-- Displaying a line of text -->
7
8    <html xmlns = "http://www.w3.org/1999/xhtml">
9       <head>
10          <title>A First Program in JavaScript</title>
11
12          <script type = "text/javascript">
13             <!--
14             document.writeln(
15                "<h1>Welcome to JavaScript Programming!</h1>" );
16             // -->
17          </script>
18
19       </head><body></body>
20    </html>
```

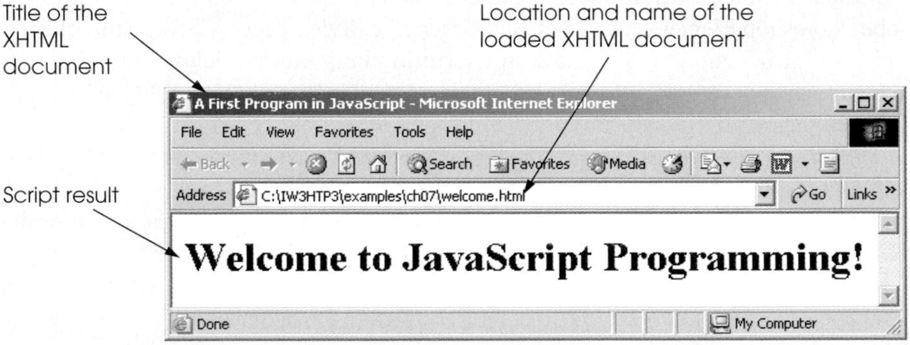

Title of the XHTML document

Location and name of the loaded XHTML document

Script result

A First Program in JavaScript - Microsoft Internet Explorer

File   Edit   View   Favorites   Tools   Help

Back   →   ·   Search   Favorites   Media

Address   C:\IW3HTP3\examples\ch07\welcome.html   Go   Links »

Welcome to JavaScript Programming!

Done   My Computer

Fig. 7.1   First program in JavaScript.

This program illustrates several important JavaScript features. We consider each line of the XHTML document and script in detail. As in the preceding chapters, we have given each XHTML document line numbers for the reader's convenience; the line numbers are not part of the XHTML document or of the JavaScript programs. Lines 14–15 do the "real work" of the script, namely, displaying the phrase Welcome to JavaScript Programming! in the Web page. However, let us consider each line in order.

Line 9 indicates the beginning of the <head> section of the XHTML document. For the moment, the JavaScript code we write will appear in the <head> section. The browser interprets the contents of the <head> section first, so the JavaScript programs we write there will execute before the <body> of the XHTML document displays. In later chapters on JavaScript and in the chapters on dynamic HTML, we illustrate **inline scripting**, in which JavaScript code is written in the <body> of an XHTML document.

Line 11 is simply a blank line to separate the <script> tag in line 12 from the other XHTML elements. This effect helps the script stand out in the XHTML document and makes the document easier to read.

Good Programming Practice 7.1

Place a blank line before `<script>` and after `</script>` to separate the script from the surrounding XHTML elements and to make it stand out in the document.

Line 12 uses the **`<script>`** tag to indicate to the browser that the text which follows is part of a script. The **`type`** attribute specifies the type of file as well as the **scripting language** used in the script—in this case, a `text` file written in `javascript`. Both Microsoft Internet Explorer and Netscape use JavaScript as the default scripting language. [*Note*: Even though Microsoft calls the language JScript, the `type` attribute specifies `javascript`, to adhere to the ECMAScript standard.]

Line 13 contains the XHTML comment tag `<!--`. Some older Web browsers do not support scripting. In such browsers, the actual text of a script often will display in the Web page. To prevent this from happening, many script programmers enclose the script code in an XHTML comment, so that browsers which do not support scripts ignore the script. The syntax used is as follows:

```
<script type = "text/javascript">
   <!--
   script code here
   // -->
</script>
```

When a browser that does not support scripts encounters the preceding code, it ignores the `<script>` and `</script>` tags and the script code in the XHTML comment. Browsers that do support scripting will interpret the JavaScript code as expected. [*Note*: Some browsers require the **JavaScript single-line comment** `//` (see Section 7.3 for an explanation) before the ending XHTML comment delimiter (`-->`) to interpret the script properly.]

Portability Tip 7.1

Some browsers do not support the `<script>`...`</script>` tags. If your document is to be rendered with such browsers, enclose the script code between these tags in an XHTML comment, so that the script text does not get displayed as part of the Web page.

Lines 14–15 instruct the browser's JavaScript interpreter to perform an **action**, namely, to display in the Web page the **string** of characters contained between the **double quotation (")** marks. A string is sometimes called a **character string**, a **message** or a **string literal**. We refer to characters between double quotation marks generically as strings. Individual white space characters between words in a string are not ignored by the browser. However, if consecutive spaces appear in a string, browsers condense them to a single space. Also, in most cases, browsers ignore leading white space characters (i.e., white space at the beginning of a string).

Software Engineering Observation 7.1

Strings in JavaScript can be enclosed in either double quotation marks (") or single quotation marks (').

Lines 14–15 use the browser's **`document` object**, which represents the XHTML document the browser is currently displaying. The `document` object allows a script programmer to specify text to display in the XHTML document. The browser contains a complete set of objects that allow script programmers to access and manipulate every element of an XHTML document. In the next several chapters, we overview some of these objects. Chapters 13–18 provide in-depth coverage of many more objects that a script programmer can manipulate.

An object resides in the computer's memory and contains information used by the script. The term **object** normally implies that **attributes** (**data**) and **behaviors** (**methods**) are associated with the object. The object's methods use the attributes' data to perform useful actions for the **client of the object** (i.e., the script that calls the methods). A method may require additional information (**arguments**) to perform its action; this information is enclosed in parentheses after the name of the method in the script. In lines 14–15, we call the `document` object's `writeln` **method** to write a line of XHTML markup in the XHTML document. The parentheses following the method name `writeln` contain the arguments that method `writeln` requires (in this case, the string of XHTML that the browser is to display). Method `writeln` instructs the browser to display the argument string. If the string contains XHTML elements, the browser interprets these elements and renders them on the screen. In this example, the browser displays the phrase `Welcome to JavaScript Programming!` as an `h1`-level XHTML heading, because the phrase is enclosed in an `h1` element.

The code elements in lines 14–15, including `document.writeln`, its argument in the parentheses (the string) and the **semicolon** (`;`), together are called a **statement**. Every statement should end with a semicolon (also known as the **statement terminator**), although this practice is not required by JavaScript. Line 17 indicates the end of the script.

Good Programming Practice 7.2

Always include a semicolon at the end of a statement to terminate the statement. This notation clarifies where one statement ends and the next statement begins.

Common Programming Error 7.1

Forgetting the ending `</script>` *tag for a script may prevent the browser from interpreting the script properly and may prevent the XHTML document from loading properly.*

The `</head>` tag in line 19 indicates the end of the `<head>` section. Also in line 19, the tags `<body>` and `</body>` specify that this XHTML document has an empty body—no XHTML appears in the `body` element. Line 20 indicates the end of this XHTML document.

We are now ready to view our XHTML in Internet Explorer. Open the XHTML document in Internet Explorer by following the procedure outlined in Section 4.2 of Chapter 4. If the script contains no syntax errors, it should produce the output shown in Fig. 7.1.

Common Programming Error 7.2

JavaScript is case sensitive. Not using the proper uppercase and lowercase letters is a syntax *error. A syntax error occurs when the script interpreter cannot recognize a statement. The interpreter normally issues an error message to help the programmer locate and fix the incorrect statement. Syntax errors are violations of the rules of the programming language. The interpreter notifies you of a syntax error when it attempts to execute the statement containing the error. The JavaScript interpreter in Internet Explorer reports all syntax errors by indicating in a separate popup window that a* "runtime error" *has occurred (i.e., a problem occurred while the interpreter was running the script). Note: To enable this feature in IE6, select* **Internet Options...** *from the* **Tools** *menu. In the* **Internet Options** *dialog that appears, select the* **Advanced** *tab and click the checkbox labelled* **Display a notification about every script error** *under the* **Browsing** *category.*

Error-Prevention Tip 7.1

When the interpreter reports a syntax error, the error may not be on the line number indicated by the error message. First, check the line for which the error was reported. If that line does not contain errors, check the preceding several lines in the script.

A script can display `Welcome to JavaScript Programming!` several ways. Figure 7.2 uses two JavaScript statements to produce one line of text in the XHTML document. This example also displays the text in a different color, using the CSS `color` property.

```
1  <?xml version = "1.0"?>
2  <!DOCTYPE html PUBLIC "-//W3C//DTD XHTML 1.0 Strict//EN"
3     "http://www.w3.org/TR/xhtml1/DTD/xhtml1-strict.dtd">
4
5  <!-- Fig. 7.2: welcome2.html              -->
6  <!-- Printing a Line with Multiple Statements -->
7
8  <html xmlns = "http://www.w3.org/1999/xhtml">
9     <head>
10        <title>Printing a Line with Multiple Statements</title>
11
12        <script type = "text/javascript">
13           <!--
14           document.write( "<h1 style = \"color: magenta\">" );
15           document.write( "Welcome to JavaScript " +
16              "Programming!</h1>" );
17           // -->
18        </script>
19
20     </head><body></body>
21  </html>
```

Fig. 7.2   Printing on one line with separate statements.

Most of this XHTML document is identical to Fig. 7.1, so we concentrate only on lines 14–16 of Fig. 7.2, which display one line of text in the XHTML document. The first statement uses `document` method **write** to display a string. Unlike `writeln`, `write` does not position the output cursor in the XHTML document at the beginning of the next line after writing its argument. [*Note*: The output cursor keeps track of where the next character appears in the XHTML document, not where the next character appears in the Web page as rendered by the browser.] The next character written in the XHTML document appears immediately after the last character written with `write`. Thus, when lines 15–16 execute, the first character written, "W," appears immediately after the last character displayed with write (the > character inside the right double quote in line 14). Each write or writeln statement resumes writing characters where the last write or writeln statement stopped writing characters. So, after a writeln statement, the next output appears on the beginning of the next line. In effect, the two statements in lines 14–16 result in one line of XHTML text. Remember that statements in JavaScript are separated by semicolons (;). Therefore, lines 15–16 represent one statement. JavaScript allows large statements to be split over many lines. However, you cannot split a statement in the middle of a string. The + operator in line 15 joins two strings together and is explained in more detail later in this chapter.

Common Programming Error 7.3

Splitting a statement in the middle of a string is a syntax error.

Note that the characters \" (in line 14) are not displayed in the browser. The **backslash** (\) in a string is an **escape character**. It indicates that a "special" character is to be used in the string. When a backslash is encountered in a string of characters, the next character is combined with the backslash to form an **escape sequence**. The escape sequence \" is the **double-quote character**, which causes a double-quote character to be inserted into the string. We will use this escape sequence to insert double quotes around the attribute value for style. We discuss escape sequences in greater detail momentarily.

It is important to note that the preceding discussion has nothing to do with the actual rendering of the XHTML text. Remember that the browser does not create a new line of text unless the browser window is too narrow for the text being rendered, or unless the browser encounters an XHTML element that explicitly starts a new line—for example, <br /> to start a new line, <p> to start a new paragraph. To see the actual text written by the write and writeln methods, select the **View** menu's **Source** option in your browser.

Common Programming Error 7.4

Many people confuse the writing of XHTML text with the rendering of XHTML text. Writing XHTML text creates the XHTML that will be rendered by the browser for presentation to the user.

In the next example, we demonstrate that a single statement can cause the browser to display multiple lines through by using line-break XHTML tags (<br />) throughout the string of XHTML text in a write or writeln method call. Figure 7.3 demonstrates the use of line-break XHTML tags. Lines 13–14 produce three separate lines of text when the browser renders the XHTML document.

```
1   <?xml version = "1.0"?>
2   <!DOCTYPE html PUBLIC "-//W3C//DTD XHTML 1.0 Strict//EN"
3       "http://www.w3.org/TR/xhtml1/DTD/xhtml1-strict.dtd">
4
5   <!-- Fig. 7.3: welcome3.html   -->
6   <!-- Printing Multiple Lines   -->
7
8   <html xmlns = "http://www.w3.org/1999/xhtml">
9       <head><title>Printing Multiple Lines</title>
```

Fig. 7.3   Printing on multiple lines with a single statement. (Part 1 of 2.)

```
10
11          <script type = "text/javascript">
12             <!--
13             document.writeln( "<h1>Welcome to<br />JavaScript" +
14                "<br />Programming!</h1>" );
15             // -->
16          </script>
17
18      </head><body></body>
19  </html>
```

Fig. 7.3   Printing on multiple lines with a single statement. (Part 2 of 2.)

The first several programs in this chapter display text in the XHTML document. Sometimes it is useful to display information in windows called **dialogs** (or **dialog boxes**) that "pop up" on the screen to grab the user's attention. Dialogs typically display important messages to users browsing the Web page. JavaScript allows you easily to display a dialog box containing a message. The program in Fig. 7.4 displays Welcome to JavaScript Programming! as three lines in a predefined dialog called an **alert** dialog.

```
 1  <?xml version = "1.0"?>
 2  <!DOCTYPE html PUBLIC "-//W3C//DTD XHTML 1.0 Strict//EN"
 3     "http://www.w3.org/TR/xhtml1/DTD/xhtml1-strict.dtd">
 4
 5  <!-- Fig. 7.4: welcome4.html                    -->
 6  <!-- Printing multiple lines in a dialog box -->
 7
 8  <html xmlns = "http://www.w3.org/1999/xhtml">
 9     <head><title>Printing Multiple Lines in a Dialog Box</title>
10
11     <script type = "text/javascript">
12        <!--
13           window.alert( "Welcome to\nJavaScript\nProgramming!" );
14        // -->
15     </script>
16
17  </head>
```

Fig. 7.4   Alert dialog displaying multiple lines. (Part 1 of 2.)

```
18
19      <body>
20          <p>Click Refresh (or Reload) to run this script again.</p>
21      </body>
22  </html>
```

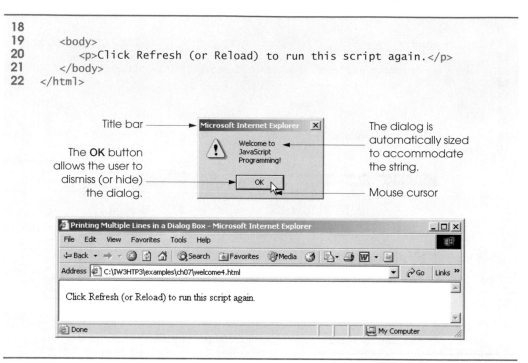

Fig. 7.4   Alert dialog displaying multiple lines. (Part 2 of 2.)

Line 13 in the script uses the browser's **window** object to display an alert dialog. The argument to the window object's **alert** method is the string to display. Executing the preceding statement displays the dialog shown in the first window of Fig. 7.4. The **title bar** of the dialog contains the string **Microsoft Internet Explorer** to indicate that the browser is presenting a message to the user. The dialog provides an **OK** button that allows the user to **dismiss** (i.e., **hide**) the dialog by clicking the button. To dismiss the dialog, position the **mouse cursor** (also called the **mouse pointer**) over the **OK** button and click the mouse.

Common Programming Error 7.5

Dialogs display plain text; they do not render XHTML. Therefore, specifying XHTML elements as part of a string to be displayed in a dialog results in the actual characters of the tags being displayed.

Note that the alert dialog contains three lines of plain text. Normally, a dialog displays the characters in a string exactly as they appear between the double quotes. Note, however, that the dialog does not display the characters \n. The escape sequence \n is the **newline character**. In a dialog, the newline character causes the **cursor** (i.e., the current screen position indicator) to move to the beginning of the next line in the dialog. Some other common escape sequences are listed in Fig. 7.5. The \n, \t and \r escape sequences in the table do not affect XHTML rendering unless they are in a **pre element** (this element displays the text between its tags in a fixed-width font exactly as it is formatted between the tags, including leading white space characters and consecutive white space characters). The other escape sequences result in characters that will be displayed in plain text dialogs and in XHTML.

Escape sequence	Description
\n	New line. Position the screen cursor at the beginning of the next line.
\t	Horizontal tab. Move the screen cursor to the next tab stop.
\r	Carriage return. Position the screen cursor to the beginning of the current line; do not advance to the next line. Any characters output after the carriage return overwrite the characters previously output on that line.
\\	Backslash. Used to represent a backslash character in a string.
\"	Double quote. Used to represent a double-quote character in a string contained in double quotes. For example,

```
window.alert( "\"in quotes\"" );
```

displays `"in quotes"` in an `alert` dialog.

\'	Single quote. Used to represent a single-quote character in a string. For example,

```
window.alert( '\'in quotes\'' );
```

displays `'in quotes'` in an `alert` dialog.

Fig. 7.5   Some common escape sequences.

7.3 Obtaining User Input with prompt Dialogs

Scripting gives Web page authors the ability to generate part or all of a Web page's content at the time it is shown to the user. A script can adapt the content based on input from the user or other variables, such as the time of day or the type of browser used by the client. Such Web pages are said to be **dynamic**, as opposed to static, since their content has the ability to change. The next two subsections use scripts to demonstrate dynamic Web pages.

7.3.1 Dynamic Welcome Page

Our next script builds on prior scripts to create a dynamic welcome page that obtains the user's name, then displays it on the page. The script uses another predefined dialog box from the window object—a **prompt** dialog—which allows the user to input a value that the script can use. The program asks the user to input a name, then displays the name in the XHTML document. Figure 7.6 presents the script and sample output. [*Note*: In later JavaScript chapters, we will obtain input via GUI components in XHTML forms, as introduced in Chapter 5.]

```
1   <?xml version = "1.0"?>
2   <!DOCTYPE html PUBLIC "-//W3C//DTD XHTML 1.1//EN"
3       "http://www.w3.org/TR/xhtml11/DTD/xhtml11.dtd">
4
5   <!-- Fig. 7.6: welcome5.html -->
6   <!-- Using Prompt Boxes        -->
```

Fig. 7.6   Prompt box used on a welcome screen. (Part 1 of 2.)

```
7
8    <html xmlns = "http://www.w3.org/1999/xhtml">
9       <head>
10         <title>Using Prompt and Alert Boxes</title>
11
12         <script type = "text/javascript">
13            <!--
14            var name; // string entered by the user
15
16            // read the name from the prompt box as a string
17            name = window.prompt( "Please enter your name", "GalAnt" );
18
19            document.writeln( "<h1>Hello, " + name +
20               ", welcome to JavaScript programming!</h1>" );
21            // -->
22         </script>
23
24      </head>
25
26      <body>
27      <p>Click Refresh (or Reload) to run this script again.</p>
28      </body>
29    </html>
```

Fig. 7.6   Prompt box used on a welcome screen. (Part 2 of 2.)

Line 14 is a **declaration** that contains the JavaScript **keyword** var. Keywords are words that have special meaning in JavaScript. The keyword **var** at the beginning of the statement indicates that the word name is a **variable**. A variable is a location in the computer's memory where a value can be stored for use by a program. All variables have a name, type and value, and should be declared with a var statement before they are used in a program. Although using var to declare variables is not required, we will see in Chapter 10, JavaScript: Functions, that var sometimes ensures proper behavior of a script.

The name of a variable can be any valid **identifier**. An identifier is a series of characters consisting of letters, digits, underscores (_) and dollar signs ($) that does not begin with a digit and is not a reserved JavaScript keyword. [*Note*: A complete list of keywords can be found in Chapter 8.] An identifier also may not contain any spaces. Some valid identifiers are `Welcome`, `$value`, `_value`, `m_inputField1` and `button7`. The name `7button` is not a valid identifier, because it begins with a digit, and the name `input field` is not a valid identifier, because it contains a space. Remember that JavaScript is **case sensitive**—uppercase and lowercase letters are considered to be different characters, so `name`, `Name` and `NAME` are different identifiers.

Good Programming Practice 7.3

Choosing meaningful variable names helps a script to be "self-documenting" (i.e., easy to understand by simply reading the script, rather than having to read manuals or extended comments).

Good Programming Practice 7.4

By convention, variable-name identifiers begin with a lowercase first letter. Every word in the name after the first word should begin with a capital first letter. For example, identifier `itemPrice` *has a capital P in its second word,* `Price`.

Common Programming Error 7.6

Splitting a statement in the middle of an identifier is normally a syntax error.

Declarations, like statements, end with a semicolon (;) and can be split over several lines with each variable in the declaration separated by a comma—known as a **comma-separated list** of variable names. Several variables may be declared either in one declaration or in multiple declarations. For example, to declare five variables we could write five declarations, one for each variable, but a single declaration in a program is more concise.

Programmers often indicate the purpose of each variable in the program by placing a JavaScript comment at the end of each line in the declaration. In line 14, a **single-line comment** that begins with the characters `//` states the purpose of the variable in the script. This form of comment is called a single-line comment because it terminates at the end of the line in which it appears. A `//` comment can begin at any position in a line of JavaScript code and continues until the end of the line. Comments do not cause the browser to perform any action when the script is interpreted; rather, comments are ignored by the JavaScript interpreter.

Good Programming Practice 7.5

Some programmers prefer to declare each variable on a separate line. This format allows for easy insertion of a descriptive comment next to each declaration.

Another comment notation facilitates the writing of **multi-line comments**. For example,

```
/* This is a multi-line
   comment. It can be
   split over many lines. */
```

is a multi-line comment spread over several lines. Such comments begin with delimiter `/*` and end with delimiter `*/`. All text between the delimiters of the comment is ignored by the interpreter.

Common Programming Error 7.7

Forgetting one of the delimiters of a multi-line comment is a syntax error.

Common Programming Error 7.8

Nesting multi-line comments (i.e., placing a multi-line comment between the delimiters of another multi-line comment) is a syntax error.

JavaScript adopted comments delimited with /* and */ from the C programming language and single-line comments delimited with // from the C++ programming language. JavaScript programmers generally prefer C++-style single-line comments over C-style comments. Throughout this book, we use C++-style single-line comments.

Line 16 is a comment indicating the purpose of the statement in the next line. Line 17 calls the window object's prompt method, which displays the dialog in Fig. 7.7. The dialog allows the user to enter a string representing the user's name.

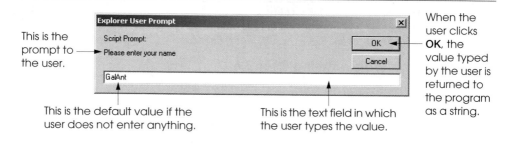

This is the prompt to the user.

When the user clicks **OK**, the value typed by the user is returned to the program as a string.

This is the default value if the user does not enter anything.

This is the text field in which the user types the value.

Fig. 7.7   Prompt dialog displayed by the window object's prompt method.

The first argument to prompt tells a user what to type in the text field. This message is called a **prompt** because it directs the user to take a specific action. The optional second argument is the default string displayed in the text field; if the second argument is not supplied, the text field does not display a default value. The user types characters in the text field, then clicks the **OK** button to submit the string to the program. [*Note*: If you type, but nothing appears in the text field, position the mouse pointer in the text field and click the left mouse button to activate the text field.] Unfortunately, JavaScript does not provide a simple form of input that is analogous to writing a line of text with document.write and document.writeln. For this reason, we normally receive input from a user through a GUI component such as the prompt dialog, as in this program, or through an XHTML form GUI component, as we will see in later chapters.

Technically, the user can type anything in the text field of the prompt dialog. For this program, anything the user enters is considered the name, even if it is not a valid name. If the user clicks the **Cancel** button, no string value is sent to the program. Instead, the prompt dialog submits the value **null**, a JavaScript keyword signifying that a variable has no value. Note that null is not a string literal, but rather a predefined term indicating the absence of value. Writing a null value to the document, however, displays the word null in the Web page.

The statement in line 17 **assigns** the value returned by the window object's prompt method (a string containing the characters typed by the user) to variable name by using the

assignment operator, =. The statement is read as, "name gets the value returned by `window.prompt( "Please enter your name", "GalAnt" )`." The = operator is called a **binary operator** because it has two **operands**—name and the result of the expression `window.prompt( "Please enter your name", "GalAnt" )`. This entire statement is called an **assignment statement** because it assigns a value to a variable. The expression to the right of the assignment operator is always evaluated first.

Good Programming Practice 7.6

Place spaces on either side of a binary operator. This format makes the operator stand out and makes the program more readable.

Lines 19–20 use `document.writeln` to display the new welcome message. The expression inside the parentheses uses the operator + to "add" a string (the literal `"<h1>Hello, "`), the variable name (the string that the user entered in line 17) and another string (the literal `", welcome to JavaScript programming!</h1>"`). JavaScript has a version of the + operator for **string concatenation** that enables a string and a value of another data type (including another string) to be combined. The result of this operation is a new (and normally longer) string. If we assume that name contains the string literal `"GalAnt"`, the expression evaluates as follows: JavaScript determines that the two operands of the first + operator (the string `"<h1>Hello, "` and the value of variable name) are both strings and concatenates the two into one string. Next, JavaScript determines that the two operands of the second + operator (the result of the first concatenation operation, the string `"<h1>Hello, GalAnt"`, and the string `", welcome to JavaScript programming!</h1>"`) are both strings and concatenates the two. This results in the string `"<h1>Hello, GalAnt, welcome to JavaScript programming!</h1>"`. The browser renders this string as part of the XHTML document. Note that the space between `Hello,` and `GalAnt` is part of the string `"<h1>Hello, "`.

As we will illustrate later, the + operator used for string concatenation can convert other variable types to strings if necessary. String concatenation occurs between two strings. Thus JavaScript must convert other variable types to strings before it can proceed with the operation. For example, if a variable age has an integer value equal to 21, then the expression `"my age is "` + age evaluates to the string `"my age is 21"`. JavaScript converts age to a string and concatenates it with the existing string literal `"my age is "`.

Common Programming Error 7.9

Confusing the + operator used for string concatenation with the + operator used for addition can lead to strange results. For example, assuming that integer variable y has the value 5, the expression "y + 2 = " + y + 2 results in "y + 2 = 52", not "y + 2 = 7", because first the value of y is concatenated with the string "y + 2 = ", then the value 2 is concatenated with the new, larger string "y + 2 = 5". The expression "y + 2 = " + (y + 2) produces the desired result.

After the browser interprets the `<head>` section of the XHTML document (which contains the JavaScript), it then interprets the `<body>` of the XHTML document (lines 26–28) and renders the XHTML. If you click your browser's **Refresh** (or **Reload**) button, the browser will reload the XHTML document, so that you can execute the script again and change the name. [*Note*: In some cases, it may be necessary to hold down the *Shift* key while clicking your browser's **Refresh** (or **Reload**) button, to ensure that the XHTML document reloads properly. Browsers often save a recent copy of a page in memory, and holding the *Shift* key forces the browser to download the most recent version of a page.]

7.3.2 Adding Integers

Our next script illustrates another use of `prompt` dialogs to obtain input from the user. Figure 7.8 inputs two **integers** (whole numbers, such as 7, −11, 0 and 31914) typed by a user at the keyboard, computes the sum of the values and displays the result.

```
1   <?xml version = "1.0"?>
2   <!DOCTYPE html PUBLIC "-//W3C//DTD XHTML 1.0 Strict//EN"
3      "http://www.w3.org/TR/xhtml1/DTD/xhtml1-strict.dtd">
4
5   <!-- Fig. 7.8: addition.html -->
6   <!-- Addition Program        -->
7
8   <html xmlns = "http://www.w3.org/1999/xhtml">
9      <head>
10        <title>An Addition Program</title>
11
12        <script type = "text/javascript">
13           <!--
14           var firstNumber,    // first string entered by user
15               secondNumber,   // second string entered by user
16               number1,        // first number to add
17               number2,        // second number to add
18               sum;            // sum of number1 and number2
19
20           // read in first number from user as a string
21           firstNumber =
22              window.prompt( "Enter first integer", "0" );
23
24           // read in second number from user as a string
25           secondNumber =
26              window.prompt( "Enter second integer", "0" );
27
28           // convert numbers from strings to integers
29           number1 = parseInt( firstNumber );
30           number2 = parseInt( secondNumber );
31
32           // add the numbers
33           sum = number1 + number2;
34
35           // display the results
36           document.writeln( "<h1>The sum is " + sum + "</h1>" );
37           // -->
38        </script>
39
40     </head>
41     <body>
42        <p>Click Refresh (or Reload) to run the script again</p>
43     </body>
44   </html>
```

Fig. 7.8   Addition script "in action." (Part 1 of 2.)

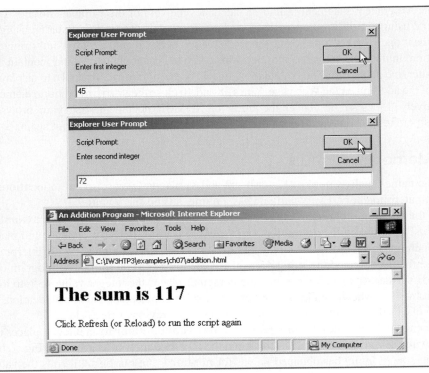

Fig. 7.8   Addition script "in action." (Part 2 of 2.)

Lines 14–18 declare the variables `firstNumber`, `secondNumber`, `number1`, `number2` and `sum`. Single-line comments state the purpose of each of these variables. Lines 21–22 employ a `prompt` dialog to allow the user to enter a string representing the first of the two integers that will be added. The script assigns the first value entered by the user to the variable `firstNumber`. Lines 25–26 display a `prompt` dialog to obtain the second number to add and assign this value to the variable `secondNumber`.

As in the preceding example, the user can type anything in the text field of the `prompt` dialog. For this program, if the user either types a noninteger value or clicks the **Cancel** button, a runtime logic error will occur, and the sum of the two values will appear in the XHTML document as **NaN** (meaning **not a number**). In Chapter 12, JavaScript: Objects, we discuss the `Number` object and its methods that can determine whether a value is not a number.

Recall that a `prompt` dialog returns the value typed by the user to the program as a string. Lines 29–30 convert the two strings input by the user to integer values that can be used in a calculation. Function **parseInt** converts its string argument to an integer. Line 29 assigns to the variable `number1` the integer that function `parseInt` returns. Line 30 assigns an integer value to variable `number2` in a similar manner. Any subsequent references to `number1` and `number2` in the program use these integer values. [*Note*: We refer to `parseInt` as a **function** rather than a **method** because we do not precede the function call with an object name (such as `document` or `window`) and a dot (`.`). The term method means that the function belongs to a particular object. For example, method `writeln` belongs to the `document` object and method `prompt` belongs to the `window` object.]

The assignment statement in line 33 calculates the sum of the variables number1 and number2 using the **addition operator**, +, and assigns the result to variable sum by using the assignment operator, =. Notice that the + operator can perform both addition and string concatenation. In this case, the + operator performs addition because both operands contain integers. After line 33 performs this calculation, line 36 uses document.writeln to display the result of the addition on the Web page. Lines 38 and 40 close the script and head elements, respectively. Lines 41–43 render the body of XHTML document. Use your browser's **Refresh** or **Reload** button to reload the XHTML document and run the script again.

7.4 Memory Concepts

Variable names such as number1, number2 and sum actually correspond to **locations** in the computer's memory. Every variable has a **name**, a **type** and a **value**.

In the addition program in Fig. 7.8, when line 29 executes, the string firstNumber (previously entered by the user in a prompt dialog) is converted to an integer and placed into a memory location to which the name number1 has been assigned by the interpreter. Suppose the user entered the string 45 as the value for firstNumber. The program converts firstNumber to an integer, and the computer places the integer value 45 into location number1, as shown in Fig. 7.9. Whenever a value is placed in a memory location, the value replaces the previous value in that location. The previous value is lost.

When line 30 executes, the program converts secondNumber to an integer, places that integer value, 72, into location number2 and the memory appears as shown in Fig. 7.10. Once the program has obtained values for number1 and number2, it adds the values and places the sum into variable sum. The statement

```
sum = number1 + number2;
```

performs the addition and also replaces sum's previous value. After sum is calculated, the memory appears as shown in Fig. 7.11. Note that the values of number1 and number2 appear exactly as they did before they were used in the calculation of sum. These values were used, but not destroyed, when the computer performed the calculation. When a value is read from a memory location, the process is **nondestructive**.

---

number1 | 45 |

Fig. 7.9   Memory location showing the name and value of variable number1.

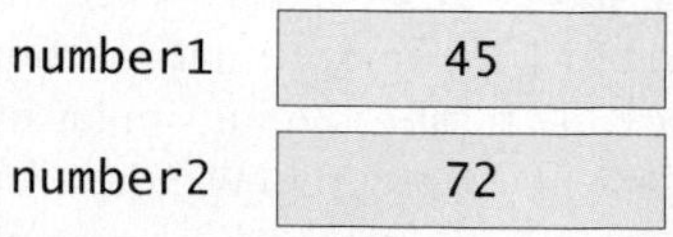

number1 | 45 |

number2 | 72 |

Fig. 7.10   Memory locations after values for variables number1 and number2 have been input.

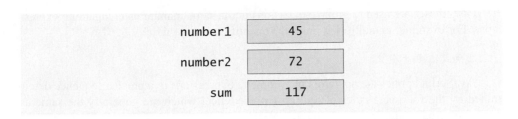

Fig. 7.11   Memory locations after calculating the sum of number1 and number2.

7.5 Arithmetic

Many scripts perform arithmetic calculations. Figure 7.12 summarizes the **arithmetic operators**. Note the use of various special symbols not used in algebra. The **asterisk** (*) indicates multiplication; the **percent sign** (%) is the **remainder operator**, which will be discussed shortly. The arithmetic operators in Fig. 7.12 are binary operators, because each operates on two operands. For example, the expression sum + value contains the binary operator + and the two operands sum and value.

JavaScript operation	Arithmetic operator	Algebraic expression	JavaScript expression
Addition	+	$f + 7$	f + 7
Subtraction	–	$p - c$	p - c
Multiplication	*	bm	b * m
Division	/	$x / y \ or \ \dfrac{x}{y} \ or \ x \div y$	x / y
Remainder	%	$r \bmod s$	r % s

Fig. 7.12   Arithmetic operators.

JavaScript provides the remainder operator, %, which yields the remainder after division. [*Note*: The % operator is known as the modulus operator in some programming languages.] The expression x % y yields the remainder after x is divided by y. Thus, 17 % 5 yields 2 (i.e., 17 divided by 5 is 3, with a remainder of 2), and 7.4 % 3.1 yields 1.2. In later chapters, we consider many interesting applications of the remainder operator, such as determining whether one number is a multiple of another. There is no arithmetic operator for exponentiation in JavaScript. (Chapter 9 shows how to perform exponentiation in JavaScript.)

Arithmetic expressions in JavaScript must be written in **straight-line form** to facilitate entering programs into the computer. Thus, expressions such as "a divided by b" must be written as a / b, so that all constants, variables and operators appear in a straight line. The following algebraic notation is generally not acceptable to computers:

$$\frac{a}{b}$$

Parentheses are used to group expressions in the same manner as in algebraic expressions. For example, to multiply a times the quantity b + c we write:

    a * (b + c)

JavaScript applies the operators in arithmetic expressions in a precise sequence determined by the following **rules of operator precedence**, which are generally the same as those followed in algebra:

1. Multiplication, division and remainder operations are applied first. If an expression contains several multiplication, division and remainder operations, operators are applied from left to right. Multiplication, division and remainder operations are said to have the same level of precedence.

2. Addition and subtraction operations are applied next. If an expression contains several addition and subtraction operations, operators are applied from left to right. Addition and subtraction operations have the same level of precedence.

The rules of operator precedence enable JavaScript to apply operators in the correct order. When we say that operators are applied from left to right, we are referring to the **associativity** of the operators—the order in which operators of equal priority are evaluated. We will see that some operators associate from right to left. Figure 7.13 summarizes the rules of operator precedence. The table in Fig. 7.13 will be expanded as additional JavaScript operators are introduced. A complete precedence chart is included in Appendix C.

Operator(s)	Operation(s)	Order of evaluation (precedence)
*, / or %	Multiplication Division Remainder	Evaluated second. If there are several such operations, they are evaluated from left to right.
+ or –	Addition Subtraction	Evaluated last. If there are several such operations, they are evaluated from left to right.

Fig. 7.13   Precedence of arithmetic operators.

Now, in light of the rules of operator precedence, let us consider several algebraic expressions. Each example lists an algebraic expression and the equivalent JavaScript expression.

The following is an example of an arithmetic mean (average) of five terms:

Algebra: $m = \dfrac{a + b + c + d + e}{5}$

JavaScript: m = (a + b + c + d + e) / 5;

The parentheses are required to group the addition operators, because division has higher precedence than addition. The entire quantity (a + b + c + d + e) is to be divided by 5. If the parentheses are erroneously omitted, we obtain a + b + c + d + e / 5, which evaluates as

$$a + b + c + d + \frac{e}{5}$$

and would not lead to the correct answer.

The following is an example of the equation of a straight line:

Algebra: $y = mx + b$

JavaScript: y = m * x + b;

No parentheses are required. The multiplication operator is applied first, because multiplication has a higher precedence than addition. The assignment occurs last, because it has a lower precedence than multiplication and addition.

The following example contains remainder (%), multiplication, division, addition and subtraction operations:

Algebra: $z = pr\%q + w/x - y$

JavaScript: z = p * r % q + w / x - y;

The circled numbers under the statement indicate the order in which JavaScript applies the operators. The multiplication, remainder and division operations are evaluated first in left-to-right order (i.e., they associate from left to right), because they have higher precedence than addition and subtraction. The addition and subtraction operations are evaluated next. These operations are also applied from left to right.

To develop a better understanding of the rules of operator precedence, consider the evaluation of a second-degree polynomial ($y = ax^2 + bx + c$):

y = a * x * x + b * x + c;

The circled numbers under the preceding statement indicate the order in which JavaScript applies the operators. There is no arithmetic operator for exponentiation in JavaScript; x^2 is represented as x * x.

Suppose that a, b, c and x are initialized as follows: a = 2, b = 3, c = 7 and x = 5. Figure 7.14 illustrates the order in which the operators are applied in the preceding second-degree polynomial.

As in algebra, it is acceptable to place unnecessary parentheses in an expression to make the expression clearer. Such unnecessary parentheses are also called **redundant parentheses**. For example, the preceding assignment statement might be parenthesized as follows:

y = (a * x * x) + (b * x) + c;

Good Programming Practice 7.7

Using parentheses for complex arithmetic expressions, even when the parentheses are not necessary, can make the arithmetic expressions easier to read.

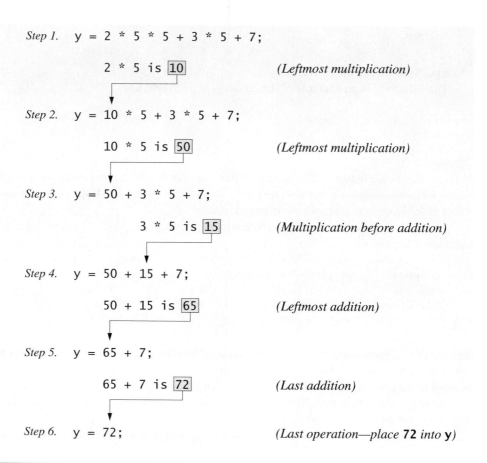

Step 1. y = 2 * 5 * 5 + 3 * 5 + 7;

2 * 5 is 10   *(Leftmost multiplication)*

Step 2. y = 10 * 5 + 3 * 5 + 7;

10 * 5 is 50   *(Leftmost multiplication)*

Step 3. y = 50 + 3 * 5 + 7;

3 * 5 is 15   *(Multiplication before addition)*

Step 4. y = 50 + 15 + 7;

50 + 15 is 65   *(Leftmost addition)*

Step 5. y = 65 + 7;

65 + 7 is 72   *(Last addition)*

Step 6. y = 72;   *(Last operation—place **72** into **y**)*

Fig. 7.14   Order in which a second-degree polynomial is evaluated.

7.6 Decision Making: Equality and Relational Operators

This section introduces a version of JavaScript's **if** statement that allows a program to make a decision based on the truth or falsity of a **condition**. If the condition is met (i.e., the condition is **true**), the statement in the body of the if statement is executed. If the condition is not met (i.e., the condition is **false**), the statement in the body of the if statement is not executed. We will see an example shortly. [*Note*: Other versions of the if statement are introduced in Chapter 8.]

Conditions in if statements can be formed by using the **equality operators** and **relational operators** summarized in Fig. 7.15. The relational operators all have the same level of precedence and associate from left to right. The equality operators both have the same level of precedence, which is lower than the precedence of the relational operators. The equality operators also associate from left to right.

Common Programming Error 7.10

It is a syntax error if the operators ==, !=, >= and <= contain spaces between their symbols, as in = =, ! =, > = and < =, respectively.

Standard algebraic equality operator or relational operator	JavaScript equality or relational operator	Sample JavaScript condition	Meaning of JavaScript condition
Equality operators			
=	==	x == y	x is equal to y
≠	!=	x != y	x is not equal to y
Relational operators			
>	>	x > y	x is greater than y
<	<	x < y	x is less than y
≥	>=	x >= y	x is greater than or equal to y
≤	<=	x <= y	x is less than or equal to y

Fig. 7.15   Equality and relational operators.

Common Programming Error 7.11

Reversing the operators !=, >= and <=, as in =!, => and =<, respectively, is a syntax error.

Common Programming Error 7.12

Confusing the equality operator, ==, with the assignment operator, =, is a logic error. The equality operator should be read as "is equal to," and the assignment operator should be read as "gets" or "gets the value of." Some people prefer to read the equality operator as "double equals" or "equals equals."

The script in Fig. 7.16 uses four `if` statements to display a time-sensitive greeting on a welcome page. The script obtains the local time from the user's computer and converts it to a 12-hour clock format. Using this value, the script displays an appropriate greeting for the current time of day. The script and sample output are shown in Fig. 7.16.

```
1   <?xml version = "1.0"?>
2   <!DOCTYPE html PUBLIC "-//W3C//DTD XHTML 1.1//EN"
3       "http://www.w3.org/TR/xhtml11/DTD/xhtml11.dtd">
4
5   <!-- Fig. 7.16: welcome6.html    -->
6   <!-- Using Relational Operators -->
7
8   <html xmlns = "http://www.w3.org/1999/xhtml">
9      <head>
10         <title>Using Relational Operators</title>
11
12         <script type = "text/javascript">
13            <!--
14            var name, // string entered by the user
15               now = new Date(),       // current date and time
16               hour = now.getHours(); // current hour (0-23)
```

Fig. 7.16   Using equality and relational operators. (Part 1 of 2.)

```
17
18              // read the name from the prompt box as a string
19              name = window.prompt( "Please enter your name", "GalAnt" );
20
21              // determine whether it is morning
22              if ( hour < 12 )
23                  document.write( "<h1>Good Morning, " );
24
25              // determine whether the time is PM
26              if ( hour >= 12 )
27              {
28                  // convert to a 12 hour clock
29                  hour = hour - 12;
30
31                  // determine whether it is before 6 PM
32                  if ( hour < 6 )
33                      document.write( "<h1>Good Afternoon, " );
34
35                  // determine whether it is after 6 PM
36                  if ( hour >= 6 )
37                      document.write( "<h1>Good Evening, " );
38              }
39
40              document.writeln( name +
41                  ", welcome to JavaScript programming!</h1>" );
42              // -->
43          </script>
44
45      </head>
46
47      <body>
48          <p>Click Refresh (or Reload) to run this script again.</p>
49      </body>
50      </html>
```

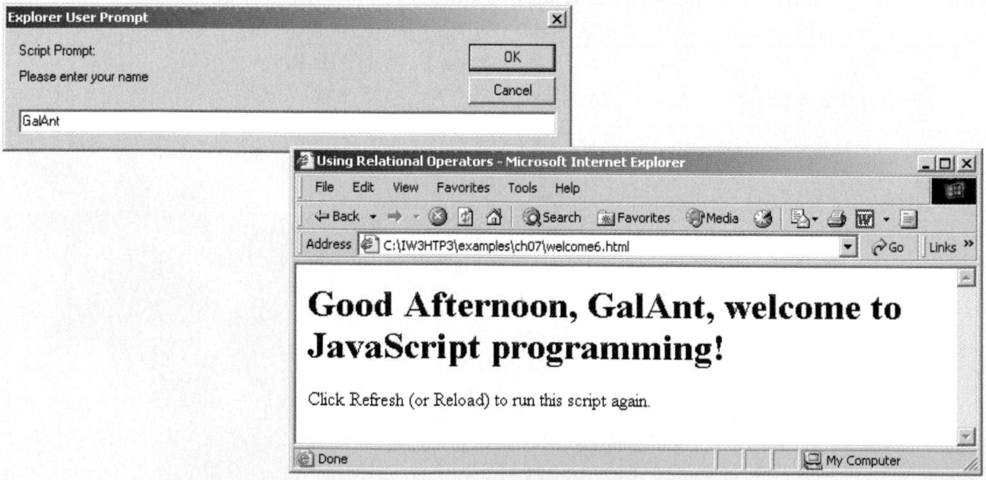

Fig. 7.16   Using equality and relational operators. (Part 2 of 2.)

Lines 14–16 declare the variables used in the script. Remember that variables may be declared in one declaration or in multiple declarations. If more than one variable is declared in a single declaration (as in this example), the names are separated by commas (,). This list of names is referred to as a comma-separated list. Once again, note the comment at the end of each line, indicating the purpose of each variable in the program. Also note that some of the variables are assigned a value in the declaration. JavaScript allows you to assign a value to a variable when the variable is declared.

Line 15 sets the variable now to a new **Date** object, which contains information about the current local time. In Section 7.2, we introduced the document object, an object that encapsulates data pertaining to the current Web page. Programmers may choose to use other objects to perform specific tasks or obtain particular pieces of information. Here, we use JavaScript's built-in Date object to acquire the current local time. We create a new instance of an object by using the **new** operator followed by the type of the object, Date, and a pair of parentheses. Some objects require that arguments be placed in the parentheses to specify details about the object to be created. In this case, we leave the parentheses empty to create a default Date object containing information about the current date and time. After line 15 executes, the variable now refers to the new Date object. [*Note*: We did not need to use the new operator when we used the document and window objects because these objects always are created by the browser.] Line 16 sets the variable hour to an integer equal to the current hour (in a 24-hour clock format) returned by the Date object's getHours method. Please refer to Chapter 12 for a more detailed discussion of the Date object's attributes and methods, and of objects in general. As in the preceding example, the script uses window.prompt to allow the user to enter a name to display as part of the greeting (line 19).

To display the correct time-sensitive greeting, the script must determine whether the user is visiting the page during the morning, afternoon or evening. The first if statement (lines 22–23) compares the value of variable hour with the integer value 12. If hour is less than 12, then the user is visiting the page during the morning, and the statement at line 23 outputs the string "Good morning". If this condition is not met, line 23 is not executed. Line 26 determines whether hour is greater than or equal to 12. If hour is greater than or equal to 12, then the user is visiting the page in either the afternoon or the evening. Lines 27–38 execute to further determine the appropriate greeting. If hour is less than 12, then the JavaScript interpreter does not execute these lines and continues to line 40.

The brace { in line 27 begins a block of statements (lines 27–38) that are all executed together if hour is greater than or equal to 12. Line 29 subtracts 12 from hour, converting the current hour from a 24-hour clock format to a 12-hour clock format. The if statement (line 32) determines whether hour is now less than 6. If it is, then the time is between noon and 6 PM, and line 33 outputs the string "Good Afternoon". If hour is greater than or equal to 6, the time is between 6 PM and midnight, and the script outputs the greeting "Good Evening" (lines 36–37). The brace } in line 38 ends the block of statements associated with the if statement in line 26. Note that if statements can be **nested**, i.e., one if statement can be placed inside another if statement. The if statements that determine whether the user is visiting the page in the afternoon or the evening (lines 32–33 and lines 36–37) only execute if the script has already established that hour is greater than or equal to 12 (line 26). If the script has already determined the current time of day to be morning, these additional comparisons are not performed. (Please refer to Chapter 8 for a more in-depth discussion of nested if statements.) Finally, lines 40–41 display the remaining part of the greeting, which does not depend on the time of day.

Note the indentation of the if statements throughout the program. Such indentation enhances program readability.

Good Programming Practice 7.8

Indent the statement in the body of an if statement to make the body of the statement stand out and to enhance program readability.

Good Programming Practice 7.9

Place only one statement per line in a program. This format enhances program readability.

Common Programming Error 7.13

Forgetting the left and right parentheses for the condition in an if statement is a syntax error. The parentheses are required.

Note that there is no semicolon (;) at the end of the first line of each if statement. Including such a semicolon would result in a logic error at execution time. For example,

```
if ( hour < 12 ) ;
    document.write( "<h1>Good Morning, " );
```

would actually be interpreted by JavaScript erroneously as

```
if ( hour < 12 )
    ;

document.write( "<h1>Good Morning, " );
```

where the semicolon on the line by itself—called the **empty statement**—is the statement to execute if the condition in the if statement is true. When the empty statement executes, no task is performed in the program. The program then continues with the next statement, which executes regardless of whether the condition is true or false.

Common Programming Error 7.14

Placing a semicolon immediately after the right parenthesis of the condition in an if statement is normally a logic error. The semicolon would cause the body of the if statement to be empty, so the if statement itself would perform no action, regardless of whether its condition is true. Worse yet, the intended body statement of the if statement would now become a statement in sequence after the if statement and would always be executed.

Common Programming Error 7.15

Leaving out a condition in a series of if statements is a logic error. For instance, checking if hour is greater than 12 or less than 12, but not if hour is equal to 12, would mean that the script takes no action when hour is equal to 12. Always be sure to handle every possible condition.

Note the use of spacing in Fig. 7.16. Remember that white space characters, such as tabs, new lines and spaces, are normally ignored by the browser. So, statements may be split over several lines and may be spaced according to the programmer's preferences without affecting the meaning of a program. However, it is incorrect to split identifiers and string literals. Ideally, statements should be kept small, but it is not always possible to do so.

Good Programming Practice 7.10

A lengthy statement may be spread over several lines. If a single statement must be split across lines, choose breaking points that make sense, such as after a comma in a comma-separated list or after an operator in a lengthy expression. If a statement is split across two or more lines, indent all subsequent lines.

The chart in Fig. 7.17 shows the precedence of the operators introduced in this chapter. The operators are shown from top to bottom in decreasing order of precedence. Note that all of these operators, with the exception of the assignment operator, =, associate from left to right. Addition is left associative, so an expression like x + y + z is evaluated as if it had been written as (x + y) + z. The assignment operator, =, associates from right to left, so an expression like x = y = 0 is evaluated as if it had been written as x = (y = 0), which first assigns the value 0 to variable y and then assigns the result of that assignment, 0, to x.

Operators	Associativity	Type
* / %	left to right	multiplicative
+ -	left to right	additive
< <= > >=	left to right	relational
== !=	left to right	equality
=	right to left	assignment

Fig. 7.17   Precedence and associativity of the operators discussed so far.

Good Programming Practice 7.11

Refer to the operator precedence chart when writing expressions containing many operators. Confirm that the operators in the expression are performed in the order in which you expect them to be performed. If you are uncertain about the order of evaluation in a complex expression, use parentheses to force the order, exactly as you would do in algebraic expressions. Be sure to observe that some operators, such as assignment (=), associate from right to left rather than from left to right.

We have introduced many important features of JavaScript, including how to display data, how to input data from the keyboard, how to perform calculations and how to make decisions. In Chapter 8, we build on the techniques of Chapter 7 as we introduce structured programming. You will become more familiar with indentation techniques. We will study how to specify and vary the order in which statements are executed; this order is called the flow of control.

7.7 Web Resources

There are a tremendous number of resources for JavaScript programmers on the Web. This section lists a variety of JavaScript, JScript and ECMAScript resources available and provides a brief description of each. Additional resources for these topics are presented in the subsequent chapters on JavaScript and in other chapters as necessary.

www.ecma-international.org/publications/standards/ECMA-262.htm
This site is the home of the ECMAScript standard that underlies both JavaScript and JScript.

msdn.microsoft.com/library/en-us/script56/html/
vtoriMicrosoftWindowsScriptTechnologies.asp
The Microsoft *Windows Script Technologies* page includes an overview of JScript, complete with tutorials, FAQs, demos, tools for downloading and newsgroups.

www.webteacher.com/javascript
Webteacher.com is an excellent source for tutorials that focus on teaching with detailed explanations and examples. This site is particularly useful for nonprogrammers.

wsabstract.com
Website Abstraction is devoted to JavaScript and provides specialized tutorials and many free scripts. This site is good for beginners, as well as people with prior experience who are looking for help in a specific area of JavaScript.

www.webdeveloper.com/javascript
WebDeveloper.com provides tutorials, tools, and links to many free scripts.

SUMMARY

- The JavaScript language facilitates a disciplined approach to the design of computer programs that enhance Web pages.

- JScript is Microsoft's version of JavaScript—a scripting language that is standardized by ECMA International as ECMAScript.

- The spacing displayed by a browser in a Web page is determined by the XHTML elements used to format the page.

- Often, JavaScripts appear in the <head> section of the XHTML document.

- The browser interprets the contents of the <head> section first.

- The <script> tag indicates to the browser that the text that follows is part of a script. Attribute type specifies the scripting language used in the script—such as javascript.

- A string of characters can be contained between double (") or single (') quotation marks.

- A string is sometimes called a character string, a message or a string literal.

- The browser's document object represents the XHTML document currently being displayed in the browser. The document object allows a script programmer to specify XHTML text to be displayed in the XHTML document.

- The browser contains a complete set of objects that allow script programmers to access and manipulate every element of an XHTML document.

- An object resides in the computer's memory and contains information used by the script. The term object normally implies that attributes (data) and behaviors (methods) are associated with the object. The object's methods use the attributes' data to perform useful actions for the client of the object—the script that calls the methods.

- The document object's writeln method writes a line of XHTML text in the XHTML document.

- The parentheses following the name of a method contain the arguments that the method requires to perform its task (or its action).

- Using writeln to write a line of XHTML text into a document does not guarantee that a corresponding line of text will appear in the XHTML document. The text displayed is dependent on the contents of the string written, which is subsequently rendered by the browser. The browser will interpret the XHTML elements as it normally does to render the final text in the document.

- Every statement should end with a semicolon (also known as the statement terminator), although none is required by JavaScript.

- JavaScript is case sensitive. Not using the proper uppercase and lowercase letters is a syntax error.

- Sometimes it is useful to display information in windows called dialogs that "pop up" on the screen to grab the user's attention. Dialogs are typically used to display important messages to the user browsing the Web page. The browser's `window` object uses method `alert` to display an alert dialog. Method `alert` requires as its argument the string to be displayed.

- When a backslash is encountered in a string of characters, the next character is combined with the backslash to form an escape sequence. The escape sequence \n is the newline character. It causes the cursor in the XHTML document to move to the beginning of the next line in the dialog.

- Keywords are words with special meaning in JavaScript.

- The keyword `var` is used to declare the names of variables. A variable is a location in the computer's memory where a value can be stored for use by a program. All variables have a name, type and value, and should be declared with a `var` statement before they are used in a program.

- A variable name can be any valid identifier consisting of letters, digits, underscores (_) and dollar signs ($) that does not begin with a digit and is not a reserved JavaScript keyword.

- Declarations end with a semicolon (;) and can be split over several lines, with each variable in the declaration separated by a comma (forming a comma-separated list of variable names). Several variables may be declared in one declaration or in multiple declarations.

- Programmers often indicate the purpose of each variable in the program by placing a JavaScript comment at the end of each line in the declaration. A single-line comment begins with the characters // and terminates at the end of the line. Comments do not cause the browser to perform any action when the script is interpreted; rather, comments are ignored by the JavaScript interpreter.

- Multi-line comments begin with delimiter /* and end with delimiter */. All text between the delimiters of the comment is ignored by the compiler.

- The `window` object's `prompt` method displays a dialog into which the user can type a value. The first argument is a message (called a prompt) that directs the user to take a specific action. The optional second argument is the default string to display in the text field.

- A variable is assigned a value with an assignment statement, using the assignment operator, =. The = operator is called a binary operator, because it has two operands.

- The `null` keyword signifies that a variable has no value. Note that `null` is not a string literal, but rather a predefined term indicating the absence of value. Writing a `null` value to the document, however, displays the word "null".

- Function `parseInt` converts its string argument to an integer.

- JavaScript has a version of the + operator for string concatenation that enables a string and a value of another data type (including another string) to be concatenated.

- Variable names correspond to locations in the computer's memory. Every variable has a name, a type and a value.

- When a value is placed in a memory location, the value replaces the previous value in that location. When a value is read out of a memory location, the process is nondestructive.

- The arithmetic operators are binary operators, because they each operate on two operands.

- Parentheses can be used to group expressions as in algebra.

- Operators in arithmetic expressions are applied in a precise sequence determined by the rules of operator precedence.

- When we say that operators are applied from left to right, we are referring to the associativity of the operators. Some operators associate from right to left.

- JavaScript's if statement allows a program to make a decision based on the truth or falsity of a condition. If the condition is met (i.e., the condition is true), the statement in the body of the if statement is executed. If the condition is not met (i.e., the condition is false), the statement in the body of the if statement is not executed.

- Conditions in if statements can be formed by using the equality operators and relational operators.

TERMINOLOGY

\" double-quote escape sequence
\n new line escape sequence
addition operator (+)
alert dialog
alert method of the window object
argument to a method
arithmetic expression in straight-line form
arithmetic operator
assignment operator (=)
assignment statement
attribute
automatic conversion
backslash (\) escape character
behavior
binary operator
blank line
case sensitive
character string
client of an object
comma-separated list
comment
condition
data
decision making
declaration
dialog
division operator (/)
document object
double quotation (") marks
ECMA International
ECMAScript
empty statement
equality operators
error message
escape sequence
false
function
identifier
if statement
inline scripting

integer
interpreter
JavaScript
JavaScript interpreter
JScript
keyword
level of precedence
location in the computer's memory
logic error
meaningful variable name
method
remainder operator (%)
multi-line comment (/* and */)
multiplication operator (*)
name of a variable
NaN (not a number)
new operator
newline character (\n)
null
object
operand
operator associativity
operator precedence
parentheses
parseInt function
perform an action
program
prompt
prompt dialog
prompt method of the window object
redundant parentheses
relational operator
remainder after division
rules of operator precedence
runtime error
script
script element
scripting language
semicolon (;) statement terminator
single quotation (') mark

single-line comment (//)	type of a variable
statement	value of a variable
string concatenation	`var` keyword
string concatenation operator (+)	variable
string literal	violation of the language rules
string of characters	white space character
subtraction operator (-)	whole number
syntax error	`window` object
text field	`write` method of the `document` object
true	`writeln` method of the `document` object
`type` attribute of the `<script>` tag	

SELF-REVIEW EXERCISES

7.1 Fill in the blanks in each of the following statements:
  a) _____ begins a single-line comment.
  b) Every statement should end with a(n) _____.
  c) The _____ statement is used to make decisions.
  d) _____, _____, _____ and _____ are known as white space.
  e) The _____ object displays `alert` dialogs and `prompt` dialogs.
  f) _____ are words that are reserved for use by JavaScript.
  g) Methods _____ and _____ of the _____ object write XHTML text into an XHTML document.

7.2 State whether each of the following is *true* or *false*. If *false*, explain why.
  a) Comments cause the computer to print the text after the `//` on the screen when the program is executed.
  b) JavaScript considers the variables `number` and `NuMbEr` to be identical.
  c) The remainder operator (%) can be used only with numeric operands.
  d) The arithmetic operators `*`, `/`, `%`, `+` and `-` all have the same level of precedence.
  e) Method `parseInt` converts an integer to a string.

7.3 Write JavaScript statements to accomplish each of the following tasks:
  a) Declare variables `c`, `thisIsAVariable`, `q76354` and `number`.
  b) Display a dialog asking the user to enter an integer. Show a default value of 0 in the text field.
  c) Convert a string to an integer, and store the converted value in variable `age`. Assume that the string is stored in `stringValue`.
  d) If the variable `number` is not equal to 7, display `"The variable number is not equal to 7"` in a message dialog.
  e) Output a line of XHTML text that will display the message `"This is a JavaScript program"` on one line in the XHTML document.
  f) Output a line of XHTML text that will display the message `"This is a JavaScript program"` on two lines in the XHTML document. Use only one statement.

7.4 Identify and correct the errors in each of the following statements:
  a) `if ( c < 7 );`
        `window.alert( "c is less than 7" );`
  b) `if ( c => 7 )`
        `window.alert( "c is equal to or greater than 7" );`

7.5 Write a statement (or comment) to accomplish each of the following tasks:
  a) State that a program will calculate the product of three integers.

b) Declare the variables x, y, z and `result`.

c) Declare the variables `xVal`, `yVal` and `zVal`.

d) Prompt the user to enter the first value, read the value from the user and store it in the variable `xVal`.

e) Prompt the user to enter the second value, read the value from the user and store it in the variable `yVal`.

f) Prompt the user to enter the third value, read the value from the user and store it in the variable `zVal`.

g) Convert `xVal` to an integer, and store the result in the variable x.

h) Convert `yVal` to an integer, and store the result in the variable y.

i) Convert `zVal` to an integer, and store the result in the variable z.

j) Compute the product of the three integers contained in variables x, y and z, and assign the result to the variable `result`.

k) Write a line of XHTML text containing the string `"The product is "` followed by the value of the variable `result`.

7.6 Using the statements you wrote in Exercise 7.5, write a complete program that calculates and prints the product of three integers.

ANSWERS TO SELF-REVIEW EXERCISES

7.1 a) `//`. b) Semicolon (`;`). c) `if`. d) Blank lines, space characters, newline characters and tab characters. e) `window`. f) Keywords. g) `write`, `writeln`, `document`.

7.2 a) False. Comments do not cause any action to be performed when the program is executed. They are used to document programs and improve their readability. b) False. JavaScript is case sensitive, so these variables are distinct. c) True. d) False. The operators `*`, `/` and `%` are on the same level of precedence, and the operators `+` and `-` are on a lower level of precedence. e) False. Function `parseInt` converts a string to an integer value.

7.3
a) `var c, thisIsAVariable, q76354, number;`

b) `value = window.prompt( "Enter an integer", "0" );`

c) `var age = parseInt( stringValue );`

d) `if ( number != 7 )`
   `    window.alert( "The variable number is not equal to 7" );`

e) `document.writeln( "This is a JavaScript program" );`

f) `document.writeln( "This is a<br />JavaScript program" );`

7.4
a) Error: There should not be a semicolon after the right parenthesis of the condition in the `if` statement.
   Correction: Remove the semicolon after the right parenthesis. [*Note:* The result of this error is that the output statement is executed whether or not the condition in the `if` statement is true. The semicolon after the right parenthesis is considered an empty statement—a statement that does nothing.]

b) Error: The relational operator `=>` is incorrect.
   Correction: Change `=>` to `>=`.

7.5
a) `// Calculate the product of three integers`

b) `var x, y, z, result;`

c) `var xVal, yVal, zVal;`

d) `xVal = window.prompt( "Enter first integer:", "0" );`

e) `yVal = window.prompt( "Enter second integer:", "0" );`

f) `zVal = window.prompt( "Enter third integer:", "0" );`

g) `x = parseInt( xVal );`

```
h) y = parseInt( yVal );
i) z = parseInt( zVal );
j) result = x * y * z;
k) document.writeln( "<h1>The product is " + result + "</h1>" );
```

7.6　　The program is as follows:

```
1   <?xml version = "1.0"?>
2   <!DOCTYPE html PUBLIC "-//W3C//DTD XHTML 1.0 Strict//EN"
3      "http://www.w3.org/TR/xhtml1/DTD/xhtml1-strict.dtd">
4
5   <!-- Exercise 7.6: product.html -->
6
7   <html xmlns = "http://www.w3.org/1999/xhtml">
8      <head>
9         <title>Product of Three Integers</title>
10
11        <script type = "text/javascript">
12           <!--
13           // Calculate the product of three integers
14           var x, y, z, result;
15           var xVal, yVal, zVal;
16
17           xVal = window.prompt( "Enter first integer:", "0" );
18           yVal = window.prompt( "Enter second integer:", "0" );
19           zVal = window.prompt( "Enter third integer:", "0" );
20
21           x = parseInt( xVal );
22           y = parseInt( yVal );
23           z = parseInt( zVal );
24
25           result = x * y * z;
26           document.writeln( "<h1>The product is " +
27              result + "<h1>" );
28           // -->
29        </script>
30
31     </head><body></body>
32  </html>
```

EXERCISES

7.7　　Fill in the blanks in each of the following statements:

    a)　_____ are used to document a program and improve its readability.

    b)　A dialog capable of receiving input from the user is displayed with method _____ of object _____.

    c)　A JavaScript statement that makes a decision is the _____ statement.

    d)　Calculations are normally performed by _____ statements.

    e)　A dialog capable of showing a message to the user is displayed with method _____ of object _____.

7.8　　Write JavaScript statements that accomplish each of the following tasks:

    a)　Display the message "Enter two numbers" using the window object.

    b)　Assign the product of variables b and c to variable a.

    c) State that a program performs a sample payroll calculation [*Hint*: Use text that helps to document a program.]

7.9 State whether each of the following is *true* or *false*. If *false*, explain why.

    a) JavaScript operators are evaluated from left to right.

    b) The following are all valid variable names: `_under_bar_`, `m928134`, `t5`, `j7`, `her_sales$`, `his_$account_total`, `a`, `b$`, `c`, `z`, `z2`.

    c) A valid JavaScript arithmetic expression with no parentheses is evaluated from left to right.

    d) The following are all invalid variable names: `3g`, `87`, `67h2`, `h22`, `2h`.

7.10 Fill in the blanks in each of the following statements:

    a) What arithmetic operations have the same precedence as multiplication? _____.

    b) When parentheses are nested, which set of parentheses is evaluated first in an arithmetic expression? _____.

    c) A location in the computer's memory that may contain different values at various times throughout the execution of a program is called a _____.

7.11 What displays in the message dialog when each of the given JavaScript statements is performed? Assume that $x = 2$ and $y = 3$.

    a) `window.alert( "x = " + x );`

    b) `window.alert( "The value of x + x is " + ( x + x ) );`

    c) `window.alert( "x =" );`

    d) `window.alert( ( x + y ) + " = " + ( y + x ) );`

7.12 Which of the following JavaScript statements contain variables whose values are destroyed (i.e., changed or replaced)?

    a) `p = i + j + k + 7;`

    b) `window.alert( "variables whose values are destroyed" );`

    c) `window.alert( "a = 5" );`

    d) `stringVal = window.prompt( "Enter string:" );`

7.13 Given $y = ax^3 + 7$, which of the following are correct JavaScript statements for this equation?

    a) `y = a * x * x * x + 7;`

    b) `y = a * x * x * (x + 7);`

    c) `y = (a * x) * x * (x + 7);`

    d) `y = (a * x) * x * x + 7;`

    e) `y = a * (x * x * x) + 7;`

    f) `y = a * x * (x * x + 7);`

7.14 State the order of evaluation of the operators in each of the following JavaScript statements, and show the value of x after each statement is performed.

    a) `x = 7 + 3 * 6 / 2 - 1;`

    b) `x = 2 % 2 + 2 * 2 - 2 / 2;`

    c) `x = ( 3 * 9 * ( 3 + ( 9 * 3 / ( 3 ) ) ) );`

7.15 Write a script that displays the numbers 1 to 4 on the same line, with each pair of adjacent numbers separated by one space. Write the program using the following methods:

    a) Using one `document.writeln` statement.

    b) Using four `document.write` statements.

7.16 Write a script that asks the user to enter two numbers, obtains the two numbers from the user and outputs text that displays the sum, product, difference and quotient of the two numbers. Use the techniques shown in Fig. 7.8.

7.17 Write a script that asks the user to enter two integers, obtains the numbers from the user and outputs XHTML text that displays the larger number followed by the words "is larger" in an in-

formation message dialog. If the numbers are equal, output XHTML text that displays the message
"These numbers are equal." Use the techniques shown in Fig. 7.16.

7.18   Write a script that takes three integers from the user and displays the sum, average, product,
smallest and largest of the numbers in an alert dialog.

7.19   Write a script that gets from the user the radius of a circle and outputs XHTML text that displays the circle's diameter, circumference and area. Use the constant value 3.14159 for π. Use the
GUI techniques shown in Fig. 7.8. [*Note*: You may also use the predefined constant Math.PI for the
value of π. This constant is more precise than the value 3.14159. The Math object is defined by Java-
Script and provides many common mathematical capabilities.] Use the following formulas (*r* is the
radius): *diameter = 2r, circumference = 2πr, area = πr²*.

7.20   Write a script that outputs XHTML text that displays in the XHTML document a rectangle,
an oval, an arrow and a diamond using asterisks (*), as follows [*Note*: Use the <pre> and </pre>
tags to specify that the asterisks should be displayed using a fixed-width font]:

```
*********         ***              *              *
*       *       *     *          ***            *   *
*       *      *       *        *****          *     *
*       *      *       *          *           *       *
*       *      *       *          *          *         *
*       *      *       *          *           *       *
*       *      *       *          *            *     *
*       *       *     *           *             *   *
*********         ***             *                *
```

7.21   Modify the program you created in Exercise 7.20 by removing the <pre> and </pre> tags.
Does the program display the shapes exactly as in Exercise 7.20?

7.22   What does the following code print?

```
document.writeln( "*\n**\n***\n****\n*****" );
```

7.23   What does the following code print?

```
document.writeln( "*" );
document.writeln( "***" );
document.writeln( "*****" );
document.writeln( "****" );
document.writeln( "**" );
```

7.24   What does the following code print?

```
document.write( "*<br />" );
document.write( "***<br />" );
document.write( "*****<br />" );
document.write( "****<br />" );
document.writeln( "**" );
```

7.25   What does the following code print?

```
document.write( "*<br />" );
document.writeln( "***" );
document.writeln( "*****" );
document.write( "****<br />" );
document.writeln( "**" );
```

7.26   Write a script that reads five integers and determines and outputs XHTML text that displays the largest and smallest integers in the group. Use only the programming techniques you learned in this chapter.

7.27   Write a script that reads an integer and determines and outputs XHTML text that displays whether it is odd or even. [*Hint*: Use the remainder operator. An even number is a multiple of 2. Any multiple of 2 leaves a remainder of zero when divided by 2.]

7.28   Write a script that reads in two integers and determines and outputs XHTML text that displays whether the first is a multiple of the second. [*Hint*: Use the remainder operator.]

7.29   Write a script that outputs XHTML text that displays in the XHTML document a checkerboard pattern, as follows:

7.30   Write a script that inputs five numbers and determines and outputs XHTML text that displays the number of negative numbers input, the number of positive numbers input and the number of zeros input.

7.31   Using only the programming techniques you learned in this chapter, write a script that calculates the squares and cubes of the numbers from 0 to 10 and outputs XHTML text that displays the resulting values in an XHTML table format, as follows:

number	square	cube
0	0	0
1	1	1
2	4	8
3	9	27
4	16	64
5	25	125
6	36	216
7	49	343
8	64	512
9	81	729
10	100	1000

[*Note*: This program does not require any input from the user.]

JavaScript: Control Statements I

Objectives

- To understand basic problem-solving techniques.
- To be able to develop algorithms through the process of top-down, stepwise refinement.
- To be able to use the if and if...else selection statements to choose among alternative actions.
- To be able to use the while repetition statement to execute statements in a script repeatedly.
- To understand counter-controlled repetition and sentinel-controlled repetition.
- To be able to use the increment, decrement and assignment operators.

Let's all move one place on.
Lewis Carroll

The wheel is come full circle.
William Shakespeare

How many apples fell on Newton's head before he took the hint!
Robert Frost

8.1 Introduction

Before writing a script to solve a problem, it is essential to have a thorough understanding of the problem and a carefully planned approach to solving the problem. When writing a script, it is equally essential to understand the types of building blocks that are available and to employ proven program-construction principles. In this chapter and in Chapter 9, we discuss these issues in our presentation of the theory and principles of structured programming. The techniques you will learn here are applicable to most high-level languages, including JavaScript.

8.2 Algorithms

Any computing problem can be solved by executing a series of actions in a specific order. A **procedure** for solving a problem in terms of

1. the **actions** to be executed, and
2. the **order** in which the actions are to be executed

is called an **algorithm**. The following example demonstrates that correctly specifying the order in which the actions are to execute is important.

Consider the "rise-and-shine algorithm" followed by one junior executive for getting out of bed and going to work: (1) get out of bed, (2) take off pajamas, (3) take a shower, (4) get dressed, (5) eat breakfast, (6) carpool to work. This routine gets the executive to work well prepared to make critical decisions. Suppose, however, that the same steps are performed in a slightly different order: (1) get out of bed, (2) take off pajamas, (3) get dressed, (4) take a shower, (5) eat breakfast, (6) carpool to work. In this case, our junior executive shows up for work soaking wet. Specifying the order in which statements are to be executed in a computer program is called **program control**. In this chapter and Chapter 9, we investigate the program-control capabilities of JavaScript.

8.3 Pseudocode

Pseudocode is an artificial and informal language that helps programmers develop algorithms. The pseudocode we present here is useful for developing algorithms that will be converted to structured portions of JavaScript programs. Pseudocode is similar to everyday English; it is convenient and user friendly, although it is not an actual computer programming language.

Software Engineering Observation 8.1

Pseudocode is often used to "think out" a program during the program-design process. Then the pseudocode program is converted to a programming language such as JavaScript.

The style of pseudocode we present consists purely of characters, so that programmers may conveniently type pseudocode in an editor program. The computer can produce a fresh printed copy of a pseudocode program on demand. Carefully prepared pseudocode may be converted easily to a corresponding JavaScript program. This process is done in many cases simply by replacing pseudocode statements with their JavaScript equivalents. In this chapter, we give several examples of pseudocode.

Pseudocode normally describes only executable statements—the actions that are performed when the program is converted from pseudocode to JavaScript and is run. Declarations are not executable statements. For example, the declaration

```
var value1;
```

instructs the JavaScript interpreter to reserve space in memory for the variable value1. This declaration does not cause any action—such as input, output or a calculation—to occur when the script executes. Some programmers choose to list variables and mention the purpose of each variable at the beginning of a pseudocode program.

8.4 Control Structures

Normally, statements in a program execute one after the other in the order in which they are written. This process is called **sequential execution**. Various JavaScript statements we will soon discuss enable the programmer to specify that the next statement to execute may not be the next one in sequence. This is known as **transfer of control**.

During the 1960s, it became clear that the indiscriminate use of transfers of control was the root of much difficulty experienced by software development groups. The finger of blame was pointed at the **goto statement**, which allows the programmer to specify a transfer of control to one of a wide range of possible destinations in a program. The notion of so-called **structured programming** became almost synonymous with "**goto** elimination." JavaScript does not have a goto statement.

The research of Bohm and Jacopini demonstrated that programs could be written without goto statements.[1] The challenge of the era for programmers was to shift their styles to "goto-less programming." It was not until the 1970s that programmers started taking structured programming seriously. The results were impressive, as software development groups reported reduced development times, more frequent on-time delivery of systems and more frequent within-budget completion of software projects. The key to these successes is that structured programs are clearer, easier to debug and modify and more likely to be bug free in the first place.

Bohm and Jacopini's work demonstrated that all programs could be written in terms of only three **control structures**, namely the **sequence structure**, the **selection structure** and the **repetition structure**. The sequence structure is built into JavaScript. Unless directed otherwise, the computer executes JavaScript statements one after the other in the order in which they are written (i.e., in sequence). The **flowchart** segment of Fig. 8.1 illustrates a typical sequence structure in which two calculations are performed in order.

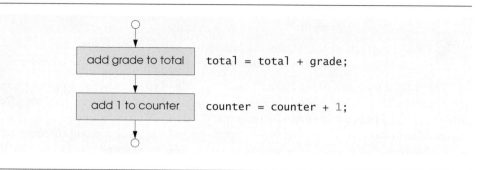

Fig. 8.1   Flowcharting JavaScript's sequence structure.

A **flowchart** is a graphical representation of an algorithm or of a portion of an algorithm. Flowcharts are drawn using certain special-purpose symbols, such as rectangles, diamonds, ovals and small circles; these symbols are connected by arrows called **flowlines**, which indicate the order in which the actions of the algorithm execute.

Like pseudocode, flowcharts often are useful for developing and representing algorithms, although pseudocode is strongly preferred by many programmers. Flowcharts show clearly how control structures operate; that is all we use them for in this text. The reader should carefully compare the pseudocode and flowchart representations of each control structure.

Consider the flowchart segment for the sequence structure on the left side of Fig. 8.1. We use the **rectangle symbol** (or **action symbol**) to indicate any type of action, including a calculation or an input/output operation. The flowlines in the figure indicate the order in which the actions are performed—the first action adds grade to total, then the second action adds 1 to counter. JavaScript allows us to have as many actions as we want in a sequence structure. Anywhere a single action may be placed, as we will soon see, we may place several actions in sequence.

In a flowchart that represents a complete algorithm, an **oval symbol** containing the word "Begin" is the first symbol used; an oval symbol containing the word "End" indicates where the algorithm ends. In a flowchart that shows only a portion of an algorithm, as in

---

1.   Bohm, C., and G. Jacopini, "Flow Diagrams, Turing Machines, and Languages with Only Two Formation Rules," *Communications of the ACM*, Vol. 9, No. 5, May 1966, pp. 336–371.

Fig. 8.1, the oval symbols are omitted in favor of using **small circle symbols**, also called **connector symbols**.

Perhaps the most important flowcharting symbol is the **diamond symbol**, also called the **decision symbol**, which indicates that a decision is to be made. We discuss the diamond symbol in the next section.

JavaScript provides three types of selection structures; we discuss each in this chapter and in Chapter 9. The **if** selection statement performs (selects) an action if a condition is true or skips the action if the condition is false. The **if...else** selection statement performs an action if a condition is true and performs a different action if the condition is false. The **switch** selection statement (Chapter 9) performs one of many different actions, depending on the value of an expression.

The if statement is called a **single-selection structure** because it selects or ignores a single action (or, as we will soon see, a single group of actions). The if...else statement is a **double-selection structure** because it selects between two different actions (or groups of actions). The switch statement is a **multiple-selection structure** because it selects among many different actions (or groups of actions).

JavaScript provides four repetition structure types, namely **while**, **do...while**, **for** and **for...in**. (do...while and for are covered in Chapter 9; for...in is covered in Chapter 11.) Each of the words if, else, switch, while, do, for and in is a JavaScript **keyword**. These words are reserved by the language to implement various features, such as JavaScript's control structures. Keywords cannot be used as identifiers (e.g., for variable names). A complete list of JavaScript keywords is shown in Fig. 8.2.

Common Programming Error 8.1

Using a keyword as an identifier is a syntax error.

JavaScript Keywords				
break	case	catch	continue	default
delete	do	else	finally	for
function	if	in	instanceof	new
return	switch	this	throw	try
typeof	var	void	while	with
Keywords that are reserved but not used by JavaScript				
abstract	boolean	byte	char	class
const	debugger	double	enum	export
extends	final	float	goto	implements
import	int	interface	long	native
package	private	protected	public	short
static	super	synchronized	throws	transient
volatile				

Fig. 8.2   JavaScript keywords.

As we have shown, JavaScript has only eight control structures: sequence, three types of selection and four types of repetition. Every program is formed by combining as many of each type of control structure as is appropriate for the algorithm the program implements. As with the sequence structure in Fig. 8.1, we will see that each control structure is flowcharted with two small circle symbols, one at the entry point to the control structure and one at the exit point.

Single-entry/single-exit control structures make it easy to build programs; the control structures are attached to one another by connecting the exit point of one control structure to the entry point of the next. This process is similar to the way in which a child stacks building blocks, so we call it **control-structure stacking**. We will learn that there is only one other way in which control structures may be connected—**control-structure nesting**. Thus, algorithms in JavaScript programs are constructed from only eight different types of control structures combined in only two ways.

8.5 if Selection Statement

A selection structure is used to choose among alternative courses of action in a program. For example, suppose that the passing grade on an examination is 60 (out of 100). Then the pseudocode statement

> *If student's grade is greater than or equal to 60*
>   *Print "Passed"*

determines whether the condition "student's grade is greater than or equal to 60" is true or false. If the condition is true, then "Passed" is printed, and the next pseudocode statement in order is "performed" (remember that pseudocode is not a real programming language). If the condition is false, the print statement is ignored, and the next pseudocode statement in order is performed. Note that the second line of this selection structure is indented. Such indentation is optional, but it is highly recommended, because it emphasizes the inherent structure of structured programs. The JavaScript interpreter ignores white space characters—blanks, tabs and new lines used for indentation and vertical spacing. Programmers insert these white space characters to enhance program clarity.

Good Programming Practice 8.1

Consistently applying reasonable indentation conventions throughout your programs improves program readability. We suggest a fixed-size tab of about 1/4 inch or three spaces per indent.

The preceding pseudocode *If* statement can be written in JavaScript as

```
if ( studentGrade >= 60 )
    document.writeln( "Passed" );
```

Note that the JavaScript code corresponds closely to the pseudocode. This similarity is the reason that pseudocode is a useful program-development tool. The statement in the body of the `if` statement outputs the character string `"Passed"` in the XHTML document.

The flowchart in Fig. 8.3 illustrates the single-selection `if` statement. This flowchart contains what is perhaps the most important flowcharting symbol—the **diamond symbol** (or **decision symbol**), which indicates that a decision is to be made. The decision symbol contains an expression, such as a condition, that can be either **true** or **false**. The decision symbol has two flowlines emerging from it. One indicates the path to follow in the program when the expression in the symbol is true; the other indicates the path to follow in the program when the expression is false. A decision can be made on any expression that evaluates to a value of JavaScript's boolean type (i.e., any expression that evaluates to `true` or `false`).

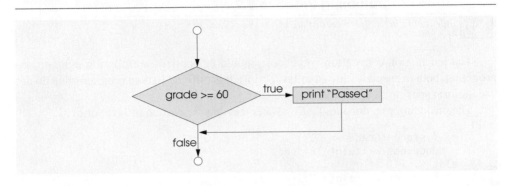

Fig. 8.3   Flowcharting the single-selection `if` statement.

Software Engineering Observation 8.2

In JavaScript, any nonzero numeric value in a condition evaluates to `true`, and 0 evaluates to `false`. For strings, any string containing one or more characters evaluates to `true`, and the empty string (the string containing no characters) evaluates to `false`. Also, a variable that has been declared with `var` but has not been assigned a value evaluates to `false`.

Note that the `if` statement is a single-entry/single-exit control structure. We will soon learn that the flowcharts for the remaining control structures also contain (besides small circle symbols and flowlines) only rectangle symbols, to indicate the actions to be performed, and diamond symbols, to indicate decisions to be made. This type of flowchart represents the **action/decision model of programming**.

We can envision eight bins, each containing only the control structures of one of the eight types. These control structures are empty. Nothing is written in the rectangles or in the diamonds. The programmer's task, then, is to assemble a program from as many of each type of control structure as the algorithm demands, combining the control structures in only two possible ways (stacking or nesting), then filling in the actions and decisions in a manner appropriate for the algorithm. We will discuss the variety of ways in which actions and decisions may be written.

8.6 `if...else` Selection Statement

The `if` selection statement performs an indicated action only when the condition evaluates to `true`; otherwise, the action is skipped. The `if...else` selection statement allows the programmer to specify that a different action is to be performed when the condition is true than when the condition is false. For example, the pseudocode statement

> *If student's grade is greater than or equal to 60*
>> *Print "Passed"*
> *Else*
>> *Print "Failed"*

prints Passed if the student's grade is greater than or equal to 60 and prints Failed if the student's grade is less than 60. In either case, after printing occurs, the next pseudocode statement in sequence (i.e., the next statement after the whole if...else structure) is performed. Note that the body of the *Else* part of the structure is also indented.

Good Programming Practice 8.2

Indent both body statements of an if...else statement.

The indentation convention you choose should be applied carefully throughout your programs (both in pseudocode and in JavaScript). It is difficult to read programs that do not use uniform spacing conventions.

The preceding pseudocode *If...Else* statement may be written in JavaScript as

```
if ( studentGrade >= 60 )
    document.writeln( "Passed" );
else
    document.writeln( "Failed" );
```

The flowchart in Fig. 8.4 nicely illustrates the flow of control in the if...else statement. Once again, note that the only symbols in the flowchart (besides small circles and arrows) are rectangles (for actions) and a diamond (for a decision). We continue to emphasize this action/decision model of computing. Imagine again a deep bin containing as many empty double-selection structures as might be needed to build a JavaScript algorithm. The programmer's job is to assemble the selection structures (by stacking and nesting) with other control structures required by the algorithm and to fill in the empty rectangles and empty diamonds with actions and decisions appropriate to the algorithm's implementation.

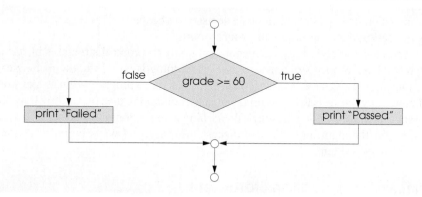

Fig. 8.4   Flowcharting the double-selection if...else statement.

JavaScript provides an operator, called the **conditional operator (?:)**, that is closely related to the if...else statement. The operator ?: is JavaScript's only **ternary operator**—it takes three operands. The operands together with the ?: form a **conditional expression**. The first operand is a boolean expression, the second is the value for the conditional expression if the condition evaluates to true and the third is the value for the conditional expression if the condition evaluates to false. For example, the statement

```
document.writeln(
   studentGrade >= 60 ? "Passed" : "Failed" );
```

contains a conditional expression that evaluates to the string `"Passed"` if the condition `studentGrade >= 60` is true and evaluates to the string `"Failed"` if the condition is false. Thus, this statement with the conditional operator performs essentially the same operation as the preceding if...else statement. The precedence of the conditional operator is low, so the entire conditional expression is normally placed in parentheses to ensure that it evaluates correctly.

Nested **if...else** statements test for multiple cases by placing if...else statements inside if...else statements. For example, the following pseudocode statement will print A for exam grades greater than or equal to 90, B for grades in the range 80 to 89, C for grades in the range 70 to 79, D for grades in the range 60 to 69 and F for all other grades:

> *If student's grade is greater than or equal to 90*
> 　　*Print "A"*
> *Else*
> 　　*If student's grade is greater than or equal to 80*
> 　　　　*Print "B"*
> 　　*Else*
> 　　　　*If student's grade is greater than or equal to 70*
> 　　　　　　*Print "C"*
> 　　　　*Else*
> 　　　　　　*If student's grade is greater than or equal to 60*
> 　　　　　　　　*Print "D"*
> 　　　　　　*Else*
> 　　　　　　　　*Print "F"*

This pseudocode may be written in JavaScript as

```
if ( studentGrade >= 90 )
   document.writeln( "A" );
else
   if ( studentGrade >= 80 )
      document.writeln( "B" );
   else
      if ( studentGrade >= 70 )
         document.writeln( "C" );
      else
         if ( studentGrade >= 60 )
            document.writeln( "D" );
         else
            document.writeln( "F" );
```

If `studentGrade` is greater than or equal to 90, the first four conditions will be true, but only the `document.writeln` statement after the first test will execute. After that particular `document.writeln` executes, the `else` part of the outer if...else statements is skipped.

Good Programming Practice 8.3

If there are several levels of indentation, each level should be indented the same additional amount of space.

Most JavaScript programmers prefer to write the preceding if structure as

```
if ( grade >= 90 )
   document.writeln( "A" );
else if ( grade >= 80 )
   document.writeln( "B" );
else if ( grade >= 70 )
   document.writeln( "C" );
else if ( grade >= 60 )
   document.writeln( "D" );
else
   document.writeln( "F" );
```

The two forms are equivalent. The latter form is popular because it avoids the deep indentation of the code to the right. Such deep indentation often leaves little room on a line, forcing lines to be split and decreasing program readability.

It is important to note that the JavaScript interpreter always associates an else with the previous if, unless told to do otherwise by the placement of braces ({}). This situation is referred to as the **dangling-else problem**. For example,

```
if ( x > 5 )
   if ( y > 5 )
      document.writeln( "x and y are > 5" );
else
   document.writeln( "x is <= 5" );
```

appears to indicate with its indentation that if x is greater than 5, the if structure in its body determines whether y is also greater than 5. If so, the body of the nested if structure outputs the string "x and y are > 5". Otherwise, it *appears* that if x is not greater than 5, the else part of the if...else structure outputs the string "x is <= 5".

Beware! The preceding nested if statement does not execute as it appears. The interpreter actually interprets the preceding statement as

```
if ( x > 5 )
   if ( y > 5 )
      document.writeln( "x and y are > 5" );
   else
      document.writeln( "x is <= 5" );
```

in which the body of the first if statement is a nested if...else statement. This statement tests whether x is greater than 5. If so, execution continues by testing whether y is also greater than 5. If the second condition is true, the proper string—"x and y are > 5"—is displayed. However, if the second condition is false, the string "x is <= 5" is displayed, even though we know that x is greater than 5.

To force the preceding nested if statement to execute as it was intended originally, the statement must be written as follows:

```
if ( x > 5 )
{
   if ( y > 5 )
      document.writeln( "x and y are > 5" );
}
else
   document.writeln( "x is <= 5" );
```

The braces ({}) indicate to the interpreter that the second if statement is in the body of the first if statement and that the else is matched with the first if statement. In Exercises 8.21 and 8.22, you will investigate the dangling-else problem further.

The if selection statement expects only one statement in its body. To include several statements in the body of an if, enclose the statements in braces ({ and }). A set of statements contained within a pair of braces is called a **block** (sometimes known as a **compound statement**).

Software Engineering Observation 8.3

A block can be placed anywhere in a program that a single statement can be placed.

Software Engineering Observation 8.4

Unlike individual statements, a block does not end with a semicolon. However, each statement within the braces of a block should end with a semicolon.

The following example includes a block in the else part of an if...else statement:

```
if ( grade >= 60 )
    document.writeln( "Passed" );
else
{
    document.writeln( "Failed<br />" );
    document.writeln( "You must take this course again." );
}
```

In this case, if grade is less than 60, the program executes both statements in the body of the else and prints

```
Failed.
You must take this course again.
```

Note the braces surrounding the two statements in the else clause. These braces are important. Without them, the statement

```
document.writeln( "You must take this course again." );
```

would be outside the body of the else part of the if and would execute regardless of whether the grade is less than 60.

Common Programming Error 8.2

Forgetting one or both of the braces that delimit a block can lead to syntax errors or logic errors.

Syntax errors (e.g., when one brace in a block is left out of the program) are caught by the interpreter when it attempts to interpret the code containing the syntax error. A **logic error** (e.g., the one caused when both braces around a block are left out of the program) also has its effect at execution time. A **fatal logic error** causes a program to fail and terminate prematurely. A **nonfatal logic error** allows a program to continue executing, but the program produces incorrect results.

Software Engineering Observation 8.5

Just as a block can be placed anywhere a single statement can be placed, it is also possible to have no statement at all (the empty statement) in such places. The empty statement is represented by placing a semicolon (;) where a statement would normally be.

Common Programming Error 8.3

Placing a semicolon after the condition in an if structure leads to a logic error in single-selection if structures and a syntax error in double-selection if structures (if the if part contains a nonempty body statement).

Good Programming Practice 8.4

Some programmers prefer to type the beginning and ending braces of blocks before typing the individual statements within the braces. This procedure helps the programmers avoid omitting one or both of the braces.

8.7 while Repetition Statement

A **repetition structure** (also known as a **loop**) allows the programmer to specify that a script is to repeat an action while some condition remains true. The pseudocode statement

> *While there are more items on my shopping list*
> *Purchase next item and cross it off my list*

describes the repetition that occurs during a shopping trip. The condition "there are more items on my shopping list" may be true or false. If it is true, then the action "Purchase next item and cross it off my list" is performed. This action will be performed repeatedly while the condition remains true. The statement(s) contained in the *While* repetition structure constitute the body of the *While*. The body of a loop such as the *While* structure may be a single statement or a block. Eventually, the condition becomes false (i.e., when the last item on the shopping list has been purchased and crossed off the list). At this point, the repetition terminates, and the first pseudocode statement after the repetition structure executes.

Common Programming Error 8.4

Not providing in the body of a while statement an action that eventually causes the condition in the while statement to become false is a logic error. Normally, such a repetition structure will never terminate—an error called an "infinite loop." Browsers handle infinite loops differently. For example, Internet Explorer allows the user to terminate the script containing the infinite loop.

Common Programming Error 8.5

Remember that JavaScript is a case-sensitive language. In code, spelling the keyword while with an uppercase W, as in While, is a syntax error. All of JavaScript's reserved keywords, such as while, if and else, contain only lowercase letters.

As an example of a while statement, consider a program segment designed to find the first power of 2 larger than 1000. Variable **product** begins with the value 2. The statement is as follows:

```
var product = 2;

while ( product <= 1000 )
   product = 2 * product;
```

When the while statement finishes executing, **product** contains the result 1024. The flowchart in Fig. 8.5 illustrates the flow of control of the preceding while repetition statement. Once again, note that (besides small circles and arrows) the flowchart contains only a rectangle symbol and a diamond symbol.

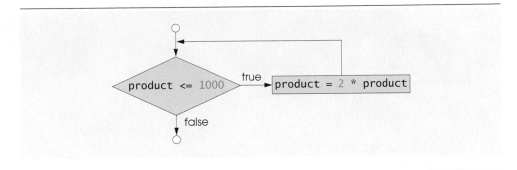

Fig. 8.5   Flowcharting the `while` repetition statement.

When the script enters the `while` statement, `product` is 2. The script repeatedly multiplies variable `product` by 2, so `product` takes on the values 4, 8, 16, 32, 64, 128, 256, 512 and 1024 successively. When `product` becomes 1024, the condition `product <= 1000` in the `while` statement becomes `false`. This terminates the repetition, with 1024 as `product`'s final value. Execution continues with the next statement after the `while` statement. [*Note*: If a `while` statement's condition is initially `false`, the body statement(s) will never execute.]

The flowchart clearly shows the repetition. The flowline emerging from the rectangle wraps back to the decision, which the script tests each time through the loop until the decision eventually becomes false. At this point, the `while` statement exits, and control passes to the next statement in the program.

8.8 Formulating Algorithms: Case Study 1 (Counter-Controlled Repetition)

To illustrate how to develop algorithms, we solve several variations of a class-averaging problem. Consider the following problem statement:

> *A class of ten students took a quiz. The grades (integers in the range 0 to 100) for this quiz are available to you. Determine the class average on the quiz.*

The class average is equal to the sum of the grades divided by the number of students (10 in this case). The algorithm for solving this problem on a computer must input each of the grades, perform the averaging calculation and display the result.

Let us use pseudocode to list the actions to execute and specify the order in which the actions should execute. We use **counter-controlled repetition** to input the grades one at a time. This technique uses a variable called a **counter** to control the number of times a set of statements executes. In this example, repetition terminates when the counter exceeds 10. In this section, we present a pseudocode algorithm (Fig. 8.6) and the corresponding program (Fig. 8.7). In the next section, we show how to develop pseudocode algorithms. Counter-controlled repetition often is called **definite repetition**, because the number of repetitions is known before the loop begins executing.

Note the references in the algorithm to a total and a counter. A **total** is a variable in which a script accumulates the sum of a series of values. A counter is a variable a script uses to count—in this case, to count the number of grades entered. Variables that store totals should normally be initialized to zero before they are used in a program.

Set total to zero
Set grade counter to one

While grade counter is less than or equal to ten
    Input the next grade
    Add the grade into the total
    Add one to the grade counter

Set the class average to the total divided by ten
Print the class average

Fig. 8.6   Pseudocode algorithm that uses counter-controlled repetition to solve
              the class-average problem.

```
1   <?xml version = "1.0"?>
2   <!DOCTYPE html PUBLIC "-//W3C//DTD XHTML 1.0 Strict//EN"
3      "http://www.w3.org/TR/xhtml1/DTD/xhtml1-strict.dtd">
4
5   <!-- Fig. 8.7: average.html -->
6   <!-- Class Average Program  -->
7
8   <html xmlns = "http://www.w3.org/1999/xhtml">
9      <head>
10        <title>Class Average Program</title>
11
12        <script type = "text/javascript">
13           <!--
14           var total,          // sum of grades
15               gradeCounter,   // number of grades entered
16               gradeValue,     // grade value
17               average,        // average of all grades
18               grade;          // grade typed by user
19
20           // Initialization Phase
21           total = 0;          // clear total
22           gradeCounter = 1;   // prepare to loop
23
24           // Processing Phase
25           while ( gradeCounter <= 10 ) {  // loop 10 times
26
27              // prompt for input and read grade from user
28              grade = window.prompt( "Enter integer grade:", "0" );
29
30              // convert grade from a string to an integer
31              gradeValue = parseInt( grade );
32
33              // add gradeValue to total
34              total = total + gradeValue;
35
```

Fig. 8.7   Counter-controlled repetition to calculate a class average. (Part 1 of 2.)

```
36             // add 1 to gradeCounter
37             gradeCounter = gradeCounter + 1;
38          }
39
40          // Termination Phase
41          average = total / 10;  // calculate the average
42
43          // display average of exam grades
44          document.writeln(
45             "<h1>Class average is " + average + "</h1>" );
46          // -->
47       </script>
48
49    </head>
50    <body>
51       <p>Click Refresh (or Reload) to run the script again<p>
52    </body>
53 </html>
```

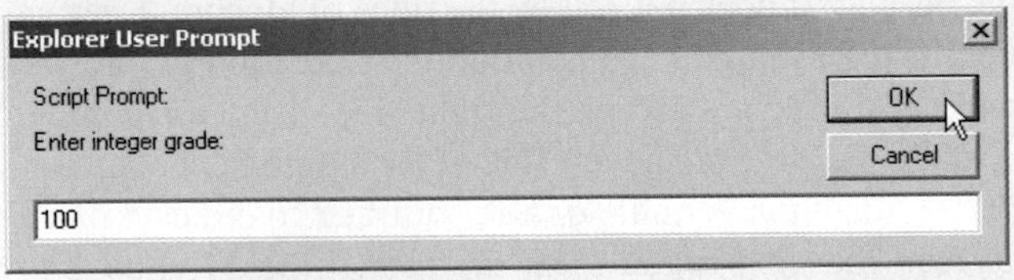
Explorer User Prompt
Script Prompt:
Enter integer grade:
OK
Cancel
100

This dialog is displayed 10 times. User input is 100, 88, 93, 55, 68, 77, 83, 95, 73 and 62.

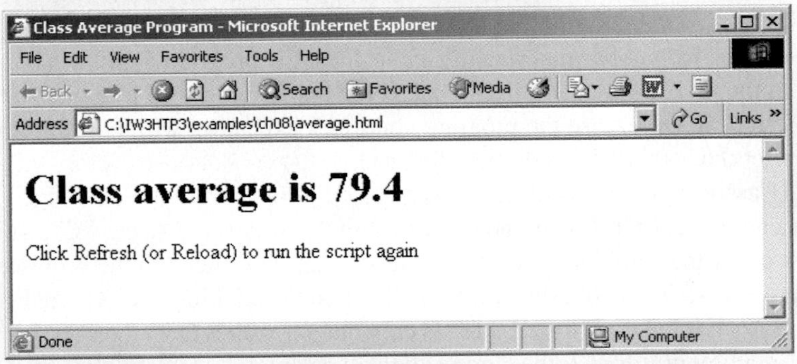
Class Average Program - Microsoft Internet Explorer
File Edit View Favorites Tools Help
Back Search Favorites Media
Address C:\IW3HTP3\examples\ch08\average.html
Go Links
Class average is 79.4
Click Refresh (or Reload) to run the script again
Done
My Computer

Fig. 8.7 Counter-controlled repetition to calculate a class average. (Part 2 of 2.)

Good Programming Practice 8.5

Variables to be used in calculations should be initialized before their use.

Lines 14–18 declare variables `total`, `gradeCounter`, `gradeValue`, `average` and `grade`. The variable `grade` will store the string the user types into the `prompt` dialog. The variable `gradeValue` will store the integer value of the `grade` the user enters in a `prompt` dialog.

Lines 21–22 are assignment statements that initialize `total` to `0` and `gradeCounter` to `1`. Note that variables `total` and `gradeCounter` are initialized before they are used in a calculation. Uninitialized variables used in calculations result in logic errors and produce the value `NaN` (not a number).

Common Programming Error 8.6

Not initializing a variable that will be used in a calculation results in a logic error. You must initialize the variable before it is used in a calculation.

Error-Prevention Tip 8.1

Initialize variables that will be used in calculations to avoid subtle errors.

Line 25 indicates that the `while` statement continues iterating while the value of `gradeCounter` is less than or equal to 10. Line 28 corresponds to the pseudocode statement *"Input the next grade."* The statement displays a `prompt` dialog with the prompt `"Enter integer grade:"` on the screen.

After the user enters the `grade`, line 31 converts it from a string to an integer. We must convert the string to an integer in this example; otherwise, the addition statement in line 34 will be a string-concatenation statement rather than a numeric sum.

Next, the program updates the `total` with the new `gradeValue` entered by the user. Line 34 adds `gradeValue` to the previous value of `total` and assigns the result to `total`. This statement seems a bit strange, because it does not follow the rules of algebra. Keep in mind that JavaScript operator precedence evaluates the addition (+) operation before the assignment (=) operation. The value of the expression on the right side of the assignment operator always replaces the value of the variable on the left side of the assignment operator.

The program now is ready to increment the variable `gradeCounter` to indicate that a grade has been processed and to read the next grade from the user. Line 37 adds 1 to `gradeCounter`, so the condition in the `while` statement will eventually become `false` and terminate the loop. After this statement executes, the program continues by testing the condition in the `while` statement in line 25. If the condition is still true, the statements in lines 28–37 repeat. Otherwise the program continues execution with the first statement in sequence after the body of the loop (i.e., line 41).

Line 41 assigns the results of the average calculation to variable `average`. Lines 44–45 write a line of XHTML text in the document that displays the string `"Class average is "` followed by the value of variable `average` as an `<h1>` head in the browser.

Execute the script in Internet Explorer by double clicking the XHTML document (from Windows Explorer). This script reads only integer values from the user. In the sample program execution in Fig. 8.7, the sum of the values entered (100, 88, 93, 55, 68, 77, 83, 95, 73 and 62) is 794. Although the script reads only integers, the averaging calculation in the program does not produce an integer. Rather, the calculation produces a **floating-point number** (i.e., a number containing a decimal point). The average of the 10 integers input by the user in this example is 79.4.

Software Engineering Observation 8.6

If the string passed to `parseInt` contains a floating-point numeric value, `parseInt` simply truncates the floating-point part. For example, the string "27.95" results in the integer 27, and the string "–123.45" results in the integer –123. If the string passed to `parseInt` is not a numeric value, `parseInt` returns NaN (not a number).

JavaScript actually represents all numbers as floating-point numbers in memory. Floating-point numbers often develop through division, as shown in this example. When we divide 10 by 3, the result is 3.3333333…, with the sequence of 3s repeating infinitely. The computer allocates only a fixed amount of space to hold such a value, so the stored floating-point value can be only an approximation. Despite the fact that floating-point numbers are not always 100% precise, they have numerous applications. For example, when we speak of a "normal" body temperature of 98.6, we do not need to be precise to a large number of digits. When we view the temperature on a thermometer and read it as 98.6, it may actually be 98.5999473210643. The point here is that few applications require high-precision floating-point values, so calling this number simply 98.6 is fine for most applications.

Common Programming Error 8.7

Using floating-point numbers in a manner that assumes they are represented precisely can lead to incorrect results. Real numbers are represented only approximately by computers. For example, no fixed-size floating-point representation of π can ever be precise, because π is a transcendental number whose value cannot be expressed as digits in a finite amount of space.

8.9 Formulating Algorithms with Top-Down, Stepwise Refinement: Case Study 2 (Sentinel-Controlled Repetition)

Let us generalize the class-average problem. Consider the following problem:

> *Develop a class-averaging program that will process an arbitrary number of grades each time the program is run.*

In the first class-average example, the number of grades (10) was known in advance. In this example, no indication is given of how many grades the user will enter. The program must process an arbitrary number of grades. How can the program determine when to stop the input of grades? How will it know when to calculate and display the class average?

One way to solve this problem is to use a special value called a **sentinel value** (also called a **signal value**, a **dummy value** or a **flag value**) to indicate the end of data entry. The user types in grades until all legitimate grades have been entered. Then the user types the sentinel value to indicate that the last grade has been entered. Sentinel-controlled repetition is often called **indefinite repetition**, because the number of repetitions is not known before the loop begins executing.

Clearly, one must choose a sentinel value that cannot be confused with an acceptable input value. Because grades on a quiz are normally nonnegative integers from 0 to 100, –1 is an acceptable sentinel value for this problem. Thus, an execution of the class-average program might process a stream of inputs such as 95, 96, 75, 74, 89 and –1. The program would compute and print the class average for the grades 95, 96, 75, 74 and 89 (–1 is the sentinel value, so it should not enter into the average calculation).

Common Programming Error 8.8

Choosing a sentinel value that is also a legitimate data value results in a logic error and may prevent a sentinel-controlled loop from terminating properly.

We approach the class-average program with a technique called **top-down, stepwise refinement**, a technique that is essential to the development of well-structured algorithms. We begin with a pseudocode representation of the **top**:

> *Determine the class average for the quiz*

The top is a single statement that conveys the overall purpose of the program. As such, the top is, in effect, a complete representation of a program. Unfortunately, the top rarely conveys a sufficient amount of detail from which to write the JavaScript algorithm. Therefore we must begin a refinement process. First, we divide the top into a series of smaller tasks and list them in the order in which they need to be performed, creating the following **first refinement**:

> *Initialize variables*
> *Input, sum up and count the quiz grades*
> *Calculate and print the class average*

Here, only the sequence structure is used; the steps listed are to be executed in order, one after the other.

Software Engineering Observation 8.7

Each refinement, as well as the top itself, is a complete specification of the algorithm; only the level of detail varies.

To proceed to the next level of refinement (the **second refinement**), we commit to specific variables. We need a running total of the numbers, a count of how many numbers have been processed, a variable to receive the string representation of each grade as it is input, a variable to store the value of the grade after it is converted to an integer and a variable to hold the calculated average. The pseudocode statement

> *Initialize variables*

may be refined as follows:

> *Initialize total to zero*
> *Initialize gradeCounter to zero*

Note that only the variables *total* and *gradeCounter* are initialized before they are used; the variables *average*, *grade* and *gradeValue* (for the calculated average, the user input and the integer representation of the *grade*, respectively) need not be initialized, because their values are determined as they are calculated or input.

The pseudocode statement

> *Input, sum up and count the quiz grades*

requires a repetition structure (a loop) that successively inputs each grade. We do not know in advance how many grades are to be processed, so we will use sentinel-controlled repetition. The user at the keyboard will enter legitimate grades, one at a time. After entering the last legitimate grade, the user will enter the sentinel value. The program will test for the sentinel value after the user enters each grade and will terminate the loop when the sentinel value is encountered. The second refinement of the preceding pseudocode statement is then

> *Input the first grade (possibly the sentinel)*
> *While the user has not as yet entered the sentinel*
>   *Add this grade into the running total*
>   *Add one to the grade counter*
>   *Input the next grade (possibly the sentinel)*

Note that in pseudocode, we do not use braces around the pseudocode that forms the body of the *While* structure. We simply indent the pseudocode under the *While*, to show that it belongs to the body of the *While*. Remember, pseudocode is only an informal program-development aid.

The pseudocode statement

> *Calculate and print the class average*

may be refined as follows:

> *If the counter is not equal to zero*
> > *Set the average to the total divided by the counter*
> > *Print the average*
>
> *Else*
> > *Print "No grades were entered"*

Note that we are testing for the possibility of division by zero—a **logic error** that, if undetected, would cause the program to produce invalid output. The complete second refinement of the pseudocode algorithm for the class-average problem is shown in Fig. 8.8.

Initialize total to zero
Initialize gradeCounter to zero

Input the first grade (possibly the sentinel)
While the user has not as yet entered the sentinel
> *Add this grade into the running total*
> *Add one to the grade counter*
> *Input the next grade (possibly the sentinel)*

If the counter is not equal to zero
> *Set the average to the total divided by the counter*
> *Print the average*

Else
> *Print "No grades were entered"*

Fig. 8.8   Sentinel-controlled repetition to solve the class-average problem.

Error-Prevention Tip 8.2

When performing division by an expression whose value could be zero, explicitly test for this case, and handle it appropriately in your program (e.g., by printing an error message) rather than allow the division by zero to occur.

Good Programming Practice 8.6

Include completely blank lines in pseudocode programs to make the pseudocode more readable. The blank lines separate pseudocode control structures and separate the phases of the programs.

Software Engineering Observation 8.8

Many algorithms can be divided logically into three phases: an initialization phase that initializes the program variables, a processing phase that inputs data values and adjusts program variables accordingly and a termination phase that calculates and prints the results.

The pseudocode algorithm in Fig. 8.8 solves the more general class-averaging problem. This algorithm was developed after only two refinements. Sometimes more refinements are necessary.

Software Engineering Observation 8.9

The programmer terminates the top-down, stepwise refinement process after specifying the pseudocode algorithm in sufficient detail for the programmer to convert the pseudocode to a JavaScript program. Then, implementing the JavaScript program will normally be straightforward.

Good Programming Practice 8.7

When converting a pseudocode program to JavaScript, keep the pseudocode in the JavaScript program as comments.

Software Engineering Observation 8.10

Experience has shown that the most difficult part of solving a problem on a computer is developing the algorithm for the solution. Once a correct algorithm is specified, the process of producing a working JavaScript program from the algorithm is normally straightforward.

Software Engineering Observation 8.11

Many experienced programmers write programs without ever using program-development tools like pseudocode. As they see it, their ultimate goal is to solve the problem on a computer, and writing pseudocode merely delays the production of final outputs. Although this approach may work for simple and familiar problems, it can lead to serious errors in large, complex projects.

Figure 8.9 shows the JavaScript program and a sample execution. Although each grade is an integer, the averaging calculation is likely to produce a number with a decimal point (a real number).

In this example, we see that control structures may be stacked on top of one another (in sequence) just as a child stacks building blocks. The `while` statement (lines 33–46) is followed immediately by an `if...else` statement (lines 49–57) in sequence. Much of the code in this program is identical to the code in Fig. 8.7, so we concentrate in this example on the new features.

Line 23 initializes `gradeCounter` to 0, because no grades have been entered yet. Remember that the program uses sentinel-controlled repetition. To keep an accurate record of the number of grades entered, the script increments `gradeCounter` only after processing a valid grade value.

```
 1   <?xml version = "1.0"?>
 2   <!DOCTYPE html PUBLIC "-//W3C//DTD XHTML 1.0 Strict//EN"
 3      "http://www.w3.org/TR/xhtml1/DTD/xhtml1-strict.dtd">
 4
 5   <!-- Fig. 8.9: average2.html         -->
 6   <!-- Sentinel-controlled Repetition -->
 7
 8   <html xmlns = "http://www.w3.org/1999/xhtml">
 9      <head>
10         <title>Class Average Program:
11            Sentinel-controlled Repetition</title>
12
```

Fig. 8.9   Sentinel-controlled repetition to calculate a class average. (Part 1 of 3.)

```
13          <script type = "text/javascript">
14             <!--
15             var gradeCounter,    // number of grades entered
16                 gradeValue,      // grade value
17                 total,           // sum of grades
18                 average,         // average of all grades
19                 grade;           // grade typed by user
20
21             // Initialization phase
22             total = 0;           // clear total
23             gradeCounter = 0;    // prepare to loop
24
25             // Processing phase
26             // prompt for input and read grade from user
27             grade = window.prompt(
28                 "Enter Integer Grade, -1 to Quit:", "0" );
29
30             // convert grade from a string to an integer
31             gradeValue = parseInt( grade );
32
33             while ( gradeValue != -1 ) {
34                // add gradeValue to total
35                total = total + gradeValue;
36
37                // add 1 to gradeCounter
38                gradeCounter = gradeCounter + 1;
39
40                // prompt for input and read grade from user
41                grade = window.prompt(
42                    "Enter Integer Grade, -1 to Quit:", "0" );
43
44                // convert grade from a string to an integer
45                gradeValue = parseInt( grade );
46             }
47
48             // Termination phase
49             if ( gradeCounter != 0 ) {
50                average = total / gradeCounter;
51
52                // display average of exam grades
53                document.writeln(
54                    "<h1>Class average is " + average + "</h1>" );
55             }
56             else
57                document.writeln( "<p>No grades were entered</p>" );
58             // -->
59          </script>
60       </head>
61
62       <body>
63          <p>Click Refresh (or Reload) to run the script again</p>
64       </body>
65    </html>
```

Fig. 8.9   Sentinel-controlled repetition to calculate a class average. (Part 2 of 3.)

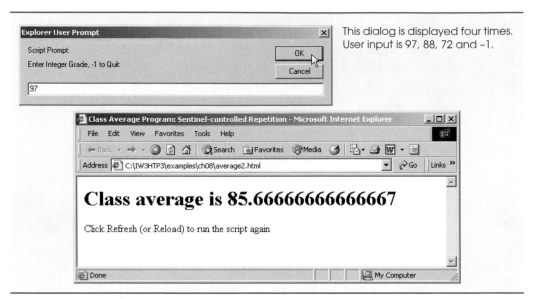

Fig. 8.9   Sentinel-controlled repetition to calculate a class average. (Part 3 of 3.)

Note the difference in program logic for sentinel-controlled repetition as compared with the counter-controlled repetition in Fig. 8.7. In counter-controlled repetition, we read a value from the user during each iteration of the while statement's body for the specified number of iterations. In sentinel-controlled repetition, we read one value (lines 27–28) and convert it to an integer (line 31) before the program reaches the while statement. The script uses this value to determine whether the program's flow of control should enter the body of the while statement. If the while statement's condition is false (i.e., the user typed the sentinel as the first grade), the script ignores the body of the while statement (i.e., no grades were entered). If, on the other hand, the condition is true, the body begins execution and processes the value entered by the user (i.e., adds the value to the total in line 35). After processing the value, the script increments gradeCounter by 1 (line 38), inputs the next grade from the user (lines 41–42) and converts the grade to an integer (line 45), before the end of the while statement's body. When the script reaches the closing right brace (}) of the body in line 46, execution continues with the next test of the condition of the while statement (line 33), using the new value just entered by the user to determine whether the while statement's body should execute again. Note that the next value always is input from the user immediately before the script evaluates the condition of the while statement. This order allows us to determine whether the value just entered by the user is the sentinel value *before* processing it (i.e., adding it to the total). If the value entered is the sentinel value, the while statement terminates and the script does not add the value to the total.

Good Programming Practice 8.8

In a sentinel-controlled loop, the prompts requesting data entry should explicitly remind the user what the sentinel value is.

Note the block in the while loop in Fig. 8.9. Without the braces, the last four statements in the body of the loop would fall outside of the loop, causing the computer to interpret the code incorrectly, as follows:

```
while ( gradeValue != -1 )
   // add gradeValue to total
   total = total + gradeValue;

// add 1 to gradeCounter
gradeCounter = gradeCounter + 1;

// prompt for input and read grade from user
grade = window.prompt(
   "Enter Integer Grade, -1 to Quit:", "0" );

// convert grade from a string to an integer
gradeValue = parseInt( grade );
```

This interpretation would cause an infinite loop in the program if the user does not input the sentinel -1 as the input value in lines 27–28 (i.e., before the `while` statement).

Common Programming Error 8.9

Omitting the braces that delineate a block can lead to logic errors such as infinite loops.

8.10 Formulating Algorithms with Top-Down, Stepwise Refinement: Case Study 3 (Nested Control Structures)

Let us work through another complete problem. We will once again formulate the algorithm using pseudocode and top-down, stepwise refinement, and we will write a corresponding JavaScript program.

Consider the following problem statement:

> *A college offers a course that prepares students for the state licensing exam for real estate brokers. Last year, several of the students who completed this course took the licensing examination. Naturally, the college wants to know how well its students did on the exam. You have been asked to write a program to summarize the results. You have been given a list of these 10 students. Next to each name is written a 1 if the student passed the exam and a 2 if the student failed.*

> *Your program should analyze the results of the exam as follows:*

> 1. *Input each test result (i.e., a 1 or a 2). Display the message "Enter result" on the screen each time the program requests another test result.*

> 2. *Count the number of test results of each type.*

> 3. *Display a summary of the test results indicating the number of students who passed and the number of students who failed.*

> 4. *If more than eight students passed the exam, print the message "Raise tuition."*

After reading the problem statement carefully, we make the following observations about the problem:

1. The program must process test results for 10 students. A counter-controlled loop will be used.

2. Each test result is a number—either a 1 or a 2. Each time the program reads a test result, the program must determine whether the number is a 1 or a 2. We test for a 1 in our algorithm. If the number is not a 1, we assume that it is a 2. (An exercise at the end of the chapter considers the consequences of this assumption.)

3. Two counters are used to keep track of the exam results—one to count the number of students who passed the exam and one to count the number of students who failed the exam.

After the program processes all the results, it must decide whether more than eight students passed the exam. Let us proceed with top-down, stepwise refinement. We begin with a pseudocode representation of the top:

> *Analyze exam results and decide whether tuition should be raised*

Once again, it is important to emphasize that the top is a complete representation of the program, but that several refinements are necessary before the pseudocode can be evolved naturally into a JavaScript program. Our first refinement is as follows:

> *Initialize variables*
> *Input the ten exam grades and count passes and failures*
> *Print a summary of the exam results and decide whether tuition should be raised*

Here, too, even though we have a complete representation of the entire program, further refinement is necessary. We now commit to specific variables. Counters are needed to record the passes and failures; a counter will be used to control the looping process, and a variable is needed to store the user input. The pseudocode statement

> *Initialize variables*

may be refined as follows:

> *Initialize passes to zero*
> *Initialize failures to zero*
> *Initialize student to one*

Note that only the counters for the number of passes, the number of failures and the number of students are initialized. The pseudocode statement

> *Input the ten quiz grades and count passes and failures*

requires a loop that successively inputs the result of each exam. Here, it is known in advance that there are precisely 10 exam results, so counter-controlled looping is appropriate. Inside the loop (i.e., **nested** within the loop), a double-selection structure will determine whether each exam result is a pass or a failure and will increment the appropriate counter accordingly. The refinement of the preceding pseudocode statement is then

> *While student counter is less than or equal to ten*
> > *Input the next exam result*
>
> > *If the student passed*
> > > *Add one to passes*
> > *Else*
> > > *Add one to failures*
>
> > *Add one to student counter*

Note the use of blank lines to set off the *If...Else* control structure to improve program readability. The pseudocode statement

> *Print a summary of the exam results and decide whether tuition should be raised*

may be refined as follows:

> *Print the number of passes*
> *Print the number of failures*
> *If more than eight students passed*
>   *Print "Raise tuition"*

The complete second refinement appears in Fig. 8.10. Note that blank lines are also used to set off the *While* statement for program readability.

Initialize passes to zero
Initialize failures to zero
Initialize student to one

While student counter is less than or equal to ten
   Input the next exam result

   If the student passed
      Add one to passes
   Else
      Add one to failures

   Add one to student counter

Print the number of passes
Print the number of failures
If more than eight students passed
   Print "Raise tuition"

Fig. 8.10   Examination-results problem pseudocode.

This pseudocode is now refined sufficiently for conversion to JavaScript. The JavaScript program and two sample executions are shown in Fig. 8.11.

```
1   <?xml version = "1.0"?>
2   <!DOCTYPE html PUBLIC "-//W3C//DTD XHTML 1.0 Strict//EN"
3      "http://www.w3.org/TR/xhtml1/DTD/xhtml1-strict.dtd">
4
5   <!-- Fig. 8.11: analysis.html -->
6   <!-- Analyzing Exam Results   -->
7
8   <html xmlns = "http://www.w3.org/1999/xhtml">
9      <head>
10        <title>Analysis of Examination Results</title>
11
12        <script type = "text/javascript">
13           <!--
14           // initializing variables in declarations
15           var passes = 0,      // number of passes
16               failures = 0,    // number of failures
17               student = 1,     // student counter
18               result;          // one exam result
```

Fig. 8.11   Examination-results calculation program in JavaScript. (Part 1 of 3.)

```
19
20              // process 10 students; counter-controlled loop
21              while ( student <= 10 ) {
22                 result = window.prompt(
23                    "Enter result (1=pass,2=fail)", "0" );
24
25                 if ( result == "1" )
26                    passes = passes + 1;
27                 else
28                    failures = failures + 1;
29
30                 student = student + 1;
31              }
32
33              // termination phase
34              document.writeln( "<h1>Examination Results</h1>" );
35              document.writeln(
36                 "Passed: " + passes + "<br />Failed: " + failures );
37
38              if ( passes > 8 )
39                 document.writeln( "<br />Raise Tuition" );
40              // -->
41           </script>
42
43        </head>
44        <body>
45           <p>Click Refresh (or Reload) to run the script again</p>
46        </body>
47     </html>
```

This dialog is displayed 10 times.
User input is 1, 2, 1, 1, 1, 1, 1, 1, 1
and 1.

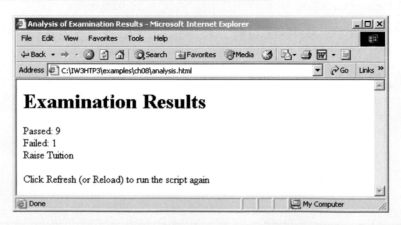

Fig. 8.11   Examination-results calculation program in JavaScript. (Part 2 of 3.)

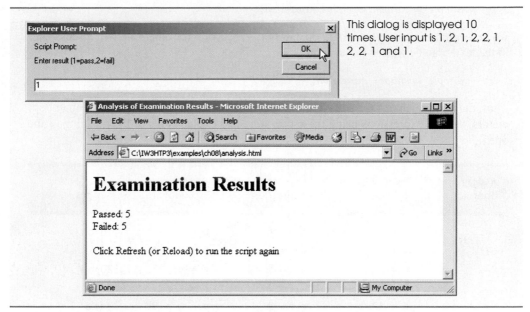

This dialog is displayed 10 times. User input is 1, 2, 1, 2, 2, 1, 2, 2, 1 and 1.

Fig. 8.11   Examination-results calculation program in JavaScript. (Part 3 of 3.)

Lines 15–18 declare the variables used to process the examination results. Note that JavaScript allows variable initialization to be incorporated into declarations (`passes` is assigned 0, `failures` is assigned 0 and `student` is assigned 1). Some programs may require initialization at the beginning of each repetition; such initialization would normally occur in assignment statements.

The processing of the exam results occurs in the `while` statement in lines 21–31. Note that the `if…else` statement in lines 25–28 in the loop tests only whether the exam result was 1; it assumes that all other exam results are 2. Normally, you should validate the values input by the user (i.e., determine whether the values are correct). In the exercises, we ask you to modify this example to validate the input values to ensure that they are either 1 or 2.

Good Programming Practice 8.9

When inputting values from the user, validate the input to ensure that it is correct. If an input value is incorrect, prompt the user to input the value again.

8.11 Assignment Operators

JavaScript provides several assignment operators (called **compound assignment operators**) for abbreviating assignment expressions. For example, the statement

```
c = c + 3;
```

can be abbreviated with the **addition assignment operator, +=,** as

```
c += 3;
```

The += operator adds the value of the expression on the right of the operator to the value of the variable on the left of the operator and stores the result in the variable on the left of the operator. Any statement of the form

$$variable = variable\ operator\ expression;$$

where *operator* is one of the binary operators +, -, *, / or % (or others we will discuss later in the text), can be written in the form

$$variable\ operator=\ expression;$$

Thus, the assignment c += 3 adds 3 to c. Figure 8.12 shows the arithmetic assignment operators, sample expressions using these operators and explanations of the meaning of the operators.

Assignment operator	Initial value of variable	Sample expression	Explanation	Assigns
+=	c = 3	c += 7	c = c + 7	10 to c
-=	d = 5	d -= 4	d = d - 4	1 to d
*=	e = 4	e *= 5	e = e * 5	20 to e
/=	f = 6	f /= 3	f = f / 3	2 to f
%=	g = 12	g %= 9	g = g % 9	3 to g

Fig. 8.12   Arithmetic assignment operators.

Performance Tip 8.1

Programmers can write programs that execute a bit faster when the abbreviated assignment operators are used, because the variable on the left side of the assignment does not have to be evaluated twice.

Performance Tip 8.2

Many of the performance tips we mention in this text result in only nominal improvements, so the reader may be tempted to ignore them. Significant performance improvement often is realized when a supposedly nominal improvement is placed in a loop that may repeat a large number of times.

8.12 Increment and Decrement Operators

JavaScript provides the unary **increment operator** (++) and **decrement operator** (--), (summarized in Fig. 8.13). If a variable c is incremented by 1, the increment operator, ++, can be used rather than the expression c = c + 1 or c += 1. If an increment or decrement operator is placed before a variable, it is referred to as the **preincrement** or **predecrement operator**, respectively. If an increment or decrement operator is placed after a variable, it is referred to as the **postincrement** or **postdecrement operator**, respectively.

Preincrementing (or predecrementing) a variable causes the program to increment (decrement) the variable by 1, then use the new value of the variable in the expression in which it appears. Postincrementing (postdecrementing) the variable causes the program to use the current value of the variable in the expression in which it appears, then increment (decrement) the variable by 1.

Operator	Called	Sample expression	Explanation
++	preincrement	++a	Increment a by 1, then use the new value of a in the expression in which a resides.
++	postincrement	a++	Use the current value of a in the expression in which a resides, then increment a by 1.
--	predecrement	--b	Decrement b by 1, then use the new value of b in the expression in which b resides.
--	postdecrement	b--	Use the current value of b in the expression in which b resides, then decrement b by 1.

Fig. 8.13 increment and decrement operators.

The script in Fig. 8.14 demonstrates the difference between the preincrementing version and the postincrementing version of the ++ increment operator. Postincrementing the variable c causes it to be incremented after it is used in the document.writeln method call (line 20). Preincrementing the variable c causes it to be incremented before it is used in the document.writeln method call (line 27). The program displays the value of c before and after the ++ operator is used. The decrement operator (--) works similarly.

```
1   <?xml version = "1.0"?>
2   <!DOCTYPE html PUBLIC "-//W3C//DTD XHTML 1.0 Strict//EN"
3      "http://www.w3.org/TR/xhtml1/DTD/xhtml1-strict.dtd">
4
5   <!-- Fig. 8.14: increment.html               -->
6   <!-- Preincrementing and Postincrementing -->
7
8   <html xmlns = "http://www.w3.org/1999/xhtml">
9      <head>
10         <title>Preincrementing and Postincrementing</title>
11
12         <script type = "text/javascript">
13            <!--
14            var c;
15
16            c = 5;
17            document.writeln( "<h3>Postincrementing</h3>" );
18            document.writeln( c );                  // print 5
19            // print 5 then increment
20            document.writeln( "<br />" + c++ );
21            document.writeln( "<br />" + c );    // print 6
22
23            c = 5;
24            document.writeln( "<h3>Preincrementing</h3>" );
25            document.writeln( c );                  // print 5
26            // increment then print 6
27            document.writeln( "<br />" + ++c );
```

Fig. 8.14 Preincrementing and postincrementing. (Part 1 of 2.)

```
28            document.writeln( "<br />" + c );    // print 6
29            // -->
30        </script>
31
32    </head><body></body>
33  </html>
```

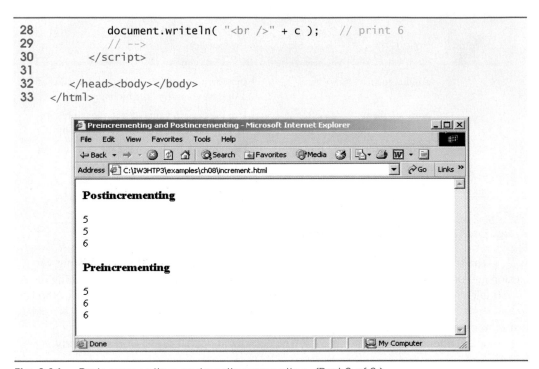

Fig. 8.14 Preincrementing and postincrementing. (Part 2 of 2.)

 Good Programming Practice 8.10

For readability, unary operators should be placed next to their operands, with no intervening spaces.

The three assignment statements in Fig. 8.11 (lines 26, 28 and 30, respectively),

```
passes = passes + 1;
failures = failures + 1;
student = student + 1;
```

can be written more concisely with assignment operators as

```
passes += 1;
failures += 1;
student += 1;
```

with preincrement operators as

```
++passes;
++failures;
++student;
```

or with postincrement operators as

```
passes++;
failures++;
student++;
```

It is important to note here that when incrementing or decrementing a variable in a statement by itself, the preincrement and postincrement forms have the same effect, and the predecrement and postdecrement forms have the same effect. It is only when a variable appears in the context of a larger expression that preincrementing the variable and post-incrementing the variable have different effects. Predecrementing and postdecrementing behave similarly.

Common Programming Error 8.10

Attempting to use the increment or decrement operator on an expression other than a left-hand-value expression is a syntax error. A left-hand-value expression is a variable or expression that can appear on the left side of an assignment operation. For example, writing ++(x + 1) is a syntax error, because (x + 1) is not a left-hand-value expression.

Figure 8.15 lists the precedence and associativity of the operators introduced up to this point. The operators are shown from top to bottom in decreasing order of precedence. The second column describes the associativity of the operators at each level of precedence. Notice that the conditional operator (?:), the unary operators increment (++) and decrement (--) and the assignment operators =, +=, -=, *=, /= and %= associate from right to left. All other operators in the operator precedence table (Fig. 8.15) associate from left to right. The third column names the groups of operators.

Operator	Associativity	Type
++ --	right to left	unary
* / %	left to right	multiplicative
+ -	left to right	additive
< <= > >=	left to right	relational
== !=	left to right	equality
?:	right to left	conditional
= += -= *= /= %=	right to left	assignment

Fig. 8.15   Precedence and associativity of the operators discussed so far.

8.13 Note on Data Types

Unlike its predecessor languages C, C++ and Java, JavaScript does not require variables to have a declared type before they can be used in a program. A variable in JavaScript can contain a value of any data type, and in many situations, JavaScript automatically converts between values of different types for you. For this reason, JavaScript is referred to as a **loosely typed language**. When a variable is declared in JavaScript, but is not given a value, the variable has an **undefined** value. Attempting to use the value of such a variable is normally a logic error.

When variables are declared, they are not assigned default values, unless specified otherwise by the programmer. To indicate that a variable does not contain a value, you can assign the value `null` to the variable.

8.14 Web Resources

There are a tremendous number of resources for JavaScript programmers on the Web. This section lists a few JavaScript and ECMAScript resources available and provides a brief description of each. Additional resources for these topics are presented at the end of other JavaScript chapters as necessary.

www.javascriptmall.com
The *JavaScript Mall* provides free scripts, FAQs, tools for Web pages and a JavaScript tutorial.

developer.netscape.com/tech/javascript
This *JavaScript Reference* provides JavaScript documentation, FAQs, recommended books, newsgroups and much more.

www.mozilla.org/js/language
The *JavaScript Language Resources* page contains technical documentation of the ECMAScript standard, on which JavaScript is based.

SUMMARY

- Any computing problem can be solved by executing a series of actions in a specific order.
- A procedure for solving a problem in terms of the actions to execute and the order in which the actions are to execute is called an algorithm.
- Specifying the order in which statements are to be executed in a computer program is called program control.
- Pseudocode is an artificial and informal language that helps programmers develop algorithms.
- Carefully prepared pseudocode may be converted easily to a corresponding JavaScript program.
- Pseudocode normally describes only executable statements—the actions that are performed when the program is converted from pseudocode to JavaScript and executed.
- Normally, statements in a program execute one after the other, in the order in which they are written. This process is called sequential execution.
- Various JavaScript statements enable the programmer to specify that the next statement to be executed may be other than the next one in sequence. This process is called transfer of control.
- All programs can be written in terms of only three control structures, namely, the sequence structure, the selection structure and the repetition structure.
- A flowchart is a graphical representation of an algorithm or of a portion of an algorithm. Flowcharts are drawn using certain special-purpose symbols, such as rectangles, diamonds, ovals and small circles; these symbols are connected by arrows called flowlines, which indicate the order in which the actions of the algorithm execute.
- JavaScript provides three selection structures. The `if` statement either performs (selects) an action if a condition is true or skips the action if the condition is false. The `if...else` statement performs an action if a condition is true and performs a different action if the condition is false. The `switch` statement performs one of many different actions, depending on the value of an expression.
- JavaScript provides four repetition statements, namely, `while`, `do...while`, `for` and `for...in`.
- Keywords cannot be used as identifiers (e.g., for variable names).
- Single-entry/single-exit control structures make it easy to build programs. Control structures are attached to one another by connecting the exit point of one control structure to the entry point of the next. This procedure is called control-structure stacking. There is only one other way control structures may be connected: control-structure nesting.

- The JavaScript interpreter ignores white space characters: blanks, tabs and newlines used for indentation and vertical spacing. Programmers insert white space characters to enhance program clarity.
- A decision can be made on any expression that evaluates to a value of JavaScript's boolean type (i.e., any expression that evaluates to `true` or `false`).
- The indentation convention you choose should be carefully applied throughout your programs. It is difficult to read programs that do not use uniform spacing conventions.
- The conditional operator (`?:`) is closely related to the `if...else` statement. Operator `?:` is JavaScript's only ternary operator—it takes three operands. The operands together with the `?:` operator form a conditional expression. The first operand is a boolean expression, the second is the value for the conditional expression if the condition evaluates to true and the third is the value for the conditional expression if the condition evaluates to false.
- Nested `if...else` statements test for multiple cases by placing `if...else` statements inside other `if...else` structures.
- The JavaScript interpreter always associates an `else` with the previous `if`, unless told to do otherwise by the placement of braces (`{}`).
- The `if` selection statement expects only one statement in its body. To include several statements in the body of an `if` statement, enclose the statements in braces (`{` and `}`). A set of statements contained within a pair of braces is called a block (sometimes known as a compound statement).
- A logic error has its effect at execution time. A fatal logic error causes a program to fail and terminate prematurely. A nonfatal logic error allows a program to continue executing, but the program produces incorrect results.
- A repetition structure allows the programmer to specify that an action is to be repeated while some condition remains true.
- Counter-controlled repetition is often called definite repetition, because the number of repetitions is known before the loop begins executing.
- Uninitialized variables used in mathematical calculations result in logic errors and produce the value `NaN` (not a number).
- JavaScript represents all numbers as floating-point numbers in memory. Floating-point numbers often develop through division. The computer allocates only a fixed amount of space to hold such a value, so the stored floating-point value can only be an approximation.
- In sentinel-controlled repetition, a special value called a sentinel value (also called a signal value, a dummy value or a flag value) indicates the end of data entry. Sentinel-controlled repetition often is called indefinite repetition, because the number of repetitions is not known in advance.
- It is necessary to choose a sentinel value that cannot be confused with an acceptable input value.
- Top-down, stepwise refinement is a technique essential to the development of well-structured algorithms. The top is a single statement that conveys the overall purpose of the program. As such, the top is, in effect, a complete representation of a program. The stepwise refinement process divides the top into a series of smaller tasks. The programmer terminates the top-down, stepwise refinement process when the pseudocode algorithm is specified in sufficient detail for the programmer to be able to convert the pseudocode to a JavaScript program.
- JavaScript provides the arithmetic assignment operators +=, -=, *=, /= and %=, which abbreviate certain common types of expressions.
- The increment operator, ++, and the decrement operator, --, increment or decrement a variable by 1, respectively. If the operator is prefixed to the variable, the variable is incremented or decremented by 1, then used in its expression. If the operator is postfixed to the variable, the variable is used in its expression, then incremented or decremented by 1.

- JavaScript does not require variables to have a type before they can be used in a program. A variable in JavaScript can contain a value of any data type, and in many situations, JavaScript automatically converts between values of different types for you. For this reason, JavaScript is referred to as a loosely typed language.

- When a variable is declared in JavaScript, but is not given a value, it has an undefined value. Attempting to use the value of such a variable is normally a logic error.

- When variables are declared, they are not assigned default values, unless specified otherwise by the programmer. To indicate that a variable does not contain a value, you can assign the value null to it.

TERMINOLOGY

-- operator
?: operator
++ operator
action
action/decision model
algorithm
arithmetic assignment operators:
    +=, -=, *=, /= and %=
block
body of a loop
compound statement
conditional expression
conditional operator (?:)
control structure
control-structure nesting
control-structure stacking
counter-controlled repetition
decision
decrement operator (--)
definite repetition
double-selection structure
empty statement (;)
flowchart
if selection statement
if...else selection statement
increment operator (++)
indefinite repetition
infinite loop
initialization

logic error
loop counter
loop-continuation condition
nested control structures
null
postdecrement operator
postincrement operator
predecrement operator
preincrement operator
program control
pseudocode
repetition
repetition structure
selection
selection structure
sentinel value
sentinel-controlled repetition
sequence structure
sequential execution
single-entry/single-exit control structure
single-selection structure
stacked control structure
structured programming
syntax error
ternary operator
top-down, stepwise refinement
unary operator
while repetition statement
white space character

SELF-REVIEW EXERCISES

8.1   Fill in the blanks in each of the following statements:

    a) All programs can be written in terms of three types of control structures: _____, _____ and _____.

    b) The _____ double-selection statement is used to execute one action when a condition is true and another action when that condition is false.

    c) Repeting a set of instructions a specific number of times is called _____ repetition.

    d) When it is not known in advance how many times a set of statements will be repeated, a _____ value can be used to terminate the repetition.

8.2 Write four JavaScript statements that each add 1 to variable x, which contains a number.

8.3 Write JavaScript statements to accomplish each of the following tasks:
    a) Assign the sum of x and y to z, and increment the value of x by 1 after the calculation. Use only one statement.
    b) Test whether the value of the variable `count` is greater than 10. If it is, print `"Count is greater than 10"`.
    c) Decrement the variable x by 1, then subtract it from the variable `total`. Use only one statement.
    d) Calculate the remainder after q is divided by `divisor`, and assign the result to q. Write this statement in two different ways.

8.4 Write a JavaScript statement to accomplish each of the following tasks:
    a) Declare variables `sum` and x.
    b) Assign `1` to variable x.
    c) Assign `0` to variable `sum`.
    d) Add variable x to variable `sum`, and assign the result to variable `sum`.
    e) Print `"The sum is: "`, followed by the value of variable `sum`.

8.5 Combine the statements that you wrote in Exercise 8.4 into a JavaScript program that calculates and prints the sum of the integers from 1 to 10. Use the `while` statement to loop through the calculation and increment statements. The loop should terminate when the value of x becomes 11.

8.6 Determine the value of each variable after the calculation is performed. Assume that, when each statement begins executing, all variables have the integer value 5.
    a) `product *= x++;`
    b) `quotient /= ++x;`

8.7 Identify and correct the errors in each of the following segments of code:
    a) `while ( c <= 5 ) {`
            `product *= c;`
            `++c;`
    b) `if ( gender == 1 )`
            `document.writeln( "Woman" );`
       `else;`
            `document.writeln( "Man" );`

8.8 What is wrong with the following `while` repetition statement?
    `while ( z >= 0 )`
       `sum += z;`

ANSWERS TO SELF-REVIEW EXERCISES

8.1 a) Sequence, selection and repetition. b) `if...else.` c) Counter-controlled (or definite). d) Sentinel, signal, flag or dummy.

8.2 `x = x + 1;`
    `x += 1;`
    `++x;`
    `x++;`

8.3 a) `z = x++ + y;`
    b) `if ( count > 10 )`
            `document.writeln( "Count is greater than 10" );`

       c) `total -= --x;`
       d) `q %= divisor;`
          `q = q % divisor;`

8.4   a) `var sum, x;`
       b) `x = 1;`
       c) `sum = 0;`
       d) `sum += x;` or `sum = sum + x;`
       e) `document.writeln( "The sum is: " + sum );`

8.5   The solution is as follows:

```
1   <?xml version = "1.0"?>
2   <!DOCTYPE html PUBLIC "-//W3C//DTD XHTML 1.0 Transitional//EN"
3       "http://www.w3.org/TR/xhtml1/DTD/xhtml1-transitional.dtd">
4
5   <!-- Exercise 8.5: ex08_05.html -->
6
7   <html xmlns = "http://www.w3.org/1999/xhtml">
8       <head><title>Sum the Integers from 1 to 10</title>
9
10          <script type = "text/javascript">
11              <!--
12              var sum, x;
13
14              x = 1;
15              sum = 0;
16
17              while ( x <= 10 ) {
18                  sum += x;
19                  ++x;
20              }
21
22              document.writeln( "The sum is: " + sum );
23              // -->
24          </script>
25
26      </head><body></body>
27   </html>
```

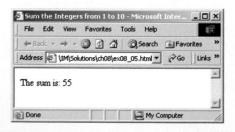

8.6   a) `product = 25, x = 6;`
       b) `quotient = 0.833333..., x = 6;`

8.7   a) Error: Missing the closing right brace of the `while` body.
          Correction: Add closing right brace after the statement `++c;`.

     b) Error: The semicolon after `else` results in a logic error. The second output statement will always be executed.

          Correction: Remove the semicolon after `else`.

8.8   The value of the variable z is never changed in the body of the `while` statement. Therefore, if the loop-continuation condition (z >= 0) is true, an infinite loop is created. To prevent the creation of the infinite loop, z must be decremented so that it eventually becomes less than 0.

EXERCISES

8.9   Identify and correct the errors in each of the following segments of code [*Note*: There may be more than one error in each piece of code]:

     a)
```
if ( age >= 65 );
    document.writeln( "Age greater than or equal to 65" );
else
    document.writeln( "Age is less than 65" );
```

     b)
```
var x = 1, total;
while ( x <= 10 ) {
    total += x;
    ++x;
}
```

     c)
```
While ( x <= 100 )
    total += x;
    ++x;
```

     d)
```
while ( y > 0 ) {
    document.writeln( y );
    ++y;
```

8.10   What does the following program print?

```
1   <?xml version = "1.0"?>
2   <!DOCTYPE html PUBLIC "-//W3C//DTD XHTML 1.0 Transitional//EN"
3       "http://www.w3.org/TR/xhtml1/DTD/xhtml1-transitional.dtd">
4
5   <html xmlns="http://www.w3.org/1999/xhtml">
6       <head><title>Mystery Script</title>
7
8           <script type = "text/javascript">
9               <!--
10              var y, x = 1, total = 0;
11
12              while ( x <= 10 ) {
13                  y = x * x;
14                  document.writeln( y + "<br />" );
15                  total += y;
16                  ++x;
17              }
18
19              document.writeln( "<br />Total is " + total );
20              // -->
21          </script>
22
23      </head><body></body>
24  </html>
```

For Exercises 8.11–8.14, perform each of the following steps:
  a) Read the problem statement.
  b) Formulate the algorithm using pseudocode and top-down, stepwise refinement.
  c) Write a JavaScript program.
  d) Test, debug and execute the JavaScript program.
  e) Process three complete sets of data.

8.11   Drivers are concerned with the mileage obtained by their automobiles. One driver has kept track of several tankfuls of gasoline by recording the number of miles driven and the number of gallons used for each tankful. Develop a JavaScript program that will take as input the miles driven and gallons used (both as integers) for each tankful. The program should calculate and output XHTML text that displays the number of miles per gallon obtained for each tankful and prints the combined number of miles per gallon obtained for all tankfuls up to this point. Use `prompt` dialogs to obtain the data from the user.

8.12   Develop a JavaScript program that will determine whether a department-store customer has exceeded the credit limit on a charge account. For each customer, the following facts are available:
  a) Account number
  b) Balance at the beginning of the month
  c) Total of all items charged by this customer this month
  d) Total of all credits applied to this customer's account this month
  e) Allowed credit limit

The program should input each of these facts from a `prompt` dialog as an integer, calculate the new balance (= *beginning balance + charges – credits*), display the new balance and determine whether the new balance exceeds the customer's credit limit. For customers whose credit limit is exceeded, the program should output XHTML text that displays the message "Credit limit exceeded."

8.13   A large company pays its salespeople on a commission basis. The salespeople receive $200 per week, plus 9% of their gross sales for that week. For example, a salesperson who sells $5000 worth of merchandise in a week receives $200 plus 9% of $5000, or a total of $650. You have been supplied with a list of the items sold by each salesperson. The values of these items are as follows:

Item	Value
1	239.99
2	129.75
3	99.95
4	350.89

Develop a program that inputs one salesperson's items sold for last week, calculates the salesperson's earnings and outputs XHTML text that displays the salesperson's earnings.

8.14   Develop a JavaScript program that will determine the gross pay for each of three employees. The company pays "straight time" for the first 40 hours worked by each employee and pays "time and a half" for all hours worked in excess of 40 hours. You are given a list of the employees of the company, the number of hours each employee worked last week and the hourly rate of each employee. Your program should input this information for each employee, determine the employee's gross pay and output XHTML text that displays the employee's gross pay. Use `prompt` dialogs to input the data.

8.15   The process of finding the largest value (i.e., the maximum of a group of values) is used frequently in computer applications. For example, a program that determines the winner of a sales contest would input the number of units sold by each salesperson. The salesperson who sells the most units wins the contest. Write a pseudocode program and then a JavaScript program that inputs a series of 10 single-digit numbers as characters, determines the largest of the numbers and outputs a message that displays the largest number. Your program should use three variables as follows:

     a) `counter`: A counter to count to 10 (i.e., to keep track of how many numbers have been input and to determine when all 10 numbers have been processed);

     b) `number`: The current digit input to the program;

     c) `largest`: The largest number found so far.

8.16   Write a JavaScript program that uses looping to print the following table of values. Output the results in an XHTML table.

```
N       10*N     100*N    1000*N
1       10       100      1000
2       20       200      2000
3       30       300      3000
4       40       400      4000
5       50       500      5000
```

8.17   Using an approach similar to that in Exercise 8.15, find the *two* largest values among the 10 digits entered. [*Note*: You may input each number only once.]

8.18   Modify the program in Fig. 8.11 to validate its inputs. For every value input, if the value entered is other than 1 or 2, keep looping until the user enters a correct value.

8.19   What does the following program print?

```
1   <?xml version = "1.0"?>
2   <!DOCTYPE html PUBLIC "-//W3C//DTD XHTML 1.0 Transitional//EN"
3       "http://www.w3.org/TR/xhtml1/DTD/xhtml1-transitional.dtd">
4
5   <html xmlns = "http://www.w3.org/1999/xhtml">
6       <head><title>Mystery Script</title>
7
8           <script type = "text/javascript">
9               <!--
10              var count = 1;
11
12              while ( count <= 10 ) {
13                  document.writeln(
14                      count % 2 == 1 ? "****<br />" : "+++++++++<br />" );
15                  ++count;
16              }
17              // -->
18          </script>
19
20      </head><body></body>
21   </html>
```

8.20   What does the following program print?

```
1   <?xml version = "1.0"?>
2   <!DOCTYPE html PUBLIC "-//W3C//DTD XHTML 1.0 Transitional//EN"
3       "http://www.w3.org/TR/xhtml1/DTD/xhtml1-transitional.dtd">
4
5   <html xmlns = "http://www.w3.org/1999/xhtml">
```

(Part 1 of 2.)

```
 6          <head><title>Mystery Script</title>
 7
 8          <script type = "text/javascript">
 9             <!--
10             var row = 10, column;
11
12             while ( row >= 1 ) {
13                column = 1;
14
15                while ( column <= 10 ) {
16                   document.write( row % 2 == 1 ? "<" : ">" );
17                   ++column;
18                }
19
20                --row;
21                document.writeln( "<br />" );
22             }
23             // -->
24          </script>
25
26       </head><body></body>
27    </html>
```

(Part 2 of 2.)

8.21   *(Dangling-Else Problem)* Determine the output for each of the given segments of code when
x is 9 and y is 11, and when x is 11 and y is 9. Note that the interpreter ignores the indentation in a
JavaScript program. Also, the JavaScript interpreter always associates an else with the previous if,
unless told to do otherwise by the placement of braces ({}). The programmer may not be sure at first
glance which if an else matches. This situation is referred to as the "dangling-else" problem. We
have eliminated the indentation from the given code to make the problem more challenging. [*Hint:*
Apply the indentation conventions you have learned.]

```
a)  if ( x < 10 )
    if ( y > 10 )
    document.writeln( "*****<br />" );
    else
    document.writeln( "#####<br />" );
    document.writeln( "$$$$$<br />" );
b)  if ( x < 10 ) {
    if ( y > 10 )
    document.writeln( "*****<br />" );
    }
    else {
    document.writeln( "#####<br />" );
    document.writeln( "$$$$$<br />" );
    }
```

8.22   *(Another Dangling-Else Problem)* Modify the given code to produce the output shown in
each part of this problem. Use proper indentation techniques. You may not make any changes other
than inserting braces and changing the indentation of the code. The interpreter ignores indentation in
a JavaScript program. We have eliminated the indentation from the given code to make the problem
more challenging. [*Note:* It is possible that no modification is necessary for some of the segments of
code.]

```
if ( y == 8 )
if ( x == 5 )
document.writeln( "@@@@@<br />" );
else
document.writeln( "#####<br />" );
document.writeln( "$$$$$<br />" );
document.writeln( "&&&&&<br />" );
```

a) Assuming that x = 5 and y = 8, the following output is produced:

    @@@@@
    $$$$$
    &&&&&

b) Assuming that x = 5 and y = 8, the following output is produced:

    @@@@@

c) Assuming that x = 5 and y = 8, the following output is produced:

    @@@@@
    &&&&&

d) Assuming that x = 5 and y = 7, the following output is produced [*Note*: The last three output statements after the else statements are all part of a block]:

    #####
    $$$$$
    &&&&&

8.23   Write a script that reads in the size of the side of a square and outputs XHTML text that displays a hollow square of that size constructed of asterisks. Use a prompt dialog to read the size from the user. Your program should work for squares of all side sizes between 1 and 20.

8.24   A palindrome is a number or a text phrase that reads the same backward and forward. For example, each of the following five-digit integers is a palindrome: 12321, 55555, 45554 and 11611. Write a script that reads in a five-digit integer and determines whether it is a palindrome. If the number is not five digits long, output XHTML text that displays an alert dialog indicating the problem to the user. Allow the user to enter a new value after dismissing the alert dialog.

8.25   Write a script that outputs XHTML text that displays the following checkerboard pattern:

    * * * * * * * *
     * * * * * * * *
    * * * * * * * *
     * * * * * * * *
    * * * * * * * *
     * * * * * * * *
    * * * * * * * *
     * * * * * * * *

Your program may use only three output statements, one of the form

```
document.write( "* " );
```

one of the form

```
document.write( " " );
```

and one of the form

```
document.writeln();
```

You may use XHTML tags (e.g., <pre>) for alignment purposes.

[*Hint*: Repetition structures are required in this exercise.]

8.26   Write a script that outputs XHTML text that keeps displaying in the browser window the multiples of the integer 2, namely 2, 4, 8, 16, 32, 64, etc. Your loop should not terminate (i.e., you should create an infinite loop). What happens when you run this program?

8.27   A company wants to transmit data over the telephone, but it is concerned that its phones may be tapped. All of its data is transmitted as four-digit integers. It has asked you to write a program that will encrypt its data so that the data may be transmitted more securely. Your script should read a four-digit integer entered by the user in a **prompt** dialog and encrypt it as follows: Replace each digit by *(the sum of that digit plus 7) modulus 10*. Then swap the first digit with the third, and swap the second digit with the fourth. Then output XHTML text that displays the encrypted integer.

8.28   Write a program that inputs an encrypted four-digit integer (from Exercise 8.27) and decrypts it to form the original number.

JavaScript: Control Statements II

Objectives

- To be able to use the `for` and `do...while` repetition statements to execute statements in a program repeatedly.
- To understand multiple selection using the `switch` selection statement.
- To be able to use the `break` and `continue` program-control statements.
- To be able to use the logical operators.

Who can control his fate?
William Shakespeare

The used key is always bright.
Benjamin Franklin

9.1 Introduction

Chapter 8 began our introduction to the types of building blocks that are available for problem solving and used them to employ proven program-construction principles. In this chapter, we continue our presentation of the theory and principles of structured programming by introducing JavaScripts's remaining control statements (with the exception of for...in, which is presented in Chapter 11). As in Chapter 8, the JavaScript techniques you will learn here are applicable to most high-level languages. In later chapters, we will see that the control structures we study in this chapter and Chapter 8 are helpful in manipulating objects.

9.2 Essentials of Counter-Controlled Repetition

Counter-controlled repetition requires:

1. The *name* of a control variable (or loop counter).

2. The *initial value* of the control variable.

3. The *increment* (or *decrement*) by which the control variable is modified each time through the loop (also known as *each iteration of the loop*).

4. The condition that tests for the *final value* of the control variable to determine whether looping should continue.

To see the four elements of counter-controlled repetition, consider the simple script shown in Fig. 9.1, which displays lines of XHTML text that illustrate the seven different font sizes supported by XHTML. The declaration in line 14 *names* the control variable (`counter`), reserves space for it in memory and sets it to an *initial value* of 1. Declarations that include initialization are, in effect, executable statements.

The declaration and initialization of `counter` could also have been accomplished by the following declaration and statement:

```
1   <?xml version = "1.0"?>
2   <!DOCTYPE html PUBLIC "-//W3C//DTD XHTML 1.0 Strict//EN"
3       "http://www.w3.org/TR/xhtml1/DTD/xhtml1-strict.dtd">
4
5   <!-- Fig. 9.1: WhileCounter.html   -->
6   <!-- Counter-Controlled Repetition -->
7
8   <html xmlns = "http://www.w3.org/1999/xhtml">
9      <head>
10         <title>Counter-Controlled Repetition</title>
11
12         <script type = "text/javascript">
13            <!--
14            var counter = 1;              // initialization
15
16            while ( counter <= 7 ) {      // repetition condition
17               document.writeln( "<p style = \"font-size: " +
18                  counter + "ex\">XHTML font size " + counter +
19                  "ex</p>" );
20               ++counter;                 // increment
21            }
22            // -->
23         </script>
24
25      </head><body></body>
26   </html>
```

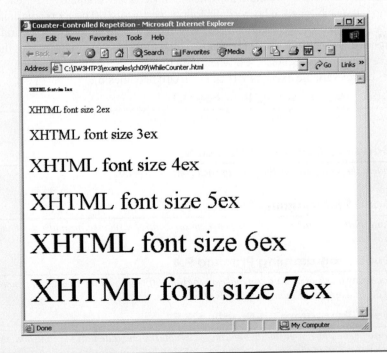

Fig. 9.1   Counter-controlled repetition.

```
var counter;           // declare counter
counter = 1;           // initialize counter to 1
```

The declaration is not executable, but the assignment statement is. We use both methods of initializing variables throughout the book.

Lines 17–19 in the `while` statement write a paragraph element consisting of the string "XHTML `font size`" concatenated with the control variable `counter`'s value, which represents the font size. An inline CSS `style` attribute sets the `font-size` property to the value of `counter` concatenated to `ex`. Note the use of the escape sequence \", which is placed around attribute `style`'s value. Because the double-quote character delimits the beginning and end of a string literal in JavaScript, it cannot be used in the contents of the string unless it is preceded by a \ to create the escape sequence \". For example, if `counter` is 5, the preceding statement produces the markup

```
<p style = "font-size: 5ex">XHTML font size 5ex</p>
```

XHTML allows either single quotes (') or double quotes (") to be placed around the value specified for an attribute. JavaScript allows single quotes to be placed in a string literal. Thus, we could have placed single quotes around the `font-size` property to produce equivalent XHTML output without the use of escape sequences.

Common Programming Error 9.1

Placing a double-quote (") character inside a string literal that is delimited by double quotes causes a runtime error when the script is interpreted. To be displayed as part of a string literal, a double-quote (") character must be preceded by a \ to form the escape sequence \".

Line 20 in the `while` statement *increments* the control variable by 1 for each iteration of the loop (i.e., each time the body of the loop is performed). The loop-continuation condition (line 16) in the `while` statement tests whether the value of the control variable is less than or equal to 7 (the *final value* for which the condition is `true`). Note that the body of this `while` statement executes even when the control variable is 7. The loop terminates when the control variable exceeds 7 (i.e., `counter` becomes 8).

Good Programming Practice 9.1

Use integer values to control the counting of loops.

Good Programming Practice 9.2

Indent the statements in the body of each control structure.

Good Programming Practice 9.3

Put a blank line before and after each major control structure, to make it stand out in the program.

Good Programming Practice 9.4

Too many levels of nesting can make a program difficult to understand. As a general rule, try to avoid using more than three levels of nesting.

Good Programming Practice 9.5

Vertical spacing above and below control structures and indentation of the bodies of control structures within the headers of the control structure give programs a two-dimensional appearance that enhances readability.

9.3 for Repetition Statement

The **for repetition statement** handles all the details of counter-controlled repetition. Figure 9.2 illustrates the power of the for statement by reimplementing the script of Fig. 9.1.

```
1   <?xml version = "1.0"?>
2   <!DOCTYPE html PUBLIC "-//W3C//DTD XHTML 1.0 Strict//EN"
3      "http://www.w3.org/TR/xhtml1/DTD/xhtml1-strict.dtd">
4
5   <!-- Fig. 9.2: ForCounter.html                        -->
6   <!-- Counter-Controlled Repetition with for statement -->
7
8   <html xmlns = "http://www.w3.org/1999/xhtml">
9      <head>
10        <title>Counter-Controlled Repetition</title>
11
12        <script type = "text/javascript">
13           <!--
14           // Initialization, repetition condition and
15           // incrementing are all included in the for
16           // statement header.
17           for ( var counter = 1; counter <= 7; ++counter )
18              document.writeln( "<p style = \"font-size: " +
19                 counter + "ex\">XHTML font size " + counter +
20                 "ex</p>" );
21           // -->
22        </script>
23
24     </head><body></body>
25  </html>
```

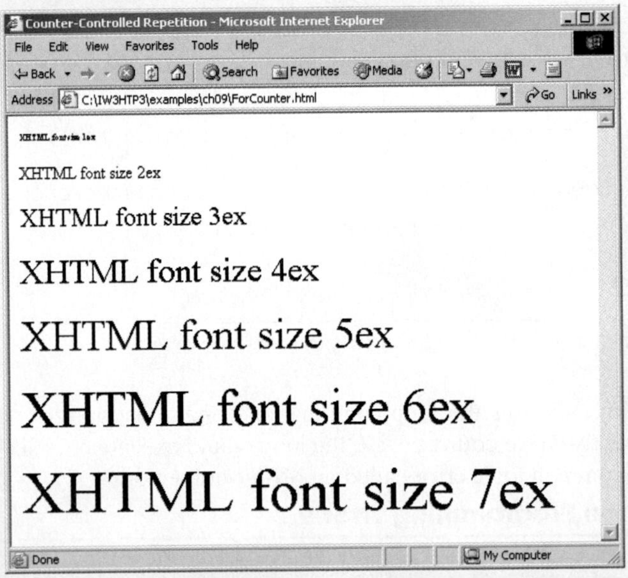

Fig. 9.2   Counter-controlled repetition with the for statement.

When the `for` statement begins executing (line 17), the control variable `counter` is declared and is initialized to 1 (i.e., the first statement of the `for` statement declares the control variable's *name* and provides the control variable's *initial value*). Next, the loop-continuation condition, `counter <= 7`, is checked. The condition contains the *final value* (7) of the control variable. The initial value of `counter` is 1. Therefore, the condition is satisfied (i.e., `true`), so the body statement (lines 18–20) writes a paragraph element in the XHTML document. Then, variable `counter` is incremented in the expression `++counter` and the loop continues execution with the loop-continuation test. The control variable is now equal to 2, so the final value is not exceeded and the program performs the body statement again (i.e., performs the next iteration of the loop). This process continues until the control variable `counter` becomes 8, at which point the loop-continuation test fails and the repetition terminates.

The program continues by performing the first statement after the `for` statement. (In this case, the script terminates, because the interpreter reaches the end of the script.)

Note that `counter` is declared inside the `for` statement in this example, but this practice is not required. Variable `counter` could have been declared before the `for` statement or not declared at all. Remember that JavaScript does not explicitly require variables to be declared before they are used. If a variable is used without being declared, the JavaScript interpreter creates the variable at the point of its first use in the script.

Figure 9.3 takes a closer look at the `for` statement of Fig. 9.2. The `for` statement's first line (including the keyword `for` and everything in parentheses after `for`) is often called the **`for` statement header**. Note that the `for` statement "does it all"—it specifies each of the items needed for counter-controlled repetition with a control variable. If there is more than one statement in the body of the `for` statement, braces (`{` and `}`) are required to define the body of the loop.

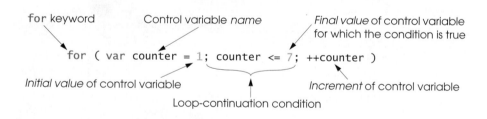

Fig. 9.3   `for` statement header components.

Note that Fig. 9.3 uses the loop-continuation condition `counter <= 7`. If the programmer incorrectly wrote `counter < 7`, the loop would execute only six times. This is an example of the common logic error called an **off-by-one error**.

Common Programming Error 9.2

Using an incorrect relational operator or an incorrect final value of a loop counter in the condition of a `while`, `for` or `do...while` statement can cause an off-by-one error or an infinite loop.

Good Programming Practice 9.6

Using the final value in the condition of a `while` *or* `for` *statement and using the <= relational operator will help avoid off-by-one errors. For a loop used to print the values 1 to 10, for example, the initial value of* `counter` *should be one, and the loop-continuation condition should be* `counter <= 10` *rather than* `counter < 10` *(which is an off-by-one error) or* `counter < 11` *(which is correct). Many programmers, however, prefer so-called zero-based counting, in which, to count 10 times through the loop,* `counter` *would be initialized to zero and the loop-continuation test would be* `counter < 10`.

The general format of the `for` statement is

```
for ( initialization; loopContinuationTest; increment )
    statement;
```

where the *initialization* expression names the loop's control variable and provides its initial value, *loopContinuationTest* is the expression that tests the loop-continuation condition (containing the final value of the control variable for which the condition is true), and *increment* is an expression that increments the control variable. The `for` statement can be represented by an equivalent `while` statement, with *initialization*, *loopContinuationTest* and *increment* placed as follows:

```
initialization;

while ( loopContinuationTest ) {
    statement;
    increment;
}
```

There is an exception to this rule that we will discuss in Section 9.7.

If the *initialization* expression in the `for` statement's header is the first definition of the control variable, the control variable can still be used after the `for` statement in the script. The part of a script in which a variable name can be used is known as the variable's **scope**. Scope is discussed in detail in Chapter 10, JavaScript: Functions.

Good Programming Practice 9.7

Place only expressions involving the control variable in the initialization and increment sections of a `for` *statement. Manipulations of other variables should appear either before the loop (if they execute only once, like initialization statements) or in the loop body (if they execute once per iteration of the loop, like incrementing or decrementing statements).*

The three expressions in the `for` statement are optional. If *loopContinuationTest* is omitted, JavaScript assumes that the loop-continuation condition is `true`, thus creating an infinite loop. One might omit the *initialization* expression if the control variable is initialized elsewhere in the program before the loop. One might omit the *increment* expression if the increment is calculated by statements in the body of the `for` statement or if no increment is needed. The increment expression in the `for` statement acts like a stand-alone statement at the end of the body of the `for` statement. Therefore, the expressions

```
counter = counter + 1
counter += 1
```

```
++counter
counter++
```

are all equivalent in the incrementing portion of the for statement. Many programmers prefer the form counter++. This is because the incrementing of the control variable occurs after the body of the loop is executed, and therefore the postincrementing form seems more natural. Preincrementing and postincrementing both have the same effect in our example because the variable being incremented does not appear in an expression. The two semicolons in the for statement are required.

Common Programming Error 9.3

Using commas instead of the two required semicolons in the header of a for statement is a syntax error.

Common Programming Error 9.4

Placing a semicolon immediately to the right of the right parenthesis of the header of a for statement makes the body of that for statement an empty statement. This code normally results in a logic error.

The initialization, loop-continuation condition and increment portions of a for statement can contain arithmetic expressions. For example, assume that x = 2 and y = 10. If x and y are not modified in the body of the loop, then the statement

```
for ( var j = x; j <= 4 * x * y; j += y / x )
```

is equivalent to the statement

```
for ( var j = 2; j <= 80; j += 5 )
```

The "increment" of a for statement may be negative, in which case it is really a decrement and the loop actually counts downward.

If the loop-continuation condition initially is false, the body of the for statement is not performed. Instead, execution proceeds with the statement following the for statement.

The control variable frequently is printed or used in calculations in the body of a for statement, but it does not have to be. Very often, the control variable is used for controlling repetition but never mentioned in the body of the for statement.

Error-Prevention Tip 9.1

Although the value of the control variable can be changed in the body of a for loop, avoid changing it, because doing so can lead to subtle errors.

The for statement is flowcharted much like the while statement. For example, Fig. 9.4 shows the flowchart of the for statement

```
for ( var counter = 1; counter <= 7; ++counter )
    document.writeln( "<p style = \"font-size: " +
        counter + "ex\">XHTML font size " + counter +
        "ex</p>" );
```

This flowchart makes it clear that the initialization occurs only once and that incrementing occurs *after* each execution of the body statement. Note that, besides small circles and arrows, the flowchart contains only rectangle symbols and a diamond symbol.

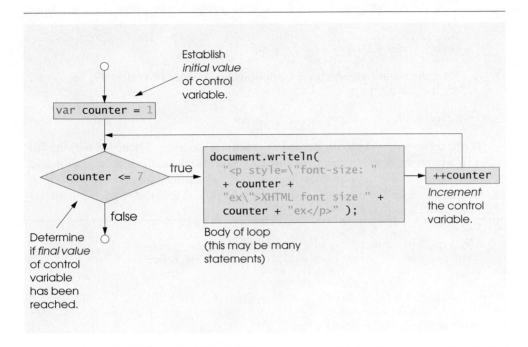

Fig. 9.4   `for` repetition statement flowchart.

9.4 Examples Using the `for` Statement

The examples in this section show methods of varying the control variable in a `for` statement. In each case, we write the appropriate `for` header. Note the change in the relational operator for loops that decrement the control variable.

Common Programming Error 9.5

Not using the proper relational operator in the loop-continuation condition of a loop that counts downward (e.g., using `i <= 1` in a loop that counts down to 1) is usually a logic error that will yield incorrect results when the program runs.

a) Vary the control variable from 1 to 100 in increments of 1.

```
for ( var i = 1; i <= 100; ++i )
```

b) Vary the control variable from 100 to 1 in increments of –1 (i.e., decrements of 1).

```
for ( var i = 100; i >= 1; --i )
```

c) Vary the control variable from 7 to 77 in steps of 7.

```
for ( var i = 7; i <= 77; i += 7 )
```

d) Vary the control variable from 20 to 2 in steps of –2.

```
for ( var i = 20; i >= 2; i -= 2 )
```

e) Vary the control variable over the following sequence of values: 2, 5, 8, 11, 14, 17, 20.

```
for ( var j = 2; j <= 20; j += 3 )
```

f) Vary the control variable over the following sequence of values: 99, 88, 77, 66, 55, 44, 33, 22, 11, 0.

```
for ( var j = 99; j >= 0; j -= 11 )
```

The next two scripts demonstrate the for repetition statement. Figure 9.5 uses the for statement to sum the even integers from 2 to 100. Note that the increment expression adds 2 to the control variable number after the body executes during each iteration of the loop. The loop terminates when number has the value 102 (which is not added to the sum).

```
1   <?xml version = "1.0"?>
2   <!DOCTYPE html PUBLIC "-//W3C//DTD XHTML 1.0 Strict//EN"
3      "http://www.w3.org/TR/xhtml1/DTD/xhtml1-strict.dtd">
4
5   <!-- Fig. 9.5: Sum.html                          -->
6   <!-- Using the for repetition statement -->
7
8   <html xmlns = "http://www.w3.org/1999/xhtml">
9      <head>
10         <title>Sum the Even Integers from 2 to 100</title>
11
12         <script type = "text/javascript">
13            <!--
14            var sum = 0;
15
16            for ( var number = 2; number <= 100; number += 2 )
17               sum += number;
18
19            document.writeln( "The sum of the even integers " +
20               "from 2 to 100 is " + sum );
21            // -->
22         </script>
23
24      </head><body></body>
25   </html>
```

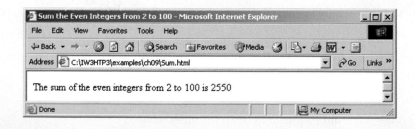

Fig. 9.5   Summation with for.

Note that the body of the for statement in Fig. 9.5 actually could be merged into the rightmost (increment) portion of the for header by using a **comma**, as follows:

```
for ( var number = 2; number <= 100; sum += number, number += 2)
   ;
```

Similarly, the initialization sum = 0 could be merged into the initialization section of the for statement.

Good Programming Practice 9.8

Although statements preceding a for and in the body of a for can often be merged into the for header, avoid doing so, because it makes the program more difficult to read.

Good Programming Practice 9.9

For clarity, limit the size of control-structure headers to a single line, if possible.

The next example computes compound interest (compounded yearly) using the for statement. Consider the following problem statement:

A person invests $1000.00 in a savings account yielding 5% interest. Assuming that all the interest is left on deposit, calculate and print the amount of money in the account at the end of each year for 10 years. Use the following formula to determine the amounts:

$$a = p \left(1 + r\right)^{n}$$

where

p is the original amount invested (i.e., the principal)
r is the annual interest rate
n is the number of years
a is the amount on deposit at the end of the nth year.

This problem involves a loop that performs the indicated calculation for each of the 10 years the money remains on deposit. Figure 9.6 presents the solution to this problem, displaying the results in a table.

```
1   <?xml version = "1.0"?>
2   <!DOCTYPE html PUBLIC "-//W3C//DTD XHTML 1.0 Strict//EN"
3      "http://www.w3.org/TR/xhtml1/DTD/xhtml1-strict.dtd">
4
5   <!-- Fig. 9.6: Interest.html              -->
6   <!-- Using the for repetition statement -->
7
8   <html xmlns = "http://www.w3.org/1999/xhtml">
9      <head>
10         <title>Calculating Compound Interest</title>
11
12         <script type = "text/javascript">
13            <!--
14            var amount, principal = 1000.0, rate = .05;
15
```

Fig. 9.6   Compound interest calculation with for loop. (Part 1 of 2.)

```
16            document.writeln(
17               "<table border = \"1\" width = \"100%\">" );
18            document.writeln(
19               "<caption>Calculating Compound Interest</caption>" );
20            document.writeln(
21               "<thead><tr><th align = \"left\">Year</th>" );
22            document.writeln(
23               "<th align = \"left\">Amount on deposit</th>" );
24            document.writeln( "</tr></thead>" );
25
26            for ( var year = 1; year <= 10; ++year ) {
27               amount = principal * Math.pow( 1.0 + rate, year );
28               document.writeln( "<tbody><tr><td>" + year +
29                  "</td><td>" + Math.round( amount * 100 ) / 100 +
30                  "</td></tr>" );
31            }
32
33            document.writeln( "</tbody></table>" );
34            // -->
35         </script>
36
37      </head><body></body>
38   </html>
```

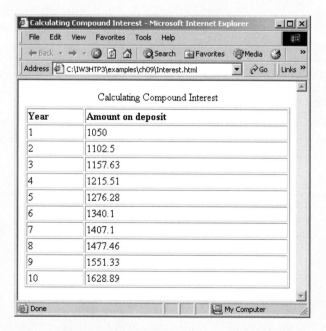

Fig. 9.6   Compound interest calculation with `for` loop. (Part 2 of 2.)

Line 14 declares three variables and initializes `principal` to `1000.0` and `rate` to `.05`. Lines 16–17 write an XHTML `<table>` tag that has a `border` of 1 and a `width` of 100% (the table uses the entire width of the browser window). After lines 16–17 write the initial attributes of the `table` element, lines 18–19 write the `caption` that summarizes the table's content. Lines 20–21 create the table's header (`<thead>`), a row (`<tr>`) and a table heading (`<th>`) that left aligns "`Year.`" Lines 22–24 create a table heading for "`Amount on deposit`" and write the closing `</tr>` and `</thead>` tags.

The `for` statement (lines 26–31) executes its body 10 times, varying control variable `year` from 1 to 10 in increments of 1 (note that `year` represents n in the problem statement). JavaScript does not include an exponentiation operator. Instead, we use the **Math** object's **pow** method for this purpose. `Math.pow(x, y)` calculates the value of x raised to the yth power. Method `Math.pow` takes two numbers as arguments and returns the result.

Line 27 performs the calculation given in the problem statement

$$a = p\,(1 + r)^{\,n}$$

where a is `amount`, p is `principal`, r is `rate` and n is `year`.

Lines 28–30 write a line of XHTML markup that creates another row in the table. The first column is the current `year` value, and the second column is the result of the expression

```
Math.round( amount * 100 ) / 100
```

which multiplies the current value of `amount` by 100 to convert the value from dollars to cents, then uses the `Math` object's **round** method to round the value to the closest integer. The result is divided by 100, to produce a dollar value that has a maximum of two digits to the right of the decimal point. Unlike many other programming languages, JavaScript does not provide numeric-formatting capabilities that allow you to precisely control the display format of a number. When the loop terminates, line 33 writes the closing `</tbody>` and `</table>` tags.

Variables `amount`, `principal` and `rate` represent numbers in this script. Remember that JavaScript represents all numbers as floating-point numbers. This feature is convenient in this example, because we are dealing with fractional parts of dollars and need a type that allows decimal points in its values. Unfortunately, floating-point numbers can cause trouble. Here is a simple example of what can go wrong when using floating-point numbers to represent dollar amounts (assuming that dollar amounts are displayed with two digits to the right of the decimal point): Two dollar amounts stored in the machine could be 14.234 (which would normally be rounded to 14.23 for display purposes) and 18.673 (which would normally be rounded to 18.67 for display purposes). When these amounts are added, they produce the internal sum 32.907, which would normally be rounded to 32.91 for display purposes. Thus your printout could appear as

```
   14.23
 + 18.67
 ───────
   32.91
```

but a person adding the individual numbers as printed would expect the sum to be 32.90! You have been warned!

9.5 `switch` Multiple-Selection Statement

Previously, we discussed the `if` single-selection statement and the `if...else` double-selection statement. Occasionally, an algorithm will contain a series of decisions in which a variable or expression is tested separately for each of the values it may assume, and different actions are taken for each value. JavaScript provides the `switch` multiple-selection statement to handle such decision making. The script in Fig. 9.7 demonstrates one of three different XHTML list formats determined by the value the user enters.

```
1   <?xml version = "1.0"?>
2   <!DOCTYPE html PUBLIC "-//W3C//DTD XHTML 1.0 Strict//EN"
3       "http://www.w3.org/TR/xhtml1/DTD/xhtml1-strict.dtd">
4
5   <!-- Fig. 9.7: SwitchTest.html  -->
6   <!-- Using the switch statement -->
7
8   <html xmlns = "http://www.w3.org/1999/xhtml">
9      <head>
10         <title>Switching between XHTML List Formats</title>
11
12         <script type = "text/javascript">
13            <!--
14            var choice,              // user's choice
15                startTag,            // starting list item tag
16                endTag,              // ending list item tag
17                validInput = true,   // indicates if input is valid
18                listType;            // list type as a string
19
20            choice = window.prompt( "Select a list style:\n" +
21               "1 (bullet), 2 (numbered), 3 (lettered)", "1" );
22
23            switch ( choice ) {
24               case "1":
25                  startTag = "<ul>";
26                  endTag = "</ul>";
27                  listType = "<h1>Bullet List</h1>";
28                  break;
29               case "2":
30                  startTag = "<ol>";
31                  endTag = "</ol>";
32                  listType = "<h1>Ordered List: Numbered</h1>";
33                  break;
34               case "3":
35                  startTag = "<ol type = \"A\">";
36                  endTag = "</ol>";
37                  listType = "<h1>Ordered List: Lettered</h1>";
38                  break;
39               default:
40                  validInput = false;
41            }
42
43            if ( validInput == true ) {
44               document.writeln( listType + startTag );
45
46               for ( var i = 1; i <= 3; ++i )
47                  document.writeln( "<li>List item " + i + "</li>" );
```

Fig. 9.7   `switch` multiple-selection statement. (Part 1 of 3.)

```
48
49              document.writeln( endTag );
50          }
51          else
52              document.writeln( "Invalid choice: " + choice );
53          // -->
54      </script>
55
56    </head>
57    <body>
58      <p>Click Refresh (or Reload) to run the script again</p>
59    </body>
60  </html>
```

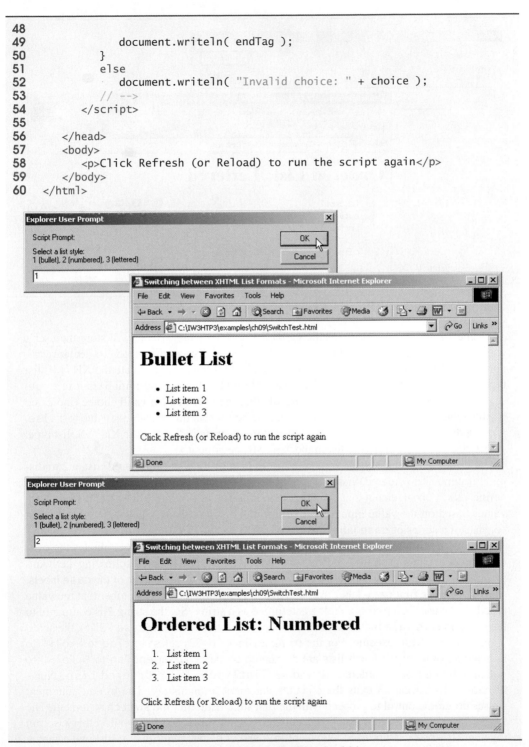

Fig. 9.7   switch multiple-selection statement. (Part 2 of 3.)

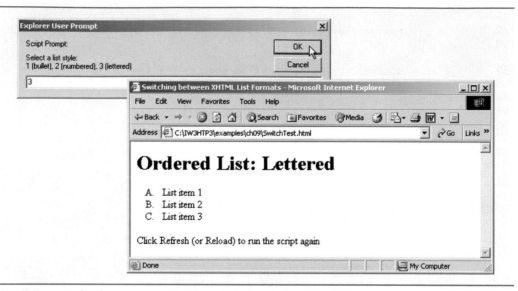

Fig. 9.7   switch multiple-selection statement. (Part 3 of 3.)

Line 14 in the script declares the variable `choice`. This variable will store the user's choice, which determines what type of XHTML list to display. Lines 15–16 declare variables `startTag` and `endTag`, which store the XHTML tags that indicate the XHTML list type the user chooses. Line 17 declares variable `validInput` and initializes it to `true`. The script uses this variable to determine whether the user made a valid choice (indicated by the value of `true`). If a choice is invalid, the script sets this variable's value to `false`. Line 18 declares variable `listType`, which stores a string indicating the XHTML list type. This string appears before the list in the XHTML document.

Lines 20–21 prompt the user to enter a 1 to display a bullet (unordered) list, a 2 to display a numbered (ordered) list and a 3 to display a lettered (ordered) list. Lines 23–41 define a `switch` statement that assigns to the variables `startTag`, `endTag` and `listType` values based on the value input by the user in the `prompt` dialog. The `switch` statement consists of a series of **case labels** and an optional **default case**.

When the flow of control reaches the `switch` statement, the script evaluates the **controlling expression** (`choice` in this example) in the parentheses following keyword `switch`. The value of this expression is compared with the value in each of the `case` labels, starting with the first `case` label. Assume that the user entered 2. Remember that the value typed by the user in a `prompt` dialog is returned as a string. So, the string 2 is compared to the string in each `case` in the `switch` statement. If a match occurs (`case "2":`), the statements for that `case` execute. For the string 2 (lines 30–32) set `startTag` to "`<ol>`" to indicate an ordered list (such lists are numbered by default), set `endTag` to "`</ol>`" to indicate the end of an ordered list and set `listType` to "`<h1>Ordered List: Numbered</h1>`". Line 33 exits the `switch` statement immediately. The `break` statement causes program control to proceed with the first statement after the `switch` statement. The `break` statement is used because the `cases` in a `switch` statement would otherwise run together. If `break` is not used anywhere in a `switch` statement, then each time a match occurs in the statement, the statements for all the remaining `cases` execute. If no match occurs between the controlling expression's value and a `case` label, the `default` case executes and sets variable `validInput` to `false`.

Next, the flow of control continues with the `if` statement in line 43, which tests variable `validInput` to determine whether its value is `true`. If so, lines 44–49 write the `listType`, the `startTag`, three list items (`<li>`) and the `endTag`. Otherwise, the script writes text in the XHTML document indicating that an invalid choice was made.

Each `case` can have multiple actions (statements). The `switch` statement is different from other statements in that braces are not required around multiple actions in a `case` of a `switch`. The general `switch` statement (i.e., using a `break` in each `case`) is flowcharted in Fig. 9.8. [*Note*: As an exercise, flowchart the general `switch` statement without `break` statements.]

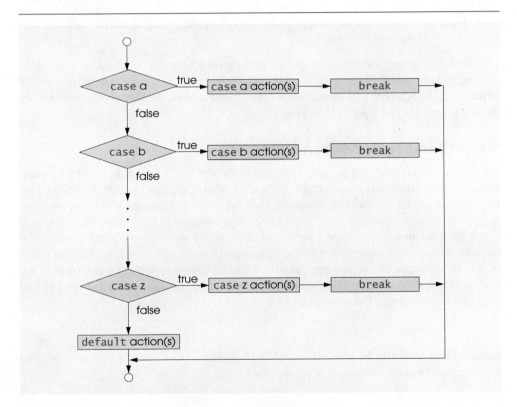

Fig. 9.8   `switch` multiple-selection statement.

The flowchart makes it clear that each `break` statement at the end of a `case` causes control to exit from the `switch` statement immediately. The `break` statement is not required for the last `case` in the `switch` statement (or the `default` case, when it appears last), because program control automatically continues with the next statement after the `switch` statement.

Common Programming Error 9.6

*Forgetting a **break** statement when one is needed in a **switch** statement is a logic error.*

Good Programming Practice 9.10

Provide a `default` case in `switch` statements. Cases not explicitly tested in a `switch` statement without a `default` case are ignored. Including a `default` case focuses the programmer on processing exceptional conditions. However, there are situations in which no `default` processing is needed.

Good Programming Practice 9.11

Although the `case` clauses and the `default` case clause in a `switch` statement can occur in any order, it is a good programming practice to place the `default` clause last.

Good Programming Practice 9.12

In a `switch` statement, when the `default` clause is listed last, the `break` for that `case` statement is not required. Some programmers include this `break` for clarity and for symmetry with other `cases`.

Note that having several `case` labels listed together (e.g., `case 1: case 2:` with no statements between the cases) simply means that the same set of actions is to occur for each of the cases. Again, note that, besides small circles and arrows, the flowchart contains only rectangle symbols and diamond symbols.

9.6 do...while Repetition Statement

The `do...while` repetition statement is similar to the `while` statement. In the `while` statement, the loop-continuation test occurs at the beginning of the loop, before the body of the loop executes. The `do...while` statement tests the loop-continuation condition *after* the loop body executes; therefore, *the loop body always executes at least once.* Please refer to Fig. 9.20 at the end of the chapter for a flowchart of this statement. When a `do...while` terminates, execution continues with the statement after the `while` clause. Note that it is not necessary to use braces in a `do...while` statement if there is only one statement in the body. However, the braces usually are included, to avoid confusion between the `while` and `do...while` statements. For example,

```
while ( condition )
```

normally is regarded as the header to a `while` statement. A `do...while` statement with no braces around a single-statement body appears as

```
do
    statement;
while ( condition );
```

which can be confusing. The last line—`while( condition );`—may be misinterpreted by the reader as a `while` statement containing an empty statement (the semicolon by itself). Thus, to avoid confusion, the `do...while` statement with one statement is often written as follows:

```
do {
    statement;
} while ( condition );
```

Good Programming Practice 9.13

Some programmers always include braces in a do...while statement even if they are not necessary. This procedure helps eliminate ambiguity between the while statement and the do...while statement containing one statement.

Common Programming Error 9.7

Infinite loops are caused when the loop-continuation condition never becomes false in a while, for or do...while statement. To prevent this, make sure that there is not a semicolon immediately after the header of a while or for statement. In a counter-controlled loop, make sure that the control variable is incremented (or decremented) in the body of the loop. In a sentinel-controlled loop, make sure that the sentinel value is eventually input.

The script in Fig. 9.9 uses a do...while statement to display each of the six different XHTML header types (h1 through h6). Line 14 declares control variable counter and initializes it to 1. Upon entering the do...while statement, lines 17–19 write a line of XHTML text in the document. The value of control variable counter is used both to create the starting and ending header tags (e.g., <h1> and </h1>) and to create the line of text to display (e.g., This is an h1 level heading). Line 21 increments the counter before the loop-continuation test occurs at the bottom of the loop.

The do...while flowchart in Fig. 9.10 makes it clear that the loop-continuation test does not occur until the action executes at least once.

```
1    <?xml version = "1.0"?>
2    <!DOCTYPE html PUBLIC "-//W3C//DTD XHTML 1.0 Strict//EN"
3       "http://www.w3.org/TR/xhtml1/DTD/xhtml1-strict.dtd">
4
5    <!-- Fig. 9.9: DoWhileTest.html    -->
6    <!-- Using the do...while statement -->
7
8    <html xmlns = "http://www.w3.org/1999/xhtml">
9       <head>
10          <title>Using the do...while Repetition Statement</title>
11
12          <script type = "text/javascript">
13             <!--
14             var counter = 1;
15
16             do {
17                document.writeln( "<h" + counter + ">This is " +
18                   "an h" + counter + " level head" + "</h" +
19                   counter + ">" );
20
21                ++counter;
22             } while ( counter <= 6 );
23             // -->
24          </script>
25
26       </head><body></body>
27    </html>
```

Fig. 9.9   do...while repetition statement. (Part 1 of 2.)

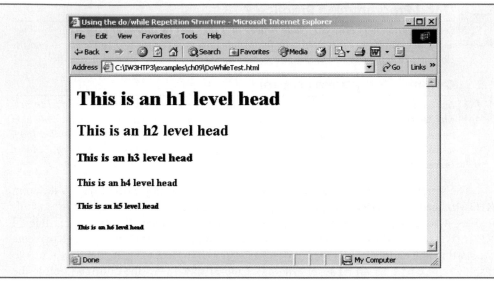

Fig. 9.9   do...while repetition statement. (Part 2 of 2.)

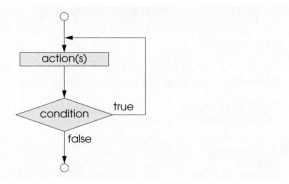

Fig. 9.10   do...while repetition statement flowchart.

9.7 break and continue Statements

The **break** and **continue** statements alter the flow of control. The break statement, when executed in a while, for, do...while or switch statement, causes immediate exit from the statement. Execution continues with the first statement after the structure. The break statement is commonly used to escape early from a loop or to skip the remainder of a switch statement (as in Fig. 9.7). Figure 9.11 demonstrates the break statement in a for repetition statement.

```
1   <?xml version = "1.0"?>
2   <!DOCTYPE html PUBLIC "-//W3C//DTD XHTML 1.0 Strict//EN"
3       "http://www.w3.org/TR/xhtml1/DTD/xhtml1-strict.dtd">
```

Fig. 9.11   break statement in a for statement. (Part 1 of 2.)

```
4
5    <!-- Fig. 9.11: BreakTest.html    -->
6    <!-- Using the break statement    -->
7
8    <html xmlns = "http://www.w3.org/1999/xhtml">
9       <head>
10         <title>
11            Using the break Statement in a for Statement
12         </title>
13
14         <script type = "text/javascript">
15            <!--
16            for ( var count = 1; count <= 10; ++count ) {
17               if ( count == 5 )
18                  break;   // break loop only if count == 5
19
20               document.writeln( "Count is: " + count + "<br />" );
21            }
22
23            document.writeln(
24               "Broke out of loop at count = " + count );
25            // -->
26         </script>
27
28      </head><body></body>
29   </html>
```

Fig. 9.11   break statement in a for statement. (Part 2 of 2.)

During each iteration of the for statement in lines 16–21, the script writes the value of count in the XHTML document. When the if statement in line 17 detects that count is 5, the break in line 18 executes. This statement terminates the for statement, and the program proceeds to line 23 (the next statement in sequence immediately after the for statement), where the script writes the value of count when the loop terminated (i.e., 5). The loop executes its body only four times.

The continue statement, when executed in a while, for or do…while statement, skips the remaining statements in the body of the statement and proceeds with the next iteration of the loop. In while and do…while statements, the loop-continuation test evaluates immediately after the continue statement executes. In for statements, the increment expression executes, then the loop-continuation test evaluates. This is the one case in which for and while differ. Improper placement of continue before the increment in a while may result in an infinite loop.

Figure 9.12 uses continue in a for statement to skip the document.writeln statement in line 21 when the if statement in line 17 determines that the value of count is 5. When the continue statement executes, the script skips the remainder of the for statement's body. Program control continues with the increment of the for statement's control variable, followed by the loop-continuation test to determine whether the loop should continue executing.

Good Programming Practice 9.14

Some programmers feel that break and continue violate structured programming. They do not use break and continue because the effects of these statements can be achieved by structured programming techniques.

Performance Tip 9.1

The break and continue statements, when used properly, perform faster than the corresponding structured techniques.

Software Engineering Observation 9.1

There is a tension between achieving quality software engineering and achieving the best-performing software. Often, one of these goals is achieved at the expense of the other. For all but the most performance-intensive situations, the following rule of thumb should be followed: First make your code simple, readable and correct; then make it fast and small, but only if necessary.

```
1   <?xml version = "1.0"?>
2   <!DOCTYPE html PUBLIC "-//W3C//DTD XHTML 1.0 Strict//EN"
3       "http://www.w3.org/TR/xhtml1/DTD/xhtml1-strict.dtd">
4
5   <!-- Fig. 9.12: ContinueTest.html  -->
6   <!-- Using the break statement      -->
7
8   <html xmlns = "http://www.w3.org/1999/xhtml">
9       <head>
10          <title>
11             Using the continue Statement in a for Statement
12          </title>
13
14          <script type = "text/javascript">
15             <!--
16             for ( var count = 1; count <= 10; ++count ) {
17                if ( count == 5 )
18                   continue;  // skip remaining code in loop
19                              // only if count == 5
20
21                document.writeln( "Count is: " + count + "<br />" );
22             }
23
```

Fig. 9.12   continue statement in a for statement. (Part 1 of 2.)

```
24              document.writeln( "Used continue to skip printing 5" );
25              // -->
26          </script>
27
28      </head><body></body>
29  </html>
```

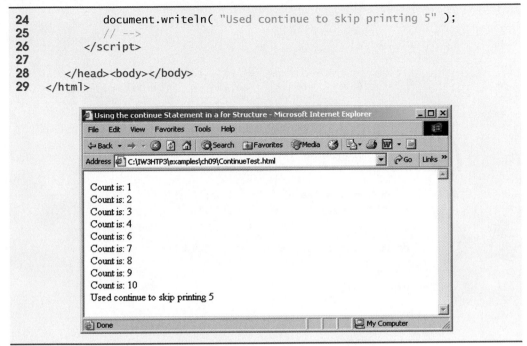

Fig. 9.12   `continue` statement in a `for` statement. (Part 2 of 2.)

9.8 Labeled break and continue Statements

The `break` statement can break out of an immediately enclosing `while`, `for`, `do...while` or `switch` statement. To break out of a nested set of structures, you can use the **labeled break statement**. This statement, when executed in a `while`, `for`, `do...while` or `switch` statement, causes immediate exit from that statement and any number of enclosing repetition statements; program execution resumes with the first statement after the enclosing **labeled statement** (a statement preceded by a label). The labeled statement can be a compound statement (a set of statements enclosed in curly braces, {}). Labeled `break` statements commonly are used to terminate nested looping structures containing `while`, `for`, `do...while` or `switch` statements. Figure 9.13 demonstrates the labeled `break` statement in a nested `for` statement.

```
1   <?xml version = "1.0"?>
2   <!DOCTYPE html PUBLIC "-//W3C//DTD XHTML 1.0 Strict//EN"
3       "http://www.w3.org/TR/xhtml1/DTD/xhtml1-strict.dtd">
4
5   <!-- Fig. 9.13: BreakLabelTest.html         -->
6   <!-- Using the break statement with a Label -->
7
8   <html xmlns = "http://www.w3.org/1999/xhtml">
9       <head>
10          <title>Using the break Statement with a Label</title>
```

Fig. 9.13   Labeled `break` statement in a nested `for` statement. (Part 1 of 2.)

```
11
12          <script type = "text/javascript">
13             <!--
14          stop: {     // labeled block
15             for ( var row = 1; row <= 10; ++row ) {
16                for ( var column = 1; column <= 5 ; ++column ) {
17
18                   if ( row == 5 )
19                      break stop; // jump to end of stop block
20
21                   document.write( "* " );
22                }
23
24                document.writeln( "<br />" );
25             }
26
27             // the following line is skipped
28             document.writeln( "This line should not print" );
29          }
30
31          document.writeln( "End of script" );
32             // -->
33          </script>
34
35       </head><body></body>
36    </html>
```

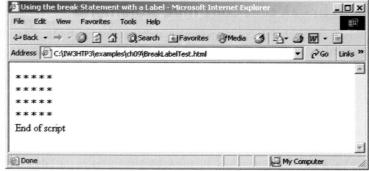

Fig. 9.13   Labeled break statement in a nested for statement. (Part 2 of 2.)

The labeled block (lines 14–29) begins with a **label** (an identifier followed by a colon). Here, we use the label stop:. The block is enclosed between the braces at the end of line 14 and in line 29, and includes both the nested for statement starting in line 15 and the document.writeln statement in line 28. When the if statement in line 18 detects that row is equal to 5, the statement in line 19 executes. This statement terminates both the for statement in line 16 and its enclosing for statement in line 15, and the program proceeds to the statement in line 31 (the first statement in sequence after the labeled block). The inner for statement executes its body only four times. Note that the document.writeln statement in line 28 never executes, because it is included in the labeled block and the outer for statement never completes.

The `continue` statement proceeds with the next iteration (repetition) of the immediately enclosing `while`, `for` or `do...while` statement. The **labeled `continue` statement**, when executed in a repetition statement (`while`, `for` or `do...while`), skips the remaining statements in the structure's body and any number of enclosing repetition statements, then proceeds with the next iteration of the enclosing **labeled repetition statement** (a repetition statement preceded by a label). In labeled `while` and `do...while` statements, the loop-continuation test evaluates immediately after the `continue` statement executes. In a labeled `for` statement, the increment expression executes, then the loop-continuation test evaluates. Figure 9.14 uses the labeled `continue` statement in a nested `for` statement to cause execution to continue with the next iteration of the outer `for` statement.

The labeled `for` statement (lines 14–26) starts with the `nextRow` label in line 14. When the `if` statement in line 20 in the inner `for` statement detects that `column` is greater than `row`, line 21 executes and program control continues with the increment of the control variable of the outer `for` loop. Even though the inner `for` statement counts from 1 to 10, the number of * characters output on a row never exceeds the value of `row`.

```
1   <?xml version = "1.0"?>
2   <!DOCTYPE html PUBLIC "-//W3C//DTD XHTML 1.0 Strict//EN"
3      "http://www.w3.org/TR/xhtml1/DTD/xhtml1-strict.dtd">
4
5   <!-- Fig. 9.14: ContinueLabelTest.html -->
6   <!-- Using the continue statement        -->
7
8   <html xmlns = "http://www.w3.org/1999/xhtml">
9      <head>
10        <title>Using the continue Statement with a Label</title>
11
12        <script type = "text/javascript">
13           <!--
14        nextRow:    // target label of continue statement
15           for ( var row = 1; row <= 5; ++row ) {
16              document.writeln( "<br />" );
17
18              for ( var column = 1; column <= 10; ++column ) {
19
20                 if ( column > row )
21                    continue nextRow; // next iteration of
22                                      // labeled loop
23
24                 document.write( "* " );
25              }
26           }
27           // -->
28        </script>
29
30     </head><body></body>
31   </html>
```

Fig. 9.14   Labeled `continue` statement in a nested `for` statement. (Part 1 of 2.)

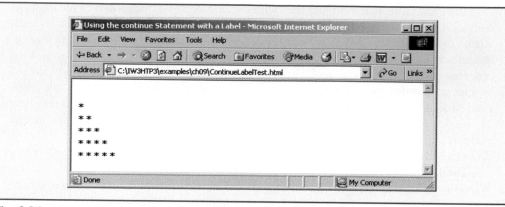

Fig. 9.14   Labeled `continue` statement in a nested `for` statement. (Part 2 of 2.)

9.9 Logical Operators

So far, we have studied only such **simple conditions** as `count <= 10`, `total > 1000` and `number != sentinelValue`. These conditions were expressed in terms of the relational operators `>`, `<`, `>=` and `<=` and in terms of the equality operators `==` and `!=`. Each decision tested one condition. To test multiple conditions in the process of making a decision, we performed these tests in separate statements or in nested `if` or `if...else` statements.

JavaScript provides **logical operators** that can be used to form more complex conditions by combining simple conditions. The logical operators are **&& (logical AND)**, **|| (logical OR)** and **! (logical NOT**, also called **logical negation**). We consider examples of each of these operators.

Suppose that, at some point in a program, we wish to ensure that two conditions are *both* `true` before we choose a certain path of execution. In this case, we can use the logical `&&` operator, as follows:

```
if ( gender == 1 && age >= 65 )
   ++seniorFemales;
```

This `if` statement contains two simple conditions. The condition `gender == 1` might be evaluated to determine, for example, whether a person is a female. The condition `age >= 65` is evaluated to determine whether a person is a senior citizen. The two simple conditions are evaluated first, because the precedences of `==` and `>=` are both higher than the precedence of `&&`. The `if` statement then considers the combined condition

```
gender == 1 && age >= 65
```

This condition is `true` *if and only if* both of the simple conditions are `true`. Finally, if this combined condition is indeed `true`, the count of `seniorFemales` is incremented by 1. If either or both of the simple conditions are `false`, the program skips the incrementing and proceeds to the statement following the `if` statement. The preceding combined condition can be made more readable by adding redundant parentheses:

```
( gender == 1 ) && ( age >= 65 )
```

The table in Fig. 9.15 summarizes the `&&` operator. The table shows all four possible combinations of `false` and `true` values for *expression1* and *expression2*. Such tables are often called **truth tables**. JavaScript evaluates to `false` or `true` all expressions that include relational operators, equality operators and/or logical operators.

expression1	expression2	expression1 && expression2
`false`	`false`	`false`
`false`	`true`	`false`
`true`	`false`	`false`
`true`	`true`	`true`

Fig. 9.15   Truth table for the && (logical AND) operator.

Now let us consider the `||` (logical OR) operator. Suppose we wish to ensure that either *or* both of two conditions are `true` before we choose a certain path of execution. In this case, we use the `||` operator, as in the following program segment:

```
if ( semesterAverage >= 90 || finalExam >= 90 )
    document.writeln( "Student grade is A" );
```

This statement also contains two simple conditions. The condition `semesterAverage >= 90` is evaluated to determine whether the student deserves an "A" in the course because of a solid performance throughout the semester. The condition `finalExam >= 90` is evaluated to determine whether the student deserves an "A" in the course because of an outstanding performance on the final exam. The `if` statement then considers the combined condition

```
semesterAverage >= 90 || finalExam >= 90
```

and awards the student an "A" if either or both of the simple conditions are `true`. Note that the message `"Student grade is A"` is *not* printed only when both of the simple conditions are `false`. Figure 9.16 is a truth table for the logical OR operator (`||`).

expression1	expression2	expression1 || expression2
`false`	`false`	`false`
`false`	`true`	`true`
`true`	`false`	`true`
`true`	`true`	`true`

Fig. 9.16   Truth table for the || (logical OR) operator.

The && operator has a higher precedence than the `||` operator. Both operators associate from left to right. An expression containing && or `||` operators is evaluated only until truth or falsity is known. Thus, evaluation of the expression

```
gender == 1 && age >= 65
```

will stop immediately if `gender` is not equal to 1 (i.e., the entire expression is `false`) and continues if `gender` is equal to 1 (i.e., the entire expression could still be `true` if the condition `age >= 65` is `true`). This performance feature for evaluation of logical AND and logical OR expressions is called **short-circuit evaluation**.

JavaScript provides the `!` (logical negation) operator to enable a programmer to "reverse" the meaning of a condition (i.e., a `true` value becomes `false`, and a `false` value becomes `true`). Unlike the logical operators `&&` and `||`, which combine two conditions (i.e., they are binary operators), the logical negation operator has only a single condition as an operand (i.e., it is a unary operator). The logical negation operator is placed before a condition to choose a path of execution if the original condition (without the logical negation operator) is `false`, as in the following program segment:

```
if ( ! ( grade == sentinelValue ) )
    document.writeln( "The next grade is " + grade );
```

The parentheses around the condition `grade == sentinelValue` are needed, because the logical negation operator has a higher precedence than the equality operator. Figure 9.17 is a truth table for the logical negation operator.

expression	! expression
false	true
true	false

Fig. 9.17   Truth table for operator `!` (logical negation).

In most cases, the programmer can avoid using logical negation by expressing the condition differently with an appropriate relational or equality operator. For example, the preceding statement may also be written as follows:

```
if ( grade != sentinelValue )
    document.writeln( "The next grade is " + grade );
```

This flexibility can help a programmer express a condition in a more convenient manner.

The script in Fig. 9.18 demonstrates all the logical operators by producing their truth tables. The script produces an XHTML table containing the results.

In the output of Fig. 9.18, the strings `"false"` and `"true"` indicate `false` and `true` for the operands in each condition. The result of the condition is shown as `true` or `false`. Note that when you add a boolean value to a string, JavaScript automatically adds the string "`false`" or "`true`", depending on the boolean value. Lines 14–42 build an XHTML table containing the results.

An interesting feature of JavaScript is that most non-boolean values can be converted to a boolean `true` or `false` value. Nonzero numeric values are considered to be `true`. The numeric value zero is considered to be `false`. Any string that contains characters is considered to be `true`. The empty string (i.e., the string containing no characters) is considered to be `false`. The value `null` and variables that have been declared but not initialized are considered to be `false`. All objects (e.g., the browser's `document` and `window` objects and JavaScript's `Math` object) are considered to be `true`.

Figure 9.19 shows the precedence and associativity of the JavaScript operators introduced up to this point. The operators are shown from top to bottom in decreasing order of precedence.

```
1   <?xml version = "1.0"?>
2   <!DOCTYPE html PUBLIC "-//W3C//DTD XHTML 1.0 Strict//EN"
3       "http://www.w3.org/TR/xhtml1/DTD/xhtml1-strict.dtd">
4
5   <!-- Fig. 9.18: LogicalOperators.html  -->
6   <!-- Demonstrating Logical Operators    -->
7
8   <html xmlns = "http://www.w3.org/1999/xhtml">
9      <head>
10         <title>Demonstrating the Logical Operators</title>
11
12         <script type = "text/javascript">
13            <!--
14            document.writeln(
15               "<table border = \"1\" width = \"100%\">" );
16
17            document.writeln(
18               "<caption>Demonstrating Logical " +
19               "Operators</caption" );
20
21            document.writeln(
22               "<tr><td width = \"25%\">Logical AND (&&)</td>" +
23               "<td>false && false: " + ( false && false ) +
24               "<br />false && true: " + ( false && true ) +
25               "<br />true && false: " + ( true && false ) +
26               "<br />true && true: " + ( true && true ) +
27               "</td>" );
28
29            document.writeln(
30               "<tr><td width = \"25%\">Logical OR (||)</td>" +
31               "<td>false || false: " + ( false || false ) +
32               "<br />false || true: " + ( false || true ) +
33               "<br />true || false: " + ( true || false ) +
34               "<br />true || true: " + ( true || true ) +
35               "</td>" );
36
37            document.writeln(
38               "<tr><td width = \"25%\">Logical NOT (!)</td>" +
39               "<td>!false: " + ( !false ) +
40               "<br />!true: " + ( !true ) + "</td>" );
41
42            document.writeln( "</table>" );
43            // -->
44         </script>
45
46      </head><body></body>
47   </html>
```

Fig. 9.18 Logical operators used in a JavaScript. (Part 1 of 2.)

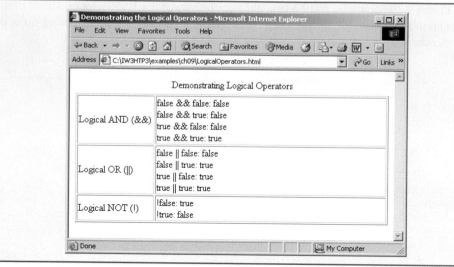

Fig. 9.18   Logical operators used in a JavaScript. (Part 2 of 2.)

Operator	Associativity	Type
++ -- !	right to left	unary
* / %	left to right	multiplicative
+ -	left to right	additive
< <= > >=	left to right	relational
== !=	left to right	equality
&&	left to right	logical AND
||	left to right	logical OR
?:	right to left	conditional
= += -= *= /= %=	right to left	assignment

Fig. 9.19   Precedence and associativity of the operators discussed so far.

9.10 Summary of Structured Programming

Just as architects design buildings by employing the collective wisdom of their profession, so should programmers design programs. Our field is younger than architecture, and our collective wisdom is considerably sparser. We have learned that structured programming produces programs that are easier to understand than unstructured programs and thus are easier to test, debug, modify and even prove correct in a mathematical sense.

Flowcharts reveal the structured nature of programs or the lack thereof. Connecting individual flowchart symbols arbitrarily can lead to unstructured programs. Therefore, the programming profession has chosen to combine flowchart symbols to form a limited set of control structures and to build structured programs by properly combining control structures in two simple ways.

For simplicity, only single-entry/single-exit control structures are used—that is, there is only one way to enter and one way to exit each control structure. Connecting control structures in sequence to form structured programs is simple: The exit point of one control structure is connected to the entry point of the next control structure (i.e., the control structures are simply placed one after another in a program). We have called this process **control structure stacking**. The rules for forming structured programs also allow for control structures to be nested. Figure 9.20 summarizes JavaScript's control structures. Small circles are used in the figure to indicate the single entry point and the single exit point of each structure.

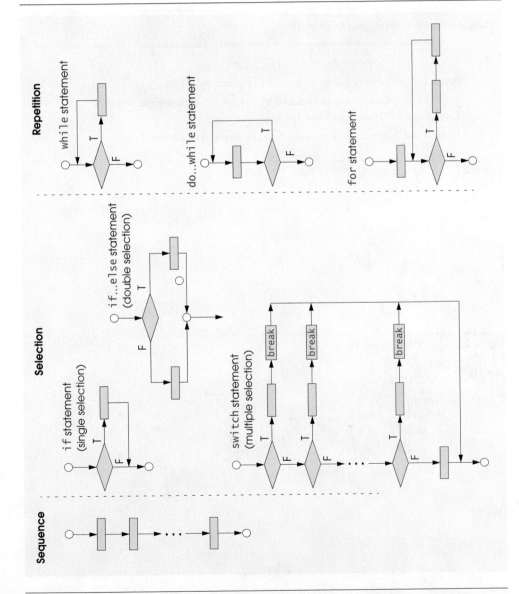

Fig. 9.20   Single-entry/single-exit sequence, selection and repetition structures.

Figure 9.21 shows the rules for forming properly structured programs. The rules assume that the rectangle flowchart symbol may be used to indicate any action, including input/output. [*Note*: An oval flowchart symbol indicates the beginning and end of a process.]

Applying the rules in Fig. 9.21 always results in structured flowchart with a neat, building-block-like appearance. For example, repeatedly applying rule 2 to the simplest flowchart (Fig. 9.22) results in a structured flowchart containing many rectangles in sequence (Fig. 9.23). Note that Rule 2 generates a stack of control structures; so let us call rule 2 the **stacking rule**.

Rules for Forming Structured Programs

1) Begin with the "simplest flowchart" (Fig. 9.22).

2) Any rectangle (action) can be replaced by two rectangles (actions) in sequence.

3) Any rectangle (action) can be replaced by any control structure (sequence, if, if...else, switch, while, do...while or for).

4) Rules 2 and 3 may be applied as often as you like and in any order.

Fig. 9.21   Forming rules for structured programs.

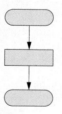

Fig. 9.22   Simplest flowchart.

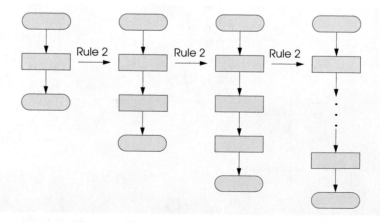

Fig. 9.23   Repeatedly applying Rule 2 of Fig. 9.21 to the simplest flowchart.

Rule 3 is called the **nesting rule**. Repeatedly applying Rule 3 to the simplest flowchart results in a flowchart with neatly nested control structures. For example, in Fig. 9.24, the rectangle in the simplest flowchart is first replaced with a double-selection (if...else) structure. Then Rule 3 is applied again to both of the rectangles in the double-selection structure by replacing each of these rectangles with double-selection structures. The dashed box around each of the double-selection structures represents the rectangle in the original simplest flowchart that was replaced.

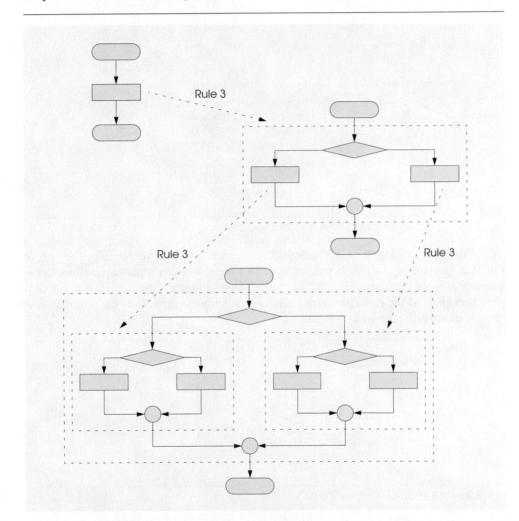

Fig. 9.24   Applying Rule 3 of Fig. 9.21 to the simplest flowchart.

Rule 4 generates larger, more involved and more deeply nested structures. The flowcharts that emerge from applying the rules in Fig. 9.21 constitute the set of all possible structured flowcharts and thus the set of all possible structured programs.

The beauty of the structured approach is that we use only seven simple single-entry/single-exit pieces and assemble them in only two simple ways. Figure 9.25 shows the kinds of stacked building blocks that emerge from applying Rule 2 and the kinds of nested building blocks that emerge from applying Rule 3. The figure also shows the kind of overlapped building blocks that cannot appear in structured flowcharts (because of the elimination of the goto statement).

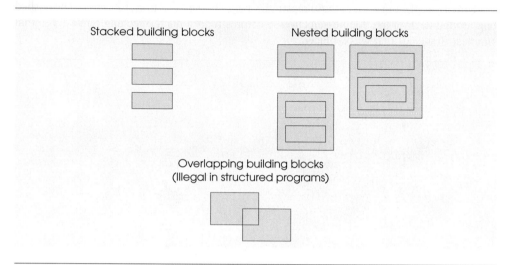

Fig. 9.25   Stacked, nested and overlapped building blocks.

If the rules in Fig. 9.21 are followed, an unstructured flowchart (like the one in Fig. 9.26) cannot be created. If you are uncertain about whether a particular flowchart is structured, apply the rules of Fig. 9.21 in reverse to try to reduce the flowchart to the simplest flowchart. If the flowchart is reducible to the simplest flowchart, the original flowchart is structured; otherwise, it is not.

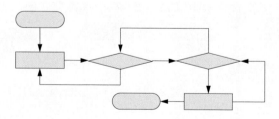

Fig. 9.26   Unstructured flowchart.

Structured programming promotes simplicity. Bohm and Jacopini have given us the result that only three forms of control are needed:

- sequence
- selection
- repetition

Sequence is trivial. Selection is implemented in one of three ways:

- **if** statement (single selection)
- **if...else** statement (double selection)
- **switch** statement (multiple selection)

In fact, it is straightforward to prove that the **if** statement is sufficient to provide any form of selection; everything that can be done with the **if...else** statement and the **switch** statement can be implemented by combining **if** statements (although perhaps not as smoothly).

Repetition is implemented in one of four ways:

- **while** statement
- **do...while** statement
- **for** statement
- **for...in** statement (discussed in Chapter 11)

It is straightforward to prove that the **while** statement is sufficient to provide any form of repetition. Everything that can be done with the **do...while** statement and the **for** statement can be done with the **while** statement (although perhaps not as elegantly).

Combining these results illustrates that any form of control ever needed in a JavaScript program can be expressed in terms of:

- sequence
- **if** statement (selection)
- **while** statement (repetition)

These control structures can be combined in only two ways—stacking and nesting. Indeed, structured programming promotes simplicity.

In this chapter, we have discussed the composition of programs from control structures containing actions and decisions. In Chapter 10, we will introduce another program-structuring unit, called the **function**. We will learn to compose large programs by combining functions that are composed of control structures. We will also discuss how functions promote software reusability.

9.11 Web Resources

www.w3schools.com/js/js_looping.asp
The *W3Schools* Web site offers several JavaScript tutorials based on W3C standards, including this tutorial on looping with the **for**, **while** and **do...while** control structures.

www.devguru.com/Technologies/ecmascript/quickref/javascript_intro.html
The *DevGuru JavaScript Quick Reference* offers a comprehensive guide to JavaScript/JScript/ECMAScript and includes additional examples of the control structures and other language features presented in this book.

SUMMARY

- Counter-controlled repetition requires the name of a control variable (or loop counter), the initial value of the control variable, the increment (or decrement) by which the control variable is modified each time through the loop (also known as *each iteration of the loop*) and the condition that tests for the final value of the control variable to determine whether looping should continue.

- The double-quote character cannot be used in the contents of a string unless it is preceded by a \, to create the escape sequence \".
- The for repetition statement handles all the details of counter-controlled repetition.
- JavaScript does not require variables to be declared before they are used. If a variable is used without being declared, the JavaScript interpreter creates the variable at the point of its first use in a script.
- The for statement's first line (including the keyword for and everything in parentheses after for) is often called the for statement header.
- Braces ({ and }) are required to define the body of a for loop with multiple statements in its body.
- The general format of the header for a for statement is

      for (*initialization*; *loopContinuationTest*; *increment*)
          statement;

  where the *initialization* expression names the loop's control variable and provides its initial value, the *loopContinuationTest* expression is the loop-continuation condition and *increment* is an expression that increments the control variable.
- In most cases, the for statement can be represented by an equivalent while statement, with *initialization*, *loopContinuationTest* and *increment* placed as follows:

      initialization;

      while (*loopContinuationTest*) {
          statement;
          increment;
      }

- The three expressions in the for statement are optional. If *loopContinuationTest* is omitted, the loop-continuation condition is true, thus creating an infinite loop. Omit the *initialization* expression if the control variable is initialized in the program before the loop. Omit the *increment* expression if the increment is calculated in the body of the for statement or if no increment is needed.
- The increment expression in a for statement acts like a stand-alone statement at the end of the for statement's body.
- The initialization, loop-continuation condition and increment portions of a for statement can contain arithmetic expressions.
- The "increment" of a for statement may be negative, in which case it is really a decrement and the loop actually counts downward.
- If the loop-continuation condition is initially false, the body of the for statement is not performed.
- JavaScript does not include an exponentiation operator. The Math object's pow method calculates the value of x raised to the yth power and returns the result.
- The Math object's round method rounds its argument to the closest integer.
- The switch multiple-selection statement handles a series of decisions in which a variable or expression is tested separately for each of the values it may assume, and different actions are taken, depending on the value.
- The switch statement consists of a series of case labels and an optional default case. When the flow of control reaches the switch statement, the controlling expression in the parentheses following keyword switch is evaluated. The value of this expression is compared with the value in each of the case labels, starting with the first case label. If a match occurs, the statements for

that `case` are executed. If no match occurs between the controlling expression's value and the value in a `case` label, the statements in the `default` case execute.

- Each `case` can have multiple actions (statements). The `switch` statement is different from other structures in that braces are not required around multiple actions in a `case` of a `switch`.

- The `break` statement at the end of a `case` causes control to immediately exit the `switch` statement. The `break` statement is not required for the last `case` (or the `default` case when it appears last), because program control automatically continues with the next statement after the `switch` statement.

- Listing several `case` labels together means that the same action is to occur for each of the cases.

- The `do`…`while` statement tests the loop-continuation condition after the body of the loop is performed; therefore, the body of the loop is always executed at least once.

- Braces are not necessary in the `do`…`while` statement if there is only one statement in the body. The braces are usually included to avoid confusion between the `while` and `do`…`while` statements.

- The `break` statement, when executed in a `while`, `for`, `do`…`while` or `switch` statement, causes immediate exit from that structure.

- The `continue` statement, when executed in a `while`, `for` or `do`…`while` statement, skips the remaining statements in the body of that statement and proceeds with the next iteration of the loop.

- The labeled `break` statement, when executed in a `while`, `for`, `do`…`while` or `switch` statement, causes immediate exit from that statement and any number of enclosing repetition statements; program execution resumes with the first statement after the enclosing labeled (compound) statement.

- The labeled `continue` statement, when executed in a repetition statement (`while`, `for` or `do`…`while`), skips the remaining statements in that statement's body and in any number of enclosing repetition statements and proceeds with the next iteration of the enclosing labeled loop.

- JavaScript provides the logical operators `&&` (logical AND), `||` (logical OR) and `!` (logical NOT), which may be used to form more complex conditions by combining simple conditions.

- A logical AND (`&&`) condition is `true` if and only if both of its operands are `true`. A logical OR (`||`) condition is `true` if either or both of its operands are `true`.

- An expression containing `&&` or `||` operators is evaluated only until its truth or falsity is known. This performance feature is called short-circuit evaluation.

- The unary logical negation (`!`) operator reverses the meaning of a condition.

- JavaScript uses only single-entry/single-exit control structures—that is, there is only one way to enter and one way to exit each control structure.

- Structured programming promotes simplicity. Any form of control ever needed in a program can be expressed in terms of the sequence structure, the `if` statement (selection) or the `while` statement (repetition). These control structures can be combined in only two ways—stacking and nesting.

- Selection is implemented in one of three ways: the `if` statement (single selection), the `if`…`else` statement (double selection) or the `switch` statement (multiple selection).

- Repetition is implemented in one of four ways: the `while` statement, the `do`…`while` statement, the `for` statement or the `for/in` statement.

TERMINOLOGY

`!` operator	`case` label
`&&` operator	`continue`
`||` operator	counter-controlled repetition
`break`	`default` case in `switch`

definite repetition	loop-continuation condition
do...while repetition statement	multiple selection
for repetition statement	nested control structure
infinite loop	off-by-one error
labeled break statement	repetition structure
labeled block	scroll box
labeled continue statement	scrollbar
labeled repetition statement	short-circuit evaluation
logical AND (&&)	single-entry/single-exit control structure
logical negation (!)	stacked control structure
logical operator	switch selection statement
logical OR (||)	while repetition statement

SELF-REVIEW EXERCISES

9.1   State whether each of the following is *true* or *false*. If *false*, explain why.
  a) The default case is required in the switch selection statement.
  b) The break statement is required in the default case of a switch selection statement.
  c) The expression (x > y && a < b) is true if either x > y is true or a < b is true.
  d) An expression containing the || operator is true if either or both of its operands is true.

9.2   Write a JavaScript statement or a set of statements to accomplish each of the following tasks:
  a) Sum the odd integers between 1 and 99. Use a for statement. Assume that the variables sum and count have been declared.
  b) Calculate the value of 2.5 raised to the power of 3. Use the pow method.
  c) Print the integers from 1 to 20 by using a while loop and the counter variable x. Assume that the variable x has been declared, but not initialized. Print only five integers per line. [*Hint*: Use the calculation x % 5. When the value of this expression is 0, use document.write("<br />") to output a line break in the XHTML document.]
  d) Repeat Exercise 9.2 (c), but using a for statement.

9.3   Find the error in each of the following code segments, and explain how to correct it:
  a)
```
x = 1;
while ( x <= 10 );
    x++;
}
```
  b)
```
for ( y = .1; y != 1.0; y += .1 )
    document.write( y + " " );
```
  c)
```
switch ( n ) {
    case 1:
        document.writeln( "The number is 1" );
    case 2:
        document.writeln( "The number is 2" );
        break;
    default:
        document.writeln( "The number is not 1 or 2" );
        break;
}
```
  d) The following code should print the values from1 to 10:
```
n = 1;
while ( n < 10 )
    document.writeln( n++ );
```

ANSWERS TO SELF-REVIEW EXERCISES

9.1 a) False. The `default` case is optional. If no default action is needed, then there is no need for a `default` case. b) False. The `break` statement is used to exit the `switch` statement. The `break` statement is not required for the last case in a `switch` statement. c) False. Both of the relational expressions must be true in order for the entire expression to be true when using the `&&` operator. d) True.

9.2 a)
```
sum = 0;
for ( count = 1; count <= 99; count += 2 )
    sum += count;
```
b) `Math.pow( 2.5, 3 )`
c)
```
x = 1;
while ( x <= 20 ) {
    document.write( x + " " );
    if ( x % 5 == 0 )
        document.write( "<br />" );
    ++x;
}
```
d)
```
for ( x = 1; x <= 20; x++ ) {
    document.write( x + " " );

    if ( x % 5 == 0 )
        document.write( "<br />" );
}
```

or

```
for ( x = 1; x <= 20; x++ )

    if ( x % 5 == 0 )
        document.write( x + "<br />" );
    else
        document.write( x + " " );
```

9.3 a) Error: The semicolon after the `while` header causes an infinite loop, and there is a missing left brace.
   Correction: Replace the semicolon by a {, or remove both the ; and the }.
   b) Error: Using a floating-point number to control a `for` repetition statement may not work, because floating-point numbers are represented approximately by most computers.
   Correction: Use an integer, and perform the proper calculation to get the values you desire:
```
for ( y = 1; y != 10; y++ )
    document.writeln( y / 10 );
```
   c) Error: Missing `break` statement in the statements for the first `case`.
   Correction: Add a `break` statement at the end of the statements for the first `case`. Note that this missing statement is not necessarily an error if the programmer wants the statement of `case 2:` to execute every time the `case 1:` statement executes.
   d) Error: Improper relational operator used in the `while` repetition-continuation condition.
   Correction: Use <= rather than <, or change 10 to 11.

EXERCISES

9.4 Find the error in each of the following segments of code. [*Note:* There may be more than one error.]
   a)
```
For ( x = 100, x >= 1, x++ )
    document.writeln( x );
```

b) The following code should print whether integer value is odd or even:

```
switch ( value % 2 ) {
    case 0:
        document.writeln( "Even integer" );
    case 1:
        document.writeln( "Odd integer" );
}
```

c) The following code should output the odd integers from 19 to 1:

```
for ( x = 19; x >= 1; x += 2 )
    document.writeln( x );
```

d) The following code should output the even integers from 2 to 100:

```
counter = 2;
do {
    document.writeln( counter );
    counter += 2;
} While ( counter < 100 );
```

9.5   What does the following script do?

```
1   <?xml version = "1.0"?>
2   <!DOCTYPE html PUBLIC "-//W3C//DTD XHTML 1.0 Strict//EN"
3       "http://www.w3.org/TR/xhtml1/DTD/xhtml1-strict.dtd">
4
5   <html xmlns = "http://www.w3.org/1999/xhtml">
6       <head><title>Mystery</title>
7           <script type = "text/javascript">
8               <!--
9               document.writeln( "<table>" );
10
11              for ( var i = 1; i <= 10; i++ ) {
12                  document.writeln( "<tr>" );
13
14                  for ( var j = 1; j <= 5; j++ )
15                      document.writeln( "<td>(" + i + ", " + j + ")</td>" );
16
17                  document.writeln( "</tr>" );
18              }
19
20              document.writeln( "</table>" );
21              // -->
22          </script>
23
24      </head><body></body>
25  </html>
```

9.6   Write a script that finds the smallest of several integers. Assume that the first value read specifies the number of values to be input from the user.

9.7   Write a script that calculates the product of the odd integers from 1 to 15 and then outputs XHTML text that displays the results.

9.8   Modify the compound-interest program in Fig. 9.6 to repeat its steps for interest rates of 5, 6, 7, 8, 9 and 10%. Use a for loop to vary the interest rate.

9.9   Write a script that outputs XHTML to display the given patterns separately, one below the other. Use for loops to generate the patterns. All asterisks (*) should be printed by a single statement of the form `document.write( "*" );` (this causes the asterisks to print side by side). A statement of the form `document.writeln( "<br />" );` can be used to position to the next line. A statement of the form `document.write( " " );` can be used to display a space (needed for the last two patterns). There should be no other output statements in the program. [*Hint*: The last two patterns require that each line begin with an appropriate number of blanks. You may need to use the XHTML `<pre></pre>` tags.]

```
(a)              (b)                  (c)                  (d)
*                **********           **********                    *
**               *********            *********                    **
***              ********             ********                    ***
****             *******              *******                    ****
*****            ******               ******                    *****
******           *****                *****                    ******
*******          ****                 ****                    *******
********          ***                  ***                    ********
*********          **                   **                    *********
**********          *                    *                    **********
```

9.10 One interesting application of computers is the drawing of graphs and bar charts (sometimes called **histograms**). Write a script that reads five numbers between 1 and 30. For each number read, output XHTML text that displays a line containing the same number of adjacent asterisks. For example, if your program reads the number 7, it should output XHTML text that displays `*******`.

9.11 (*"The Twelve Days of Christmas" Song*) Write a script that uses repetition and `switch` statements to print the song "The Twelve Days of Christmas." One `switch` statement should be used to print the day (i.e., "First," "Second," etc.). A separate `switch` statement should be used to print the remainder of each verse. You can find the words at the site

       `www.santas.net/twelvedaysofchristmas.htm`

9.12 A mail-order house sells five different products whose retail prices are as follows: product 1, $2.98; product 2, $4.50; product 3, $9.98; product 4, $4.49; and product 5, $6.87. Write a script that reads a series of pairs of numbers as follows:
     a) Product number
     b) Quantity sold for one day

Your program should use a `switch` statement to help determine the retail price for each product and should calculate and output XHTML that displays the total retail value of all the products sold last week. Use a `prompt` dialog to obtain the product number from the user. Use a sentinel-controlled loop to determine when the program should stop looping and display the final results.

9.13 Assume that i = 1, j = 2, k = 3 and m = 2. What does each of the given statements print? Are the parentheses necessary in each case?
     a) `document.writeln( i == 1 );`
     b) `document.writeln( j == 3 );`
     c) `document.writeln( i >= 1 && j < 4 );`
     d) `document.writeln( m <= 99 && k < m );`
     e) `document.writeln( j >= i || k == m );`
     f) `document.writeln( k + m < j || 3 - j >= k );`
     g) `document.writeln( !( k > m ) );`

9.14 Modify Exercise 9.9 to combine your code from the four separate triangles of asterisks into a single script that prints all four patterns side by side, making clever use of nested `for` loops.

```
*                 **********  **********                     *
**                *********    *********                    **
***               ********      ********                   ***
****              *******        *******                  ****
*****             ******          ******                 *****
******            *****            *****                ******
*******           ****              ****               *******
********          ***                ***              ********
*********         *                    **            *********
**********        *                      *           **********
```

9.15   *(De Morgan's Laws)* In this chapter, we have discussed the logical operators **&&**, **||** and **!**. De Morgan's Laws can sometimes make it more convenient for us to express a logical expression. These laws state that the expression ! (*condition1* && *condition2*) is logically equivalent to the expression (!*condition1* || !*condition2*). Also, the expression ! (*condition1* || *condition2*) is logically equivalent to the expression (!*condition1* && !*condition2*). Use De Morgan's Laws to write equivalent expressions for each of the following, and then write a program to show that the original expression and the new expression are equivalent in each case:

 a) ! (x < 5) && ! (y >= 7)
 b) ! (a == b) || ! (g != 5)
 c) ! ((x <= 8) && (y > 4))
 d) ! ((i > 4) || (j <= 6))

9.16   Write a script that prints the following diamond shape:

```
    *
   ***
  *****
 *******
*********
 *******
  *****
   ***
    *
```

You may use output statements that print a single asterisk (*), a single space or a single newline character. Maximize your use of repetition (with nested `for` statements), and minimize the number of output statements.

9.17   Modify the program you wrote in Exercise 9.16 to read an odd number in the range 1 to 19. This number specifies the number of rows in the diamond. Your program should then display a diamond of the appropriate size.

9.18   A criticism of the `break` statement and the `continue` statement is that each is unstructured. Actually, `break` statements and `continue` statements can always be replaced by structured statements, although coding the replacement can be awkward. Describe in general how you would remove any `break` statement from a loop in a program and replace it with some structured equivalent. [*Hint*: The `break` statement "jumps out of" a loop from the body of that loop. The other way to leave is by failing the loop-continuation test. Consider using in the loop-continuation test a second test that indicates "early exit because of a 'break' condition."] Use the technique you develop here to remove the `break` statement from the program in Fig. 9.11.

9.19   What does the following script do?

```
1   <?xml version = "1.0"?>
2   <!DOCTYPE html PUBLIC "-//W3C//DTD XHTML 1.0 Strict//EN"
3       "http://www.w3.org/TR/xhtml1/DTD/xhtml1-strict.dtd">
4
5   <html xmlns = "http://www.w3.org/1999/xhtml">
6       <head><title>Mystery</title>
7           <script type = "text/javascript">
8               <!--
9               for ( var i = 1; i <= 5; i++ ) {
10                  for ( var j = 1; j <= 3; j++ ) {
11                      for ( var k = 1; k <= 4; k++ )
12                          document.write( "*" );
13                      document.writeln( "<br />" );
14                  }
15                  document.writeln( "<br />" );
16              }
17              // -->
18          </script>
19
20      </head><body></body>
21  </html>
```

9.20   Describe in general how you would remove any `continue` statement from a loop in a program and replace it with some structured equivalent. Use the technique you develop to remove the `continue` statement from the program in Fig. 9.12.

9.21   Given the following `switch` statement:

```
1   switch ( k ) {
2       case 1:
3           break;
4       case 2:
5       case 3:
6           ++k;
7           break;
8       case 4:
9           --k;
10          break;
11      default:
12          k *= 3;
13  }
14
15  x = k;
```

What values are assigned to x when k has values of 1, 2, 3, 4 and 10?

10

JavaScript: Functions

Objectives

- To understand how to construct programs modularly from small pieces called functions.
- To be able to create new functions.
- To understand the mechanisms used to pass information between functions.
- To introduce simulation techniques that use random-number generation.
- To understand how the visibility of identifiers is limited to specific regions of programs.

Form ever follows function.
Louis Sullivan

E pluribus unum.
(One composed of many.)
Virgil

O! call back yesterday, bid time return.
William Shakespeare

Call me Ishmael.
Herman Melville

When you call me that, smile.
Owen Wister

Outline

10.1 Introduction

Most computer programs that solve real-world problems are much larger than the programs presented in the first few chapters of this book. Experience has shown that the best way to develop and maintain a large program is to construct it from small, simple pieces, or **modules**. This technique is called **divide and conquer**. This chapter describes many key features of JavaScript that facilitate the design, implementation, operation and maintenance of large scripts.

10.2 Program Modules in JavaScript

Modules in JavaScript are called **functions**. JavaScript programs are written by combining new functions that the programmer writes with "prepackaged" functions and objects available in JavaScript. The prepackaged functions that belong to JavaScript objects (such as `Math.pow` and `Math.round`, introduced previously) are often called **methods**. The term method implies that the function belongs to a particular object; however, the terms function and method can be used interchangeably. We will refer to functions that belong to a particular JavaScript object as methods; all others are referred to as functions.

JavaScript provides several objects that have a rich collection of methods for performing common mathematical calculations, string manipulations, date and time manipulations, and manipulations of collections of data called **Arrays**. These objects make the programmer's job easier, because they provide many of the capabilities programmers need. Some common predefined objects of JavaScript and their methods are discussed in Chapter 11, JavaScript: Arrays, and Chapter 12, JavaScript: Objects.

 Good Programming Practice 10.1

Familiarize yourself with the rich collection of objects and methods provided by JavaScript.

Software Engineering Observation 10.1

Avoid reinventing the wheel. If possible, use JavaScript objects, methods and functions instead of writing new functions. This practice reduces script-development time and helps prevent the introduction of new errors.

Portability Tip 10.1

Using the methods built into JavaScript objects helps make scripts more portable.

Performance Tip 10.1

Do not try to rewrite existing methods of JavaScript objects to make them more efficient. You usually will not be able to increase the performance of the methods.

The programmer can write functions to define specific tasks that may be used at many points in a script. These functions are referred to as **programmer-defined functions**. The actual statements defining the function are written only once and are hidden from other functions.

A function is **invoked** (i.e., made to perform its designated task) by a **function call**. The function call specifies the function name and provides information (as **arguments**) that the called function needs to perform its task. A common analogy for this structure is the hierarchical form of management. A boss (the **calling function**, or **caller**) asks a worker (the **called function**) to perform a task and **return** (i.e., report back) the results when the task is done. The boss function does not know how the worker function performs its designated tasks. The worker may call other worker functions, and the boss will be unaware of this situation. We will soon see how this "hiding" of implementation details promotes good software engineering. Figure 10.1 shows the boss function communicating with several worker functions in a hierarchical manner. Note that worker1 acts as a "boss" function to worker4 and worker5, and worker4 and worker5 report back to worker1. Relationships among functions may be other than the hierarchical structure shown in this figure.

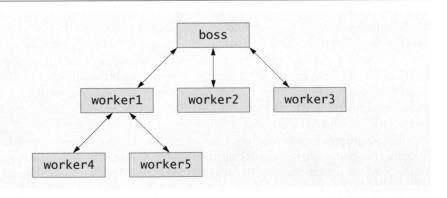

Fig. 10.1   Hierarchical boss-function/worker-function relationship.

Functions (and methods) are invoked by writing the name of the function (or method), followed by a left parenthesis, followed by the argument(s) of the function (or method), if any, followed by a right parenthesis. For example, a programmer desiring to convert a string stored in variable `inputValue` to a floating-point number and add it to variable `total`, might write

```
total += parseFloat( inputValue );
```

When this statement executes, JavaScript function **parseFloat** converts the string contained in the parentheses (stored in variable `inputValue` in this case) to a floating-point value and adds value to `total`. The variable `inputValue` is the argument of the `parse-Float` function. Function `parseFloat` takes a string representation of a floating-point number as an argument and returns the corresponding floating-point numeric value.

Function (and method) arguments may be constants, variables or expressions. If `s1 = "22.3"` and `s2 = "45"`, then the statement

```
total += parseFloat( s1 + s2 );
```

evaluates the expression `s1 + s2`, concatenates the strings `s1` and `s2` (resulting in the string `"22.345"`), converts the result into a floating-point number and adds the floating-point number to variable `total`.

10.3 Programmer-Defined Functions

Functions allow the programmer to modularize a program. All variables declared in function definitions are **local variables**—this means that they are known only in the function in which they are defined. Most functions have a list of **parameters** that provide the means for communicating information between functions via function calls. A function's parameters are also considered to be local variables. When a function is called, the arguments in the function call are assigned to the corresponding parameters in the function definition.

There are several reasons for modularizing a program with functions. The divide-and-conquer approach makes program development more manageable. Another reason is **software reusability** (i.e., using existing functions as building blocks to create new programs). With good function naming and definition, programs can be created from standardized functions rather than built by using customized code. For example, we did not have to define how to convert strings to integers and floating-point numbers—JavaScript already provides function `parseInt` to convert a string to an integer and function `parseFloat` to convert a string to a floating-point number. A third reason is to avoid repeating code in a program. Code that is packages as a function can be executed from several locations in a program by calling the function.

Error-Prevention Tip 10.1

Copying the same code in multiple parts of a program is a common source of bugs

Software Engineering Observation 10.2

Each function should perform a single, well-defined task, and the name of the function should express that task effectively. This promotes software reusability.

Software Engineering Observation 10.3

If a function's task cannot be expressed concisely, perhaps the function is performing too many different tasks. It is usually best to break such a function into several smaller functions.

10.4 Function Definitions

Each script we have presented thus far in the text has consisted of a series of statements and control structures in sequence. These scripts have been executed as the browser loads the Web page and evaluates the <head> section of the page. We now consider how programmers write their own customized functions and call them in a script.

Programmer-Defined Function *square*

Consider a script (Fig. 10.2) that uses a function square to calculate the squares of the integers from 1 to 10. [*Note*: We continue to show many examples in which the body element of the XHTML document is empty and the document is created directly by JavaScript. In later chapters, we show many examples in which JavaScripts interact with the elements in the body of a document.]

```
1   <?xml version = "1.0"?>
2   <!DOCTYPE html PUBLIC "-//W3C//DTD XHTML 1.0 Strict//EN"
3     "http://www.w3.org/TR/xhtml1/DTD/xhtml1-strict.dtd">
4
5   <!-- Fig. 10.2: SquareInt.html -->
6   <!-- Square function            -->
7
8   <html xmlns = "http://www.w3.org/1999/xhtml">
9     <head>
10       <title>A Programmer-Defined square Function</title>
11
12       <script type = "text/javascript">
13         <!--
14         document.writeln(
15           "<h1>Square the numbers from 1 to 10</h1>" );
16
17         // square the numbers from 1 to 10
18         for ( var x = 1; x <= 10; ++x )
19           document.writeln( "The square of " + x + " is " +
20             square( x ) + "<br />" );
21
22         // The following square function's body is executed
23         // only when the function is explicitly called.
24
25         // square function definition
26         function square( y )
27         {
28           return y * y;
29         }
30         // -->
31       </script>
32
33     </head><body></body>
34   </html>
```

Fig. 10.2   Programmer-defined function square. (Part 1 of 2.)

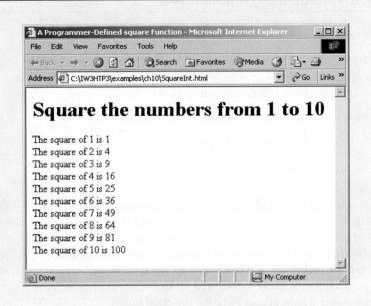

Fig. 10.2   Programmer-defined function `square`. (Part 2 of 2.)

The `for` statement in lines 18–20 outputs XHTML that displays the results of squaring the integers from 1 to 10. Each iteration of the loop calculates the `square` of the current value of control variable `x` and outputs the result by writing a line in the XHTML document. Function `square` is invoked, or **called**, in line 20 with the expression `square( x )`. When program control reaches this expression, the program calls function `square` (defined in lines 26–29). The `()` represent the **function-call operator**, which has high precedence. At this point, the program makes a copy of the value of `x` (the argument) and program control transfers to the first line of function `square`. Function `square` receives the copy of the value of `x` and stores it in the parameter `y`. Then `square` calculates `y * y`. The result is passed back to the point in line 20 where `square` was invoked. Lines 19–20 concatenate `"The square of "`, the value of `x`, `" is "`, the value returned by function `square` and a `<br />` tag and write that line of text in the XHTML document. This process is repeated 10 times.

The definition of function `square` (lines 26–29) shows that `square` expects a single parameter `y`. Function `square` uses this name in its body to manipulate the value passed to `square` from line 20. The **return statement** in `square` passes the result of the calculation `y * y` back to the calling function. Note that JavaScript keyword `var` is not used to declare variables in the parameter list of a function.

Common Programming Error 10.1

Using the JavaScript `var` keyword to declare a variable in a function parameter list results in a JavaScript runtime error.

In this example, function `square` follows the rest of the script. When the `for` statement terminates, JavaScript will not continue to flow sequentially into function `square`. A function must be called explicitly for the code in its body to execute. Thus, when the `for` statement terminates in this example, the script terminates.

Good Programming Practice 10.2

Place a blank line between function definitions to separate the functions and enhance program readability.

Software Engineering Observation 10.4

Statements that are enclosed in the body of a function definition are not executed by the Java-Script interpreter unless the function is invoked explicitly.

The format of a function definition is

```
function function-name( parameter-list )
{
    declarations and statements
}
```

The *function-name* is any valid identifier. The *parameter-list* is a comma-separated list containing the names of the parameters received by the function when it is called (remember that the arguments in the function call are assigned to the corresponding parameter in the function definition). There should be one argument in the function call for each parameter in the function definition. If a function does not receive any values, the *parameter-list* is empty (i.e., the function name is followed by an empty set of parentheses). The *declarations* and *statements* within braces form the **function body**.

Common Programming Error 10.2

Forgetting to return a value from a function that is supposed to return a value is a logic error.

Common Programming Error 10.3

Placing a semicolon after the right parenthesis enclosing the parameter list of a function definition results in a JavaScript runtime error.

Common Programming Error 10.4

Redefining a function parameter as a local variable in the function is a logic error.

Common Programming Error 10.5

Passing to a function an argument that is not compatible with the corresponding parameter's expected type is a logic error and may result in a JavaScript runtime error.

Good Programming Practice 10.3

Although it is not incorrect to do so, do not use the same name for an argument passed to a function and the corresponding parameter in the function definition. Using different names avoids ambiguity.

Good Programming Practice 10.4

Choosing meaningful function names and meaningful parameter names makes programs more readable and helps avoid excessive use of comments.

Software Engineering Observation 10.5

A function should usually be no longer than one printed page. Better yet, a function should usually be no longer than half a printed page. Regardless of how long a function is, it should perform one task well. Small functions promote software reusability.

Software Engineering Observation 10.6

Scripts should be written as collections of small functions. This practice makes programs easier to write, debug, maintain and modify.

Software Engineering Observation 10.7

A function requiring a large number of parameters may be performing too many tasks. Consider dividing the function into smaller functions that perform the separate tasks. The function header should fit on one line, if possible.

Software Engineering Observation 10.8

Modularizing programs in a neat, hierarchical manner promotes good software engineering—sometimes, however, at the expense of performance.

Performance Tip 10.2

A heavily modularized program—as compared with a monolithic (i.e., one-piece) program without functions—may make too many function calls, and this will consume execution time and space on a computer's processor(s). But monolithic programs are difficult to program, test, debug, maintain and evolve. So modularize your programs judiciously, always keeping in mind the delicate balance between performance and good software engineering.

Error-Prevention Tip 10.2

Small functions are easier to test, debug and understand than large ones.

There are three ways to return control to the point at which a function was invoked. If the function does not return a result, control returns when the program reaches the function-ending right brace or by executing the statement

```
return;
```

If the function does return a result, the statement

```
return expression;
```

returns the value of *expression* to the caller. When a `return` statement is executed, control returns immediately to the point at which the function was invoked.

Programmer-Defined Function `maximum`

The script in our next example (Fig. 10.3) uses a programmer-defined function called `maximum` to determine and return the largest of three floating-point values.

```
1   <?xml version = "1.0"?>
2   <!DOCTYPE html PUBLIC "-//W3C//DTD XHTML 1.0 Strict//EN"
3      "http://www.w3.org/TR/xhtml1/DTD/xhtml1-strict.dtd">
4
5   <!-- Fig. 10.3: maximum.html -->
6   <!-- Maximum function          -->
7
8   <html xmlns = "http://www.w3.org/1999/xhtml">
```

Fig. 10.3 Programmer-defined `maximum` function. (Part 1 of 3.)

```
 9      <head>
10        <title>Finding the Maximum of Three Values</title>
11
12        <script type = "text/javascript">
13          <!--
14          var input1 =
15             window.prompt( "Enter first number", "0" );
16          var input2 =
17             window.prompt( "Enter second number", "0" );
18          var input3 =
19             window.prompt( "Enter third number", "0" );
20
21          var value1 = parseFloat( input1 );
22          var value2 = parseFloat( input2 );
23          var value3 = parseFloat( input3 );
24
25          var maxValue = maximum( value1, value2, value3 );
26
27          document.writeln( "First number: " + value1 +
28             "<br />Second number: " + value2 +
29             "<br />Third number: " + value3 +
30             "<br />Maximum is: " + maxValue );
31
32          // maximum method definition (called from line 25)
33          function maximum( x, y, z )
34          {
35             return Math.max( x, Math.max( y, z ) );
36          }
37          // -->
38        </script>
39
40      </head>
41      <body>
42        <p>Click Refresh (or Reload) to run the script again</p>
43      </body>
44   </html>
```

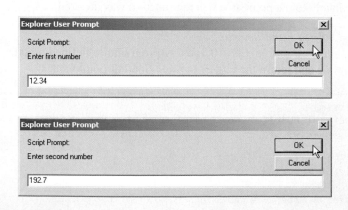

Fig. 10.3   Programmer-defined `maximum` function. (Part 2 of 3.)

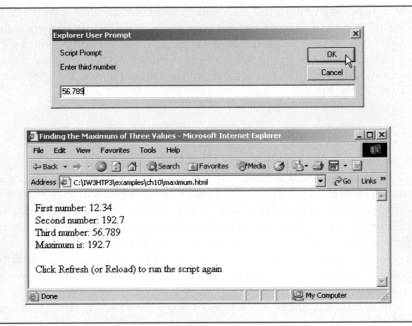

Fig. 10.3   Programmer-defined `maximum` function. (Part 3 of 3.)

The three floating-point values are input by the user via `prompt` dialogs (lines 14–19). Lines 21–23 use function `parseFloat` to convert the strings input by the user to floating-point values. The statement in line 25 passes the three floating-point values to function `maximum` (defined in lines 33–36), which determines the largest floating-point value. This value is returned to line 25 by the `return` statement in function `maximum`. The value returned is assigned to variable `maxValue`. Lines 27–30 concatenate and display the three floating-point values input by the user and the `maxValue`.

Note the implementation of the function `maximum` (lines 33–36). The first line indicates that the function's name is `maximum` and that the function takes three parameters (`x`, `y` and `z`) to accomplish its task. Also, the body of the function contains the statement which returns the largest of the three floating-point values, using two calls to the `Math` object's `max` method. First, method `Math.max` is invoked with the values of variables `y` and `z` to determine the larger of the two values. Next, the value of variable `x` and the result of the first call to `Math.max` are passed to method `Math.max`. Finally, the result of the second call to `Math.max` is returned to the point at which `maximum` was invoked (i.e., line 25). Note once again that the script terminates before sequentially reaching the definition of function `maximum`. The statement in the body of function `maximum` executes only when the function is invoked from line 25.

10.5 Random-Number Generation

We now take a brief and, it is hoped, entertaining diversion into a popular programming application, namely simulation and game playing. In this section and the next section, we will develop a nicely structured game-playing program that includes multiple functions. The program uses most of the control structures we have studied thus far.

There is something in the air of a gambling casino that invigorates people, from the high-rollers at the plush mahogany-and-felt craps tables to the quarter poppers at the one-armed bandits. It is the **element of chance**, the possibility that luck will convert a pocketful of money into a mountain of wealth. The element of chance can be introduced through the `Math` object's **random** method. (Remember, we are calling `random` a method because it belongs to the `Math` object.)

Consider the following statement:

```
var randomValue = Math.random();
```

Method `random` generates a floating-point value from 0.0 up to, but not including, 1.0. If `random` truly produces values at random, then every value from 0.0 up to, but not including, 1.0 has an equal **chance** (or **probability**) of being chosen each time `random` is called.

The range of values produced directly by `random` is often different than what is needed in a specific application. For example, a program that simulates coin tossing might require only 0 for heads and 1 for tails. A program that simulates rolling a six-sided die would require random integers in the range from 1 to 6. A program that randomly predicts the next type of spaceship, out of four possibilities, that will fly across the horizon in a video game might require random integers in the range 0–3 or 1–4.

To demonstrate method `random`, let us develop a program (Fig. 10.4) that simulates 20 rolls of a six-sided die and displays the value of each roll. We use the multiplication operator (*) with `random` as follows:

```
Math.floor( 1 + Math.random() * 6 )
```

First, the preceding expression multiplies the result of a call to `Math.random()` by 6 to produce a number in the range 0.0 up to, but not including, 6.0. This is called **scaling** the range of the random numbers. The number 6 is called the **scaling factor**. Next, we add 1 to the result to **shift** the range of numbers to produce a number in the range 1.0 up to, but not including, 7.0. Finally, we use method **Math.floor** to *round* the result down to the closest integer value in the range 1 to 6. `Math` method `floor` rounds its floating-point number argument to the closest integer not greater than the argument's value—for example 1.75 is rounded to 1, and –1.25 is rounded to –2. Figure 10.4 confirms that the results are in the range 1 to 6.

```
1    <?xml version = "1.0"?>
2    <!DOCTYPE html PUBLIC "-//W3C//DTD XHTML 1.0 Strict//EN"
3        "http://www.w3.org/TR/xhtml1/DTD/xhtml1-strict.dtd">
4
5    <!-- Fig. 10.4: RandomInt.html         -->
6    <!-- Demonstrating the Random method -->
7
8    <html xmlns = "http://www.w3.org/1999/xhtml">
9        <head>
10           <title>Shifted and Scaled Random Integers</title>
11
12           <script type = "text/javascript">
13              <!--
```

Fig. 10.4   Random integers, shifting and scaling. (Part 1 of 2.)

```
14              var value;
15
16          document.writeln(
17              "<table border = \"1\" width = \"50%\">" );
18          document.writeln(
19              "<caption>Random Numbers</caption><tr>" );
20
21          for ( var i = 1; i <= 20; i++ ) {
22              value = Math.floor( 1 + Math.random() * 6 );
23              document.writeln( "<td>" + value + "</td>" );
24
25              // write end and start <tr> tags when
26              // i is a multiple of 5 and not 20
27              if ( i % 5 == 0 && i != 20 )
28                  document.writeln( "</tr><tr>" );
29          }
30
31          document.writeln( "</tr></table>" );
32          // -->
33      </script>
34
35  </head>
36  <body>
37      <p>Click Refresh (or Reload) to run the script again</p>
38  </body>
39  </html>
```

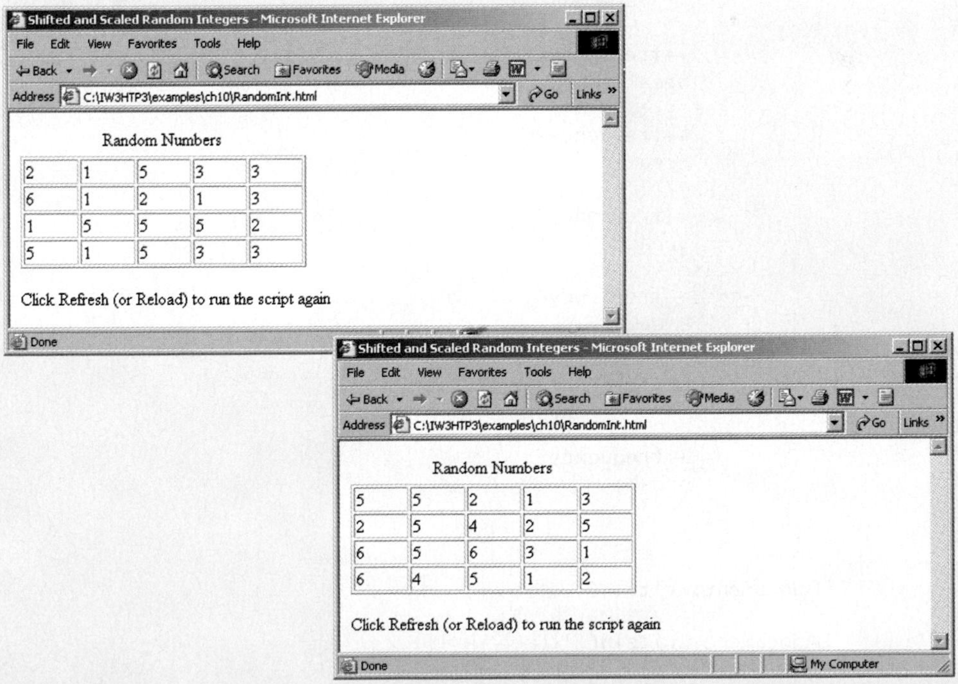

Fig. 10.4 Random integers, shifting and scaling. (Part 2 of 2.)

To show that these numbers occur with approximately equal likelihood, let us simulate 6000 rolls of a die with the program in Fig. 10.5. Each integer from 1 to 6 should appear approximately 1000 times. Use your browser's **Refresh** (or **Reload**) button to execute the script again.

```
1   <?xml version = "1.0"?>
2   <!DOCTYPE html PUBLIC "-//W3C//DTD XHTML 1.0 Strict//EN"
3       "http://www.w3.org/TR/xhtml1/DTD/xhtml1-strict.dtd">
4
5   <!-- Fig. 10.5: RollDie.html -->
6   <!-- Rolling a Six-Sided Die -->
7
8   <html xmlns = "http://www.w3.org/1999/xhtml">
9       <head>
10          <title>Roll a Six-Sided Die 6000 Times</title>
11
12          <script type = "text/javascript">
13             <!--
14             var frequency1 = 0, frequency2 = 0,
15                 frequency3 = 0, frequency4 = 0,
16                 frequency5 = 0, frequency6 = 0, face;
17
18             // summarize results
19             for ( var roll = 1; roll <= 6000; ++roll ) {
20                 face = Math.floor( 1 + Math.random() * 6 );
21
22                 switch ( face ) {
23                     case 1:
24                         ++frequency1;
25                         break;
26                     case 2:
27                         ++frequency2;
28                         break;
29                     case 3:
30                         ++frequency3;
31                         break;
32                     case 4:
33                         ++frequency4;
34                         break;
35                     case 5:
36                         ++frequency5;
37                         break;
38                     case 6:
39                         ++frequency6;
40                         break;
41                 }
42             }
43
44             document.writeln( "<table border = \"1\"" +
45                 "width = \"50%\">" );
46             document.writeln( "<thead><th>Face</th>" +
47                 "<th>Frequency<th></thead>" );
```

Fig. 10.5   Rolling a six-sided die 6000 times. (Part 1 of 2.)

```
48          document.writeln( "<tbody><tr><td>1</td><td>" +
49              frequency1 + "</td></tr>" );
50          document.writeln( "<tr><td>2</td><td>" + frequency2 +
51              "</td></tr>" );
52          document.writeln( "<tr><td>3</td><td>" + frequency3 +
53              "</td></tr>" );
54          document.writeln( "<tr><td>4</td><td>" + frequency4 +
55              "</td></tr>" );
56          document.writeln( "<tr><td>5</td><td>" + frequency5 +
57              "</td></tr>" );
58          document.writeln( "<tr><td>6</td><td>" + frequency6 +
59              "</td></tr></tbody></table>" );
60          // -->
61       </script>
62
63    </head>
64    <body>
65       <p>Click Refresh (or Reload) to run the script again</p>
66    </body>
67 </html>
```

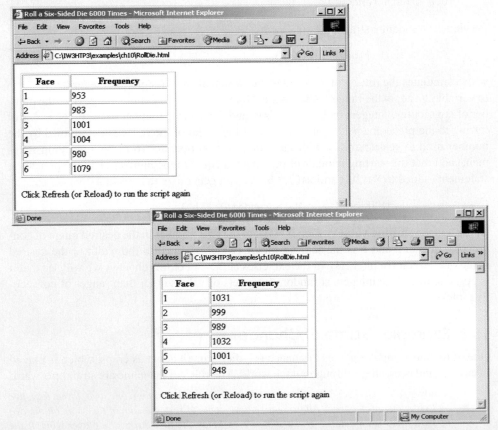

Fig. 10.5   Rolling a six-sided die 6000 times. (Part 2 of 2.)

As the output of the program shows, we used `Math` method `random` and the scaling and shifting techniques of the previous example to simulate the rolling of a six-sided die. Note that we used nested control structures to determine the number of times each side of the six-sided die occurred. Lines 14–16 declare and initialize counter variables to keep track of the number of times each of the six die values appears. Line 16 also declares a variable to store the face value of the die at each of the 6000 rolls. The `for` loop in lines 19–42 iterates 6000 times. During each iteration of the loop, line 20 produces a value from 1 to 6, which is stored in `face`. The nested `switch` statement in lines 22–41 uses the `face` value that was randomly chosen as its controlling expression. Based on the value of `face`, the program increments one of the six counter variables during each iteration of the loop. Note that no `default` case is provided in this `switch` statement, because the statement in line 20 only produces only the values 1, 2, 3, 4, 5 and 6. In this example, the `default` case would never execute. After we study `Arrays` in Chapter 11, we will discuss how to replace the entire `switch` statement in this program with a single-line statement.

Run the program several times, and observe the results. Note that the program produces different random numbers each time the script executes, so the results should vary.

The values returned by `random` are always in the range

$$0.0 \leq \text{Math.random()} < 1.0$$

Previously, we demonstrated the statement

```
face = Math.floor( 1 + Math.random() * 6 );
```

which simulates the rolling of a six-sided die, which always assigns an integer (at random) to variable `face`, in the range $1 \leq \text{face} \leq 6$. Note that the width of this range (i.e., the number of consecutive integers in the range) is 6, and the starting number in the range is 1. Referring to the preceding statement, we see that the width of the range is determined by the number used to scale `random` with the multiplication operator (6 in the preceding statement) and that the starting number of the range is equal to the number (1 in the preceding statement) added to `Math.random() * 6`. We can generalize this result as

```
face = Math.floor( a + Math.random() * b );
```

where `a` is the **shifting value** (which is equal to the first number in the desired range of consecutive integers) and `b` is the **scaling factor** (which is equal to the width of the desired range of consecutive integers). In the exercises at the end of this chapter, we will see that it is possible to choose integers at random from sets of values other than ranges of consecutive integers.

10.6 Example: Game of Chance

One of the most popular games of chance is a dice game known as craps, which is played in casinos and back alleys throughout the world. The rules of the game are straightforward:

> *A player rolls two dice. Each die has six faces. These faces contain one, two, three, four, five and six spots, respectively. After the dice have come to rest, the sum of the spots on the two upward faces is calculated. If the sum is 7 or 11 on the first throw, the player wins. If the sum is 2, 3 or 12 on the first throw (called "craps"), the player loses (i.e., the "house" wins). If the sum is 4, 5, 6, 8, 9 or 10 on the first throw, that sum becomes the player's*

"point." To win, you must continue rolling the dice until you "make your point" (i.e., roll your point value). The player loses by rolling a 7 before making the point.

The script in Fig. 10.6 simulates the game of craps.

```
1   <?xml version = "1.0"?>
2   <!DOCTYPE html PUBLIC "-//W3C//DTD XHTML 1.0 Transitional//EN"
3       "http://www.w3.org/TR/xhtml1/DTD/xhtml1-transitional.dtd">
4
5   <!-- Fig. 10.6: Craps.html -->
6   <!-- Craps Program          -->
7
8   <html xmlns = "http://www.w3.org/1999/xhtml">
9      <head>
10        <title>Program that Simulates the Game of Craps</title>
11
12        <script type = "text/javascript">
13           <!--
14           // variables used to test the state of the game
15           var WON = 0, LOST = 1, CONTINUE_ROLLING = 2;
16
17           // other variables used in program
18           var firstRoll = true,              // true if first roll
19               sumOfDice = 0,                 // sum of the dice
20               myPoint = 0, // point if no win/loss on first roll
21               gameStatus = CONTINUE_ROLLING; // game not over yet
22
23           // process one roll of the dice
24           function play()
25           {
26              if ( firstRoll ) {          // first roll of the dice
27                 sumOfDice = rollDice();
28
29                 switch ( sumOfDice ) {
30                    case 7: case 11:           // win on first roll
31                       gameStatus = WON;
32                       // clear point field
33                       document.craps.point.value = "";
34                       break;
35                    case 2: case 3: case 12: // lose on first roll
36                       gameStatus = LOST;
37                       // clear point field
38                       document.craps.point.value = "";
39                       break;
40                    default:                      // remember point
41                       gameStatus = CONTINUE_ROLLING;
42                       myPoint = sumOfDice;
43                       document.craps.point.value = myPoint;
44                       firstRoll = false;
45                 }
46              }
47              else {
48                 sumOfDice = rollDice();
```

Fig. 10.6   Craps game simulation. (Part 1 of 5.)

```
49
50                         if ( sumOfDice == myPoint ) // win by making point
51                            gameStatus = WON;
52                         else
53                            if ( sumOfDice == 7 )     // lose by rolling 7
54                               gameStatus = LOST;
55                      }
56
57                      if ( gameStatus == CONTINUE_ROLLING )
58                         window.status = "Roll again";
59                      else {
60                         if ( gameStatus == WON )
61                            window.status = "Player wins. " +
62                               "Click Roll Dice to play again.";
63                         else
64                            window.status = "Player loses. " +
65                               "Click Roll Dice to play again.";
66
67                         firstRoll = true;
68                      }
69                   }
70
71                   // roll the dice
72                   function rollDice()
73                   {
74                      var die1, die2, workSum;
75
76                      die1 = Math.floor( 1 + Math.random() * 6 );
77                      die2 = Math.floor( 1 + Math.random() * 6 );
78                      workSum = die1 + die2;
79
80                      document.craps.firstDie.value = die1;
81                      document.craps.secondDie.value = die2;
82                      document.craps.sum.value = workSum;
83
84                      return workSum;
85                   }
86                   // -->
87                </script>
88
89          </head>
90          <body>
91             <form name = "craps" action = "">
92                <table border = "1">
93                <caption>Craps</caption>
94                <tr><td>Die 1</td>
95                   <td><input name = "firstDie" type = "text" />
96                   </td></tr>
97                <tr><td>Die 2</td>
98                   <td><input name = "secondDie" type = "text" />
99                   </td></tr>
100               <tr><td>Sum</td>
101                  <td><input name = "sum" type = "text" />
```

Fig. 10.6   Craps game simulation. (Part 2 of 5.)

```
102                    </td></tr>
103            <tr><td>Point</td>
104                <td><input name = "point" type = "text" />
105                </td></tr>
106            <tr><td><input type = "button" value = "Roll Dice"
107                onclick = "play()" /></td></tr>
108            </table>
109        </form>
110    </body>
111 </html>
```

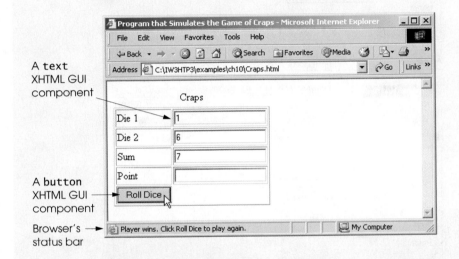

A **text**
XHTML GUI
component

A **button**
XHTML GUI
component

Browser's
status bar

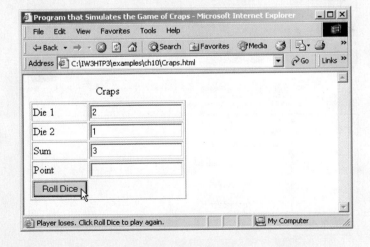

Fig. 10.6   Craps game simulation. (Part 3 of 5.)

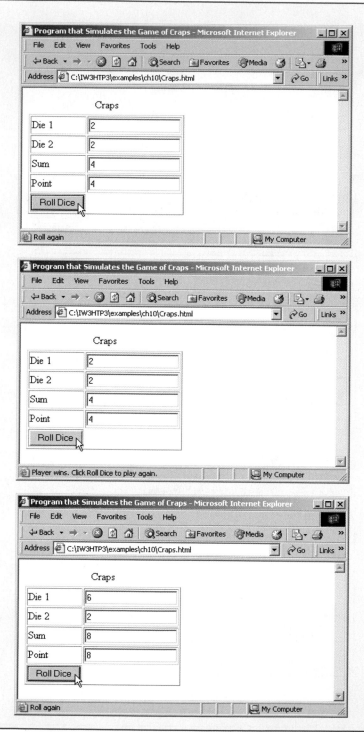

Fig. 10.6   Craps game simulation. (Part 4 of 5.)

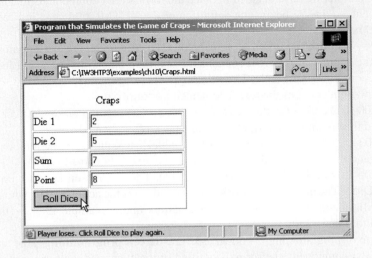

Fig. 10.6   Craps game simulation. (Part 5 of 5.)

Note that the player must roll two dice on the first and all subsequent rolls. When you execute the script, click the **Roll Dice** button to play the game. The **status bar** in the lower-left corner of the browser window displays the results of each roll. The screen captures show four separate executions of the script (a win and a loss on the first roll, and a win and a loss after the first roll).

Until now, all user interactions with scripts have been through either a `prompt` dialog (in which the user types an input value for the program) or an `alert` dialog (in which a message is displayed to the user, and the user can click **OK** to dismiss the dialog). Although these dialogs are valid ways to receive input from a user and to display messages in a Java-Script program, they are fairly limited in their capabilities. A `prompt` dialog can obtain only one value at a time from the user, and a message dialog can display only one message.

More frequently, multiple inputs are received from the user at once via an XHTML **form** (such as one in which the user enters name and address information) or to display many pieces of data at once (e.g., the values of the dice, the sum of the dice and the point in this example). To begin our introduction to more elaborate user interfaces, this program uses an XHTML form (discussed in Chapter 5) and a new graphical user interface concept: GUI **event handling**. This example is our first in which the JavaScript executes in response to the user's interaction with a GUI component in an XHTML form. This interaction causes an **event**. Scripts often are used to respond to events.

Before we discuss the script code, we discuss the `body` element (lines 90–110) of the XHTML document. The GUI components in this section are used extensively in the script.

Line 91 begins the definition of an XHTML `form` element with its **name** attribute set to `craps`. The `name` attribute `craps` enables script code to refer to the elements of the form. This attribute helps a script distinguish between multiple forms in the same XHTML document. Similarly, the `name` attribute is specified for each GUI component in the form, so that the script code can refer to each GUI component individually. Valid XHTML code requires that every `form` contain an `action` attribute. This form does not post its informa-tion to a Web server, so the empty string, `""`, is used.

In this example, we have decided to place the form's GUI components in an XHTML table element, so line 92 begins the definition of the XHTML table and indicates that it has a 1-pixel border.

Lines 94–96 define the first row of the table. The column on the left contains the text Die 1, and the column on the right contains the text field named firstDie. Lines 97–99 define the second row of the table. The column on the left contains the text Die 2, and the column on the right contains the text field named secondDie.

Lines 100–102 define the third row of the table. The column on the left contains the text Sum, and the column on the right contains the text field named sum.

Lines 103–105 define the fourth row of the table. The column on the left contains the text Point, and the column on the right contains the text field named point.

Lines 106–107 define the last row of the table. The column on the left contains the button **Roll Dice**. The button's **onclick** attribute indicates the action to take when the user of the XHTML document clicks the **Roll Dice** button. In this example, clicking the button causes a call to function play.

This style of programming is known as **event-driven programming**—the user interacts with a GUI component, the script is notified of the event and the script processes the event. The user's interaction with the GUI "drives" the program. The clicking of the button is known as the **event**. The function that is called when an event occurs is known as an **event-handling function** or **event handler**. When a GUI event occurs in a form, the browser calls the specified event-handling function. Before any event can be processed, each GUI component must know which event-handling function will be called when a particular event occurs. Most XHTML GUI components have several different event types. The event model is discussed in detail in Chapter 14, Dynamic HTML: Event Model. By specifying onclick = "play()" for the **Roll Dice** button, we enable the browser to **listen for events** (button-click events in particular). This **registers the event handler** for the GUI component. (We also like to call the line on which it occurs the **start listening line**, because the browser is now listening for button-click events from the button.) If no event handler is specified for the **Roll Dice** button, the script will not respond when the user presses the button. Lines 108–109 end the table and form elements, respectively.

The game is reasonably involved. The player may win or lose on the first roll, or may win or lose on any roll. Line 15 creates variables that define the three game states—game won, game lost and continue rolling the dice. Unlike many other programming languages, JavaScript does not provide a mechanism to define a **constant** (i.e., a variable whose value cannot be modified). For this reason, we use all capital letters for these variable names, to indicate that we do not intend to modify their values and to make them stand out in the code.

Good Programming Practice 10.5
Use only uppercase letters (with underscores between words) in the names of variables that should be used as constants. This format makes such variables stand out in a program.

Good Programming Practice 10.6
Use meaningfully named variables rather than constants (such as 2) to make programs more readable.

Lines 18–21 declare several variables that are used throughout the script. Variable firstRoll indicates whether the next roll of the dice is the first roll in the current game. Variable sumOfDice maintains the sum of the dice from the last roll. Variable myPoint stores the point if the player does not win or lose on the first roll. Variable gameStatus keeps track of the current state of the game (WON, LOST or CONTINUE_ROLLING).

We define a function rollDice (lines 72–85) to roll the dice and to compute and display their sum. Function rollDice is defined once, but is called from two places in the program (lines 27 and 48). Function rollDice takes no arguments, so it has an empty parameter list. Function rollDice returns the sum of the two dice.

The user clicks the **Roll Dice** button to roll the dice. This action invokes function play (lines 24–69) of the script. Function play checks the variable firstRoll (line 26) to determine whether it is true or false. If it is true, the roll is the first roll of the game. Line 27 calls rollDice, which picks two random values from 1 to 6, displays the value of the first die, the value of the second die and the sum of the dice in the first three text fields and returns the sum of the dice. (We will discuss function rollDice in detail shortly.) After the first roll has taken place, the nested switch statement in line 29 determines whether the game is won or lost, or whether it should continue with another roll. After the first roll, if the game is not over, sumOfDice is saved in myPoint and displayed in the text field point in the XHTML form. Note how the text field's value is changed in lines 33, 38 and 43. The expression

```
document.craps.point.value
```

accesses the **value** property of the text field point. The value property specifies the text to display in the text field. To access this property, we specify the name of the form (craps) that contains the text field, followed by a **dot** (.), followed by the name of the text field (point) we would like to manipulate. The preceding expression uses **dot notation** to access the point member of the craps form. Similarly, the second use of dot notation accesses the value member (or property) of the point text field. Actually, we will see in the chapters on Dynamic HTML that every element of an XHTML document is accessible in a manner similar to that shown here.

The program proceeds to the nested if...else statement in line 57, which sets the window object's status property (window.status in lines 58, 61 and 64) to

```
Roll again.
```

if gameStatus is equal to CONTINUE, to

```
Player wins. Click Roll Dice to play again.
```

if gameStatus is equal to WON and to

```
Player loses. Click Roll Dice to play again.
```

if gameStatus is equal to LOST. The window object's status property displays the string assigned it in the status bar of the browser. If the game is won or lost, line 67 sets first-Roll to true to indicate that the next roll of the dice begins the next game.

The program then waits for the user to click the button **Roll Dice** again. Each time the user clicks **Roll Dice**, the program calls function play, which, in turn, calls the rollDice function to produce a new value for sumOfDice. If sumOfDice matches myPoint, gameStatus is set to WON, the if...else statement in line 57 executes and the game is complete. If sum is equal to 7, gameStatus is set to LOST, the if...else statement in line 57 executes and the game is complete. Clicking the **Roll Dice** button starts a new game. The program updates the four text fields in the XHTML form with the new values of the dice and the sum on each roll, and updates the text field `point` each time a new game begins.

Function `rollDice` (lines 72–85) defines its own local variables `die1`, `die2` and `workSum` in line 74. These variables are defined inside the body of `rollDice`, so they are known only in that function. If these three variable names are used elsewhere in the program, they will be entirely separate variables in memory. Lines 76–77 pick two random values in the range 1 to 6 and assign them to variables `die1` and `die2`, respectively. Lines 80–82 assign the values of `die1`, `die2` and `workSum` to the corresponding text fields in the XHTML form `craps`. Note that the integer values are converted automatically to strings when they are assigned to each text field's `value` property. Line 84 returns the value of `workSum` for use in function `play`.

Software Engineering Observation 10.9

Variables that are defined inside the body of a function are known only in that function. If the same variable names are used elsewhere in the program, they will be entirely separate variables in memory.

Note the interesting use of the various program-control mechanisms we have discussed. The craps program uses two functions—`play` and `rollDice`—and the `switch`, `if...else` and nested `if` statements. Note also the use of multiple `case` labels in the `switch` statement to execute the same statements (lines 30 and 35). In the exercises at the end of this chapter, we investigate various interesting characteristics of the game of craps.

Error-Prevention Tip 10.3

Initializing variables when they are declared in functions helps the programmer avoid incorrect results and interpret messages warning of uninitialized data.

10.7 Another Example: Random Image Generator

Random numbers are used in many Web applications. For example, as we learned in the preceding section, they are necessary for simulating randomness in online games. Web content that varies randomly adds dynamic, interesting effects to a page. In the next example, we build a **random image generator**, a script that displays a randomly selected image every time the page that contains the script is loaded.

For the script in Fig. 10.7 to function properly, the directory containing the file `RandomPicture.html` must also contain seven images with integer file names (i.e., `1.gif`, `2.gif`, ..., `7.gif`). The Web page containing this script displays one of these seven images, selected at random, each time the page loads.

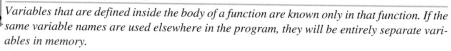

```
1    <?xml version = "1.0"?>
2    <!DOCTYPE html PUBLIC "-//W3C//DTD XHTML 1.1//EN"
3        "http://www.w3.org/TR/xhtml11/DTD/xhtml11.dtd">
4
5    <!-- Fig. 10.7: RandomPicture.html    -->
6    <!-- Randomly displays one of 7 images -->
7
```

Fig. 10.7   Random image generation using `Math.random`. (Part 1 of 2.)

```
8    <html xmlns = "http://www.w3.org/1999/xhtml">
9       <head>
10         <title>Random Image Generator</title>
11
12         <script type = "text/javascript">
13            <!--
14            document.write ( "<img src = \"" +
15               Math.floor( 1 + Math.random() * 7 ) +
16               ".gif\" width = \"105\" height = \"100\" />" );
17            // -->
18         </script>
19
20      </head>
21
22      <body>
23         <p>Click Refresh (or Reload) to run the script again</p>
24      </body>
25   </html>
```

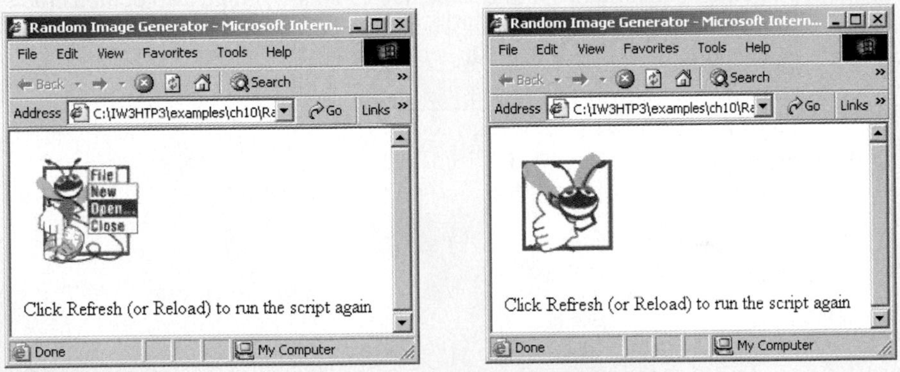

Fig. 10.7 Random image generation using `Math.random`. (Part 2 of 2.)

Lines 14–16 randomly select an image to display on a Web page. This `document.write` statement creates an image tag in the Web page with the `src` attribute set to a random integer from 1 to 7, concatenated with `".gif"`. Recall from Section 10.5 that to obtain a random integer from 1 to 7, we use the `Math.random` method, a shifting value of 1 and a scaling factor of 7. Thus, the script dynamically sets the source of the image tag to the name of one of the image files in the current directory. The rest of the image tag is constant and ensures that the width and height of the image remain the same. This allows the script to choose any image without altering the appearance of the Web page. [*Note*: All seven image files used in this example are the same original size, so the dimensions of the `img` element can be held constant without distorting any of the images.]

10.8 Scope Rules

Chapters 7 through 9 used identifiers for variable names. The attributes of variables include name, value and data type (e.g., string, number or boolean). We also use identifiers as names for user-defined functions. Each identifier in a program also has a scope.

The **scope** of an identifier for a variable or function is the portion of the program in which the identifier can be referenced. **Global variables** or **script-level variables** (i.e., variables declared in the head element of the XHTML document) are accessible in any part of a script and are said to have **global scope**. Thus every function in the script can potentially use the variables.

Identifiers declared inside a function have **function** (or **local**) **scope** and can be used only in that function. Function scope begins with the opening left brace ({) of the function in which the identifier is declared and ends at the terminating right brace (}) of the function. Local variables of a function and function parameters have function scope. If a local variable in a function has the same name as a global variable, the global variable is "hidden" from the body of the function.

Good Programming Practice 10.7

Avoid local-variable names that hide global-variable names. This can be accomplished by avoiding the use of duplicate identifiers in a script.

The script in Fig. 10.8 demonstrates the **scope rules** that resolve conflicts between global variables and local variables of the same name. This example also demonstrates the event **onload**, which calls an event handler when the <body> of the XHTML document is completely loaded into the browser window.

```
1   <?xml version = "1.0"?>
2   <!DOCTYPE html PUBLIC "-//W3C//DTD XHTML 1.0 Strict//EN"
3      "http://www.w3.org/TR/xhtml1/DTD/xhtml1-strict.dtd">
4
5   <!-- Fig. 10.8: scoping.html    -->
6   <!-- Local and Global Variables -->
7
8   <html xmlns = "http://www.w3.org/1999/xhtml">
9      <head>
10        <title>A Scoping Example</title>
11
12        <script type = "text/javascript">
13           <!--
14           var x = 1;       // global variable
15
16           function start()
17           {
18              var x = 5;    // variable local to function start
19
20              document.writeln( "local x in start is " + x );
21
22              functionA(); // functionA has local x
23              functionB(); // functionB uses global variable x
24              functionA(); // functionA reinitializes local x
25              functionB(); // global variable x retains its value
26
27              document.writeln(
28                 "<p>local x in start is " + x + "</p>" );
29           }
```

Fig. 10.8   Scoping example. (Part 1 of 2.)

```
30
31        function functionA()
32        {
33           var x = 25;   // initialized each time
34                         // functionA is called
35
36           document.writeln( "<p>local x in functionA is " +
37                             x + " after entering functionA" );
38           ++x;
39           document.writeln( "<br />local x in functionA is " +
40              x + " before exiting functionA" + "</p>" );
41        }
42
43        function functionB()
44        {
45           document.writeln( "<p>global variable x is " + x +
46              " on entering functionB" );
47           x *= 10;
48           document.writeln( "<br />global variable x is " +
49              x + " on exiting functionB"  + "</p>" );
50        }
51        // -->
52     </script>
53
54  </head>
55  <body onload = "start()"></body>
56  </html>
```

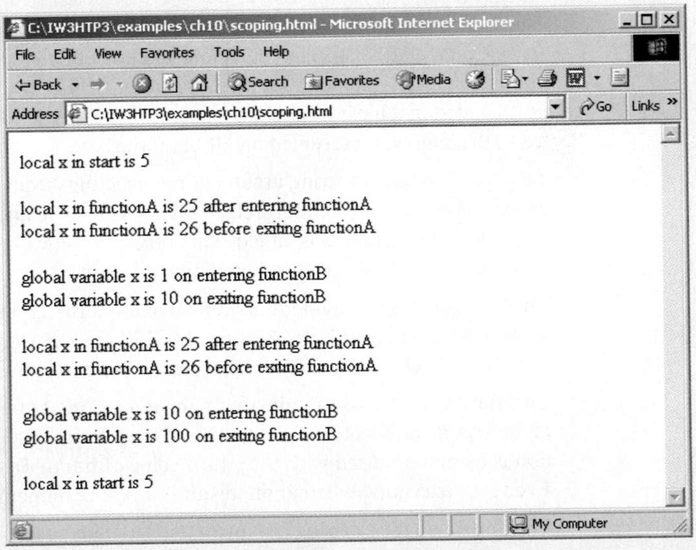

Fig. 10.8 Scoping example. (Part 2 of 2.)

Global variable x (line 14) is declared and initialized to 1. This global variable is hidden in any block (or function) that declares a variable named x. Function start (line 16) declares a local variable x (line 18) and initializes it to 5. This variable is output in a line of XHTML text to show that the global variable x is hidden in start. The script defines two other functions—functionA and functionB—that each take no arguments and return nothing. Each function is called twice from function start.

Function functionA defines local variable x (line 33) and initializes it to 25. When functionA is called, the variable is output in a line of XHTML text to show that the global variable x is hidden in functionA; then the variable is incremented and output in a line of XHTML text again before the function is exited. Each time this function is called, local variable x is re-created and initialized to 25.

Function functionB does not declare any variables. Therefore, when it refers to variable x, the global variable x is used. When functionB is called, the global variable is output in a line of XHTML text, multiplied by 10 and output in a line of XHTML text again before the function is exited. The next time function functionB is called, the global variable has its modified value, 10. Finally, the program outputs local variable x in start in a line of XHTML text again, to show that none of the function calls modified the value of x in start, because the functions all referred to variables in other scopes.

10.9 JavaScript Global Functions

JavaScript provides seven functions that are available globally in a JavaScript. We have already used two of these functions—parseInt and parseFloat. The global functions are summarized in Fig. 10.9.

Global function	Description
escape	This function takes a string argument and returns a string in which all spaces, punctuation, accent characters and any other character that is not in the ASCII character set (see Appendix D, ASCII Character Set) are encoded in a hexadecimal format (see Appendix E, Number Systems) that can be represented on all platforms.
eval	This function takes a string argument representing JavaScript code to execute. The JavaScript interpreter evaluates the code and executes it when the eval function is called. This function allows JavaScript code to be stored as strings and executed dynamically.
isFinite	This function takes a numeric argument and returns true if the value of the argument is not NaN, Number.POSITIVE_INFINITY or Number.NEGATIVE_INFINITY; otherwise, the function returns false.
isNaN	This function takes a numeric argument and returns true if the value of the argument is not a number; otherwise, it returns false. The function is commonly used with the return value of parseInt or parseFloat to determine whether the result is a proper numeric value.
parseFloat	This function takes a string argument and attempts to convert the beginning of the string into a floating-point value. If the conversion is unsuccessful, the function returns NaN; otherwise, it returns the converted value (e.g., parseFloat("abc123.45") returns NaN, and parseFloat("123.45abc") returns the value 123.45).

Fig. 10.9   JavaScript global functions. (Part 1 of 2.)

Global function	Description
parseInt	This function takes a string argument and attempts to convert the beginning of the string into an integer value. If the conversion is unsuccessful, the function returns NaN; otherwise, it returns the converted value (e.g., parseInt("abc123") returns NaN, and parseInt("123abc") returns the integer value 123). This function takes an optional second argument, from 2 to 36, specifying the **radix** (or **base**) of the number. Base 2 indicates that the first argument string is in **binary** format, base 8 indicates that the first argument string is in **octal** format and base 16 indicates that the first argument string is in **hexadecimal** format. See Appendix E, Number Systems, for more information on binary, octal and hexadecimal numbers.
unescape	This function takes a string as its argument and returns a string in which all characters previously encoded with escape are decoded.

Fig. 10.9   *JavaScript global functions. (Part 2 of 2.)*

Actually, the global functions in Fig. 10.9 are all part of JavaScript's **Global object**. The Global object contains all the global variables in the script, all the user-defined functions in the script and all the functions listed in Fig. 10.9. Because global functions and user-defined functions are part of the Global object, some JavaScript programmers refer to these functions as **methods**. We will use the term method only when referring to a function that is called for a particular object (e.g., Math.random()). As a JavaScript programmer, you do not need to use the Global object directly; JavaScript uses it for you.

10.10 Recursion

The programs we have discussed thus far are generally structured as functions that call one another in a disciplined, hierarchical manner. For some problems, however, it is useful to have functions call themselves. A **recursive function** is a function that calls itself, either directly, or indirectly through another function. Recursion is an important topic discussed at length in upper-level computer science courses. In this section, we present a simple example of recursion. Figure 10.12 (at the end of Section 10.11) summarizes the recursion examples and exercises in the book.

We consider recursion conceptually first; then we examine several programs containing recursive functions. Recursive problem-solving approaches have a number of elements in common. A recursive function is called to solve a problem. The function actually knows how to solve only the simplest case(s), or **base case(s)**. If the function is called with a base case, the function returns a result. If the function is called with a more complex problem, the function divides the problem into two conceptual pieces—a piece that the function knows how to process (the base case) and a piece that the function does not know how to process. To make recursion feasible, the latter piece must resemble the original problem, but be a slightly simpler or slightly smaller version of the original problem. Because this new problem looks like the original problem, the function invokes (calls) a fresh copy of itself to go to work on the smaller problem; this invocation is referred to as a **recursive call**, or the **recursion step**. The recursion step also normally includes the keyword `return`, because its result will be combined with the portion of the problem the function knew how to solve to form a result that will be passed back to the original caller.

The recursion step executes while the original call to the function is still open (i.e., it has not finished executing). The recursion step can result in many more recursive calls as the function divides each new subproblem into two conceptual pieces. For the recursion eventually to terminate, each time the function calls itself with a slightly simpler version of the original problem, the sequence of smaller and smaller problems must converge on the base case. At that point, the function recognizes the base case, returns a result to the previous copy of the function and a sequence of returns ensues up the line until the original function call eventually returns the final result to the caller. This process sounds exotic when compared with the conventional problem solving we have performed to this point. As an example of these concepts at work, let us write a recursive program to perform a popular mathematical calculation.

The factorial of a nonnegative integer n, written $n!$ (and pronounced "n factorial"), is the product

$$n \cdot (n - 1) \cdot (n - 2) \cdot \ldots \cdot 1$$

where $1!$ is equal to 1 and $0!$ is defined as 1. For example, $5!$ is the product $5 \cdot 4 \cdot 3 \cdot 2 \cdot 1$, which is equal to 120.

The factorial of an integer (`number` in the following example) greater than or equal to zero can be calculated **iteratively** (nonrecursively) using a `for` statement, as follows:

```
var factorial = 1;

for ( var counter = number; counter >= 1; --counter )
    factorial *= counter;
```

A recursive definition of the factorial function is arrived at by observing the following relationship:

$$n! = n \cdot (n - 1)!$$

For example, $5!$ is clearly equal to 5 * 4!, as is shown by the following equations:

$$5! = 5 \cdot 4 \cdot 3 \cdot 2 \cdot 1$$
$$5! = 5 \cdot (4 \cdot 3 \cdot 2 \cdot 1)$$
$$5! = 5 \cdot (4!)$$

The evaluation of $5!$ would proceed as shown in Fig. 10.10. Figure 10.10 (a) shows how the succession of recursive calls proceeds until $1!$ is evaluated to be 1, which terminates the recursion. Figure 10.10 (b) shows the values returned from each recursive call to its caller until the final value is calculated and returned.

Figure 10.11 uses recursion to calculate and print the factorials of the integers 0 to 10. The recursive function `factorial` first tests (line 26) to see if a terminating condition is `true` (i.e., if `number` less than or equal to 1). If `number` is indeed less than or equal to 1, `factorial` returns 1, no further recursion is necessary and the function returns. If `number` is greater than 1, line 29 expresses the problem as the product of `number` and the value returned by a recursive call to `factorial` evaluating the factorial of `number` - 1. Note that `factorial( number - 1 )` is a slightly simpler problem than the original calculation, `factorial( number )`.

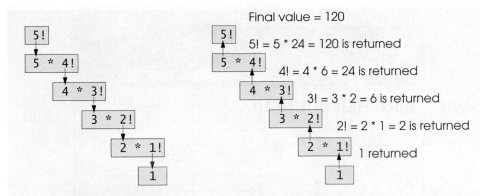

(a) Procession of recursive calls.   (b) Values returned from each recursive call.

Fig. 10.10   Recursive evaluation of *5!*.

```
1    <?xml version = "1.0"?>
2    <!DOCTYPE html PUBLIC "-//W3C//DTD XHTML 1.0 Strict//EN"
3       "http://www.w3.org/TR/xhtml1/DTD/xhtml1-strict.dtd">
4
5    <!-- Fig. 10.11: FactorialTest.html -->
6    <!-- Recursive factorial example      -->
7
8    <html xmlns = "http://www.w3.org/1999/xhtml">
9       <head>
10          <title>Recursive Factorial Function</title>
11
12          <script language = "javascript">
13             document.writeln( "<h1>Factorials of 1 to 10</h1>" );
14             document.writeln(
15                "<table border = '1' width = '100%'>" );
16
17             for ( var i = 0; i <= 10; i++ )
18                document.writeln( "<tr><td>" + i + "!</td><td>" +
19                   factorial( i ) + "</td></tr>" );
20
21             document.writeln( "</table>" );
22
23             // Recursive definition of function factorial
24             function factorial( number )
25             {
26                if ( number <= 1 )  // base case
27                   return 1;
28                else
29                   return number * factorial( number - 1 );
30             }
31          </script>
32       </head><body></body>
33    </html>
```

Fig. 10.11   Factorial calculation with a recursive function. (Part 1 of 2.)

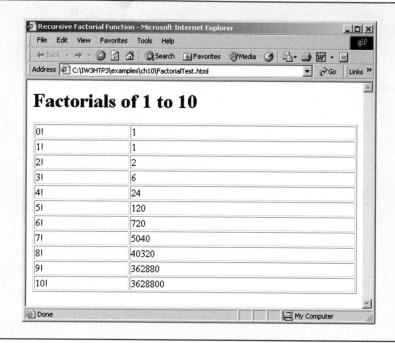

Fig. 10.11   Factorial calculation with a recursive function. (Part 2 of 2.)

Function `factorial` (lines 24–30) receives as its argument the value for which to calculate the factorial. As can be seen in the screen capture in Fig. 10.11, factorial values become large quickly. Because JavaScript uses floating-point numeric representations, we are able to calculate factorials of larger numbers.

Common Programming Error 10.6

Forgetting to return a value from a recursive function when one is needed results in a logic error.

Common Programming Error 10.7

Omitting the base case and writing the recursion step incorrectly so that it does not converge on the base case are both errors that will cause infinite recursion, eventually exhausting memory. This situation is analogous to the problem of an infinite loop in an iterative (nonrecursive) solution.

Error-Prevention Tip 10.4

Internet Explorer displays a message when a script takes an unusually long time to execute. This information allows the user of the Web page to recover from a script that contains an infinite loop or infinite recursion.

10.11 Recursion vs. Iteration

In the preceding section, we studied a function that can easily be implemented either recursively or iteratively. In this section, we compare the two approaches and discuss why a programmer might choose one approach over the other in a particular situation.

Both iteration and recursion are based on a control statement: Iteration uses a repetition statement (e.g., `for`, `while` or `do…while`); recursion uses a selection statement (e.g., `if`, `if…else` or `switch`). Both iteration and recursion involve repetition: Iteration explicitly uses a repetition statement; recursion achieves repetition through repeated function calls. Iteration and recursion each involve a termination test: Iteration terminates when the loop-continuation condition fails; recursion terminates when a base case is recognized. Iteration with counter-controlled repetition and recursion both gradually approach termination: Iteration keeps modifying a counter until the counter assumes a value that makes the loop-continuation condition fail; recursion keeps producing simpler versions of the original problem until the base case is reached. Both iteration and recursion can occur infinitely: An infinite loop occurs with iteration if the loop-continuation test never becomes false; infinite recursion occurs if the recursion step does not reduce the problem each time via a sequence that converges on the base case or if the base case is incorrect.

Recursion has many negatives. It repeatedly invokes the mechanism and, consequently, the overhead of function calls. This effect can be expensive in terms of processor time and memory space. Each recursive call causes another copy of the function (actually, only the function's variables) to be created; this effect can consume a considerable amount of memory. Iteration, on the other hand, normally occurs within a function, thereby omitting the overhead of repeated function calls and extra memory assignment. So why choose recursion?

Software Engineering Observation 10.10

Any problem that can be solved recursively can also be solved iteratively (nonrecursively). A recursive approach is normally chosen in preference to an iterative approach when the recursive approach more naturally mirrors the problem and results in a program that is easier to understand and debug. Another reason to choose a recursive solution is that an iterative solution may not be apparent.

Performance Tip 10.3

Avoid using recursion in performance-oriented situations. Recursive calls take time and consume additional memory.

Common Programming Error 10.8

Accidentally having a nonrecursive function call itself, either directly, or indirectly through another function, can cause infinite recursion.

Most programming textbooks introduce recursion much later than we have done here. We feel that recursion is so rich and complex a topic that it is better to introduce it earlier and spread examples of it over the remainder of the JavaScript chapters. Figure 10.12 summarizes the recursion examples and exercises that are provided in the text.

Let us reconsider some observations we make repeatedly throughout the book. Good software engineering is important. High performance is often important. Unfortunately, these goals are often at odds with one another. Good software engineering is key to making more manageable the task of developing larger and more complex software systems. High performance in these systems is key to realizing the systems of the future, which will make ever greater computing demands on hardware. Where do functions fit in here?

Software Engineering Observation 10.11

Modularizing programs in a neat, hierarchical manner promotes good software engineering, sometimes at the expense of performance.

Chapter	Recursion examples and exercises
10	Factorial function Sum of two integers Multiply two integers Raising an integer to an integer power Visualizing recursion
12	Printing a string input at the keyboard backward
13	Navigating the object hierarchy in Dynamic HTML

Fig. 10.12   Recursion examples and exercises in the text.

 Performance Tip 10.4

A heavily modularized program—as compared with a monolithic (i.e., one-piece) program without functions—may make a large number of function calls that consume execution time and space on a computer's processor(s). But monolithic programs are difficult to program, test, debug, maintain and evolve. So modularize your programs judiciously, always keeping in mind the delicate balance between performance and good software engineering.

10.12 Web Resources

www.citycat.ru/doc/JavaScript/intro/script.htm
JavaScript - Intro by Voodoo teaches how to program in JavaScript.

www.xs4all.nl/~ppk/js/function.html
This site provides a tutorial on JavaScript functions.

www.w3schools.com/js/js_functions.asp
This URL provides an introduction to JavaScript functions.

SUMMARY

- Experience has shown that the best way to develop and maintain a large program is to construct it from small, simple pieces, or modules. This technique is called divide and conquer.

- Modules in JavaScript are called functions. JavaScript programs are written by combining new functions that the programmer writes with "prepackaged" functions and objects available in JavaScript.

- The prepackaged functions that belong to JavaScript objects are often called methods. The term method implies that the function belongs to a particular object.

- The programmer can write programmer-defined functions to define specific tasks that may be used at many points in a script. The actual statements defining the function are written only once and are hidden from other functions.

- A function is invoked by a function call. The function call specifies the function name and provides information (as arguments) that the called function needs to do its task.

- Functions allow the programmer to modularize a program.

- All variables declared in function definitions are local variables—they are known only in the function in which they are defined.

- Most functions have parameters that provide the means for communicating information between functions via function calls. A function's parameters are also considered to be local variables.

- The divide-and-conquer approach to program development makes program development more manageable.
- Using existing functions as building blocks with which to create new programs promotes software reusability. With good function naming and definition, programs can be created from standardized functions rather than be built by using customized code.
- The `return` statement passes the result of a function call back to the calling function.
- The format of a function definition is

```
function function-name( parameter-list )
{
    declarations and statements
}
```

The *function-name* is any valid identifier. The *parameter-list* is a comma-separated list containing the names of the parameters received by the function when it is called. There should be one argument in the function call for each parameter in the function definition. If a function does not receive any values, the *parameter-list* is empty (i.e., the function name is followed by an empty set of parentheses). The *declarations* and *statements* within braces form the function body.

- There are three ways to return control to the point at which a function was invoked. If the function does not return a result, control is returned when the function-ending right brace is reached or by executing the statement

```
return;
```

- If the function does return a result, the statement

```
return expression;
```

returns the value of *expression* to the caller. When a `return` statement is executed, control returns immediately to the point at which the function was invoked.

- The `Math` object `max` method determines the larger of its two argument values.
- `Math` method `floor` rounds its floating-point number argument to the closest integer not greater than its argument's value.
- The values produced directly by the `Math` object `random` method are always in the range

```
0.0 ≤ Math.random() < 1.0
```

- We can generalize picking a random number from a range of values by writing

```
value = Math.floor( a + Math.random() * b );
```

where `a` is the shifting value (the first number in the desired range of consecutive integers) and `b` is the scaling factor (the width of the desired range of consecutive integers).

- Graphical-user-interface event handling enables JavaScript code to execute in response to the user's interaction with a GUI component in an XHTML form. This interaction causes an event. Scripts are often used to respond to events.
- Specifying the `name` attribute of an XHTML `<form>` enables script code to refer to the elements of the form. This attribute helps a script distinguish between multiple forms in the same XHTML document. Similarly, the `name` attribute is specified for each GUI component in the form, so the script code can individually refer to each GUI component.
- An XHTML button's attribute `onclick` indicates the action to take when the user clicks the button.

- When the user interacts with a GUI component, the script is notified of the event and processes the event. The user's interaction with the GUI "drives" the program. This style of programming is known as event-driven programming.

- The clicking of the button (or any other GUI interaction) is known as the event. The function that is called when an event occurs is known as an event-handling function, or event handler. When a GUI event occurs in a form, the browser automatically calls the specified event-handling function.

- The `value` property specifies the text to display in an XHTML text-field GUI component.

- Dot notation is used to access properties (e.g., the value of an input box on an XHTML form).

- Each identifier in a program has a scope.

- The scope of an identifier for a variable or function is the portion of the program in which the identifier can be referenced. The scopes for an identifier are global scope and function (or local) scope.

- Global variables defined in the `head` element of the XHTML document are accessible in any part of a script and are said to have global scope.

- Identifiers declared inside a function have function (or local) scope. Function scope begins with the opening left brace (`{`) of the function in which the identifier is declared and ends at the terminating right brace (`}`) of the function. Local variables of a function and function parameters have function scope.

- If a local variable in a function has the same name as a global variable, the global variable is "hidden" from the body of the function.

- Event `onload` calls an event handler when the `<body>` of the XHTML document is loaded into the browser.

- Function `escape` takes a string argument and returns a string in which all spaces, punctuation, accent characters and any other character that is not in the ASCII character set are encoded in a hexadecimal format that can be represented on all platforms.

- Function `eval` takes a string argument representing JavaScript code to execute. The JavaScript interpreter evaluates the code and executes it when the `eval` function is called.

- Function `isFinite` takes a numeric argument and returns `true` if the value of the argument is not NaN, `Number.POSITIVE_INFINITY` or `Number.NEGATIVE_INFINITY`; otherwise, the function returns `false`.

- Function `isNaN` takes a numeric argument and returns `true` if the value of the argument is not a number; otherwise, the function returns `false`.

- Function `parseFloat` takes a string argument and attempts to convert the beginning of the string into a floating-point value. If the conversion is not successful, the function returns NaN; otherwise, it returns the converted value.

- Function `parseInt` takes a string argument and attempts to convert the beginning of the string into an integer value. If the conversion is not successful, the function returns NaN; otherwise, it returns the converted value. This function takes an optional second argument between 2 and 36 specifying the radix (or base) of the number.

- Function `unescape` takes a string as its argument and returns a string in which all characters that were previously encoded with `escape` are decoded.

- JavaScript's global functions are all part of the `Global` object, which also contains all the global variables in the script and all the user-defined functions in the script.

- A recursive function is a function that calls itself, either directly or indirectly.

- If a recursive function is called with a base case, the function returns a result. If the function is called with a more complex problem, the function divides the problem into two or more conceptual pieces—a piece that the function knows how to do, and a slightly smaller version of the original problem. Because this new problem looks like the original problem, the function launches a recursive call to work on the smaller problem.

- For recursion to terminate, each time the recursive function calls itself with a slightly simpler version of the original problem, the sequence of smaller and smaller problems must converge on the base case. When the function recognizes the base case, the result is returned to the previous function call, and a sequence of returns ensues all the way up the line until the original call of the function eventually returns the final result.

- Both iteration and recursion are based on a control structure: Iteration uses a repetition structure; recursion uses a selection structure.

- Both iteration and recursion involve repetition: Iteration explicitly uses a repetition structure; recursion achieves repetition through repeated function calls.

- Iteration and recursion each involve a termination test: Iteration terminates when the loop-continuation condition fails; recursion terminates when a base case is recognized.

- Iteration and recursion can occur infinitely: An infinite loop occurs with iteration if the loop-continuation test never becomes false; infinite recursion occurs if the recursion step does not reduce the problem in a manner that converges on the base case.

- Recursion repeatedly invokes the mechanism and, consequently, the overhead of function calls. This effect can be expensive in term of both processor time and memory space.

TERMINOLOGY

argument in a function call
base case
block
call a function
called function
caller
calling function
compound statement
converge on the base case
copy of a value
divide and conquer
dot (.)
dot notation
escape function
eval function
event
event handler
event-driven programming
field-access operator (.)
floor method of the Math object
function
function argument
function body
function call
function definition
function keyword
function name

function parameter
function scope
function-call operator ()
Global object
global scope
global variable
invoke a function
isFinite function
isNaN function
local scope
local variable
max method of the Math object
method
modularize a program
module
name attribute of an XHTML <form>
onclick attribute
onload attribute
parameter in a function definition
parseFloat function
parseInt function
programmer-defined function
random method of the Math object
random-number generation
recursion
recursive function
recursive step

respond to an event
return statement
scaling
scaling factor
scope
script-level variable
shifting value

side effect
signature
simulation
software engineering
software reusability
unescape function
value property of an XHTML text field

SELF-REVIEW EXERCISES

10.1 Fill in the blanks in each of the following statements:
   a) Program modules in JavaScript are called _____.
   b) A function is invoked with a(n) _____.
   c) A variable known only within the function in which it is defined is called a(n) _____.
   d) The _____ statement in a called function can be used to pass the value of an expression back to the calling function.
   e) The keyword _____ indicates the beginning of a function definition.

10.2 For the given program, state the scope (either global scope or function scope) of each of the following elements:
   a) The variable x.
   b) The variable y.
   c) The function cube.
   d) The function output.

```
1    <?xml version = "1.0"?>
2    <!DOCTYPE html PUBLIC "-//W3C//DTD XHTML 1.0 Transitional//EN"
3       "http://www.w3.org/TR/xhtml1/DTD/xhtml1-transitional.dtd">
4
5    <!-- Exercise 10.2: cube.html -->
6
7    <html xmlns = "http://www.w3.org/1999/xhtml">
8       <head>
9          <title>Scoping</title>
10
11         <script type = "text/javascript">
12            <!--
13            var x;
14
15            function output()
16            {
17               for ( var x = 1; x <= 10; x++ )
18                  document.writeln( cube( x ) + "<br />" );
19            }
20
21            function cube( y )
22            {
23               return y * y * y;
24            }
25            // -->
26         </script>
27
28      </head><body onload = "output()"></body>
29   </html>
```

10.3   Fill in the blanks in each of the following statements:
   a) Programmer-defined functions, global variables and JavaScript's global functions are all part of the _____ object.
   b) Function _____ determines if its argument is or is not a number.
   c) Function _____ takes a string argument and returns a string in which all spaces, punctuation, accent characters and any other character that is not in the ASCII character set are encoded in a hexadecimal format.
   d) Function _____ takes a string argument representing JavaScript code to execute.
   e) Function _____ takes a string as its argument and returns a string in which all characters that were previously encoded with `escape` are decoded.

10.4   Fill in the blanks in each of the following statements:
   a) The _____ of an identifier is the portion of the program in which the identifier can be used.
   b) The three ways to return control from a called function to a caller are _____, _____ and _____.
   c) The _____ function is used to produce random numbers.
   d) Variables declared in a block or in a function's parameter list are of _____ scope.

10.5   Locate the error in each of the following program segments and explain how to correct it:
   a)
```
method g()
{
    document.writeln( "Inside method g" );
}
```
   b)
```
// This function should return the sum of its arguments
function sum( x, y )
{
    var result;
    result = x + y;
}
```
   c)
```
function f( a );
{
    document.writeln( a );
}
```

10.6   Write a complete JavaScript program to prompt the user for the radius of a sphere, and call function `sphereVolume` to calculate and display the volume of the sphere. Use the statement

```
volume = ( 4.0 / 3.0 ) * Math.PI * Math.pow( radius, 3 );
```

to calculate the volume. The user should input the radius through an XHTML text field in a `<form>` and click an XHTML button to initiate the calculation.

ANSWERS TO SELF-REVIEW EXERCISES

10.1   a) functions. b) function call. c) local variable. d) `return`. e) `function`.

10.2   a) Global scope. b) Function scope. c) Global scope. d) Global scope.

10.3   a) `Global`. b) `isNaN`. c) `escape`. d) `eval`. e) `unescape`.

10.4   a) scope. b) `return;` or `return` *expression*; or encountering the closing right brace of a function. c) `Math.random`. d) local.

10.5   a) Error: `method` is not the keyword used to begin a function definition.
           Correction: Change `method` to `function`.
       b) Error: The function is supposed to return a value, but does not.

Correction: Delete variable `result`, and either place the statement
```
return x + y;
```
in the function or add the following statement at the end of the function body:
```
return result;
```
c) Error: The semicolon after the right parenthesis that encloses the parameter list.
   Correction: Delete the semicolon after the right parenthesis of the parameter list.

10.6   The following solution calculates the volume of a sphere using the radius entered by the user.

```
1   <?xml version = "1.0"?>
2   <!DOCTYPE html PUBLIC "-//W3C//DTD XHTML 1.0 Transitional//EN"
3      "http://www.w3.org/TR/xhtml1/DTD/xhtml1-transitional.dtd">
4
5   <!-- Exercise 10.6: volume.html -->
6
7   <html xmlns = "http://www.w3.org/1999/xhtml">
8      <head>
9         <title>Calculating Sphere Volumes</title>
10
11         <script type = "text/javascript">
12            <!--
13            function displayVolume()
14            {
15               var radius = parseFloat( myForm.radiusField.value );
16               window.status = "Volume is " + sphereVolume( radius );
17            }
18
19            function sphereVolume( r )
20            {
21               return ( 4.0 / 3.0 ) * Math.PI * Math.pow( r, 3 );
22            }
23            // -->
24         </script>
25
26      </head>
27
28      <body>
29         <form name = "myForm" action = "">
30            Enter radius of sphere<br />
31            <input name = "radiusField" type = "text" />
32            <input name = "calculate" type = "button" value =
33               "Calculate" onclick = "displayVolume()" />
34         </form>
35      </body>
36   </html>
```

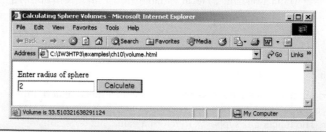

EXERCISES

10.7   Write a script that uses a function `circleArea` to prompt the user for the radius of a circle and to calculate and print the area of the circle.

10.8   A parking garage charges a $2.00 minimum fee to park for up to three hours. The garage charges an additional $0.50 per hour for each hour *or part thereof* in excess of three hours. The maximum charge for any given 24-hour period is $10.00. Assume that no car parks for longer than 24 hours at a time. Write a script that calculates and displays the parking charges for each customer who parked a car in this garage yesterday. You should input from the user the hours parked for each customer. The program should display the charge for the current customer and should calculate and display the running total of yesterday's receipts. The program should use the function `calculateCharges` to determine the charge for each customer. Use the techniques described in Self-Review Exercise 10.6 to obtain the input from the user.

10.9   Write function `distance` that calculates the distance between two points (*x1*, *y1*) and (*x2*, *y2*). All numbers and return values should be floating-point values. Incorporate this function into a script that enables the user to enter the coordinates of the points through an XHTML form.

10.10   Answer each of the following questions:
   a) What does it mean to choose numbers "at random"?
   b) Why is the `Math.random` function useful for simulating games of chance?
   c) Why is it often necessary to scale and/or shift the values produced by `Math.random`?
   d) Why is computerized simulation of real-world situations a useful technique?

10.11   Write statements that assign random integers to the variable *n* in the following ranges:
   a) $1 \leq n \leq 2$
   b) $1 \leq n \leq 100$
   c) $0 \leq n \leq 9$
   d) $1000 \leq n \leq 1112$
   e) $-1 \leq n \leq 1$
   f) $-3 \leq n \leq 11$

10.12   For each of the following sets of integers, write a single statement that will print a number at random from the set:
   a) 2, 4, 6, 8, 10.
   b) 3, 5, 7, 9, 11.
   c) 6, 10, 14, 18, 22.

10.13   Write a function `integerPower( base, exponent )` that returns the value of

$$base^{exponent}$$

For example, `integerPower( 3, 4 )` = 3 * 3 * 3 * 3. Assume that `exponent` is a positive, nonzero integer and `base` is an integer. Function `integerPower` should use a `for` or `while` statement to control the calculation. Do not use any math library functions. Incorporate this function into a script that reads integer values from an XHTML form for `base` and `exponent` and performs the calculation with the `integerPower` function. The XHTML form should consist of two text fields and a button to initiate the calculation. The user should interact with the program by typing numbers in both text fields and then clicking the button.

10.14   Write a function `multiple` that determines, for a pair of integers, whether the second integer is a multiple of the first. The function should take two integer arguments and return `true` if the second is a multiple of the first, and `false` otherwise. Incorporate this function into a script that inputs a series of pairs of integers (one pair at a time). The XHTML form should consist of two text fields and a button to initiate the calculation. The user should interact with the program by typing numbers in both text fields, and then clicking the button.

10.15 Write a script that inputs integers (one at a time) and passes them one at a time to function `isEven`, which uses the modulus operator to determine whether an integer is even. The function should take an integer argument and return `true` if the integer is even and `false` otherwise. Use sentinel-controlled looping and a `prompt` dialog.

10.16 Write a function `squareOfAsterisks` that displays a solid square of asterisks whose side is specified in integer parameter `side`. For example, if `side` is 4, the function displays

```
****
****
****
****
```

Incorporate this function into a script that reads an integer value for `side` from the user at the keyboard and performs the drawing with the `squareOfAsterisks` function.

10.17 Modify the function created in Exercise 10.16 to form the square out of whatever character is contained in parameter `fillCharacter`. Thus, if `side` is 5 and `fillCharacter` is #, the function should print

```
#####
#####
#####
#####
#####
```

10.18 Write program segments that accomplish each of the following tasks:
   a) Calculate the integer part of the quotient when integer a is divided by integer b.
   b) Calculate the integer remainder when integer a is divided by integer b.
   c) Use the program pieces developed in parts (a) and (b) to write a function `displayDigits` that receives an integer between 1 and 99999 and prints it as a series of digits, each pair of which is separated by two spaces. For example, the integer 4562 should be printed as

      4   5   6   2.
   d) Incorporate the function developed in part (c) into a script that inputs an integer from a `prompt` dialog and invokes `displayDigits` by passing to the function the integer entered.

10.19 Implement the following functions:
   a) Function `celsius` returns the Celsius equivalent of a Fahrenheit temperature, using the calculation

$$C = 5.0 / 9.0 * (F - 32);$$

   b) Function `fahrenheit` returns the Fahrenheit equivalent of a Celsius temperature, using the calculation

$$F = 9.0 / 5.0 * C + 32;$$

   c) Use these functions to write a script that enables the user to enter either a Fahrenheit or a Celsius temperature and displays the Celsius or Fahrenheit equivalent.

Your XHTML document should contain two buttons—one to initiate the conversion from Fahrenheit to Celsius and one to initiate the conversion from Celsius to Fahrenheit.

10.20 Write a function `minimum3` that returns the smallest of three floating-point numbers. Use the `Math.min` function to implement `minimum3`. Incorporate the function into a script that reads three values from the user and determines the smallest value. Display the result in the status bar.

10.21 An integer number is said to be a **perfect number** if its factors, including 1 (but not the number itself), sum to the number. For example, 6 is a perfect number, because $6 = 1 + 2 + 3$. Write a function `perfect` that determines whether parameter `number` is a perfect number. Use this function in a script that determines and displays all the perfect numbers between 1 and 1000. Print the factors of each perfect number to confirm that the number is indeed perfect. Challenge the computing power of your computer by testing numbers much larger than 1000. Display the results in a `<textarea>`.

10.22 An integer is said to be **prime** if it is greater than 1 and divisible only by 1 and itself. For example, 2, 3, 5 and 7 are prime, but 4, 6, 8 and 9 are not.

    a) Write a function that determines whether a number is prime.

    b) Use this function in a script that determines and prints all the prime numbers between 1 and 10,000. How many of these 10,000 numbers do you really have to test before being sure that you have found all the primes? Display the results in a `<textarea>`.

    c) Initially, you might think that $n/2$ is the upper limit for which you must test to see whether a number is prime, but you only need go as high as the square root of n. Why? Rewrite the program, and run it both ways. Estimate the performance improvement.

10.23 Write a function that takes an integer value and returns the number with its digits reversed. For example, given the number 7631, the function should return 1367. Incorporate the function into a script that reads a value from the user. Display the result of the function in the status bar.

10.24 The **greatest common divisor** (GCD) of two integers is the largest integer that evenly divides each of the two numbers. Write a function `gcd` that returns the greatest common divisor of two integers. Incorporate the function into a script that reads two values from the user. Display the result of the function in the browser's status bar.

10.25 Write a function `qualityPoints` that inputs a student's average and returns 4 if the student's average is 90–100, 3 if the average is 80–89, 2 if the average is 70–79, 1 if the average is 60–69 and 0 if the average is lower than 60. Incorporate the function into a script that reads a value from the user. Display the result of the function in the browser's status bar.

10.26 Write a script that simulates coin tossing. Let the program toss the coin each time the user clicks the **Toss** button. Count the number of times each side of the coin appears. Display the results. The program should call a separate function `flip` that takes no arguments and returns `false` for tails and `true` for heads. [*Note*: If the program realistically simulates the coin tossing, each side of the coin should appear approximately half the time.]

10.27 Computers are playing an increasing role in education. Write a program that will help an elementary-school student learn multiplication. Use `Math.random` to produce two positive one-digit integers. It should then display a question such as

```
How much is 6 times 7?
```

The student then types the answer into a text field. Your program checks the student's answer. If it is correct, display the string `"Very good!"` in the browser's status bar, and generate a new question. If the answer is wrong, display the string `"No. Please try again."` in the browser's status bar, and let the student try the same question again repeatedly until the student finally gets it right. A separate function should be used to generate each new question. This function should be called once when the script begins execution and each time the user answers the question correctly.

10.28 The use of computers in education is referred to as **computer-assisted instruction** (CAI). One problem that develops in CAI environments is student fatigue. This problem can be eliminated by varying the computer's dialogue to hold the student's attention. Modify the program in Exercise 10.27 to print one of a variety of comments for each correct answer and each incorrect answer. The set of responses for correct answers is as follows:

```
Very good!
Excellent!
Nice work!
Keep up the good work!
```

The set of responses for incorrect answers is as follows:

```
No. Please try again.
Wrong. Try once more.
Don't give up!
No. Keep trying.
```

Use random-number generation to choose a number from 1 to 4 that will be used to select an appropriate response to each answer. Use a `switch` statement to issue the responses.

10.29 More sophisticated computer-assisted instruction systems monitor the student's performance over a period of time. The decision to begin a new topic is often based on the student's success with previous topics. Modify the program in Exercise 10.28 to count the number of correct and incorrect responses typed by the student. After the student answers 10 questions, your program should calculate the percentage of correct responses. If the percentage is lower than 75%, print `Please ask your instructor for extra help`, and reset the program so another student can try it.

10.30 Write a script that plays a "guess the number" game as follows: Your program chooses the number to be guessed by selecting a random integer in the range 1 to 1000. The script displays the prompt `Guess a number between 1 and 1000` next to a text field. The player types a first guess into the text field and clicks a button to submit the guess to the script. If the player's guess is incorrect, your program should display `Too high. Try again.` or `Too low. Try again.` in the browser's status bar to help the player "zero in" on the correct answer and should clear the text field so the user can enter the next guess. When the user enters the correct answer, display `Congratulations. You guessed the number!` in the status bar, and clear the text field so the user can play again. [*Note*: The guessing technique employed in this problem is similar to a **binary search**, which we discuss in Chapter 11, Arrays.]

10.31 Modify the program of Exercise 10.30 to count the number of guesses the player makes. If the number is 10 or fewer, display `Either you know the secret or you got lucky!` If the player guesses the number in 10 tries, display `Ahah! You know the secret!` If the player makes more than 10 guesses, display `You should be able to do better!` Why should it take no more than 10 guesses? Well, with each good guess, the player should be able to eliminate half of the numbers. Now show why any number 1 to 1000 can be guessed in 10 or fewer tries.

10.32 Exercises 10.27 through 10.29 developed a computer-assisted instruction program to teach an elementary-school student multiplication. This exercise suggests enhancements to that program.
   a) Modify the program to allow the user to enter a grade-level capability. A grade level of 1 means to use only single-digit numbers in the problems, a grade level of 2 means to use numbers as large as two digits, and so on.
   b) Modify the program to allow the user to pick the type of arithmetic problems he or she wishes to study. An option of 1 means addition problems only, 2 means subtraction problems only, 3 means multiplication problems only, 4 means division problems only and 5 means to intermix randomly problems of all these types.

10.33 Modify the craps program in Fig. 10.6 to allow wagering. Initialize variable `bankBalance` to 1000 dollars. Prompt the player to enter a `wager`. Check that the `wager` is less than or equal to bankBalance and, if not, have the user reenter wager until a valid wager is entered. After a valid wager is entered, run one game of craps. If the player wins, increase bankBalance by wager, and print the new bankBalance. If the player loses, decrease bankBalance by wager, print the new bankBalance, check whether bankBalance has become zero and, if so, print the message Sorry. You busted! As the game progresses, print various messages to create some chatter, such as Oh, you're going for broke, huh? or Aw c'mon, take a chance! or You're up big. Now's the time to cash in your chips!. Implement the chatter as a separate function that randomly chooses the string to display.

10.34 Write a recursive function power(base, exponent) that, when invoked, returns

$$base^{\,exponent}$$

for example, power(3, 4) = 3 * 3 * 3 * 3. Assume that exponent is an integer greater than or equal to 1. (*Hint:* The recursion step would use the relationship

$$base^{\,exponent} = base \cdot base^{\,exponent-1}$$

and the terminating condition occurs when exponent is equal to 1, because

$$base^{1} = base$$

Incorporate this function into a script that enables the user to enter the base and exponent.)

10.35 *(Visualizing Recursion)* It is interesting to watch recursion in action. Modify the factorial function in Fig. 10.11 to display its local variable and recursive-call parameter. For each recursive call, display the outputs on a separate line and add a level of indentation. Do your utmost to make the outputs clear, interesting and meaningful. Your goal here is to design and implement an output format that helps a person understand recursion better. You may want to add such display capabilities to the many other recursion examples and exercises throughout the text.

10.36 What does the following function do?

```
// Parameter b must be a positive
// integer to prevent infinite recursion


function mystery( a, b )
{
   if ( b == 1 )
      return a;
   else
      return a + mystery( a, b - 1 );
}
```

10.37 Find the error in the following recursive function, and explain how to correct it:

```
function sum( n )
{
   if ( n == 0 )
      return 0;
   else
      return n + sum( n );
}
```

JavaScript: Arrays

Objectives

- To introduce the array data structure.
- To understand the use of arrays to store, sort and search lists and tables of values.
- To understand how to declare an array, initialize an array and refer to individual elements of an array.
- To be able to pass arrays to functions.
- To be able to search and sort an array.
- To be able to declare and manipulate multi-dimensional arrays.

With sobs and tears he sorted out
Those of the largest size . . .
Lewis Carroll

Attempt the end, and never stand to doubt;
Nothing's so hard, but search will find it out.
Robert Herrick

Now go, write it before them in a table,
and note it in a book.
Isaiah 30:8

'Tis in my memory lock'd,
And you yourself shall keep the key of it.
William Shakespeare

11.1 Introduction

This chapter serves as an introduction to the important topic of data structures. **Arrays** are data structures consisting of related data items (sometimes called **collections** of data items). JavaScript arrays are "dynamic" entities in that they can change size after they are created. Many of the techniques demonstrated in this chapter are used frequently in the chapters on Dynamic HTML as we introduce the collections that allow a script programmer to manipulate every element of an XHTML document dynamically.

11.2 Arrays

An array is a group of memory locations that all have the same name and normally are of the same type (although this attribute is not required in JavaScript). To refer to a particular location or element in the array, we specify the name of the array and the **position number** of the particular element in the array.

Figure 11.1 shows an array of integer values named c. This array contains 12 **elements**. Any one of these elements may be referred to by giving the name of the array followed by the position number of the element in square brackets ([]). The first element in every array is the **zeroth element**. Thus, the first element of array c is referred to as c[0], the second element of array c is referred to as c[1], the seventh element of array c is referred to as c[6] and, in general, the ith element of array c is referred to as c[i-1]. Array names follow the same conventions as other identifiers.

The position number in square brackets is called a **subscript** (or an **index**). A subscript must be an integer or an integer expression. If a program uses an expression as a subscript, then the expression is evaluated to determine the value of the subscript. For example, if we assume that variable a is equal to 5 and that variable b is equal to 6, then the statement

```
c[ a + b ] += 2;
```

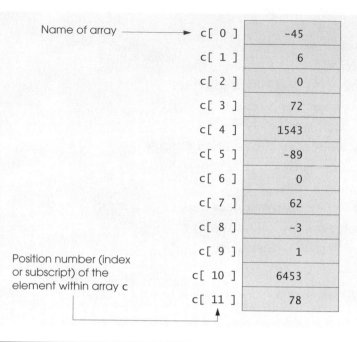

Name of array

Position number (index or subscript) of the element within array c

Fig. 11.1   Array with 12 elements.

adds 2 to array element c[11]. Note that a subscripted array name is a **left-hand-side expression**—it can be used on the left side of an assignment to place a new value into an array element.

Let us examine array c in Fig. 11.1 more closely. The array's **name** is c. The **length** of array c is 12 and is determined by the following expression:

```
c.length
```

Every array in JavaScript *knows* its own length. The array's 12 elements are referred to as c[0], c[1], c[2], ..., c[11]. The **value** of c[0] is –45, the value of c[1] is 6, the value of c[2] is 0, the value of c[7] is 62 and the value of c[11] is 78. To calculate the sum of the values contained in the first three elements of array c and store the result in variable sum, we would write

```
sum = c[ 0 ] + c[ 1 ] + c[ 2 ];
```

To divide the value of the seventh element of array c by 2 and assign the result to the variable x, we would write

```
x = c[ 6 ] / 2;
```

Common Programming Error 11.1

It is important to note the difference between the "seventh element of the array" and "array element seven." Because array subscripts begin at 0, the seventh element of the array has a subscript of 6, while array element seven has a subscript of 7 and is actually the eighth element of the array. This confusion is a source of "off-by-one" errors.

The brackets that enclose the array subscript are a JavaScript operator. Brackets have the same level of precedence as parentheses. The chart in Fig. 11.2 shows the precedence and associativity of the operators introduced to this point in the text. They are shown from top to bottom in decreasing order of precedence, alongside their associativity and type.

Operators	Associativity	Type
() [] .	left to right	highest
++ -- !	right to left	unary
* / %	left to right	multiplicative
+ -	left to right	additive
< <= > >=	left to right	relational
== !=	left to right	equality
&&	left to right	logical AND
||	left to right	logical OR
?:	right to left	conditional
= += -= *= /= %=	right to left	assignment

Fig. 11.2   Precedence and associativity of the operators discussed so far.

11.3 Declaring and Allocating Arrays

Arrays occupy space in memory. Actually, an array in JavaScript is an **Array object**. The programmer uses **operator new** to allocate dynamically (request memory for) the number of elements required by each array. Operator new creates an object as the program executes by obtaining enough memory to store an object of the type specified to the right of new. The process of creating new objects is also known as **creating an instance** or **instantiating an object**, and operator new is known as the **dynamic memory allocation operator**. Arrays are allocated with new because arrays are considered to be objects, and all objects must be created with new. To allocate 12 elements for integer array c, use the statement

```
var c = new Array( 12 );
```

The preceding statement can also be performed in two steps, as follows:

```
var c;                    // declares the array
c = new Array( 12 );      // allocates the array
```

When arrays are allocated, the elements are not initialized.

Common Programming Error 11.2

Assuming that the elements of an array are initialized when the array is allocated may result in logic errors.

Memory may be reserved for several arrays by using a single declaration. The following declaration reserves 100 elements for array b and 27 elements for array x:

```
var b = new Array( 100 ), x = new Array( 27 );
```

11.4 Examples Using Arrays

This section presents several examples of creating and manipulating arrays.

Creating and Initializing Arrays

The script in Fig. 11.3 uses operator new to allocate an Array of five elements and an empty array. The script demonstrates initializing an Array of existing elements and also shows that an Array can grow dynamically to accommodate new elements. The Array's values are displayed in XHTML tables. [*Note*: Many of the scripts in this chapter are executed in response to the <body>'s onload event.]

```
1   <?xml version = "1.0"?>
2   <!DOCTYPE html PUBLIC "-//W3C//DTD XHTML 1.0 Strict//EN"
3      "http://www.w3.org/TR/xhtml1/DTD/xhtml1-strict.dtd">
4
5   <!-- Fig. 11.3: InitArray.html -->
6   <!-- Initializing an Array       -->
7
8   <html xmlns = "http://www.w3.org/1999/xhtml">
9      <head>
10         <title>Initializing an Array</title>
11
12         <script type = "text/javascript">
13            <!--
14            // this function is called when the <body> element's
15            // onload event occurs
16            function initializeArrays()
17            {
18               var n1 = new Array( 5 );    // allocate 5-element Array
19               var n2 = new Array();        // allocate empty Array
20
21               // assign values to each element of Array n1
22               for ( var i = 0; i < n1.length; ++i )
23                  n1[ i ] = i;
24
25               // create and initialize five-elements in Array n2
26               for ( i = 0; i < 5; ++i )
27                  n2[ i ] = i;
28
29               outputArray( "Array n1 contains", n1 );
30               outputArray( "Array n2 contains", n2 );
31            }
32
33            // output "header" followed by a two-column table
34            // containing subscripts and elements of "theArray"
35            function outputArray( header, theArray )
36            {
37               document.writeln( "<h2>" + header + "</h2>" );
38               document.writeln( "<table border = \"1\" width =" +
39                  "\"100%\">" );
40
```

Fig. 11.3   Initializing the elements of an array. (Part 1 of 2.)

```
41          document.writeln( "<thead><th width = \"100\"" +
42             "align = \"left\">Subscript</th>" +
43             "<th align = \"left\">Value</th></thead><tbody>" );
44
45          for ( var i = 0; i < theArray.length; i++ )
46             document.writeln( "<tr><td>" + i + "</td><td>" +
47                theArray[ i ] + "</td></tr>" );
48
49          document.writeln( "</tbody></table>" );
50       }
51       // -->
52    </script>
53
54    </head><body onload = "initializeArrays()"></body>
55 </html>
```

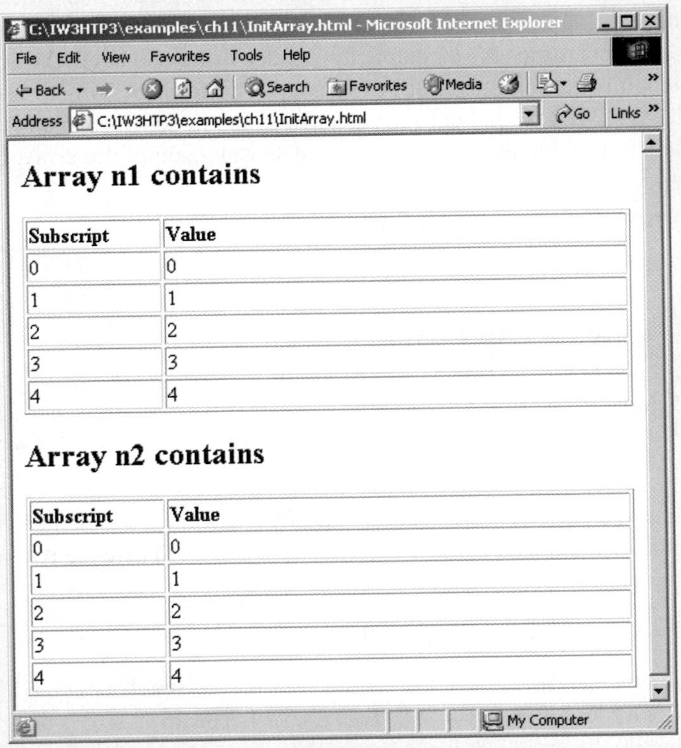

Fig. 11.3   Initializing the elements of an array. (Part 2 of 2.)

Function `initializeArrays` (defined in lines 16–31) is called by the browser as the event handler for the `<body>`'s `onload` event. Line 18 creates Array `n1` as an array of five elements. Line 19 creates Array `n2` as an empty array.

Lines 22–23 use a `for` statement to initialize the elements of `n1` to their subscript numbers (0 to 4). Note the use of zero-based counting (remember, array subscripts start at 0) so that the loop can access every element of the array. Note too the use of the expression `n1.length` in the condition for the `for` statement to determine the length of the array. In this example, the length of the array is 5, so the loop continues executing as long as the value of control variable i is less than 5. For a five-element array, the subscript values are 0 through 4, so using the less than operator, <, guarantees that the loop does not attempt to access an element beyond the end of the array.

Lines 26–27 use a for statement to add five elements to the Array n2 and initialize each element to its subscript number (0 to 4). Note that Array n2 grows dynamically to accommodate the values assigned to each element of the array.

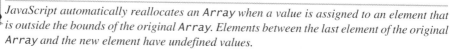

Software Engineering Observation 11.1

JavaScript automatically reallocates an Array when a value is assigned to an element that is outside the bounds of the original Array. Elements between the last element of the original Array and the new element have undefined values.

Lines 29–30 invoke function outputArray (defined in lines 35–50) to display the contents of each array in an XHTML table. Function outputArray receives two arguments—a string to be output before the XHTML table that displays the contents of the array and the array to output. Lines 37–43 output the header string and begin the definition of the XHTML table with two columns: Subscript and Value. Lines 45–47 use a for statement to output XHTML text that defines each row of the table. Once again, note the use of zero-based counting so that the loop can access every element of the array. Line 49 terminates the definition of the XHTML table.

Common Programming Error 11.3

Referring to an element outside the Array bounds is normally a logic error.

Error-Prevention Tip 11.1

When using subscripts to loop through an Array, the subscript should never go below 0 and should always be less than the number of elements in the Array (i.e., one less than the size of the Array). Make sure that the loop-terminating condition prevents the access of elements outside this range.

If the values of an Array's elements are known in advance, the elements of the Array can be allocated and initialized in the declaration of the array. There are two ways in which the initial values can be specified. The statement

```
var n = [ 10, 20, 30, 40, 50 ];
```

uses a comma-separated **initializer list** enclosed in square brackets ([and]) to create a five-element Array with subscripts of 0, 1, 2, 3 and 4. The array size is determined by the number of values in the initializer list. Note that the preceding declaration does not require the new operator to create the Array object—this functionality is provided by the interpreter when it encounters an array declaration that includes an initializer list. The statement

```
var n = new Array( 10, 20, 30, 40, 50 );
```

also creates a five-element array with subscripts of 0, 1, 2, 3 and 4. In this case, the initial values of the array elements are specified as arguments in the parentheses following new Array. The size of the array is determined by the number of values in parentheses. It is also possible to reserve a space in an Array for a value to be specified later by using a comma as a **place holder** in the initializer list. For example, the statement

```
var n = [ 10, 20, , 40, 50 ];
```

creates a five-element array with no value specified for the third element (n[2]).

Initializing Arrays with Initializer Lists

The script in Fig. 11.4 creates three Array objects to demonstrate initializing arrays with initializer lists (lines 18–21) and displays each array in an XHTML table using the same function outputArray discussed in Fig. 11.3. Note that when Array integers2 is displayed in the Web page, the elements with subscripts 1 and 2 (the second and third elements of the array) appear in the Web page as undefined. These elements are the two elements of the array for which we did not supply values in the declaration in line 21 in the script.

```
1   <?xml version = "1.0"?>
2   <!DOCTYPE html PUBLIC "-//W3C//DTD XHTML 1.0 Strict//EN"
3       "http://www.w3.org/TR/xhtml1/DTD/xhtml1-strict.dtd">
4
5   <!-- Fig. 11.4: InitArray2.html            -->
6   <!-- Initializing an Array with a Declaration -->
7
8   <html xmlns = "http://www.w3.org/1999/xhtml">
9      <head>
10         <title>Initializing an Array with a Declaration</title>
11
12         <script type = "text/javascript">
13            <!--
14            function start()
15            {
16               // Initializer list specifies number of elements and
17               // value for each element.
18               var colors = new Array( "cyan", "magenta",
19                  "yellow", "black" );
20               var integers1 = [ 2, 4, 6, 8 ];
21               var integers2 = [ 2, , , 8 ];
22
23               outputArray( "Array colors contains", colors );
24               outputArray( "Array integers1 contains", integers1 );
25               outputArray( "Array integers2 contains", integers2 );
26            }
27
28            // output "header" followed by a two-column table
29            // containing subscripts and elements of "theArray"
30            function outputArray( header, theArray )
31            {
32               document.writeln( "<h2>" + header + "</h2>" );
33               document.writeln( "<table border = \"1\"" +
34                  "width = \"100%\">" );
35               document.writeln( "<thead><th width = \"100\" " +
36                  "align = \"left\">Subscript</th>" +
37                  "<th align = \"left\">Value</th></thead><tbody>" );
38
```

Fig. 11.4   Initializing the elements of an array. (Part 1 of 2.)

```
39              for ( var i = 0; i < theArray.length; i++ )
40                 document.writeln( "<tr><td>" + i + "</td><td>" +
41                    theArray[ i ] + "</td></tr>" );
42
43              document.writeln( "</tbody></table>" );
44           }
45           // -->
46        </script>
47
48     </head><body onload = "start()"></body>
49  </html>
```

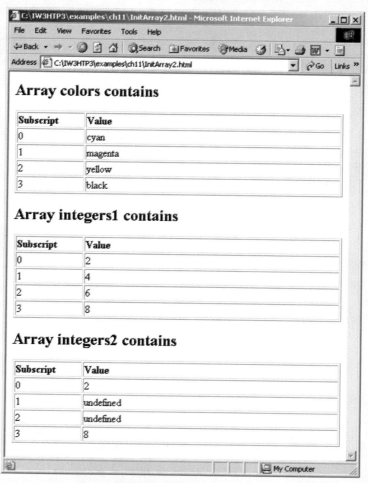

Fig. 11.4   Initializing the elements of an array. (Part 2 of 2.)

Summing the Elements of an Array with for and for...in

The script in Fig. 11.5 sums the values contained in the 10-element integer array called `theArray`, which is declared, allocated and initialized in line 16 of function `start` (lines 14–26). When the Web page loads, the script calls function `start` in response to the

<body>'s onload event. The statement in line 20 in the body of the first for loop does the
totaling. It is important to remember that the values supplied as initializers for array the-
Array would normally be read into the program. For example, in a script, the user could
enter the values through an XHTML form.

```
1    <?xml version = "1.0"?>
2    <!DOCTYPE html PUBLIC "-//W3C//DTD XHTML 1.0 Strict//EN"
3       "http://www.w3.org/TR/xhtml1/DTD/xhtml1-strict.dtd">
4
5    <!-- Fig. 11.5: SumArray.html       -->
6    <!-- Summing Elements of an Array -->
7
8    <html xmlns = "http://www.w3.org/1999/xhtml">
9       <head>
10         <title>Sum the Elements of an Array</title>
11
12         <script type = "text/javascript">
13            <!--
14            function start()
15            {
16               var theArray = [ 1, 2, 3, 4, 5, 6, 7, 8, 9, 10 ];
17               var total1 = 0, total2 = 0;
18
19               for ( var i = 0; i < theArray.length; i++ )
20                  total1 += theArray[ i ];
21
22               document.writeln( "Total using subscripts: " + total1 );
23
24               for ( var element in theArray )
25                  total2 += theArray[ element ];
26
27               document.writeln( "<br />Total using for...in: " +
28                  total2 );
29            }
30            // -->
31         </script>
32
33      </head><body onload = "start()"></body>
34   </html>
```

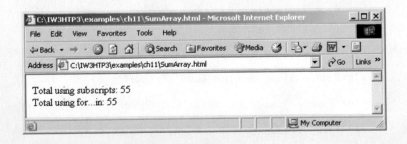

Fig. 11.5   Calculating the sum of the elements of an array.

In this example, we introduce JavaScript's **for…in** statement, which enables a script to perform a task **for each element in an array** (or, as we will see in the chapters on Dynamic HTML, for each element in a collection). This process is also known as **iterating over the elements of an array**. Lines 24–25 show the syntax of a for…in statement. Inside the parentheses, we declare the element variable used to select each element in the object to the right of keyword in (theArray in this case). When using for…in, JavaScript automatically determines the number of elements in the array. As the JavaScript interpreter iterates over theArray's elements, variable element is assigned a value that can be used as a subscript for theArray. In the case of an Array, the value assigned is a subscript in the range from 0 up to, but not including, theArray.length. Each value is added to total2 to produce the sum of the elements in the array.

Error-Prevention Tip 11.2

When iterating over all the elements of an Array, use a for…in statement to ensure that you manipulate only the existing elements of the Array. Note that a for…in statement skips any undefined elements within the array.

Using the Elements of an Array as Counters

In Chapter 10, we indicated that there is a more elegant way to implement the dice-rolling program in Fig. 10.5. The program rolled a single six-sided die 6000 times and used a switch statement to total the number of times each value was rolled. An array version of this script is shown in Fig. 11.6. The switch statement in lines 22–41 of Fig. 10.5 is replaced by line 19 of this program. This line uses the random face value as the subscript for the array frequency to determine which element to increment during each iteration of the loop. Because the random-number calculation in line 18 produces numbers from 1 to 6 (the values for a six-sided die), the frequency array must be large enough to allow subscript values of 1 to 6. The smallest number of elements required for an array to have these subscript values is seven elements (subscript values from 0 to 6). In this program, we ignore element 0 of array frequency and use only the elements that correspond to values on the sides of a die. Also, lines 28–30 of this program replace lines 48–59 in Fig. 10.5. Because we can loop through array frequency to help produce the output, we do not have to enumerate each XHTML table row as we did in Fig. 10.5.

```
 1   <?xml version = "1.0"?>
 2   <!DOCTYPE html PUBLIC "-//W3C//DTD XHTML 1.0 Strict//EN"
 3      "http://www.w3.org/TR/xhtml1/DTD/xhtml1-strict.dtd">
 4
 5   <!-- Fig. 11.6: RollDie.html          -->
 6   <!-- Roll a Six-Sided Die 6000 Times -->
 7
 8   <html xmlns = "http://www.w3.org/1999/xhtml">
 9      <head>
10         <title>Roll a Six-Sided Die 6000 Times</title>
11
12         <script type = "text/javascript">
13            <!--
14               var face, frequency = [ , 0, 0, 0, 0, 0, 0 ];
15
```

Fig. 11.6   Dice-rolling program using arrays instead of a switch. (Part 1 of 2.)

```
16          // summarize results
17          for ( var roll = 1; roll <= 6000; ++roll ) {
18             face = Math.floor( 1 + Math.random() * 6 );
19             ++frequency[ face ];
20          }
21
22          document.writeln( "<table border = \"1\"" +
23             "width = \"100%\">" );
24          document.writeln( "<thead><th width = \"100\"" +
25             " align = \"left\">Face<th align = \"left\">" +
26             "Frequency</th></thead><tbody>" );
27
28          for ( face = 1; face < frequency.length; ++face )
29             document.writeln( "<tr><td>" + face + "</td><td>" +
30                frequency[ face ] + "</td></tr>" );
31
32          document.writeln( "</tbody></table>" );
33          // -->
34       </script>
35
36    </head>
37    <body>
38       <p>Click Refresh (or Reload) to run the script again</p>
39    </body>
40 </html>
```

Face	Frequency
1	1029
2	1062
3	966
4	951
5	968
6	1024

Click Refresh (or Reload) to run the script again

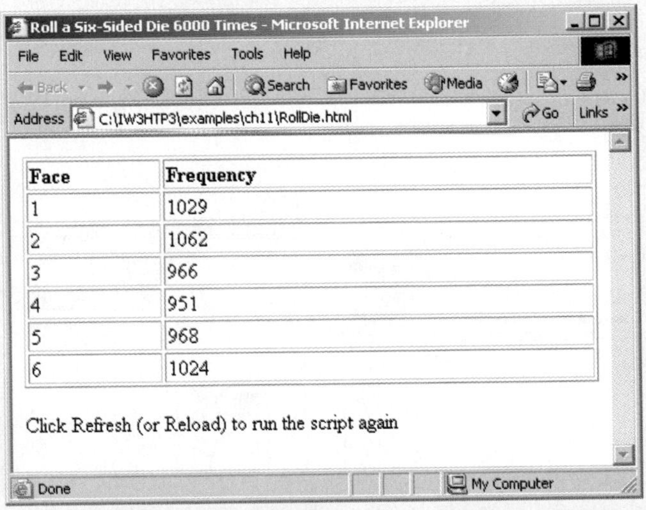

Fig. 11.6   Dice-rolling program using arrays instead of a `switch`. (Part 2 of 2.)

11.5 Random Image Generator Using Arrays

In Chapter 10, we created a random image generator that required image files to be named 1.gif, 2.gif, ..., 7.gif. In this example (Fig. 11.7), we create a more elegant random image generator that does not require the image file names to be integers. This version of the random image generator uses an array `pictures` to store the names of the image files as strings. The script generates a random integer and uses it as a subscript into the pictures array. The script outputs an XHTML img element whose src attribute contains the image file name located in the randomly selected position in the pictures array.

```
1    <?xml version = "1.0"?>
2    <!DOCTYPE html PUBLIC "-//W3C//DTD XHTML 1.1//EN"
3       "http://www.w3.org/TR/xhtml11/DTD/xhtml11.dtd">
4
5    <!-- Fig. 11.7: RandomPicture2.html    -->
6    <!-- Randomly displays one of 7 images -->
7
8    <html xmlns = "http://www.w3.org/1999/xhtml">
9       <head>
10          <title>Random Image Generator</title>
11
12          <script type = "text/javascript">
13             <!--
14             var pictures =
15                [ "CPE", "EPT", "GPP", "GUI", "PERF", "PORT", "SEO" ];
16
17             document.write ( "<img src = \"" +
18                pictures[ Math.floor( Math.random() * 7 ) ] +
19                ".gif\" width = \"105\" height = \"100\" />" );
20             // -->
21          </script>
22
23       </head>
24
25       <body>
26          <p>Click Refresh (or Reload) to run the script again</p>
27       </body>
28    </html>
```

Fig. 11.7   Random image generation using arrays.

The script declares the array pictures in lines 14–15 and initializes it with the names of seven image files. Lines 17–19 create the img tag that displays the random image on the Web page. Line 17 opens the img tag and begins the src attribute. Line 18 generates a random integer from 0 to 6 as an index into the `pictures` array, the result of which is a randomly selected image file name. The expression

```
pictures[ Math.floor( Math.random() * 7 ) ]
```

evaluates to a string from the `pictures` array, which then is written to the document (line 18). Line 19 completes the `img` tag with the extension of the image file (`.gif`) and the width and height of the image. Internet Explorer displays the image after the entire `img` tag is written to the document.

11.6 References and Reference Parameters

Two ways to pass arguments to functions (or methods) in many programming languages are **pass-by-value** and **pass-by-reference**. When an argument is passed to a function by value, a *copy* of the argument's value is made and is passed to the called function. In Java-Script, numbers and boolean values are passed to functions by value.

Error-Prevention Tip 11.3

With pass-by-value, changes to the copy of the called function do not affect the original variable's value in the calling function. This prevents the accidental side effects that so greatly hinder the development of correct and reliable software systems.

With pass-by-reference, the caller gives the called function direct access to the caller's data and allows it to modify the data if it so chooses. This procedure is accomplished by passing to the called function the actual **location in memory** (also called the **address**) where the data resides. Pass-by-reference can improve performance because it can eliminate the overhead of copying large amounts of data, but it can weaken security because the called function can access the caller's data. In JavaScript, all objects (and thus all `Arrays`) are passed to functions by reference.

Software Engineering Observation 11.2

Unlike some other languages, JavaScript does not allow the programmer to choose whether to pass each argument by value or by reference. Numbers and boolean values are passed by value. Objects are not passed to functions; rather, references to objects are passed to functions. When a function receives a reference to an object, the function can manipulate the object directly.

Software Engineering Observation 11.3

When returning information from a function via a `return` statement, numbers and boolean values are always returned by value (i.e., a copy is returned), and objects are always returned by reference (i.e., a reference to the object is returned).

To pass a reference to an object into a function, simply specify the reference name in the function call. Normally, the reference name is the identifier that the program uses to manipulate the object. Mentioning the reference by its parameter name in the body of the called function actually refers to the original object in memory, and the original object can be accessed directly by the called function.

`Arrays` are objects in JavaScript, so `Arrays` are passed to a function by reference—a called function can access the elements of the caller's original `Arrays`. The name of an array actually is a reference to an object that contains the array elements and the `length` variable, which indicates the number of elements in the array. In the next section, we demonstrate pass-by-value and pass-by-reference, using arrays.

Performance Tip 11.1

Passing arrays by reference makes sense for performance reasons. If arrays were passed by value, a copy of each element would be passed. For large, frequently passed arrays, this procedure would waste time and would consume considerable storage for the array copies.

11.7 Passing Arrays to Functions

To pass an array argument to a function, specify the name of the array (a reference to the array) without brackets. For example, if array `hourlyTemperatures` has been declared as

```
var hourlyTemperatures = new Array( 24 );
```

then the function call

```
modifyArray( hourlyTemperatures );
```

passes array `hourlyTemperatures` to function `modifyArray`. As stated in Section 11.2, every array object in JavaScript *knows* its own size (via the `length` attribute). Thus, when we pass an array object into a function, we do not pass the size of the array separately as an argument. In fact, Fig. 11.3 illustrated this concept when we passed `Arrays n1` and `n2` to function `outputArray` to display each `Array`'s contents.

Although entire arrays are passed by reference, *individual numeric and boolean array elements are passed by value exactly as simple numeric and boolean variables are passed* (the objects referred to by individual elements of an `Array` of objects are still passed by reference). Such simple single pieces of data are called **scalars**, or **scalar quantities**. To pass an array element to a function, use the subscripted name of the element as an argument in the function call.

For a function to receive an `Array` through a function call, the function's parameter list must specify a parameter that will refer to the `Array` in the body of the function. Unlike other programming languages, JavaScript does not provide a special syntax for this purpose. JavaScript simply requires that the identifier for the `Array` be specified in the parameter list. For example, the function header for function `modifyArray` might be written as

```
function modifyArray( b )
```

indicating that `modifyArray` expects to receive a parameter named b (the argument supplied in the calling function must be an `Array`). Arrays are passed by reference, and therefore when the called function uses the array name b, it refers to the actual array in the caller (array `hourlyTemperatures` in the preceding call).

Software Engineering Observation 11.4

JavaScript does not check the number of arguments or types of arguments that are passed to a function. It is possible to pass any number of values to a function. JavaScript will attempt to perform conversions when the values are used.

The script in Fig. 11.8 demonstrates the difference between passing an entire array and passing an array element. [*Note*: Function `start` (defined in lines 15–37) is called in response to the `<body>`'s `onload` event.]

```
 1  <?xml version = "1.0"?>
 2  <!DOCTYPE html PUBLIC "-//W3C//DTD XHTML 1.0 Strict//EN"
 3      "http://www.w3.org/TR/xhtml1/DTD/xhtml1-strict.dtd">
 4
 5  <!-- Fig. 11.8: PassArray.html -->
 6  <!-- Passing Arrays                -->
 7
 8  <html xmlns = "http://www.w3.org/1999/xhtml">
 9     <head>
10        <title>Passing Arrays and Individual Array
11              Elements to Functions</title>
12
13        <script type = "text/javascript">
14           <!--
15           function start()
16           {
17              var a = [ 1, 2, 3, 4, 5 ];
18
19              document.writeln( "<h2>Effects of passing entire " +
20                 "array by reference</h2>" );
21              outputArray(
22                 "The values of the original array are: ", a );
23
24              modifyArray( a );  // array a passed by reference
25
26              outputArray(
27                 "The values of the modified array are: ", a );
28
29              document.writeln( "<h2>Effects of passing array " +
30                 "element by value</h2>" +
31                 "a[3] before modifyElement: " + a[ 3 ] );
32
33              modifyElement( a[ 3 ] );
34
35              document.writeln(
36                 "<br />a[3] after modifyElement: " + a[ 3 ] );
37           }
38
39           // outputs "header" followed by the contents of "theArray"
40           function outputArray( header, theArray )
41           {
42              document.writeln(
43                 header + theArray.join( " " ) + "<br />" );
44           }
45
46           // function that modifies the elements of an array
47           function modifyArray( theArray )
48           {
49              for ( var j in theArray )
50                 theArray[ j ] *= 2;
51           }
52
```

Fig. 11.8   Passing arrays and individual array elements to functions. (Part 1 of 2.)

```
53              // function that attempts to modify the value passed
54              function modifyElement( e )
55              {
56                  e *= 2;
57                  document.writeln( "<br />value in modifyElement: " + e );
58              }
59              // -->
60          </script>
61
62      </head><body onload = "start()"></body>
63  </html>
```

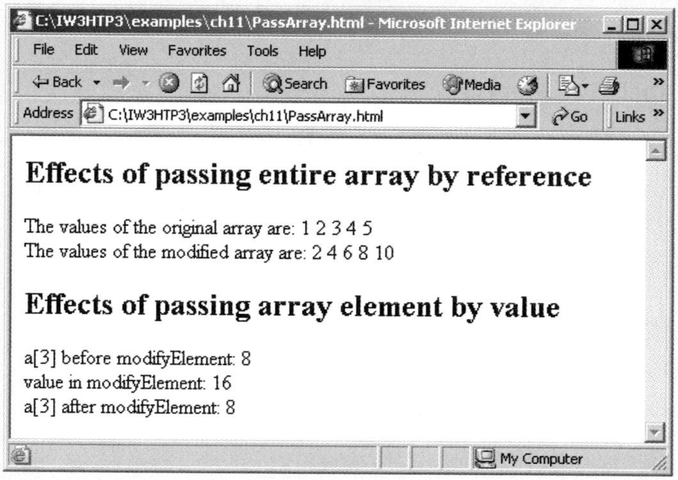

Fig. 11.8   Passing arrays and individual array elements to functions. (Part 2 of 2.)

The statement in lines 21–22 invokes function `outputArray` to display the contents of array a before it is modified. Function `outputArray` (defined in lines 40–44) receives a string to output and the array to output. The statement in lines 42–43 uses `Array` method **join** to create a string containing all the elements in `theArray`. Method `join` takes as its argument a string containing the **separator** that should be used to separate the elements of the array in the string that is returned. If the argument is not specified, the empty string is used as the separator.

Line 24 invokes function `modifyArray` (lines 47–51) and passes it array a. The `modifyArray` function multiplies each element by 2. To illustrate that array a's elements were modified, the statement in lines 26–27 invokes function `outputArray` again to display the contents of array a after it is modified. As the screen capture shows, the elements of a are indeed modified by `modifyArray`.

To show the value of a[3] before the call to `modifyElement`, lines 29–31 output the value of a[3] (as well as other information). Line 33 invokes `modifyElement` (lines 54–58) and passes a[3] as the argument. Remember that a[3] actually is one integer value in the array a. Also remember that numeric values and boolean values are always passed to functions by value. Therefore, a copy of a[3] is passed. Function `modifyElement` multiplies its argument by 2 and stores the result in its parameter e. The parameter of function `modifyElement` is a local variable in that function, so when the function terminates, the local variable is no longer accessible. Thus, when control is returned to start, the unmodified value of a[3] is displayed by the statement in lines 35–36.

11.8 Sorting Arrays

Sorting data (putting data in some particular order, such as ascending or descending) is one of the most important computing functions. A bank sorts all checks by account number so that it can prepare individual bank statements at the end of each month. Telephone companies sort their lists of accounts by last name and, within that, by first name, to make it easy to find phone numbers. Virtually every organization must sort some data—in many cases, massive amounts of data. Sorting data is an intriguing problem that has attracted some of the most intense research efforts in the field of computer science.

The Array object in JavaScript has a built-in method **sort** for sorting arrays. Figure 11.9 demonstrates the Array object's sort method.

```
1   <?xml version = "1.0"?>
2   <!DOCTYPE html PUBLIC "-//W3C//DTD XHTML 1.0 Strict//EN"
3       "http://www.w3.org/TR/xhtml1/DTD/xhtml1-strict.dtd">
4
5   <!-- Fig. 11.9: Sort.html -->
6   <!-- Sorting an Array         -->
7
8   <html xmlns = "http://www.w3.org/1999/xhtml">
9      <head>
10         <title>Sorting an Array with Array Method sort</title>
11
12         <script type = "text/javascript">
13            <!--
14            function start()
15            {
16               var a = [ 10, 1, 9, 2, 8, 3, 7, 4, 6, 5 ];
17
18               document.writeln( "<h1>Sorting an Array</h1>" );
19               outputArray( "Data items in original order: ", a );
20               a.sort( compareIntegers );  // sort the array
21               outputArray( "Data items in ascending order: ", a );
22            }
23
24            // outputs "header" followed by the contents of "theArray"
25            function outputArray( header, theArray )
26            {
27               document.writeln( "<p>" + header +
28                  theArray.join( " " ) + "</p>" );
29            }
30
31            // comparison function for use with sort
32            function compareIntegers( value1, value2 )
33            {
34               return parseInt( value1 ) - parseInt( value2 );
35            }
36            // -->
```

Fig. 11.9   Sorting an array with sort. (Part 1 of 2.)

```
37          </script>
38
39      </head><body onload = "start()"></body>
40  </html>
```

Fig. 11.9   Sorting an array with sort. (Part 2 of 2.)

By default, Array method sort (with no arguments) uses string comparisons to determine the sorting order of the Array elements. The strings are compared by the ASCII values of their characters. [*Note*: String comparison is discussed in more detail in Chapter 12, JavaScript: Objects.] In this example, we would like to sort an array of integers.

Method sort takes as its optional argument the name of a function (called the **comparator function**) that compares its two arguments and returns one of the following:

- a negative value if the first argument is less than the second argument
- zero if the arguments are equal, or
- a positive value if the first argument is greater than the second argument

This example uses function compareIntegers (defined in lines 32–35) as the comparator function for method sort. It calculates the difference between the integer values of its two arguments (function parseInt ensures that the arguments are handled properly as integers). If the first argument is less than the second argument, the difference will be a negative value. If the arguments are equal, the difference will be zero. If the first argument is greater than the second argument, the difference will be a positive value.

Line 20 invokes Array object a's sort method and passes function compareIntegers as an argument. In JavaScript, functions are considered to be data and can be assigned to variables and passed to functions like any other data. Here, method sort receives function compareIntegers as an argument, then uses the function to compare elements of the Array a to determine their sorting order.

Software Engineering Observation 11.5

Functions in JavaScript are considered to be data. Therefore, functions can be assigned to variables, stored in Arrays and passed to functions just like other data types.

11.9 Searching Arrays: Linear Search and Binary Search

Often, a programmer will be working with large amounts of data stored in arrays. It may be necessary to determine whether an array contains a value that matches a certain **key value**.

The process of locating a particular element value in an array is called **searching**. In this section we discuss two searching techniques—the simple **linear search** technique (Fig. 11.10) and the more efficient **binary search** (Fig. 11.11) technique.

Searching an Array with Linear Search

In the script in Fig. 11.10, function `linearSearch` (defined in lines 38–45) uses a `for` statement containing an `if` statement to compare each element of an array with a search key (lines 40–42). If the search key is found, the function returns the subscript value (line 42) of the element to indicate the exact position of the search key in the array. [*Note:* The loop in the `linearSearch` function terminates, and the function returns control to the caller as soon as the `return` statement in its body executes.] If the search key is not found, the function returns a value of -1. The function returns the value -1 because it is not a valid subscript number.

```
1   <?xml version = "1.0"?>
2   <!DOCTYPE html PUBLIC "-//W3C//DTD XHTML 1.0 Strict//EN"
3      "http://www.w3.org/TR/xhtml1/DTD/xhtml1-strict.dtd">
4
5   <!-- Fig. 11.10: LinearSearch.html -->
6   <!-- Linear Search of an Array      -->
7
8   <html xmlns = "http://www.w3.org/1999/xhtml">
9      <head>
10         <title>Linear Search of an Array</title>
11
12         <script type = "text/javascript">
13            <!--
14            var a = new Array( 100 );  // create an Array
15
16            // fill Array with even integer values from 0 to 198
17            for ( var i = 0; i < a.length; ++i )
18               a[ i ] = 2 * i;
19
20            // function called when "Search" button is pressed
21            function buttonPressed()
22            {
23               var searchKey = searchForm.inputVal.value;
24
25               // Array a is passed to linearSearch even though it
26               // is a global variable. Normally an array will
27               // be passed to a method for searching.
28               var element = linearSearch( a, parseInt( searchKey ) );
29
30               if ( element != -1 )
31                  searchForm.result.value =
32                     "Found value in element " + element;
33               else
34                  searchForm.result.value = "Value not found";
35            }
36
```

Fig. 11.10 Linear search of an array. (Part 1 of 2.)

```
37              // Search "theArray" for the specified "key" value
38              function linearSearch( theArray, key )
39              {
40                 for ( var n = 0; n < theArray.length; ++n )
41                    if ( theArray[ n ] == key )
42                       return n;
43
44                 return -1;
45              }
46              // -->
47           </script>
48
49        </head>
50
51        <body>
52           <form name = "searchForm" action  = "">
53              <p>Enter integer search key<br />
54              <input name = "inputVal" type = "text" />
55              <input name = "search" type = "button" value = "Search"
56                    onclick = "buttonPressed()" /><br /></p>
57
58              <p>Result<br />
59              <input name = "result" type = "text" size = "30" /></p>
60           </form>
61        </body>
62     </html>
```

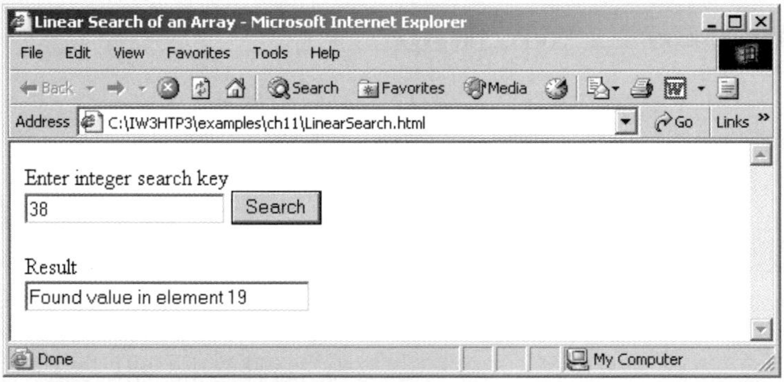

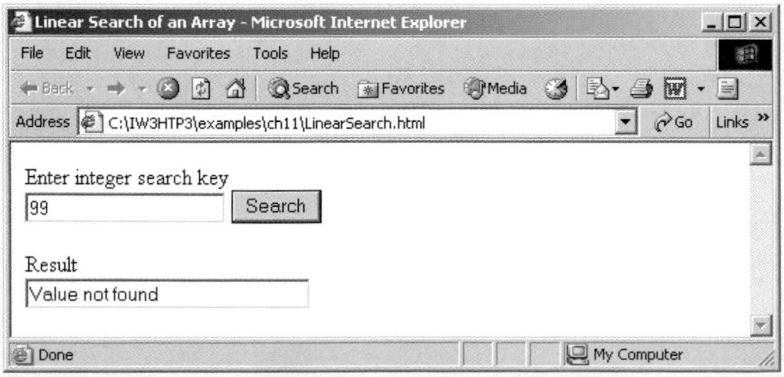

Fig. 11.10 Linear search of an array. (Part 2 of 2.)

If the array being searched is not in any particular order, it is just as likely that the value will be found in the first element as the last. On average, therefore, the program will have to compare the search key with half the elements of the array.

The program contains a 100-element array (defined in line 14) filled with the even integers from 0 to 198. The user types the search key in a text field (defined in the XHTML form in lines 52–60) and clicks the **Search** button to start the search. [*Note*: The array is passed to `linearSearch` even though the array is a global script variable. We do this because arrays are normally passed to functions for searching.]

Searching an Array with Binary Search
The linear-search method works well for small arrays or for unsorted arrays. However, for large arrays, linear searching is inefficient. If the array is sorted, the high-speed binary-search technique can be used.

After each comparison, the binary search algorithm eliminates half of the elements in the array being searched. The algorithm locates the middle array element and compares it to the search key. If they are equal, the search key has been found and the subscript of that element is returned. Otherwise, the problem is reduced to searching half of the array. If the search key is less than the middle array element, the first half of the array is searched; otherwise, the second half of the array is searched. If the search key is not the middle element in the specified subarray (piece of the original array), the algorithm is repeated on one quarter of the original array. The search continues until the search key is equal to the middle element of a subarray or until the subarray consists of one element that is not equal to the search key (i.e., the search key is not found).

In a worst-case scenario, searching an array of 1023 elements will take only 10 comparisons using a binary search. Repeatedly dividing 1024 by 2 (because after each comparison we are able to eliminate half of the array) yields the values 512, 256, 128, 64, 32, 16, 8, 4, 2 and 1. The number 1024 (2^{10}) is divided by 2 only ten times to get the value 1. Dividing by 2 is equivalent to one comparison in the binary search algorithm. An array of one million elements takes a maximum of 20 comparisons to find the key. An array of 1 billion elements takes a maximum of 30 comparisons to find the key. When searching a sorted array, this is a tremendous increase in performance over the linear search that required comparing the search key to an average of half the elements in the array. For a 1-billion-element array, this is the difference between an average of 500 million comparisons and a maximum of 30 comparisons! The maximum number of comparisons needed for the binary search of any sorted array is the exponent of the first power of 2 greater than the number of elements in the array.

Figure 11.11 presents the iterative version of function `binarySearch` (lines 42–66). Function `binarySearch` is called from line 32 of function `buttonPressed` (lines 20–39)—the event handler for the **Search** button in the XHTML form. Function `binarySearch` receives two arguments—an array called `theArray` (the array to search) and `key` (the search key). The array is passed to `binarySearch` even though the array is global variable. Once again, we do this because an array is normally passed to a function for searching. If `key` matches the `middle` element of a subarray (line 57), `middle` (the subscript of the current element) is returned, to indicate that the value was found and the search is complete. If `key` does not match the `middle` element of a subarray, the `low` subscript or the `high` subscript (both declared in the function) is adjusted, so that a smaller subarray can be searched. If `key` is less than the middle element (line 59), the `high` subscript is set to middle - 1 and the search is continued on the elements from low to middle - 1. If key is greater than the middle element (line 61), the low subscript is set to middle + 1 and the search is continued on the elements from middle + 1 to high. These comparisons are performed by the nested if...else statement in lines 57–62.

```
1    <?xml version = "1.0"?>
2    <!DOCTYPE html PUBLIC "-//W3C//DTD XHTML 1.0 Transitional//EN"
3       "http://www.w3.org/TR/xhtml1/DTD/xhtml1-transitional.dtd">
4
5    <!-- Fig. 11.11 : BinarySearch.html -->
6    <!-- Binary search                   -->
7
8    <html xmlns = "http://www.w3.org/1999/xhtml">
9       <head>
10          <title>Binary Search</title>
11
12          <script type = "text/javascript">
13             <!--
14             var a = new Array( 15 );
15
16             for ( var i = 0; i < a.length; ++i )
17                a[ i ] = 2 * i;
18
19             // function called when "Search" button is pressed
20             function buttonPressed()
21             {
22                var searchKey = searchForm.inputVal.value;
23
24                searchForm.result.value =
25                   "Portions of array searched\n";
26
27                // Array a is passed to binarySearch even though it
28                // is a global variable. This is done because
29                // normally an array is passed to a method
30                // for searching.
31                var element =
32                   binarySearch( a, parseInt( searchKey ) );
33
34                if ( element != -1 )
35                   searchForm.result.value +=
36                      "\nFound value in element " + element;
37                else
38                   searchForm.result.value += "\nValue not found";
39             }
40
41             // Binary search
42             function binarySearch( theArray, key )
43             {
44                var low = 0;                      // low subscript
45                var high = theArray.length - 1;  // high subscript
46                var middle;                       // middle subscript
47
```

Fig. 11.11 Binary search of an array. (Part 1 of 3.)

```
48                while ( low <= high ) {
49                    middle = ( low + high ) / 2;
50
51                    // The following line is used to display the
52                    // part of theArray currently being manipulated
53                    // during each iteration of the binary
54                    // search loop.
55                    buildOutput( theArray, low, middle, high );
56
57                    if ( key == theArray[ middle ] )  // match
58                        return middle;
59                    else if ( key < theArray[ middle ] )
60                        high = middle - 1; // search low end of array
61                    else
62                        low = middle + 1; // search high end of array
63                }
64
65                return -1;    // searchKey not found
66            }
67
68            // Build one row of output showing the current
69            // part of the array being processed.
70            function buildOutput( theArray, low, mid, high )
71            {
72                for ( var i = 0; i < theArray.length; i++ ) {
73                    if ( i < low || i > high )
74                        searchForm.result.value += "      ";
75                    // mark middle element in output
76                    else if ( i == mid )
77                        searchForm.result.value += theArray[ i ] +
78                            ( theArray[ i ] < 10 ? "*  " : "* " );
79                    else
80                        searchForm.result.value += theArray[ i ] +
81                            ( theArray[ i ] < 10 ? "   " : "  " );
82                }
83
84                searchForm.result.value += "\n";
85            }
86            // -->
87        </script>
88    </head>
89
90    <body>
91        <form name = "searchForm" action = "">
92            <p>Enter integer search key<br />
93            <input name = "inputVal" type = "text" />
94            <input name = "search" type = "button" value =
95                "Search" onclick = "buttonPressed()" /><br /></p>
96            <p>Result<br />
97            <textarea name = "result" rows = "7" cols = "60">
98            </textarea></p>
99        </form>
100    </body>
```

Fig. 11.11   Binary search of an array. (Part 2 of 3.)

101 `</html>`

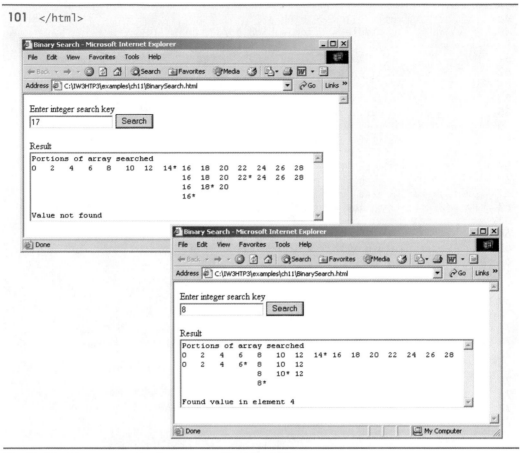

Fig. 11.11 Binary search of an array. (Part 3 of 3.)

This program uses a 15-element array (defined at line 14). The first power of 2 greater than the number of elements is 16 (2^4), so `binarySearch` requires at most four comparisons to find the `key`. To illustrate this, line 55 calls method `buildOutput` (declared in lines 70–85) to output each subarray during the binary-search process. Method `build-Output` marks the middle element in each subarray with an asterisk (*) to indicate the element with which the `key` is compared. No matter what search key is entered, each search in this example results in a maximum of four lines of output—one per comparison.

11.10 Multidimensional Arrays

Multidimensional arrays with two subscripts often are used to represent **tables** of values consisting of information arranged in **rows** and **columns**. To identify a particular table element, we must specify the two subscripts; by convention, the first identifies the element's row, and the second identifies the element's column. Arrays that require two subscripts to identify a particular element are called **two-dimensional arrays**. Note that multidimensional arrays can have more than two subscripts. JavaScript does not support multidimensional arrays directly, but does allow the programmer to specify one-dimensional arrays whose elements are also one-dimensional arrays, thus achieving the same effect. Figure 11.12 illustrates a two-dimensional array a, that contains three rows and four columns (i.e., a three-by-four array). In general, an array with *m* rows and *n* columns is called an ***m*-by-*n* array**.

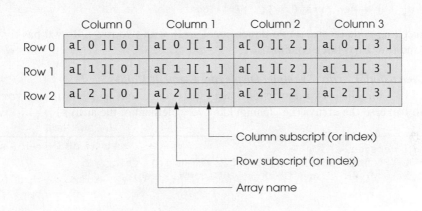

Fig. 11.12 Two-dimensional array with three rows and four columns.

Every element in array a is identified in Fig. 11.12 by an element name of the form a[i][j]; a is the name of the array, and i and j are the subscripts that uniquely identify the row and column, respectively, of each element in a. Note that the names of the elements in the first row all have a first subscript of 0; the names of the elements in the fourth column all have a second subscript of 3.

Arrays of One-Dimensional Arrays

Multidimensional arrays can be initialized in declarations like a one-dimensional array. Array b with two rows and two columns could be declared and initialized with the statement

```
var b = [ [ 1, 2 ], [ 3, 4 ] ];
```

The values are grouped by row in square brackets. So 1 and 2 initialize b[0][0] and b[0][1], and 3 and 4 initialize b[1][0] and b[1][1]. The interpreter determines the number of rows by counting the number of sub initializer lists (represented by sets of square brackets) in the main initializer list. The interpreter determines the number of columns in each row by counting the number of initializer values in the sub initializer list for that row.

Two-Dimensional Arrays with Rows of Different Lengths

Multidimensional arrays are maintained as arrays of arrays. The declaration

```
var b = [ [ 1, 2 ], [ 3, 4, 5 ] ];
```

creates array b with row 0 containing two elements (1 and 2) and row 1 containing three elements (3, 4 and 5).

Creating Two-Dimensional Arrays with *new*

A multidimensional array in which each row has a different number of columns can be allocated dynamically, as follows:

```
var b;
b = new Array( 2 );        // allocate rows
b[ 0 ] = new Array( 5 );   // allocate columns for row 0
b[ 1 ] = new Array( 3 );   // allocate columns for row 1
```

The preceding code creates a two-dimensional array with two rows. Row 0 has five columns, and row 1 has three columns.

Two-Dimensional Array Example: Displaying Element Values

Figure 11.13 initializes two-dimensional arrays in declarations and uses nested for...in loops to **traverse the arrays** (i.e., manipulate every element of the array).

```
 1   <?xml version = "1.0"?>
 2   <!DOCTYPE html PUBLIC "-//W3C//DTD XHTML 1.0 Strict//EN"
 3      "http://www.w3.org/TR/xhtml1/DTD/xhtml1-strict.dtd">
 4
 5   <!-- Fig. 11.13: InitArray3.html          -->
 6   <!-- Initializing Multidimensional Arrays -->
 7
 8   <html xmlns = "http://www.w3.org/1999/xhtml">
 9      <head>
10         <title>Initializing Multidimensional Arrays</title>
11
12         <script type = "text/javascript">
13            <!--
14            function start()
15            {
16               var array1 = [ [ 1, 2, 3 ],       // first row
17                              [ 4, 5, 6 ] ];      // second row
18               var array2 = [ [ 1, 2 ],           // first row
19                              [ 3 ],              // second row
20                              [ 4, 5, 6 ] ];      // third row
21
22               outputArray( "Values in array1 by row", array1 );
23               outputArray( "Values in array2 by row", array2 );
24            }
25
26            function outputArray( header, theArray )
27            {
28               document.writeln( "<h2>" + header + "</h2><tt>" );
29
30               for ( var i in theArray ) {
31
32                  for ( var j in theArray[ i ] )
33                     document.write( theArray[ i ][ j ] + " " );
34
35                  document.writeln( "<br />" );
36               }
```

Fig. 11.13   Initializing multidimensional arrays. (Part 1 of 2.)

```
37
38                   document.writeln( "</tt>" );
39            }
40         // -->
41      </script>
42
43   </head><body onload = "start()"></body>
44   </html>
```

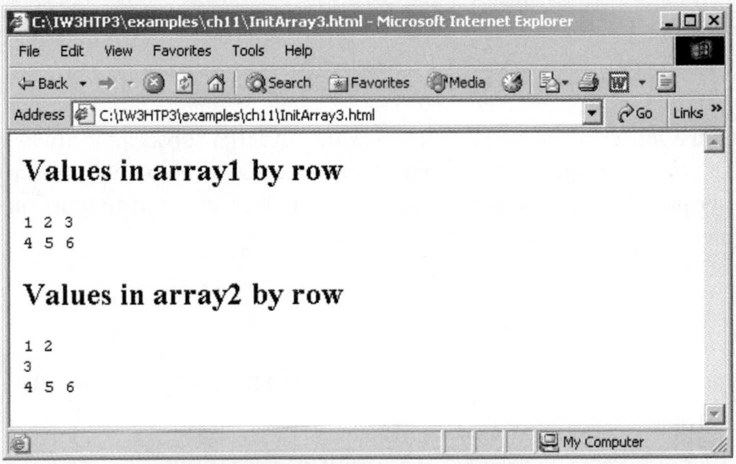

Fig. 11.13 Initializing multidimensional arrays. (Part 2 of 2.)

The program declares two arrays in function `start` (which is called in response to the `<body>`'s `onload` event). The declaration of `array1` (lines 16–17) provides six initializers in two sublists. The first sublist initializes the first row of the array to the values 1, 2 and 3; the second sublist initializes the second row of the array to the values 4, 5 and 6. The declaration of `array2` (lines 18–20) provides six initializers in three sublists. The sublist for the first row explicitly initializes the first row to have two elements, with values 1 and 2, respectively. The sublist for the second row initializes the second row to have one element, with value 3. The sublist for the third row initializes the third row to the values 4, 5 and 6.

Function `start` calls function `outputArray` from lines 22–23 to display each array's elements in the Web page. Function `outputArray` (lines 26–39) receives two arguments—a string `header` to output before the array and the array to output (called `theArray`). Note the use of a nested `for...in` statement to output the rows of each two-dimensional array. The outer `for...in` statement iterates over the rows of the array. The inner `for...in` statement iterates over the columns of the current row being processed. The nested `for...in` statement in this example could have been written with `for` statements, as follows:

```
for ( var i = 0; i < theArray.length; ++i ) {

    for ( var j = 0; j < theArray[ i ].length; ++j )
        document.write( theArray[ i ][ j ] + " " );

    document.writeln( "<br />" );
}
```

In the outer `for` statement, the expression `theArray.length` determines the number of rows in the array. In the inner `for` statement, the expression `theArray[i].length` determines the number of columns in each row of the array. This condition enables the loop to determine, for each row, the exact number of columns.

Common Multidimensional-Array Manipulations with for and for...in Statements
Many common array manipulations use `for` or `for...in` repetition statements. For example, the following `for` statement sets all the elements in the third row of array `a` in Fig. 11.12 to zero:

```
for ( var col = 0; col < a[ 2 ].length; ++col )
   a[ 2 ][ col ] = 0;
```

We specified the *third* row; therefore, we know that the first subscript is always 2 (0 is the first row and 1 is the second row). The `for` loop varies only the second subscript (i.e., the column subscript). The preceding `for` statement is equivalent to the assignment statements

```
a[ 2 ][ 0 ] = 0;
a[ 2 ][ 1 ] = 0;
a[ 2 ][ 2 ] = 0;
a[ 2 ][ 3 ] = 0;
```

The following `for...in` statement is also equivalent to the preceding `for` statement:

```
for ( var col in a[ 2 ] )
   a[ 2 ][ col ] = 0;
```

The following nested `for` statement determines the total of all the elements in array `a`:

```
var total = 0;

for ( var row = 0; row < a.length; ++row )

   for ( var col = 0; col < a[ row ].length; ++col )
      total += a[ row ][ col ];
```

The `for` statement totals the elements of the array, one row at a time. The outer `for` statement begins by setting the `row` subscript to 0, so that the elements of the first row may be totaled by the inner `for` statement. The outer `for` statement then increments `row` to 1, so that the elements of the second row can be totaled. Then the outer `for` statement increments `row` to 2, so that the elements of the third row can be totaled. The result can be displayed when the nested `for` statement terminates. The preceding `for` statement is equivalent to the following `for...in` statement:

```
var total = 0;

for ( var row in a )

   for ( var col in a[ row ] )
      total += a[ row ][ col ];
```

11.11 Building an Online Quiz

Online quizzes and polls are popular Web applications often used for educational purposes or just for fun. Web developers typically build quizzes using simple XHTML forms and grade the quizzes with JavaScript. Arrays allow a programmer to represent several possible answer choices in a single data structure. Figure 11.14 contains an online quiz consisting of one question. The quiz page contains one of the tip icons used throughout this book and an XHTML form in which the user identifies the type of tip the image represents by selecting one of four radio buttons. After the user selects one of the radio button choices and submits the form, the script determines whether the user selected the correct type of tip to match the mystery image. The JavaScript function that checks the user's answer combines several of the concepts from the current chapter and previous chapters in a concise and useful script.

```
1   <?xml version = "1.0" encoding = "utf-8"?>
2   <!DOCTYPE html PUBLIC "-//W3C//DTD XHTML 1.1//EN"
3      "http://www.w3.org/TR/xhtml11/DTD/xhtml11.dtd">
4
5   <!-- Fig. 11.14: quiz.html -->
6   <!-- Online Quiz            -->
7
8   <html xmlns = "http://www.w3.org/1999/xhtml">
9   <head>
10  <title>Online Quiz</title>
11
12  <script type = "text/JavaScript">
13
14     function checkAnswers()
15     {
16        // determine whether the answer is correct
17        if ( myQuiz.radiobutton[ 1 ].checked )
18           document.write( "Congratulations, your answer is correct" );
19        else // if the answer is incorrect
20           document.write( "Your answer is incorrect. Please try again" );
21     }
22
23  </script>
24
25  </head>
26
27  <body>
28     <form id = "myQuiz" action = "JavaScript:checkAnswers()">
29        <p>Select the name of the tip that goes with the image shown:<br />
30           <img src="EPT.gif" width="108" height="100" alt="mystery tip"/>
31           <br />
32
33           <input type = "radio" name = "radiobutton" value = "CPE" />
34           <label>Common Programming Error</label>
35
36           <input type = "radio" name = "radiobutton" value = "EPT" />
37           <label>Error-Prevention Tip</label>
38
39           <input type = "radio" name = "radiobutton" value = "PERF" />
40           <label>Performance Tip</label>
41
```

Fig. 11.14 Online quiz graded with JavaScript. (Part 1 of 2.)

```
42            <input type = "radio" name = "radiobutton" value = "PORT" />
43            <label>Portability Tip</label><br />
44
45            <input type = "submit" name = "submit" value = "Submit" />
46            <input type = "reset" name = "reset" value = "Reset" />
47         </p>
48      </form>
49   </body>
50   </html>
```

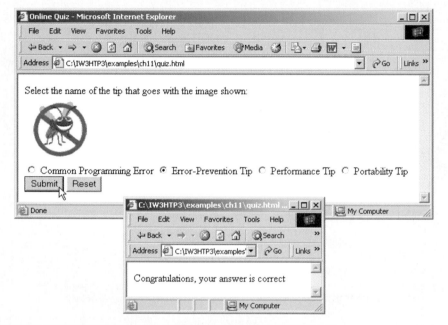

Fig. 11.14   Online quiz graded with JavaScript. (Part 2 of 2.)

Before we discuss the script code, we first discuss the body element (lines 27–49) of the XHTML document. The GUI components in the body play an important role in the script.

Lines 28–48 define the form that presents the quiz to users. Line 28 begins the form element and specifies the attribute action to be "JavaScript:checkAnswers()", indicating that the interpreter should execute the JavaScript function checkAnswers (lines 14–21) when the user submits the form (i.e., clicks the **Submit** button or presses *Enter*).

Line 30 adds the tip image to the page. Lines 33–43 display the radio buttons and corresponding labels that display possible answer choices. Note that all the radio buttons share the name radiobutton. Lines 45–46 add the submit and reset buttons to the page.

We now examine the script used to check the answer submitted by the user. Lines 14–21 declare the function checkAnswers that contains all the JavaScript required to grade the quiz. The if...else statement in lines 17–20 determines whether the user answered the question correctly. The image that the user is asked to identify is the Error-Prevention Tip icon. Thus the correct answer to the quiz corresponds to the second radio button.

A group of XHTML radio buttons is represented in JavaScript by an array whose name is equal to the value of the name attribute assigned to each of the radio buttons in the group.

In the current example, the radio buttons share the name `radiobutton` (lines 33–43), so an array named `radiobutton` contains information about their status. The radio buttons are part of the XHTML form `myQuiz`, so we access their corresponding array using dot notation as `myQuiz.radiobutton`. The array element `myQuiz.radiobutton[ 1 ]` corresponds to the correct answer (i.e., the second radio button).

Line 17 determines whether the property **checked** of the second radio button is `true`. Property `checked` of a radio button is `true` when the radio button is selected, and it is `false` when the radio button is not selected. Recall that only one radio button may be selected at any given time. If property `myQuiz.radiobutton[ 1 ].checked` is `true`, indicating that the correct answer is selected, the script displays a congratulatory message in the browser window (line 18). If property `checked` of the radio button is `false`, then the script outputs an alternate message (line 20).

11.12 Web Resources

`www.pageresource.com/jscript/jarray.htm`
This site discusses JavaScript arrays.

`hotwired.lycos.com/webmonkey/98/04/index1a_page8.html?tw=programming`
Thau's JavaScript Tutorial introduces JavaScript arrays.

SUMMARY

- Arrays are data structures consisting of related data items (sometimes called collections).

- Arrays are dynamic entities, in that they can change size after they are created.

- An array is a group of memory locations that all have the same name and are normally of the same type (although this attribute is not required).

- To refer to a particular location or element in an array, specify the name of the array and the position number of the element in the array.

- The first element in every array is the zeroth element.

- The length of an array is determined by *arrayName*.`length`.

- An array in JavaScript is an `Array` object. Operator `new` is used to dynamically allocate the number of elements required by an array. Operator `new` creates an object as the program executes, by obtaining enough memory to store an object of the type specified to the right of `new`.

- The process of creating new objects is also known as creating an instance, or instantiating an object, and operator `new` is known as the dynamic memory allocation operator.

- An array can be initialized with a comma-separated initializer list enclosed in square brackets (`[` and `]`). The array size is determined by the number of values in the initializer list. When using an initializer list in an array declaration, the `new` operator is not required to create the `Array` object— this operator is provided by the interpreter.

- It is possible to reserve a space in an `Array` for a value to be specified later by using a comma as a place holder in the initializer list.

- JavaScript's `for...in` statement enables a script to perform a task `for` each element `in` an array. This process is also known as iterating over the elements of an array.

- The basic syntax of a `for...in` statement is

        for (var *element* in *arrayName*)
            statement

where element is the name of the variable to which the for…in statement assigns a subscript number and arrayName is the array over which to iterate.

- When a value is assigned to an element that is outside the current bounds of the Array, JavaScript allocates more memory so that the Array will contain the appropriate number of elements. The new elements of the array are not initialized.

- Two ways to pass arguments to functions (or methods) in many programming languages are pass-by-value and pass-by-reference.

- When an argument is passed to a function by value, a copy of the argument's value is made and passed to the called function. Numbers and boolean values are passed by value.

- With pass-by-reference, the caller gives the called function the ability to access the caller's data directly and modify it. This procedure is accomplished by passing to the called function the location or address in memory where the data resides. All objects and Arrays are passed by reference.

- To pass a reference to an object into a function, specify the name of the reference in the function call. The name of the reference is the identifier that is used to manipulate the object in the program.

- The name of an array is actually a reference to an object that contains the elements of the array and the length variable, which indicates the number of elements in the array.

- Putting data in some particular order, such as ascending or descending, is called sorting the data.

- The Array object in JavaScript has a built-in method, sort, for sorting arrays. By default, Array method sort uses string comparisons to determine the sorting order of the elements of the Array.

- Method sort takes as its optional argument the name of a comparator function, which returns a negative value if its first argument is less than its second argument, zero if the arguments are equal or a positive value if its first argument is greater than its second argument.

- The process of locating a particular element value (the key value) in an array is called searching.

- A linear search compares each element of an array with a search key. If the search key is found, the linear search normally returns the subscript for the element, to indicate the exact position of the search key in the array. If the search key is not found, the linear search normally returns -1.

- If the array being searched with a linear search is not in any particular order, it is just as likely that the value will be found in the first element as the last. On average, the program has to compare the search key with half the elements of the array.

- If an array is sorted, the binary search technique can be used to locate a search key. The binary search algorithm eliminates half of the elements in the array being searched after each comparison. The algorithm locates the middle array element and compares it to the search key. If they are equal, the search key has been found and the subscript of that element is returned. Otherwise, the problem is reduced to searching half of the array. If the search key is less than the middle array element, the first half of the array is searched; otherwise, the second half of the array is searched.

- The maximum number of comparisons needed for the binary search of any sorted array is the exponent of the first power of 2 greater than the number of elements in the array.

- Multidimensional arrays with two subscripts are often used to represent tables of values consisting of information arranged in rows and columns. Two subscripts identify a particular table element; the first identifies the element's row, and the second identifies the element's column.

- Arrays requiring two subscripts to identify a particular element are called two-dimensional arrays. Multidimensional arrays can have more than two subscripts.

- JavaScript does not support multidimensional arrays directly, but does allow one-dimensional arrays whose elements are also one-dimensional arrays, thus achieving the same effect.

- In general, an array with m rows and n columns is called an m-by-n array.

- Multidimensional arrays can be initialized with initializer lists. The compiler determines the number of rows by counting the number of subinitializer lists (represented by sets of square brackets) in the main initializer list. The compiler determines the number of columns in each row by counting the number of initializer values in the subinitializer list for the row.

- A group of XHTML radio buttons is represented by a JavaScript array with the same name as the `name` attribute assigned to each of the radio buttons in the group.

- Property `checked` of a radio button is true when the radio button is selected, and it is false when the radio button is not selected.

TERMINOLOGY

`a[i]`	linear search of an array
`a[i][j]`	location in an array
array	*m*-by-*n* array
array initializer list	multidimensional array
`Array` object	name of an array
binary search	off-by-one error
bounds of an array	one-dimensional array
`checked` property of a radio button	pass-by-reference
column subscript	pass-by-value
comma-separated initializer list	passing arrays to functions
comparator function	place holder in an initializer list (,)
creating an instance	position number of an element
data structure	reserve a space in an `Array`
declare an array	row subscript
dynamic memory allocation operator (`new`)	search key
element of an array	searching an array
`for...in` repetition statement	`sort` method of the `Array` object
index of an element	sorting an array
initialize an array	square brackets `[]`
initializer	subscript
initializer list	table of values
instantiating an object	tabular format
iterating over an array's elements	two-dimensional array
`join` method	value of an element
left-hand-side expression	zeroth element
`length` of an `Array`	

SELF-REVIEW EXERCISES

11.1 Fill in the blanks in each of the following statements:
  a) Lists and tables of values can be stored in _____.
  b) The elements of an array are related by the fact that they normally have the same _____.
  c) The number used to refer to a particular element of an array is called its _____.
  d) The process of putting the elements of an array in order is called _____ the array.
  e) Determining whether an array contains a certain key value is called _____ the array.
  f) An array that uses two subscripts is referred to as a(n) _____ array.

11.2 State whether each of the following is *true* or *false*. If *false*, explain why.
  a) An array can store many different types of values.

   b) An array subscript should normally be a floating-point value.
   c) An individual array element that is passed to a function and modified in it will contain
      the modified value when the called function completes execution.

11.3 Write JavaScript statements (regarding array `fractions`) to accomplish each of the following tasks:
   a) Declare an array with 10 elements, and initialize the elements of the array to 0.
   b) Refer to the fourth element of the array.
   c) Refer to array element 4.
   d) Assign the value `1.667` to array element 9.
   e) Assign the value `3.333` to the seventh element of the array.
   f) Sum all the elements of the array, using a `for...in` statement. Define variable x as a con-
      trol variable for the loop.

11.4 Write JavaScript statements (regarding array `table`) to accomplish each of the following
tasks:
   a) Declare and create the array with three rows and three columns.
   b) Display the number of elements.
   c) Use a `for...in` statement to initialize each element of the array to the sum of its sub-
      scripts. Assume that the variables x and y are declared as control variables.

11.5 Find the error(s) in each of the following program segments, and correct them.
   a) Assume that `var b = new Array( 10 );`
      ```
      for ( var i = 0; i <= b.length; ++i )
         b[ i ] = 1;
      ```
   b) Assume that `var a = [ [ 1, 2 ], [ 3, 4 ] ];`
      ```
      a[ 1, 1 ] = 5;
      ```

ANSWERS TO SELF-REVIEW EXERCISES

11.1 a) Arrays. b) Name. c) Subscript. d) Sorting. e) Searching. f) Two-dimensional.

11.2 a) True. b). False. An array subscript must be an integer or an integer expression. c) False.
Individual primitive-data-type elements are passed by value. If a reference to an array is passed, then
modifications to the elements of the array are reflected in the original element of the array. Also, an
individual element of an object type passed to a function is passed by reference, and changes to the
object will be reflected in the original array element.

11.3 a) `var fractions = [ 0, 0, 0, 0, 0, 0, 0, 0, 0, 0 ];`
   b) `fractions[ 3 ]`
   c) `fractions[ 4 ]`
   d) `fractions[ 9 ] = 1.667;`
   e) `fractions[ 6 ] = 3.333;`
   f) ```
      var total = 0;
      for (var x in fractions)
         total += fractions[x];
      ```

**11.4**  a) ```
      var table = new Array( new Array( 3 ), new Array( 3 ),
         new Array( 3 ) );
      ```
   b) ```
      document.write("total: " + (table.length *
         table[i].length * table[i][j].length));
      ```
   c) ```
      for ( var x in table )
         for ( var y in table[ x ] )
            table[ x ][ y ] = x + y;
      ```

11.5 a) Error: Referencing an array element outside the bounds of the array (b[10]). [*Note*: This error is actually a logic error, not a syntax error.] Correction: Change the <= operator to <. b) Error: The array subscripting is done incorrectly. Correction: Change the statement to a[1][1] = 5;.

EXERCISES

11.6 Fill in the blanks in each of the following statements:
  a) JavaScript stores lists of values in _____.
  b) The names of the four elements of array p are _____, _____, _____ and _____.
  c) In a two-dimensional array, the first subscript identifies the _____ of an element, and the second subscript identifies the _____ of an element.
  d) An *m*-by-*n* array contains _____ rows, _____ columns and _____ elements.
  e) The name the element in row 3 and column 5 of array d is _____.
  f) The name of the element in the third row and fifth column of array d is _____.

11.7 State whether each of the following is *true* or *false*. If *false*, explain why.
  a) To refer to a particular location or element within an array, we specify the name of the array and the value of the element.
  b) A variable declaration reserves space for an array.
  c) To indicate that 100 locations should be reserved for integer array p, the programmer should write the declaration
     p[100];
  d) A JavaScript program that initializes the elements of a 15-element array to zero must contain at least one for statement.
  e) A JavaScript program that totals the elements of a two-dimensional array must contain nested for statements.

11.8 Write JavaScript statements to accomplish each of the following tasks:
  a) Display the value of the seventh element of array f.
  b) Initialize each of the five elements of one-dimensional array g to 8.
  c) Total the elements of array c, which contains 100 numeric elements.
  d) Copy 11-element array a into the first portion of array b, which contains 34 elements.
  e) Determine and print the smallest and largest values contained in 99-element floating-point array w.

11.9 Consider a two-by-three array t that will store integers.
  a) Write a statement that declares and creates array t.
  b) How many rows does t have?
  c) How many columns does t have?
  d) How many elements does t have?
  e) Write the names of all the elements in the second row of t.
  f) Write the names of all the elements in the third column of t.
  g) Write a single statement that sets the elements of t in row 1 and column 2 to zero.
  h) Write a series of statements that initializes each element of t to zero. Do not use a repetition structure.
  i) Write a nested for statement that initializes each element of t to zero.
  j) Write a series of statements that determines and prints the smallest value in array t.
  k) Write a statement that displays the elements of the first row of t.
  l) Write a statement that totals the elements of the fourth column of t.
  m) Write a series of statements that prints the array t in neat, tabular format. List the column subscripts as headings across the top, and list the row subscripts at the left of each row.

11.10 Use a one-dimensional array to solve the following problem: A company pays its salespeople on a commission basis. The salespeople receive $200 per week plus 9% of their gross sales for that week. For example, a salesperson who grosses $5000 in sales in a week receives $200 plus 9% of $5000, or a total of $650. Write a script (using an array of counters) that obtains the gross sales for each employee through an XHTML form and determines how many of the salespeople earned salaries in each of the following ranges (assume that each salesperson's salary is truncated to an integer amount):

    a) $200–299
    b) $300–399
    c) $400–499
    d) $500–599
    e) $600–699
    f) $700–799
    g) $800–899
    h) $900–999
    i) $1000 and over

11.11 Write statements that perform the following operations for a one-dimensional array:

    a) Set the 10 elements of array counts to zeros.
    b) Add 1 to each of the 15 elements of array bonus.
    c) Display the five values of array bestScores, separated by spaces.

11.12 Use a one-dimensional array to solve the following problem: Read in 20 numbers, each of which is between 10 and 100. As each number is read, print it only if it is not a duplicate of a number that has already been read. Provide for the "worst case," in which all 20 numbers are different. Use the smallest possible array to solve this problem.

11.13 Label the elements of three-by-five two-dimensional array sales to indicate the order in which they are set to zero by the following program segment:

```
for ( var row in sales )
   for ( var col in sales[ row ] )
      sales[ row ][ col ] = 0;
```

11.14 Write a script to simulate the rolling of two dice. The script should use Math.random to roll the first die and again to roll the second die. The sum of the two values should then be calculated. [*Note*: Since each die can show an integer value from 1 to 6, the sum of the values will vary from 2 to 12, with 7 being the most frequent sum, and 2 and 12 the least frequent sums. Figure 11.15 shows the 36 possible combinations of the two dice. Your program should roll the dice 36,000 times. Use a one-dimensional array to tally the numbers of times each possible sum appears. Display the results in an XHTML table. Also determine whether the totals are reasonable (e.g., there are six ways to roll a 7, so approximately 1/6 of all the rolls should be 7).]

11.15 Write a script that runs 1000 games of craps and answers the following questions:

    a) How many games are won on the first roll, second roll, ..., twentieth roll and after the twentieth roll?
    b) How many games are lost on the first roll, second roll, ..., twentieth roll and after the twentieth roll?
    c) What are the chances of winning at craps? [*Note*: You should discover that craps is one of the fairest casino games. What do you suppose this means?]
    d) What is the average length of a game of craps?
    e) Do the chances of winning improve with the length of the game?

11.16 (*Airline Reservations System*) A small airline has just purchased a computer for its new automated reservations system. You have been asked to program the new system. You are to write a program to assign seats on each flight of the airline's only plane (capacity: 10 seats).

Fig. 11.15 Thirty-six possible outcomes of rolling two dice.

Your program should display the following menu of alternatives: `Please type 1 for "First Class"` and `Please type 2 for "Economy"`. If the person types 1, your program should assign a seat in the first-class section (seats 1–5). If the person types 2, your program should assign a seat in the economy section (seats 6–10). Your program should print a boarding pass indicating the person's seat number and whether it is in the first-class or economy section of the plane.

Use a one-dimensional array to represent the seating chart of the plane. Initialize all the elements of the array to 0 to indicate that all the seats are empty. As each seat is assigned, set the corresponding elements of the array to 1 to indicate that the seat is no longer available.

Your program should, of course, never assign a seat that has already been assigned. When the first-class section is full, your program should ask the person if it is acceptable to be placed in the economy section (and vice versa). If yes, then make the appropriate seat assignment. If no, then print the message `"Next flight leaves in 3 hours."`

11.17 Use a two-dimensional array to solve the following problem: A company has four salespeople (1 to 4) who sell five different products (1 to 5). Once a day, each salesperson passes in a slip for each different type of product actually sold. Each slip contains

1. the salesperson number,
2. the product number, and
3. the total dollar value of the product sold that day.

Thus, each salesperson passes in between zero and five sales slips per day. Assume that the information from all of the slips for last month is available. Write a script that will read all this information for last month's sales and summarize the total sales by salesperson by product. All totals should be stored in the two-dimensional array `sales`. After processing all the information for last month, display the results in an XHTML table format, with each of the columns representing a different salesperson and each of the rows representing a different product. Cross-total each row to get the total sales of each product for last month; cross-total each column to get the total sales by salesperson for last month. Your tabular printout should include these cross-totals to the right of the totaled rows and to the bottom of the totaled columns.

11.18 (*Turtle Graphics*) The Logo language, which is popular among young computer users, made the concept of **turtle graphics** famous. Imagine a mechanical turtle that walks around the room under the control of a JavaScript program. The turtle holds a pen in one of two positions, up or down. When the pen is down, the turtle traces out shapes as it moves; when the pen is up, the turtle moves about freely without writing anything. In this problem, you will simulate the operation of the turtle and create a computerized sketchpad as well.

Use a 20-by-20 array floor that is initialized to zeros. Read commands from an array that contains them. Keep track of the current position of the turtle at all times and of whether the pen is currently up or down. Assume that the turtle always starts at position (0,0) of the floor, with its pen up. The set of turtle commands your script must process are as follows:

Command	Meaning
1	Pen up
2	Pen down
3	Turn right
4	Turn left
5,10	Move forward 10 spaces (or a number other than 10)
6	Print the 20-by-20 array
9	End of data (sentinel)

Suppose that the turtle is somewhere near the center of the floor. The following "program" would draw and print a 12-by-12 square, and then leave the pen in the up position:

```
2
5,12
3
5,12
3
5,12
3
5,12
1
6
9
```

As the turtle moves with the pen down, set the appropriate elements of array floor to 1s. When the 6 command (print) is given, display an asterisk or some other character of your choosing wherever there is a 1 in the array. Wherever there is a zero, display a blank. Write a script to implement the turtle-graphics capabilities discussed here. Write several turtle-graphics programs to draw interesting shapes. Add other commands to increase the power of your turtle-graphics language.

11.19 *(The Sieve of Eratosthenes)* A prime integer is an integer greater than 1 that is evenly divisible only by itself and 1. The Sieve of Eratosthenes is an algorithm for finding prime numbers. It operates as follows:

a) Create an array with all elements initialized to 1 (true). Array elements with prime subscripts will remain as 1. All other array elements will eventually be set to zero.

b) Set the first two elements to zero, since 0 and 1 are not prime. Starting with array subscript 2, every time an array element is found whose value is 1, loop through the remainder of the array and set to zero every element whose subscript is a multiple of the subscript for the element with value 1. For array subscript 2, all elements beyond 2 in the array that are multiples of 2 will be set to zero (subscripts 4, 6, 8, 10, etc.); for array subscript 3, all elements beyond 3 in the array that are multiples of 3 will be set to zero (subscripts 6, 9, 12, 15, etc.); and so on.

When this process is complete, the array elements that are still set to 1 indicate that the subscript is a prime number. These subscripts can then be printed. Write a script that uses an array of 1000 elements to determine and print the prime numbers between 1 and 999. Ignore element 0 of the array.

11.20 (*Simulation: The Tortoise and the Hare*) In this problem, you will re-create one of the truly great moments in history, namely the classic race of the tortoise and the hare. You will use random-number generation to develop a simulation of this memorable event.

Our contenders begin the race at square 1 of 70 squares. Each square represents a possible position along the race course. The finish line is at square 70. The first contender to reach or pass square 70 is rewarded with a pail of fresh carrots and lettuce. The course weaves its way up the side of a slippery mountain, so occasionally the contenders lose ground.

There is a clock that ticks once per second. With each tick of the clock, your script should adjust the position of the animals according to the following rules:

Animal	Move type	Percentage of the time	Actual move
Tortoise	Fast plod	50%	3 squares to the right
	Slip	20%	6 squares to the left
	Slow plod	30%	1 square to the right
Hare	Sleep	20%	No move at all
	Big hop	20%	9 squares to the right
	Big slip	10%	12 squares to the left
	Small hop	30%	1 square to the right
	Small slip	20%	2 squares to the left

Use variables to keep track of the positions of the animals (i.e., position numbers are 1–70). Start each animal at position 1 (i.e., the "starting gate"). If an animal slips left before square 1, move the animal back to square 1.

Generate the percentages in the preceding table by producing a random integer i in the range $1 \leq i \leq 10$. For the tortoise, perform a "fast plod" when $1 \leq i \leq 5$, a "slip" when $6 \leq i \leq 7$ and a "slow plod" when $8 \leq i \leq 10$. Use a similar technique to move the hare.

Begin the race by printing

    BANG !!!!!
    AND THEY'RE OFF !!!!!

Then, for each tick of the clock (i.e., each repetition of a loop), print a 70-position line showing the letter T in the position of the tortoise and the letter H in the position of the hare. Occasionally, the contenders will land on the same square. In this case, the tortoise bites the hare, and your script should print OUCH!!! beginning at that position. All print positions other than the T, the H or the OUCH!!! (in case of a tie) should be blank.

After each line is printed, test whether either animal has reached or passed square 70. If so, print the winner, and terminate the simulation. If the tortoise wins, print TORTOISE WINS!!! YAY!!! If the hare wins, print Hare wins. Yuck! If both animals win on the same tick of the clock, you may want to favor the turtle (the "underdog"), or you may want to print It's a tie. If neither animal wins, perform the loop again to simulate the next tick of the clock. When you are ready to run your script, assemble a group of fans to watch the race. You'll be amazed at how involved your audience gets!

Later in the book, we introduce a number of Dynamic HTML capabilities, such as graphics, images, animation and sound. As you study those features, you might enjoy enhancing your tortoise-and-hare contest simulation.

12

JavaScript: Objects

Objectives

- To understand object-based programming terminology and concepts.
- To understand encapsulation and data hiding.
- To appreciate the value of object orientation.
- To be able to use the JavaScript objects `Math`, `String`, `Date`, `Boolean` and `Number`.
- To be able to use the browser's `document` and `window` objects.
- To be able to use cookies.

My object all sublime
I shall achieve in time.
W. S. Gilbert

Is it a world to hide virtues in?
William Shakespeare

Good as it is to inherit a library, it is better to collect one.
Augustine Birrell

A philosopher of imposing stature doesn't think in a vacuum.
Even his most abstract ideas are, to some extent, conditioned
by what is or is not known in the time when he lives.
Alfred North Whitehead

Outline

12.1 Introduction

Most of the JavaScript programs demonstrated to this point illustrate basic computer programming concepts. These programs provide you with the foundation you need to build powerful and complex scripts as part of your Web pages. As you proceed beyond this chapter, you will use JavaScript to manipulate every element of an XHTML document from a script.

This chapter presents a more formal treatment of **objects**. The chapter overviews—and serves as a reference for—several of JavaScript's built-in objects and demonstrates many of their capabilities. In the chapters on Dynamic HTML that follow this chapter, you will be introduced to many objects provided by the browser that enable scripts to interact with the elements of an XHTML document.

12.2 Thinking About Objects

Now we begin our introduction to objects. We will see that objects are a natural way of thinking about the world and of writing scripts that manipulate XHTML documents.

In Chapters 7–11, we used built-in JavaScript objects—Math and Array—and objects provided by the Web browser—document and window—to perform tasks in our scripts. JavaScript uses objects to perform many tasks and therefore is referred to as an **object-based programming language**. As we have seen, JavaScript also uses constructs from the "conventional" structured programming methodology supported by many other programming languages. The first six JavaScript chapters concentrated on these conventional parts of JavaScript because they are important components of all JavaScript programs.

This section introduces the basic concepts (i.e., "object think") and terminology (i.e., "object speak") of object-based programming, so that we can properly refer to the object-based concepts as we encounter them in the remainder of the text.

Let us start by introducing some of the key terminology of object orientation. Look around you in the real world. Everywhere you look you see them—objects! People, animals, plants, cars, planes, buildings, computers and the like. Humans think in terms of objects. We have the marvelous ability of **abstraction**, which enables us to view screen images as objects such as people, planes, trees and mountains rather than as individual dots of color (called **pixels**, for "picture elements"). We can, if we wish, think in terms of beaches rather than grains of sand, forests rather than trees and houses rather than bricks.

We might be inclined to divide objects into two categories—animate objects and inanimate objects. Animate objects are "alive" in some sense. They move around and do things. Inanimate objects, like towels, seem not to do much at all. They just kind of "sit around." All objects, however, do have some things in common. They all have **attributes**, such as size, shape, color, weight and the like; and they all exhibit **behaviors**—for example, a ball rolls, bounces, inflates and deflates; a baby cries, sleeps, crawls, walks and blinks; a car accelerates, decelerates, brakes and turns; a towel absorbs water.

Humans learn about objects by studying their attributes and observing their behaviors. Different objects can have similar attributes and can exhibit similar behaviors. Comparisons can be made, for example, between babies and adults and between humans and chimpanzees. Cars, trucks, little red wagons and skateboards have much in common.

Objects **encapsulate** data (attributes) and methods (behavior); the data and methods of an object are tied together intimately. Objects have the property of **information hiding**. Programs communicate with objects through well-defined **interfaces**. Normally, the implementation details of objects are hidden within the objects themselves.

Most of the readers of this book drive (or have driven) an automobile—a perfect example of an object. Surely it is possible to drive an automobile effectively without knowing the details of how engines, transmissions and exhaust systems work internally. Millions of human years of research and development have been performed for automobiles and have resulted in extremely complex objects containing thousands of parts (attributes). All of this complexity is hidden (encapsulated) from the driver. As drivers we only sees the friendly user interfaces of behaviors that enable us to make the car go faster by pressing the gas pedal, go slower by pressing the brake pedal, turn left or right by turning the steering wheel, go forward or backward by selecting the gear and turn on and off by turning the key in the ignition.

Like the designers of an automobile, the designers of World Wide Web browsers have defined a set of objects that encapsulate the elements of an XHTML document and expose to a JavaScript programmer the attributes and behaviors that enable a JavaScript program to interact with (or script) the elements (objects) in an XHTML document. The browser's `window` object provides attributes and behaviors that enable a script to manipulate a browser window. A string assigned to the `window` object's `status` property (attribute) is displayed in the status bar of the browser window. The `window` object's `alert` method (behavior) allows the programmer to display a message in a separate window. We will soon see that the browser's `document` object contains attributes and behaviors that provide access to every element of an XHTML document. Similarly, JavaScript provides objects that encapsulate various capabilities in a script. For example, the JavaScript `Array` object provides attributes and behaviors that enable a script to manipulate a collection of data. The `Array` object's `length` property (attribute) contains the number of elements in the `Array`. The `Array` object's `sort` method (behavior) orders the elements of the `Array`.

Indeed, with object technology, we will build most future software by combining standardized, interchangeable parts called objects. These parts allow programmers to create new programs without having to reinvent the wheel. Objects will allow programmers to speed and enhance the quality of future software development efforts.

12.3 Math Object

The `Math` object's methods allow the programmer to perform many common mathematical calculations. As shown previously, an object's methods are called by writing the name of the object followed by a dot (.) and the name of the method. In parentheses following the method name is the argument (or a comma-separated list of arguments) to the method. For example, a programmer desiring to calculate and display the square root of `900.0` might write

```
document.writeln( Math.sqrt( 900.0 ) );
```

When this statement executes, it calls method `Math.sqrt` to calculate the square root of the number contained in the parentheses (`900.0`). The number `900.0` is the argument of the `Math.sqrt` method. The preceding statement would display `30.0`. Invoking the `sqrt` method of the `Math` object is also referred to as **sending the `sqrt` message to `Math` object**. Similarly, invoking the `writeln` method of the `document` object is also referred to as **sending the `writeln` message to the `document` object**. Some `Math` object methods are summarized in Fig. 12.1.

Method	Description	Example
abs(x)	absolute value of x	abs(7.2) is 7.2 abs(0.0) is 0.0 abs(-5.6) is 5.6
ceil(x)	rounds x to the smallest integer not less than x	ceil(9.2) is 10.0 ceil(-9.8) is -9.0
cos(x)	trigonometric cosine of x (x in radians)	cos(0.0) is 1.0
exp(x)	exponential method e^x	exp(1.0) is 2.71828 exp(2.0) is 7.38906
floor(x)	rounds x to the largest integer not greater than x	floor(9.2) is 9.0 floor(-9.8) is -10.0
log(x)	natural logarithm of x (base e)	log(2.718282) is 1.0 log(7.389056) is 2.0

Fig. 12.1 Math object methods. (Part 1 of 2.)

Method	Description	Example
max(x, y)	larger value of x and y	max(2.3, 12.7) is 12.7 max(-2.3, -12.7) is -2.3
min(x, y)	smaller value of x and y	min(2.3, 12.7) is 2.3 min(-2.3, -12.7) is -12.7
pow(x, y)	x raised to power y (x^y)	pow(2.0, 7.0) is 128.0 pow(9.0, .5) is 3.0
round(x)	rounds x to the closest integer	round(9.75) is 10 round(9.25) is 9
sin(x)	trigonometric sine of x (x in radians)	sin(0.0) is 0.0
sqrt(x)	square root of x	sqrt(900.0) is 30.0 sqrt(9.0) is 3.0
tan(x)	trigonometric tangent of x (x in radians)	tan(0.0) is 0.0

Fig. 12.1   Math object methods. (Part 2 of 2.)

Common Programming Error 12.1

Forgetting to invoke a Math method by preceding the method name with the object name Math and a dot (.) is an error.

Software Engineering Observation 12.1

The primary difference between invoking a function and invoking a method is that an object name and a dot are not required to call the function.

The Math object also defines several commonly used mathematical constants, summarized in Fig. 12.2. [*Note*: By convention, the names of constants are written in all uppercase letters so they stand out in a program.]

Good Programming Practice 12.1

Use the mathematical constants of the Math object rather than explicitly typing the numeric value of the constant.

Constant	Description	Value
Math.E	Base of a natural logarithm (*e*).	Approximately 2.718.
Math.LN2	Natural logarithm of 2.	Approximately 0.693.
Math.LN10	Natural logarithm of 10.	Approximately 2.302.
Math.LOG2E	Base 2 logarithm of *e*.	Approximately 1.442.
Math.LOG10E	Base 10 logarithm of *e*.	Approximately 0.434.

Fig. 12.2   Properties of the Math object. (Part 1 of 2.)

Constant	Description	Value
Math.PI	π—the ratio of a circle's circumference to its diameter.	Approximately 3.141592653589793.
Math.SQRT1_2	Square root of 0.5.	Approximately 0.707.
Math.SQRT2	Square root of 2.0.	Approximately 1.414.

Fig. 12.2 Properties of the Math object. (Part 2 of 2.)

12.4 String Object

In this section, we introduce JavaScript's string- and character-processing capabilities. The techniques discussed here are appropriate for processing names, addresses, credit card information, and similar items.

12.4.1 Fundamentals of Characters and Strings

Characters are the fundamental building blocks of JavaScript programs. Every program is composed of a sequence of characters grouped together meaningfully that is interpreted by the computer as a series of instructions used to accomplish a task.

A string is a series of characters treated as a single unit. A string may include letters, digits and various **special characters**, such as +, -, *, /, and $. JavaScript supports the set of characters called **Unicode**®, which represents a large portion of the world's commercially viable languages. (We discuss Unicode in detail in Appendix F.) A string is an object of type String. **String literals** or **string constants** (often called **anonymous String objects**) are written as a sequence of characters in double quotation marks or single quotation marks, as follows:

```
"John Q. Doe"            (a name)
'9999 Main Street'       (a street address)
"Waltham, Massachusetts" (a city and state)
'(201) 555-1212'         (a telephone number)
```

A String may be assigned to a variable in a declaration. The declaration

```
var color = "blue";
```

initializes variable color with the String object containing the string "blue". Strings can be compared with the relational operators (<, <=, > and >=) and the equality operators (== and !=).

12.4.2 Methods of the String Object

The String object encapsulates the attributes and behaviors of a string of characters. The String object provides many methods (behaviors) for selecting characters from a string, combining strings (called **concatenation**), obtaining substrings of a string, searching for substrings within a string, tokenizing strings (i.e., splitting strings into individual words) and converting strings to all uppercase or lowercase letters. The String object also provides several methods that generate XHTML tags. Figure 12.3 summarizes many `String` methods. Figures 12.4–12.7 demonstrate some of these methods.

Method	Description
charAt(*index*)	Returns a string containing the character at the specified *index*. If there is no character at the *index*, `charAt` returns an empty string. The first character is located at *index* 0.
charCodeAt(*index*)	Returns the Unicode value of the character at the specified *index*. If there is no character at the *index*, `charCodeAt` returns NaN (not a number).
concat(*string*)	Concatenates its argument to the end of the string that invokes the method. The string invoking this method is not modified; instead a new `String` is returned. This method is the same as adding two strings with the string concatenation operator + (e.g., `s1.con-cat( s2 )` is the same as `s1 + s2`).
fromCharCode(*value1*, *value2*, ...)	Converts a list of Unicode values into a string containing the corresponding characters.
indexOf(*substring*, *index*)	Searches for the first occurrence of *substring* starting from position *index* in the string that invokes the method. The method returns the starting index of *substring* in the source string or –1 if *substring* is not found. If the *index* argument is not provided, the method begins searching from index 0 in the source string.
lastIndexOf(*substring*, *index*)	Searches for the last occurrence of *substring* starting from position *index* and searching toward the beginning of the string that invokes the method. The method returns the starting index of *substring* in the source string or –1 if *substring* is not found. If the *index* argument is not provided, the method begins searching from the end of the source string.
slice(*start*, *end*)	Returns a string containing the portion of the string from index *start* through index *end*. If the *end* index is not specified, the method returns a string from the *start* index to the end of the source string. A negative *end* index specifies an offset from the end of the string starting from a position one past the end of the last character (so –1 indicates the last character position in the string).
split(*string*)	Splits the source string into an array of strings (tokens) where its *string* argument specifies the delimiter (i.e., the characters that indicate the end of each token in the source string).
substr(*start*, *length*)	Returns a string containing *length* characters starting from index *start* in the source string. If *length* is not specified, a string containing characters from *start* to the end of the source string is returned.
substring(*start*, *end*)	Returns a string containing the characters from index *start* up to but not including index *end* in the source string.

Fig. 12.3   `String` object methods. (Part 1 of 2.)

Method	Description
toLowerCase()	Returns a string in which all uppercase letters are converted to lowercase letters. Non-letter characters are not changed.
toUpperCase()	Returns a string in which all lowercase letters are converted to uppercase letters. Non-letter characters are not changed.
toString()	Returns the same string as the source string.
valueOf()	Returns the same string as the source string.
Methods that generate XHTML tags	
anchor(*name*)	Wraps the source string in an anchor element (`<a></a>`) with *name* as the anchor name.
blink()	Wraps the source string in a `<blink></blink>` element.
fixed()	Wraps the source string in a `<tt></tt>` element.
link(*url*)	Wraps the source string in an anchor element (`<a></a>`) with *url* as the hyperlink location.
strike()	Wraps the source string in a `<strike></strike>` element.
sub()	Wraps the source string in a `<sub></sub>` element.
sup()	Wraps the source string in a `<sup></sup>` element.

Fig. 12.3   `String` object methods. (Part 2 of 2.)

12.4.3 Character-Processing Methods

The script in Fig. 12.4 demonstrates some of the `String` object's character-processing methods, including **charAt** (returns the character at a specific position), **charCodeAt** (returns the Unicode value of the character at a specific position), **fromCharCode** (returns a string created from a series of Unicode values), **toLowerCase** (returns the lowercase version of a string) and **toUpperCase** (returns the uppercase version of a string).

```
1   <?xml version = "1.0"?>
2   <!DOCTYPE html PUBLIC "-//W3C//DTD XHTML 1.0 Strict//EN"
3       "http://www.w3.org/TR/xhtml1/DTD/xhtml1-strict.dtd">
4
5   <!-- Fig. 12.4: CharacterProcessing.html -->
6   <!-- Character Processing Methods          -->
7
8   <html xmlns = "http://www.w3.org/1999/xhtml">
9      <head>
10        <title>Character Processing Methods</title>
11
12        <script type = "text/javascript">
13           <!--
14           var s = "ZEBRA";
```

Fig. 12.4   String methods `charAt`, `charCodeAt`, `fromCharCode`, `toLowercase` and `toUpperCase`. (Part 1 of 2.)

```
15            var s2 = "AbCdEfG";
16
17            document.writeln( "<p>Character at index 0 in '" +
18               s + "' is " + s.charAt( 0 ) );
19            document.writeln( "<br />Character code at index 0 in '"
20               + s + "' is " + s.charCodeAt( 0 ) + "</p>" );
21
22            document.writeln( "<p>'" +
23               String.fromCharCode( 87, 79, 82, 68 ) +
24               "' contains character codes 87, 79, 82 and 68</p>" )
25
26            document.writeln( "<p>'" + s2 + "' in lowercase is '" +
27               s2.toLowerCase() + "'" );
28            document.writeln( "<br />'" + s2 + "' in uppercase is '"
29               + s2.toUpperCase() + "'</p>" );
30            // -->
31         </script>
32
33      </head><body></body>
34   </html>
```

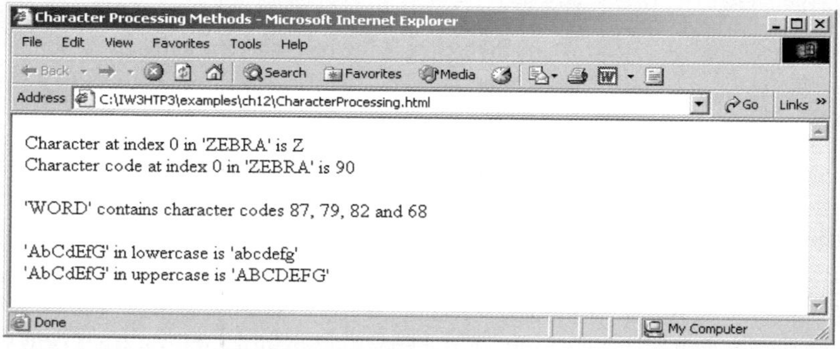

Fig. 12.4   String methods `charAt`, `charCodeAt`, `fromCharCode`, `toLowercase` and `toUpperCase`. (Part 2 of 2.)

Lines 17–18 display the first character in `String s` ("ZEBRA") using `String` method `charAt`. Method **charAt** returns a string containing the character at the specified index (0 in this example). Indices for the characters in a string start at 0 (the first character) and go up to (but do not include) the string's `length` (i.e., if the string contains five characters, the indices are 0 through 4). If the index is outside the bounds of the string, the method returns an empty string.

Lines 19–20 display the character code for the first character in `String s` ("ZEBRA") by calling `String` method **charCodeAt**. Method `charCodeAt` returns the Unicode value of the character at the specified index (0 in this example). If the index is outside the bounds of the string, the method returns NaN.

`String` method **fromCharCode** receives as its argument a comma-separated list of Unicode values and builds a string containing the character representation of those Unicode values. Lines 22–24 display the string "WORD," which consists of the character codes 87, 79, 82 and 68. Note that the `String` object calls method `fromCharCode`, rather than a specific `String` variable. Appendix D, ASCII Character Set, contains the character codes

ASCII character set—a subset of the Unicode character set (Appendix F) that contains only Western characters.

The statements in lines 26–27 and 28–29 use String methods **toLowerCase** and **toUpperCase** to display versions of String s2 ("AbCdEfG") in all lowercase letters and all uppercase letters, respectively.

12.4.4 Searching Methods

Being able to search for a character or a sequence of characters in a string is often useful. For example, if you are creating your own word processor, you may want to provide a capability for searching through the document. The script in Fig. 12.5 demonstrates the String object methods **indexOf** and **lastIndexOf** that search for a specified substring in a string. All the searches in this example are performed on the global string letters (initialized in line 16 with "abcdefghijklmnopqrstuvwxyzabcdefghijklm" in the script).

```
1   <?xml version = "1.0"?>
2   <!DOCTYPE html PUBLIC "-//W3C//DTD XHTML 1.0 Strict//EN"
3      "http://www.w3.org/TR/xhtml1/DTD/xhtml1-strict.dtd">
4
5   <!-- Fig. 12.5: SearchingStrings.html -->
6   <!-- Searching Strings                  -->
7
8   <html xmlns = "http://www.w3.org/1999/xhtml">
9      <head>
10        <title>
11           Searching Strings with indexOf and lastIndexOf
12        </title>
13
14        <script type = "text/javascript">
15           <!--
16           var letters = "abcdefghijklmnopqrstuvwxyzabcdefghijklm";
17
18           function buttonPressed()
19           {
20              searchForm.first.value =
21                 letters.indexOf( searchForm.inputVal.value );
22              searchForm.last.value =
23                 letters.lastIndexOf( searchForm.inputVal.value );
24              searchForm.first12.value =
25                 letters.indexOf( searchForm.inputVal.value, 12 );
26              searchForm.last12.value =
27                 letters.lastIndexOf(
28                    searchForm.inputVal.value, 12 );
29           }
30           // -->
31        </script>
32
33     </head>
34     <body>
35        <form name = "searchForm" action = "">
```

Fig. 12.5 String searching with indexOf and lastIndexOf. (Part 1 of 2.)

```
36            <h1>The string to search is:<br />
37               abcdefghijklmnopqrstuvwxyzabcdefghijklm</h1>
38            <p>Enter substring to search for
39            <input name = "inputVal" type = "text" />
40            <input name = "search" type = "button" value = "Search"
41               onclick = "buttonPressed()" /><br /></p>
42
43            <p>First occurrence located at index
44            <input name = "first" type = "text" size = "5" />
45            <br />Last occurrence located at index
46            <input name = "last" type = "text" size = "5" />
47            <br />First occurrence from index 12 located at index
48            <input name = "first12" type = "text" size = "5" />
49            <br />Last occurrence from index 12 located at index
50            <input name = "last12" type = "text" size = "5" /></p>
51         </form>
52      </body>
53   </html>
```

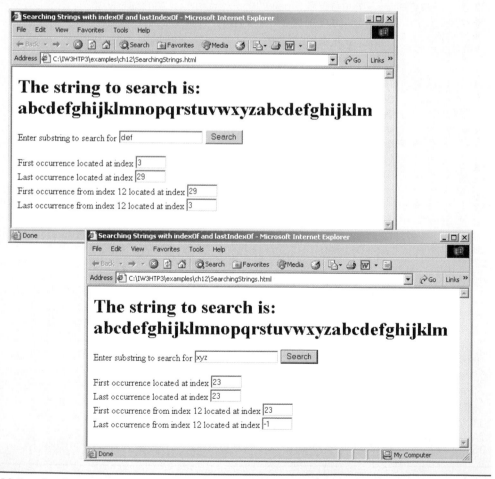

Fig. 12.5   String searching with indexOf and lastIndexOf. (Part 2 of 2.)

The user types a substring in the XHTML form `searchForm`'s `inputVal` text field and presses the **Search** button to search for the substring in `letters`. Clicking the **Search** button calls function `buttonPressed` (defined in lines 18–29) to respond to the `onclick` event and perform the searches. The results of each search are displayed in the appropriate text field of `searchForm`.

Lines 20–21 use `String` method `indexOf` to determine the location of the first occurrence in string `letters` of the string `searchForm.inputVal.value` (i.e., the string the user typed in the `inputVal` text field). If the substring is found, the index at which the first occurrence of the substring begins is returned; otherwise, –1 is returned.

Lines 22–23 use `String` method `lastIndexOf` to determine the location of the last occurrence in `letters` of the string in `inputVal`. If the substring is found, the index at which the last occurrence of the substring begins is returned; otherwise, –1 is returned.

Lines 24–25 use `String` method `indexOf` to determine the location of the first occurrence in string `letters` of the string in the `inputVal` text field, starting from index 12 in `letters`. If the substring is found, the index at which the first occurrence of the substring (starting from index 12) begins is returned; otherwise, –1 is returned.

Lines 26–28 use `String` method `lastIndexOf` to determine the location of the last occurrence in `letters` of the string in the `inputVal` text field, starting from index 12 in `letters`. If the substring is found, the index at which the first occurrence of the substring (starting from index 12) begins is returned; otherwise, –1 is returned.

Software Engineering Observation 12.2

String methods `indexOf` and `lastIndexOf`, with their optional second argument (the starting index from which to search), are particularly useful for continuing a search through a large amount of text.

12.4.5 Splitting Strings and Obtaining Substrings

When you read a sentence, your mind breaks it into individual words, or **tokens,** each of which conveys meaning to you. The process of breaking a string into tokens is called **tokenization.** Interpreters also perform tokenization. They break up statements into such individual pieces as keywords, identifiers, operators and other elements of a programming language. Figure 12.6 demonstrates `String` method **split**, which breaks a string into its component tokens. Tokens are separated from one another by **delimiters,** typically white-space characters such as blanks, tabs, newlines and carriage returns. Other characters may also be used as delimiters to separate tokens. The XHTML document displays a form containing a text field where the user types a sentence to tokenize. The results of the tokenization process are displayed in an XHTML `textarea` GUI component. The script also demonstrates `String` method **substring**, which returns a portion of a string.

```
1   <?xml version = "1.0"?>
2   <!DOCTYPE html PUBLIC "-//W3C//DTD XHTML 1.0 Strict//EN"
3       "http://www.w3.org/TR/xhtml1/DTD/xhtml1-strict.dtd">
4
5   <!-- Fig. 12.6: SplitAndSubString.html -->
6   <!-- String Method split and substring -->
```

Fig. 12.6   `String` object methods `split` and `substring`. (Part 1 of 2.)

```
7
8    <html xmlns = "http://www.w3.org/1999/xhtml">
9       <head>
10          <title>String Method split and substring</title>
11
12          <script type = "text/javascript">
13             <!--
14             function splitButtonPressed()
15             {
16                var strings = myForm.inputVal.value.split( " " );
17                myForm.output.value = strings.join( "\n" );
18
19                myForm.outputSubstring.value =
20                   myForm.inputVal.value.substring( 0, 10 );
21             }
22             // -->
23          </script>
24       </head>
25
26    <body>
27       <form name = "myForm" action = "">
28          <p>Enter a sentence to split into words<br />
29          <input name = "inputVal" type = "text" size = "40" />
30          <input name = "splitButton" type = "button" value =
31             "Split" onclick = "splitButtonPressed()" /></p>
32
33          <p>The sentence split into words is<br />
34          <textarea name = "output" rows = "8" cols = "34">
35          </textarea></p>
36
37          <p>The first 10 characters of the input string are
38          <input name = "outputSubstring" type = "text"
39             size = "15" /></p>
40       </form>
41    </body>
42    </html>
```

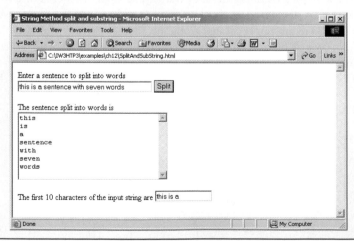

Fig. 12.6   String object methods split and substring. (Part 2 of 2.)

The user types a sentence into form myForm's inputVal text field and presses the **Split** button to tokenize the string. Function splitButtonPressed (defined in lines 14–21) handles splitButton's onclick event.

Line 16 calls String method split to tokenize myForm.inputVal.value, which contains the string the user entered. The argument to method split is the **delimiter string**—the string that determines the end of each token in the original string. In this example, the space character delimits the tokens. The delimiter string can contain multiple characters that should be used as delimiters. Method split returns an array of strings containing the tokens. Line 17 uses Array method join to combine the strings in array strings and separate each string with a newline character (\n). The resulting string is assigned to the value property of the XHTML form's output GUI component (an XHTML textarea).

Lines 19–20 use String method substring to obtain a string containing the first 10 characters of the string the user entered in text field inputVal. The method returns the substring from the **starting index** (0 in this example) up to but not including the **ending index** (10 in this example). If the ending index is greater than the length of the string, the substring returned includes the characters from the starting index to the end of the original string.

12.4.6 XHTML Markup Methods

The script in Fig. 12.7 demonstrates the String object's methods that generate XHTML markup tags. When a String object invokes a markup method, the method wraps the String's contents in the appropriate XHTML tag. These methods are particularly useful for generating XHTML dynamically during script processing.

```
1   <?xml version = "1.0"?>
2   <!DOCTYPE html PUBLIC "-//W3C//DTD XHTML 1.0 Strict//EN"
3      "http://www.w3.org/TR/xhtml1/DTD/xhtml1-strict.dtd">
4
5   <!-- Fig. 12.7: MarkupMethods.html          -->
6   <!-- XHTML markup methods of the String object -->
7
8   <html xmlns = "http://www.w3.org/1999/xhtml">
9      <head>
10        <title>XHTML Markup Methods of the String Object</title>
11
12        <script type = "text/javascript">
13           <!--
14           var anchorText = "This is an anchor",
15               blinkText = "This is blinking text",
16               fixedText = "This is monospaced text",
17               linkText = "Click here to go to anchorText",
18               strikeText = "This is strike out text",
19               subText = "subscript",
20               supText = "superscript";
21
22           document.writeln( anchorText.anchor( "top" ) );
23           document.writeln( "<br />" + blinkText.blink() );
```

Fig. 12.7   String object XHTML markup methods. (Part 1 of 2.)

```
24            document.writeln( "<br />" + fixedText.fixed() );
25            document.writeln( "<br />" + strikeText.strike() );
26            document.writeln(
27               "<br />This is text with a " + subText.sub() );
28            document.writeln(
29               "<br />This is text with a " + supText.sup() );
30            document.writeln(
31               "<br />" + linkText.link( "#top" ) );
32            // -->
33         </script>
34
35      </head><body></body>
36   </html>
```

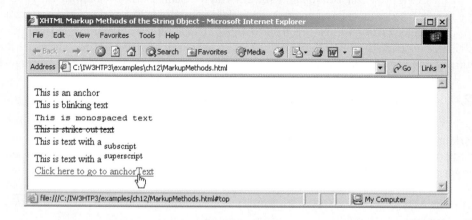

Fig. 12.7   String object XHTML markup methods. (Part 2 of 2.)

Lines 14–20 define the strings that call each of the XHTML markup methods of the String object. Line 22 uses String method **anchor** to format the string in variable anchorText ("This is an anchor") as

```
<a name = "top">This is an anchor</a>
```

The name of the anchor is the argument to the method. This anchor will be used later in the example as the target of a hyperlink.

Line 23 calls String method **blink** to make the string blink in the Web page by formatting the string in variable blinkText ("This is blinking text") as

```
<blink>This is blinking text</blink>
```

[*Note*: The blink tag works in most versions of Netscape and in the Mozilla Web browser. Internet Explorer, however, and many other browsers do not support blink.]

Line 24 uses String method **fixed** to display text in a fixed-width font by formatting the string in variable fixedText ("This is monospaced text") as

```
<tt>This is monospaced text</tt>
```

Line 25 uses `String` method **strike** to display text with a line through it by formatting the string in variable `strikeText` ("This is strike out text") as

```
<strike>This is strike out text</strike>
```

Lines 26–27 use `String` method **sub** to display subscript text by formatting the string in variable `subText` ("subscript") as

```
<sub>subscript</sub>
```

Note that the resulting line in the XHTML document displays the word `subscript` smaller than the rest of the line and slightly below the line. Lines 28–29 call `String` method **sup** to display superscript text by formatting the string in variable `supText` ("superscript") as

```
<sup>superscript</sup>
```

Note that the resulting line in the XHTML document displays the word `superscript` smaller than the rest of the line and slightly above the line.

Lines 30–31 use `String` method **link** to create a hyperlink by formatting the string in variable `linkText` ("Click here to go to anchorText") as

```
<a href = "#top">Click here to go to anchorText</a>
```

The target of the hyperlink (`#top` in this example) is the argument to the method and can be any URL. In this example, the hyperlink target is the anchor created in line 22. If you make your browser window short and scroll to the bottom of the Web page, then click this link, the browser will reposition to the top of the Web page.

12.5 Date Object

JavaScript's **Date** object provides methods for date and time manipulations. Date and time processing can be performed based on the computer's **local time zone** or based on World Time Standard's **Coordinated Universal Time** (abbreviated **UTC**)—formerly called **Greenwich Mean Time (GMT)**. Most methods of the `Date` object have a local time zone and a UTC version. The methods of the `Date` object are summarized in Fig. 12.8.

Method	Description
`getDate()` `getUTCDate()`	Returns a number from 1 to 31 representing the day of the month in local time or UTC.
`getDay()` `getUTCDay()`	Returns a number from 0 (Sunday) to 6 (Saturday) representing the day of the week in local time or UTC.
`getFullYear()` `getUTCFullYear()`	Returns the year as a four-digit number in local time or UTC.
`getHours()` `getUTCHours()`	Returns a number from 0 to 23 representing hours since midnight in local time or UTC.
`getMilliseconds()` `getUTCMilliSeconds()`	Returns a number from 0 to 999 representing the number of milliseconds in local time or UTC, respectively. The time is stored in hours, minutes, seconds and milliseconds.

Fig. 12.8   `Date` object methods. (Part 1 of 3.)

Method	Description
`getMinutes()` `getUTCMinutes()`	Returns a number from 0 to 59 representing the minutes for the time in local time or UTC.
`getMonth()` `getUTCMonth()`	Returns a number from 0 (January) to 11 (December) representing the month in local time or UTC.
`getSeconds()` `getUTCSeconds()`	Returns a number from 0 to 59 representing the seconds for the time in local time or UTC.
`getTime()`	Returns the number of milliseconds between January 1, 1970 and the time in the `Date` object.
`getTimezoneOffset()`	Returns the difference in minutes between the current time on the local computer and UTC—previously known as Greenwich Mean Time (GMT).
`setDate( val )` `setUTCDate( val )`	Sets the day of the month (1 to 31) in local time or UTC.
`setFullYear( y, m, d )` `setUTCFullYear( y, m, d )`	Sets the year in local time or UTC. The second and third arguments representing the month and the date are optional. If an optional argument is not specified, the current value in the `Date` object is used.
`setHours( h, m, s, ms )` `setUTCHours( h, m, s, ms )`	Sets the hour in local time or UTC. The second, third and fourth arguments, representing the minutes, seconds and milliseconds, are optional. If an optional argument is not specified, the current value in the `Date` object is used.
`setMilliSeconds( ms )` `setUTCMilliseconds( ms )`	Sets the number of milliseconds in local time or UTC.
`setMinutes( m, s, ms )` `setUTCMinutes( m, s, ms )`	Sets the minute in local time or UTC. The second and third arguments, representing the seconds and milliseconds, are optional. If an optional argument is not specified, the current value in the `Date` object is used.
`setMonth( m, d )` `setUTCMonth( m, d )`	Sets the month in local time or UTC. The second argument, representing the date, is optional. If the optional argument is not specified, the current date value in the `Date` object is used.
`setSeconds( s, ms )` `setUTCSeconds( s, ms )`	Sets the second in local time or UTC. The second argument, representing the milliseconds, is optional. If this argument is not specified, the current millisecond value in the `Date` object is used.
`setTime( ms )`	Sets the time based on its argument—the number of elapsed milliseconds since January 1, 1970.
`toLocaleString()`	Returns a string representation of the date and time in a form specific to the computer's locale. For example, September 13, 2001 at 3:42:22 PM is represented as *09/13/01 15:47:22* in the United States and *13/09/01 15:47:22* in Europe.

Fig. 12.8   Date object methods. (Part 2 of 3.)

Method	Description
toUTCString()	Returns a string representation of the date and time in the form: *19 Sep 2001 15:47:22 UTC*
toString()	Returns a string representation of the date and time in a form specific to the locale of the computer (*Mon Sep 19 15:47:22 EDT 2001* in the United States).
valueOf()	The time in number of milliseconds since midnight, January 1, 1970.

Fig. 12.8   Date object methods. (Part 3 of 3.)

The script of Fig. 12.9 demonstrates many of the local time zone methods in Fig. 12.8. Line 14 creates a new **Date** object. The **new** operator allocates the memory for the **Date** object. The empty parentheses indicate a call to the **Date** object's **constructor** with no arguments. A constructor is an initializer method for an object. Constructors are called automatically when an object is allocated with **new**. The **Date** constructor with no arguments initializes the local computer's **Date** object with the current date and time.

```
1   <?xml version = "1.0"?>
2   <!DOCTYPE html PUBLIC "-//W3C//DTD XHTML 1.0 Strict//EN"
3       "http://www.w3.org/TR/xhtml1/DTD/xhtml1-strict.dtd">
4
5   <!-- Fig. 12.9: DateTime.html -->
6   <!-- Date and Time Methods    -->
7
8   <html xmlns = "http://www.w3.org/1999/xhtml">
9       <head>
10          <title>Date and Time Methods</title>
11
12          <script type = "text/javascript">
13              <!--
14              var current = new Date();
15
16              document.writeln(
17                  "<h1>String representations and valueOf</h1>" );
18              document.writeln( "toString: " + current.toString() +
19                  "<br />toLocaleString: " + current.toLocaleString() +
20                  "<br />toUTCString: " + current.toUTCString() +
21                  "<br />valueOf: " + current.valueOf() );
22
23              document.writeln(
24                  "<h1>Get methods for local time zone</h1>" );
25              document.writeln( "getDate: " + current.getDate() +
26                  "<br />getDay: " + current.getDay() +
27                  "<br />getMonth: " + current.getMonth() +
28                  "<br />getFullYear: " + current.getFullYear() +
29                  "<br />getTime: " + current.getTime() +
```

Fig. 12.9   Date and time methods of the Date object. (Part 1 of 3.)

```
30              "<br />getHours: " + current.getHours() +
31              "<br />getMinutes: " + current.getMinutes() +
32              "<br />getSeconds: " + current.getSeconds() +
33              "<br />getMilliseconds: " +
34              current.getMilliseconds() +
35              "<br />getTimezoneOffset: " +
36              current.getTimezoneOffset() );
37
38          document.writeln(
39              "<h1>Specifying arguments for a new Date</h1>" );
40          var anotherDate = new Date( 2001, 2, 18, 1, 5, 0, 0 );
41          document.writeln( "Date: " + anotherDate );
42
43          document.writeln(
44              "<h1>Set methods for local time zone</h1>" );
45          anotherDate.setDate( 31 );
46          anotherDate.setMonth( 11 );
47          anotherDate.setFullYear( 2001 );
48          anotherDate.setHours( 23 );
49          anotherDate.setMinutes( 59 );
50          anotherDate.setSeconds( 59 );
51          document.writeln( "Modified date: " + anotherDate );
52          // -->
53      </script>
54
55    </head><body></body>
56 </html>
```

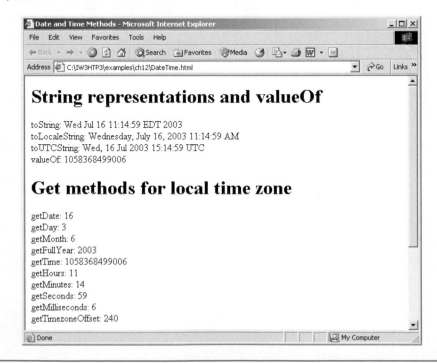

Fig. 12.9   Date and time methods of the `Date` object. (Part 2 of 3.)

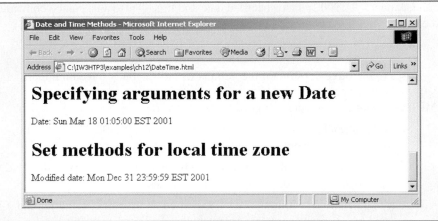

Fig. 12.9   Date and time methods of the Date object. (Part 3 of 3.)

Software Engineering Observation 12.3

*When an object is allocated with **new**, the object's constructor is called automatically to initialize the object before it is used in the program.*

Lines 18–21 demonstrate the methods toString, toLocaleString, toUTCString and valueOf. Note that method valueOf returns a large integer value representing the total number of milliseconds between midnight, January 1, 1970 and the date and time stored in Date object current.

Lines 25–36 demonstrate the Date object's *get* methods for the local time zone. Note that method getFullYear returns the year as a four-digit number. Note as well that method getTimeZoneOffset returns the difference in minutes between the local time zone and UTC time (i.e., a difference of four hours in our time zone when this example was executed).

Line 40 demonstrates creating a new Date object and supplying arguments to the Date constructor for *year*, *month*, *date*, *hours*, *minutes*, *seconds* and *milliseconds*. Note that the *hours*, *minutes*, *seconds* and *milliseconds* arguments are all optional. If any one of these arguments is not specified, a zero is supplied in its place. For the *hours*, *minutes* and *seconds* arguments, if the argument to the right of any of these arguments is specified, it too must be specified (e.g., if the *minutes* argument is specified, the *hours* argument must be specified; if the *milliseconds* argument is specified, all the arguments must be specified).

Lines 45–50 demonstrate the Date object *set* methods for the local time zone. Date objects represent the month internally as an integer from 0 to 11. These values are off by one from what you might expect (i.e., 1 for January, 2 for February, …, and 12 for December). When creating a Date object, you must specify 0 to indicate January, 1 to indicate February, …, and 11 to indicate December.

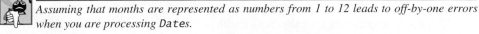

Common Programming Error 12.2

Assuming that months are represented as numbers from 1 to 12 leads to off-by-one errors when you are processing Dates.

The Date object provides two other methods that can be called without creating a new Date object—**Date.parse** and **Date.UTC**. Method Date.parse receives as its argument a string representing a date and time, and returns the number of milliseconds between midnight, January 1, 1970 and the specified date and time. This value can be converted to a `Date` object with the statement

```
var theDate = new Date( numberOfMilliseconds );
```

which passes to the `Date` constructor the number of milliseconds since midnight, January 1, 1970 for the `Date` object.

Method `parse` converts the string using the following rules:

- Short dates can be specified in the form MM-DD-YY, MM-DD-YYYY, MM/DD/YY or MM/DD/YYYY. The month and day are not required to be two digits.

- Long dates that specify the complete month name (e.g., "January"), date and year can specify the month, date and year in any order.

- Text in parentheses within the string is treated as a comment and ignored. Commas and white space characters are treated as delimiters.

- All month and day names must have at least two characters. The names are not required to be unique. If the names are identical, the name is resolved as the last match (e.g., "Ju" represents "July" rather than "June").

- If the name of the day of the week is supplied, it is ignored.

- All standard time zones (e.g., EST for Eastern Standard Time), Coordinated Universal Time (UTC) and Greenwich Mean Time (GMT) are recognized.

- When specifying hours, minutes and seconds, separate each by colons.

- When using a 24-hour-clock format, "PM" should not be used for times after 12 noon.

`Date` method UTC returns the number of milliseconds between midnight, January 1, 1970 and the date and time specified as its arguments. The arguments to the UTC method include the required *year*, *month* and *date*, and the optional *hours*, *minutes*, *seconds* and *milliseconds*. If any of the *hours*, *minutes*, *seconds* or *milliseconds* arguments is not specified, a zero is supplied in its place. For the *hours*, *minutes* and *seconds* arguments, if the argument to the right of any of these arguments in the argument list is specified, that argument must also be specified (e.g., if the *minutes* argument is specified, the *hours* argument must be specified; if the *milliseconds* argument is specified, all the arguments must be specified). As with the result of `Date.parse`, the result of `Date.UTC` can be converted to a `Date` object by creating a new `Date` object with the result of `Date.UTC` as its argument.

12.6 Boolean and Number Objects

JavaScript provides the **Boolean** and **Number** objects as object **wrappers** for boolean `true`/`false` values and numbers, respectively. These wrappers define methods and properties useful in manipulating boolean values and numbers. Wrappers provide added functionality for working with simple data types.

When a JavaScript program requires a boolean value, JavaScript automatically creates a `Boolean` object to store the value. JavaScript programmers can create `Boolean` objects explicitly with the statement

```
var b = new Boolean( booleanValue );
```

The constructor argument *booleanValue* specifies whether the value of the `boolean` object should be `true` or `false`. If *booleanValue* is `false`, 0, `null`, `Number.NaN` or an empty string (`""`), or if no argument is supplied, the new `Boolean` object contains `false`. Otherwise, the new `Boolean` object contains `true`. Figure 12.10 summarizes the methods of the `Boolean` object.

Method	Description
toString()	Returns the string `"true"` if the value of the `Boolean` object is true; otherwise, returns the string `"false"`.
valueOf()	Returns the value `true` if the `Boolean` object is `true`; otherwise, returns `false`.

Fig. 12.10 `Boolean` object methods.

JavaScript automatically creates `Number` objects to store numeric values in a JavaScript program. JavaScript programmers can create a `Number` object with the statement

```
var n = new Number( numericValue );
```

The constructor argument *numericValue* is the number to store in the object. Although you can explicitly create `Number` objects, normally the JavaScript interpreter creates them as needed. Figure 12.11 summarizes the methods and properties of the `Number` object.

Method or Property	Description
toString(*radix*)	Returns the string representation of the number. The optional *radix* argument (a number from 2 to 36) specifies the number's base. For example, radix 2 results in the binary representation of the number, 8 results in the octal representation, 10 results in the decimal representation and 16 results in the hexadecimal representation. See Appendix E, Number Systems for a review of the binary, octal, decimal and hexadecimal number systems.
valueOf()	Returns the numeric value.
Number.MAX_VALUE	This property represents the largest value that can be stored in a JavaScript program—approximately 1.79E+308
Number.MIN_VALUE	This property represents the smallest value that can be stored in a JavaScript program—approximately 2.22E–308
Number.NaN	This property represents *not a number*—a value returned from an arithmetic expression that does not result in a number (e.g., the expression `parseInt( "hello" )` cannot convert the string `"hello"` into a number, so `parseInt` would return `Number.NaN`. To determine whether a value is NaN, test the result with function `isNaN`, which returns `true` if the value is NaN; otherwise, it returns `false`.

Fig. 12.11 `Number` object methods and properties. (Part 1 of 2.)

Method or Property	Description
Number.NEGATIVE_INFINITY	
	This property represents a value less than -Number.MAX_VALUE.
Number.POSITIVE_INFINITY	
	This property represents a value greater than Number.MAX_VALUE.

Fig. 12.11 Number object methods and properties. (Part 2 of 2.)

12.7 document Object

JavaScript provides the **document** object for manipulating the document that is currently visible in the browser window. The document object has many useful properties and methods, such as methods document.write and document.writeln, which have both been used in prior JavaScript examples. Figure 12.12 shows the methods and properties of the document objects that are used in this chapter. A more comprehensive list of properties and methods can be found at the JavaScript reference URL located in Section 12.11, Web Resources.

Method or Property	Description
write(*string*)	Writes the string to the XHTML document as XHTML code.
writeln(*string*)	Writes the string to the XHTML document as XHTML code and adds a newline character at the end.
document.cookie	This property is a string containing the values of all the cookies stored on the user's computer for the current document. See Section 12.9, Using Cookies.
document.lastModified	This property is the date and time that this document was last modified.

Fig. 12.12 Important document object methods and properties.

12.8 window Object

JavaScript's **window** object provides methods for manipulating browser windows. The following script shows many of the commonly used properties and methods of the window object and uses them to create an interesting Web site that spans multiple browser windows. Figure 12.13 allows the user to create a new, fully customized browser window by completing an XHTML form and clicking the **Submit** button. The script also allows the user to add text to the new window and redirect the window to a different URL.

```
1    <?xml version = "1.0" encoding = "utf-8"?>
2    <!DOCTYPE html PUBLIC "-//W3C//DTD XHTML 1.1//EN"
3       "http://www.w3.org/TR/xhtml11/DTD/xhtml11.dtd">
4
5    <!-- Fig. 12.13: window.html  -->
6    <!-- Using the Window Object  -->
7
8    <html xmlns = "http://www.w3.org/1999/xhtml">
9    <head>
10   <title>Using the Window Object</title>
11
12   <script type = "text/javascript">
13      <!--
14      var childWindow; // variable to control the child window
15
16      function createChildWindow()
17      {
18         // these variables all contain either "yes" or "no"
19         // to enable or disable a feature in the child window
20         var toolBar // specify if toolbar will appear in child window
21         var menuBar; // specify if menubar will appear in child window
22         var location; // specify if address bar will appear in child window
23         var scrollBars; // specify if scrollbars will appear in child window
24         var status; // specify if status bar will appear in child window
25         var resizable; // specify if the child window will be resizable
26
27         // determine whether the Tool Bar checkbox is checked
28         if ( toolBarCheckBox.checked )
29            toolBar = "yes";
30         else
31            toolBar = "no";
32
33         // determine whether the Menu Bar checkbox is checked
34         if ( menuBarCheckBox.checked )
35            menuBar = "yes";
36         else
37            menuBar = "no";
38
39         // determine whether the Address Bar checkbox is checked
40         if ( locationCheckBox.checked )
41            location = "yes";
42         else
43            location = "no";
44
45         // determine whether the Scroll Bar checkbox is checked
46         if ( scrollBarsCheckBox.checked )
47            scrollBars = "yes";
48         else
49            scrollBars = "no";
50
51         // determine whether the Status Bar checkbox is checked
52         if ( statusCheckBox.checked )
53            status = "yes";
```

Fig. 12.13 Using the window object to create and modify child windows. (Part 1 of 4.)

```
54          else
55              status = "no";
56
57          // determine whether the Resizable checkbox is checked
58          if ( resizableCheckBox.checked )
59              resizable = "yes";
60          else
61              resizable = "no";
62
63          // display window with selected features
64          childWindow = window.open( "", "", "resizable = " + resizable +
65              ", toolbar = " + toolBar + ", menubar = " + menuBar +
66              ", status = " + status + ", location = " + location +
67              ", scrollbars = " + scrollBars );
68
69          // disable buttons
70          closeButton.disabled = false;
71          modifyButton.disabled = false;
72          getURLButton.disabled = false;
73          setURLButton.disabled = false;
74       } // end function createChildWindow
75
76       // insert text from the textbox into the child window
77       function modifyChildWindow()
78       {
79          if ( childWindow.closed )
80              alert( "You attempted to interact with a closed window" );
81          else
82              childWindow.document.write( textForChild.value );
83       } // end function modifyChildWindow
84
85       // close the child window
86       function closeChildWindow()
87       {
88          if ( childWindow.closed )
89              alert( "You attempted to interact with a closed window" );
90          else
91              childWindow.close();
92
93          closeButton.disabled = true;
94          modifyButton.disabled = true;
95          getURLButton.disabled = true;
96          setURLButton.disabled = true;
97       } // end function closeChildWindow
98
99       // copy the URL of the child window into the parent window's myChildURL
100      function getChildWindowURL()
101      {
102         if ( childWindow.closed )
103             alert( "You attempted to interact with a closed window" );
104         else
105             myChildURL.value = childWindow.location;
106      } // end function getChildWindowURL
```

Fig. 12.13 Using the `window` object to create and modify child windows. (Part 2 of 4.)

```
107
108     // set the URL of the child window to the URL
109     // in the parent window's myChildURL
110     function setChildWindowURL()
111     {
112        if ( childWindow.closed )
113           alert( "You attempted to interact with a closed window" );
114        else
115           childWindow.location = myChildURL.value;
116     } // end function setChildWindowURL
117     //-->
118  </script>
119
120  </head>
121
122  <body>
123  <h1>Hello, This is the main window</h1>
124  <p>Please check the features to enable for the child window<br/>
125     <input id = "toolBarCheckBox" type = "checkbox" value = ""
126        checked = "checked" />
127        <label>Tool Bar</label>
128     <input id = "menuBarCheckBox" type = "checkbox" value = ""
129        checked = "checked" />
130        <label>Menu Bar</label>
131     <input id = "locationCheckBox" type = "checkbox" value = ""
132        checked = "checked" />
133        <label>Address Bar</label><br/>
134     <input id = "scrollBarsCheckBox" type = "checkbox" value = ""
135        checked = "checked" />
136        <label>Scroll Bars</label>
137     <input id = "statusCheckBox" type = "checkbox" value = ""
138        checked = "checked" />
139        <label>Status Bar</label>
140     <input id = "resizableCheckBox" type = "checkbox" value = ""
141        checked = "checked" />
142        <label>Resizable</label><br/></p>
143
144  <p>Please enter the text that you would like to display
145     in the child window<br/>
146     <input id = "textForChild" type = "text"
147        value = "<h1> Hello, I am a child window</h1> <br\>"/>
148     <input id = "createButton" type = "button"
149        value = "Create Child Window" onclick = "createChildWindow()" />
150     <input id= "modifyButton" type = "button" value = "Modify Child Window"
151        onclick = "modifyChildWindow()" disabled = "disabled"/>
152     <input id = "closeButton" type = "button" value = "Close Child Window"
153        onclick = "closeChildWindow()" disabled = "disabled"/></p>
154
155  <p>The other window's URL is: <br/>
156     <input id = "myChildURL" type = "text" value = "./"/>
157     <input id = "setURLButton" type = "button" value = "Set Child URL"
158        onclick = "setChildWindowURL()" disabled = "disabled"/>
```

Fig. 12.13 Using the window object to create and modify child windows. (Part 3 of 4.)

```
159        <input id = "getURLButton" type = "button" value = "Get URL From Child"
160           onclick = "getChildWindowURL()" disabled = "disabled"/></p>
161
162  </body>
163  </html>
```

Initially empty
child window

Child window
after being
modified by the
main window

Fig. 12.13 Using the window object to create and modify child windows. (Part 4 of 4.)

The script starts in line 12. Line 14 declares a variable to refer to the new window. We will refer to the new window as the **child window** because it is created and controlled by the main, or **parent**, window in this script. Lines 16–74 define the function `createChild-Window`, which determines the features that have been selected by the user and creates a child window with those features (but does not add any content to the window). Lines 20–25 declare several variables to store the status of the checkboxes on the page. Lines 28–61 set each variable to `"yes"` or `"no"` based on whether the corresponding checkbox is checked or unchecked. The statement in lines 64–67 uses the `window` object's `open` method to create the requested child window. Method `open` has three parameters. The first parameter is the URL of the page to open in the new window, and the second parameter is the title of the window. In our example, we pass `window.open` empty strings as the first two parameter values because we want the new window to open a blank page with no title. The third parameter is a string of comma-separated, all-lowercase feature names, each followed by an = sign and either `"yes"` or `"no"` to determine whether that feature should be displayed in the new window. If any of these parameters are omitted, the browser will default to a new window containing an empty page, no title and all features visible. Lines 70–73 enable the buttons for manipulating the child window—these are initially disabled when the page loads.

Lines 77–83 define the function `modifyChildWindow`, which adds a line of text to the content of the child window. In line 79, the script determines whether the child window is closed. Function `modifyChildWindow` uses property `childWindow.closed` to obtain a boolean value that is `true` if `childWindow` is closed and `false` if the window is still open. If the window is closed, an alert box is displayed notifying the user that the window is currently closed and cannot be modified. If the child window is open, line 82 obtains text from the `textForChild` textbox (lines 146–147) in the XHTML form in the parent window and uses the child's `document.write` method to write this text to the child window.

Function `closeChildWindow` (lines 86–97) also determines whether the child window is closed before proceeding. If the child window is not open, the script displays an alert box telling the user that the window is already closed. If the child window is open, line 91 closes it using the `childWindow.close` method. Lines 93–96 disable the buttons that interact with the child window.

Function `getChildWindowUrl` (lines 100–106) obtains the URL displayed in the child window and copies it into the `myChildURL` textbox in the parent window. The function first determines the status of the window. If the child is closed, then the script displays an alert box to the user. If the window is still open, then the script copies property `childWindow.location`—which contains a string representation of the window's current URL—to the `myChildURL` textbox in the parent window.

Software Engineering Observation 12.4

window.location is a property that always contains a string representation of the URL displayed in the current window. Most Web browsers will only allow a script to access the window.location property of another window if the script is running on the same Web site as the page in the other window.

Function `setChildWindowURL` (lines 110–116) copies the contents of the `myChildURL` textbox to the `location` property of the child window. If the child window is open, line 115 sets property `location` of the child window to the string in the myChildURL textbox. This action changes the URL of the child window and is equivalent to typing a new URL into the window's address bar and clicking **Go**.

The script ends in line 118. Lines 122–162 contain the body of the XHTML document, comprising a form that contains checkboxes, buttons, textboxes and form field labels. The script uses the form elements defined in the body to obtain input from the user. In lines 149, 151, 153, 158 and 160, the Web page specifies the onclick attribute of an XHTML button. The property onclick defines what will occur when the user clicks the button. In this example, each button is set to call a corresponding JavaScript function when clicked. Line 163 closes the XHTML document.

Figure 12.14 contains a list of some commonly used methods and properties of the window object.

Method or Property	Description
open(*url*, *name*, *options*)	Creates a new window with the URL of the window set to *url*, the name set to *name*, and the visible features set by the string passed in as *option*.
prompt(*prompt*, *default*)	Displays a dialog box asking the user for input. The text of the dialog is *prompt*, and the default value is set to *default*.
close()	Closes the current window and deletes its object from memory.
focus()	This method gives focus to the window (i.e., puts the window in the foreground, on top of any other open browser windows).
blur()	This method takes focus away from the window (i.e., puts the window in the background).
window.document	This property contains the document object representing the document currently inside the window.
window.closed	This property contains a boolean value that is set to true if the window is closed, and false if it is not.
window.opener	This property contains the window object of the window that opened the current window, if such a window exists.

Fig. 12.14   Important window object methods and properties.

12.9 Using Cookies

Cookies provide Web developers with a tool for personalizing Web pages. A **cookie** is a piece of data that is stored on the user's computer to maintain information about the client during and between browser sessions. A Web site may store a cookie on the client's computer to record user preferences or other information that the Web site can retrieve during the client's subsequent visits. For example, a Web site can retrieve the user's name from a cookie and use it to display a personalized greeting.

Microsoft Internet Explorer stores cookies as small text files on the client's hard drive. When a user visits a Web site, the browser locates any cookies written by scripts on that site and makes them available to any scripts located on the site. Note that cookies may only be accessed by scripts located on the server from which they originated (i.e., a cookie set by a script on `amazon.com` can only be read by other scripts on `amazon.com`).

Cookies are accessible in JavaScript through the `document` object's **cookie** property. JavaScript treats a cookie as a string of text. Any standard string function or method can manipulate a cookie. A cookie has the syntax "*identifier=value*", where *identifier* is any valid JavaScript variable identifier, and *value* is the value of the cookie variable. When multiple cookies exist for one Web site, *identifier-value* pairs are separated by semicolons in the `document.cookie` string.

Cookies differ from ordinary strings in that each cookie has an expiration date after which the Web browser deletes it. This date can be defined by setting the **expires** property in the cookie string. If a cookie's expiration date is not set, then the cookie expires by default after the user closes the browser window. A cookie can be deleted immediately by setting the `expires` property to a date and time in the past.

Figure 12.15 uses a cookie to store the user's name and displays a personalized greeting. This example improves upon the functionality in the dynamic welcome page example of Fig. 7.6 by requiring the user to enter a name only during the first visit to the Web page. On each subsequent visit, the script can display the user name that is stored in the cookie.

Line 12 is the beginning of the script. Lines 14–15 declare the variables needed to obtain the time, and line 16 declares the variable that stores the name of the user. Lines 18–29 contain the same `if...else` statement used in Fig. 7.6 to display a time-sensitive greeting.

```
1   <?xml version = "1.0"?>
2   <!DOCTYPE html PUBLIC "-//W3C//DTD XHTML 1.1//EN"
3      "http://www.w3.org/TR/xhtml11/DTD/xhtml11.dtd">
4
5   <!-- Fig. 12.15: cookie.html -->
6   <!-- Using Cookies           -->
7
8   <html xmlns = "http://www.w3.org/1999/xhtml">
9      <head>
10        <title>Using Cookies</title>
11
12        <script type = "text/javascript">
13           <!--
14           var now = new Date(); // current date and time
15           var hour = now.getHours(); // current hour (0-23)
16           var name;
17
18           if ( hour < 12 ) // determine whether it is morning
19              document.write( "<h1>Good Morning, " );
20           else
21           {
22              hour = hour - 12; // convert from 24 hour clock to PM time
23
24              // determine whether it is afternoon or evening
```

Fig. 12.15   Using cookies to store user identification data. (Part 1 of 3.)

```
25                if ( hour < 6 )
26                    document.write( "<h1>Good Afternoon, " );
27                else
28                    document.write( "<h1>Good Evening, " );
29            }
30
31            // determine whether there is a cookie
32            if ( document.cookie )
33            {
34                // convert escape characters in the cookie string to their
35                // english notation
36                var myCookie = unescape( document.cookie );
37
38                // split the cookie into tokens using = as delimiter
39                var cookieTokens = myCookie.split( "=" );
40
41                // set name to the part of the cookie that follows the = sign
42                name = cookieTokens[ 1 ];
43            }
44            else
45            {
46                // if there was no cookie then ask the user to input a name
47                name = window.prompt( "Please enter your name", "GalAnt" );
48
49                // escape special characters in the name string
50                // and add name to the cookie
51                document.cookie = "name=" + escape( name );
52            }
53
54            document.writeln(
55                name + ", welcome to JavaScript programming! </h1>" );
56            document.writeln( "<a href= \" JavaScript:wrongPerson() \" > " +
57                "Click here if you are not " + name + "</a>" );
58
59            // reset the document's cookie if wrong person
60            function wrongPerson()
61            {
62                // reset the cookie
63                document.cookie= "name=null;" +
64                    " expires=Thu, 01-Jan-95 00:00:01 GMT";
65
66                // after removing the cookie reload the page to get a new name
67                location.reload();
68            }
69
70            // -->
71        </script>
72    </head>
73
74    <body>
75        <p>Click Refresh (or Reload) to run the script again</p>
76    </body>
77 </html>
```

Fig. 12.15 Using cookies to store user identification data. (Part 2 of 3.)

Fig. 12.15 Using cookies to store user identification data. (Part 3 of 3.)

Lines 32–69 contain the code used to manipulate the cookie. Line 32 determines whether a cookie exists on the client computer. The expression `document.cookie` evaluates to `true` if a cookie exists. If a cookie does not exist, then the script prompts the user to enter a name (line 47). The script creates a cookie containing the string `"name="`, followed by a copy of the user's name produced by the built-in JavaScript function **escape** (line 51). The function `escape` converts any non-alphanumeric characters, such as spaces and semicolons, in a string to their equivalent **hexadecimal escape sequences** of the form "*%XX*," where *XX* is the two-digit hexadecimal ASCII value of a special character. For example, if `name` contains the value `"Luna Tic"`, the statement `escape( name )` evaluates to `"Luna%20Tic"`, because the hexadecimal ASCII value of a blank space is 20. It is a good idea to always escape cookie values before writing them to the client. This conversion prevents any special characters in the cookie from being misinterpreted as having a special meaning in the code, rather than being a character in a cookie value. For instance, a semicolon in a cookie value could be misinterpreted as a semicolon separating two adjacent *identifier-value* pairs. Applying the function **unescape** to cookies when they are read out of the `document.cookie` string converts the hexadecimal escape sequences back to English characters for display in a Web page.

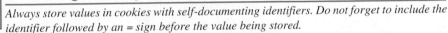

Good Programming Practice 12.2

Always store values in cookies with self-documenting identifiers. Do not forget to include the identifier followed by an = sign before the value being stored.

If a cookie exists (i.e., the user has been to the page before), then the script **parses** the user name out of the cookie string and stores it in a local variable. Parsing generally refers to the act of splitting a string into smaller, more useful components. Line 36 uses the JavaScript function `unescape` to replace all the escape sequences in the cookie with their equivalent English-language characters. The script stores the unescaped cookie value in the variable myCookie (line 36) and uses the JavaScript function split (line 39), introduced in Section 12.4.5, to break the cookie into identifier and value pieces. At this point in the script, myCookie contains a string of the form "name=*value*". We call split on myCookie with = as the delimiter to obtain the cookieTokens array, with the first element equal to the name of the identifier and the second element equal to the value of the identifier. Line 42 assigns the value of the second element in the cookieTokens array (i.e., the actual value stored in the cookie) to the variable name. Lines 54–55 add the personalized greeting to the Web page using the user's name stored in the cookie.

The Web page provides users with the option of resetting the cookie, which is useful in case someone new is using the computer. Lines 56–57 create a hyperlink that, when clicked, calls the JavaScript function wrongPerson (lines 60–68). Lines 63–64 set the cookie name to null and the expires property to January 1, 1995 (though any date in the past will suffice). Internet Explorer detects that the expires property is set to a date in the past and deletes the cookie from the user's computer. The next time this page loads, no cookie will be found. The **reload** method of the location object forces the page to refresh, and, unable to find an existing cookie, the script prompts the user to enter a new name.

12.10 Final JavaScript Example

The past few chapters have explored many interesting JavaScript concepts and how they can be applied on the Web. The next JavaScript example combines many of these concepts into a single Web page. Figure 12.16 uses functions, cookies, arrays, loops, the Date object, the window object and the document object to create a sample welcome screen containing a personalized greeting, a short quiz, a random image and a random quotation. We have seen all of these concepts before, but this example illustrates how they work together on one Web page.

```
1   <?xml version = "1.0"?>
2   <!DOCTYPE html PUBLIC "-//W3C//DTD XHTML 1.1//EN"
3       "http://www.w3.org/TR/xhtml11/DTD/xhtml11.dtd">
4
5   <!-- Fig. 12.16: final.html   -->
6   <!-- Putting It All Together -->
7
8   <html xmlns = "http://www.w3.org/1999/xhtml">
9      <head>
10        <title>Putting It All Together</title>
11
12        <script type = "text/javascript">
13           <!--
14           var now = new Date(); // current date and time
15           var hour = now.getHours(); // current hour
16
17           // array with names of the images that will be randomly selected
18           var pictures =
19              [ "CPE", "EPT", "GPP", "GUI", "PERF", "PORT", "SEO" ];
20
```

Fig. 12.16 Rich welcome page using several JavaScript concepts. (Part 1 of 5.)

```
21        // array with the quotes that will be randomly selected
22        var quotes = [ "Form ever follows function.<br/>" +
23           " Louis Henri Sullivan", "E pluribus unum." +
24           " (One composed of many.) <br/> Virgil", "Is it a" +
25           " world to hide virtues in?<br/> William Shakespeare" ];
26
27        // write the current date and time to the web page
28        document.write( "<p>" + now.toLocaleString() + "<br/></p>" );
29
30        // determine whether it is morning
31        if ( hour < 12 )
32           document.write( "<h2>Good Morning, " );
33        else
34        {
35           hour = hour - 12; // convert from 24 hour clock to PM time
36
37           // determine whether it is afternoon or evening
38           if ( hour < 6 )
39              document.write( "<h2>Good Afternoon, " );
40           else
41              document.write( "<h2>Good Evening, " );
42        }
43
44        // determine whether there is a cookie
45        if ( document.cookie )
46        {
47           // convert escape characters in the cookie string to their
48           // english notation
49           var myCookie = unescape( document.cookie );
50
51           // split the cookie into tokens using = as delimiter
52           var cookieTokens = myCookie.split( "=" );
53
54           // set name to the part of the cookie that follows the = sign
55           name = cookieTokens[ 1 ];
56        }
57        else
58        {
59           // if there was no cookie then ask the user to input a name
60           name = window.prompt( "Please enter your name", "GalAnt" );
61
62           // escape special characters in the name string
63           // and add name to the cookie
64           document.cookie = "name =" + escape( name );
65        }
66
67        // write the greeting to the page
68        document.writeln(
69           name + ", welcome to JavaScript programming!</h2>" );
70
71        // write the link for deleting the cookie to the page
72        document.writeln( "<a href = \" JavaScript:wrongPerson() \" > " +
73           "Click here if you are not " + name + "</a><br/>" );
```

Fig. 12.16 Rich welcome page using several JavaScript concepts. (Part 2 of 5.)

```
74
75            // write the random image to the page
76            document.write ( "<img src = \"" +
77                pictures[ Math.floor( Math.random() * 7 ) ] +
78                ".gif\" width= \" 105 \" height= \" 100 \" /> <br/>" );
79
80            // write the random quote to the page
81            document.write ( quotes[ Math.floor( Math.random() * 3 ) ] );
82
83            // create a window with all the quotes in it
84            function allQuotes()
85            {
86               // create the child window for the quotes
87               quoteWindow = window.open( "", "", "resizable=yes, toolbar" +
88                  "=no, menubar=no, status=no, location=no," +
89                  " scrollBars=yes" );
90               quoteWindow.document.write( "<p>" )
91
92               // loop through all quotes and write them in the new window
93               for ( var i = 0; i < quotes.length; i++ )
94                  quoteWindow.document.write( ( i + 1 ) + ".) " +
95                     quotes[ i ] + "<br/><br/>");
96
97               // write a close link to the new window
98               quoteWindow.document.write( "</p><br/><a href = \" " +
99                  "JavaScript:window.close()\">" +
100                  " Close this window </a>" )
101            }
102
103            // reset the document's cookie if wrong person
104            function wrongPerson()
105            {
106               // reset the cookie
107               document.cookie= "name=null;" +
108                  " expires=Thu, 01-Jan-95 00:00:01 GMT";
109
110               // after removing the cookie reload the page to get a new name
111               location.reload();
112            }
113
114            // open a new window with the quiz2.html file in it
115            function openQuiz()
116            {
117               window.open( "quiz2.html", "", "resizable = yes, " +
118                  "toolbar = no, menubar = no, status = no, " +
119                  "location = no, scrollBars = no");
120            }
121         // -->
122         </script>
123
124    </head>
125
126    <body>
```

Fig. 12.16   Rich welcome page using several JavaScript concepts. (Part 3 of 5.)

```
127         <p><a href = "JavaScript:allQuotes()">View all quotes</a></p>
128
129         <p id = "quizSpot">
130            <a href = "JavaScript:openQuiz()">Please take our quiz</a></p>
131
132         <script type = "text/javascript">
133            // variable that gets the last midification date and time
134            var modDate = new Date( document.lastModified );
135
136            // write the last modified date and time to the page
137            document.write ( "This page was last modified " +
138               modDate.toLocaleString() );
139         </script>
140
141      </body>
142   </html>
```

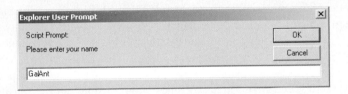

Fig. 12.16   Rich welcome page using several JavaScript concepts.   (Part 4 of 5.)

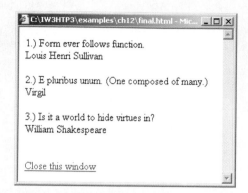

Fig. 12.16   Rich welcome page using several JavaScript concepts. (Part 5 of 5.)

The script that builds most of this page starts in line 12. Lines 14–15 declare variables needed for determining the time of day. Lines 18–25 create two arrays from which content is randomly selected. This Web page contains both an image (whose file name is randomly selected from the `pictures` array) and a quote (whose text is randomly selected from the `quotes` array). Line 28 writes the user's local date and time to the Web page using the `Date` object's `toLocaleString` method. Lines 30–42 display a time-sensitive greeting using the same code as Fig. 7.6. The script either uses an existing cookie to obtain the user's name (lines 45–56) or prompts the user for a name, which the script then stores in a new cookie (lines 57–65). Lines 68–69 write the greeting to the Web page, and lines 72–73 produce the link for resetting the cookie. This is the same code used in Fig. 12.15 to manipulate cookies. Lines 76–81 write the random image and random quote to the Web page. The script chooses each by randomly selecting an index into each array. This code is similar to the code used in Fig. 11.7 to display a random image using an array.

The `allQuotes` function (lines 84–101) uses the `window` object and a `for` loop to open a new window containing all the quotes in the `quotes` array. Lines 87–89 create a new window called `quoteWindow`. The script does not assign a URL or a title to this window, but it does specify the window features to display. Line 90 opens a new paragraph in `quoteWindow`. A `for` loop (lines 93–95) traverses the quotes array and writes each quote to `quoteWindow`. Lines 98–100 close the paragraph in `quoteWindow`, insert a new line and add a link at the bottom of the page that allows the user to close the window. Note that function `allQuotes` generates a Web page and opens it in an entirely new window with JavaScript.

Function `wrongPerson` (lines 104–112) resets the cookie storing the user's name. This function is identical to function `wrongPerson` in Fig. 12.15.

Function `openQuiz` (lines 115–120) opens a new window to display a sample quiz. Using the `window.open` method, the script creates a new window containing `quiz2.html` (lines 117–119). We discuss `quiz2.html` later in this section.

The primary script ends in line 122, and the body of the XHTML document begins in line 126. Line 127 creates the link that calls function `allQuotes` when clicked. Lines 129–130 create a paragraph element containing the attribute `id = "quizSpot"`. This paragraph contains a link that calls function `openQuiz`.

Lines 132–139 contain a second script. This script appears in the body of the XHTML document because it adds a dynamic footer to the page, which must appear after the static XHTML content contained in the first part of the body. This script creates another instance of the Date object, but the date is set to the last modified date and time of the XHTML document, rather than the current date and time (line 134). The script obtains the last modified date and time using property `document.lastModified`. Lines 137–138 add this information to the Web page. Note that the last modified date and time appear at the bottom of the page, after the rest of the body content. If this script were in the head element, this information would be displayed before the entire body of the XHTML document. Lines 139–142 close the `script`, the body and the XHTML document.

The quiz used in this example is in a separate XHTML document named `quiz2.html` (Fig. 12.17). This document is similar to `quiz.html` in Chapter 11 (Fig. 11.14). The quiz in this example differs from the quiz in Chapter 11 in that it shows the result in the main window in the example, whereas the earlier quiz example displays the result in the same window as the quiz. After clicking the **Submit** button in the quiz window, the main window changes to reflect that the quiz was taken, and the quiz window closes.

Lines 17–23 of this script check the user's answer and output the result to the main window. Lines 18–19 use `window.opener` to write to the main window. The property **window.opener** always contains a reference to the window that opened the current window, if such a window exists. Line 18 writes to property `window.opener.quizSpot.inner-Text`. Recall that `quizSpot` is the `id` of the paragraph element in the main window that contains the link to open the quiz. Property **innerText** refers to the text inside this paragraph element (i.e., the text between `<p>` and `</p>`). Modifying this property replaces the current text with the new text in the Web browser. Thus, when lines 18–19 execute, the link in the main window disappears, and the string `"Congratulations, your answer is correct."` appears. Lines 21–23 modify `window.opener.quizSpot.innerHTML`. Property **inner-HTML** is similar to `innerText`, but it refers to the XHTML code inside the paragraph element. Modifying this property dynamically changes the XHTML code in the paragraph. When lines 21–23 execute, the contents of the main window's `quizSpot` paragraph are replaced with the string `"Your answer is incorrect. Please try again"`, followed by a link to try the quiz again.

After checking the quiz answer, the script gives focus to the main window (i.e., puts the main window in the foreground, on top of any other open browser windows) using the method **focus** of the main window's `window` object. The property `window.opener` references the main window, so `window.opener.focus()` (line 25) gives the main window focus, allowing the user to see the changes made to the text of the main window's `quizSpot` paragraph. Finally, the script closes the quiz window using method `window.close` (line 26).

```
1   <?xml version = "1.0" encoding = "utf-8"?>
2   <!DOCTYPE html PUBLIC "-//W3C//DTD XHTML 1.1//EN"
3      "http://www.w3.org/TR/xhtml11/DTD/xhtml11.dtd">
4
5   <!-- Fig. 12.17: quiz2.html -->
6   <!-- Online Quiz                -->
```

Fig. 12.17   Online quiz in a child window. (Part 1 of 3.)

```
7
8    <html xmlns = "http://www.w3.org/1999/xhtml">
9    <head>
10   <title>Online Quiz</title>
11
12   <script type = "text/JavaScript">
13      <!--
14      function checkAnswers()
15      {
16         // determine whether the answer is correct
17         if ( myQuiz.radiobutton[ 1 ].checked )
18            window.opener.quizSpot.innerText =
19               "Congratulations, your answer is correct";
20         else // if the answer is incorrect
21            window.opener.quizSpot.innerHTML = "Your answer is incorrect." +
22               " Please try again <br /> <a href= \" JavaScript:openQuiz()" +
23               " \" > Please take our quiz</a>";
24
25         window.opener.focus();
26         window.close();
27      } // end checkAnswers function
28      //-->
29   </script>
30
31   </head>
32
33   <body>
34      <form id = "myQuiz" action = "JavaScript:checkAnswers()">
35         <p>Select the name of the tip that goes with the image shown:<br />
36            <img src = "EPT.gif" width = "108" height = "100"
37               alt = "mystery tip"/>
38            <br />
39
40            <input type = "radio" name = "radiobutton" value = "CPE" />
41            <label>Common Programming Error</label>
42
43            <input type = "radio" name = "radiobutton" value = "EPT" />
44            <label>Error-Prevention Tip</label>
45
46            <input type = "radio" name = "radiobutton" value = "PERF" />
47            <label>Performance Tip</label>
48
49            <input type = "radio" name = "radiobutton" value = "PORT" />
50            <label>Portability Tip</label><br />
51
52            <input type = "submit" name = "Submit" value = "Submit" />
53            <input type = "reset" name = "reset" value = "Reset" />
54         </p>
55      </form>
56   </body>
57   </html>
```

Fig. 12.17   Online quiz in a child window. (Part 2 of 3.)

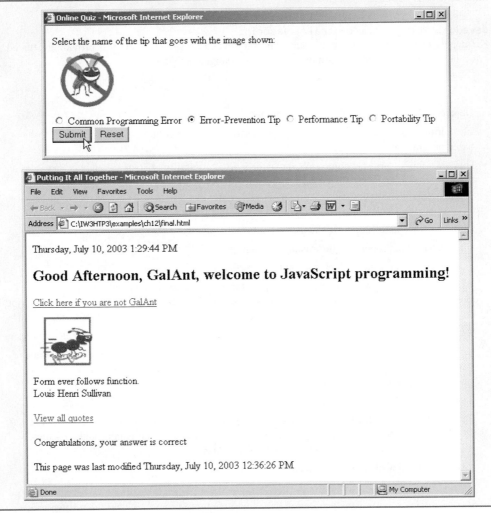

Fig. 12.17   Online quiz in a child window. (Part 3 of 3.)

Lines 29–31 close the `script` and `head` elements of the XHTML document. Line 33 opens the `body` of the XHTML document. The `body` contains the `form`, image, text labels and radio buttons that comprise the quiz. Lines 55–57 close the `form`, the `body` and the XHTML document.

12.11 Web Resources

www.javascript.com
JavaScript.com provides JavaScript tips and articles.

www.iboost.com/build/programming/js/tutorial/885.htm
This page provides a tutorial on JavaScript objects.

www.javascriptsearch.com
This site provides a variety of JavaScript examples.

`www.aljavascripts.com`
This site provides JavaScript examples, links, tutorials and tools.

`devedge.netscape.com/central/javascript`
Netscape's *JavaScript Central* site contains links to several JavaScript references providing detailed information on JavaScript's built-in objects and other language features.

SUMMARY

- Objects are a natural way of thinking about the world.

- JavaScript uses objects to perform many tasks, and therefore is commonly referred to as an object-based programming language.

- Humans think in terms of objects. We have the marvelous ability of abstraction, which enables us to view screen images as objects such as people, planes, trees and mountains rather than as individual dots of color (called pixels for "picture elements"). All objects have attributes and exhibit behaviors. Humans learn about objects by studying their attributes and observing their behaviors.

- Objects encapsulate data (attributes) and methods (behavior).

- Objects have the property of information hiding.

- Programs communicate with objects by using well-defined interfaces.

- World Wide Web browsers have a set of objects that encapsulate the elements of an XHTML document and expose to a JavaScript programmer attributes and behaviors that enable a JavaScript program to interact with (or script) the elements (i.e., objects) in an XHTML document.

- `Math` object methods allow programmers to perform many common mathematical calculations.

- An object's methods are called by writing the name of the object followed by a dot operator (`.`) and the name of the method. In parentheses following the method name is the argument (or a comma-separated list of arguments) to the method.

- Invoking (or calling) a method of an object is called "sending a message to the object."

- Characters are the fundamental building blocks of JavaScript programs. Every program is composed of a sequence of characters grouped together meaningfully that is interpreted by the computer as a series of instructions used to accomplish a task.

- A string is a series of characters treated as a single unit.

- A string may include letters, digits and various special characters, such as +, -, *, /, and $.

- String literals or string constants (often called anonymous `String` objects) are written as a sequence of characters in double quotation marks or single quotation marks.

- String method `charAt` returns the character at a specific index in a string. Indices for the characters in a string start at 0 (the first character) and go up to (but do not include) the string's `length` (i.e., if the string contains five characters, the indices are 0 through 4). If the index is outside the bounds of the string, the method returns an empty string.

- String method `charCodeAt` returns the Unicode value of the character at a specific index in a string. If the index is outside the bounds of the string, the method returns NaN. `String` method `fromCharCode` creates a string from a list of Unicode values.

- String method `toLowerCase` returns the lowercase version of a string. `String` method `toUpperCase` returns the uppercase version of a string.

- String method `indexOf` determines the location of the first occurrence of its argument in the string used to call the method. If the substring is found, the index at which the first occurrence of the substring begins is returned; otherwise, `-1` is returned. This method receives an optional second argument specifying the index from which to begin the search.

- `String` method `lastIndexOf` determines the location of the last occurrence of its argument in the string used to call the method. If the substring is found, the index at which the first occurrence of the substring begins is returned; otherwise, `-1` is returned. This method receives an optional second argument specifying the index from which to begin the search.

- The process of breaking a string into tokens is called tokenization. Tokens are separated from one another by delimiters, typically white-space characters such as blank, tab, newline and carriage return. Other characters may also be used as delimiters to separate tokens.

- `String` method `split` breaks a string into its component tokens. The argument to method `split` is the delimiter string—the string that determines the end of each token in the original string. Method `split` returns an array of strings containing the tokens.

- `String` method `substring` returns the substring from the starting index (its first argument) up to but not including the ending index (its second argument). If the ending index is greater than the length of the string, the substring returned includes the characters from the starting index to the end of the original string.

- `String` method `anchor` wraps the string that calls the method in XHTML element `<a></a>` with the `name` of the anchor supplied as the argument to the method.

- `String` method `blink` makes a string blink in a Web page by wrapping the string that calls the method in a `<blink></blink>` XHTML element.

- `String` method `fixed` displays text in a fixed-width font by wrapping the string that calls the method in a `<tt></tt>` XHTML element.

- `String` method `strike` displays struck-out text (i.e., text with a line through it) by wrapping the string that calls the method in a `<strike></strike>` XHTML element.

- `String` method `sub` displays subscript text by wrapping the string that calls the method in a `<sub></sub>` XHTML element.

- `String` method `sup` displays superscript text by wrapping the string that calls the method in a `<sup></sup>` XHTML element.

- `String` method `link` creates a hyperlink by wrapping the string that calls the method in XHTML element `<a></a>`. The target of the hyperlink (i.e, value of the `href` property) is the argument to the method and can be any URL.

- JavaScript's `Date` object provides methods for date and time manipulations.

- Date and time processing can be performed based either on the computer's local time zone or on World Time Standard's Coordinated Universal Time (abbreviated UTC)—formerly called Greenwich Mean Time (GMT).

- Most methods of the `Date` object have a local time zone and a UTC version.

- `Date` method `parse` receives as its argument a string representing a date and time and returns the number of milliseconds between midnight, January 1, 1970 and the specified date and time.

- `Date` method UTC returns the number of milliseconds between midnight, January 1, 1970 and the date and time specified as its arguments. The arguments to the UTC method include the required year, month and date, and the optional hours, minutes, seconds and milliseconds. If any of the hours, minutes, seconds or milliseconds arguments is not specified, a zero is supplied in its place. For the hours, minutes and seconds arguments, if the argument to the right of any of these arguments is specified, that argument must also be specified (e.g., if the minutes argument is specified, the hours argument must be specified; if the milliseconds argument is specified, all the arguments must be specified).

- JavaScript provides the `Boolean` and `Number` objects as object wrappers for boolean `true`/`false` values and numbers, respectively.

- When a boolean value is required in a JavaScript program, JavaScript automatically creates a `Boolean` object to store the value.
- JavaScript programmers can create `Boolean` objects explicitly with the statement

  `var b = new Boolean( ` *booleanValue* ` );`

  The argument *booleanValue* specifies whether the value of the `Boolean` object should be `true` or `false`. If *booleanValue* is `false`, `0`, `null`, `Number.NaN` or the empty string (`""`), or if no argument is supplied, the new `Boolean` object contains `false`. Otherwise, the new `Boolean` object contains `true`.
- JavaScript automatically creates `Number` objects to store numeric values in a JavaScript program.
- JavaScript programmers can create a `Number` object with the statement

  `var n = new Number( ` *numericValue* ` );`

  The argument *numericValue* is the number to store in the object. Although you can explicitly create `Number` objects, normally they are created when needed by the JavaScript interpreter.
- JavaScript provides the `document` object for manipulating the document that is currently visible in the browser window.
- JavaScript's `window` object provides methods for manipulating browser windows.
- A cookie is a piece of data that is stored on the user's computer to maintain information about the client during and between browser sessions.
- Cookies are accessible in JavaScript through the `document` object's `cookie` property.
- A cookie has the syntax "*identifier=value*", where *identifier* is any valid JavaScript variable identifier, and *value* is the value of the cookie variable. When multiple cookies exist for one Web site, *identifier-value* pairs are separated by semicolons in the `document.cookie` string.
- The `expires` property in a cookie string sets an expiration date after which the Web browser deletes the cookie. If a cookie's expiration date is not set, then the cookie expires by default after the user closes the browser window. A cookie can be deleted immediately by setting the `expires` property to a date and time in the past.

TERMINOLOGY

abs method of `Math`	cos method of `Math`
abstraction	date
anchor method of `String`	`Date` object
anonymous `String` object	delimiter
attribute	`document` object
behavior	E property of `Math`
blink method of `String`	empty string
`Boolean` object	encapsulation
bounds of the string	escape function
ceil method of `Math`	exp method of `Math`
character	fixed method of `String`
charAt method of `String`	floor method of `Math`
charCodeAt method of `String`	focus method of `window`
close method of `window`	fromCharCode method of `String`
concat method of `String`	getDate method of `Date`
cookie	getDay method of `Date`
Coordinated Universal Time (UTC)	getFullYear method of `Date`

valueOf method of String   window object
well-defined interfaces   wrap in XHTML tags

SELF-REVIEW EXERCISE

12.1   Fill in the blanks in each of the following statements:
a) Because JavaScript uses objects to perform many tasks, JavaScript is commonly referred to as a(n) _____.
b) All objects have _____ and exhibit _____.
c) The methods of the _____ object allow programmers to perform many common mathematical calculations.
d) Invoking (or calling) a method of an object is referred to as _____.
e) String literals or string constants are written as a sequence of characters in _____ or _____.
f) Indices for the characters in a string start at _____.
g) String methods _____ and _____ search for the first and last occurrences of a substring in a String, respectively.
h) The process of breaking a string into tokens is called _____.
i) String method _____ formats a String as a hyperlink.
j) Date and time processing can be performed based on the _____ or on World Time Standard's _____.
k) Date method _____ receives as its argument a string representing a date and time, and returns the number of milliseconds between midnight, January 1, 1970 and the specified date and time.

ANSWERS TO SELF-REVIEW EXERCISE

12.1   a) object-based programming language. b) attributes, behaviors. c) Math. d) sending a message to the object. e) double quotation marks, single quotation marks. f) 0. g) indexOf, lastIndexOf. h) tokenization. i) link. j) computer's local time zone, Coordinated Universal Time (UTC). k) parse.

EXERCISES

12.2   Write a script that tests whether the examples of the Math method calls shown in Fig. 12.1 actually produce the indicated results.

12.3   Write a script that tests as many of the Math library functions in Fig. 12.1 as you can. Exercise each of these functions by having your program display tables of return values for several argument values in an XHTML textarea.

12.4   Math method floor may be used to round a number to a specific decimal place. For example, the statement

```
y = Math.floor( x * 10 + .5 ) / 10;
```

rounds x to the tenths position (the first position to the right of the decimal point). The statement

```
y = Math.floor( x * 100 + .5 ) / 100;
```

rounds x to the hundredths position (i.e., the second position to the right of the decimal point). Write a script that defines four functions to round a number x in various ways:
a) roundToInteger(number)
b) roundToTenths(number)

     c) `roundToHundredths( number )`

     d) `roundToThousandths( number )`

For each value read, your program should display the original value, the number rounded to the nearest integer, the number rounded to the nearest tenth, the number rounded to the nearest hundredth and the number rounded to the nearest thousandth.

12.5   Modify the solution to Exercise 12.4 to use `Math` method `round` instead of method `floor`.

12.6   Write a script that uses relational and equality operators to compare two `String`s input by the user through an XHTML form. Output in an XHTML `textarea` whether the first string is less than, equal to or greater than the second.

12.7   Write a script that uses random number generation to create sentences. Use four arrays of strings called `article`, `noun`, `verb` and `preposition`. Create a sentence by selecting a word at random from each array in the following order: `article`, `noun`, `verb`, `preposition`, `article` and `noun`. As each word is picked, concatenate it to the previous words in the sentence. The words should be separated by spaces. When the final sentence is output, it should start with a capital letter and end with a period.

The arrays should be filled as follows: the `article` array should contain the articles `"the"`, `"a"`, `"one"`, `"some"` and `"any"`; the `noun` array should contain the nouns `"boy"`, `"girl"`, `"dog"`, `"town"` and `"car"`; the `verb` array should contain the verbs `"drove"`, `"jumped"`, `"ran"`, `"walked"` and `"skipped"`; the `preposition` array should contain the prepositions `"to"`, `"from"`, `"over"`, `"under"` and `"on"`.

The program should generate 20 sentences to form a short story and output the result to an XHTML `textarea`. The story should begin with a line reading `"Once upon a time..."` and end with a line reading `"THE END"`.

12.8   *(Limericks)* A limerick is a humorous five-line verse in which the first and second lines rhyme with the fifth, and the third line rhymes with the fourth. Using techniques similar to those developed in Exercise 12.7, write a script that produces random limericks. Polishing this program to produce good limericks is a challenging problem, but the result will be worth the effort!

12.9   *(Pig Latin)* Write a script that encodes English-language phrases in pig Latin. Pig Latin is a form of coded language often used for amusement. Many variations exist in the methods used to form pig Latin phrases. For simplicity, use the following algorithm:

To form a pig Latin phrase from an English-language phrase, tokenize the phrase into an array of words using `String` method `split`. To translate each English word into a pig Latin word, place the first letter of the English word at the end of the word and add the letters "ay." Thus the word "jump" becomes "umpjay," the word "the" becomes "hetay" and the word "computer" becomes "omputercay." Blanks between words remain as blanks. Assume the following: The English phrase consists of words separated by blanks, there are no punctuation marks and all words have two or more letters. Function `printLatinWord` should display each word. Each token (i.e., word in the sentence) is passed to method `printLatinWord` to print the pig Latin word. Enable the user to input the sentence through an XHTML form. Keep a running display of all the converted sentences in an XHTML `textarea`.

12.10   Write a script that inputs a telephone number as a string in the form `(555) 555-5555`. The script should use `String` method `split` to extract the area code as a token, the first three digits of the phone number as a token and the last four digits of the phone number as a token. Display the area code in one text field and the seven-digit phone number in another text field.

12.11   Write a script that inputs a line of text, tokenizes it with `String` method `split` and outputs the tokens in reverse order.

12.12   Write a script that inputs text from an XHTML form and outputs it in uppercase and lowercase letters.

12.13   Write a script that inputs several lines of text and a search character and uses `String` method `indexOf` to determine the number of occurrences of the character in the text.

12.14   Write a script based on the program in Exercise 12.13 that inputs several lines of text and uses `String` method `indexOf` to determine the total number of occurrences of each letter of the alphabet in the text. Uppercase and lowercase letters should be counted together. Store the totals for each letter in an array, and print the values in tabular format in an XHTML `textarea` after the totals have been determined.

12.15   Write a script that reads a series of strings and outputs in an XHTML `textarea` only those strings beginning with the character "b."

12.16   Write a script that reads a series of strings and outputs in an XHTML `textarea` only those strings ending with the characters "ED."

12.17   Write a script that inputs an integer code for a character and displays the corresponding character.

12.18   Modify your solution to Exercise 12.17 so that it generates all possible three-digit codes in the range 000 to 255 and attempts to display the corresponding characters. Display the results in an XHTML `textarea`.

12.19   Write your own version of the `String` method `indexOf` and use it in a script.

12.20   Write your own version of the `String` method `lastIndexOf` and use it in a script.

12.21   Write a program that reads a five-letter word from the user and produces all possible three-letter words that can be derived from the letters of the five-letter word. For example, the three-letter words produced from the word "bathe" include the commonly used words "ate," "bat," "bet," "tab," "hat," "the" and "tea." Output the results in an XHTML `textarea`.

12.22   *(Printing Dates in Various Formats)* Dates are printed in several common formats. Write a script that reads a date from an XHTML form and creates a `Date` object in which to store it. Then use the various methods of the `Date` object that convert `Date`s into strings to display the date in several formats.

SPECIAL SECTION: CHALLENGING STRING-MANIPULATION EXERCISES

The preceding exercises are keyed to the text and designed to test the reader's understanding of fundamental string-manipulation concepts. This section includes a collection of intermediate and advanced string-manipulation exercises. The reader should find these problems challenging, yet entertaining. The problems vary considerably in difficulty. Some require an hour or two of program writing and implementation. Others are useful for lab assignments that might require two or three weeks of study and implementation. Some are challenging term projects.

12.23   *(Text Analysis)* The availability of computers with string-manipulation capabilities has resulted in some rather interesting approaches to analyzing the writings of great authors. Much attention has been focused on whether William Shakespeare really wrote the works attributed to him. Some scholars believe there is substantial evidence indicating that Christopher Marlowe actually penned these masterpieces. Researchers have used computers to find similarities in the writings of these two authors. This exercise examines three methods for analyzing texts with a computer.

    a)   Write a script that reads several lines of text from the keyboard and prints a table indicating the number of occurrences of each letter of the alphabet in the text. For example, the phrase

```
To be, or not to be: that is the question:
```

    contains one "a," two "b's," no "c's," etc.

b) Write a script that reads several lines of text and prints a table indicating the number of one-letter words, two-letter words, three-letter words, etc., appearing in the text. For example, the phrase

```
Whether 'tis nobler in the mind to suffer
```

contains

Word length	Occurrences
1	0
2	2
3	1
4	2 (including 'tis)
5	0
6	2
7	1

c) Write a script that reads several lines of text and prints a table indicating the number of occurrences of each different word in the text. The first version of your program should include the words in the table in the same order in which they appear in the text. For example, the lines

```
To be, or not to be: that is the question:
Whether 'tis nobler in the mind to suffer
```

contain the word "to" three times, the word "be" twice, and the word "or" once. A more interesting (and useful) printout should then be attempted in which the words are sorted alphabetically.

12.24 *(Check Protection)* Computers are frequently employed in check-writing systems such as payroll and accounts payable applications. Many strange stories circulate regarding weekly paychecks being printed (by mistake) for amounts in excess of $1 million. Incorrect amounts are printed by computerized check-writing systems because of human error and/or machine failure. Systems designers build controls into their systems to prevent erroneous checks from being issued.

Another serious problem is the intentional alteration of a check amount by someone who intends to cash a check fraudulently. To prevent a dollar amount from being altered, most computerized check-writing systems employ a technique called *check protection.*

Checks designed for imprinting by computer contain a fixed number of spaces in which the computer may print an amount. Suppose a paycheck contains eight blank spaces in which the computer is supposed to print the amount of a weekly paycheck. If the amount is large, then all eight of those spaces will be filled, for example:

```
1,230.60  (check amount)
--------
12345678  (position numbers)
```

On the other hand, if the amount is less than $1000, then several of the spaces would ordinarily be left blank. For example,

```
    99.87
 --------
12345678
```

contains three blank spaces. If a check is printed with blank spaces, it is easier for someone to alter the amount of the check. To prevent a check from being altered, many check-writing systems insert *leading asterisks* to protect the amount as follows:

```
***99.87
 --------
12345678
```

Write a script that inputs a dollar amount to be printed on a check, and then prints the amount in check-protected format with leading asterisks if necessary. Assume that nine spaces are available for printing the amount.

12.25 *(Writing the Word Equivalent of a Check Amount)* Continuing the discussion in the preceding exercise, we reiterate the importance of designing check-writing systems to prevent alteration of check amounts. One common security method requires that the check amount be written both in numbers and spelled out in words. Even if someone is able to alter the numerical amount of the check, it is extremely difficult to change the amount in words.

Many computerized check-writing systems do not print the amount of the check in words. Perhaps the main reason for this omission is the fact that most high-level languages used in commercial applications do not contain adequate string-manipulation features. Another reason is that the logic for writing word equivalents of check amounts is somewhat involved.

Write a script that inputs a numeric check amount and writes the word equivalent of the amount. For example, the amount 112.43 should be written as

```
ONE HUNDRED TWELVE and 43/100
```

12.26 *(Morse Code)* Perhaps the most famous of all coding schemes is the Morse code, developed by Samuel Morse in 1832 for use with the telegraph system. The Morse code assigns a series of dots and dashes to each letter of the alphabet, each digit and a few special characters (e.g., period, comma, colon and semicolon). In sound-oriented systems, the dot represents a short sound and the dash represents a long sound. Other representations of dots and dashes are used with light-oriented systems and signal-flag systems.

Separation between words is indicated by a space or, quite simply, by the absence of a dot or dash. In a sound-oriented system, a space is indicated by a short period of time during which no sound is transmitted. The international version of the Morse code appears in Fig. 12.18.

Write a script that reads an English-language phrase and encodes it in Morse code. Also write a program that reads a phrase in Morse code and converts the phrase into the English-language equivalent. Use one blank between each Morse-coded letter and three blanks between each Morse-coded word.

12.27 *(Metric Conversion Program)* Write a script that will assist the user with metric conversions. Your program should allow the user to specify the names of the units as strings (e.g., centimeters, liters, grams, for the metric system and inches, quarts, pounds, for the English system) and should respond to simple questions such as

```
"How many inches are in 2 meters?"
"How many liters are in 10 quarts?"
```

Your program should recognize invalid conversions. For example, the question

```
"How many feet in 5 kilograms?"
```

is not a meaningful question because `"feet"` is a unit of length whereas `"kilograms"` is a unit of mass.

Character	Code	Character	Code
A	.–	T	–
B	–...	U	..–
C	–.–.	V	...–
D	–..	W	.––
E	.	X	–..–
F	..–.	Y	–.––
G	––.	Z	––..
H	....		
I	..	Digits	
J	.–––	1	.––––
K	–.–	2	..–––
L	.–..	3	...––
M	––	4	....–
N	–.	5	.....
O	–––	6	–....
P	.––.	7	––...
Q	––.–	8	–––..
R	.–.	9	––––.
S	...	0	–––––

Fig. 12.18 Letters of the alphabet as expressed in international Morse code.

12.28 *(Project: A Spell Checker)* Many popular word-processing software packages have built-in spell checkers.

In this project, you are asked to develop your own spell-checker utility. We make suggestions to help get you started. You should then consider adding more capabilities. Use a computerized dictionary (if you have access to one) as a source of words.

Why do we type so many words with incorrect spellings? In some cases, it is because we simply do not know the correct spelling, so we make a best guess. In some cases, it is because we transpose two letters (e.g., "defualt" instead of "default"). Sometimes we double-type a letter accidentally (e.g., "hanndy" instead of "handy"). Sometimes we type a nearby key instead of the one we intended (e.g., "biryhday" instead of "birthday"). And so on.

Design and implement a spell-checker application in JavaScript. Your program should maintain an array wordList of strings. Enable the user to enter these strings.

Your program should ask a user to enter a word. The program should then look up the word in the wordList array. If the word is present in the array, your program should print "Word is spelled correctly."

If the word is not present in the array, your program should print "word is not spelled correctly." Then your program should try to locate other words in wordList that might be the word the user intended to type. For example, you can try all possible single transpositions of adjacent letters to discover that the word "default" is a direct match to a word in wordList. Of course, this implies that your program will check all other single transpositions, such as "edfault," "dfeault," "deafult," "defalut" and "defautl." When you find a new word that matches one in `wordList`, print that word in a message, such as "`Did you mean "default?"`"

Implement other tests, such as replacing each double letter with a single letter and any other tests you can develop, to improve the value of your spell checker.

12.29 *(Project: Crossword Puzzle Generator)* Most people have worked a crossword puzzle, but few have ever attempted to generate one. Generating a crossword puzzle is suggested here as a string-manipulation project requiring substantial sophistication and effort.

There are many issues the programmer must resolve to get even the simplest crossword puzzle generator program working. For example, how does one represent the grid of a crossword puzzle in the computer? Should one use a series of strings, or should double-subscripted arrays be used?

The programmer needs a source of words (i.e., a computerized dictionary) that can be directly referenced by the program. In what form should these words be stored to facilitate the complex manipulations required by the program?

The really ambitious reader will want to generate the clues portion of the puzzle, in which the brief hints for each across word and each down word are printed for the puzzle worker. Merely printing a version of the blank puzzle itself is not a simple problem.

13

Dynamic HTML: Object Model and Collections

Objectives

- To use the Dynamic HTML Object Model and scripting to create dynamic Web pages.
- To understand the Dynamic HTML object hierarchy.
- To use the `all` and `children` collections to enumerate all of the XHTML elements of a Web page.
- To use dynamic styles and dynamic positioning.
- To use the `frames` collection to access objects in a separate frame on your Web page.
- To use the `navigator` object to determine which browser is being used to access your page.

Absolute freedom of navigation upon the seas...
Woodrow Wilson

Our children may learn about heroes of the past. Our task is to make ourselves architects of the future.
Jomo Mzee Kenyatta

The complex is made over into the simple, the hypothetical into the dogmatic, and the relative into an absolute.
Walter Lippmann

The thing that impresses me most about America is the way parents obey their children.
Duke of Windsor

The test of greatness is the page of history.
William Hazlitt

Outline

13.1 Introduction

In this chapter we introduce the Dynamic HTML Object Model.[1] The object model allows Web authors to control the presentation of their pages and gives them access to all the elements on their Web page. The whole Web page—elements, forms, frames, tables, etc.—is represented in an object hierarchy. Using scripting, an author is able to retrieve and modify any properties or attributes of the Web page dynamically.

This chapter begins by examining several of the objects available in the object hierarchy. Toward the end of the chapter, there is a diagram of the extensive object hierarchy, with explanations of the various objects and properties and links to Web sites with further information on the topic.

Software Engineering Observation 13.1

With Dynamic HTML, XHTML elements can be treated as objects, and attributes of XHTML elements can be treated as properties of those objects. Then, objects can be scripted (through their `id` attributes) with languages like JavaScript and VBScript to achieve dynamic effects.

13.2 Object Referencing

The simplest way to reference an element is by using the element's `id` attribute. The element is represented as an object, and its various XHTML attributes become properties that can be manipulated by scripting. Figure 13.1 uses this technique to read the **innerText** property of a p element.

---

1. Microsoft Dynamic HTML (discussed in Chapters 13–16 and Chapters 30–31) and Netscape Dynamic HTML are incompatible. In this book, we focus on Microsoft Dynamic HTML. We have tested all of the Dynamic HTML examples in Microsoft Internet Explorer 6 and Netscape® 7.1. All of the examples execute in Microsoft Internet Explorer; most do not execute in Netscape 7.1. We have posted the testing results at www.deitel.com. The Macromedia® Flash™ material we present in Chapters 17 and 18 executes properly in both of the latest Microsoft and Netscape browsers and enables you to achieve many of the effects of Dynamic HTML.

```
1   <?xml version = "1.0"?>
2   <!DOCTYPE html PUBLIC "-//W3C//DTD XHTML 1.0 Strict//EN"
3      "http://www.w3.org/TR/xhtml1/DTD/xhtml1-strict.dtd">
4
5   <!-- Fig. 13.1: reference.html  -->
6   <!-- Object Model Introduction -->
7
8   <html xmlns = "http://www.w3.org/1999/xhtml">
9      <head>
10         <title>Object Model</title>
11
12         <script type = "text/javascript">
13            <!--
14            function start()
15            {
16               alert( pText.innerText );
17               pText.innerText = "Thanks for coming.";
18            }
19            // -->
20         </script>
21
22      </head>
23
24      <body onload = "start()">
25         <p id = "pText">Welcome to our Web page!</p>
26      </body>
27   </html>
```

Fig. 13.1   Object referencing with the Dynamic HTML Object Model.

Line 24 uses the **onload** event to call the JavaScript start function (lines 14–18) when document loading completes. (Events are covered in depth in the next chapter.) Function start displays an alert box containing the value of pText.innerText. The object pText refers to the p element whose id is set to pText (line 25). The innerText property of the object refers to the text contained in that element (Welcome to our Web page!). When the user clicks **OK**, line 17 sets the innerText property of pText to a different value. Changing the text displayed on screen in this manner is an example of a Dynamic HTML capability called **dynamic content**.

13.3 Collections all and children

Included in the Dynamic HTML Object Model is the notion of **collections**, which basically are arrays of related objects on a page. There are several special collections in the object model (several collections are listed in Fig. 13.10 and Fig. 13.11 at the end of this chapter). The Dynamic HTML Object Model includes the **all** collection, which is a collection (or array) of all the XHTML elements in a document, in the order in which they appear. This provides an easy way of referring to any specific element, especially if it does not have an id. The script in Fig. 13.2 iterates through the all collection and displays the list of XHTML elements on the page by writing to the **innerHTML** property of a p element.

 Portability Tip 13.1

The all collection is a Microsoft-specific collection. Scripts using the all collection may not work properly on non-Microsoft browsers.

```
1    <?xml version = "1.0"?>
2    <!DOCTYPE html PUBLIC "-//W3C//DTD XHTML 1.0 Strict//EN"
3       "http://www.w3.org/TR/xhtml1/DTD/xhtml1-strict.dtd">
4
5    <!-- Fig 13.2: all.html          -->
6    <!-- Using the all collection -->
7
8    <html xmlns = "http://www.w3.org/1999/xhtml">
9       <head>
10          <title>Object Model</title>
11
12          <script type = "text/javascript">
13             <!--
14             var elements = "";
15
16             function start()
17             {
18                for ( var loop = 0; loop < document.all.length; ++loop )
19                   elements += "<br />" + document.all[ loop ].tagName;
20
21                pText.innerHTML += elements;
22                alert( elements );
23             }
24             // -->
25          </script>
26       </head>
27
28       <body onload = "start()">
29          <p id = "pText">Elements on this Web page:</p>
```

Fig. 13.2   Looping through the all collection. (Part 1 of 2.)

```
30        </body>
31   </html>
```

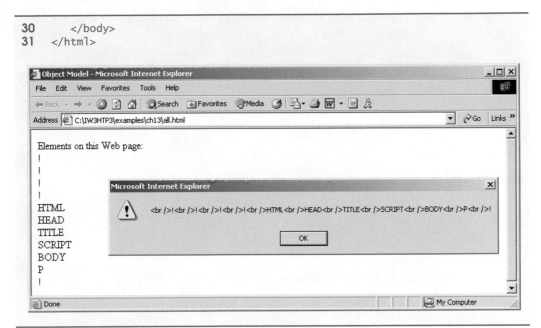

Fig. 13.2   Looping through the `all` collection. (Part 2 of 2.)

Lines 18–19 in function **start** loop through the elements of the `all` collection and display each element's name. Like an array, a collection begins at element 0, and specific elements in a collection can be referenced using a subscript (or index) in square brackets (`[]`). The `all` collection is a property of the **document** object (discussed in more detail later in this chapter). The **length** property of the `all` collection (and other collections) specifies the number of elements in the collection. For each element in the collection, we append to **elements** the name of the XHTML element (determined with the **tagName** property). When the loop terminates, we write the names of the elements to **pText.innerHTML**—the **innerHTML** property is similar to the **innerText** property, but it can include XHTML formatting. Note that line 1, lines 2–3 and all the comment elements are represented with a **tagName** property of ! in the output.

When we use the **document.all** collection, we refer to all the XHTML elements in the document. However, every element has its own `all` collection, consisting of all the elements contained within that element. For example, the body element's `all` collection contains the p element in line 29, but not the **title** element in line 10 (which is part of the head element's `all` collection).

A collection similar to the `all` collection is the **children** collection, which for a specific element contains that element's child elements (or direct descendants in the hierarchy). For example, an **html** element has only two children—the **head** element and the body element. The body element may contain several children of its own, such as p elements. The **children** collection provides an easy way to navigate the object hierarchy of elements in an XHTML document.

Figure 13.3 uses the **children** collection to walk through all the elements in the document. When you look at the script in this XHTML document, do you notice anything different about its use of functions as compared to the uses of functions in our prior scripts?

The difference is that function `child` (lines 16–33) uses recursion to call itself in line 25 in the program. Recursion was introduced in Chapter 10.

```
1   <?xml version = "1.0"?>
2   <!DOCTYPE html PUBLIC "-//W3C//DTD XHTML 1.0 Strict//EN"
3      "http://www.w3.org/TR/xhtml1/DTD/xhtml1-strict.dtd">
4
5   <!-- Fig 13.3: children.html -->
6   <!-- The children collection -->
7
8   <html xmlns = "http://www.w3.org/1999/xhtml">
9      <head>
10        <title>Object Model</title>
11
12        <script type = "text/javascript">
13           <!--
14           var elements = "<ul>";
15
16           function child( object )
17           {
18              var loop = 0;
19
20              elements += "<li>" + object.tagName + "<ul>";
21
22              for ( loop = 0; loop < object.children.length; loop++ )
23              {
24                 if ( object.children[ loop ].children.length )
25                    child( object.children[ loop ] );
26                 else
27                    elements += "<li>" +
28                       object.children[ loop ].tagName +
29                       "</li>";
30              }
31
32              elements += "</ul>" + "</li>";
33           }
34           // -->
35        </script>
36     </head>
37
38     <body onload = "child( document.all[ 4 ] );
39        myDisplay.outerHTML += elements;
40        myDisplay.outerHTML += '</ul>';">
41
42        <p>Welcome to our <strong>Web</strong> page!</p>
43
44        <p id = "myDisplay">
45           Elements on this Web page:
46        </p>
47
48     </body>
49   </html>
```

Fig. 13.3   Navigating the object hierarchy using collection `children`. (Part 1 of 2.)

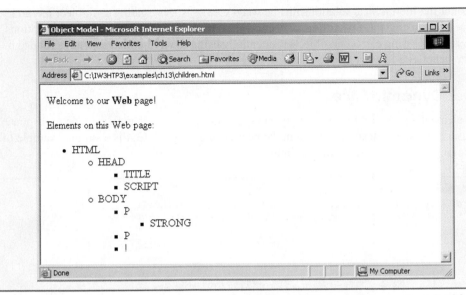

Fig. 13.3 Navigating the object hierarchy using collection `children`. (Part 2 of 2.)

Function `child` uses recursion to view all the elements on the page and output them in a hierarchical manner—it starts at the level of the `html` element (`document.all[ 4 ]` in line 38), which is the fifth element on the page, and begins walking through all the children of that element. If it encounters an element that has its own children (line 24), it recursively calls the `child` function, passing the child element through which the function should loop in the recursive call. As that loop finishes, the loop which called it proceeds to the next element in its own array of `children`. We use the `tagName` property to gather the names of the tags we encounter while looping through the document, and we place them in the string `elements`. The script adds `ul` and `li` tags to display the elements in a hierarchical manner on the page. Note that the string `elements` initially contains an opening `ul` tag to display the page's object hierarchy in an unordered list (line 14). Child elements are recursively added to the hierarchy as list items, and a nested unordered list is created to contain the children of each encountered element (line 20). Line 32 closes the nested `ul` tag and the `li` tag of the current child element.

When the original call to function `child` completes, line 39 concatenates the string `elements` to the `outerHTML` property of the p element `myDisplay`. Line 40 further adds to `myDisplay.outerHTML` a closing `ul` tag to match the `ul` tag initially present in `elements`. Property `outerHTML` is similar to property `innerHTML` introduced in the preceding example, but it includes the enclosing XHTML tags (tags `<p id = "myDisplay">` and `</p>` in this case) as well as the content inside them. When the `body` of the page loads completely, the `myDisplay` paragraph contains the dynamically generated object hierarchy of the page.

The `all` collection and the `children` collection provide valuable ways to examine and manipulate the elements of an XHTML document. Choosing which collection to use in a specific application depends largely on the order in which the elements need to be handled. Remember that the `all` collection simply contains objects for XHTML elements in the order in which the elements appear, whereas the `children` collection takes into account the hierarchical relationships between elements. Navigating the object hierarchy recursively using the `children` collection may be better suited for some applications, whereas accessing elements' objects sequentially using the `all` collection may prove to be more beneficial in other applications.

13.4 Dynamic Styles

An element's style can be changed dynamically. Often such a change is made in response to user events, which are discussed in the next chapter. Figure 13.4 is a simple example of changing styles in response to user input.

```
1   <?xml version = "1.0"?>
2   <!DOCTYPE html PUBLIC "-//W3C//DTD XHTML 1.0 Strict//EN"
3      "http://www.w3.org/TR/xhtml1/DTD/xhtml1-strict.dtd">
4
5   <!-- Fig. 13.4: dynamicstyle.html -->
6   <!-- Dynamic Styles             -->
7
8   <html xmlns = "http://www.w3.org/1999/xhtml">
9      <head>
10         <title>Object Model</title>
11
12         <script type = "text/javascript">
13            <!--
14            function start()
15            {
16               var inputColor = prompt(
17                  "Enter a color name for the " +
18                  "background of this page", "" );
19               document.body.style.backgroundColor = inputColor;
20            }
21            // -->
22         </script>
23      </head>
24
25      <body onload = "start()">
26         <p>Welcome to our Web site!</p>
27      </body>
28   </html>
```

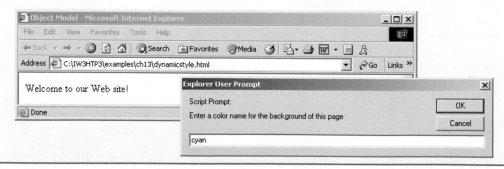

Fig. 13.4   Dynamic styles. (Part 1 of 2.)

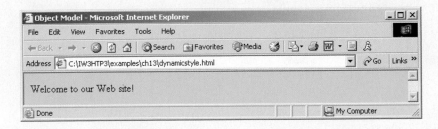

Fig. 13.4   Dynamic styles. (Part 2 of 2.)

Function `start` (lines 14–20) `prompts` the user to enter a color name, then sets the background color to that value. [*Note:* An error occurs if the value entered is not a valid color. See Appendix B, XHTML Colors, for further information.] We refer to the background color as `document.body.style.backgroundColor`—the `body` property of the `document` object refers to the `body` element. We then use the `style` property (a property of most XHTML elements) to set the `background-color` CSS property. (This is referred to as `backgroundColor` in JavaScript, to avoid confusion with the subtraction (-) operator. This naming convention is consistent for most CSS properties. For example, `borderWidth` correlates to the `border-width` CSS property, and `fontFamily` correlates to the `font-family` CSS property.)

The Dynamic HTML Object Model also allows you to change the `class` attribute of an element—instead of changing many individual styles at a time, you can have preset style classes for easily altering element styles. Figure 13.5 prompts the user to enter the name of a style class, and then changes the screen text to that style.

```
1   <?xml version = "1.0"?>
2   <!DOCTYPE html PUBLIC "-//W3C//DTD XHTML 1.0 Strict//EN"
3       "http://www.w3.org/TR/xhtml11/DTD/xhtml1-strict.dtd">
4
5   <!-- Fig. 13.5: dynamicstyle2.html -->
6   <!-- More Dynamic Styles           -->
7
8   <html xmlns = "http://www.w3.org/1999/xhtml">
9       <head>
10          <title>Object Model</title>
11
12          <style type = "text/css">
13
14              .bigText    { font-size: 3em;
15                            font-weight: bold }
16
17              .smallText { font-size: .75em }
18
19          </style>
20
21          <script type = "text/javascript">
22              <!--
```

Fig. 13.5   Dynamic styles in action. (Part 1 of 2.)

```
23          function start()
24          {
25              var inputClass = prompt(
26                 "Enter a className for the text " +
27                 "(bigText or smallText)", "" );
28              pText.className = inputClass;
29          }
30          // -->
31      </script>
32  </head>
33
34  <body onload = "start()">
35      <p id = "pText">Welcome to our Web site!</p>
36  </body>
37  </html>
```

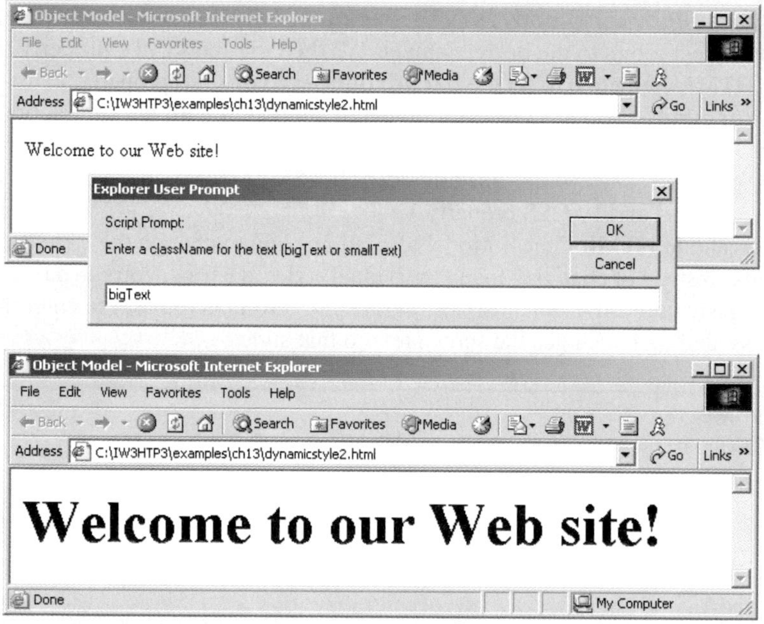

Fig. 13.5 Dynamic styles in action. (Part 2 of 2.)

As in the preceding example, we prompt the user for information—in this case, we ask for the name of a style class to apply, either bigText or smallText. [*Note*: CSS style class names are case-sensitive.] Once we have this information, we then use the class-Name property to change the style class of pText (line 28).

13.5 Dynamic Positioning

Another important feature of Dynamic HTML is **dynamic positioning**, which enables XHTML elements to be positioned with scripting. This is done by declaring an element's CSS position property to be either absolute or relative, and then moving the element by manipulating any of the top, left, right or bottom CSS properties.

The example in Fig. 13.6 demonstrates dynamic positioning, dynamic styles and dynamic content—we vary the position of the element on the page by accessing its CSS `left` attribute, we use scripting to vary the `color`, `fontFamily` and `fontSize` attributes, and we use the element's `innerHTML` property to alter the content of the element.

```
1   <?xml version = "1.0"?>
2   <!DOCTYPE html PUBLIC "-//W3C//DTD XHTML 1.0 Strict//EN"
3      "http://www.w3.org/TR/xhtml1/DTD/xhtml1-strict.dtd">
4
5   <!-- Fig. 13.6: dynamicposition.html -->
6   <!-- Dynamic Positioning            -->
7
8   <html xmlns = "http://www.w3.org/1999/xhtml">
9      <head>
10         <title>Dynamic Positioning</title>
11
12         <script type = "text/javascript">
13            <!--
14            var speed = 5;
15            var count = 10;
16            var direction = 1;
17            var firstLine = "Text growing";
18            var fontStyle = [ "serif", "sans-serif", "monospace" ];
19            var fontStylecount = 0;
20
21            function start()
22            {
23               window.setInterval( "run()", 100 );
24            }
25
26            function run()
27            {
28               count += speed;
29
30               if ( ( count % 200 ) == 0 ) {
31                  speed *= -1;
32                  direction = !direction;
33
34                  pText.style.color =
35                     ( speed < 0 ) ? "red" : "blue" ;
36                  firstLine =
37                     ( speed < 0 ) ? "Text shrinking" : "Text growing";
38                  pText.style.fontFamily =
39                     fontStyle[ ++fontStylecount % 3 ];
40               }
41
42               pText.style.fontSize = count / 3;
43               pText.style.left = count;
44               pText.innerHTML = firstLine + "<br /> Font size: " +
45                  count + "px";
46            }
47            // -->
```

Fig. 13.6 Dynamic positioning. (Part 1 of 2.)

```
48          </script>
49      </head>
50
51      <body onload = "start()">
52          <p id = "pText" style = "position: absolute; left: 0;
53              font-family: serif; color: blue">
54          Welcome!</p>
55      </body>
56  </html>
```

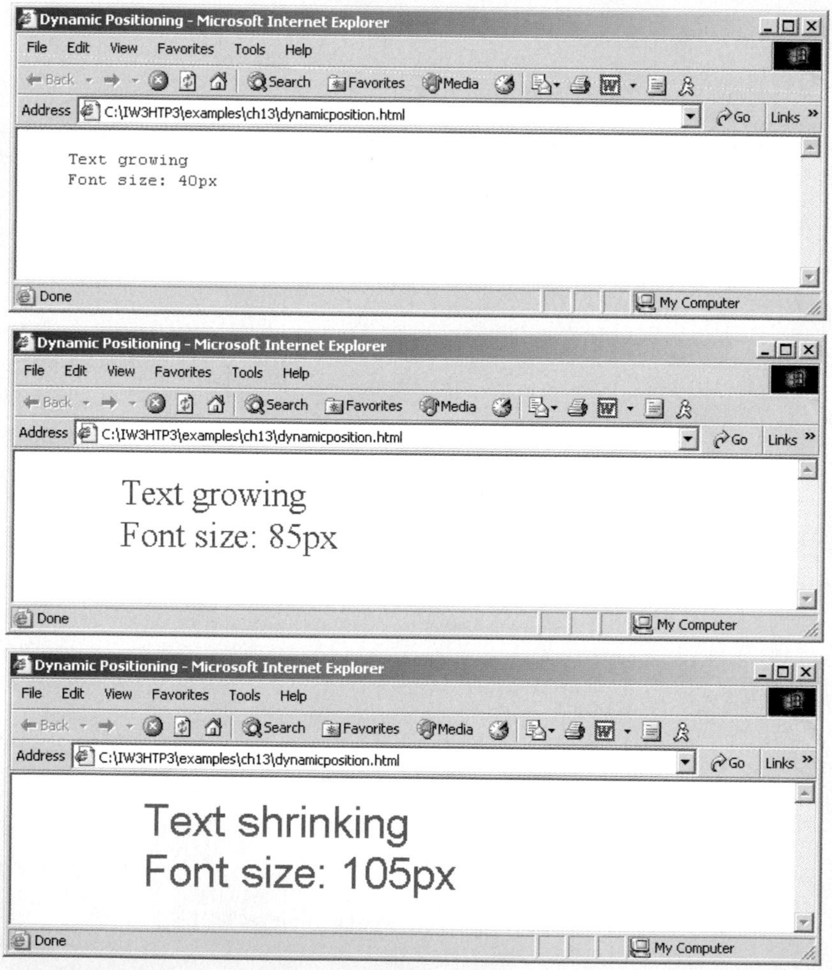

Fig. 13.6   Dynamic positioning. (Part 2 of 2.)

To continuously update the p element's content, in line 23 we use a new function, **setInterval**. This function takes two parameters—a function name, and how often to execute the function (in this case, every 100 milliseconds). A similar JavaScript function is **setTimeout**, which takes the same parameters but instead waits the specified amount of time before calling the named function only once. There are also JavaScript functions for stopping either of these two timers—the `clearTimeout` and `clearInterval` functions. To stop a specific timer, the parameter you pass to either of these functions should be the value that the corresponding set time function returned. For example, if you started a `setTimeout` timer with

```
timer1 = window.setTimeout( "timedFunction()", 2000 );
```

you could then stop the timer by calling

```
window.clearTimeout( timer1 );
```

which would stop the timer before it fired.

13.6 Using the `frames` Collection

One problem that you might run into while developing applications is communication between frames. The referencing we have used certainly allows for access to objects and XHTML elements on the same page, but what if those elements and objects are in different frames? Figure 13.7 and Fig. 13.8 solve this problem by using the `frames` collection.

```
1   <?xml version = "1.0"?>
2   <!DOCTYPE html PUBLIC "-//W3C//DTD XHTML 1.0 Frameset//EN"
3       "http://www.w3.org/TR/xhtml1/DTD/xhtml1-frameset.dtd">
4
5   <!-- Fig. 13.7: index.html      -->
6   <!-- Using the frames collection -->
7
8   <html xmlns = "http://www.w3.org/1999/xhtml">
9      <head>
10         <title>Frames collection</title>
11      </head>
12
13      <frameset rows = "100, *">
14         <frame src = "top.html" name = "upper" />
15         <frame src = "" name = "lower" />
16      </frameset>
17
18   </html>
```

Fig. 13.7   `frameset` file for cross-frame scripting.

```
1   <?xml version = "1.0"?>
2   <!DOCTYPE html PUBLIC "-//W3C//DTD XHTML 1.0 Strict//EN"
3       "http://www.w3.org/TR/xhtml1/DTD/xhtml1-strict.dtd">
4
5   <!-- Fig. 13.8: top.html      -->
6   <!-- Cross-frame scripting -->
7
8   <html xmlns = "http://www.w3.org/1999/xhtml">
9      <head>
```

Fig. 13.8   Accessing other frames. (Part 1 of 2.)

```
10          <title>The frames collection</title>
11
12          <script type = "text/javascript">
13             <!--
14             function start()
15             {
16                var text = prompt( "What is your name?", "" );
17                parent.frames( "lower" ).document.write(
18                   "<h1>Hello, " + text + "</h1>" );
19             }
20             // -->
21          </script>
22       </head>
23
24       <body onload = "start()">
25          <h1>Cross-frame scripting!</h1>
26       </body>
27    </html>
```

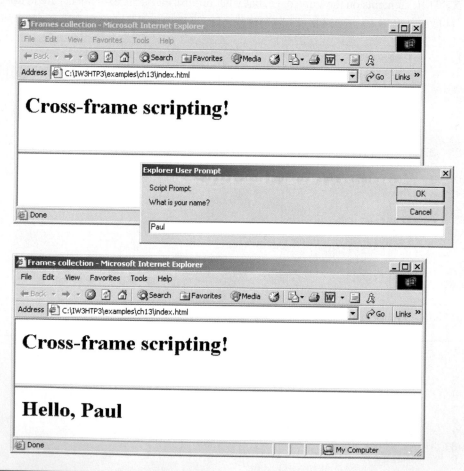

Fig. 13.8   Accessing other frames. (Part 2 of 2.)

Lines 17–18 (Fig. 13.8) apply changes to the lower frame. To reference the lower frame, we first reference the `parent` frame of the current frame, then use the `frames` collection. We use a new notation here—`frames( "lower" )`—to refer to the element in the frames collection with an `id` or `name` of lower. The `<frame>` tag for the lower frame appears second in the XHTML file of Fig. 13.7, so the frame is second in the `frames` collection. We then use the familiar `document.write` method in that frame to update it with the user input from our `prompt` in line 16 of Fig. 13.8.

Error-Prevention Tip 13.1

Internet Explorer 6 only allows cross-frame scripting between pages under the same domain (i.e., the same Web server). This precaution ensures that a Web page cannot be modified from outside its domain. If script interaction is attempted between pages under different domains, Internet Explorer will display a permission error. For instance, an error will occur if a page at aol.com *(in one frame) attempts to alter prices listed on a page at* amazon.com *(in a different frame) because the pages are under different domains.*

13.7 navigator Object

One of the most appealing aspects of the Internet is its diversity. Unfortunately, standards are sometimes compromised because of this diversity. The two most popular browsers currently on the market, Netscape and Microsoft's Internet Explorer, have many features that give the Web author great control over the browser, but many of their features are incompatible. Each, however, supports the `navigator` object, which contains information about the Web browser that is viewing the page. This allows Web authors to determine which browser the user has—this is especially important when the page uses browser-specific features, because it allows the author to redirect users to pages that their browsers can display properly. Figure 13.9 demonstrates a way to determine the type of browser that requests the document `navigator.html` and appropriately redirects users to either an Internet Explorer or Netscape-compatible (i.e., Netscape, Mozilla, etc.) version of the page.

```
1   <?xml version = "1.0"?>
2   <!DOCTYPE html PUBLIC "-//W3C//DTD XHTML 1.0 Strict//EN"
3       "http://www.w3.org/TR/xhtml1/DTD/xhtml1-strict.dtd">
4
5   <!-- Fig 13.9: navigator.html   -->
6   <!-- Using the navigator object -->
7
8   <html xmlns = "http://www.w3.org/1999/xhtml">
9      <head>
10         <title>The navigator Object</title>
11
12         <script type = "text/javascript">
13            <!--
14            function start()
15            {
16               if (navigator.appName=="Microsoft Internet Explorer")
17               {
18                  if ( navigator.appVersion.substring( 1, 0 ) >= "4" )
19                     document.location = "newIEversion.html";
```

Fig. 13.9   Using the `navigator` object to redirect users. (Part 1 of 2.)

```
20                 else
21                     document.location = "oldIEversion.html";
22                 }
23             else
24                 document.location = "NSversion.html";
25             }
26         // -->
27     </script>
28 </head>
29
30 <body onload = "start()">
31     <p>Redirecting your browser to the appropriate page,
32     please wait...</p>
33 </body>
34 </html>
```

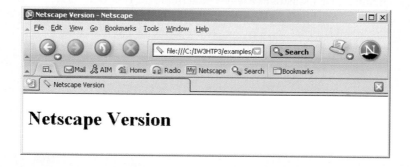

Fig. 13.9   Using the `navigator` object to redirect users. (Part 2 of 2.)

When the page loads, the `onload` event calls function `start` (lines 14–25), which checks the value of the property `navigator.appName`. This property of the `navigator` object contains the name of the browser application (for IE, this property is `"Microsoft Internet Explorer"`; for Netscape, it is `"Netscape"`). If the browser viewing this page is not Internet Explorer, in line 24 we redirect the browser to the document "NSversion.html" by assigning the document name to property `document.location`—the URL of the document being viewed. When a script assigns `document.location` a new URL, the browser immediately switches Web pages.

Line 18 checks the version of an IE browser with the `navigator.appVersion` property. The value of `appVersion` is not a simple integer, however—it is a string containing other information, such as the operating system of the user's computer. For example, the `appVersion` of IE6 on Windows XP is

```
4.0 (compatible; MSIE 6.0; Windows NT 5.0)
```

Therefore, the script uses method `substring` to retrieve the first character of the string, which is the actual version number. If the version number is 4 or greater, we redirect to `newIEversion.html`. Otherwise, we redirect the browser to `oldIEversion.html`.

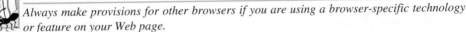

Portability Tip 13.2

Always make provisions for other browsers if you are using a browser-specific technology or feature on your Web page.

As we see here, the `navigator` object is crucial in providing browser-specific pages so that as many users as possible can view your site properly. A similar technique to the one shown here can be used to detect the use of other browsers, too, such as Opera. Please see `javascriptkit.com/javatutors/navigator.shtml` for information on using the `navigator` object to detect other browsers.

13.8 Summary of the DHTML Object Model

As you have seen in the preceding sections, the objects and collections supported by Internet Explorer allow the script programmer tremendous flexibility in manipulating the elements of a Web page. We have shown how to access the objects in a page, how to navigate the objects in a collection, how to change element styles dynamically and how to change the position of elements dynamically.

The Dynamic HTML Object Model provided by Internet Explorer allows a script programmer to access every element in an XHTML document. Literally every element in a document is represented by a separate object. The diagram in Fig. 13.10 shows many of the important objects and collections supported in Internet Explorer. The table in Fig. 13.11 provides a brief description of each object and collection in the diagram in Fig. 13.10.

For a comprehensive listing of all the objects and collections supported by Internet Explorer, browse the Microsoft *HTML and DHTML Reference* Web site,

```
msdn.microsoft.com/workshop/author/dhtml/reference/
dhtml_reference_entry.asp
```

This site provides detailed information on HTML, Dynamic HTML and Cascading Style Sheets technologies. The *DHTML References* section of this site provides detailed descriptions of every object, event and collection used in DHTML.

Another valuable Web resource is the W3C's *Document Object Model (DOM) Specifications* site,

```
www.w3.org/DOM/DOMTR
```

which provides technical reports on the standard Document Object Model that underlies Microsoft's Dynamic HTML. This site presents the W3C standards that make cross-browser and cross-platform scripting of XHTML documents possible.

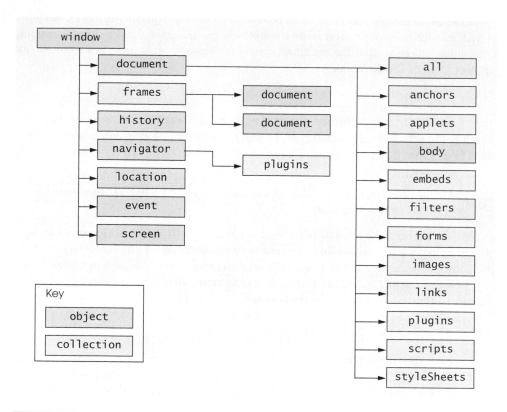

Fig. 13.10   DHTML Object Model.

Object or collection	Description
Objects	
window	Represents the browser window and provides access to the document object contained in the window. If the window contains frames a separate window object is created automatically for each frame, to provide access to the document rendered in the frame. Frames are considered to be sub-windows in the browser.
document	Represents the XHTML document rendered in a window. The document object provides access to every element in the XHTML document and allows dynamic modification of the XHTML document.
body	Provides access to the body element of an XHTML document.
history	Keeps track of the sites visited by the browser user. The object provides a script programmer with the ability to move forward and backward through the visited sites, but for security reasons does not allow the actual site URLs to be manipulated.

Fig. 13.11   Objects in the Internet Explorer 6 Object Model. (Part 1 of 2.)

Object or collection	Description
navigator	Contains information about the Web browser, such as the name of the browser, the version of the browser, the operating system on which the browser is running and other information that can help a script writer customize the user's browsing experience.
location	Contains the URL of the rendered document. When this object is set to a new URL, the browser immediately switches (navigates) to the new location.
event	Can be used in an event handler to obtain information about the event that occurred (e.g., the mouse *x-y* coordinates during a mouse event).
screen	Contains information about the computer screen for the computer on which the browser is running. Information such as the width and height of the screen in pixels can be used to determine the size at which elements should be rendered in a Web page.
Collections	
all	Many objects have an all collection that provides access to every element contained in the object. For example, the body object's all collection provides access to every element in the body element of an XHTML document.
anchors	Collection contains all the anchor elements (a) that have a name or id attribute. The elements appear in the collection in the order they were defined in the XHTML document.
applets	Contains all the applet elements in the XHTML document. Currently, the most common applet elements are Java™ applets.
embeds	Contains all the embed elements in the XHTML document.
forms	Contains all the form elements in the XHTML document. The elements appear in the collection in the order they were defined in the XHTML document.
frames	Contains window objects that represent each frame in the browser window. Each frame is treated as its own subwindow.
images	Contains all the img elements in the XHTML document. The elements appear in the collection in the order they were defined in the XHTML document.
links	Contains all the anchor elements (a) with an href property. This collection also contains all the area elements that represent links in an image map.
plugins	Like the embeds collection, this collection contains all the embed elements in the XHTML document.
scripts	Contains all the script elements in the XHTML document.
styleSheets	Contains styleSheet objects that represent each style element in the XHTML document and each style sheet included in the XHTML document via link.

Fig. 13.11   Objects in the Internet Explorer 6 Object Model. (Part 2 of 2.)

SUMMARY

- The Dynamic HTML Object Model gives Web authors great control over the presentation of their pages by giving them access to all the elements on their Web page. The whole Web page—elements, forms, frames, tables, etc.—is represented in an object hierarchy. Using scripting, an author is able to retrieve and modify any properties or attributes of the Web page dynamically.

- The simplest way to reference an element is by its `id` attribute. The element is represented as an object, and its various XHTML attributes become properties that can be manipulated by scripting.

- The `innerText` property of the object refers to the text contained in the element.

- Changing the text displayed on screen is a Dynamic HTML ability called dynamic content.

- Collections are basically arrays of related objects on a page. There are several special collections in the object model.

- The `all` collection contains all the XHTML elements in a document.

- The `length` property of the a collection specifies the size of the collection.

- Property `innerHTML` is similar to property `innerText`, but it can include XHTML formatting.

- Every element has its own `all` collection consisting of all the elements contained in the element.

- The `children` collection of an element contains only the element's direct child elements. For example, an `html` element has only two children: the `head` element and the `body` element.

- The `tagName` property contains the name of the tags we encounter while looping through the document, to place them in the string `elements`.

- The `outerHTML` property is similar to the `innerHTML` property, but it includes the enclosing XHTML tags as well as the content inside them.

- The `className` property of an element is used to change the element's style class.

- An important feature of Dynamic HTML is dynamic positioning, in which XHTML elements can be positioned with scripting. This is done by declaring an element's CSS `position` property to be either `absolute` or `relative`, and then moving the element by manipulating any of the `top`, `left`, `right` or `bottom` CSS properties.

- Function `setInterval` takes two parameters—a function name and how often to call it.

- Function `setTimeout` takes the same parameters as `setInterval`, but instead waits the specified amount of time before calling the named function only once.

- There are also JavaScript functions for stopping the `setTimeout` and `setInterval` timers—the `clearTimeout` and `clearInterval` functions. To stop a specific timer, the parameter you pass to either of these functions should be the value that the corresponding set time function returns.

- The `frames` collections contains all the frames in a document.

- The `navigator` object contains information about the Web browser that is viewing the page. This allows Web authors to determine which browser the user has.

- The `navigator.appName` property contains the name of the application—for IE, this property is `"Microsoft Internet Explorer"`, for Netscape, it is `"Netscape"`.

- The version of the browser is accessible through the `navigator.appVersion` property. The value of `appVersion` is not a simple integer, however—it is a string containing other information, such as the current operating system. The `navigator` object is crucial in providing browser-specific pages so that as many users as possible can view your site properly.

TERMINOLOGY

all collection of an element
background-color CSS property
base case
body property of document object
bottom CSS property
children collection
className property
clearInterval JavaScript function
clearTimeout JavaScript function
collection
document object
document.all.length
dynamic content
Dynamic HTML Object Model
dynamic positioning
dynamic style
fontSize property
id attribute
innerHTML property
innerText property

iteration
JavaScript
left CSS property
length property of a collection
loop through a collection
object referencing
onload event
outerHTML property
position: absolute
position: relative
prompt dialog
reference an object
right CSS property
setInterval JavaScript function
setTimeout JavaScript function
style object
tagName property
top CSS property
window.setInterval
window.setTimeout

SELF-REVIEW EXERCISES

13.1   State whether each of the following is *true* or *false*. If *false*, explain why.
  a) An XHTML element may be referred to in JavaScript by its id attribute.
  b) Only the document object has an all collection.
  c) An element's tag is accessed with the tagName property.
  d) You can change an element's style class dynamically with the style property.
  e) The frames collection contains all the frames on a page.
  f) The setTimeout method calls a function repeatedly at a set time interval.
  g) The browser object is often used to determine which Web browser is viewing the page.
  h) The browser may be sent to a new URL by setting the document.url property.
  i) Collection links contains all the links in a document with specified name or id attributes.

13.2   Fill in the blanks for each of the following statements.
  a) The _____ property refers to the text inside an element.
  b) The _____ property refers to the text inside an element, including XHTML tags.
  c) The _____ property refers to the text and XHTML inside an element *and* the enclosing XHTML tags.
  d) The _____ property contains the number of elements in a collection.
  e) An element's CSS position property must be set to _____ or _____ in order to reposition it dynamically.
  f) The _____ property contains the name of the browser viewing the Web page.
  g) The _____ property contains the version of the browser viewing the Web page.
  h) The _____ collection contains all the img elements on a page.
  i) The _____ object contains information about the sites that a user previously visited.
  j) CSS properties may be accessed using the _____ object.

ANSWERS TO SELF-REVIEW EXERCISES

13.1   a) True. b) False. All elements have an `all` collection. c) True. d) False. This is done with the `className` property. e) True. f) False. the `setInterval` method does this. g) False. the `navigator` object does this. h) False. Use the `document.location` object to send the browser to a different URL. i) False. The `anchors` collection contains all links in a document.

13.2   a) `innerText`. b) `innerHTML`. c) `outerHTML`. d) `length`. e) `absolute`, `relative`. f) `navigator.appName`. g) `navigator.appVersion`. h) `images`. i) `history`. j) `style`.

EXERCISES

13.3   Modify Fig.13.9 to display a greeting to the user which contains the name and version of the user's browser.

13.4   Use the `screen` object to get the size of the user's screen, then use this information to place an image (using dynamic positioning) in the middle of the page. [*Note*: This exercise assumes that the user's browser window is maximized to the full width of the screen.]

13.5   Write a script that loops through the elements in a page and places enclosing `<strong>...</strong>` tags around all the text inside all the p elements.

13.6   Write a script that prints out the length of all the JavaScript collections on a page.

13.7   Create a Web page in which users are allowed to select their favorite layout and formatting through the use of the `className` property.

13.8   (*15 Puzzle*) Write a Web page that enables the user to play the game of 15. There is a 4-by-4 board (implemented as an XHTML table) for a total of 16 slots. One of the slots is empty. The other slots are occupied by 15 tiles, randomly numbered from 1 through 15. Any tile next to the currently empty slot can be moved into the currently empty slot by clicking on the tile. Your program should create the board with the tiles out of order. The user's goal is to arrange the tiles in sequential order row by row. Using the DHTML Object Model and the `onclick` event, write a script that allows the user to swap the positions of the open position and an adjacent tile. [*Hint*: The `onclick` event should be specified for each table cell.]

13.9   Modify your solution to Exercise 13.8 to determine when the game is over, then prompt the user to determine whether to play again. If so, scramble the numbers.

13.10   Modify your solution to Exercise 13.9 to use an image that is split into 16 equally sized pieces. Discard one of the pieces and randomly place the other 15 pieces in the XHTML table.

14

Dynamic HTML: Event Model

Objectives

- To understand the notion of events, event handlers and event bubbling.
- To be able to create event handlers that respond to mouse and keyboard events.
- To be able to use the **event** object to be made aware of and, ultimately, respond to user actions.
- To understand how to recognize and respond to the most popular events.

The wisest prophets make sure of the event first.
Horace Walpole

Do you think I can listen all day to such stuff?
Lewis Carroll

The user should feel in control of the computer; not the other way around. This is achieved in applications that embody three qualities: responsiveness, permissiveness, and consistency.
Inside Macintosh, Volume 1
Apple Computer, Inc., 1985

We are responsible for actions performed in response to circumstances for which we are not responsible.
Allan Massie

14.1 Introduction

We have seen that XHTML pages can be controlled via scripting. Dynamic HTML with the **event model** exists so that scripts can respond to user interactions and change the page accordingly. This makes Web applications more responsive and user friendly and can reduce server load—a concern we will learn more about in the second half of this book.

With the event model, scripts can respond to a user who is moving the mouse, scrolling up or down the screen or entering keystrokes. Content becomes more dynamic, while interfaces become more intuitive.

In this chapter, we discuss how to use the event model to respond to user actions. We give examples of event handling for 10 of the most common and useful events, which range from mouse capture to error handling to form processing. For example, we use the onreset event to prompt a user to confirm that a form is to be reset. Included at the end of the chapter is a table of all DHTML events.

14.2 Event onclick

One of the most common events is onclick. When the user clicks a specific item with the mouse, the onclick event **fires**. With JavaScript, we are able to respond to onclick and other events. Figure 14.1 is an example of simple event handling for the onclick event.

The script beginning in lines 15–16 introduces a new notation. Using the for property of the script element allows you to specify the element to which the script applies. In this case, para represents the p element in line 26. When the event specified in the event attribute occurs for the element with id specified in the for attribute, the statements in the script execute. Line 26 sets the id for the p element to para. Attribute id specifies a unique identifier for an XHTML element. When the onclick event for this element fires, the script in lines 15–20 executes.

```
1   <?xml version = "1.0"?>
2   <!DOCTYPE html PUBLIC "-//W3C//DTD XHTML 1.0 Transitional//EN"
3       "http://www.w3.org/TR/xhtml1/DTD/xhtml1-transitional.dtd">
4
5   <!-- Fig 14.1: onclick.html          -->
6   <!-- Demonstrating the onclick event -->
7
8   <html xmlns = "http://www.w3.org/1999/xhtml">
9      <head>
10         <title>DHTML Event Model - onclick</title>
11
12         <!-- The for attribute declares the script for -->
13         <!-- a certain element, and the event for a    -->
14         <!-- certain event.                            -->
15         <script type = "text/javascript" for = "para"
16            event = "onclick">
17            <!--
18            alert( "Hi there" );
19            // -->
20         </script>
21      </head>
22
23      <body>
24
25         <!-- The id attribute gives a unique identifier -->
26         <p id = "para">Click on this text!</p>
27
28         <!-- You can specify event handlers inline -->
29         <input type = "button" value = "Click Me!"
30            onclick = "alert( 'Hi again' )" />
31
32      </body>
33   </html>
```

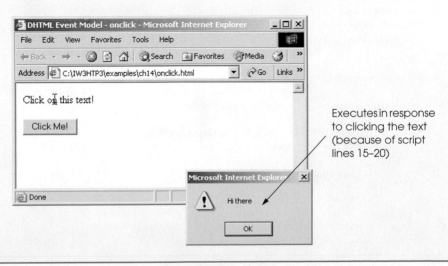

Executes in response
to clicking the text
(because of script
lines 15–20)

Fig. 14.1   Triggering an **onclick** event. (Part 1 of 2.)

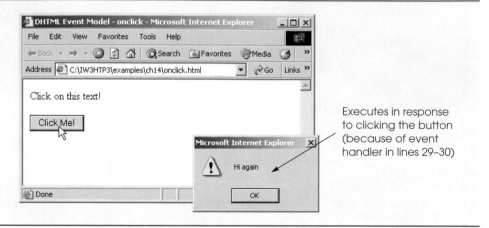

Executes in response
to clicking the button
(because of event
handler in lines 29–30)

Fig. 14.1   Triggering an `onclick` event. (Part 2 of 2.)

Another way to handle events is with inline scripting. Lines 29–30 specify the event as an XHTML attribute. This syntax associates the script directly with the `input` element. Inline scripting like this is often used to pass a value associated with the clicked element, to an event handler.

14.3 Event `onload`

The `onload` event fires whenever an element finishes loading successfully (i.e., all its children are loaded). Frequently, this event is used in the `body` element to initiate a script after the page loads into the client. Figure 14.2 uses the `onload` event for this purpose. The script called by the `onload` event updates a timer that indicates how many seconds have elapsed since the document was loaded.

```
1    <?xml version = "1.0"?>
2    <!DOCTYPE html PUBLIC "-//W3C//DTD XHTML 1.0 Strict//EN"
3       "http://www.w3.org/TR/xhtml1/DTD/xhtml1-strict.dtd">
4
5    <!-- Fig. 14.2: onload.html        -->
6    <!-- Demonstrating the onload event -->
7
8    <html xmlns = "http://www.w3.org/1999/xhtml">
9       <head>
10          <title>DHTML Event Model - onload</title>
11          <script type = "text/javascript">
12             <!--
13             var seconds = 0;
14
15             function startTimer() {
16                // 1000 milliseconds = 1 second
17                window.setInterval( "updateTime()", 1000 );
18             }
```

Fig. 14.2   Demonstrating the `onload` event. (Part 1 of 2.)

```
19
20          function updateTime() {
21              seconds++;
22              soFar.innerText = seconds;
23          }
24          // -->
25      </script>
26  </head>
27
28  <body onload = "startTimer()">
29
30      <p>Seconds you have spent viewing this page so far:
31      <strong id = "soFar">0</strong></p>
32
33  </body>
34  </html>
```

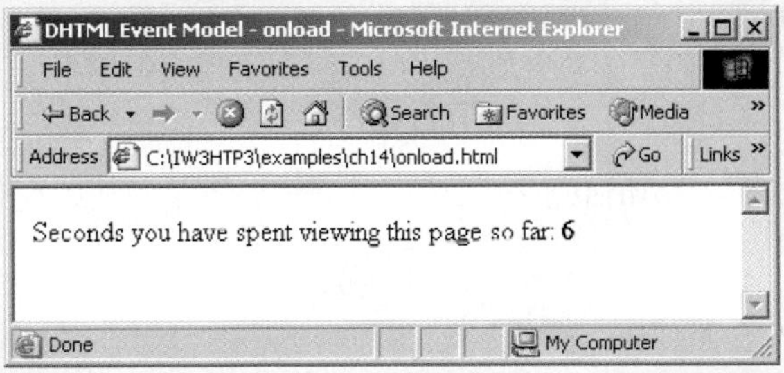

Fig. 14.2   Demonstrating the `onload` event. (Part 2 of 2.)

Our reference to the `onload` event occurs in line 28. After the `body` section loads, the browser triggers the `onload` event. This calls function `startTimer` (lines 15–18), which in turn uses method `window.setInterval` to specify that function `updateTime` should be called every 1000 milliseconds. Other uses of the `onload` event are to open a popup window once your page has loaded and to trigger a script when an image or Java applet loads.

14.4 Error Handling with onerror

The Web is a dynamic medium. Sometimes a script refers to objects that existed at a specified location when the script was written, but the location changes at a later time, rendering the script invalid. The error dialog presented by the browser in such a case can be confusing to the user. To prevent this dialog box from displaying and to handle errors more elegantly, scripts can use the `onerror` event to execute specialized error-handling code. Figure 14.3 uses the `onerror` event to launch a script that writes error messages to the status bar of the browser. [*Note*: This program works correctly only if "Script debugging" is disabled in Internet Explorer. In the **Tools** menu's **Internet Options** dialog, click the **Advanced** tab, and select **Disable script debugging** under **Browsing**.]

Line 15 indicates that function `handleError` (defined in lines 24–34) should execute when an `onerror` event occurs in the `window` object. The misspelled function name (`alrrt`) in line 18 intentionally creates an error; the code in line 15 then calls function `handleError`.

```
1   <?xml version = "1.0"?>
2   <!DOCTYPE html PUBLIC "-//W3C//DTD XHTML 1.0 Transitional//EN"
3      "http://www.w3.org/TR/xhtml1/DTD/xhtml1-transitional.dtd">
4
5   <!-- Fig 14.3: onerror.html             -->
6   <!-- Demonstrating the onerror event   -->
7
8   <html xmlns = "http://www.w3.org/1999/xhtml">
9      <head>
10        <title>DHTML Event Model - onerror</title>
11        <script type = "text/javascript">
12           <!--
13           // Specify that if an onerror event is triggered
14           // in the window function handleError should execute
15           window.onerror = handleError;
16
17           function doThis() {
18              alrrt( "hi" ); // alert misspelled, creates an error
19           }
20
21           // The ONERROR event passes three values to the
22           // function: the name of the error, the url of
23           // the file, and the line number.
24           function handleError( errType, errURL, errLineNum )
25           {
26              // Writes to the status bar at the
27              // bottom of the window.
28              window.status = "Error: " + errType + " on line " +
29                 errLineNum;
30
31              // Returning a value of true cancels the
32              // browser's reaction.
33              return true;
34           }
35           // -->
36        </script>
37     </head>
38
39     <body>
40
41        <input id = "mybutton" type = "button" value = "Click Me!"
42           onclick = "doThis()" />
43
44     </body>
45   </html>
```

Fig. 14.3   Handling script errors by handling an **onerror** event. (Part 1 of 2.)

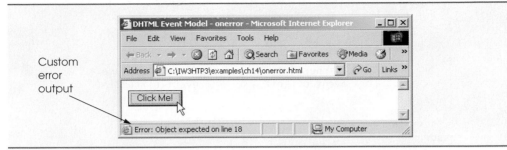

Custom
error
output

Fig. 14.3   Handling script errors by handling an `onerror` event. (Part 2 of 2.)

The `handleError` function (lines 24–34) accepts three parameters from the `onerror` event, which is one of the few events that passes parameters to an event handler. The parameters are the type of error that occurred, the URL of the file that had the error and the line number on which the error occurred. Lines 28–29 use the parameters passed to the function to write information about the scripting error to the status bar at the bottom of the browser window.

Line 33 returns `true` to the event handler to indicate that the error has been handled. This prevents the browser's default response (the dialog we wish to circumvent) from being displayed. Returning `false` indicates that the error has not been handled and causes the default response to occur. If you are using an advanced feature of JavaScript, chances are that some browsers will be unable to view your site properly. In these cases, error handling is particularly useful. If a browser triggers an `onerror` event, your Web page can provide a custom message to the user such as "Your browser does not support some features on this site. It may not render correctly."

 Error-Prevention Tip 14.1

Error handling can be used to prevent incompatible browsers from complaining about scripts they cannot process. Still, testing a Web page on different browsers and accounting for browser differences in advance is the best way to reduce errors.

14.5 Tracking the Mouse with Event onmousemove

Event `onmousemove` fires repeatedly whenever the user moves the mouse over the Web page. Figure 14.4 uses this event to update a coordinate display that gives the position of the mouse in the coordinate system of the object containing the mouse cursor.

```
1    <?xml version = "1.0"?>
2    <!DOCTYPE html PUBLIC "-//W3C//DTD XHTML 1.0 Transitional//EN"
3       "http://www.w3.org/TR/xhtml1/DTD/xhtml1-transitional.dtd">
4
5    <!-- Fig. 14.4: onmousemove.html        -->
6    <!-- Demonstrating the onmousemove event -->
7
8    <html xmlns = "http://www.w3.org/1999/xhtml">
9       <head>
10          <title>DHTML Event Model - onmousemove event</title>
```

Fig. 14.4   Demonstrating the `onmousemove` event. (Part 1 of 2.)

```
11          <script type = "text/javascript">
12             <!--
13             function updateMouseCoordinates()
14             {
15                coordinates.innerText = event.srcElement.tagName +
16                   " (" + event.offsetX + ", " + event.offsetY + ")";
17             }
18             // -->
19          </script>
20       </head>
21
22       <body style = "back-groundcolor: wheat"
23          onmousemove = "updateMouseCoordinates()">
24
25          <span id = "coordinates">(0, 0)</span><br />
26          <img src = "deitel.gif" style = "position: absolute;
27             top: 100; left: 100" alt = "Deitel" />
28
29       </body>
30    </html>
```

Updated text
(keeps changing
as you move the
mouse)

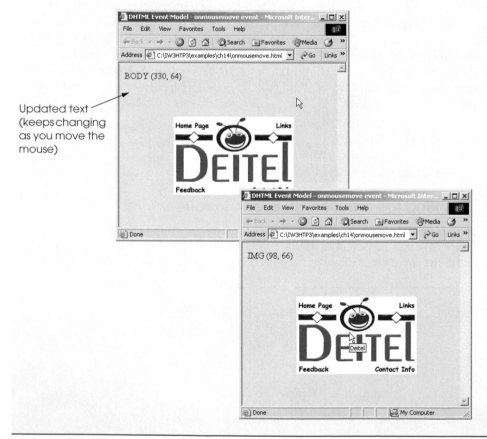

Fig. 14.4   Demonstrating the **onmousemove** event. (Part 2 of 2.)

Our event handling in this example occurs in lines 15–16. The `event` object (line 15) contains information about the triggered event. Property `srcElement` references the element that triggered the event. The script uses `tagName` to retrieve the element's name and display it in the `innerText` (line 15) of the `span` called `coordinates` (line 25).

The **offsetX** and **offsetY** properties of the `event` object give the location of the mouse cursor relative to the top-left corner of the object on which the event was triggered. Note that when you move the cursor over the image, the coordinate display changes to the image's coordinate system. This is because the `onmousemove` event occurs over the image. Figure 14.5 lists several other `event` object properties. The properties of the `event` object contain information about any events that occur on your page and are used to create Web pages that are truly dynamic and responsive to the user.

Property of `event`	Description
`altkey`	This value is `true` if the *Alt* key was pressed when event fired.
`button`	Returns which mouse button was pressed by user (1: left-mouse button, 2: right-mouse button, 3: left and right buttons, 4: middle button, 5: left and middle buttons, 6: right and middle buttons, 7: all three buttons).
`cancelBubble`	Set to `false` to prevent this event from bubbling (see Section 14.9, Event Bubbling).
`clientX`/`clientY`	The coordinates of the mouse cursor inside the client area (i.e., the active area where the Web page is displayed, excluding scrollbars, navigation buttons, etc.).
`ctrlKey`	This value is `true` if the *Ctrl* key was pressed when event fired.
`offsetX`/`offsetY`	Coordinates of the mouse cursor relative to the object that fired the event.
`propertyName`	The name of the property that changed in this event.
`recordset`	A reference to a data field's recordset (see Chapter 16, Data Binding).
`returnValue`	Set to `false` to cancel the default browser action.
`screenX`/`screenY`	The coordinates of the mouse cursor on the screen coordinate system.
`shiftKey`	This value is `true` if the *Shift* key was pressed when event fired.
`srcElement`	A reference to the object that fired the event.
`type`	The name of the event that fired.
`x`/`y`	The coordinates of the mouse cursor relative to this element's parent element.

Fig. 14.5　Some `event` object properties.

14.6 Rollovers with onmouseover and onmouseout

Two more events fired by mouse movements are `onmouseover` and `onmouseout`. When the mouse cursor moves over an element, an `onmouseover` event occurs for that element. When the mouse cursor leaves the element, an `onmouseout` event occurs for that element. Figure 14.6 uses these events to achieve a **rollover effect** that updates text when the mouse cursor moves over it. We also introduce a technique for creating rollover images.

To create a rollover effect for the image in the table caption, lines 15–18 create two new JavaScript `Image` objects—`captionImage1` and `captionImage2`. Image `caption-Image2` displays when the mouse hovers over the image. Image `captionImage1` displays when the mouse is outside the image. The script sets the `src` properties of each `Image` in lines 16 and 18. Creating `Image` objects preloads the images (i.e., loads the images in advance), so the browser does not need to download the rollover image the first time the script indicates to display the image. If the image is large or the connection is slow, downloading causes a noticeable delay in the image update.

```
1   <?xml version = "1.0"?>
2   <!DOCTYPE html PUBLIC "-//W3C//DTD XHTML 1.0 Strict//EN"
3      "http://www.w3.org/TR/xhtml1/DTD/xhtml1-strict.dtd">
4
5   <!-- Fig 14.6: onmouseoverout.html       -->
6   <!-- Events onmouseover and onmouseout -->
7
8   <html xmlns = "http://www.w3.org/1999/xhtml">
9      <head>
10        <title>
11           DHTML Event Model - onmouseover and onmouseout
12        </title>
13        <script type = "text/javascript">
14           <!--
15           captionImage1 = new Image();
16           captionImage1.src = "caption1.gif";
17           captionImage2 = new Image();
18           captionImage2.src = "caption2.gif";
19
20           function mOver()
21           {
22              if ( event.srcElement.id == "tableCaption" ) {
23                 event.srcElement.src = captionImage2.src;
24                 return;
25              }
26
27              // If the element which triggered onmouseover has
28              // an id, change its color to its id.
29              if ( event.srcElement.id )
30                 event.srcElement.style.color =
31                    event.srcElement.id;
32           }
33
34           function mOut()
35           {
36              if ( event.srcElement.id == "tableCaption" ) {
37                 event.srcElement.src = captionImage1.src;
38                 return;
39              }
40
41              // If it has an id, change the text inside to the
42              // text of the id.
```

Fig. 14.6   Events `onmouseover` and `onmouseout`. (Part 1 of 4.)

```
43                if ( event.srcElement.id )
44                    event.srcElement.innerText = event.srcElement.id;
45             }
46
47          document.onmouseover = mOver;
48          document.onmouseout = mOut;
49          // -->
50       </script>
51    </head>
52
53    <body style = "background-color: wheat">
54
55       <h1>Guess the Hex Code's Actual Color</h1>
56
57       <p>Can you tell a color from its hexadecimal RGB code
58       value? Look at the hex code, guess the color. To see
59       what color it corresponds to, move the mouse over the
60       hex code. Moving the mouse out will display the color
61       name.</p>
62
63       <table style = "width: 50%; border-style: groove;
64          text-align: center; font-family: monospace;
65          font-weight: bold">
66
67          <caption>
68             <img src = "caption1.gif" id = "tableCaption"
69                alt = "Table Caption" />
70          </caption>
71
72          <tr>
73             <td id = "Black">#000000</td>
74             <td id = "Blue">#0000FF</td>
75             <td id = "Magenta">#FF00FF</td>
76             <td id = "Gray">#808080</td>
77          </tr>
78          <tr>
79             <td id = "Green">#008000</td>
80             <td id = "Lime">#00FF00</td>
81             <td id = "Maroon">#800000</td>
82             <td id = "Navy">#000080</td>
83          </tr>
84          <tr>
85             <td id = "Olive">#808000</td>
86             <td id = "Purple">#800080</td>
87             <td id = "Red">#FF0000</td>
88             <td id = "Silver">#C0C0C0</td>
89          </tr>
90          <tr>
91             <td id = "Cyan">#00FFFF</td>
92             <td id = "Teal">#008080</td>
93             <td id = "Yellow">#FFFF00</td>
94             <td id = "White">#FFFFFF</td>
95          </tr>
```

Fig. 14.6   Events onmouseover and onmouseout. (Part 2 of 4.)

```
96              </table>
97
98          </body>
99      </html>
```

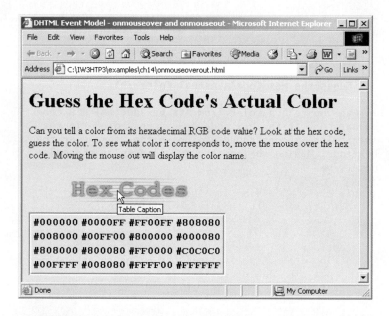

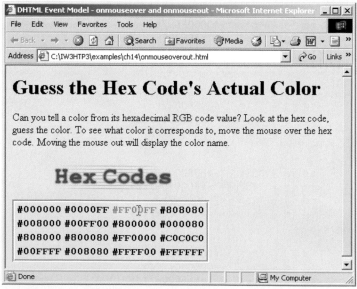

Fig. 14.6   Events **onmouseover** and **onmouseout**. (Part 3 of 4.)

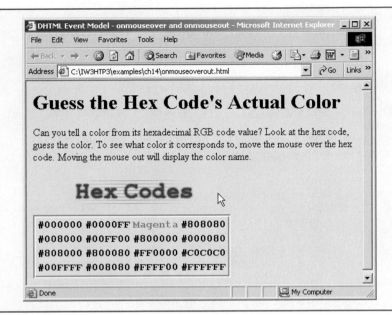

Fig. 14.6   Events onmouseover and onmouseout. (Part 4 of 4.)

Lines 22–25 in the mOver function handle the onmouseover event for the image by setting its src attribute (event.srcElement.src) to the src property of the appropriate Image object (captionImage2.src). The same task occurs with captionImage1 in the mOut function (lines 34–39).

The script handles the onmouseover event for the table cells in lines 29–31. As mentioned earlier, the event object contains information about the triggered event. In particular, the id property of the srcElement object is the id attribute of that element. This code tests whether an id is specified, and, if it is, the code changes the color of the element to match the color name in the id. As you can see in the code for the table (lines 63–96), each td element containing a color code has an id attribute set to one of the 16 basic XHTML colors.

Lines 43–44 handle the onmouseout event by changing the text in the table cell the mouse cursor just left to match the color that it represents.

14.7 Form Processing with onfocus and onblur

The onfocus and onblur events are particularly useful when dealing with form elements that allow user input (Fig. 14.7). The onfocus event fires when an element gains focus (i.e., when the user clicks a form field or uses the *Tab* key to move between form elements), and onblur fires when an element loses focus, which occurs when another control gains the focus. In line 30, the script changes the text inside the text box in the upper-right corner based on the messageNum passed to helpText (lines 28–31). The elements of the form, for example in lines 39–40, each pass a different value to the helpText function when they gain focus and the onfocus event is fired. When elements lose focus, they all pass the value 6 to helpText so that helpBox can display the default message, which is stored in the last element of the array.

```
1   <?xml version = "1.0"?>
2   <!DOCTYPE html PUBLIC "-//W3C//DTD XHTML 1.0 Transitional//EN"
3      "http://www.w3.org/TR/xhtml1/DTD/xhtml1-transitional.dtd">
4
5   <!-- Fig. 14.7: onfocusblur.html                         -->
6   <!-- Demonstrating the onfocus and onblur events    -->
7
8   <html xmlns = "http://www.w3.org/1999/xhtml">
9      <head>
10         <title>DHTML Event Model - onfocus and onblur</title>
11         <script type = "text/javascript">
12            <!--
13            var helpArray =
14               [ "Enter your name in this input box.",
15                 "Enter your email address in this input box, " +
16                 "in the format user@domain.",
17                 "Check this box if you liked our site.",
18                 "In this box, enter any comments you would " +
19                 "like us to read.",
20                 "This button submits the form to the " +
21                 "server-side script",
22                 "This button clears the form",
23                 "This textarea provides context-sensitive " +
24                 "help. Click on any input field or use the TAB " +
25                 "key to get more information about the " +
26                 "input field." ];
27
28            function helpText( messageNum )
29            {
30               myForm.helpBox.value = helpArray[ messageNum ];
31            }
32            // -->
33         </script>
34      </head>
35
36      <body>
37
38         <form id = "myForm" action = "">
39            Name: <input type = "text" name = "name"
40               onfocus = "helpText(0)" onblur = "helpText(6)" /><br />
41            Email: <input type = "text" name = "email"
42               onfocus = "helpText(1)" onblur = "helpText(6)" /><br />
43            Click here if you like this site
44            <input type = "checkbox" name = "like" onfocus =
45               "helpText(2)" onblur = "helpText(6)" /><br /><hr />
46
47            Any comments?<br />
48            <textarea name = "comments" rows = "5" cols = "45"
49               onfocus = "helpText(3)" onblur = "helpText(6)"></textarea>
50            <br />
51            <input type = "submit" value = "Submit" onfocus =
52               "helpText(4)" onblur = "helpText(6)" />
```

Fig. 14.7   Events onfocus and onblur. (Part 1 of 2.)

```
53                 <input type = "reset" value = "Reset" onfocus =
54                     "helpText(5)" onblur = "helpText(6)" />
55
56                 <textarea name = "helpBox" style = "position: absolute;
57                     right: 0; top: 0" readonly = "true" rows = "4" cols = "45">
58     This textarea provides context-sensitive help. Click on any input field
59     or use the Tab key to get more information about the input field.
60             </textarea>
61         </form>
62
63     </body>
64 </html>
```

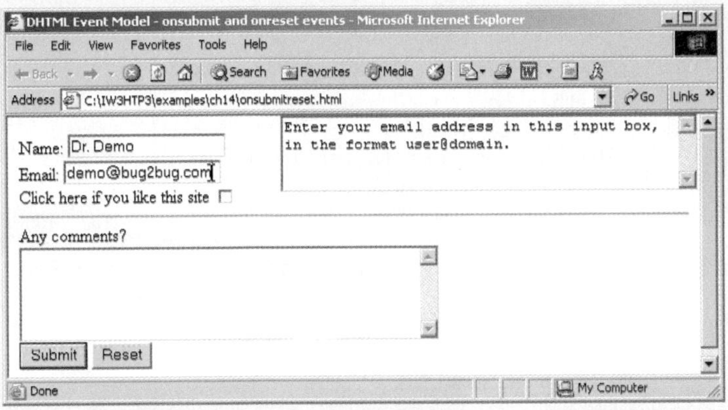

Fig. 14.7   Events onfocus and onblur. (Part 2 of 2.)

14.8 More Form Processing with onsubmit and onreset

Two more useful events for processing forms are onsubmit and onreset. These events fire when a form is submitted or reset, respectively (Fig. 14.8). The function formSubmit (lines 35–40) executes in response to the user submitting the form (i.e., clicking the **Submit** button or pressing the *Enter* key). Line 36 sets the event's returnValue property to false, which cancels the default action of the event on the element (i.e., for the browser to submit the form). Line 38 pops up a dialog asking the user to confirm the action about to take place. If the user clicks **OK**, function confirm returns true. Line 39 then sets the returnValue back to true, because the user has confirmed that the form should indeed be submitted. If the user clicks **Cancel**, confirm returns false, and the form is not submitted. [*Note*: When the confirmation dialog pops up, focus shifts from the clicked button to the dialog. Thus, the button's onblur event fires, and the text in the helpBox text area returns to the default text until the confirmation dialog closes and focus returns to the button.] Function formReset (lines 42–47) behaves similarly to formSubmit.

```
1   <?xml version = "1.0"?>
2   <!DOCTYPE html PUBLIC "-//W3C//DTD XHTML 1.0 Transitional//EN"
3       "http://www.w3.org/TR/xhtml1/DTD/xhtml1-transitional.dtd">
```

Fig. 14.8   Events onsubmit and onreset. (Part 1 of 3.)

```
4
5    <!-- Fig 14.8: onsubmitreset.html                      -->
6    <!-- Demonstrating the onsubmit and onreset events -->
7
8    <html xmlns = "http://www.w3.org/1999/xhtml">
9       <head>
10         <title>
11            DHTML Event Model - onsubmit and onreset events
12         </title>
13         <script type = "text/javascript">
14            <!--
15            var helpArray =
16               [ "Enter your name in this input box.",
17                 "Enter your email address in this input box, " +
18                 "in the format user@domain.",
19                 "Check this box if you liked our site.",
20                 "In this box, enter any comments you would " +
21                 "like us to read.",
22                 "This button submits the form to the " +
23                 "server-side script",
24                 "This button clears the form",
25                 "This textarea provides context-sensitive " +
26                 "help. Click on any input field or use the Tab " +
27                 "key to get more information about " +
28                 "the input field." ];

30            function helpText( messageNum )
31            {
32               myForm.helpBox.value = helpArray[ messageNum ];
33            }

35            function formSubmit() {
36               window.event.returnValue = false;
37
38               if ( confirm ( "Are you sure you want to submit?" ) )
39                  window.event.returnValue = true;
40            }

42            function formReset() {
43               window.event.returnValue = false;
44
45               if ( confirm( "Are you sure you want to reset?" ) )
46                  window.event.returnValue = true;
47            }
48            // -->
49         </script>
50      </head>
51
52      <body>
53
54            <form id = "myForm" onsubmit = "formSubmit()"
55               onreset = "formReset()" action = "">
```

Fig. 14.8   Events onsubmit and onreset. (Part 2 of 3.)

```
56              Name: <input type = "text" name = "name"
57                 onfocus =  "helpText(0)" onblur = "helpText(6)" /><br />
58              Email: <input type = "text" name = "email"
59                 onfocus = "helpText(1)" onblur = "helpText(6)" /><br />
60              Click here if you like this site
61              <input type = "checkbox" name = "like" onfocus =
62                 "helpText(2)" onblur = "helpText(6)" /><hr />
63
64              Any comments?<br />
65              <textarea name = "comments" rows = "5" cols = "45"
66                 onfocus = "helpText(3)" onblur = "helpText(6)"></textarea>
67              <br />
68              <input type = "submit" value = "Submit" onfocus =
69                 "helpText(4)"  onblur = "helpText(6)" />
70              <input type = "reset" value = "Reset" onfocus =
71                 "helpText(5)" onblur = "helpText(6)" />
72
73              <textarea name = "helpBox" style = "position: absolute;
74                  right:0; top: 0" readonly = "true" rows = "4" cols = "45">
75  This textarea provides context-sensitive help. Click on any input field
76  or use the Tab key to get more information about the input field.
77              </textarea>
78          </form>
79
80      </body>
81  </html>
```

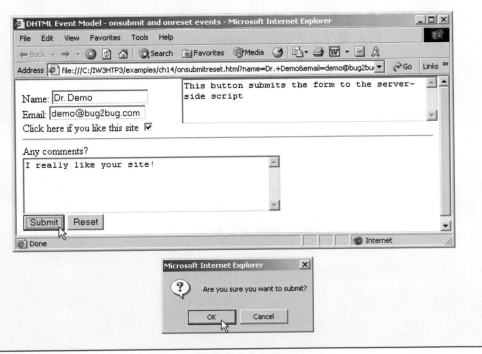

Fig. 14.8 Events onsubmit and onreset. (Part 3 of 3.)

14.9 Event Bubbling

Event bubbling is the process whereby events fired in child elements "bubble" up to their parent elements. When a child event is fired, the event is first delivered to the child's event handler, then to the parent's event handler. This might result in event handling that was not intended. If you intend to handle an event in a child element, you might need to cancel the bubbling of the event in the child element's event-handling code by using the `cancelBubble` property of the `event` object, as shown in Fig. 14.9.

Clicking the first p element (line 34) first triggers a call to `paragraphClick` with a `false` argument, then, because line 27 registers the `onclick` event for the `document`, `documentClick` is also called. This occurs because the `onclick` event bubbles up to the document level. This is probably not the desired result. Clicking the second p element (line 35) passes a value of `true` to function `paragraphClick`, so that the `if` statement in line 23 executes its body, which disables the event bubbling for this event by setting the `cancelBubble` property of the `event` object to `true`.

```
1   <?xml version = "1.0"?>
2   <!DOCTYPE html PUBLIC "-//W3C//DTD XHTML 1.0 Strict//EN"
3      "http://www.w3.org/TR/xhtml1/DTD/xhtml1-strict.dtd">
4
5   <!-- Fig 14.9: bubbling.html   -->
6   <!-- Disabling event bubbling -->
7
8   <html xmlns = "http://www.w3.org/1999/xhtml">
9      <head>
10         <title>DHTML Event Model - Event Bubbling</title>
11
12         <script type = "text/javascript">
13            <!--
14            function documentClick()
15            {
16               alert( "You clicked in the document" );
17            }
18
19            function paragraphClick( value )
20            {
21               alert( "You clicked the text" );
22
23               if ( value )
24                  event.cancelBubble = true;
25            }
26
27            document.onclick = documentClick;
28            // -->
29         </script>
30      </head>
31
32      <body>
33
```

Fig. 14.9   Event bubbling. (Part 1 of 2.)

```
34        <p onclick = "paragraphClick( false )">Click here!</p>
35        <p onclick = "paragraphClick( true )">Click here, too!</p>
36    </body>
37 </html>
```

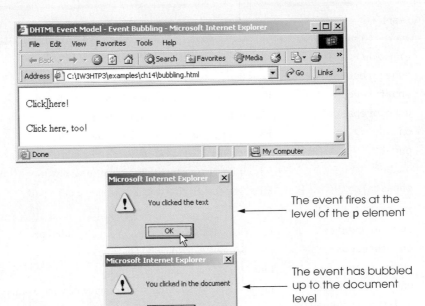

The event fires at the level of the **p** element

The event has bubbled up to the document level

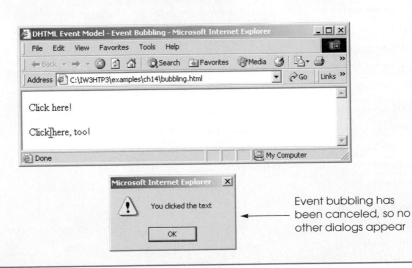

Event bubbling has been canceled, so no other dialogs appear

Fig. 14.9　Event bubbling. (Part 2 of 2.)

Common Programming Error 14.1

Forgetting to cancel event bubbling when necessary may cause unexpected results in your scripts.

14.10 More DHTML Events

The events we covered in this chapter are among the most commonly used. The remaining DHTML events and their descriptions are listed in Fig. 14.10.

Event	Description
Clipboard events	
onbeforecut	Fires before a selection is cut to the clipboard.
onbeforecopy	Fires before a selection is copied to the clipboard.
onbeforepaste	Fires before a selection is pasted from the clipboard.
oncopy	Fires when a selection is copied to the clipboard.
oncut	Fires when a selection is cut to the clipboard.
onabort	Fires if image transfer has been interrupted by user.
onpaste	Fires when a selection is pasted from the clipboard.
Data binding events	
onafterupdate	Fires immediately after a databound object has been updated.
onbeforeupdate	Fires before a data source is updated.
oncellchange	Fires when a data source has changed.
ondataavailable	Fires when new data from a data source become available.
ondatasetchanged	Fires when content at a data source has changed.
ondatasetcomplete	Fires when transfer of data from the data source has completed.
onerrorupdate	Fires if an error occurs while updating a data field.
onrowenter	Fires when a new row of data from the data source is available.
onrowexit	Fires when a row of data from the data source has just finished.
onrowsdelete	Fires when a row of data from the data source is deleted.
onrowsinserted	Fires when a row of data from the data source is inserted.
Keyboard events	
onhelp	Fires when the user initiates help (i.e., by pressing the *F1* key).
onkeydown	Fires when the user pushes down a key.
onkeypress	Fires when the user presses a key.
onkeyup	Fires when the user ends a key press.
marquee events	
onbounce	Fires when a scrolling `marquee` bounces back in the other direction.
onfinish	Fires when a `marquee` finishes its scrolling.
onstart	Fires when a `marquee` begins a new loop.
Mouse events	
oncontextmenu	Fires when the context menu is shown (right-click).

Fig. 14.10 Dynamic HTML events. (Part 1 of 2.)

Event	Description
ondblclick	Fires when the mouse is double clicked.
ondrag	Fires during a mouse drag.
ondragend	Fires when a mouse drag ends.
ondragenter	Fires when something is dragged onto an area.
ondragleave	Fires when something is dragged out of an area.
ondragover	Fires when a drag is held over an area.
ondragstart	Fires when a mouse drag begins.
ondrop	Fires when a mouse button is released over a valid target during a drag.
onmousedown	Fires when a mouse button is pressed down.
onmouseup	Fires when a mouse button is released.
Miscellaneous events	
onafterprint	Fires immediately after the document prints.
onbeforeeditfocus	Fires before an element gains focus for editing.
onbeforeprint	Fires before a document is printed.
onbeforeunload	Fires before a document is unloaded (i.e., the window was closed or a link was clicked).
onchange	Fires when a new choice is made in a `select` element, or when a text input is changed and the element loses focus.
onfilterchange	Fires when a filter changes properties or finishes a transition (see Chapter 15, Dynamic HTML: Filters and Transitions).
onlosecapture	Fires when the `releaseCapture` method is invoked.
onpropertychange	Fires when the property of an object is changed.
onreadystatechange	Fires when the `readyState` property of an element changes.
onreset	Fires when a form resets (i.e., the user clicks a reset button).
onresize	Fires when the size of an object changes (i.e., the user resizes a window or frame).
onscroll	Fires when a window or frame is scrolled.
onselect	Fires when a text selection begins (applies to `input` or `textarea`).
onselectstart	Fires when the object is selected.
onstop	Fires when the user stops loading the object.
onunload	Fires when a page is about to unload.

Fig. 14.10 Dynamic HTML events. (Part 2 of 2.)

14.11 Web Resources

msdn.microsoft.com/workshop/author/dhtml/reference/events.asp
Microsoft's *DHTML Events* site provides a comprehensive reference on events in Dynamic HTML.

wsabstract.com/dhtmltutors/domevent1.shtml
This *JavaScript Kit* tutorial introduces event handling in the DOM (Document Object Model), as supported by both Internet Explorer 5+ and Netscape 6+.

SUMMARY

- The event model allows scripts to respond to user actions and change a page accordingly. This makes Web applications responsive and user friendly and can greatly lessen server load but can cause compatibility problems.

- With the event model, scripts can respond to a user moving the mouse, scrolling up or down the screen or entering keystrokes. Content becomes more dynamic, and interfaces become more intuitive.

- One of the most common events is onclick. When the user clicks the mouse, onclick fires.

- Using the for property of the script element allows you to specify the element to which the script applies. When the event specified in the event attribute occurs for the element with id specified in the for attribute, the designated script runs.

- Specifying an event as an XHTML attribute allows you to insert script directly into your XHTML. Inline scripting is usually used to pass a value (to a event handler) based on the element that was clicked.

- The onload event fires whenever an element finishes loading successfully and is often used in the body element to initiate scripts as soon as the page has been loaded into the client.

- You can use the onerror event to write error-handling code.

- The syntax window.onerror = *functionName* specifies that *functionName* runs if the onerror event is triggered in the window object.

- Error handlers can accept three parameters from the onerror event (one of the few events that passes parameters to an event handler). The onerror event passes the type of error that occurred, the URL of the file that had the error and the line number on which the error occurred.

- Returning true in an error handler prevents the browser from displaying an error dialog.

- Writing a function to ignore other script errors is not a good idea—try writing scripts that adjust or stop their actions if an error in loading the page has been detected.

- Event onmousemove fires constantly whenever the mouse is in motion.

- The event object contains information about the triggered event.

- Property srcElement of the event object refers to the element that triggered the event.

- The offsetX and offsetY properties of the event object give the location of the mouse cursor relative to the top-left corner of the object on which the event was triggered.

- Note that when you move the mouse cursor over an element like an image, the offsetX and offsetY properties change to the element's coordinate system.

- Whenever the mouse cursor moves over an element, it fires event onmouseover for that element. Once the mouse cursor leaves the element, an onmouseout event is fired.

- Events onfocus and onblur fire when an element gains or loses focus, respectively.

- The events onsubmit and onreset fire when a form is submitted or reset, respectively.

- The code window.event.returnValue = false cancels the default browser action.

- Event bubbling is the process whereby events fired in child elements "bubble" up to their parent elements for handling. If you intend to handle an event in a child element, you might need to cancel the bubbling of that event in the child element's event-handling code by using the cancelBubble property of the event object.

TERMINOLOGY

altKey property of event object
button property of event object
cancelBubble property of event object
clientX property of event object
clientY property of event object
confirm method of window object
ctrlKey property of event object
Dynamic HTML event model
event attribute of script element
event bubbling
event handler
event model
event object (property of the window object)
events in DHTML
fire an event
for attribute of script element
innerText property of an XHTML element
keyboard event
mouse event
offsetX property of event object
offsetY property of event object
onafterprint event
onafterupdate event
onbeforecopy event
onbeforecut event
onbeforeeditfocus event
onbeforepaste event
onbeforeprint event
onbeforeunload event
onbeforeupdate event
onblur event
onbounce event
oncellchange event
onchange event
onclick event
oncontextmenu event
oncopy event
oncut event
ondataavailable event
ondatasetchanged event
ondatasetcomplete event
ondblclick event
ondrag event
ondragend event
ondragenter event
ondragleave event
ondragover event

ondragstart event
ondrop event
onerrorupdate event
onfinish event
onfocus event
onhelp event
onkeydown event
onkeypress event
onkeyup event
onload event
onlosecapture event
onmousedown event
onmousemove event
onmouseout event
onmouseover event
onmouseup event
onpaste event
onpropertychange event
onreadystatechange event
onreset event
onresize event
onrowexit event
onrowsdelete event
onrowsinserted event
onscroll event
onselect event
onselectstart event
onstart event
onstop event
onsubmit event
onunload event
position of the mouse cursor
propertyName property of event object
returnValue property of event
screenX property of event
screenY property of event
setInterval method of window object
shiftkey property of event
srcElement property of event
status bar at bottom of a window
status property of window object
Tab key to switch between fields on a form
tagName property of event object
trigger an event
type property of event
x property of event object
y property of event object

SELF-REVIEW EXERCISES

14.1   Fill in the blanks in each of the following statements:

a) The state of three special keys can be retrieved by using the event object. These keys are _____, _____ and _____.

b) If a child element does not handle an event, _____ lets the event rise through the object hierarchy.

c) Using the _____ property of the script element allows you to specify the element to which the script applies.

d) The _____ property of the event object specifies whether to continue bubbling the current event.

e) Setting window.event.returnValue to _____ cancels the default browser action for the event.

f) In an event handler, the reference for the id of an element that fired an event is _____.

g) Three events that fire when the user clicks the mouse are _____, _____ and _____.

14.2   State whether each of the following is *true* or *false*. If the statement is *false*, explain why.

a) The onload event fires whenever an element starts loading successfully.

b) The onclick event fires when the user clicks the mouse on an element.

c) It is generally a good idea to include a function in your document that will ignore other script errors.

d) When using the rollover effect with images, it is a good programming practice to create image objects that preload the desired images.

e) Returning true in an error handler prevents the browser from displaying an error dialog.

ANSWERS TO SELF-REVIEW EXERCISES

14.1   a) *Ctrl, Alt* and *Shift.* b) event bubbling. c) for. d) returnValue. e) false. f) event.srcElement.id. g) onclick, onmousedown, onmouseup.

14.2   a) False. The onload event fires whenever an element *finishes* loading successfully. b) True. c) False. it is not a good idea to write a function that ignores other script errors; instead, you should try writing a script that adjusts or stops the actions if an error has occurred when loading a page. d) True. e) True.

EXERCISES

14.3   Write an error handler that changes the alt text of an image to "Error Loading" if the image loading is not completed.

14.4   You have a server-side script that cannot handle any ampersands (&) in the form data. Write a function that converts all ampersands in a form field to " and " when the field loses focus (onblur).

14.5   Write a function that responds to a click anywhere on the page by displaying an alert dialog. Display the event name if the user held *Shift* during the mouse click. Display the element name that triggered the event if the user held *Ctrl* during the mouse click.

14.6   Use CSS absolute positioning, onmousemove and event.x/event.y to have a sentence of text follow the mouse as the user moves the mouse over the Web page. Disable this feature if the user double clicks (ondblclick).

14.7   Modify Exercise 14.6 to have an image follow the mouse as the user moves the mouse over the Web page.

14.8   Add two elements to Fig. 14.9 that users can click. Use the `deitel.gif` image file as the first element. When the user clicks the image, display an `alert` dialog box with the text "you clicked the image." For the second element, create a one-row table containing a text string. Set the table border to 1. When the user clicks the table element, display an `alert` dialog box containing "you clicked the table." In the two accompanying functions, set each event object to `true`.

Dynamic HTML: Filters and Transitions

Objectives

- To use filters to achieve special effects.
- To combine filters to achieve an even greater variety of special effects.
- To be able to create animated visual transitions between Web pages.
- To be able to modify filters dynamically, using DHTML.

. . . as through a filter, before the clear product emerges.
F. Scott Fitzgerald

There is strong shadow where there is much light.
Johann Wolfgang von Goethe

When all things are equal, translucence in writing is more effective than transparency, just as glow is more revealing than glare.
James Thurber

. . . one should disdain the superficial and let the true beauty of one's soul shine through.
Fran Lebowitz

Modernity exists in the form of a desire to wipe out whatever came earlier, in the hope of reaching at least a point that could be called a true present, a point of origin that marks a new departure.
Paul de Man

Outline

15.1 Introduction

Just a few years ago, it would not have been realistic to offer the kinds of dramatic visual effects you will see in this chapter, because desktop computer processing power was insufficient. Today, with powerful processors, these visual effects are realizable without delays. Just as you expect to see dramatic visual effects on TV weather reports, Web users appreciate visual effects when browsing Web pages.

In the past, achieving these kinds of effects, if you could get them at all, demanded frequent trips back and forth to the server. With the consequent delays, the beauty of the effects was lost.

Performance Tip 15.1

With Dynamic HTML, many visual effects are implemented directly in the client-side browser (Internet Explorer 6 for this book), so no server-side processing delays are incurred. The DHTML code that initiates these effects is generally quite small and is coded directly into the XHTML Web page.

You will be able to achieve many effects, such as transitioning between pages with **random dissolves** and **horizontal and vertical blinds** effects similar to those you find in slide presentation software packages. You can convert colored images to gray in response to user actions; this could be used, for example, to indicate that some option is not currently selectable. You can make letters **glow** for emphasis. You can create **drop shadows** to give text a three-dimensional appearance. You can **blur** text or an image to give it the illusion of motion. You can even combine effects to generate a greater variety of visual results.

In this chapter, we discuss both **filters** and **transitions**. Filters and transitions are specified with the **CSS `filter` property**. Applying filters to text and images causes changes that are persistent. Transitions are temporary; applying a transition allows you to transfer from one page to another with a pleasant visual effect, such as a random dissolve. Filters and transitions do not add content to your pages—rather, they present existing content in an engaging manner to capture the user's attention.

Each of the visual effects achievable with filters and transitions is programmable, so these effects can be adjusted dynamically by programs that respond to user-initiated events, such as mouse clicks and keystrokes. Filters and transitions are so easy to use that virtually any Web page designer or programmer can incorporate these effects with minimal effort.

Look-and-Feel Observation 15.1

Experiment by applying combinations of filters to the same element. You may discover some eye-pleasing effects that are particularly appropriate for your applications.

Look-and-Feel Observation 15.2

Some Web page visitors may find the use of too many filters and transitions to be excessive and distracting. Be sure that the DHTML used on a page enhances, not diminishes, the existing site content.

Part of the beauty of DHTML filters and transitions is that they are built right into Internet Explorer. You do not need to spend time working with sophisticated graphics packages, preparing images that will be downloaded (slowly) from servers. When Internet Explorer renders your page, it applies all the special effects and does this while running on the client computer, without lengthy waits for files to download from the server.

Look-and-Feel Observation 15.3

DHTML's effects are programmable. They can be applied dynamically to elements of your pages in response to user events, such as mouse clicks and keystrokes.

Software Engineering Observation 15.1

Filters and transitions can be applied to all block-level elements such as div or p. They can be applied to an inline-level element such as strong or em, however, only if the element has its height or width CSS property set.

Portability Tip 15.1

Filters and transitions are Microsoft technologies available only in Windows-based versions of Internet Explorer 6. Do not use these capabilities if you are writing for other browsers. [Note: For portability, many of the same effects can be achieved with Macromedia Flash (Chapters 17–18).]

15.2 Flip Filters: `flipv` and `fliph`

The **flipv** and **fliph** filters mirror text or images vertically and horizontally. Figure 15.1 demonstrates these effects, using both filters to flip text.

```
1   <?xml version = "1.0"?>
2   <!DOCTYPE html PUBLIC "-//W3C//DTD XHTML 1.0 Strict//EN"
3       "http://www.w3.org/TR/xhtml1/DTD/xhtml1-strict.dtd">
4
5   <!-- Fig. 15.1: flip.html    -->
6   <!-- Using the flip filters -->
7
```

Fig. 15.1   Using the `flipv` and `fliph` filters. (Part 1 of 2.)

```
8    <html xmlns = "http://www.w3.org/1999/xhtml">
9       <head>
10         <title>The flip filter</title>
11
12         <style type = "text/css">
13            body  { background-color: #CCFFCC }
14
15            table { font-size: 3em;
16                    font-family: Arial, sans-serif;
17                    background-color: #FFCCCC;
18                    border-style: ridge ;
19                    border-collapse: collapse }
20
21            td    { border-style: groove;
22                    padding: 1ex }
23         </style>
24      </head>
25
26      <body>
27
28         <table>
29
30            <tr>
31               <!-- Filters are applied in style declarations -->
32               <td style = "filter: fliph">Text</td>
33               <td>Text</td>
34            </tr>
35
36            <tr>
37               <!-- More than one filter can be applied at once -->
38               <td style = "filter: flipv fliph">Text</td>
39               <td style = "filter: flipv">Text</td>
40            </tr>
41
42         </table>
43
44      </body>
45   </html>
```

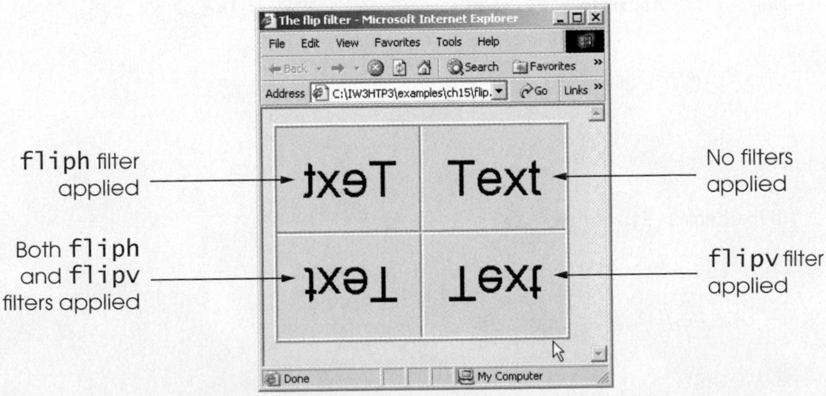

Fig. 15.1 Using the flipv and fliph filters. (Part 2 of 2.)

Line 32 applies a filter using the `style` attribute. The value of the `filter` property is the name of the filter. In this case, the filter is `fliph`, which flips the affected object horizontally.

Line 38 applies more than one filter at once by specifying multiple filters separated by spaces as the value of the `filter` attribute. In this case, the `flipv` filter is also applied, which vertically flips the object to which the filter is applied.

15.3 Transparency with the chroma Filter

The **chroma** filter applies **transparency effects** dynamically, without using a graphics editor to hard-code transparency into the image. Figure 15.2 alters the transparency of an image, using object model scripting based on a user selection from a `select` element.

```
1   <?xml version = "1.0"?>
2   <!DOCTYPE html PUBLIC "-//W3C//DTD XHTML 1.0 Transitional//EN"
3      "http://www.w3.org/TR/xhtml1/DTD/xhtml1-transitional.dtd">
4
5   <!-- Fig 15.2: chroma.html                              -->
6   <!-- Applying transparency using the chroma filter   -->
7
8   <html xmlns = "http://www.w3.org/1999/xhtml">
9      <head>
10         <title>Chroma Filter</title>
11
12         <script type = "text/javascript">
13            <!--
14            function changecolor( theColor )
15            {
16               if ( theColor ) {
17                  // if the user selected a color, parse the
18                  // value to hex and set the filter color.
19                  chromaImg.filters( "chroma" ).color = theColor;
20                  chromaImg.filters( "chroma" ).enabled = true;
21               }
22               else // if the user selected "None",
23                  // disable the filter.
24                  chromaImg.filters( "chroma" ).enabled = false;
25            }
26            // -->
27         </script>
28      </head>
29
30      <body>
31
32         <h1>Chroma Filter:</h1>
33
34         <img id = "chromaImg" src = "trans.gif" style =
35            "position: absolute; filter: chroma"  alt =
36            "Transparent Image" />
37
38         <form action = "">
```

Fig. 15.2   Changing values of the chroma filter. (Part 1 of 2.)

```
39              <!-- The onchange event fires when -->
40              <!-- a selection is changed        -->
41              <select onchange = "changecolor( this.value )">
42                 <option value = "">None</option>
43                 <option value = "#00FFFF">Cyan</option>
44                 <option value = "#FFFF00">Yellow</option>
45                 <option value = "#FF00FF">Magenta</option>
46                 <option value = "#000000" selected = "selected">
47                    Black</option>
48              </select>
49           </form>
50
51       </body>
52   </html>
```

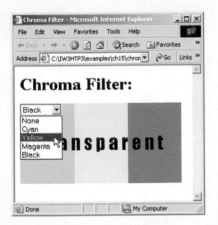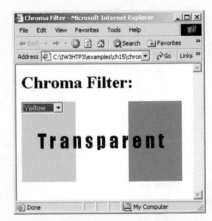

Fig. 15.2   Changing values of the `chroma` filter. (Part 2 of 2.)

Line 19 sets the filter properties dynamically using JavaScript. In this case, the value of the `select` drop-down list (lines 41–48) is a string containing the color value. This value is passed as an argument to function `changecolor` (lines 14–25).

Line 20 turns on the filter. Each filter has a property named `enabled`. If this property is set to `true`, the filter is applied. If it is set to `false`, the filter is not applied. Line 24 indicates that the filter is disabled if the user selected **None** (line 42) from the drop-down list.

Line 41 introduces the event **onchange**. This event fires whenever the `value` of a form field changes. In this example, an `onchange` event occurs when the user makes a new selection in the `colorSelect` drop-down list. The expression `this.value` represents the currently selected value in the `select` GUI component, which is passed to function `changeColor`.

15.4 Creating Image masks

Applying the **mask** filter to an image allows you to create an effect in which an element's background is a solid color and its foreground is transparent, so the image or color behind it shows through. This is known as an **image mask**. Figure 15.3 adds the `mask` filter to a `div` element (lines 20–26) which overlaps an image (lines 28–29). The foreground of the div element (the h1 text inside it) is transparent, so you can see the background image through the letters in the foreground. Line 21 sets the color parameter for the mask filter. Parameters are always specified in the format param = value.

```
1   <?xml version = "1.0"?>
2   <!DOCTYPE html PUBLIC "-//W3C//DTD XHTML 1.0 Transitional//EN"
3       "http://www.w3.org/TR/xhtml1/DTD/xhtml1-transitional.dtd">
4
5   <!-- Fig 15.3: mask.html           -->
6   <!-- Placing a mask over an image -->
7
8   <html xmlns = "http://www.w3.org/1999/xhtml">
9       <head>
10          <title>Mask Filter</title>
11      </head>
12
13      <body>
14
15          <h1>Mask Filter</h1>
16
17          <!-- Filter parameters are specified in parentheses, -->
18          <!-- in the form param1 = value1, param2 = value2,   -->
19          <!-- etc.                                            -->
20          <div style = "position: absolute; top: 125; left: 20;
21              filter: mask( color = #CCFFFF )">
22          <h1 style = "font-family: Courier, monospace">
23          AaBbCcDdEeFfGgHhIiJj<br />
24          KkLlMmNnOoPpQqRrSsTt
25          </h1>
26          </div>
27
28          <img src = "gradient.gif" width = "400" height = "200"
29              alt = "Image with Gradient Effect" />
30      </body>
31  </html>
```

Fig. 15.3   Using the mask filter.

15.5 Miscellaneous Image Filters: `invert`, `gray` and `xray`

The three image filters discussed in this section apply simple image effects to images or text. The **invert** filter applies a **negative image effect**—dark areas become light and light areas become dark. The **gray** filter applies a **grayscale image effect**, in which all color is stripped from the image and all that remains is brightness data. The **xray** filter applies an x-ray effect, which basically is an inversion of the grayscale effect. Figure 15.4 demonstrates applying these filters, alone and in combination, to a simple image. Each of our filters in lines 26–41 applies a separate image effect to hc.jpg.

```
1   <?xml version = "1.0"?>
2   <!DOCTYPE html PUBLIC "-//W3C//DTD XHTML 1.0 Strict//EN"
3       "http://www.w3.org/TR/xhtml1/DTD/xhtml1-strict.dtd">
4
5   <!-- Fig 15.4: misc.html                                    -->
6   <!-- Image filters to invert, grayscale or xray an image -->
7
8   <html xmlns = "http://www.w3.org/1999/xhtml">
9      <head>
10        <title>Misc. Image filters</title>
11
12        <style type = "text/css">
13           .cap { font-weight: bold;
14                  background-color: #DDDDAA;
15                  text-align: center }
16        </style>
17     </head>
18
19     <body>
20        <table class = "cap">
21           <tr>
22              <td>Normal</td>
23              <td>Grayscale</td>
24           </tr>
25           <tr>
26              <td><img src = "hc.jpg" alt =
27                    "normal scenic view" /></td>
28              <td><img src = "hc.jpg" style = "filter: gray"
29                    alt = "gray scenic view"/>
30              </td>
31           </tr>
32           <tr>
33              <td>Xray</td>
34              <td>Invert</td>
35           </tr>
36           <tr>
37              <td><img src = "hc.jpg" style = "filter: xray"
38                    alt = "xray scenic view"/>
39              </td>
40              <td><img src = "hc.jpg" style = "filter: invert"
41                    alt = "inverted scenic view"/>
42              </td>
```

Fig. 15.4   Filters `invert`, `gray` and `xray`. (Part 1 of 2.)

```
43              </tr>
44          </table>
45
46      </body>
47  </html>
```

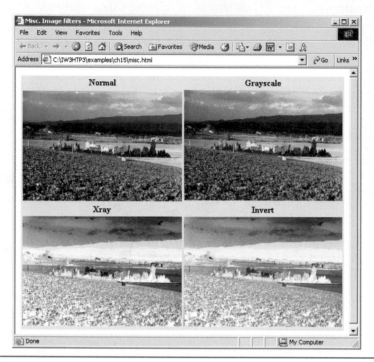

Fig. 15.4   Filters `invert`, `gray` and `xray`. (Part 2 of 2.)

 Look-and-Feel Observation 15.4

A good use of the `invert` filter is to signify that something has just been clicked or selected.

15.6 Adding shadows to Text

A simple filter that adds depth to your text is the **shadow** filter. This filter creates a shadowing effect that gives your text a three-dimensional appearance (Fig. 15.5).

```
1   <?xml version = "1.0"?>
2   <!DOCTYPE html PUBLIC "-//W3C//DTD XHTML 1.0 Strict//EN"
3       "http://www.w3.org/TR/xhtml1/DTD/xhtml1-strict.dtd">
4
5   <!-- Fig 15.5: shadow.html      -->
6   <!-- Applying the shadow filter -->
7
8   <html xmlns = "http://www.w3.org/1999/xhtml">
```

Fig. 15.5   Applying a **shadow** filter to text. (Part 1 of 2.)

```
9      <head>
10         <title>Shadow Filter</title>
11
12         <script type = "text/javascript">
13            <!--
14            var shadowDirection = 0;
15
16            function start()
17            {
18               window.setInterval( "runDemo()", 500 );
19            }
20
21            function runDemo()
22            {
23               shadowText.innerText =
24                  "Shadow Direction: " + shadowDirection % 360;
25               shadowText.filters( "shadow" ).direction =
26                  ( shadowDirection % 360 );
27               shadowDirection += 45;
28            }
29            // -->
30         </script>
31      </head>
32
33      <body onload = "start()">
34
35         <h1 id = "shadowText" style = "position: absolute; top: 25;
36            left: 25; padding: 10; filter: shadow( direction = 0,
37            color = red )">Shadow Direction: 0</h1>
38      </body>
39   </html>
```

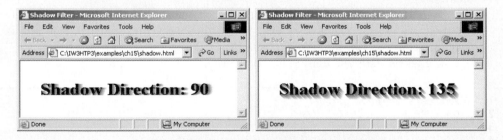

Fig. 15.5   Applying a **shadow** filter to text. (Part 2 of 2.)

Lines 35–37 apply the shadow filter to text. Property direction of the shadow filter determines in which direction the shadow effect is applied—this can be set to one of eight directions expressed in angular notation: 0 (up), 45 (above-right), 90 (right), 135 (below-right), 180 (below), 225 (below-left), 270 (left) and 315 (above-left). Property color specifies the color of the shadow that is applied to the text. Lines 23–27 in function run-Demo cycle through the direction property values from 0 to 315, and update property innerText of the h1 element (shadowText) to match the current shadow direction.

Note that we apply a padding CSS style to the h1 element (line 36). Otherwise, the shadow effect is partially cut off by the border of the element. Increasing the padding provides greater distance between the text and the border of the element, allowing the full effect to be displayed.

Software Engineering Observation 15.2

Some filters may be cut off by element edges—make sure to increase the padding in the element if this happens.

15.7 Creating Gradients with alpha

In Chapter 3, we saw a brief example of the gradient effect, which is a gradual progression from a starting color to a target color. Internet Explorer 6 allows you to create the same effect dynamically using the **alpha** filter (Fig. 15.6). The alpha filter is also used for transparency effects not achievable with the chroma filter.

Lines 26–29 apply the alpha filter to a div element containing an image. The style property of the filter determines in what opacity style is applied. Opacity refers to the color saturation of an image. The various style values create different transitions from opaque to transparent. A style value of 0 applies **uniform opacity**, a value of 1 applies a **linear gradient**, a value of 2 applies a **circular gradient** and a value of 3 applies a **rectangular gradient**.

The opacity and finishopacity properties are both percentages that determine at what percent opacity the specified gradient starts and finishes, respectively. Additional attributes are startX, startY, finishX and finishY. These specify at what x-y coordinates the gradient starts and finishes in that element.

```
1   <?xml version = "1.0"?>
2   <!DOCTYPE html PUBLIC "-//W3C//DTD XHTML 1.0 Strict//EN"
3      "http://www.w3.org/TR/xhtml1/DTD/xhtml1-strict.dtd">
4
5   <!-- Fig 15.6: alpha.html                        -->
6   <!-- Applying the alpha filter to an image -->
7
8   <html xmlns = "http://www.w3.org/1999/xhtml">
9      <head>
10         <title>Alpha Filter</title>
11      <script type = "text/javascript">
12         <!--
13         function run()
14         {
```

Fig. 15.6   Applying the alpha filter. (Part 1 of 3.)

```
15              pic.filters( "alpha" ).opacity = opacityButton.value;
16              pic.filters( "alpha" ).finishopacity =
17                 opacityButton2.value;
18              pic.filters( "alpha" ).style = styleSelect.value;
19           }
20           // -->
21       </script>
22       </head>
23
24       <body>
25
26          <div id = "pic"
27              style = "position: absolute; left:0; top: 0;
28                       filter: alpha( style = 2, opacity = 100,
29                       finishopacity = 0 )">
30             <img src = "flag.gif" alt = "Flag" />
31          </div>
32
33          <table style = "position: absolute; top: 250; left: 0;
34             background-color: #CCFFCC" border = "1">
35
36             <tr>
37                <td>Opacity (0-100):</td>
38                <td><input type = "text" id = "opacityButton"
39                   size = "3" maxlength = "3" value = "100" /></td>
40             </tr>
41
42             <tr>
43                <td>FinishOpacity (0-100):</td>
44                <td><input type = "text" id = "opacityButton2"
45                   size = "3" maxlength = "3" value = "0" /></td>
46             </tr>
47
48             <tr>
49                <td>Style:</td>
50                <td><select id = "styleSelect">
51                   <option value = "1">Linear</option>
52                   <option value = "2" selected = "selected">
53                      Circular</option>
54                   <option value = "3">Rectangular</option>
55                   </select></td>
56             </tr>
57
58             <tr>
59                <td align = "center" colspan = "2">
60                   <input type = "button" value = "Apply"
61                      onclick = "run()" />
62                </td>
63             </tr>
64          </table>
65
66       </body>
67    </html>
```

Fig. 15.6   Applying the alpha filter. (Part 2 of 3.)

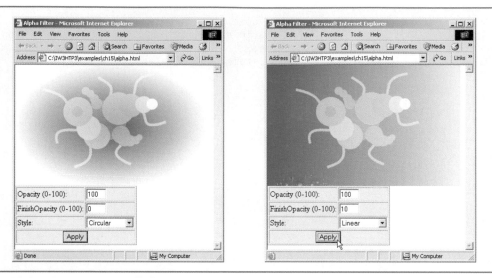

Fig. 15.6   Applying the `alpha` filter. (Part 3 of 3.)

15.8 Making Text `glow`

The **glow** filter adds an aura of color around text. The color and strength can both be specified, as demonstrated in Fig. 15.7.

```
1   <?xml version = "1.0"?>
2   <!DOCTYPE html PUBLIC "-//W3C//DTD XHTML 1.0 Transitional//EN"
3      "http://www.w3.org/TR/xhtml1/DTD/xhtml1-transitional.dtd">
4
5   <!-- Fig 15.7: glow.html        -->
6   <!-- Applying the glow filter -->
7
8   <html xmlns = "http://www.w3.org/1999/xhtml">
9      <head>
10        <title>Glow Filter</title>
11        <script type = "text/javascript">
12           <!--
13           var strengthIndex = 1;
14           var counter = 1;
15           var upDown = true;
16           var colorArray = [ "FF0000", "FFFF00", "00FF00",
17              "00FFFF", "0000FF", "FF00FF" ];
18           function apply()
19           {
20              glowSpan.filters( "glow" ).color =
21                 parseInt( glowColor.value, 16 );
22              glowSpan.filters( "glow" ).strength =
23                 glowStrength.value;
24           }
25
```

Fig. 15.7   Applying changes to the `glow` filter. (Part 1 of 3.)

```
26          function startdemo()
27          {
28              window.setInterval( "rundemo()", 150 );
29          }
30
31          function rundemo()
32          {
33              if ( upDown ) {
34                  glowSpan.filters( "glow" ).strength =
35                      strengthIndex++;
36              }
37              else {
38                  glowSpan.filters( "glow" ).strength =
39                      strengthIndex--;
40              }
41
42              if ( strengthIndex == 1 ) {
43                  upDown = !upDown;
44                  counter++;
45                  glowSpan.filters( "glow" ).color =
46                      parseInt( colorArray[ counter % 6 ], 16 );
47              }
48
49              if ( strengthIndex == 10 ) {
50                  upDown = !upDown;
51              }
52          }
53          // -->
54      </script>
55   </head>
56
57   <body style = "background-color: #00AAAA">
58      <h1>Glow Filter:</h1>
59
60      <span id = "glowSpan" style = "position: absolute;
61          left: 200;top: 100; padding: 5; filter: glow(
62          color = red, strength = 5 ); font-size: 2em">
63          Glowing Text
64      </span>
65
66      <table border = "1" style = "background-color: #CCFFCC">
67          <tr>
68              <td>Color (Hex)</td>
69              <td><input id = "glowColor" type = "text" size = "6"
70                  maxlength = "6" value = "FF0000" /></td>
71          </tr>
72          <tr>
73              <td>Strength (1-255)</td>
74              <td><input id = "glowStrength" type = "text"
75                  size = "3" maxlength = "3" value = "5" />
76              </td>
77          </tr>
```

Fig. 15.7   Applying changes to the glow filter. (Part 2 of 3.)

```
78              <tr>
79                <td colspan = "2">
80                  <input type = "button" value = "Apply"
81                    onclick = "apply()" />
82                  <input type = "button" value = "Run Demo"
83                    onclick = "startdemo()" /></td>
84              </tr>
85            </table>
86
87      </body>
88    </html>
```

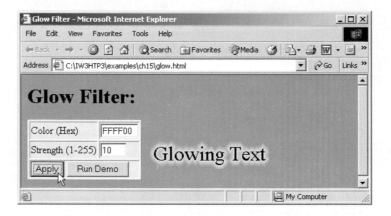

Fig. 15.7 Applying changes to the glow filter. (Part 3 of 3.)

Lines 16–17 establish an array of color values to cycle through in the demo. Lines 45–46 change the color attribute of the glow filter based on counter, which is incremented (line 44) every time the value of strengthIndex becomes 1. We use the parseInt function (line 46) to assign a proper hexadecimal value (taken from the colorArray we declared in lines 16–17) to the color property.

Lines 33–40 increment or decrement the strength property of the glow filter based on the value of upDown, which is toggled in the if statements in lines 42 and 49 when strengthIndex reaches either 1 or 10.

Clicking the **Run Demo** button starts a cycle that oscillates the filter strength, cycling through the colors in colorArray after every loop.

 Common Programming Error 15.1

When the glow filter is set to a large strength, the effect is often cut off by the edges of the element. Add CSS padding to prevent this.

15.9 Creating Motion with blur

The **blur** filter creates an illusion of motion by blurring text or images in a certain direction. As we see in Fig. 15.8, the blur filter can be applied in any of eight directions, and its strength can vary.

```
1   <?xml version = "1.0"?>
2   <!DOCTYPE html PUBLIC "-//W3C//DTD XHTML 1.0 Transitional//EN"
3      "http://www.w3.org/TR/xhtml1/DTD/xhtml1-transitional.dtd">
4
5   <!-- Fig 15.8: blur.html -->
6   <!-- The blur filter     -->
7
8   <html xmlns = "http://www.w3.org/1999/xhtml">
9      <head>
10        <title>Blur Filter</title>
11        <script type = "text/javascript">
12           <!--
13           var strengthIndex = 1;
14           var blurDirection = 0;
15           var upDown = 0;
16           var timer;
17
18           function reBlur()
19           {
20              blurImage.filters( "blur" ).direction =
21                 document.forms( "myForm" ).Direction.value;
22              blurImage.filters( "blur" ).strength =
23                 document.forms( "myForm" ).Strength.value;
24              blurImage.filters( "blur" ).add =
25                 document.forms( "myForm" ).AddBox.checked;
26           }
27
28           function startDemo()
29           {
30              timer = window.setInterval( "runDemo()", 5 );
31           }
32
33           function runDemo( )
34           {
35              document.forms( "myForm" ).Strength.value =
36                 strengthIndex;
37              document.forms( "myForm" ).Direction.value =
38                 ( blurDirection % 360 );
39
40              if ( strengthIndex == 35 || strengthIndex == 0 )
41                 upDown = !upDown;
42
43              blurImage.filters( "blur" ).strength =
44                 ( upDown ? strengthIndex++ : strengthIndex-- );
45
46              if ( strengthIndex == 0 )
47                 blurImage.filters( "blur" ).direction =
48                    ( ( blurDirection += 45 ) % 360 );
49           }
50           // -->
51        </script>
52     </head>
53
```

Fig. 15.8   Using the `blur` filter. (Part 1 of 3.)

```
54    <body>
55       <form name = "myForm" action = "">
56
57       <table border = "1" style = "background-color: #CCFFCC">
58       <caption>Blur filter controls</caption>
59
60          <tr>
61             <td>Direction:</td>
62             <td><select name = "Direction">
63                <option value = "0">above</option>
64                <option value = "45">above-right</option>
65                <option value = "90">right</option>
66                <option value = "135">below-right</option>
67                <option value = "180">below</option>
68                <option value = "225">below-left</option>
69                <option value = "270">left</option>
70                <option value = "315">above-left</option>
71             </select></td>
72          </tr>
73
74          <tr>
75             <td>Strength:</td>
76             <td><input name = "Strength" size = "3" type = "text"
77                maxlength = "3" value = "0" /></td>
78          </tr>
79
80          <tr>
81             <td>Add original?</td>
82             <td><input type = "checkbox" name = "AddBox" /></td>
83          </tr>
84
85          <tr>
86             <td align = "center" colspan = "2">
87                <input type = "button" value = "Apply"
88                   onclick = "reBlur();" /></td>
89          </tr>
90
91          <tr>
92             <td colspan = "2">
93             <input type = "button" value = "Start demo"
94                onclick = "startDemo();" />
95             <input type = "button" value = "Stop demo"
96                onclick = "window.clearInterval( timer );" /></td>
97          </tr>
98
99       </table>
100      </form>
101
102      <div id = "blurImage" style = "position: absolute;
103         top: 0; left: 300; padding: 0; filter: blur(
104         add = 0, direction = 0, strength = 0 );
105         background-color: white;">
```

Fig. 15.8   Using the blur filter. (Part 2 of 3.)

```
106                    <img align = "middle" src = "shapes.gif"
107                        alt = "Shapes" />
108            </div>
109
110        </body>
111    </html>
```

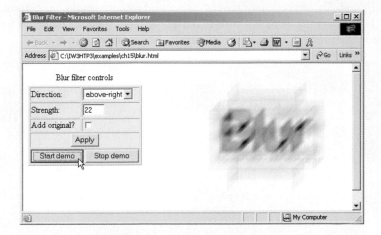

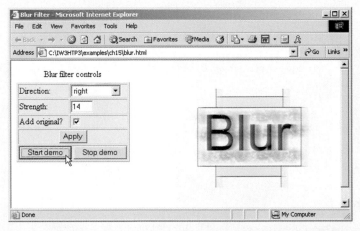

Fig. 15.8   Using the `blur` filter. (Part 3 of 3.)

The three properties of the `blur` filter are **add**, **direction** and **strength**. The add property, when set to `true`, adds a copy of the original image over the blurred image, creating a more subtle blurring effect; Fig. 15.8 demonstrates the contrast between setting this to `true` and to `false`.

The `direction` property determines in which direction the `blur` filter is applied. This is expressed in angular form (as we saw in Fig. 15.5 with the `shadow` filter). The `strength` property determines how strong the blurring effect is.

Lines 24–25 assign to the `add` property of the `blur` filter the boolean `checked` property of the **Add original?** checkbox—if the box is checked, the value is `true`.

Lines 47–48 increment the direction property whenever the strength of the blur filter is 0 (i.e., whenever an iteration has completed). The value assigned to the direction property cycles through all the multiples of 45 between 0 and 360.

15.10 Using the wave Filter

The **wave** filter allows you to apply **sine-wave distortions** to text and images on your Web pages (Fig. 15.9). The wave filter, as seen in lines 35–36, has many properties. The add property, like the blur filter, adds a copy of the text or image underneath the filtered effect. The add property is useful only when applying the wave filter to images.

```
1   <?xml version = "1.0"?>
2   <!DOCTYPE html PUBLIC "-//W3C//DTD XHTML 1.0 Transitional//EN"
3      "http://www.w3.org/TR/xhtml1/DTD/xhtml1-transitional.dtd">
4
5   <!-- Fig 15.9: wave.html        -->
6   <!-- Applying the wave filter -->
7
8   <html xmlns = "http://www.w3.org/1999/xhtml">
9      <head>
10        <title>Wave Filter</title>
11
12        <script type = "text/javascript">
13           <!--
14           var wavePhase = 0;
15
16           function start()
17           {
18              window.setInterval( "wave()", 5 );
19           }
20
21           function wave()
22           {
23              wavePhase++;
24              flag.filters( "wave" ).phase = wavePhase;
25           }
26           // -->
27        </script>
28     </head>
29
30     <body onload = "start();">
31
32        <span id = "flag"
33           style = "align: center; position: absolute;
34           left: 30; padding: 15;
35           filter: wave(add = 0, freq = 1, phase = 0,
36              strength = 10); font-size: 2em">
37        Here is some waaaavy text
38        </span>
39
40     </body>
41  </html>
```

Fig. 15.9 Adding a wave filter to text. (Part 1 of 2.)

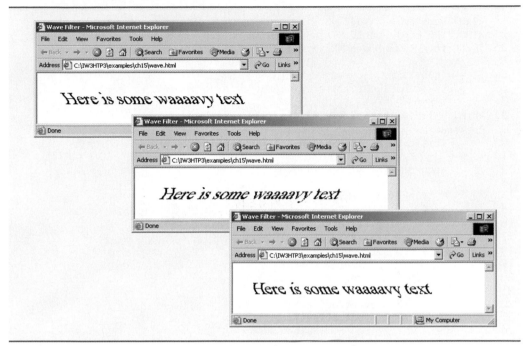

Fig. 15.9   Adding a **wave** filter to text. (Part 2 of 2.)

Performance Tip 15.2

*Applying the **wave** filter to images is processor intensive—if your viewers have inadequate processor power, your pages may act sluggishly on their systems.*

The `freq` property determines the **frequency of the wave** applied—that is, how many complete sine waves are applied in the affected area. Increasing this property creates a more pronounced wave effect, but makes the text harder to read.

The `phase` property indicates the **phase shift of the wave**. Increasing this property does not modify any physical attributes of the wave, but merely shifts it in space. This property is useful for creating a gentle waving effect, as we do in this example. The last property, `strength`, is the amplitude of the sine wave that is applied. In the script, lines 23–24, increment the `phase` shift of the wave in every call to the `wave` function.

15.11 Advanced Filters: dropShadow and light

Two filters that apply advanced image processing effects are the **dropShadow** and **light** filters. The `dropShadow` filter, as you can probably tell, applies an effect similar to the drop shadow we applied to our images with Photoshop Elements in Chapter 3—it creates a blacked-out version of the image, and places it behind the image, offset by a specified number of pixels.

The `light` filter is the most powerful and advanced filter available in Internet Explorer 6. It allows you to simulate the effect of a light source shining on your page. With scripting, this filter can be used with dazzling results. Fig. 15.10 combines these two filters to create an interesting effect.

```
1   <?xml version = "1.0"?>
2   <!DOCTYPE html PUBLIC "-//W3C//DTD XHTML 1.0 Transitional//EN"
3      "http://www.w3.org/TR/xhtml1/DTD/xhtml1-transitional.dtd">
4
5   <!-- Fig. 15.10: dropshadow.html                          -->
6   <!-- Using the light filter with the dropshadow filter  -->
7
8   <html xmlns = "http://www.w3.org/1999/xhtml">
9      <head>
10        <title>DHTML dropShadow and light Filters</title>
11
12        <script type = "text/javascript">
13           <!--
14           function setlight( )
15           {
16              dsImg.filters( "light" ).addPoint( 150, 150,
17                 125, 255, 255, 255, 100 );
18           }
19
20           function run()
21           {
22              eX = event.offsetX;
23              eY = event.offsetY;
24
25              xCoordinate = Math.round(
26                 eX-event.srcElement.width / 2, 0. );
27              yCoordinate = Math.round(
28                 eY-event.srcElement.height / 2, 0 );
29
30              dsImg.filters( "dropShadow" ).offx =
31                 xCoordinate / -3;
32              dsImg.filters( "dropShadow" ).offy =
33                 yCoordinate / -3;
34
35              dsImg.filters( "light" ).moveLight(
36                 0, eX, eY, 125, 1 );
37           }
38           // -->
39        </script>
40     </head>
41
42     <body onload = "setlight()" style = "background-color: green">
43
44        <img id = "dsImg" src = "circle.gif"
45           style = "top: 100; left: 100; filter: dropShadow(
46           offx = 0, offy = 0, color = black ) light()"
47           onmousemove = "run()" alt = "Circle Image" />
48
49     </body>
50  </html>
```

Fig. 15.10 Applying light filter with a dropShadow. (Part 1 of 2.)

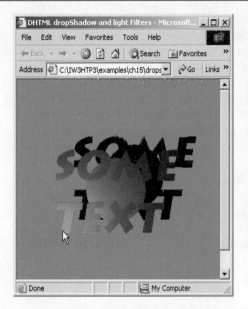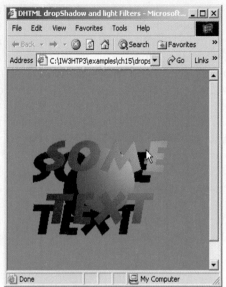

Fig. 15.10 Applying light filter with a dropShadow. (Part 2 of 2.)

Let us begin by examining the dropShadow filter. In lines 44–47, we apply the drop-Shadow filter to our image. The offx and offy properties determine the number of pixels by which the drop shadow is offset. The color property specifies the color of the drop shadow. Note that we also declare the light filter in line 46, although we do not give it any initial parameters—all the parameters and methods of the light filter are set by scripting. Lines 16–17 call the addPoint method of the light filter. This adds a **point light source**—a source of light which emanates from a single point and radiates in all directions. The first two parameters (150, 150) set the *x-y* coordinates at which to add the point source. In this case we place the source at the center of the image, which is 300-by-300 pixels. The next parameter (125) sets the **height** of the point source. This simulates how far above the surface the light is situated. Small values create a small but high-intensity circle of light on the image, while large values cast a circle of light which is darker, but spreads over a greater distance. The next three parameters (255, 255, 255) specify the color of the light in RGB format. In this case we set the light to a color of white. The last value (100) is a strength percentage—we set our light in this case to radiate with 100% strength.

This point light source creates a pleasant lighting effect, but it is static. We can use scripting to animate the light source in response to user actions. We use the onmousemove event (line 47) to have the light source follow the mouse cursor as the user moves it over the image. The run function (lines 20–37) animates both the dropshadow filter and the light filter in response to user actions. First we set the variables xCoordinate and yCoordinate to the distance between the current cursor position (eX and eY, which were set to event.offsetX and event.offsetY in lines 22–23) and the middle of the image (event.srcElement.width / 2 or event.srcElement.height / 2). Lines 20–33 set the offx and offy properties of the dropShadow filter relative to the current *x-y* coordinates of the image. We divide by -3 to create an effect of height (shadows cast by objects far from light sources only move a small amount when the light source moves by a larger amount). Note that the negative number causes the drop shadow to be applied in the opposite direction from the mouse movement.

Lines 35–36 then call the moveLight method to update the position of the light source as well. The first parameter (0) is the index of the light source on the page. Multiple light sources have index numbers assigned to them in the order in which they are added. The next two parameters (event.offsetX, event.offsetY) specify the *x-y* coordinates to which we should move the light source. We use the offsetX and offsetY properties of the event object to move the light source to the current mouse cursor position over the image. The next parameter (125) specifies the height to which we move the light source. In this case, we keep the light source at the same level as when we declared it. The last parameter (1) indicates that the values we are using are absolute. To move the light source by relative amounts instead, use a value of 0 for the last parameter of the moveLight function.

As you can see, combining the dropShadow and light filters creates a stunning effect that responds to user actions. The point source is not the only type of light source available for the light filter. Figure 15.11 demonstrates the use of a **cone light source** for illuminating an image.

```
1    <?xml version = "1.0"?>
2    <!DOCTYPE html PUBLIC "-//W3C//DTD XHTML 1.0 Transitional//EN"
3        "http://www.w3.org/TR/xhtml1/DTD/xhtml1-transitional.dtd">
4
5    <!-- Fig 15.11: conelight.html          -->
6    <!-- Automating the cone light source -->
7
8    <html xmlns = "http://www.w3.org/1999/xhtml">
9        <head><title>Cone lighting</title>
10
11       <script type = "text/javascript">
12           var upDown = true;
13           var counter = 0;
14           var moveRate = -2;
15
16           function setLight()
17           {
18               marquee.filters( "light" ).addCone( 0, marquee.height,
19                   8, marquee.width / 2, 30, 255, 150, 255, 50, 15 );
20               marquee.filters( "light" ).addCone( marquee.width,
21                   marquee.height, 8, 200, 30, 150, 255, 255, 50, 15 );
22               marquee.filters( "light" ).addCone( marquee.width / 2,
23                   marquee.height, 4, 200, 100, 255, 255, 150, 50, 50 );
24
25               window.setInterval( "display()", 100 );
26           }
27
28           function display()
29           {
30               counter++;
31
```

Fig. 15.11 Dynamic cone source lighting. (Part 1 of 2.)

```
32              if ( ( counter % 30 ) == 0 )
33                  upDown = !upDown;
34
35              if ( ( counter % 10 ) == 0 )
36                  moveRate *= -1;
37
38              if ( upDown ) {
39                  marquee.filters( "light" ).moveLight(
40                      0, -1, -1, 3, 0 );
41                  marquee.filters( "light" ).moveLight(
42                      1, 1, -1, 3, 0 );
43                  marquee.filters( "light" ).moveLight(
44                      2, moveRate, 0, 3, 0);
45              }
46              else {
47                  marquee.filters( "light" ).moveLight(
48                      0, 1, 1, 3, 0 );
49                  marquee.filters( "light" ).moveLight(
50                      1, -1, 1, 3, 0 );
51                  marquee.filters( "light" ).moveLight(
52                      2, moveRate, 0, 3, 0) ;
53              }
54          }
55      </script>
56      </head>
57      <body style = "background-color: #000000"
58          onload = "setLight()">
59
60          <img id = "marquee" src = "marquee.gif"
61              style = "filter: light; position: absolute; left: 25;
62              top: 25" alt = "Deitel movie marquee" />
63
64      </body>
65  </html>
```

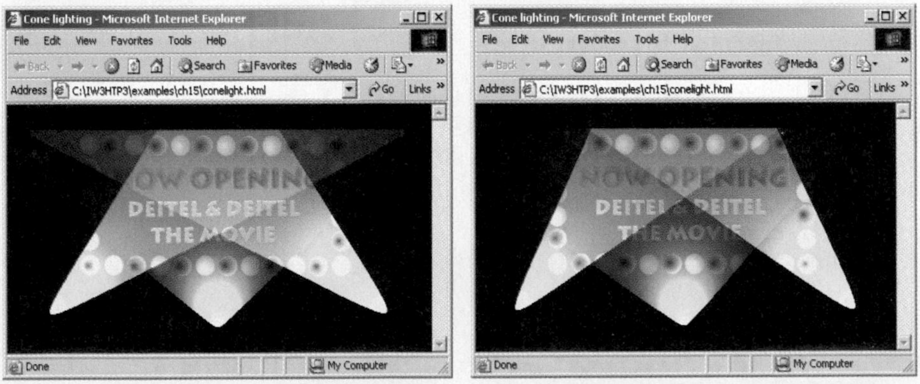

Fig. 15.11 Dynamic cone source lighting. (Part 2 of 2.)

Lines 18–19 add our first cone light source, using the addCone method. The parameters of this method are similar to the addPoint method. The first two parameters specify the *x-y* coordinates of the light source, and the third parameter specifies the simulated height above the page at which the light should be placed. The next two parameters (`mar-quee.width` / 2, 30) are new—they specify the *x-y* coordinates at which the cone source is targeted. The next three parameters (255, 150, 255) specify the RGB value of the light's color, just as we did in the `addPoint` method. The next parameter (50) specifies the strength of the cone source in a percentage (also equivalent to the strength parameter in the `addPoint` method). The last value (15) specifies the **spread** of the light source in degrees (this can be set in the range 0–90). In this case we set the spread of the cone to 15 degrees, illuminating a relatively narrow area.

In lines 39–40, we use the `moveLight` method once again. When used on cone sources, the `moveLight` method moves the target of the light. In this case, we set the last parameter to 0 to move the light by a relative amount, not an absolute amount, as we did in Fig 15.10.

15.12 `blendTrans` Transition

The transitions included with Internet Explorer 6 give the author control of many scriptable PowerPoint type effects. Transitions are set as values of the `filter` CSS property, just as regular filters are. We then use scripting to begin the transition. Figure 15.12 is a simple example of the **blendTrans** transition, which creates a smooth fade-in/fade-out effect.

```
1   <?xml version = "1.0"?>
2   <!DOCTYPE html PUBLIC "-//W3C//DTD XHTML 1.0 Strict//EN"
3       "http://www.w3.org/TR/xhtml1/DTD/xhtml1-strict.dtd">
4
5   <!-- Fig 15.12: blendtrans.html -->
6   <!-- Blend transition            -->
7
8   <html xmlns = "http://www.w3.org/1999/xhtml">
9       <head>
10          <title>Using blendTrans</title>
11
12          <script type = "text/javascript">
13              <!--
14              function blendOut()
15              {
16                  textInput.filters( "blendTrans" ).apply();
17                  textInput.style.visibility = "hidden";
18                  textInput.filters( "blendTrans" ).play();
19              }
20              // -->
21          </script>
22      </head>
23
24      <body>
25
26          <div id = "textInput" onclick = "blendOut()" style =
27              "width: 300; filter: blendTrans( duration = 3 )">
28              <h1>Some fading text</h1>
29          </div>
```

Fig. 15.12 Using the `blendTrans` transition. (Part 1 of 2.)

```
30
31        </body>
32    </html>
```

Fig. 15.12 Using the blendTrans transition. (Part 2 of 2.)

Lines 26–27 set the filter to blendTrans and the duration parameter to 3 seconds. The duration attribute determines how long the transition takes. When the user clicks the text, lines 16–18 invoke two methods of blendTrans. The apply method (line 16) initializes the transition for the affected element. Once this is done, we set the visibility of the element to hidden. Next, we call method play (line 18) which causes the text to transition to the specified visibility.

Figure 15.13 is a more complex example of the blendTrans transition. We use this to transition between two separate images.

We begin by placing two overlapping images on the page, with ids image1 and image2 (lines 53–63). The body tag's onload event (line 49) calls function blend (lines 16–28) as the body loads. The blend function checks the value of the whichImage variable, and, because it is set to true, begins a fade transition on image1. Because there are two images in the same place, when image1 fades out, it appears that image2 fades in to replace it. When the transition is complete, image1's onfilterchange event (line 60) fires. This calls function reBlend (lines 30–43), which in lines 33–34 changes the zIndex (the JavaScript version of the z-index CSS property) of image1 so that it is now below image2. Once this is done, the image is made visible again. The function then toggles the whichImage property and calls function blend so that the whole process starts again, now transitioning from image2 back to image1.

```
1     <?xml version = "1.0"?>
2     <!DOCTYPE html PUBLIC "-//W3C//DTD XHTML 1.0 Transitional//EN"
3         "http://www.w3.org/TR/xhtml1/DTD/xhtml1-transitional.dtd">
4
5     <!-- Fig 15.13: blendtrans2.html -->
6     <!-- Blend Transition              -->
7
8     <html xmlns = "http://www.w3.org/1999/xhtml">
9         <head>
10            <title>Blend Transition II</title>
11
12            <script type = "text/javascript">
13                <!--
```

Fig. 15.13 Blending between images with blendTrans. (Part 1 of 3.)

```
14              var whichImage = true;
15
16              function blend()
17              {
18                  if ( whichImage ) {
19                      image1.filters( "blendTrans" ).apply();
20                      image1.style.visibility = "hidden";
21                      image1.filters( "blendTrans" ).play();
22                  }
23                  else {
24                      image2.filters( "blendTrans" ).apply();
25                      image2.style.visibility = "hidden";
26                      image2.filters( "blendTrans" ).play();
27                  }
28              }
29
30              function reBlend( fromImage )
31              {
32                  if ( fromImage ) {
33                      image1.style.zIndex -= 2;
34                      image1.style.visibility = "visible";
35                  }
36                  else {
37                      image1.style.zIndex += 2;
38                      image2.style.visibility = "visible";
39                  }
40
41                  whichImage = !whichImage;
42                  blend();
43              }
44              // -->
45          </script>
46      </head>
47
48      <body style = "color: darkblue; background-color: lightblue"
49          onload = "blend()">
50
51          <h1>Blend Transition Demo</h1>
52
53          <img id = "image2" src = "cool12.jpg"
54          onfilterchange = "reBlend( false )"
55          style = "position: absolute; left: 50; top: 50;
56          width: 300; filter: blendTrans( duration = 4 );
57          z-index: 1" alt = "First Transition Image"  />
58
59          <img id = "image1" src = "cool8.jpg"
60              onfilterchange = "reBlend( true )"
61              style = "position: absolute; left: 50; top: 50;
62              width: 300; filter: blendTrans( duration = 4 );
63              z-index: 2" alt = "Second Transition Image"  />
64
65      </body>
66  </html>
```

Fig. 15.13 Blending between images with **blendTrans**. (Part 2 of 3.)

Fig. 15.13 Blending between images with `blendTrans`. (Part 3 of 3.)

15.13 revealTrans Transition

The **revealTrans** filter allows you to create professional-style transitions, from **box out** to **random dissolve**. Figure 15.14 cycles through all 24 of these, transitioning from one image to another.

```
1   <?xml version = "1.0"?>
2   <!DOCTYPE html PUBLIC "-//W3C//DTD XHTML 1.0 Transitional//EN"
3      "http://www.w3.org/TR/xhtml1/DTD/xhtml1-transitional.dtd">
4
5   <!-- Fig. 15.14: revealtrans.html   -->
6   <!-- Cycling through 24 transitions -->
7
8   <html xmlns = "http://www.w3.org/1999/xhtml">
9      <head>
10         <title>24 DHTML Transitions</title>
11
12      <script type = "text/javascript">
13         <!--
14         var transitionName =
15           ["Box In", "Box Out",
16            "Circle In", "Circle Out",
17            "Wipe Up", "Wipe Down", "Wipe Right", "Wipe Left",
18            "Vertical Blinds", "Horizontal Blinds",
19            "Checkerboard Across", "Checkerboard Down",
20            "Random Dissolve",
21            "Split Vertical In", "Split Vertical Out",
22            "Split Horizontal In", "Split Horizontal Out",
23            "Strips Left Down", "Strips Left Up",
24            "Strips Right Down", "Strips Right Up",
25            "Random Bars Horizontal", "Random Bars Vertical",
26            "Random" ];
27
28         var counter = 0;
29         var whichImage = true;
30
31         function blend()
32         {
33            if ( whichImage ) {
34               image1.filters( "revealTrans" ).apply();
35               image1.style.visibility = "hidden";
36               image1.filters( "revealTrans" ).play();
37            }
38            else {
39               image2.filters( "revealTrans" ).apply();
40               image2.style.visibility = "hidden";
41               image2.filters( "revealTrans" ).play();
42            }
43         }
44
45         function reBlend( fromImage )
46         {
47            counter++;
48
49            if ( fromImage ) {
50               image1.style.zIndex -= 2;
51               image1.style.visibility = "visible";
```

Fig. 15.14   Transitions using revealTrans. (Part 1 of 3.)

```
52              image2.filters( "revealTrans" ).transition =
53                 counter % 24;
54           }
55           else {
56              image1.style.zIndex += 2;
57              image2.style.visibility = "visible";
58              image1.filters( "revealTrans" ).transition =
59                 counter % 24;
60           }
61
62           whichImage = !whichImage;
63           blend();
64           transitionDisplay.innerHTML = "Transition " +
65              counter % 24 + ": " + transitionName[ counter % 24 ];
66        }
67        // -->
68     </script>
69     </head>
70
71     <body style = "color: white; background-color: lightcoral"
72           onload = "blend()">
73
74        <img id = "image2" src = "icontext.gif"
75              style = "position: absolute; left: 10; top: 10;
76              width: 300; z-index:1; visibility: visible;
77              filter: revealTrans( duration = 2, transition = 0 )"
78              onfilterchange = "reBlend( false )" alt =
79              "Programming Tips" />
80
81        <img id = "image1" src = "icons2.gif"
82              style = "position: absolute; left: 10; top: 10;
83              width: 300; z-index:1; visibility: visible;
84              filter: revealTrans( duration = 2, transition = 0 )"
85              onfilterchange = "reBlend( true )" alt = "Icons" />
86
87        <div id = "transitionDisplay" style = "position: absolute;
88           top: 70; left: 80">Transition 0: Box In</div>
89
90     </body>
91     </html>
```

Fig. 15.14 Transitions using revealTrans. (Part 2 of 3.)

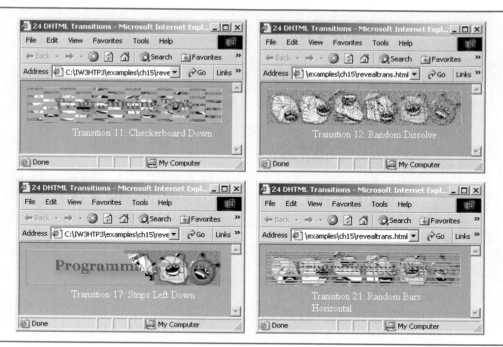

Fig. 15.14   Transitions using `revealTrans`. (Part 3 of 3.)

The script in this example is almost the same as the script in the `blendTrans` example. In lines 52–53, we set the `transition` property of the image, which determines what visual transition is used here. There are 24 different visual transitions (their names are listed in the `transitionName` array) for updating the `div` element `transitionDisplay` (lines 87–88).

SUMMARY

- Applying filters to text and images causes changes that are persistent.
- Transitions are temporary phenomena; applying a transition allows you to transfer from one page to another with a pleasant visual effect, such as a random dissolve.
- Filters and transitions do not add content to your pages—rather, they present existing content in an engaging manner to help hold the user's attention.
- Each of the visual effects achievable with filters and transitions is programmable, so these effects can be adjusted dynamically by programs that respond to user-initiated events like mouse clicks and keystrokes.
- When Internet Explorer renders your page, it applies all the special effects and does this while running on the client computer without lengthy waits for files to download from the server.
- The `flipv` and `fliph` filters mirror text or images vertically and horizontally, respectively.
- Filters are applied in the `style` attribute. The `filter` property's value is the name of the filter.
- More than one filter can be applied at once. Enter multiple filters as values of the `filter` attribute, separated by spaces.
- The `chroma` filter applies transparency effects dynamically, without using a graphics editor to hard-code transparency into the image.

- Use the `parseInt` function to convert a string to a hexadecimal integer for setting the `color` property of the `chroma` filter. The second parameter of `parseInt` specifies the base of the integer.

- Each filter has a property named `enabled`. If this property is set to `true`, the filter is applied. If it is set to `false`, the filter is not applied.

- The `onchange` event fires whenever the `value` of a form field changes.

- Applying the `mask` filter to an image allows you to create an image mask, in which an element's background is a solid color and its foreground is transparent to the image or color behind it.

- Parameters for filters are always specified in the format `param = value`.

- The `invert` filter applies a negative image effect—dark areas become light, and light areas become dark.

- The `gray` filter applies a grayscale image effect, in which all color is stripped from the image and all that remains is brightness data.

- The `xray` filter applies an x-ray effect which is basically just an inversion of the grayscale effect.

- A simple filter that adds depth to your text is the `shadow` filter. This filter creates a shadowing effect that gives your text a three-dimensional look. The `direction` property of the `shadow` filter determines in which direction the shadow effect will be applied—this can be set to any of eight directions, expressed in angular notation: 0 (up), 45 (above-right), 90 (right), 135 (below-right), 180 (below), 225 (below-left), 270 (left) and 315 (above-left). The `color` property of the `shadow` filter specifies the color of the shadow that is applied to the text.

- Internet Explorer 6 allows you to create gradient effects dynamically, using the `alpha` filter. The `style` property of the filter determines in what style the opacity is applied, a value of 0 applies uniform opacity, a value of 1 applies a linear gradient, a value of 2 applies a circular gradient and a value of 3 applies a rectangular gradient. The `opacity` and `finishopacity` properties are percentages determining at what percent opacity the specified gradient will start and finish, respectively. Additional attributes are `startX`, `startY`, `finishX` and `finishY`. These allow you to specify at what *x-y* coordinates the gradient starts and finishes in that element.

- The `glow` filter allows you to add an aura of color around your text. The `color` and `strength` can both be specified.

- The `blur` filter creates an illusion of motion by blurring text or images in a certain direction. The `blur` filter can be applied in any of eight directions, and its strength can vary. The `add` property, when set to `true`, adds a copy of the original image over the blurred image, creating a more subtle blurring effect. The `direction` property determines in which direction the `blur` filter will be applied. This is expressed in angular form (as with the `shadow` filter). The `strength` property determines how strong the blurring effect is.

- The `wave` filter allows you to apply sine-wave distortions to text and images on your Web pages.

- The `add` property, as in the case of the `blur` filter, adds a copy of the text or image, but underneath the filtered effect. The `add` property is useful when applying the `wave` filter to images. The `freq` property determines the frequency of the wave applied—that is, how many complete sine waves are applied in the affected area. Increasing this property would create a more pronounced wave effect, but makes the text harder to read. The `phase` property indicates the phase shift of the wave. Increasing this property does not modify any physical attributes of the wave, but merely shifts it in space. This property is useful for creating a gentle waving effect. The last property, `strength`, is the amplitude of the sine wave that is applied.

- The `dropShadow` filter creates a blacked-out version of the image, and places it behind the image, offset by a specified number of pixels.

- The `offx` and `offy` properties of the `dropShadow` filter determine by how many pixels the drop shadow offsets. The `color` property specifies the color of the drop shadow.

- The light filter is one of the most powerful and advanced filters available in Internet Explorer 6. It allows you to simulate the effect of a light source shining on your page.

- The light filter's addPoint method adds a point light source—a source of light which emanates from a single point and radiates in all directions. The first two parameters set the x-y coordinates at which to add the point source. The next parameter sets the height of the point source. This simulates how far above the surface the light is situated. Small values create a small but high-intensity circle of light on the image, while large values cast a circle of light which is darker, but spreads over a greater distance. The next three parameters specify the RGB value of the light in decimal. The last parameter is a strength percentage.

- The moveLight method updates the position of a light source. The first parameter is the index of the light source on the page. Multiple light sources have index numbers assigned to them in the order they are added. The next two parameters specify the x-y coordinates to which we should move the light source. The next parameter specifies the height to which we move the light source. Setting the last parameter to 1 indicates that the values we are using are absolute. To move your light source by relative amounts instead, use a value of 0 for the last parameter of the moveLight function.

- The parameters of the addCone method are similar to the addPoint method. The first two parameters specify the x-y coordinates of the light source, and the third parameter specifies the simulated height above the page at which the light should be placed. The next two parameters specify the x-y coordinates at which the cone source is targeted. The next three parameters specify the RGB value of the light which is cast, just as in the addPoint method. The next parameter specifies the strength of the cone source in a percentage. The last value specifies the spread of the light source in degrees (this can be set in the range 0–90).

- The transitions included with Internet Explorer 6.0 give the author control of scriptable PowerPoint type effects. Transitions are set as values of the filter CSS property, just as regular filters are.

- The duration parameter of blendTrans determines how long the transition will take.

- The apply method initializes the transition for the affected element. The play method then begins the transition.

- The revealTrans filter allows you to transition using professional-style transitions, from Box Out to Random Dissolve. The transition property determines what visual transition is used. There are 24 different visual transitions.

TERMINOLOGY

add property of blur filter	filter:blur
add property of wave filter	filter:chroma
addCone method of light filter	filter:dropshadow
addPoint method of light filter	filter:fliph
alpha filter	filter:flipv
blendTrans filter	filter:glow
blur filter	filter:gray
chroma filter	filter:invert
circular gradient	filter:light
color property of chroma filter	filter:mask
enabled property of each filter	filter:shadow
fade-in/fade-out effect	filter:wave
filter	filter:xray
filter property with style attribute	finishopacity property of alpha filter
filter strength	finishx property of alpha filter
filter:alpha	finishy property of alpha filter

flipH filter
flipV filter
freq property of wave filter
glow filter
gradient
gray filter
grayscale image effect
height of light source
horizontal blinds transition
illusion of motion by blurring
image mask
invert filter
color property of dropshadow filter
color property of glow filter
color property of shadow filter
combining filters
cone light source
CSS filter property
direction property of blur filter
direction property of shadow filter
dropShadow filter
duration of blendTrans filter
light filter
linear opacity
mask filter
moveLight property of light filter
negative image effect with invert filter
offx property of dropshadow filter

offy property of dropshadow filter
opacity property of alpha filter
padding (CSS)
phase property of wave filter
phase shift of a wave
point light source
radial opacity
random dissolve transition
rectangular opacity
revealTrans filter
shadow filter
sine-wave distortion
spread of cone light source
startx property of alpha filter
starty property of alpha filter
strength property of blur filter
strength property of glow filter
strength property of wave filter
style property of alpha filter
three-dimensional effect with shadow filter
transition effect
transparency effect
uniform opacity
vertical blinds transition
visibility
visual filter
wave filter
xray filter

SELF-REVIEW EXERCISES

15.1   State whether the following are *true* or *false*. If *false*, explain why.
   a) You can determine the strength of the shadow filter.
   b) The flip filter flips text horizontally.
   c) The mask filter makes the foreground of an element transparent.
   d) The freq property of the wave filter determines how many sine waves are applied to that element.
   e) Increasing the margin of an element prevents the glow filter from being clipped by the element's border.
   f) The apply method begins a transition.
   g) The invert filter creates a negative image effect.
   h) The add property of the blur filter adds a duplicate image below the affected image.

15.2   Fill in the blanks in the following statements:
   a) You must use the _____ function when passing a string (not hexadecimal) value to the color property.
   b) The last parameter of the moveLight method determines whether the move is _____ or _____.
   c) The amplitude of the wave filter is controlled by the _____ property.
   d) There are _____ directions in which the blur filter can be applied.
   e) There are two coordinate pairs in the parameters of the light filter's addCone method: the _____ and the _____.

f) There are _____ different transition styles for the revealTrans transition.

g) The two properties of the dropShadow filter that specify the offset of the shadow are _____ and _____.

h) The four possible opacity attributes of the alpha filter are _____, _____, _____ and _____.

i) The _____ filter creates a grayscale version of the affected image.

ANSWERS TO SELF-REVIEW EXERCISES

15.1   a) False; there is no strength property for the shadow filter. You can only determine the color and direction of the shadow filter. b) False; the fliph filter flips text horizontally. c) True. d) True. e) False; increasing the padding of an element prevents clipping. f) False; the play method begins a transition. g) True. h) True.

15.2   a) parseInt. b) relative, absolute. c) strength. d) eight. e) source, target. f) 24. g) offx, offy. h) uniform, linear, circular, rectangular. i) gray.

EXERCISES

15.3   Create a Web page that applies the invert filter to an image if the user moves the mouse over it.

15.4   Create a Web page that applies the glow filter to a hyperlink if the user moves the mouse over the link.

15.5   Write a script that blurs images and slowly unblurs them when they are finished loading into the browser (use event onload for the image).

15.6   Write a script that creates a cone light filter that tracks mouse movements across the page.

15.7   Write a script that uses the blendTrans filter to transition into an image after the image fully loads (use event onload for the image).

15.8   Write a script that changes the attributes of an alpha filter every 20 seconds (see setInterval in Chapter 13). Change both the color and the style of the alpha filter every time.

15.9   *(Slide Show)* Use the revealTrans filter to present your own slide show in a Web page. On each transition, display a new image.

15.10   *(Image Selector)* Design a Web page that allows the user to choose from a series of images and to view the image in color and in grayscale.

16

Dynamic HTML:
Data Binding with
Tabular Data Control

Objectives

- To understand Dynamic HTML's notion of data binding and how to bind data to XHTML elements.
- To be able to sort and filter data directly on the client without involving the server.
- To be able to bind a `table` and other XHTML elements to data source objects (DSOs).
- To be able to filter data to select only records appropriate for a particular application.
- To be able to navigate backward and forward through a database with the `Move` methods.

Let's look at the record.
Alfred Smith

It is a capital mistake to theorize before one has data.
Sir Arthur Conan Doyle

The more the data banks record about each one of us, the less we exist.
Marshall McLuhan

Poor fellow, he suffers from files.
Aneurin Bevan

Outline

16.1 Introduction

This is one of the most important chapters for people who will build substantial, real-world, Web-based applications. Businesses and organizations thrive on data. Dynamic HTML helps Web application developers produce more responsive data-intensive applications.

Performance Tip 16.1

Before Dynamic HTML, the kinds of data manipulations we discuss in this chapter had to be done on the server, increasing the server load and the network load and resulting in choppy application responsiveness. With Dynamic HTML, these manipulations, such as sorting and filtering data, can now be done directly on the client without involving the server and the network.

With **data binding**, data need no longer reside exclusively on the server. Data can be maintained on the client, in a manner that distinguishes it from the XHTML markup on the page. Typically, data is sent to the client. All subsequent manipulations then take place on the data directly on the client, thus eliminating server activity and network delays.

Performance Tip 16.2

With Dynamic HTML (rather than server-based database processing) it is more likely that a larger amount of data will be sent to the client on the first request. This initial downloading of the data by Internet Explorer is performed in a manner that enables processing to begin immediately on the portion of the data that has arrived.

With the kind of data-binding technology we discuss in this chapter, changes to data made on the client do not propagate back to the server. This is not a problem for a great many popular applications. If you do need to access the database directly and want the changes that you make on the client actually to update the original database, you can use the server-side techniques we demonstrate in Chapters 23–27 and Chapters 33–37 (on the CD).

Once it is available on the client, the data can be sorted and filtered in various ways. We present examples of each of these operations.

To bind external data to XHTML elements, Internet Explorer employs software capable of connecting the browser to live data sources. These are known as **Data Source Objects** (DSOs). There are several DSOs available in IE6—in this chapter we discuss the most popular DSO—the **Tabular Data Control (TDC)**.

Software Engineering Observation 16.1

Data-bound properties can be modified with Dynamic HTML even after the browser renders the page.

16.2 Simple Data Binding

The Tabular Data Control is an ActiveX control that is added to a page with the `object` element. Data is stored in a separate file (e.g., Fig. 16.1) and not embedded in the XHTML document. Figure 16.2 demonstrates a simple use of data binding with the TDC to update the contents of a `span` element. The data file used by this example is listed in Fig. 16.1.

```
1   @ColorName@|@ColorHexRGBValue@
2   @aqua@|@#00FFFF@
3   @black@|@#000000@
4   @blue@|@#0000FF@
5   @fuchsia@|@#FF00FF@
6   @gray@|@#808080@
7   @green@|@#008000@
8   @lime@|@#00FF00@
9   @maroon@|@#800000@
10  @navy@|@#000080@
11  @olive@|@#808000@
12  @purple@|@#800080@
13  @red@|@#FF0000@
14  @silver@|@#C0C0C0@
15  @teal@|@#008080@
16  @yellow@|@#FFFF00@
17  @white@|@#FFFFFF@
```

Fig. 16.1   XHTML color table data (`HTMLStandardColors.txt`).

```
1   <?xml version = "1.0"?>
2   <!DOCTYPE html PUBLIC "-//W3C//DTD XHTML 1.0 Strict//EN"
3       "http://www.w3.org/TR/xhtml1/DTD/xhtml1-strict.dtd">
4
5   <!-- Fig 16.2: introdatabind.html              -->
6   <!-- Simple data binding and recordset manipulation -->
7
8   <html xmlns = "http://www.w3.org/1999/xhtml">
9      <head>
10        <title>Intro to Data Binding</title>
11
12        <!-- This object element inserts an ActiveX control -->
13        <!-- for handling and parsing our data. The PARAM   -->
14        <!-- tags give the control starting parameters       -->
15        <!-- such as URL.                                     -->
16        <object id = "Colors"
17           classid = "CLSID:333C7BC4-460F-11D0-BC04-0080C7055A83">
18           <param name = "DataURL" value =
19              "HTMLStandardColors.txt" />
```

Fig. 16.2   Simple data binding. (Part 1 of 3.)

```
20          <param name = "UseHeader" value = "TRUE" />
21          <param name = "TextQualifier" value = "@" />
22          <param name = "FieldDelim" value = "|" />
23       </object>
24
25       <script type = "text/javascript">
26          <!--
27          var recordSet = Colors.recordset;
28
29          function displayRecordNumber()
30          {
31             if ( !recordSet.EOF )
32                recordNumber.innerText =
33                   recordSet.absolutePosition;
34             else
35                recordNumber.innerText = " ";
36          }
37
38          function forward()
39          {
40             recordSet.MoveNext();
41
42             if ( recordSet.EOF )
43                recordSet.MoveFirst();
44
45             colorSample.style.backgroundColor =
46                colorRGB.innerText;
47             displayRecordNumber();
48          }
49          // -->
50       </script>
51    </head>
52
53    <body onload = "displayRecordNumber()" onclick = "forward()">
54
55       <h1>XHTML Color Table</h1>
56       <h3>Click anywhere in the browser window
57          to move forward in the recordset.</h3>
58       <p><strong>Color Name: </strong>
59       <span id = "colorId" style = "font-family: monospace"
60          datasrc = "#Colors" datafld = "ColorName"></span><br />
61
62       <strong>Color RGB Value: </strong>
63       <span id = "colorRGB" style = "font-family: monospace"
64          datasrc = "#Colors" datafld = "ColorHexRGBValue">
65       </span><br />
66
67       Currently viewing record number
68       <span id = "recordNumber" style = "font-weight: 900">
69       </span><br />
70
71       <span id = "colorSample" style = "background-color: aqua;
72          color: 888888; font-size: 30pt">Color Sample
```

Fig. 16.2 Simple data binding. (Part 2 of 3.)

```
73          </span></p>
74
75      </body>
76  </html>
```

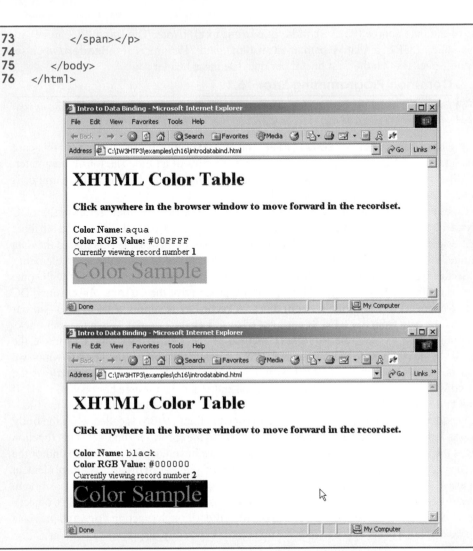

Fig. 16.2   Simple data binding. (Part 3 of 3.)

Line 1 of Fig. 16.1 begins our data file with a **header row**. This row specifies the names of the columns of data (`ColorName` and `ColorHexRGBValue`). Data in each field is enclosed in **text qualifiers** (@) and each field is separated with a **field delimiter** (|). Lines 21–22 in Fig. 16.2 indicate to the Tabular Data Control the text qualifier and field delimiter symbols chosen for use in this data source.

The `object` element (lines 16–23 in Fig. 16.2) inserts the Tabular Data Control—one of the Microsoft ActiveX controls built into Internet Explorer 6. Attribute `classid` specifies the ActiveX control to add to the Web page—here we use the `classid` of the Tabular Data Control (i.e., the fixed value of `CLSID:333C7BC4-460F-11D0-BC04-0080C7055A83`). Each ActiveX control has a unique `classid`.

The `param` tag specifies parameters for the object in the `object` element. Attribute `name` is the parameter name, and attribute `value` is the value. Parameter `DataURL` is the

URL of the data source (HTMLStandardColors.txt). [*Note*: The DataURL can be any fully qualified URL, a relative path or an absolute path.] Parameter UseHeader, when set to true, specifies that the first line of our data file has a header row.

Common Programming Error 16.1

Forgetting to set the UseHeader parameter to TRUE when you have a header row in your data source is an error that can cause problems in referencing columns.

The third parameter, TextQualifier, sets the **text qualifier** of our data (in this case to @). A text qualifier is the character placed on both ends of a field. The fourth parameter, FieldDelim, sets the field delimiter of our data (in this case to |). The field delimiter is the character separating different data fields.

Lines 59–60 bind the data to a span element. The datasrc attribute refers to the TDC object's id (Colors, in this case) preceded by a hash mark (#), and the datafld attribute specifies the name of the field to bind it to (ColorName, in this case). This places the data contained in the first **record** (i.e., row) of the ColorName column into the span element.

So far, we only have a static display of data. We can update it dynamically with some simple scripting. Line 27 assigns the recordset property of the Colors object (our TDC object element) to the variable recordSet. A **recordset** is simply a set of data—in our case, it is the data from our HTMLStandardColors.txt data source. When the user clicks in the page, line 41 calls the **MoveNext** method of the recordSet object to move the recordset to the next row in the data source. This automatically updates the span to which we bound our data. Note that line 42 determines whether the boolean EOF property of the recordSet is true. If true, it indicates that the end of the data source has been reached. If EOF is true, line 43 calls the **MoveFirst** method to move to the first recordset in the file.

The function displayRecordNumber (defined in lines 29–36) is called when the body loads (as indicated by line 53) or whenever we move in the recordset (line 47). This function updates the record number displayed on the page. If we have not yet reached the end of the data, lines 32–33 change the innerText property of the recordNumber span element (defined in lines 68–69) such that this element's text correctly reflects our current position in the recordset (i.e., the value of the absolutePosition property of the recordSet object). If we have somehow moved past the end of the recordset (though function forward prevents this), we display a blank space to indicate no record is currently displayed.

Common Programming Error 16.2

Trying to use the MoveNext or MovePrevious methods past the boundaries of the data source is a JavaScript error.

16.3 Moving within a Recordset

Most applications will probably need more functionality than simply moving forward in a recordset. Figure 16.3 demonstrates creating a user interface for navigating the data source of Fig. 16.1.

The switch in lines 31–64 evaluates the value passed to move when the user clicks one of the buttons in lines 93–103. The two new functions we use are **MoveLast** and **MovePrevious**, which move to the last recordset and the preceding recordset, respectively. Lines 43 and 54 determine if the beginning (BOF) or end (EOF) of the recordset has been reached. If so, the recordset moves to the last or first record, respectively.

```
1   <?xml version = "1.0"?>
2   <!DOCTYPE html PUBLIC "-//W3C//DTD XHTML 1.0 Transitional//EN"
3       "http://www.w3.org/TR/xhtml1/DTD/xhtml1-transitional.dtd">
4
5   <!-- Fig 16.3: moving.html       -->
6   <!-- Moving through a recordset -->
7
8   <html xmlns = "http://www.w3.org/1999/xhtml">
9       <head>
10          <title>Dynamic Recordset Viewing</title>
11          <object id = "Colors"
12              classid = "CLSID:333C7BC4-460F-11D0-BC04-0080C7055A83">
13              <param name = "DataURL" value =
14                  "HTMLStandardColors.txt" />
15              <param name = "UseHeader" value = "TRUE" />
16              <param name = "TextQualifier" value = "@" />
17              <param name = "FieldDelim" value = "|" />
18          </object>
19
20          <script type = "text/javascript">
21              <!--
22              var recordSet = Colors.recordset;
23
24              function update()
25              {
26                  h1Title.style.color = colorRGB.innerText;
27              }
28
29              function move( whereTo )
30              {
31                  switch ( whereTo ) {
32
33                      case "first":
34                          recordSet.MoveFirst();
35                          update();
36                          break;
37
38                      // If recordset is at beginning, move to end.
39                      case "previous":
40
41                          recordSet.MovePrevious();
42
43                          if ( recordSet.BOF )
44                              recordSet.MoveLast();
45
46                          update();
47                          break;
48
49                      // If recordset is at end, move to beginning.
50                      case "next":
51
52                          recordSet.MoveNext();
53
```

Fig. 16.3   Moving through a recordset using JavaScript. (Part 1 of 3.)

```
54                          if ( recordSet.EOF )
55                             recordSet.MoveFirst();
56
57                          update();
58                          break;
59
60                      case "last":
61                          recordSet.MoveLast();
62                          update();
63                          break;
64              }
65          }
66          // -->
67       </script>
68
69       <style type = "text/css">
70          input { background-color: khaki;
71                  color: green;
72                  font-weight: bold }
73       </style>
74    </head>
75
76    <body style = "background-color: darkkhaki">
77
78       <h1 style = "color: black" id = "h1Title">
79          XHTML Color Table</h1>
80       <span style = "position: absolute; left: 200; width: 270;
81          border-style: groove; text-align: center;
82          background-color: cornsilk; padding: 10">
83       <strong>Color Name: </strong>
84       <span id = "colorName" style = "font-family: monospace"
85          datasrc = "#Colors" datafld = "ColorName">ABC</span>
86       <br />
87
88       <strong>Color RGB Value: </strong>
89       <span id = "colorRGB" style = "font-family: monospace"
90          datasrc = "#Colors" datafld = "ColorHexRGBValue">ABC
91       </span><br />
92
93       <input type = "button" value = "First"
94          onclick = "move( 'first' );" />
95
96       <input type = "button" value = "Previous"
97          onclick = "move( 'previous' );" />
98
99       <input type = "button" value = "Next"
100         onclick = "move( 'next' );" />
101
102      <input type = "button" value = "Last"
103         onclick = "move( 'last' );" />
104      </span>
105
106   </body>
```

Fig. 16.3   Moving through a recordset using JavaScript. (Part 2 of 3.)

107 </html>

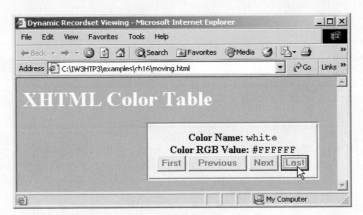

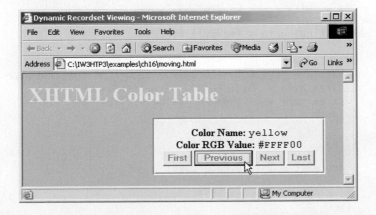

Fig. 16.3   Moving through a recordset using JavaScript. (Part 3 of 3.)

16.4 Binding to an `img`

Many different types of XHTML elements can be bound to data sources. One of the more interesting elements in which to bind data is the `img` element. Figure 16.4 lists a data source that contains image file names. Figure 16.5 binds an `img` element to the data source shown in Fig. 16.4.

Lines 59–60 bind the data source to an `img` element. When binding to an `img` element, changing the recordset updates the `src` attribute of the image. The script used to move through the recordset in this example is almost identical to that of the previous example. Clicking any of the navigation buttons in this example, however, changes the image displayed on screen, rather than the background color of the page.

```
1   image
2   numbers/0.gif
3   numbers/1.gif
4   numbers/2.gif
5   numbers/3.gif
6   numbers/4.gif
7   numbers/5.gif
8   numbers/6.gif
9   numbers/7.gif
10  numbers/8.gif
11  numbers/9.gif
```

Fig. 16.4   `images.txt` data source file for Fig. 16.5.

```
1   <?xml version = "1.0"?>
2   <!DOCTYPE html PUBLIC "-//W3C//DTD XHTML 1.0 Transitional//EN"
3      "http://www.w3.org/TR/xhtml1/DTD/xhtml1-transitional.dtd">
4
5   <!-- Fig. 16.5: bindimg.html  -->
6   <!-- Binding data to an image -->
7
8   <html xmlns = "http://www.w3.org/1999/xhtml">
9      <head>
10        <title>Binding to a img</title>
11
12        <object id = "Images"
13           classid = "CLSID:333C7BC4-460F-11D0-BC04-0080C7055A83">
14           <param name = "DataURL" value = "images.txt" />
15           <param name = "UseHeader" value = "True" />
16        </object>
17
18        <script type = "text/javascript">
19           <!--
20           recordSet = Images.recordset;
21
22           function move( whereTo )
23           {
```

Fig. 16.5   Binding data to an `img` element. (Part 1 of 3.)

```
24              switch( whereTo ) {
25
26                  case "first":
27                      recordSet.MoveFirst();
28                      break;
29
30                  case "previous":
31
32                      recordSet.MovePrevious();
33
34                      if ( recordSet.BOF )
35                          recordSet.MoveLast();
36
37                      break;
38
39                  case "next":
40
41                      recordSet.MoveNext();
42
43                      if ( recordSet.EOF )
44                          recordSet.MoveFirst();
45
46                      break;
47
48                  case "last":
49                      recordSet.MoveLast();
50                      break;
51              }
52          }
53          // -->
54      </script>
55  </head>
56
57  <body>
58
59      <img datasrc = "#Images" datafld = "image" alt = "Image"
60          style = "position: relative; left: 45px" /><br />
61
62      <input type = "button" value = "First"
63        onclick = "move( 'first' );" />
64
65      <input type = "button" value = "Previous"
66        onclick = "move( 'previous' );" />
67
68      <input type = "button" value = "Next"
69        onclick = "move( 'next' );" />
70
71      <input type = "button" value = "Last"
72        onclick = "move( 'last' );" />
73
74  </body>
75  </html>
```

Fig. 16.5   Binding data to an img element. (Part 2 of 3.)

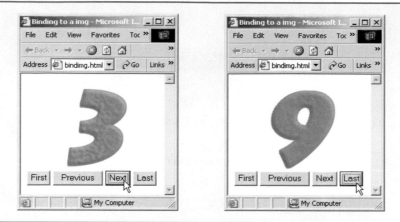

Fig. 16.5   Binding data to an `img` element. (Part 3 of 3.)

16.5 Binding to a `table`

Binding data to a `table` element is perhaps the most important feature of data binding. This is done somewhat differently from the data binding we have seen so far. Figure 16.6 binds the data in Fig. 16.1 to a `table` element.

```
1   <?xml version = "1.0"?>
2   <!DOCTYPE html PUBLIC "-//W3C//DTD XHTML 1.0 Strict//EN"
3       "http://www.w3.org/TR/xhtml1/DTD/xhtml1-strict.dtd">
4
5   <!-- Fig. 16.6: tablebind.html       -->
6   <!-- Using Data Binding with tables -->
7
8   <html xmlns = "http://www.w3.org/1999/xhtml">
9       <head>
10          <title>Data Binding and Tables</title>
11          <object id = "Colors"
12            classid = "CLSID:333C7BC4-460F-11D0-BC04-0080C7055A83">
13            <param name = "DataURL" value =
14                "HTMLStandardColors.txt" />
15            <param name = "UseHeader" value = "TRUE" />
16            <param name = "TextQualifier" value = "@" />
17            <param name = "FieldDelim" value = "|" />
18          </object>
19       </head>
20
21       <body style = "background-color: darkseagreen">
22
23          <h1>Binding Data to a <code>table</code></h1>
24
25          <table datasrc = "#Colors" style = "border-style: ridge;
26              border-color: darkseagreen;
27              background-color: lightcyan">
```

Fig. 16.6   Binding data to a `table` element. (Part 1 of 2.)

```
28
29          <thead>
30          <tr style = "background-color: mediumslateblue">
31             <th>Color Name</th>
32             <th>Color RGB Value</th>
33          </tr>
34          </thead>
35
36          <tbody>
37             <tr style = "background-color: lightsteelblue">
38                <td><span datafld = "ColorName"></span></td>
39                <td><span datafld = "ColorHexRGBValue"
40                   style = "font-family: monospace"></span></td>
41             </tr>
42          </tbody>
43
44       </table>
45
46    </body>
47 </html>
```

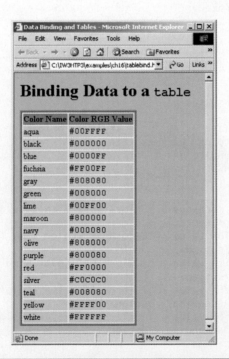

Fig. 16.6   Binding data to a `table` element. (Part 2 of 2.)

Lines 25–27 begin binding to the table by adding the `datasrc` attribute to the opening `table` tag. We complete the data binding in lines 38–39 by adding the `datafld` attribute to `span` elements that reside in the table cells. Note that in the file we only have one row of table cells—Internet Explorer iterates through the data file and creates a table row for each record it finds.

16.6 Sorting table Data

If you are manipulating a large data source, your client will probably need some way to sort the data. This is accomplished with the **Sort** property of the TDC (Fig. 16.7).

```
1    <?xml version = "1.0"?>
2    <!DOCTYPE html PUBLIC "-//W3C//DTD XHTML 1.0 Strict//EN"
3       "http://www.w3.org/TR/xhtml1/DTD/xhtml1-strict.dtd">
4
5    <!-- Fig 16.7: sorting.html -->
6    <!-- Sorting table data      -->
7
8    <html xmlns = "http://www.w3.org/1999/xhtml">
9       <head>
10          <title>Data Binding and Tables</title>
11          <object id = "Colors"
12             classid = "CLSID:333C7BC4-460F-11D0-BC04-0080C7055A83">
13             <param name = "DataURL" value =
14                "HTMLStandardColors.txt" />
15             <param name = "UseHeader" value = "TRUE" />
16             <param name = "TextQualifier" value = "@" />
17             <param name = "FieldDelim" value = "|" />
18          </object>
19       </head>
20
21       <body style = "background-color: darkseagreen">
22
23          <h1>Sorting Data</h1>
24
25          <table datasrc = "#Colors" style = "border-style: ridge;
26             border-color: darkseagreen;
27             background-color: lightcyan">
28             <caption>
29             Sort by:
30
31             <select onchange = "Colors.Sort = this.value;
32                Colors.Reset();">
33                <option value = "ColorName">Color Name (Ascending)
34                   </option>
35                <option value = "-ColorName">Color Name (Descending)
36                   </option>
37                <option value = "ColorHexRGBValue">Color RGB Value
38                   (Ascending)</option>
39                <option value = "-ColorHexRGBValue">Color RGB Value
40                   (Descending)</option>
41             </select>
42             </caption>
43
44             <thead>
45             <tr style = "background-color: mediumslateblue">
46                <th>Color Name</th>
47                <th>Color RGB Value</th>
48             </tr>
```

Fig. 16.7   Sorting data in a table. (Part 1 of 2.)

```
49              </thead>
50
51              <tbody>
52              <tr style = "background-color: lightsteelblue">
53                  <td><span datafld = "ColorName"></span></td>
54                  <td><span datafld = "ColorHexRGBValue"
55                      style = "font-family: monospace"></span></td>
56              </tr>
57              </tbody>
58
59          </table>
60
61      </body>
62  </html>
```

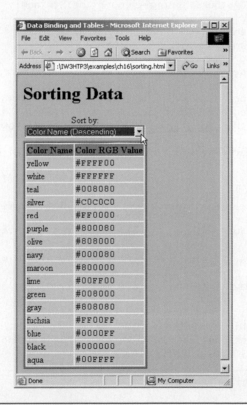

Fig. 16.7   Sorting data in a `table`. (Part 2 of 2.)

Lines 31–32 set up the `onchange` event that will enable us to sort our data by specifying the value of the TDC's `Sort` property (i.e., `Colors.Sort`). This example sets property `Sort` to the value of the selected `option` tag (`this.value`) when the `onchange` event is fired. JavaScript keyword `this` refers to the element in which the statement resides (i.e., the `select` element). Therefore, the `value` property refers to the currently selected `option` tag. After setting the `Sort` property to the specific column to use for sorting, we invoke the `Reset` method of the TDC to display the data in its new order.

Lines 33–40 set the `value` attributes of the `option` tags to the column names in our data file. By default, a column is sorted in ascending order. To sort in descending order, the column name is preceded by a minus sign (`-`).

16.7 Advanced Sorting and Filtering

The TDC can sort data containing multiple columns (Fig. 16.8). Combined with **filtering** (i.e., selecting data that meets a specific criteria), this provides a powerful means of data rendering. The example of Fig. 16.9 displays a grid of data pertaining to books and allows the user to sort by one or more columns in either ascending or descending order to obtain a customized view of the data. A user also can choose to filter by selected data.

```
1   @Title:String@|@Authors:String@|@Copyright:String@|
2   @Edition:String@|@Type:String@
3   @C How to Program@|@Deitel,Deitel@|@1992@|@1@|@BK@
4   @C How to Program@|@Deitel,Deitel@|@1994@|@2@|@BK@
5   @C++ How to Program@|@Deitel,Deitel@|@1994@|@1@|@BK@
6   @C++ How to Program@|@Deitel,Deitel@|@1998@|@2@|@BK@
7   @Java How to Program@|@Deitel,Deitel@|@1997@|@1@|@BK@
8   @Java How to Program@|@Deitel,Deitel@|@1998@|@2@|@BK@
9   @Java How to Program@|@Deitel,Deitel@|@2000@|@3@|@BK@
10  @Visual Basic 6 How to Program@|@Deitel,Deitel,Nieto@|@1999@|
11  @1@|@BK@
12  @Internet and World Wide Web How to Program@|@Deitel,Deitel@|
13  @2000@|@1@|@BK@
14  @The Complete C++ Training Course@|@Deitel,Deitel@|@1996@|
15  @1@|@BKMMCD@
16  @The Complete C++ Training Course@|@Deitel,Deitel@|@1998@|
17  @2@|@BKMMCD@
18  @The Complete Java Training Course@|@Deitel,Deitel@|@1997@|
19  @1@|@BKMMCD@
20  @The Complete Java Training Course@|@Deitel,Deitel@|@1998@|
21  @2@|@BKMMCD@
22  @The Complete Java Training Course@|@Deitel,Deitel@|@2000@|
23  @3@|@BKMMCD@
24  @The Complete Visual Basic 6 Training Course@|
25  @Deitel,Deitel,Nieto@|@1999@|@1@|@BKMMCD@
26  @The Complete Internet and World Wide Web Programming Training
Course@|@Deitel,Deitel@|@2000@|@1@|@BKMMCD@
```

Fig. 16.8   `DBPublications.txt` data file for Fig. 16.9.

```
1   <?xml version = "1.0"?>
2   <!DOCTYPE html PUBLIC "-//W3C//DTD XHTML 1.0 Strict//EN"
3      "http://www.w3.org/TR/xhtml1/DTD/xhtml1-strict.dtd">
4
5   <!-- Fig 16.9: advancedsort.html -->
6   <!-- Sorting and filtering data -->
7
8   <html xmlns = "http://www.w3.org/1999/xhtml">
```

Fig. 16.9   Advanced sorting and filtering. (Part 1 of 6.)

```
9    <head>
10       <title>Data Binding - Sorting and Filtering</title>
11
12       <object id = "Publications"
13          classid = "CLSID:333C7BC4-460F-11D0-BC04-0080C7055A83">
14          <param name = "DataURL" value = "DBPublications.txt" />
15          <param name = "UseHeader" value = "TRUE" />
16          <param name = "TextQualifier" value = "@" />
17          <param name = "FieldDelim" value = "|" />
18          <param name = "Sort" value = "+Title" />
19       </object>
20
21       <style type = "text/css">
22
23          a       { font-size: 9pt;
24                    text-decoration: underline;
25                    cursor: hand;
26                    color: blue }
27
28          caption { cursor: hand; }
29
30          span    { cursor: hand; }
31
32       </style>
33
34       <script type = "text/javascript">
35          <!--
36          var sortOrder;
37
38          function reSort( column, order )
39          {
40             if ( order )
41                sortOrder = "";
42             else
43                sortOrder = "-";
44
45             if ( event.ctrlKey ) {
46                Publications.Sort += "; " + sortOrder + column;
47                Publications.Reset();
48             }
49             else {
50                Publications.Sort = sortOrder + column;
51                Publications.Reset();
52             }
53
54             spanSort.innerText = "Current sort: " +
55                Publications.Sort;
56          }
57
58          function filter( filterText, filterColumn )
59          {
60             Publications.Filter = filterColumn + "=" +
61                filterText;
```

Fig. 16.9   Advanced sorting and filtering. (Part 2 of 6.)

```
62                Publications.Reset();
63                spanFilter.innerText =
64                   "Current filter: " + Publications.Filter;
65             }
66
67          function clearAll()
68          {
69                Publications.Sort = " ";
70                spanSort.innerText = "Current sort: None";
71                Publications.Filter = " ";
72                spanFilter.innerText = "Current filter: None";
73                Publications.Reset();
74          }
75          // -->
76       </script>
77    </head>
78
79    <body>
80       <h1>Advanced Sorting</h1>
81       <p>Click the link next to a column head to sort by that
82       column. To sort by more than one column at a time, hold
83       down Ctrl while you click another sorting link. Click
84       any cell to filter by the data of that cell. To clear
85       filters and sorts, click the green caption bar.</p>
86
87       <table datasrc = "#Publications" border = "1"
88          cellspacing = "0" cellpadding = "2" style =
89          "background-color: papayawhip;">
90
91          <caption style = "background-color: lightgreen;
92             padding: 5" onclick = "clearAll()">
93             <span id = "spanFilter" style = "font-weight: bold;
94                background-color: lavender">Current filter: None
95                </span>
96             <span id = "spanSort" style = "font-weight: bold;
97                background-color: khaki">Current sort: None</span>
98          </caption>
99
100         <thead>
101         <tr>
102            <th>Title <br />
103               (<a onclick = "reSort( 'Title', true )">
104                  Ascending</a>
105               <a onclick = "reSort( 'Title', false )">
106                  Descending</a>)
107            </th>
108
109            <th>Authors <br />
110               (<a onclick = "reSort( 'Authors', true )">
111                  Ascending</a>
112               <a onclick = "reSort( 'Authors', false )">
113                  Descending</a>)
114            </th>
```

Fig. 16.9   Advanced sorting and filtering. (Part 3 of 6.)

```
115
116             <th>Copyright <br />
117                (<a onclick = "reSort( 'Copyright', true )">
118                   Ascending</a>
119                <a onclick = "reSort( 'Copyright', false )">
120                   Descending</a>)
121             </th>
122
123             <th>Edition <br />
124                (<a onclick = "reSort( 'Edition', true )">
125                   Ascending</a>
126                <a onclick = "reSort( 'Edition', false )">
127                   Descending</a>)
128             </th>
129
130             <th>Type <br />
131                (<a onclick = "reSort( 'Type', true )">
132                   Ascending</a>
133                <a onclick = "reSort( 'Type', false )">
134                   Descending</a>)
135             </th>
136          </tr>
137          </thead>
138
139          <tr>
140             <td><span datafld = "Title" onclick =
141                "filter( this.innerText, 'Title' )"></span>
142             </td>
143
144             <td><span datafld = "Authors" onclick =
145                "filter( this.innerText, 'Authors')"></span>
146             </td>
147
148             <td><span datafld = "Copyright" onclick =
149                "filter( this.innerText, 'Copyright' )"></span>
150             </td>
151
152             <td><span datafld = "Edition" onclick =
153                "filter( this.innerText, 'Edition' )"></span>
154             </td>
155
156             <td><span datafld = "Type" onclick =
157                "filter( this.innerText, 'Type' )"></span>
158             </td>
159
160          </tr>
161
162       </table>
163
164    </body>
165 </html>
```

Fig. 16.9   Advanced sorting and filtering. (Part 4 of 6.)

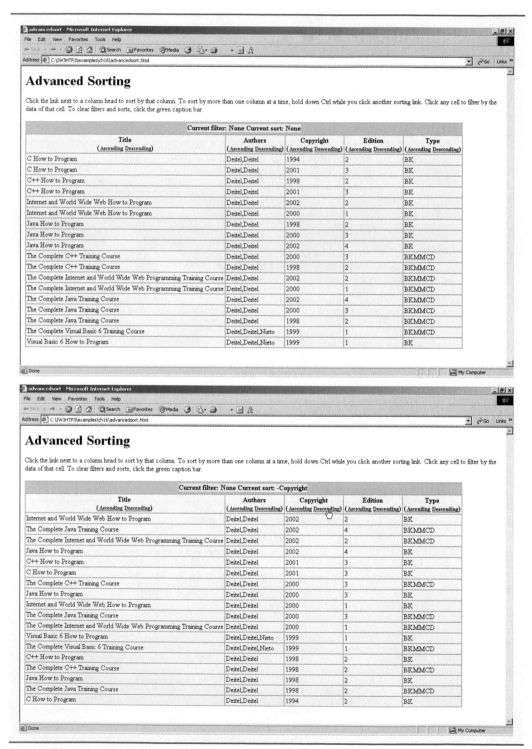

Fig. 16.9   Advanced sorting and filtering. (Part 5 of 6.)

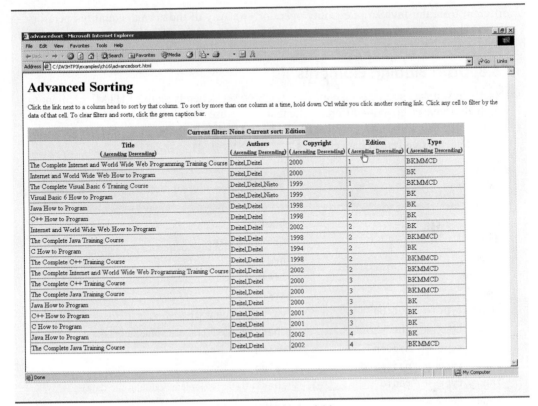

Fig. 16.9   Advanced sorting and filtering. (Part 6 of 6.)

Line 18 of Fig. 16.9 sets the Sort property of the TDC using a param tag. This provides the initial sorting order (in this case, alphabetically by Title). Lines 28 and 30 introduce the cursor CSS attribute, which specifies what the mouse cursor looks like when hovering over an object. In this case we set the property to hand (the same hand that appears when you move your cursor over a link). This lets the user know that a span is clickable when the cursor is moved over it.

When a user clicks the word **Ascending** or **Descending** in any of the column heads, the table resorts by that column. To do this, each column head has an associated onclick event that calls the reSort function, passing the name of the column to sort and a boolean value that specifies the sort order (true for ascending, false for descending).

The user can sort by multiple columns by holding *Ctrl* while clicking a link. Line 45 checks the boolean value event.ctrlKey, which returns true if *Ctrl* was pressed when the event was triggered. If the user did press *Ctrl*, line 46 adds another sort criterion to property Sort, separated from the first by a semicolon ("; ").

The Filter property filters out all records that do not have a cell matching the specified text. In this example, the user can click any cell to filter by the text inside that cell. Any cell, when clicked, calls the filter function, passing as parameters the text of the cell (this.innerText) and the column by which to filter. In the filter function, lines 60–61 set the Filter property of the TDC to the column and text by which the column should be filtered. In this case, the filter tests for equality using the equality operator = (which is different from the JavaScript equality operator ==). Any of the normal equality operators (=, <>) and relational operators (>, <, >=, <=) may be used for filtering.

16.8 Data Binding Elements

Exactly how a data source is displayed by the browser depends on the XHTML element to which the data is bound—different elements may use the data for different purposes. Figure 16.10 lists some elements that can be bound to data with the TDC, and the attributes of the elements that reflect data changes.

Element	Bindable Property/Attribute
a	href
div	Contained text
frame	href
iframe	href
img	src
input type = "button"	value (button text)
input type = "checkbox"	checked (use a boolean value in the data)
input type = "hidden"	value
input type = "password"	value
input type = "radio"	checked (use a boolean value in the data)
input type = "text"	value
marquee	Contained text
param	value
select	Selected option
span	Contained text
table	Cell elements
textarea	Contained text (value)

Fig. 16.10 XHTML elements that allow data binding.

16.9 Web Resources

www.microsoft.com/data
The Microsoft *Data Access Technologies* Web site provides information about Microsoft database access strategies and data source objects.

www.microsoft.com/mind/0797/databinding.asp
This article presents an overview of data-binding capabilities in Dynamic HTML.

SUMMARY

- With data binding, data need no longer reside exclusively on the server. Data can be maintained on the client in a manner that distinguishes it from the XHTML code on the page.

- Once the data is available on the client, the Web application designer can provide various functionality, especially the ability to sort and filter the data in various ways.
- The Tabular Data Control (TDC) is an ActiveX control that can be added to the page with an `object` tag.
- When a Web page is loaded with data-bound elements, the client retrieves the data from the data source specified by the TDC. The data is then formatted for display on the Web page and remains accessible on the client.
- A header row in a data source specifies the names of the columns. The data in each field can be encapsulated in text qualifiers, and the fields are separated with a field delimiter.
- An `object` tag inserts an ActiveX Tabular Data Control. The `classid` attribute specifies the ActiveX control identifier.
- The `param` tag specifies parameters for the object in the `object` tag. The `name` attribute is the parameter name, and the `value` attribute is the value. The `DataURL` parameter is the URL of the data source. The `UseHeader` parameter specifies that the first line of the data file is to have a header row when set to `true`. The `TextQualifier` parameter sets the text qualifier of the data. The `FieldDelim` parameter sets the field delimiter of the data.
- The `datasrc` attribute refers to the `id` of the TDC object, and the `datafld` attribute specifies the name of the field to which it is bound.
- The `MoveNext` method moves the current recordset forward by one row, automatically updating the bound element.
- The `EOF` property indicates whether the recordset has reached the end of the data source.
- The `MoveFirst` method moves the recordset to the first row in the file.
- The `BOF` property indicates whether the recordset is before the first row of the data source.
- When binding to an `img` element, changing the recordset updates the `src` attribute of the image.
- To bind to a table, add the `datasrc` attribute to the opening `table` tag. Then add the `datafld` attribute to `span` tags that reside in the table cells. Internet Explorer iterates through the data file, and creates a table row for each row it finds.
- The `Sort` property of the ActiveX control determines the column by which the data is sorted. Once the `Sort` property is set, call the `Reset` method to display the data in its new sort order. By default, a column will be sorted in ascending order—to sort in descending order, the column name is preceded by a minus sign (-).
- Setting the `Sort` property of the TDC using a `param` tag instead of scripting is useful for providing an initial sorting order.
- The `cursor` CSS attribute specifies what the mouse cursor will look like when hovering over an object. The value `hand` makes the mouse look like the same hand that appears when you move your cursor over a link.
- The boolean value `event.ctrlKey` returns `true` if *Ctrl* was held down when the event was triggered.
- An additional sort criterion can be added to the `Sort` property, separated from the first by a semicolon.
- The `Filter` property allows you to filter out all records that do not have a cell that matches the text you specify.
- Any of the equality operators (=, <>) and relational operators (>, <, >=, <=) can be used for filtering data in the TDC.

TERMINOLOGY

ActiveX control

ascending sort order

binding

BOF (beginning-of-file) property of `recordset`

bound element

`classid` property

column in a database

current record of a recordset

data binding

data source

data source object (DSO)

database

data-bound element

`datafld` attribute

`datasrc` attribute

`DataURL` property of Tabular Data Control

descending sort order

DSO (data source object)

EOF (end-of-file) property of `recordset`

field delimiter

field of a record

`FieldDelim` property of Tabular Data Control

filter data

`Filter` property of Tabular Data Control

header row

minus sign (–) for descending sort order

`MoveFirst` method of `recordset`

`MoveLast` method of `recordset`

`MoveNext` method of `recordset`

`MovePrevious` method of `recordset`

multicolumn sort

record

recordset

sort in ascending order

sort in descending order

`Sort` property of Tabular Data Control

Tabular Data Control (TDC)

text qualifier

`TextQualifer` property of TDC

`UseHeader` property of Tabular Data Control

SELF-REVIEW EXERCISES

16.1   State whether each of the following is *true* or *false*. If *false*, explain why.
   a) A TDC recordset is one row of data.
   b) You can bind any XHTML element to data sources.
   c) The `classid` attribute for the TDC never changes.
   d) `span` elements display bound data as inner text.
   e) `img` elements display bound data as `alt` text.
   f) You separate multiple sort criteria of the `Sort` property with a comma (,).
   g) The equality operator (=) is the only operator that can be used in filtering data.
   h) Calling `MoveNext` when EOF is true will move the recordset to the first row of data.
   i) Calling `MoveLast` when EOF is true causes an error.

16.2   Fill in the blank for each of the following statements:
   a) When binding data to a table, the _____ attribute is placed in the opening `<table>` tag, and the _____ attribute is placed inside the table cells.
   b) The TDC is a(n) _____ control.
   c) To sort in descending order, precede the sort criterion with a(n) _____.
   d) To display data with recently applied sorting, call the _____ method.
   e) The _____ parameter specifies that the data source has a header row.
   f) A(n) _____ encloses data in each field of a data source, and a(n) _____ separates fields in a data source.
   g) The _____ CSS property changes the appearance of the mouse cursor.

ANSWERS TO SELF-REVIEW EXERCISES

16.1   a) False. A TDC recordset contains all the rows of data in a data source. b) False; only some XHTML elements may be bound to data. c) True. d) True. e) False; data bound to `img` elements affects the `src` attribute of that `img`. f) False; you separate them with a semicolon (;). g) False; any of the equality operators or relational operators can be used. h) False; this causes an error. i) False; the recordset moves to the last row of data.

16.2   a) `datasrc, datafld`. b) ActiveX. c) minus sign, (-). d) `Reset`. e) `UseHeader`. f) text qualifier, field delimiter. g) `cursor`.

EXERCISES

16.3   Create a data source file with two columns: one for URLs, and one for URL descriptions. Bind the first column to an a element on a page and the second to a span element contained within the a element.

16.4   Bind the data source file you created in Exercise 16.3 to a `table` to create a table of clickable links.

16.5   Add a drop-down `select` list to Fig. 16.9 that allows you to choose the binary operator used for filter matching, from any of =, >, <, >= or <=.

16.6   Create a data source with a set of name/password pairs. Bind these fields to an `input type = "text"` and `input type = "password"` and provide navigation buttons to allow the user to move throughout the data source.

16.7   Apply the transitions you learned in Chapter 15 to Fig. 16.5 to create a virtual slide show out of a set of images whose names are bound to a TDC.

16.8   Modify the table binding example in Fig. 16.6 to store the names and phone numbers of between five and ten of your friends. Change the text file's name to `friends.txt`. The left column should be titled "Friends" and the right column should be titled "Phone Numbers."

Macromedia Flash™ MX 2004: Building Interactive Animations

Objectives

- To learn Flash MX 2004 multimedia development.
- To learn Flash animation techniques.
- To learn ActionScript 2.0, Flash's object-oriented programming language.
- To create an animation that preloads objects into a Flash movie.
- To add sound to Flash movies.
- To embed a Flash movie into a Web page.

A flash and where previously the brain held a dead fact, the soul grasps a living truth! At moments we are all artists.
Arnold Bennett

All the world's a stage, and all the men and women merely players; they have their exits and their entrances; and one man in his time plays many parts. . .
William Shakespeare

Science and technology and the various forms of art, all unite humanity in a single and interconnected system.
Zhores Aleksandrovich Medvedev

Music has charms to soothe a savage breast,
To soften rocks, or bend a knotted oak.
William Congreve

The true art of memory is the art of attention.
Samuel Johnson

Outline

17.1 Introduction

Macromedia *Flash MX 2004* is a commercial application that developers use to produce interactive, animated **movies**. Flash can be used to create Web-based banner advertisements, interactive Web sites, games and Web-based applications with stunning graphics and multimedia effects. An advantage Flash has over other multimedia-development applications is that it provides tools for drawing graphics, generating animation and adding sound and video. Flash movies can be embedded in Web pages, placed on CD-ROMs as independent applications or converted into standalone, executable programs.

Another advantage of using Flash to produce interactive content is that Flash includes tools for coding in its scripting language, **ActionScript 2.0**. ActionScript, which is similar to JavaScript, is the enabling technology for Flash interactivity.

To play Flash movies, the **Flash Player plug-in** must be installed in your Web browser. This plug-in has several versions, the most recent of which is version 7. Netscape versions 4.02 and higher and Microsoft Internet Explorer versions 4 and higher include the Flash Player plug-in. Other products with which the plug-in is bundled include several versions of Microsoft Windows (98SE, Me, NT 4, 2000 and XP), AOL 5.0 and higher and various Macintosh software products. According to Macromedia's statistics, more than 97% of Web users (approximately 436 million people) can view Flash movies without ever having to download the plug-in because it is bundled with software that they already own.[1] The plug-in can be downloaded from:

> www.macromedia.com/software/flashplayer

There are ways to detect whether a user has the appropriate plug-in to view Flash content. Macromedia provides a tool called the Flash Deployment Kit which contains files that work together to detect whether a suitable version of Macromedia Flash Player is installed in a user's Web browser. This kit may be downloaded from:

> www.macromedia.com/support/flash/player/flash_deployment_readme

This chapter provides an introduction to building Flash movies. You will create interactive buttons, add sound to movies, create special graphic effects and integrate ActionScript in movies.

A 30-day trial version of Flash MX 2004 is included on the CD that accompanies the book. This is a fully functional version of Flash MX 2004, which can be used for 30 days after the software is first installed.[2] To follow along with the examples in this chapter, please install this software before continuing. Detailed installation instructions are available on the CD. [*Note*: Do not change your computer's clock settings after installing Flash. Doing so causes the 30-day trial to expire immediately, disabling the program. Reinstalling Flash will not reactivate the program.]

Flash MX 2004 is available in two editions: Flash MX 2004 and Flash MX 2004 Professional. The Professional edition provides additional tools for database connectivity and for creating more powerful stand-alone applications. The trial software allows users to try out both editions. This chapter and its examples are based on the standard edition. We recommend choosing this edition during the trial software installation. If at anytime you want to try the Professional edition, you may do so by choosing **Switch to Flash MX Professional 2004...** from the **Help** menu.

17.2 Flash Movie Development

Once Flash MX 2004 is installed, open the program. Flash's **Start Page** appears by default. The **Start Page** contains options such as **Open a Recent Item** and **Create from Template**. The bottom of the page contains links to useful help topics and tutorials. [*Note*: For additional help, refer to Flash's **Help** panel or **Help** menu.] To create a blank Flash document, click **Flash Document** under the **Create New** heading. Flash opens a new file called **Untitled-1** in the Flash development environment (Fig. 17.1).

---

1. Flash Player statistics from Macromedia's Flash Player Penetration Survey Web site. <www.macromedia.com/software/flash/survey>.
2. Users of the trial version of Flash MX 2004 should be sure to open existing Flash .fla files from within the Flash application (by choosing **Open...** from its **File** menu). Attempting to open Flash files directly from My Computer or Windows Explorer may result in an error in the trial version. Users of the registered version of the software should not experience this problem.

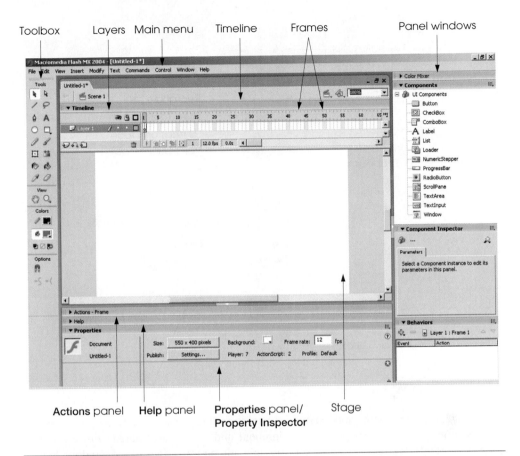

Fig. 17.1   Flash MX development environment.

The largest element in the development environment is the movie **stage**. The stage is the white area in which a developer places graphic elements during movie development. Only objects in this area will appear in the final movie. Directly above the stage is the **time-line**. The timeline represents the time period over which a movie runs. The timeline is divided into increments called **frames**, which are represented by gray and white rectangles. Each frame depicts a moment in time during the movie, into which the developer can insert movie elements.

The development environment contains several windows that provide options and tools for the creation of Flash movies. Many of these tools are located in the **toolbox**, the vertical window located along the left side of the development environment. The toolbox (Fig. 17.2) is divided into four sections, each containing tools and functions that help the developer create Flash movies. The **Tools** section contains tools that select, add and remove graphics from Flash movies. The **View** section contains two tools that determine what portion of the stage is visible at any time. The **Colors** section provides colors for shapes, lines and filled areas. The **Options** section contains settings for the **active tool** (i.e., the tool that is highlighted and is in use). A developer can make a tool behave differently by selecting a new mode from the **Options** section of the toolbox.

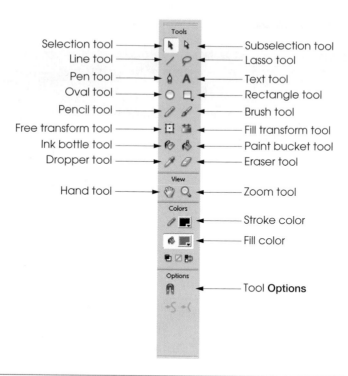

Fig. 17.2   Flash MX Toolbox.

Application windows called **panels** organize frequently used movie options. Panel options modify the size, shape, color, alignment and effects associated with a movie's graphic elements. By default, panels line the right and bottom edges of the window. Panels may be placed anywhere in the development environment by clicking and dragging the tab at the left edge of their light blue title bars.

The context-sensitive **Properties** panel (frequently referred to as the **Property Inspector**) is located at the bottom of the screen by default. This panel displays various information about the currently selected object. It is Flash's most useful tool for viewing and altering an object's properties.

The **Color Mixer**, **Actions**, **Components**, **Components Inspector**, **Behaviors**, and **Help** panels also appear in the development environment by default. A developer can access different panels by selecting them from the **Window** menu. To save a customized panel layout, select **Save Panel Layout…** from the **Window** menu. Select **Panel Sets** from the **Window** menu to load a saved panel layout or to restore the default panel layout.

17.3 Learning Flash with Hands-On Examples

The best way to learn Flash is to create complete Flash movies. The first example demonstrates how to create an interactive, animated button. ActionScript code will enable the button to produce a random text string each time the button is clicked. The following steps describe how to create a Flash movie file and customize the movie settings. Open a new Flash movie by selecting **New** from the **File** menu. In the **New Document** dialog (Fig. 17.3), select

General tab   Templates tab

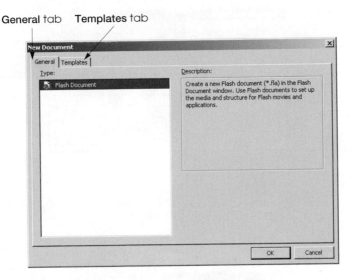

Fig. 17.3   New Document dialog.

Flash Document under the **General** tab and click **OK**. Next, choose **Save As...** from the **File** menu, and save the movie as CeoAssistant.fla. The .fla file extension is a Flash-specific extension for editable movies.

Good Programming Practice 17.1

Save each project with a meaningful name in its own folder. Creating a new folder for each movie helps keep projects organized. Also, Flash does not have an auto-save option, so remember to save your movies frequently.

Right click the stage to open a menu containing different movie options. Select **Document Properties...** to display the **Document Properties** dialog (Fig. 17.4). This dialog can also be accessed by selecting **Document...** from the **Modify** menu. Settings such as the **Frame rate**, **Dimensions** and **Background color** are configured in this dialog.

Frame rate sets the speed at which movie frames display. A higher frame rate causes more frames to be displayed in a given unit of time (the standard measurement is seconds), thus creating a faster movie. The frame rate for Flash movies on the Web is generally between 5 and 15 frames per second (**fps**). Flash's default frame rate is 12 fps. For this example, set the **Frame Rate** to **10** frames per second.

Performance Tip 17.1

Larger frame rates increase the amount of information to process, thus increasing the movie's file size. Be especially aware of file sizes when catering to low bandwidth Web users.

The **Background color** determines the color of the stage. Click the **Background color** box (called a **swatch**) to select the background color. A new dialog opens presenting a Web-safe palette. Web-safe palettes and color selection are discussed in detail in Chapter 3. Note that the mouse pointer changes into an eyedropper, which indicates that the developer may select a color. Choose a light blue color with the color-selection eyedropper (Fig. 17.5).

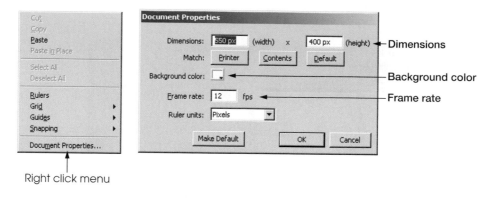

Right click menu

Fig. 17.4   Flash MX **Document Properties** dialog.

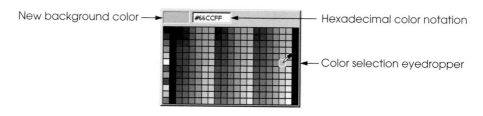

Fig. 17.5   Selecting a background color.

The box in the upper-left corner of the dialog displays the new background color. The **hexadecimal notation** for the selected color appears beside this box. The hexadecimal notation is the color code that a Web browser uses to render color. Hexadecimal notation is discussed in detail in Appendix E, Number Systems.

Dimensions define the size of the movie as it displays on the screen. For this example, set the movie **width** to **200** pixels and the movie **height** to **180** pixels. Click **OK** to apply the changes in the movie settings.

 Software Engineering Observation 17.1

The number of pixels per unit measure is called the resolution. The resolution of a Flash movie is always equal to the resolution of the monitor on which the movie displays.

 Software Engineering Observation 17.2

A movie's contents are not resized by changing the size of the movie stage.

With the new dimensions, the stage appears smaller. Select the **zoom** tool from the toolbox (Fig. 17.2) and click the stage once to enlarge it to 200% of its size (i.e., zoom in). The current zoom percentage appears in the upper-right corner of the viewing environment. Editing a movie with small dimensions is easier when the stage is enlarged. Press the *Alt* key while clicking the zoom tool to reduce the size of the work area (i.e., zoom out). Select the **hand** tool from the toolbox, and drag the stage to the center of the editing area. The hand tool may be accessed at any time by holding down the *spacebar* key.

17.3.1 Creating a Shape with the Oval Tool

Flash provides several editing tools and options for creating graphics. Flash has an advantage over most other graphic applications in that it creates shapes using **vectors**. Vectors are mathematical equations that Flash uses to define size, shape and color. Some graphics applications create **raster graphics** or **bitmapped graphics**.

When vector graphics are saved, they are stored using equations. Raster graphics are defined by areas of colored **pixels**—the unit of measurement for most computer monitors. Raster graphics typically have larger file sizes because the computer saves the information for every pixel. Vector and raster graphics also differ in their resizability. Vector graphics can be resized without losing clarity, whereas raster graphics lose clarity as they are enlarged or reduced. Chapter 3 provides a detailed discussion of vector and raster graphics in Section 3.3.

The next step is to create the interactive button out of a circular shape. A developer creates shapes by clicking and dragging with the shape tools. Select the oval tool from the toolbox. We use this tool to specify the button area. Every shape has a **stroke color** and a **fill color**. The stroke color is the color of a shape's outline, and the fill color is the color that fills the shape. Click the swatches in the **Colors** section of the toolbox (Fig. 17.6) to set the fill color to red and the stroke color to black. Select the colors from the Web-safe palette or enter their hexadecimal values.

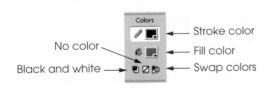

Fig. 17.6   Setting the fill and stroke colors.

Clicking the **black and white** button resets the stroke color to black and the fill color to white. A shape can be created without a fill or stroke color by selecting the **no color** option when you select either the stroke or fill swatch. Selecting the **swap colors** option switches the stroke and fill colors.

Create the oval anywhere on the stage by clicking and dragging with the oval tool while pressing the *Shift* key. The *Shift* key **constrains** the oval's proportions to have equal height and width (i.e., a circle). The same technique creates a square with the rectangle tool or draws a straight line with the pencil tool. Drag the mouse until the circle is approximately the size of a dime, then release the mouse button.

Note that when the shape is drawn, a dot appears in frame 1, the first frame of the timeline. This dot signifies a **keyframe** (Fig. 17.7), which indicates a point of change in a timeline. Whenever a shape is drawn in an empty frame, a keyframe is created.

The shape's fill and stroke may be edited individually. Click the red area with the **selection** tool (black arrow) to select the circle fill. A grid of white dots appears over an object when it is selected (Fig. 17.8). Click the black stroke around the circle while pressing the *Shift* key to add to this selection. A developer also can make multiple selections by clicking and dragging with the selection tool to draw a selection box around specific items.

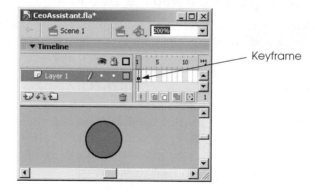

Fig. 17.7   Keyframe added to the timeline.

Fig. 17.8   Making multiple selections with the selection tool.

A shape's size can be modified with the **Property Inspector** (**Properties** panel) when the shape is selected (Fig. 17.9). The **Property Inspector** should be open by default. If it is not open, open it by selecting **Properties** from the **Window** menu or pressing *Ctrl+F3*.

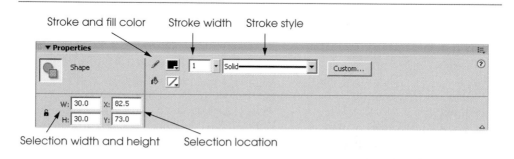

Fig. 17.9   Modifying the size of a shape with the **Property Inspector**.

Set the width and height of the circle by typing **30** into the **W:** text field and **30** into the **H:** text field. Entering an equal width and height maintains a **constrained aspect ratio** while changing the circle's size. A constrained aspect ratio maintains an object's proportions as it is resized. Press *Enter* to apply these values.

The next step is to modify the shape's color. We will apply a **gradient fill**. Gradient fills are gradual progressions of color. Open the **Color Swatches** panel, either by selecting **Color Swatches** from the **Design Panels** sub-menu of the **Window** menu, or pressing *Ctrl+F9*. The **Color Swatches** panel provides four **radial gradients** and three **linear gradients**, although a developer also can create and edit gradients with the **Color Mixer** panel.

Click outside the circle with the selection tool to deselect the circle. Now, select only the red fill with the selection tool. Change the fill color by clicking the red radial gradient fill in the **Color Swatches** panel. The gradient fills are located at the bottom of the **Color Swatches** panel (Fig. 17.10). The circle should now have a red radial gradient fill with a black stroke surrounding it.

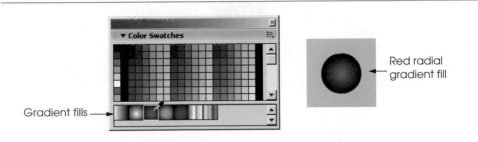

Fig. 17.10   Choosing a gradient fill.

17.3.2 Adding Text to a Button

Button titles communicate a button's function to the user. The easiest way to create a title is with the **text** tool. Create a button title by selecting the text tool and clicking the center of the button. Next, type **GO** in capital letters. Highlight the text with the text tool. Once text is selected, a developer can change the font, text size and font color with the **Property Inspector** (Fig. 17.11). Select a sans-serif font, such as **Arial** or **Verdana**, from the font drop-down list.

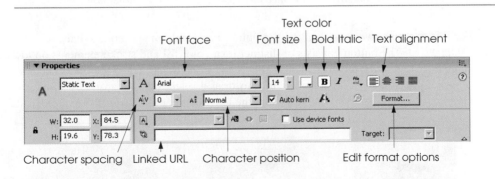

Fig. 17.11   Setting the font face, size, weight and color with the **Property Inspector**.

Look-and-Feel Observation 17.1

Sans-serif fonts, such as Arial, Helvetica and Verdana, are easier to read on a computer monitor, and therefore ensure better usability.

Set the font size to **14** pt either by typing the size into the font height field or by pressing the arrow button next to the font height field revealing the **size selection slider**. The size selection slider is a vertical slider that, when moved, changes the font size. Set the font weight to bold by clicking the bold button. Finally, change the font color by clicking the text color swatch and selecting white from the palette.

If the text does not appear in the correct location, drag it to the center of the button with the selection tool. The button is almost complete and should now look similar to Fig. 17.12.

Fig. 17.12 Adding text to the button.

17.3.3 Converting a Shape into a Symbol

A Flash movie consists of a **parent movie** and **symbols**. The parent movie, sometimes called a **scene**, contains the entire movie, including all graphics and symbols. The parent movie may contain several symbols that are reusable movie elements, such as **graphics**, **buttons** and **movie clips**. A parent movie timeline can contain numerous symbols, each with its own timeline and properties. A parent movie may have several **instances** of any given symbol (i.e., the same symbol appears multiple times in one movie). A developer can edit symbols independently of the parent movie by using the symbol's **editing stage**. The editing stage is separate from the parent movie stage and only contains one symbol.

 Good Programming Practice 17.2

Reusing symbols can drastically reduce file size, thereby allowing faster downloads.

For this example, we must convert the button into a button symbol so that it can be made interactive. The button consists of distinct text, color fill and stroke elements on the parent stage. These items are combined and treated as one object when the button is converted into a symbol. Use the selection tool to drag a **selection box** around the button, selecting the button fill, the button stroke and the text all at one time (Fig. 17.13).

Fig. 17.13 Selecting an object with the selection tool.

Now, select **Convert to Symbol...** from the **Modify** menu or use the shortcut *F8* on the keyboard. This opens the **Convert to Symbol** dialog, in which a developer sets the properties of a new symbol (Fig. 17.14).

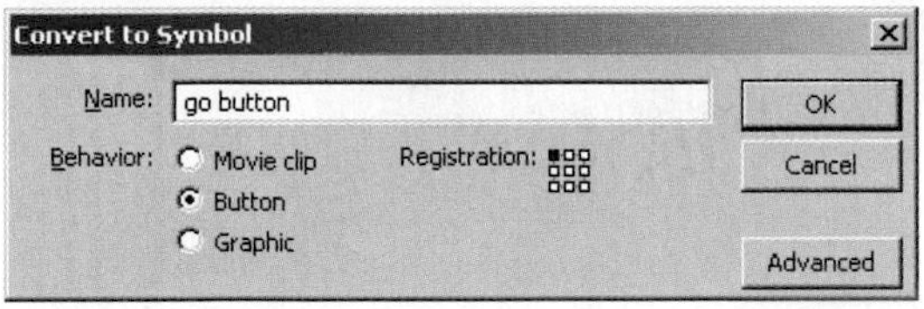

Fig. 17.14 Creating a new symbol with the **Convert to Symbol** dialog.

Every symbol in a Flash movie must have a unique name. It is a good idea to name symbols by their contents or function because this makes them easier to identify and reuse. Enter the name **go button** into the **Name** field of the **Convert to Symbol** dialog. The **Behavior** option determines the symbol's function in the movie.

In Flash, we can create three different types of symbols—movie clips, buttons and graphics. The behavior of a **movie clip symbol** is similar to that of the parent movie and ideal for recurring animations. **Graphic symbols** are ideal for static images and basic animations. **Button symbols** are objects that perform button actions, such as **rollovers** and hyperlinking. A rollover is an action that changes the appearance of a button when the mouse passes over it. For this example, select **Button** as the type of symbol and click **OK**. The button should now be surrounded by a blue box with crosshairs in the upper-left corner, indicating that the button is a symbol. Use the selection tool to drag the button to the lower-right corner of the stage.

The **Library** panel (Fig. 17.15) stores every symbol present in a movie and is accessed through the **Window** menu or by the shortcuts *Ctrl+L* or *F11*. Multiple instances of a symbol can be placed in a movie by dragging and dropping the symbol from the **Library** panel onto the stage.

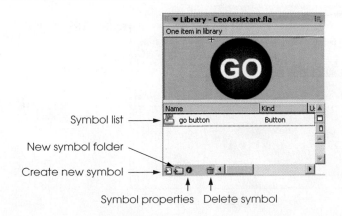

Fig. 17.15 **Library** panel.

The **Movie Explorer** displays the movie structure and is accessed by selecting **Movie Explorer** from the **Other Panels** sub-menu of the **Window** menu or by pressing *Alt+F3* (Fig. 17.16). The **Movie Explorer** panel illustrates the relationship between the parent movie (**Scene 1**), and its symbols.

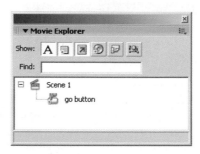

Fig. 17.16   Movie Explorer for `CeoAssistant.fla`.

17.3.4 Editing Button Symbols

The next step in our hands-on example is to make the button symbol interactive. The different components of a button symbol, such as its fill and type, may be edited in the symbol's editing stage. The developer may access a symbol's editing stage by double clicking the symbol in the **Library** or by pressing the **Edit Symbols** button and selecting the symbol name (Fig. 17.17). The separate pieces that make up the button (i.e., the text, the color fill and the stroke) can all be changed in the editing stage. A button symbol's timeline contains four frames, one for each of the button states (up, over and down) and one for the hit area.

The **up state** (indicated by the **Up** frame on screen) is the default state before the user presses the button or rolls over it with the mouse. Control shifts to the **over state** (i.e., the

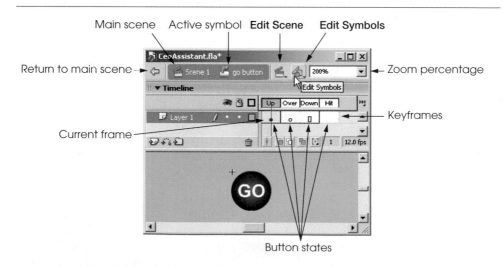

Fig. 17.17   Modifying button states with a button's editing stage.

Over frame) when the user rolls over the button with the mouse cursor. The button's **down state** (i.e., the **Down** frame) plays when a user presses a button. Developers can create interactive, user-responsive buttons by customizing the appearance of a button in each of these states. Graphic elements in the **hit state** (i.e., the **Hit** frame) are not visible when viewing the movie; they exist simply to define the active area of the button (i.e., the area that can be clicked). The hit state will be discussed more in Section 17.7, Creating a Web-Site Introduction.

By default, buttons only have the up state activated when they are created. The developer may activate other states by adding keyframes to the other three frames. Keyframes, discussed in the next section, determine how a button reacts when it is rolled over or clicked with the mouse.

17.3.5 Adding Keyframes

Keyframes determine different points of change in a Flash movie and appear in the timeline as gray with a black dot. By adding keyframes to a button symbol's timeline, the developer can control how the button reacts to user input. The following step shows how to create a button rollover. A rollover is added by inserting a keyframe in the button's **Over** frame, then changing the button's appearance in that frame. Right click the **Over** frame and select **Insert Keyframe** from the resulting menu or press *F6* (Fig. 17.18).

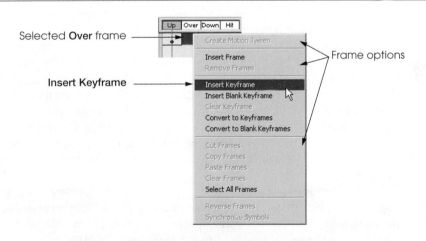

Fig. 17.18 Inserting a keyframe.

Select the **Over** frame and click outside the button area with the selection tool to deselect the button's components. Change the color of the button in the over state from red gradient fill to green gradient fill by reselecting only the fill portion of the button with the selection tool. Select the green gradient fill in the **Color Swatches** panel to change the color of the button in the over state. Changing the color of the button in the over state does not affect the color of the button in the up state. Now, when the user moves the cursor over the button (in the up state) the button animation is replaced by the animation in the over state. Here, we only change the button's color, but we could have created an entirely new animation in the over state. The button will now change from red to green when the user rolls over the button with the mouse. The button will return to red when the mouse is no longer positioned over the button.

17.3.6 Adding Sound to a Button

The next step is to add a sound effect that plays when a user clicks the button. Flash imports sounds in the WAV (Windows), AIFF (Macintosh) or MP3 formats. Several button sounds are available free for download from sites such as Flashkit (www.flashkit.com) and Muinar (www.sounds.muinar.com). For this example, download the **cash register** sound in WAV format from

> www.flashkit.com/soundfx/Industrial_Commercial/Cash

Click the **Download** link to download the sound from this site. This link opens a new Web page from which the user chooses the sound format. Choose **WAV** as the file format by clicking the **WAV** link. This link begins the download process. Select **Save** in the **File Download** dialog and save the file to the same folder as CeoAssistant.fla. Downloaded sound files usually are compressed as **ZIP archive** files. An archiving program such as *WinZip* can extract the sound file from the archive. WinZip is available as a trial download from www.winzip.com. Once WinZip is installed on a computer, extract a ZIP file by right clicking the file name in Windows Explorer and, in the resulting menu, selecting **Extract To Folder** from the **WinZip** sub-menu. This menu item extracts the sound file and saves it in the same folder as the ZIP archive. The WinZip Web site provides detailed instructions on how to use WinZip to compress and extract files.

Once the sound file is extracted, it can be imported into Flash. Import the sound into the **Library** by choosing **Import to Library** from the **Import** sub-menu of the **File** menu. Select **All Formats** in the **Files of type** field of the **Import** dialog so that all available files are displayed. Select the sound file and press the **Open** button. This imports the sound file and places it in the movie's **Library**, making it available to use in the movie.

A developer can add sound to a movie by placing the sound clip in a keyframe or over a series of frames. For this example, we add the sound to the button's down state so that the sound plays when the user presses the button. Select the button's **Down** frame and press *F6* to add a keyframe.

Add the sound to the **Down** keyframe by dragging it from the **Library** to the stage. Open the **Property Inspector** and select the **Down** frame in the timeline to define the sound's properties in the movie. To make sure the desired sound has been added to the keyframe, choose the sound file name from the **Sound** drop-down list. This list contains all the sounds that have been added to the movie. Make sure the **Sync** field is set to **Event** so that the sound plays when the user clicks the button. If the **Down** frame has a blue wave or line through it, the sound effect has been added to the button (Fig. 17.19).

The next step is to optimize the sound for the Web. Double click the sound icon in the **Library** panel to open the **Sound Properties** dialog (Fig. 17.20). The settings in this dialog change the way that the sound is saved in the final movie. Different settings are optimal for different sounds and different audiences. For this example, set the **Compression** type to **Raw**, which does not compress the sound, making it appropriate for short sound clips. If the sound clip is long, choose **APDCM** (**Adaptive Differential Pulse Code Modulation**) as the compression type to reduce file size. When a developer changes the **Compression** type from **Default**, the **Sample Rate** and **Preprocessing** options appear in the dialog.

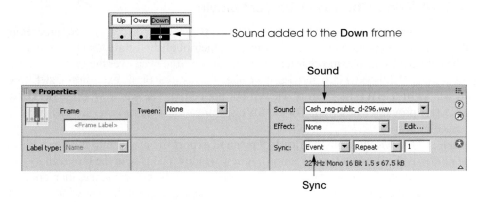

Fig. 17.19   Adding sound to a button.

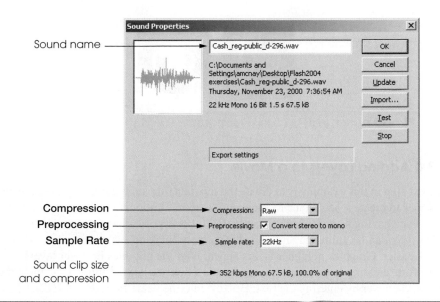

Fig. 17.20   Optimizing sound with the **Sound Properties** dialog.

The **Sample Rate** of a sound clip is the sound's frequency, which controls the sound's playback quality. Set the **Sample Rate** to **11kHz** or **22kHz** to reduce the size of the sound file while maintaining sound clarity. The **Preprocessing** option converts stereo to mono sound. For low-quality sounds, it is a good idea to select this option because it reduces the audio file size. Press **OK** to apply these settings.

The sound clip is now optimized for use on the Web. Return to the parent movie by pressing the **Edit Scene** button and selecting **Scene 1** or by clicking **Scene 1** at the top of the movie window.

Performance Tip 17.2

A sample rate of 11kHz or higher is good for voice audio. Music should have a sample rate of 22kHz or higher to maintain sound quality.

17.3.7 Verifying Changes with Test Movie

It is a good idea to make sure that movie components function correctly before proceeding further with development. Movies can be viewed in their **published state** with the Flash Player. The published state of a movie is how it would appear if viewed over the Web or with the Flash Player. Published Flash movies have the Shockwave Flash extension **.swf** (pronounced "swiff"). SWF files can be viewed but not edited. The site **www.openswf.org/spec.html** provides a description of the SWF specification. Other Flash file extensions are discussed in Section 17.4.

Select **Test Movie** from the **Control** menu to **export** the movie into the Flash Player (*Ctrl+Enter* is the shortcut for this action). A new window opens with the movie in its published state. Move the cursor over the **GO** button to view the color change, then click the button to play the sound (Fig. 17.21). To return to the stage, close the test window. If the button's color does not change, return to the button's editing stage to make sure that the correct steps were followed.

Up state ──→   ←── Over state

Fig. 17.21   **GO** button in its up and over states.

17.3.8 Adding Layers to a Movie

The next step in this example is to create the movie's title animation. It is a good idea for a developer to create a new **layer** for new movie items. A movie can be composed of many layers, each having its own attributes and effects. Layers organize different movie elements so that they can be animated and edited separately, making the composition of complex movies easier. Graphics in higher layers appear over the graphics in lower layers.

Before creating a new title layer, double click the text: **Layer 1** in the timeline. Rename the layer by entering the text: **Button** into the name field (Fig. 17.22).

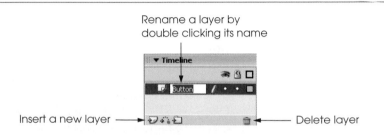

Rename a layer by
double clicking its name

Insert a new layer ──→   ←── Delete layer

Fig. 17.22   Renaming a layer.

Create a new layer for the title animation by clicking the insert layer button or by selecting **Layer** from the **Timeline** sub-menu of the **Insert** menu. The insert layer button places a layer named **Layer 2** above the selected layer. Change the name of **Layer 2** to **Title**. Activate the new layer by clicking its name.

Good Programming Practice 17.3

Always give movie layers descriptive names. Descriptive names are especially helpful when working with many layers.

Select the text tool to create the title text. Click with the type tool in the center of the stage towards the top. Use the **Property Inspector** to set the font to **Arial**, the text color to navy blue (hexadecimal value #000099) and the font size to **20** pt (Fig. 17.23). Set the text alignment to center by clicking the center justify button.

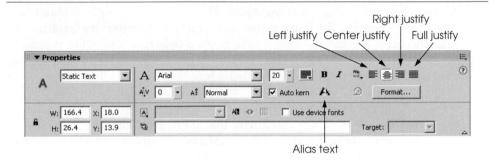

Fig. 17.23 Setting text alignment with the **Property Inspector**.

Type the title **CEO Assistant 1.0** (Fig. 17.24). The text may appear to have jagged edges, which can be remedied by deselecting the **alias text** button in the **Property Inspector** to turn on anti-aliasing. **Anti-aliasing** smooths edges on scalable fonts and other graphics by blending the color of the edge pixels with the color of the background on which the text is placed.

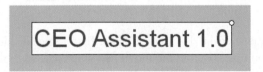

Fig. 17.24 Creating a title with the text tool.

After applying anti-aliasing, click the selection tool. A blue box should appear around the text, indicating that it is a **grouped object**. This text is a grouped object because each letter is a part of a text string and cannot be edited independently. Text can be ungrouped or regrouped for color editing, shape modification or animation (as we will see in a later example). However, once text has been ungrouped, it may not be edited with the text tool.

17.3.9 Animating Text with Tweening

Animations in Flash are created by inserting keyframes into the timeline. Each keyframe represents a significant change in the position or appearance of the animated object.

A developer may use several methods to animate objects in Flash. One method is to create a series of successive keyframes in the timeline. Modifying the animated object in each keyframe creates an animation as the movie plays. Another method is to insert a keyframe later in the timeline representing the final appearance and position of the object, then create a **tween** between the two keyframes. Tweening, also known as **morphing**, is an automated process in which Flash creates the intermediate steps of the animation between two keyframes.

Performance Tip 17.3

Tweened animations have smaller file sizes than frame-by-frame animations because Flash stores only the keyframe information. Tweened animation may have only two keyframes whereas frame-by-frame animation would require 20 or 30 keyframes.

Flash provides two methods to tween objects. **Shape tweening** morphs an object from one shape to another shape. For instance, the word "star" could morph into the shape of a star. Shape tweening can only be applied to ungrouped objects, not symbols or grouped objects. Be sure to ungroup text before attempting to create a shape tween. **Motion tweening** moves objects around the stage. Motion tweening can be applied to symbols or grouped objects.

At this point in the development of the example movie, only frame 1 is occupied in each layer. Keyframes must be designated in the timeline before adding the motion tween. Click frame 15 in the **Title** layer and press *F6* to add a new keyframe. All the intermediate frames in the timeline should turn gray, indicating that they are active (Fig. 17.25). Until the motion tween is added, each active frame contains the same image as the first frame.

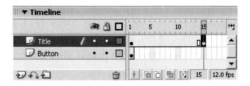

Fig. 17.25 Adding a keyframe to create an animation.

The button disappears from the movie after the first frame because only the first frame is active in the button layer. Before the movie is completed, we will move the button to frame 15 of its layer so that the button appears once the animation stops.

We now create a motion tween by modifying the position of the title text. Select frame 1 of the **Title** layer and select the title text with the selection tool. Drag the title text directly above the stage. When the motion tween is added, the title will move onto the stage. Add the motion tween by right clicking frame 1 in the **Title** layer. Then select **Create Motion Tween** from the **Insert** menu. Tweens also can be added using the **Property Inspector**. Frames 2–14 should turn blue, with an arrow pointing from the keyframe in frame 1 to the keyframe in frame 15 (Fig. 17.26).

Test the movie again with the Flash Player by pressing *Ctrl+Enter* to view the new animation. Note that the animation continues to loop—all Flash movies loop by default. Adding the ActionScript **method stop** to the last frame in the movie stops the movie from looping. For this example, click frame 15 of the **Title** layer, and open the **Actions** panel (Fig. 17.27). The **Actions** panel is used to add actions (i.e., scripted behaviors) to symbols and frames.

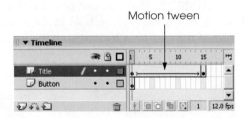

Fig. 17.26 Creating a motion tween.

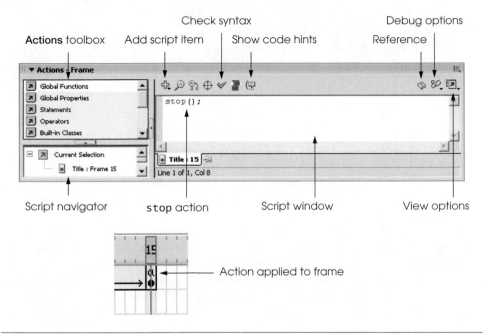

Fig. 17.27 Adding ActionScript to a frame with the **Actions** panel.

Minimize the **Actions** panel by clicking the down arrow in its title bar. The small letter **a** in frame 15 of the **Title** layer indicates the new action. Test the movie again in the Flash Player. Now, the animation should play only once.

The next step is to move the button to frame 15 so that it appears only at the end of the movie. Add a keyframe to frame 15 of the **Button** layer. A copy of the button should appear in the new keyframe. Select the button in the first frame and delete it by pressing the *Delete* key. The button will now only appear in the keyframe at the end of the movie.

17.3.10 Adding a Text Field

The final component of our movie is a **text field**, which contains a string of text that changes every time the user presses the button. A variable name is given to the text field so that ActionScript added to the button can control its contents.

Create a layer named **Advice** for the new text field, and add a keyframe to frame 15 of the **Advice** layer. Select the text tool and create the text field by clicking and dragging with the mouse in the stage (Fig. 17.28). Place the text field directly below the title. Set the text font to **Courier New, 12 pt** and the style to bold in the **Property Inspector**. The developer can alter the size of the text field by dragging the **anchor** that appears in its upper-right corner.

Fig. 17.28 Creating a text field.

We will now assign a variable name to the text field. Select the text field and open the **Property Inspector** (Fig. 17.29). The **Property Inspector** contains several options for modifying text fields. The top-left field contains the different types of text fields. **Static Text**, the default setting for this panel, creates text that does not change. The second option, **Dynamic Text**, creates text that can be changed or determined by outside variables through ActionScript. When a developer selects this text type, new options appear below this field. The line type drop-down list specifies the text field size as either a single line or multiple lines of text. The **Var** field allows the developer to give the text field a variable name. Then, by incorporating this variable into a script, the developer can control the text box contents. For example, if the text field variable name is `newText`, the developer could write a script setting `newText` equal to a string or a function output. The third text type, **Input Text**, creates a text field into which the viewers of the movie can input their own text.

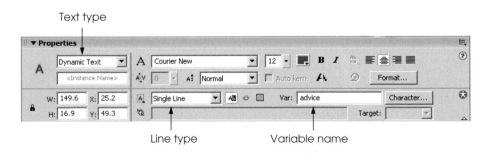

Fig. 17.29 Creating a dynamic text field with the **Property Inspector**.

For this example, select **Dynamic Text** as the text type. Set the line type to **Single Line** and enter `advice` as the variable name. This variable will be incorporated into a script later in this example.

17.3.11 Adding ActionScript

All the movie objects are now in place, so CEO Assistant 1.0 is almost complete. The final step is to add ActionScript to the button, enabling the script to change the contents of the text field every time a user clicks the button. Our script calls a built-in Flash function to generate a random number. This random number corresponds to a message in a list of possible messages to display. [*Note*: The ActionScript in this chapter has been formatted to conform with the code-layout conventions of this book. The Flash application may produce code that is formatted differently.]

Make sure that you are working in frame 15 of the **Button** layer. Select the **GO** button on the stage and open the **Actions** panel.

We want the action to occur when the user clicks the button. To achieve this, press the add button, labeled **+**, and select **Global Functions** from the resulting pop-up menu. Then, select **Movie Clip Control** from the **Global Functions** menu. In the resulting submenu, select **on**. Select **press** from the code hint menu or enter it directly in the script window (Fig. 17.30). press is now the event for the on event handler. The code hint menu can be accessed any time while in the script window by pressing the **show code hint** button in the **Actions** panel.

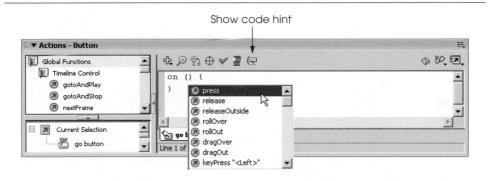

Fig. 17.30   Adding an action to a button with the **Actions** panel.

The ActionScript window contains the code

```
on ( press ) {
}
```

The on (press) action specifies that an action is performed when the user clicks the button. The next step is to add the code to define the result of the press event. Click the cursor within the curly braces of the on function and create a new line by pressing *Enter*. Click the **+** button and select **Statements**. Then, in the **Variables** submenu select **var**. Create a new variable named randomNumber by typing randomNumber, followed by an equals sign (=). The code should now look like

```
on ( press ) {
    var randomNumber =
}
```

The value assigned to randomNumber is designated after the =. For this example, we use a function that chooses a random number from 0 to 4. To insert the function click the

+ button and select **Functions** from the **Deprecated** sub-menu. Choose **random** and enter the number 5 inside the parentheses. The number inside the parentheses sets the argument for function `random`. The code should now read:

```
on ( press ) {
    var randomNumber = random ( 5 );
}
```

Common Programming Error 17.1

ActionScript is case sensitive. Be aware of the case when entering arguments or variable names.

Each time a user presses the button, the value of the variable `randomNumber` is set to a new random number between 0 and 4. This random number determines the text string that appears in the text field. A series of `if` statements sets the text field's value according to the value of `randomNumber`. [*Note*: For more on `if` statements, refer to Chapter 8, JavaScript: Control Structures I.]

On a new line in the `on` function, type the code

```
if ( randomNumber == 0 ) {
}
```

so that the full code reads

```
on ( press ) {
    var randomNumber = random ( 5 );

    if ( randomNumber == 0 ) {
    }
}
```

We use `if…else` statements to cause different text to appear in the `advice` text field depending on the value of the variable `randomNumber`. The code currently causes an action to be performed only if `randomNumber` is equal to 0.

Common Programming Error 17.2

When testing equality, use the == operator. The = operator assigns a value to a variable; it does not test equality.

Next, we add four nested `if` statements following the initial `if` statement. Five equality tests are needed to perform five different actions, each corresponding to one of the possible values of the random number. Add the appropriate `if` statements so the code appears as follows:

```
on ( press ) {
    set ( randomNumber, random ( 5 ) );

    if ( randomNumber == 0 ) {
    } else if ( randomNumber == 1 ) {
    } else if ( randomNumber == 2 ) {
    } else if ( randomNumber == 3 ) {
    } else if ( randomNumber == 4 ) {
    }
}
```

For these numbers to produce text in the text field, actions must be added to each branch of the if...else statement. Within the curly braces of the first if statement, add the code

```
advice = "Hire Someone!";
```

Each time randomNumber is set to 0, the advice text field will read **Hire Someone!**. Add similar code to each if statement, giving the variable advice a new string value each time. The code should now resemble the following, though the advice string value may vary:

```
on ( press ) {
    var randomNumber = random ( 5 );

    if ( randomNumber == 0 ) {
        advice = "Hire Someone!";
    } else if ( randomNumber == 1 ) {
        advice = "Buy a Yacht!";
    } else if ( randomNumber == 2 ) {
        advice = "Buy Stock!";
    } else if ( randomNumber == 3 ) {
        advice = "Go Golfing!";
    } else if ( randomNumber == 4 ) {
        advice = "Hold A Meeting!";
    }
}
```

If you feel ambitious, increase the number of advice statements by making the argument for the random function larger and adding more if statements. Minimize the **Actions** panel to continue.

Congratulations! You have now completed building CEO Assistant 1.0. After testing the movie with the Flash Player, return to the main window and save the file.

17.4 Creating a Projector (.exe) File with Publish

Flash movies must be **published** for users to view them outside Flash MX environment and Flash player. This section discusses the more common methods of publishing Flash movies. The Flash **Publish** operation is similar to the **Export** command in other programs, but it has more advanced features. For this example, we want to publish in two formats, Flash and **Windows Projector**, which creates a standard Windows-executable file. Select **Publish Settings...** from the **File** menu to open the **Publish Settings** dialog.

Select the **Flash** and **Windows Projector** checkboxes and uncheck all the others. Then click the **Flash** tab at the top of the dialog. This section of the dialog allows the developer to choose the Flash settings. Flash movies may be published in a different Flash version to enable support by older Flash players. Bear in mind some elements of ActionScript 2.0 are not supported by older players, so choose a version with care. Click **OK** to enable the new publishing settings. Publish the movie in both formats by selecting **Publish** from the **File** menu. When the publish function is complete, the directory in which you save the movie will have two new files (Fig. 17.31).

As we can see in the Ceo Assistant 1.0 example, Flash is a feature-rich program. We have only begun to use Flash to its full potential. ActionScript can create sophisticated

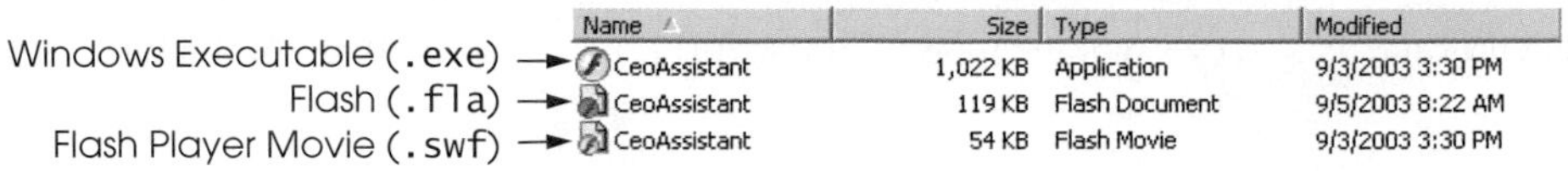

	Name ⋏	Size	Type	Modified
Windows Executable (.exe) →	CeoAssistant	1,022 KB	Application	9/3/2003 3:30 PM
Flash (.fla) →	CeoAssistant	119 KB	Flash Document	9/5/2003 8:22 AM
Flash Player Movie (.swf) →	CeoAssistant	54 KB	Flash Movie	9/3/2003 3:30 PM

Fig. 17.31 Published Flash files.

programs and interactive movies. It also enables Flash to interact with ASP.NET (Chapters 23–24), CGI (Chapter 25), PHP (Chapter 26), ColdFusion (Chapter 27) and JavaScript (Chapters 7–12), making it a program that integrates smoothly into a Web environment.

17.5 Manually Embedding a Flash Movie in a Web Page

An important aspect of Web development is ensuring browser compatibility. Flash movies have the same appearance in any browser with the Flash Player plug-in. Embedding a Flash SWF file into an XHTML Web document enables Web browsers to display Flash content. However, to ensure that a Flash movie is visible in both Microsoft Internet Explorer and Netscape, two different tags must be placed in the Web document to embed the Flash movie. Flash movies are added to a Web site with the **object** and **embed** elements. The **object** element allows the movie to be viewed with Internet Explorer, and **embed** makes the movie viewable in Netscape. Figure 17.32 presents an example of source code to embed a Flash movie in a Web document so that it displays in both Internet Explorer and Netscape.

```
1   <?xml version = "1.0"?>
2   <!DOCTYPE html PUBLIC "-//W3C//DTD XHTML 1.0 Transitional//EN"
3      "http://www.w3.org/TR/xhtml1/DTD/xhtml1-transitional.dtd">
4
5   <!-- Fig. 17.32: embedFlash.html              -->
6   <!-- Embedding a Flash movie into a Web site -->
7
8   <html xmlns = "http://www.w3.org/1999/xhtml">
9
10     <head>
11        <title>Adding Flash to your Web site</title>
12     </head>
13
14     <body>
15
16        <!-- The following object tag tells the    -->
17        <!-- Microsoft Internet Explorer browser to -->
18        <!-- play the Flash movie and where to find -->
19        <!-- the Flash Player plug-in if it is not  -->
20        <!-- installed.                             -->
21
22        <object classid =
23           "clsid:d27cdb6e-ae6d-11cf-96b8-444553540000"
24           codebase = "http://download.macromedia.com/pub/shockwave/
25           cabs/flash/swflash.cab#version=7,0,0,0">
26           <param name = "movie" value = "CeoAssistant.swf" />
```

Fig. 17.32 Embedding a Flash movie into a Web site. (Part 1 of 2.)

```
27
28          <!-- The following embed tag tells the Netscape -->
29          <!-- browser to play the Flash movie and where  -->
30          <!-- to find the Flash Player plug-in if it is   -->
31          <!-- not installed.                              -->
32
33          <embed src = "CeoAssistant.swf" pluginspage =
34             "http://www.macromedia.com/go/getflashplayer">
35          </embed>
36
37          <!-- Non-Flash viewing page content -->
38          <noembed>
39             This Web site contains the CEO Assistant 1.0
40             Flash movie. You must have the Flash Player
41             plug-in to view the Flash movie.
42          </noembed>
43
44       </object>
45
46    </body>
47 </html>
```

Fig. 17.32   Embedding a Flash movie into a Web site. (Part 2 of 2.)

The `object` element in Fig. 17.32 has several attributes. For a developer to properly embed the movie, the `classid` and `codebase` attributes must appear exactly as shown in lines 22–25. The `codebase` attribute prompts users to download the plug-in if they do not have it. It is also important to place the `embed` element inside the `object` element. Microsoft Internet Explorer ignores tags placed inside the `object` element. Netscape reads only the `embed` element; it ignores the `object` element. The `noembed` element in lines 38–42 provides alternative content for those without the Flash Player. Any XHTML elements can be placed within the `noembed` element.

Flash movies can also be published directly in HTML format. Select **Publish Settings...** from the **File** menu and select the **HTML** checkbox. Publish the movie again. The folder containing the movie will now contain an HTML file with the Flash movie embedded in it. This page can be used as is, or its code can be copied into another HTML or XHTML document.

Good Programming Practice 17.4

It is not necessary to transfer the `.fla` version of your Flash movie to a Web server unless you want other users to be able to download the editable version of the movie.

17.6 Creating Special Effects with Flash

The following sections introduce a variety of special effects using more advanced Flash capabilities. By completing the preceding example, you should understand basic movie development. The next sections cover many additional topics, from importing bitmaps to creating animations that preload Web pages.

17.6.1 Importing and Manipulating Bitmaps

Some of the examples in this chapter require importing bitmap images and other media into a Flash movie. The importing process is similar for all types of media, including images, sound and video. The following example shows how to import an image into a Flash movie.

Begin by creating a new Flash document. The image we are going to import is located on the CD-ROM included with this book. Once the CD-ROM is loaded, return to Flash and select **Import to Stage...** from **Import** sub-menu of the **File** menu. Browse to the Chapter 17 examples folder on the CD-ROM, then open the folder labeled images. Select bug.bmp and click **OK** to continue. A bug image should appear on the stage. The **Library** panel stores imported images. Developers can convert imported images into editable shapes by selecting the image and pressing *Ctrl+B* or by choosing **Break Apart** from the **Modify** menu. Once an imported image is broken apart, it may be shape tweened or edited with **editing tools** such as the lasso, paint bucket, eraser and paintbrush. The editing tools are found in the toolbox and apply changes to a shape.

Clicking and dragging to draw with the **lasso tool** selects areas of shapes. The color of a selected area may be changed or moved. Click and drag with the lasso tool to draw the boundaries of the selection. As with the button in the last example, when a developer selects a shape area, a mesh of white dots covers the selection. Once an area is selected, its color may be changed by selecting a new fill color with the fill swatch or by clicking the selection with the paint bucket tool. The lasso tool has different options (located in the **Options** section of the toolbox) including **magic wand** and **polygonal mode**. The magic wand option changes the lasso tool into the magic wand tool, which selects areas of similar colors. The polygonal lasso selects straight-edged areas.

The **eraser tool** removes shape areas when a developer clicks and drags the tool across an area. A developer can change the eraser size using the tool options. Other options include settings that make the tool erase only fills or strokes.

The **paintbrush tool** applies color in the same way that the eraser removes color. The paintbrush color is selected with the fill swatch. The paintbrush tool options include **paint behind**, which sets the tool to paint only in areas with no color information; **paint selection**, which paints only areas that have been selected; and **paint inside**, which paints inside a line boundary.

Each of these tools can create original graphics. Experiment with the different tools to change the shape and color of the imported bug graphic.

Portability Tip 17.1

When building Flash movies, try to use the smallest possible file size and Web-safe colors, ensuring that most people can view the movie regardless of bandwidth, processor speed or monitor resolution.

17.6.2 Creating an Advertisement Banner with Masking

Masking hides portions of layers. A **masking layer** hides objects in the layers beneath it, revealing only the areas that can be seen through the shape of the mask. Items drawn on a masking layer define the mask's shape and cannot be seen in the final movie. The next example, which builds a Web site banner, shows how to use masking frames to add animation and color effects to text.

Create a new Flash document and set the size of the stage to **470** pixels wide by **60** pixels high. Create three layers named **top**, **middle** and **bottom** according to their positions in the layer hierarchy. These names help track the masked layer and the visible layers. The **top** layer contains the mask, the **middle** layer becomes the masked animation and the **bottom** layer contains an imported bitmapped logo. Import the graphic bug_apple.bmp (found on the CD-ROM in the images folder of the Chapter 17 examples folder) into the first frame of the **top** layer, using the method described in the preceding section. This image will appear too large to fit in the stage area. Select the image with the selection tool and align it with the upper-left corner of the stage. Then select the **free transform tool** in the toolbox (Fig. 17.33).

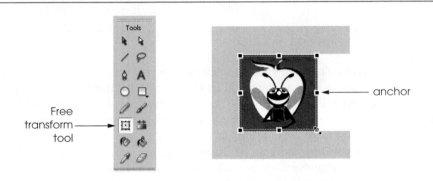

Fig. 17.33 Resizing an image with the free transform tool.

The free transform tool allows us to resize an image. When an object is selected with this tool, **anchors** appear around its corners and sides. Click and drag an anchor to resize the image in any direction. Hold down the *Shift* key while clicking and dragging the lower-right anchor upwards until the image fits on the stage. Holding down the *Shift* key while dragging a corner anchor ensures that the image maintains the original height and width ratio.

Use the text tool to add text to frame 1 of the **top** layer. Use **Verdana, 28** pt **bold** as the font. Select a blue text color, and make sure that **Static Text** is selected in the **Property Inspector**. Type the banner text, making sure that the text fits inside the stage area, and use the selection tool to position the text next to the image. This text becomes the object that masks an animation.

We must convert the text into a shape before converting it to a mask. Click the text field with the selection tool to ensure that it is active and select **Break Apart** twice from the **Modify** menu. Breaking the text apart once converts each letter into its own text field. Breaking it apart again converts the letters into shapes that cannot be edited with the text tool, but can be manipulated as regular graphics.

Copy the contents of the **top** layer to the **bottom** layer before creating the mask, so that the text remains visible when the mask is added. Right click frame 1 of the **top** layer, and select **Copy Frames** from the resulting menu. Paste the contents of the **top** layer into frame 1 of the **bottom** layer by right clicking frame 1 and selecting **Paste Frames** from the menu. This shortcut pastes the frame's contents in the very same position as the original frame. Delete the extra copy of the bug image by selecting the bug image in the **top** layer with the selection tool and pressing the *Delete* key.

The next step is to create the animated graphic that the type in the **top** layer masks. Click in the first frame of the **middle** layer and use the oval tool to draw an oval that is taller than the text. The oval does not need to fit inside the banner area. Set the oval stroke to **no color** by clicking the stroke swatch and selecting the **No Color** option (Fig. 17.34). Set the fill color to the rainbow gradient, found at the bottom of the **Color Swatches** panel.

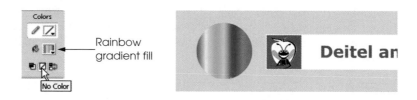

Rainbow
gradient fill

No Color

Fig. 17.34 Creating the oval graphic.

Select the oval by clicking it with the selection tool, and convert the circle to a symbol by pressing *F8*. Name the symbol **oval** and set the behavior to **Graphic**. When the banner is complete, the oval will move across the stage; however, it will be visible only through the text mask in the **top** layer. Move the circle just outside the left edge of the stage, indicating the point at which the circle begins its animation. Create a keyframe in frame 20 of the **middle** layer and another in frame 40. These keyframes indicate the different locations of the **oval** symbol during the animation. Click frame 20 and move the circle just outside the right side of the banner to indicate the animation's next key position. Do not move the position of the **oval** graphic in frame 40 so that the circle will return to its original position at the end of the animation. Create the first part of the animation by right clicking frame 1 of the **middle** layer and choosing **Create Motion Tween** from the menu. Repeat this step for frame 20 of the **middle** layer, making the **oval** symbol move from left to right and back. Add keyframes to frame 40 of both the **top** and **bottom** layers so that the other movie elements appear throughout the movie.

Now that all the supporting movie elements are in place, the next step is the application of the masking effect. This is accomplished by right clicking the **top** layer and selecting **Mask** from the resulting menu (Fig. 17.35). Adding a mask to the **top** layer masks only the items in the layer directly below it (the **middle** layer), causing the bug logo in the **bottom** layer to be visible while obscuring the animation in the **middle** layer.

Now that the movie is complete, save it as `banner.fla` and test it with the Flash Player. The rainbow oval is visible through the text as it animates from left to right. The text in the bottom layer is visible in the portions not containing the rainbow (Fig. 17.36).

17.6.3 Adding Online Help to Forms

In this section, we build on Flash techniques introduced earlier in this chapter, including tweening, masking, importing sound and bitmapped images and writing ActionScript. In the following example, we apply these various techniques to create an online form that offers interactive help. The interactive help consists of animations that appear when a user presses buttons located next to the form fields. Each button contains a script that triggers an animation, and each animation provides the user with information regarding the form field that corresponds to the pressed button.

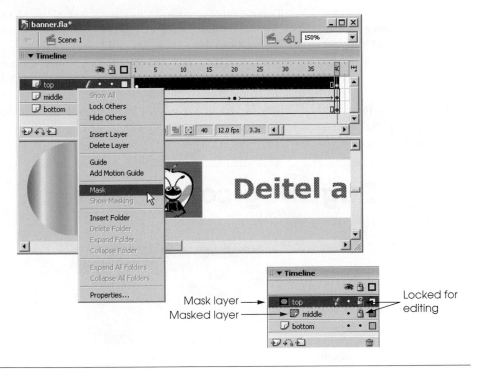

Fig. 17.35   Creating a mask layer.

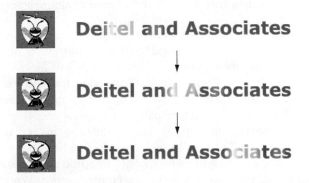

Fig. 17.36   Completed banner.

Each animation is a movie clip symbol that is placed in a separate frame and layer of the parent movie. Adding a `stop` action to frame 1 pauses the movie until the user presses a button. The `press` event makes the movie skip ahead in the timeline so that the corresponding animation plays.

Begin by creating a new movie, using default movie size settings. The first layer will contain the site name, form title and form captions. Change the name of **Layer 1** to **text**. Add a `stop` action to frame 1 of the text layer. Create the site name as static text in the **text** layer using a large, bold font, and place the title at the top of the page. Next, place the form name **Registration Form** as static text beneath the site name, using the same font, but in a smaller size and different color. The final text element added to this layer is the text box containing the form labels. Create a text box, and enter the text: `Name:`, `Member #:` and `Password:`, pressing *Enter* after entering each label to put it on a different line. Next, adjust the value of the **Line Spacing** field (the amount of space between lines of text) found by clicking the **Format...** button in the **Property Inspector**. Change the form field caption line spacing to **22** in the **Format Options** dialog (Fig. 17.37) and set the text alignment (found in the **Property Inspector**) to right justify.

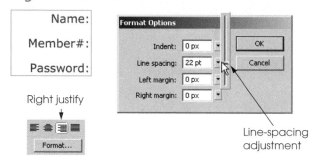

Fig. 17.37 Adjusting the line spacing with the **Format Options** dialog.

We will now create the form fields for our help form. The first step in the production of these form fields is to create a new layer named **form**. In the **form** layer, draw a rectangle that is roughly the same height as the caption text. This rectangle will serve as a background for the form text fields. The **Round Rectangle Radius** option, found in the **Options** section of the toolbox, can be employed to round the corners of the rectangle. In this example, we set the corner radius to **5** (Fig. 17.38). Feel free to experiment with other shapes and colors.

The next step is to convert the rectangle into a symbol so that it may be reused in the movie. Select the rectangle fill and stroke with the selection tool and press *F8* to convert the selection to a symbol. Set the symbol behavior to **Graphic** and name the symbol **form field**. This symbol should be positioned next to the **Name:** caption. When the symbol is in place, open the **Library** panel by pressing *Ctrl+L*, select the **form** layer and drag two copies of the **form field** symbol from the **Library** onto the stage. This will create two new instances of this symbol. Use the selection tool to align the fields with their corresponding captions. For more precise alignment, select the desired object with the selection tool and press the arrow key on the keyboard in the direction you want to move the object. After aligning the **form field** symbols, the movie should resemble Fig. 17.39.

We will now add **input text fields** to our movie. An input text field is a text field into which the user can type text. Select the text tool and, using the **Property Inspector**, set the font to **Verdana**, **16** pt, with dark blue as the color. In the text type pull-down menu in the **Property Inspector**, select **Input Text** (Fig. 17.40). Then, click and drag in the stage

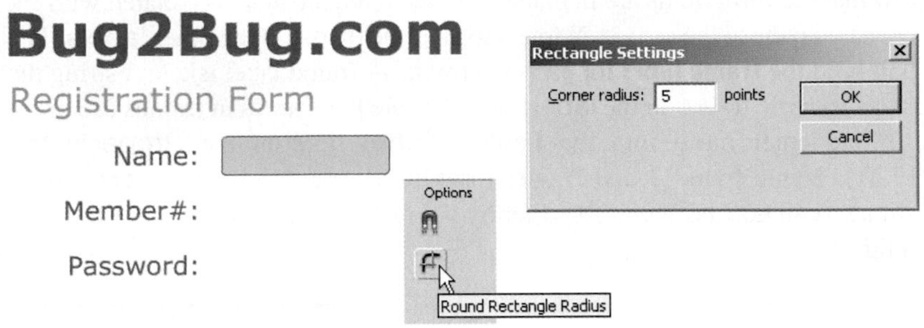

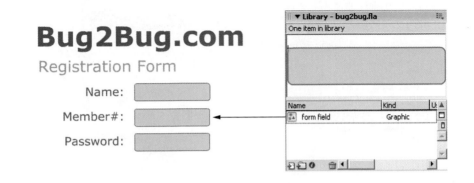

Fig. 17.38 Creating a rectangle with rounded corners.

Fig. 17.39 Creating multiple instances of a symbol with the **Library** panel.

to create a text field slightly smaller than the **form field** symbol we just created. With the selection tool, position the text field over the instance of the **form field** symbol associated with the name. Create a similar text field for member number and password. Select the password text field, and select **Password** in the line type pull-down menu in the **Property Inspector**. Selecting **Password** causes any text entered into the field by the user to appear as an asterisk (*). We have now created all the input text fields for our help form. In this example, we will not actually process the text entered into these fields. Using advanced ActionScript, we could give each input text field a variable name, and send the values of these variables to a server-side script for processing.

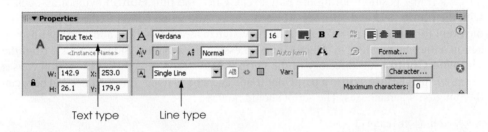

Fig. 17.40 Input and password text field creation.

Now that the form fields are in place, we can create the help associated with each field. Add two new layers to the movie. Name one layer **button** and the other **labels**. The **labels** layer will hold the **frame label** for each keyframe. A frame label is a text string that corresponds to a specific frame. In the **labels** layer, create keyframes in frames 2, 3 and 4. Select frame 2 and enter `name` into the **Frame Label** field in the **Property Inspector** (Fig. 17.41). Name frame 3 and frame 4 `memberNumber` and `password`, respectively. These frames can now be accessed either by number or name. We will use the labels again later in this example.

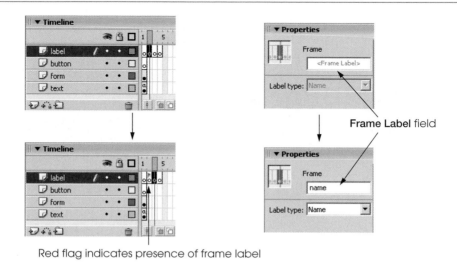

Fig. 17.41   Adding **Frame Labels** using the **Property Inspector**.

In frame 1 of the **button** layer, create a small circular button containing a question mark. Position it next to the **name** field. When the button is complete, select all the button's pieces with the selection tool, and press *F8* to convert the shape into a button symbol named **helpButton**. Drag two more instances of the **helpButton** symbol from the **Library** panel onto the stage next to each of the form fields.

These buttons trigger animations that provide information about their corresponding form fields. A script is added to each button, which causes the **playhead** to jump to a particular frame when a user presses the button. The playhead is a counter that shows the movie's frame position during the play cycle. Click the **helpButton** symbol associated with the **name** field and open the **Actions** panel. Add an on action to the button, setting the event for the action as `release`. On a new line in the on function, add a `gotoAndStop` action, either by typing it in directly, or by pressing the **+** button and selecting it from the **Timeline Control** sub-directory of the **Global Functions** directory. This action causes the movie playhead to skip to a particular frame and stop playing. Enter `"name"` in between the function's parentheses. The script should now read

```
on ( release ) {
   gotoAndStop( "name" );
}
```

This script causes the playhead to advance to the frame labeled name and stop when a user presses the button. [*Note:* We could also have entered gotoAndStop(2), referenced by frame number, in place of gotoAndStop("name").] Add the same actions to the buttons associated with the **Member #** field and the **Password** field, changing the frame labels to memberNumber and password, respectively. Each button now has an action that points to a distinct frame in the timeline. We will next add the interactive help animations to these frames.

The animation associated with each of the buttons is created as a movie clip symbol that is inserted into the parent movie at the correct frame. For instance, the animation associated with the **Password** field is placed in frame 4 so that when the button is pressed, the gotoAndStop action skips to the frame containing the correct animation. When the user clicks the button, a help rectangle will fly open and display the purpose of the associated field.

Each movie clip should be created as a **new symbol** so that it can be edited without affecting the parent movie. Select **New Symbol...** from the **Insert** menu (or use the shortcut *Ctrl+F8*), name the symbol **nameWindow** and set the behavior to **Movie Clip**. Press **OK** to open the symbol's stage and timeline.

The next step is to create the interactive help animation. This animation contains text that describes the form field. Before adding the text, we are going to create a small background animation that we will position behind the text. Begin by changing the name of **layer 1** to **background**. Draw a dark blue rectangle with no border. This rectangle can be of any size because we will customize its proportions with the **Property Inspector**. Select the rectangle with the selection tool, then open the **Property Inspector**. Set the **W:** field to **200** and the **H:** field to **120**, to define the rectangle's size. Next, center the rectangle by entering **–100** and **–60** into the **x** and **y** fields, respectively (Fig. 17.42).

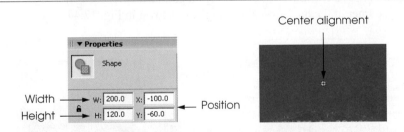

Fig. 17.42 Centering an image on the stage with the **Property Inspector**.

Now that the rectangle is correctly positioned, we can begin to create its animation. Add keyframes to frames 5 and 10 of the **background** layer. Use the **Property Inspector** to change the size of the rectangle in frame 5, setting its height to **5.0**. Next, right click frame 5 and select **Copy Frames**. Then right click frame 1 and select **Paste Frames**. While in frame 1, change the width of the rectangle to **5**.

The animation is created by applying shape tweening to frames 1 and 5. Recall that shape tweening morphs one shape into another. The shape tween causes the dot in frame 1 to grow into a line by frame 5, then into a rectangle in frame 10. Select frame 1 and apply the shape tween by selecting **Shape** from the **Tween** drop-down list in the **Property Inspector**. Shape tweens appear green in the timeline (Fig. 17.43). Follow the same procedure for frame 5.

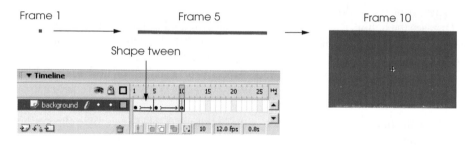

Fig. 17.43 Creating a shape tween.

Now that this portion of the animation is complete, it may be tested on the stage by pressing *Enter*. The animation should appear as the dot from frame 1 growing into a line by frame 5 and subsequently into a rectangle by frame 10.

The next step is to add a mock form field to this animation which demonstrates what the user would type in the actual field. Add two new layers above the **background** layer, named **field** and **text**. The **field** layer contains a mock form field, and the **text** layer contains the help information.

First, create an animation similar to the growing rectangle we just created for the mock form field. Add a keyframe to frame 10 in both the **field** and **text** layers. Fortunately, we have a form field already created as a symbol. Select frame 10 of the **field** layer, and drag the **form field** symbol from the **Library** panel onto the stage, placing the **form field** symbol within the current movie clip. Symbols may be embedded in one another; however, they cannot be placed within themselves (i.e., an instance of the **form field** symbol cannot be dragged onto the **form field** symbol editing stage). Align the **form field** symbol with the upper-left corner of the background rectangle, as shown in Fig. 17.44.

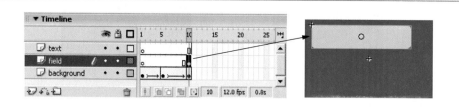

Fig. 17.44 Adding the **field** symbol to the **nameWindow** movie clip.

Next, set the end of this movie clip by adding keyframes to the **background** and **field** layers in frame 40. Also add keyframes to frames 20 and 25 of the **field** layer. These keyframes define intermediate points in the animation. Refer to Figure 17.45 for correct keyframe positioning.

The next step in creating the animation is to make the **form field** symbol grow in size. Select frame 20 of the **field** layer, which contains only the **form field** symbol. Next open the **Transform** panel, found in the **Design Panels** sub-menu of the **Window** menu. The **Transform** panel, like the **Property Inspector**, can be used to change an object's size. Check the **Constrain** checkbox to constrain the object's proportions as it is resized. Selecting this option causes the **scale factor** to be equal in the height and width fields. The

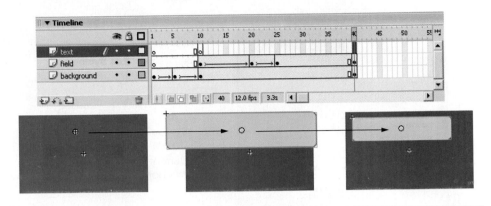

Fig. 17.45   Creating an animation with the **form field** symbol.

scale factor measures the change in proportion. Set the scale factor for the width and height to **150%**, and press *Enter* to apply the changes. Repeat the previous step for frame 10 of the **field** layer, but scale the **form field** symbol down to **0%**.

The symbol's animation is created by adding a motion tween. Adding the tween to **field** layer frames 10 and 20 will cause the form field symbol to grow from 0% of the original size to 150%, then to 100%. Figure 17.45 illustrates this portion of the animation.

It is necessary to add text to the movie clip which helps the user understand the purpose of the corresponding text field. We will set text to appear over the **form field** symbol as an example to the user. The text that appears below the **form field** symbol tells the user what should be typed in the text field.

The next step is to add the descriptive text. First insert a keyframe in frame 25 of the **text** layer. Use the text tool with white, Arial, 16 pt text, to type the help information for the **Name** field. This text will appear in the help window. For instance, our example gives the following directions for the **Name** field: **Enter your name in this field. First name, Last name**. Align this text with the left side of the rectangle. Next, add a keyframe to frame 40 of this layer, causing the text to appear throughout the animation.

Next, duplicate this movie clip so that it may be customized and reused for the other two help button animations. Open the **Library** panel and right click the **nameWindow** movie clip. Select **Duplicate** from the resulting menu, and name the new clip **passwordWindow**. Repeat this step once more, and name the third clip **memberWindow** (Fig. 17.46).

It is necessary to customize the duplicated movie clips so their text reflects the corresponding form fields. To begin, open the **memberWindow** editing stage by pressing the **Edit Symbols** button, which is found in the upper-right corner of the editing environment, and selecting **memberWindow** from the list of available symbols (Fig. 17.46). Select frame 25 of the **text** layer and change the form field description with the text tool so that the box contains the directions for the **Member #** form field. Copy the text in frame 25 by selecting it with the text tool and using the shortcut *Ctrl+C*. Click frame 40 of the **text** layer, which contains the old text. Highlight the old text with the text tool, and use the shortcut *Ctrl+V* to paste the copied text into this frame. Repeat these steps for the **passwordWindow** movie clip so that each clip contains the necessary information to help the user to fill out the form. [*Note*: Changing a symbol's function or appearance in its editing stage updates the symbol in the parent movie.]

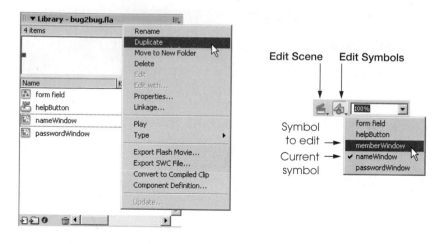

Fig. 17.46 Duplicating movie clip symbols with the **Library** panel.

The following steps further customize the help boxes for each form field. Open the **nameWindow** symbol's editing stage by clicking the **Edit Symbols** button (Fig. 17.46) and selecting **nameWindow**. Add a new layer to this symbol called **typedText** above **text** layer. This layer contains an animation that simulates the typing of text into the form field. Insert a keyframe in frame 25. Select this frame and use the text tool to create a text box on top of the **form field** symbol. Make sure the text type is **Static Text**, and type the name **John Doe** in the text box.

The following frame-by-frame animation creates the appearance of the name being typed into the field. Add a keyframe to frame 40 to indicate the end of the animation. Then add new keyframes to frames 26–31. Each keyframe contains a new letter being typed in the sequence, so when the playhead advances, new letters appear. Select the **John Doe** text in frame 25 and delete everything except the first **J** with the text tool. Next, select frame 26 and delete all of the characters except the **J** and the **o**. This step must be repeated for all subsequent keyframes up to frame 31, each keyframe containing one more letter than the last (Fig. 17.47). Frame 31 should show the entire name. When this process is complete, press *Enter* to preview the frame-by-frame typing animation.

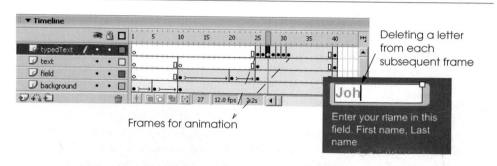

Fig. 17.47 Creating a frame-by-frame animation.

Create the same type of animation for both the **passwordWindow** and the **member-Window** movie clips, using suitable words. For example, we use asterisks for the **pass-wordWindow** movie clip and six numbers for the **memberWindow** movie clip. Add a `stop` action to frame 40 of all three movie clips so that the animations play only once.

The movie clips are now ready to be added to the parent movie. Click the **Edit Scene** button next to the **Edit Symbols** button, and select **Scene 1** to return to the parent movie. Before inserting the movie clips, add the following layers to the timeline: **nameMovie**, **memberMovie** and **passwordMovie**, one layer for each of the movie clips. Add a keyframe in frame 2 of the **nameMovie** layer.

Now we will place the movie clips in the correct position in the parent movie. Select frame 2 of the **nameMovie** layer. Recall that the ActionScript for each help button contains the script

```
on ( release ) {
    gotoAndStop( frameLabel );
}
```

in which *frameLabel* is `name`, `memberNumber` or `password`, depending on the button. This script causes the playhead to skip to the specified frame and stop. Placing the movie clips in the correct frames causes the playhead to skip to the desired frame, play the animation and stop. This effect is created by selecting frame 2 of the **nameMovie** layer and dragging the **nameWindow** movie clip onto the stage. Align the movie clip with the button next to the **Name** field, placing it halfway between the button and the right edge of the stage.

The preceding step is repeated twice for the other two movie clips so that they appear in the correct frames. Add a keyframe to frame 3 of the **memberMovie** layer and drag the **memberWindow** movie clip onto the stage. Position this clip in the same manner as the previous clip. Repeat this step for the **passwordWindow** movie clip, dragging it into frame 4 of the **passwordMovie** layer.

When all of the movie clips are placed, the parent movie is almost complete. Finish the movie by adding keyframes to frame 4 of the **form**, **text** and **button** layers, ensuring that the fields, field names, buttons and titles appear after a help button is pressed.

The movie is now complete. Press *Ctrl+Enter* to preview it with the Flash Player. If the triggered animations do not appear in the correct locations, return to the parent movie and adjust their position. The final movie is displayed in Fig. 17.48.

In our example, we have added a picture beneath the text layer. Movies can be enhanced in many ways, such as by changing colors and fonts or by adding pictures. Our movie (`bug2bug.fla`) can be found in the Chapter 17 examples directory on the CD-ROM that accompanies this book. If you want to use our symbols to recreate the movie, select **Open External Library...** from the **Import** sub-menu of the **File** menu and open `bug2bug.fla`. The **Open External Library...** option allows a developer to reuse symbols from another movie.

17.7 Creating a Web-Site Introduction

Flash is becoming an important tool for e-businesses. Many organizations use Flash to create Web-site introductions, product demos and Web applications. Others use Flash to build games and interactive entertainment in an effort to attract new visitors. However, these types of applications can take a long time to load, causing visitors—especially those with

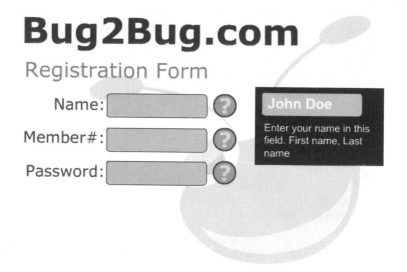

Fig. 17.48 Bug2Bug.com help form.

slow connections—to leave the site. One way to alleviate this problem is to provide visitors with an animated Flash introduction that draws and keeps their attention. Flash animations are ideal for amusing visitors while conveying information as the rest of a page downloads "behind the scenes."

A **preloader** is a simple animation that plays while the rest of the Web page is loading. Several techniques are used to create animation preloaders. The following example creates an animation preloader that uses ActionScript to pause the movie at a particular frame until all the movie elements have loaded.

To start building the animation preloader, create a new Flash document, maintaining the default size, and setting the background color to a light yellow. The first step involves the construction of the movie pieces that will be loaded later in the process. Create four new layers, one for each of the loaded objects. Rename **Layer 3** to **C++**, **Layer 4** to **IW3** and **Layer 5** to **Java**. **Layer 1** will contain the movie's ActionScript, so name it **actions.** Because **Layer 2** contains the introductory animation, rename this layer **animation**.

The pre-loaded objects we use in this example are animated movie clip symbols. Create the first symbol by clicking frame 2 of the **C++** layer, inserting a keyframe, and creating a new movie clip symbol named **cbook**. When the symbol's editing stage opens, import the image `chtp.gif` (found in the `images` folder in the Chapter 17 examples directory). Place a keyframe in frame 20 of **Layer 1**, and add a `stop` action to this frame. The animation in this example is produced with the motion tween **rotate** option, which causes an object to spin on its axis. Create a motion tween in frame 1 with the **Property Inspector**, setting the **Rotate** option to **CCW** (counter-clockwise) and the **times** field to **2** (Fig. 17.49). This causes the image `chtp.gif` to spin two times counter-clockwise over a period of 20 frames.

After returning to the parent movie, drag and drop a copy of the **cbook** symbol onto the stage in frame 2 of the **C++** layer. Move this symbol to the left side of the stage.

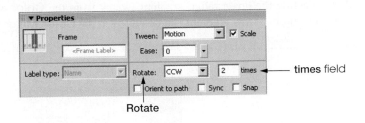

Fig. 17.49 Creating a rotating object with the motion tween **Rotate** option.

Build a similar movie clip for the **Java** and **IW3** layers, using the file java.gif and iw3.gif to create the symbols. Name the symbol for the **Java** layer **jbook** and the **IW3** symbol **ibook** to identify the symbols with their contents. In the main scene, create a keyframe in frame 8 of the **Java** layer, and place the **jbook** symbol in the center of the stage. Insert the **ibook** symbol in a keyframe in frame 14 of the **IW3** layer, and position it to the right of the **jbook** symbol. Make sure to leave some space between these symbols so that they will not overlap when they spin (Fig. 17.50).

Fig. 17.50 Inserted movie clips.

Now that the loading objects have been placed, it is time to create the preloading animation. By placing the preloading animation in the frame preceding the frame that contains the objects, we can use ActionScript to pause the movie until the objects have loaded. Begin by adding a stop action to frame 1 of the **actions** layer. Select frame 1 of the **animation** layer and create another new movie-clip symbol named **loader**. Use the text tool with a medium-sized sans-serif font, and place the word **Loading** in the center of the symbol's editing stage. This title indicates to the user that objects are loading. Insert a keyframe into frame 14 and rename this layer **load**.

Create a new layer called **orb** to contain the animation. Draw a circle with no stroke about the size of a quarter above the word **Loading**. Give the circle a green radial gradient fill by selecting the green radial gradient swatch from the **Color Mixer** panel for the fill color. The colors of this gradient can be edited in the **Color Mixer** panel (Fig. 17.51).

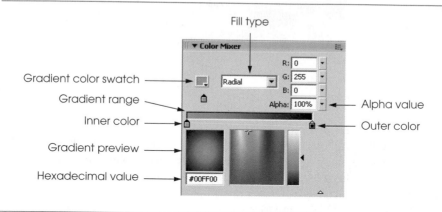

Fig. 17.51   Changing gradient colors with the **Color Mixer** panel.

The block farthest to the left on the **gradient range** indicates the innermost color of the radial gradient, whereas the block farthest to the right indicates the outermost color of the radial gradient. Click the green block (left) to reveal the **gradient color** swatch. Click the swatch and select a medium blue as the inner color of the gradient. Select the black, outer color box (right) and change its color to white. Deselect the circle by clicking on a blank portion of the stage. Note that a white ring appears around the circle due to the colored background. To make the circle fade into the background, we adjust its **alpha** value. Alpha is a value between 0 and 100% that corresponds to a color's transparency or opacity. An alpha value of 0% appears transparent, whereas a value of 100% appears completely opaque. Select the circle again and click on the right gradient box (white). Adjust the value of the **Alpha** field in the **Color Mixer** panel to 0%. Deselect the circle. It should now appear to fade into the background.

The rate of progression in a gradient can also be changed by sliding the color boxes. Select the circle again. Slide the left color box to the middle so that the gradient contains more blue than transparent white. Intermediate colors may be added to the gradient range by clicking beneath the bar, next to one of the existing color boxes. Click to the left of the blue, inner color box to add a new color box (Fig. 17.52). Slide the new color box to the left and change its color to a darker blue. Any color box may be removed from a gradient by clicking and dragging it downward off the gradient range.

Insert keyframes into frame 7 and 14 of the **orb** layer. Select the circle in frame 7 with the selection tool. In the **Color Mixer** panel change the alpha of evert color box to 0%. Select frame 1 in the **Timeline** and add shape tween. Change the value of the **Ease** field in the **Property Inspector** to –100. **Ease** controls the rate of change during tween animation. Negative values cause the animated change to be gradual at the beginning and become increasingly drastic. Positive values cause the animation to change quickly in the first frames, becoming less drastic as the animation progresses. Add shape tween to frame 7 and set the **Ease** value to 100. The animation is now complete and may be previewed by pressing *Enter*. The circle should now appear to pulse.

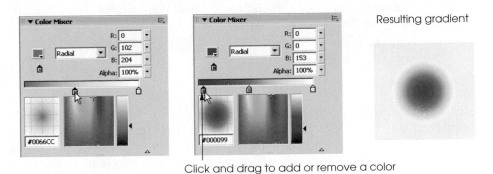

Click and drag to add or remove a color

Fig. 17.52 Adding an intermediate color to a gradient.

Before inserting the movie clip into the parent movie, we are going to create a **hypertext linked button** that will enable the user to skip over the animations to the final destination. Add a new layer called **link** to the **loader** symbol with keyframes in frames 1 and 14. Using the text tool, place the words **skip directly to Deitel Web site** below **Loading** in a smaller font size. Select the words with the selection tool and convert them into a button symbol named **skip**. Converting the text into a button simulates a text hyperlink created with XHTML. Double click the words to open the **skip** button's editing stage. For this example, we are going to edit only the hit state. When a button is created from a shape, the button's hit area is, by default, the area of the shape. It is important to change the hit state of a button created from text so that it includes the spaces between the letters; otherwise, the link will work only when the user hovers over a letter's area. Place a keyframe in the hit state. Use the rectangle tool to draw the hit area of the button, covering the entire length and height of the text. This rectangle is not visible in the final movie, because it defines only the hit area (Fig. 17.53).

Up state   Hit state

Fig. 17.53 Defining the hit area of a button.

The button is activated by giving it an action that links it to another Web page. After returning to the **loader** movie clip editing stage, right click the **skip** button and open the **Actions** dialog. Add an **on** action to the button and set the event to `release.` In the body of the **on** function, and add the action `getURL`, found in the **Browser/Network** sub-directory of the **Global Functions** directory. This call creates a hyperlink which directs the user to a new page or site. The code now reads

```
on ( release ) {
    getURL ( );
}
```

The URL is specified as the argument to function `getURL`. Enter `"http://www.deitel.com"` as the URL, followed by a comma. After the comma, write `"_blank"` to signify that a new browser window displaying the Deitel Web site should open when the user presses the button. The code now reads

```
on ( release ) {
    getURL ( "http://www.deitel.com", "_blank" );
}
```

Return to the parent movie by clicking **Scene 1** directly above the timeline, next to the name of the current symbol. Drag and drop a copy of the **loader** movie clip from the **Library** panel into frame 1 of the **animation** layer, and center it on the stage.

The process is nearly complete. Right click the **loader** movie clip and open the **Actions** panel. The following actions direct the movie clip to play until all the parent movie's objects are loaded. Select onClipEvent from the **Movie Clip Control** sub-directory of the **Global Functions** directory. Insert enterFrame in between the parentheses. The onClipEvent action responds to particular events that occur when the movie is played with the Flash Player. The enterFrame event occurs every time the playhead enters a new frame. Since this movie's frame rate is 12fps (frames per second), the enterFrame event will occur 12 times each second. The code now reads:

```
onClipEvent ( enterFrame ) {
}
```

The next action added to this sequence is an if statement. The condition of the if statement will be used to determine how many frames of the movie are **loaded**. Flash movies load frame by frame. Frames that contain complex images take longer to load. Flash will continue playing the current frame until the next frame has loaded. For our movie, if the number of frames loaded is greater than or equal to 21, then the movie is completely loaded and so it will move to frame 2 and continue to play. If the number of frames loaded is less than 21, then the current movie clip continues to play. Add an if statement in the body of the onClipEvent function. As the condition for the if statement, write _root._framesloaded >= 21. Property _root references the main timeline. When adding code to an object, we often want to refer to other objects or the main movie timeline. Any variable following the dot (.) of "_root." refers to the main timeline. The _framesloaded property determines the number of frames that have been loaded in a movie. Use >= as the operator and 21 as the comparative value to determine whether the number of frames loaded is greater than 21. The code now reads

```
onClipEvent ( enterFrame ) {
    if ( _root._framesloaded >= 21 ) {
    }
}
```

In the if statement's body, add the code _root.gotoAndPlay(2). When the if statement's condition is true, the movie will begin playing the loaded images in the second frame of the main movie timeline (because of the _root.). The final script for this movie clip reads

```
onClipEvent ( enterFrame ) {
    if ( _root._framesloaded >= 21 ) {
    _root.gotoAndPlay ( 2 );
    }
}
```

Create one more layer in the parent movie, and name the layer **title**. Add a keyframe to frame 2 of this layer, and use the text tool to create a title for the rotating text books. Below the title, create another text hyperlink button to the Deitel Web site. The simplest way to do this is to duplicate the existing **skip** button and modify the text. Right click the **skip** symbol in the **Library** panel, and select **Duplicate**. Rename the new button **visit** by right clicking **skip copy** in the **Library** panel and selecting **Rename**. Place the **visit** symbol in frame 2 of the **title** layer. Double click the **visit** button and edit the text to say **Visit the Deitel Web site**. Add an empty frame to frame 21 of each layer, except the **animation** layer, by right clicking frame 21 and selecting **Insert Frame** for each layer. Now the animations will run throughout the movie. Add keyframes to each frame of the **title** layer and manipulate the text to create a typing effect similar to the one we created in the bug2bug example.

The final step is to add a `stop` action to frame 21 of the **actions** layer to prevent the movie from repeating. The movie is now complete. Test the movie with the Flash Player (Fig. 17.54). When viewed in the testing window, the loading sequence will only play for one frame because your processor loads all the frames (`_framesloaded == 21`) almost instantly. Flash can simulate how a movie would appear to an online user, though. While still in the testing window, select **56K** from the **Download Settings** sub-menu of the **View** menu. Also, select and **Bandwidth Profiler** from the **View** menu. Then select **Simulate Download** from the **View** menu or press *Ctrl+Enter*. The testing stage should now simulate the movie as it would appear for someone with a 56K modem. The graph at the top of the window displays the amount of bandwidth required to load each frame.

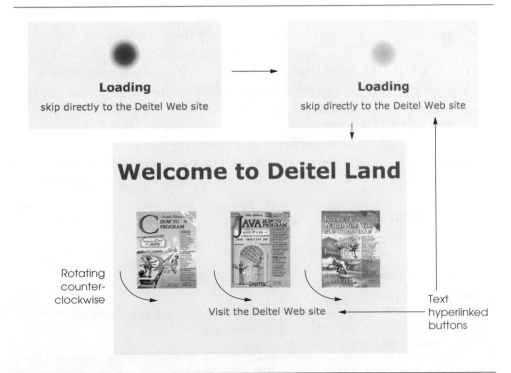

Fig. 17.54 Creating an animation to preload images.

17.8 ActionScript

Figure 17.55 lists common Flash ActionScript 2.0 functions. By attaching these functions to frames and symbols, you can build some fairly complex Flash movies.

Action	Description
goto	Jump to a frame or scene in another part of the movie.
play	Start a movie at certain points at which the movie may have been stopped.
stop	Stop a movie.
toggleHighQuality	Turn anti-aliasing on and off. When it is turned off, the movie is able to play faster, but renders with rough edges.
stopAllSounds	Stop the sound track without affecting the movie.
getURL	Load a URL into a new or existing browser window.
FSCommand	Insert JavaScript or other scripting languages into a Flash movie.
loadMovie/ unloadMovie	Load a SWF or JPEG file into the Flash Player from the current movie. Can also load another SWF into a particular movie.
ifFrameLoaded	Check whether certain frames have been loaded.
onClipEvent	Assigns actions to a movie clip based on specific events. The events include load, unLoad, enterFrame, mouseUp, mouseDown, mouseMove, keyUp, keyDown and data.
on	Assign actions such as Press, Release and RollOver to a button.
if	Set up condition statements that run only when the condition is true.
while/do while	Run a collection of statements while a condition statement is true.
setProperty	Change the attributes of a movie clip while the movie plays.
duplicateMovieClip/ removeMovieClip	Dynamically add a movie clip to a movie or remove a clip from a movie.
startDrag/stopDrag	Move a movie clip while the movie is running.
trace	Display programming notes or variable values while testing a movie.
// (comment)	Keep track of personal notes in a frame or action for future reference.

Fig. 17.55 Additional ActionScript functions.

17.9 Web Resources

www.macromedia.com
Macromedia specializes in tools for creating multimedia-rich Web sites. Free 30-day trial versions of its multimedia authoring tools are available at this site.

www.macromedia.com/software/flash
Macromedia's Flash site contains detailed product information, product support, tutorials, sample files and a showcase of professional Web sites built with Flash. The most recent version of the Flash 30-day trial software is available at this site.

`www.actionscripts.org`
An online community that offers Flash tutorials for all levels. The community also provides free sounds, fonts and open source code for Flash developers. Its forums provide open discussions about Flash topics between developers.

`www.flashkit.com`
Geared to Flash developers and enthusiasts. It has several forums covering various Flash topics.

`www.moock.org`
Provides helpful information on ActionScript and links to other ActionScript resources. It also offers professional Flash production tips and sample `.fla` files which may be downloaded for learning purposes.

`www.openswf.org`
Provides discussion about SWF tools and open source SWF creation links to SWF resources.

`www.webmonkey.com/multimedia/shockwave_flash`
WebMonkey offers information on many facets of Web design and development, including Flash and Shockwave.

`www.shockwave.com`
The *Shockwave* Web site contains a variety of Web-based games, cartoons and music. The site was created with Macromedia authoring tools, including Flash.

SUMMARY

- Macromedia Flash MX 2004 is a commercial application for creating interactive, animated movies.
- Flash movies may be embedded in Web pages, placed on CD-ROMs as independent applications or converted into stand-alone, executable programs.
- Web users need the Flash Player plug-in to view Flash movies; most users already have it.
- When the program opens, Flash creates a new file called **Untitled-1**, by default.
- The tools are located in the vertical window (called the toolbox) along the left side of the development environment.
- Panels modify the attributes for symbols, tools and shapes.
- The `.fla` file extension is a Flash-specific extension for editable movies.
- The **Document Properties** dialog sets properties such as the **Frame rate**, **Dimensions** and **Background color**.
- The **Frame rate** of a movie is a movie's speed.
- The **Dimensions** define the size of the movie as it appears on the screen.
- The **Background color** is the color of the movie background and is selected by clicking the background color box (called a swatch).
- Shapes are created by clicking and dragging with the shape tools. By default, shapes are created with a stroke (border) and a fill. A shape's fill and stroke may be edited individually.
- Gradient fills are gradual progressions of color.
- Use the text tool in conjunction with the **Property Inspector** to create text.
- The selection tool selects and moves objects.
- Symbols are the reusable elements of a Flash movies, such as graphics, buttons and movie clips, that make the movies interactive.
- Flash movies consist of a parent movie and symbols. The parent movie is the main movie.
- Editing stages for symbols are separate from the parent movie and may be accessed separately.

- The timeline for the parent movie may contain several symbols, each of which has its own timelines and properties.
- A Flash movie may have several instances of a particular symbol, meaning that the same symbol may appear several times.
- Every symbol in a Flash movie must have a unique name. The symbol behavior determines how a symbol performs in a movie.
- The **Library** panel provides an inventory of every symbol in the movie. Multiple instances of a certain symbol can be placed in a movie by dragging and dropping it from the **Library** panel onto the stage.
- The timeline for a button symbol contains four frames, one for each of the button's states (up, over and down) and one for the hit area.
- Keyframes indicate points of change in the timeline of a layer.
- Movies can be viewed in their published state with the Flash Player. Published Flash movies have the file extension .swf, which stands for Shockwave file.
- Shockwave files are read only, meaning that they can be viewed but not edited.
- A movie can be composed of many layers, each having its own attributes and effects.
- Tweening is a morphing process in which Flash creates all the intermediate steps of the animation between two keyframes.
- Shape tweening morphs an object from one shape to another. Shape tweening cannot be performed on symbols or grouped objects, only ungrouped objects.
- Motion tweening moves objects on the stage and can only be performed on symbols or grouped objects.
- ActionScript, the programming language of Flash, is similar to JavaScript.
- The text type determines a text field's interaction.
- A text field is created with the text tool by clicking and dragging with the mouse.
- Imported images are graphic symbols and can be accessed from the **Library** panel.
- Editable shapes may be shape tweened or edited with editing tools.
- When an image is selected with the free transform tool, anchors appear around the corners and sides of the image. When clicked and dragged, they resize the image.
- Breaking apart text converts the letters into shapes, causing them to be uneditable with the text tool.
- Adding a mask to a layer masks the items in the layer directly beneath it.
- Interactive help forms may be created with Flash.
- The gotoAndPlay action causes the movie to advance to a particular frame and play.
- Shape tweens appear green in the timeline.
- Frame-by-frame animations are created as a succession of keyframes.
- Preloading animations use ActionScript to pause the movie at a particular frame until all of the elements of the movie have loaded.
- Frames or groups of frames can be given a label.
- The **Rotate** option for motion tweening spins a object on its axis in a particular direction over the length of the animation.
- The rate of progression in a gradient may be changed by sliding the inner or outer color boxes in the **Color Mixer** panel.
- An image's transparency can be adjusted with the **Alpha** field in the **Color Mixer** panel.

- The **Ease** value in the **Property Inspector** controls the progressive rate of tween animation.
- Converting text into a button simulates a text hyperlink created with XHTML.
- The getURL action creates a hyperlink directing the user to a new page or site.
- When testing a movie, select **Simulate Download** from the **view** menu to view the movie at the connection speed selected in the **Download Settings** sub-menu.

TERMINOLOGY

ActionScript 2.0
active tool
alpha value
selection tool
Background Color
Bandwidth Profiler
break apart
button state
button symbol
constrained proportions
convert to symbol
Copy Frames
Document Properties dialog
dynamic text
Ease
editing stage
embed tag
eraser tool
event
export to Flash Player
expression
file size
fill color
Flash Player plug-in
frame
frame label
Frame Rate
function
getURL
goto
gradient
graphic symbol
grouped object
hand tool

Import
insert layer
instance
keyframe
layer
Library panel
masking
motion tween
movie
movie clip symbol
Movie Explorer
noembed tag
object tag
oval tool
parent movie
Paste Frame
playhead
Property Inspector
Publish
random
rectangle tool
scale option
scene
selection tool
shape tween
stage
stop
symbol
Test Movie
text field
text tool
timeline
tweening
zoom tool

SELF-REVIEW EXERCISES

17.1   Fill in the blanks in each of the following statements:
  a) Macromedia Flash's _____ feature draws the in-between frames of an animation.
  b) Graphics, buttons and movie clips are all types of _____.
  c) The two types of tweening in Macromedia Flash are _____ tweening and _____ tweening.

d) Macromedia Flash's scripting language is called _____.

e) The area in which the movie is created is called the _____.

f) Holding down the *Shift* key while drawing with the oval tool draws a perfect _____.

g) Morphing one shape into another over a period of time requires _____.

h) By default, shapes in Flash are created with a(n) _____ and a(n) _____.

i) _____ tell Flash how a shape or symbol should look at the beginning and end of an animation.

j) A graphic's transparency can be altered by adjusting its _____.

17.2   State whether each of the following is *true* or *false*. If *false*, explain why.

a) A Macromedia Flash button's hit state is entered when the button is clicked.

b) To draw a straight line in Flash, hold down the *Shift* key while drawing with the pencil tool.

c) Motion tweening moves objects within the stage.

d) The more frames you give to an animation, the slower it is.

e) Setting the argument of Flash's `random` function to 5 tells the function to generate a number between 1 and 5.

f) The maximum number of layers allowed in a movie is ten.

g) Flash can shape tween only one shape per layer.

h) When a new layer is created, it is placed above the selected layer.

i) The lasso tool selects objects by drawing free-hand or straight-edge selection areas.

j) The **Ease** value controls an object's transparency during motion tween.

ANSWERS TO SELF-REVIEW EXERCISES

17.1   a) tweening. b) symbols. c) shape, motion. d) ActionScript. e) stage. f) circle. g) shape tweening. h) fill, stroke. i) keyframes. j) alpha value.

17.2   a) False. The down state is entered when the button is clicked. b) True. c) True. d) True. e) False. Setting the argument of Flash's `random` function to 5 tells the function to generate a number between 0 and 4. f) False. Flash allows an unlimited number of layers for each movie. g) False. Flash can tween as many shapes as there are on a layer. The effect is usually better when the shapes are placed on their own layers. h) True. i) True. j) False. The **Ease** value controls the progressive rate of animation (increasing or decreasing) of tween animation.

EXERCISES

17.3   Using the combination of one movie clip symbol and one button symbol to create a navigation bar that contains four buttons, make the buttons trigger an animation (contained in the movie clip) when the user rolls over the buttons with the mouse. Link the four buttons to `www.nasa.gov`, `www.w3c.org`, `www.flashkit.com` and `www.cnn.com`.

17.4   Download and import five WAV files from `www.coolarchive.com`. Create five buttons, each activating a different sound when it is pressed.

17.5   Create an animated mask that acts as a spotlight on an image. First, import the file `arches.jpg` from the `images` folder in the Chapter 17 examples directory. Then, change the background color of the movie to black. Animate the mask in the layer above to create a spotlight effect.

17.6   Create a text "morph" animation using a shape tween. Make the text that appears in the first frame of the animation change into a shape in the last frame. Make the text and the shape different colors.

17.7   Give a brief description of the following terms:

a) playhead.

b) symbol.

     c) tweening.
     d) ActionScript.
     e) **Frame rate**.
     f) **Library** panel.
     g) masking.
     h) Context-sensitive **Property Inspector**.
     i) **Bandwidth Profiler**.
     j) **Frame Label**.

17.8   Describe what the following file extensions are used for in Flash movie development.
     a) `.fla`
     b) `.swf`
     c) `.exe`
     d) `.html`

18

Macromedia Flash™ MX 2004: Building an Interactive Game

Objectives

- To learn advanced ActionScript in Flash MX 2004.
- To build on Flash skills learned in Chapter 17.
- To create a functional, interactive Flash application.

Knowledge must come through action.
Sophocles

It is circumstance and proper timing that give an action its character and make it either good or bad.
Agesilaus

Life's but a walking shadow, a poor player that struts and frets his hour upon the stage and then is heard no more: it is a tale told by an idiot, full of sound and fury, signifying nothing.
William Shakespeare

Come, Watson, come! The game is afoot.
Sir Arthur Conan Doyle

Cannon to right of them,
Cannon to left of them,
Cannon in front of them
Volley'd and thunder'd.
Alfred, Lord Tennyson

Outline

18.1 Introduction

While Macromedia *Flash MX 2004* is useful for creating short animations, it is also capable of building larger, interactive applications. In this chapter, we present a case study in which we build a fully functional interactive game. Open `fullcannon.swf` from the Chapter 18 examples directory and test the completed game. In the cannon game, the player has a limited amount of time to hit every part of a moving target. Hitting the target increases the remaining time, and either missing the target or hitting the blocker decreases it. Some elements of the fullcannon.swf game are not discussed in the body of this chapter, but are presented as supplementary exercises. Completing this case study will sharpen the Flash skills acquired in Chapter 17 and introduce more advanced ActionScript. For this case study, we assume that the student is comfortable with the material in Chapter 17.

18.2 Object-Oriented Programming

ActionScript 2.0 is an **object-oriented** scripting language that closely resembles JavaScript. Knowledge gained from the JavaScript treatment in Chapters 7–12 will help you understand the ActionScript used in this case study.

In ActionScript, we encounter **classes**. A class is a collection of characteristics known as **properties** and behaviors known as **methods**. We can create our own classes or use any of Flash's predefined classes. A symbol stored in the **Library** is a class. A class can be used to create many **instances** or **objects** of a class. For example, when you created the rotating-book movie clips in the preloader exercise in Chapter 17, you created a class. Dragging a symbol from the **Library** onto the stage created an instance (object) of the class. Multiple instances of one class can exist on the stage at the same time. Any changes made to an individual instance (resizing, rotating, etc.) affect only that one instance. Changes made to a class (accessed through the **Library**), however, affect every instance of the class. The concepts of class and instance will become clearer as we move through the chapter.

18.3 Objects in Flash

Before we begin the case study, we introduce Flash's object-oriented programming through a brief example. This section demonstrates dynamic positioning in Flash.

Start by creating a new Flash document. On the stage, draw a black box and convert it to a movie clip symbol. Drag another instance of the movie clip from the **Library** onto the stage. Each instance of the symbol has an **instance name**, which can be altered with the **Property Inspector**'s **Instance Name** field. Change the instance names of the two boxes to **box1** and **box2**. Select **box1** and open the **Actions** panel. Add the script:

```
on( press )
{
    box2._x -= 5; // decreases box2._x value by 5
} //end of on( press )
```

Properties **_x** and **_y** refer to the *x*- and *y*-coordinates of an object. The function on(press) is called every time the user clicks **box1**. Test the movie and note that nothing happens when you click either box. The script is trying to find an instance named **box2** within the **box1** object. However, **box2** is not part of **box1**; each box is a separate object in the movie's main timeline.

Now adjust the code to read:

```
on( press )
{
    _root.box2._x -= 5; // decreases box2._x value by 5
} //end of on( press )
```

Test the movie again. Each time **box1** is clicked, **box2** should move to the left. The property **_root** references the main timeline object, which contains **box2**. If we think of a movie as consisting of levels, **box1** and **box2** are on the same level—one below the main timeline. To access **box2** from **box1**, we must first move up a level to the main timeline that contains the two objects, using the **_root** property, then down a level to the **box2** instance, which is a member of the timeline object.

18.4 Preliminary Instructions and Notes

Open the template file named `cannontemplate.fla` from the Chapter 18 directory on the CD-ROM accompanying the book.[1] We will build our game from this template. For this case study, the graphics have already been created so that we can focus on ActionScript. We created all the images using Flash. Chapter 17 provides a detailed coverage of Flash's graphical capabilities. Take a minute to familiarize yourself with the symbols in the **Library**. Note that the **target** movie clip has movie clips within it. Also, the **ball, sounds, text** and **scoreText** movie clips have `stop` actions and labels already in place. Throughout the game, we will play different sections of these movie clips by referencing their frame labels. The `stop` action at the end of each section ensures that only the desired animation will be played.

18.4.1 Manual Coding

At this point, we assume that the reader is reasonably proficient at adding ActionScript to an object or frame. From now on, we will ask you to manually enter code into the **Actions** panel, rather than using Flash's code directories. If you have a question about ActionScript that is not answered in this book, select **ActionScript Dictionary** from the **Help** menu. Flash's help section provides a detailed list of ActionScript's capabilities. The **Help** menu should not be necessary for this case study, as all the code is explained, but this resource will prove to be valuable in the future.

18.4.2 Labeling Frames

Before writing any ActionScript to build the game, we must label each frame in the main timeline to represent its purpose in the game. Open `cannontemplate.fla` and add a keyframe to frames 2 and 3 of the **Labels** layer. Select the first frame of the **Labels** layer and enter **intro** into the **Frame Label** field in the **Property Inspector**. A flag should appear in the corresponding box in the **timeline**. Label the second frame **game** and the third frame **end**. These labels will provide useful references as we create the game.

18.4.3 Using the Actions Layer

In our game, we will use an **Actions** layer to hold any ActionScript attached to a specific frame. ActionScript programmers often create an **Actions** layer to divide larger applications into more manageable pieces. Add a `stop` action to all three frames in the **Actions** layer.

---

1. Users of the trial version of Flash MX 2004 should be sure to open existing Flash `.fla` files from within the Flash application (by choosing **Open...** from its **File** menu). Attempting to open Flash files directly from My Computer or Windows Explorer may result in an error in the trial version. Users of the registered version of the software should not experience this problem.

18.5 Adding a Start Button

Most games start with an introduction animation. In this section, we create a simple starting frame for our game.

Select the first frame of the **Intro/End** layer. From the **Library**, drag the **introText** movie clip and the **Play** button onto the stage. The **Play** button comes from Flash's built-in **Buttons** library, found under **Common Libraries** in the **Other Panels** sub-menu of the **Window** menu. Resize the **Play** button's width and height to 320 and 90, respectively. Arrange the two objects vertically with the text on top (Fig. 18.1). Do not worry that the text is almost invisible when deselected; it will fade in when the movie is viewed.

Fig. 18.1   Positioning the **introText** movie clip and **Play** button.

Test the movie. The text effects were created by manipulating alpha and gradient values with shape tweening. Feel free to explore the different symbols in the **Library** to see how they were created.

Select the **Play** button and add the script:

```
on( release )
{
   // plays frame labelled game in main timeline
   gotoAndPlay( "game" );
} //end of on( release )
```

When the **Play** button is clicked, the movie will now play the second frame, labeled **game**.

18.6 Creating Moving Objects

18.6.1 Adding the Target

In our game, the user's goal is to hit a moving target. In this section, we create the moving target. Drag an instance of the **target** movie clip from the **Library** to the second frame of the **Target** layer. Using the **Property Inspector**, position the target at the **x** and **y** coordinates 510 and 320, respectively. The coordinate (0, 0) is situated in the upper-left-hand corner of the screen, so the target should appear near the lower-right-hand corner of the stage. Give the **target** symbol the instance name **target** and open its **Actions** panel. Add the script:

```
onClipEvent( load )
{
    // initializes three variables
    direction = 1;
    speed = 5;
    hitCounter = 0;
} // end of onClipEvent( load )
```

onClipEvent(*event*) is an **event handler** that detects when the specified *event* occurs. onClipEvent(load) runs when the clip containing this symbol first loads. It creates and initializes three variables that apply to the **target** object. The variable direction indicates the direction in which the **target** object is moving at any time in the game. This variable will be set to either -1 (up) or 1 (down). The variable speed determines how quickly the **target** object moves. We will discuss the hitCounter variable later.

On a new line in the **Actions** panel, add the code presented in Fig. 18.2. [*Note*: Code formatting and line numbers will not necessarily coincide with the formatting and numbers of the code viewed in Flash. Code has been formatted here to match the conventions of this book.] This code causes the **target** symbol to oscillate (i.e., move up and down) continuously between the top and bottom of the stage. The onClipEvent(enterFrame) event handler executes every time the playhead enters a new frame. With a frame rate of 24 frames per second (**fps**), the code within the onClipEvent handler will execute 24 times per second.

```
1   onClipEvent( enterFrame )
2   {
3       // changes direction based on location
4       if ( this._y > 325 ) {
5           direction = -1;
6       } else if ( this._y < 75 ) {
7           direction = 1;
8       } // end if...else if statement
9
10      // increases the target's y coordinate by
11      // speed times direction ( 1 or -1 )
12      this._y += speed * direction;
13
14  } // end of onClipEvent( enterFrame )
```

Fig. 18.2   Making an object in Flash oscillate.

The if...else statement (lines 4–8) sets direction to -1 (up) when the target is at the bottom of the screen and 1 (down) when it is at the top of the screen, causing the target to change direction when it reaches either boundary. Keyword **this** (line 4) always references the symbol instance to which the current ActionScript code is attached (in this case, the **target**). While it is not always necessary to use the keyword this, we will always use it to maintain clarity in our code. Thus the conditional expression this._y > 325 (line 4) is true when the target's y-coordinate is greater than 325. [*Note*: The property _y refers specifically to the y-coordinate of the small white circle that appears on the main stage.] Since the stage is 400 pixels high and the target is 180 pixels high (half of which is below it's y-coordinate), when the target's y-coordinate is equal to 325, the bottom end of the target is

15 pixels past the bottom of the stage. Comparable logic applies to when the target is at the top of the stage. When the target has crossed one of the boundaries, we update `direction` to cause the target to reverse.

Line 12 causes the target to move, changing its *y*-coordinate by the number of pixels equal to `direction` times `speed`. Recall that we initialized `speed` to 5 in the target's `onClipEvent( load )` event handler, and `direction` is either -1 or 1. Also recall that *x-y* coordinate (0, 0) is in the upper-left corner of the stage, so decreasing the *y*-coordinate moves the target up, and increasing the *y*-coordinate moves the target down. Test the movie to see the target oscillate between the top and bottom of the stage.

18.6.2 Adding the Blocker

An additional moving object is used to block the ball and add an additional degree of difficulty to our game. Select the second frame of the **Blocker** layer and drag an instance of the **blocker** object from the **Library** onto the stage. Set the **blocker** instance's *x-* and *y*-coordinates to 390 and 320, respectively. Copy all the script from the **target** object's **Actions** panel and paste it in the blocker's **Actions** panel. Change the value of variable `speed` to 2 in the event handler `onClipEvent( load )`. Note that we employ identical logic to make each moving object oscillate between the top and bottom of the stage. The only difference in this code is that we program the blocker to move slower. The blocker's code should now resemble that in Fig. 18.3. Test the movie. The blocker and target should both oscillate at different speeds (Fig. 18.4).

18.7 Adding the Rotating Cannon

Many Flash applications include animation that responds to mouse cursor motions. In this section, we discuss how to make the cannon's barrel follow the cursor, allowing the user to aim at the moving target. The skills learned in this section can be used to create many effects that respond to cursor movements.

```
1   onClipEvent( load )
2   {
3      // initializes two variables
4      direction = 1;
5      speed = 2;
6   } // end of onClipEvent( enterFrame )
7
8   onClipEvent( enterFrame )
9   {
10     // changes direction based on location
11     if ( this._y > 325 ) {
12        direction = -1;
13     } else if ( this._y < 75 ) {
14        direction = 1;
15     } // end of if...else if
16     this._y += speed * direction;
17  } // end of onClipEvent( enterFrame )
```

Fig. 18.3   Adding oscillation to the **blocker** object.

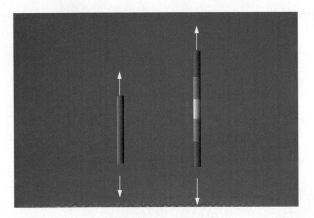

Fig. 18.4   Oscillating blocker and target.

Start by selecting the second frame of the **Cannon** layer and dragging the **cannon** object from the **Library** onto the stage. Set its x- and y-coordinates to 0 and 179.4, respectively. The cannon should appear in the middle of the stage's left edge (Fig. 18.5).

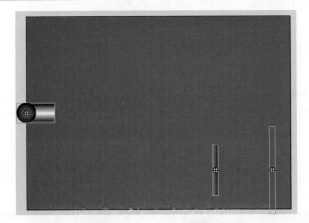

Fig. 18.5   Cannon position.

18.7.1 Coding the Cannon's Rotation

Select the cannon and open its **Actions** panel. Add the code in Fig. 18.6. This script should rotate the cannon barrel to point toward the cursor. The event handler `onClipEvent(` `mouseMove )` executes every time the mouse moves. Thus this code executes continuously (except when the mouse is completely motionless), causing the cannon to always point toward the mouse cursor. The code creates two variables, `x` and `y`, and assigns them to the mouse's x- and y-coordinates, respectively (lines 4–5). `_root` must precede `_xmouse` and `_ymouse` to get the mouse's coordinates relative to the main stage. The `if` statement's condition (line 8) is true only if the mouse is within the stage. If the cursor is within the stage, the code adjusts the cannon's rotation so that it points toward the cursor (lines 11–12). The property **_rotation** (line 12) controls an object's rotation, assuming its natural orientation to be 0 degrees.

```
1   onClipEvent( mouseMove )
2   {
3       // sets x and y to corresponding cursor position on stage
4       x = _root._xmouse;
5       y = _root._ymouse;
6
7       // determines whether the cursor is in stage (width: 550 height: 400)
8       if ( x > 0 && y > 0 && x < 550 && y < 400 ) {
9
10          // adjusts the cannon's rotation based on cursor position.
11          angle = Math.atan2( ( y - 200 ), x );
12          this._rotation = angle * ( 180 / Math.PI );
13      } // end of if statement
14  } // end of onClipEvent( mouseMove )
```

Fig. 18.6   Rotating the **cannon** object.

ActionScript's **Math** object contains various mathematical methods and properties that are useful when performing complex operations. For a full list of the Math object's components, refer to Flash's ActionScript dictionary. We will use the Math object to help us compute the rotation angle required to point the cannon toward the cursor.

First, we need to find the cursor's coordinates relative to the cannon. Subtracting 200 from the cursor's *y*-coordinate gives us the cursor's vertical position, assuming (0, 0) lies is located at the cannon's center (Fig. 18.7). We then set up a simple trigonometric equation to find the desired angle of rotation. Note the right triangle created by the cannon and the cursor in Fig. 18.7. From trigonometry, we know that the tangent of angle α equals the length of side *y* divided by side *x*: $tan(\alpha) = y/x$. We want the value of α, though, not the value of $tan(\alpha)$. Since the arc tangent is the inverse of the tangent, we can rewrite this equation as $\alpha = arctan(y/x)$. The Math object provides us with an arc tangent method: Math.atan2(y / x). This method returns a value, in radians, equal to the angle opposite

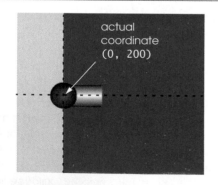
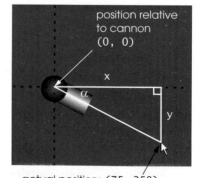

actual position: (75, 250)
position relative to cannon: (75, 50)

Fig. 18.7   Geometry of the **cannon** object.

side y and adjacent to side x. Radians are a type of angle measurement similar to degrees that range from 0 to 2π instead of 0 to 360. To convert from radians to degrees, we multiply by *180 / π*. `Math.PI` provides us with the constant value of π. To find the angle of the cannon, we first find the value of the angle between the cannon and the cursor in radians, using the method `Math.atan2`, and then convert the result to degrees (lines 11–12). Since this rotation adjustment is performed every time the mouse moves within the stage, the cannon barrel appears to constantly point at the cursor. Test the movie to observe this effect.

Error-Prevention Tip 18.1

If your code is not working properly and no error message displays, make sure that every variable points to the correct object. One incorrect `this` *or* `_root` *can prevent an entire function from operating correctly.*

18.7.2 Hiding the Cannon Layer

We will not make any other changes to the **Cannon** layer. Hide the **Cannon** layer by selecting the **show/hide** selector (dot) in the portion of the **Timeline** to the right of the layer name (Fig. 18.8). A red **x** should appear in place of the dot to indicate that the layer is invisible for editing. The layer will still be visible when the movie is viewed. Clicking the show/hide **x** again makes the **Cannon** layer visible.

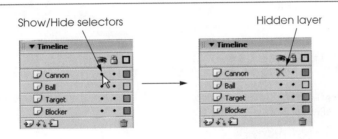

Fig. 18.8   Show/hide layers.

18.8 Adding the Cannon Ball

In this section, we add the cannon ball to our game. Drag the **ball** symbol from the **Library** on to the stage in frame 2 of the **Ball** layer. Notice that the ball instance appears as a small white circle on the stage. This circle is Flash's default appearance for a movie clip that has no graphic in its first frame. Set the ball's instance name to **ball** and adjust its *x*- and *y*-coordinates to 0 and 200, respectively. The ball will appear hidden beneath the cannon when the movie is viewed, because it is on a lower layer.

18.8.1 Initializing the Ball's Motion Variables

Open the ball's **Actions** panel and add the code:

```
onClipEvent( load )
{
    // initializes four variables
    fire = false;
    exploding = false;
```

```
        fireRatio = 0;
        speed = 30;
    } // end of onClipEvent( load )
```

This code initializes four variables: `fire`, `exploding`, `fireRatio` and `speed`. Variable `fire` and `exploding` are set to `false` to signify that the ball is in its resting state (i.e., it is not in flight) and is not exploding. Later, we will set `exploding` to `true` to play a brief explosion animation when the ball hits either the target or the blocker. Variables `fireRatio` and `speed` will determine the ball's firing direction and speed, respectively.

On a new line, enter the code presented in Fig. 18.9. This code executes every time the user clicks the mouse. The `if` statement (lines 8–13) allows the user to fire the ball only if the cannon ball is not currently in flight (`!fire`) and not exploding (`!exploding`). If both of these conditions are `false`, and the mouse is within the stage (line 9), `fire` is set to true (line 11). Variable `fireRatio` is set to the mouse's *y*-coordinate divided by its *x*-coordinate, relative to the cannon (line 12). We will use the `fireRatio` again in the next section to determine the angle at which the ball fires.

```
1   onClipEvent( mouseDown )
2   {
3       // sets x and y to corresponding cursor position on stage
4       x = _root._xmouse;
5       y = _root._ymouse;
6
7       // fires ball if conditions are true
8       if ( ( !fire ) && ( !exploding ) &&
9           x > 0 && y > 0 && x < 550 && y < 400 ) {
10
11          fire = true;
12          fireRatio = ( y - 200 ) / x;
13      } // end of if statement
14  } // end of onClipEvent( mouseDown )
```

Fig. 18.9   Setting the **ball** object's fire ratio.

18.8.2 Scripting the Ball's Motion

On a new line in the ball's **Actions** panel, write the code in Fig. 18.10. This code contains an `if...else` statement to determine how to script the ball's motion such that the ball travels along a straight line in the direction the cannon was pointing when the shot was fired.

```
1   onClipEvent( enterFrame )
2   {
3       // changes the fired bullet's position
4       if ( ( !exploding ) && fire ) {
5           this._x += speed;
6           this._y += speed * fireRatio;
7
8       // returns ball to starting position
9       } else if ( ( !exploding ) && ( !fire ) ) {
```

Fig. 18.10   Moving the fired **ball** object. (Part 1 of 2.)

```
10            this._x = 0;
11            this._y = 200;
12         } // end of if statement
13      } // end of onClipEvent( enterFrame )
```

Fig. 18.10 Moving the fired **ball** object. (Part 2 of 2.)

For the first condition to be true, the ball must not be exploding and must have been fired already (line 4). If these two conditions are satisfied, the code increments the ball's *x*-coordinate by speed and its *y*-coordinate by speed * fireRatio. Remember that fire-Ratio equals (y - 200) / x, where y and x are the cursor's coordinates when the ball is fired. Since the ball's *x*-coordinate increases by variable speed, we can use fireRatio to determine the change in the ball's *y*-coordinate. The expression speed * fireRatio gives the appropriate change in y based on the given change in x (speed). This code moves the ball along a straight-line path between the cannon and the mouse's position when fired. Since this function executes 24 times per second, the ball travels continuously in a straight line until fire is set to false. As we will soon see, fire becomes false when the ball goes off the stage or hits either the blocker or the target. If the ball is not moving or exploding (line 9), it will return to its original position underneath the cannon (lines 10–11). Test the movie and try clicking the stage. The ball should shoot only once because we have not yet added code that resets variable fire to false.

18.9 Adding Sound and Text Objects to the Movie

Next, we add sound and text to our movie. Add a keyframe to frame 2 of the **Text** layer and drag the **text** symbol from the **Library** onto the stage. Note that the **text** object, like the ball, is represented by a small white dot. This dot will not appear when the movie is viewed. Position the **text** symbol in the center of the stage at coordinate (275, 200), and name the instance **text**. Add a keyframe to the second frame of the **Sound** and **ScoreText** layers, and add an instance of the **sound** and **scoreText** objects, respectively. Center both objects in the stage and give them instance names matching their symbol names: **sound** and **scoreText**. Lock the layers by clicking the **lock/unlock** selector (dot) to the right of the layer name in the timeline (Fig. 18.11). When a layer is locked, its elements are visible, but they cannot be edited. This allows a developer to use one layer's elements as visual references for designing another layer, while ensuring that no elements are moved unintentionally. To unlock a layer, click the lock symbol to the right of the layer name in the **Timeline**.

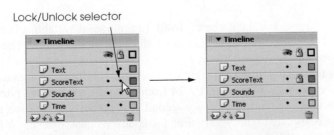

Fig. 18.11 Lock/unlock layers.

All the necessary sound and text has now been added to the game. In the next section, we will add the time counter to our game.

18.10 Adding the Time Counter

The cannon game's difficulty lies in the limited amount of time given to the player to hit every piece of the target. Time, whether increasing or decreasing, is an important aspect of many games and applications. In this section, we discuss adding a time counter that decreases as the game progresses.

18.10.1 Adding the Time Box

In the cannon game, the player has a limited amount of time to destroy every section of the target. The current amount of time remaining appears in a dynamic text box in the bottom-left corner of the screen. Add a keyframe to frame 2 of the **Time** layer and add an instance of the **time** symbol. Position it at coordinate (25, 340), which should be in the lower-left corner of the stage. Name the instance **timeBox**. Open the **time** symbol from the **Library** and select the text field. In the **Property Inspector**, change the text type to **Dynamic Text** and name the instance **timeText**. Return to the main scene. Select the **timeBox** instance and add the ActionScript presented in Fig. 18.12 to the **timeBox** instance's **Actions** panel.

```
1   onClipEvent( load )
2   {
3       // initializes variable time
4       time = 10;
5   } // end of onClipEvent( load )
6
7   onClipEvent( enterFrame )
8   {
9       // decreases time and changes text in timeBox
10      time -= ( 1 / 24 );
11      this.timeText.text = "TIME :" + parseInt( time );
12
13      // plays end sequence
14      if ( time < 0 ) {
15          _global.winner = false;
16          _root.gotoAndPlay( "end" );
17      } // end of if statement
18  } // end of onClipEvent( enterFrame )
```

Fig. 18.12 Time-decrease code.

The event handler `onClipEvent( load )` initializes a variable `time` to 10 (line 4). This variable will hold the remaining time throughout the game. The event handler `onClipEvent( enterFrame )` (lines 7–18) first decrements `time` by 1 / 24 and then displays the new time in the **timeText** text box (lines 10–11). Since the movies plays at a rate of 24 frames per second, subtracting 1 / 24 from `time` at each `enterFrame` event has the net effect of decreasing `time` by 1 every second. The property `text` (line 11) refers to the text in the `timeText` text field. Every time the code executes, `"TIME:  "` followed by the current value of variable `time` is written in the `timeText` field. The + means that the string `"TIME:  "` is **concatenated**, or combined, with variable `time`'s value. Since we want the time to appear as a whole number, we use parseInt(*value*), which converts the *value* within its parentheses to an integer (line 11).

The if statement in line 14 executes when time runs out and initializes a **global** variable winner to false (line 15). A global variable can be accessed from anywhere in the movie without using a reference path to a specific symbol or _root. Initializing or changing the value of a global variable, however, requires using the _global reference so as not to be confused with initializing a local variable. From now on, we can determine whether _global.winner is true or false simply by referring to this variable as winner from anywhere in our movie.

Line 16 plays the frame labeled **end** in the main timeline. We discuss the end sequence animation in the next subsection. Test the movie. The time should decrease from 10 to 0. When the time reaches 0, the **end** frame should play.

18.10.2 Creating a Final Animation Sequence

Real-world games generally have a final animation sequence that informs the user of the outcome of the game. In this section, we create a final animation sequence for our game.

First, insert a keyframe in frame 3 of the **Text** layer. Next, select the **Actions** layer (also in the third frame) and open its **Actions** panel. There should already be a stop action applied to this frame. Add the code:

```
if ( winner )
{
   // plays win sequence
   _root.text.gotoAndPlay( "win" );
} else {
   // plays lose sequence
   _root.text.gotoAndPlay( "lose" );
} // end of if statement
```

This if...else refers to the global variable winner, which is set to true or false depending on the outcome of the game. If true, the portion of the **text** instance labeled **win** plays, otherwise the section labeled **lose** plays. Test the movie again. When the time runs out, the text **Game Over**, which appears in the section labeled **lose**, should appear on a blank stage.

18.11 Detecting a Miss

We will now add code to the **ball** instance that detects when the ball has been fired off the stage. Select the ball in the second frame of the **Ball** layer and open its **Actions** panel. In the event handler onClipEvent(enterFrame), add the code presented in Fig. 18.13.

```
1   if ( this._x < 0 || this._y < 0 || this._x > 550 || this._y > 400 )
2   {
3      // setting fire to false returns ball to original position
4      fire = false;
5
```

Fig. 18.13 Miss detection in Flash. (Part 1 of 2.)

```
6      // plays appropriate sound and score sequences
7      _root.text.gotoAndPlay( "miss" );
8      _root.scoreText.gotoAndPlay( "minusTwo" );
9      _root.sound.gotoAndPlay( "miss" );
10
11     // changes variable time in timeBox
12     _root.textBox.time -= 2;
13  } // end of if statement
```

Fig. 18.13 Miss detection in Flash. (Part 2 of 2.)

The || operator in the if statement (line 1) behaves the same as the logical OR operator (||) in JavaScript. If any of the conditions connected by the || operator are true, the entire condition is true. The condition determines whether the ball travels outside the bounds of the stage. If it does, the shot is considered a miss. A miss sets fire to false (line 4) and deducts two from the variable time in the **timeBox** (line 12). Setting fire to false returns the ball to its starting position and plays a series of effects, including the text for a miss, the text indicating that two seconds were lost and the miss sound (lines 7–9). To play these effects, we must reference the appropriate movie clips using the _root property (because these actions appear in the **ball**'s **Actions** panel) and indicate the frame label to play. Open the **sound**, **text** and **scoreText** symbols from the **Library** to see how their frames are labeled. At the end of each labeled section a stop action ensures that only the specified section plays. Test the movie with your computer's sound turned on. At this point, every fired ball should travel off the stage and count as a miss. In the next few sections, we discuss how to add features that allow the user to gain time and win the game.

18.12 Creating a Function

In Flash, we often want to create our own **functions**. A function is a block of code that can be called multiple times. Functions are commonly used when a specific task needs to be repeated many times in different parts of the movie. In Flash, a function is bound to the object in which it is created. It is also possible to create a **global function**, which is accessible from any part of a movie. In this section, we discuss creating and using functions in Flash.

We now create a global function that is called every time the ball makes contact with the blocker or the target. Our function can be passed **parameters** (**arguments**) and **return values**, both of which will be discussed more in the following sections. Select the **ball** instance in the second frame and open its **Actions** panel. On a new line in the onClip-Event(load) event handler, add the code presented in Fig. 18.14.

```
1   _global.ballContact = function( timeChange )
2   {
3       // determines whether ball has been fired and is not exploding
4       if ( ( !exploding ) && ( fire ) ) {
5
6           // adjusts variables to play exploding sequence
7           exploding = true;
8           fire = false;
```

Fig. 18.14 Function creation in Flash. (Part 1 of 2.)

```
 9        _root.timeBox.time += timeChange;
10        _root.ball.gotoAndPlay( "explode" );
11
12        // plays appropriate sound and text based on timeChange
13        if ( timeChange < 0 ) {
14            _root.sound.gotoAndPlay( "blocked" );
15            _root.text.gotoAndPlay( "blocked" );
16
17            if ( timeChange == -5 ) {
18                _root.scoreText.gotoAndPlay( "minusFive" );
19            } // end of if statement
20
21        } else if ( timeChange >= 0 ) {
22            _root.sound.gotoAndPlay( "hit" );
23            _root.text.gotoAndPlay( "hit" );
24
25            if ( timeChange == 5 ) {
26               _root.scoreText.gotoAndPlay( "plusFive" );
27            } else if ( timeChange == 10 ) {
28               _root.scoreText.gotoAndPlay( "plusTen" );
29            } else if ( timeChange == 20 ) {
30               _root.scoreText.gotoAndPlay( "plus20" );
31            } // end of if...else if statement
32        }// end of if...else if statement.
33
34        return true;
35    }// end of if statement
36
37    return false;
38 }// end of function
```

Fig. 18.14 Function creation in Flash. (Part 2 of 2.)

This code creates a global function named ballContact (line 1) using the **function** action. The function action is passed a parameter timeChange that is used in the function's code to modify the amount of time remaining. In the next section, we discuss how to detect a collision between the ball and another object. Each time such a collision occurs, we call ballContact and pass it the appropriate value for timeChange. For instance, if the ball hits an object such that the time should decrease by 5, we would write ballContact(-5).

Every time the function ballContact is called, it detects whether the ball has been fired and is not currently exploding (line 4). If so, the code makes the ball stop moving and plays a brief exploding animation by setting exploding to true and fire to false (lines 7–10). The code also changes the value of variable time in the **timeBox** to reflect the desired change (line 9).

An if...else statement (lines 13–32) determines whether the time is decreasing or increasing (based on the value of timeChange) and plays the appropriate sound and text. The function returns true (line 34) if it has performed these tasks; otherwise, it returns false (line 37). We will revisit this return value later. In the next section, we discuss how to detect collisions between objects.

18.13 Adding Collision Detectors

18.13.1 Adding Collision Detection to the Blocker

Flash has a built-in **collision detection** method that determines whether two objects are overlapping. The method *object1*.hitTest(*object2*) returns true if any part of *object1* overlaps *object2*. Many games must detect collisions between moving objects to control game play or add realistic effects. For example, if two players in a sports game run into each other, they might react by falling down. In this game, we rely on collision detection simply to determine if a shot fired hits either the blocker or the target.

Select the **blocker** instance in frame 2 of the **Blocker** layer and open its **Actions** panel. Find the event handler onClipEvent(enterFrame) and, on a new line, add the code:

```
if ( this.hitTest( _root.ball ) )
{
   // runs function ballContact()
   ballContact( -5 );
} // end of if statement
```

The property this indicates that the first object in the collision test is the blocker to which this code is attached. The second object is the **ball** instance. If the **ball** overlaps the **blocker**, then hitTest returns true and the ballContact function is called. Remember that the parameter within the parentheses determines the change in time. A blocked hit corresponds to a time decrease of five. Select the **ball** instance and find the ballContact function. Trace the code, assuming that timeChange is set to -5.

Test the movie, and shoot the ball at the blocker. The time should decrease by five. The ball should stay in the position where it hit the blocker, even after the exploding animation is played. The function ballContact set the ball's variable exploding to true. We have not yet written code that sets it back to false. The ball will return to its original position only if it is not exploding. Open the **ball** symbol's editing stage from the **Library** and select the last frame of the **Actions** layer. On a new line in the **Actions** panel, enter the code: _root.ball.exploding = false;. Test the movie again. The ball should now disappear after its exploding animation, allowing multiple shots to be taken. In the next section, we add similar collision detection to the target.

18.13.2 Adding Collision Detection to the Target

In this section, we add code to the **target** that increases the player's remaining time each time the target is hit. Open the **target** object's editing stage from the **Library** panel. Note that the **target** object comprises three symbols: **targetCenter** (white), **targetMiddle** (gray), and **targetOut** (white). Select one of the red **targetOut** instances and add the script presented in Fig. 18.15.

```
1  onClipEvent( enterFrame )
2  {
3     newHit = false;
4
```

Fig. 18.15 Collision detection in Flash. (Part 1 of 2.)

```
5        // tests for collision
6        if ( this.hitTest( _root.ball ) ) {
7
8            // newHit will be true if ballContact() returns true
9            newHit = ballContact( 5 );
10
11           // determines whether newHit is true
12           if ( newHit ) {
13
14               // increments hitCounter and plays target's hit animation
15               _root.target.hitCounter += 1;
16               this.gotoAndPlay( "hit" );
17           } // end of if statement
18       } // end of if statement
19   } // end of onClipEvent( enterFrame )
```

Fig. 18.15   Collision detection in Flash. (Part 2 of 2.)

In this code, we first initialize the variable newHit to false (line 3). Line 9 calls the function ballContact with a parameter value of 5 to indicate that five seconds should be added to player's remaining time. Line 9 also sets newHit equal to ballContact's return value. Remember that ballContact returns true if the ball has been fired and is not currently exploding. If newHit is true, the code increments hitCounter by one and plays **targetOut**'s hit animation (lines 12–17). Open **targetOut**'s editing stage and go to its animation labeled **hit**. Note that the last frame of the hit animation contains no graphic, making the **targetOut** instance effectively disappear when hit.

Return to the **target** object's editing stage. Copy the code from the **targetOut** instance to the other four instances that make up the target. Change the time increase to 10 for the two **targetMiddle** (gray) instances and 20 for the **targetCenter** (white) instance. Return to the main scene and test the movie. The target blocks should disappear when hit by the ball. The user can now gain time by hitting the target. In the next section, we add the final lines of code to our game.

18.14 Finishing the Game

We will now add the final code that determines whether the player has won or lost. Select the **target** instance in the second frame of the **Target** layer and open its **Actions** panel. Find the onClipEvent(enterFrame) event handler and, on a new line, add the code:

```
if ( hitCounter >= 5 )
{
    // initializes variable winner and plays frame labelled "end"
    _global.winner = true;
    _root.gotoAndPlay( "end" );
} // end of if statement
```

Remember that each time a piece of the target is hit, we increment the variable hitCounter by one. Once hitCounter is greater than or equal to 5, the player has destroyed the entire target. In this case, the global variable winner is set to true and the frame labeled **end** is played. Setting winner to true will cause the text sequence labeled **win** to play in the **end** frame. Open the **text** symbol's editing stage from the **Library**. An action that plays the frame labeled **intro** in the main scene has already been attached to the last frame of the sections labeled **win** and **lose**. These actions, which were included in the original `cannontemplate.fla` file, cause the game to restart after the final text animation is played.

Return to the main scene and test your movie. To change the game's difficulty, adjust the variable `speed` in either the **blocker** or the **target**. Adjusting the time change in the `timeBox` instance also changes the difficulty (a smaller decrement gives more time).

Congratulations! You have created an interactive Flash game. Publish the game and play the completed version. Move on to the exercises at the end of the chapter to improve the game and add additional levels.

18.15 ActionScript 2.0 Elements Introduced in This Chapter

Figure 18.16 lists the Flash ActionScript 2.0 elements introduced in this chapter, which are useful in building complex Flash movies.

Action	Description
object.`_x`	Property that refers to *object*'s x-coordinate.
object.`_y`	Property that refers to *object*'s y-coordinate.
`_xmouse`	Property that gives the mouse's x-coordinate.
`_ymouse`	Property that gives the mouse's y-coordinate.
object.`_rotation`	Property that refers to the rotation of *object*.
`text`	Property that refers to the text in a text field.
`this`	References the object to which the code is attached.
`_root`	Creates a reference path that starts at the main timeline.
`_global`	Declares a global variable or function.
`function()`	Declares a function.
object1.`hitTest(` *object2* `)`	Returns true if *object1* and *object2* are overlapping.
`parseInt(` *n* `)`	Returns number *n* without decimals.
`onClipEvent(` *event* `)`	Event handler that detects when the specified *event*, such as `load`, `enterFrame` or `mouseMove`, occurs.
`Math`	Built in object that contains useful methods and properties (refer to Flash's ActionScript Dictionary for a full list).

Fig. 18.16   ActionScript 2.0 elements.

SUMMARY

- ActionScript 2.0 is an object-oriented scripting language.
- ActionScript contains classes, which are collections of characteristics known as properties and behaviors known as methods. We can create our own classes or use any of Flash's predefined classes.
- A class can be used to create many instances or objects of a class. Dragging its symbol from the **Library** onto the stage created an instance (object) of the class. There can be multiple instances

(objects) of one class on the stage. Any changes made to an individual instance (resizing, rotating, etc.) affect only that one instance.

- Property `_root` references the main timeline object.
- ActionScript programmers often create an **Actions** layer to divide larger applications into more manageable pieces.
- `onClipEvent( event )` is an event handler that detects when the specified *event* occurs.
- The keyword `this` references the instance to which it is attached. While it is not always necessary to use the keyword `this`, it helps maintain clarity in code.
- Many Flash applications contain animation that responds to cursor motions.
- The event handler `onClipEvent( mouseMove )` executes every time the mouse moves.
- The property `_rotation` controls an object's rotation, assuming its natural orientation to be 0 degrees, increasing clockwise.
- Flash's `Math` object contains various mathematical methods and properties that are useful when performing complex operations.
- A small white circle is Flash's default appearance for a movie clip that has no graphic in its first frame. The circle will not be visible when the movie is viewed.
- To hide a layer, click the show/hide selector (dot) in the portion of the timeline containing the layer name. A red **x** should appear through the dot to indicate that the layer is invisible for editing. The layer will still be visible when the movie is viewed. Clicking the show/hide **x** again will make the layer visible.
- To lock a layer, click the lock/unlock selector (dot) to the right of the layer name in the timeline. When a layer is locked, its elements are visible, but cannot be edited. To unlock a layer, click the lock symbol to the right of the layer name in the timeline.
- Time, whether increasing or decreasing, is an important aspect of many games and applications.
- A global variable can be accessed from anywhere in a movie without a reference path. Initializing or changing the value of a global variable, however, requires using the `_global` reference path.
- Real-world games generally have a final animation sequence that informs the user of the outcome of their game.
- In Flash, a programmer often wants to create new functions. A function is a block of code that carries out a specific task and can be called multiple times. In Flash, a function is bound to the object in which it is created.
- It is possible to create a global function that is accessible from anywhere in our movie.
- Flash has a built-in collision detection method that determines whether or not two objects are overlapping. The method *object1*.`hitTest`(*object2*) returns `true` if any part of *object1* and *object2*'s fields (represented by the blue, outlined square) overlap.

TERMINOLOGY

&& operator
|| operator
_global
_root
_rotation
ActionScript 2.0
ActionScript Dictionary
Buttons library

class
collision detection
Common Libraries
event handler
frame label
function
global function
global variable

hitTest collision detection method

instance

instance name

Library

lock/unlock layer

method

object

onClipEvent event handler

oscillation (oscillating object)

parameter

rotation (rotating object)

show/hide layer

symbol

text property

this

SELF-REVIEW EXERCISES

18.1   State whether each of the following is *true* or *false*. If *false*, explain why.
   a)   ActionScript 2.0 is an object-oriented scripting language that contains methods and classes.
   b)   There can be multiple instances of one symbol.
   c)   Variables in one movie clip cannot be accessed or changed from another movie clip.
   d)   Locking a layer is the same as hiding it, except that a hidden layer can still be edited.
   e)   New functions can never be created in Flash. We must rely on Flash's predefined functions.

18.2   Fill in the blanks for each of the following statements.
   a)   Property _____ accesses the main timeline object.
   b)   Keyword _____ accesses the object to which the code is attached.
   c)   A movie clip with no animation in its first frame appears as a(n) _____.
   d)   A(n) _____ variable or function can be accessed from anywhere in a movie without referencing a specific path.
   e)   Flash has a built-in _____ method that returns true when two objects overlap.

ANSWERS TO SELF-REVIEW EXERCISES

18.1   a) True. b) True. c) False. Using the property _root references the main timeline object, from which another movie clip in the movie can be accessed. d) False. Neither locked nor hidden layers can be edited. Locked layers are visible, though, whereas hidden layers are not. e) False. New functions can be created using the function() action.

18.2   a) _root. b) this. c) small white circle. d) global. e) collision detection.

EXERCISES

18.3   Add an **instructions** button to the **intro** frame of the main scene. Make it play a brief movie clip explaining the rules of the game. The instructions should not interfere with the actual game play.

18.4   Use Flash's random(n) function (discussed in Chapter 17) to assign a random speed between 1 and 4 to the blocker, and a speed between 5 and 7 to the target. Remember that random(n) returns a random integer between 0 and n.

18.5   Add a text field to the **end** frame that displays the player's final score (i.e., the time remaining) if the player wins. Output different phrases depending on the player's final score (e.g, 1–10: nice job, 11–15: Great!, 16–20: Amazing!). [*Hint*: Create a new global variable finalTime if the player wins. Think about creating an if...else statement to determine which text phrase to use based on finalTime.]

18.6   Add a second level to the game with two blockers instead of one. Try to do this without adding a fourth frame to the timeline. Instead, create a duplicate **blocker** symbol and modify it to appear invisible at first. Think about reversing the process we used to make the sections of the **target** invisible. The final score should be a combination of first- and second-round scores. [*Hint*: Create a global variable `level` that stores the current level (i.e., 1 or 2). Make the second blocker visible only if `level == 2`.]

18.7   Give a brief description of the following terms:
  a) Lock/unlock
  b) Instance
  c) Collision detection
  d) `_x` and `_y`
  e) `onClipEvent( event )`
  f) Function

19

Macromedia Dreamweaver® MX 2004

Objectives

- To be able to use Dreamweaver MX 2004 effectively.
- To develop Web pages in a visual environment.
- To insert images and links into Web pages.
- To use Dreamweaver to create XHTML elements such as tables and forms.
- To be able to insert scripts into Dreamweaver pages.
- To be able to use Dreamweaver's site-management capabilities.

We must select the illusion which appeals to our temperament, and embrace it with passion, if we want to be happy.
Cyril Connolly

The symbolic view of things is a consequence of long absorption in images. Is sign language the real language of Paradise?
Hugo Ball

What you see is what you get (WYSIWYG).
Anonymous

All human knowledge takes the form of interpretation.
Walter Benjamin

Outline

19.1 Introduction

In this chapter we discuss Macromedia's *Dreamweaver MX 2004*. Perhaps the most popular visual HTML editor, Dreamweaver MX 2004 is a versatile tool with an interface similar to that of Macromedia's *Flash MX 2004* (Chapters 17–18).

A fully functional, 30–day trial version of Dreamweaver is included on the CD that accompanies this book. The software will become disabled 30 days after installation. Please install the software before continuing in this chapter. Detailed installation instructions are available on the CD. [*Note*: Do not alter the computer's clock settings during the trial period. Doing so causes the 30-day trial to end immediately, rendering the software unusable. Reinstalling Dreamweaver will not reactivate the program.]

Dreamweaver can more easily perform many of the tasks already discussed in previous chapters. It can insert and edit text, as well as create more complex XHTML elements, such as tables, forms, frames and much more. For a complete list and description of Dreamweaver's XHTML tags, open the **Reference** panel by selecting **Reference** from the **Window** menu. Select the desired XHTML element from the **Tag** pull-down list in the **Reference** panel.

19.2 Macromedia Dreamweaver MX 2004

Upon starting Dreamweaver for the first time, the **Workspace Setup** dialog appears. The **Workspace Setup** dialog offers two selections, **Designer** and **Coder**, which determine the arrangement of the Dreamweaver editing environment. Select **Designer** and click **OK**. Dreamweaver then displays the default **Start Page**, which offers various options, such as **Open a Recent Item**, **Create New** and **Dreamweaver tutorial**. Click the **HTML** option under the **Create New** heading to open a blank page in the default viewing mode (Fig. 19.1). This is a **WYSIWYG (What You See Is What You Get)** display. Unlike editors that simply display XHTML code, Dreamweaver renders XHTML elements exactly as a browser would. This enables you to design your Web pages as they will be seen on the Web.

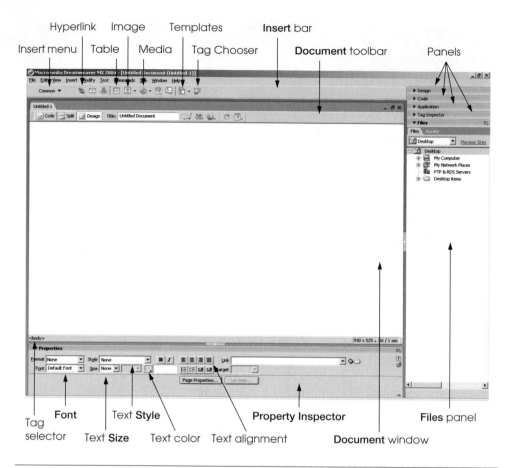

Insert menu   Hyperlink   Image   Templates   **Insert** bar
             Table   Media   Tag Chooser   **Document** toolbar   Panels

Tag selector   **Font**   Text **Style**   **Property Inspector**   **Files** panel
             Text **Size**   Text color   Text alignment   **Document** window

Fig. 19.1   Dreamweaver editing environment.

We will now re-create the book's first XHTML example (Fig. 4.1) using Dream-weaver. First, create a new document by selecting **New...** from the **File** menu. In the **New Document** dialog, select **Basic page** from the **Category** list, and **HTML** from the **Basic page** list. Also, check the **Make document XHTML compliant** checkbox in the lower-left corner to force Dreamweaver to generate XHTML-compliant code. Click the **Create** button to open the new document.

Type

```
Welcome to XHTML!
```

in the **Document** window. Dreamweaver encloses this text in a paragraph (p) element for proper formatting. Note that XHTML tags are not visible in the **Design** view. We will switch to the **Code** view in a moment to see the code that Dreamweaver generates. Now, to insert a title as we did in Fig. 4.1, right click in the **Document** window, and select **Page Properties...** from the pop-up menu to view the **Page Properties** dialog (Fig. 19.2).

The **Category** list lets the user specify which page properties are displayed. Select **Title/Encoding** from the **Category** list and enter **Internet and WWW How to Pro-**

gram into the **Title** field. Clicking **OK** inserts a `<title>` tag with the corresponding title text inside the head element in your XHTML code. Your page now appears exactly as it is in Fig. 4.1, shown here in Dreamweaver's WYSIWYG display instead of the browser window (Fig. 19.3). To view your page in a browser, press *F12* or select **Preview in Browser** from the **File** menu.

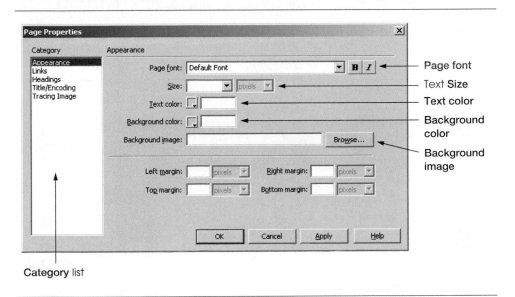

Fig. 19.2   Page Properties dialog.

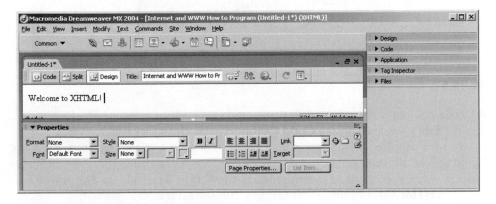

Fig. 19.3   Example of Fig. 4.1 in Dreamweaver.

Now that you have seen a basic example of WYSIWYG editing, remember that you are still programming in XHTML. To view or edit your XHTML directly, click the **Code** button in the **Document** toolbar (Fig. 19.4). Note the different colors of the code that appears (Fig. 19.5). Dreamweaver automatically color-codes XHTML to make viewing easier. The tag names, tag attributes, attribute values and page text are all displayed in different colors.

File name

Code and design view

View options

View in browser

Untitled-1*

◇ Code   Split   Design   Title: Internet and WWW How to Pr

Code view   **Design** view   Page title   File management

Refresh **Design** view

Fig. 19.4   **Document** toolbar.

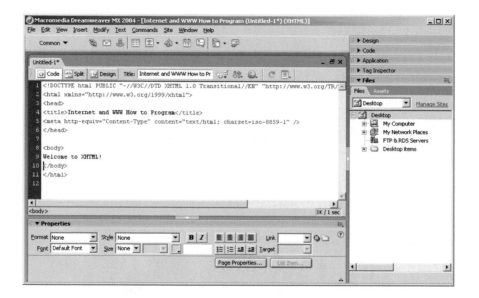

Fig. 19.5   **Code** view.

The code-coloring scheme can be accessed (and modified) by selecting **Preferences...** from the **Edit** menu and clicking **Code Coloring** in the **Category** list.

To save your file, click **Save** in the **File** menu or press *Ctrl+S*. The **Save As** dialog should appear, allowing you to specify a file name, type and location (Fig. 19.6). Create a folder in your C: drive named **Dreamweaver sites**. Type main into the **File name** field and select **HTML Documents** as the file type. Dreamweaver adds a .htm file-name extension if no extension is specified.

19.3 Text Styles

In Dreamweaver, we can alter text properties with the **Text** menu or the **Property Inspector**. Using these tools, we can quickly apply header tags (<h1>, <h2>, etc.), list tags (<ol>, <ul>) and several other tags used for stylizing text. Text can also be aligned left, right or centered, increased or decreased in size, indented and colored.

Fig. 19.6   Save As dialog.

Create a new document and type the text, as shown in the screen capture of Fig. 19.7, into the **Document** window. Drag the mouse to highlight one line at a time and select the corresponding header tag from the **Format** pull-down menu in the **Property Inspector**. Then, highlight all the text by pressing *Ctrl+A*, and click the align center button in the **Property Inspector**. The resulting XHTML produced by Dreamweaver is shown in Fig. 19.7.

As you can see, Dreamweaver is prone to produce somewhat inefficient code. In this case, using **Cascading Style Sheets** (**CSS**) to center the text would have been more efficient. Dreamweaver provides powerful tools to add CSS to pages, though this feature of the application is not covered in this chapter. Please refer to

www.macromedia.com/devnet/mx/dreamweaver/css.html

for information on using CSS in Dreamweaver.

```
1   <?xml version="1.0" encoding="iso-8859-1"?>
2   <!DOCTYPE html PUBLIC "-//W3C//DTD XHTML 1.0 Transitional//EN" "http://
3   www.w3.org/TR/xhtml1/DTD/xhtml1-transitional.dtd">
4   <head>
5   <html xmlns="http://www.w3.org/1999/xhtml">
6   <head>
7   <title>Untitled Document</title>
8   <meta http-equiv="Content-Type" content="text/html; charset=iso-8859-1" />
9   </head>
10  <body>
11  <h1 align="center">Level 1 Header</h1>
12  <h2 align="center">Level 2 Header</h2>
13  <h3 align="center">Level 3 Header</h3>
14  <h4 align="center">Level 4 Header</h4>
15  <h5 align="center">Level 5 Header</h5>
16  <h6 align="center">Level 6 Header</h6>
17  </body>
18  </html>
```

Fig. 19.7   Applying header tags and centering using Dreamweaver. (Part 1 of 2.)

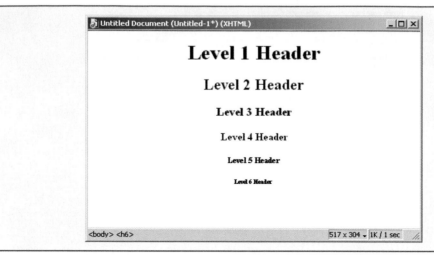

Fig. 19.7   Applying header tags and centering using Dreamweaver. (Part 2 of 2.)

Software Engineering Observation 19.1

Dreamweaver uses a wide variety of techniques to manipulate text that sometimes produce inefficient code. Make sure to check the code often to know exactly the kind of XHTML Dreamweaver is producing. Thorough knowledge of a page and what XHTML elements are present is necessary for advanced scripting.

Dreamweaver is capable of much more extensive text formatting. Perhaps you need to place a mathematical formula on your Web page. For example, type

```
e = mc2
```

in the window, then highlight the text. You can now change the formatting of the equation by selecting **Style** from the **Text** menu, and selecting **Code**. The **Text** menu contains many useful text-formatting options. The **Code** option applies a `code` element to the highlighted text, which designates formulas or computer code. Click the **Code** button in the **Document** toolbar to view the code, and find the 2 in the equation. Surround the 2 with a `<sup>...</sup>` tag. The `<sup>...</sup>` tag formats encompassed text as a superscript. Notice that after typing `<sup>` Dreamweaver inserts a matching end tag (`</sup>`). Click the **Design** button in the **Document** toolbar to view the fully formatted text.

You can also access most of the elements in the **Text** menu by right clicking highlighted text. The formula can be further emphasized by selecting a **Color...** attribute from the **Text** menu.

Good Programming Practice 19.1

When you press Enter *after typing text, Dreamweaver will enclose that text in a new set of* `<p>...</p>` *tags. If you want to insert only a* `<br />` *tag into a page, hold down* Shift *while pressing* Enter.

Good Programming Practice 19.2

You can manipulate the properties of almost any element displayed in the Dreamweaver window by right clicking an element and selecting its properties from the menu that pops up.

The **Property Inspector** is also useful for creating lists. Try entering the contents of a shopping list, as shown in Fig. 19.8, and applying the **Unordered List** style. Apply an h2 element to the title of the list.

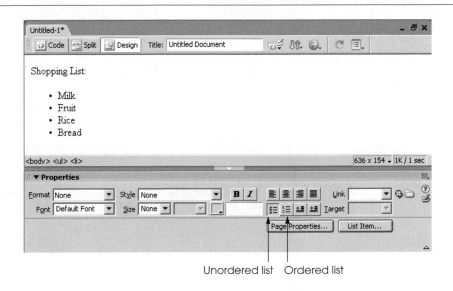

Fig. 19.8　List creation in Dreamweaver.

Select **List** from the **Text** menu for more list-related tags, such as the definition list (`<dl>`). There are two list elements in a **definition list**—the defined term (`<dt>`) and the definition data (`<dd>`). Figure 19.9 shows the formatting produced by a definition list and the code Dreamweaver uses to produce it.

To apply the definition list as shown, select **Definition List** from the **List** submenu of the **Text** menu. In the **Document** window, type the first term you want to define. When you press *Enter*, Dreamweaver changes the style to match that of a definition. Pressing *Enter* again lets you enter another defined term. The bold style of the defined terms is applied by clicking the **Bold** button in the **Property Inspector**, which applies the strong element.

```
1   <dl>
2      <dt><strong>FTP</strong></dt>
3      <dd>File Transfer Protocol</dd>
4      <dt><strong>GIF</strong></dt>
5      <dd>Graphics Interchange Format</dd>
6      <dt><strong>XHTML</strong></dt>
7      <dd>HyperText Markup Language</dd>
8      <dt><strong>PNG</strong></dt>
9      <dd>Portable Network Graphics</dd>
10  </dl>
```

Fig. 19.9　Definition list inserted using the **Text** menu. (Part 1 of 2.)

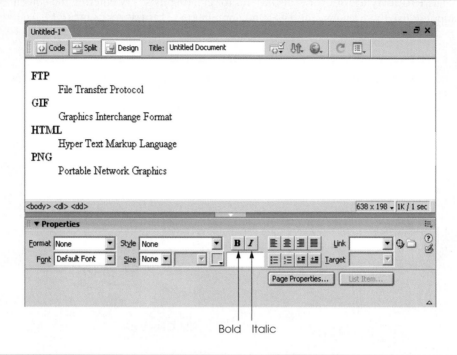

Fig. 19.9   Definition list inserted using the **Text** menu. (Part 2 of 2.)

19.4 Images and Links

Inserting images using Dreamweaver is simply a matter of clicking a button and selecting an image to insert. Open the **Select Image Source** dialog (Fig. 19.10) either by selecting **Image** from the **Insert** menu, clicking the **Image** button in the **Insert** bar, or pressing *Ctrl+Alt+I*. Browse your local hard drive directory for a JPEG, GIF or PNG image. (For more information on image types, please refer to Chapter 3.) You can view the image's URL in the **URL** field.

Software Engineering Observation 19.2

When you insert a local image into an unsaved document, Dreamweaver sets an absolute path, such as file:///C|/Dreamweaver sites/camel.gif. *Saving the document sets the image source to a relative path, starting at the folder in which the document is saved (e.g.,* camel.gif).

After inserting your image, select it in the **Document** window and create a hyperlink using the **Link** field in the **Property Inspector** (Fig. 19.11). Type in the URL to which the hyperlink will point. Dreamweaver adds a border = 0 attribute to the <img> tag, removing the blue rectangle that would normally appear around the image.

You can also change other image attributes in the **Property Inspector**. Try resizing the image using the height and width fields, and changing its alignment in the **Align** pull-down menu.

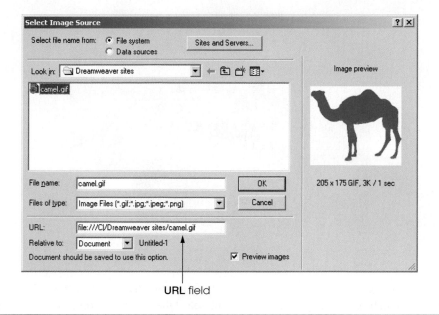

URL field

Fig. 19.10   Image source selection in Dreamweaver.

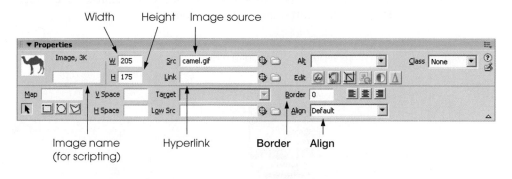

Fig. 19.11   Image properties in the **Property Inspector**.

19.5 Symbols and Lines

Dreamweaver allows you to insert characters that are not located on the standard keyboard. These characters are accessed by selecting **HTML** in the **Insert** menu, and then selecting **Special Characters**. Select **Other...** from the **Special Characters** submenu to view the **Insert Other Character** dialog, which contains a list of various characters (Fig. 19.12).

In the next example, we demonstrate how these symbols can be used in a Web page, along with Dreamweaver's **horizontal rule** feature. Begin by typing

    10 ÷ 5 =

Use the **Insert Other Character** dialog to insert the division symbol. Then, select **HTML** from the **Insert** menu in the **Insert** bar and click the **Horizontal Rule** button (Fig. 19.13).

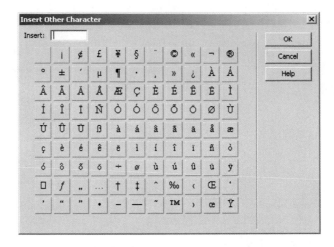

Fig. 19.12   Insert Other Characters dialog.

This action will insert a line (hr element) onto the page directly below the cursor's position. The line should be selected by default; if it is not, select the line by clicking it once. Using the **Property Inspector**, set the width to **60** pixels by entering **60** in the **W** field and selecting **pixels** from the pull-down menu directly to its left (Fig. 19.14). Make the line **5** pixels high by entering **5** in the **H** field. Select **Left** from the **Align** pull-down menu.

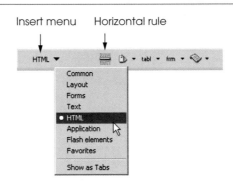

Fig. 19.13   Using the **Insert** menu to alter the **Insert** bar's appearance.

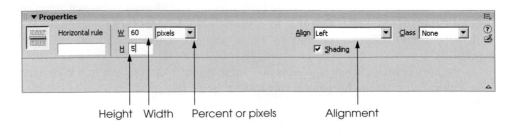

Fig. 19.14   Horizontal Rule properties.

On a new line, type the following text

2

Insert another horizontal rule below the 2. Set its height to 10 pixels and width to 100%. The page should now resemble Fig. 19.15.

Fig. 19.15 Special characters and hr elements in Dreamweaver.

19.6 Tables

As useful as tables are, they often are time-consuming and confusing to code accurately by hand in XHTML. Dreamweaver offers easy-to-use table-editing commands. Open the **Table** dialog by selecting **Table** from the **Insert** menu, clicking the **Table** button in the **Common Insert** bar, or pressing *Ctrl+Alt+T*. The **Table** dialog (Fig. 19.16) allows us to select the number of rows and columns, the overall width of the table and several other related settings.

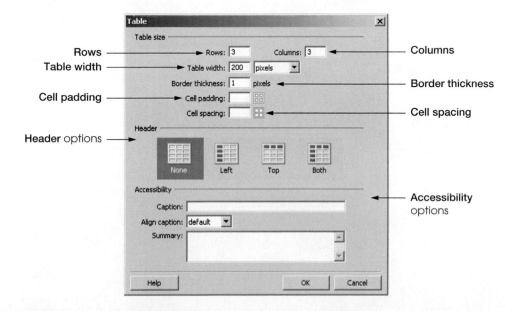

Fig. 19.16 Insert **Table** dialog.

Figure 19.17 is a simple table with two rows and two columns, created in Dreamweaver. Once the table is placed, you can manipulate its size. Click in a cell and press **<td>** in the **tag selector** at the bottom of the **Document** window to select that cell. Pressing the *Delete* key removes the cell from the table. You can highlight two adjacent cells by clicking **<tr>** in the tag selector. Clicking the **Merge Cells** button in the **Property Inspector** while two cells are selected combines the cells into one (Fig. 19.18). Dreamweaver uses the `colspan` and `rowspan` attributes of the <td> tag to merge cells. Select a cell and click the **Split Cell** button in the **Property Inspector** to open the **Split Cell** dialog, which allows you to divide the selected cell into any number of rows or columns (Fig. 19.19).

The **Property Inspector** allows us to manipulate the selected table, or a portion of the table. While a cell is selected, its text attributes can be adjusted just as we did earlier in the chapter. In addition, background and border colors can be assigned to cells, groups of cells or an entire table. We can adjust a cell's height and width in the **Property Inspector**. To manually adjust a cell's size, you can also click and drag its border lines.

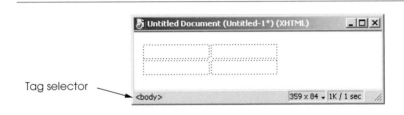

Fig. 19.17 Table with two rows and two columns.

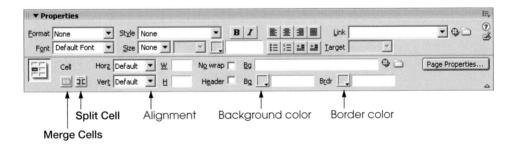

Fig. 19.18 Table **Property Inspector**.

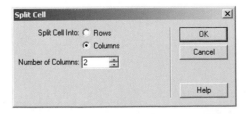

Fig. 19.19 Split Cell dialog.

We will now recreate the table of Fig. 5.2. Begin by making a table four rows high and five columns wide that spans 90% of the page with a border thickness of one pixel. Click the top-left cell, hold down the *Shift* key and click the cell directly below it. This will select the top two leftmost cells. Merge them by right clicking in either cell and selecting **Merge Cells** from the **Table** option in the pop-up menu (Fig. 19.20).

To make space for the title of the table, select the top three cells (again using the *Shift* key) and merge them together. Repeat this process for the rest of the cells, so that they resemble the table layout in Fig. 19.21. Then, type in the text and insert the image.

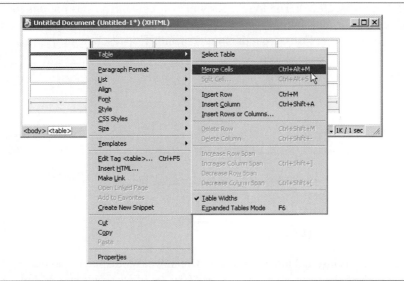

Fig. 19.20 Merging.

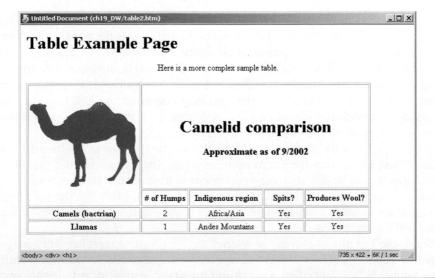

Fig. 19.21 Almost completed table.

To increase the visual appeal of the table, add color by selecting the desired cells and adjusting their background color in the **Property Inspector**. The size of rows and columns also can be adjusted by changing the **H** (height) and **W** (width) field values in the **Property Inspector** or by clicking and dragging the boundaries between cells.

19.7 Forms

All the necessary XHTML coding needed for creating a feedback form or any other forms can be done in Dreamweaver. To insert a form, first select **Forms** from the insert menu in the **Insert** bar (Fig. 19.22). The **Insert** bar will now contain various options for creating forms. Click the left-most button to insert an empty form into the document. Forms can also be inserted by selecting **Form** from the **Insert** menu's **Form** submenu.

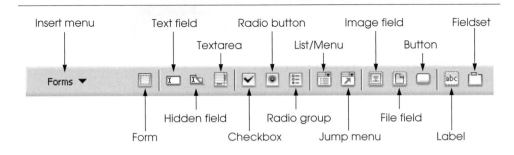

Fig. 19.22   Forms Insert bar.

After a form is inserted into a document, Dreamweaver displays a dotted line to delineate the bounds of the form. Any form objects (i.e., text fields, buttons, etc.) placed inside this dotted line will be part of the same `form` element in the XHTML code that Dreamweaver generates.

We can modify the properties of a form by clicking anywhere inside the dotted line that delineates the form, then clicking **<form#**_name_**>** (where _name_ is the `name` of the `form` element) in the tag selector at the bottom of the **Document** window. Dreamweaver assigns default names to forms in sequential order (i.e., the first form inserted is named **form1**, the second form is named **form2** and so on). The **Form name** field in the **Property Inspector** assigns a name to a form. The **Property Inspector** can also be used to set the **Action** and **Method** attributes of the form, which are required for server-side processing. Server-side technology is discussed later in this book.

A text field is easily inserted by clicking the text field button in the **Insert** bar or by selecting **Text Field** from the **Form** submenu of the **Insert** menu. Once placed, a text field's attributes can by adjusted using the **Property Inspector**. Its `name`, `id` and `value` attributes can be set along with the `size` and `maxlength` (Fig. 19.23). The text field type also can be set to **Multi line**, allowing multiple lines of text, or **Password**, making all entered text appear as an asterisk (*).

Scrollable **Textarea**s also can be selected from the **Form Insert** bar. Their properties are almost identical to those of a text field, except that they have the additional attributes for the number of lines (specified in the **Num Lines** field in the **Property Inspector**) and **Wrap** (i.e., how the text area handles lines of text that exceed its width).

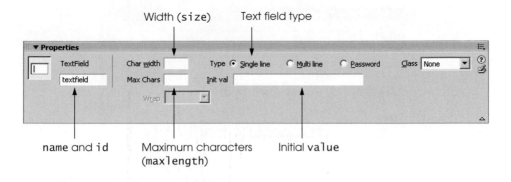

Fig. 19.23 Text field **Property Inspector**.

A drop-down select menu can be added by clicking the **List/Menu** button in the **Insert** bar. To add entries and values to the list or menu, click the **List Values...** button in the **Property Inspector** (Fig. 19.24). In the **List Values** dialog, you can add entries by pressing the **+** button, and remove entries by pressing the **–** button. Each entry has an **Item Label** and a **Value.** An entry can be made the default selection by selecting it in the **Initially selected** list in the **Property Inspector**.

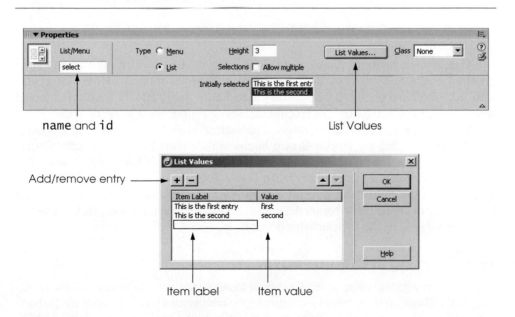

Fig. 19.24 **List Values** dialog box.

Now that we have discussed the basics of forms in Dreamweaver, we are ready to create a form that could be used on any Web site—a "rate my Web site" form. To start, insert a form into a new page, followed by text fields, menus and text. The elements should appear as in Fig. 19.25.

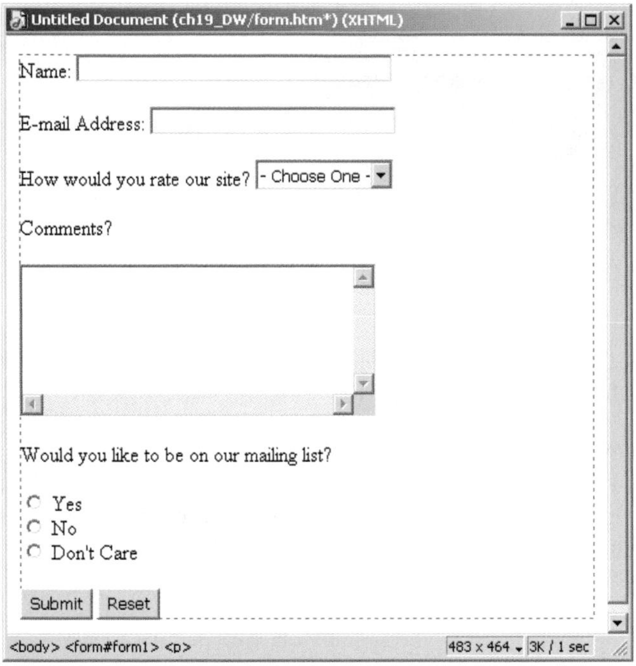

Fig. 19.25 Completed form.

Make the text fields the proper width by adjusting the **Char width** value in the **Property Inspector**. Now select the drop-down menu to the right of the text **How would you rate our site?** and click the **List Values...** button in the **Property Inspector** to add appropriate entries to the list (e.g., **Excellent**, **Good**, **Fair**, **Poor** and **Terrible**).

This example has three radio buttons, all contained in the same group. To add a group of radio buttons, click the **Radio Group** button in the **Insert** bar. In the **Radio Group** dialog, specify the **Name** of the group, and each radio button's **Label** and **Value**. The **Radio Group** dialog works similarly to the **List Values** dialog.

To create the **Reset** and **Submit** buttons, click the **Button** selection in the **Insert** bar. The **Label** of each new button defaults to **Submit**, but can be changed to **Reset** or any other value using the **Property Inspector**.

19.8 Scripting in Dreamweaver

Dreamweaver also allows us to add JavaScript to our pages. JavaScript can be added manually in the **Code** view, or automatically using the **Behaviors** panel. To open the **Behaviors** panel, either select **Behaviors** from the **Window** menu, or press *Shift+F3*. The **Behaviors** panel appears as a tab option in the **Tag** panel (Fig. 19.26).

The **Behaviors** panel allows us to add commands to elements of a Web page that trigger various JavaScript actions in response to browser events. To add an action, select an element on the page. Click the **+** button in the **Behaviors** panel to display a pop-up menu of applicable actions. The pop-up menu offers several pre-defined JavaScript actions, such as **Go To URL** or **Popup Message**. A developer also can manually write an action by

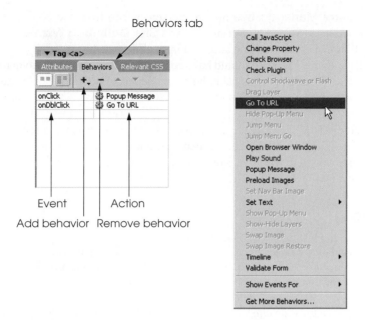

Fig. 19.26 **Behaviors** panel and menu to add behaviors.

selecting **Call JavaScript** from the pop-up menu and entering the desired code into the **Call JavaScript** dialog. Selecting **Get More Behaviors...** opens a Web page that provides options to download or purchase additional behaviors. After completing the dialog associated with the selected action, the action and a default event appear in the **Behaviors** panel. A developer can change the event that triggers this action by clicking the event field and choosing an event from the drop-down list that appears.

Dreamweaver also supports several server-side scripting languages, discussed later in the book, such as ASP.NET, ColdFusion, JSP and PHP. Server-side scripting elements, such as **Databases** and **Bindings**, can be accessed in the **Window** menu. Tags of the various languages can also be selected from the **Tag Chooser**, which is accessed by selecting **Tag...** from the **Insert** menu. Dreamweaver only allows the user to add scripting elements where applicable.

19.9 Site Management

In this book, we focus primarily on the skills and technologies involved in creating individual Web pages. As a result, we do not spend much time discussing complete **Web sites**. A Web site is a group of Web pages that typically interact with one another and are located on a **server**. Creating an effective Web site is a difficult process, requiring planning, effort and time.

Dreamweaver is a powerful tool for creating and maintaining a Web site. To create a site using Dreamweaver, first open the **Files** panel either by selecting **Files** from the **Window** menu or by pressing *F8*. Click the **Manage Sites...** link in the **Files** panel's drop-down list to open the **Manage Sites** dialog. From this dialog, a developer can access previously created Web sites or create new ones. To create a new Web site, click the

New… button in the **Manage Sites** dialog and select **Site** from the pop-up list. Then, follow the instructions provided by Dreamweaver's **Site Definition Wizard**. Once completed, all site files can be viewed and accessed in the **File** panel.

In general, pages in a Web site should have consistent colors and styles to maintain site uniformity. Dreamweaver's **Assets** panel holds elements common to a Web site, such as pictures, colors and links. Open the **Assets** panel by selecting **Assets** from the **Window** menu or pressing *F11*.

While Dreamweaver is a valuable aid in Web-site creation, it is not a replacement for thorough knowledge of XHTML and the related scripting languages taught in this book. Be sure to familiarize yourself with these other technologies before using Dreamweaver to accelerate the development process.

19.10 Web Resources

`www.macromedia.com/devnet/mx/dreamweaver`
Macromedia's *Dreamweaver Developer Center* contains numerous tutorials and sample files intended for beginner, intermediate and expert users. This site explores some of the more advanced features of Dreamweaver in addition to the topics covered in this chapter.

`www.macromedia.com/software/dreamweaver`
This site contains detailed product information, software downloads and links to featured sites created with Dreamweaver MX 2004.

SUMMARY

- *Dreamweaver MX 2004* can insert text and font changes, as well as create more complex XHTML elements, such as tables, forms, frames and much more.

- Dreamweaver is a WYSIWYG (What You See Is What You Get) editor—it renders XHTML elements exactly as a browser would.

- Dreamweaver will automatically enclose text in a paragraph (p) element for proper formatting.

- To view your page in a browser, press *F12* or select **Preview in Browser** from the **File** menu.

- To view or edit your XHTML directly, click the **Code** button in the **Document** toolbar.

- XHTML is automatically color coded when viewed in Dreamweaver's code editor.

- To save your file, click **Save** in the **File** menu or press *Ctrl + S*. Select **HTML Documents** as the file type in the **Save As** dialog to create an HTML document.

- We can alter text with the **Text** menu or the **Property Inspector**. Using these tools, we can quickly apply header tags (<h1>, <h2>, etc.), list tags (<ol>, <ul>) and several other tags used for stylizing text. Text can also be aligned left, right or centered, increased or decreased in size, indented and colored.

- To create a new document, select **New…** from the **File** menu. In the **New Document** dialog, select **Basic page** from the **Category** list, and **HTML** from the **Basic page** list. Check the **Make Document XHTML Compliant** checkbox to make Dreamweaver's code XHTML compliant.

- The **Text** menu contains many useful text-formatting options. Most of the elements in the **Text** menu can be accessed by right clicking highlighted text.

- Click the **Code** button in the **Document** toolbar to view the document code. Click the **Design** button in the **Document** toolbar to view a page as it would appear in a Web browser.

- By default, Dreamweaver will enclose the text you type in a new set of <p>…</p> tags when you press *Enter*. If you want to insert only a <br /> tag into a page, hold down *Shift* and press *Enter*.

- Almost any element displayed in Dreamweaver can be edited by right clicking the element and selecting its properties from the pop-up menu.
- The **Property Inspector** is useful for creating lists. Select **List** from the **Text** menu for list-related tags, such as the definition list (<dl>). There are two list elements in a definition list—the defined term (<dt>) and the definition data (<dd>).
- When you insert a local image into an unsaved document using the **Browse…** button, Dreamweaver sets an absolute path, such as file:///C|/Dreamweaver sites/camel.gif. Saving the document sets the image source to a relative path, starting at the folder in which the document is saved.
- Create a hyperlink by typing the URL to which the hyperlink will point in the **Link** field in the **Property Inspector**.
- Image attributes can be changed in the **Property Inspector**.
- Dreamweaver provides characters that are not located on the standard keyboard, accessed by selecting **Special Characters** from the **Insert** menu.
- Click the **Horizontal Rule** button in the **Insert** panel or select **Horizontal Rule** from the **Insert** menu to add an hr element. Its properties can be adjusted in the **Property Inspector**.
- Tables are often time consuming and confusing to code accurately by hand in XHTML. To create a table using Dreamweaver, select **Table** from the **Insert** menu, click the **Table** button in the **Insert** bar, or press *Ctrl + Alt + T*.
- The tag selector at the bottom of the **Document** window is used to select elements in a page.
- The **Property Inspector** allows us to manipulate the selected table or portion of a table. The **Merge Cells** and **Split Cell** buttons are two of the table-editing elements found in the **Property Inspector**.
- Hold down the *Shift* key to select multiple cells.
- All the necessary XHTML coding needed for installing a feedback and other forms can be done in Dreamweaver.
- Selecting **Forms** from the **Insert** menu displays various options for creating forms.
- After a form is inserted into a document, Dreamweaver displays a dotted line to delineate the bounds of the form. Any form objects (e.g., text fields, buttons, etc.) placed inside this dotted line will be part of the same form element in the XHTML code that Dreamweaver generates.
- The **Property Inspector** can be used to set the **Action** and **Method** attributes of a form, which are required for server-side processing.
- Clicking the text field button in the **Insert** bar creates a text field. A text field's attributes can by adjusted using the **Property Inspector**. Scrollable text areas can also be inserted using the **Form Insert** bar.
- A drop-down select menu is added by clicking the **List/Menu** button in the **Insert** bar. To add entries and values to the list or menu, click the **List Values** button in the **Property Inspector**.
- To add a group of radio buttons, click the **Radio Group** button in the **Insert** bar. In the **Radio Group** dialog, specify the name of the group, and each radio button's label and value.
- To create the **Reset** and **Submit** buttons, click the **Button** selection in the **Insert** bar. The **Label** of the placed button defaults to **Submit**, but can be changed to **Reset** or **None** using the **Property Inspector**.
- JavaScript can be added manually in the code view, or automatically using the **Behaviors** panel, opened either by selecting **Behaviors** from the **Window** menu or by pressing *Shift + F3*. The **Behaviors** panel appears as a tab option in the **Tag** panel.
- To add an event using the **Behaviors** panel, select an element on your page and click the **+** button. A pop-up menu appears that displays the events applicable to the selected element.

- Dreamweaver supports several scripting languages, such as ASP, ColdFusion, JSP and PHP. Some of these languages' elements accessed in the **Window** menu.

- Dreamweaver is a powerful tool for creating and maintaining a Web site. To create a site using Dreamweaver, open the **Files** panel by selecting **Files** from the **Window** menu. Then click the **Manage Sites...** link in the **Site** panel's drop-down list. Click **New...** in the **Manage Site** dialog.

- Pages in a Web site should have consistent colors and styles to maintain site uniformity. Dreamweaver's **Assets** panel holds common site elements. Open the **Assets** panel by pressing *F11* or selecting **Assets** from the **Window** menu.

TERMINOLOGY

Assets panel
Background Color
Behaviors panel
Button button
Code view
dd element (definition; <dd>...</dd>)
Design view
dl element (definition list; <dl>...</dl>)
Document toolbar
Document window
dt element (defined term; <dt>...</dt>)
Files panel
Font field in **Property Inspector**
Form button in **Insert** bar
Form tab in **Insert** bar
From Location in Image
Horizontal Rule button in **Insert** bar
Hyperlink field in the **Property Inspector**
Image button in **Insert** bar

Insert bar
Insert menu
List Values button
List/Menu button
Manage Sites dialog
Merge Cells button
Page Property... dialog
Property Inspector
Preview in Browser
Save in **File** menu
File Panel
Special Characters
Split Cell button in **Property Inspector**
Style in **Text** menu
Table button in **Insert** bar
Tag selector
Text Field button
WYSIWYG (What You See Is What You Get)

SELF-REVIEW EXERCISES

19.1 State whether each of the following is *true* or *false*. If *false*, explain why.
   a) Dreamweaver renders XHTML elements correctly in its WYSIWYG display.
   b) Dreamweaver allows Web page authors to insert images simply by clicking a button and selecting an image to insert.
   c) Dreamweaver requires the user to manually write special characters into the code.
   d) Dreamweaver delineates a form element in the WYSIWYG editor with a dotted line.
   e) Dreamweaver can be used to create only XHTML documents.

19.2 Fill in the blanks for each of the following statements.
   a) A(n) _____ editor renders Web page elements exactly as a browser would.
   b) The _____ allows us to adjust the selected element's attributes.
   c) Dreamweaver's _____ option combines selected table cells into one cell.
   d) The _____ panel allows a developer to add JavaScript to an XHTML document.

ANSWERS TO SELF-REVIEW EXERCISES

19.1 a) True. b) True. c) False. Selecting **Special Characters** from **HTML** sub-menu of the **Insert** menu provides a list of special characters. d) True. e) False. Dreamweaver supports several server-side scripting languages, such as ASP.NET, ColdFusion, JSP and PHP.

19.2   a) WYSIWYG (What You See Is What You Get).   b) **Property Inspector**.   c) **Merge Cells**. d) **Behaviors**.

EXERCISES

19.3   Create the following table using Dreamweaver:

```
┌─────────────────────────────────────────────────────────┐
│ 🔲 Untitled Document (ch19_DW/exercise_table.htm) (XHTML)  _□×│
├─────────────────────────────────────────────────────────┤
│                                                          │
│                                                          │
├─────────────────────────────────────────────────────────┤
│ <body>                              608 x 120 ▾ 1K / 1 sec │
└─────────────────────────────────────────────────────────┘
```

19.4   Create the following form using Dreamweaver:

```
┌─────────────────────────────────────────────────────────┐
│ 🔲 Untitled Document (ch19_DW/exercise_form1.htm) (XHTML) _□×│
├─────────────────────────────────────────────────────────┤
│ Please enter your information:                           │
│                                                          │
│      Name:          E-mail          ZIP code:            │
│   ┌──────────┐   ┌──────────┐    ┌──────────┐            │
│   └──────────┘   └──────────┘    └──────────┘            │
│   Yes ☐ No ☐     Yes ☐ No ☐      Yes ☐ No ☐               │
│                                                          │
│ Gender:                                                  │
│                                                          │
│   ○ Male                                                 │
│   ○ Female                                               │
│   ○ No Answer                                            │
│   ┌────────┐ ┌───────┐                                   │
│   │ Submit │ │ Reset │                                   │
│   └────────┘ └───────┘                                   │
├─────────────────────────────────────────────────────────┤
│ <body>                              608 x 324 ▾ 2K / 1 sec │
└─────────────────────────────────────────────────────────┘
```

19.5   Add a feature to your solution to Exercise 19.4 that displays an `alert` dialog reading "`form submitted`" when the user clicks the **Submit** button, and an `alert` dialog "`form reset`" appear when the user clicks the **Reset** button.

19.6   Create a personal Web page using Dreamweaver that features an image and a list of interests. Experiment with different text-formatting options. Link the image to your favorite Web site.

20

Extensible Markup Language (XML)

Objectives

- To understand XML.
- To be able to mark up data using XML.
- To become familiar with the types of markup languages created with XML.
- To understand the relationships among DTDs, Schemas and XML.
- To understand the fundamentals of DOM-based and SAX-based parsing.
- To understand the concept of an XML namespace.
- To be able to create simple XSL documents.
- To become familiar with Web services and related technologies.

Knowing trees, I understand the meaning of patience.
Knowing grass, I can appreciate persistence.
Hal Borland

Like everything metaphysical, the harmony between thought and reality is to be found in the grammar of the language.
Ludwig Wittgenstein

Outline

20.1 Introduction

The **World Wide Web Consortium's** (**W3C**) **XML Working Group** developed **XML** (**Extensible Markup Language**), which is derived from **Standard Generalized Markup Language** (**SGML**), in 1996. XML is a widely supported **open technology** (i.e., nonproprietary technology) for electronic data exchange and storage. XML is actually a language used to create other markup languages to describe data in a structured manner.

XML documents contain only data, not formatting instructions, so applications that process XML documents must decide how to manipulate or display the document's data. For example, a PDA (personal digital assistant) may render an XML document differently than a wireless phone or a desktop computer. Programmers use **Extensible Stylesheet Language** (**XSL**) to specify rendering instructions for different platforms.

XML permits document authors to create markup for virtually any type of information. This extensibility enables document authors to create entirely new markup languages for describing data such as mathematical formulas, chemical molecular structures, music, news and recipes. Some XML-based markup languages include XHTML (Chapters 4 and 5), MathML (for mathematics), VoiceXML™ (for speech), SMIL™ (Synchronous Multimedia Integration Language—for multimedia presentations), CML (Chemical Markup

Language—for chemistry) and XBRL (Extensible Business Reporting Language—for financial data exchange). These markup languages are called XML **vocabularies**.

XML elements describe data, so XML-processing programs can search, sort, manipulate and render XML documents using technologies such as the Extensible Stylesheet Language (XSL). Some other XML-related technologies are XPath (a language for accessing parts of an XML document), XSL-FO (an XML vocabulary used to describe document formatting) and XSLT (a language for transforming XML documents into other XML documents).

XML documents are highly portable. Viewing or modifying an XML document— which typically ends with the `.xml` filename extension—does not require special software. Any text editor that supports ASCII/Unicode characters can open XML documents for viewing and editing. One important characteristic of XML is that it is both human readable and machine readable.

Processing an XML document requires a software program called an **XML parser** (or **XML processor**). Most XML parsers are available at no charge and for a variety of programming languages (e.g., Java, Perl, C++). Parsers check an XML document's syntax and enable software programs to process marked-up data. XML parsers can support the **Document Object Model** (**DOM**) or the **Simple API for XML** (**SAX**).

DOM-based parsers build tree structures containing XML document data in memory. SAX-based parsers process XML documents and generate events when the parser encounters tags, text, comments, and so on. These events contain data from the XML document. Software programs can "listen" for these events to obtain data from the XML document. Several Independent Software Vendors (ISVs) have developed XML parsers. In Section 20.7 and Section 20.8 we discuss DOM and SAX, respectively.

An XML document can reference a **Document Type Definition** (**DTD**) or a **schema** that defines the proper structure of the XML document. When an XML document references a DTD or a schema, some parsers (called **validating parsers**) can read the DTD/schema and check that the XML document follows the structure defined by the DTD/schema. If the XML document conforms to the DTD/schema (i.e., the document has the appropriate structure), the XML document is **valid**. We discuss DTDs and schemas in Section 20.4. Parsers that cannot check for document conformity against DTDs/schemas are **nonvalidating parsers**. If an XML parser (validating or nonvalidating) can process an XML document successfully, that XML document is **well formed** (i.e., it is syntactically correct). By definition, a valid XML document also is well formed. Some programs (e.g., an XSLT) are designed to navigate an XML document's structure. Validating an XML document ensures that a program navigates a well-formed document. However, it is possible to run an XSL on an XML document without validating the XML document.

20.2 Structuring Data

In this section and throughout this chapter, we create our own XML markup. With XML, a document author can create elements that describe data precisely. As in the XHTML markup seen throughout the book, tags delimit the start and end of each element in an XML document.

XML Markup for a News Article
In Fig. 20.1, we mark up a simple news article using tags. The tags used in the example do not come from any specific markup language. Instead, we chose the tag names and markup structure that best describe the data. A programmer can invent tags to mark up data.

```
1   <?xml version = "1.0"?>
2
3   <!-- Fig. 20.1: article.xml      -->
4   <!-- Article structured with XML -->
5
6   <article>
7
8      <title>Simple XML</title>
9
10     <date>July 15, 2003</date>
11
12     <author>
13        <firstName>Carpenter</firstName>
14        <lastName>Cal</lastName>
15     </author>
16
17     <summary>XML is pretty easy.</summary>
18
19     <content>Once you have mastered XHTML, XML is easily
20        learned. You must remember that XML is not for
21        displaying information but for managing information.
22     </content>
23
24  </article>
```

Fig. 20.1   News article marked up with XML.

We begin with the optional **XML declaration** in line 1. Value **version** indicates the XML version to which the document conforms. The current XML standard is version 1.0. The World Wide Web Consortium may release new versions of XML as it evolves to meet the requirements of different fields.

Good Programming Practice 20.1

Always include an XML declaration.

Common Programming Error 20.1

Placing whitespace characters before the XML declaration is an error.

Common Programming Error 20.2

XML is case sensitive. Using the wrong case for an XML tag is a syntax error.

Common Programming Error 20.3

In an XML document, each start tag must have a matching end tag.

Common Programming Error 20.4

Not enclosing attribute values in either double quotes ("") or single quotes (' ') is an error in XML.

Comments (lines 3–4) in XML use the same syntax as XHTML. Every XML document must contain exactly one **root element** that encompasses all other elements. In

Fig. 20.1, `article` (line 6) is the root element. The lines that precede the root element are the XML **prolog**. The prolog in this example is lines 1–5. XML element and attribute names can be of any length and may contain letters, digits, underscores, hyphens and periods. However, XML names must begin with either a letter or an underscore.

Common Programming Error 20.5

Using either a space or a tab in an XML element or attribute name is an error.

Good Programming Practice 20.2

XML element and attribute names should be meaningful and human readable. For example, use <address> instead of <adr>.

Common Programming Error 20.6

Attempting to create more than one root element is an error.

Element `title` (line 8) contains text that describes the article's title (i.e., Simple XML). Similarly, `date` (line 10), `author` (lines 12–15), `summary` (line 17) and `content` (lines 19–22) contain text that describes the date, author, summary and content of the document, respectively.

Any element (e.g., `article` or `author`) that contains other elements is a **container element**. Elements inside a container element are **child elements** (or **children**) of that container element.

Note that the XML document in Fig. 20.1 does not contain formatting information for the article. This is because XML is a technology for structuring data. Formatting and displaying data from an XML document are application specific. For example, when Internet Explorer 6 (IE6) loads an XML document, its parser **MSXML** parses and displays the document. Figure 20.2 shows `article.xml` (Fig. 20.1) displayed in IE6. Note that what IE6 displays is virtually identical to the listing in Fig. 20.1—because an XML document does not

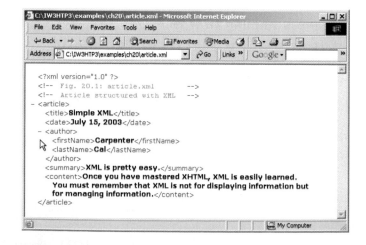

Fig. 20.2   IE6 displaying `article.xml`. (Part 1 of 2.)

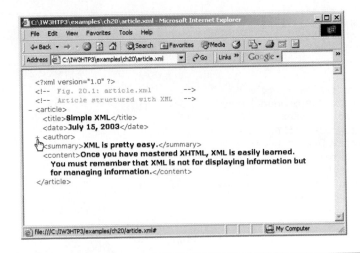

Fig. 20.2   IE6 displaying `article.xml`. (Part 2 of 2.)

contain formatting information. We will discuss how to format data in an XML document when we study the Extensible Stylesheet Language (XSL) later in this chapter (Section 20.9).

Note the minus sign (–) and plus sign (+) in Fig. 20.2. IE6 places these symbols next to every container element. A minus sign indicates that IE6 is displaying the container element's child elements. Clicking the minus sign next to an element causes IE6 to hide the container element's children and replaces the minus sign with a plus sign. Clicking the plus sign next to an element causes IE6 to display the container element's children and replaces the plus sign with a minus sign.

XML Markup for a Business Letter

Now that we have seen a simple XML document, let us examine a slightly more complex XML document that marks up a business letter (Fig. 20.3). As in the preceding example, we begin the document with the XML declaration in line 1. This explicitly states the XML version to which the document conforms.

```
1   <?xml version = "1.0"?>
2
3   <!-- Fig. 20.3: letter.xml            -->
4   <!-- Business letter formatted with XML   -->
5
6   <!DOCTYPE letter SYSTEM "letter.dtd">
7
8   <letter>
9
10     <contact type = "from">
11        <name>John Doe</name>
12        <address1>123 Main St.</address1>
13        <address2></address2>
14        <city>Anytown</city>
15        <state>Anystate</state>
```

Fig. 20.3   Business letter marked up as XML. (Part 1 of 3.)

```
16        <zip>12345</zip>
17        <phone>555-1234</phone>
18        <flag gender = "M"/>
19     </contact>
20
21     <contact type = "to">
22        <name>Joe Schmoe</name>
23        <address1>Box 12345</address1>
24        <address2>15 Any Ave.</address2>
25        <city>Othertown</city>
26        <state>Otherstate</state>
27        <zip>67890</zip>
28        <phone>555-4321</phone>
29        <flag gender = "M"/>
30     </contact>
31
32     <salutation>Dear Sir:</salutation>
33
34     <paragraph>It is our privilege to inform you about our new
35        database managed with XML. This new system allows
36        you to reduce the load of your inventory list server by
37        having the client machine perform the work of sorting
38        and filtering the data.</paragraph>
39     <closing>Sincerely</closing>
40     <signature>Mr. Doe</signature>
41
42  </letter>
```

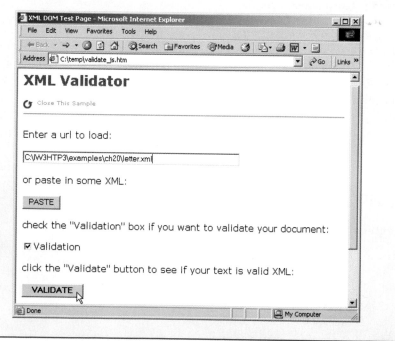

Fig. 20.3   Business letter marked up as XML. (Part 2 of 3.)

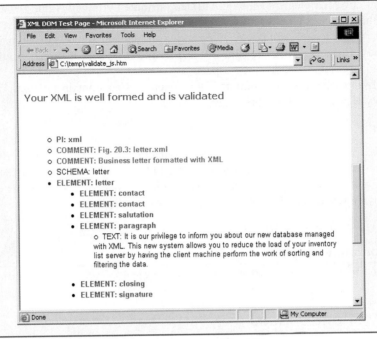

Fig. 20.3　Business letter marked up as XML. (Part 3 of 3.)

Line 6 specifies that this XML document references a **document type definition** (**DTD**). DTDs define the structural rules for an XML document. An XML document does not require a DTD, but validating XML parsers can use a DTD to ensure that an XML document has the proper structure. The DTD reference (line 6) contains three items: the name of the root element that the DTD specifies (`letter`), the keyword **SYSTEM** (which denotes an **external DTD**—a DTD declared in a separate file), and the DTD's name and location (i.e., `letter.dtd` in the current directory). DTD documents typically end with the **.dtd** extension. We discuss DTDs and `letter.dtd` in detail in Section 20.4.

The output of Fig. 20.3 shows the results of validating the document using Microsoft's **XML Validator**. Several tools (many of which are free) exist that check a document's conformity to DTDs and schemas (discussed in Section 20.4). Visit `www.w3.org/XML/Schema.html` for a list of validating tools. Microsoft's XML Validator is available free of charge from

```
msdn.microsoft.com/downloads/samples/Internet/xml/
xml_validator/sample.asp
```

 Common Programming Error 20.7

Overlapping XML tags is a syntax error. For example, `<x><y>hello</x></y>` is illegal.

Root element `letter` (lines 8–42) contains child elements `contact`, `salutation`, `paragraph`, `closing` and `signature`. A contact element stores the contact's name, address and phone number. The first `contact` element (lines 10–19) has attribute `type` with value `from`, which indicates that this `contact` element identifies the letter's sender.

The second `contact` element (lines 21–30) has attribute `type` with value `to`, which indicates that this `contact` element identifies the letter's recipient. Element `salutation` (line 32) marks up the letter's salutation. A `paragraph` element (lines 34–38) marks up the letter's body. Elements `closing` (line 39) and `signature` (line 40) mark up the closing sentence and the author's signature, respectively.

Line 18 introduces **empty element** `flag`, which does not contain any text. An example of an empty element is the line break tag

```
<br />
```

in XHTML. Empty element `flag` indicates a contact's gender. This attribute allows us to address the recipient correctly either as Mr. (if gender is `"M"`) or Ms. (if gender is `"F"`). Document authors can close an empty element either by placing a slash at the end of the element (as shown in line 18) or by writing a closing tag explicitly, as in

```
<flag gender = "F"></flag>
```

Common Programming Error 20.8

Not terminating an empty element with a closing tag or a forward slash (/) is a syntax error.

20.3 XML Namespaces

XML allows document authors to create custom elements. This extensibility can result in **naming collisions** (i.e., different elements that each have the same name) among elements in an XML document. For example, we may use the element **book** to mark up data about a Deitel publication. A stamp collector may use the element **book** to mark up data about a book of stamps. Using both of these elements in the same document would create a naming collision, making it difficult to determine which kind of data each element contained.

An XML **namespace** is a collection of element and attribute names. Each namespace has a unique name that provides a means for document authors to unambiguously refer to elements with the same name (i.e., prevent collisions). For example,

```
<subject>Math</subject>
```

and

```
<subject>Thrombosis</subject>
```

use element `subject` to mark up a piece of data. However, in the first case the subject is something one studies in school, whereas in the second case the subject is in the field of medicine. Namespaces can differentiate these two `subject` elements. For example

```
<school:subject>Math</school:subject>
```

and

```
<medical:subject>Thrombosis</medical:subject>
```

Both `school` and `medical` are **namespace prefixes**. A document author places a namespace prefix and colon (`:`) before an element or attribute name to specify the namespace for that element or attribute. Each namespace prefix has a corresponding **uni-**

form resource identifier (URI) that uniquely identifies the namespace. A URI is simply a string of text for differentiating names. A URI can refer to a document, a resource or anything on the Web either by name or address. For example, the string `urn:deitel:book` could be a URI for a namespace that contains elements and attributes related to Deitel & Associates, Inc., publications. Document authors can create their own namespace prefixes using virtually any name except the reserved namespace **xml**.

Do not confuse URLs with URIs. URLs are a subset of URIs that locate resources based on a network filename concept. A URL is a path to a file on the World Wide Web. A URI is simply a name.

Common Programming Error 20.9

Attempting to create a namespace prefix xml in any mixture of cases is an error.

Figure 20.4 demonstrates namespaces. In this document, namespaces differentiate two distinct elements: the `file` element related to text and the one related to images.

```
1   <?xml version = "1.0"?>
2
3   <!-- Fig. 20.4 : namespace.xml -->
4   <!-- Demonstrating Namespaces  -->
5
6   <text:directory xmlns:text = "urn:deitel:textInfo"
7      xmlns:image = "urn:deitel:imageInfo">
8
9      <text:file filename = "book.xml">
10        <text:description>A book list</text:description>
11     </text:file>
12
13     <image:file filename = "funny.jpg">
14        <image:description>A funny picture</image:description>
15        <image:size width = "200" height = "100"/>
16     </image:file>
17
18  </text:directory>
```

Fig. 20.4   Listing for `namespace.xml`.

Software Engineering Observation 20.1
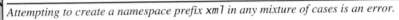

Attributes do not require namespace prefixes, because each attribute is part of an element that specifies the namespace prefix.

Lines 6–7 use the XML-namespace reserved attribute **xmlns** to create two namespace prefixes—**text** and **image**—and assign URIs to them. The element **directory** (line 6) is the root element and contains the other elements. It is a part of the text namespace

Document authors must provide a unique URI to ensure that a namespace is unique. Here we use `urn:deitel:textInfo` and `urn:deitel:imageInfo` as URIs for the **text** and **image** namespace prefixes, respectively. Document authors commonly use **Universal Resource Locators (URLs)** for URIs because the domain names (e.g., `deitel.com`) in URLs must be unique. For example, lines 6–7 could have used the namespace URIs

```
<text:directory xmlns:text =
   "http://www.deitel.com/xmlns-text"
   xmlns:image = "http://www.deitel.com/xmlns-image">
```

where URLs related to the Deitel & Associates, Inc., Web site (www.deitel.com) serve as URIs for the text and image namespace prefixes. The parser does not visit these URLs, nor do these URLs represent actual Web pages. They simply represent a unique series of characters for differentiating URI names. Any string can represent a URI. For example, our image namespace could be hgjfkdlsa4556, and thus our assignment prefix would be

```
xmlns:image = "hgjfkdlsa4556"
```

Lines 9–11 use the namespace prefix text for elements file and description. Note that the end tags also specify the namespace prefix text. Lines 13–16 apply namespace prefix image to elements file, description and size.

To eliminate the need to place namespace prefixes in each element, document authors may specify a **default namespace** for an element and its children. Figure 20.5 demonstrates using a default namespace (urn:deitel:textInfo) for element directory.

```
1   <?xml version = "1.0"?>
2
3   <!-- Fig. 20.5 : defaultnamespace.xml -->
4   <!-- Using Default Namespaces         -->
5
6   <directory xmlns = "urn:deitel:textInfo"
7      xmlns:image = "urn:deitel:imageInfo">
8
9      <file filename = "book.xml">
10        <description>A book list</description>
11     </file>
12
13     <image:file filename = "funny.jpg">
14        <image:description>A funny picture</image:description>
15        <image:size width = "200" height = "100"/>
16     </image:file>
17
18  </directory>
```

Fig. 20.5   Using default namespaces.

We declare a default namespace by using keyword xmlns and specifying the namespace URI (line 6). Once this default namespace is in place, elements that are declared under the default namespace and their children do not need namespace prefixes to be part of the default namespace. Any element that specifies a namespace prefix is not part of the default namespace. Element file (lines 9–11) is in the urn:deitel:textInfo namespace, which is the default namespace. Compare this to Fig. 20.4, where we had to prefix the file and description elements with the namespace prefix text (lines 9–11).

Element file (lines 13–16) uses the namespace prefix image to indicate that this element is in the urn:deitel:imageInfo namespace, not the default namespace.

XML-based languages, such as XML Schema (Section 20.4.2), Extensible Stylesheet Language (Section 20.9) and SOAP (Section 20.10), often use namespaces.

20.4 Document Type Definitions (DTDs) and Schemas

In this section, we discuss two types of documents for specifying XML document structure: Document Type Definitions (DTDs) and schemas. We present DTDs and schemas in Section 20.4.1 and Section 20.4.2, respectively.

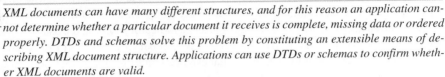

Software Engineering Observation 20.2

XML documents can have many different structures, and for this reason an application cannot determine whether a particular document it receives is complete, missing data or ordered properly. DTDs and schemas solve this problem by constituting an extensible means of describing XML document structure. Applications can use DTDs or schemas to confirm whether XML documents are valid.

Software Engineering Observation 20.3

*Many organizations and individuals are creating DTDs and XML schemas for a broad range of applications (e.g., financial transactions, medical prescriptions). These collections—called **repositories**—often are available free for download from the Web.*

20.4.1 Document Type Definitions

In Fig. 20.3, we presented a simple business letter marked up with XML. The DTD in Fig. 20.6 specifies the business letter's list of element types, attributes and their relationships to one another. A DTD enables an XML parser to verify whether an XML document is **valid** (i.e., its elements contain the proper attributes in the proper sequence). DTDs allow indepen-

```
1   <!-- Fig. 20.6: letter.dtd        -->
2   <!-- DTD document for letter.xml -->
3
4   <!ELEMENT letter ( contact+, salutation, paragraph+,
5      closing, signature )>
6
7   <!ELEMENT contact ( name, address1, address2, city, state,
8      zip, phone, flag )>
9   <!ATTLIST contact type CDATA #IMPLIED>
10
11  <!ELEMENT name ( #PCDATA )>
12  <!ELEMENT address1 ( #PCDATA )>
13  <!ELEMENT address2 ( #PCDATA )>
14  <!ELEMENT city ( #PCDATA )>
15  <!ELEMENT state ( #PCDATA )>
16  <!ELEMENT zip ( #PCDATA )>
17  <!ELEMENT phone ( #PCDATA )>
18  <!ELEMENT flag EMPTY>
19  <!ATTLIST flag gender (M | F) "M">
20
21  <!ELEMENT salutation ( #PCDATA )>
22  <!ELEMENT closing ( #PCDATA )>
23  <!ELEMENT paragraph ( #PCDATA )>
24  <!ELEMENT signature ( #PCDATA )>
```

Fig. 20.6　Business letter DTD.

dent user groups to check document structure and to exchange data in a standardized format. A DTD expresses the set of rules for document structure using an **EBNF (Extended Backus-Naur Form) grammar**. Line 6 in Fig. 20.3 references this DTD.

Line 4's **ELEMENT element type declaration** defines the rules for the element `letter`. In this case, `letter` contains one or more `contact` elements, one `salutation` element, one or more `paragraph` elements, one `closing` element and one `signature` element, in that sequence. The plus sign (+) occurrence indicator specifies that the DTD allows one or more occurrences of an element. Other occurrence indicators include the asterisk (*), which indicates an optional element that can occur any number of times, and the question mark (?), which indicates an optional element that can occur at most once. If an element does not have an occurrence indicator, the DTD allows exactly one occurrence.

The `contact` element definition (line 7) specifies that element `contact` contains child elements `name`, `address1`, `address2`, `city`, `state`, `zip`, `phone` and `flag`—in that order. The DTD requires exactly one occurrence of each of these elements.

Line 9 uses the **ATTLIST attribute-list declaration** to define an attribute (i.e., `type`) for the `contact` element. Keyword **#IMPLIED** specifies that if the parser finds a `contact` element without a `type` attribute, it can choose an arbitrary value for the attribute or ignore the attribute, and the document will be valid. The XML document is also valid if a `contact` element does not have a `type` attribute. Other types of default values include **#REQUIRED** and **#FIXED**. Keyword #REQUIRED specifies that the attribute must be present in the element, and keyword #FIXED specifies that the attribute (if present) must have the given fixed value. For example,

```
<!ATTLIST address zip #FIXED "01757">
```

indicates that attribute `zip` must have the value `01757` for the document to be valid. If the attribute is not present, the parser, by default, uses the fixed value that the `ATTLIST` declaration specifies. Keyword **CDATA** specifies that attribute `type` contains **character data**, which indicates that the parser will not process the data, but will pass the data to the application without modification.

Software Engineering Observation 20.4

DTD syntax does not provide a mechanism for describing an element's (or attribute's) data type. For example, a DTD cannot specify that a particular element or attribute can contain only integer data.

Keyword **#PCDATA** (line 11) specifies that the element can contain **parsed character data** (i.e., text). Parsable character data should not contain markup characters, such as less than (<), greater than (>) and ampersand (&). The document author should replace any markup character with its corresponding entity (i.e., <, > or &). See Appendix A for a list of character entities.

Line 18 creates an empty element named `flag`. Keyword **EMPTY** specifies that the element does not contain any data. Attributes commonly contain data that the empty element describes (e.g., the `gender` attribute of empty element `flag`).

Common Programming Error 20.10

If a document references a DTD and contains any element or attribute that the DTD does not define, the document is invalid.

Common Programming Error 20.11

Using markup characters (e.g., <, > and &) in attribute values is an error. Attribute values can contain ampersands (&) only for inserting entities (e.g., <). A literal ampersand, as in XHTML, can be expressed as &.

20.4.2 W3C XML Schema Documents

In this section, we introduce **schemas** for specifying XML document structure and validating XML documents. Many developers in the XML community believe that DTDs are not flexible enough to meet today's programming needs. For example, programs cannot manipulate DTDs in the same manner as XML documents because DTDs are not themselves XML documents. These and other limitations have led to the development of schemas.

Unlike DTDs, schemas do not use EBNF grammar. Instead, schemas use XML syntax and are actually XML documents that programs can manipulate. Like DTDs, schemas require validating parsers.

In this section, we focus on the W3C's **XML Schema**. For the latest information on W3C XML Schema, visit www.w3.org/XML/Schema.

Software Engineering Observation 20.5

XML Schema defines a DTD to which schemas must conform. Validating parsers include this DTD for validating schemas.

A DTD describes an XML document's structure, not the content of its elements. For example,

```
<quantity>5</quantity>
```

contains character data. If the document that contains element `quantity` references a DTD, an XML parser can validate the document to confirm that this element indeed does contain PCDATA content, but the parser cannot validate that the content is numeric; DTDs do not provide such capability. So, unfortunately, the parser also considers markup such as

```
<quantity>hello</quantity>
```

to be valid. The application that uses the XML document that contains this markup would need to test that the data in element `quantity` is numeric and take appropriate action if it is not.

XML Schema enables schema authors to specify that element `quantity`'s data must be numeric. In validating the XML document against this schema, the parser can determine that `5` conforms and `hello` does not. An XML document that conforms to a schema document is **schema valid**, and a document that does not conform is invalid.

Software Engineering Observation 20.6

Schemas are XML documents that reference DTDs, and therefore they themselves must be valid.

Figure 20.7 shows a schema-valid XML document named `book.xml`, and Fig. 20.8 shows the pertinent XML Schema document (`book.xsd`) that defines the structure for `book.xml`. Although schema authors can use virtually any filename extension, schemas commonly use the **.xsd** extension. To ensure that the XML document in Fig. 20.7 conforms to the schema in Fig. 20.8, we used an online XSD schema validator at http://apps.gotdotnet.com/xmltools/xsdvalidator

We used XSV (XML Schema Validator), an open-source schema validator, to validate the
Schema document itself, book.xsd, and produce the output shown in Fig. 20.8. An online
form-based version of this validator is available at www.w3.org/2001/03/webdata/xsv.

```
1    <?xml version = "1.0"?>
2
3    <!-- Fig. 20.7 : book.xml        -->
4    <!-- Book list marked up as XML -->
5
6    <deitel:books xmlns:deitel = "http://www.deitel.com/booklist">
7       <book>
8          <title>XML How to Program</title>
9       </book>
10      <book>
11         <title>C How to Program</title>
12      </book>
13      <book>
14         <title>Java How to Program</title>
15      </book>
16      <book>
17         <title>C++ How to Program</title>
18      </book>
19      <book>
20         <title>Perl How to Program</title>
21      </book>
22   </deitel:books>
```

Fig. 20.7   Schema-valid XML document.

```
1    <?xml version = "1.0"?>
2
3    <!-- Fig. 20.8 : book.xsd          -->
4    <!-- Simple W3C XML Schema document -->
5
6    <schema xmlns = "http://www.w3.org/2001/XMLSchema"
7            xmlns:deitel = "http://www.deitel.com/booklist"
8            targetNamespace = "http://www.deitel.com/booklist">
9
10      <element name = "books" type = "deitel:BooksType"/>
11
12      <complexType name = "BooksType">
13         <sequence>
14            <element name = "book" type = "deitel:SingleBookType"
15                      minOccurs = "1" maxOccurs = "unbounded"/>
16         </sequence>
17      </complexType>
18
19      <complexType name = "SingleBookType">
20         <sequence>
```

Fig. 20.8   XML Schema document for book.xml. (Part 1 of 2.)

```
21              <element name = "title" type = "string"/>
22          </sequence>
23      </complexType>
24
25   </schema>
```

```
Target: file:///usr/local/XSV/xsvlog/@11038.1uploaded
   (Real name: C:\IW3HTP3\examples\ch 20\book.xsd)
docElt: {http://www.w3.org/2001/XMLSchema}schema
Validation was strict, starting with type [Anonymous]
The schema(s) used for schema-validation had no errors
No schema-validity problems were found in the target
```

Fig. 20.8   XML Schema document for `book.xml`. (Part 2 of 2.)

Figure 20.7 contains markup describing several Deitel & Associates, Inc. books. The `books` element (line 6) must have the namespace prefix `deitel` because the `books` element is a part of the `http://www.deitel.com/booklist` namespace. Note that we also define the namespace prefix `deitel` in the same line.

Figure 20.8 presents the XML Schema document that specifies the structure of `book.xml` (Fig. 20.7). XML Schema documents always use the standard namespace URI **http://www.w3.org/2001/XMLSchema**. Root element **schema** contains elements that define the XML document structure. Line 7 binds the URI `http://www.deitel.com/booklist` to namespace prefix `deitel`. Line 8 specifies the **targetNamespace**, which is the namespace of the XML vocabulary that this schema defines.

In XML Schema, the **element** tag (line 10) defines an element to be included in the XML document structure. In other words, `element` specifies the actual *elements* that can be used to mark up data. Attributes **name** and **type** specify the `element`'s name and data type, respectively. Possible data types include XML Schema-defined types (e.g., `string`, `double`) and user-defined types (e.g., `BooksType`, which is defined in lines 12–17). XML Schema provides a large number of built-in simple types, such as **date** for dates, **int** for integers, **double** for floating-point numbers and **time** for times. An element's data type indicates the data that the element may contain.

Two categories of data types exist in XML Schema: **simple types** and **complex types**. Simple types and complex types differ in one way: Simple types cannot contain attributes or child elements; complex types can.

In this example, `books` is defined as an element of data type `deitel:BooksType` (line 10). `BooksType` is a user-defined type in the `http://www.deitel.com/booklist` namespace and therefore must have the namespace prefix `deitel`. It is not an existing XML Schema data type.

Recall that any element (e.g., `books`) that contains attributes or child elements must be of a complex type. Lines 12–17 use element **complexType** to define `BooksType` as a complex type that has a child element named `book`. The `sequence` element (line 13–16) allows a programmer to specify the sequential order in which child elements must appear. The `element` tag (lines 14–15) nested within the `complexType` element indicates that an element of type `BooksType` (e.g., `books`) can contain child elements named `book` of type `deitel:SingleBookType`. Attribute **minOccurs** = "1" specifies that elements of type `BooksType` must contain a minimum of one `book` element. Attribute **maxOccurs**, with value **unbounded** (line 15), specifies that elements of type BooksType may have any number of book child elements.

Lines 19–23 define a complex type called SingleBookType. Line 21 defines element title to be of simple type **string**. Recall that elements of a simple type cannot contain attributes or child elements. The closing schema tag (line 25) declares the end of the XML Schema document.

Good Programming Practice 20.3

W3C XML Schema authors use URI www.w3.org/2001/XMLSchema when referring to the XML Schema namespace.

We now take a closer look at types in XML Schema. Every element in XML Schema has some type. Possible types include the built-in data types provided by XML Schema (e.g., date, time, int, string) or user-defined types (e.g., SingleBookType in Fig. 20.8).

Recall that all types in XML Schema are classified as either simple or complex. Every simple type defines a **restriction** on a built-in schema data type (e.g., string, float, time) or a restriction of a user-defined type. A restriction limits the possible values that an element can hold.

Complex types are divided into two groups. Complex types can have either **simple content** or **complex content**. Both simple content and complex content can contain attributes, but only complex content can have child elements. While complex types with simple content must be extended or restricted, complex types with complex content do not have this limitation. The Schema document in Fig. 20.9 creates both simple types and complex types. The XML instance document in Fig. 20.10 follows the structure defined in the Fig. 20.9 schema to describe parts of a laptop computer.

```
1   <?xml version = "1.0"?>
2
3   <!-- Fig 20.9 : computer.xsd -->
4   <!-- W3C XML Schema document -->
5
6   <schema xmlns = "http://www.w3.org/2001/XMLSchema"
7           xmlns:computer = "http://www.deitel.com/computer"
8           targetNamespace = "http://www.deitel.com/computer">
9
10      <simpleType name = "gigahertz">
11         <restriction base = "decimal">
12            <minInclusive value = "2.1"/>
13         </restriction>
14      </simpleType>
15
16      <complexType name = "CPU">
17         <simpleContent>
18            <extension base = "string">
19               <attribute name = "model" type = "string"/>
20            </extension>
21         </simpleContent>
22      </complexType>
23
```

Fig. 20.9   XML Schema document for laptop.xml. (Part 1 of 2.)

```
24      <complexType name = "portable">
25         <all>
26            <element name = "processor" type = "computer:CPU"/>
27            <element name = "monitor" type = "int"/>
28            <element name = "CPUSpeed" type = "computer:gigahertz"/>
29            <element name = "RAM" type = "int"/>
30         </all>
31         <attribute name = "manufacturer" type = "string"/>
32      </complexType>
33
34      <element name = "laptop" type = "computer:portable"/>
35
36   </schema>
```

Fig. 20.9   XML Schema document for `laptop.xml`. (Part 2 of 2.)

Line 6 declares the default namespace to be the standard XML Schema namespace (i.e., any elements without a prefix are assumed to be in the XML Schema namespace). Line 7 binds the namespace prefix `computer` to the namespace `http://www.deitel.com/computer`, which line 8 indicates is the namespace being defined in the current document.

In designing the XML tags for describing laptop computers, first we create a simple type in lines 10–14 using the **`simpleType`** element. We name this `simpleType giga-hertz` because it will be used to describe the clock speed of the processor in gigahertz. Simple types are restrictions of a type typically called a **base type**. Line 11 declares the base type. For this `simpleType`, the base type is `decimal`, and we restrict the value to be at least `2.1` by using the **`minInclusive`** element in line 12.

We then declare a `complexType` that has `simpleContent` (lines 16–22). Remember that a complex type with simple content cannot have child elements but can have attributes. Also recall that complex types with simple content must extend or restrict some data type or user-defined type. The **`extension`** element with attribute **`base`** (line 18) sets the base type to `string`. In this `complexType` we **extend** the base type `string` with an attribute. The **`attribute`** element (line 19) gives the `complexType` an attribute named `model` of type `string`. Thus an element of type CPU must contain `string` text and may contain a `model` attribute that is also of type `string`.

Lastly we define the type `portable`, which is a `complexType` with `complexContent` (line 24–32). Complex types with complex content are allowed to have child elements and attributes. The element **`all`** (line 25) encloses those elements that must each be included once in the corresponding XML instance document. These elements can be included in any order. This complex type holds four elements: `processor`, `monitor`, `CPUSpeed` and `RAM`. These elements are given types CPU, `int`, `gigahertz` and `int`, respectively. When using the types CPU and `gigahertz`, we must include the namespace prefix `computer` because these user-defined types are part of the `computer` namespace (`http://www.deitel.com/com-puter`)—the namespace defined in the current document (line 8). Also, `portable` contains an attribute defined in line 31. The `attribute` tag indicates that elements of type `portable` contain an attribute of type `string` named `manufacturer`.

Line 34 declares the actual element that uses the three types defined in the schema. The element is called `laptop` and is of type `portable`. We must use the namespace prefix `computer` in front of `portable`.

We have created a tag named laptop that contains elements processor, monitor, CPUSpeed and RAM, and an attribute manufacturer. Putting it all together, Fig. 20.10 uses the laptop element tag defined in the schema.

Line 6 declares the namespace prefix computer. The laptop element requires this prefix because it is part of the http://www.deitel.com/computer namespace. Line 7 defines the laptop's manufacturer attribute, and lines 9–12 use the element tags defined in the schema.

```
1   <?xml version = "1.0"?>
2
3   <!-- Fig 20.10 : laptop.xml              -->
4   <!-- Laptop components marked up as XML -->
5
6   <computer:laptop xmlns:computer = "http://www.deitel.com/computer"
7                    manufacturer = "IBM">
8
9       <processor model = "Centrino">Intel</processor>
10      <monitor>17</monitor>
11      <CPUSpeed>2.4</CPUSpeed>
12      <RAM>256</RAM>
13
14  </computer:laptop>
```

Fig. 20.10 XML document using the laptop tag defined in computer.xsd.

20.5 XML Vocabularies

XML allows authors to create their own tags to describe data precisely. People and organizations in various fields of study have created many different kinds of XML for structuring data. Some of these markup languages are: **MathML (Mathematical Markup Language)**, **Scalable Vector Graphics (SVG)**, **Wireless Markup Language (WML)**, **Extensible Business Reporting Language (XBRL)**, **Extensible User Interface Language (XUL)** and **Product Data Markup Language (PDML)**. Two other examples of XML vocabularies are W3C XML Schema and the Extensible Stylesheet Language (XSL), which we discuss in Section 20.4 and Section 20.9, respectively. The following subsections describe MathML and other custom markup languages.

20.5.1 MathML™

Until recently, computers typically required specialized software packages such as TeX and LaTeX for displaying complex mathematical expressions. This section introduces MathML, which the W3C developed for describing mathematical notations and expressions. One application that can parse and render MathML is the W3C's *Amaya*™ browser/editor, which can be downloaded at no charge from

> www.w3.org/Amaya/User/BinDist.html

This Web page contains download links for the Windows 98/NT/2000/XP, Mac OS X, Linux and Solaris™ platforms. Amaya documentation and installation notes also are available at the W3C Web site.

MathML markup describes mathematical expressions for display. MathML is divided into two types of markup: **content** markup and **presentation** markup. Content markup provides tags that embody mathematical concepts. Content MathML allows programmers to write mathematical notation specific to different areas of mathematics. For instance, the multiplication symbol has one meaning in set theory and another meaning in linear algebra. Content MathML distinguishes between different uses of the same symbol. Programmers can take content MathML markup, discern mathematical context and evaluate the marked-up mathematical operations. Presentation MathML is directed towards formatting and displaying mathematical notation. We focus on Presentation MathML in the MathML examples. Figure 20.11 uses MathML to mark up a simple expression.

```
1   <?xml version="1.0"?>
2   <!DOCTYPE html PUBLIC "-//W3C//DTD XHTML 1.0 Transitional//EN"
3       "http://www.w3.org/TR/xhtml1/DTD/xhtml1-transitional.dtd">
4
5   <!-- Fig. 20.11: mathml1.html -->
6   <!-- Simple MathML           -->
7
8   <html xmlns="http://www.w3.org/1999/xhtml">
9
10      <head><title>Simple MathML Example</title></head>
11
12      <body>
13
14          <math xmlns = "http://www.w3.org/1998/Math/MathML">
15
16              <mrow>
17                  <mn>2</mn>
18                  <mo>+</mo>
19                  <mn>3</mn>
20                  <mo>=</mo>
21                  <mn>5</mn>
22              </mrow>
23
24          </math>
25
26      </body>
27  </html>
```

Fig. 20.11 Expression marked up with MathML and displayed in the Amaya browser. (Courtesy of World Wide Web Consortium (W3C).)

We embed the MathML content into an XHTML file by using a `math` element with the default namespace `http://www.w3.org/1998/Math/MathML` (line 14). The **mrow** element (line 16) is a container element for expressions that contain more than one element. In this case, the `mrow` element contains five children. The **mn** element (line 17) marks up a number. The **mo** element (line 18) marks up an operator (e.g., +). Using this markup, we define the expression 2+3=5, which a MathML browser could display.

Let us now consider using MathML to mark up an algebraic equation that uses exponents and arithmetic operators (Fig. 20.12).

```
1    <?xml version="1.0"?>
2    <!DOCTYPE html PUBLIC "-//W3C//DTD XHTML 1.0 Transitional//EN"
3        "HTTP://WWW.W3.ORG/TR/XHTML1/DTD/XHTML1-TRANSITIONAL.DTD">
4
5    <!-- FIG. 20.12: mathml2.html -->
6    <!-- Simple MathML            -->
7
8    <html xmlns="http://www.w3.org/1999/xhtml">
9
10       <head><title>Algebraic MathML Example</title></head>
11
12       <body>
13
14          <math xmlns = "http://www.w3.org/1998/Math/MathML">
15             <mrow>
16
17                <mrow>
18                   <mn>3</mn>
19                   <mo>&InvisibleTimes;</mo>
20
21                   <msup>
22                      <mi>x</mi>
23                      <mn>2</mn>
24                   </msup>
25
26                </mrow>
27
28                <mo>+</mo>
29                <mi>x</mi>
30                <mo>-</mo>
31
32                <mfrac>
33                   <mn>2</mn>
34                   <mi>x</mi>
35                </mfrac>
36
37                <mo>=</mo>
38                <mn>0</mn>
39
40             </mrow>
41          </math>
```

Fig. 20.12 Algebraic equation marked up with MathML and displayed in the Amaya browser. (Courtesy of World Wide Web Consortium (W3C).) (Part 1 of 2.)

```
42
43      </body>
44   </html>
```

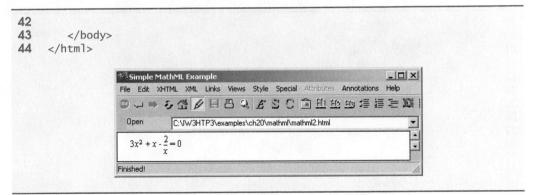

Fig. 20.12 Algebraic equation marked up with MathML and displayed in the Amaya
browser. (Courtesy of World Wide Web Consortium (W3C).) (Part 2 of 2.)

Element `mrow` behaves like parentheses, which allow the document author to group
related elements properly. Line 19 uses entity reference **⁢** to indicate a
multiplication operation without explicit **symbolic representation** (i.e., the multiplication
symbol does not appear between the 3 and x). For exponentiation, line 21 uses the **msup**
element, which represents a superscript. This `msup` element has two children—the expression to be superscripted (i.e., the base) and the superscript (i.e., the exponent). Correspond-
ingly, the **msub** element represents a subscript. To display variables such as x, line 22 uses
identifier element mi.

To display a fraction, line 32 uses element **mfrac**. Lines 33–34 specify the numerator
and the denominator for the fraction. If either the numerator or the denominator contains
more than one element, it must appear in an `mrow` element.

Figure 20.13 marks up a calculus expression that contains an integral symbol and a
square-root symbol.

```
 1   <?xml version = "1.0"?>
 2   <!DOCTYPE html PUBLIC "-//W3C//DTD XHTML 1.0 Transitional//EN"
 3       "http://www.w3.org/TR/xhtml1/DTD/xhtml1-transitional.dtd">
 4
 5   <!-- Fig. 20.13 mathml3.html        -->
 6   <!-- Calculus example using MathML -->
 7
 8   <html xmlns="http://www.w3.org/1999/xhtml">
 9
10      <head><title>Calculus MathML Example</title></head>
11
12      <body>
13
14         <math xmlns = "http://www.w3.org/1998/Math/MathML">
15            <mrow>
16               <msubsup>
17
18                  <mo>&Integral;</mo>
```

Fig. 20.13 Calculus expression marked up with MathML and displayed in the Amaya
browser. (Courtesy of World Wide Web Consortium (W3C).) (Part 1 of 2.)

```
19                       <mn>0</mn>
20
21                       <mrow>
22                           <mn>1</mn>
23                           <mo>-</mo>
24                           <mi>y</mi>
25                       </mrow>
26
27                   </msubsup>
28
29               <msqrt>
30                   <mrow>
31
32                       <mn>4</mn>
33                       <mo>&InvisibleTimes;</mo>
34
35                       <msup>
36                           <mi>x</mi>
37                           <mn>2</mn>
38                       </msup>
39
40                       <mo>+</mo>
41                       <mi>y</mi>
42
43                   </mrow>
44               </msqrt>
45
46               <mo>&delta;</mo>
47               <mi>x</mi>
48           </mrow>
49       </math>
50     </body>
51 </html>
```

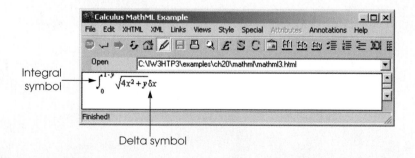

Integral symbol

Delta symbol

Fig. 20.13 Calculus expression marked up with MathML and displayed in the Amaya browser. (Courtesy of World Wide Web Consortium (W3C).) (Part 2 of 2.)

The **entity ∫** (line 18) represents the integral symbol, while the msubsup element (line 16) specifies the subscript and superscript. Element mo marks up the integral operator. Element msubsup requires three child elements—an operator (e.g., the integral entity), the subscript expression (line 19) and the superscript expression (lines 21–25). Element mn (line 19) marks up the number (i.e., 0) that represents the subscript. Element mrow marks up the expression (i.e., 1-y) that specifies the superscript expression

Element **msqrt** (lines 29–44) represents a square root expression. Line 30 uses element mrow to group the expression contained in the square root. Line 46 introduces entity **δ** for representing a lowercase delta symbol. Delta is an operator, so line 46 places this entity in element mo. To see other operations and symbols in MathML, visit www.w3.org/Math.

20.5.2 Chemical Markup Language (CML)

Chemical Markup Language (CML) is an XML vocabulary for representing molecular and chemical information. Many previous methods for storing this type of information (e.g., special file types) inhibited document reuse. CML takes advantage of XML's portability to enable document authors to use and reuse molecular information without corrupting important data in the process. Although many readers will not know the chemistry required for a full understanding of the example in this section, we feel that CML illustrates the purpose of XML.

Document authors can edit and view CML using the *Jumbo browser* (available at www.xml-cml.org) or the *Jmol* browser (available at jmol.sourceforge.net). To test this example, we recommend using Jmol. Download the file jmol-7.zip (the latest version at the time of publication) from

```
http://sourceforge.net/project/showfiles.php?group_id=23629
```

If necessary, download the *WinZip* archive utility from www.winzip.com, and extract the downloaded file. Double click the file jmol.jar in the extracted jmol-7 directory to run the application. [*Note*: Jmol requires Java 1.2 or later. If Java is not installed on your system, please go to www.java.com and click the **Get It Now** button. Follow the on-screen instructions to install Java.] Figure 20.14 shows an ammonia molecule marked up in CML and viewed in Jmol.

```
1   <?xml version = "1.0" ?>
2
3   <!-- Fig. 20.14 : ammonia.xml -->
4   <!-- Structure of ammonia -->
5
6   <molecule id = "ammonia">
7
8      <atomArray>
9
10        <stringArray builtin = "id" >
11           Nitrogen Hydrogen1 Hydrogen2 Hydrogen3
12        </stringArray>
13
14        <stringArray builtin = "elementType">
15           N H H H
16        </stringArray>
```

Fig. 20.14   CML markup for ammonia molecule rendered by Jmol. (Courtesy of the Jmol Project.) (Part 1 of 2.)

```
17
18          <floatArray builtin = "x3">
19              -0.7 -1.3 -1.2 -0.7
20          </floatArray>
21
22          <floatArray builtin = "y3">
23              -0.0 0.2 0.8 -0.9
24          </floatArray>
25
26          <floatArray builtin = "z3">
27              0.0 -0.9 0.6 0.6
28          </floatArray>
29
30      </atomArray>
31
32  </molecule>
```

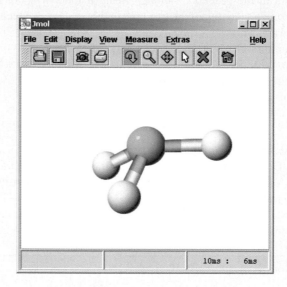

Fig. 20.14 CML markup for ammonia molecule rendered by Jmol. (Courtesy of the Jmol Project.) (Part 2 of 2.)

Line 6 defines an ammonia molecule using element `molecule`. Attribute `id` identifies this molecule as `ammonia`. A molecule is composed of atoms. The `atomArray` element is used to specify one or more atoms that comprise the molecule. Lines 10–12 use element `stringArray` and assign `id` to attribute `builtin` to specify the `ids` of the atoms that make up the molecule. Ammonia contains one nitrogen atom and three hydrogen atoms.

Lines 14–16 specify the actual type of each atom. The allowed values of `element-Type` include every element on the periodic table.

Lines 18–20 use element `floatArray` with attribute `builtin` assigned to the value `x3` to specify a list of floating-point numbers. Each number defines the *x*-coordinate of each atom. The first value (-0.7) is the *x*-coordinate of the first atom (nitrogen), the second value (1.3) is the *x*-coordinate of the second atom (the first hydrogen atom) and so forth.

Lines 22–24 use element `floatArray` with attribute `builtin` assigned to the value y3 to define the *y*-coordinates, and lines 26-28 define the *z*-coordinates.

20.5.3 MusicXML

MusicXML is the most successful standard in music notation and performance since MIDI. MIDI focuses on music performance, whereas MusicXML focuses on music distribution. MusicXML simplifies the exchange of musical scores over the Internet. It is also a format for translating between the many other popular music formats, such as SharpEye, TaBazar and MuseData. Recordare (`www.recordare.com`) developed MusicXML to mark up all types of music from classical to folk and pop.

MusicXML is defined with a DTD. Currently, XML Schema is the W3C recommendation, not DTD. However, Recordare started MusicXML when DTD was the W3C recommendation. MusicXML relies heavily upon elements rather than attributes to hold musical information. Elements inherently are more structured than attributes. Because music is very structured, using elements to define music is natural and improves readability.

MusicXML also improves music analysis (i.e., finding the highest note in a song) and takes advantage of many XML languages and tools. The descriptiveness of MusicXML, combined with its wide-ranging acceptance, will facilitate the distribution of musical scores and parts over the Internet.

Figure 20.15 shows an example of MusicXML markup displayed in MakeMusic!'s *Finale*® *2003* music notation editing software. Additional songs marked up in MusicXML are available for download at `www.recordare.com/xml/samples.html`. To play these songs, or to play your own MusicXML-marked music, download and install the Finale 2003 demo available at `www.finalemusic.com/finale/demo.asp`. Then download and install the *Dolet for Finale* plug-in from `www.musicxml.org/downloads.html#Finale` before continuing. Dolet for Finale is a plug-in that allows users to import MusicXML into Finale and is required to test the following example.

To play a MusicXML file, open Finale and create a new song file by clicking **Default Document** in the **New** sub-menu in the **File** menu. Then select **MusicXML Import** from the **Plug-ins** menu. Open your song and press the green arrow to listen. The short tune rendered in Fig. 20.15, `tune.xml`, is located on the CD-ROM in the Chapter 20 examples directory.

Fig. 20.15 MusicXML markup rendered by Finale 2003. (Courtesy of MakeMusic!® Inc.)

20.5.4 RSS

RSS stands for RDF (Resource Description Framework) Site Summary and is also known as Rich Site Summary and Really Simple Syndication. RSS is a popular and simple XML format designed to share headlines and Web content between Web sites. You can view various RSS formatted headlines and content at www.brokenvaporware.com/ht/rss.

Figure 20.16 shows a sample **RSS 2.0** file. Several other RSS standards also exist (e.g., RSS 0.91, 0.92, 0.93, 0.94 and 1.0). An RSS validator is available at feeds.archive.org/validator.

```
1   <?xml version = "1.0" ?>
2
3   <!-- Fig. 20.16 deitel.rss   -->
4   <!-- RSS feed                 -->
5
6   <rss version = "2.0">
7      <channel>
8         <title>Deitel</title>
9         <link>http://www.deitel.com</link>
10        <description>CS textbooks</description>
11        <language>en-us</language>
12        <item>
13           <title>Simply VB How To Program</title>
14           <description>
15              This book combines the DEITEL signature live-code approach
16              with a new application-driven methodology, in which readers
17              build real-world applications that incorporate Visual
18              Basic .NET programming fundamentals.
19           </description>
20           <link>
21              http://www.deitel.com/books/downloads.html#vbnetHTP2
22           </link>
23        </item>
24        <item>
25           <title>Visual C++ </title>
26           <description>
27              For experienced programmers. Pictures of pyramids
28              on the cover.
29           </description>
30           <link>
31              http://www.deitel.com/books/vbnetFEP1
32           </link>
33        </item>
34     </channel>
35  </rss>
```

Fig. 20.16   RSS 2.0 feed.

An RSS file, also called an **RSS feed**, consists of a container **rss** element that denotes the RSS version (line 6) and container **channel** elements (line 7). RSS feeds can then contain several descriptive tags (lines 8–11) and **item** elements (lines 12–33) that concisely describe the news or information. Each item element has a **title** element (like a headline), a **description** element (a description of the content), and a **link** element (a link to the actual content).

It is a Web author's task to update and maintain a feed for others to view, manipulate, and put on their site. Feeds are placed online and accessed like a Web page or XML file. A large compilation of RSS feeds is available at `www.syndic8.com/feeds`. Typically, an XSLT or some server-side script is used to request and parse the RSS feed for viewing or including on a Web site.

By providing up-to-date, free and linkable content for anyone to use, RSS provides a way for Web-site developers to obtain more traffic. It also allows users to get news and information from a variety of providers easily and reduces content development time. RSS simplifies importing information from portals, Weblogs and news sites. For instance, news service Slashdot has an RSS feed at `http://slashdot.org/slashdot.rss`. Any piece of information can be syndicated via RSS, not just news. After putting information in RSS format an RSS program can check the feed for changes and react to them.

Many RSS programs are available. An **aggregator** is one type of RSS program. It keeps tracks of many RSS feeds and brings together information from the separate feeds. Aggregators can also sort and sift through many RSS feeds to find pertinent information. Newzcrawler is one such aggregator (`www.newzcrawler.com/downloads.shtml`).

20.5.5 Other Markup Languages

Literally hundreds of markup languages derive from XML. Every day developers find new uses for XML. In Fig. 20.17, we summarize some of these markup languages.

Markup language	Description
VoiceXML™	The VoiceXML Forum founded by AT&T, IBM, Lucent and Motorola developed VoiceXML. It provides interactive voice communication between humans and computers through a telephone, PDA (personal digital assistant) or desktop computer. IBM's VoiceXML SDK can process VoiceXML documents. Visit `www.voicexml.org` for more information on VoiceXML. We introduce VoiceXML in Chapter 29, Accessibility.
Synchronous Multimedia Integration Language (SMIL™)	SMIL is an XML vocabulary for multimedia presentations. The W3C was the primary developer of SMIL, with contributions from some companies. Visit `www.w3.org/AudioVideo` for more on SMIL. We introduce SMIL in Chapter 28, Multimedia.
Research Information Exchange Markup Language (RIXML)	RIXML, developed by a consortium of brokerage firms, marks up investment data. Visit `www.rixml.org` for more information on RIXML.
ComicsML	A language developed by Jason MacIntosh for marking up comics. Visit `www.jmac.org/projects/comics_ml` for more information on ComicsML.

Fig. 20.17   Various markup languages derived from XML. (Part 1 of 2.)

Markup language	Description
Geography Markup Language (GML)	OpenGIS developed the Geography Markup Language to describe geographic information. Visit `www.opengis.org` for more information on GML.
Extensible User Interface Language (XUL)	The Mozilla Project created the Extensible User Interface Language for describing graphical user interfaces in a platform-independent way.

Fig. 20.17   Various markup languages derived from XML. (Part 2 of 2.)

20.6 Document Object Model (DOM)

Although an XML document is a text file, retrieving data from the document using traditional sequential file-access techniques is neither practical nor efficient, especially for adding and removing elements dynamically. As mentioned earlier, when a DOM parser successfully parses an XML document, it creates a tree structure in memory that contains the document's data. Figure 20.18 shows the tree structure for the document `article.xml` discussed in Fig. 20.1. This hierarchical tree structure is a **Document Object Model (DOM) tree**. Each tag name (e.g., `article`, `date`, `firstName`) represents a **node**. A node that contains other nodes (called **child nodes** or **children**) is called a **parent node** (e.g., `author`). A parent node can have many children, but a child node can have only one parent node. Nodes that are peers (e.g., `firstName` and `lastName`) are called **sibling nodes**. A node's **descendant nodes** include its children, its children's children and so on. A node's **ancestor nodes** include its parent, its parent's parent and so on.

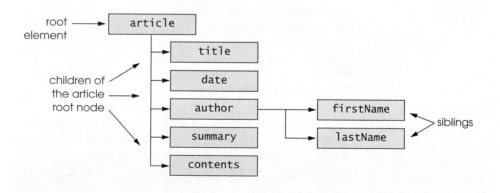

Fig. 20.18   Tree structure for `article.xml`.

The DOM has a single **root node**, which contains all the other nodes in the document. For example, the root node for `article.xml` (Fig. 20.1) contains a node for the XML declaration (line 1), two nodes for the comments (lines 3–4) and a node for the root element `article` (line 6).

Each node is an object that has properties, methods and events. Properties associated with a node include names, values and child nodes. Methods enable programs to create, delete and append nodes, load XML documents, and so on. An XML parser exposes these methods as a programmatic library called an **Application Programming Interface (API)**.

20.7 DOM Methods

To introduce document manipulation with the XML Document Object Model, we provide a simple scripting example that uses JavaScript and Microsoft's MSXML parser that is built into IE6. This example takes the XML document `article.xml` (Fig. 20.1) that marks up an article and uses the DOM API to display the document's element names and values. Figure 20.19 lists the JavaScript code that manipulates this XML document and displays its content in an XHTML page.

```
1   <?xml version="1.0"?>
2   <!DOCTYPE html PUBLIC "-//W3C//DTD XHTML 1.0 Transitional//EN"
3      "http://www.w3.org/TR/xhtml1/DTD/xhtml1-transitional.dtd">
4   <html xmlns="http://www.w3.org/1999/xhtml">
5
6   <!-- Fig. 20.19: DOMExample.html -->
7   <!-- DOM with JavaScript          -->
8
9      <head>
10        <title>A DOM Example</title>
11     </head>
12
13     <body>
14
15     <script type = "text/javascript" language = "JavaScript">
16        <!--
17        var xmlDocument = new ActiveXObject( "Microsoft.XMLDOM" );
18
19        xmlDocument.load( "article.xml" );
20
21        // get the root element
22        var element = xmlDocument.documentElement;
23
24        document.writeln(
25           "<p>Here is the root node of the document: " +
26           "<strong>" + element.nodeName + "</strong>" +
27           "<br />The following are its child elements:" +
28           "</p><ul>" );
29
30        // traverse all child nodes of root element
31        for ( var i = 0; i < element.childNodes.length; i++ ) {
32           var curNode = element.childNodes.item( i );
33
34           // print node name of each child element
35           document.writeln( "<li><strong>" + curNode.nodeName
36              + "</strong></li>" );
37        }
```

Fig. 20.19 Traversing `article.xml` with JavaScript. (Part 1 of 2.)

```
38
39        document.writeln( "</ul>" );
40
41        // get the first child node of root element
42        var currentNode = element.firstChild;
43
44        document.writeln( "<p>The first child of root node is: " +
45           "<strong>" + currentNode.nodeName + "</strong>" +
46           "<br />whose next sibling is:" );
47
48        // get the next sibling of first child
49        var nextSib = currentNode.nextSibling;
50
51        document.writeln( "<strong>" + nextSib.nodeName +
52           "</strong>.<br />Value of <strong>" +
53           nextSib.nodeName + "</strong> element is: " );
54
55        var value = nextSib.firstChild;
56
57        // print the text value of the sibling
58        document.writeln( "<em>" + value.nodeValue + "</em>" +
59           "<br />Parent node of <strong>" + nextSib.nodeName +
60           "</strong> is: <strong>" +
61           nextSib.parentNode.nodeName + "</strong>.</p>" );
62        -->
63     </script>
64
65     </body>
66  </html>
```

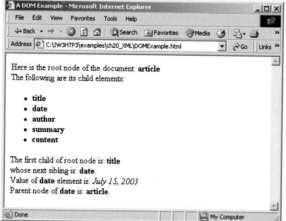

Fig. 20.19 Traversing `article.xml` with JavaScript. (Part 2 of 2.)

Line 17 uses the JavaScript `ActiveXObject` class to instantiate (i.e., create) a Microsoft XML Document Object Model object and assign it to the reference `xmlDocument`. This object represents an XML-document DOM tree and provides methods for manipulating its data. The statement merely creates the object, which does not yet refer to any specific XML document.

Line 19 calls the method **load** to load `article.xml` (Fig. 20.1) into memory. The MSXML parser parses the XML document and stores it in memory as a tree structure.

Line 22 assigns the root element node (i.e., `article`) to variable `element`. Property **documentElement** corresponds to the root element in the document (e.g., `article`), which is important because this element is the reference point for retrieving all the other nodes in the document.

Line 26 places the name of the root element in XHTML element `strong` and writes this string to the browser for rendering. Property **nodeName** corresponds to the name of an element, attribute, or so on. In this particular case, `element` refers to the root node named `article`.

Lines 31–37 loop through the root node's children using property **childNodes**. `element.childNodes` is a **NodeList**. A NodeList is a collection of nodes. Property **length** returns the number of children in the root element.

Calling method **item** (line 32) accesses individual child nodes. Each node has an integer index (starting at zero) based on the order in which the node occurs in the XML document. For example, in Fig. 20.1, `title` has index 0, `date` has index 1, and so on. Line 32 calls method `item` to obtain the child node at index `i` and assigns the node to `curNode`.

Line 42 retrieves the root node's first child node (i.e., `title`) using property **firstChild**. The expression in line 42 is a more concise alternative to

```
var currentNode = element.childNodes.item( 0 );
```

Elements `title`, `date`, `author`, `summary` and `content` are all sibling nodes. Property **nextSibling** returns a node's next sibling. Line 49 assigns `currentNode`'s (i.e., `title`'s) next sibling node (i.e., `date`) to reference `nextSib`.

In addition to elements and attributes, text (e.g., `Simple XML` in line 8 of Fig. 20.1) also is a node. Line 55 assigns `nextSib`'s (i.e., `date`'s) first child node to `value`. In this case, the first child node is a text node. In line 58, property **nodeValue** retrieves the value of this text node. A text node's value is simply the text that the node contains. Element nodes have a value of **null** (i.e., no value). Line 61 retrieves and displays `nextSib`'s (i.e., `date`'s) parent node (i.e., `article`). Property **parentNode** returns a node's parent node.

The tables in Figs. 20.20–20.26 describe important DOM methods. The primary DOM objects are **Node** (a node in the tree), **NodeList** (an ordered set of nodes), **NamedNodeMap** (an unordered set of nodes), **Document** (the document), **Element** (an element node), **Attr** (an attribute node), **Text** (a text node) and **Comment** (a comment node). Some methods of these objects are described in the tables.

Method	Description
getNodeType	Returns an integer representing the node type.
getNodeName	Returns the name of the node. If the node does not have a name, a string consisting of # followed by the type of the node is returned.

Fig. 20.20 Node object methods. (Part 1 of 2.)

Method	Description
getNodeValue	Returns a string or null depending on the node type.
getParentNode	Returns the parent node.
getChildNodes	Returns a NodeList (Fig. 20.21) with all the children of the node.
getFirstChild	Returns the first child in the NodeList.
getLastChild	Returns the last child in the NodeList.
getPreviousSibling	Returns the node preceding this node, or null.
getNextSibling	Returns the node following this node, or null.
getAttributes	Returns a NamedNodeMap (Fig. 20.22) containing the attributes for this node.
insertBefore	Inserts the node (passed as the first argument) before the existing node (passed as the second argument). If the new node is already in the tree, it is removed before insertion. The same behavior is true for other methods that add nodes.
replaceChild	Replaces the second argument node with the first argument node.
removeChild	Removes the child node passed to it.
appendChild	Appends the node passed to it to the list of child nodes.
getElementsByTagName	Returns a NodeList of all the nodes in the subtree with the name specified as the first argument ordered as they would be encountered in a preorder traversal. An optional second argument specifies either the direct child nodes (0) or any descendant (1).
getChildAtIndex	Returns the child node at the specified index in the child list.
addText	Appends the string passed to it to the last Node if it is a Text node, otherwise creates a new Text node for the string and adds it to the end of the child list.
isAncestor	Returns true if the node passed is a parent of the node or is the node itself.

Fig. 20.20 Node object methods. (Part 2 of 2.)

Method	Description
item	Passed an index number, returns the element node at that index. Indices range from 0 to $length - 1$.
getLength	Returns the total number of nodes in the list.

Fig. 20.21 NodeList object methods.

Method	Description
getNamedItem	Returns either a node in the NamedNodeMap with the specified name or null.
setNamedItem	Stores a node passed to it in the NamedNodeMap. Two nodes with the same name cannot be stored in the same NamedNodeMap.
removeNamedItem	Removes a specified node from the NamedNodeMap.
getLength	Returns the total number of nodes in the NamedNodeMap.
getValues	Returns a NodeList containing all the nodes in the NamedNodeMap.

Fig. 20.22 NamedNodeMap object methods.

Method	Description
getDocumentElement	Returns the root node of the document.
createElement	Creates and returns an element node with the specified tag name.
createAttribute	Creates and returns an attribute node with the specified name and value.
createTextNode	Creates and returns a text node that contains the specified text.
createComment	Creates a comment to hold the specified text.

Fig. 20.23 Document methods.

Method	Description
getTagName	Returns the name of the element.
setTagName	Changes the name of the element to the specified name.
getAttribute	Returns the value of the specified attribute.
setAttribute	Changes the value of the attribute passed as the first argument to the value passed as the second argument.
removeAttribute	Removes the specified attribute.
getAttributeNode	Returns the specified attribute node.
setAttributeNode	Adds a new attribute node with the specified name.

Fig. 20.24 Element methods.

Method	Description
getValue	Returns the specified attribute's value.
setValue	Changes the value of the attribute to the specified value.
getName	Returns the name of the attribute.

Fig. 20.25 Attr methods.

Method	Description
getData	Returns the data contained in the node (text or comment).
setData	Sets the node's data.
getLength	Returns the number of characters contained in the node.

Fig. 20.26 Text and Comment methods.

20.8 Simple API for XML (SAX)

Members of the XML-DEV mailing list developed the **Simple API for XML (SAX)**, which they released in May, 1998. SAX is an alternative method for parsing XML documents that uses an **event-based model**—**SAX-based parsers** generate notifications called **events** as the parser parses the document. Software programs can "listen" for these events to retrieve specified data from the document. For example, a program that builds mailing lists might read name and address information from an XML document that contains much more than just mailing address information (e.g., birthdays, phone numbers, e-mail addresses). Such a program could use a SAX parser to parse the document, and might listen only for events that contain name and address information. If this program used a DOM parser, the parser would load every element and attribute into memory, and the program would have to traverse the DOM tree to locate the relevant address information.

SAX and DOM provide dramatically different APIs for accessing XML document information. Each API has advantages and disadvantages. DOM is a tree-based model that stores the document's data in a hierarchy of nodes. After parsing is completed, programs can access data quickly, because all the document's data is in memory. DOM also provides facilities for adding or removing nodes, which enables programs to modify XML documents easily.

SAX-based parsers invoke **listener methods** when the parser encounters markup. With this event-based model, the SAX-based parser does not create a tree structure to store the XML document's data—instead, the parser passes data to the application from the XML document as it finds the data. This results in better performance and less memory overhead than with DOM-based parsers. In fact, many DOM parsers use SAX parsers "under the hood" to retrieve data from a document for building the DOM tree in memory. Many programmers find it easier to traverse and manipulate XML documents using the DOM tree structure. Programs typically use SAX parsers for reading XML documents that the program will not modify. SAX-based parsers are available for several programming languages, such as Java, Perl, Python and C++. Please visit `www.saxproject.org` for further information on SAX and how it is currently being used.

Performance Tip 20.1

SAX-based parsing is often more efficient than DOM-based parsing when processing large XML documents, because SAX-based parsers do not load entire XML documents into memory at once.

Performance Tip 20.2

SAX-based parsing is an efficient means of parsing documents that only need to be parsed once.

Performance Tip 20.3

DOM-based parsing is often more efficient than SAX-based parsing when a program must quickly and repeatedly retrieve information from the document.

Performance Tip 20.4

Programs that must conserve memory commonly use SAX-based parsers.

20.9 Extensible Stylesheet Language (XSL)

Extensible Stylesheet Language (**XSL**) documents specify how programs should render XML document data. XSL is a group of three technologies: **XSL-FO** (**XSL Formatting Objects**), **XSLT** (**XSL Transformations**) and **XPath**. XSL-FO is a vocabulary for specifying formatting. XSLT is a language for transforming XML into other formats and XPath is a syntax for accessing parts of an XML document. The relationship between XML and XSL is similar to the relationship between XHTML and Cascading Style Sheets (CSS), although XSL is much more powerful than CSS. Document authors also can use CSS to specify formatting information for XML documents. A subset of XSL—XSL Transformations—provides elements that define rules for transforming data from one XML document to produce a different XML document (e.g., XHTML). By convention, XSL documents have the filename extension **.xsl**.

Software Engineering Observation 20.7

XSL enables document authors to separate data presentation from data description.

Transforming an XML document using XSLT involves two tree structures: the **source tree** (i.e., the XML document to be transformed) and the **result tree** (i.e., the XML document to be created). **XPath** is used to locate parts of the **source tree** document that match **templates** defined in the XSL stylesheet. When there is a match (i.e., a node matches a template), the matching template executes and adds its result to the **result tree**. When there are no more **matches**, the XSLT has transformed a **source tree** into the **result tree**. The XSLT does not go through every node of the source tree; it selectively navigates the source tree using XPath's `select` and `match` attributes. For the XSLT to function, the source tree must be properly structured. Schemas, DTDs and validating parsers can validate document structure before using XPath and XSLTs. The table in Fig. 20.27 lists some commonly used XSL elements.

Element	Description
`<xsl:apply-templates>`	Applies the templates of the XSL document to the children of the current node.
`<xsl:apply-templates match = "expression">`	Applies the templates of the XSL document to the children of *expression*. The value of the attribute `match` (i.e., *expression*) must be an XPath expression that specifies elements.

Fig. 20.27 XSL stylesheet elements. (Part 1 of 2.)

Element	Description
`<xsl:template>`	Contains rules to apply when a specified node is matched.
`<xsl:value-of select = "`*expression*`">`	Selects the value of an XML element and adds it to the output tree of the transformation. The required `select` attribute contains an XPath expression.
`<xsl:for-each select = "`*expression*`">`	Applies a template to every node selected by the XPath specified by the `select` attribute.
`<xsl:sort select = "`*expression*`">`	Used as a child element of an `<xsl:apply-templates>` or `<xsl:for-each>` element. Sorts the nodes selected by the `<apply-template>` or `<for-each>` element so that the nodes are processed in sorted order.
`<xsl:output>`	Has various attributes to define the format (e.g., xml, html), version (e.g., 1.2, 2.0), document type and media type of the output document. This tag is a top-level element, which means that it can be used only as a child element of a `stylesheet`.
`<xsl:copy>`	Adds the current node to the output tree.

Fig. 20.27   XSL stylesheet elements. (Part 2 of 2.)

A Simple XSL Example

Figure 20.28 lists an XML document that marks up various sports. The output shows the results of the transformation (specified in the XSLT template of Fig. 20.29) rendered by Internet Explorer 6.[1] We discuss the specific XSL document that performs the transformation in Fig. 20.29.

```
1   <?xml version = "1.0"?>
2   <?xml:stylesheet type = "text/xsl" href = "games.xsl"?>
3
4   <!-- Fig. 20.28 : games.xml -->
5   <!-- Sports Database          -->
6
7   <sports>
8
9      <game id = "783">
10        <name>Cricket</name>
11
12        <paragraph>
13           Popular in Commonwealth nations.
14        </paragraph>
15     </game>
```

Fig. 20.28   XML document containing a list of sports. (Part 1 of 2.)

---

1.   The examples in this section require MSXML 3.0 or higher to run. This program is included in Internet Explorer 6. For information on downloading and installing MSXML for use in a previous version of IE, please visit Microsoft's *XML General Downloads* site, `msdn.microsoft.com/downloads/list/xmlgeneral.asp`.

```
16
17      <game id = "239">
18         <name>Baseball</name>
19
20         <paragraph>
21             Popular in America.
22         </paragraph>
23      </game>
24
25      <game id = "418">
26         <name>Soccer (Football)</name>
27
28         <paragraph>
29             Popular sport in the world.
30         </paragraph>
31      </game>
32
33   </sports>
```

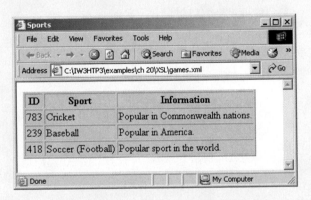

Fig. 20.28   XML document containing a list of sports. (Part 2 of 2.)

Line 2 is a **processing instruction (PI)** that references the XSL stylesheet
games.xsl. Its **type** attribute specifies that games.xsl is a text/xsl file. A processing
instruction is an application-specific piece of information embedded in an XML document.
The characters **<?** and **?>** delimit a processing instruction. The processing instruction of
line 2 provides application-specific information to whatever XML processor the application
uses. Processing instructions consist of a **PI target** (e.g., xml:stylesheet) and a **PI
value** (e.g., type = "text/xsl" href = "games.xsl"). A browser such as Internet
Explorer uses this processing instruction to determine the XSL transformation to apply to
the XML document. When games.xml is opened in the browser, the processing instruction
tells it to apply games.xsl to itself and output the result.

 Portability Tip 20.1

*Processing instructions allow document authors to embed application-specific information
in an XML document without affecting its portability.*

Figure 20.29 shows an XSL document for transforming the structured data of the XML
document of Fig. 20.28 into an XHTML document for presentation.

```
 1   <?xml version = "1.0"?>
 2
 3   <!-- Fig. 20.29 : games.xsl        -->
 4   <!-- A simple XSLT transformation    -->
 5
 6   <!-- reference XSL stylesheet URI    -->
 7   <xsl:stylesheet version = "1.0"
 8      xmlns:xsl = "http://www.w3.org/1999/XSL/Transform">
 9
10      <xsl:output method = "html" omit-xml-declaration = "no"
11         doctype-system =
12            "http://www.w3.org/TR/xhtml1/DTD/xhtml1-strict.dtd"
13         doctype-public = "-//W3C//DTD XHTML 1.0 Strict//EN"/>
14
15      <xsl:template match = "/">
16
17         <html xmlns="http://www.w3.org/1999/xhtml">
18
19            <head>
20               <title>Sports</title>
21            </head>
22
23            <body>
24
25               <table border = "1" bgcolor = "cyan">
26
27                  <thead>
28
29                     <tr>
30                        <th>ID</th>
31                        <th>Sport</th>
32                        <th>Information</th>
33                     </tr>
34
35                  </thead>
36
37                  <!-- insert each name and paragraph element value  -->
38                  <!-- into a table row.                             -->
39                  <xsl:for-each select = "/sports/game">
40
41                     <tr>
42                        <td><xsl:value-of select = "@id"/></td>
43                        <td><xsl:value-of select = "name"/></td>
44                        <td><xsl:value-of select = "paragraph"/></td>
45                     </tr>
46
47                  </xsl:for-each>
48
49               </table>
50
51            </body>
52
53         </html>
```

Fig. 20.29 Using XSLT to create elements and attributes. (Part 1 of 2.)

```
54
55      </xsl:template>
56
57  </xsl:stylesheet>
```

Fig. 20.29   Using XSLT to create elements and attributes. (Part 2 of 2.)

Lines 7–8 use the **stylesheet** start tag—which begins the XSL stylesheet. Line 8 binds namespace prefix **xsl** to the URI http://www.w3.org/1999/XSL/Transform, which uniquely identifies the XSL namespace.

Lines 10–13 use element **xsl:output** to write an XHTML document type declaration to the result tree. Attribute **omit-xml-declaration** specifies whether the transformation should write the XML declaration to the result tree. In this case we do not omit the XML declaration. Attributes **doctype-system** and **doctype-public** specify the DTD system and public values for the resulting document, respectively.

XSLT uses **templates** to describe how to transform particular nodes from the source tree into the result tree. A template is applied to nodes that are specified in the required **match** attribute. Line 15 uses the **match** attribute to select the **document root** (i.e., the conceptual part of the document that contains the root element and everything below it) of the XML source document (i.e., game.xml). The XPath character / always selects the document root element. In XPath, a beginning / specifies that we are using absolute addressing. In Fig. 20.28, the child nodes of the document root are the processing instruction node (line 2), the two comment nodes (lines 4–5) and the sports element node (line 7). Because the template **matches** some node (it matches the root node), the contents of the template are now added to the result tree. So far, the result tree only contains the **doctype** definitions.

The MSXML processor writes the XHTML in lines 17–35 (Fig. 20.29) to the result tree exactly as it appears in the XSLT document. Now the result tree consists of the doctype definition and the XHTML code from lines 17–35. Line 39 uses element **xsl:for-each** to iterate through the source XML document and search for game elements. The xsl:for-each element is similar to JavaScript's for...in statement. Attribute **select** is an XPath expression that specifies the set of nodes (called the **node set**) on which the xsl:for-each operates. The first forward slash means that we are using absolute addressing (i.e., we are starting from the root and defining paths down the source tree). The forward slash between sports and game indicates that game is a child node of sports. Thus, the xsl:for-each finds game nodes that are children of the sports node. In this document there is only one sports node, which is also the document root node. After it finds the elements that match the selection criteria, the xsl:for-each processes each element with the code in lines 41–45 (these lines produce one row in a table each time they execute) and places the result of lines 41–45 in the result tree.

Line 42 uses element **value-of** to retrieve attribute id's value and place it in a td element in the result tree. The XPath symbol @ specifies that id is an attribute node of the context node game. Lines 43–44 place the name and paragraph element values in td elements and insert those elements in the result tree. When an XPath expression has no beginning forward slash, the expression is using **relative addressing**. Omitting the beginning forward slash tells the **<xsl:value-of select>** statements to search for name and paragraph elements that are children of the context node, not the root node. The current context node is `game`, which does indeed have an `id` attribute, a `name` child element and a `paragraph` child element.

Using XSLT to Sort and Format Data

Figure 20.30 presents an XML document (`sorting.xml`) that marks up information about a book. Line 6 references the XSL stylesheet `sorting.xsl` (Fig. 20.31). Line 6 contains a processing instruction (PI), which is application-specific information embedded in an XML document.

```
1   <?xml version = "1.0"?>
2
3   <!-- Fig. 20.30 : sorting.xml          -->
4   <!-- Usage of elements and attributes -->
5
6   <?xml:stylesheet type = "text/xsl" href = "sorting.xsl"?>
7
8   <book isbn = "999-99999-9-X">
9      <title>Deitel&apos;s XML Primer</title>
10
11     <author>
12        <firstName>Paul</firstName>
13        <lastName>Deitel</lastName>
14     </author>
15
16     <chapters>
17        <frontMatter>
18           <preface pages = "2"/>
19           <contents pages = "5"/>
20           <illustrations pages = "4"/>
21        </frontMatter>
22
23        <chapter number = "3" pages = "44">
24           Advanced XML</chapter>
25        <chapter number = "2" pages = "35">
26           Intermediate XML</chapter>
27        <appendix number = "B" pages = "26">
28           Parsers and Tools</appendix>
29        <appendix number = "A" pages = "7">
30           Entities</appendix>
31        <chapter number = "1" pages = "28">
32           XML Fundamentals</chapter>
33     </chapters>
34
35     <media type = "CD"/>
36  </book>
```

Fig. 20.30 XML document containing book information.

Figure 20.31 presents an XSL document (`sorting.xsl`) for transforming `sorting.xml` (Fig. 20.30) to XHTML. Recall that the XSL document navigates a source tree and builds a result tree. In this example, the source tree is XML and the output tree is XHTML. Line 15 of Fig. 20.31 matches the root element of the document in Fig. 20.30.

Line 16 outputs an `html` tag to the result tree. The `<xsl:apply-templates/>` tag (line 17) specifies that the XML processor (MSXML) should apply the `xsl:templates` defined in this XSL document to the current node's (i.e., the document root's) children. Lines 21–82 specify a template that matches element `book`. The template indicates how to format the information contained in `book` elements of `sorting.xml` (Fig. 20.30) as XHTML.

Lines 23–24 create the title for the XHTML document. We use the book's ISBN (from attribute `isbn`) and the contents of element `title` to create the title string (**ISBN 999-99999-9-X - Deitel's XML Primer**).

Lines 30–31 create a header element that displays the book's author. The context node to determine where to obtain the name is `book`. `author/lastName` uses a relative location path (note that it does not have a beginning forward slash). Thus it treats the context node (i.e., `book`) as the root and looks for `lastName` nodes with `author` parents. So the XPath expression `author/firstName` selects the author's first name, and the expression `author/lastName` selects the author's last name.

Performance Tip 20.5

Using a client Web browser (e.g., Internet Explorer 6) to process XSL documents conserves server resources.

```
1    <?xml version = "1.0"?>
2
3    <!-- Fig. 20.31 : sorting.xsl                          -->
4    <!-- Transformation of Book information into XHTML -->
5
6    <xsl:stylesheet version = "1.0"
7       xmlns:xsl = "http://www.w3.org/1999/XSL/Transform">
8
9       <xsl:output method = "html" omit-xml-declaration = "no"
10
11          doctype-system =
12             "http://www.w3.org/TR/xhtml1/DTD/xhtml1-strict.dtd"
13          doctype-public = "-//W3C//DTD XHTML 1.0 Strict//EN"/>
14
15       <xsl:template match = "/">
16          <html xmlns = "http://www.w3.org/1999/xhtml">
17             <xsl:apply-templates/>
18          </html>
19       </xsl:template>
20
21       <xsl:template match = "book">
22          <head>
23             <title>ISBN <xsl:value-of select = "@isbn"/> -
24                <xsl:value-of select = "title"/></title>
25          </head>
26
27          <body>
28             <h1><xsl:value-of select = "title"/></h1>
29
30             <h2>by <xsl:value-of select = "author/lastName"/>,
31                <xsl:value-of select = "author/firstName"/></h2>
```

Fig. 20.31   XSL document that transforms `sort.xml` into XHTML. (Part 1 of 3.)

```
32
33                    <table border = "1">
34                        <xsl:for-each select = "chapters/frontMatter/*">
35                            <tr>
36                                <td align = "right">
37                                    <xsl:value-of select = "name()"/>
38                                </td>
39
40                                <td>
41                                    ( <xsl:value-of select = "@pages"/> pages )
42                                </td>
43                            </tr>
44                        </xsl:for-each>
45
46                        <xsl:for-each select = "chapters/chapter">
47                            <xsl:sort select = "@number" data-type = "number"
48                                order = "ascending"/>
49                            <tr>
50                                <td align = "right">
51                                    Chapter <xsl:value-of select = "@number"/>
52                                </td>
53
54                                <td>
55                                    <xsl:value-of select = "text()"/>
56                                    ( <xsl:value-of select = "@pages"/> pages )
57                                </td>
58                            </tr>
59                        </xsl:for-each>
60                        <xsl:for-each select = "chapters/appendix">
61                            <xsl:sort select = "@number" data-type = "text"
62                                order = "ascending"/>
63                            <tr>
64                                <td align = "right">
65                                    Appendix <xsl:value-of select = "@number"/>
66                                </td>
67
68                                <td>
69                                    <xsl:value-of select = "text()"/>
70                                    ( <xsl:value-of select = "@pages"/> pages )
71                                </td>
72                            </tr>
73                        </xsl:for-each>
74                    </table>
75
76                    <br />Pages:
77                        <xsl:variable name = "pagecount"
78                            select = "sum(chapters//*/@pages)"/>
79                        <xsl:value-of select = "$pagecount"/>
80                    <br />Media Type: <xsl:value-of select = "media/@type"/>
81                </body>
82        </xsl:template>
83
84    </xsl:stylesheet>
```

Fig. 20.31 XSL document that transforms `sort.xml` into XHTML. (Part 2 of 3.)

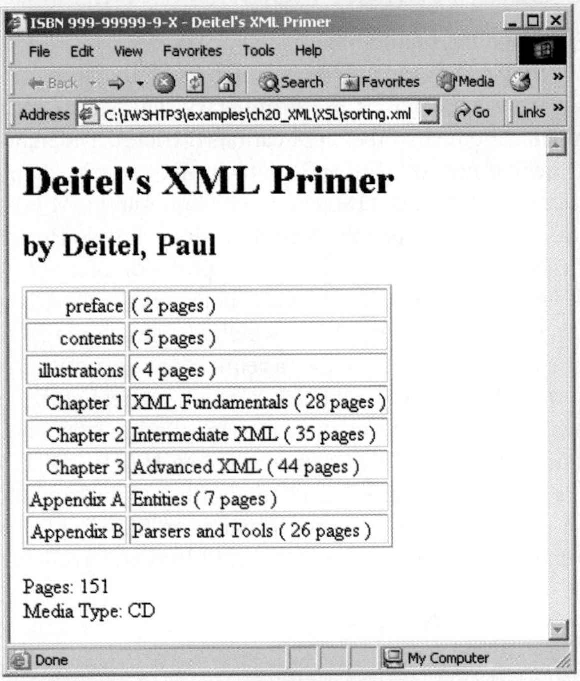

Fig. 20.31   XSL document that transforms `sort.xml` into XHTML. (Part 3 of 3.)

Line 34 selects each child element (indicated by an asterisk) of `frontMatter`. Line 37 calls **function name** to retrieve the current node's element name (e.g., `preface`). This function applies to a **node-set** object: the result of an XPath location path (e.g., `/chapter/frontMatter`). The current node is the context node specified in the `xsl:for-each` element (line 34). Line 41 retrieves the value of the `pages` attribute of the current node.

Line 46 selects each `chapter` element. Lines 47–48 use **element xsl:sort** to sort `chapter`s by number in ascending order. Attribute `select` selects the value of attribute `number` in context node `chapter`. Attribute **data-type** specifies a numeric sort, and attribute **order** specifies `ascending` order. Attribute `data-type` also accepts the value **"text"** (line 61), and attribute `order` also accepts the value **"descending"**. Line 55 uses the `text` node-set function to get the text between the `chapter` tags. Lines 60–73 perform similar tasks for each `appendix`.

Lines 77–78 use an **XSL variable** to store the value of the book's page count and output the page count to the result tree. Attribute `name` specifies the variable's name (i.e., `pagecount`), and attribute `select` assigns a value to the variable. Function **sum** (line 78) totals the values for all `page` attribute values. The two slashes between `chapters` and `*` indicate a **recursive descent**—the MSXML processor will search all descendant nodes of `chapters` for elements that contain an attribute named `pages`. The XPath expression

```
//*
```

selects all the nodes in an XML document. Line 79 retrieves the value of the newly created XSL variable `pagecount` by placing a dollar sign in front of its name.

20.10 Simple Object Access Protocol (SOAP)

Many applications use the Internet to transfer data. Some of these applications run on clients with little processing power and thus have to invoke methods on other machines to process data. Many of these applications use proprietary data specifications and protocols, which makes communication with other applications difficult. The majority of these applications also reside behind network firewalls, which often restrict data communication to and from the application. IBM, Lotus Development Corporation, Microsoft, DevelopMentor and Userland Software developed the **Simple Object Access Protocol** (**SOAP**) to address these problems. SOAP is an XML-based protocol that allows applications to communicate easily over the Internet using XML documents called **SOAP messages**.

A SOAP message contains an **envelope**, which is a structure that describes a method call. A SOAP message's body contains either a **request** or a **response**. A request message's body contains a **Remote Procedure Call** (**RPC**), which is a request for another machine to perform a task. The RPC specifies the method to be invoked and any parameters the method takes. The application sends the SOAP message via an HTTP POST. A SOAP response message is an HTTP response document that contains the results from the method call (e.g., return values, error messages). For more information on SOAP, please refer to the W3C Recommendation entitled "SOAP Version 1.2 Part 0: Primer," available at `www.w3.org/TR/soap12-part0`.

20.11 Web Services

Web services encompass a set of related standards that can enable two computer applications to communicate and exchange data over the Internet. The data is passed back and forth using standard protocols such as HTTP, the same protocol used to transfer ordinary Web pages. Web services operate using open, text-based standards that enable components written in different languages and on different platforms to communicate. They are ready-to-use pieces of software on the Internet. XML, SOAP, **Web Services Description Language** (**WSDL**) and **Universal Description, Discovery and Integration** (**UDDI**) are the standards on which Web services rely. XML is used to create markup languages and describe data. XML allows groups to standardize data markup and formatting. SOAP enables data transfer between distributed systems on a network. WSDL is an XML-based description language. It is used to describe a Web service so that other applications can understand and access the methods the service provides. UDDI is another XML-based format that enables developers and businesses to publish and locate Web services on a network. Figure 20.32 shows how the different technologies interact.

Open standards enable businesses (running different platforms) to communicate and transfer data without designing costly platform-specific software. Web services improve collaborative software development by allowing developers to create applications by combining code written in any language on any platform. Also, Web services promote **modular** programming. Each specific function in an application can be exposed as a separate Web service. With separate Web service components, individuals or businesses can create their own unique applications by mixing and matching Web services that provide the functionality they need. **Modularization** is less error prone and promotes software reuse.

A Web service can be as trivial as multiplying two numbers together or as complicated as the functions carried out by an entire **customer relationship management** (**CRM**) soft-

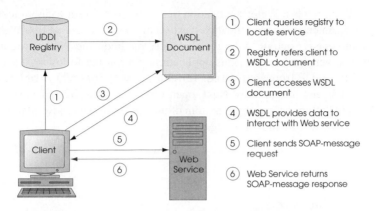

Fig. 20.32 SOAP, UDDI and WSDL in a Web service interaction.

ware system. For example, tracking the location and status of a FedEx package is a Web service (`fedex.com/us/tracking`).

Some e-commerce Web sites allow independent developers to harness the power of their existing technologies by exposing certain functions of their sites as Web services. For example, the online retailer Amazon.com allows developers to build online stores that search Amazon's product databases and display detailed product information via Amazon.com Web Services (`www.amazon.com/gp/aws/landing.html`). The Google search engine also can be integrated with other functionality through the Google Web APIs (`www.google.com/apis`), which connect to Google's indices of Web sites using Web services. Amazon.com and Google provide access to their sites' features through SOAP and other standard protocols in exchange for increased exposure.

For additional information on Web services, please visit `www.w3.org/2002/WS`. Also, see Chapter 23, ASP.NET, for an example of building a Web service using ASP.NET and XML technologies.

20.12 Water™ XML-Based Programming Language

Water is a general-purpose programming language that simplifies XML and Web services programming. Building Web services typically requires knowledge of XHTML, a scripting language, a database language and a server-side programming language. Water can perform the tasks of all these individual technologies.

Water represents all objects and data as XML. As an XML-based programming language, Water simplifies converting data to and from XML. It also brings object-oriented programming to XML.

Water's syntax (**ConciseXML**) is a superset of XML syntax and is compatible with XML. XHTML is a subset of XML, and XML is a subset of ConciseXML; consequently, any XHTML program is also a Water program. ConciseXML simplifies the description of data and logic. In addition, ConciseXML is less verbose than XML. Thus ConciseXML files are smaller than XML files that contain similar data. More information about Water can be found at `www.waterlanguage.org`. This Web site provides chapters from a book written by the creators of Water and offers a free, trial version of Clear Methods Steam, an IDE (integrated development environment) used to write Water-based services and applications.

Figure 20.33 presents a Water application that prompts the user to input text and outputs the text in a sentence. This application has two methods that create two Web pages—one for input and one for output. After running these methods, the Water program sets up and accesses a server that executes this application. To run the following example, first download the Steam IDE from `www.waterlanguage.org/install.html` and install it following the on-screen instructions. Next, open `concatenate.h2o` in Steam and click the green **Execute** button located at the bottom of the application window. This will run the example in your browser as shown in Fig. 20.33.

```
1   <!-- 20.33: concatenate.h2o              -->
2   <!-- Form Input and Output with Water -->
3
4   <defclass concatenate>
5      <defmethod start>
6         <FORM action = "/putTogether">
7            Type in a subject: <INPUT name = "word1"/>
8            Type in a verb: <INPUT name = "word2"/>
9            <INPUT type = "submit"/>
10        </FORM>
11     </defmethod>
12
13     <defmethod putTogether word1 word2>
14        <vector word1 " " word2 "."/>
15     </defmethod>
16  </defclass>
17
18  <server concatenate port = 9090/>
19  <open_browser_window "http://localhost:9090"/>
```

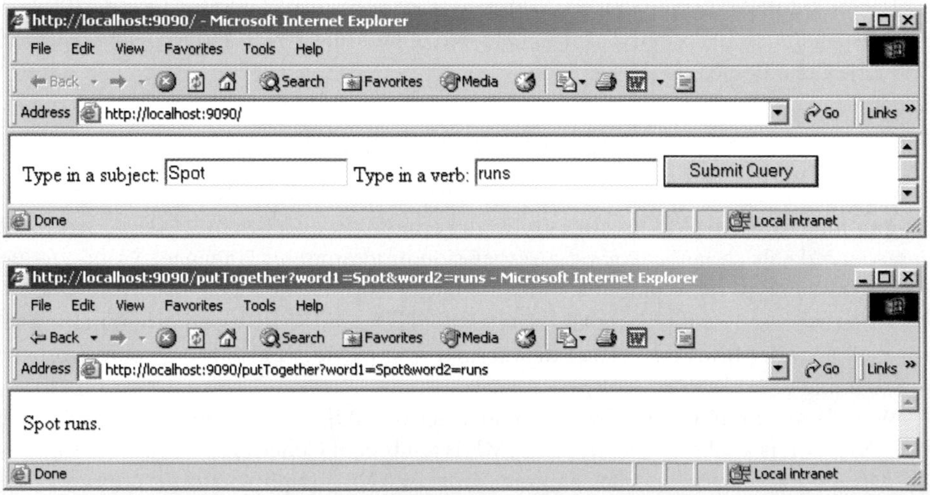

Fig. 20.33 Water program that performs simple input and output.

Lines 4–16 define a class called **concatenate**. The class is our entire application. All the content in the **defclass** will be executed when the class is called. Line 5 declares a method using **defmethod** and names it **start.** Method start is not given any parameters. Lines 6–10 create a form using XHTML tags. The **action** attribute of the **FORM** element (line 6) specifies the method that the server executes when the user clicks the submit button. When the user clicks submit, the form will call method **putTogether**. Method start returns the form as a **hypertext object**. We do not have to write the XHTML code for the actual output because the server implicitly converts **hypertext objects** (e.g., the form) to XHTML with a **to_html** function.

Line 13 declares method putTogether, which has two parameters: **word1** and **word2**. word1 and word2 are associated with the inputs of the form in method start. The body of method putTogether (line 14) creates a vector that contains word1, a space, word2 and a period. A **vector** is a resizable array. putTogether returns this vector as a hypertext object.

Line 18 uses the **server** tag to create a **server** on the user's machine at the given port (i.e., 9090). The server *serves* the application concatenate. Line 19 then opens a browser that accesses the server created in line 18. When the server is accessed, it executes the code specified in the server tag (i.e., concatenate). By default, the server looks for and calls a method named start. So the first page is the form defined in method start. When the user clicks on the **Submit Query** button, the form calls the method associated with its action attribute (i.e., putTogether). The method putTogether is passed word1 and word2. putTogether creates the second page and outputs the contents of the vector (i.e., word1, a space, word2 and a period). Once again, we do not have to write the XHTML code for the actual output because the server converts the hypertext objects (e.g., the form and the vector) to XHTML. Sample input and output are shown in Fig. 20.33.

20.13 Web Resources

www.w3.org/xml
The W3C (World Wide Web Consortium) works to develop common protocols to ensure interoperability on the Web. Their XML page includes information about upcoming events, publications, software and discussion groups. Visit this site to read about the latest developments in XML.

www.xml.org
xml.org is a reference for XML, DTDs, schemas and namespaces.

www.w3.org/style/XSL
Provides information on XSL, including what is new in XSL, learning XSL, XSL-enabled tools, XSL specification, FAQs, XSL history and more.

www.w3.org/TR
W3C technical reports and publications page. Contains links to working drafts, proposed recommendations, recommendations and more.

xml.apache.org
The Apache XML Web site provides many resources related to XML, including tools and downloads.

www.xmlbooks.com
Contains a list of recommended XML books by Charles Goldfarb, one of the original designers of GML (General Markup Language), from which SGML was derived.

www.xmlsoftware.com
The site contains links for downloading XML-related software. Downloads include XML browsers, conversion tools, database systems, DTD editors, XML editors and more.

www.xml-zone.com
The *Development Exchange XML Zone* is a complete resource for XML information. It includes FAQ, news, articles, links to other XML sites and newsgroups.

`wdvl.internet.com/Authoring/Languages/XML`
The Web Developer's Virtual Library XML site includes tutorials, FAQ, the latest news and extensive links to XML sites and software downloads.

`www.xml.com`
Visit `XML.com` for the latest news and information about XML, conference listings, links to XML Web resources organized by topic, tools and more.

`msdn.microsoft.com/xml/default.asp`
The MSDN Online XML Development Center features articles on XML, Ask the Experts chat sessions, samples and demos, newsgroups and other helpful information.

`www.oasis-open.org/cover/xml.html`
The SGML/XML Web Page is an extensive resource that includes links to FAQs, online resources, industry initiatives, demos, conferences and tutorials.

`www.gca.org/whats_xml/default.htm`
The GCA site has an XML glossary, list of books, brief descriptions of the draft standards for XML and links to online drafts.

`www.xmlinfo.com`
XMLINFO is a resource site with tutorials, a list of recommended books, documentation, discussion forums and more.

`www.ibm.com/developer/xml`
The IBM XML Zone site is a great resource for developers. You will find news, tools, a library, case studies, events and information about standards.

`developer.netscape.com/tech/xml/index.html`
The XML and Metadata Developer Central site has demos, technical notes and news articles related to XML.

`www.projectcool.com/developer/xmlz`
The Project Cool Developer Zone site includes several tutorials covering introductory through advanced XML.

`www.ucc.ie/xml`
This site is a detailed XML FAQ with responses to some popular questions. Submit your own questions through the site.

`www.xml-cml.org`
This site is a resource for the Chemical Markup Language (CML). It includes a FAQ list, documentation, software and XML links.

`backend.userland.com/rss`
Provides information about using RSS and SOAP to access content from `userland.com`.

`www.w3.org/2002/ws`
This site has detailed information about the development and standards of Web service and its related technologies.

`www.oasis-open.org`
The Organization of the Advancement of Structured Information Standards is a key standards body working to develop Web services specifications.

`www.clearmethods.com`
Clear Methods, Inc. provides Steam, an interactive development environment (IDE) that includes tools for the Steam platform. It provides an environment to write, run and debug Water programs.

`www.textuality.com/xml`
This site contains FAQs and the Lark nonvalidating XML parser.

`www.zvon.org`
This site provides an XML tutorial and documentation for XML vocabularies.

SUMMARY

- XML is a widely supported, open technology (i.e., nonproprietary technology) for data exchange.

- XML permits document authors to create their own markup for virtually any type of information. This extensibility enables document authors to create new markup languages to describe specific types of data, including mathematical formulas, chemical molecular structures, music and recipes.

- XML documents are highly portable. Opening an XML document does not require special software—any text editor that supports ASCII/Unicode characters will suffice. One important characteristic of XML is that it is both human readable and machine readable.

- Processing an XML document—which typically ends with the `.xml` extension—requires a software program called an XML parser (or XML processor). XML parsers check an XML document's syntax and can support the Document Object Model (DOM) or the Simple API for XML (SAX) API.

- DOM-based parsers build a tree structure containing the XML document's data in memory. This allows programs to manipulate the document's data. SAX-based parsers process the document and generate events as they encounter tags, text, comments, and so forth. These events contain data from the XML document.

- An XML document optionally can reference an external document that defines the XML document's structure. This optional document can be either a Document Type Definition (DTD) or a schema.

- If an XML document conforms to its DTD or schema, then the XML document is valid. Parsers that cannot check for document conformity against the DTD/Schema are nonvalidating parsers. If an XML parser (validating or nonvalidating) can successfully process an XML document that does not have a DTD/Schema, the XML document is well formed (i.e., it is syntactically correct). By definition, a valid XML document is also a well-formed document.

- The `ATTLIST` attribute-list declaration in a DTD defines an attribute. Keyword `#IMPLIED` specifies that if the parser finds an element without the attribute, it can choose an arbitrary value or can ignore the attribute. Keyword `#REQUIRED` specifies that the attribute must be in the document, and keyword `#FIXED` specifies that the attribute must have the given fixed value. Keyword `CDATA` specifies that an attribute contains a string that the parser should not process as markup. Keyword `EMPTY` specifies that the element does not contain any text.

- Keyword `#PCDATA` specifies that the element can store parsed character data (i.e., text). Parsable character data should not contain markup. Document authors should replace the characters less than (<), greater than (>) and ampersand (&) with their entities (i.e., `&lt;`, `&gt;` and `&amp;`).

- Schemas use XML syntax and are XML documents that programs can manipulate (e.g., add elements, remove elements) like any other XML document.

- In XML Schema, the `element` tag defines an element to be included in an XML document structure. Attributes `name` and `type` specify the `element`'s name and data type, respectively. Any element that contains attributes or child elements must define a type—called a complex type—that defines each attribute and child element.

- Attribute `minOccurs` specifies the minimum number of occurrences for an element. Attribute `maxOccurs` specifies the maximum number of occurrences for an element.

- A simple type element, such as xsd:string, cannot contain attributes and child elements.

- XML allows document authors to create their own tags, so naming collisions (i.e., different elements that have the same name) can occur. Namespaces enable document authors to prevent collisions among elements in an XML document.

- Namespace prefixes prepended to element and attribute names specify the namespace in which the element or attribute can be found. Each namespace prefix has a corresponding uniform resource identifier (URI) that uniquely identifies the namespace. By definition, a URI is a series of characters that differentiates names. Document authors can create their own namespace prefixes. Document authors can use virtually any namespace prefix, except the reserved namespace prefix xml.

- To eliminate the need to place a namespace prefix in each element, authors may specify a default namespace for an element and all of its child elements.

- MathML markup describes mathematical expressions.

- Chemical Markup Language (CML) marks up molecular and chemical information.

- MusicXML provides markup for musical notation. It simplifies the exchange of musical scores over the Internet. It is also a format for translating between the many other popular music formats.

- RSS is a popular, simple XML format designed to share headlines and Web content.

- The characters *<?* and *?>* delimit processing instructions (PIs), which are items of application-specific information embedded in an XML document. A processing instruction consists of a PI target and a PI value.

- A DOM tree has a single root node that contains all the other nodes in the document. Each node is an object that has properties, methods and events. Properties associated with a node provide access to the node's name, value, and child nodes. Methods allow developers to create, delete and append nodes, load XML documents, and so on. The XML parser exposes these methods and properties as a programmatic library called an Application Programming Interface (API).

- A node that contains other nodes (called child nodes) is a parent node. Nodes that are peers are sibling nodes. A node's descendent nodes include its children, its children's children and so on. A node's ancestor nodes include its parent, its parent's parent and so on.

- SAX is an alternative method for parsing XML documents that uses an event-based model—SAX-based parsers generate notifications called events as the parser parses the document. Software programs can "listen" for these events to retrieve specified data from the document.

- Extensible Stylesheet Language (XSL) documents specify how programs should render an XML document data. A subset of XSL—XSL Transformations (XSLT)—provides elements that define rules for transforming data from one XML document to produce another XML document (e.g., XHTML).

- Transforming an XML document using XSLT involves two tree structures—the source tree (i.e., the XML document being transformed) and the result tree (i.e., the XML document being created).

- The Simple Object Access Protocol (SOAP) is an XML-based protocol that allows applications to communicate easily over the Internet using XML documents called SOAP messages. Every SOAP message contains an envelope—a structure for describing a method call. A SOAP message's body contains either a request or a response.

- Web services encompass a set of related standards that can enable computer applications to communicate and exchange data over the Internet.

- XML, SOAP, Web Services Description Language (WSDL) and Universal Description, Discovery and Integration (UDDI) are the main standards on which Web services rely.

- Water is a general-purpose programming language for XML and Web services. It is an alternative to many of the technologies required to build Web applications.

TERMINOLOGY

absolute addressing

aggregator

ancestor node

asterisk (*) occurrence indicator

`ATTLIST`

attribute node

`CDATA`

child node

`childNodes` property (`documentElement`)

`complexType` element

container element

context node

default namespace

descendant node

`doctype-public` attribute (`xsl:output`)

`doctype-system` attribute (`xsl:output`)

`documentElement` object

document root

Document Object Model (DOM)

Document Type Definition (DTD)

DOM API (Application Programming Interface)

DOM-based XML parser

`ELEMENT` element

element type declaration

empty element

`EMPTY` keyword

event

Extended Backus-Naur Form (EBNF) grammar

Extensible Markup Language (XML)

Extensible Stylesheet Language (XSL)

Extensible Stylesheet Language
    Transformations (XSLT)

`extension` element

external DTD

feed

`firstChild` property (`NodeList`)

`foreach` statement

forward slash

`#IMPLIED`

Independent Software Vendor (ISV)

invalid document

`item` method (`childNodes`)

`language` attribute (`script`)

`length` property (`NodeList`)

`load` method (`xmlDocument`)

`match` attribute (`xsl:template`)

modular

MSXML parser

`name` node-set function

namespace prefix

node

node-set

node-set function

nonvalidating XML parser

`null`

occurrence indicator

`order` attribute

parent node

parsed character data

parser

`#PCDATA`

PI target

PI value

plus sign (+) occurrence indicator

processing instruction (PI)

prolog

question mark (?) occurrence indicator

RDF Site Summary (RSS)

Really Simple Syndication (RSS)

recursive descent

relative addressing

request message (SOAP)

Resource Description Framework (RDF)

response message (SOAP)

restriction

result tree

Rich Site Summary (RSS)

root element

root node

SAX-based parser

`schema` element

schema-valid document

`select` attribute (`xsl:value-of`)

sibling node

Simple Object Access Protocol (SOAP)

Simple API for XML (SAX)

`sum` function

`SYSTEM`

`targetNamespace` attribute (`schema` element)

text node

tree-based model

Universal Description, Discovery and
    Integration (UDDI)

valid document

validating XML parser

Water

Web services

Web Services Description Language (WSDL)

well-formed document
XML declaration
.xml file extension
xml namespace
XML Schema
XML Validator
XML version
xmlns reserved attribute
.xsd extension

.xsl extension
<xsl:apply-templates>
<xsl:copy>
<xsl:for-each select = "*expression*">
<xsl:sort select = "*expression*">
<xsl:template>
<xsl:value-of select = "*expression*">
XSL variable

SELF-REVIEW EXERCISES

20.1 Which of the following are valid XML element names?
a) yearBorn
b) year.Born
c) year Born
d) year-Born1
e) 2_year_born
f) --year/born
g) year*born
h) .year_born
i) _year_born_
j) y_e-a_r-b_o-r_n

20.2 State whether the following are *true* or *false*. If *false*, explain why.
a) XML is a technology for creating markup languages.
b) Forward and backward slashes (/ and \) delimit XML markup text.
c) All XML start tags must have corresponding end tags.
d) Parsers check an XML document's syntax and may support the Document Object Model or the Simple API for XML.
e) URIs are strings that identify resources such as files, images, services and electronic mailboxes.
f) When creating new XML tags, document authors must use the set of XML tags that the W3C provides.
g) The pound character (#), dollar sign ($), ampersand (&), greater-than (>) and less-than (<) are examples of XML reserved characters.

20.3 Fill in the blanks for each of the following statements:
a) MathML element _____ defines a mathematical operator.
b) _____ help avoid naming collisions.
c) _____ embed application-specific information into an XML document.
d) _____ is Microsoft's XML parser.
e) XSL element _____ inserts a DOCTYPE in the result tree.
f) XML Schema documents have root element _____.
g) Element _____ marks up the ∫ MathML symbol.
h) _____ defines element attributes in a DTD.
i) XSL element _____ is the root element in an XSL document.
j) XSL element _____ selects specific XML elements using repetition.

20.4 State which of the following statements are *true* and which are *false*. If *false*, explain why.
a) XML is not case sensitive.
b) An XML document may contain only one root element.
c) XML displays information.

d) A DTD/Schema defines the presentation style of an XML document.

e) Element `xsl:for-each` is similar to JavaScript's `for...in` statement.

f) MathML is an XML vocabulary.

g) XSL is an acronym for XML Stylesheet Language.

h) The `<!ELEMENT list (item*)>` defines element `list` as containing one or more `item` elements.

i) XML documents must have the `.xml` extension.

20.5 Find the error(s) in each of the following and explain how to correct it (them).

a)
```
<job>
    <title>Manager</title>
    <task number = "42">
</job>
```

b)
```
<mfrac>
    <mi>x</mi>
    <mo>+</mo>
    <mn>4</mn>
    <mi>y</mi>
</mfrac>
```

c) `<company name = "Deitel & Associates, Inc." />`

20.6 In Fig. 20.1 we subdivided the `author` element into more detailed pieces. How would you subdivide the `date` element?

20.7 What is `#PCDATA` used for?

20.8 Write a processing instruction that includes the stylesheet `wap.xsl`.

ANSWERS TO SELF-REVIEW EXERCISES

20.1 a, b, d, i, j.

20.2 a) True. b) False. In an XML document, markup text is delimited by angle brackets (< and >) with a forward slash being used in the end tag. c) True. d) True. e) True. f) False. When creating new tags, document authors may use any valid name except the reserved word `xml` (also `XML`, `Xml`, etc.). g) False. XML reserved characters include the ampersand (&), the left-angle bracket (<) and the right-angle bracket (>) but not # and $.

20.3 a) `mo`. b) namespaces. c) processing instructions. d) MSXML. e) `xsl:output`. f) schema. g) `mo`. h) `!ATTLIST`. i) `xsl:stylesheet`. j) `xsl:for-each`.

20.4 a) False. XML is case sensitive. b) True. c) False. XML is used to organize material in a structured manner. d) False. A DTD/schema defines the structure of an XML document. e) True. f) True. g) False. XSL is an acronym for Extensible Stylesheet Language. h) False. (`item*`) defines a `list` element containing any number of optional `item` elements. i) False. An XML document can have any extension.

20.5 a) The closing `/` in the empty element is missing:
```
<task number = "42"/>
```

b) `<mrow>` tag is needed to contain *x + 4*.

c) A character entity needs to be used to represent the ampersand:
```
<company name = "Deitel &amp; Associates, Inc." />
```

20.6
```
<date>
    <month>September</month>
    <day>19</day>
    <year>2001</year>
</date>
```

20.7   #PCDATA denotes that parsed character data is contained in the element.

20.8   `<?xsl:stylesheet type = "text/xsl" href = "wap.xsl"?>`

EXERCISES

20.9   Create an XML document that marks up the nutrition facts for a package of Grandma Deitel's Cookies. A package of Grandma Deitel's Cookies has a serving size of 1 package and the following nutritional value per serving: 260 calories, 100 fat calories, 11 grams of fat, 2 grams of saturated fat, 5 milligrams of cholesterol, 210 milligrams of sodium, 36 grams of total carbohydrates, 2 grams of fiber, 15 grams of sugar and 5 grams of protein. Load the XML document in Internet Explorer 6. [*Hint*: Your markup should contain elements that describe the product name, serving size/amount, calories, sodium, cholesterol, protein, etc. Mark up each nutrition fact/ingredient listed above.]

20.10   Write an XSL stylesheet for your solution to Exercise 20.9 that displays the nutritional facts in an XHTML table.

20.11   Write a DTD for the XML document in Fig. 20.1.

20.12   Using Amaya and MathML, generate the following mathematical expressions:

a) $\displaystyle\int_{-\frac{1}{2}}^{0} 5y\delta x$

b) $y = 2x - b^3 - 6cy^{kx} + 9$

c) $x = \sqrt{(2y^{-3})} - 8y + \dfrac{\sqrt{y}}{3}$

20.13   Write an XML document that marks up the information in the following table:

Name	Job	Department	Cubicle
Joe	Programmer	Engineering	5E
Erin	Designer	Marketing	9M
Melissa	Designer	Human Resources	8H
Craig	Administrator	Engineering	4E
Eileen	Project Coordinator	Marketing	3M
Danielle	Programmer	Engineering	12E
Frank	Salesperson	Marketing	17M
Corinne	Programmer	Technical Support	19T

20.14   Write a DTD for the XML document in Exercise 20.13.

20.15   Modify your solution to Exercise 20.13 to qualify each person with a namespace prefix corresponding to his or her job. Your solution should not have the job as either an element or an attribute.

20.16   Write an XSLT document that transforms the XML document of Exercise 20.13 into an XHTML sorted list.

20.17 Write a schema that provides tags for a person's first name, last name, weight and shoe size. Weight and shoe size tags should have attributes to designate measuring systems.

20.18 Write JavaScript code that uses the DOM to replace every job description (from Exercise 20.13) that matches "Programmer" with "Developer."

20.19 Modify Fig. 20.31 (`sorting.xsl`) to sort by descending page number rather than by chapter number.

20.20 Modify Fig. 20.31 (`sorting.xsl`) to also output the total number of appendix pages.

21

Web Servers (IIS and Apache)

Objectives

- To understand a Web server's functionality.
- To introduce Microsoft Internet Information Services (IIS) and Apache Web server.
- To learn how to request documents from a Web server.

In fact, a fundamental interdependence exists between the personal right to liberty and the personal right to property.
Potter Stewart

Stop abusing my verses, or publish some of your own.
Martial

There are three difficulties in authorship: to write anything worth the publishing, to find honest men to publish it, and to get sensible men to read it.
Charles Caleb Colton

When your Daemon is in charge, do not try to think consciously. Drift, wait and obey.
Rudyard Kipling

Outline

21.1 Introduction

In this chapter, we discuss the specialized software—called a **Web server**—that responds to client requests (typically from a Web browser) by providing resources such as XHTML documents. For example, when users enter a **Uniform Resource Locator** (**URL**) address, such as www.deitel.com, into a Web browser, they are requesting a specific document from a Web server. The Web server maps the URL to a resource on the server (or to a file on the server's network) and returns the requested resource to the client. During this interaction, the Web server and the client communicate using the platform-independent **Hypertext Transfer Protocol** (**HTTP**), a protocol for transferring requests and files over the Internet (i.e., between Web servers and Web browsers).

Our Web-server discussion introduces **Microsoft Internet Information Services** (**IIS**) and the open-source **Apache Web server**. Sections 21.6 and 21.7 discuss IIS and Apache, respectively. Figure 21.1 provides details about these Web servers.

	IIS 5.0	**IIS 6.0**	**Apache Web server**
Company	Microsoft Corporation	Microsoft Corporation	Apache Software Foundation

Fig. 21.1   Web servers discussed in this chapter. (Part 1 of 2.)

	IIS 5.0	IIS 6.0	Apache Web server
Version	5.0	6.0	2.0.47
Released	2/17/00	3/28/03	7/10/03
Platforms	Windows 2000, Windows XP	Windows Server 2003	Windows NT/2000/XP, Mac OS X, Linux and other UNIX-based platforms, experimentally supports Windows 95/98
Brief description	The most popular Web server for Windows 2000.	The newest release of IIS from Microsoft.	Currently the most popular Web server.
Price	Included with Windows 2000 and Windows XP.	Included with Windows Server 2003	Freeware.

Fig. 21.1   Web servers discussed in this chapter. (Part 2 of 2.)

For illustration purposes, we use Internet Explorer 6 to various documents of various types—XHTML, ASP.NET, Perl, Python and PHP. In later chapters, we discuss the specifics of ASP.NET (Chapter 23), Perl (Chapter 25), PHP (Chapter 26) and Python (Chapter 35). This chapter concentrates on the steps for requesting documents from a Web server.

21.2 HTTP Request Types

The two most common **HTTP request types** (also known as **request methods**) are *get* and *post*. A *get* request typically **gets** (or **retrieves**) information from a server. Common uses of *get* requests are to retrieve an HTML document or an image, or to fetch search results based on a user-submitted search term. A *post* request typically **posts** (or **sends**) data to a server. Common uses of *post* requests are to send information to a server, such as authentication information or data from a form that gathers user input.

An HTTP request often posts data to a **server-side form handler** that processes the data. For example, when a user performs a search or participates in a Web-based survey, the Web server receives the information specified in the XHTML form as part of the request. *Get* requests and *post* requests can both be used to send form data to a Web server, yet each type sends the information differently.

A *get* request sends information to the server as part of the URL (e.g., `www.search-engine.com/search?`*name=value*), where `search` is the name of a server-side form handler, *name* is the `name` of a variable in an XHTML form and *value* is the value assigned to that variable. Notice the ? in the preceding URL. A ? separates the **query string** from the rest of the URL in a *get* request. A *name/value* pair is passed to the server with the *name* and the *value* separated by an equal sign (=). If more than one *name/value* pair is submitted, each pair is separated by an ampersand (&). The server uses data passed in a query string to retrieve an appropriate resource from the server. The server then sends a **response** to the client.

A *get* request may be initiated by submitting an XHTML form whose `method` attribute is set to `"get"`. Suppose a search engine's Web page contains a `form` element with the attributes method = "get" and action = "search", and that includes a text field named "searchTerm". A search for the term "Massachusetts" might send a *get* request for the URL www.searchengine.com/search?searchTerm=Massachusetts. The server would then perform a search for the value Massachusetts and return a Web page containing search results to the user. (See Chapter 2 for more information on how various search engines operate and Chapter 5 for an in-depth discussion of XHTML forms.)

A *post* request is specified in an XHTML form by the method "post". The *post* method sends form data as an HTTP message, not as part of the URL. Because a *get* request limits the query string (i.e., everything to the right of the ?) to 2048 characters, it is often necessary to send large pieces of information using the *post* method. The *post* method is also sometimes preferred because it hides the submitted data from the user by embedding it an HTTP message. If a form submits several hidden input values along with user-submitted data, the *post* method might generate the URL www.searchengine.com/search. The form data still reaches the server and is processed in a similar fashion to a *get* request, but the user does not see the exact information sent.

Software Engineering Observation 21.1

The data sent in a post *request is not part of the URL and cannot easily be seen by the user. Forms that contain many fields are submitted most often by a* post *request. Sensitive form fields, such as passwords, usually are sent using this request type.*

Browsers often **cache** (save on disk) Web pages so they can quickly reload the pages. If there are no changes between the last version stored in the cache and the current version on the Web, this helps speed up your browsing experience. The browser first asks the server if the document has changed or expired since the date the file was cached. If not, the browser loads the document from the cache. Thus, the browser minimizes the amount of data that must be downloaded for you to view a Web page. Browsers typically do not cache the server's response to a *post* request, because the next *post* might not return the same result. For example, in a survey, many users could visit the same Web page and respond to a question. The survey results could then be displayed for the user. Each new response changes the overall results of the survey.

When you use a Web-based search engine, the browser normally supplies the information you specify in an HTML form to the search engine with a *get* request. The search engine performs the search, then returns the results to you as a Web page. Such pages are often cached by the browser in case you perform the same search again. As with *post* requests, *get* requests can supply parameters as part of the request to the Web server.

21.3 System Architecture

A Web server is part of a **multi-tier application**, sometimes referred to as an ***n*-tier application**. Multi-tier applications divide functionality into separate tiers (i.e., logical groupings of functionality). Tiers can be located on the same computer or on separate computers. Figure 21.2 presents the basic structure of a three-tier application.

The **information tier** (also called the **data tier** or the **bottom tier**) maintains data for the application. This tier typically stores data in a **relational database management system (RDBMS)**. We discuss RDBMS in further detail in Chapter 22, Database: SQL, MySQL, DBI and ADO.NET. For example, a retail store may have a database for product information, such as descriptions, prices and quantities in stock. The same database also

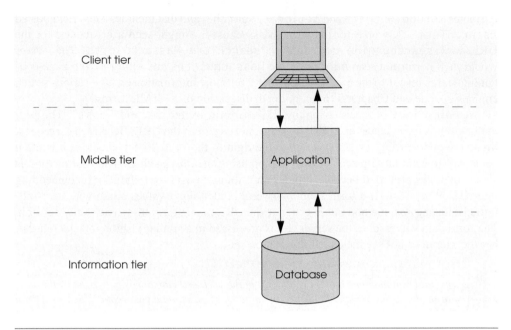

Client tier

Middle tier   Application

Information tier   Database

Fig. 21.2   Three-tier application model.

may contain customer information, such as user names, billing addresses and credit-card numbers.

The **middle tier** implements **business logic** and **presentation logic** to control interactions between application clients and application data. The middle tier acts as an intermediary between data in the information tier and the application clients. The middle-tier **controller logic** processes client requests from the top tier (e.g., a request to view a product catalog) and retrieves data from the database. The middle-tier presentation logic then processes data from the information tier and presents the content to the client. This layer often is divided into its two logical components, hence the term *n*-tier application.

Business logic in the middle tier enforces **business rules** and ensures that data is reliable (i.e., edited for appropriateness) before updating the database or presenting data to a user. Business rules dictate how clients can and cannot access application data and how applications process data. The middle tier also implements the application's presentation logic. Web applications typically present information to clients as XHTML documents (older applications present information as HTML).

The **client tier**, or **top tier**, is the application's user interface. Users interact directly with the application through the client tier, which is typically a Web browser, keyboard and mouse. The client interacts with the middle tier to make requests and to retrieve data from the information tier. The client then displays the data retrieved from the middle tier to the user. The client tier never directly interacts with the information tier.

21.4 Client-Side Scripting versus Server-Side Scripting

In earlier chapters, we focused on client-side scripting with JavaScript. Client-side scripting validates user input, accesses the browser and enhances Web pages with Dynamic HT-

ML, ActiveX controls and **Java applets** (client-side Java programs that execute in a browser). Client-side **validation** reduces the number of requests that need to be passed to the server. Interactivity allows users to make decisions, click buttons, play games, and so on—making the Web-site experience more interesting. Client-side scripts can access the browser, use features specific to the browser and manipulate browser documents.

Client-side scripting does have limitations, such as browser dependency; the browser or **scripting host** must support the scripting language. Another issue is that client-side scripts are viewable to the client (e.g., by using the **View** menu's **Source** option in Internet Explorer). Some Web developers do not advocate this because users potentially can view proprietary scripting code. Sensitive information, such as passwords or other personally-identifiable data, should not be stored or validated on the client.

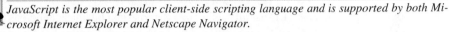

Software Engineering Observation 21.2

JavaScript is the most popular client-side scripting language and is supported by both Microsoft Internet Explorer and Netscape Navigator.

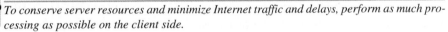

Performance Tip 21.1

To conserve server resources and minimize Internet traffic and delays, perform as much processing as possible on the client side.

Programmers have greater flexibility when using **server-side scripts**. Scripts executed on the server often generate custom responses for clients. For example, a client might connect to an airline's Web server and request a list of all flights from Boston to San Antonio between September 19th and November 5th. The server queries the database, dynamically generates XHTML content containing the flight list and sends the XHTML to the client. This technology allows clients to obtain the most current flight information from the database by connecting to an airline's Web server.

Server-side scripting languages have a wider range of programmatic capabilities than their client-side equivalents. For example, server-side scripts often can access the server's file directory structure, whereas client-side scripts cannot access the client's directories.

Server-side scripts also have access to server-side software that extends server functionality—Microsoft Web servers use **ISAPI (Internet Server Application Program Interface) Extensions** and Apache Web servers use **modules**. Components and modules range from programming language support to counting the number of Web page hits. We discuss some of these components and modules in the remaining chapters of the book.

Software Engineering Observation 21.3

Properly configured server-side scripts are not visible to the client; only XHTML and any client-side scripts are visible to the client.

21.5 Accessing Web Servers

To request documents from Web servers, users must know the machine names (called **host names**) on which the Web server software resides. Users can request documents from **local Web servers** (i.e., ones residing on users' machines) or **remote Web servers** (i.e., ones residing on different machines).

Local Web servers can be accessed in two ways: Through the machine name or through `localhost`—a host name that references the local machine. We use `localhost` in this book for demonstration purposes. To determine the machine name in Windows 98, right click **Network Neighborhood**, and select **Properties** from the context menu to display the **Network** dialog. In the **Network** dialog, click the **Identification** tab. The computer name displays in the **Computer name:** field. Click **Cancel** to close the **Network** dialog. In Windows 2000 or Windows XP, right click **My Network Places** and select **Properties** from the context menu to display the **Network and Dialup Connections** explorer. In the explorer, click **Network Identification**. The **Full computer name:** field in the **System Properties** window displays the computer name.

A remote Web server referenced by a **domain name** (e.g., `deitel` or `yahoo`) and an **Internet Protocol (IP) address** also can serve documents. A domain name represents a group of hosts on the Internet; it combines with a host name (e.g., `www`—World Wide Web) and a **top-level domain (TLD)**, such as `com`, `org` or `edu`, to form a **fully qualified host name**, which provides a user-friendly way to identify a site on the Internet. In a fully qualified host name, the TLD often describes the type of organization that owns the domain name. For example, the `com` TLD usually refers to a commercial business, whereas the `org` TLD usually refers to a nonprofit organization. In addition, each country has its own TLD, such as `cn` for China, `et` for Ethiopia, `om` for Oman and `us` for the United States.

Each fully qualified host name is assigned a unique address called an **IP address**, which is much like the street address of a house. Just as people use street addresses to locate houses or businesses in a city, computers use IP addresses to locate other computers on the Internet. A **domain name system (DNS) server**, a computer that maintains a database of host names and their corresponding IP addresses, translates the fully qualified host name to an IP address. The translation operation is referred to as a **DNS lookup**. A DNS server translates `www.deitel.com` into the IP address of the Deitel Web server. The IP address `127.0.0.1` always refers to the local Web server (i.e., `localhost`) running on the computer from where it is accessed.

21.6 Microsoft Internet Information Services (IIS)

Microsoft Internet Information Services (IIS) is an enterprise-level Web server that is included with several versions of Windows. Installing IIS on a machine allows that computer to serve documents. For instructions on how to install IIS, please visit `www.deitel.com/books/iw3HTP3/index.html`. The remainder of this section assumes that either IIS 5.0 or IIS 6.0 is installed on a system.

The following two subsections explain how to configure IIS 5.0 and IIS 6.0 to serve documents via HTTP. If you are using Windows 2000 or Windows XP, see Section 21.6.1. If you are using a version of Windows newer than Windows XP, see Section 21.6.2.

21.6.1 Microsoft Internet Information Services (IIS) 5.0

After installation, start the Internet Services Manager by opening the **Control Panel**, double clicking the **Administrative Tools** icon and double clicking the **Internet Services Manager** icon. This opens the **Internet Information Services** window (Fig. 21.3)—the administration program for IIS 5.0. Alternatively, typing `inetmgr` at the **Start** menu's **Run...** command prompt opens the **Internet Services Manager**. Place the documents that will be requested from IIS either in the **default directory** (i.e., `C:\Inetpub\wwwroot`) or in a **virtual directory**. A virtual directory is an alias for an existing directory that resides on the local

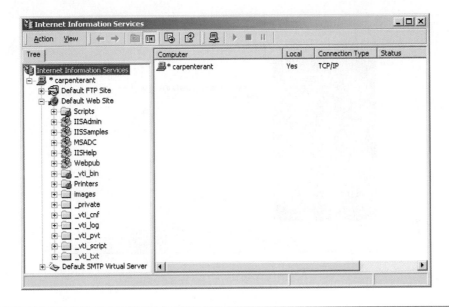

Fig. 21.3   Internet Information Services window of Internet Services Manager (IIS 5.0).

machine (e.g., C:\) or on the network. When a server is accessed from a Web browser, only the virtual directories are visible to the client.

In the **Internet Information Services** window, the left pane contains the Web server's directory structure. The name of the machine running IIS (e.g., **carpenterant**) is listed under **Internet Information Services**. Clicking the **+** symbol to the left of the machine name displays **Default FTP Site**, **Default Web Site** and **Default SMTP Virtual Server**.

The **Default FTP Site** is a **File Transfer Protocol (FTP)** site; the **Default Web Site** is an HTTP site. Although FTP and HTTP permit transferring documents between a computer and a Web server, FTP provides a faster and more persistent connection between the client and the Web server than HTTP. HTTP is used most frequently to request documents from Web servers. FTP is often used for transferring large files across the Internet. The **Default SMTP Virtual Server** allows you to create a **Simple Mail Transfer Protocol (SMTP)** server for sending **electronic mail (e-mail)**.

Expand the **Default Web Site** directory by clicking the **+** to the left of it. In this directory, we will create a virtual directory for the HTTP Web site. The **Default Web Site** sub-directories are virtual directories. Most Web documents are placed in the Web server's **Webpub** (Web publishing) directory. For this example, we create our virtual directory in the **Webpub** virtual directory. To create a virtual directory within this directory, right click **Webpub**, select **New**, then **Virtual Directory**. This starts the **Virtual Directory Creation Wizard** (Fig. 21.4), which guides users through creating a virtual directory.

To begin, click **Next** in the **Virtual Directory Creation Wizard** welcome dialog. In the **Virtual Directory Alias** dialog (Fig. 21.5), enter a name for the virtual directory and click **Next**. We use the name Chapter21Test, although the virtual directory may have any name provided that it does not conflict with an existing virtual directory name.

Fig. 21.4   **Virtual Directory Creation Wizard** welcome dialog.

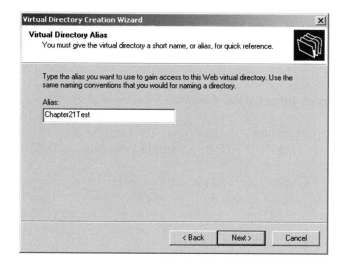

Fig. 21.5   **Virtual Directory Alias** dialog of the **Virtual Directory Creation Wizard**.

In the **Web Site Content Directory** dialog (Fig. 21.6), enter the path for the directory containing the documents that clients will view. We created a directory named C:\Chapter21Examples that serves our documents, although any existing directory would be appropriate. If necessary, select the **Browse** button to navigate to the desired directory. Click **Next**.

The **Access Permissions** dialog (Fig. 21.7) presents the virtual directory **security level** choices. Choose the access level appropriate for a Web document. The **Read** option allows users to read and download files located within the directory. The **Run scripts (such as ASP)** option allows scripts to run in the directory. The **Execute (such as ISAPI applications or CGI)** option allows applications to run in the directory. The **Write** option

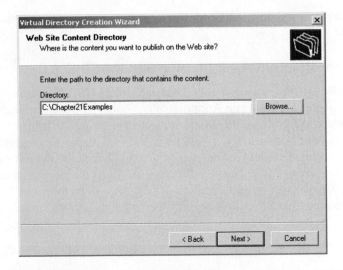

Fig. 21.6   **Web Site Content Directory** dialog of the **Virtual Directory Creation Wizard.**

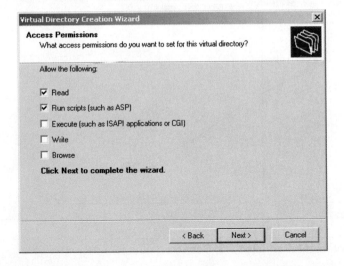

Fig. 21.7   **Access Permissions** dialog of the **Virtual Directory Creation Wizard.**

allows a Web page to write to files on the server. The **Browse** option allows users to see a full list of the files in the folder through a Web browser. By default, **Read** and **Run scripts** are enabled. Click **Next**.

Click **Finish** to complete the creation of the virtual directory and exit the **Virtual Directory Creation Wizard**. The newly created virtual directory, **Chapter21Test**, is now located under the **Webpub** virtual directory. Now the IIS server is configured to serve documents through the Chapter21Test virtual directory. The URL `http://localhost/WebPub/Chapter21Test` now references the `C:\Chapter21Examples` directory.

To start IIS so it can serve content, right click **Default Web Site** and select **Start**. If you need to stop IIS, right click **Default Web Site** (or **Default FTP site** or **Default**

SMTP Virtual Server) and select **Stop**. The Web server is not available to serve content if it is stopped.

21.6.2 Microsoft Internet Information Services (IIS) 6.0

After installation, start the **Internet Information Services (IIS) Manager** by opening the **Control Panel**, double clicking the **Administrative Tools** icon and double clicking the **Internet Information Services (IIS) Manager** icon. This opens the **Internet Information Services (IIS) Manager** window (Fig. 21.8)—the administration program for IIS 6.0. Place the documents that will be requested from IIS either in the **default directory** (i.e., C:\Inetpub\wwwroot) or in a **virtual directory**. A virtual directory is an alias for an existing directory that resides on the local machine (e.g., C:\) or on the network. When a server is being accessed from a Web browser only the virtual directories are seen by the client.

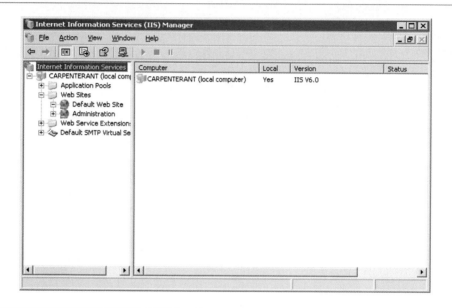

Fig. 21.8   Internet Information (IIS) Services Manager window (IIS 6.0).

In the **Internet Information Services (IIS) Manager** window, the left pane contains the Web server's directory structure. The name of the machine running IIS (e.g., **CARPENTERANT**) is listed under **Internet Information Services**. Clicking the **+** symbol to the left of the machine name displays **Application Pools**, **Web Sites**, **Web Server Extensions** and **Default SMTP Virtual Server**

The **Application Pools** and **Web Server Extensions** folders contain tools for configuring advanced features of IIS 6.0. The **Default SMTP Virtual Server** allows you to create a **Simple Mail Transfer Protocol (SMTP)** server for sending **electronic mail (e-mail)**.

Expand the **Web Sites** directory by clicking the **+** to the left of it. This should display **Default Web Site** and **Administration**. Expand the **Default Web Site** directory by clicking the **+** to the left of it. Any subdirectories in this directory refer to virtual directories. By default, none exist. For this example, we create a virtual directory from which we request our documents. To create a virtual directory, right click **Default Web Site**, select **New** and then **Virtual Directory**. This starts the **Virtual Directory Creation Wizard** (Fig. 21.9), which guides users through the virtual directory creation process.

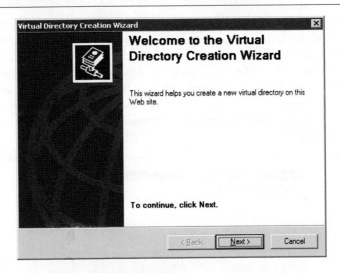

Fig. 21.9   Virtual Directory Creation Wizard welcome dialog.

To begin, click **Next** in the **Virtual Directory Creation Wizard** welcome dialog. In the **Virtual Directory Alias** dialog (Fig. 21.10), enter a name for the virtual directory and click **Next**. We use the name `Chapter21Test`, although the virtual directory may have any name provided that it does not conflict with an existing virtual directory name.

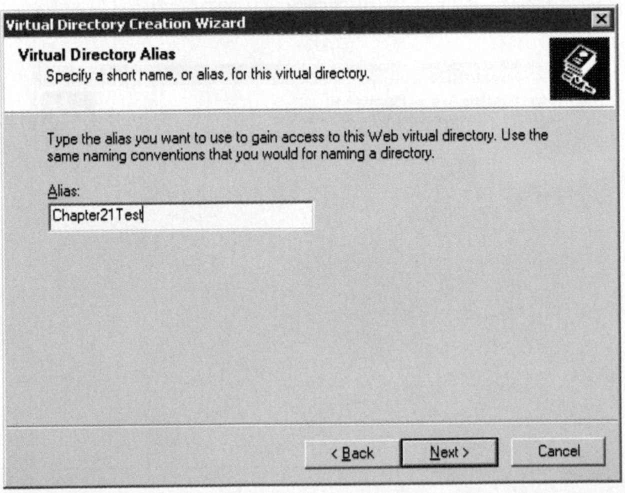

Fig. 21.10   Virtual Directory Alias dialog of the Virtual Directory Creation Wizard.

In the **Web Site Content Directory** dialog (Fig. 21.11), enter the path for the directory containing the documents that clients will view. We created a directory named `C:\Chapter21Examples` that serves our documents, although any existing directory would be appropriate. If necessary, select the **Browse** button to navigate to the desired directory. Click **Next**.

The **Access Permissions** dialog (Fig. 21.12) presents the virtual directory **security level** choices. Choose the access level appropriate for a Web document. The **Read** option allows users to read and download files located within the directory. The **Run scripts (such as ASP)** option allows scripts to run in the directory. The **Execute (such as ISAPI applications or CGI)** option allows applications to run in the directory. The **Write** option allows a Web page to write to files on the server. The **Browse** option allows users to see a full list of the files in the folder through a Web browser. By default, **Read** and **Run scripts** are enabled. Click **Next**.

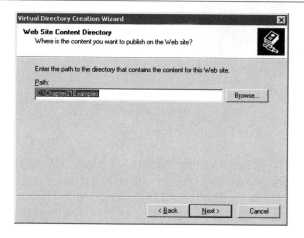

Fig. 21.11 Web Site Content Directory dialog of the Virtual Directory Creation Wizard.

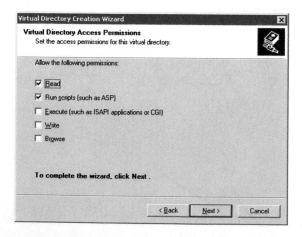

Fig. 21.12 Access Permissions dialog of the Virtual Directory Creation Wizard.

Click **Finish** to complete the creation of the virtual directory and exit the **Virtual Directory Creation Wizard**. The newly created virtual directory, `Chapter21Test`, is now located in the **Default Web Site**. Now the IIS server is configured to serve documents through the `Chapter21Test` virtual directory. The URL `http://localhost/Chapter21Test` now references the `C:\Chapter21Examples` directory.

To start IIS, right click **Default Web Site** and select **Start**. To stop IIS, right click **Default Web Site** (or **Default SMTP Virtual Server**) and select **Stop**.

21.7 Apache Web Server

The Apache Web server, maintained by the Apache Software Foundation, is currently the most popular Web server because of its stability, efficiency, portability, security and small size. It is an open-source product (i.e., software that can be freely obtained and customized) that runs on UNIX, Linux, Mac OS X, Windows and numerous other platforms.

To obtain the Apache Web server for a variety of platforms, visit `httpd.apache.org/download.cgi`. The CD that accompanies this book includes Apache 2.0.47 for Windows. For instructions on installing this version of the Apache Web server, please visit

```
http://httpd.apache.org/docs-2.0/platform/windows.html
```

After installing the Apache Web server, start the application. From the **Start** menu, select **Programs > Apache HTTPD Server > Control Apache Server > Start**. If the server starts successfully, a command-prompt window opens stating that the service is starting (Fig. 21.13). To stop the Apache Web server, from the **Start** menu, select **Programs > Apache HTTPD Server > Control Apache Server > Stop**.

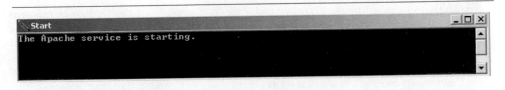

Fig. 21.13　Apache Web server starting. (Courtesy of The Apache Software Foundation, <`http://www.apache.org/`>.)

All documents that will be requested from an Apache Web server must either be in the default directory (i.e., `C:\Program Files\Apache Group\Apache2\htdocs`) or in a directory for which an Apache Web server **alias** is configured. An alias is Apache's version of a Microsoft IIS virtual directory. It is a pointer to an existing directory that resides on the local machine or on the network. We will create an alias for the examples in this chapter.

Instead of using an administrative utility or set of wizards, we configure the Apache Web server by editing the `httpd.conf` file. This file contains all the information that the Apache Web server needs to run correctly and serve Web documents. The `httpd.conf` file is located in the `conf` subdirectory of Apache's installation directory. To edit this file, either go to the `conf` directory in the Apache Web server directory and open the `httpd.conf` in a text editor, or go to the **Start** menu and select **Programs > Apache HTTP Server** [*version number*] **> Configure Apache Server > Edit the Apache httpd.conf Configuration File**. The `httpd.conf` file opens in Notepad. `httpd.conf` is a large text file with all of Apache Web server's configuration information. In this file, any line that starts with a # is a comment that explains the various configuration options.

Good Programming Practice 21.1

Place a small comment near any changes you make to the Apache httpd.conf file.

An introductory comment at the top of the `httpd.conf` file explains how the file is organized. After this comment, the configuration information starts with the most important, global settings. These should have been configured correctly by the Apache installer. Scroll down in the file until you have reached the section titled `Aliases`. This section begins with the following text:

```
# Aliases: Add here as many aliases as you need...
```

To create an alias, we add the following lines below the comment.

```
#This alias is for the examples used in Chapter 21
Alias /Chapter21Test "C:/Chapter21Examples"
```

This creates an alias called `Chapter21Test` that points to the physical directory `C:\Chapter21Examples`. We use the name `Chapter21Test`, but any name that does not conflict with an existing alias is allowed. We created a directory named `C:\Chapter21Examples` that serves our documents, although any existing directory would be appropriate. Note that in both the name of the alias and the path of the directory to which the alias points we must use forward slashes (/), not back slashes (\).

Error-Prevention Tip 21.1

If you place a forward slash (/) at the end of the alias name, Apache will require this slash to be present when a document is requested from the server. For example, if you name your alias /myExamples/, then a user request for http://localhost/myExamples will not work as expected. The user will need to request http://localhost/myExamples/ to access the alias. If the forward slash (/) is not placed at the end of the alias name, Apache will not require this slash, and will work as expected whether or not it is present in the request.

With the alias line added to the `httpd.conf` file, the Apache Web server is set up to serve our Web document from the `C:\Chapter21Examples` directory. We need to restart the server so that our changes to `httpd.conf` file will take effect. Then we will be ready to request documents from the Apache Web server. To restart the server, we must first stop it and start it again. Please refer to the beginning of this section for instructions on how to stop and start the Apache Web server.

21.8 Requesting Documents

This section demonstrates how an HTTP server responds to requests for five types of documents—XHTML, ASP.NET, Perl, PHP and Python. We discuss serving these documents using IIS and Apache Web server. We start with XHTML documents, which the server sends to the client as **static Web pages**. The server response for a given XHTML document always is the same. For each of the other four types of documents, the appropriate language interpreter or scripting engine first generates XHTML content, then transmits it to the client over HTTP. These are often referred to as **dynamic Web pages,** because the results of these requests might vary based on numerous factors, such as user input, the time of day and current database content.

[*Note*: This section discusses how to *serve* documents using a Web server; we discuss how to *create* ASP.NET, Perl, PHP and Python documents in Chapters 23, 25, 26 and 35, respectively. *To render ASP.NET, Perl, PHP and Python documents, the respective programming languages must be installed on your computer and configured to run on each server.* Visit `www.deitel.com/books/iw3HTP3/index.html` to obtain installation instructions for these various programming languages.]

21.8.1 XHTML

This section shows how to request an XHTML document from the IIS and Apache Web servers. Copy `test.html` from the Chapter 21 examples directory on the CD-ROM accompanying this book into `C:\Chapter21Examples` (or to the directory you created in Section 21.6 or 21.7). This is the directory that is referenced by our virtual directory (`Chapter21Test`). [*Note*: A file cannot be copied directly to a virtual directory because a virtual directory is only a name referring to a physical local directory.] To request the document from IIS 5.0, start the server, launch Internet Explorer and enter the XHTML document's location (i.e., `http://localhost/Webpub/Chapter21Test/test.html`) in the **Address** field. Figure 21.14 displays the result of requesting `test.html`.

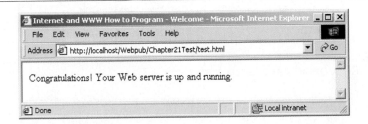

Fig. 21.14   Requesting `test.html` from IIS 5.

To request `test.html` from IIS 6.0 or Apache, start the server, launch Internet Explorer and enter the XHTML document's location (i.e., `http://localhost/Chapter21Test/test.html`) in the **Address** field. Figure 21.15 displays the result of requesting `test.html`.

Fig. 21.15   Requesting `test.html` from IIS 6 or Apache.

21.8.2 ASP.NET

In addition to XHTML documents, IIS can serve ASP.NET documents.[1] Although the Apache Web server supports older versions of ASP (if additional modules are installed), it does not support ASP.NET.

To request an ASP.NET document from IIS 5, copy the `test.aspx` file from the Chapter 21 examples directory on the CD-ROM into `C:\Chapter21Examples` (or the directory created in Section 21.6 or 21.7). To request the document from IIS 5, launch Internet Explorer and enter the ASP.NET document's location (i.e., `http://localhost/Webpub/Chapter21Test/test.aspx`) in the **Address** field. Figure 21.16 displays the result of requesting `test.aspx`.

To request `test.aspx` from IIS 6, launch Internet Explorer and enter the ASP .NET document's location (i.e., `http://localhost/Chapter21Test/test.aspx`) in the **Address** field. Figure 21.17 displays the result of requesting `test.aspx`.

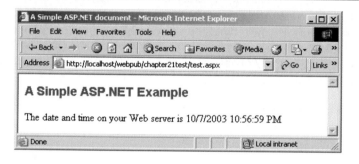

Fig. 21.16 Requesting `test.aspx` from IIS 5.

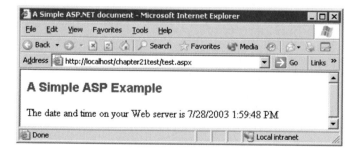

Fig. 21.17 Requesting `test.aspx` from IIS 6.

21.8.3 Perl

IIS and Apache Web servers can serve Perl-generated documents. Copy the file `test.pl` from the Chapter 21 examples directory on the CD-ROM to `C:\Chapter21Examples` (or the directory you created in Section 21.6 or 21.7). To request the document from IIS 5,

---

1. The procedures in this section also apply to IIS users serving versions of ASP (Active Server Pages) prior to .NET.

launch Internet Explorer and enter the Perl document's location (i.e., `http://local-host/Webpub/Chapter21Test/test.pl`) in the **Address** field. Figure 21.18 displays the result of requesting `test.pl`.

To request `test.pl` from IIS 6, launch Internet Explorer and enter the Perl document's location (i.e., `http://localhost/Chapter21Test/test.pl`) in the **Address** field. Figure 21.19 displays the result of requesting `test.pl`.

To request Perl-generated documents on the Apache Web server, copy the `test.pl` file from the Chapter 21 examples directory on the CD-ROM to the `cgi-bin` directory. On a Windows platform, the `cgi-bin` directory typically resides in `C:\Program Files\Apache Group\Apache2`; on a Linux platform, it resides in the `/usr/local/httpd` directory. All Perl documents must reside in the `cgi-bin` directory, because certain environment variables have been registered for this directory that help Apache recognize the Perl scripts and allow them to execute properly. To request a document, launch Internet Explorer (or your UNIX/Linux equivalent browser) and enter the Perl document's location (i.e., `http://localhost/cgi-bin/test.pl`) in the **Address** field. Figure 21.20 displays the result of requesting `test.pl`.

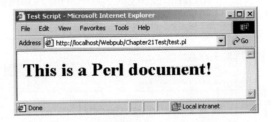

Fig. 21.18   Requesting `test.pl` from IIS 5.

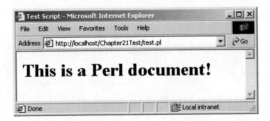

Fig. 21.19   Requesting `test.pl` from IIS 6.

Fig. 21.20   Requesting `test.pl` from Apache.

21.8.4 PHP

IIS and Apache Web servers can request PHP-generated documents. Copy the file `test.php` from the Chapter 21 examples directory on the CD-ROM into `C:\Chapter21Examples` (or the directory you created in Section 21.6 or 21.7). To request the document from IIS 5, launch Internet Explorer and enter the PHP document's location (i.e., `http://localhost/Webpub/Chapter21Test/test.php`) in the **Address** field. Figure 21.21 displays the result of requesting `test.php`.

To request `test.php` from IIS 6, launch Internet Explorer and enter the PHP document's location (i.e., `http://localhost/Chapter21Test/test.php`) in the **Address** field. Figure 21.22 displays the result of requesting `test.php`.

To request PHP-generated documents on the Apache Web server, copy the file `test.php` from the Chapter 21 examples directory on the CD-ROM to the `htdocs` directory. On a Windows platform, the `htdocs` directory typically resides in `C:\Program Files\Apache Group\Apache2`; on a Linux platform, it resides in the `/usr/local/httpd` directory. Save PHP documents in the `htdocs` directory. To request the document, launch Internet Explorer (or a UNIX/Linux equivalent browser) and enter the PHP document's location (i.e., `http://localhost/test.php`) in the **Address** field. Figure 21.23 displays the result of requesting `test.php`.

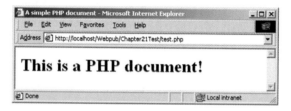

Fig. 21.21   Requesting `test.php` from IIS 5.

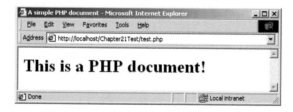

Fig. 21.22   Requesting `test.php` from IIS 6.

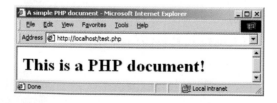

Fig. 21.23   Requesting `test.php` from Apache.

21.8.5 Python

IIS and Apache Web servers can serve Python-generated documents. Copy the file `test.py` from the Chapter 21 examples directory on the CD-ROM to `C:\Chapter21Examples` (or the directory you created in Section 21.6 or 21.7). To request the document from IIS 5, launch Internet Explorer and enter the Python document's location (i.e., `http://localhost/Webpub/Chapter21Test/test.py`) in the **Address** field. Figure 21.24 displays the result of requesting `test.py`.

Fig. 21.24   Requesting `test.py` from IIS.

To request `test.py` from IIS 6, launch Internet Explorer and enter the Python document's location (i.e., `http://localhost/Chapter21Test/test.py`) in the **Address** field. Figure 21.25 displays the result of requesting `test.py`.

Fig. 21.25   Requesting `test.py` from IIS 6.

To request Python-generated documents from the Apache Web server, copy the file `test.py` from the Chapter 21 examples directory on the CD-ROM to the `cgi-bin` directory. On a Windows platform, the `cgi-bin` directory typically resides in `C:\Program Files\Apache Group\Apache2`; on a Linux platform, it resides in the `/usr/local/httpd` directory. All Python documents must reside in the `cgi-bin` directory, because certain environment variables have been registered to help Apache recognize Python files. To request a document, launch Internet Explorer (or the UNIX/Linux equivalent browser) and enter the Python document's location in the **Address** field (i.e., `http://localhost/cgi-bin/test.py`). Figure 21.26 displays the result of requesting `test.py`.

Fig. 21.26 Requesting `test.py` from Apache.

21.9 Web Resources

This section lists several URLs for downloading Web servers and learning more about Web server technology.

`www.w3.org/Protocols`
The World Wide Web Consortium (W3C) Web site contains information on the HTTP specification. The site contains links to news, mailing lists and published articles.

`www.apache.org`
The Apache Software Foundation was created to protect the use of Apache software products. This is the home page of the Apache Software Foundation

`httpd.apache.org`
This is the product home page for the Apache Web server.

`httpd.apache.org/docs-2.0`
The *Apache HTTP Server Version 2.0 Documentation* is Apache's source for Apache Web server information.

`www.apacheweek.com`
The online magazine *Apache Week* contains articles about Apache jobs, product reviews and other information concerning Apache software.

`linuxtoday.com/stories/18780.html`
This site contains an article discussing the widespread use of the Apache Web server. It contains links to other articles that discuss Apache.

`www.iisanswers.com`
The *IIS Answers* Web site provides links to articles that discuss IIS topics. The articles cover issues from installation to security.

`www.iisadministrator.com`
The *IIS Administrator* Web site is a technical newsletter that provides tips and techniques for maintaining IIS.

SUMMARY

- Web servers respond to client requests by providing resources, such as XHTML documents.
- Web servers and clients communicate with each other via the platform-independent Hypertext Transfer Protocol (HTTP).
- The most common HTTP request types are *get* and *post*.
- An HTTP request often posts data to a server-side form handler that processes the data.

- A *get* request typically gets (or retrieves) information from a server. Common uses of *get* requests are to retrieve an HTML document or an image, or to fetch search results based on a user-submitted search term.
- A *get* request sends information to the server as part of the URL.
- A *post* request typically posts (or sends) data to a server. Common uses of *post* requests are to send information to a server, such as authentication information or data from a form that gathers user input.
- The *post* method sends form data as an HTTP message, not as part of the URL.
- Browsers often cache Web pages for quick reloading. Browsers typically do not cache the server's response to a *post* request, because the next *post* might not return the same result.
- A Web server typically is part of a multi-tier application—sometimes referred to as an *n*-tier application. A multi-tier application divides functionality into separate tiers. The three-tier application contains an information tier, a middle tier and a client tier.
- The information tier maintains data for the application in a database.
- The middle tier implements business logic and presentation logic to control interactions between application clients and application data. A Web server is a middle-tier application. This tier often is divided into its two logical components, hence the term *n*-tier application.
- The client tier is the application's user interface. The client interacts with the middle tier to make requests and to retrieve data from the information tier. The client then displays data retrieved from the middle tier to the user.
- Client-side scripting often is used for validation, interactivity, accessing the browser and enhancing a Web page with Dynamic HTML, ActiveX controls and Java applets.
- Client-side scripting has some limitations—such as browser dependency.
- Microsoft Internet Information Services (IIS) is an enterprise-level Web server.
- The Apache Web server, maintained by the Apache Software Foundation, is the most popular Web server in use today and runs on many platforms.
- A virtual directory is an alias for an existing directory on a local machine.
- In its default configuration, Apache supports Perl and Python documents stored in the `cgi-bin` directory, whereas XHTML and PHP documents are stored in the `htdocs` directory (the default Web-content directory in Apache).

TERMINOLOGY

ActiveX control
Apache Web server
bottom tier
business logic
cache
`cgi-bin` directory
client-side scripting
client tier
controller logic
data tier
DNS lookup
DNS server
domain name
domain name system (DNS)

dynamic Web page
File Transfer Protocol (FTP)
fully qualified host name
get (HTTP request)
host name
`htdocs` directory
HTTP request type
Hypertext Transfer Protocol (HTTP)
information tier
Internet Information Services (IIS)
Internet Protocol (IP) address
Java applet
local Web server
`localhost`

middle tier	security level
module	server-side form handler
multi-tier application	server-side script
n-tier application	Simple Mail Transfer Protocol (SMTP)
open source	static Web page
post (HTTP request)	top tier
presentation logic	top-level domain (TLD)
relational database management system (RDBMS)	Uniform Resource Locator (URL)
remote Web server	validation
request method	virtual directory
request type	Web server
scripting host	

SELF-REVIEW EXERCISES

21.1   State whether each of the following is *true* or *false*. If *false*, explain why.
   a) Web servers and clients communicate with each other through the platform-independent HTTP.
   b) Web servers often cache Web pages for quick reloading.
   c) The information tier implements business logic to control the type of information that is presented to a particular client.
   d) Client-side scripts can access the browser, use features specific to that browser and manipulate browser documents.
   e) A virtual directory is an alias for an existing directory on a remote machine.
   f) The Apache Web server is said to be platform-independent because it runs on various operating systems, such as UNIX, Linux and Windows.
   g) In Apache, Perl and PHP, documents are stored in the `cgi-bin` directory.
   h) IIS and Apache can serve ASP.NET, Perl, Python and PHP documents.

21.2   Fill in the blanks in each of the following statements:
   a) The two most common HTTP request types are _____ and _____.
   b) In a three-tier application, a Web server is typically part of the _____ tier.
   c) Client-side validation reduces the number of requests passed to the _____.
   d) The most popular client-side scripting language is _____.
   e) A(n) _____ translates a fully qualified host name to an IP address.
   f) _____ is a host name that references the local computer.
   g) In the Apache Web server, Python documents are stored in the _____ directory.

ANSWERS TO SELF-REVIEW EXERCISES

21.1   a.) True. b) True. c) False. The middle tier implements business logic and presentation logic to control interactions between application clients and application data. d) True. e) False. A virtual directory is an alias for an existing directory on the local machine. f) True. g) False. In Apache, Perl and Python, documents are stored in the `cgi-bin` directory. PHP documents are stored in the `htdocs` directory. h) False, IIS and Apache can serve XHTML, Perl, Python and PHP documents. The Apache Web server cannot serve ASP.NET documents, but IIS can.

21.2   a) *get, post.* b) middle. c) server. d) JavaScript. e) domain name system (DNS) server. f) `localhost.` g) `cgi-bin.`

EXERCISES

21.3   Define the following terms:
      a) HTTP.
      b) Multi-tier application.
      c) Request method.

21.4   Define the following terms:
      a) Top-level domain (TLD).
      b) Virtual directory.
      c) Web server.

21.5   In a three-tier application, explain how the middle tier (e.g., Web server) interacts with the client tier (e.g., Web browser).

21.6   Explain the difference between the *get* request type and the *post* request type. When is it ideal to use the *post* request type?

21.7   Explain how to determine the machine names of remote Web servers (in your local network).

21.8   Given that you have a document, `sample.php`, in the `C:\Exercises\Webservers` directory, explain how to request the document using:
      a) IIS.
      b) Apache.

22

Database: SQL, MySQL, DBI and ADO.NET

Objectives

- To understand the relational database model.
- To be able to write database queries using SQL (Structured Query Language).
- To understand the MySQL database server.
- To learn various database interfaces.
- To understand ADO.NET's object model.

Now go, write it before them in a table, and note it in a book, that it may be for the time to come for ever and ever.
Holy Bible: Isaiah

True art selects and paraphrases, but seldom gives a verbatim translation.
Thomas Bailey Aldrich

Get your facts first, and then you can distort them as much as you please.
Mark Twain

I like two kinds of men: domestic and foreign.
Mae West

Outline

22.1 Introduction

A **database** is an integrated collection of data. Many different strategies exist for organizing data in databases to facilitate easy access to and manipulation of the data. A **database management system (DBMS)** provides mechanisms for storing and organizing data in a manner that is consistent with the database's format. Database management systems enable programmers to access and store data without worrying about the internal representation of databases.

Today's most popular database systems are **relational databases**. Almost universally, relational databases use a language called **SQL (Structured Query Language**—pronounced as its individual letters or as "sequel") to perform **queries** (i.e., to request information that satisfies given criteria) and to manipulate data. [*Note*: The writing in this chapter assumes that SQL is pronounced as its individual letters. For this reason, we often precede SQL with the article "an" as in "an SQL database" or "an SQL statement."]

Some popular enterprise-level relational database systems include Microsoft SQL Server, Oracle™, Sybase™, DB2™, Informix™ and MySQL™. This chapter presents examples using *Microsoft Access*—a relational database system that comes with *Microsoft Office XP Professional*.

A programming language connects to, and interacts with, a relational database via an **interface**—software that facilitates communication between a database management system and a program. For example, Perl developers use the Perl DBI to interact with databases. Similarly, Python programmers use the DB-API interface, and PHP includes a dbx module to interact with other database modules. ASP.NET programmers communicate with databases and manipulate their data through Microsoft ActiveX Data Objects™ (ADO) and ADO.NET. We introduce each of these interfaces in the latter half of this chapter.

22.2 Relational Database Model

The **relational database model** is a logical representation of data that allows relationships among items of data to be considered without concern for the physical structure of the data. A relational database is composed of **tables**. Figure 22.1 shows an example table that might be used in a personnel system. The table name is `Employee`, and its primary purpose is to store the specific attributes of various employees. Tables are composed of **rows** and **columns**. This table contains six rows and five columns. The `number` column of each row in the table pictured in Fig. 22.1 is the **primary key** for referencing data in the table. A primary key is a column (or set of columns) in a table that contains unique data (i.e., data that is not duplicated in other rows of the table). This guarantees that each row can be identified by at least one unique value. Examples of primary keys are columns that contain social security numbers, employee IDs and part numbers in an inventory system. The rows in Fig. 22.1 are **ordered** by primary key. In this case, the rows are listed in increasing order (they also could be in decreasing order).

number	name	department	salary	location
23603	Jones	413	1100	New Jersey
24568	Kerwin	413	2000	New Jersey
34589	Larson	642	1800	Los Angeles
35761	Myers	611	1400	Orlando
47132	Neumann	413	9000	New Jersey
78321	Stephens	611	8500	Orlando

Row { (34589–35761)   Primary key   Column

Fig. 22.1   Relational database structure of an `Employee` table.

Each column of the table represents a different data item. Rows normally are unique (by primary key) within a table, but particular values might be duplicated in multiple rows. For example, three different rows in the `Employee` table's `Department` column contain the number 413.

Often, different users of a database are interested in different data and different relationships among the data items. Some users require only subsets of the columns. To obtain such subsets, we use SQL to specify certain data to **select** from a table. SQL provides a complete set of keywords (including **SELECT**) that enable programmers to define complex **queries** to select data from a table. The results of queries commonly are called **result sets**, **record sets** or **result tables**. Regardless of the term used to describe the results, a query always produces a table. For example, we might select data from the table in Fig. 22.1 to generate a new table containing only the location of each department. This table appears in Fig. 22.2. SQL queries are discussed in Section 22.4.

department	location
413	New Jersey
611	Orlando
642	Los Angeles

Fig. 22.2   Table formed by selecting Department and Location data from the Employee table.

22.3 Relational Database Overview: Books.mdb Database

This section provides an overview of SQL in the context of a sample Books.mdb database we created for this chapter. Before we discuss SQL, we explain the various tables of this Microsoft Access database.[1] We use this database to introduce various database concepts, including the use of SQL to manipulate and obtain useful information from the database. The Chapter 22 examples directory on the CD-ROM that accompanies this book contains the database.

The database consists of four tables: Authors, Publishers, AuthorISBN and Titles. The Authors table (described in Fig. 22.3) consists of three columns that maintain each author's unique ID number, first name and last name. Figure 22.4 contains the data from the Authors table of the Books.mdb database.

Field	Description
authorID	Author's ID number in the database. In the Books.mdb database, this Integer column is defined as **auto-increment**. For each new row inserted in this table, the database increments the authorID value, ensuring that each row has a unique authorID. This column represents the table's primary key.
firstName	Author's first name (a String).
lastName	Author's last name (a String).

Fig. 22.3   Authors table from Books.mdb.

---

1. Note that Microsoft Access refers to rows as "records" and columns as "fields."

authorID	firstName	lastName
1	Harvey	Deitel
2	Paul	Deitel
3	Tem	Nieto
4	Kate	Steinbuhler
5	Sean	Santry
6	Ted	Lin
7	Praveen	Sadhu
8	David	McPhie
9	Cheryl	Yaeger
10	Marina	Zlatkina
11	Ben	Wiedermann
12	Jonathan	Liperi

Fig. 22.4   Data from the `Authors` table of `Books.mdb`.

The `Publishers` table (Fig. 22.5) consists of two columns, representing each publisher's unique ID and name. Figure 22.6 contains the data from the `Publishers` table of the `Books.mdb` database.

Field	Description
publisherID	The publisher's ID number in the database. This auto-incremented `Integer` is the table's primary key.
publisherName	The name of the publisher (a `String`).

Fig. 22.5   `Publishers` table from `Books.mdb`.

publisherID	publisherName
1	Prentice Hall
2	Prentice Hall PTG

Fig. 22.6   Data from the `Publishers` table of `Books.mdb`.

The `AuthorISBN` table (Fig. 22.7) consists of two columns that maintain ISBN numbers for each book and the authors' ID numbers. This table helps associate the names of the authors with the titles of their books. Figure 22.8 contains a portion of the data from the `AuthorISBN` table of the `Books.mdb` database. ISBN is an abbreviation for "International Standard Book Number"—a numbering scheme by which publishers worldwide give every book a unique identification number. [*Note*: To save space, we split the contents of Fig. 22.8 into two columns, each containing the `authorID` and `isbn` columns.

Field	Description
authorID	The author's ID number, which allows the database to associate each book with a specific author. The integer ID number in this column must also appear in the `Authors` table.
isbn	The ISBN number for a book (a `String`).

Fig. 22.7   AuthorISBN table from Books.mdb.

authorID	isbn	authorID	isbn
1	0130895725	2	0139163050
1	0132261197	2	013028419x
1	0130895717	2	0130161438
1	0135289106	2	0130856118
1	0139163050	2	0130125075
1	013028419x	2	0138993947
1	0130161438	2	0130852473
1	0130856118	2	0130829277
1	0130125075	2	0134569555
1	0138993947	2	0130829293
1	0130852473	2	0130284173
1	0130829277	2	0130284181
1	0134569555	2	0130895601
1	0130829293	3	013028419x
1	0130284173	3	0130161438
1	0130284181	3	0130856118
1	0130895601	3	0134569555
2	0130895725	3	0130829293
2	0132261197	3	0130284173
2	0130895717	3	0130284181
2	0135289106	4	0130895601

Fig. 22.8   Portion of the data from AuthorISBN table in Books.mdb.

The `Titles` table (Fig. 22.9) consists of eight columns that maintain general information about the books in the database. This information includes each book's ISBN number, title, edition number, copyright year, description and publisher's ID number, as well as the

name of a file containing an image of the book cover, and finally, each book's price.
Figure 22.10 contains a portion of the data from the `Titles` table.

Field	Description
isbn	ISBN number of the book (a `String`).
title	Title of the book (a `String`).
editionNumber	Edition number of the book (a `String`).
copyright	Copyright year of the book (an `Integer`).
description	Description of the book (a `String`).
publisherID	Publisher's ID number (an `Integer`). This value must correspond to an ID number in the `Publishers` table.
imageFile	Name of the file containing the book's cover image (a `String`).
price	Suggested retail price of the book (a real number). [*Note*: The prices shown in this database are for example purposes only.]

Fig. 22.9   `Titles` table from `Books.mdb`.

isbn	title	edition-Number	publisherID	copy-right	price
0130923613	Python How to Program	1	1	2002	$69.95
0130622214	C# How to Program	1	1	2002	$69.95
0130341517	Java How to Program	4	1	2002	$69.95
0130649341	The Complete Java Training Course	4	2	2002	$109.95
0130895601	Advanced Java 2 Platform How to Program	1	1	2002	$69.95
0130308978	Internet and World Wide Web How to Program	2	1	2002	$69.95
0130293636	Visual Basic .NET How to Program	2	1	2002	$69.95
0130895636	The Complete C++ Training Course	3	2	2001	$109.95
0130895512	The Complete e-Business & e-Commerce Programming Training Course	1	2	2001	$109.95

Fig. 22.10   Portion of the data from the `Titles` table of `Books.mdb`.

Figure 22.11 illustrates the relationships among the tables in the `Books.mdb` database. We created this diagram in Microsoft Access when we designed the database. [*Note*:

Selecting **Relationships...** from the **Tools** menu in Access produces this diagram.] The header line in each table is the table's name. The column whose name appears in bold contains the table's primary key. A table's primary key uniquely identifies each row in the table. Every row must have a value in the primary key, and the value must be unique. This is known as the **Rule of Entity Integrity**. Note that the AuthorISBN table contains two columns whose names are bold. This indicates that these two columns form a **composite primary key**—each row in the table must have a unique authorID–isbn combination. For example, several rows might have an authorID of 2, and several rows might have an isbn of 0130895601, but only one row can have both an authorID of 2 and an isbn of 0130895601.

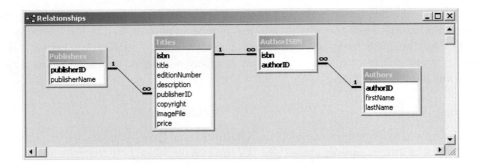

Fig. 22.11   Table relationships in Books.mdb.

Common Programming Error 22.1

Failure to provide a value for a primary key in every row breaks the Rule of Entity Integrity and causes the DBMS to report an error.

Common Programming Error 22.2

Providing duplicate values for the primary key in multiple rows causes the DBMS to report an error.

The lines connecting the tables in Fig. 22.11 represent the **relationships** among the tables. Consider the line between the Publishers and Titles tables. On the Publishers end of the line, there is a 1, and on the Titles end, there is an infinity (∞) symbol. This line indicates a **one-to-many relationship**, in which every publisher in the Publishers table can have an arbitrarily large number of books in the Titles table. Note that the relationship line links the publisherID field in the Publishers table to the publisherID field in the Titles table. In the Titles table, the publisherID field is a **foreign key**—a column or set of columns which must match the primary key of another table (e.g., publisherID in the Publishers table). Programmers specify foreign keys when creating a table. The foreign key helps maintain the **Rule of Referential Integrity**: Every foreign-key value must appear in another table's primary key. Foreign keys enable information from multiple tables to be **joined** together for analysis purposes. A one-to-many relationship exists between a primary key and its corresponding foreign keys. This means that a foreign-key value can appear many times in its own table, but must appear exactly once as the primary key of another table. The line between the tables represents the link between the foreign key in one table and the primary key in another table.

Common Programming Error 22.3

Providing a foreign key that does not appear as a primary key in another table breaks the Rule of Referential Integrity and causes the DBMS to report an error.

The line between the `AuthorISBN` and `Authors` tables indicates that, for each author in the `Authors` table, there can be an arbitrary number of ISBNs for books written by that author in the `AuthorISBN` table. The `authorID` in the `AuthorISBN` table is a foreign key for the `authorID` (the primary key) of the `Authors` table. Note, again, that the line between the tables links the foreign key in table `AuthorISBN` to the corresponding primary key in table `Authors`. The `AuthorISBN` table links information in the `Titles` and `Authors` tables.

Finally, the line between the `Titles` and `AuthorISBN` tables illustrates a one-to-many relationship; a title can be written by any number of authors. In fact, the sole purpose of the `AuthorISBN` table is to represent a many-to-many relationship between the `Authors` and `Titles` tables; an author can write any number of books, and a book can have any number of authors.

22.4 SQL (Structured Query Language)

In this section, we provide an overview of SQL (Structured Query Language) in the context of our `Books.mdb` sample database. The SQL queries discussed here form the foundation for the SQL used in the chapter examples.

Figure 22.12 lists SQL keywords programmers use in the context of SQL queries and data-manipulation statements. In the next several subsections, we discuss these SQL keywords in the context of complete SQL queries. Other SQL keywords exist, but are beyond the scope of this text. [*Note*: To locate additional information on SQL, please refer to the Internet and World Wide Web Resources at the end of the chapter.]

SQL keyword	Description
SELECT	Selects (retrieves) columns from one or more tables.
FROM	Specifies tables from which to get columns or delete rows. Required in every SELECT and DELETE statement.
WHERE	Specifies criteria that determine the rows to be retrieved.
INNER JOIN	Joins rows from multiple tables to produce a single set of rows.
GROUP BY	Specifies criteria for grouping rows.
ORDER BY	Specifies criteria for ordering rows.
INSERT	Inserts data into a specified table.
UPDATE	Updates data in a specified table.
DELETE	Deletes data from a specified table.
CREATE	Creates a new table.
DROP	Deletes an existing table.
COUNT	Returns the number of records that satisfy given search criteria.

Fig. 22.12 SQL keywords.

22.4.1 Basic SELECT Query

Let us consider several SQL queries that extract information from database Books.mdb. A typical SQL query "selects" information from one or more tables in a database. Such selections are specified by the **SELECT** keyword. The simplest format for a SELECT is:

```
SELECT * FROM tableName
```

In this query, the asterisk (*) indicates that all the columns from the *tableName* table should be selected. For example, to select the entire contents of the Authors table (i.e., all the data in Fig. 22.4), use the query:

```
SELECT * FROM Authors
```

To select specific columns from a table, replace the asterisk (*) with a comma-separated list of the column names to select. For example, to select only the columns authorID and lastName for all the rows in the Authors table, use the query

```
SELECT authorID, lastName FROM Authors
```

This query only returns the data presented in Fig. 22.13. [*Note*: If a field name contains spaces, the entire field name must be enclosed in square brackets ([]) in the query. For example, if the field name is first name, it must appear in the query as [first name].]

authorID	lastName	authorID	lastName
1	Deitel	7	Sadhu
2	Deitel	8	McPhie
3	Nieto	9	Yaeger
4	Steinbuhler	10	Zlatkina
5	Santry	11	Wiedermann
6	Lin	12	Liperi

Fig. 22.13 authorID and lastName from the Authors table.

Common Programming Error 22.4

If a program assumes that a query using the asterisk (*) to select columns always returns those columns in the same order, the program could process the result set incorrectly. If the column order in the table(s) changes, the order of the columns in the result set would change accordingly.

Performance Tip 22.1

If a program does not know the order of columns in a result set, the program must process the columns by name. This could require a linear search of the column names in the result set. If users specify the column names that they wish to select from a table (or several tables), the application receiving the result set can know the order of the columns in advance. When this occurs, the program can process the data more efficiently, because columns can be accessed directly by column number.

22.4.2 WHERE Clause

In most cases, users search a database for rows that satisfy certain **selection criteria**. Only rows that match the selection criteria are selected. SQL uses the optional **WHERE clause** to specify the selection criteria for the query. The simplest format of a query that includes selection criteria is:

```
SELECT columnName1, columnName2, ... FROM tableName WHERE criteria
```

For example, to select the `title`, `editionNumber` and `copyright` columns from those rows of table `Titles` in which the `copyright` date is than 1999, use the query more recent:

```
SELECT title, editionNumber, copyright
FROM Titles
WHERE copyright > 1999
```

Figure 22.14 shows the result set of the preceding query. [*Note*: When we construct a query for use in a server-side scripting language, we simply create a variable containing the entire query as a string of text. However, when we display queries in the text, we often use multiple lines and indentation to enhance readability.]

title	editionNumber	copyright
Internet and World Wide Web How to Program	2	2002
Java How to Program	4	2002
The Complete Java Training Course	4	2002
The Complete e-Business & e-Commerce Programming Training Course	1	2001
The Complete Internet & World Wide Web Programming Training Course	2	2001
The Complete Perl Training Course	1	2001
The Complete XML Programming Training Course	1	2001
C How to Program	3	2001
C++ How to Program	3	2001
The Complete C++ Training Course	3	2001
e-Business and e-Commerce How to Program	1	2001
Internet and World Wide Web How to Program	1	2000
The Complete Internet and World Wide Web Programming Training Course	1	2000
Java How to Program (Java 2)	3	2000
The Complete Java 2 Training Course	3	2000
XML How to Program	1	2001

Fig. 22.14   Titles with copyrights after 1999 from table `Titles`. (Part 1 of 2.)

title	editionNumber	copyright
Perl How to Program	1	2001
Advanced Java 2 Platform How to Program	1	2002
e-Business and e-Commerce for Managers	1	2000
Wireless Internet and Mobile Business How to Program	1	2001
C# How To Program	1	2002
Python How to Program	1	2002
Visual Basic .NET How to Program	2	2002

Fig. 22.14 Titles with copyrights after 1999 from table `Titles`. (Part 2 of 2.)

Performance Tip 22.2

Using selection criteria improves performance, because queries that involve such criteria normally select a subset of rows that is smaller than the entire table. Working with a smaller portion of the data is more efficient than working with the entire table.

The WHERE clause condition can contain operators <, >, <=, >=, =, <> and LIKE. Operator LIKE is used for **pattern matching** with wildcard characters **asterisk** (*) and **question mark** (?). Pattern matching allows SQL to search for similar strings that "match a pattern."

A pattern that contains an asterisk (*) searches for strings in which zero or more characters take the asterisk character's place in the pattern. For example, the following query locates the data for all authors whose last names start with the letter D:

```
SELECT authorID, firstName, lastName
FROM Authors
WHERE lastName LIKE 'D*'
```

The preceding query selects the two rows shown in Fig. 22.15, because two of the authors in our database have last names that begin with the letter D (followed by zero or more characters). The * in the WHERE clause's LIKE pattern indicates that any number of characters can appear after the letter D in the lastName field. Note that the pattern string is surrounded by single-quote characters.

authorID	firstName	lastName
1	Harvey	Deitel
2	Paul	Deitel

Fig. 22.15 Authors from the `Authors` table whose last names start with D.

Portability Tip 22.1

Not all database systems support the LIKE operator, so be sure to read the database system's documentation carefully before employing this operator.

Portability Tip 22.2

Unlike Access, standard SQL uses the % character in place of the * character in LIKE expressions.

Portability Tip 22.3

In most databases, string data is case sensitive.

Portability Tip 22.4

In some databases, table names and column names are case sensitive.

A pattern string including a question mark (?) character searches for strings in which exactly one character takes the question mark's place in the pattern. For example, the following query locates the rows of all authors whose last names start with any character (specified with ?), followed by the letter i, followed by any number of additional characters (specified with *):

```
SELECT authorID, firstName, lastName
FROM Authors
WHERE lastName LIKE '?i*'
```

The preceding query produces the table listed in Fig. 22.16; four authors in our database have last names that contain the letter i as the second letter.

authorID	firstName	lastName
3	Tem	Nieto
6	Ted	Lin
11	Ben	Wiedermann
12	Jonathan	Liperi

Fig. 22.16 Authors from table `Authors` whose last names contain i as their second letter.

Portability Tip 22.5

Unlike Access, standard SQL uses the _ character in place of the ? character in LIKE expressions.

22.4.3 ORDER BY Clause

The results of a query can be arranged in ascending or descending order using the optional **ORDER BY clause**. The simplest form of an ORDER BY clause is:

```
SELECT columnName1, columnName2, ... FROM tableName ORDER BY column ASC
SELECT columnName1, columnName2, ... FROM tableName ORDER BY column DESC
```

where ASC specifies ascending order (lowest to highest), DESC specifies descending order (highest to lowest) and *column* specifies the column that determines the sorting order.

For example, to obtain the list of authors that is arranged in ascending order by last name (Fig. 22.17), use the query:

```
SELECT authorID, firstName, lastName
FROM Authors
ORDER BY lastName ASC
```

Note that the default sorting order is ascending; therefore ASC is optional.

authorID	firstName	lastName
2	Paul	Deitel
1	Harvey	Deitel
6	Ted	Lin
12	Jonathan	Liperi
8	David	McPhie
3	Tem	Nieto
7	Praveen	Sadhu
5	Sean	Santry
4	Kate	Steinbuhler
11	Ben	Wiedermann
9	Cheryl	Yaeger
10	Marina	Zlatkina

Fig. 22.17   Authors from table `Authors` in ascending order by `lastName`.

To obtain the same list of authors arranged in descending order by last name (Fig. 22.18), use the query:

```
SELECT authorID, firstName, lastName
FROM Authors
ORDER BY lastName DESC
```

authorID	firstName	lastName
10	Marina	Zlatkina
9	Cheryl	Yaeger
11	Ben	Wiedermann
4	Kate	Steinbuhler
5	Sean	Santry
7	Praveen	Sadhu

Fig. 22.18   Authors in descending order by `lastName`. (Part 1 of 2.)

authorID	firstName	lastName
3	Tem	Nieto
8	David	McPhie
12	Jonathan	Liperi
6	Ted	Lin
2	Paul	Deitel
1	Harvey	Deitel

Fig. 22.18   Authors in descending order by `lastName`. (Part 2 of 2.)

The ORDER BY clause also can be used to order rows by multiple columns. Such queries are written in the form:

    ORDER BY *column1 sortingOrder*, *column2 sortingOrder*, ...

where *sortingOrder* is either ASC or DESC. Note that the *sortingOrder* does not have to be identical for each column. For example, the query:

```
SELECT authorID, firstName, lastName
FROM Authors
ORDER BY lastName, firstName
```

sorts all authors in ascending order by last name, then by first name. This means that if any authors have the same last name, their rows are returned sorted by first name (Fig. 22.19).

authorID	firstName	lastName
1	Harvey	Deitel
2	Paul	Deitel
6	Ted	Lin
12	Jonathan	Liperi
8	David	McPhie
3	Tem	Nieto
7	Praveen	Sadhu
5	Sean	Santry
4	Kate	Steinbuhler
11	Ben	Wiedermann
9	Cheryl	Yaeger
10	Marina	Zlatkina

Fig. 22.19   Authors from table `Authors` in ascending order by `lastName` and by `firstName`.

The WHERE and ORDER BY clauses can be combined in one query. For example, the query

```
SELECT isbn, title, editionNumber, copyright, price
FROM Titles
WHERE title
LIKE '*How to Program' ORDER BY title ASC
```

returns the ISBN, title, edition number, copyright and price of each book in the Titles table that has a title ending with "How to Program"; it lists these rows in ascending order by title. The results of the query are depicted in Fig. 22.20.

isbn	title	edition-Number	copy-right	price
0130895601	Advanced Java 2 Platform How to Program	1	2002	$69.95
0131180436	C How to Program	1	1992	$69.95
0130895725	C How to Program	3	2001	$69.95
0132261197	C How to Program	2	1994	$49.95
0130622214	C# How To Program	1	2002	$69.95
0135289106	C++ How to Program	2	1998	$49.95
0131173340	C++ How to Program	1	1994	$69.95
0130895717	C++ How to Program	3	2001	$69.95
013028419X	e-Business and e-Commerce How to Program	1	2001	$69.95
0130308978	Internet and World Wide Web How to Program	2	2002	$69.95
0130161438	Internet and World Wide Web How to Program	1	2000	$69.95
0130341517	Java How to Program	4	2002	$69.95
0136325890	Java How to Program	1	1998	$69.95
0130284181	Perl How to Program	1	2001	$69.95
0130923613	Python How to Program	1	2002	$69.95
0130293636	Visual Basic .NET How to Program	2	2002	$69.95
0134569555	Visual Basic 6 How to Program	1	1999	$69.95
0130622265	Wireless Internet and Mobile Business How to Program	1	2001	$69.95
0130284173	XML How to Program	1	2001	$69.95

Fig. 22.20   Books from table Titles whose titles end with How to Program in ascending order by title.

22.4.4 Merging Data from Multiple Tables: INNER JOIN

Database designers often **normalize** databases, i.e., split related data into separate tables to ensure that a database does not store data redundantly. For example, the Books.mdb database has tables Authors and Titles. We use an AuthorISBN table to provide "links" between authors and titles. If we did not separate this information into individual tables, we would need to include author information with each entry in the Titles table. This would result in the database storing duplicate author information for authors who wrote multiple books

Often, it is necessary for analysis purposes to merge data from multiple tables into a single set of data. Referred to as **joining** the tables, this is accomplished via an **INNER JOIN** operation in the SELECT query. An INNER JOIN merges rows from two or more tables by testing for matching values in a column that is common to the tables. The simplest format of an INNER JOIN clause is:

```
SELECT columnName1, columnName2, ...
FROM table1
INNER JOIN table2
    ON table1.columnName = table2.columnName
```

The ON part of the INNER JOIN clause specifies the columns from each table that are compared to determine which rows are combined. For example, the following query produces a list of authors accompanied by the ISBN numbers for books written by each author:

```
SELECT firstName, lastName, isbn
FROM Authors
INNER JOIN AuthorISBN
    ON Authors.authorID = AuthorISBN.authorID
ORDER BY lastName, firstName
```

The query combines the firstName and lastName columns from table Authors and the isbn column from table AuthorISBN, sorting the results in ascending order by lastName and firstName. Note the use of the syntax *tableName.columnName* in the ON part of the INNER JOIN. This syntax (called a **qualified name**) specifies the columns from each table that should be compared to join the tables. The *tableName.columnName* syntax is required if the columns have the same name in both tables. The same syntax can be used in any query to distinguish among columns in different tables that have the same name. In some database systems, qualified names that start with the database name can be used to perform cross-database queries.

Software Engineering Observation 22.1

If an SQL query includes columns from multiple tables that have the same name, the statement must precede those column names with their table names and a dot separator (e.g., Authors.authorID).

Common Programming Error 22.5

In a query, failure to provide qualified names for columns that have the same name in two or more tables is an error.

As always, the query can contain an ORDER BY clause. Figure 22.21 depicts a portion of the results of the preceding query, ordered by lastName and firstName. [*Note:* To

save space, we split the results of the query into two columns, each containing the first-
Name, lastName and isbn fields.]

firstName	lastName	isbn	firstName	lastName	isbn
Harvey	Deitel	0130895601	Harvey	Deitel	0130856118
Harvey	Deitel	0130284181	Harvey	Deitel	0130161438
Harvey	Deitel	0130284173	Harvey	Deitel	013028419x
Harvey	Deitel	0130829293	Harvey	Deitel	0139163050
Harvey	Deitel	0134569555	Harvey	Deitel	0135289106
Harvey	Deitel	0130829277	Harvey	Deitel	0130895717
Harvey	Deitel	0130852473	Harvey	Deitel	0132261197
Harvey	Deitel	0138993947	Harvey	Deitel	0130895725
Harvey	Deitel	0130125075	Paul	Deitel	0130895601
Paul	Deitel	0130284181	Paul	Deitel	0135289106
Paul	Deitel	0130284173	Paul	Deitel	0130895717
Paul	Deitel	0130829293	Paul	Deitel	0132261197
Paul	Deitel	0134569555	Paul	Deitel	0130895725
Paul	Deitel	0130829277	Tem	Nieto	0130284181
Paul	Deitel	0130852473	Tem	Nieto	0130284173
Paul	Deitel	0138993947	Tem	Nieto	0130829293
Paul	Deitel	0130125075	Tem	Nieto	0134569555
Paul	Deitel	0130856118	Tem	Nieto	0130856118
Paul	Deitel	0130161438	Tem	Nieto	0130161438
Paul	Deitel	013028419x	Tem	Nieto	013028419x
Paul	Deitel	0139163050	Sean	Santry	0130895601

Fig. 22.21 Portion of the query results for author names and the ISBN numbers of the
books they have written, sorted in ascending order by lastName and
firstName.

22.4.5 Joining Data from Tables Authors, AuthorISBN, Titles and Publishers

The Books.mdb database contains one predefined query (TitleAuthor), which selects as
its result the title, ISBN number, author's first name, author's last name, copyright year and
publisher's name for each book in the database. For books that have multiple authors, the
query produces a separate record for each author. The TitleAuthor query is shown in
Fig. 22.22. Figure 22.23 contains a portion of the query results.

We added indentation to make the query in Fig. 22.22 more readable. Let us now break
down the query into its various parts. Lines 1–3 contain a comma-separated list of the columns that the query returns; the order of the columns from left to right specifies the columns'
order in the returned table. This query selects columns title and isbn from table Titles,

```
1   SELECT Titles.title, Titles.isbn, Authors.firstName,
2          Authors.lastName, Titles.copyright,
3          Publishers.publisherName
4   FROM
5     ( Publishers INNER JOIN Titles
6        ON Publishers.publisherID = Titles.publisherID )
7     INNER JOIN
8     ( Authors INNER JOIN AuthorISBN
9        ON Authors.authorID = AuthorISBN.authorID )
10    ON Titles.isbn = AuthorISBN.isbn
11  ORDER BY Titles.title
```

Fig. 22.22   Joining tables to produce a result set in which each row contains an author, title, ISBN number, copyright and publisher name.

Title	isbn	first-Name	last-Name	copy-right	publisher-Name
Advanced Java 2 Platform How to Program	0130895601	Paul	Deitel	2002	Prentice Hall
Advanced Java 2 Platform How to Program	0130895601	Harvey	Deitel	2002	Prentice Hall
Advanced Java 2 Platform How to Program	0130895601	Sean	Santry	2002	Prentice Hall
C How to Program	0131180436	Harvey	Deitel	1992	Prentice Hall
C How to Program	0131180436	Paul	Deitel	1992	Prentice Hall
C How to Program	0132261197	Harvey	Deitel	1994	Prentice Hall
C How to Program	0132261197	Paul	Deitel	1994	Prentice Hall
C How to Program	0130895725	Harvey	Deitel	2001	Prentice Hall
C How to Program	0130895725	Paul	Deitel	2001	Prentice Hall
C# How To Program	0130622214	Tem	Nieto	2002	Prentice Hall
C# How To Program	0130622214	Paul	Deitel	2002	Prentice Hall
C# How To Program	0130622214	Cheryl	Yaeger	2002	Prentice Hall
C# How To Program	0130622214	Marina	Zlatkina	2002	Prentice Hall
C# How To Program	0130622214	Harvey	Deitel	2002	Prentice Hall
C++ How to Program	0130895717	Paul	Deitel	2001	Prentice Hall
C++ How to Program	0130895717	Harvey	Deitel	2001	Prentice Hall
C++ How to Program	0131173340	Paul	Deitel	1994	Prentice Hall
C++ How to Program	0131173340	Harvey	Deitel	1994	Prentice Hall
C++ How to Program	0135289106	Harvey	Deitel	1998	Prentice Hall
C++ How to Program	0135289106	Paul	Deitel	1998	Prentice Hall

Fig. 22.23   Portion of the result set produced by the query in Fig. 22.22. (Part 1 of 2.)

Title	isbn	first-Name	last-Name	copy-right	publisher-Name
e-Business and e-Commerce for Managers	0130323640	Harvey	Deitel	2000	Prentice Hall
e-Business and e-Commerce for Managers	0130323640	Kate	Stein-buhler	2000	Prentice Hall
e-Business and e-Commerce for Managers	0130323640	Paul	Deitel	2000	Prentice Hall
e-Business and e-Commerce How to Program	013028419X	Harvey	Deitel	2001	Prentice Hall
e-Business and e-Commerce How to Program	013028419X	Paul	Deitel	2001	Prentice Hall
e-Business and e-Commerce How to Program	013028419X	Tem	Nieto	2001	Prentice Hall

Fig. 22.23 Portion of the result set produced by the query in Fig. 22.22. (Part 2 of 2.)

columns `firstName` and `lastName` from table `Authors`, column `copyright` from table `Titles` and column `publisherName` from table `Publishers`. For the purpose of clarity, we fully qualified each column name with its table name (e.g., `Titles.isbn`).

Lines 5–10 specify the `INNER JOIN` operations used to combine information from the various tables. There are three `INNER JOIN` operations. Although an `INNER JOIN` is performed on two tables, either of those two tables can be a temporary table that is the result of another query or another `INNER JOIN`. We use parentheses to nest the `INNER JOIN` operations; SQL evaluates the innermost set of parentheses first, then moves outward. We begin with the `INNER JOIN`:

```
( Publishers INNER JOIN Titles
    ON Publishers.publisherID = Titles.publisherID )
```

which joins the `Publishers` table and the `Titles` table `ON` the condition that the `publisherID` number in each table matches. The resulting temporary table contains information about each book and its publisher.

The other nested set of parentheses contains another `INNER JOIN`:

```
( Authors INNER JOIN AuthorISBN ON
    Authors.AuthorID = AuthorISBN.AuthorID )
```

which joins the `Authors` table and the `AuthorISBN` table `ON` the condition that the `authorID` column in each table matches. Remember that the `AuthorISBN` table has multiple entries for ISBN numbers of books that have more than one author.

The third `INNER JOIN`:

```
( Publishers INNER JOIN Titles
    ON Publishers.publisherID = Titles.publisherID )
INNER JOIN
```

```
( Authors INNER JOIN AuthorISBN
   ON Authors.authorID = AuthorISBN.authorID )
ON Titles.isbn = AuthorISBN.isbn
```

joins the two temporary tables produced by the prior inner joins ON the condition that the
Titles.isbn column for each row in the first temporary table matches the corresponding
AuthorISBN.isbn column for each row in the second temporary table. The result of all
these INNER JOIN operations is a temporary table from which the appropriate columns are
selected to produce the result of the query.

Finally, line 11 of the query:

```
ORDER BY Titles.title
```

indicates that all the titles should be sorted in ascending order (the default).

22.4.6 INSERT Statement

The **INSERT** statement inserts a new row in a table. The simplest form for this statement is:

```
INSERT INTO tableName ( columnName1, columnName2, ..., columnNameN )
   VALUES ( value1, value2, ..., valueN )
```

where *tableName* is the table in which to insert the row. The *tableName* is followed by a
comma-separated list of column names in parentheses. The list of column names is followed by the SQL keyword VALUES and a comma-separated list of values in parentheses.
The specified values in this list must match the columns listed after the table name in both
order and type (e.g., if *columnName1* is specified as the firstName column, then *value1*
should be a string in single quotes representing the first name). The INSERT statement:

```
INSERT INTO Authors ( firstName, lastName )
   VALUES ( 'Sue', 'Smith' )
```

inserts a row into the Authors table. The first comma-separated list indicates that the statement provides data for the firstName and lastName columns. The corresponding values
to insert, which are contained in the second comma-separated list, are 'Sue' and 'Smith'.
We do not specify an authorID in this example because authorID is an auto-increment
column. Every new row that we add to this table is assigned a unique authorID value that
is the next value in the auto-increment sequence (i.e., 1, 2, 3, etc.). In this case, Sue Smith
would be assigned authorID number 13. Figure 22.24 shows the Authors table after we
perform the INSERT operation.

authorID	firstName	lastName
1	Harvey	Deitel
2	Paul	Deitel
3	Tem	Nieto

Fig. 22.24   Table Authors after an INSERT operation to add a row. (Part 1 of 2.)

authorID	firstName	lastName
4	Kate	Steinbuhler
5	Sean	Santry
6	Ted	Lin
7	Praveen	Sadhu
8	David	McPhie
9	Cheryl	Yaeger
10	Marina	Zlatkina
11	Ben	Wiedermann
12	Jonathan	Liperi
13	Sue	Smith

Fig. 22.24   Table `Authors` after an `INSERT` operation to add a row. (Part 2 of 2.)

Common Programming Error 22.6

SQL uses the single-quote (') character as a delimiter for strings. To specify a string containing a single quote (such as O'Malley) in SQL, the string must include two single quotes in the position where the single-quote character should appear in the string (e.g., `'O''Malley')`. *The first of the two single-quote characters acts as an escape character for the second. Failure to escape single-quote characters in a string in SQL is a syntax error.*

22.4.7 UPDATE Statement

An **UPDATE** statement modifies data in a table. The simplest form for an UPDATE statement is:

> UPDATE *tableName*
>   SET *columnName1* = *value1*,
>   *columnName2* = *value2*,
>   …,
>   *columnNameN* = *valueN*
>   WHERE *criteria*

where *tableName* is the table in which to update a row (or rows). The *tableName* is followed by keyword **SET** and a comma-separated list of column name/value pairs written in the format, *columnName = value*. The WHERE clause specifies the criteria used to determine which row(s) to update. For example, the UPDATE statement:

> UPDATE Authors
>   SET lastName = 'Jones'
>   WHERE lastName = 'Smith' AND firstName = 'Sue'

updates a row in the Authors table. The statement indicates that lastName will be assigned the new value Jones for the row in which lastName currently is equal to Smith and firstName is equal to Sue. If we knew the authorID in advance of the UPDATE operation (possibly because we searched for the record previously), the WHERE clause could be simplified as follows:

```
WHERE AuthorID = 13
```

Figure 22.25 depicts the Authors table after we perform the UPDATE operation.

authorID	firstName	lastName
1	Harvey	Deitel
2	Paul	Deitel
3	Tem	Nieto
4	Kate	Steinbuhler
5	Sean	Santry
6	Ted	Lin
7	Praveen	Sadhu
8	David	McPhie
9	Cheryl	Yaeger
10	Marina	Zlatkina
11	Ben	Wiedermann
12	Jonathan	Liperi
13	Sue	Jones

Fig. 22.25   Table Authors after an UPDATE operation to change a row.

Common Programming Error 22.7

Failure to use a WHERE clause with an UPDATE statement could lead to logic errors, since it would update all *rows in the table.*

22.4.8 DELETE Statement

An SQL **DELETE** statement removes data from a table. The simplest form for a DELETE statement is:

```
DELETE FROM tableName WHERE criteria
```

where *tableName* is the table from which to delete a row (or rows). The WHERE clause specifies the criteria used to determine which row(s) to delete. For example, the DELETE statement:

```
DELETE FROM Authors
    WHERE lastName = 'Jones' AND firstName = 'Sue'
```

deletes the row for Sue Jones from the Authors table. Figure 22.26 shows the Authors table after we perform the DELETE operation.

Common Programming Error 22.8

Multiple rows may satisfy a WHERE clause's selection criteria. When deleting rows from a database, be sure to define a WHERE clause that matches only the rows to be deleted.

authorID	firstName	lastName
1	Harvey	Deitel
2	Paul	Deitel
3	Tem	Nieto
4	Kate	Steinbuhler
5	Sean	Santry
6	Ted	Lin
7	Praveen	Sadhu
8	David	McPhie
9	Cheryl	Yaeger
10	Marina	Zlatkina
11	Ben	Wiedermann
12	Jonathan	Liperi

Fig. 22.26 Table `Authors` after a DELETE operation to remove a row.

22.5 MySQL

In 1994, TcX, a Swedish consulting firm, needed a fast and flexible way to access its tables. Unable to find a database server that could accomplish the required task adequately, Michael Widenius, the principal developer at TcX, decided to create his own database server. The resulting product was called *MySQL* (pronounced "my ess cue ell"), a robust and scalable relational database management system (RDBMS).

MySQL is a multiuser, multithreaded (i.e., allows multiple simultaneous connections) RDBMS server that uses SQL to interact with and manipulate data. [*Note*: Please visit `www.deitel.com/books/iw3HTP3/index.html` for MySQL installation instructions and helpful MySQL commands for creating, populating and deleting tables.]

The MySQL Manual (`www.mysql.com/doc`) lists numerous features that characterize MySQL. A few important features include:

1. Multithreading capabilities that enable the database to perform multiple tasks concurrently, allowing the server to process client requests efficiently.

2. Support for various programming languages (C, C++, Java, Perl, PHP, ColdFusion, Python, etc.). Later chapters demonstrate how to access a MySQL database from Perl (Chapter 25), PHP (Chapter 26) and Python (Chapter 35).

3. Implementations of MySQL are available for Windows, Mac OS X, Linux and UNIX.

4. Full support of functions and operators within the SELECT and WHERE clauses of an SQL query that allow users to manipulate data.

5. The ability to access tables from different databases by using a single query, increasing the efficiency of retrieving accurate and necessary information.

6. The ability to handle large databases (e.g., tens of thousands of tables with millions of rows).

For these reasons, MySQL is becoming the database of choice for many businesses, universities and individuals. MySQL is an open-source software product. The term **open source** refers to software that can be freely obtained and customized to fulfill corporate, educational or personal requirements. [*Note*: Under certain situations, a commercial license is required for MySQL.]

22.6 Introduction to DBI

Databases have become a crucial part of **distributed applications**—programs that divide work across multiple computer systems. For instance, one computer might be responsible for managing a Web site and another for a database management system. A distributed application uses both computers to retrieve a result set from a database and display it on another computer—typically called a client.

Relational databases (e.g., MySQL, Microsoft Access, Oracle) have many different implementations. A software program, called a **driver**, helps programs access a database. Each database implementation requires its own driver, and each driver can have a different syntax. To simplify the use of multiple databases, an **interface** provides uniform access to all database systems. Various programming languages provide programmatic libraries (called **database interfaces**) for accessing relational databases. This section provides a brief overview of database interfaces for Perl, PHP and Python (each of which is covered in detail in Chapter 25, Chapter 26 and Chapter 35, respectively). Each of the chapters on these languages demonstrates the manipulation of MySQL databases.

22.6.1 Perl Database Interface

The Perl **Database Interface** (DBI) enables users to access relational databases from Perl programs. Database vendors create drivers that can receive interactions through DBI and process them in a database-specific manner. DBI is database independent, so it allows for easy migration from one DBMS to another. DBI is the most widely used interface available for database connectivity in Perl.

DBI uses object-oriented interfaces, known as **handles**. Figure 22.27 describes three different handle types—**driver handles**, **database handles** and **statement handles**. A driver handle can be used to create any number of database handles, and a database handle can be used to create any number of statement handles.

Data object handle	Description
Driver handle	Encapsulates the driver for the database; rarely used in a Perl script.
Database handle	Encapsulates a specific connection to a database; can send SQL statements to a database.
Statement handle	Encapsulates specific SQL statements and the results returned from them.

Fig. 22.27 Data object handles for Perl DBI.

22.6.2 PHP dbx module

In PHP, an XHTML-embedded scripting language, the database interface is referred to as a **dbx module**. The dbx module does not interact with a database directly. It interacts with one of several database-specific module, which performs the actual database operations. Currently, the dbx module supports MySQL, PostgreSQL, Microsoft SQL Server, Oracle, Sybase, FrontBase and ODBC (Open Database Connectivity) databases. [*Note*: ODBC is Microsoft's original generic API for relational database access.] The seven dbx functions are listed in Fig. 22.28.

dbx function	Description
dbx_connect	Opens a connection/database.
dbx_close	Closes an open connection/database.
dbx_error	Reports any error messages from the last function call in the module.
dbx_query	Executes a query and returns the results.
dbx_sort	Sorts a result by a custom sort function.
dbx_compare	Compares two rows and sorts them.
dbx_escape_string	Escapes a string for use in an SQL query.

Fig. 22.28   Data objects for PHP **dbx** modules.

22.6.3 Python DB-API

In Python, the database interface is referred to as **DB-API** (database application programming interface). The DB-API, which consists of **Connection data objects** and **Cursor data objects**, is portable across several databases. A Python programmer creates a Connection data object using connect(*parameters*), where database-dependent *parameters* specify options for the connection to the database. Connection data objects access the database through four methods: close, commit, rollback and cursor. Figure 22.29 describes these methods.

Connection method	Description
close	Closes the connection to the database.
commit	Commits a transaction (i.e., saves changes to the database).
rollback	Exits a pending transaction without saving changes.
cursor	Returns a new Cursor object for the current connection.

Fig. 22.29   Connection data object methods for Python DB-API.

The cursor method returns Cursor data objects, which manipulate and retrieve data. Figure 22.30 lists some of the methods and attributes that constitute Cursor data objects.

Cursor method	Description
rowcount	Returns the number of rows affected by the last execute method call.
close	Closes the Cursor object.
execute(operation)	Executes a database query or statement.
executemany(operation, parameters)	Executes a database query or statement against a set of parameters.
fetchone	Returns the next row of a query result.
fetchmany(size)	Returns a set of rows—defined in the parameter—from a query result.
fetchall	Returns all the rows of a query result.

Fig. 22.30 Some Cursor data object methods for Python-API.

22.7 ADO.NET Object Model

The **ADO.NET object model** provides an API for accessing database systems programmatically. ADO.NET was created for the .NET framework and is the next generation of ActiveX Data Objects (ADO), which was designed to interact with Microsoft's Component Object Model™ (COM) framework.

The primary namespaces (i.e., groups of classes) for ADO.NET are **System.Data**, **System.Data.OleDb** and **System.Data.SqlClient**. These namespaces contain classes for working with databases and other types of data sources (e.g., XML files). Namespace System.Data is the root namespace for the ADO.NET API. Namespaces System.Data.OleDb and System.Data.SqlClient contain classes that enable programs to connect with and modify data sources. Namespace System.Data.OleDb contains classes that are designed to work with any data source, whereas the System.Data.SqlClient namespace contains classes that are optimized to work with Microsoft SQL Server 2000 databases.

Instances of class **System.Data.DataSet**, which consist of a set of **DataTable**s and relationships among them, represent a **cache** of data—data that a program stores temporarily in local memory. The structure of a **DataSet** mimics the structure of a relational database. An advantage of using class DataSet is that it is **disconnected**—the program does not need a persistent connection to the data source to work with the data in a DataSet. The program connects to the data source only during the initial population of the DataSet and then to store any changes made in it. Hence, the program does not require any active, permanent connection to the data source.

Instances of class **OleDbConnection** of namespace System.Data.OleDb represent a connection to a data source. Instances of class **OleDbDataAdapter** connect to a data source through an instance of class OleDbConnection and can populate DataSets with data from a data source.

Instances of class **OleDbCommand** of namespace System.Data.OleDb represent an arbitrary SQL command to be executed on a data source. A program can use instances of class OleDbCommand to manipulate a data source through an OleDbConnection. The programmer must close the active connection to the data source explicitly once no further changes are to be made. Unlike `DataSets`, `OleDbCommand` objects do not cache data in local memory.

In this chapter, we have introduced database management systems, the relational database model, SQL, MySQL, DBI and ADO.NET. We will use these technologies throughout the remaining chapters of the book to build interactive, database-intensive Web applications.

22.8 Web Resources

Many database-related resources are available on the Web. This section lists a variety of database resources for SQL, MySQL and ADO.NET. It also provides a brief description of each database resource.

`www.sql.org`
The `sql.org` site is an online resource that provides a tutorial on the SQL programming language. It offers links to news groups, discussion forums, free software and various database vendors.

`www.mysql.com`
The MySQL site is maintained by *MySQL AB*, the company that promotes and provides the MySQL database. The site contains product information on the MySQL database, downloads, MySQL news and future development plans.

`www.microsoft.com/sql`
The *Microsoft SQL Server 2000 Web Site* contains product information, technical support, SQL news and tips on using the SQL Server to solve business problems.

`www.microsoft.com/sql/downloads/default.asp`
Offers tools for *Microsoft's SQL Server*.

`www.postgresql.org`
The *PostgreSQL* site discusses the history of the PostgreSQL database server. It contains HTTP and FTP mirror sites, technical support, a mailing list and a download page for this open-source database.

`www.interbase.com`
Discusses *InterBase*, an open-source database server developed by *Borland*. The site provides product downloads, technical support, InterBase news and certification programs.

`www.maverick-dbms.org`
Discusses the open-source database product, *MaVerick*. You can download the product, register for a mailing list and read recent articles pertaining to MaVerick.

`www.devshed.com`
The *Developer Shed* Web site provides numerous resources on open-source products, such as MySQL, Perl, Python and PHP. It also provides news, discussion forums and tutorials for server-side and client-side technologies.

`www.cql.com`
The *CQL++* site provides information on the CQL++ open-source database product and offers the product for download.

`leap.sourceforge.net`
LEAP is an open-source RDBMS, commonly used by students and teachers as an educational tool. The site contains a mailing list, forum, downloads and LEAP news.

`www.voicenet.com/~gray/Home.html`
The site for the *SQSH* database, which is an SQL shell for UNIX and Windows platforms. You can download the latest version of the product from this site.

`msdn.microsoft.com/library/devprods/vs6/vstudio/mdac200/mdac3sc7.htm`
The *Microsoft Data Access Components* (*MDAC*) *SDK Overview* site offers references to ADO, ODBC and other database-related technologies.

`www.w3schools.com/sql`
The *SQL School* Web site provides a tutorial on basic to advanced SQL commands. The site contains a short quiz that reinforces SQL concepts.

`www.sqlmag.com`
SQL Server Magazine is an excellent SQL resource. Subscribers receive monthly issues filled with articles on SQL design and information on current developments involving SQL. Certain articles are available for free at the Web site.

SUMMARY

- Database systems provide file-processing capabilities and organize data in a manner that facilitates sophisticated queries.

- The most popular style of database system on personal computers is the relational database.

- SQL (Structured Query Language) performs relational database queries.

- A database is an integrated collection of centrally controlled data.

- A database management system (DBMS) controls the storage and retrieval of data in a database.

- A distributed database is a database that is spread throughout a network's computer systems.

- A relational database is composed of tables.

- A table is composed of rows and columns

- Each table column represents a different data item.

- Select data from the table (SELECT in SQL) to create subsets. Table data can be combined with join operations.

- A table's primary key uniquely identifies each row in the table. Every row must have a value in the primary key—Rule of Entity Integrity—and the value must be unique.

- A foreign key is a column (or set of columns) in a table which must match the primary key of another table. The foreign key helps maintain the Rule of Referential Integrity—every value in a foreign key must appear in another table's primary key. Foreign keys enable information from multiple tables to be joined and presented to the user.

- A typical SQL query "selects" information from one or more tables in a database. Such selections are coded with the SELECT keyword. The simplest form of a query is

      SELECT * FROM *TableName*

in which the asterisk (*) indicates that all the columns from *TableName* should be selected. *TableName* specifies the table in the database from which the columns will be selected. To select specific columns from a table, replace the asterisk (*) with a comma-separated list of the column names to be selected.

- SQL uses the optional WHERE clause to specify the selection criteria for the query. The simplest query with selection criteria is

      SELECT * FROM *TableName* WHERE *criteria*

The condition in the WHERE clause can contain operators <, >, <=, >=, =, <> and LIKE. Operator LIKE matches a string using the wildcard characters asterisk (*) and question mark (?).

- Query results can be arranged in ascending or descending order using the optional ORDER BY clause. The simplest form of an ORDER BY clause is

      SELECT * FROM *TableName* ORDER BY *column* ASC
      SELECT * FROM *TableName* ORDER BY *column* DESC

  in which ASC specifies ascending (lowest to highest) order, DESC specifies descending (highest to lowest) order and *column* represents the column used for sorting purposes.

- Multiple columns can order data with an ORDER BY clause in the form

      ORDER BY *column1 SortingOrder*, *column2 SortingOrder*, ...

  in which *SortingOrder* is either ASC or DESC.

- The WHERE and ORDER BY clauses can be combined in one query.

- The query syntax *TableName.columnName* distinguishes between columns with the same name that reside in different tables.

- The basic form of an INSERT SQL statement is

      INSERT INTO *TableName* (*columnName1*, *columnName2*, ...)
      VALUES ('*value1*', '*value2*', ...)

  where *TableName* is the table in which the data will be inserted. Each column name to be updated is specified in a comma-separated list in parentheses. The value for each column is specified after the SQL keyword VALUES in another comma-separated list in parentheses.

- A basic UPDATE SQL statement has the form

      UPDATE *TableName*
      SET *columnName1* = *value1*, *columnName2* = *value2*, ...
      WHERE *criteria*

  in which *TableName* is the table to update. The individual columns to update are specified (followed by an equal sign and a new value in single quotes) after the SET keyword, and the WHERE clause determines what rows to update.

- Row(s) can be permanently deleted from an existing table by using the DELETE statement. The simplest form of a DELETE statement is

      DELETE FROM *TableName* WHERE *criteria*

  in which *TableName* is the table that contains the rows to be deleted, and the WHERE clause determines the rows to be deleted.

- MySQL is a scalable, robust and enterprise-level relational database management system (RDBMS). It provides multithreading capabilities, supports a variety of programming languages and handles large databases. MySQL is not a true open-source product.

- Most databases are distributed applications—programs that divide work among multiple computer systems.

- Database interfaces are programmatic libraries that allow various programming languages to access and interact with a database.

- In Perl, the database interface is referred to as DBI. The DBI objects are known as handles. The three different handle types are driver handles, database handles and statement handles.

- The PHP database interface is referred to as a dbx module. The dbx module does not interact with a database directly. It interacts with one of several database-specific modules, which performs the actual database operations.

- The Python database interface is referred to as DB-API (database application programming interface). It uses Connection data objects and Cursor data objects to access the database.

- The primary namespaces in ADO.NET are System.Data, System.Data.OleDb and System.Data.SqlClient.

- Instances of class OleDbConnection of namespace System.Data.OleDb represent a connection to a data source. Instances of class OleDbDataAdapter connect to a data source through an instance of class OleDbConnection and can populate DataSets with data from a data source.

- Instances of class OleDbCommand of namespace System.Data.OleDb represent an arbitrary SQL operation to be executed on a data source. A program can use instances of class OleDbCommand to manipulate a data source through an OleDbConnection.

TERMINOLOGY

* Microsoft Access SQL wildcard character	INNER JOIN operator
? Microsoft Access SQL wildcard character	INSERT statement
% SQL wildcard character	LIKE operator
_ SQL wildcard character	MySQL
ActiveX Data Objects .NET (ADO.NET)	OleDbCommand class
collection	OleDBConnection class
column	OleDbDataAdapter class
Connection data object	Open Database Connectivity (ODBC)
COUNT function	ORDER BY keyword
Cursor data object	primary key
data binding	query
data source	record set
database	relational database management
database handle	system (RDBMS)
database interface (DBI)	result set
database management system (DBMS)	rollback
DataSet in ADO.NET	row
DataTable in ADO.NET	rowcount
DB-API	Rule of Entity Integrity
dbx module	Rule of Referential Integrity
DELETE statement	SELECT keyword
distributed application	SET keyword
driver handle	statement handle
execute(*operation*)	Structured Query Language (SQL)
executemany(*operation*, *parameters*)	SQL (Structured Query Language)
fetchall	System.Data namespace
fetchmany(*size*)	System.Data.DataSet class
fetchone	System.Data.OleDb namespace
field	System.Data.SqlClient namespace
foreign key	table
FROM clause	TcX
qualified name	UPDATE statement
GROUP BY clause	WHERE clause
handle	wildcard character

SELF-REVIEW EXERCISES

22.1   Fill in the blanks in each of the following statements:
  a) The most popular database query language is _____.
  b) A(n) _____ is a column in a table which matches the primary key for another table.
  c) SQL keyword _____ is followed by the selection criteria that specify the rows to select in a query.
  d) A(n) _____ is an integrated collection of centrally controlled data.
  e) The Python database interface is referred to as _____ and is composed of _____ and _____ data objects.

22.2   State whether each of the following is *true* or *false*. If *false*, explain why.
  a) A foreign key uniquely identifies each row in a table.
  b) A distributed application divides tasks across multiple computer systems.
  c) A table in a database consists of rows and records.
  d) In PHP, the dbx module interfaces directly to the database.
  e) MySQL is a non-portable database that can be used only on the Windows platform.

ANSWERS TO SELF-REVIEW EXERCISES

22.1   a) SQL. b) foreign key. c) WHERE. d) database. e) DB-API, Connection, Cursor.

22.2   a) False. A primary key uniquely identifies each row in a table. b) True. c) False. A table in a database consists of rows and columns. A record is a row. d) False. The PHP dbx module does not interact with a database directly. It interacts with one of several database-specific modules, which performs the actual database operations. e) False. MySQL is a portable database that can execute on many platforms, including Windows, Mac OS X, Linux and UNIX. Moreover, it can execute with various programming languages, such as C, C++, Java, Perl, PHP, ColdFusion and Python.

EXERCISES

22.3   Define the following terms:
  a) Database handle.
  b) Qualified name.
  c) Open source.
  d) Rule of Referential Integrity.
  e) System.Data.

22.4   Define the following SQL keywords:
  a) ASC.
  b) COUNT.
  c) INSERT.
  d) LIKE.
  e) UPDATE.

22.5   Write SQL queries for the Books.mdb database (discussed in Section 22.3) that perform each of the following tasks:
  a) Select all authors from the Authors table.
  b) Select all publishers from the Publishers table.
  c) Select a specific author and list all books for that author. Include the title, year and ISBN number. Order the information alphabetically by title.
  d) Select a specific publisher and list all books published by that publisher. Include the title, year and ISBN number. Order the information alphabetically by title.

22.6   Write SQL statements for the `Books.mdb` database (discussed in Section 22.3) that perform each of the following tasks:
   a) Add a new author to the `Authors` table.
   b) Add a new title for an author (remember that the book must have an entry in the `Author-ISBN` table). Be sure to specify the publisher of the title.
   c) Add a new publisher.

22.7   Fill in the blanks in each of the following statements:
   a) MySQL is a robust and scalable _____.
   b) The _____ PHP module consists of seven functions that interface to the database module.
   c) ADO is an acronym for _____.
   d) An instance of the ADO.NET class _____ represents a connection to a data source.

22.8   Correct each of the following SQL operations that refer to the `Books.mdb` database.
   a) `SELECT firstName FROM Author WHERE authorID = 3`.
   b) `SELECT isbn, title FROM Titles ORDER WITH title DESC`.
   c) `INSERT INTO Authors ( authorID, firstName, lastName )`
      `VALUES ( "2", "Jane", "Doe" )`.
   d) `SELECT authorID, Titles.title, Titles.copyright,`
      `          Titles.isbn`
      `FROM Titles, Authors, AuthorISBN`
      `WHERE AuthorISBN.isbn = Titles.isbn`
      `AND ( authorID = 1 )`
      `ORDER BY Titles.title`.
   e) `UPDATE Publishers`
      `WITH publisherID = 4`
      `WHERE publisherName = 'Prentice Hall'`.

ASP.NET

Objectives

- To program ASP.NET pages using JScript .NET.
- To understand how ASP.NET pages work.
- To understand the differences between client-side scripting and server-side scripting.
- To create Web services.
- To use and manipulate XML files with ASP.NET.
- To understand Web forms and code-behind files.
- To be able to use session tracking in an ASP.NET application.
- To use ActiveX Data Objects .NET (ADO.NET) to access a database.

A client is to me a mere unit, a factor in a problem.
Sir Arthur Conan Doyle

Rule One: Our client is always right.
Rule Two: If you think our client is wrong, see Rule One.
Anonymous

Protocol is everything.
Francoise Giuliani

23.1 Introduction

Interactive Web pages are created with both client- and server-side scripting. This book has focused on client-side scripting up to this point. This and the next several chapters discuss server-side technologies, which are essential to programming Internet applications. Server-side scripting uses information sent by clients, information stored on the server, information stored in the server's memory and information from the Internet to dynamically create Web pages. This and the next chapter focus on **ASP.NET**, a server-side technology that dynamically builds documents (e.g., XHTML, text, XML) in response to client requests.

ASP.NET is a compiled .NET programming platform and technology that can be used on a server to create Web applications. ASP.NET takes advantage of Microsoft's .NET Framework, which provides thousands of classes that deal with XML, text input, validation of user input, image processing and more. ASP.NET also simplifies Web Services programming (discussed in Section 23.12). ASP.NET supports over 25 programming languages, including Visual Basic .NET, C# and JScript .NET.[1] This technology also features object-oriented programming and helps separate procedure from presentation.

The examples in this chapter illustrate how ASP.NET uses server and client information to create and send dynamic Web pages to clients. Examples include a program to dis-

---

1. "Why ASP.NET?," *ASP.NET Web: The Official Microsoft ASP.NET Site* <www.asp.net/ whitepaper/whyaspnet.aspx?tabindex=0&tabid=1>.

play the time and date on a Web server, a guest book, an address form, an advertisement rotator and a database application. Chapter 24 uses the techniques presented here to construct an online message forum using ASP.NET and XML. In addition, the CD includes two bonus chapters on ASP, the predecessor to ASP.NET. [*Note*: Throughout this chapter, ASP refers to the original Active Server Pages technology, whereas ASP.NET refers to the .NET version of Active Server Pages.]

23.2 .NET Overview

Before explaining ASP.NET, we must provide a general overview of the .NET platform. A key aspect of the .NET strategy is its independence from a specific programming language. Rather than forcing developers to use a single language, Microsoft enables developers to create .NET applications in any .NET-compatible language. This means that programmers can contribute to the same application, writing code in the .NET languages (such as Visual Basic .NET, Visual C++ .NET and C#) in which they are most proficient.

Learning to program using a .NET-compatible language is relatively simple, especially for experienced programmers. Visual Basic .NET, Visual C++ .NET and JScript .NET resemble their earlier versions, whereas the new language C# (pronounced "C sharp") incorporates aspects of C++ and Java.

The .NET strategy also promotes software reuse. Microsoft's .NET Framework (discussed in Section 23.2.1) includes tools for **porting**, or adapting, existing software components (such as those written in Visual Basic 6 or Visual C++ 6) to .NET. This minimizes the need to recreate existing software components. Developers can write new components in .NET-compatible languages, then assemble applications by combining existing and new components.

Web services, which are central to the .NET initiative, extend the concept of software reuse to the Internet by allowing developers to reuse software components that reside on another machine or platform. Employing Web services as reusable building blocks, programmers can concentrate on their specialties without having to implement every component of an application. For example, a company developing an e-commerce application can subscribe to Web services that process payments and authenticate users—this enables programmers to focus on other unique aspects of the e-commerce application.

23.2.1 .NET Framework

The Microsoft **.NET Framework** is at the heart of the .NET strategy. This framework manages and executes applications, provides a class library (called the **Framework Class Library**, or **FCL**), enforces security and supplies many other programming capabilities. The FCL contains reusable components that programmers can incorporate into their applications—this makes it unnecessary for programmers to create new software entirely from the ground up. Details of the .NET Framework are found in the **Common Language Infrastructure** (**CLI**). The CLI is now an ECMA International (originally, the European Computer Manufacturers Association) standard.[2] This allows independent software vendors to create the .NET Framework for other platforms. The .NET Framework exists only for the

---

2. More information on the CLI standard can be found at `www.ecma-international.org/publications/standards/Ecma-335.htm`.

Windows platform, but is being developed for other platforms as well. Microsoft's **Shared Source CLI** is an archive of source code that provides a subset of the Microsoft .NET Framework for Windows XP, FreeBSD[3] and Mac OS X 10.2. The source code in the Shared Source CLI is written to the ECMA International CLI standard. There are also other projects underway to provide the .NET Framework to other platforms. The Mono project (www.go-mono.com) provides a subset of the .NET Framework for the UNIX and Linux operating systems, and also runs on Windows. The DotGNU Portable .NET project (www.southern-storm.com.au/portable_net.html) provides software tools that enable programmers to write .NET applications on several operating systems (although it is targeted primarily at the Linux operating system).

Another central part of the .NET framework is the **Common Language Runtime** (**CLR**), which executes programs written in any .NET-compatible programming language. .NET programs are compiled in two steps. First, a program is compiled into **Microsoft Intermediate Language** (**MSIL**), which defines instructions for the CLR. Code translated into MSIL from multiple programming languages and sources can be woven together by the CLR. MSIL then is compiled into machine code for a specific platform. Because most platforms use different machine languages, compiling first to a common format such as MSIL increases portability between platforms and interoperability between languages. MSIL allows various platforms to support .NET and, at the same time, preserve separate methods of handling memory management, security and other details.

Microsoft also offers a version of the .NET Framework called the **.NET Compact Framework**. This version enables developers to create applications for limited-resource devices, such as mobile phones and PDAs. Applications built using the Compact Framework can run on any device that has the Compact Framework installed. Users download applications onto a device through a wireless Internet connection or a connection from a PC. Once downloaded to the device, many applications do not require an Internet connection.

23.2.2 ASP (Active Server Pages) .NET

ASP.NET, another integral part of the .NET initiative, is a technology for creating dynamic Web content marked up as HTML. ASP.NET developers can create multi-tier, database-intensive applications quickly by employing .NET's object-oriented languages and the FCL's **Web controls** (technically known as **ASP.NET server controls**). Web controls look like HTML elements but are designed specifically for ASP.NET applications. ASP.NET is a sophisticated technology that includes optimizations for performance, testing and security.

ASP.NET applications consist of several file types. The first type is **.aspx**, which we refer to as **ASPX files**. These files contain the graphical user interface of a page, and may also contain the logic of the page (in the form of scripts written in a .NET-compatible language). These scripts are usually separated from the portion of the ASPX file that defines the page's GUI. ASPX files often have a corresponding **code-behind file** that contains a class written in a .NET language, such as JScript .NET. This class includes initialization code, utility methods and other supporting code that provides the ASPX file's programmatic implementation. Code-behinds help separate the business logic code from the presen-

---

3. The FreeBSD project provides a freely available and open-source UNIX-like operating system that is based on UC Berkeley's *Berkeley System Distribution* (*BSD*). For more information on BSD, visit www.freebsd.org.

tation code, but are not required in an ASP.NET application. Code-behinds written in JScript .NET typically have an `.aspx.js` extension and are usually used in the middle tier of a three-tier Web-based application. Please refer to Chapter 21 for information on three-tier applications.

Every server control in an ASP.NET page is treated as an object and run on a server. An ASP.NET page gets compiled into Microsoft Intermediate Language (MSIL) by a .NET CLR compiler. Compiling improves the performance and load time of ASP.NET pages because the MSIL code is directly executed by the runtime.

The ASP.NET pages in this chapter demonstrate communication between clients and servers via the HTTP protocol of the Web. When a server receives a client's HTTP request, the server loads the document (or page) requested by the client. XHTML documents are **static documents**—all clients see the same content when the document is requested. ASP.NET is a Microsoft technology for sending the client **dynamic Web content**, including XHTML, Dynamic HTML, client-side scripts and Java applets (i.e., client-side Java programs that are embedded in a Web page). ASP.NET processes the request (which often includes interacting with a database) and returns the results to the client—normally in the form of an HTML document, but other data formats (e.g., images, binary data) can be returned. [*Note*: Throughout this chapter, we often refer to the documents produced by ASP.NET as HTML documents, rather than XHTML documents, because the code that ASP.NET generates to display server controls is not necessarily XHTML-compliant.]

Portability Tip 23.1

An ASP.NET page that generates pure HTML may be rendered by any client browser.

Software Engineering Observation 23.1

Developers must have installed the .NET Framework to code and test ASP.NET pages.

23.3 Setup

This chapter contains examples that require either Internet Information Services (IIS) 5 or 6 to execute. Before attempting to execute any example, you should make sure IIS is running (see Chapter 21).

Creating and viewing ASP.NET pages requires the Microsoft .NET Framework and the .NET Framework System Development Kit (SDK). The SDK provides tools, examples, reference files and tutorials helpful in building .NET applications. The Framework and the SDK are included on the CD-ROM accompanying this book. Please follow the instructions available on the CD-ROM to install the software.

To execute the chapter examples, we recommend creating a virtual directory named `deitel` on your computer (see Chapter 21). Copy all the `.aspx` files from the Chapter 23 examples directory (included on the CD-ROM that accompanies this book) to the physical directory referenced by the `deitel` virtual directory. Do not copy files from subdirectories in the Chapter 23 examples directory, however. We will use these subdirectories later. Create another directory beneath the `C:\Inetpub\wwwroot` home directory of your Web server named `images`. Copy all `.gif` (or any other graphic file extension) files to `images`.

To run the Web applications on a system that uses the NTFS file system, you must set proper security permissions for the folders that contain the ASP.NET pages. To determine which file system you are using, open Windows Explorer and right click the C: drive, then select **Properties**. In the dialog that appears, select the **General** tab. The file system will be displayed in the **File system:** field. If you are using the FAT32 file system, you do not need to change any security permissions. If you are using the NTFS file system, perform the following steps to configure the appropriate security permissions. In Explorer, right click the folder that contains the Web page or application. Select **Properties** and click the **Security** tab. Click **Add** and type in **ASPNET** in the **Select Users or Groups** dialog. Click **OK**, then exit the folder's **Properties** dialog. Figure 23.1 shows the security properties menu and the **Select Users or Groups** dialog.

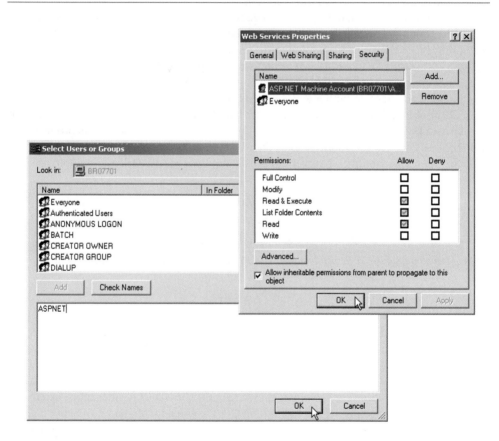

Fig. 23.1   Adding ASP.NET security permissions to a folder (on the NTFS file system).

In addition, ASP.NET virtual directories must be configured to run as applications under IIS. To configure a directory, open IIS (by running the **Internet Services Manager** from **Administrative Tools**, located in the Windows **Control Panel**) and navigate to the virtual directory that contains the ASP.NET page. Right click the directory and select **Properties**. Click the **Virtual Directory** tab, then click **Create** in the **Application Settings** portion of the **Virtual Directory** tab. Figure 23.2 shows the directory properties for a folder.

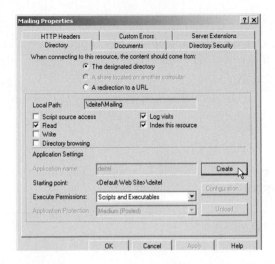

Fig. 23.2   Configuring a virtual directory as an application in IIS.

23.4 JScript .NET

In this chapter, we program ASP.NET pages using JScript .NET, the latest version of Microsoft's JScript scripting language. JScript .NET differs from both JScript and JavaScript in that it is a truly object-oriented language, whereas JScript and JavaScript are object-based, meaning that JScript .NET contains more functionality with regard to creating and using of objects. JScript .NET is backward compatible with JScript, however, and provides scripting features such as typeless programming. JScript .NET adheres to the ECMA-262 Edition 4 standard. Netscape's upcoming JavaScript 2.0 provides capabilities similar to Microsoft's JScript .NET, but it does not have the added .NET functionality. Using JScript .NET also provides access to the numerous classes found in the .NET FCL.

The advent of Web services and the increased demand for complex Web software (e.g., online banking systems) have made large, complex programs more prevalent on the Web. JScript .NET still looks like JavaScript but provides added features to simplify large-scale Web programming. JScript .NET provides classes, packages, typed variables and access to the .NET Framework.

Remember that introducing a new variable name in JavaScript implicitly declares a new variable. This implicit declaration can lead to subtle errors. Unlike the JavaScript shown in Chapters 7–12, JScript .NET enables programmers to declare the types of variables. It is good practice to declare the types of JScript variables before they are used. To specify a variable's type, place a `:`, followed by the *type* of the variable, after the variable declaration (e.g., `var number : int;`). Multiple variables can be declared in one `var` statement by separating each declaration with a comma:

```
var number : int, size : int;
```

This single line declares two integer variables: `number` and `size`.

We can also initialize variables and set the types of classes and objects when they are declared, as shown below:

```
var word = new StringBuilder() : StringBuilder;
```

This statement declares a variable word of type StringBuilder (a class provided by the FCL) and initializes it to a new StringBuilder object.

Performance Tip 23.1

Declaring variables and their types improves efficiency in JScript .NET.

23.5 A Simple ASP.NET Example

In this section, we present simple ASP.NET examples. The first example (Fig. 23.3) sends the Web server's time and date to the client as HTML markup.

```
1   <%@ Page Language="JScript" %>
2
3   <!-- Fig. 23.3: date.aspx        -->
4   <!-- A simple ASP.NET example -->
5
6   <!DOCTYPE html PUBLIC "-//W3C//DTD XHTML 1.1//EN"
7      "http://www.w3.org/TR/xhtml11/DTD/xhtml11.dtd">
8
9   <html xmlns = "http://www.w3.org/1999/xhtml">
10
11     <head>
12        <title>A Simple ASP.NET Example</title>
13        <style type = "text/css">
14           td        { background-color: black;
15                        color: yellow }
16           strong    { font-family: arial, sans-serif;
17                        font-size: 14pt; color: blue }
18           p         { font-size: 14pt }
19        </style>
20        <script runat = "server" language = "JScript">
21           var dayAndTime : DateTime = DateTime.Now;
22        </script>
23     </head>
24
25     <body>
26        <strong>A Simple ASP.NET Example</strong>
27        <p>
28           <table border = "6">
29              <tr>
30                 <td>  It is
31                    <% Response.Write( dayAndTime.ToShortTimeString() ); %>
32                 </td>
33
34                 <td> on
35                    <% Response.Write( dayAndTime.ToShortDateString() ); %>
36                 </td>
37              </tr>
38           </table>
```

Fig. 23.3   ASP.NET page that displays the time and date. (Part 1 of 2.)

```
39            </p>
40         </body>
41    </html>
```

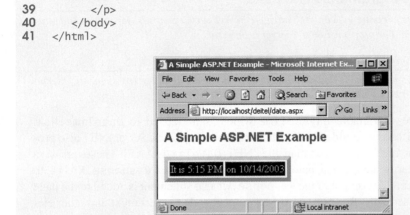

Fig. 23.3   ASP.NET page that displays the time and date. (Part 2 of 2.)

Note the **scripting delimiters <%** and **%>** (lines 31 and 35) wrapped around the JScript .NET code—these delimit the scripting code that is compiled and executed on the server, not the client. Scripts enclosed in scripting delimiters are not sent to the client. However, the scripting code inside delimiters can generate information that is sent to the client. Everything outside <% and %> is simply written to the client. Using the scripting delimiters allows programmers to dynamically output HTML to the client.

Common Programming Error 23.1
Missing the opening delimiter, <%, closing delimiter, %>, or both for server-side scripting code is an error.

Line 1 specifies settings (i.e., directives) that tell the compiler how to process the page. Directives are typically located at the top of an ASPX file. The **@ Page directive** specifies information needed by the CLR to process the file. The **Language** attribute specifies JScript .NET as the scripting language. This indicates which CLR compiler is needed to compile the scripting code. We only need to specify **"JScript"** as the name of the JScript .NET compiler. In this chapter, we use JScript .NET exclusively to develop our ASP.NET pages, although several other .NET-compatible languages may be used.

Good Programming Practice 23.1
When using JScript .NET code in an ASPX file, use the Language attribute of the @ Page directive to ensure that the code is compiled by the correct compiler.

Common Programming Error 23.2
The @ Page directive can appear only once in an ASP.NET file. By convention, the @ Page directive should appear at the top of a file, though it technically can be placed anywhere.

Lines 20–22 use a `script` element to insert JScript .NET code. Scripts in ASP.NET pages must be contained in `script` elements or within the scripting delimiters <% and %>. Attribute `runat` (line 20) with value `"server"` indicates that the script should be processed on the server. If the attribute `runat = "server"` is not included, the client tries to read the script, and unexpected results can arise.

Common Programming Error 23.3

Not including the `runat = "server"` *attribute in Web server controls, script tags and other items that should be processed on the server is an error.*

Good Programming Practice 23.2

In ASP.NET pages, methods and variables must be defined within `script` *elements. Executable code must be within* `<% %>` *blocks.*

Line 21 declares a variable `dayAndTime` which is initialized to `DateTime.Now`. **DateTime** is a .NET object provided in the .NET framework. [*Note*: JScript .NET also provides a `Date` class, but it is slower than the .NET `DateTime` class.] The expression `DateTime.Now` returns the current date and time. Line 31 uses **Response.Write** to output the current time. The output of the `Response.Write` statement is added to the page being processed. Essentially, `Response.Write` outputs code to create text and other elements to be displayed on the Web page. In this case, `Response.Write` outputs its argument `dayAndTime.ToShortTimeString()`. The method `ToShortTimeString` returns a string containing the hours, minutes and seconds corresponding to the time in a `DateTime` object.

Performance Tip 23.2

Using .NET Framework classes and libraries (e.g., `DateTime`*) instead of the objects provided by JScript .NET (e.g.,* `Date`*) improves performance in ASP.NET pages.*

Line 35 uses `Response.Write( dayAndTime.ToShortDateString() )` to output the month, the day of the month and the year of the `DateTime` object. Instead of using `Response.Write( dayAndTime.ToShortDateString() )`, we could have written

```
<% = dayAndTime.ToShortDateString() %>
```

to print out the date. The **<% = %>** construct outputs to the Web page the value that is written after the equal (=) sign. The `<% = %>` construct is commonly used to display single pieces of information. Similarly, line 31 could be changed to

```
<% = dayAndTime.ToShortTimeString() %>
```

to output the time.

Figure 23.4 shows the HTML generated by `Date.aspx` that is rendered in the client browser. This is what the user would see by selecting the **View** menu's **Source** command in Internet Explorer. As you can see, server-side scripts, unlike client-side scripts, are not viewable by the client.

```
1   <!-- Fig. 23.3: date.aspx      -->
2   <!-- A Simple ASP.NET example -->
3
4   <!DOCTYPE html PUBLIC "-//W3C//DTD XHTML 1.1//EN"
5     "http://www.w3.org/TR/xhtml11/DTD/xhtml11.dtd">
6
7   <html xmlns = "http://www.w3.org/1999/xhtml">
```

Fig. 23.4   HTML generated by Fig. 23.3. (Part 1 of 2.)

```
8
9     <head>
10       <title>A Simple ASP.NET Example</title>
11       <style type = "text/css">
12           td      { background-color: black;
13                     color: yellow }
14         strong    { font-family: arial, sans-serif;
15                     font-size: 14pt; color: blue }
16          p        { font-size: 14pt }
17       </style>
18
19     </head>
20
21     <body>
22       <strong>A Simple ASP.NET Example</strong>
23       <p>
24         <table border = "6">
25           <tr>
26             <td>
27                 It is 5:15 PM
28             </td>
29
30             <td>
31                 on 10/14/2003
32             </td>
33           </tr>
34         </table>
35       </p>
36     </body>
37   </html>
```

Fig. 23.4   HTML generated by Fig. 23.3. (Part 2 of 2.)

ASP.NET Objects

An ASP.NET application, when compiled, actually defines a class. Recall from Chapter 12 that a class contains variables and methods. The class inherits from class **Page**, provided by the .NET Framework. By inheriting from the **Page** class, the ASP.NET application gains access to several built-in objects that enable programmers to communicate with a Web browser, gather data sent by an HTTP request and distinguish between users. These objects exist in all ASP.NET pages. A programmer does not need to instantiate these objects as would be necessary for other objects. Figure 23.5 provides a brief description of the most commonly used ASP.NET objects.

Object Name	Description
Request	Used to access information passed by an HTTP request.
Response	Used to control the information sent to the client.
Server	Used to access methods and properties on the server.

Fig. 23.5   Commonly used ASP.NET objects.

The **Request object** is used to access the information passed by a *get* or *post* request. This information often consists of data provided by the user in an HTML form. The Request object provides access to information (such as cookies) that is stored on a client's machine. This object also provides access to binary information (e.g., a file upload). See Fig. 23.30 in Section 23.9 for a list of some of the Request object's properties. The **Response object** sends information, such as HTML and text, to the client. The **Server object** provides access to methods and properties on the server.

The Request, Response and Server objects that exist in ASP.NET possess functionality similar to their equivalents in ASP. In ASP.NET, however, these objects are defined as properties of the System.Web.HttpContext class.

23.6 Web Forms

ASPX files are usually referred to as **Web Forms** or **Web Form pages**, because they normally process form input. Data entered into a form can be sent to the server, processed, then sent back to the client in a different format. For example, an e-commerce site may use this to verify a customer's order information. The order information is entered into the form, then sent to the server for processing. Once the information is received, the server may return an order confirmation page, for verification purposes, that displays all the information the customer entered into the form. The first time a Web form is requested, the entire page is compiled. Later requests are served from the compiled page and do not have to be recompiled.

Technically, any text file with an .aspx extension is an ASP.NET Web Forms page. Any pure HTML page can be given an .aspx extension and run as an ASP.NET page. Web Forms contain blocks of code that are processed on the server. Including the attribute runat = "server" designates that the element should be processed by the server. Programmers customize Web Forms by adding Web controls, which include labels, text boxes, images, buttons and other GUI components. This is how the Web Form file (i.e., the ASPX file) specifies the appearance of the Web page that is sent to the client browser.

Web controls normally have the attribute runat = "server" and are included within an ASP.NET Web Form designated by the <form> tag, which also contains the attribute runat = "server". This form tag is similar to the one in XHTML except that ASP.NET's form tag does not require the attribute action or the attribute method; ASP.NET implicitly sets the form's action to the current ASP.NET page and method to "post" when the server processes the <form> tag. [*Note*: We include these optional attributes in our Web Forms examples to increase program clarity.] Each ASP.NET page can have at most one form.[4]

The <form> tag tells the server to process the form controls. Server controls on an ASP.NET Web Form persist data (i.e., maintain user input after the user leaves a page). Current Web pages that use XHTML forms alone rely on HTTP, which is **stateless**—each new request is considered separate from all other requests.

There are four different types of Web controls: **HTML server controls, Web server controls, validation controls** (also known as **validators**) and **user controls**. HTML controls are programmable HTML elements run on the server. Web server controls include form-like controls such as drop-down lists and text boxes. Validation controls are used with input controls; they provide the ability to check patterns, required fields, ranges and so on.

---

4. An exception to this rule occurs when ASP.NET applications are created for wireless devices, where multiple forms on a page are allowed.

User controls are controls created by the programmer, rather than provided by the FCL. Figure 23.6–Fig. 23.8 list some common Web controls.

HTML Server Control	Description
HtmlAnchor	Navigation link.
HtmlButton	Customizable input button.
HtmlTable	Programmatically built table.
HtmlInputFile	Handles uploading of files from client to server.
HtmlImage	Renders images.
HtmlForm	User-input form.

Fig. 23.6   HTML server controls.

Web Server Control	Description
AdRotator	Presents ad images and ad banners.
DataGrid	Displays tabular data and supports selecting, sorting and editing data.
TextBox	Enables user to enter text.
HyperLink	Creates a link to another document.
DropDownList	Provides a single-select drop-down list.
Calendar	Displays a month calendar from which users can select dates.

Fig. 23.7   Web server controls.

Server Control	Description
RequiredFieldValidator	Checks that the user does not leave a field blank.
CompareValidator	Compares an input value with another value. The value being compared to may be another control's input value.
RangeValidator	Checks that a user's entry is within a specified range.
RegularExpressionValidator	Checks that the entry matches a regular expression pattern.
ValidationSummary	Displays the validation errors for all the validation controls on a page.

Fig. 23.8   Validation server controls.

Using Basic Web Server Controls

Figure 23.9 is an ASPX page that uses a form element containing server controls <asp:TextBox>, <asp:RadioButtonList>, <asp:Button> and <asp:Label>. Recall that an ASPX page can contain only one <form runat = "server"> element.

```
1    <%@ Page Language="JScript" %>
2
3    <!DOCTYPE html PUBLIC "-//W3C//DTD XHTML 1.1//EN"
4       "http://www.w3.org/TR/xhtml11/DTD/xhtml11.dtd">
5
6    <!-- Fig. 23.9: name.aspx            -->
7    <!-- Another Simple ASP.NET example  -->
8
9    <html>
10      <head>
11         <title>Name Request</title>
12
13         <script language = "JScript" runat = "server">
14
15            function submitButton_Click(
16               sender : Object, events : EventArgs ) : void
17            {
18               if ( IsPostBack )
19               {
20                  if ( iceCream.SelectedItem == "Yes" )
21                  {
22                     message.Text = name.Text + " likes ice cream.";
23                  }
24                  else
25                  {
26                     message.Text = name.Text + " does not like ice cream.";
27                  }
28               }
29
30            } // end submitButton_Click
31         </script>
32      </head>
33
34      <body>
35         <form action = "name.aspx" method = "post" runat = "server">
36
37            Name: <asp:TextBox id = "name" runat = "server"/>
38
39            <br />
40            Do you like ice cream?
41
42            <asp:RadioButtonList id = "iceCream" runat = "server">
43               <asp:ListItem>Yes</asp:ListItem>
44               <asp:ListItem>No</asp:ListItem>
45            </asp:RadioButtonList>
46
47            <asp:Button text = "Submit" OnClick = "submitButton_Click"
48               runat = "server"/>
49
50            <br />
51            <center>
52               <h1> <asp:Label id = "message" runat = "server"/> </h1>
53            </center>
```

Fig. 23.9   ASP.NET page that processes user input. (Part 1 of 2.)

```
54
55            </form>
56        </body>
57    </html>
```

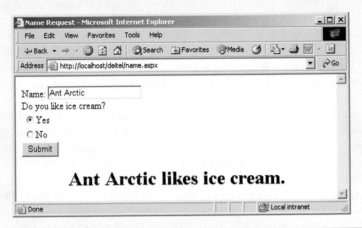

Fig. 23.9   ASP.NET page that processes user input. (Part 2 of 2.)

Lines 35–55 define a form composed of server controls. Line 35 specifies the value name.aspx (the current page) for the action attribute. ASPX pages usually contain a form that, when submitted, causes the current page to be requested again. This event is known as a **postback**. Note that all the server controls and the form contain the attribute runat = "server" to designate that these components should be processed by the server. Line 37 creates a text box, lines 42–45 create Yes and No radio buttons, lines 47–48 create a button and line 52 creates a label. Some of the controls contain an **id** attribute, used to specify a name for the control. Although these controls resemble the controls used in regular XHTML, keep in mind that they are actually objects that contain additional data and methods. These controls are created using the prefix asp, indicating that they are ASP.NET Web controls. They are actually created as objects on the server. Each object's type is specified by the text following the asp and colon (:) in that control's tag. Line 37, for instance, causes an object of type TextBox to be created on the server. This object's variables and methods can later be used to modify the page.

The button in lines 47–48 has the attribute OnClick = "submitButton_Click" to specify that when this button is clicked, the function submitButton_Click (lines 15–30) is called. This function is known as an **event handler**, because it executes in response to an action (called an **event**). In this case, the event is the clicking of a button. The action attribute of the form element indicates the .aspx file to which the form information is posted. The form's action attribute specifies that the form is to be posted to itself. [*Note*: Specifying the attributes action and method is optional in ASP.NET because the form is marked runat = "server". ASP.NET sets the action attribute to the current page and the method attribute to post by default. We include them here to increase program clarity.]

Lines 13–31 define a script. The script is written in JScript .NET and is processed by the server. We declare a function submitButton_Click that is passed two parameters: sender of type Object and events of type EventArgs. Parameter sender references the object that triggers the function, and parameter `events` contains any event parameters that accompany the `object`. In this example, we do not use the parameters. The function `submitButton_Click` does not return a value; it only modifies the text in the `message` server control (defined in line 52). Thus we declare the function to be of type `void` (line 14).

The first `if` statement (lines 18–28) determines whether the page is being loaded on a postback. **`IsPostBack`** returns a value indicating whether the page is being loaded in response to a client postback (in which case it will return the value `true`), or if it is being loaded and accessed for the first time (in which case it will return the value `false`). `IsPostBack` is a **property**. A property is a member of a class that contains functionality to *get* (retrieve) or *set* (assign a value to) a piece of data. In .NET, any class can have properties. The syntax to access a property of an object is the same as for accessing a variable of an object. The attributes of a Web control can be accessed in JScript .NET as properties of that object. We will demonstrate several properties defined in the FCL throughout this chapter.

If the page is not being loaded for the first time (i.e., `IsPostBack` returns the value `true`), the function continues with the `if...else` statement in lines 20–27. Line 20 checks the value returned from `iceCream`'s `SelectedItem` property. Recall that object `iceCream` (of type `RadioButtonList`) was created in lines 42–45. `RadioButtonList` objects contain a **`SelectedItem`** property which returns the item selected by the user (in the form of a `ListItem` object). The `Text` property of the `ListItem` is then used to access the text displayed in the selected item. If the text equals `"Yes"`, line 22 executes. If the text does not equal `"Yes"` (as occurs when the user selects **No**), line 26 executes. Lines 22 and 26 display the appropriate output based on the user's selection. Note how output is displayed on each line. On the right side of the =, variable `Text` of object `name` (the `TextBox` created in line 37) returns the name entered by the user. The name is then concatenated (using the +) with the text `" likes ice cream."` or `" does not like ice cream."`. The concatenated text is then assigned to `message`'s `Text` property. This assignment causes the text to be displayed in `Label message`, created in line 37.

Clicking the button submits the form and causes the page to be reloaded. As mentioned earlier, this is called a postback. When a postback occurs, the input parameters accompanying the request are exposed to ASP.NET scripts. This allows the values returned from the `SelectedItem` and `Text` properties to be accessed. The page is then updated, and the server controls maintain any client-entered values between trips to the server.

Using Validators

The example in Fig. 23.10 adds validation controls to the `name.aspx` example. We use a **required field validator** and a **range validator**. A required field validator ensures that a field receives input. In this example, a required field validator is attached to the `name` text box (lines 43–48). A range validator checks that input is within a specified range. In this example, we attach a range validator to the `scoops` text box (lines 70–77).

```
1    <%@ Page Language="JScript" %>
2
3    <!DOCTYPE html PUBLIC "-//W3C//DTD XHTML 1.1//EN"
4        "http://www.w3.org/TR/xhtml11/DTD/xhtml11.dtd">
5
```

Fig. 23.10 Validation controls used in a Web Form. (Part 1 of 3.)

```
6    <!-- Fig. 23.10: validation.aspx  -->
7    <!-- ASP.NET validation example    -->
8
9    <html>
10      <head>
11         <title>Validate Fields</title>
12
13         <script language = "JScript" runat = "server">
14
15            function submitButton_Click(
16               sender : Object , events : EventArgs ) : void
17            {
18               if ( IsPostBack )
19               {
20                  if ( iceCream.SelectedItem == "Yes" )
21                  {
22                     message.Text = name.Text + " likes ice cream.";
23                  }
24                  else
25                  {
26                     message.Text = name.Text + " does not like ice cream.";
27                  }
28               }
29
30            } // end submitButton_Click
31         </script>
32      </head>
33
34      <body>
35         <form action = "validation.aspx" method = "post" runat = "server">
36
37            <table>
38               <tr>
39                  <td>
40                     Name: <asp:textbox id = "name" runat = "server"/>
41                  </td>
42                  <td>
43                     <asp:RequiredFieldValidator id = "required"
44                        ControlToValidate = "name"
45                        Display = "Static"
46                        runat = "server">
47                        Please enter your name.
48                     </asp:RequiredFieldValidator>
49                  </td>
50               </tr>
51            </table>
52
53            <br />
54            Do you like ice cream?
55
56            <asp:RadioButtonList id = "iceCream" runat = "server">
57               <asp:ListItem>Yes</asp:ListItem>
58               <asp:ListItem>No</asp:ListItem>
```

Fig. 23.10 Validation controls used in a Web Form. (Part 2 of 3.)

```
59              </asp:RadioButtonList>
60
61              <br />
62              How many scoops would you like? (0-45)
63
64              <asp:TextBox id = "scoops" runat = "server" />
65
66              <br />
67              <asp:button text = "Submit" OnClick = "submitButton_Click"
68                 runat = "server"/>
69
70              <asp:RangeValidator
71                 ControlToValidate = "scoops"
72                 MinimumValue = "0"
73                 MaximumValue = "45"
74                 Type = "Integer"
75                 EnableClientScript = "false"
76                 Text = "We cannot give you that many scoops."
77                 runat = "server" />
78
79              <center>
80                 <h1> <asp:label id = "message" runat = "server"/> </h1>
81              </center>
82
83          </form>
84       </body>
85   </html>
```

Fig. 23.10   Validation controls used in a Web Form. (Part 3 of 3.)

Lines 37–51 create a table which has one row and two cells. The first cell (lines 39–41) holds the name text box. The second cell (line 42–49) contains the RequiredField-Validator control.

The RequiredFieldValidator (lines 43–48) contains the attributes id (which defines the name of the validator control), ControlToValidate (which indicates the control whose input will be validated), Display (which sets the display behavior for the validation control) and runat = "server" (which specifies that this control should be processed by the server). Legal Display attribute values are None, Static and Dynamic. Specifying Static causes the control to display an error message if validation fails. With this setting, space is reserved on the page for the message even if the input is valid. The error message (if necessary) is written between the RequiredFieldValidator opening and closing tags (line 47). The attribute value Dynamic makes the control behave the same as Static does, except that space is not reserved for the error message if no error occurs. With a value of None for Display, no error message is displayed on the page, but an error is still recorded in a log.

Several attributes control the behavior of the RangeValidator (lines 70–77): ControlToValidate indicates the id of the server control to validate; MinimumValue specifies the smallest allowed input; MaximumValue specifies the largest allowed input; Type indicates the input's allowed data type; EnableClientScript is a boolean value that specifies whether client-side validation (where the validation occurs on the client machine before the form is submitted) is enabled or not; Text is the message that is displayed when validation fails; and `runat` specifies that this control is a server control. The `RangeValidator` is associated with the `scoops` text box, expects an integer in the range 0–45 and displays the message `"We cannot give you that many scoops."` if validation fails.

If neither the `RequiredFieldValidator` nor the `RangeValidator` is satisfied (i.e., a required field has not been given input and/or a value is out of range), the server will not process *any* of the input when the user clicks **Submit**. However, if the required field (`name`) is filled but the value in `scoops` is not within the correct range, the form will process the valid input. Sample validation error messages are shown in Fig. 23.11. Figure 23.12 shows a page that passes the two validation controls.

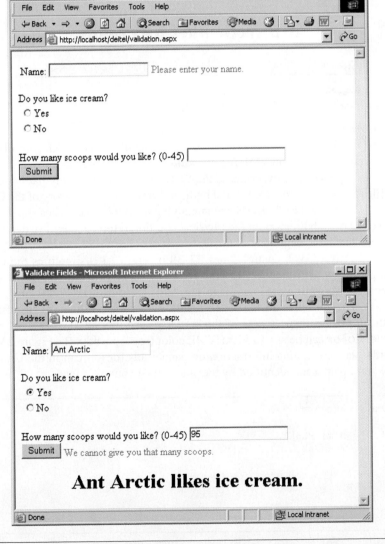

Fig. 23.11 Validation error output.

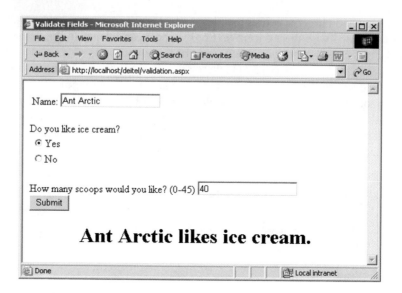

Fig. 23.12   Valid page without validation errors.

Using AdRotators

This section modifies the validation example to use an AdRotator Web control. Using advertisement data located in an XML file, the **AdRotator** control randomly selects an image to display, then generates a hyperlink to the Web page associated with that image.

All files for this example are located in the AdRotator subdirectory of the Chapter 23 examples directory on the CD-ROM accompanying the book. These files should be copied to an AdRotator subdirectory in the physical location referenced by the deitel virtual directory created at the beginning of this chapter.

The AdRotator Web control (lines 37–38 of Fig. 23.13) simplifies the creation of advertising banners. Attribute **AdvertisementFile** specifies an XML file that contains advertisement information (i.e., an image file, URL, alternate text and relative frequency for each ad). The attributes BorderColor and BorderWidth (line 38) specify the color and width (in pixels), respectively, of the border placed around the displayed banner ad. The BorderColor can be any valid XHTML color (see Appendix B). Figure 23.14 shows the file ads.xml containing information on banner ads for tourism in the United States, Germany and Spain, each identified by the appropriate country's flag.

```
1    <%@ Page Language="JScript" %>
2
3    <!DOCTYPE html PUBLIC "-//W3C//DTD XHTML 1.1//EN"
4       "http://www.w3.org/TR/xhtml11/DTD/xhtml11.dtd">
5
6    <!-- Fig. 23.13: adRotator.aspx  -->
7    <!-- ASP.NET AdRotator example  -->
8
9    <html>
```

Fig. 23.13   AdRotator control used in a Web Form. (Part 1 of 3.)

```
10      <head>
11         <title>Using An AdRotator</title>
12
13         <script language = "JScript" runat = "server">
14
15            function submitButton_Click(
16               sender : Object, events : EventArgs ) : void
17            {
18               if ( IsPostBack )
19               {
20                  if ( iceCream.SelectedItem == "Yes" )
21                  {
22                     message.Text = name.Text + " likes ice cream.";
23                  }
24                  else
25                  {
26                     message.Text = name.Text + " does not like ice cream.";
27                  }
28               }
29
30            } // end submitButton_Click
31         </script>
32      </head>
33
34      <body>
35         <form action = "adRotator.aspx" method = "post" runat = "server">
36
37            <asp:AdRotator AdvertisementFile = "ads.xml"
38               BorderColor = "black" BorderWidth = "1" runat = "server"/>
39
40            <table>
41               <tr>
42                  <td>
43                     Name: <asp:textbox id = "name" runat = "server"/>
44                  </td>
45                  <td>
46                     <asp:RequiredFieldValidator id = "required"
47                        ControlToValidate = "name"
48                        Display = "Static"
49                        runat = "server">
50                        Please enter your name.
51                     </asp:RequiredFieldValidator>
52                  </td>
53               </tr>
54            </table>
55
56            <br />
57            Do you like ice cream?
58
59            <asp:RadioButtonList id = "iceCream" runat = "server">
60               <asp:ListItem>Yes</asp:ListItem>
61               <asp:ListItem>No</asp:ListItem>
62            </asp:RadioButtonList>
```

Fig. 23.13 AdRotator control used in a Web Form. (Part 2 of 3.)

```
63
64                    <br />
65                    How many scoops would you like? (0-45)
66
67                    <asp:TextBox id = "scoops" runat = "server" />
68
69                    <br />
70                    <asp:button text = "Submit" OnClick = "submitButton_Click"
71                       runat = "server"/>
72
73                    <asp:RangeValidator
74                       ControlToValidate = "scoops"
75                       MinimumValue = "0"
76                       MaximumValue = "45"
77                       Type = "Integer"
78                       EnableClientScript = "false"
79                       Text = "We cannot give you that many scoops."
80                       runat = "server" />
81
82                    <center>
83                       <h1> <asp:label id = "message" runat = "server"/> </h1>
84                    </center>
85
86                 </form>
87             </body>
88      </html>
```

Fig. 23.13 AdRotator control used in a Web Form. (Part 3 of 3.)

```
1     <?xml version = "1.0" ?>
2
3     <!-- Fig. 23.14: ads.xml    -->
4     <!-- Flag database          -->
5
6     <Advertisements>
7
8        <Ad>
9           <ImageUrl>images/unitedstates.png</ImageUrl>
10          <NavigateUrl>http://www.usa.worldweb.com/</NavigateUrl>
11          <AlternateText>US Tourism</AlternateText>
12          <Impressions>80</Impressions>
13       </Ad>
14
15       <Ad>
16          <ImageUrl>images/germany.png</ImageUrl>
17          <NavigateUrl>http://www.germany-tourism.de/</NavigateUrl>
18          <AlternateText>German Tourism</AlternateText>
19          <Impressions>80</Impressions>
20       </Ad>
21
22       <Ad>
23          <ImageUrl>images/spain.png</ImageUrl>
```

Fig. 23.14 XML data for the AdRotator control. (Part 1 of 2.)

```
24          <NavigateUrl>http://www.tourspain.es/</NavigateUrl>
25          <AlternateText>Spanish Tourism</AlternateText>
26          <Impressions>80</Impressions>
27     </Ad>
28
29  </Advertisements>
```

Fig. 23.14 XML data for the `AdRotator` control. (Part 2 of 2.)

This XML document contains the information for each advertisement to be presented in the advertising banner. The `AdRotator` displays a random advertisement each time the page is visited. Each `Ad` element in the XML document contains information about an advertisement. The `ImageUrl` element specifies the picture that will appear in the banner. The `NavigateUrl` element specifies the URL to link to if the user clicks the ad. The `AlternateText` element specifies alternate text for the image. Finally, `Impressions` specifies the display rate in percentage of Web page hits. An ad with a relatively high `Impressions` value will be shown more often than an ad with a low value. In Fig. 23.14, all the Ads have the same `Impressions` value, so each Ad will have the same chance of being displayed. Figure 23.15 displays the output of this application. Refreshing the page causes a flag to be selected at random. This flag may or may not be the same as the flag previously displayed.

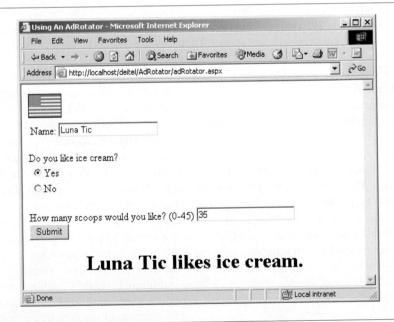

Fig. 23.15 ASPX page with an `AdRotator`.

23.7 Session Tracking

Originally, critics accused the Internet and e-business of failing to provide the kind of customized service typically experienced in brick-and-mortar stores. To address this problem, e-businesses began to establish mechanisms by which they could personalize users' browsing experiences, tailoring content to individual users while enabling them to bypass irrelevant information. Businesses achieve this level of service by tracking each customer's movement through the Internet and combining the collected data with information provided by the consumer, including billing information, personal preferences, interests and hobbies.

Personalization makes it possible for e-businesses to communicate effectively with their customers and also improves users' ability to locate desired products and services. Companies that provide content of particular interest to certain users can establish relationships with them and build on those relationships over time. Furthermore, by targeting consumers with personal offers, advertisements, promotions and services, e-businesses create customer loyalty. At such Web sites as MSN.com and CNN.com, sophisticated technology allows visitors to customize home pages to suit their individual needs and preferences. Similarly, online shopping sites often store personal information for customers and target them with notifications and special offers tailored to their interests. Such services can create customer bases that visit sites more frequently and make purchases from those sites more regularly.

A trade-off exists, however, between personalized e-business service and protection of **privacy**. Whereas some consumers embrace the idea of tailored content, others fear that the release of information that they provide to e-businesses or that is collected about them by tracking technologies will have adverse consequences on their lives. Consumers and privacy advocates ask: What if the e-business to which we give personal data sells or gives that information to another organization without our knowledge? What if we do not want our actions on the Internet—a supposedly anonymous medium—to be tracked and recorded by unknown parties? What if unauthorized parties gain access to sensitive private data, such as credit-card numbers or medical history? All these are questions that must be debated and addressed by consumers, e-businesses and lawmakers alike.

To provide personalized services to consumers, e-businesses must be able to recognize clients when they request information from a site. As we have discussed, the request/response model on which the Web operates is facilitated by HTTP. Unfortunately, HTTP is a stateless protocol—it does not support persistent connections that would enable Web servers to maintain state information regarding clients. This means that Web servers have no capacity to determine whether a request comes from a specific client or whether the same or different clients have generated a series of requests. To circumvent this problem, sites such as MSN.com and CNN.com provide mechanisms that identify individual clients. A **session ID** represents a unique client on the Internet. If the client leaves a site and returns later, the client will still be recognized as the same user. To help the server distinguish among clients, each client must identify itself to the server. The tracking of individual clients, known as **session tracking**, can be achieved in a number of ways. One popular technique involves the use of cookies (Section 23.7.1); another employs .NET's HttpSessionState object (Section 23.7.2). Additional session-tracking techniques include the use of input form elements of type "hidden" and URL rewriting. Using "hidden" form elements, a Web Form can write session-tracking data into a form in the Web page that it returns to the client in response to a prior request. When the user submits the form in the new Web page, all the form data, including the "hidden" fields, is sent to the form handler on the Web server. When a Web site employs URL rewriting, the Web Form embeds session-tracking information directly in the URLs of hyperlinks that the user clicks to send subsequent requests to the Web server.

23.7.1 Cookies

A popular way to customize interactions with Web pages is via cookies. Recall from Chapter 12 that a cookie is a text file stored by a Web site on an individual's computer that allows the site to track the individual's actions. The user's computer receives a cookie the first time the user visits the Web site; this cookie is then reactivated each time the user revisits the site. The collected information is intended to be an anonymous record containing data that are used to personalize the user's future visits to the site. For example, cookies in a shopping application might store unique identifiers for users. When a user adds items to an online shopping cart or performs another task resulting in a request to the Web server, the server receives a cookie containing the user's unique identifier. The server then uses the unique identifier to locate the shopping cart and perform any necessary processing.

In addition to identifying users, cookies also can indicate their shopping preferences. When a Web Form receives a request from a client, the Web Form could examine the cookie(s) it sent to the client during previous communications, identify the client's preferences and immediately display products that are of interest to the client.

Every HTTP-based interaction between a client and a server includes a header containing information either about the request (when the communication is from the client to the server) or about the response (when the communication is from the server to the client). When a Web Form receives a request, the header includes information such as the request type (e.g., GET) and any cookies that have been sent previously from the server to be stored on the client machine. When the server formulates its response, the header information includes any cookies the server wants to store on the client computer and other information, such as the MIME type of the response.

If the programmer of a cookie does not set an **expiration date**, the Web browser maintains the cookie for the duration of the browsing session. Otherwise, the Web browser maintains the cookie until the expiration date occurs. When the browser requests a resource from a Web server, cookies previously sent to the client by that Web server are returned to the Web server as part of the request formulated by the browser. Cookies are deleted when they expire. The expiration date of a cookie can be set in the cookie's **Expires** property.

The next Web application demonstrates the use of cookies. The Web page displays a message based on the last time the user visited the Web page. If the user has not visited the page within the last day, the page displays the message

```
This is the first time that you have visited this site today.
```

If a cookie is found indicating that the user has visited the site within the last day, the page outputs the time and date of the user's last visit. Figure 23.16 shows the Web Form code and sample output.

```
1    <%@ Page Language="JScript" Debug="true" %>
2
3    <!-- Fig. 23.16: cookie.aspx -->
4    <!-- Records last visit        -->
5
6    <html>
7       <head>
```

Fig. 23.16 Using cookies to track page visits. (Part 1 of 2.)

```
 8          <title> Simple Cookies </title>
 9
10       <script runat = "server">
11
12          function Page_Load( object : Object, events : EventArgs )
13          {
14             var lastVisit : String;
15
16             if ( Request.Cookies( "visit" ) == null )
17             {
18                welcome.Text = "This is the first time that " +
19                   "you have visited this site today";
20             }
21             else
22             {
23                lastVisit = Request.Cookies( "visit" ).Value;
24                welcome.Text = "You last visited the site at " +
25                   lastVisit + ".";
26             }
27
28             var time : DateTime = DateTime.Now;
29             Response.Cookies( "visit" ).Value = time.ToString();
30             Response.Cookies( "visit" ).Expires = time.AddDays( 1 );
31
32          } // end Page_Load
33       </script>
34    </head>
35    <body>
36       <form runat = "server">
37          <asp:label id = "welcome" runat = "server"/>
38       </form>
39    </body>
40 </html>
```

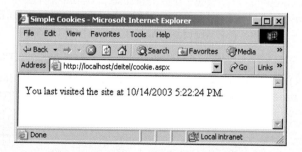

Fig. 23.16   Using cookies to track page visits. (Part 2 of 2.)

This page begins with a slightly modified @ Page directive. The attribute Debug="true" (line 1) instructs the ASP.NET compiler to enable script debugging to help pinpoint errors in code. Only one programmer-defined function appears in this script, the **Page_Load** event handler (lines 12–32). This function executes when the page loads. The function contains an if...else statement (lines 16–26) that attempts to read an existing cookie and display its value on the page. Line 16 uses the **Cookies** property of the Request object to determine whether a cookie with the name "visit" exists. If such a cookie exists, it will be returned as an object of type **HttpCookie**. Class HttpCookie contains various properties that can be used to manipulate cookies (Fig. 23.17). If no "visit" cookie is found, null is returned and lines 18–19 update the label welcome to display on the Web page that this is the user's first visit to the site on that day. The cookie will be absent if the user has never visited the page before, or if the cookie has expired. The expiration date of the cookie created in this example is set to one day in the future, so a cookie will only be present within one day of the user's last visit. If a cookie named "visit" does exist, line 23 accesses the cookie's value (via the **Value** property) and assigns the result to string lastVisit (created in line 14). The first time this page is accessed, the cookie has not yet been created, so lines 18–19 will be executed. The function will then continue in lines 28–30. Line 28 obtains the current date and time (using the expression DateTime.Now) and assigns this value to time. Line 29 then assigns the string representation of this value to the "visit" cookie. The ToString method converts a date and time to a readable string format. If the cookie has not yet been created, it will be created at this time. If the cookie already exists, its value will be updated with the current time. Line 30 changes the cookie's expiration date to one day in the future by calling the DateTime class's AddDays method.

Property	Description
Domain	Returns a String containing the cookie's domain (i.e., the domain of the Web server from which the cookie was downloaded). This determines which Web servers can receive the cookie. By default, cookies are sent to the Web server that originally sent them to the client.
Expires	Returns a DateTime object indicating when the browser can delete the cookie.
Name	Returns a String containing the cookie's name.
Path	Returns a String containing the URL prefix for the cookie. Cookies can be "targeted" to specific URLs that include directories on the Web server, enabling the programmer to specify the location of the cookie. By default, a cookie is returned to services operating in the same directory as the service that sent the cookie or a subdirectory of that directory.
Secure	Returns a Boolean value indicating whether the cookie should be transmitted through a secure protocol. The value True causes a secure protocol to be used.
Value	Returns a String containing the cookie's value.

Fig. 23.17 HttpCookie properties.

23.7.2 Session Tracking with HttpSessionState

In the previous section, we demonstrated session tracking using cookies. .NET also provides session-tracking capabilities in the Framework Class Library's **HttpSessionState** class. Figure 23.18 list some common HttpSessionState properties.

Property	Description
Count	Specifies the number of key-value pairs in the `Session` object.
IsNewSession	Indicates whether this is a new session (i.e., whether the session was created during loading of this page).
IsReadOnly	Indicates whether the `Session` object is read only.
Keys	Returns an object containing the `Session` object's keys.
SessionID	Returns the session's unique ID.
Timeout	Specifies the maximum number of minutes during which a session can be inactive (i.e., no requests are made) before the session expires. By default, this property is set to 20 minutes.

Fig. 23.18   `HttpSessionState` properties.

The next Web application (Fig. 23.19–Fig. 23.20) demonstrates session tracking. The example contains two pages. In the first page, users select their favorite programming language from a group of radio buttons, then submit the HTML form to the Web server for processing. The files for this example are located in the `Sessions` subdirectory in the Chapter 23 examples directory. To be able to run the examples, please copy the `Sessions` directory to the physical directory referenced by the `deitel` virtual directory created earlier in this chapter.

Every Web Form includes an `HttpSessionState` object, which is accessible through property **Session** of class `Page`. Throughout this section, we use property `Session` to manipulate our page's `HttpSessionState` object. When the Web page is requested, an `HttpSessionState` object is created and assigned to the `Page`'s `Session` property. We often refer to property `Session` as the `Session` object.

Software Engineering Observation 23.2

A Web Form must not use instance variables to maintain client state information, because clients accessing the Web Form in parallel might overwrite the shared instance variables. Web Forms should maintain client state information in `HttpSessionState` objects, because such objects are specific to each client.

The Web page then allows the user either to select another programming language or to view the second page in the application, which lists recommended books pertaining to the programming language that the user selected previously. When the user clicks the hyperlink, the `HttpSessionState` previously stored on the client is read and used to form the list of book recommendations.

The first page of this two-page Web site is shown in Fig. 23.19. Line 2 imports the namespace `System`. Classes of related components provided by the .NET Framework are organized and grouped together into **namespaces**. An `Import` statement makes .NET classes readily available by allowing a programmer to use a class name without specifying the namespace in front of it. To import namespaces in an `.aspx` file, we use the `@ Import` directive with an attribute `Namespace` to specify the namespace to import.

The `.aspx` file in Fig. 23.19 contains four radio buttons (lines 95–100) with values `C#`, `C++`, `C` and `Python`. The user selects a programming language by clicking one of the radio

buttons. The page also contains a **Submit** button, which, when clicked, calls
`submitButton_Click`. The `submitButton_Click` event handler (lines 62–79) stores
the user selections in the `Session` object.

```
1    <%@ Page Language="JScript" %>
2    <%@ Import Namespace="System" %>
3
4    <%-- Fig. 23.19: optionsPage.aspx                        --%>
5    <%-- Page that presents a list of language options. --%>
6
7    <!DOCTYPE html PUBLIC "-//W3C//DTD XHTML 1.1//EN"
8        "http://www.w3.org/TR/xhtml11/DTD/xhtml11.dtd">
9
10   <html>
11      <head>
12         <title>Options Page</title>
13
14         <script runat = "server">
15
16            // event handler for Load event
17            var books : Hashtable = new Hashtable();
18
19            function Page_Load( sender : Object, events : EventArgs ) : void
20            {
21               // if page is loaded due to postback, load session
22               // information, hide language options from user
23               books.Add( "C#", "0-13-062221-4" );
24               books.Add( "C++", "0-13-089571-7" );
25               books.Add( "C", "0-13-089572-5" );
26               books.Add( "Python", "0-13-092361-3" );
27
28               if ( IsPostBack )
29               {
30                  // display components that contain
31                  // session information
32                  welcomeLabel.Visible = true;
33                  languageLink.Visible = true;
34                  recommendationsLink.Visible = true;
35
36                  // hide components
37                  submitButton.Visible = false;
38                  promptLabel.Visible = false;
39                  languageList.Visible = false;
40
41                  // set labels to display Session information
42                  if ( languageList.SelectedItem != null )
43                  {
44                     welcomeLabel.Text +=
45                        languageList.SelectedItem.ToString() + ".";
46                  }
47                  else
48                  {
```

Fig. 23.19 Recording user-selected options with session tracking. (Part 1 of 4.)

```
49                        welcomeLabel.Text += "no language.";
50                    }
51
52                    idLabel.Text += "Your unique session ID is: " +
53                        Session.SessionID;
54
55                    timeoutLabel.Text += "Timeout: " +
56                        Session.Timeout + " minutes";
57                } // end if
58            } // end Page_Load
59
60            // when user clicks Submit button,
61            // store user's choice in session object
62            function submitButton_Click (
63                sender : Object, events : EventArgs ) : void
64            {
65                if ( languageList.SelectedItem != null )
66                {
67                    var language : String =
68                        languageList.SelectedItem.ToString();
69
70                    // note: must use ToString method because the hash table
71                    // stores information as objects
72                    var ISBN : String = books[ language ].ToString();
73
74                    // store in session as name-value pair
75                    // name is language chosen, value is
76                    // ISBN number for corresponding book
77                    Session.Add( language, ISBN );
78                } // end if
79            } // end submitButton_Click
80
81        </script>
82    </head>
83    <body>
84        <form id = "recommendationsPage" method = "post" runat = "server">
85            <P>
86            <asp:Label id = "promptLabel" runat = "server"
87                Font-Bold = "True">Select a programming language:
88            </asp:Label>
89            <asp:Label id = "welcomeLabel" runat = "server"
90                Font-Bold = "True" Visible = "False">
91                Welcome to Sessions! You selected
92            </asp:Label>
93            </P>
94            <P>
95            <asp:RadioButtonList id = "languageList" runat = "server">
96                <asp:ListItem Value = "C#">C#</asp:ListItem>
97                <asp:ListItem Value = "C++">C++</asp:ListItem>
98                <asp:ListItem Value = "C">C</asp:ListItem>
99                <asp:ListItem Value = "Python">Python</asp:ListItem>
100           </asp:RadioButtonList></P>
101           <P>
```

Fig. 23.19 Recording user-selected options with session tracking. (Part 2 of 4.)

```
102                    <asp:Button id = "submitButton" runat = "server"
103                       Text = "Submit" onClick = "submitButton_Click">
104                    </asp:Button>
105            </P>
106            <P>
107               <asp:Label id = "idLabel" runat = "server">
108               </asp:Label>
109            </P>
110            <P>
111               <asp:Label id = "timeoutLabel" runat = "server">
112               </asp:Label>
113            </P>
114            <P>
115               <asp:Label id = "newSessionLabel" runat = "server">
116               </asp:Label>
117            </P>
118            <P>
119               <asp:HyperLink id = "languageLink" runat = "server"
120                  NavigateUrl = "optionsPage.aspx" Visible = "False">
121                  Click here to choose another language.
122               </asp:HyperLink>
123            </P>
124            <P>
125               <asp:HyperLink id = "recommendationsLink" runat = "server"
126                  NavigateUrl = "recommendationsPage.aspx"
127                  Visible = "False">
128                  Click here to get book recommendations.
129               </asp:HyperLink>
130            </P>
131         </form>
132      </body>
133 </html>
```

Fig. 23.19 Recording user-selected options with session tracking. (Part 3 of 4.)

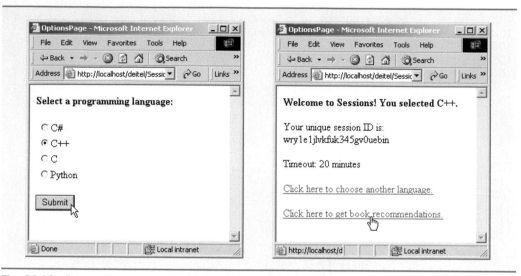

Fig. 23.19   Recording user-selected options with session tracking. (Part 4 of 4.)

Like a cookie, an `HttpSessionState` object stores name-value pairs. In session terminology, these are called **session items**, and they are placed into an `HttpSessionState` object by calling method **Add**. Line 77 calls Add to place the language and its corresponding recommended book's ISBN number into the `HttpSessionState` object. One of the primary benefits of using `HttpSessionState` objects (rather than cookies) is that `HttpSessionState` objects can store objects of any type (not just strings) as attribute values. If the application calls method Add to add an attribute that has the same name as an attribute previously stored in a session, the object associated with that attribute is replaced.

After the values are added to the `HttpSessionState` object, the application handles the postback (lines 28–57) in method `Page_Load`. Here we retrieve information about the current client's session from the `Session` object's properties and display this information in the Web page. The ASP.NET application contains information about the `HttpSessionState` object for the current client. Property **SessionID** (line 53) contains the **session's unique ID**. The first time a client connects to the Web server, a unique session ID is created for that client. When the client makes additional requests, the client's session ID is compared with the session IDs stored in the Web server's memory. Property **Timeout** (line 56) specifies the maximum amount of time that an `HttpSessionState` object can be inactive before it is discarded.

When the postback occurs, certain components are revealed (i.e., their **Visible** property is set to `true`), whereas others become hidden (i.e., their `Visible` property is set to `false`). The welcome message is displayed (line 32), and two hyperlinks located toward the bottom of the page become visible (lines 33–34). One link requests the current page (lines 119–122), and one requests `recommendations.aspx` (lines 125–129). Note that clicking the first hyperlink (i.e., the one that requests the current page) does not cause a postback to occur. The file `optionsPage.aspx` is specified in the **NavigateUrl** property of the hyperlink. When the hyperlink is clicked, this page is requested as a completely new request to allow the user to select a new programming language. After the postback, the form labels and elements are hidden (lines 37–39).

Line 17 defines `books` as a **Hashtable**, which is a data structure that stores key-value pairs. A hash table is like an associative array in which keys are mapped to array positions that store values. The program uses the key to store and retrieve the associated value in the hash table. In this example, the keys are strings that contain the programming language names, and the values are strings that contain the ISBN numbers for the recommended books. Class `Hashtable` provides method `Add`, which takes as arguments a key and a value. The value for a specific hash table entry can be obtained by indexing the hash table with the value's key. For instance,

```
books[ language ];
```

in line 72 returns the value from the key-value pair in which `language` is a key in the `books` hash table. Lines 23–26 add four programming languages and their respective ISBNs to the `Hashtable`.

As mentioned earlier, clicking the **Submit** button causes a postback to occur. As a result, the condition in the `if` statement (line 28) of the `Page_Load` event handler evaluates to `true`, and lines 32–56 execute. Line 42 determines whether the user selected a language. If so, that language is displayed in `welcomeLabel` (lines 44–45). Otherwise, text indicating that a language was not selected is displayed in `welcomeLabel` (line 49).

Additionally, clicking **Submit** causes `submitButton_Click` (lines 62–79) to be called. If the user selects a language, event handler `submitButton_Click` adds a key-value pair to our `Session` object specifying the language chosen and the ISBN number for a book on that language. Next, a postback occurs. Each time the user clicks **Submit**, `submitButton_Click` adds a new language-ISBN pair to the `HttpSessionState` object.

The user is then provided two links. The user can choose another language (i.e., return to the first page with the radio buttons) or link to `recommendationsPage.aspx` (Fig. 23.20), which displays a list of book recommendations on the basis of the user's language selections.

```
1   <%@ Page Language="JScript" %>
2
3   <%-- Fig. 23.20: recommendationsPage.aspx --%>
4   <%-- Read the users session data.           --%>
5
6   <!DOCTYPE html PUBLIC "-//W3C//DTD XHTML 1.1//EN"
7      "http://www.w3.org/TR/xhtml11/DTD/xhtml11.dtd">
8
9   <html>
10     <head>
11        <title>Recommendations Page</title>
12
13        <script runat = "server">
14
15           protected function OnInit( events : EventArgs ) : void
16           {
17              // determine if Session contains information
18              if ( Session != null )
19              {
```

Fig. 23.20 Extracting information from an `HttpSessionState` object. (Part 1 of 2.)

```
20                    // iterate through Session values,
21                    // display in ListBox
22                    for ( var i : int = 0; i < Session.Count; i++ )
23                    {
24                        // store current key in sessionName
25                        var keyName : String = Session.Keys[ i ];
26
27                        // use current key to display
28                        // Session's name/value pairs
29                        booksListBox.Items.Add( keyName +
30                            " How to Program. ISBN#: " + Session[ keyName ] );
31                    } // end for
32                }
33                else
34                {
35                    recommendationsLabel.Text = "No Recommendations";
36                    booksListBox.Visible = false;
37                }
38            } // end OnInit
39
40        </script>
41    </head>
42    <body>
43        <form id = "Form1" method = "post" runat = "server">
44            <asp:Label id = "recommendationsLabel"
45                runat = "server" Font-Bold = "True">
46                Recommendations
47            </asp:Label>
48            <br />
49            <asp:ListBox id = "booksListBox" runat = "server"
50                Width = "383px" Height = "91px">
51            </asp:ListBox>
52        </form>
53    </body>
54 </html>
```

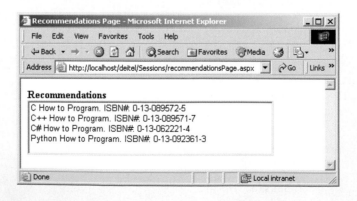

Fig. 23.20   Extracting information from an `HttpSessionState` object. (Part 2 of 2.)

The file `recommendationsPage.aspx` contains a label (lines 44–47) and a list box (lines 49–51). The label displays the text **Recommendations** if the user has selected one or more languages; otherwise, it displays **No Recommendations**. The `ListBox` Web control displays the recommendations created by the ASP.NET page's script.

Event handler **OnInit** (lines 15–38) retrieves the session information. `OnInit` is an event handler that is called when a page is initialized. If a user has never selected languages during any visit to this site, the `Session` object's **Count** property will be zero. This property indicates the number of session items contained in a `Session` object. If the `Session` object is `null` (i.e., no language has ever been selected), then we display the text **No Recommendations**.

If the user has chosen a language, the `for` statement (lines 22–31) iterates through the `Session` object. Remember that property `Count` contains the number of key-value pairs stored in this session. The value in a key-value pair is retrieved from the `Session` object by indexing the `Session` object with the key name, using the same process by which we retrieved a value from our hash table in the last section.

We access the **Keys** property of class `HttpSessionState` (line 25), which returns an object that contains all the keys in the session. This line indexes our object (as if it were an array) using the current `for` loop's control variable to retrieve the current key. Lines 29–30 add to the `ListBox` a string formed by combining the `keyName`'s value, the string " How to Program. ISBN#: " and the value from the `Session` object for which `keyName` is the key. As a result, the string `"C# How to program. ISBN: 0-13-062221-4"`, for example, appears in the `ListBox` when the user has previously selected the C# programming language on `optionsPage.aspx`.

23.8 ASP.NET and XML

ASP.NET provides classes and built-in functionality to manipulate XML files as well. In this section we create a guest book that stores posts in XML and uses an extensible stylesheet (XSL) to output the posts. Figure 23.21 shows the posts stored in XML. Please refer to Chapter 20 for more information on the XML concepts used in this section. Also note that the source files for this example are located in the `Guestbook` subdirectory of the Chapter 23 examples directory. This directory should be copied to the physical directory referenced by the `deitel` virtual directory created earlier in the chapter.

```
1    <?xml version = "1.0" ?>
2
3    <!-- Fig. 23.21: posts.xml -->
4    <!-- Guest book posts         ->
5
6    <?xml-stylesheet type = "text/xsl" href = "formatting.xsl"?>
7
8    <guestbook>
9       <post timestamp = "8/1/2003 9:41:49 AM">
10         <name>anter</name>
11         <email>ic@deitel.com</email>
12         <text>Hello! How are you today? I am fine! </text>
13      </post>
```

Fig. 23.21   Guest book post data. (Part 1 of 2.)

```
14          <post timestamp = "8/1/2003 9:40:40 AM">
15              <name>Pro Gram Fly</name>
16              <email>PGF@deitel.com</email>
17              <text>XML and ASP.NET! What a combination!</text>
18          </post>
19      </guestbook>
```

Fig. 23.21 Guest book post data. (Part 2 of 2.)

The processing instruction in line 6 tells the browser to use the XSL document `formatting.xsl` (Fig. 23.23) to display the contents of this XML file. The root element `guestbook` contains multiple child `post` elements. Each `post` element contains an attribute `timestamp` that stores the date and time when the guest book entry was posted (line 9). The `name` element stores the name of the person who posted (line 10). The `email` element stores the e-mail address of the poster (line 11). The `text` element stores the guest book message (line 12).

Figure 23.22 shows the Web Form for the guest book. Lines 2–3 import two namespaces, `System.Data` and `System.Xml`. These namespaces contain classes that enable programmers to manipulate data sources and process XML documents, respectively. This script only contains one function, `guestBookPost_Click`. This function takes the user input and adds the `post`, `name`, `email` and `text` elements to the `guestbook` node in the `posts.xml` file. The rest of the Web Form contains the user interface and input text fields.

```
1    <%@ Page Language="JScript" Debug="true" %>
2    <%@ Import Namespace="System.Data" %>
3    <%@ Import Namespace="System.Xml" %>
4
5    <!-- Fig. 23.22: guestbook.aspx              -->
6    <!-- Web Form for guest book application -->
7
8    <html>
9       <head>
10          <title>Guest Book</title>
11
12          <link rel = "stylesheet" type = "text/css"
13             href = "style.css" />
14
15          <script language = "JScript" runat = "server">
16
17             function guestBookPost_Click(
18                sender : Object, events : EventArgs ) : void
19             {
20                // Open an XML document.
21                var myDocument : XmlDocument = new XmlDocument();
22                myDocument.Load( Server.MapPath( "posts.xml" ) );
23
24                // Create XML element that will represent the post
25                var postNode : XmlElement =
26                   myDocument.CreateElement( "post" );
```

Fig. 23.22 Guest book application. (Part 1 of 3.)

```
27
28              postNode.SetAttribute( "timestamp", DateTime.Now.ToString() );
29
30              var nameNode : XmlElement =
31                 myDocument.CreateElement( "name" );
32              var emailNode : XmlElement =
33                 myDocument.CreateElement( "email" );
34              var messageNode : XmlElement =
35                 myDocument.CreateElement( "text" );
36
37              nameNode.AppendChild(
38                 myDocument.CreateTextNode( name.Text ) );
39              emailNode.AppendChild(
40                 myDocument.CreateTextNode( email.Text ) );
41              messageNode.AppendChild(
42                 myDocument.CreateTextNode( message.Text ) );
43
44              postNode.AppendChild( nameNode );
45              postNode.AppendChild( emailNode );
46              postNode.AppendChild( messageNode );
47
48              // Insert the new element into the XML tree and save
49              myDocument.DocumentElement.PrependChild( postNode );
50              myDocument.Save( Server.MapPath( "posts.xml" ) );
51
52              name.Text = "";
53              email.Text = "";
54              message.Text = "";
55
56              Response.Redirect ( "posts.xml" );
57          } // end guestBookPost_Click
58
59       </script>
60    </head>
61    <body>
62
63       <p>My Guest Book</p>
64
65       <hr />
66       <form Runat = "server">
67          <table>
68             <tr><td>Name:</td><td> <asp:TextBox ID = "name"
69                Columns = "50" Runat = "server"/></td></tr>
70             <tr><td>E-mail:</td><td><asp:TextBox ID = "email"
71                Columns = "50" Runat = "server"/></td></tr>
72          </table>
73          Message: <asp:TextBox ID = "message" TextMode = "MultiLine"
74             Columns = "50" Rows = "4" Runat = "server"/><br />
75
76          <asp:LinkButton ID = "guestBookPost"
77             OnClick = "guestBookPost_Click" Text = "Post"
78             Runat = "server" ForeColor = "Green" Font-Size = "20" />
```

Fig. 23.22   Guest book application. (Part 2 of 3.)

```
79
80              <br />
81
82              <asp:HyperLink ID = "link" NavigateUrl = "posts.xml"
83                 Text = "View" Runat = "server" ForeColor = "Green"
84                 Font-Size = "20" />
85          </form>
86      </body>
87  </html>
```

Fig. 23.22 Guest book application. (Part 3 of 3.)

The function `guestBookPost_Click` (lines 17–57) performs three tasks—it modifies the XML file, clears the input fields and redirects the user to another page. Lines 21–50 modify the XML file to include the new guest book post. First, the function creates a new XML document as an object of type **XmlDocument** (line 21). Line 22 loads the XML file in `posts.xml` by first calling method **Server.MapPath**. This method returns the physical path on the server of the file passed as an argument (in this case, `posts.xml`). This path is then passed to method **Load**, which parses the XML document, and stores the resulting data in the XmlDocument object. Once an XML document is loaded into an XmlDocument, its data can be read and manipulated programmatically. Lines 25–26 create a variable `postNode` that represents the `post` element that will hold the `name`, `email` and `text` elements. Note that XML elements are objects of type **XmlElement**. Line 26 creates this object by calling method **CreateElement** and passing it the text `"post"`. This method creates an element with the name `post`. Line 28 sets the attribute `timestamp` of the `post` element to the current date and time (using method **SetAttribute**). Lines 30–35 create the child elements of the `post` parent (i.e., `name`, `email` and `text`). Lines 37–42 create the text for the `name`, `email` and `text` elements. These values are extracted from the ASP.NET TextBoxes named `name`, `email` and `text`. To create the text for these elements, we first need to call method **CreateTextNode** (lines 38, 40 and 42). This method creates an object of type **XmlText**, which is then added to the appropriate element by calling method **AppendChild** (lines 37, 39 and 41). Lines 44–46 also use method AppendChild, this time to append the three elements to their parent node `post`. Line 49 then appends the `post` node to the `guestbook` root node. Property **DocumentElement** returns the root node, and method **PrependChild** adds the post node as the first element below the root. Line 50 saves the changes to the file `posts.xml` by calling method **Save**. Lines 52–54 clear the input TextBoxes by setting their Text properties to the empty string (i.e, `""`). Line 56 then uses `Response.Redirect` to transfer the user to `posts.xml`.

When the user's Web browser opens the file `posts.xml`, the processing instruction in line 6 of Fig. 23.21 tells the browser to use an XSL (`formatting.xsl`) that extracts the contents of the XML file and creates an XHTML page for viewing. Refer to Chapter 20 for a review of XSLs. The XSL file is shown in Fig. 23.23.

```
1   <?xml version = "1.0" ?>
2
3   <!-- Fig. 23.23: formatting.xsl                              -->
```

Fig. 23.23 XSL to transform XML guest book data into HTML. (Part 1 of 3.)

```
4    <!-- XSL document that transforms XML data to HTML  -->
5
6    <xsl:stylesheet version = "1.0"
7       xmlns:xsl = "http://www.w3.org/1999/XSL/Transform">
8
9       <xsl:output method = "html" omit-xml-declaration = "no"
10         doctype-system =
11            "http://www.w3.org/TR/xhtml1/DTD/xhtml11.dtd"
12         doctype-public = "-//W3C//DTD XHTML 1.1//EN" />
13
14      <xsl:template match = "/">
15
16         <html xmlns = "http://www.w3.org/1999/xhtml">
17            <xsl:apply-templates select = "*" />
18         </html>
19
20      </xsl:template>
21
22      <xsl:template match = "guestbook">
23
24         <head>
25            <title><xsl:value-of select = "name"/></title>
26            <link rel = "stylesheet" type = "text/css"
27               href = "style.css" />
28         </head>
29
30         <body>
31
32            <table width = "100%" cellspacing = "0"
33               cellpadding = "2">
34               <xsl:apply-templates
35                  select = "post" />
36            </table>
37
38            <p>
39               <a href = "guestbook.aspx">Post a Message!</a>
40            </p>
41
42         </body>
43
44      </xsl:template>
45
46      <xsl:template match = "post">
47
48            <tr>
49               <td class = "msgInfo">
50
51
52                  <em>   <a href = "mailto:{email}">
53                  <xsl:value-of select = "name" /> </a> </em>
54                  -
55
```

Fig. 23.23 XSL to transform XML guest book data into HTML. (Part 2 of 3.)

```
56                    <span class = "date">
57                        <xsl:value-of select = "@timestamp" />
58                    </span>
59                </td>
60            </tr>
61
62            <tr>
63                <td class = "msgText">
64                    <xsl:value-of select = "text" />
65                </td>
66            </tr>
67
68        </xsl:template>
69
70   </xsl:stylesheet>
```

Fig. 23.23   XSL to transform XML guest book data into HTML. (Part 3 of 3.)

This XSL outputs an XHTML page. Lines 10–12 declare the **doctype** of the output XHTML page. There are three templates in this XSL document. The template starting in line 14 matches the root element of the XML document. The template starting in line 22 matches the **guestbook** element, and the template starting in line 46 matches **post** elements.

The XSL begins to process the document with the template in line 14 because that template matches the document root using the XPath expression "**/**". This template creates the opening and closing **html** tags. The output from the other templates is placed between these two tags. Line 17 uses the **<xsl apply-templates>** tag to apply the other templates to all the child nodes of the context element (i.e., the document root). [*Note*: The child nodes of the document root are the two comment nodes and the **guestbook** element. Recall that the XPath expression * matches every child element.]

Next the template in line 22 matches the **guestbook** element. This template creates the **head** (lines 24–28) and the **body** (lines 30–42) of the XHTML output. At the bottom of the page, we include a link back to the Web Form page so that the user can post additional messages (line 39). This template also creates a table to hold the output of the template that matches **post** elements. Lines 34–35 apply this template.

The template that matches **post** elements appears in lines 46–68. This template extracts the post information and places it in table rows and cells. Line 52 uses an XPath expression within an XHTML element. To use an XPath expression within another markup language, the XPath expression must be surrounded by curly braces ({}). Line 52 extracts the poster's e-mail address and creates a **mailto:** link that appears as the name of the poster. Line 54 outputs a hyphen, and line 57 outputs the date and time of the post. The next table row consists of the actual guest book message.

This template is applied to all the child post elements under the guest book element, thereby creating a table with alternating rows of names and messages. When there are no more elements to process, the page is finished and the browser outputs the page. The Web form and the posts are displayed in Fig. 23.24. [*Note*: The CSS stylesheet, **style.css**, is not shown but is included in the Chapter 23 examples directory on the CD accompanying the book.]

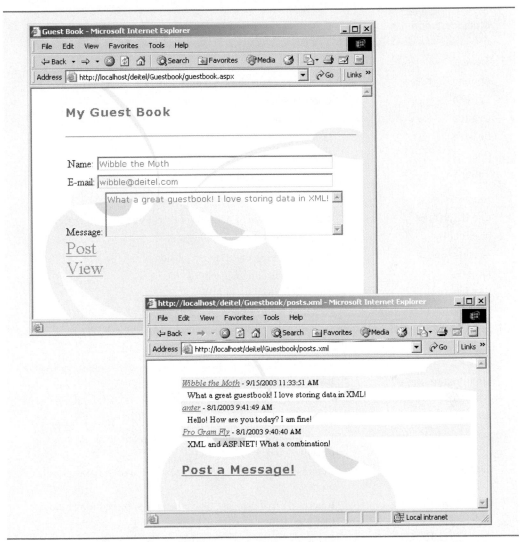

Fig. 23.24   ASP.NET page output and output of the transformation of the XML document.

23.9 Reading and Writing Text Files

ASP.NET uses the classes provided by the .NET Framework to manipulate files. The System.IO namespace contains classes that allow reading and writing to files and streams. It also provides support for manipulating directories. The FCL provides several classes that enable programmers to retrieve information from files, manipulate file paths (the string representations of directory locations on the hard disk) and perform read and write operations on data streams and files.

The FileInfo and Directory classes (Fig. 23.25–Fig. 23.26) provide methods and properties to retrieve information and perform basic operations on files and directories (e.g., create files, delete files, determine file sizes and find subdirectories).

Methods/Properties	Description
Methods	
AppendText	Creates a stream object for appending to current file.
CopyTo	Copies a file.
Create	Creates a file.
Delete	Deletes a file.
Open	Opens a file.
ToString	Returns a string that represents the full path of a file.
Properties	
CreationTime	The creation time of the current FileSystemInfo object.
Directory	An instance of the parent directory.
extension	A string that represents the extension of the file.
Exists	Boolean indicating whether the file exists.
Length	The size of the current file.

Fig. 23.25 FileInfo class methods and properties.

Methods/Properties	Description
Methods	
Exists	Determines whether the specified path refers to an existing directory on disk.
GetLastAccessTime	Returns the date and time the specified file or directory was last accessed.
GetLastWriteTime	Returns the last date and time when the specified file or directory was written.
GetLogicalDrives	Retrieves the names of the drives on the computer.
GetParent	Retrieves the parent directory of the specified path.

Fig. 23.26 Directory class methods and properties.

The classes FileStream, StreamReader and StreamWriter read and write content to and from a file. These classes are used to create objects known as streams, writers and readers that are used to manipulate files. Many specialized streams, writers and readers exist. The .NET Framework also provides TextReader, BinaryReader, XmlReader, XMLText and several other readers. Not all these classes are within the System.IO namespace; therefore you must include Import statements for the appropriate namespaces before using them. The methods and properties of some of these classes are presented in Fig. 23.27–Fig. 23.28.

Methods/Properties	Description
Methods	
Close	Closes the StreamReader and the underlying stream, then releases any system resources associated with the reader.
Peek	Returns the next available character but does not consume it.
Read	Reads the next character or next set of characters from the input stream.
ReadLine	Reads a line of characters from the current stream and returns the data as a string.
Properties	
BaseStream	The underlying stream.
CurrentEncoding	The current character encoding of the current stream.

Fig. 23.27 StreamReader class methods and properties.

Methods/Properties	Description
Methods	
Close	Closes the current StreamWriter and any underlying stream.
Flush	Clears all buffers for the current writer.
Write	Writes data to the stream.
WriteLine	Writes data to the stream data followed by a line terminator.
Properties	
AutoFlush	Gets or sets a value indicating whether the StreamWriter will flush its buffer after every Write call.
Encoding	Gets the encoding in which the output is written.

Fig. 23.28 StreamWriter class methods and properties.

Figure 23.29 is an ASP.NET page that allows users to sign up for a mailing list. It uses a text file to store names and addresses. The .NET stream classes are used to write the submitted contact information to the text file.

```
1   <%@ Page Language="JScript" %>
2   <%@ Import Namespace="System" %>
3   <%@ Import Namespace="System.Data" %>
4   <%@ Import Namespace="System.Web.UI.WebControls" %>
5   <%@ Import Namespace="System.IO" %>
6
```

Fig. 23.29 Using text files to store mailing information. (Part 1 of 5.)

```
7   <%
8       // Fig. 23.29: mailinglist.aspx
9       // A Web Form mailing list.
10  %>
11
12  <!DOCTYPE html PUBLIC "-//W3C//DTD XHTML 1.1//EN"
13      "http://www.w3.org/TR/xhtml11/DTD/xhtml11.dtd">
14
15  <html>
16      <head>
17          <title>Join our Mailing List</title>
18          <script language = "JScript" runat = "server">
19
20              var dataView : DataView;
21
22              function Page_Load (
23                  sender : Object, events : EventArgs ) : void
24              {
25                  dataView = new DataView ( new DataTable() );
26              }
27
28              function clearButton_Click(
29                  sender : Object, events : System.EventArgs ) : void
30              {
31                  nameTextBox.Text = "";
32                  emailTextBox.Text = "";
33                  cityTextBox.Text = "";
34                  stateTextBox.Text = "";
35                  addressTextBox.Text = "";
36              }
37
38              function FillMessageTable() : void
39              {
40                  var table : DataTable = dataView.Table;
41                  table.Columns.Add( "Name" );
42                  table.Columns.Add( "Address" );
43                  table.Columns.Add( "City" );
44                  table.Columns.Add( "State" );
45                  table.Columns.Add( "E-mail" );
46
47                  // open mailing list for reading
48                  var reader : StreamReader = new StreamReader(
49                      Request.PhysicalApplicationPath + "/Mailing/" +
50                      "mailinglist.txt" );
51
52                  var separator : char[] = [ '\t' ];
53
54                  // read in line from file
55                  var message : String = reader.ReadLine();
56
57                  while ( message != null ) {
58                      // split the string into its four parts
59                      var parts : String[] = message.Split( separator );
```

Fig. 23.29 Using text files to store mailing information. (Part 2 of 5.)

```
60
61                    // load data into table
62                    table.LoadDataRow( parts, true );
63
64                    // read in one line from file
65                    message = reader.ReadLine();
66                } // end while
67
68             // update grid
69             dataGrid.DataSource = table;
70             dataGrid.DataBind();
71
72             reader.Close();
73          } // end FillMessageTable
74
75          function submitButton_Click (
76             sender : Object, events: System.EventArgs ): void
77          {
78             // open stream for appending to file
79             var list : StreamWriter =
80                new StreamWriter( Request.PhysicalApplicationPath
81                + "/Mailing/" + "mailinglist.txt", true );
82
83             // write new address to file
84             list.WriteLine(
85                nameTextBox.Text + "\t" + addressTextBox.Text + "\t"
86                + cityTextBox.Text + "\t" + stateTextBox.Text  + "\t" +
87                emailTextBox.Text );
88
89             // clear textboxes and close stream
90             nameTextBox.Text = "";
91             emailTextBox.Text = "";
92             cityTextBox.Text = "";
93             stateTextBox.Text = "";
94             addressTextBox.Text = "";
95             list.Close();
96
97             FillMessageTable();
98          } // end submitButton_Click
99
100      </script>
101   </head>
102   <body>
103      <form id = "Form1" runat = "server">
104         <asp:Label id = "promptLabel" runat = "server"
105            ForeColor = "Blue" Font-Size = "X-Large">
106            Fill in the fields below to join our mailing list:
107         </asp:Label>
108         <br />
109
110         <asp:Label id = "nameLabel" runat = "server"
111            style = "position: absolute; left:107px">
112            Name:</asp:Label>
```

Fig. 23.29 Using text files to store mailing information. (Part 3 of 5.)

```
113         <asp:TextBox id = "nameTextBox" runat = "server"
114            style = "position: absolute; left:150px">
115         </asp:TextBox>
116         <br />
117
118         <asp:Label id = "addressLabel" runat = "server"
119            style = "position: absolute; left:93px">
120            Address:</asp:Label>
121         <asp:TextBox id = "addressTextBox" runat = "server"
122            style = "position: absolute; left:150px">
123         </asp:TextBox>
124         <br />
125
126         <asp:Label id = "cityLabel" runat = "server"
127            style = "position: absolute; left:119px">
128            City:</asp:Label>
129         <asp:TextBox id = "cityTextBox" runat = "server"
130            style = "position: absolute; left:150px">
131         </asp:TextBox>
132         <br />
133
134         <asp:Label id = "stateLabel" runat = "server"
135            style = "position: absolute; left:56px">
136            State/Province:
137         </asp:Label>
138         <asp:TextBox id = "stateTextBox" runat = "server"
139            style = "position: absolute; left:150px">
140         </asp:TextBox>
141         <br />
142
143         <asp:Label id = "emailLabel" runat = "server"
144            style = "position: absolute; left:105px">
145            E-mail:
146         </asp:Label>
147         <asp:TextBox id = "emailTextBox" runat = "server"
148            style = "position: absolute; left:150px">
149         </asp:TextBox>
150         <br />
151         <br />
152
153         <asp:Button id = "clearButton" runat = "server" Width = "57px"
154            style = "position: absolute; left:150px"
155            Text = "Clear" OnClick = "clearButton_Click">
156         </asp:Button>
157         <asp:Button id = "submitButton" runat = "server"
158            style = "position: absolute; left:220px"
159            Text = "Submit" OnClick = "submitButton_Click">
160         </asp:Button>
161         <br />
162         <br />
163
164         <asp:DataGrid id = "dataGrid" runat = "server"
165            HorizontalAlign = "Left" BorderColor = "#E7E7FF"
```

Fig. 23.29   Using text files to store mailing information. (Part 4 of 5.)

```
166              GridLines = "Horizontal" BackColor = "White"
167              BorderStyle = "None" CellPadding = "3">
168              <SelectedItemStyle Font-Bold = "True" ForeColor = "#F7F7F7"
169                 BackColor = "#738A9C">
170              </SelectedItemStyle>
171              <AlternatingItemStyle BackColor = "#F7F7F7">
172              </AlternatingItemStyle>
173              <ItemStyle HorizontalAlign = "Left" ForeColor = "#4A3C8C"
174                 BackColor = "#E7E7FF">
175              </ItemStyle>
176              <HeaderStyle Font-Bold = "True" ForeColor = "#F7F7F7"
177                 BackColor = "#4A3C8C">
178              </HeaderStyle>
179              <FooterStyle ForeColor = "#4A3C8C" BackColor = "#B5C7DE">
180              </FooterStyle>
181           </asp:DataGrid>
182        </form>
183
184     </body>
185  </html>
```

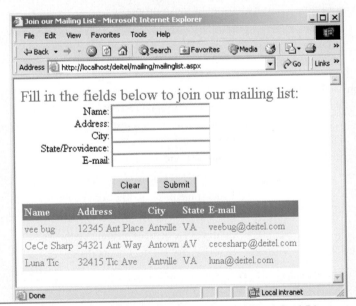

Fig. 23.29 Using text files to store mailing information. (Part 5 of 5.)

Lines 2–5 import namespaces that will be used in this page so that the long namespace prefixes (e.g., System.Web.UI.WebControls) do not have to be typed. Lines 12–13 declare the doctype of the page.

Lines 18–100 contain the script that declares variables and functions used in the page. Line 20 declares variable dataView of type **DataView**. A DataView provides a bindable (i.e., allows data binding—the ability of a control to be assigned data of various types and formats), customized view of a DataTable that can be sorted and edited. A **DataTable** is an object representing a table of data. Data binding allows programmers to easily display and manipulate data without dealing with the underlying data structures. A DataTable typically represents a table in a database. A DataTable contains a DataColumn object and a DataRow object. We use variable dataView to display the strings in a text document.

Function Page_Load in lines 22–26 executes when the page loads. This function initializes a new DataView instance using a DataTable as the data source. Function clearButton_Click (lines 28–36) executes when the user clicks the **Clear** button. This function clears the TextBoxes by setting the Text property of each to the empty string (""). The **Clear** button server control's OnClick attribute is set to this method.

Function FillMessageTable (lines 38–73) fills a DataTable. Line 40 uses the **Table** property to extract dataView's DataTable. The table is then assigned to variable table. Lines 41–45 add five columns to the data table with the names Name, Address, City, State and E-mail. To do this, each line first accesses the table's **Columns** property. This property returns the columns of the table. The **Add** method is then called, which adds a new column to the table with the specified name. Lines 48–50 use class Stream-Reader to create a new stream reader to read the information in the text file. The property **PhysicalApplicationPath** of the Request object contains the file system path of the currently executing server application's root directory. PhysicalApplicationPath is one of many properties of the Request object that provide valuable information about the client and server. Figure 23.30 lists some of these properties.

Property	Description
PhysicalApplicationPath	The file system path of the currently executing server application's root directory.
IsSecureConnection	Boolean. Determines if the request came in through SSL (Secure Sockets Layer).
UserHostAddress	Client's IP address.
UserHostName	Client's DNS host name.
HttpMethod	Request method (i.e., GET or POST).
UserAgent	Provides information about the client making the request.
Cookies	Retrieves the cookies residing on the client.
ServerVariables	Retrieves the variables about the server.

Fig. 23.30 Request object properties.

The string "/Mailing/" is added to the path (line 49) because the application and the text files are located within the Mailing subdirectory of the server application's root directory (i.e., the value provided by Request.PhysicalApplicationPath). Without the additional directory name, the stream would attempt to access a text file outside the directory Mailing. The text file is named mailinglist.txt.

When data is written to the file, tabs are inserted to separate the data. Line 52 declares a character array whose contents indicate the characters that should be recognized as delimiters (or separators) when parsing the data read from the text file. The data in our text file is only delimited by tabs, so the array separator contains only one element: '\t', the escape character signifying a tab. In line 55, the StreamReader instance (i.e., reader) reads a line from the text file (using method **ReadLine**). Thus variable message is initialized to be the first line of text in the text file. Lines 57–66 contain a while loop that reads through the entire text file, line by line. As each line is read, the **Split** method divides the line into individual strings and places each string in a string array called parts. The Split method is passed separator (the char array declared in line 52), which specifies the delimiters for the data. The Split method identifies individual strings separated by the delimiter (the tab character in this case) and returns them as an array. This array (i.e., parts) is then loaded into the table in line 62. Method **LoadDataRow** is passed two parameters. The first parameter indicates the data to load into the table, and the second parameter is a boolean that specifies whether the data table should accept changes. If the second parameter is false, any added rows are marked as new entries that need to be manually accepted. The method LoadDataRow finds and updates a specific row. If no row's data matches the data to be inserted, LoadDataRow creates a new row and inserts the data (i.e., parts). Line 65 reads the next line from the file for the next iteration of the while loop.

The table we have created is bound to the dataGrid in lines 69–70 by assigning the dataGrid's DataSource to the DataTable table. A **DataGrid** is a control that displays data from a data source (e.g., a database) in the form of a table. The DataGrid control contains built-in features that make it useful in the organizing and display of data.

The DataGrid is added in lines 164–181. Several child elements and attributes define the appearance of a DataGrid server control. Element SelectedItemStyle (lines 168–170) sets the properties for selected items in the DataGrid control. AlternatingItemStyle (lines 171–172) sets the properties for alternating items (i.e., every other item) in the DataGrid. In this example, we specify the BackColor attribute value of the AlternatingItemStyle element, which is different from the BackColor attribute value of the ItemStyle element (lines 173–175), to achieve the alternating row color effect visible in the output shown in Fig. 23.29. The HeaderStyle child element (lines 176–178) sets properties for the DataGrid's header (which appears at the top of the control), and FooterStyle sets the properties for the footer (which appears at the bottom of the control).

The reader instance is then closed in line 72. If the reader were not closed, it would maintain sole access to the stream and prohibit any other function or program from accessing its source text file.

Function submitButton_Click (lines 75–98) is called when the user clicks the **Submit** button. This function writes new data to the text file. Lines 79–81 open a StreamWriter for writing information to the text file. Lines 84–87 use method **WriteLine** to write a new line to the text file. The string to be written is composed of the user's text inputs separated by tab characters. Recall that the tab characters are used to separate the individual strings that represent the user's name, address, city, state and e-mail address to allow for easy parsing at a later time. [*Note*: The method WriteLine inserts a newline character ('\n') at the end of each line it writes, so we do not have to explicitly include the newline character in the string passed to this method.] Lines 90–95 clear the text boxes on the form to allow for new input and close the StreamWriter. The function then calls FillMessageTable to update the dataGrid with the new information for display.

The body of the Web Form contains the server controls that specify the appearance of the page. Each TextBox has a corresponding Label to indicate the text that should be entered. Lines 110–115 contain the Label and TextBox for the user's name, lines 118–

123 contain the `Label` and `TextBox` for the user's address and so on. Two buttons, marked **Clear** and **Submit**, are placed below the input text boxes on the form. These buttons are given `OnClick` attribute-value pairs that define the function to be called when each button is clicked. The input boxes are all given *x*-coordinates of `150px` to align them using absolute positioning (where controls are given an exact location in the browser, rather than a position relative to the other controls on the page). These properties are manipulated by assigning the style attributes `"position: absolute; left:150px"`. The `position` value is set to `absolute`, and the `left` value is set to `150px`.

Finally, we add the `DataGrid` server control to the page (lines 164–181). Initially, when the page is loaded and first accessed, the `DataGrid` is not visible because it has not yet been bound to any data. When the user clicks the **Submit** button, the event handler `submitButton_Click` executes and calls the function `FillMessageTable` to bind `dataGrid` to `dataTable`, which contains the information from the text file.

23.10 Connecting to a Database in ASP.NET

The next example presents a Web-based application in which a user can view a list of publications by a chosen author. The page `authors.aspx` displays a list of authors. When the user chooses an author and clicks the **Select** button, a postback occurs, and the updated page displays a table that contains the titles, ISBNs and publishers of books written by the selected author.

The information provided by this Web page is accessed through a Microsoft Access database stored in the directory containing the rest of our project. All author information is retrieved from the `Books.mdb` database. The reader can view this database by opening the `Database` directory in the Chapter 23 examples directory. To run this example, place the `Books.mdb` database file in the directory `C:\Inetpub\wwwroot\Database`. If this directory does not exist, please create it. Copy the remaining example files in the `Database` examples directory to a `Database` directory within the directory referenced by the `deitel` virtual directory. To run the examples in this section, you need Microsoft Data Access Components (MDAC) Version 2.6 or later. If you receive an error when attempting to run the examples, download the latest version of MDAC from

        `msdn.microsoft.com/downloads/list/dataaccess.asp`

Follow the instructions in the MDAC installation program. Note that finishing this setup requires the system to be restarted.

We use an **OleDbDataReader**, an object that reads data from a database. The `OleDbDataReader` is not as flexible as other readers. The object can read, but not update, data. We use `OleDbDataReader` in this example, however, because we only need to read the authors' names, and this object provides a simple way to do so.

Applications frequently use a standard sequence when accessing databases. First the program initializes the OLE DB interface. Then the page connects to a data source, executes a command (e.g., a query), processes (e.g., sorts and displays) the results and finally closes the data source so that other objects or processes can access the source.

The ASPX file (Fig. 23.31) for this page creates several controls, including a `DropDownList`, a `Button` and a `DataGrid`. Users select an author from the `DropDownList` and click **Submit**, causing a postback to occur. Recall that a `DataGrid` is a Web control that displays database information in a table. It also allows sorting of data-

base rows and columns on the client side. When the postback is handled, the DataGrid
with id set to dataGrid is filled and displays the appropriate data from the database.
Figure 23.31 presents this application.

```
1   <%@ Page Language="JScript" %>
2   <%@ Import Namespace="System" %>
3   <%@ Import Namespace="System.Data" %>
4   <%@ Import Namespace="System.Data.OleDb" %>
5   <%@ Register TagPrefix="Header" TagName="ImageHeader"
6      Src="imageHeader.ascx" %>
7
8   <!-- Fig 23.31: authors.aspx             -->
9   <!-- This page allows a user to choose an -->
10  <!-- author and display that authors name -->
11
12  <html>
13     <body>
14        <script language = "JScript" runat = "server">
15
16           function Page_Load( sender : Object, events : EventArgs )
17           {
18              if ( !IsPostBack )
19              {
20                 var dataBaseConnection : OleDbConnection = new
21                    OleDbConnection( ConfigurationSettings.AppSettings(
22                    "ConnectionString" ) );
23
24                 var queryString : System.String =
25                    "SELECT lastName, firstName FROM Authors";
26
27                 dataBaseConnection.Open();
28
29                 var dataBaseCommand : OleDbCommand =
30                    new OleDbCommand( queryString, dataBaseConnection );
31
32                 var dataReader = dataBaseCommand.ExecuteReader();
33
34                 // while we read a row from result of
35                 // query, add first item to drop down list
36                 while ( dataReader.Read() )
37                    nameList.Items.Add( dataReader.GetString( 0 ) +
38                    ", " + dataReader.GetString( 1 ) );
39
40                 // close database connection
41                 dataBaseConnection.Close();
42              }
43              else
44              {
45                 dataGrid.DataSource = GetData();
46                 dataGrid.DataBind();
47              }
48           } // end Page_Load
```

Fig. 23.31 Database access application. (Part 1 of 3.)

```
49
50            // Read a database and return the DataView
51         function GetData() : ICollection
52         {
53            var set : DataSet = new DataSet();
54
55            // establish a connection, and query the database
56            var dataBaseConnection: OleDbConnection = new
57               OleDbConnection( ConfigurationSettings.AppSettings(
58               "ConnectionString" ) );
59
60            var authorID : int = nameList.SelectedIndex + 1;
61
62            var queryString : String =
63               "SELECT Titles.Title, Titles.ISBN, " +
64               "Publishers.PublisherName FROM AuthorISBN " +
65               "INNER JOIN Titles ON AuthorISBN.ISBN = " +
66               "Titles.ISBN, Publishers WHERE " +
67               "(AuthorISBN.AuthorID = " + authorID + ")";
68
69            var dataBaseCommand : OleDbCommand =
70               new OleDbCommand( queryString, dataBaseConnection );
71
72            var dataAdapter : OleDbDataAdapter =
73               new OleDbDataAdapter( dataBaseCommand );
74
75            dataAdapter.Fill( set );
76
77            // close database connection
78            dataBaseCommand.Connection.Close();
79
80            var dataView : DataView = new DataView( set.Tables[ 0 ] );
81            dataView.Sort = "Title";
82
83            return dataView;
84         } // end GetData
85
86      </script>
87
88      <form runat = "server">
89
90         <Header:ImageHeader id = "head" runat = "server">
91         </Header:ImageHeader>
92         <br />
93
94         Authors:
95         <asp:DropDownList id = "nameList" runat = "server"
96            Width = "158px" Height = "22px">
97         </asp:DropDownList>
98         <asp:button id = "button" text = "select" runat = "server">
99         </asp:button>
100        <p>
101           <asp:DataGrid id = "dataGrid" runat = "server">
```

Fig. 23.31   Database access application. (Part 2 of 3.)

```
102                 </asp:DataGrid>
103           </p>
104
105        </form>
106     </body>
107  </html>
```

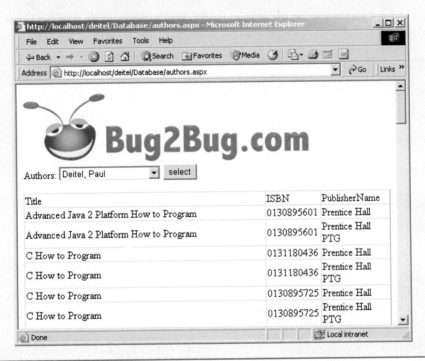

Fig. 23.31 Database access application. (Part 3 of 3.)

Lines 5–6 declare a Web user control for later use in the .aspx file. Recall that a Web user control is a custom reusable control that can be placed on an ASP.NET page like any of the built-in HTML and Web server controls. The **@ Register** directive allows programmers to declare the user controls that will be included in an .aspx file. A user control is defined in an external file saved with an **.ascx** extension. An .ascx file, as we will see in a moment, can contain the same syntax as ordinary ASP.NET Web Forms. However, since .ascx files only define individual components of a page and will never be requested by the user, they do not contain html, body or form elements. For example, a programmer might want to include a **navigation bar** (i.e., a series of buttons for navigating a Web site) on every page of a site. If the site consists of a large number of pages, adding markup to create the navigation bar for each page could be time-consuming. Moreover, if the programmer subsequently modifies the navigation bar, every page on the site that uses the navigation bar must be updated. By creating a user control, the programmer can include a navigation bar on any page using only a few lines of markup. If the navigation bar changes, only the file that defines the control needs modification, and pages that include the navigation bar will continue to refer to the now modified .ascx file.

The Web user control included in the current example displays a page header containing a logo image. Lines 5–6 define the user control's **tag name** (i.e., the name of this instance of the control) and **tag prefix**, as they will be used in the current .aspx file. We set the attribute TagName to "ImageHeader" and the attribute TagPrefix to "Header". Line 6 uses the attribute **Src** to specify the file that defines the custom control: imageHeader.ascx (Fig. 23.32). Once this Web user control is declared with the @ Register directive, it can be placed anywhere on the Web page. We add the ImageHeader element to the file in lines 90–91. When compiled by ASP.NET into output suitable for a Web browser, this element is replaced by the content of the Src file.

```
1   <%-- Fig. 23.32: imageHeader.ascx      --%>
2   <%-- Listing for the header user control --%>
3
4   <asp:Image id = "Image1" runat = "server"
5      ImageUrl = "bug2bug.png">
6   </asp:Image>
```

Fig. 23.32   User control that displays an image.

 Software Engineering Observation 23.3

Using .ascx files helps encapsulate frequently used blocks of code.

Another external file that is used in this program is a **Web.config** file. Web.config files are XML-formatted text files that reside in the Web site's root directory. Web.config files typically specify configuration settings, such as authorization settings for the Web site or the appearance of error pages. The Web.config file used in this example is shown in Fig. 23.33. This Web.config file stores only the database connection string used in lines 21–22 and lines 57–58 of Fig. 23.31. The code in Web.config (lines 5–9 of Fig. 23.33) adds an application-wide setting named ConnectionString that contains the information required by the OleDbConnection object to identify the type and location of the database. To access the value of ConnectionString, we use the command,

ConfigurationSettings.AppSettings("ConnectionString")

This value is now visible to any Web pages in the directory containing the Web.config file.

```
1    <!-- Fig 23.33: Web.config        -->
2    <!-- Web.Config Configuration File -->
3
4    <configuration>
5       <appSettings>
6          <add key = "ConnectionString"
7             value = "Provider=Microsoft.Jet.OLEDB.4.0;
8             Data Source=C:\Inetpub\wwwroot\Database\Books.mdb" />
9       </appSettings>
10   </configuration>
```

Fig. 23.33   Web.config file.

If the user is visiting authors.aspx for the first time (i.e., !IsPostBack is true), Page_Load (lines 16–48 of Fig. 23.31) loads the nameList with the first names of the authors from the database (lines 18–42). If the user has visited the site before (i.e., !IsPostBack is false), Page_Load calls GetData (which we will discuss shortly), refreshes dataGrid and rebinds dataGrid (lines 43–47).

To load the first names of the authors from the data base, Page_Load creates an **OleDbConnection** object (lines 20–22). An OleDbConnection object represents a connection to a database. The connection string, defined in the Web.config file, provides the type of connection that we are using (i.e., Microsoft.Jet.OLEDB.4.0) and the source of the data (C:\Inetpub\wwwroot\Database\Books.mdb). Because the data source is set to this location, the Books.mdb file must be placed in the C:\Inetpub\wwwroot\Database\, as mentioned earlier.

Next we create an SQL query string (line 24–25) that selects the last and first names from the Authors table of the Books.mdb database. See Chapter 22 for information on how this statement is formed. Line 27 opens the dataBaseConnection with method **Open**. Lines 29–30 create a new **OleDbCommand** object that is passed two parameters. The first parameter is the queryString, which contains the SQL to execute, and the second parameter is the database connection. Line 32 then executes this command using method **ExecuteReader**. This method returns the result of the query in the form of an OleDbDataReader, which is assigned to variable dataReader. This object holds the values (i.e., the authors' first names) that were accessed by the SQL query. A dataReader retrieves data that is accessed from a query. The dataReader's **Read** method accesses a row from the results of the query. The Read method returns false if no more rows exist to be read. It also updates the values in the dataReader to the next row, if one exists.

Lines 36–38 use the Read method to access each row of the data resulting from the query and adds each name to the nameList drop-down list. The method **GetString** returns the value in the specified column as a string. GetString(0) gets the value in column 0 (because the columns in the query results use a zero-based numbering scheme), and GetString(1) gets the value in column 1. Column 0 contains the last names, and column 1 contains the first names. Note how the names are added to nameList. We first access property **Items**, which returns an object representing all the items in nameList. We then call method **Add** to add a new item to the object returned from the Items property. The items displayed in nameList are specified by property Items, so the new item added will now be displayed in nameList.

Finally the database connection is closed in line 41. If it were not closed, other readers, writers and programs would not be able to access the database.

If the user posts back (i.e., !IsPostBack is false in line 18), a selection from the drop-down list must have been made. The Page_Load function calls GetData (line 45), which queries the database for the name selected, then binds the result to the dataGrid (line 46) using method **DataBind**. Binding the new information to the dataGrid refreshes the dataGrid and outputs the information to the user.

The GetData method (lines 51–84) begins by creating a DataSet in line 53. A **DataSet** represents a set of data and includes the tables that contain and order it, in addition to the relationships between the tables. We will make use of the DataSet shortly. Most of this method uses the same sequence of method calls as the Page_Load function to establish a database connection, query the database and close the database. Line 60 retrieves the user's selection by accessing the value of nameList.SelectedIndex. We add 1 because the nameList uses zero-based numbering, while the authorID in the database table uses numbering that starts from 1. Lines 62–67 specify a new SQL command. This query incorporates the user's drop-down list selection and selects more columns from the database than the former query. The query

```
SELECT Titles.Title, Titles.ISBN, Publishers.PublisherName
FROM AuthorISBN
INNER JOIN Titles ON AuthorISBN.ISBN = Titles.ISBN, Publishers
WHERE ( AuthorISBN.AuthorID = authorID )
```

selects the Title and ISBN of the book from the Titles table and the PublisherName from the Publishers table. The INNER JOIN SQL operator returns all the rows from both tables (AuthorISBN and Titles) when there is a match. The ON keyword specifies the join condition. In this query, we select rows where the AuthorISBN.AuthorID equals Titles.ISBN. The WHERE keyword determines the rows to be retrieved. The WHERE condition specifies that only rows where AuthorISBN.authorID = authorID are to be retrieved (i.e., rows where the authorID stored in the database equals the authorID of the author selected by the user). Lines 69–70 create an OleDbCommand object representing this SQL command, and assign this OleDbCommand to dataBaseCommand.

Lines 72–73 create an object of type OleDbDataAdapter. An **OleDbDataAdapter** is used to retrieve information from a database and place the resulting information in a DataSet. Line 75 calls the OleDbDataAdapter class's **Fill** method to load the DataSet object set (declared in line 53) with data returned from the SQL command. We then close the database connection (line 78) and declare a DataView object (line 80). A **DataView** enables the creation of different views of the data stored in a DataTable. Essentially, it presents the data in a table that can be manipulated (e.g., sorted). Line 80 loads the first table of our DataSet into the DataView using property **Tables**. There is only one table returned from our SQL query, so we simply access the first table using the index 0. We then sort the dataView by title (line 81) using method **Sort**, and return the dataView (line 83).

Lines 88–105 create the ASP.NET Web Form used to select the author whose books are to be displayed. Initially, the DataGrid does not appear on the screen because it has not yet been bound to any information. After a postback, the dataGrid becomes bound to the results of the database query and presents them in a clear and readable manner.

23.11 Code-Behind Approach

ASP.NET supports two methods of adding scripts to make static content dynamic. The first method (i.e., the inline code method) embeds scripts within script elements in the .aspx file, as we have seen up until this point. An alternative approach is to use the **code-behind**

method. This approach further separates the graphical user interface (GUI) of an ASP.NET page from the dynamic scripts (e.g., JScript .NET or C# code) that control the behavior of the application. Using code-behinds enables the presentation code and programming logic to be placed in their own files. The approach allows the look and feel of a page to be modified easily without disrupting the "code behind" the page, and vice versa. ASP.NET pages (with `.aspx` extensions) implement the Web site GUI, while JScript .NET code-behind files (with `.aspx.js` extensions) handle the pages' event handlers and logic.

A code-behind, unlike prior scripts, is not included in the `.aspx` file and must be compiled first. Then the `.aspx` file can call methods from the binary **dynamic link library (DLL)** that the compiler creates. A DLL is a library of functions or data that can be used by an application. Using the code-behind model ensures that every file is written either entirely in JScript .NET or entirely using XHTML and ASP.NET Web Form controls. This section modifies the `AdRotator` example to use the code-behind approach.

All the files for this example are located in the `CodeBehind` subdirectory of the Chapter 23 examples directory on the CD-ROM accompanying the book. Copy the `Code-Behind` directory to the physical location referenced by the `deitel` virtual directory created at the beginning of this chapter. The GUI (i.e., the `.aspx` file) is shown in Fig. 23.34. This `.aspx` file is similar to the `adRotator.aspx` file in Fig. 23.13. There are two differences—the new directive in lines 1–2 and the lack of any JScript .NET code, which are required changes to use the code-behind approach.

```
1   <%@ Page Language="JScript"
2       Src="adRotator.aspx.js" Inherits="MyCodeBehind" %>
3
4   <!DOCTYPE html PUBLIC "-//W3C//DTD XHTML 1.1//EN"
5       "http://www.w3.org/TR/xhtml11/DTD/xhtml11.dtd">
6
7   <!-- Fig. 23.34: adRotator.aspx   -->
8   <!-- ASP.NET AdRotator example    -->
9
10  <html>
11     <head>
12        <title>Using An AdRotator</title>
13     </head>
14
15     <body>
16        <form action = "adRotator.aspx" method = "post" runat = "server">
17
18           <asp:AdRotator AdvertisementFile = "ads.xml"
19              BorderColor = "black" BorderWidth = "1" runat = "server"/>
20
21           <table>
22              <tr>
23                 <td>
24                    Name: <asp:TextBox id = "name" runat = "server"/>
25                 </td>
26                 <td>
27                    <asp:RequiredFieldValidator id = "requiredCheck"
28                       ControlToValidate = "name"
```

Fig. 23.34 Web Form page for use with code-behind. (Part 1 of 2.)

```
29                          Display = "Static"
30                          runat = "server">
31                          Please enter your name.
32                       </asp:RequiredFieldValidator>
33                   </td>
34                </tr>
35             </table>
36
37             <br />
38             Do you like ice cream?
39
40             <asp:RadioButtonList id = "iceCream" runat = "server">
41                <asp:ListItem>Yes</asp:ListItem>
42                <asp:ListItem>No</asp:ListItem>
43             </asp:RadioButtonList>
44
45             <br />
46             How many scoops would you like? (0-45)
47
48             <asp:TextBox id = "scoops" runat = "server" />
49
50             <br />
51             <asp:button text = "Submit" OnClick = "submitButton_Click"
52                runat = "server"/>
53
54             <asp:RangeValidator id = "rangeCheck"
55                ControlToValidate = "scoops"
56                MinimumValue = "0"
57                MaximumValue = "45"
58                Type = "Integer"
59                EnableClientScript = "false"
60                Text = "We cannot give you that many scoops."
61                runat = "server" />
62
63             <center>
64                <h1> <asp:label id = "message" runat = "server"/> </h1>
65             </center>
66
67          </form>
68       </body>
69    </html>
```

Fig. 23.34 Web Form page for use with code-behind. (Part 2 of 2.)

Lines 1–2 contain the @ Page directive. The attribute Inherits indicates a code-behind class from which the page is to inherit properties and methods. Attribute Src specifies the name of the file containing the code-behind class that will be compiled when the page is requested. The attribute Language specifies the programming language used (e.g., JScript .NET, VB.NET, or C#).

The JScript .NET code, previously embedded in the adRotator.aspx file, has been moved to the code-behind file, which has an .aspx.js extension (Fig. 23.35). Lines 5–7 contain import statements. Import statements are placed before the class definition and enable developers to access parts of the .NET Framework easily.

The code-behind file (Fig. 23.35) defines a class called MyCodeBehind (line 9). Recall that a class contains variables and methods. The extends keyword specifies that class MyCodeBehind *extends* class Page. A class that extends another page inherits the properties and methods of that class. Some properties inherited from class Page are IsValid and IsPostBack, which are boolean properties that indicate, respectively, whether a page satisfies all validators and has been posted back.

```
1   // Fig 23.35: adRotator.aspx.js
2   // Code-behind for the adRotator.aspx
3   // user interface.
4
5   import System;
6   import System.Web.UI;
7   import System.Web.UI.WebControls;
8
9   public class MyCodeBehind extends Page
10  {
11      protected var name : TextBox;
12      protected var scoops : TextBox;
13      protected var iceCream : RadioButtonList;
14      protected var message : Label;
15
16      public function submitButton_Click(
17          sender : Object, events : EventArgs ) : void
18      {
19          if ( IsPostBack )
20          {
21              if ( iceCream.SelectedItem == "Yes" )
22              {
23                  message.Text = name.Text + " likes ice cream.";
24              }
25              else
26              {
27                  message.Text = name.Text + " does not like ice cream.";
28              }
29          }
30      } // end submitButton_Click
31  } // end class MyCodeBehind
```

Fig. 23.35 Code-behind file for the adRotator.aspx Web Form page.

We will explain how to run this application shortly. Note that the function submitButton_Click from Fig. 23.9 has been placed in the class MyCodeBehind (lines 16–30). This function has not been altered from the earlier example. Lines 11–14 declare the variables that are used in the script. These variables correspond to Web controls in the .aspx GUI file. Each variable declaration is preceded by the keyword protected, which makes the variables visible only to the class to which they belong (i.e., MyCodeBehind) and any derived classes (i.e., classes that extend MyCodeBehind).

For the code to work, the code-behind file must be compiled into a DLL. The DLL created from our code-behind will contain the single submitButton_Click function and variables. Integrated desktop environments (IDEs), such as Visual Studio .NET, which are designed to simplify ASP.NET page coding, seamlessly handle the compilation of code-behind files. Since we are not using an IDE, we must compile the code-behind in the Windows command prompt.

The Microsoft .NET SDK provides many tools and compilers for creating ASP.NET pages. To use the tools, the user must set the appropriate PATH, INCLUDE and LIB environment variables in *each* command-prompt session. To set the environment variables, open a command-prompt session and run the sdkvars.bat program located in the C:\Program Files\Microsoft.NET\SDK\v1.1\Bin directory. To run this program, type

```
C:\Program Files\Microsoft.NET\SDK\v1.1\Bin\sdkvars.bat
```

at the command prompt and press *Enter*, or navigate to the directory noted above using the cd command, then type sdkvars.bat and press *Enter*. Note that the Microsoft.NET\ SDK directory differs from the Microsoft.NET\Framework directory, which will exist in your system root directory (i.e., C:\WINDOWS or C:\WINNT). If you have Visual Studio .NET, replace Microsoft.NET with the directory for the latest version of Visual Studio .NET on your system.

After running the .bat file, create a subdirectory named **bin** in the directory that contains the code-behind. We will place the compiler's output for the code-behind file in this directory. Next, in the command prompt, navigate to the directory where the code-behind is located. Use the cd command followed by a subdirectory to change directories. The command cd .. navigates up a directory level. Type

```
jsc /t:library /out:bin\codebehind.dll adRotator.aspx.js
```

at the command prompt and press *Enter* to compile the code-behind. The command jsc specifies that we are executing the JScript .NET compiler. The command-line flag /t:library is short for /target:library. The target specifies the type of output file (e.g., exe, winexe or library). Libraries are typically DLLs. The command line flag / out:bin\codebehind.dll specifies the name and location for the output file to be created by the compiler. This command names the output codebehind.dll and specifies that it should be created in the bin subdirectory. The file that we are compiling (adRotator.aspx.js) is specified at the end of the command. Figure 23.36 shows the output in the command prompt.

Fig. 23.36   Using the command prompt to compile the code-behind.

Once the code-behind file has been compiled, we can run the example. Figure 23.37 shows the output of adRotator.aspx written with the code-behind method. The page's @ Page directive informs ASP.NET where to find the compiled code-behind file. The output and functionality of the page are identical to the page written using the in-line code approach.

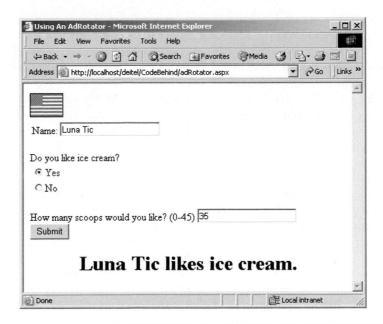

Fig. 23.37 Output of `AdRotator.aspx` using the code-behind method.

23.12 ASP.NET Web Services

A Web service (sometimes called an XML Web service) is an application that enables distributed computing by allowing one machine to call methods on other machines via common data formats and protocols such as XML and HTTP. In .NET and other frameworks these method calls are implemented using the Simple Object Access Protocol (SOAP), an XML-based protocol describing how to mark up requests and responses so that they can be transferred via protocols such as HTTP. Using SOAP, applications represent and transmit data in a standardized format—XML. See Chapter 20 for further details on how XML and SOAP operate. The underlying implementation of the Web service is irrelevant to clients using the Web service.

Microsoft is encouraging software vendors and e-businesses to deploy Web services. As larger numbers of people worldwide connect to the Internet, the concept of applications that call methods across a network becomes more practical. Earlier in this text, we delineated the merits of object-oriented programming. Web services represent the next step in object-oriented programming: Instead of developing software from a small number of class libraries provided at one location, programmers can access countless libraries in multiple locations. This technology also makes it easier for businesses to collaborate and grow together. By purchasing Web services that are relevant to their businesses, companies that create applications can spend less time coding and more time developing new products. In addition, e-businesses can employ Web services to provide their customers with an enhanced shopping experience. Let us look at an online music store as a simple example. The store's Web site provides links to various CDs, enabling users to purchase the CDs or to obtain information about the artists. Another company that sells concert tickets provides a Web service that displays the dates of upcoming concerts by various artists, then allows users to buy concert tickets. By deploying the concert-ticket Web service on its site, the online music store can provide an additional service to its customers that will likely result in increased traffic to its site. The company that sells concert tickets also benefits from the business relationship. In addition to selling more tickets, it receives revenue from the online music store for the use of its Web service.

The .NET framework provides a simple way to create Web services like the one discussed in this example. In this section, we explore the steps involved in the creation of Web services. Because we are only introducing Web services in this text, we will not create an application that uses the Web service.

Defining the Web Service

A Web service is a class stored on one machine that can be accessed by another machine over a network. Because of this relationship, the machine on which the Web service resides is commonly referred to as a **remote machine**. The application that desires access to the Web service sends a method call and its arguments to the remote machine, which processes the call and sends a response to the caller. This kind of distributed computing can benefit various systems, including slow systems, those with limited amounts of memory or resources, those without access to certain data and those lacking the code necessary to perform specific computations. Another advantage of Web services is that code and data can be stored on another computer. For instance, a Web service can be defined at one location to execute several common queries to a database. Not only does the Web service define the necessary code for the client, but the database is stored on the same machine as the Web service. The client does not need to access or store the database on its machine.

A Web service is, in its simplest form, a class. Normally, when we want to include a class in an application, we define it in the application or add a reference to the compiled class. As a result, all the pieces of our application reside on one machine. When we are using Web services, the class we wish to include in our project is instead stored on a remote machine—a compiled version of this class will not be placed in the current application.

Methods in a Web service are executed through a **Remote Procedure Call** (RPC). These methods are often referred to as **Web-service methods**. To specify that a method is a Web-service method, we must declare the method with attribute **WebMethod** (of the **WebMethodAttribute** class). **Attributes** are identifiers that specify additional information in a declaration. Attributes are used to define the underlying behavior of classes, methods or variables. The code that defines an attribute is applied at run time. Declaring a method with this attribute makes the method accessible to other classes through an RPC. The declaration of a Web-service method with attribute **WebMethod** is known as **exposing** a Web-service method, and enables it to be called remotely.

 Common Programming Error 23.4

Trying to call a remote method in a Web service where the method is not declared with the **WebMethod** *attribute is a compile-time error.*

Method calls to and responses from Web services are transmitted via SOAP. This means that any client capable of generating and processing SOAP messages can use a Web service, regardless of the language in which the Web service is written.

Web services have important implications for **business-to-business (B2B) transactions**—that is, transactions that occur between two or more businesses. Now businesses are able to conduct their transactions via Web services rather than custom-created applications—a much simpler and more efficient means of conducting business. Because Web services and SOAP are platform independent, companies can collaborate and use each other's Web services without worrying about the compatibility of technologies or programming languages. In this way, Web services are an inexpensive, readily available solution to facilitate B2B transactions.

Like an ASP.NET Web application, a Web service in .NET can have two parts—an **ASMX** file (with an **.asmx** extension) and a code-behind file. The ASMX file can be viewed in any Web browser and contains valuable information about the Web service, such as descriptions of Web-service methods and ways to test them. The implementation for the methods that the Web service encompasses can be located in the ASMX file or the code-behind file. Figure 23.38 shows an ASMX file that defines a Web-service class.

```
1   <%@ WebService Language="JScript" Class="NumberService" %>
2
3   // Fig. 23.38: number.asmx
4   // A simple Web Service
5
6   import System;
7   import System.Web.Services;
8
9   public class NumberService extends WebService
10  {
11      // Determines whether all the characters in a String are digits
12      WebMethod public function isNum( number : String ) : Boolean
13      {
14          var digitArray : char[];
15          digitArray = number.ToCharArray();
16
17          for ( var i : int = 0; i < digitArray.Length ; i++ )
18          {
19              if ( !Char.IsDigit( digitArray[ i ] ) )
20              {
21                  return false;
22              }
23          }
24
25          return true;
26      } // end isNum
27
28      WebMethod public function Add( a : float, b : float) : float {
29          return a + b;
30      }
31  } // end class NumberService
```

Fig. 23.38 ASP.NET Web service.

The information in line 1 is mandatory. This declaration tells the `.asmx` handler which class to inspect for Web methods and the language in which the file will be compiled. In this example, we have a class called `NumberService`, and the attribute `language` is set to `"JScript"`. Line 6 imports the .NET `System` namespace, which contains classes that define commonly used values and data types, event handlers and attributes. In line 7, we import the .NET `System.Web.Services` namespace, which contains classes that enable you to create XML Web services using ASP.NET and XML Web service clients.

Line 9 declares a class `NumberService` which extends `WebService` (i.e., class `NumberService` inherits the attributes and methods of class `WebService`). XML Web services can derive from the `WebService` class to get access to the ASP.NET `WebMethodAttribute` class, which provides the `WebMethod` attribute that must be applied to any method exposed over the Web.

Line 12 declares a function `isNum` that takes a `String number` as an argument and returns a `Boolean`. The function determines whether `number` represents a non-negative integer. Defining the function as `public` allows any other class to call and use it. Adding `WebMethod` to the front of the function declaration exposes the function (i.e., allows it to be called from remote Web clients).

Lines 14–15 declare a character array `digitArray` and initialize it to hold the characters in the argument `number`. Lines 17–23 determine whether each character in the string is a digit. If the script finds a non-digit character, the method returns `false`; if every character is a digit, the method returns `true`. Lines 28–30 declare another function that is included in the Web service. This method simply adds two `float`s and returns the sum.

Viewing the Web Service
As mentioned, opening an `.asmx` file in a Web browser displays descriptions of Web-service methods and provides ways to test them. Figure 23.39 shows `number.asmx` as it is rendered in Internet Explorer.

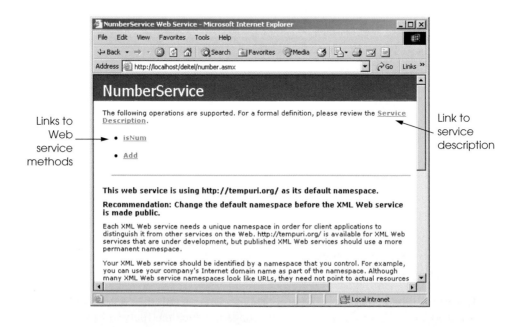

Links to Web service methods

Link to service description

Fig. 23.39 ASMX file rendered in Internet Explorer.

The top of the page provides a link to the Web service's **Service Description**. A service description is an XML document that conforms to the **Web Service Description Language (WSDL)**, an XML vocabulary that defines the methods that the Web service makes available and the ways in which clients can interact with them. The WSDL document also specifies lower-level information that the client might need, such as the required formats for requests and responses. Client programs can use the service description to confirm the correctness of calls to Web methods. When a user clicks the **Service Description** link at the top of the `.asmx` page, a WSDL document is displayed that defines the service description for this Web service (Fig. 23.40).

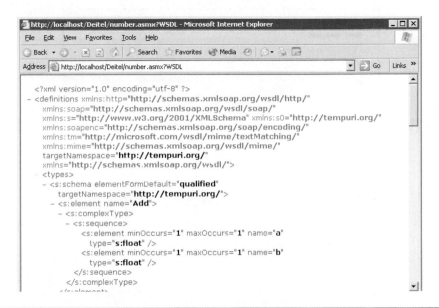

Fig. 23.40   Service description for a Web service.

Below the **Service Description** link, the Web page shown in Fig. 23.39 lists the methods that the Web service provides (i.e., all the methods in the application that are declared with `WebMethod`). Clicking any method name requests a test page (Fig. 23.41) that explains the method's arguments. The test page also allows users to test the method by entering the proper parameters and clicking **Invoke**. Below the **Invoke** button, the page displays sample request and response messages using SOAP, HTTP GET and HTTP POST. These protocols are the three options for sending and receiving messages in Web services. The protocol used for request and response messages is sometimes known as the Web service's **wire protocol** or **wire format**, because the wire format specifies how information is sent "along the wire."

Users can test the `isNum` method by entering **Value**s in the **number:** field, then clicking **Invoke**. The method executes, and a new Web-browser window opens to display an XML document containing the result (Fig. 23.42). Now that we have a Web service that has been tested, clients can write applications that call our Web-service method from across the Internet.

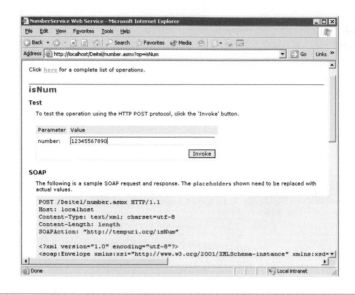

Fig. 23.41   Invoking a method of a Web service from a Web browser.

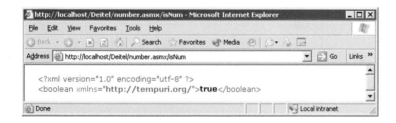

Fig. 23.42   Results of invoking a Web-service method from a Web browser.

Error-Prevention Tip 23.2

Using the ASMX page of a Web service to test and debug methods makes that Web service more reliable and robust; it also reduces the likelihood that clients using the Web service will encounter errors.

This chapter has introduced ASP.NET, JScript .NET and the .NET Framework. Students should now be able to create dynamic Web forms that respond to user input, use code-behinds, create Web services, manipulate text files, track and maintain a user's session information and interact with a server-side database from a Web form. ASP.NET and the .NET Framework offer many additional classes and much advanced functionality that goes far beyond what has been covered here. Please explore the URLs in the Web Resources section if you are interested in further study of ASP.NET.

23.13 Web Resources

`www.asp.net`
The Microsoft site overviews ASP.NET and provides a link for downloading ASP.NET. This site includes the IBuySpy e-commerce storefront example that uses ASP.NET. Links to the Amazon and Barnes & Noble Web sites, where the user can purchase books, also are included.

`www.asp101.com/aspdotnet/aspplus/index.asp`
Overviews ASP.NET and includes articles, code examples and links to ASP.NET resources. The code samples demonstrate the use of cookies in an ASP.NET application and show how to establish a connection to a database—two key capabilities of multi-tier applications.

`www.411asp.net`
Provides programmers with ASP .NET tutorials and code samples. The community page allows programmers to ask questions, answer questions and post messages.

`www.aspfree.com`
Provides free ASP.NET demos and source code. The site also provides a list of articles for various topics and a FAQs page.

`www.aspng.com`
Offers tutorials, links and recommendations for books on ASP.NET. Links to different mailing lists also are provided, organized by topic. This site also contains articles related to many ASP. NET topics, such as "Performance Tips and Tricks."

`www.aspnetfaq.com`
Provides answers to FAQs about ASP. NET.

`www.123aspx.com`
Offers a directory of links to ASP .NET resources. It also includes daily and weekly newsletters.

`msdn.microsoft.com/netframework`
Articles, examples, libraries, and APIs about the .NET framework

`www.xmlforasp.net`
Provides articles and tutorials on XML and ASP.NET.

`www.ondotnet.com/topics/dotnet/asp.net`
Provides articles written by programmers about ASP.NET development.

SUMMARY

- Server-side scripting uses information sent by clients, information stored on the server, information stored in the server's memory and information from the Internet to dynamically create Web pages.
- ASP.NET is a compiled .NET programming framework and technology that can be used on a server to create Web applications.
- ASP.NET takes advantage of Microsoft's .NET Framework, which provides thousands of classes.
- A key aspect of the .NET strategy is its independence from a specific programming language.
- Microsoft's .NET Framework includes tools for porting, or adapting, existing software components to .NET.
- The FCL contains reusable components that programmers can incorporate into their applications—this makes it unnecessary to create new software entirely from the ground up.
- ASP.NET developers can create multi-tier, database-intensive applications quickly by employing .NET's object-oriented languages and the FCL's Web controls.
- Web controls look like HTML elements but are designed specifically for ASP.NET applications.
- ASPX files contain the GUI of a page, and may also contain the logic of the page.

- ASPX files often have a corresponding code-behind file that contains the ASPX file's programmatic implementation.
- Every element in an ASP.NET page is treated as an object and run on a server.
- An ASP.NET page gets compiled. Compiling improves the performance and load time of ASP.NET pages because the code is directly executed rather than interpreted.
- JScript .NET is Microsoft's latest version of its JScript scripting language. JScript .NET is a truly object-oriented language. Using JScript .NET provides access to the numerous classes found in the FCL.
- Scripts in ASP.NET pages must be contained in `script` elements or between the scripting delimiters <% and %>.
- Attribute `runat` with value `"server"` indicates that the script should be processed on the server.
- An ASP.NET application, when compiled, actually defines a class. The class inherits from class `Page`, provided by the .NET Framework. By inheriting from the `Page` class, the ASP.NET application gains access to several built-in objects.
- The `Request` object is used to access the information passed by a *get* or *post* request.
- The `Response` object sends information, such as XHTML and text, to the client.
- The `Server` object provides access to methods and properties on the server.
- ASPX files are sometimes referred to as Web Forms or Web Form pages.
- Programmers customize Web Forms by adding Web controls.
- Server controls on an ASP.NET Web Form persist data.
- HTML controls are programmable HTML elements run on the server.
- Validation controls are used with input controls; they provide the ability to check patterns, required fields, ranges and so on.
- User controls are controls created by the programmer rather than the FCL.
- ASPX pages usually contain a form that, when submitted, causes the current page to be requested again. This event is known as a postback.
- An event handler is a function that executes in response to an action (called an event).
- The `action` attribute of the `form` element indicates the `.aspx` file to which the form information is `posted`.
- Property `IsPostBack` returns a value indicating whether the page is being loaded in response to a client postback.
- A required field validator ensures that a field receives input.
- A range validator checks that input is within a specified range.
- The `id` attribute of a Web control defines the name of the control.
- The `AdRotator` Web control simplifies the creation of advertising banners, using advertisement data located in an XML file.
- Personalization makes it possible for e-businesses to communicate effectively with their customers and also improves users' ability to locate desired products and services. To provide personalized services to consumers, e-businesses must be able to recognize clients when they request information from a site.
- A session ID represents a unique client on the Internet. If the client leaves a site and returns later, the client will still be recognized as the same user.
- The tracking of individual clients is known as session tracking.

- A cookie is a text file stored by a Web site on an individual's computer that allows the site to track the actions of the visitor.
- When the browser requests a resource from a Web server, cookies previously sent to the client by that Web server are returned to the Web server as part of the request formulated by the browser.
- The Page_Load event handler executes when an ASPX page loads.
- The Cookies property of the Request object can be used to retrieve cookies from the user's machine.
- In .NET, cookies are represented as objects of type HttpCookie. Class HttpCookie has various properties that can be used to manipulate cookies.
- .NET provides session-tracking capabilities in the FCL's HttpSessionState class. Every Web Form includes an HttpSessionState object, which is accessible through property Session of class Page.
- Like a cookie, an HttpSessionState object stores name-value pairs. In session terminology, these are called session items.
- HttpSessionState objects can store any type of object as an attribute value.
- Property SessionID contains the session's unique ID. The first time a client connects to the Web server, a unique session ID is created for that client. When the client makes additional requests, the client's session ID is compared with the session IDs stored in the Web server's memory.
- OnInit is an event handler that is called when a page is initialized.
- In .NET, XML documents are represented as objects of type XmlDocument.
- Method Load of class XmlDocument parses an XML document. Once an XML document is loaded into an XmlDocument, its data can be read and manipulated programmatically.
- In .NET, XML elements are objects of type XmlElement, which can be created by calling method CreateElement.
- A DataView provides a bindable, customized view of a DataTable that can be sorted and edited.
- A DataTable is an object representing a table of data.
- Data binding allows programmers to easily display and manipulate data without dealing with the underlying data structures.
- Property PhysicalApplicationPath of the Request object contains the file system path of the currently executing server application's root directory.
- Method ReadLine of class StreamReader reads a line from a text file.
- The method LoadDataRow finds and updates a specific row of a DataTable.
- A DataGrid is a control that displays data from a data source (e.g., a database) in the form of a table.
- Method WriteLine of class StreamWriter is used to write a line of text to a file.
- An OleDbDataReader is an object that reads data from a database.
- The @ Register directive allows programmers to declare the user controls that will be included in an ASPX file.
- A user control is defined in an external file saved with an .ascx extension. Using .ascx files helps encapsulate frequently used blocks of code.
- Web.config files are XML-formatted text files that reside in the Web site's root directory. Web.config files typically specify configuration settings, such as authorization settings for the Web site or the appearance of error pages.
- An OleDbConnection object represents a connection to a database.

- A database connection is opened by calling method `Open` of class `OleDbConnection`.
- `OleDbCommand` objects represent SQL commands to be executed on a data source.
- Method `ExecuteReader` returns the result of a query in the form of an `OleDbDataReader`.
- Method `Read` of class `OleDbDataReader` accesses a row from the results of the query.
- A `DataSet` represents a set of data and includes the tables that contain and order the data, in addition to the relationships between the tables.
- An `OleDbDataAdapter` is an object used to retrieve information from a database and place it in a `DataSet`.
- A `DataView` enables the creation of different views of the data stored in a `DataTable`.
- Using code-behinds enables the presentation code and programming logic to be placed in separate files.
- A code-behind must be compiled before the page is accessed. Then the `.aspx` file can call methods from the binary dynamic link library (DLL) that the compiler creates.
- A Web service is a class stored on one machine that can be accessed on another machine over a network. Because of this relationship, the machine on which the Web service resides is commonly referred to as a remote machine.
- Methods in a Web service are executed through a Remote Procedure Call (RPC). These methods are often referred to as Web-service methods.
- To specify that a method is a Web-service method, we must declare it with attribute `WebMethod`.
- The declaration of a Web-service method with attribute `WebMethod` is known as exposing a Web-service method, and enables it to be called remotely.
- A Web service in .NET has two parts—an ASMX file and a code-behind file.
- A Web service's service description is an XML document that conforms to the Web Service Description Language (WSDL), an XML vocabulary that defines the methods that the Web service makes available and the ways in which clients can interact with those methods.

TERMINOLOGY

`<% %>` scripting delimiters
Add method of `DataTable.Columns`
Add method of the `Items` property
`AdRotator` control
advertisement
`AdvertisementFile` attribute of the
    `AdRotator` control
`AppendChild` method of class `XmlElement`
`.ascx` file extension
ASMX file
`.asmx` file extension
ASP.NET
ASP.NET server control
ASP.NET user control
ASP.NET Web service
ASPX file
`.aspx` file extension
`.aspx.js` file extension
attribute

Berkeley System Distribution (BSD)
brick-and-mortar store
Business-to-Business (B2B)
client
code-behind file
`Columns` property of class `DataTable`
Common Language Infrastructure (CLI)
Common Language Runtime (CLR)
`Cookies` property of `Request` object
`Counts` property of class `HttpSessionState`
`CreateElement` method of class
    `XmlDocument`
`CreateTextNode` method of class
    `XmlDocument`
`DataBind` method of class `DataGrid`
`DataGrid` control
`DataSet` class
`DataTable` class
`DataView` class

wire format
wire protocol
WriteLine method of class StreamWriter

XmlDocument object
XmlElement class
XmlText class

SELF-REVIEW EXERCISES

23.1 State whether each of the following is *true* or *false*. If *false*, explain why.
a) JScript .NET is the only language that can be used in an ASP.NET page.
b) ASP.NET Web Form file names typically end in .aspx.
c) Only Microsoft Internet Explorer can render an ASP.NET page.
d) The <%@ Page Language="JScript" %> statement can go anywhere in an ASP.NET file.
e) An ASP.NET page can contain an unlimited number of Web Forms.
f) Code-behinds help separate the business logic code from presentation.
g) ASP.NET includes built-in classes that allow interaction with XML documents.
h) The @ Register directive allows programmers to declare instances of custom user controls that will be included in an external .ascx file.
i) Property PostBack returns a value indicating whether the page is being loaded in response to a client postback.
j) ASP.NET is an interpreted .NET programming platform and technology that can be used on a server to create Web applications.

23.2 Fill in the blanks for each of the following statements:
a) Directive _____ informs the ASP.NET compiler of the programing language used.
b) Session variables retain their value for the duration of the _____.
c) Classes of related components provided by the .NET Framework are organized and grouped together into _____.
d) A(n) _____ is a Web control that displays database information in a table and allows paging and sorting of database rows and columns on the client side.
e) _____ files are XML-formatted text files that reside in the Web site's root directory and typically specify configuration settings for the site.
f) _____ returns the file system path of the server application's root directory.
g) The _____ Web control simplifies the creation of advertising banners, using advertisement data located in an XML file.
h) A(n) _____ object represents a connection to a database.
i) Every Web Form includes an HttpSessionState object, which is accessible through property _____ of class Page.
j) _____ controls are used with input controls; they provide the ability to check for patterns, required fields, ranges and the like.

ANSWERS TO SELF-REVIEW EXERCISES

23.1 a) False. ASP.NET pages can be programmed in any of the .NET-compatible programming languages (e.g., JScript .NET, VB.NET and C#). b) True. c) False. Most browsers can render HTML rendered by an ASP.NET page. d) True. However, <%@ Page Language="JScript" %> is placed at the top of a file by convention. e) False. An ASP.NET page can contain at most one Web Form. f) True. g) True. h) True. i) False. Property IsPostBack returns a value indicating whether the page is being loaded in response to a client postback. j) False. ASP.NET is a compiled .NET programming platform and technology that can be used on a server to create Web applications.

23.2 a) @ Page. b) session (which usually ends when the user closes the Web browser). c) namespaces. d) DataGrid. e) Web.config. f) Request.PhysicalApplicationPath. g) AdRotator. h) OleDbConnection. i) Session. j) Validation.

EXERCISES

23.3   What does the following code segment do?

```
1    <html>
2       <head>
3          <script language = "JScript" runat = "server">
4
5             function submitButton_Click(
6                sender : Object, events : EventArgs ) : void
7             {
8                var myDocument : XmlDocument = new XmlDocument();
9                myDocument.Load( Server.MapPath( "accounts.xml" ) );
10
11               var userNode : XmlElement =
12                  myDocument.CreateElement( "user" );
13               var nameNode : XmlElement =
14                  myDocument.CreateElement( "name" );
15               var passwordNode : XmlElement =
16                  myDocument.CreateElement( "password" );
17
18               nameNode.AppendChild(
19                  myDocument.CreateTextNode( name.Text ) );
20               passwordNode.AppendChild(
21                  myDocument.CreateTextNode( password.Text ) );
22
23               userNode.AppendChild( nameNode );
24               userNode.AppendChild( passwordNode );
25
26               myDocument.DocumentElement.AppendChild( userNode );
27               myDocument.Save( Server.MapPath( "accounts.xml" ) );
28
29               name.Text = "";
30               password.Text = "";
31            } // end submitButton_Click
32
33         </script>
34      </head>
35      <body>
36
37         <form runat = "server">
38
39            <p>Please enter a name:
40            <asp:TextBox id = "name" runat = "server" /></p>
41
42            <p>Please enter a password:
43            <asp:TextBox id = "password" runat = "server" /></p>
44
45            <asp:Button text = "Submit" runat = "server"
46               OnClick = "submitButton_Click" />
47
48         </form>
49
50      </body>
51   </html>
```

23.4   Find the error(s) in the following program segment, and correct it (them).

```
<asp:RadioButtonList id = "languageList">
    <asp:ListItem Value = "C#">C#</asp:ListItem>
    <asp:ListItem Value = "C++">C++</asp:ListItem>
    <asp:ListItem Value = "C">C</asp:ListItem>
    <asp:ListItem Value = "Python">Python
</asp:RadioButtonList>
```

23.5   Create a Web form that uses validation controls to check the user's input. The Web form should have the same appearance as the form shown in Fig. 23.43. Each text box should have a corresponding `RequiredFieldValidator`. The **Card number:** text box should use a `RegularExpressionValidator` to check that only digits were entered (dashes and spaces should not be allowed). The **Expiration (MM/YY):** text box should use a `RegularExpressionValidator` check that the input matches MM/YY. [*Hint:* Create the `RegularExpressionValidators` as we created `RequiredFieldValidators` earlier in the chapter, and set their `ControlToValidate` attributes to the text boxes for the card number and expiration date. For the `RegularExpressionValidator` that will validate the card number, set the validator's `ValidationExpression` attribute to `"^\d+$"`. For the `RegularExpressionValidator` that will validate the expiration date, set the validator's `ValidationExpression` attribute to `"\d{2}/\d{2}"`. These values are known as regular expressions, a subject that will be discussed later in the book.]

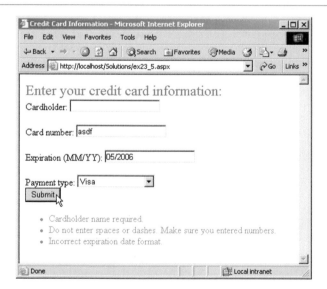

Fig. 23.43   Validation control output.

Set each validator's `Display` attribute to `"None"`. Add a `ValidationSummary` control at the end of the form, setting its `id` attribute to `"summary"` and its `runat` attribute to `"server"`. This causes all error messages to be displayed in a summary at the end of the page.

23.6   Modify the database example from Section 23.10 so that the `DataGrid` shows the description of the book instead of the publisher, as pictured in Fig. 23.44. Also, modify the `DataGrid` so that it has a background color of `"#7CFC00"`, where every other row has the background color `"#90EE90"`. Have the `DataGrid`'s header display with a background color of `"#006400"` and a foreground color of `"#FFFFFF"` (white). Set the text in the header to display in bold.

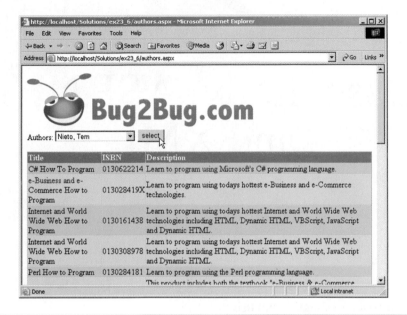

Fig. 23.44 Sample display of first and last names, and book description.

23.7   Modify Section 23.9's mailing list application to use the code-behind approach.

23.8   Create a navigation bar Web user control with four buttons. The buttons do not need to have any functionality (i.e., no actions need to occur when they are clicked). The buttons should appear as in Fig. 23.45.

23.9   Using cookies, create a page that displays the number of times a user has accessed it, as pictured in Fig. 23.46. At the top of the page, include the Web user control created in the preceding exercise. For the purposes of this exercise, have the value in the cookie increased only if the page is *not* being accessed due to a postback (this will prevent the cookie value from being increased each time a button is clicked).

Fig. 23.45 Navigation bar.

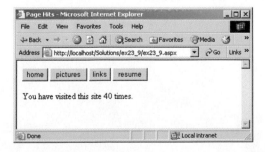

Fig. 23.46 Application displays the number of times a page has been accessed.

24

Case Study: ASP.NET and XML

Objectives

- To create a Web-based message forum using ASP.NET Pages.
- To use XML with ASP.NET.
- To be able to add new forums.
- To be able to post messages to the message forum.
- To use .NET Framework classes to manipulate XML documents.
- To use XSLT to transform XML documents.

If any man will draw up his case, and put his name at the foot of the first page, I will give him an immediate reply. Where he compels me to turn over the sheet, he must wait my leisure.
Lord Sandwich

They also serve who only stand and wait.
John Milton

A fair request should be followed by a deed in silence.
Dante Alighieri

24.1 Introduction

In this chapter, we use XML and ASP.NET to create one of the most popular types of Web sites—a **message forum**. Message forums are "virtual" bulletin boards where various topics are discussed. Common features of message forums include discussion groups, questions and answers and general comments. Many Web sites host message forums. In particular,

```
messages.yahoo.com
web.eesite.com/forums
groups.google.com
```

are popular sites that host message forums.

In this case study, users can post messages and create new forums. This chapter assumes you are familiar with the concepts presented in Chapter 20 and Chapter 23.

24.2 Setup and Message Forum Documents

In this section, we provide the setup instructions for executing the case study. The case study requires the following software:

1. Microsoft Internet Information Services (IIS) 5 or 6.

2. Internet Explorer 6 (for XML and XSLT processing).

3. MSXML 3.0 or higher (included with IE 6).

Copy the files from the Chapter 24 examples directory (on the CD-ROM that accompanies this book) to a directory named Forums within the directory referenced by the deitel virtual directory (created in Chapter 23). If the deitel virtual directory does not exist, please create it now. These directories must be located within the IIS Web root directory (e.g., C:\Inetpub\wwwroot). [*Note*: Either IIS 5 or 6 must be installed; otherwise, this directory will not exist. This directory must also have permission to write to the files in the application, so that users can post messages and add forums. Follow the steps in the beginning of Section 23.3 to add the **ASPNET** user to the Forums folder. If your system uses the NTFS file system, select the **Security** tab of this folder's **Properties** dialog, and check the **Write** check box in the **Allow** column for the **ASPNET** user (the left check box in the last row of check boxes in Fig. 23.1). See Section 23.3 for more information on determining which type of file system you are using.]

Each of the files and documents used in this case study is summarized in Fig. 24.1 and will be discussed later in the chapter.

The main page, `default.aspx`, displays the list of available message forums, which are stored in the XML document `forums.xml`. The document `forums.xsl` creates hyperlinks in the `default.aspx` page to each of the forums listed in `forums.xml`. The ASP.NET document `default.aspx` also contains a link to `addForum.aspx`, which adds a new forum to the listing of forums in `forums.xml` and creates a new XML document to store the messages in this forum (e.g., `forum2.xml`).

Each XML message forum document (e.g., `forumASP.xml`) is transformed into an XHTML document using the XSLT document `formatting.xsl`. CSS document `style.css` formats the XHTML for display. New messages are posted to a forum by `addPost.aspx`. Each forum page (produced from the corresponding XML document transformed by the XSLT document) presents a hyperlink to `addPost.aspx`. Some of these key interactions between documents are illustrated in Fig. 24.2.

File Name	Description
`default.aspx`	Main page, providing navigational links to the forums.
`addForum.aspx`	Adds a forum.
`addPost.aspx`	Adds a message to a forum.
`forums.xml`	XML document listing all available forums and their filenames.
`forumASP.xml`	Sample message forum.
`forums.xsl`	XSL for transforming forum listing into XHTML.
`formatting.xsl`	Document for transforming message forums into XHTML.
`style.css`	Style sheet for formatting the message forum site.

Fig. 24.1   Message forum documents.

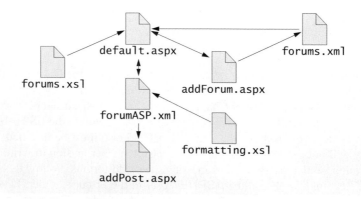

Fig. 24.2   Interactions between message forum documents.

24.3 Forum Navigation

This section introduces the documents that organize and display the message forums. Figure 24.3 lists the XML document (forums.xml) that marks up each message forum.

```
1   <?xml version = "1.0"?>
2
3   <!-- Fig. 24.3: forums.xml      -->
4   <!-- Creating the ASP.NET forum -->
5
6   <forums>
7
8       <forum filename = "forumASP.xml">ASP.NET Forum</forum>
9
10  </forums>
```

Fig. 24.3   XML document that marks up the message forums.

Root element forums can hold any number of forum elements. We provide an initial forum named forumASP.xml. An individual message forum is marked up, using element forum. Attribute filename stores the name of the XML document that contains the forum's messages and markup. The **content** (i.e., the text between the opening and closing tags) of the forum element holds the forum's title.

We will discuss how forums.xml is manipulated momentarily. Figure 24.4 shows the ASP.NET page (default.aspx) that displays the list of message forums contained in forums.xml. CSS document style.css (Fig. 24.14) is applied to the HTML sent to the Web browser.

```
1   <%@ Page Language="JScript" %>
2   <%@ Import Namespace="System" %>
3   <%@ Import Namespace="System.Data" %>
4   <%@ Import Namespace="System.Xml" %>
5
6   <!-- Fig. 24.4: default.aspx -->
7   <!-- Forum home page.        -->
8
9   <!DOCTYPE html PUBLIC "-//W3C//DTD XHTML 1.1//EN"
10      "http://www.w3.org/TR/xhtml11/DTD/xhtml11.dtd">
11
12  <html xmlns = "http://www.w3.org/1999/xhtml">
13
14      <head>
15          <title>Deitel Message Forums</title>
16          <link rel = "stylesheet" type = "text/css"
17              href = "style.css" />
18      </head>
19
20      <body>
21          <h1>Deitel Message Forums</h1>
22          <p><strong>Available Forums</strong></p>
```

Fig. 24.4   Message forum main page. (Part 1 of 2.)

```
23
24          <form runat = "server">
25             <ul>
26                <asp:Xml runat = "server"
27                   DocumentSource = "forums.xml"
28                   TransformSource = "forums.xsl" />
29             </ul>
30          </form>
31
32          <p><strong>Forum Management</strong></p>
33
34          <ul>
35             <li><a href = "addForum.aspx">Add a Forum</a></li>
36          </ul>
37
38          <strong>If you do not see changes, please
39             <a href = "JavaScript:window.location.reload()">Refresh</a>
40             the page.</strong>
41       </body>
42    </html>
```

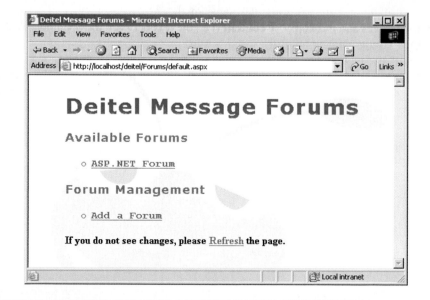

Fig. 24.4   Message forum main page. (Part 2 of 2.)

This form uses an **Xml** Web server control in lines 26–28. This control displays an XML document or the results of an XSL transformation. It is especially useful for extracting small amounts of data from an XML file and embedding the output within the rest of the ASPX page.

Attribute **DocumentSource** (line 27) specifies a path to an XML file to display, and attribute **TransformSource** (line 28) specifies an XSLT document (e.g., forums.xsl) that tranforms and formats the output. In this example, DocumentSource and TransformSource use relative addresses to locate the XML file and the XSLT, respectively.

The bottom of the page offers the user a link to add a forum (line 35). We discuss the file `addForum.aspx` later in the chapter. Lines 38–40 provide a link to refresh the page, which may be necessary to view the latest posts.

The `forums.xsl` (Fig. 24.5) file transforms the list of forums contained within `forums.xml` as XML data into XHTML list items. This stylesheet contains only one template. This template, declared in lines 10–16, creates links to the XML files that contain the listed forums' messages. The text of each link is a forum name, and each link appears as a list item (`li` element). Recall that we include the `ul` (unordered list) element in lines 25–29 in `default.aspx` (Fig. 24.4), the document where the result of the transformation will go. Therefore, `forums.xsl` only generates `li` elements. A valid unordered list with one or more list items will appear when `default.aspx` is rendered by the browser.

```
1   <?xml version = "1.0"?>
2
3   <!-- Fig. 24.5: forums.xsl            -->
4   <!-- XSL document that transforms -->
5   <!-- forums XML data to XHTML         -->
6
7   <xsl:transform version = "1.0"
8       xmlns:xsl = "http://www.w3.org/1999/XSL/Transform">
9
10      <xsl:template match = "forum">
11          <li>
12              <a href = "{@filename}">
13                  <xsl:value-of select = "." />
14              </a>
15          </li>
16      </xsl:template>
17
18  </xsl:transform>
```

Fig. 24.5   XSL to transform XML forums into unsorted list elements.

The template outputs a list (`li` element) containing a link for each `forum` element. The attribute `href` of the link is assigned the value of the attribute `filename` of the `forum` element in the XML document (i.e., `forums.xml`). To extract the `filename`, we use the XPath character `@`. Also note that the XPath expression `@filename` must be contained in curly braces (`{}`) to distinguish it from the surrounding XHTML. The resulting link text only contains the value of `filename`, not the curly braces. We use the `<xsl:value-of>` tag to extract the content of the `forum` element. The required attribute `select` set to `"."` selects the current context node (i.e., the content of a `forum` element). The XPath expression `"."` is short for `self::node()`, which also refers to the current context node.

24.4 Adding Forums

In this section, we discuss the documents used to add new forums. Each new forum XML document has a structure similar to the sample forum XML document shown in Fig. 24.6. This document contains a `stylesheet` processing instruction (line 6) that references `formatting.xsl` (discussed in Section 24.5). When the browser opens this XML file, it applies `formatting.xsl` to the file and outputs the results. The root element `forum` has an attribute `filename` set to the name of the XML file that contains the messages for the forum (i.e., the current file). Every `forum` element contains exactly one child element `name` and multiple `message` elements that contain information specific to each message. The XML file for each forum is created and modified by an ASP.NET script using .NET Framework classes and methods to generate the XML, resulting in line spacing and formatting that varies slightly from the format used throughout this book. [*Note*: The XHTML comments in the file shown were manually inserted.]

```xml
1   <?xml version="1.0"?>
2
3   <!-- Fig. 24.6: forumASP.xml -->
4   <!-- Sample ASP.NET forum     -->
5
6   <?xml-stylesheet type = 'text/xsl' href = 'formatting.xsl'?>
7   <forum filename="forumASP.xml">
8      <name>ASP.NET Forum</name>
9      <message timestamp="8/13/2003 2:03:07 PM">
10        <user>D. Bug</user>
11        <title>I Love ASP.NET</title>
12        <text>Everyone should use ASP.NET.</text>
13     </message>
14     <message timestamp="8/13/2003 2:03:38 PM">
15        <user>Ms. Quito</user>
16        <title>ASP.NET and XML</title>
17        <text>What a powerful combination. Try it!</text>
18     </message>
19     <message timestamp="8/13/2003 2:04:08 PM">
20        <user>Sarge Ant</user>
21        <title>ASP.NET</title>
22        <text>This army ant uses ASP.NET in boot camp.</text>
23     </message>
24  </forum>
```

Fig. 24.6   Sample forum XML file.

Figure 24.7 presents the ASP.NET page (`addForum.aspx`) that enables users to create new forums. It employs a form to obtain user input about the new forum, then creates the appropriate new forum XML file containing a welcome message and adds a `forum` element to `forums.xml`.

This page performs two tasks. First, it displays the form that gets the new forum's information (lines 98–145). Second, it provides the function for creating an XML forum file with a message and adding a new forum to `forums.xml` (lines 20–80).

The form contains five text boxes and two buttons for user input. Clicking the **Submit** button executes the `submitButton_Click` function, which creates the XML file to store the messages for the new forum. As we will see in a moment, this function also adds an initial posting to the file and updates the `forums.xml` file listing all the existing forums. The **Clear** button calls function `clearButton_Click` (lines 82–90) to clear the text boxes by setting each of their `Text` properties to the empty string (`""`).

Function `submitButton_Click` (lines 20–80) performs the actions required to add a new forum. The function first creates a new XML file to store the messages in the new forum. Next, an initial message is added to the forum by adding a `message` element containing the user input on the form. Finally the script updates `forums.xml` to include the new forum.

```
1   <%@ Page Language="JScript" Debug="true" %>
2   <%@ Import Namespace="System.Data" %>
3   <%@ Import Namespace="System.Xml" %>
4
5   <!-- Fig. 24.7: addForum.aspx        -->
6   <!-- Adds a forum and creates the -->
7   <!-- first message in that forum. -->
8
9   <!DOCTYPE html PUBLIC "-//W3C//DTD XHTML 1.1//EN"
10      "http://www.w3.org/TR/xhtml11/DTD/xhtml11.dtd">
11
12  <html xmlns = "http://www.w3.org/1999/xhtml">
13      <head>
14          <title>Add a Forum</title>
15          <link rel = "stylesheet"
16              type = "text/css" href = "style.css" />
17
18          <script language = "JScript" runat = "server">
19
20              function submitButton_Click( sender : Object,
21                  events : EventArgs ) : void
22              {
23                  // create file to hold messages for the new forum
24
25                  var physicalPath : String = Server.MapPath( "" );
26                  physicalPath = physicalPath + "\\" + fileBox.Text;
27
28                  var writer : XmlTextWriter =
29                      new XmlTextWriter( physicalPath, null );
30
31                  // indent the file automatically
32                  writer.Formatting = Formatting.Indented;
33
34                  writer.WriteStartDocument();
35
36                  // create processing instruction
37                  var PI : String = "type = 'text/xsl' href = 'formatting.xsl'";
38                  writer.WriteProcessingInstruction( "xml-stylesheet", PI );
39
40                  // write the root element
41                  writer.WriteStartElement( "forum" );
42
43                  // give forum an attribute filename
44                  writer.WriteAttributeString( "filename", fileBox.Text );
45                  writer.WriteElementString( "name", nameBox.Text );
46                  writer.WriteStartElement( "message" );
47                  writer.WriteAttributeString(
```

Fig. 24.7 ASP.NET page to add a forum. (Part 1 of 4.)

```
48              "timestamp", DateTime.Now.ToString() );
49
50          writer.WriteElementString( "user", userBox.Text );
51          writer.WriteElementString( "title", titleBox.Text );
52          writer.WriteElementString( "text", textBox.Text );
53
54          // end the message element
55          writer.WriteEndElement();
56
57          // end the root element
58          writer.WriteFullEndElement();
59
60          writer.Close();
61
62          // add element to forums.xml
63
64          // open an XML document.
65          var forums : XmlDocument = new XmlDocument();
66          forums.Load( Server.MapPath( "forums.xml" ) );
67
68          // create XML element that will represent the post
69          var forumNode : XmlElement = forums.CreateElement( "forum" );
70
71          forumNode.SetAttribute( "filename", fileBox.Text );
72          forumNode.AppendChild(
73             forums.CreateTextNode( nameBox.Text ) );
74
75          // insert the new element into the XML tree and save
76          forums.DocumentElement.AppendChild( forumNode );
77          forums.Save( Server.MapPath( "forums.xml" ) );
78
79          Response.Redirect( "default.aspx" );
80       } // end submitButton_Click
81
82       function clearButton_Click( sender : Object,
83          events : EventArgs ) : void
84       {
85          nameBox.Text = "";
86          fileBox.Text = "";
87          userBox.Text = "";
88          titleBox.Text = "";
89          textBox.Text = "";
90       } // end clearButton_Click
91
92    </script>
93 </head>
94
95 <body>
96    <p>Create a Forum</p>
97
98    <form runat = "server">
99
100       <h2>
```

Fig. 24.7 ASP.NET page to add a forum. (Part 2 of 4.)

```
101                    Forum Name:<br />
102                    <asp:TextBox id = "nameBox" runat = "server"
103                       columns = "50">
104                    </asp:TextBox>
105             </h2>
106
107             <h2>
108                    Forum File Name:<br />
109                    <asp:TextBox id = "fileBox" runat = "server"
110                       columns = "50">
111                    </asp:TextBox>
112             </h2>
113
114             <h2>
115                 User:<br />
116                    <asp:TextBox id = "userBox" runat = "server"
117                       columns = "50">
118                    </asp:TextBox>
119             </h2>
120
121             <h2>
122                 Message Title:<br />
123                    <asp:TextBox id = "titleBox" runat = "server"
124                       columns = "50">
125                    </asp:TextBox>
126             </h2>
127
128             <h2>
129                 Message Text:<br />
130                    <asp:TextBox id = "textBox" runat = "server" rows = "5"
131                       textmode = "multiline" columns = "50">
132                    </asp:TextBox>
133             </h2>
134
135             <h2>
136                 <asp:Button id = "submitButton" OnClick = "submitButton_Click"
137                    Text = "Submit" runat = "server"
138                    style = "position: absolute; left:100px" />
139
140                 <asp:Button id = "clearButton" OnClick = "clearButton_Click"
141                    Text = "Clear" runat = "server"
142                    style = "position: absolute; left:180px" />
143             </h2>
144
145         </form>
146         <br />
147         <p>
148             <br />
149             <a href = "default.aspx">Return to Main Page</a>
150         </p>
151
152     </body>
153 </html>
```

Fig. 24.7   ASP.NET page to add a forum. (Part 3 of 4.)

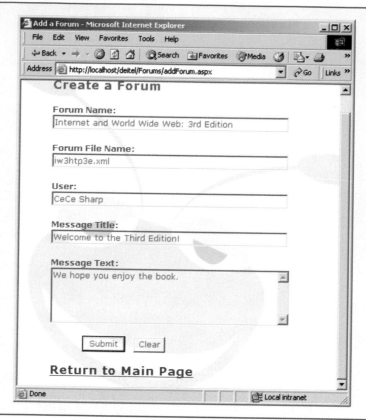

Fig. 24.7   ASP.NET page to add a forum. (Part 4 of 4.)

Before we discuss how to create the new XML file, we must explain a little about different types of file paths (i.e., location on disk). Each file on a Web server can be accessed either through a **virtual path** or through a **physical path**. For example, in the URL

        http://www.deitel.com/books/index.html

`books/index.html` is the virtual path. This is a path to the file `index.html` in the virtual directory `books` located on the Web server hosted by `www.deitel.com`. It is the path that is observed by a user on the Web. The physical path refers to the physical location of a file in memory on the machine running the Web server (i.e., the actual drive letter, directory and filename of the file). This information is typically hidden from users. For example,

        C:\Inetpub\wwwroot\deitel\books\index.html

might be the physical path to the same file that the above virtual path refers.

Some objects and methods require the use of physical paths to identify files. For instance, loading XML documents, connecting to databases and opening text files require that files be specified using physical paths. Since the physical path can be difficult to determine, we use the `Server` method `MapPath`, which takes one argument, a virtual path, and returns the corresponding physical path as a string.

In this example, we need to create a new XML file in the current working directory (i.e., the directory where our scripts reside). Thus the script calls MapPath with an empty string (the virtual path to the current directory) as the single argument (line 25). This function call returns the physical path of the directory where this script is located and where we want to write our new file. Line 26 then constructs the exact physical path of the file to be created by concatenating the directory's physical path with a backslash character (\) and the desired filename specified by the user (i.e., the value of fileBox.Text). [*Note*: We must escape the backslash character with an additional backslash (i.e., "\\"). Writing a single backslash in quotation marks (i.e., "\") would result in an error, as the backslash would escape the closing quotation mark, and the string would not be terminated correctly.]

We use the XmlTextWriter class in the .NET System.XML namespace to create and write to the new XML file. The **XmlTextWriter** class has methods and properties for writing XML to a file. An XmlTextWriter adds content to an XML file sequentially (i.e., from the top of the file to the bottom). For example, a programmer would first add the XML version, any processing instructions, the root element, any attributes for the root element, any children of the root element and finally a closing tag for the root element. The XmlTextWriter class contains methods specifically designed to add the different types of XML elements.

Lines 28–29 create an instance of XmlTextWriter called writer. The XmlText-Writer constructor (i.e., the special method used to create an XmlTextWriter) is passed the physical path where the new XML document should be created. The second argument, null, specifies the encoding of the output. Passing null for this argument gives the resulting XML file the default encoding, UTF-8, and omits the encoding attribute from the processing instruction.

Since the new XML forum file does not yet exist, the text writer first creates a new file in the location specified in the constructor. Line 32 sets property **Formatting** to **Formatting.Indented**, indicating that the writer should indent the XML content written to the file. The resulting content will be indented without any programmer effort. Line 34 writes the start of document (i.e., <?xml version = "1.0"?>), using method **WriteStartDocument**. Line 37 declares and initializes PI, which represents the processing instruction. Line 38 then writes a processing instruction to the XML file using method **WriteProcessingInstruction**. This method takes two arguments—the name of the processing instruction (i.e., xml-stylesheet) and the actual processing instruction. The resulting processing instruction is output as

```
<?xml-stylesheet type='text/xsl' href='formatting.xsl'?>
```

Line 41 then writes the first element and names it forum, using method **WriteStartElement**. Line 44 adds the forum element attribute filename and assigns it to the text in fileBox, using method **WriteAttributeString**. Line 45 gives the element forum a child element name that marks up the text in nameBox. The XmlTextWriter method **WriteElementString** creates the opening and closing tags of the element name and inserts the value of nameBox.Text between them. Line 46 creates the opening tag for an element message, but does not create any content, nor does it output the closing message tag. Recall that the message element will contain three child elements and an attribute. Lines 47–48 gives message an attribute timestamp assigned to the current date and time. The method DateTime.Now produces the date and time, and calling the method ToString on this result converts the date and time to a string. We combine these calls into one expression: `DateTime.Now.ToString()`. We could alternatively have stored the `DateTime` object returned by `DateTime.Now` in a temporary variable, then called the `ToString` method of this object to achieve the same result.

Lines 50–52 add three child elements to the `message` element: `user`, `title` and `text`, which markup `userBox.Text`, `titleBox.Text` and `textBox.Text`, respectively. **`WriteEndElement`** (line 55) closes the most recently declared unclosed element (i.e., `message`) by outputting `/>`. Line 58 uses **`WriteFullEndElement`** to write a full closing tag (e.g., `</forum>`) to close the root element. This method always writes the full closing tag, as opposed to the method `WriteEndElement`, which closes empty elements with a `/>` (e.g., `<br />`). Line 60 closes `writer` (using method **`Close`**), since we now have a complete XML document.

The second part of the function `submitButton_Click` adds the new forum to the list of forums contained within `forums.xml` (lines 65–77). Line 65 declares a new `XmlDocument` instance named `forums`, and line 66 loads the file `forums.xml` into this object. Line 69 creates a new element node named `forum`, which will be inserted into `forums.xml` to represent the new forum. Line 71 gives the `forum` element an attribute `filename` set to `fileBox.Text`. Lines 72–73 add content (i.e., the name of the forum from `nameBox.Text`) to the `forum` element. Line 76 adds the newly constructed `forum` element to the document root element (`forums`), and line 77 saves the changes to the `forums.xml` file. Line 79 sends the user back to the main page (`default.aspx`).

Figure 24.8 shows the main page after a new forum (i.e., **Internet and World Wide Web: 3rd Edition**) has been added to the message board, and Fig. 24.9 shows the initial content of that forum.

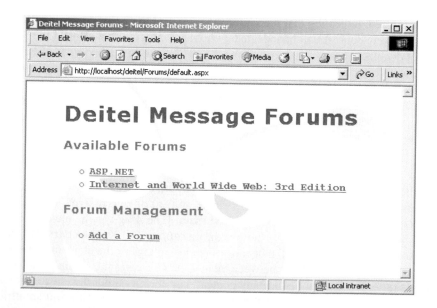

Fig. 24.8   New forum on the message board.

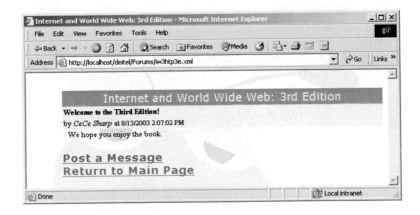

Fig. 24.9   Initial content of the newly added forum.

24.5 Forum XML Documents

In the previous section, Fig. 24.6 presented an XML document (i.e., `forumASP.xml`) that contains the properties and messages of a sample forum. Figure 24.10 presents the XSLT document that transforms each forum XML document (e.g., `forumASP.xml`) to XHTML.

```
1   <?xml version = "1.0"?>
2
3   <!-- Fig. 24.10: formatting.xsl                    -->
4   <!-- XSL document that transforms XML data to XHTML -->
5
6   <xsl:stylesheet version = "1.0"
7      xmlns:xsl = "http://www.w3.org/1999/XSL/Transform">
8
9      <xsl:output method = "html" omit-xml-declaration = "no"
10        doctype-system =
11           "http://www.w3.org/TR/xhtml1/DTD/xhtml1-strict.dtd"
12        doctype-public = "-//W3C//DTD XHTML 1.0 Strict//EN" />
13
14     <xsl:template match = "/">
15
16        <html xmlns = "http://www.w3.org/1999/xhtml">
17           <xsl:apply-templates select = "*" />
18        </html>
19
20     </xsl:template>
21
22     <xsl:template match = "forum">
23
24        <head>
25           <title><xsl:value-of select = "name" /></title>
26           <link rel = "stylesheet" type = "text/css"
27              href = "style.css" />
28        </head>
```

Fig. 24.10   XSLT to transform XML forum document into XHTML. (Part 1 of 3.)

```
29
30          <body>
31
32              <table width = "100%" cellspacing = "0"
33                 cellpadding = "2">
34                 <tr>
35                    <td class = "forumTitle">
36                       <xsl:value-of select = "name" />
37                    </td>
38                 </tr>
39              </table>
40
41              <table width = "100%" cellspacing = "0"
42                 cellpadding = "2">
43                 <xsl:apply-templates
44                    select = "message" />
45              </table>
46
47              <p>
48                 <a>
49                    <xsl:attribute name = "href">
50                       addPost.aspx?file=<xsl:value-of
51                       select = "@filename" />
52                    </xsl:attribute>
53                    Post a Message</a><br />
54                 <a href = "default.aspx">Return to Main Page</a>
55              </p>
56              <strong>If you do not see changes, please
57                 <a href = "JavaScript:window.location.reload()">Refresh</a>
58                 the page.</strong>
59          </body>
60
61      </xsl:template>
62
63      <xsl:template match = "message">
64
65          <tr>
66             <td class = "msgTitle">
67                <xsl:value-of select = "title" />
68             </td>
69          </tr>
70
71          <tr>
72             <td class = "msgInfo">
73                by
74                <em><xsl:value-of select = "user" /></em>
75                at
76                <span class = "date">
77                   <xsl:value-of select = "@timestamp" />
78                </span>
79             </td>
80          </tr>
81
```

Fig. 24.10   XSLT to transform XML forum document into XHTML. (Part 2 of 3.)

```
82              <tr>
83                  <td class = "msgText">
84                      <xsl:value-of select = "text" />
85                  </td>
86              </tr>
87
88          </xsl:template>
89
90      </xsl:stylesheet>
```

Fig. 24.10 XSLT to transform XML forum document into XHTML. (Part 3 of 3.)

The stylesheet `formatting.xsl` creates an XHTML document that contains one table to display the title of the forum and another table with alternating rows of message properties and message bodies (i.e., the actual messages posted). The XSLT contains three templates. One template (lines 14–20) matches the document root (using attribute `match = "/"`), produces the `html` element and applies templates to the rest of the document.

The template that matches element `forum` (lines 22–61) creates the `head` and `body` elements of the resulting XHTML page. Line 36 extracts the `name` element of the forum and places it in a table. This table serves as the page header. The table created in lines 41–45 will contain the forum's messages. Lines 43–44 apply templates to `message` elements. The template that matches `message` elements appears in lines 63–88. This template extracts the message title (line 67) and places it in a table row. The `message` template extracts the user name (line 74) and `timestamp` attribute (line 77), and placing these values in another table row. Finally, the template outputs the message `text` (line 84) in a third table row.

Lines 47–58 of the `forum` matching template produce the page footer, to appear below all the messages in the forum. Lines 48–53 write an `a` (anchor) element to the result tree (i.e., the XHTML page being constructed). XSLT element **`xsl:attribute`** adds an attribute named `href` to the `a` element and assigns this attribute the value of attribute `filename` concatenated to `addPost.asp?file=`. Adding information to a URL is a common method of transferring data between pages. In `addPost.aspx`, we will use this information (e.g., `file=forumASP.xml`) to determine which forum XML file should be modified when the new message is added. Lines 56–58 provide a link to refresh the page.

Figure 24.11 shows the XHTML document that is rendered by Internet Explorer 6 when `forumASP.xml` is transformed by `formatting.xsl`.[1] [*Note*: We have reformatted and edited the XHTML output for presentation purposes.] We can see that the templates in `formatting.xsl` have extracted the data from `forumASP.xml` to produce a clear and stylized XHTML page showing the contents of the forum. Lines 69–70 provide a link to `addPost.aspx`, along with the name of the file to which the new message will be added.

---

1. To view the resulting XHTML in your browser, go to msdn.microsoft.com/downloads/list/xmlgeneral.asp and click on the **Internet Explorer Tools for Validating XML and Viewing XSLT Output** link. Follow the installation directions provided, then open a browser to http://localhost/deitel/Forums/forumASP.xml. Right-click on the page and select **View XSL Output**.

```
1   <!DOCTYPE html PUBLIC "-//W3C//DTD XHTML 1.0 Strict//EN"
2      "http://www.w3.org/TR/xhtml1/DTD/xhtml1-strict.dtd">
3
4   <!-- Fig. 24.11: forumASP-output.html                        -->
5   <!-- XHTML produced by applying formatting.xsl to forumASP.xml -->
6
7   <html xmlns = "http://www.w3.org/1999/xhtml">
8
9      <head xmlns = "">
10        <title>ASP.NET Forum</title>
11        <link rel = "stylesheet" type = "text/css" href = "style.css">
12     </head>
13
14     <body xmlns = "">
15        <table width = "100%" cellspacing = "0" cellpadding = "2">
16           <tr>
17              <td class = "forumTitle">ASP.NET Forum</td>
18           </tr>
19        </table>
20
21        <table width = "100%" cellspacing = "0" cellpadding = "2">
22           <tr>
23              <td class = "msgTitle">I Love ASP.NET</td>
24           </tr>
25           <tr>
26              <td class = "msgInfo">
27                 by
28                 <em>D. Bug</em>
29                 at
30                 <span class = "date">8/13/2003 2:03:07 PM</span>
31              </td>
32           </tr>
33           <tr>
34              <td class = "msgText">Everyone should use ASP.NET.</td>
35           </tr>
36           <tr>
37              <td class = "msgTitle">ASP.NET and XML</td>
38           </tr>
39           <tr>
40              <td class = "msgInfo">
41                 by
42                 <em>Ms. Quito</em>
43                 at
44                 <span class = "date">8/13/2003 2:03:38 PM</span>
45              </td>
46           </tr>
47           <tr>
48              <td class = "msgText">What a powerful combination. Try it!
49              </td>
50           </tr>
51           <tr>
52              <td class = "msgTitle">ASP.NET</td>
53           </tr>
```

Fig. 24.11   Output of the transformation of the forum XML document. (Part 1 of 2.)

```
54              <tr>
55                  <td class = "msgInfo">
56                      by
57                      <em>Sarge Ant</em>
58                      at
59                      <span class = "date">8/13/2003 2:04:08 PM</span>
60                  </td>
61              </tr>
62              <tr>
63                  <td class = "msgText">This army ant uses ASP.NET in boot camp.
64                  </td>
65              </tr>
66          </table>
67
68          <p>
69              <a href = "addPost.aspx?file=forumASP.xml">
70                  Post a Message</a><br>
71              <a href = "default.aspx">Return to Main Page</a><br>
72          </p>
73
74          <strong>If you do not see changes, please
75              <a href = "JavaScript:window.location.reload()">Refresh</a>
76              the page.</strong>
77
78      </body>
79  </html>
```

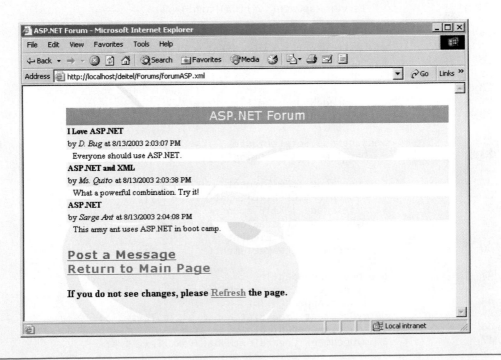

Fig. 24.11 Output of the transformation of the forum XML document. (Part 2 of 2.)

24.6 Posting Messages

In this section, we present the ASP.NET document `addPost.aspx` (Fig. 24.12), which posts messages to a forum. This ASP.NET uses much of the same functionality as `addForum.aspx`. The code is also similar to the mailing list application in Section 23.9.

```
1   <%@ Page Language="JScript" Debug="true" %>
2   <%@ Import Namespace="System.Data" %>
3   <%@ Import Namespace="System.Xml" %>
4
5   <!-- Fig. 24.12: addPost.aspx -->
6   <!-- Adds a post to a forum    -->
7
8   <html>
9      <head>
10        <title>Add a message</title>
11
12        <link rel = "stylesheet" type = "text/css"
13           href = "style.css" />
14
15        <script language = "JScript" runat = "server">
16
17           function submitButton_Click( sender : Object,
18              events : EventArgs ) : void
19           {
20              var virtualPath : String = Request.QueryString( "file" );
21              var physicalPath : String =
22                 Server.MapPath( virtualPath );
23
24              // open an XML document
25              var myDocument : XmlDocument = new XmlDocument();
26              myDocument.Load( physicalPath );
27
28              // create XML element that will represent the post
29              var messageNode : XmlElement =
30                 myDocument.CreateElement( "message" );
31
32              messageNode.SetAttribute( "timestamp",
33                 DateTime.Now.ToString() );
34
35              var userNode : XmlElement =
36                 myDocument.CreateElement( "user" );
37              var titleNode : XmlElement =
38                 myDocument.CreateElement( "title" );
39              var textNode : XmlElement =
40                 myDocument.CreateElement( "text" );
41
42              userNode.AppendChild(
43                 myDocument.CreateTextNode( user.Text ) );
44              titleNode.AppendChild(
45                 myDocument.CreateTextNode( title.Text ) );
46              textNode.AppendChild(
47                 myDocument.CreateTextNode( text.Text ) );
```

Fig. 24.12 Adding a message to a forum. (Part 1 of 3.)

```
48
49                    messageNode.AppendChild( userNode );
50                    messageNode.AppendChild( titleNode );
51                    messageNode.AppendChild( textNode );
52
53                    // insert the new element into the XML tree and save
54                    myDocument.DocumentElement.AppendChild( messageNode );
55                    myDocument.Save( physicalPath );
56
57                    Response.Redirect( virtualPath );
58              } // end submitButton_Click
59
60              function clearButton_Click( sender : Object,
61                 events : EventArgs ) : void
62              {
63                 user.Text = "";
64                 title.Text = "";
65                 text.Text = "";
66              } // end clearButton_Click
67
68        </script>
69     </head>
70     <body>
71
72        <p>My Message Forum</p>
73
74        <hr />
75        <form runat = "server">
76           <p>
77              User: <br />
78              <asp:TextBox id = "user" Columns = "50" runat = "server" />
79           </p>
80           <p>
81              Message Title: <br />
82              <asp:TextBox id = "title" Columns = "50" runat = "server" />
83           </p>
84           <p>
85              Message: <br />
86              <asp:TextBox id = "text" TextMode = "multiLine" Columns = "50"
87                 Rows = "4" runat = "server" />
88           </p>
89           <p>
90              <asp:Button id = "submitButton" OnClick = "submitButton_Click"
91                 Text = "Submit" runat = "server"
92                 style = "position: absolute; left:100px" />
93
94              <asp:Button id = "clearButton" OnClick = "clearButton_Click"
95                 Text = "Clear" runat = "server"
96                 style = "position: absolute; left:180px" />
97           </p>
98           <br />
99           <p>
100             <br />
```

Fig. 24.12 Adding a message to a forum. (Part 2 of 3.)

```
101                     <a href = "default.aspx">Return to Main Page</a>
102              </p>
103           </form>
104
105       </body>
106   </html>
```

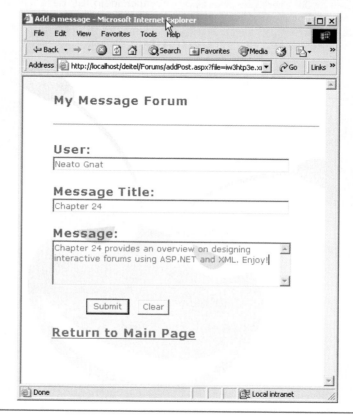

Fig. 24.12 Adding a message to a forum. (Part 3 of 3.)

Recall that the **Post a Message** link on each forum page contains

    ?file=*filename*

appended to the value of the `href` attribute, where *filename* is the name of the file that stores the forum's messages. The portion of the URL after the question mark is often called the **query string**. The query string contains variables and values separated by equals signs that need to be passed from one page to another. Multiple *variable=value* pairs are separated by the ampersand character (**&**). **Request.QueryString** provides access to variables passed through the query string. For example, in line 20 of the current example, the statement `Request.QueryString( "file" )` returns the value of `file` in the query string (e.g., `forumASP.xml`).

Line 20 declares a variable `virtualPath` as a string to store the value of `file`. This avoids repeated use of the `Request.QueryString` and could improve application performance. Lines 21–22 get the physical path from the virtual path (i.e., the value of `file` passed in the URL). Lines 25–27 create and load the XML document. We then create a `message` element with three child nodes: `user`, `title` and `text` (lines 29–51) using the same techniques as we employed to construct the new `forum` node in `addForum.aspx` (Fig. 24.7). Line 54 adds the new `message` node to the document, and line 55 saves the changes to the XML file. After the post has been added to the forum, the script redirects the user (line 59) to the forum page itself (i.e., the URL in `virtualPath`).

The remainder of the script in Fig. 24.12 contains the function `clearButton_Click` (lines 60–66), which clears the form fields when the user clicks the **Clear** button. Lines 75–103 create the form that users use to input their names and the text and title of new messages to post. Figure 24.13 shows the result of posting a new message to the **Internet and World Wide Web: 3rd Edition** forum.

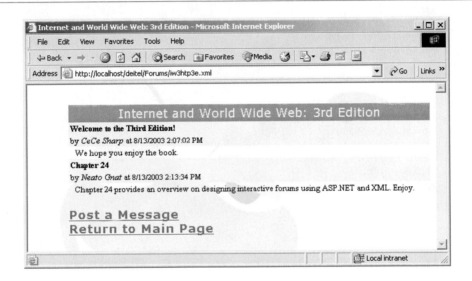

Fig. 24.13 Contents of the **Internet and World Wide Web: 3rd Edition** forum.

24.7 CSS Document for Forum Pages

In this section, we present an additional document used in the case study. Figure 24.14 lists the CSS document (`style.css`) that formats all documents in the forum application.

```
1   /* Fig. 24.14: style.css */
2   /* Stylesheet for forums */
3
4   h1
5   {
6       color: #330099;
7       letter-spacing: 2px;
8       font-family: Verdana, Geneva, Arial, Helvetica, sans-serif;
```

Fig. 24.14 CSS document for forums. (Part 1 of 3.)

```
 9          background-color: transparent;
10      }
11
12      h2
13      {
14          color: #6633FF;
15          font-family: Verdana, Geneva, Arial, Helvetica, sans-serif;
16          font-size: small;
17          background-color: transparent;
18      }
19
20      p
21      {
22          font-family: Verdana, Geneva, Arial, Helvetica, sans-serif;
23          color: #336666;
24          letter-spacing: 1px;
25          font-size: larger;
26          font-weight: bold;
27          background-color: transparent;
28      }
29
30      body
31      {
32          background-image: url(bug2.gif);
33          background-repeat: no-repeat;
34          margin-top: 5%;
35          background-position: 25%;
36          margin-left: 10%;
37      }
38
39      li
40      {
41          font-family: "Courier New", Courier, monospace;
42          font-weight: bolder;
43          list-style-type: circle;
44          color: #3333FF;
45          background-color: transparent;
46      }
47
48      input
49      {
50          background-color: transparent;
51          color: #336666;
52          font-family: Verdana, Geneva, Arial, Helvetica, sans-serif;
53      }
54
55      textarea
56      {
57          background-color: transparent;
58          color: #336666;
59          font-family: Verdana, Geneva, Arial, Helvetica, sans-serif;
60      }
61
```

Fig. 24.14   CSS document for forums. (Part 2 of 3.)

```
62   .forumTitle
63   {
64      color: #FFFFCC;
65      font-size: 14pt;
66      font-family: Verdana, Geneva, Arial, Helvetica, sans-serif;
67      text-align: center;
68      background-color: #6666CC;
69   }
70
71   .msgTitle
72   {
73      background: #FFFFCC;
74      color: black;
75      font-size: 10pt;
76      font-weight: bold;
77   }
78
79   .msgInfo
80   {
81      background: #FFFFCC;
82      color: black;
83      font-size: 10pt;
84   }
85
86   .msgPost
87   {
88      background: silver;
89      color: black;
90      font-size: 8pt;
91   }
92
93   .msgText
94   {
95      font-size: 10pt;
96      padding-left: 10px;
97   }
98
99   .date
100  {
101     font-size: 8pt;
102  }
```

Fig. 24.14 CSS document for forums. (Part 3 of 3.)

24.8 Web Resources

aspnet.4guysfromrolla.com/
Lists different ways to extract XML data from an ASP.NET page.

www.15seconds.com/focus/XML.htm
The *ASPWatch* site contains many articles on integrating ASP with various technologies. This section focuses on ASP and XML.

msdn.microsoft.com/library/default.asp
Provides extensive resources and articles on Microsoft technologies such as .NET, ASP.NET and Windows Forms.

`www.xmlforasp.net`
The *XML for ASP.NET Developers* site offers a large collection of articles, example code and online tutorials.

SUMMARY

- Message forums are "virtual" bulletin boards where various topics are discussed.

- Common features of message forums include discussion groups, questions and answers and general comments.

- The `Xml` Web server control displays an XML document or the results of an XSL transformation.

- Attribute `DocumentSource` of an `Xml` Web control specifies the path of an XML file to display.

- Attribute `TransformSource` of an `Xml` Web control specifies an XSLT document that tranforms and formats the output.

- The XPath expression `"."` is short for `self::node()`, which also refers to the current context node.

- Each file on a Web server can be accessed either through a virtual path or through a physical path.

- A virtual path is the path to a file's virtual directory on the Web server. This is the path that is observed by a user on the Web.

- The physical path refers to the physical location of a file in memory on the machine running the Web server. This information is typically hidden from users.

- Some objects and methods require the use of physical paths to identify files.

- Method `Server.MapPath` takes one argument, a virtual path, and returns the corresponding physical path as a string.

- The `XmlTextWriter` class has methods and properties for writing XML to a file.

- The `XmlTextWriter` constructor is passed the physical path where the new XML document should be created. The second argument specifies the encoding of the output.

- Method `WriteStartDocument` of class `XmlTextWriter` outputs the start of the XML document.

- Method `WriteProcessingInstruction` of class `XmlTextWriter` writes a processing instruction to the XML file.

- Method `WriteStartElement` of class `XmlTextWriter` writes the start element of the XML file.

- Method `WriteAttributeString` of class `XmlTextWriter` adds an attribute (and a value for that attribute) to the current element.

- Method `WriteElementString` of class `XmlTextWriter` creates the opening and closing tags of an element and inserts a value between them.

- Method `WriteEndElement` of class `XmlTextWriter` closes the most recently declared unclosed element by outputting `/>`.

- Method `WriteFullEndElement` of class `XmlTextWriter` writes a full closing tag to close the root element.

- XSLT element `xsl:attribute` adds an attribute named `href` to the `<a>` tag.

- Adding information to a URL is a common method of transferring data between pages.

- The portion of the URL after the question mark is often called the query string.

- The query string contains variables and values separated by equals signs that need to be passed from one page to another.

- `Request.QueryString` provides access to variables passed through the query string.

TERMINOLOGY

`Close` method of class `XmlTextWriter`

discussion group

`DocumentSource` attribute of `Xml` Web control

`Formatting` property of class `XmlTextWriter`

`Formatting.Indented` value to indent XML content

`MapPath` method of the `Server` object

message forum

physical path

query string

`Request.QueryString`

`TransformSource` attribute of `Xml` Web control

virtual path

`WriteAttributeString` method of class `XmlTextWriter`

`WriteElementString` method of class `XmlTextWriter`

`WriteEndElement` method of class `XmlTextWriter`

`WriteFullEndElement` method of class `XmlTextWriter`

`WriteProcessingInstruction` method of class `XmlTextWriter`

`WriteStartDocument` of class `XmlTextWriter`

`WriteStartElement` method of class `XmlTextWriter`

`Xml` Web server control

`XmlTextWriter` class

`xsl:attribute`

SELF-REVIEW EXERCISES

24.1　What does the XML server control (i.e., `asp:Xml`) do?

24.2　To create child element nodes for elements in an XML document, what needs to be done?

ANSWERS TO SELF-REVIEW EXERCISES

24.1　The `asp:Xml` control displays an XML document or the results of an XSL transformation in an ASP.NET page. It is especially useful for extracting small amounts of data from an XML file and embedding the output within the rest of a Web Form page.

24.2　To create element nodes, call the `XmlDocument` object's method `CreateElement`, with the name of the element to be created as a parameter. Next, method `AppendChild` is called on the element to which the new element is to be a child, with the child element as the parameter.

EXERCISES

24.3　Modify this chapter's code so that the user can enter a home page URL to be posted with a message. When displaying a message, the home page URL should appear in a link next to the message. If the user does not input a Web site, do not display the link.

24.4　Modify this chapter's code so that the user can enter an e-mail address. When displaying the message, a `mailto:` link should appear in the message header. If the user does not input an address, do not display the link.

24.5　Add required field validators to this chapter's code.

24.6　Modify the solution to Exercise 24.5 to include a regular expression validator. Ensure that the user enters a filename with an `.xml` extension when adding a forum. Set the validator's `ValidationExpression` attribute to `".*\.[xX][mM][lL]"`.

25

Perl and CGI (Common Gateway Interface)

Objectives

- To understand basic Perl programming.
- To understand the Common Gateway Interface.
- To understand string processing and regular expressions in Perl.
- To be able to read and write cookies.
- To be able to construct programs that interact with MySQL databases.

This is the common air that bathes the globe.
Walt Whitman

The longest part of the journey is said to be the passing of the gate.
Marcus Terentius Varro

Railway termini. . . are our gates to the glorious and the unknown. Through them we pass out into adventure and sunshine, to them, alas! we return.
E. M. Forster

There comes a time in a man's life when to get where he has to go—if there are no doors or windows—he walks through a wall.
Bernard Malamud

You ought to be able to show that you can do it a good deal better than anyone else with the regular tools before you have a license to bring in your own improvements.
Ernest Hemingway

25.1 Introduction

Practical Extraction and Report Language (Perl) is one of the most widely used languages for Web programming today. Larry Wall began developing this high-level programming language in 1987 while working at Unisys. His initial intent was to create a programming language to monitor large software projects and generate reports. Wall wanted to create a language that would be more powerful than shell scripting and more flexible than C, a language with rich text-processing capabilities and, most of all, a language that would make common programming tasks straightforward and easy. In this chapter, we discuss Perl 5.8 and examine several practical examples that use Perl for Internet programming.

The **Common Gateway Interface (CGI)** is a standard interface through which users interact with applications on Web servers. Thus, CGI provides a way for clients (e.g., Web browsers) to interface indirectly with applications on the Web server. Because CGI is an interface, it cannot be programmed directly; a script or executable program (commonly called a **CGI script**) must be executed to interact with it. While CGI scripts can be written in many different programming languages, Perl is commonly used because of its power, its flexibility and the availability of preexisting scripts.

Figure 25.1 illustrates the interaction between client and server when the client requests a document that references a CGI script. Often, CGI scripts process information (e.g., a search-engine query, a credit-card number) gathered from a form. For example, a CGI script might verify credit-card information and notify the client of the results (i.e., accepted or rejected). Permission is granted within the Web server (usually by the **Webmaster** or the author of the Web site) for specific programs on the server to be executed. These programs are typically designated with a certain filename extension (e.g., `.cgi` or `.pl`) or located within a special directory (e.g., `cgi-bin`). After the application output is sent to the server through CGI, the results may be sent to the client. Information received by the client is usually an HTML or XHTML document, but may contain images, streaming audio, Macromedia Flash files (see Chapters 17–18), XML (see Chapter 20), and so on.

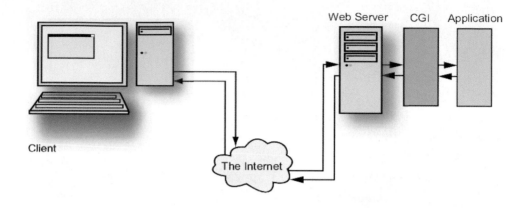

Fig. 25.1   Data path of a typical CGI-based application.

Applications typically interact with the user through **standard input** and **standard output**. Standard input is the stream of information received by a program from a user, typically through the keyboard, but also possibly from a file or another input device. Standard output is the information stream presented to the user by an application; it is typically displayed on the screen, but may be printed or written to a file.

For CGI scripts, the standard output is redirected (or **piped**) through the Common Gateway Interface to the server and then sent over the Internet to a Web browser for rendering. If the server-side script is programmed correctly, the output will be readable by the client. Usually, the output is an HTML or XHTML document that is rendered by a Web browser.

25.2 Perl

With the advent of the World Wide Web and Web browsers, the Internet gained tremendous popularity. This greatly increased the volume of requests users made for information from Web servers. It became evident that the degree of interactivity between the user and the server would be crucial. The power of the Web resides not only in serving content to users, but also in responding to requests from users and generating dynamic content. The framework for such communication already existed through CGI. Most of the information users send to servers is text; thus Perl was a logical choice for programming the server side of interactive Web-based applications. Perl possesses simple, yet powerful, text-processing capabilities and is arguably the most popular CGI scripting language. The Perl community, headed by Wall (who currently works for O'Reilly & Associates as a Perl developer and researcher), continuously works to evolve the language, keeping it competitive with newer server-side technologies, such as PHP (see Chapter 26).

To run the Perl scripts in this chapter, Perl must first be installed on your system. *ActivePerl* is the industry-standard Perl distribution for Windows, Solaris and Linux platforms and is available as a free download from www.activestate.com/Products/ActivePerl. Installation instructions can be found at aspn.activestate.com/ASPN/docs/ActivePerl/install.html. Please visit www.perl.com to find information on obtaining and installing Perl on other platforms.

Printing a Line of Text

Figure 25.2 presents a simple Perl program that writes the text "Welcome to Perl!" to the screen. The program does not interact with the Common Gateway Interface and therefore is not a CGI script. Our initial examples are command-line programs that illustrate fundamental Perl programming.

```
1   #!C:\Perl\bin\perl
2   # Fig. 25.2: fig25_02.pl
3   # A first program in Perl.
4
5   print( "Welcome to Perl!\n" );
```

```
Welcome to Perl!
```

Fig. 25.2   Simple Perl program.

Lines 2–3 use the Perl **comment character** (#) to instruct the interpreter to ignore everything on the current line following the #. This syntax allows programmers to write descriptive comments in their programs. The exception to this rule is the **"shebang" construct** (#!) in line 1. On UNIX systems, this line indicates the path to the Perl interpreter (e.g., #!/usr/bin/perl). On other systems (e.g., Windows), the line may be ignored or may indicate to the server (e.g., Apache) that a Perl program follows the statement.

Good Programming Practice 25.1

While not all servers require the "shebang" construct (#!), it is good practice to include it for program portability.

Common Programming Error 25.1

Some systems require that the shebang construct indicate the path to the Perl interpreter. If this path is incorrect, the program might not run. For Windows, this path is normally #!C:\Perl\bin\perl. For Unix, the path is normally #!/usr/bin/perl. If you are unsure where the Perl interpreter is, do a search for perl and use the path found in the shebang construct.

The comment (line 2) indicates that the file name of the program is fig25_02.pl. Perl program file names typically end with the .pl extension. The program can be executed by running the Perl interpreter from the command prompt (e.g., the Command Prompt in Windows 2000/XP or the MS-DOS Prompt in older versions of Windows). Refer to "Running a Perl Script" later in this section to learn more about how to execute this example.

Line 5 calls function **print** to write text to the screen. Note that because Perl is case sensitive, writing Print or PRINT instead of print yields an error. The text "Welcome to Perl!\n" is enclosed in quotes and is called a **string**. The last portion of the string— the newline **escape sequence**, \n—moves the output cursor to the next line. The semicolon (;) at the end of line 5 terminates the Perl statement. Note that the argument passed to function print (i.e., the string that we wish to print) is enclosed in parentheses (). The parentheses are not required; however, we suggest that you use parentheses as often as possible in your programs to maintain clarity. In this example, we use parentheses to indicate what we want printed. We will demonstrate the use of parentheses throughout the chapter.

Common Programming Error 25.2

Forgetting to terminate a statement with a ; is a syntax error in most cases.

Running a Perl Script

To run `fig25_02.pl`, we must first open the Windows command prompt. Click the **Start** button and click **Run....** Type **cmd** in the **Open:** text field. This opens the command-prompt window. At the command prompt, type

    cd *examplesFolder*

where *examplesFolder* is the full path of the folder containing the Chapter 25 examples (e.g., `C:\IW3HTP3\examples\ch25examples`). This folder path should now appear to the left of the blinking cursor to indicate that any commands we type will be executed in that location. Type at the command prompt

    perl fig25_02.pl

where `perl` is the interpreter and `fig25_02.pl` is the script. Alternatively, you could type

    perl -w fig25_02.pl

which instructs the Perl interpreter to output warnings to the screen if it finds potential bugs in your code.

On Windows systems, a Perl script may also be executed by double clicking its program icon. The program window closes automatically once the script terminates, and any screen output is lost. For this reason, it is usually better to run a script from the command prompt.

Error-Prevention Tip 25.1

When running a Perl script from the command line, always use the -w option. Otherwise, the program may seem to execute correctly even though there is actually something wrong with the source code. The -w option displays warnings encountered while executing a Perl program.

Perl Variables and Data Types

Perl has built-in data types (Fig. 25.3) that represent different kinds of data. Note that each variable name has a specific character (i.e., **$**, **@** or **%**) preceding it. For example, the $ character specifies that the variable contains a **scalar** value (i.e., strings, integer numbers, float-

Data type	Format for variable names of this type	Description
Scalar	*$scalarname*	Can be a string, an integer number, a floating-point number or a reference.
Array	*@arrayname*	An ordered list of scalar variables that can be accessed using integer indices.
Hash	*%hashname*	An unordered set of scalar variables whose values are accessed using unique scalar values (i.e., strings) called **keys**.

Fig. 25.3   Perl data types.

ing-point numbers and references). The script `fig25_04.pl` (Fig. 25.4) demonstrates the manipulation of scalar variables.

Common Programming Error 25.3

Failure to place a preceding $ character before a scalar variable name is a syntax error.

```perl
1   #!C:\Perl\bin\perl
2   # Fig. 25.4: fig25_04.pl
3   # Program to illustrate the use of scalar variables.
4
5   $number = 5;
6   print( "The value of variable \$number is: $number\n\n" );
7
8   $number += 5;
9   print( "Variable \$number after adding 5 is: $number\n" );
10
11  $number *= 2;
12  print( "Variable \$number after multiplying by 2 is: " );
13  print( "$number\n\n\n" );
14
15  # using an uninitialized variable in the context of a string
16  print( "Using a variable before initializing: $variable\n\n" );
17
18  # using an uninitialized variable in a numeric context
19  $test = $undefined + 5;
20  print( "Adding uninitialized variable \$undefined " );
21  print( "to 5 yields: $test\n" );
22
23  # using strings in numeric contexts
24  $string = "A string value";
25  $number += $string;
26  print( "Adding a string to an integer yields: $number\n" );
27
28  $string2 = "15charactersand1";
29  $number2 = $number + $string2;
30  print( "Adding $number to string \"$string2\" yields: " );
31  print( "$number2\n" );
```

```
The value of variable $number is: 5

Variable $number after adding 5 is: 10
Variable $number after multiplying by 2 is: 20


Using a variable before initializing:

Adding uninitialized variable $undefined to 5 yields: 5
Adding a string to an integer yields: 20
Adding 20 to string "15charactersand1" yields: 35
```

Fig. 25.4   Using scalar variables.

In Perl, a variable is created the first time it is encountered by the interpreter. Line 5 creates a variable with name `$number` and sets its value to 5. Line 6 calls function `print` to write text followed by the value of `$number`. Note that the actual value of `$number` is printed, rather than the string `"$number"`; when a variable is encountered inside a double-quoted (`""`) string, Perl uses a process called **interpolation** to replace the variable with its associated data. Note that we avoid interpolation and actually print the string `"$number"` in the first part of line 6 by immediately preceding the dollar sign with a backslash character (`\`). The string `"\$number"` is interpreted as the dollar-sign character followed by the string `number`, rather than as the variable `$number`. See the last paragraph of this section for more on printing special characters. Line 8 adds 5 to `$number`, which results in the value 10 being stored in `$number`. Note that we use an **assignment operator** (`+=`) to yield an expression equivalent to `$number = $number + 5`, which adds 5 to the value of `$number` and stores the result in `$number`. Assignment operators (i.e., `+=`, `-=`, `*=` and `/=`) are syntactical shortcuts. In line 11, we use the multiplication assignment operator, `*=`, to multiply `$number` by 2 and store the result in `$number`.

Error-Prevention Tip 25.2

Function `print` can be used to display the value of a variable at a particular point during a program's execution. This is often helpful in debugging a program.

In Perl, uninitialized variables have the value **undef**, which evaluates to different values depending on the variable's context. When `undef` is used in a numeric context (e.g., `$undefined` in line 19), it evaluates to 0. In contrast, when it is interpreted in a string context (e.g., `$variable` in line 16), `undef` evaluates to the empty string (`""`).

Lines 24–31 show the results of evaluating strings in a numeric context. Unless a string begins with a digit, it is evaluated as `undef` in a numeric context. If it begins with a digit, every character up to, but not including, the first nondigit character is evaluated as a number, and the remaining characters are ignored. For example, the string `"A string value"` (line 24) does not begin with a digit and therefore evaluates to `undef`. Because `undef` evaluates to 0, variable `$number`'s value is unchanged. The string `"15charactersand1"` (line 28) begins with a digit and is interpreted as 15. The character 1 on the end is ignored, because there are nondigit characters preceding it. Evaluating a string in numeric context does not actually change the value of the string. This rule is shown by line 31's output, which prints the original string as `"15charactersand1"` and the result of adding this string to the integer value 20 as 35.

The programmer does not need to differentiate between numeric and string data types, because the interpreter's evaluation of scalar variables depends on the context in which they are used.

Common Programming Error 25.4

Using an uninitialized variable might make a numerical calculation incorrect. For example, multiplying a number by an uninitialized variable results in 0.

Error-Prevention Tip 25.3

While it is not always necessary to initialize variables before using them, errors can be avoided by doing so. Many Perl programmers place the statements `use strict` and `use warnings` at the top of their programs to catch such errors. For simplicity, we will not initialize variables before using them in this chapter.

Creating and Manipulating Arrays

Perl provides the capability to store data in arrays. Arrays are divided into **elements**, each containing a scalar value. The script `fig25_05.pl` (Fig. 25.5) demonstrates some techniques for array initialization and manipulation.

```
1   #!C:\Perl\bin\perl
2   # Fig. 25.5: fig25_05.pl
3   # Program to demonstrate arrays in Perl.
4
5   @array = ( "Bill", "Bobby", "Sue", "Michelle" );
6
7   print( "The array contains: @array\n" );
8   print( "Printing array outside of quotes: ", @array, "\n\n" );
9
10  print( "Third element: $array[ 2 ]\n" );
11
12  $number = 3;
13  print( "Fourth element: $array[ $number ]\n\n" );
14
15  @array2 = ( 'A' .. 'Z' );
16  print( "The range operator is used to create a list of\n" );
17  print( "all capital letters from A to Z:\n" );
18  print( "@array2 \n\n" );
19
20  $array3[ 3 ] = "4th";
21  print( "Array with just one element initialized: @array3 \n\n" );
22
23  print( 'Printing literal using single quotes: ' );
24  print( '@array and \n', "\n" );
25
26  print( "Printing literal using backslashes: " );
27  print( "\@array and \\n\n" );
```

```
The array contains: Bill Bobby Sue Michelle
Printing array outside of quotes: BillBobbySueMichelle

Third element: Sue
Fourth element: Michelle

The range operator is used to create a list of
all capital letters from A to Z:
A B C D E F G H I J K L M N O P Q R S T U V W X Y Z

Array with just one element initialized:    4th

Printing literal using single quotes: @array and \n
Printing literal using backslashes: @array and \n
```

Fig. 25.5   Using arrays.

Line 5 initializes array `@array` to contain the strings `"Bill"`, `"Bobby"`, `"Sue"` and `"Michelle"`. In Perl, all array variable names must be preceded by the @ symbol. Parentheses are necessary to group the strings in the array assignment; this group of elements surrounded by parentheses is called a **list**. In assigning the list to @array, each person's name is stored in an individual array element with a unique integer index value, starting at 0. Like JavaScript arrays, arrays in Perl use a zero-based numbering scheme.

Common Programming Error 25.5

Although lists in Perl may seem similar to arrays, they are not. A list is simply a group of elements surrounded by parentheses and does not contain the entire functionality of an array. You can access individual elements in a list using square brackets (i.e., subscript notation), but you cannot assign a new value to an element; lists are immutable.

When printing an array inside double quotes (line 7), the array element values are printed with only one space separating them. The values are separated by whatever is in special variable $", which, by default, is a space. If this value were changed to the letter "a", all the array elements would be printed with the character "a" between them. If the array name is not enclosed in double quotes when it is printed (line 8), the interpreter prints the element values without inserting spaces between them.

Line 10 demonstrates how individual array elements are accessed using square brackets ([]). As mentioned previously, if we use the @ character followed by the array name, we reference the array as a whole. But if the name of the array is prefixed by the $ character and followed by an index number in square brackets (as in line 10), it refers instead to an individual element of the array that is a scalar value. Line 13 demonstrates the use of a variable as the index number. The value of $array[$number] is used to get the value of the fourth element of the array.

Line 15 initializes array @array2 to contain the capital letters A to Z inclusive. The **range operator** (..) specifies that all values between uppercase A and uppercase Z are to be placed in the array. The range operator can be used to create a consecutive series of values, such as 1 through 15 or a through z.

The Perl interpreter handles memory management. Therefore, it is not necessary to specify an array's size. If a value is assigned to a position outside the range of the array or to an uninitialized array, the interpreter automatically extends the array range to include the new element. Elements that are added by the interpreter during an adjustment of the range are initialized to the undef value. Line 20 assigns a value to the fourth element in the uninitialized array @array3. The interpreter recognizes that memory has not been allocated for this array and creates new memory for the array. The interpreter then sets the value of the first three elements to undef and the value of the fourth element to the string "4th". When the array is printed, the first three undef values are treated as empty strings and printed with a space between each. This accounts for the three extra spaces in the output before the string "4th".

To print special characters like \, @, $ and " and not have the interpreter treat them as an escape sequence, array or variable, Perl provides two options. The first is to **print** (lines 23–24) the characters as a **literal string** (i.e., a string enclosed in single quotes). When strings are inside single quotes, the interpreter treats the string literally and does not attempt to interpret any escape sequence or variable substitution. The second choice is to use the backslash character (line 26–27) to **escape** special characters.

25.3 String Processing and Regular Expressions

One of Perl's most powerful capabilities is the processing of textual data easily and efficiently, which allows for straightforward searching, substitution, extraction and concatenation of strings. Text manipulation in Perl is usually done with a **regular expression**—a series of characters that serves as a pattern-matching template (or search criterion) in strings, text files and databases. This feature allows complicated searching and string processing to be performed using relatively simple expressions.

Comparing Strings

Many string-processing tasks can be accomplished by using Perl's **equality** and **comparison** operators (Fig. 25.6, `fig25_06.pl`). Line 5 declares and initializes array `@fruits`. Operator qw ("quote word") takes the content inside the parentheses and creates a comma-separated list, with each element wrapped in double quotes. In this example, qw(apple orange banana) is equivalent to ("apple", "orange", "banana").

```
1   #!C:\Perl\bin\perl
2   # Fig. 25.6: fig25_06.pl
3   # Program to demonstrate the eq, ne, lt, gt operators.
4
5   @fruits = qw( apple orange banana );
6
7   foreach $item ( @fruits ) {
8
9      if ( $item eq "banana" ) {
10         print( "String '$item' matches string 'banana'\n" );
11      }
12
13      if ( $item ne "banana" ) {
14         print( "String '$item' does not match string 'banana'\n" );
15      }
16
17      if ( $item lt "banana" ) {
18         print( "String '$item' is less than string 'banana'\n" );
19      }
20
21      if ( $item gt "banana" ) {
22         print( "String '$item' is greater than string 'banana'\n" );
23      }
24   }
```

```
String 'apple' does not match string 'banana'
String 'apple' is less than string 'banana'
String 'orange' does not match string 'banana'
String 'orange' is greater than string 'banana'
String 'banana' matches string 'banana'
```

Fig. 25.6   Using the eq, ne, lt and gt operators.

Lines 7–24 demonstrate our first example of Perl **control statements**. The **foreach** statement (line 7) iterates sequentially through the elements in `@fruits`. Each element's value is assigned to variable `$item`, and the body of the `foreach` executes once for each element in the array. Note that a semicolon does not terminate the `foreach`.

Line 9 introduces the **if** statement. Parentheses surround the condition being tested, and mandatory curly braces surround the block of code that is executed when the condition is true. In Perl, any scalar except the number 0, the string "0" and the empty string (i.e., `undef` values) is defined as true. In our example, when the `$item`'s content is tested against "banana" (line 9) for equality, the condition evaluates to true, and the **print** function (line 10) executes.

The remaining `if` statements (lines 13, 17 and 21) demonstrate the other string comparison operators. Operators `ne`, `lt` and `gt` test strings for inequality, less-than and greater-than, respectively. These operators are used only with strings. When comparing numeric values, operators `==`, `!=`, `<`, `<=`, `>` and `>=` are used.

Common Programming Error 25.6

Using == for string comparisons or eq for numerical comparisons can result in errors in the program.

Common Programming Error 25.7

While the number 0 and the string "0" evaluate to false in Perl if statements, other string values that might look like zero ("0.0") evaluate to true.

Regular Expressions

For more powerful string comparisons, Perl provides the **match operator** (m/*pattern*/ or /*pattern*/), which uses regular expressions to search a string for a specified *pattern*. Figure 25.7 uses the match operator to perform a variety of regular-expression tests.

```
1   #!C:\Perl\bin\perl
2   # Fig 25.7: fig25_07.pl
3   # Searches using the matching operator and regular expressions.
4
5   $search = "Now is is the time";
6   print( "Test string is: '$search'\n\n" );
7
8   if ( $search =~ /Now/ ) {
9      print( "String 'Now' was found.\n" );
10  }
11
12  if ( $search =~ /^Now/ ) {
13     print( "String 'Now' was found at the beginning of the line." );
14     print( "\n" );
15  }
16
17  if ( $search =~ /Now$/ ) {
18     print( "String 'Now' was found at the end of the line.\n" );
19  }
20
21  if ( $search =~ /\b ( \w+ ow ) \b/x ) {
22     print( "Word found ending in 'ow': $1 \n" );
23  }
24
25  if ( $search =~ /\b ( \w+ ) \s ( \1 ) \b/x ) {
26     print( "Repeated words found: $1 $2\n" );
27  }
28
```

Fig. 25.7   Using the matching operator. (Part 1 of 2.)

```
29   @matches = ( $search =~ / \b ( t \w+ ) \b /gx );
30   print( "Words beginning with 't' found: @matches\n" );
```

```
Test string is: 'Now is is the time'

String 'Now' was found.
String 'Now' was found at the beginning of the line.
Word found ending in 'ow': Now
Repeated words found: is is
Words beginning with 't' found: the time
```

Fig. 25.7   Using the matching operator. (Part 2 of 2.)

We begin by assigning the string "Now is is the time" to variable $search (line 5). The expression in line 8 uses the match operator to search for the **literal characters** Now inside variable $search. The m character preceding the slashes of the m// operator is optional in most cases and thus is omitted here.

The match operator takes two operands. The first operand is the regular-expression pattern to search for (Now), which is placed between the slashes of the m// operator. The second operand is the string within which to search, which is assigned to the match operator using the =~ operator. The =~ operator is sometimes called a **binding operator** because it binds whatever is on its left side to a regular-expression operator on its right.

In our example, the pattern Now is found in the string "Now is is the time". The match operator returns true, and the body of the if statement is executed. In addition to literal characters like Now, which match only themselves, regular expressions can include special characters called **metacharacters**, which specify patterns or contexts that cannot be defined using literal characters. For example, the **caret metacharacter** (^) matches the beginning of a string. The next regular expression (line 12) searches the beginning of $search for the pattern Now.

The $ metacharacter searches the end of a string for a pattern (line 17). The pattern Now is not found at the end of $search, so the body of the if statement (line 18) is not executed. Note that Now$ is not a variable; it is a search pattern that uses $ to search for Now at the end of a string.

The condition in line 21 searches (from left to right) for the first word ending with the letters ow. As in strings, backslashes in regular expressions escape characters with special significance. For example, the \b expression does not match the literal characters "\b." Instead, the expression matches any **word boundary**. A word boundary is a boundary between an **alphanumeric character** (0–9, a–z, A–Z and the underscore character) and something that is not an alphanumeric character. The expression inside the parentheses, \w+ ow, indicates that we are searching for patterns ending in ow. The first part, \w+, is a combination of **\w** (an escape sequence that matches a single alphanumeric character) and the **+ modifier**, which is a **quantifier** that instructs Perl to match the preceding character one or more times. Thus, \w+ matches one or more alphanumeric characters. The characters ow are taken literally. Collectively, the expression /\b (\w+ ow) \b/ matches one or more alphanumeric characters ending with ow, with word boundaries at the beginning and end. See Fig. 25.8 for a description of several Perl regular-expression quantifiers and Fig. 25.9 for a list of regular-expression metacharacters.

Quantifier	Matches
{n}	Exactly n times
{m,n}	Between m and n times inclusive
{n,}	n or more times
+	One or more times (same as {1,})
*	Zero or more times (same as {0,})
?	One or zero times (same as {0,1})

Fig. 25.8   Some of Perl's quantifiers.

Symbol	Matches	Symbol	Matches
^	Beginning of line	\d	Digit (i.e., 0 to 9)
$	End of line	\D	Nondigit
\b	Word boundary	\s	Whitespace
\B	Nonword boundary	\S	Nonwhitespace
\w	Word (alphanumeric) character	\n	Newline
\W	Nonword character	\t	Tab

Fig. 25.9   Some of Perl's metacharacters.

The parentheses that surround \w+ ow in line 21 (Fig. 25.7) indicate that the text matching the pattern is to be saved in a special Perl variable. The parentheses (line 21 of Fig. 25.7) cause Now to be stored in variable $1. Multiple sets of parentheses may be used in regular expressions, where each match results in a new Perl variable ($1, $2, $3, etc.). The value matched in the first set of parentheses is stored in variable $1, the value matched in the second set of parentheses is stored in variable $2, and so on.

Adding **modifying characters** after a regular expression refines the pattern-matching process. Modifying characters (Fig. 25.10) placed to the right of the forward slash that delimits the regular expression instruct the interpreter how to treat the preceding expression. For example, the i after the regular expression

```
/computer/i
```

tells the interpreter to ignore case when searching, thus matching computer, COMPUTER, Computer, CoMputER, etc.

When added to the end of a regular expression, the x modifying character indicates that whitespace characters in the regular expression are to be ignored. This allows programmers to add space characters to their regular expressions for readability without affecting the search. If the expression were written as

```
$search =~ /\b ( \w+ ow ) \b/
```

Modifying character	Purpose
g	Performs a global search; finds and returns all matches, not just the first one found.
i	Ignores the case of the search string (case insensitive).
m	The string is evaluated as if it had multiple lines of text (i.e., newline characters are not ignored).
s	Ignores the newline character and treats it as whitespace. The text is seen as a single line.
x	All whitespace characters in the regular expression are ignored when searching the string.

Fig. 25.10 Some of Perl's modifying characters.

without the **x** modifying character, then the script would be searching for a word boundary, two spaces, one or more alphanumeric characters, one space, the characters **ow**, two spaces and a word boundary. The expression would not match **$search**'s value.

The condition in line 25 uses the **memory function** (i.e., parentheses) in a regular expression. The first parenthetical expression matches any string containing one or more alphanumeric characters. The expression **\1** then evaluates to the word that was matched in the first parenthetical expression. The regular expression searches for two identical consecutive words separated by a whitespace character (**\s**), in this case "**is is**."

Line 29 searches for words beginning with the letter **t** in the string **$search**. Modifying character **g** indicates a global search—a search that does not stop after the first match is found. The array **@matches** is assigned the value of a list of all matching words.

25.4 Viewing Client/Server Environment Variables

Knowing information about a client's execution environment allows system administrators to provide client-specific information. **Environment variables** contain information about the execution environment in which a script is being run, such as the type of Web browser used, the HTTP host and the HTTP connection. A Web server might use this information to generate client-specific Web pages.

Until now, we have written simple Perl applications that output to the local user's screen. Through CGI, we can communicate with the Web server and its clients, allowing us to use the Internet as a method of input and output for our Perl applications. In order to run Perl scripts as CGI applications, a Web server must be installed and configured correctly for your system. See Chapter 21, Web Servers (IIS and Apache), and www.deitel.com for information on installing and setting up a Web server.

We place our CGI programs in the cgi-bin folder. If this directory does not exist, create it in the Web server's root directory. Recall that, by default, the Web server's root directory is C:\Inetpub\wwwroot under IIS and C:\Program Files\Apache Group\Apache2 under Apache. The Web server must be configured correctly to allow files in the cgi-bin directory to run as scripts. The Web server also must be running for CGI programs to execute. Please consult your Web server's documentation for additional configuration details. Copy the remaining .pl files and the password.txt file from the Chapter 25 examples directory to the cgi-bin directory. Other important files (.html files, .shtml files, etc.) normally are placed in the Web server's root directory. All image (.gif) files should be placed in an images folder within the Web server's root directory for the examples in this chapter to display properly.

CGI Script that Displays Environment Variables

In Fig. 25.11, we present our first CGI program. When creating dynamic Web pages in Perl, we output XHTML by using print statements. The XHTML generated in this program displays the client's environment variables. The **use directive** (line 5) instructs Perl programs to include the contents (e.g., functions) of predefined packages called **modules**. The **CGI module**, for example, contains useful functions for CGI scripting in Perl, including functions that return strings representing XHTML (or HTML) tags and HTTP headers. With the use directive, we can specify which functions we would like to import from a particular module. In line 5, we use the **import tag :standard** to import a predefined set of standard functions. We use several of these functions in the following examples.

```
1   #!C:\Perl\bin\perl
2   # Fig. 25.11: fig25_11.pl
3   # Program to display CGI environment variables.
4
5   use CGI qw( :standard );
6
7   $dtd =
8   "-//W3C//DTD XHTML 1.0 Transitional//EN\"
9       \"http://www.w3.org/TR/xhtml1/DTD/xhtml1-transitional.dtd";
10
11  print( header() );
12
13  print( start_html( { dtd => $dtd,
14          title => "Environment Variables..." } ) );
15
16  print( "<table style = \"border: 0; padding: 2;
17          font-weight: bold\">" );
18
19  print( Tr( th( "Variable Name" ),
20          th( "Value" ) ) );
21
22  print( Tr( td( hr() ), td( hr() ) ) );
23
24  foreach $variable ( sort( keys( %ENV ) ) ) {
25
26     print( Tr( td( { style => "background-color: #11bbff" },
27                  $variable ),
28              td( { style => "font-size: 12pt" },
29                      $ENV{ $variable } ) ) );
30
31     print( Tr( td( hr() ), td( hr() ) ) );
32  }
33
```

Fig. 25.11 Displaying CGI environment variables. (Part 1 of 2.)

```
34    print( "</table>" );
35    print( end_html() );
```

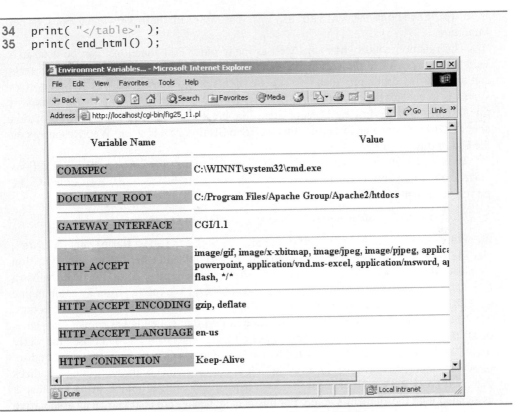

Fig. 25.11　Displaying CGI environment variables. (Part 2 of 2.)

Line 11 instructs the Perl script to print a valid **HTTP header**, using function **header** from the CGI library. Browsers use HTTP headers to determine how to handle incoming data. The header function returns the string "Content-type: text/ html\n\n", indicating to the client that what follows is XHTML. The text/html portion of the header indicates that the browser must display the returned information as an XHTML document. Standard output is redirected when a CGI script executes, so the function print outputs to the user's Web browser.

In lines 13–14, we begin to write XHTML to the client by using the **start_html** function. This function prints the document type definition for this document, as well as several opening XHTML tags (<html>, <head>, <title>, etc., up to the opening <body> tag). Note that certain information is specified within curly braces ({}). In many CGI module functions, additional information (e.g., attributes) can be specified within curly braces. The print function in lines 13–14 displays the result returned by start_html. Each argument within the curly braces is in the form of a *key–value* pair. A **key** (or **value name**) is assigned a value using the **arrow operator** (=>), where the key is to the left of the arrow and the value is to the right. The first argument consists of the key dtd and the value $dtd. When we include the **dtd** argument in the function start_html, the default document type definition is changed from HTML's DTD to the value of $dtd. This adds the proper XHTML DTD (specified in lines 7–9) to this file. The **title** argument specifies the value that goes between the opening and closing <title> tags. In this example, the title of the Web page is set to "Environment Variables...". The order of these key–value pairs is not important.

The function start_html, as well as many other Perl functions, can be used in a variety of ways. All of the arguments to start_html are optional, and some arguments can be specified differently than how we see in this program. A good way to find correct syntax is to consult the book *Official Guide to Programming with CGI.pm: The Standard for Building Web Scripts* by Lincoln Stein (the creator of the CGI library). Information about CGI is also available on the Internet. (See Section 25.11, Wide Web Resources, at the end of this chapter.)

In lines 19–20, we have two more CGI.pm functions—**Tr** and **th**. These functions place their arguments between table row tags and table header tags, respectively. The print statement outputs

```
<tr><th>Variable Name</th><th>Value</th></tr>
```

Function th is called twice, with the arguments "Variable Name" and "Value", causing both of these values to be surrounded by start and end table header tags. Function Tr places these two header tags inside <tr> start and end tags. [*Note*: This function has a capital "T" because Perl already contains an operator tr.] We call function Tr again in line 22 with the **hr** and **td** functions, in order to print a row of horizontal rules within <td> tags.

The **%ENV hash** is a built-in data structure in Perl that contains the names and values of all the environment variables. The foreach statement in lines 24–32 uses the %ENV hash. The **hash** data type is designated by the % character and represents an unordered set of scalar-value pairs. Unlike an array, which accesses elements through integer indices (e.g., $array[2]), each element in a hash is accessed using a unique string **key** that is associated with the element's value. For this reason, hashes are also known as **associative arrays**, because the keys and values are associated in pairs. Hash values are accessed using the syntax $hashName{ keyName }. In this example, each key in hash %ENV is the name of an environment variable name (e.g., HTTP_HOST). When this value is used as the key in the %ENV hash, the variable's value is returned.

Function **keys** returns an unordered array containing all the keys in the %ENV hash (line 24), as hash elements have no defined order. We call function **sort** to order the array of keys alphabetically. Finally, the foreach iterates sequentially through the array returned by sort, repeatedly assigning the current key's value to scalar $variable. Lines 26–31 execute for each element in the array of key values. In lines 26–29, we output a new row for the table, containing the name of the environment variable ($variable) in one column and the value for the variable ($ENV{ $variable }) in the next. We call function td in line 26 and use curly-brace notation to specify the value for the attribute style. In line 28, we use the hash notation again to specify a style attribute. Line 35 calls the function **end_html**, which returns the closing tags for the page (</body> and </html>).

25.5 Form Processing and Business Logic

XHTML forms enable Web pages to collect data from users and send it to a Web server for processing by server-side programs and scripts. This allows users to purchase products, send and receive Web-based e-mail, participate in polls and perform many other tasks. This type of Web communication allows users to interact with the server and is vital to Web development.

Figure 25.12 uses an XHTML form to collect information about users before adding them to a mailing list. This type of registration form could be used by a software company to obtain profile information before allowing the user to download software.

```
1   <!DOCTYPE html PUBLIC "-//W3C//DTD XHTML 1.0 Transitional//EN"
2      "http://www.w3.org/TR/xhtml1/DTD/xhtml1-transitional.dtd">
3
4   <!-- Fig. 25.12: fig25_12.html -->
5
6   <html>
7      <head>
8         <title>Sample form to take user input in XHTML</title>
9      </head>
10
11     <body style = "font-face: arial; font-size: 12pt">
12
13        <div style = "font-size: 14pt; font-weight: bold">
14              This is a sample registration form.
15        </div>
16
17        <br />
18        Please fill in all fields and click Register.
19
20        <form method = "post" action = "/cgi-bin/fig25_13.pl">
21
22           <img src = "images/user.gif" /><br />
23
24           <div style = "color: blue" >
25              Please fill out the fields below.<br />
26           </div>
27
28           <img src = "images/fname.gif" />
29           <input type = "text" name = "fname" /><br />
30           <img src = "images/lname.gif" />
31           <input type = "text" name = "lname" /><br />
32           <img src = "images/email.gif" />
33           <input type = "text" name = "email" /><br />
34           <img src = "images/phone.gif" />
35           <input type = "text" name = "phone" /><br />
36
37           <div style = "font-size: 10pt">
38              Must be in the form (555)555-5555.<br /><br />
39           </div>
40
41           <img src = "images/downloads.gif" /><br />
42           <div style = "color: blue">
43              Which book would you like information about?<br />
44           </div>
45
46           <select name = "book">
47              <option>Internet and WWW How to Program 3e</option>
48              <option>C++ How to Program 4e</option>
```

Fig. 25.12 XHTML document with an interactive form. (Part 1 of 2.)

```
49              <option>Java How to Program 5e</option>
50              <option>XML How to Program 1e</option>
51          </select><br /><br />
52
53          <img src = "images/os.gif" /><br />
54          <div style = "color: blue">
55              Which operating system are you currently using?
56          </div><br />
57
58          <input type = "radio" name = "os"
59              value = "Windows XP" checked />
60          Windows XP<input type = "radio"
61              name = "os" value = "Windows 2000" />
62          Windows 2000<input type = "radio"
63              name = "os" value = "Windows 98/me" />
64          Windows 98/me<br /><input type = "radio"
65              name = "os" value = "Linux" />
66          Linux<input type = "radio" name = "os"
67              value = "Other" />
68          Other<br /><input type = "submit"
69              value = "Register" />
70      </form>
71  </body>
72 </html>
```

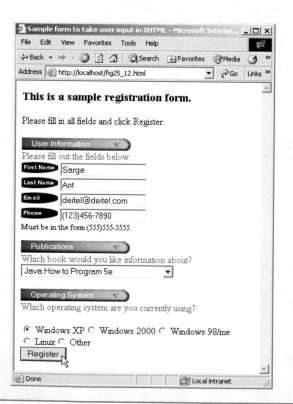

Fig. 25.12 XHTML document with an interactive form. (Part 2 of 2.)

Line 21 contains a form element which indicates that, when the user clicks **Register**, the form information is posted to the server. The attribute action = "/cgi-bin/fig25_13.pl" directs the server to execute the fig25_13.pl Perl script (located in the cgi-bin directory) to process the posted form data. We assign a unique name (e.g., email in line 33) to each of the form's input fields. When **Register** is clicked, each field's name and value are sent to the script fig25_13.pl, which can then access the submitted value for each specific field.

Good Programming Practice 25.2

Use meaningful XHTML object names for input fields. This practice makes Perl programs easier to understand when processing form data.

The program in Fig. 25.13 processes the data posted by fig25_12.html and sends a Web-page response back to the client. Function **param** (lines 8–13) is part of the Perl CGI module and retrieves values from a form field's value. For example, in line 35 of Fig. 25.12, an XHTML form text field is created with the name phone. In line 12 of Fig. 25.13, we access the value that the user entered for that field by calling param("phone") and assign the value returned to variable $phone.

Line 24 determines whether the phone number entered by the user is valid. In this case, *(555)555-5555* is the only acceptable format. Validating information is crucial when you are maintaining a database, and a great way to do this is by using regular expressions. Validation ensures, for example, that data is stored in the proper format in a database and that credit-card numbers contain the proper number of digits before they are encrypted for submission to a merchant. This script implements the **business logic**, or **business rules**, of our application.

```
1   #!C:\Perl\bin\perl
2   # Fig. 25.13: fig25_13.pl
3   # Program to read information sent to the server
4   # from the form in the fig25_12.html document.
5
6   use CGI qw( :standard );
7
8   $os = param( "os" );
9   $firstName = param( "fname" );
10  $lastName = param( "lname" );
11  $email = param( "email" );
12  $phone = param( "phone" );
13  $book = param( "book" );
14
15  $dtd =
16  "-//W3C//DTD XHTML 1.0 Transitional//EN\"
17     \"http://www.w3.org/TR/xhtml1/DTD/xhtml1-transitional.dtd";
18
19  print( header() );
20
21  print( start_html( { dtd => $dtd,
22                       title => "Form Results" } ) );
23
24  if ( $phone =~ / ^ \( \d{3} \) \d{3} - \d{4} $ /x ) {
25     print( "Hi " );
```

Fig. 25.13 Script to process user data from fig25_12.html. (Part 1 of 3.)

```perl
26      print( span( { style => "color: blue; font-weight: bold" },
27                      $firstName ) );
28      print( "!" );
29
30      print( "\nThank you for completing the survey." );
31      print( br(), "You have been added to the " );
32
33      print( span( { style => "color: blue; font-weight: bold" },
34                      $book ) );
35      print( " mailing list.", br(), br() );
36
37      print( span( { style => "font-weight: bold" },
38                      "The following information has
39                      been saved in our database: " ), br() );
40
41      print( table(
42              Tr( th( { style => "background-color: #ee82ee" },
43                      "Name" ),
44                  th( { style => "background-color: #9370db" },
45                      "E-mail" ),
46                  th( { style => "background-color: #4169e1" },
47                      "Phone" ),
48                  th( { style => "background-color: #40e0d0" },
49                      "OS" ) ),
50
51              Tr( { style => "background-color: #c0c0c0" },
52                  td( "$firstName $lastName" ),
53                  td( $email ),
54                  td( $phone ),
55                  td( $os ) ) ) );
56
57      print( br() );
58
59      print( div( { style => "font-size: x-small" },
60              "This is only a sample form. You have not been
61              added to a mailing list." ) );
62   }
63   else {
64      print( div( { style => "color: red; font-size: x-large" },
65              "INVALID PHONE NUMBER" ), br() );
66
67      print( "A valid phone number must be in the form " );
68      print( span( { style => "font-weight: bold" },
69                      "(555)555-5555." ) );
70
71      print( div( { style => "color: blue" },
72              "Click the Back button, and enter a
73              valid phone number and resubmit." ) );
74      print( br(), br() );
75      print( "Thank you." );
76   }
77
78   print( end_html() );
```

Fig. 25.13 Script to process user data from `fig25_12.html`. (Part 2 of 3.)

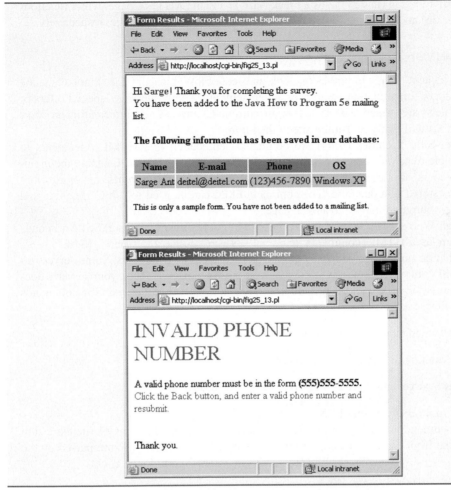

Fig. 25.13   Script to process user data from `fig25_12.html`. (Part 3 of 3.)

    The `if` condition in line 24 uses a regular expression to validate the phone number. The expression "`\(`" matches the opening parenthesis of the phone number. Because we want to match the literal character (, we must escape its normal meaning by using the \ character. This sequence must be followed by three digits (`\d{3}`), a closing parenthesis, three digits, a hyphen and finally, four more digits. Note that we use the ^ and $ metacharacters to ensure that there are no extra characters at the beginning or end of the string.

    If the regular expression is matched, then the phone number is valid, and a Web page is sent, thanking the user for completing the form. If the user posts an invalid phone number, the **else** (lines 63–76) executes, instructing the user to enter a valid phone number.

Good Programming Practice 25.3

Use business logic to ensure that invalid information is not stored in a database.

The **br** function (line 31) adds a break (<br />) to the XHTML page, while functions **span** (line 26) and **div** (line 59) add span and div elements to the page, respectively.

25.6 Server-Side Includes

Dynamic content greatly improves the look-and-feel of a Web page. Pages that include the current date or time, rotating banners or advertisements, a daily message, special offers or company news are attractive because they are current. Clients see new information on every visit and thus will likely revisit the site in the future.

Server-Side Includes (SSIs) are commands embedded in XHTML documents to create simple dynamic content. SSI commands like **ECHO** and **INCLUDE** enable the inclusion on Web pages of content that is constantly changing (i.e., the current time) or information that is stored in a database. The command **EXEC** can be used to run CGI scripts and embed their output directly into a Web page.

Not all Web servers support the available SSI commands. Therefore, SSI commands are written as XHTML comments (e.g., <!--#ECHO VAR="DOCUMENT_NAME" -->). Servers that do not recognize these commands treat them as comments. Some servers do support SSI commands, but only if they are configured to do so. Check your server's documentation for instructions on how to configure your server to process SSI commands properly. Please refer to

```
httpd.apache.org/docs/howto/ssi.html
```

if you are running the Apache Web server, or

```
perl.xotechnologies.net/tutorials/SSI/SSI.htm
```

if you are running a version of IIS.

A document containing SSI commands is typically given the **.shtml** file extension (the **s** at the front of the extension stands for **server**). The **.shtml** files are parsed by the server. The server executes the SSI commands and writes output to the client.

 Performance Tip 25.1

Parsing XHTML documents on a server can dramatically increase the load on the server. To increase the performance of a heavily loaded server, limit the use of server-side includes.

Figure 25.14 implements a **Web page hit counter**. Each time a client requests the document, the counter is incremented by 1. The Perl script **fig25_15.pl** manipulates the counter.

```
1   <!DOCTYPE html PUBLIC "-//W3C//DTD XHTML 1.0 Strict//EN"
2       "http://www.w3.org/TR/xhtml1/DTD/xhtml1-strict.dtd">
3
4   <!-- Fig. 25.14: fig25_14.shtml -->
5
6   <html>
7       <head>
```

Fig. 25.14 Incorporating a Web-page hit counter and displaying environment variables, using server-side includes. (Part 1 of 3.)

```
 8          <title>Using Server-Side Includes</title>
 9      </head>
10
11      <body>
12          <h3 style = "text-align: center">
13              Using Server-Side Includes
14          </h3>
15
16          <!--#EXEC CGI="/cgi-bin/fig25_15.pl" --><br />
17
18          The Greenwich Mean Time is
19          <span style = "color: blue">
20              <!--#ECHO VAR="DATE_GMT" -->.
21          </span><br />
22
23          The name of this document is
24          <span style = "color: blue">
25              <!--#ECHO VAR="DOCUMENT_NAME" -->.
26          </span><br />
27
28          The local date is
29          <span style = "color: blue">
30              <!--#ECHO VAR="DATE_LOCAL" -->.
31          </span><br />
32
33          This document was last modified on
34          <span style = "color: blue">
35              <!--#ECHO VAR="LAST_MODIFIED" -->.
36          </span><br />
37
38          Your current IP Address is
39          <span style = "color: blue">
40              <!--#ECHO VAR="REMOTE_ADDR" -->.
41          </span><br />
42
43          My server name is
44          <span style = "color: blue">
45              <!--#ECHO VAR="SERVER_NAME" -->.
46          </span><br />
47
48          And I am using the
49          <span style = "color: blue">
50              <!--#ECHO VAR="SERVER_SOFTWARE" -->
51              Web Server.
52          </span><br />
53
54          You are using
55          <span style = "color: blue">
56              <!--#ECHO VAR="HTTP_USER_AGENT" -->.
57          </span><br />
58
59          This server is using
```

Fig. 25.14 Incorporating a Web-page hit counter and displaying environment variables, using server-side includes. (Part 2 of 3.)

```
60          <span style = "color: blue">
61             <!--#ECHO VAR="GATEWAY_INTERFACE" -->.
62          </span><br />
63
64          <br /><br />
65          <div style = "text-align: center;
66                        font-size: xx-small">
67             <hr />
68             This document was last modified on
69             <!--#ECHO VAR="LAST_MODIFIED" -->.
70          </div>
71       </body>
72    </html>
```

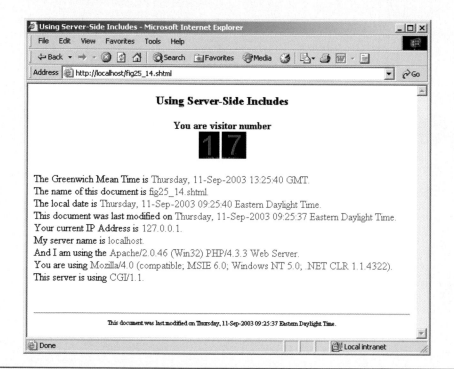

Fig. 25.14 Incorporating a Web-page hit counter and displaying environment variables, using server-side includes. (Part 3 of 3.)

Line 16 of the `fig25_14.shtml` script executes the `fig25_15.pl` script, using the EXEC command. Before the XHTML document is sent to the client, the SSI command is executed, and any script output is sent to the client.

Line 20 uses the **ECHO command** to display variable information. The ECHO command is followed by the **keyword VAR** and the name of the variable. For example, **variable DATE_GMT** contains the current date and time in Greenwich Mean Time (GMT). In line 25, the name of the current document is included in the XHTML page with the **DOCUMENT_NAME variable**. The **DATE_LOCAL variable** inserts the date in line 30 in local format—different formats are used around the world.

Figure 25.15 (`fig25_15.pl`) introduces file input and output in Perl. Line 8 opens (for input) the file `counter.dat`, which contains the number of hits to date for the `fig25_14.shtml` Web page. Function **open** is called to create a **filehandle** to refer to the file during the execution of the script. In this example, the file opened is assigned a filehandle named COUNTREAD.

```perl
1   #!C:\Perl\bin\perl
2   # Fig. 25.15: fig25_15.pl
3   # Program to track the number of times
4   # a Web page has been accessed.
5
6   use CGI qw( :standard );
7
8   open( COUNTREAD, "counter.dat" );
9   $data = <COUNTREAD>;
10  $data++;
11  close( COUNTREAD );
12
13  open( COUNTWRITE, ">counter.dat" );
14  print( COUNTWRITE $data );
15  close( COUNTWRITE );
16
17  print( header(), "<div style = \"text-align: center;
18                                 font-weight: bold\">" );
19  print( "You are visitor number", br() );
20
21  for ( $count = 0; $count < length( $data ); $count++ ) {
22     $number = substr( $data, $count, 1 );
23     print( img( { src => "images/$number.gif" } ), "\n" );
24  }
25
26  print( "</div>" );
```

Fig. 25.15 Perl script for counting Web page hits.

Line 9 uses the **diamond operator**, <>, to read one line of the file referred to by filehandle COUNTREAD and assign it to the variable $data. When the diamond operator is used in a scalar context, only one line is read. If assigned to an array, each line from the file is assigned to a successive element of the array. Because the file `counter.dat` contains only one line (in this case, only one number), the variable $data is assigned the value of that number in line 9. Line 10 then increments $data by 1. If the file does not yet exist when we try to open it, $data is assigned the value `undef`, which will be evaluated as 0 and incremented to 1 in line 10. In line 11, the connection to `counter.dat` is terminated by calling function **close**.

Now that the counter has been incremented for this hit, we write it back to the `counter.dat` file. In line 13, we open the `counter.dat` file for writing by preceding the file name with a > **character** (this is called **write mode**). This immediately truncates (i.e., discards) any data in that file. If the file does not exist, Perl creates a new one with the specified name. The first argument (COUNTWRITE) specifies the filehandle that will be used to refer to the file. Perl also provides an **append mode** (>>) for appending to the end of a file.

After line 13 executes, data can be written to the file `counter.dat`. Line 14 writes the counter number back to the file `counter.dat`. The first argument to `print` indicates the filehandle that refers to the file where data is written. If no filehandle is specified, `print` writes to standard out (`STDOUT`). Note that we need to use a space, rather than a comma, to separate the filehandle from the data. Line 15 closes the connect to the file `counter.dat`.

Lines 21–24 use a **for** statement to iterate through each digit of the number scalar `$data`. The `for` statement syntax consists of three semicolon-separated statements in parentheses, followed by a body delimited by curly braces. In our example, we iterate until `$count` is equal to `length( $data )`. Function **length** returns the length of a character string, so the `for` iterates once for each digit in the variable `$data`. For instance, if `$data` stores the value `"32"`, then the `for` iterates twice, first to process the value `"3"`, and second to process the value `"2"`. In the first iteration, `$count` equals 0 (as initialized in line 21), and the second time `$count` will equal 1. This is because the value of `$count` will be incremented for each loop (as specified by the statement `$count++`, also in line 21). For each iteration, we obtain the current digit by calling function **substr**. The first parameter passed to function `substr` specifies the string from which to obtain a substring. The second parameter specifies the offset, in characters, from the beginning of the string, so an offset of 0 returns the first character, 1 returns the second and so forth. The third argument specifies the length of the substring to be obtained (one character in this case). The `for` then assigns each digit (possibly from a multiple-digit number) to the scalar variable `$number`. Each digit's corresponding image is displayed using the **img** function (line 23).

Good Programming Practice 25.4

When opening a text file to read its contents, open the file in read-only mode. Opening the file in other modes increases the risk of overwriting the data accidentally.

Good Programming Practice 25.5

Always close files as soon as you are finished with them.

It is important in this example to think about file permissions and security. This program may not run correctly if the user's default settings do not allow scripts to manipulate files. To resolve this issue, the user can change the permissions in the folder where `counter.dat` resides so that all users have **Write** access. Check your Web server's documentation for instructions on configuring file permissions. The user should be aware that giving users **Write** access poses a security risk to the system. Security details are covered in Chapter 38, e-Business & e-Commerce.

25.7 Verifying a Username and Password

It is often desirable to have a **private Web site** that is visible only to certain people. Implementing privacy generally involves username and password verification. Figure 25.16 is an XHTML form that queries the user for a username and a password. It posts the fields `username` and `password` to the Perl script `fig25_17.pl` upon submission of the form. For simplicity, this example does not encrypt the data before sending it to the server.

The script `fig25_17.pl` (Fig. 25.17) is responsible for verifying the username and password of the client by crosschecking against values from a database. The database of valid users and their passwords is a simple text file: `password.txt` (Fig. 25.18).

```
1    <!DOCTYPE html PUBLIC "-//W3C//DTD XHTML 1.0 Strict//EN"
2       "http://www.w3.org/TR/xhtml1/DTD/xhtml1-strict.dtd">
3
4    <!-- Fig. 25.16: fig25_16.html -->
5
6    <html>
7       <head>
8          <title>Verifying a username and a password</title>
9       </head>
10
11      <body>
12         <p>
13            <div style = "font-family = arial">
14               Type in your username and password below.
15            </div><br />
16
17            <div style = "color: #0000ff; font-family: arial;
18                          font-weight: bold; font-size: small">
19               Note that the password will be sent as plain text.
20            </div>
21         </p>
22
23         <form action = "/cgi-bin/fig25_17.pl" method = "post">
24
25            <table style = "background-color: #dddddd">
26               <tr>
27                  <td style = "font-face: arial;
28                               font-weight: bold">Username:</td>
29               </tr>
30               <tr>
31                  <td>
32                     <input name = "username" />
33                  </td>
34               </tr>
35               <tr>
36                  <td style = "font-face: arial;
37                               font-weight: bold">Password:</td>
38               </tr>
39               <tr>
40                  <td>
41                     <input name = "password" type = "password" />
42                  </td>
43               </tr>
44               <tr>
45                  <td>
46                     <input type = "submit" value = "Enter" />
47                  </td>
48               </tr>
49            </table>
50         </form>
51      </body>
52   </html>
```

Fig. 25.16   XHTML form for submitting a username and a password to a Perl script. (Part 1 of 2.)

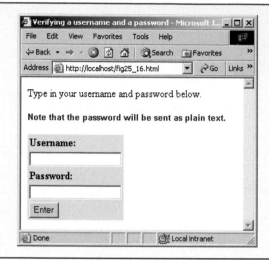

Fig. 25.16 XHTML form for submitting a username and a password to a Perl script. (Part 2 of 2.)

In line 14 of `fig25_17.pl`, we open the file `password.txt` (Fig. 25.18) for reading and assign it to the filehandle `FILE`. To verify that the file was opened successfully, a test is performed using the **logical OR operator** (`||`). Operator `||` returns true if either the left condition or the right condition evaluates to true. If the condition on the left evaluates to true, then the condition on the right is not evaluated. In this case, the function **die** executes only if **open** returns false, indicating that the file did not open properly. Function `die` displays an error message and terminates program execution.

```
1   #!C:\Perl\bin\perl
2   # Fig. 25.17: fig25_17.pl
3   # Program to search a database for usernames and passwords.
4
5   use CGI qw( :standard );
6
7   $dtd =
8   "-//W3C//DTD XHTML 1.0 Transitional//EN\"
9      \"http://www.w3.org/TR/xhtml1/DTD/xhtml1-transitional.dtd";
10
11  $testUsername = param( "username" );
12  $testPassword = param( "password" );
13
14  open( FILE, "password.txt" ) ||
15     die( "The database could not be opened." );
16
17  while ( $line = <FILE> ) {
18     chomp( $line );
19     ( $username, $password ) = split( ",", $line );
20
```

Fig. 25.17 Script to analyze the username and password submitted from an XHTML form. (Part 1 of 3.)

```
21      if ( $testUsername eq $username ) {
22         $userVerified = 1;
23
24         if ( $testPassword eq $password ) {
25            $passwordVerified = 1;
26            last;
27         }
28      }
29   }
30
31   close( FILE );
32
33   print( header() );
34   print( start_html( { dtd => $dtd,
35                        title => "Password Analyzed" } ) );
36
37   if ( $userVerified && $passwordVerified ) {
38      accessGranted();
39   }
40   elsif ( $userVerified && !$passwordVerified ) {
41      wrongPassword();
42   }
43   else {
44      accessDenied();
45   }
46
47   print( end_html() );
48
49   sub accessGranted
50   {
51      print( div( { style => "font-face: arial;
52                             color: blue;
53                             font-weight: bold" },
54         "Permission has been granted,
55         $username.", br(), "Enjoy the site." ) );
56   }
57
58   sub wrongPassword
59   {
60      print( div( { style => "font-face: arial;
61                             color: red;
62                             font-weight: bold" },
63         "You entered an invalid password.", br(),
64         "Access has been denied." ) );
65   }
66
67   sub accessDenied
68   {
69      print( div( { style => "font-face: arial;
70                             color: red;
71                             font-size: larger;
72                             font-weight: bold" },
```

Fig. 25.17 Script to analyze the username and password submitted from an XHTML form. (Part 2 of 3.)

```
73              "You have been denied access to this site." ) );
74   }
```

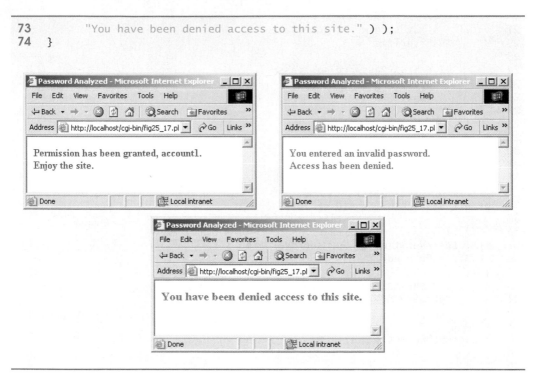

Fig. 25.17 Script to analyze the username and password submitted from an XHTML form. (Part 3 of 3.)

```
1    account1,password1
2    account2,password2
3    account3,password3
4    account4,password4
5    account5,password5
6    account6,password6
7    account7,password7
8    account8,password8
9    account9,password9
10   account10,password10
```

Fig. 25.18 Database `password.txt` containing usernames and passwords.

Good Programming Practice 25.6

Function `die` is useful to handle situations in which a program cannot continue. Rather than resulting in program errors, function `die` will cause the program to end with a message explaining the situation to the user.

The **while** statement (lines 17–29) repeatedly executes the code enclosed in curly braces until the condition in parentheses evaluates to false. In this case, the test condition assigns the next unread line of **password.txt** to $line and evaluates to true as long as a line from the file is successfully read. When the end of the file is reached, <FILE> returns false and the loop terminates.

Each line in `password.txt` (Fig. 25.18) consists of an account name and password pair, separated by a comma, and followed by a newline character. For each line read, function **chomp** is called (line 18) to remove the newline character at the end of the line. Then `split` is called to divide the string into substrings at the specified separator or **delimiter** (in this case, a comma). For example, the `split` of the first line in `password.txt` returns the list (`"account1"`, `"password1"`). The syntax

```
( $username, $password ) = split( ",", $line );
```

sets `$username` and `$password` to the first and second elements returned by `split` (`account1` and `password1`), respectively.

If the username entered is equivalent to the one we have read from the text file, the condition in line 21 returns true. The `$userVerified` variable is then set to 1. Next, the value of `$testPassword` is tested against the value in the `$password` variable (line 24). If the password matches, the `$passwordVerified` variable is set to 1. In this case, because a successful username-password match has been found, the **last** statement, used to exit a repetition structure prematurely, allows us to exit the `while` loop immediately in line 26.

We are finished reading from `password.txt`, so we `close` the file in line 31. Line 37 checks whether both the username and the password were verified, using the Perl **logical AND operator (&&)**. If both conditions are true (i.e., if both variables evaluate to nonzero values), then the function `accessGranted` is called (lines 49–56), which sends a Web page to the client, indicating a successful login. Otherwise, the condition in the `elsif` (line 40) is tested to determine whether the user was verified but not the password. In this case, the function `wrongPassword` is called (lines 58–65). The unary **logical negation operator** (`!`) is used in line 40 to negate the value of `$passwordVerified` and test whether it is false. If the user is not recognized, function `accessDenied` is called, and a message indicating that permission has been denied is sent to the client (lines 67–74).

Perl allows programmers to define their own **functions** or **subroutines**. Keyword `sub` begins a function definition (lines 49, 58 and 67), and curly braces delimit the function body. To call a function (i.e., to execute the code within the function definition), use the function's name, followed by a pair of parentheses (line 38, 41 and 44).

25.8 Using DBI to Connect to a Database

Database connectivity allows system administrators to maintain information on user accounts, passwords, credit-card information, mailing lists, product inventory and similar matters. Databases allow companies to enter the world of electronic commerce and maintain crucial data. For more information on databases, please refer to Chapter 22.

To access various relational databases in Perl, we need an interface (in the form of software) that allows us to connect to and execute SQL operations (queries). The **Perl DBI (Database Interface)** allows us to do this. This interface was created to access different types of databases uniformly. In this section, we access and manipulate a MySQL database containing information on several of Deitel & Associates, Inc.'s publications.

The examples in this section require that MySQL (`www.mysql.org`) be installed. Please refer to the MySQL installation instructions posted at `www.deitel.com/books/iw3HTP3/index.html`. The Perl **DBI** module and the MySQL driver, **DBD::mysql** (specified in lines 6–7 of Fig. 25.19), are also required.

If you are using ActiveState Perl, you can download these files using the *Perl Package Manager* (PPM), which is part of ActiveState Perl. Using PPM, you can download and install Perl modules and packages (provided that you are connected to the Internet at the time you are running the program). To use PPM, type ppm at the command prompt. This command starts the package manager in **interactive mode**, providing you with the ppm> prompt. Type install DBI and press *Enter* to install DBI. To install the MySQL driver, type install DBD-mysql and press *Enter*. [*Note*: The specific package to install is named DBD-mysql, whereas the driver itself is referred to as DBD::mysql.] If you do not have the Perl Package Manager, you can search for the module or package on *CPAN*, the *Comprehensive Perl Archive Network* (www.cpan.org).

The final step in setting up a computer to run the following example is to copy the database books to the computer. This database is located in the Chapter 25 examples directory on the CD-ROM that accompanies this book. The examples directory contains a subfolder named books, which contains all the required database files. In your mysql directory (e.g., C:\mysql), a data directory exists, which contains MySQL databases. Each subfolder in the data directory represents a database and contains all the files that comprise that database. Copy the books folder into this data directory.

In Fig. 25.19, the client selects an author from a drop-down list (the authors are numbered by their ID value). When **Get Info** is clicked, the chosen author and the author's ID are posted to the Perl script in Fig. 25.20 that queries the database for all books published by that author. The results are displayed in an XHTML table. To create and execute SQL queries, we create DBI objects known as **handles**. Database handles create and manipulate a connection to a database, while **statement handles** create and submit SQL to a database.

```
1   #!C:\Perl\bin\perl
2   # Fig. 25.19: fig25_19.pl
3   # CGI program that generates a list of authors.
4
5   use CGI qw( :standard );
6   use DBI;
7   use DBD::mysql;
8
9   $dtd =
10  "-//W3C//DTD XHTML 1.0 Transitional//EN\"
11     \"http://www.w3.org/TR/xhtml1/DTD/xhtml1-transitional.dtd";
12
13  print( header() );
14
15  print( start_html( { dtd => $dtd,
16                       title => "Authors" } ) );
17
18  # connect to "books" database, no password needed
19  $databaseHandle = DBI->connect( "DBI:mysql:books",
20                       "root", "", { RaiseError => 1 } );
21
22  # retrieve the names and IDs of all authors
23  $query = "SELECT FirstName, LastName, AuthorID
24          FROM Authors ORDER BY LastName";
```

Fig. 25.19 Perl script that queries a MySQL database for authors. (Part 1 of 2.)

```
25
26   # prepare the query for execution, then execute it
27   # a prepared query can be executed multiple times
28   $statementHandle = $databaseHandle->prepare( $query );
29   $statementHandle->execute();
30
31   print( h2( "Choose an author:" ) );
32
33   print( start_form( { action => 'fig25_20.pl' } ) );
34
35   print( "<select name = \"author\">\n" );
36
37   # drop-down list contains the author and ID number
38   # method fetchrow_array returns a single row from the result
39   while ( @row = $statementHandle->fetchrow_array() ) {
40      print( "<option>" );
41      print( "$row[ 2 ]. $row[ 1 ], $row[ 0 ]" );
42      print( "</option>" );
43   }
44
45   print( "</select>\n" );
46
47   print( submit( { value => 'Get Info' } ) );
48   print( end_form(), end_html() );
49
50   # clean up -- close the statement and database handles
51   $databaseHandle->disconnect();
52   $statementHandle->finish();
```

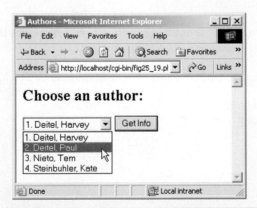

Fig. 25.19 Perl script that queries a MySQL database for authors. (Part 2 of 2.)

In lines 19–20, we connect to the database by calling DBI method **connect**. The first argument specifies the data source (i.e., the database). Note that we first specify the interface name (DBI), followed by a colon (:), then the database driver (mysql), followed by another colon and the name of the data source (books). The second argument specifies the user, and the third argument specifies the password for the database. This database does not require a username or password, so we simply use the empty string (""). The fourth argument ({ RaiseError => 1 }) is used for error checking. If an error occurs when trying to connect to the database, function die is called and passed an error message. Setting this hash reference to 1 is like setting a variable to true—this value "turns on" the error checking, saving the programmer from writing extra code to handle the problem or from having the program crash unexpectedly. If the connection succeeds, function connect returns a database handle that is assigned to $databaseHandle.

In this example, we query the database for the names and IDs of the authors. We create this query in lines 23–24. In line 28, we use our database handle to prepare the query (using the method **prepare**). This method prepares the database driver for a statement that can be executed multiple times. The statement handle returned is assigned to $statement-Handle. We execute the query by calling method **execute** in line 29.

Once the query has been executed, we can access the results by calling method **fetchrow_array** (line 39). Each call to this function returns the next set of data in the resulting table until there are no data sets left. A data set, or a row in the resulting table, contains one of the elements that satisfies the query. For example, in the first program, a query is executed that returns the ID and name of each author. This query creates a table that contains two columns, one for the author's ID and one for the author's name. A row contains the ID and name of a specific author. Each row is returned as an array and assigned to @row. We print these values as list options in lines 40–42. The option chosen is sent as the parameter "author" (line 35) to the Perl script in Fig. 25.20. In lines 51–52, we close the database connection (using method **disconnect**), and we specify that we are finished with this query by calling method **finish**. This function closes the statement handle and frees memory, especially if the resulting table is large.

 Look-and-Feel Observation 25.1

Using tables to output fields in a database neatly organizes information into rows and columns.

Figure 25.20 presents the script fig25_20.pl, which queries the database for information about the specified author.

```perl
1   #!C:\Perl\bin\perl
2   # Fig. 25.20: fig25_20.pl
3   # CGI program to query a MySQL database.
4
5   use CGI qw( :standard );
6   use DBI;
7   use DBD::mysql;
8
9   $dtd =
10  "-//W3C//DTD XHTML 1.0 Transitional//EN\"
11      \"http://www.w3.org/TR/xhtml1/DTD/xhtml1-transitional.dtd";
12
13  print( header() );
14
15  # retrieve author's ID and name from the posted form
16  $authorID = substr( param( "author" ), 0, 1 );
17  $authorName = substr( param( "author" ), 3 );
18
```

Fig. 25.20   Perl script that queries a MySQL database for author information. (Part 1 of 3.)

```perl
19   print( start_html( { dtd => $dtd,
20                        title => "Books by $authorName" } ) );
21
22   $databaseHandle = DBI->connect( "DBI:mysql:books",
23                        "root", "", { RaiseError => 1 } );
24
25   # use AuthorID to find all the ISBNs related to this author
26   $query1 = "SELECT ISBN FROM AuthorISBN
27            WHERE AuthorID = $authorID";
28
29   $statementHandle1 = $databaseHandle->prepare( $query1 );
30   $statementHandle1->execute();
31
32   print( h2( "$authorName" ) );
33
34   print( "<table border = 1>" );
35   print( th( "Title" ), th( "ISBN" ), th( "Publisher" ) );
36
37   while ( @isbn = $statementHandle1->fetchrow_array() ) {
38      print( "<tr>\n" );
39
40      # use ISBN to find the corresponding title
41      $query2 = "SELECT Title, PublisherID FROM titles
42               WHERE ISBN = \'$isbn[ 0 ]\'";
43      $statementHandle2 = $databaseHandle->prepare( $query2 );
44      $statementHandle2->execute();
45      @title_publisherID = $statementHandle2->fetchrow_array();
46
47      # use PublisherID to find the corresponding PublisherName
48      $query3 = "SELECT PublisherName FROM Publishers
49               WHERE PublisherID = \'$title_publisherID[ 1 ]\'";
50
51      $statementHandle3 = $databaseHandle->prepare( $query3 );
52      $statementHandle3->execute();
53      @publisher = $statementHandle3->fetchrow_array();
54
55
56      # print resulting values
57      print( td( $title_publisherID[ 0 ] ), "\n" );
58      print( td( $isbn[ 0 ] ), "\n" );
59      print( td( $publisher[ 0 ] ), "\n" );
60
61      print( "</tr>" );
62
63      $statementHandle2->finish();
64      $statementHandle3->finish();
65   }
66
67   print( "</table>" );
68
69   print( end_html() );
70
71   $databaseHandle->disconnect();
```

Fig. 25.20 Perl script that queries a MySQL database for author information. (Part 2 of 3.)

```
72    $statementHandle1->finish();
```

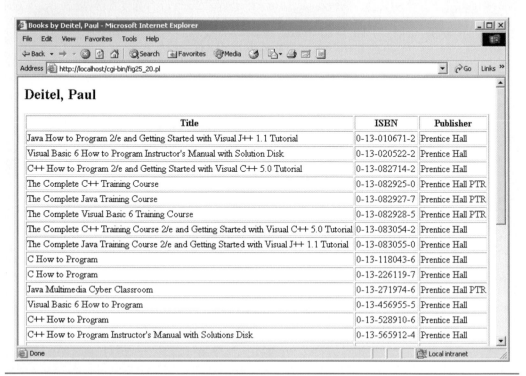

Fig. 25.20 Perl script that queries a MySQL database for author information. (Part 3 of 3.)

This program creates an XHTML page that displays the title of each book written by the current author, along with the ISBN number and book publisher. To obtain this information, we need the author's ID number, because the `AuthorISBN` table contains a field for the author's ID, not the author's name. Recall that the author's ID was submitted to this script by `fig25_19.pl`. The ID is the numerical value that precedes the author's name in the `author` parameter. To retrieve the ID and author name, we call method `substr` in lines 16–17. This statement returns the first character in the string (an offset of zero indicates the beginning of the string), which contains the ID value. In line 17, we specify an offset of three, because the author's name begins after the third character. Note that in this call we do not specify a length, because we want all the characters from the offset to the end of the string.

After connecting to the database, we specify and execute our first query in lines 26–30. This query returns all the ISBN numbers for the specified author. We place these values in a table. In line 37, we begin a `while` loop that iterates through each row matched by the query. The rows are retrieved by calling `fetchrow_array`, which returns the current data set as an array. When there are no more data sets to return, the condition evaluates to false. Within the loop, we use the ISBNs to obtain the title and publisher values for the current table row. The query in lines 41–45 uses the ISBN value to determine the book's title and the publisher's ID number. The next query (lines 48–53) uses the publisher's ID to determine the name of the publisher. These values are `printed` in lines 57–59.

25.9 Cookies and Perl

Cookies maintain **state information** for each client who uses a Web browser. Preserving this information allows data and settings to be retained even after the execution of a CGI script has ended. Cookies are used to record preferences (or other information) for the next time the client visits a Web site. For example, many Web sites use cookies to store each client's postal zip code. The zip code is used when the client asks a Web page to send, for instance, current weather information or news updates for the client's region. On the server side, cookies may be used to track information about client activity in order to determine which sites are visited most frequently or how effective certain advertisements and products are.

Microsoft Internet Explorer stores cookies as small text files saved on the client's hard drive. The data stored in the cookies is sent back to the server whenever the user requests a Web page from that server. The server can then serve XHTML content to the client that is specific to the information stored in the cookie.

Writing Cookies

Figure 25.21 uses a script to write a cookie to a client's machine. The `fig25_21.html` file is used to display an XHTML form that allows a user to enter a name, height and favorite color. When the user clicks the **Write Cookie** button, the `fig25_22.pl` script (Fig. 25.22) executes.

Good Programming Practice 25.7

Personal identifying information, such as credit-card numbers and passwords, should not be stored using cookies. Cookies cannot be used to retrieve information such as e-mail addresses or other data stored on the hard drive of a client's computer.

```
1    <!DOCTYPE html PUBLIC "-//W3C//DTD XHTML 1.0 Strict//EN"
2       "http://www.w3.org/TR/xhtml1/DTD/xhtml1-strict.dtd">
3
4    <!-- Fig. 25.21: fig25_21.html -->
5
6    <html>
7       <head>
8          <title>Writing a cookie to the client computer</title>
9       </head>
10
11      <body style = "font-face: arial">
12          <div style = "font-size: large;
13                          font-weight: bold">
14             Click Write Cookie to save your cookie data.
15          </div><br />
16
17          <form method = "post" action = "cgi-bin/fig25_22.pl"
18                style = "font-weight: bold">
19             Name:<br />
20             <input type = "text" name = "name" /><br />
21             Height:<br />
22             <input type = "text" name = "height" /><br />
23             Favorite Color:<br />
24             <input type = "text" name = "color" /><br />
```

Fig. 25.21 XHTML document to read in cookie data from the user. (Part 1 of 2.)

```
25              <input type = "submit" value = "Write Cookie" />
26          </form>
27        </font>
28      </body>
29  </html>
```

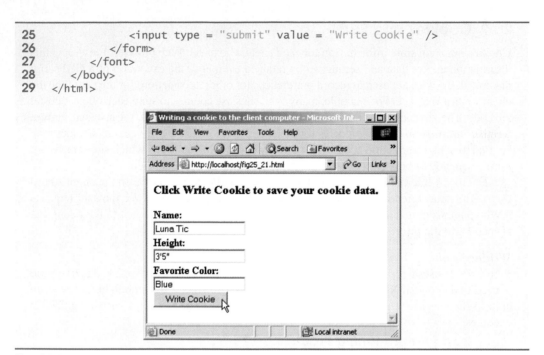

Fig. 25.21 XHTML document to read in cookie data from the user. (Part 2 of 2.)

```
1   #!C:\Perl\bin\perl
2   # Fig. 25.22: fig25_22.pl
3   # Program to write a cookie to a client's machine.
4
5   use CGI qw( :standard );
6
7   $name = param( "name" );
8   $height = param( "height" );
9   $color = param( "color" );
10
11  $expires = gmtime( time() + 86400 );
12
13  print( "Set-Cookie: Name=$name; expires=$expires; path=\n" );
14  print( "Set-Cookie: Height=$height; expires=$expires; path=\n" );
15  print( "Set-Cookie: Color=$color; expires=$expires; path=\n" );
16
17  $dtd =
18  "-//W3C//DTD XHTML 1.0 Transitional//EN\"
19      \"http://www.w3.org/TR/xhtml1/DTD/xhtml1-transitional.dtd";
20
21  print( header() );
22  print( start_html( { dtd => $dtd,
23                       title => "Cookie Saved" } ) );
24
25  print <<End_Data;
26  <div style = "font-face: arial; font-size: larger">
```

Fig. 25.22 Writing a cookie to the client. (Part 1 of 2.)

```
27       The cookie has been set with the following data:
28   </div><br /><br />
29
30   <span style = "color: blue">
31   Name: <span style = "color: black">$name</span><br />
32   Height: <span style = "color: black">$height</span><br />
33   Favorite Color:</span>
34
35   <span style = "color: $color"> $color</span><br />
36   <br />Click <a href = "fig25_25.pl">here</a>
37   to read saved cookie.
38   End_Data
39
40   print( end_html() );
```

Fig. 25.22 Writing a cookie to the client. (Part 2 of 2.)

The fig25_22.pl script (Fig. 25.22) reads the data sent from the client in lines 7–9. Line 11 declares and initializes variable $expires to contain the expiration date of the cookie. The browser deletes a cookie after it expires. This script dynamically sets the cookie's expiration date to be one day in the future (i.e., the cookie will be deleted one day after it is created). Function **time** returns the current date and time as a measure of the number of seconds since the epoch (i.e., January 1, 1970 on most systems, but January 1, 1904 on Mac OS). Adding 86400 to this value produces a date and time that is exactly one day ahead of the current date and time (86400 seconds = 60 seconds/minute x 60 minutes/hour $\times$ 24 hours/day). A measure of the date and time as the number of seconds since the epoch cannot be used to specify a cookie's expiration date, however. Function **gmtime** converts this representation of the date and time to a string representation of the date and time (e.g., "Thu Aug 14 12:00:00 2003"), localized to Coordinated Universal Time (abbreviated UTC)—formerly Greenwich Mean Time (GMT). The script assigns this string to the variable $expires to set the cookie's expiration date to be exactly 24 hours from the moment the cookie is created.

Lines 13–15 call function print to output the cookie information. We use the **Set-Cookie: header** to indicate that the browser should store the incoming data in a cookie. The header sets three attributes for each cookie: A name-value pair containing the data to be stored, the expiration date and the URL path of the server domain over which the cookie is valid. For this example, no path is given, making the cookie readable from anywhere within the server's domain. Lines 21–40 create a Web page indicating that the cookie has been written to the client.

In lines 25–38 we see our first **"here" document**. Line 25 instructs the Perl interpreter to print the subsequent lines verbatim (after variable interpolation) until it reaches the End_Data label (line 38). This label consists simply of the identifier End_Data, placed at the beginning of a line, with no whitespace characters preceding it, and followed immediately with a newline. "Here" documents are often used in CGI programs to eliminate the need to call function print repeatedly. Note that we use functions in the CGI library, as well as "here" documents, to create a clean program.

If the client is an Internet Explorer browser, cookies are stored in the Cookies directory on the client's machine. Figure 25.23 shows the contents of this directory on Windows prior to the execution of fig25_22.pl. After the cookie is written, an additional text file is added to this list. The file luna tic@localhost[1].txt can be seen in the Cookies directory in Fig. 25.24. The domain for which the cookie is valid is localhost. The username luna tic, however, is only part of name of the file Internet Explorer uses to store the cookie and is not actually a part of the cookie itself. Therefore, a remote server cannot access the username.

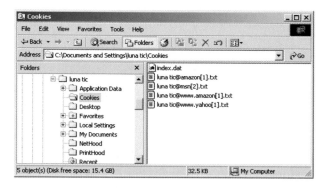

Fig. 25.23 Cookies directory before a cookie is written.

Fig. 25.24 Cookies directory after a cookie is written.

Reading an Existing Cookie

Figure 25.25 (`fig25_25.pl`) reads the cookie written in Fig. 25.22 and displays the information in a table. Environment variable **HTTP_COOKIE** contains the client's cookies. Line 25 calls subroutine `readCookies` (lines 37–47) and places the returned value into hash `%cookies`. The user-defined subroutine `readCookies` splits the environment variable containing the cookie information into separate cookies (using `split`) and stores them as distinct elements in `@cookieArray` (line 39). For each cookie in `@cookieArray`, we call `split` again to obtain the original name-value pair, which, in turn, is stored in `%cookieHash` in line 43.

```perl
1   #!C:\Perl\bin\perl
2   # Fig. 25.25: fig25_25.pl
3   # program to read cookies from the client's computer.
4
5   use CGI qw( :standard );
6
7   $dtd =
8   "-//W3C//DTD XHTML 1.0 Transitional//EN\"
9      \"http://www.w3.org/TR/xhtml1/DTD/xhtml1-transitional.dtd";
10
11  print( header() );
12  print( start_html( { dtd => $dtd,
13                       title => "Read Cookies" } ) );
14
15  print( div( { style => "font-face: arial;
16                          font-size: larger;
17                          font-weight: bold" },
18          "The following data is saved in a
19           cookie on your computer." ), br() );
20
21  print( "<table style = \"background-color: #aaaaaa\"
22                 border = 5 cellpadding = 10
23                 cellspacing = 0>" );
24
25  %cookies = readCookies();
26  $color = $cookies{ Color };
27
28  foreach $cookieName ( "Name", "Height", "Color" ) {
29     print( Tr( td( { style => "background-color: $color" },
30                  $cookieName ),
31              td( $cookies{ $cookieName } ) ) );
32  }
33
34  print( "<table>" );
35  print( end_html() );
36
37  sub readCookies
38  {
39     @cookieArray = split( "; ", $ENV{ 'HTTP_COOKIE' } );
40
41     foreach ( @cookieArray ) {
42        ( $cookieName, $cookieValue ) = split( "=", $_ );
```

Fig. 25.25 Output displaying the cookie's content. (Part 1 of 2.)

```
43            $cookieHash{ $cookieName } = $cookieValue;
44       }
45
46       return %cookieHash;
47   }
```

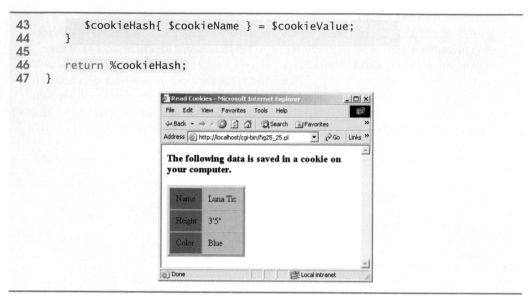

Fig. 25.25 Output displaying the cookie's content. (Part 2 of 2.)

The `split` function in line 42 makes reference to a variable named `$_`. The special Perl variable `$_` is used as a default argument for many Perl functions. In this case, because no variable was provided in the `foreach` loop (line 41), `$_` is used by default. Thus, in this example, `$_` is assigned the value of the current element of `@cookieArray` as a `foreach` statement iterates through it.

Once `%cookieHash` has been created, line 46 returns it from the function (using the `return` keyword), and `%cookies` is assigned this value in line 25. A `foreach` loop (lines 28–32) then iterates through the hash with the given key names, printing the key and value for the data from the cookie in an XHTML table.

Be aware that users can disable cookies on their machines. There are a few ways to handle this issue, but the most basic is to create a file similar to a cookie that would be stored on the server's computer rather than the client's computer. For more information, the reader can visit the Web sites listed at the end of this chapter.

25.10 Operator Precedence Chart

This section contains the operator precedence chart for Perl (Fig. 25.26). The operators are shown in decreasing order of precedence, from top to bottom.

Operator	Type	Associativity
terms and list operators	`print @array` or `sort (4, 2, 7)`	left to right
`->`	member access	left to right

Fig. 25.26 Perl operator precedence chart. (Part 1 of 3.)

Operator	Type	Associativity
++ --	increment decrement	none
**	exponentiation	right to left
! ~ \ + -	logical NOT bitwise one's complement reference unary plus unary minus	right to left
=~ !~	matching negated match	left to right
* / % x	multiplication division modulus repetition	left to right
+ - .	addition subtraction string concatenation	left to right
<< >>	left shift right shift	left to right
named unary operators	unary operators—e.g., -e (filetest)	none
< > <= >= lt gt le ge	numerical less than numerical greater than numerical less than or equal to numerical greater than or equal to string less than string greater than string less than or equal to string greater than or equal to	none
== != <=> eq ne cmp	numerical equality numerical inequality numerical comparison (returns –1, 0 or 1) string equality string inequality string comparison (returns –1, 0 or 1)	none
&	bitwise AND	left to right
| ^	bitwise inclusive OR bitwise exclusive OR	left to right
&&	logical AND	left to right
||	logical OR	left to right
..	range operator	none

Fig. 25.26 Perl operator precedence chart. (Part 2 of 3.)

Operator	Type	Associativity
?:	conditional operator	right to left
= += -= *= /= %= **= .= x= &= |= ^= <<= >>= &&= ||=	assignment addition assignment subtraction assignment multiplication assignment division assignment modulus assignment exponentiation assignment string concatenation assignment repetition assignment bitwise AND assignment bitwise inclusive OR assignment bitwise exclusive OR assignment left shift assignment right shift assignment logical AND assignment logical OR assignment	right to left
, =>	expression separator; returns value of last expression expression separator; groups two expressions	left to right
not	logical NOT	right to left
and	logical AND	left to right
or xor	logical OR logical exclusive OR	left to right

Fig. 25.26 Perl operator precedence chart. (Part 3 of 3.)

25.11 Web Resources

There is a strongly established Perl community online that has made available a wealth of information on the Perl language, Perl modules and CGI scripting.

www.perl.com

Perl.com: The Source for Perl is the first place to look for information about Perl. The home page provides up-to-date news on Perl, answers to frequent questions about Perl and an impressive collection of links to Perl resources on the Internet. The links include sites for Perl software, tutorials, user groups and demos.

www.pm.org

This site is the home page of *Perl Mongers*, a group dedicated to supporting the Perl community. The site is helpful in finding others in the Perl community with whom to converse; Perl Mongers has established Perl user groups around the globe.

www.perl.org

This Perl Mongers site is a great one-stop resource for developers. Resources include documentation, links to several other Perl sites and mailing lists.

www.activestate.com

From this site you can download ActivePerl—the Perl 5.8 implementation for Windows.

`www.cpan.org`
The *Comprehensive Perl Archive Network* includes an extensive listing of Perl-related information.

`www.perl.com/CPAN/scripts/index.html`
This site is the scripts index from the CPAN archive. You will find a wealth of scripts written in Perl.

`www.speakeasy.org/~cgires`
This site is a collection of tutorials and scripts that can provide a thorough understanding of CGI.

`www.perlarchive.com`
This site features a large number of scripts and guides, as well as a learning center that includes helpful articles.

`www.cgi.resourceindex.com`
General CGI site including scripts, a list of freelance CGI programmers, documentation, job listings and several other resources.

`www.cgi101.com`
CGI 101 is a site for those looking to improve their programming ability through familiarity with CGI. The site contains a six-chapter class outlining techniques for CGI programming in the Perl language. The class includes both basic and advanced scripts, with working examples. Also available at the site are script libraries and links to other helpful sources.

`www.freeperlcode.com`
This site provides a help guide and access to several Perl scripts that can be easily downloaded and installed.

`www.jmarshall.com/easy/cgi`
This site provides a good, brief explanation of CGI for those with programming experience.

`www.wdvl.com/Authoring/Languages/Perl`
This site contains many links to Perl resources.

`www.wdvl.com/Authoring/CGI`
The *Web Developer's Virtual Library* provides tutorials for learning both CGI and Perl.

`www.perlmonth.com`
Perlmonth is a monthly online periodical devoted to Perl, with featured articles from professional programmers. This site is a good source for those who use Perl frequently and wish to keep up on the latest developments.

`tpj.com`
The Perl Journal is a large magazine dedicated to Perl. Subscribers are provided with up-to-date Perl news and articles, on the Internet or in printed form.

`www.1024kb.net/index.html?./texts/perlnet.html`
This page provides a brief tutorial on Perl network programming for those who already know the language. The tutorial uses code examples to explain the basics of network communication.

`www.w3.org/CGI`
The World Wide Web Consortium page on CGI is concerned with CGI security issues. This page provides links to CGI specifications, as indicated by the National Center for Supercomputing Applications (NCSA).

SUMMARY

- The Common Gateway Interface (CGI) is a standard protocol through which applications interact with Web servers. CGI provides a way for clients to interface indirectly with applications on the Web server.
- Because CGI is an interface, it cannot be programmed directly; a script or executable program (commonly called a CGI script) must be executed to interact with it.

- CGI scripts often process information gathered from a form. These programs are typically designated with a certain filename extension (e.g., .cgi or .pl) or located within a special directory (e.g., cgi-bin). After the application output is sent to the server through CGI, the results may be sent to the client.

- Standard input is the stream of information received by a program from a user, typically through the keyboard, but also possibly from a file or another input device.

- Standard output is the information stream presented to the user by an application; it is typically displayed on the screen, but may also be printed by a printer, written to a file, etc.

- The Perl comment character (#) instructs the interpreter to ignore everything on the current line following the #. The exception to this rule is the "shebang" construct (#!). On Unix systems, this line indicates the path to the Perl interpreter. On other systems, the line may be ignored or may indicate to the server that a Perl program follows the statement.

- Perl program file names typically end with the .pl extension. Programs can be executed by running the Perl interpreter from the command-line prompt (e.g., the Command Prompt in Windows).

- Using the -w option when running a Perl program instructs the interpreter to output warnings to the screen if it finds bugs in your code.

- Function print is used to output text.

- Text surrounded by quotes is called a string.

- Escape sequences can be used to output special characters, such as newlines.

- Semicolons (;) are used to terminate Perl statements.

- Perl has built-in data types that represent different kinds of data, including scalar, hash and array.

- The $ character specifies that a variable contains a scalar value.

- The @ character specifies that a variable contains an array, while the % character specifies that a variable contains a hash.

- In Perl, a variable is created the first time it is encountered by the interpreter.

- When a variable is encountered inside a double-quoted ("") string, Perl uses a process called interpolation to replace the variable with its associated data.

- In Perl, uninitialized variables have the value undef, which can be evaluated differently depending on context. When undef is found in a numeric context, it evaluates to 0. When it is interpreted in a string context, undef evaluates to the empty string ("").

- Unless a string begins with a digit, it is evaluated as undef in a numeric context. If the string does begin with a digit, every character up to the first nondigit character is evaluated as a number, and the remaining characters are ignored.

- The programmer does not need to differentiate between numeric and string data types because the interpreter evaluates scalar variables depending on the context in which they are used.

- Several values can be stored in arrays, which are divided into elements, each containing a scalar value. Array variable names are preceded by the @ symbol.

- When printing an array inside double quotes, the array element values are printed with only one space separating them.

- Individual array elements are accessed using square brackets ([]). If the array name is prefaced by the $ character and followed by an index number in square brackets, it refers instead to an individual array element, which is a scalar value.

- The range operator (..) is used to specify all the values in a range.

- It is not necessary to specify an array's size. The Perl interpreter recognizes that memory has not been allocated for this array and creates new memory automatically.

- When strings are inside single quotes, the interpreter treats the string literally and does not attempt to interpret any escape sequence or variable substitution.
- Text manipulation in Perl is usually done with regular expressions—a series of characters that serve as pattern-matching templates in strings, text files and databases.
- Operator qw ("quote word") takes the contents inside the parentheses and creates a comma-separated list with each element wrapped in double quotes.
- The `foreach` statement iterates sequentially through the elements in a specified array or the elements in a range of values.
- The `if` statement is used to execute code depending on a specified condition.
- In Perl, anything except the number 0, the string "0" and the empty string (i.e., `undef` values) is defined as true.
- Operators ne, lt and gt test strings for equality, less than and greater than, respectively. These operators are used only with strings. When comparing numeric values, operators ==, !=, <, <=, > and >= are used.
- Perl provides the match operator (m/*pattern*/ or /*pattern*/), which uses regular expressions to search a string for a specified *pattern*.
- The match operator takes two operands. The first operand is the regular-expression pattern for which to search; it is placed between the slashes of the m// operator. The second operand is the string to search within; it is assigned to the match operator by using the =~ (binding) operator.
- Regular expressions can include special characters, called metacharacters, that can specify patterns or contexts that cannot be defined using literal characters.
- The caret metacharacter (∧) searches the beginning of a string for a pattern.
- The $ metacharacter searches the end of a string for a pattern.
- The \b expression matches any word boundary.
- The + modifier is a quantifier that instructs Perl to match the preceding character one or more times.
- Parentheses indicate that the text matching the pattern is to be saved in a special Perl variable.
- Modifying characters placed to the right of the forward slash that delimits a regular expression instruct the interpreter to treat the expression in different ways.
- Placing an i after the regular expression tells the interpreter to ignore case when searching.
- Placing an x after the regular expression indicates that whitespace characters are to be ignored.
- Modifying character g indicates a global search—a search that does not stop after the first match is found.
- Environment variables contain information about the environment in which a script is being run.
- The use directive directs Perl programs to include the contents of predefined packages, called modules.
- The CGI module contains many useful functions for CGI scripting in Perl.
- With the use directive, we can specify an import tag to include a predefined set of functions.
- We usually specify the import tag :standard when importing the CGI.pm module to specify the standard CGI functions.
- Function header directs the Perl program to output a valid HTTP header.
- The start_html function begins the output of XHTML. This function will print the document type definition for this document, as well as several opening XHTML tags.
- When using many of the functions in the CGI module, attribute information can be specified within curly braces.

- Each argument within the curly braces is in the form of a key–value pair. A key (or value name) is assigned a value using the arrow operator (=>), where the key is to the left of the arrow, and the value is to the right.

- Function Tr contains its arguments within table row tags.

- Function th contains its arguments within table header tags.

- Function hr creates horizontal rules.

- Function td contains its arguments within table data tags.

- The hash data type is designated by the % character and represents an unordered set of scalar-value pairs.

- Each element in a hash is accessed by using a unique key that is associated with a value.

- Hash values are accessed by using the syntax $hashName{ keyName }.

- Function keys returns an array of all the keys from a specified hash in no specific order because elements have no defined order.

- We use function sort to order the array of keys alphabetically.

- The %ENV hash is a built-in table that contains the names and values of all the environment variables.

- Function end_html outputs the closing tags for a page (</body> and </html>).

- Function param is used to retrieve values from form field elements.

- Regular expressions can be used to validate information in a CGI script. The design of verifying information is called business logic (also called business rules).

- Function br adds a break (<br />) to the XHTML page.

- Function span adds span elements to a page.

- Function div adds div elements to a page.

- Server-side includes (SSIs) are commands embedded in HTML documents to allow simple dynamic content creation.

- The command EXEC can be used to run CGI scripts and embed their output directly into a Web page. Before the XHTML document is sent to the client, the SSI command EXEC is executed and any script output is sent to the client.

- A document containing SSI commands is typically given the .shtml file extension. The .shtml files are parsed by the server.

- The ECHO command is used to display variable information. It is followed by the keyword VAR and the name of the variable.

- The variable DATE_GMT contains the current date and time in Greenwich Mean Time (GMT).

- The name of the current document is specified as the DOCUMENT_NAME variable.

- The DATE_LOCAL variable inserts the date.

- Function open is called to open a file and create a filehandle to be associated with the file.

- The diamond operator (<>) is used to read input from the user or a file. When the diamond operator is used in a scalar context, only one line is read. When the operator is used in list context, all the input (or the entire file) is read and assigned to values in the list.

- We open a file for writing by preceding the file name with a > character. Perl also provides an append mode (>>) for appending to the end of a file.

- A for statement is similar to a foreach statement. It iterates through a set of values, specified in parentheses after the keyword for. Within the parentheses, three statements are used to indicate the values through which the structure will iterate.

- Function `length` returns the length of a character string.

- Function `substr` is used to identify a specified substring.

- The `img` function is used to display images.

- Function `die` displays an error message and terminates the program.

- Function `chomp` removes the newline character from the end of a string, if a newline exists.

- Function `split` divides a string into substrings at the specified separator or delimiter.

- The `last` statement is used to exit a loop structure once a desired condition has been satisfied.

- Perl allows programmers to define their own functions or subroutines. Keyword `sub` begins a function definition, and curly braces delimit the function body.

- Database connectivity allows system administrators to maintain crucial data.

- The Perl Database Interface (DBI) allows access to various relational databases in a uniform manner.

- The Perl `DBI` module and the MySQL driver, `DBD::mysql` are required to access and manipulate a MySQL database from a Perl program.

- The Perl Package Manager (PPM) is designed so that the user can easily download and install several Perl modules and packages. Perl modules and packages can also be found on the Comprehensive Perl Archive Network (CPAN).

- To create and execute SQL queries, we create DBI objects known as handles.

- Database handles create and manipulate a connection to a database.

- Statement handles create and submit SQL to a database.

- Method `connect` in module `DBI` sets up a database connection and returns a database handle.

- A database handle is used to prepare a database query (using the method `prepare` in module `DBI`). This method prepares the database driver for a query that can be executed multiple times.

- We execute a query by calling method `execute` in module `DBI`.

- Once a query has been executed, we can access the results using the method `fetchrow_array` in module `DBI`. Each call to this function returns the next set of data in the resulting table until there are no data sets left.

- A database connection can be closed using method `disconnect` in module `DBI`.

- We can indicate that we are no longer using a query by calling method `finish` in module `DBI`.

- Cookies maintain state information for each client who uses a Web browser. Microsoft Internet Explorer stores cookies as small text files saved on the client's hard drive.

- Function `time` returns the current date and time as a measure of the number of seconds since the epoch (i.e., January 1, 1970 on most systems, but January 1, 1904 on Mac OS).

- Function `gmtime` converts a date and time from a measure of seconds since the epoch to a string representation of the date and time, localized to Coordinated Universal Time (abbreviated UTC)— formerly Greenwich Mean Time (GMT).

- We use the `Set-Cookie:` header to indicate that the browser should store the incoming data in a cookie.

- A "here" document is used to output a string verbatim. The string is specified as all the text from the beginning of the document to the closing identifier.

- Environment variable `HTTP_COOKIE` contains the client's cookies.

- The special variable `$_` is used as a default argument for many Perl functions.

TERMINOLOGY

!= operator
$ metacharacter
$ type symbol
$_ special variable
% type symbol
* quantifier
? quantifier
@ type symbol
\b metacharacter
\B metacharacter
\d metacharacter
\D metacharacter
\n escape sequence
\n metacharacter
\s metacharacter
\S metacharacter
\t metacharacter
\w metacharacter
\W metacharacter
\w pattern
^ metacharacter
{} curly braces in CGI.pm functions
{m,n} quantifier
{n,} quantifier
{n} quantifier
+ quantifier
< operator
<= operator
<> diamond operator
== operator
> operator
> write mode
>= operator
>> append mode
alphanumeric character
Apache Web server
append mode (>>)
array
assignment operator
associative array
binding operator (=~)
br function
built-in metacharacter
business logic
business rules
.cgi file extension
CGI module
CGI script
CGI tutorial

cgi-bin directory
chomp function
close function
comment character (#)
Common Gateway Interface (CGI)
comparison operator
Comprehensive Perl Archive Network (CPAN)
connect method
cookie
Cookies directory
database connectivity
database handle
DATE_GMT variable
DATE_LOCAL variable
DBD::mysql driver
DBI module
delimiter
diamond operator (<>)
die function
disconnect method
div function
DOCUMENT_NAME variable
dtd argument in start_html function
ECHO command
elements in an array
empty string
end_html function
%ENV hash
environment variable
equality operators
escape sequence
escaping special characters
EXEC command
execute method
fetchrow_array method
filehandle
finish method
for statement
foreach statement
forms
function
g modifying character
gt operator
handle
hash
header function
hr function
HTTP connection
HTTP header

HTTP host
HTTP_COOKIE environment variable
HTTP_HOST environment variable
i modifying character
if statement
img function
import tag
INCLUDE command
interactive mode
interpolation
keys (in a hash)
keys function
last statement
length function
list
literal character
logical AND (&&) operator
logical negation (!) operator
logical OR (||) operator
lt operator
m modifying character
m//
match operator (m//)
metacharacter
modifying character
module
MySQL database
mysql directory
MySQL driver
ne operator
numeric context
open function
param function
Perl (Practical Extraction and Report Language)
perl command
.pl file extension
Perl interpreter
Perl Package Manager (PPM)
piping
post method
ppm method
prepare method
print function
private Web site

quantifier
qw operator
range operator (..)
read-only mode
redirection
regular expression
return keyword
s modifying character
scalar
scalar value
semicolons (;) to terminate statement
Server-Side Include (SSI)
Set-Cookie: header
shebang construct (#!)
.shtml file extension
sort function
span function
split function
SQL query string
SSI (Server-Side Include)
:standard import tag
standard input (STDIN)
standard output (STDOUT)
start_html function
state information
statement handle
string context
sub keyword
subroutine
substr method
td function
th function
title argument in start_html function
tr operator
Tr function
undef value
Unisys
use directive
VAR keyword
-w command-line option in Perl
while statement
word boundary
write mode (>)
x modifying character

SELF-REVIEW EXERCISES

25.1 Fill in the blanks in the following statements.
  a) The _____ Protocol is used by Web browsers and Web servers to communicate with each other.
  b) Typically, all CGI programs reside in directory _____.

c) To output warnings as a Perl program executes, the _____ command-line option should be used.

d) The three data types in Perl are _____, _____ and _____.

e) _____ are divided into individual elements that can each contain an individual scalar variable.

f) To test the equality of two strings, operator _____ should be used.

g) Business _____ is used to ensure that invalid data are not entered into a database.

h) _____ allow Webmasters to include the current time, date or even the contents of a different HTML document.

i) The _____ statement iterates once for each element in a list or array.

j) Many Perl functions take special variable _____ as a default argument.

25.2 State whether each of the following is *true* or *false*. If *false*, explain why.

a) Documents containing server-side includes must have a file extension of .SSI in order to be parsed by the server.

b) A valid HTTP header must be sent to the client to ensure that the browser correctly displays the information.

c) The numerical equality operator, eq, is used to determine whether two numbers are equal.

d) The ∧ metacharacter is used to match the beginning of a string.

e) Perl has a built-in binding operator, =, that tests whether a matching string is found within a variable.

f) Cookies can read information, such as e-mail addresses and personal files, from a client's hard drive.

g) An example of a valid HTTP header is Content-type text\html.

h) CGI environment variables contain such information as the type of Web browser the client is running.

i) The characters \w in a regular expression match only a letter or number.

j) CGI is a programming language that can be used in conjunction with Perl to program for the Web.

ANSWERS TO SELF-REVIEW EXERCISES

25.1 a) Hypertext Transfer. b) cgi-bin. c) -w. d) scalar variable, array, hash. e) Arrays. f) eq. g) logic (or rules). h) Server-side includes. i) foreach. j) $_.

25.2 a) False. Documents containing server-side includes usually have a file extension of .shtml. b) True. c) False. The numerical equality operator is ==. d) True. e) False. The built-in binding operator is =~. f) False. Cookies do not have access to private information, such as e-mail addresses or private data, stored on the hard drive. g) False. A valid HTTP header might be: Content-type: text/html. h) True. i) False. \w also matches the underscore character. j) False. CGI is an interface, not a programming language.

EXERCISES

25.3 How can a Perl program determine the type of browser a Web client is using?

25.4 Describe how input from an HTML form is retrieved in a Perl program.

25.5 How does a Web browser determine how to handle or display incoming data?

25.6 What is the terminology for a command that is embedded in an HTML document and parsed by a server prior to being sent?

25.7　Write a Perl program named ex25_07.pl that creates a scalar variable $states with the value "Mississippi Alabama Texas Massachusetts Kansas". Using only the techniques discussed in this chapter, write a program that does the following:

  a) Search for a word in scalar $states that ends in xas. Store this word in element 0 of an array named @statesArray.

  b) Search for a word in $states that begins with k and ends in s. Perform a case-insensitive comparison. Store this word in element 1 of @statesArray.

  c) Search for a word in $states that begins with M and ends in s. Store this in element 2 of the array.

  d) Search for a word in $states that ends in a. Store this word in element 3 of the array.

  e) Search for a word in $states at the beginning of the string that starts with M. Store this word in element 4 of the array.

  f) Output the array @statesArray to the screen.

25.8　In this chapter, we have presented CGI environment variables. Develop a program that determines whether the client is using Internet Explorer. If so, determine the version number, and send this information back to the client.

25.9　Modify the programs and documents in Figs. 25.12 and 25.13 to save information sent to the server in a text file.

25.10　Write a Perl program that tests whether an e-mail address is input correctly. A valid e-mail address contains a series of characters followed by the @ character and a domain name.

25.11　Using CGI environment variables, write a program that logs the IP addresses (obtained with the REMOTE_ADDR CGI environment variable) that request information from the Web server.

25.12　Modify the programs in Figs. 25.19 and 25.20 so that there is another column in the resulting table. Each element in the column will be a button that, when clicked, will display a third Web page with a description of the current book. To do this in a straightforward manner, you should create a third program that will query the database for the book's description. This program will be called when one of the buttons is clicked.

26

PHP

Objectives

- To understand PHP data types, operators, arrays and control statements.
- To understand string processing and regular expressions in PHP.
- To construct programs that process form data.
- To be able to read and write client data using cookies.
- To construct programs that interact with MySQL databases.

Conversion for me was not a Damascus Road experience. I slowly moved into an intellectual acceptance of what my intuition had always known.
Madeleine L'Engle

Be careful when reading health books; you may die of a misprint.
Mark Twain

Reckoners without their host must reckon twice.
John Heywood

There was a door to which I found no key; There was the veil through which I might not see.
Omar Khayyam

Outline

26.1 Introduction

PHP, or **PHP: Hypertext Preprocessor**, is quickly becoming one of the most popular server-side scripting languages for creating dynamic Web pages. PHP was created in 1994 by Rasmus Lerdorf (who currently works for Linuxcare, Inc. as a senior open-source researcher) to track users at his Web site.[1] In 1995, Lerdorf released it as a package called the "Personal Home Page Tools." PHP 2 featured built-in database support and form handling. In 1997, PHP 3 was released, featuring a rewritten parser, which substantially increased performance and led to an explosion in PHP use. It is estimated that over 13 million domains now use PHP. The release of PHP 4, which features the new *Zend Engine* and is considerably faster and more powerful than its predecessor, has further increased PHP's popularity.[2] PHP 5 is currently in beta and features the *Zend Engine 2*, which provides further increases in speed and functionality. More information about the Zend Engine can be found at `www.zend.com`.

PHP is an **open-source** technology that is supported by a large community of users and developers. Open-source software provides developers with access to the software's source code and free redistribution rights. PHP is platform independent; implementations exist for all major UNIX, Linux and Windows operating systems. PHP also supports a large number of databases, including MySQL.

After introducing the basics of the scripting language, we discuss viewing environment variables. Knowing information about a client's execution environment allows dynamic content to be sent to the client. We then discuss form processing and business logic, which are vital to e-commerce applications. We provide an example of implementing a private Web site through username and password verification. Next, we build a three-tier Web-

---

1. S.S. Bakken, et al., "Introduction to PHP," 17 April 2000 `<www.zend.com/zend/hof/rasmus.php>`.
2. S.S. Bakken, et al., "A Brief History of PHP," January 2001 `<www.php.net/manual/en/intro-history.php>`.

based application that queries a MySQL database. We also show how Web sites use cookies to store information on the client that will be retrieved during a client's subsequent visits to a Web site. Finally, we revisit the form-processing example to demonstrate some of PHP's more dynamic capabilities.

26.2 PHP

The power of the Web resides not only in serving content to users, but also in responding to requests from users and generating Web pages with dynamic content. Interactivity between the user and the server has become a crucial part of Web functionality. While other languages can perform this function as well, PHP was written specifically for interacting with the Web.

PHP code is embedded directly into XHTML documents. This allows the document author to write XHTML in a clear, concise manner, without having to use multiple `print` statements, as is necessary with other CGI-based languages.

PHP script file names usually end with `.php`, although a server can be configured to handle other file extensions. To run a PHP script, PHP must first be installed on your system. PHP 4.3.3 is available on the CD-ROM accompanying this book. Please refer to the PHP installation and configuration instructions available on the CD-ROM. The most recent version of PHP always can be downloaded from `www.php.net/downloads.php`, and the latest installation instructions are available at `www.php.net/manual/en/installation.php`. Although PHP can be used from the command line, a Web server is necessary to take full advantage of the scripting language. Before continuing, please copy the `.php`, `.html` and `.txt` files and the `images` directory from the Chapter 26 examples directory on the CD-ROM to the Web server's root directory (e.g., `C:\Inetpub\wwwroot` for IIS or `C:\Program Files\Apache Group\Apache2\htdocs` for Apache).

Simple PHP Program
Figure 26.1 presents a simple PHP program that displays a welcome message.

```
1   <!DOCTYPE html PUBLIC "-//W3C//DTD XHTML 1.0 Strict//EN"
2      "http://www.w3.org/TR/xhtml1/DTD/xhtml1-strict.dtd">
3
4   <!-- Fig. 26.1: first.php -->
5   <!-- Our first PHP script -->
6
7   <?php
8      $name = "LunaTic";    // declaration
9   ?>
10
11  <html xmlns = "http://www.w3.org/1999/xhtml">
12     <head>
13        <title>A simple PHP document</title>
14     </head>
15
16     <body style = "font-size: 2em">
17        <p>
```

Fig. 26.1   Simple PHP program. (Part 1 of 2.)

```
18          <strong>
19
20              <!-- print variable name's value -->
21              Welcome to PHP, <?php print( "$name" ); ?>!
22          </strong>
23       </p>
24    </body>
25 </html>
```

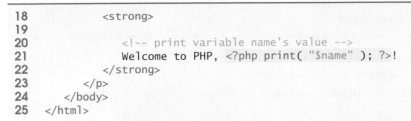

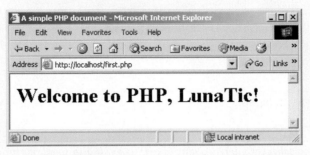

Fig. 26.1   Simple PHP program. (Part 2 of 2.)

In PHP, code is inserted between the scripting delimiters **<?php** and **?>**. PHP code can be placed anywhere in XHTML markup, as long as the code is enclosed in these scripting delimiters. Line 8 declares variable $name and assigns to it the string "LunaTic". All variables are preceded by a **$** and are created the first time they are encountered by the PHP interpreter. PHP statements are terminated with a **semicolon (;)**.

Common Programming Error 26.1

Failing to precede a variable name with a $ is a syntax error.

Common Programming Error 26.2

Variable names in PHP are case sensitive. Failure to use the proper mixture of cases is a syntax error.

Common Programming Error 26.3

Forgetting to terminate a statement with a semicolon (;) is a syntax error.

Line 8 contains a **one-line comment**, which begins with two **forward slashes (//)**. Text to the right of the slashes is ignored by the interpreter. One-line comments can also begin with the pound sign (#). Multiline comments begin with delimiter **/*** and end with delimiter ***/**.

Line 21 outputs the value of variable $name by calling function print. The actual value of $name is printed, instead of "$name". When a variable is encountered inside a double-quoted ("") string, PHP **interpolates** the variable. In other words, PHP inserts the variable's value where the variable name appears in the string. Thus, variable $name is replaced by LunaTic for printing purposes. PHP variables are "**multitype**," meaning that they can contain different types of data (e.g., **integers**, **doubles** or **strings**) at different times. Figure 26.2 introduces these data types.

Data type	Description
int, integer	Whole numbers (i.e., numbers without a decimal point).
float, double	Real numbers (i.e., numbers containing a decimal point).
string	Text enclosed in either single (' ') or double ("") quotes.
bool, Boolean	True or false.
array	Group of elements of the same type.
object	Group of associated data and methods.
Resource	An external data source.
NULL	No value.

Fig. 26.2 PHP data types.

Good Programming Practice 26.1

Whitespace enhances the readability of PHP code. It also simplifies programming and debugging.

Converting Between PHP Data Types

Conversion between different data types may be necessary when performing arithmetic operations with variables. In PHP, data-type conversion can be performed by passing the data type as an argument to function **settype**. Figure 26.3 demonstrates type conversion of the PHP data types introduced in Fig. 26.2.

```
1   <!DOCTYPE html PUBLIC "-//W3C//DTD XHTML 1.0 Transitional//EN"
2      "http://www.w3.org/TR/xhtml1/DTD/xhtml1-transitional.dtd">
3
4   <!-- Fig. 26.3: data.php              -->
5   <!-- Demonstration of PHP data types -->
6
7   <html xmlns = "http://www.w3.org/1999/xhtml">
8      <head>
9         <title>PHP data types</title>
10     </head>
11
12     <body>
13
14        <?php
15
16           // declare a string, double and integer
17           $testString = "3.5 seconds";
18           $testDouble = 79.2;
19           $testInteger = 12;
20        ?>
21
22        <!-- print each variable's value -->
23        <?php print( $testString ); ?> is a string.<br />
```

Fig. 26.3 Type conversion. (Part 1 of 2.)

```
24        <?php print( $testDouble ); ?> is a double.<br />
25        <?php print( $testInteger ); ?> is an integer.<br />
26
27        <br />
28        Now, converting to other types:<br />
29        <?php
30
31          // call function settype to convert variable
32          // testString to different data types
33          print( "$testString" );
34          settype( $testString, "double" );
35          print( " as a double is $testString <br />" );
36          print( "$testString" );
37          settype( $testString, "integer" );
38          print( " as an integer is $testString <br />" );
39          settype( $testString, "string" );
40          print( "Converting back to a string results in
41             $testString <br /><br />" );
42
43          $data = "98.6 degrees";
44
45          // use type casting to cast variables to a
46          // different type
47          print( "Now using type casting instead: <br />
48             As a string - " . (string) $data .
49             "<br />As a double - " . (double) $data .
50             "<br />As an integer - " . (integer) $data );
51        ?>
52     </body>
53  </html>
```

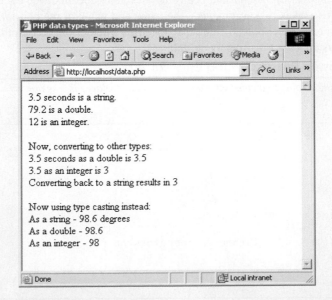

Fig. 26.3   Type conversion. (Part 2 of 2.)

Lines 17–19 of Fig. 26.3 assign a string to variable $testString, a floating-point number to variable $testDouble and an integer to variable $testInteger. Variables are converted to the data type of the value they are assigned. For example, variable $testString becomes a string when assigned the value "3.5 seconds". Lines 23–25 print the value of each variable. Note that enclosing a variable name in double quotes in a print statement is optional. Lines 34–39 call function settype to modify the data type of each variable. Function settype takes two arguments—the variable whose data type is to be changed and the variable's new data type. Calling function settype can result in loss of data. For example, doubles are truncated when they are converted to integers. When converting between a string and a number, PHP uses the value of the number that appears at the beginning of the string. If no number appears at the beginning of the string, the string evaluates to 0. In line 34, the string "3.5 seconds" is converted to a double, resulting in the value 3.5 being stored in variable $testString. In line 37, double 3.5 is converted to integer 3. When we convert this variable to a string (line 39), the variable's value becomes "3".

Another option for conversion between types is **casting** (or **type casting**). Unlike settype, casting does not change a variable's content. Rather, type casting creates a temporary copy of a variable's value in memory. Lines 47–50 cast variable $data's value to a string, a double and an integer. Casting is necessary when a specific data type is required for an arithmetic operation.

The **concatenation operator** (.) concatenates strings. This combines multiple strings in the same print statement (lines 47–50). A print statement may be split over multiple lines; everything that is enclosed in the parentheses, terminated by a semicolon, is sent to the client.

Arithmetic Operators

PHP provides a variety of arithmetic operators, which we demonstrate in Fig. 26.4. Line 14 declares variable $a and assigns it the value 5. Line 18 calls function define to create a **named constant**. A constant is a value that cannot be modified once it is declared. Function define takes two arguments—the name and value of the constant. An optional third argument accepts a boolean value that specifies whether the constant is case insensitive—constants are case sensitive by default.

Common Programming Error 26.4

Assigning a value to a constant after a constant is declared is a syntax error.

```
1    <!DOCTYPE html PUBLIC "-//W3C//DTD XHTML 1.0 Transitional//EN"
2        "http://www.w3.org/TR/xhtml1/DTD/xhtml1-transitional.dtd">
3
4    <!-- Fig. 26.4: operators.php    -->
5    <!-- Demonstration of operators -->
6
7    <html xmlns = "http://www.w3.org/1999/xhtml">
8       <head>
9          <title>Using arithmetic operators</title>
10      </head>
11
12      <body>
```

Fig. 26.4   Using PHP's arithmetic operators. (Part 1 of 3.)

```php
13          <?php
14             $a = 5;
15             print( "The value of variable a is $a <br />" );
16
17             // define constant VALUE
18             define( "VALUE", 5 );
19
20             // add constant VALUE to variable $a
21             $a = $a + VALUE;
22             print( "Variable a after adding constant VALUE
23                is $a <br />" );
24
25             // multiply variable $a by 2
26             $a *= 2;
27             print( "Multiplying variable a by 2 yields $a <br />" );
28
29             // test if variable $a is less than 50
30             if ( $a < 50 )
31                print( "Variable a is less than 50 <br />" );
32
33             // add 40 to variable $a
34             $a += 40;
35             print( "Variable a after adding 40 is $a <br />" );
36
37             // test if variable $a is 50 or less
38             if ( $a < 51 )
39                print( "Variable a is still 50 or less<br />" );
40
41             // test if variable $a is between 50 and 100, inclusive
42             elseif ( $a < 101 )
43                print( "Variable a is now between 50 and 100,
44                   inclusive<br />" );
45             else
46                print( "Variable a is now greater than 100
47                   <br />" );
48
49             // print an uninitialized variable
50             print( "Using a variable before initializing:
51                $nothing <br />" );
52
53             // add constant VALUE to an uninitialized variable
54             $test = $num + VALUE;
55             print( "An uninitialized variable plus constant
56                VALUE yields $test <br />" );
57
58             // add a string to an integer
59             $str = "3 dollars";
60             $a += $str;
61             print( "Adding a string to variable a yields $a
62                <br />" );
63          ?>
64       </body>
65    </html>
```

Fig. 26.4   Using PHP's arithmetic operators. (Part 2 of 3.)

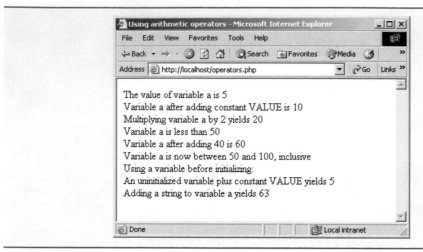

Fig. 26.4   Using PHP's arithmetic operators. (Part 3 of 3.)

Line 21 adds constant VALUE to variable $a, which is a typical use of arithmetic operators. Line 26 uses the **assignment operator** *= to yield an expression equivalent to $a = $a * 2 (thus assigning $a the value 20). These assignment operators (i.e., +=, -=, *= and /=) are syntactical shortcuts. Line 34 adds 40 to the value of variable $a.

In PHP, uninitialized variables have the value **undef**, which evaluates to different values, depending on its context. For example, when undef is used in a numeric context (e.g., $num in line 54), it evaluates to 0. In contrast, when undef is interpreted in a string context (e.g., $nothing in line 51), it evaluates to an **empty string ("")**.

Error-Prevention Tip 26.1

Always initialize variables before using them. Doing so helps avoid subtle errors.

Strings are converted to integers when they are used in arithmetic operations (lines 59–60). In line 60, the string value "3 dollars" is converted to the integer 3 before being added to integer variable $a.

Error-Prevention Tip 26.2

Function print can be used to display the value of a variable at a particular point during a program's execution. This is often helpful in debugging a script.

Common Programming Error 26.5

Using an uninitialized variable might result in an incorrect numerical calculation. For example, multiplying a number by an uninitialized variable results in 0.

PHP **keywords** (such as if...elseif...else) are reserved for implementing language features. Figure 26.5 contains a list of frequently used PHP keywords.

Initializing and Manipulating Arrays

PHP provides the capability to store data in arrays. Arrays are divided into **elements** that behave as individual variables. Array names, like other variables, begin with the $ symbol. Script arrays.php (Fig. 26.6) demonstrates initializing and manipulating arrays.

PHP keywords

and	do	for	include	require	true
break	else	foreach	list	return	var
case	elseif	function	new	static	virtual
class	extends	global	not	switch	xor
continue	false	if	or	this	while
default					

Fig. 26.5   PHP keywords.

Individual array elements are accessed by following the array-variable name with an index enclosed in braces ([]). If a value is assigned to an array that does not exist, then the array is created (line 18). Likewise, assigning a value to an element where the index is omitted appends a new element to the end of the array (line 21). The for loop (lines 24–25) prints each element's value. Function **count** returns the total number of elements in the array. Since array indices start at 0, the index of the last element is one less than the total number of elements. In this example, the for loop terminates once the counter ($i) is equal to the number of elements in the array.

Line 31 demonstrates a second method of initializing arrays. Function **array** returns an array that contains the arguments passed to it. The first item in the list is stored as the first array element, the second item is stored as the second array element and so on. Lines 32–33 use another for loop to print out each array element's value.

In addition to integer indices, arrays can have nonnumeric indices (lines 39–41). For example, indices ArtTic, LunaTic and GalAnt are assigned the values 21, 18 and 23, respectively. PHP provides functions for **iterating** through the elements of an array (lines 45–46). Each array has a built-in **internal pointer**, which points to the array element currently being referenced. Function **reset** sets the internal pointer to the first element of the array. Function **key** returns the index of the element currently referenced by the internal pointer, and function **next** moves the internal pointer to the next element. The for loop continues to execute as long as function key returns an index. Function next returns false when there are no additional elements in the array. When this occurs, function key cannot return an index, and the for loop terminates. Line 47 prints the index and value of each element.

```
1   <!DOCTYPE html PUBLIC "-//W3C//DTD XHTML 1.0 Transitional//EN"
2      "http://www.w3.org/TR/xhtml1/DTD/xhtml1-transitional.dtd">
3
4   <!-- Fig. 26.6: arrays.php -->
5   <!-- Array manipulation      -->
6
7   <html xmlns = "http://www.w3.org/1999/xhtml">
8      <head>
9         <title>Array manipulation</title>
10     </head>
11
12     <body>
```

Fig. 26.6   Array manipulation. (Part 1 of 3.)

```php
13    <?php
14
15        // create array first
16        print( "<strong>Creating the first array</strong>
17           <br />" );
18        $first[ 0 ] = "zero";
19        $first[ 1 ] = "one";
20        $first[ 2 ] = "two";
21        $first[] = "three";
22
23        // print each element's index and value
24        for ( $i = 0; $i < count( $first ); $i++ )
25           print( "Element $i is $first[$i] <br />" );
26
27        print( "<br /><strong>Creating the second array
28           </strong><br />" );
29
30        // call function array to create array second
31        $second = array( "zero", "one", "two", "three" );
32        for ( $i = 0; $i < count( $second ); $i++ )
33           print( "Element $i is $second[$i] <br />" );
34
35        print( "<br /><strong>Creating the third array
36           </strong><br />" );
37
38        // assign values to non-numerical indices
39        $third[ "ArtTic" ] = 21;
40        $third[ "LunaTic" ] = 18;
41        $third[ "GalAnt" ] = 23;
42
43        // iterate through the array elements and print each
44        // element's name and value
45        for ( reset( $third ); $element = key( $third );
46           next( $third ) )
47           print( "$element is $third[$element] <br />" );
48
49        print( "<br /><strong>Creating the fourth array
50           </strong><br />" );
51
52        // call function array to create array fourth using
53        // string indices
54        $fourth = array(
55           "January"   => "first",    "February" => "second",
56           "March"     => "third",    "April"    => "fourth",
57           "May"       => "fifth",    "June"     => "sixth",
58           "July"      => "seventh",  "August"   => "eighth",
59           "September" => "ninth",    "October"  => "tenth",
60           "November"  => "eleventh", "December" => "twelfth"
61        );
62
63        // print each element's name and value
64        foreach ( $fourth as $element => $value )
65           print( "$element is the $value month <br />" );
```

Fig. 26.6   Array manipulation. (Part 2 of 3.)

```
66        ?>
67     </body>
68   </html>
```

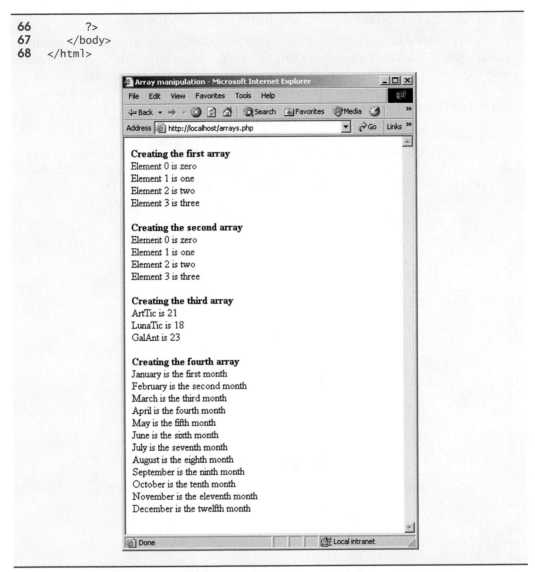

Fig. 26.6   Array manipulation. (Part 3 of 3.)

Function `array` can also be used to initialize arrays with string indices. In order to override the automatic numeric indexing performed by function `array`, use operator `=>`, as demonstrated in lines 54–61. The value to the left of the operator is the array index, and the value to the right is the element's value. An array with string indices also is called an **associative array**.

The **foreach** loop (lines 64–65) is a control statement that is specially designed for iterating through arrays. The syntax for a `foreach` loop starts with the array to iterate through, followed by the keyword **as**, followed by the variables to receive the index and the value for each element. We use the `foreach` loop to `print` each element and value of array `$fourth`.

26.3 String Processing and Regular Expressions

PHP processes text data easily and efficiently, enabling straightforward searching, substitution, extraction and concatenation of strings. Text manipulation in PHP is usually done with **regular expressions**—a series of characters that serve as pattern-matching templates (or search criteria) in strings, text files and databases. This feature allows complex searching and string processing to be performed using relatively simple expressions.

Comparing Strings

Many string-processing tasks are accomplished by using PHP's **equality** and **comparison** operators (Fig. 26.7). Line 16 declares and initializes array `$fruits` by calling function `array`. The `for` loop (line 19) iterates through each element in the `$fruits` array.

```
1    <!DOCTYPE html PUBLIC "-//W3C//DTD XHTML 1.0 Transitional//EN"
2       "http://www.w3.org/TR/xhtml1/DTD/xhtml1-transitional.dtd">
3
4    <!-- Fig. 26.7: compare.php -->
5    <!-- String Comparison       -->
6
7    <html xmlns = "http://www.w3.org/1999/xhtml">
8       <head>
9          <title>String Comparison</title>
10      </head>
11
12      <body>
13         <?php
14
15            // create array fruits
16            $fruits = array( "apple", "orange", "banana" );
17
18            // iterate through each array element
19            for ( $i = 0; $i < count( $fruits ); $i++ ) {
20
21               // call function strcmp to compare the array element
22               // to string "banana"
23               if ( strcmp( $fruits[ $i ], "banana" ) < 0 )
24                  print( $fruits[ $i ]." is less than banana " );
25               elseif ( strcmp( $fruits[ $i ], "banana" ) > 0 )
26                  print( $fruits[ $i ].
27                     " is greater than banana " );
28               else
29                  print( $fruits[ $i ]." is equal to banana " );
30
31               // use relational operators to compare each element
32               // to string "apple"
33               if ( $fruits[ $i ] < "apple" )
34                  print( "and less than apple! <br />" );
35               elseif ( $fruits[ $i ] > "apple" )
36                  print( "and greater than apple! <br />" );
37               elseif ( $fruits[ $i ] == "apple" )
38                  print( "and equal to apple! <br />" );
```

Fig. 26.7   Using the string comparison operators. (Part 1 of 2.)

```
39
40                }
41          ?>
42       </body>
43    </html>
```

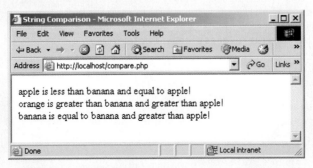

Fig. 26.7   Using the string comparison operators. (Part 2 of 2.)

Lines 23 and 25 call function **strcmp** to compare two strings. If the first string alphabetically precedes the second string, then -1 is returned. If the strings are equal, then 0 is returned. If the first string alphabetically follows the second string, then 1 is returned. Lines 23–29 compare each element to the string **"banana"**, printing the elements that are greater than, less than and equal to the string.

Relational operators (==, !=, <, <=, > and >=) can also be used to compare strings. Lines 33–38 use relational operators to compare each element of the array to the string **"apple"**. These operators are also used for numerical comparison with integers and doubles.

Using Regular Expressions

For more powerful string comparisons, PHP provides functions **ereg** and **preg_match**, which use regular expressions to search a string for a specified pattern. Function ereg uses **Portable Operating System Interface (POSIX) extended regular expressions,** whereas function preg_match provides **Perl-compatible regular expressions**. POSIX-extended regular expressions are a standard to which PHP regular expressions conform. In this section, we use function ereg. Perl regular expressions are more widely used than POSIX regular expressions. Support for Perl regular expressions also eases migration from Perl to PHP. For more information on Perl regular expressions, see Chapter 25. Consult PHP's documentation for a list of differences between the Perl and PHP implementations. Figure 26.8 demonstrates some of PHP's regular expression capabilities.

We begin by assigning the string **"Now is the time"** to variable **$search** (line 14). Line 19's condition calls function ereg to search for the **literal characters** Now inside variable $search. If the pattern is found, ereg returns true, and line 20 prints a message indicating that the pattern was found. We use single quotes ('') inside the print statement to emphasize the search pattern. Anything enclosed within single quotes is not **interpolated**. For example, '$name' in a print statement would output $name, not variable $name's value. Function ereg takes two arguments—a regular expression pattern to search for (Now) and the string to search. Although case mixture and whitespace are typically significant in patterns, PHP provides function **eregi** for specifying case-insensitive pattern matches.

```
1   <!DOCTYPE html PUBLIC "-//W3C//DTD XHTML 1.0 Transitional//EN"
2      "http://www.w3.org/TR/xhtml1/DTD/xhtml1-transitional.dtd">
3
4   <!-- Fig. 26.8: expression.php -->
5   <!-- Using regular expressions -->
6
7   <html xmlns = "http://www.w3.org/1999/xhtml">
8      <head>
9         <title>Regular expressions</title>
10     </head>
11
12     <body>
13        <?php
14           $search = "Now is the time";
15           print( "Test string is: '$search'<br /><br />" );
16
17           // call function ereg to search for pattern 'Now'
18           // in variable search
19           if ( ereg( "Now", $search ) )
20              print( "String 'Now' was found.<br />" );
21
22           // search for pattern 'Now' in the beginning of
23           // the string
24           if ( ereg( "^Now", $search ) )
25              print( "String 'Now' found at beginning
26                 of the line.<br />" );
27
28           // search for pattern 'Now' at the end of the string
29           if ( ereg( "Now$", $search ) )
30              print( "String 'Now' was found at the end
31                 of the line.<br />" );
32
33           // search for any word ending in 'ow'
34           if ( ereg( "[[:<:]]([a-zA-Z]*ow)[[:>:]]", $search,
35              $match ) )
36              print( "Word found ending in 'ow': " .
37                 $match[ 1 ] . "<br />" );
38
39           // search for any words beginning with 't'
40           print( "Words beginning with 't' found: " );
41
42           while ( eregi( "[[:<:]](t[[:alpha:]]+)[[:>:]]",
43              $search, $match ) ) {
44              print( $match[ 1 ] . " " );
45
46              // remove the first occurrence of a word beginning
47              // with 't' to find other instances in the string
48              $search = ereg_replace( $match[ 1 ], "", $search );
49           }
50
51           print( "<br />" );
52        ?>
53     </body>
```

Fig. 26.8   Regular expressions in PHP. (Part 1 of 2.)

54   `</html>`

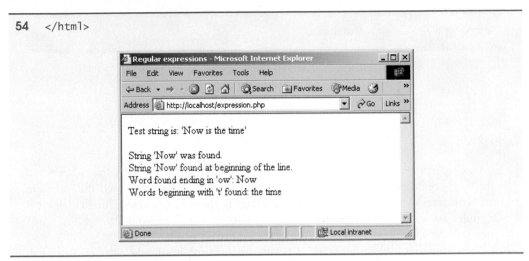

Fig. 26.8   Regular expressions in PHP. (Part 2 of 2.)

In addition to literal characters, regular expressions can include special characters that specify patterns. For example, the **caret (^) special character** matches the beginning of a string. Line 24 searches the beginning of `$search` for the pattern Now.

The characters **$**, **^** and **.** are part of a special set of characters called **metacharacters**. A **dollar sign ($)** searches for the specified pattern at the end of the string (line 29). The pattern Now is not found at the end of `$search`, so the body of the `if` statement (lines 30–31) is not executed. Note that Now$ is not a variable; it is a pattern that uses $ to search for the characters Now at the end of a string. Another special character is the period (`.`), which matches any single character.

Lines 34–35 search (from left to right) for the first word ending with the letters ow. **Bracket expressions** are lists of characters enclosed in braces (`[ ]`) that match a single character from the list. Ranges can be specified by supplying the beginning and the end of the range separated by a dash (`-`). For instance, the bracket expression `[a-z]` matches any lowercase letter, and `[A-Z]` matches any uppercase letter. In this example, we combine the two to create an expression that matches any letter. The special bracket expressions `[[:<:]]` and `[[:>:]]` match the beginning and end of a word, respectively.

The expression inside the parentheses, `[a-zA-Z]*ow`, matches any word ending in ow. It uses the **quantifier** `*` to match the preceding pattern zero or more times. Thus, `[a-zA-Z]*ow` matches any number of characters followed by the literal characters ow. Some PHP quantifiers are listed in Fig. 26.9.

Quantifier	Matches
{n}	Exactly n times.
{m,n}	Between m and n times inclusive.
{n,}	n or more times.

Fig. 26.9   Some PHP quantifiers. (Part 1 of 2.)

Quantifier	Matches
+	One or more times (same as {1,}).
*	Zero or more times (same as {0,}).
?	Zero or one time (same as {0,1}).

Fig. 26.9   Some PHP quantifiers. (Part 2 of 2.)

Placing a pattern in parentheses stores the matched string in the array that is specified in the third argument to function ereg. The first parenthetical pattern matched is stored in the second array element, the second in the third array element and so on. The first element (i.e., index 0) stores the string matched for the entire pattern. The parentheses in lines 34–35 result in Now being stored in variable $match[1].

Searching for multiple instances of a pattern in a string is slightly more complicated, because the ereg function matches only the first instance of the pattern. To find multiple instances of a given pattern, we must remove any matched instances before calling ereg again. Lines 42–49 use a while loop and the **ereg_replace** function to find all the words in the string that begins with t. We will say more about this function momentarily.

The pattern used in this example, [[:<:]](t[[:alpha:]]+)[[:>:]], matches any word beginning with the character t followed by one or more characters. The example uses the **character class** [[:alpha:]] to recognize any alphabetic character. This is equivalent to the [a-zA-Z] bracket expression that was used earlier. Figure 26.10 lists some character classes that can be matched with regular expressions.

Character class	Description
alnum	Alphanumeric characters (i.e., letters [a-zA-Z] or digits [0-9]).
alpha	Word characters (i.e., letters [a-zA-Z]).
digit	Digits.
space	Whitespace.
lower	Lowercase letters.
upper	Uppercase letters.

Fig. 26.10   Some PHP character classes.

The quantifier + matches one or more instances of the preceding expression. The result of the match is stored in $match[1]. Once a match is found, we print it in line 44. We then remove it from the string in line 48, using function ereg_replace. Function ereg_replace takes three arguments—the pattern to match, a string to replace the matched string and the string to search. The modified string is returned. Here, we search for the word that we matched with the regular expression, replace the word with an empty string, then assign the result back to $search. This allows us to match any other words beginning with the character t in the string.

26.4 Viewing Client/Server Environment Variables

Knowledge of a client's execution environment is useful to system administrators who want to provide client-specific information. **Environment variables** contain information about a script's environment, such as the client's Web browser, the HTTP host and the HTTP connection.

Figure 26.11 lists some global arrays. Figure 26.12 generates an XHTML document that displays the values of the client's environment variables in a table. PHP stores the environment variables and their values in the **$_ENV array**. Iterating through this array allows us to view all the client's environment variables. [*Note*: The output of this example will vary from system to system.] In lines 19–22, we use a foreach loop to print out the $key and $value of each element in the $_ENV array.

Variable name	Description
$_SERVER	Data about the currently running server.
$_ENV	Data about the client's environment.
$_GET	Data posted to the server by the get method.
$_POST	Data posted to the server by the post method.
$_COOKIE	Data contained in cookies on the client's computer.
$GLOBALS	Array containing all global variables.

Fig. 26.11 Some useful global arrays.

```
1   <!DOCTYPE html PUBLIC "-//W3C//DTD XHTML 1.0 Transitional//EN"
2       "http://www.w3.org/TR/xhtml1/DTD/xhtml1-transitional.dtd">
3
4   <!-- Fig. 26.11: env.php                          -->
5   <!-- Program to display environment variables -->
6
7   <html xmlns = "http://www.w3.org/1999/xhtml">
8       <head>
9           <title>Environment Variables</title>
10      </head>
11
12      <body>
13          <table border = "0" cellpadding = "2" cellspacing = "0"
14              width = "100%">
15          <?php
16
17              // print the key and value for each element
18              // in the $_ENV array
19              foreach ( $_ENV as $key => $value )
20                  print( "<tr><td bgcolor = \"#11bbff\">
21                      <strong>$key</strong></td>
22                      <td>$value</td></tr>" );
23          ?>
```

Fig. 26.12 Displaying environment variables. (Part 1 of 2.)

```
24              </table>
25          </body>
26      </html>
```

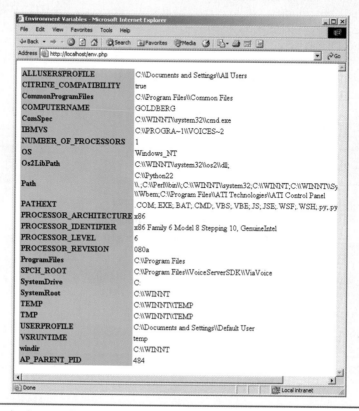

Fig. 26.12 Displaying environment variables. (Part 2 of 2.)

26.5 Form Processing and Business Logic

XHTML forms enable Web pages to collect data from users and send it to a Web server for processing. Interaction of this kind between users and Web servers is vital to e-commerce applications. Such capabilities allow users to purchase products, request information, send and receive Web-based e-mail, perform online paging and take advantage of various other online services. Figure 26.13 uses an XHTML form to collect information about users for the purpose of adding them to a mailing list. The type of registration form in this example could be used by a software company to acquire profile information before allowing users to download software.

```
1   <!DOCTYPE html PUBLIC "-//W3C//DTD XHTML 1.0 Transitional//EN"
2       "http://www.w3.org/TR/xhtml1/DTD/xhtml1-transitional.dtd">
3
4   <!-- Fig. 26.13: form.html                              -->
```

Fig. 26.13 XHTML form for gathering user input. (Part 1 of 3.)

```
5    <!-- Form for use with the form.php program -->
6
7    <html xmlns = "http://www.w3.org/1999/xhtml">
8       <head>
9          <title>Sample form to take user input in XHTML</title>
10      </head>
11
12      <body>
13
14         <h1>This is a sample registration form.</h1>
15         Please fill in all fields and click Register.
16
17         <!-- post form data to form.php -->
18         <form method = "post" action = "form.php">
19            <img src = "images/user.gif" alt = "User" /><br />
20            <span style = "color: blue">
21               Please fill out the fields below.<br />
22            </span>
23
24            <!-- create four text boxes for user input -->
25            <img src = "images/fname.gif" alt = "First Name" />
26            <input type = "text" name = "fname" /><br />
27
28            <img src = "images/lname.gif" alt = "Last Name" />
29            <input type = "text" name = "lname" /><br />
30
31            <img src = "images/email.gif" alt = "Email" />
32            <input type = "text" name = "email" /><br />
33
34            <img src = "images/phone.gif" alt = "Phone" />
35            <input type = "text" name = "phone" /><br />
36
37            <span style = "font-size: 10pt">
38               Must be in the form (555)555-5555</span>
39            <br /><br />
40
41            <img src = "images/downloads.gif"
42               alt = "Publications" /><br />
43
44            <span style = "color: blue">
45               Which book would you like information about?
46            </span><br />
47
48            <!-- create drop-down list containing book names -->
49            <select name = "book">
50               <option>Internet and WWW How to Program 3e</option>
51               <option>C++ How to Program 4e</option>
52               <option>Java How to Program 5e</option>
53               <option>XML How to Program 1e</option>
54            </select>
55            <br /><br />
56
57            <img src = "images/os.gif" alt = "Operating System" />
```

Fig. 26.13 XHTML form for gathering user input. (Part 2 of 3.)

```
58              <br /><span style = "color: blue">
59                  Which operating system are you currently using?
60              <br /></span>
61
62              <!-- create five radio buttons -->
63              <input type = "radio" name = "os" value = "Windows XP"
64                  checked = "checked" />
65                  Windows XP
66
67              <input type = "radio" name = "os" value =
68                  "Windows 2000" />
69                  Windows 2000
70
71              <input type = "radio" name = "os" value =
72                  "Windows 98" />
73                  Windows 98<br />
74
75              <input type = "radio" name = "os" value = "Linux" />
76                  Linux
77
78              <input type = "radio" name = "os" value = "Other" />
79                  Other<br />
80
81              <!-- create a submit button -->
82              <input type = "submit" value = "Register" />
83          </form>
84
85      </body>
86  </html>
```

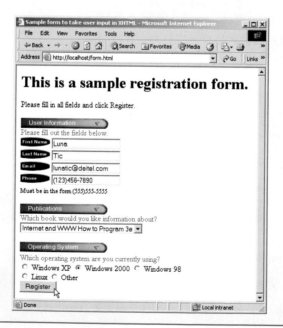

Fig. 26.13   XHTML form for gathering user input. (Part 3 of 3.)

The `action` attribute of the `form` element (line 18) indicates that when the user clicks the **Register** button, the `form` data will be `posted` to `form.php` (Fig. 26.14) for processing. Using **method = "post"** appends form data to the browser request that contains the protocol (i.e., HTTP) and the requested resource's URL. Scripts located on the Web server's machine (or on a machine accessible through the network) can access the form data sent as part of the request.

We assign a unique `name` (e.g., `email`) to each of the `form`'s `input` fields. When **Register** is clicked, each field's `name` and `value` are sent to the Web server. Script `form.php` can then access the value for each specific field through the **superglobal array $_POST**. Superglobal arrays are associative arrays predefined by PHP that hold variables acquired from the user input, the environment or the Web server and are accessible in any variable scope. The $_ENV array used in Fig. 26.12 is another example of a superglobal array. $_POST contains key-value pairs corresponding to name-value pairs for variables submitted through the form. [*Note*: The superglobal array **$_GET** would contain these key-value pairs if the form had been submitted using the HTTP *get* method.] Figure 26.14 (`form.php`) processes the data `posted` by `form.html` and sends XHTML back to the client.

Good Programming Practice 26.2

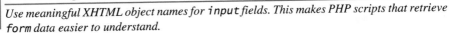

Use meaningful XHTML object names for `input` fields. This makes PHP scripts that retrieve form data easier to understand.

```
1   <!DOCTYPE html PUBLIC "-//W3C//DTD XHTML 1.0 Transitional//EN"
2      "http://www.w3.org/TR/xhtml1/DTD/xhtml1-transitional.dtd">
3
4   <!-- Fig. 26.14: form.php                             -->
5   <!-- Read information sent from form.html -->
6
7   <html xmlns = "http://www.w3.org/1999/xhtml">
8      <head>
9         <title>Form Validation</title>
10     </head>
11
12     <body style = "font-family: arial,sans-serif">
13
14        <?php
15           extract( $_POST );
16
17           // determine whether phone number is valid and print
18           // an error message if not
19           if ( !ereg( "^\([0-9]{3}\)[0-9]{3}-[0-9]{4}$",
20              $phone ) ){
21
22              print( "<p><span style = \"color: red;
23                 font-size: 2em\">
24                 INVALID PHONE NUMBER</span><br />
25                 A valid phone number must be in the form
26                 <strong>(555)555-5555</strong><br />
27                 <span style = \"color: blue\">
28                 Click the Back button, enter a valid phone
```

Fig. 26.14 Obtaining user input through forms. (Part 1 of 3.)

```
29              number and resubmit.<br /><br />
30              Thank You.</span></p></body></html>" );
31
32                  die(); // terminate script execution
33          }
34      ?>
35
36      <p>Hi
37          <span style = "color: blue">
38              <strong>
39                  <?php print( "$fname" ); ?>
40              </strong>
41          </span>.
42          Thank you for completing the survey.<br />
43
44          You have been added to the
45          <span style = "color: blue">
46              <strong>
47                  <?php print( "$book " ); ?>
48              </strong>
49          </span>
50          mailing list.
51      </p>
52      <strong>The following information has been saved
53          in our database:</strong><br />
54
55      <table border = "0" cellpadding = "0" cellspacing = "10">
56          <tr>
57              <td bgcolor = "#ffffaa">Name </td>
58              <td bgcolor = "#ffffbb">Email</td>
59              <td bgcolor = "#ffffcc">Phone</td>
60              <td bgcolor = "#ffffdd">OS</td>
61          </tr>
62
63          <tr>
64              <?php
65
66                  // print each form field's value
67                  print( "<td>$fname $lname</td>
68                      <td>$email</td>
69                      <td>$phone</td>
70                      <td>$os</td>" );
71              ?>
72          </tr>
73      </table>
74
75      <br /><br /><br />
76      <div style = "font-size: 10pt; text-align: center">
77          This is only a sample form.
78          You have not been added to a mailing list.
79      </div>
80  </body>
81 </html>
```

Fig. 26.14 Obtaining user input through forms. (Part 2 of 3.)

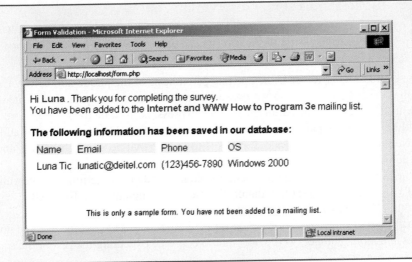

Fig. 26.14 Obtaining user input through forms. (Part 3 of 3.)

Function **extract(** *associativeArray* **)** (line 15) creates a variable-value pair corresponding to each key-value pair in the *associativeArray* (i.e., $_POST), creating variables whose respective names and values correspond to the names and values of each posted form field. For example, in line 32 of Fig. 26.13, an XHTML text box is created and given the name email. In line 68 of our PHP script (Fig. 26.14), after having called function extract, we access the field's value by using variable $email. Elements in the superglobal array $_POST also can be accessed using standard array notation. For example, we could have accessed the form field email's value by referring to $_POST['email'].

Portability Tip 26.1

In PHP versions 4.2 and higher, the directive register_globals *is set to* Off *by default for security reasons. Turning off* register_globals *means that all variables sent from an XHTML form to a PHP document now must be accessed using the appropriate superglobal array (*$_POST *or* $_GET*). With this directive turned* On*, as was the case by default in PHP versions prior to 4.2, PHP creates an individual global variable corresponding to each form field.*

Software Engineering Observation 26.1

Using function extract *to initialize variables from the superglobal arrays* $_POST *and* $_GET *is not recommended in a script on a Web site dealing with private or sensitive material. It is more secure to access each element in the superglobal array directly, using the* array[key] *notation.*

In lines 19–20, we determine whether the phone number entered by the user is valid. In this case, the phone number must begin with an opening parenthesis, followed by an area code, a closing parenthesis, an exchange, a hyphen and a line number. It is crucial to validate information that will be entered into databases or used in mailing lists. For example, validation can be used to ensure that credit-card numbers contain the proper number of digits before the numbers are encrypted to a merchant. This script implements the **business logic**, or **business rules**, of our application.

Software Engineering Observation 26.2

Use business logic to ensure that invalid information is not stored in databases. When possible, validate form data with JavaScript to conserve server resources. Some data, such as passwords, must be validated on the server side.

The expression \(matches the opening parenthesis of the phone number. We want to match the literal character (, so we **escape** its normal meaning by preceding it with the backslash character (\). The parentheses in the expression must be followed by three digits ([0-9]{3}), a closing parenthesis, three more digits, a literal hyphen and four additional digits. Note that we use the ∧ and $ symbols to ensure that no extra characters appear at either end of the string.

If the regular expression is matched, the phone number is determined to be valid, and an XHTML document is sent that thanks the user for completing the form. Otherwise, the body of the **if** statement is executed, and an error message is printed.

Function **die** (line 32) terminates script execution. In this case, if the user did not enter a correct telephone number, we do not want to continue executing the rest of the script, so we call function **die**.

Error-Prevention Tip 26.3

Be sure to close any open XHTML tags before calling function die(). Not doing so could produce invalid XHTML output that will not display properly. die() has an optional parameter that specifies a message to output when exiting, so one method of closing tags is to call die("</body></html>").

26.6 Verifying a Username and Password

It is often desirable to have a **private Web site** that is accessible only to certain individuals. Implementing privacy generally involves username and password verification. Figure 26.15 presents an XHTML **form** that queries the user for a username and a password. Fields USERNAME and PASSWORD are posted to the PHP script **password.php** for verification. For simplicity, we do not encrypt the data before sending it to the server. For more information regarding PHP encryption functions, visit

www.php.net/manual/en/ref.mcrypt.php

```
1   <!DOCTYPE html PUBLIC "-//W3C//DTD XHTML 1.0 Transitional//EN"
2      "http://www.w3.org/TR/xhtml1/DTD/xhtml1-transitional.dtd">
3
4   <!-- Fig. 26.15: password.html                          -->
5   <!-- XHTML form sent to password.php for verification -->
6
7   <html xmlns = "http://www.w3.org/1999/xhtml">
8      <head>
9         <title>Verifying a username and a password.</title>
10
11         <style type = "text/css">
12            td { background-color: #DDDDDD }
13         </style>
14      </head>
```

Fig. 26.15 XHTML form for obtaining a username and password. (Part 1 of 3.)

```
15
16      <body style = "font-family: arial">
17         <p style = "font-size: 13pt">
18            Type in your username and password below.
19            <br />
20            <span style = "color: #0000FF; font-size: 10pt;
21               font-weight: bold">
22               Note that password will be sent as plain text
23            </span>
24         </p>
25
26         <!-- post form data to password.php -->
27         <form action = "password.php" method = "post">
28            <br />
29
30            <table border = "0" cellspacing = "0"
31               style = "height: 90px; width: 123px;
32               font-size: 10pt" cellpadding = "0">
33
34               <tr>
35                  <td colspan = "3">
36                     <strong>Username:</strong>
37                  </td>
38               </tr>
39
40               <tr>
41                  <td colspan = "3">
42                     <input size = "40" name = "USERNAME"
43                        style = "height: 22px; width: 115px" />
44                  </td>
45               </tr>
46
47               <tr>
48                  <td colspan = "3">
49                     <strong>Password:</strong>
50                  </td>
51               </tr>
52
53               <tr>
54                  <td colspan = "3">
55                     <input size = "40" name = "PASSWORD"
56                        style = "height: 22px; width: 115px"
57                        type = "password" />
58                  <br/></td>
59               </tr>
60
61               <tr>
62                  <td colspan = "1">
63                     <input type = "submit" name = "Enter"
64                        value = "Enter" style = "height: 23px;
65                        width: 47px" />
66                  </td>
67                  <td colspan = "2">
```

Fig. 26.15   XHTML form for obtaining a username and password. (Part 2 of 3.)

```
68                  <input type = "submit" name = "NewUser"
69                     value = "New User"
70                     style = "height: 23px" />
71                 </td>
72               </tr>
73             </table>
74           </form>
75         </body>
76      </html>
```

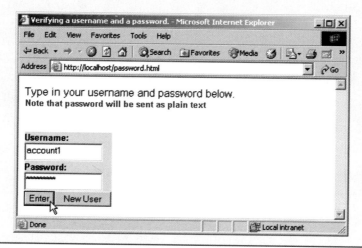

Fig. 26.15   XHTML form for obtaining a username and password. (Part 3 of 3.)

Script `password.php` (Fig. 26.16) verifies the client's username and password by querying a database. The valid user list and each user's respective password are contained in a simple text file named `password.txt` (Fig. 26.17). Existing users are validated against this text file, and new users are appended to it.

```
1   <!DOCTYPE html PUBLIC "-//W3C//DTD XHTML 1.0 Transitional//EN"
2      "http://www.w3.org/TR/xhtml1/DTD/xhtml1-transitional.dtd">
3
4   <!-- Fig. 26.16: password.php                        -->
5   <!-- Searching a database for usernames and passwords. -->
6
7   <html xmlns = "http://www.w3.org/1999/xhtml">
8      <head>
9         <?php
10           extract( $_POST );
11
12           // check if user has left USERNAME or PASSWORD field blank
13           if ( !$USERNAME || !$PASSWORD ) {
14              fieldsBlank();
15              die();
16           }
```

Fig. 26.16   Verifying a username and password. (Part 1 of 4.)

```
17
18          // check if the New User button was clicked
19      if ( isset( $NewUser ) ) {
20
21          // open password.txt for writing using append mode
22      if ( !( $file = fopen( "password.txt",
23        "a" ) ) ) {
24
25          // print error message and terminate script
26          // execution if file cannot be opened
27          print( "<title>Error</title></head><body>
28            Could not open password file
29            </body></html>" );
30          die();
31      }
32
33          // write username and password to file and
34          // call function userAdded
35      fputs( $file, "$USERNAME,$PASSWORD\n" );
36      userAdded( $USERNAME );
37      }
38      else {
39
40          // if a new user is not being added, open file
41          // for reading
42      if ( !( $file = fopen( "password.txt",
43        "r" ) ) ) {
44          print( "<title>Error</title></head>
45            <body>Could not open password file
46            </body></html>" );
47          die();
48      }
49
50      $userVerified = 0;
51
52          // read each line in file and check username
53          // and password
54      while ( !feof( $file ) && !$userVerified ) {
55
56          // read line from file
57          $line = fgets( $file, 255 );
58
59          // remove newline character from end of line
60          $line = chop( $line );
61
62          // split username and password
63          $field = split( ",", $line, 2 );
64
65          // verify username
66          if ( $USERNAME == $field[ 0 ] ) {
67              $userVerified = 1;
68
```

Fig. 26.16   Verifying a username and password. (Part 2 of 4.)

```
69              // call function checkPassword to verify
70              // user's password
71              if ( checkPassword( $PASSWORD, $field )
72                 == true )
73                 accessGranted( $USERNAME );
74              else
75                 wrongPassword();
76           }
77        }
78
79        // close text file
80        fclose( $file );
81
82        // call function accessDenied if username has
83        // not been verified
84        if ( !$userVerified )
85           accessDenied();
86     }
87
88     // verify user password and return a boolean
89     function checkPassword( $userpassword, $filedata )
90     {
91        if ( $userpassword == $filedata[ 1 ] )
92           return true;
93        else
94           return false;
95     }
96
97     // print a message indicating the user has been added
98     function userAdded( $name )
99     {
100       print( "<title>Thank You</title></head>
101          <body style = \"font-family: arial;
102          font-size: 1em; color: blue\">
103          <strong>You have been added
104          to the user list, $name.
105          <br />Enjoy the site.</strong>" );
106    }
107
108    // print a message indicating permission
109    // has been granted
110    function accessGranted( $name )
111    {
112       print( "<title>Thank You</title></head>
113          <body style = \"font-family: arial;
114          font-size: 1em; color: blue\">
115          <strong>Permission has been
116          granted, $name. <br />
117          Enjoy the site.</strong>" );
118    }
119
```

Fig. 26.16 Verifying a username and password. (Part 3 of 4.)

```
120            // print a message indicating password is invalid
121         function wrongPassword()
122         {
123            print( "<title>Access Denied</title></head>
124               <body style = \"font-family: arial;
125               font-size: 1em; color: red\">
126               <strong>You entered an invalid
127               password.<br />Access has
128               been denied.</strong>" );
129         }
130
131            // print a message indicating access has been denied
132         function accessDenied()
133         {
134            print( "<title>Access Denied</title></head>
135               <body style = \"font-family: arial;
136               font-size: 1em; color: red\">
137               <strong>
138               You were denied access to this server.
139               <br /></strong>" );
140         }
141
142            // print a message indicating that fields
143            // have been left blank
144         function fieldsBlank()
145         {
146            print( "<title>Access Denied</title></head>
147               <body style = \"font-family: arial;
148               font-size: 1em; color: red\">
149               <strong>
150               Please fill in all form fields.
151               <br /></strong>" );
152         }
153      ?>
154   </body>
155 </html>
```

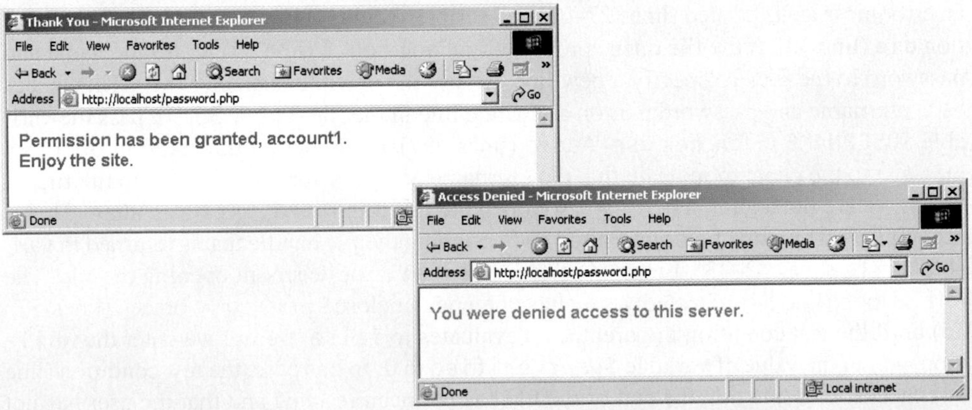

Fig. 26.16 Verifying a username and password. (Part 4 of 4.)

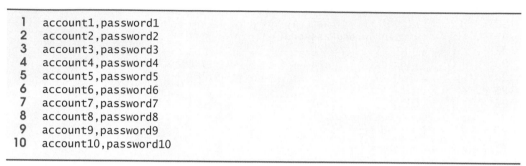

```
 1   account1,password1
 2   account2,password2
 3   account3,password3
 4   account4,password4
 5   account5,password5
 6   account6,password6
 7   account7,password7
 8   account8,password8
 9   account9,password9
10   account10,password10
```

Fig. 26.17 Database `password.txt` containing usernames and passwords.

First, lines 13–16 check whether the user has submitted a form without specifying a username or password. Variable names, when preceded by the **logical negation operator** (!), return `true` if they are empty or are set to 0. **Logical operator OR** (||) returns `true` if either of the operands returns `true` (i.e., if either of the variables is empty or is set to 0). If this is the case, function `fieldsBlank` (lines 144–152) is called, which notifies the client that all form fields must be completed.

We determine whether we are adding a new user (line 19 in Fig. 26.16) by calling **function isset** to test whether variable `$NewUser` has been set. When submitting the XHTML form in `password.html`, the user clicks either the **New User** or **Enter** button. After calling function `extract`, either variable `$NewUser` or variable `$Enter` is created, depending on which button the user clicked. If variable `$NewUser` has been set, lines 22–36 execute. If this variable has not been set, we assume that the user has pressed the **Enter** button, and lines 42–75 execute.

To add a new user, we open the file `password.txt` by calling function **fopen** and assigning the file handle that is returned to variable `$file` (lines 22–23). A **file handle** is a number assigned to the file by the Web server for purposes of identification. Function `fopen` takes two arguments—the name of the file and the mode in which to open it. The possible modes include **r** (read), **w** (write) and **a** (append). Here, we open the file in **a** (append) mode, which opens it for writing, but does not write over the previous contents of the file. If an error occurs in opening the file, function `fopen` does not return a file handle, an error message is printed (lines 27–29) and script execution is terminated by calling function **die** (line 30). If the file opens properly, function `fputs` (line 35) writes the name and password to the file. To specify a new line, we use the newline character (\n). This places each username and password pair on a separate line in the file. In line 36, we pass the variable `$USERNAME` to function `userAdded` (lines 98–106). Function `userAdded` prints a message to the client to indicate that the username and password were added to the file.

If we are not adding a new user, we open the file `password.txt` for reading. This is accomplished by using function `fopen` and assigning the file handle that is returned to variable `$file` (lines 42–43). Lines 44–47 execute if an error occurs in opening the file. The `while` loop (line 54) repeatedly executes the code enclosed in its curly braces (lines 57–75) until the test condition in parentheses evaluates to `false`. Before we enter the `while` loop, we set the value of variable `$userVerified` to 0. In this case, the test condition (line 54) checks to ensure that the end of the file has not been reached and that the user has not been found in the password file. **Logical operator AND (&&)** connects the two conditions. Function **feof**, which determines whether we have reached the end of the specified file, preceded by the logical negation operator (!), returns `true` when there are more lines to be read. When the logical negation operator (!) is applied to the `$userVerified` variable, `true` is returned if the variable is empty or is set to 0.

Each line in `password.txt` consists of a username and password pair that is separated by a comma and followed by a newline character. A line from this file is read using function `fgets` (line 57) and is assigned to variable `$line`. Function `fgets` takes two arguments—the file handle to read, and the maximum number of characters to read. The function reads until a newline character is encountered, the end of the file is encountered or the number of characters read reaches one less than the number specified in the second argument.

For each line read, function **chop** is called (line 60) to remove the newline character from the end of the line. Then function **split** is called to divide the string into substrings at the specified separator, or **delimiter** (in this case, a comma). For example, function `split` returns an array containing ("account1" and "password1") from the first line in `password.txt`. This array is assigned to variable `$field`.

Line 66 determines whether the username entered by the user matches the one returned from the text file (stored in the variable `$field[ 0 ]`). If the condition evaluates to `true`, then the `$userVerified` variable is set to 1, and lines 71–75 execute. Otherwise, the script continues looping through the password file. In line 71, function `checkPassword` (lines 89–95) is called to verify the user's password. Variables `$PASSWORD` and `$field` are passed to the function. Function `checkPassword` compares the user's password to the password in the file. If they match, `true` is returned (line 92), whereas `false` is returned if they do not (line 94). If the condition evaluates to `true`, then function `accessGranted` (lines 110–118) is invoked. Variable `$USERNAME` is passed to the function, and a message notifies the client that permission has been granted. However, if the condition evaluates to `false`, function `wrongPassword` (lines 121–129) is invoked, which notifies the client that an invalid password was entered.

When the `while` loop is complete, either as a result of matching a username or of reaching the end of the file, we are finished reading from `password.txt`. We call function `fclose` (line 80) to close the file. Line 84 checks whether the `$userVerified` variable is empty or has a value of 0, which indicates that the username and password pair was not found in the `password.txt` file. If this returns `true`, function `accessDenied` (lines 132–140) is called. This function notifies the client that access to the server has been denied.

26.7 Connecting to a Database

Databases enable companies to enter the world of e-commerce by maintaining crucial data. Database connectivity allows system administrators to maintain and update such information as user accounts, passwords, credit-card numbers, mailing lists and product inventories. PHP offers built-in support for a wide variety of databases. In this example, we use MySQL. MySQL (located on the CD-ROM accompanying this book) must be installed before running this example. See www.deitel.com/books/iw3HTP3/index.html for instructions on installing and configuring MySQL. Then copy the `Products` directory from the Chapter 26 examples directory on the CD-ROM to the `data` directory located in the directory where MySQL is installed (e.g., `C:\MySQL\data`).

In this example, the client selects a database field name that is sent to the Web server. The PHP script is then executed; the script builds the select query, queries the database and sends a record set in the form of XHTML to the client. The rules and syntax for writing such a query string are discussed in Chapter 22.

Figure 26.18 (`data.html`) is a Web page that `post`s form data containing a database column to the server. PHP script `database.php` (Fig. 26.19) processes the form data.

```
1   <!DOCTYPE html PUBLIC "-//W3C//DTD XHTML 1.0 Transitional//EN"
2      "http://www.w3.org/TR/xhtml1/DTD/xhtml1-transitional.dtd">
3
4   <!-- Fig. 26.18: data.html      -->
5   <!-- Querying a MySQL Database -->
6
7   <html xmlns = "http://www.w3.org/1999/xhtml">
8      <head>
9         <title>Sample Database Query</title>
10     </head>
11
12     <body style = "background-color: #F0E68C">
13        <h2 style = "font-family: arial color: blue">
14           Querying a MySQL database.
15        </h2>
16
17        <form method = "post" action = "database.php">
18           <p>Select a field to display:
19
20              <!-- add a select box containing options -->
21              <!-- for SELECT query                    -->
22              <select name = "select">
23                 <option selected = "selected">*</option>
24                 <option>ID</option>
25                 <option>Title</option>
26                 <option>Category</option>
27                 <option>ISBN</option>
28              </select>
29           </p>
30
31           <input type = "submit" value = "Send Query"
32              style = "background-color: blue;
33              color: yellow; font-weight: bold" />
34        </form>
35     </body>
36  </html>
```

Fig. 26.18   Form to query a MySQL database.

```
1    <!DOCTYPE html PUBLIC "-//W3C//DTD XHTML 1.0 Transitional//EN"
2       "http://www.w3.org/TR/xhtml1/DTD/xhtml1-transitional.dtd">
3
4    <!-- Fig. 26.19: database.php          -->
5    <!-- Program to query a database and -->
6    <!-- send results to the client.       -->
7
8    <html xmlns = "http://www.w3.org/1999/xhtml">
9       <head>
10         <title>Search Results</title>
11      </head>
12
13      <body style = "font-family: arial, sans-serif"
14         style = "background-color: #F0E68C">
15         <?php
16
17            extract( $_POST );
18
19            // build SELECT query
20            $query = "SELECT " . $select . " FROM Books";
21
22            // Connect to MySQL
23            if ( !( $database = mysql_connect( "localhost",
24               "httpd", "" ) ) )
25               die( "Could not connect to database" );
26
27            // open Products database
28            if ( !mysql_select_db( "Products", $database ) )
29               die( "Could not open Products database" );
30
31            // query Products database
32            if ( !( $result = mysql_query( $query, $database ) ) ) {
33               print( "Could not execute query! <br />" );
34               die( mysql_error() );
35            }
36         ?>
37
38         <h3 style = "color: blue">
39         Search Results</h3>
40
41         <table border = "1" cellpadding = "3" cellspacing = "2"
42            style = "background-color: #ADD8E6">
43
44            <?php
45
46               // fetch each record in result set
47               for ( $counter = 0;
48                  $row = mysql_fetch_row( $result );
49                  $counter++ ){
50
51                  // build table to display results
52                  print( "<tr>" );
53
```

Fig. 26.19 Querying a database and displaying the results. (Part 1 of 2.)

```
54                      foreach ( $row as $key => $value )
55                          print( "<td>$value</td>" );
56
57                      print( "</tr>" );
58                  }
59
60              mysql_close( $database );
61          ?>
62
63      </table>
64
65      <br />Your search yielded <strong>
66      <?php print( "$counter" ) ?> results.<br /><br /></strong>
67
68      <h5>Please email comments to
69          <a href = "mailto:deitel@deitel.com">
70              Deitel and Associates, Inc.
71          </a>
72      </h5>
73
74      </body>
75  </html>
```

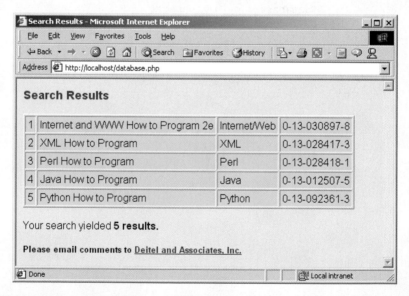

Fig. 26.19   Querying a database and displaying the results. (Part 2 of 2.)

Line 17 (Fig. 26.18) creates an XHTML `form`, specifying that the data submitted from the `form` will be sent to script `database.php` (Fig. 26.19). Lines 22–28 add a select box to the `form`, set the name of the select box to `select`, and set its default selection to `*`. This value specifies that all rows are to be retrieved from the database. Each database column is set as an option in the select box.

Script `database.php` (Fig. 26.19) is responsible for building an SQL query with the specified field name and sending it to the database management system. Line 20 concatenates the posted field name to a SELECT query. Line 23 calls function **mysql_connect** to connect to the MySQL database. We pass three arguments to function mysql_connect—the server's host name, a username and a password. This function returns a **database handle**—a reference to the object that is used to represent PHP's connection to the database—which we assign to variable $database. If the connection to MySQL fails, function die is called, which outputs an error message and terminates the script. Line 28 calls function **mysql_select_db** to specify the database to be queried (in this case, Products). Function die is called if the database cannot be opened. To query the database, line 32 calls function **mysql_query**, specifying the query string and the database to query. Function mysql_query returns an object containing the result of the query, which we assign to variable $result. If the query of the database fails, a message is output to the client indicating that the query failed to execute. Function die is then called, accepting function **mysql_error** as a parameter instead of a string message. In the event that the query fails, function mysql_error returns any error strings from the database. Function mysql_query can also be used to execute SQL statements, such as INSERT or DELETE, that do not return results.

Lines 47–58 use a for loop to iterate through each record in the result set while constructing an XHTML table from the results. The loop condition calls function **mysql_fetch_row** to return an array containing the values for each column of each row in the result of our query ($result). The array is then stored in variable $row. Lines 54–55 use a foreach loop to construct individual cells for each of the columns in the row. The foreach loop takes the name of the array ($row), iterates through each index value of the array ($key) and stores the value in variable $value. Each element of the array is then printed as an individual cell. For each row retrieved, variable $counter is incremented by one. When the end of the result has been reached, undef (false) is returned by function mysql_fetch_row, which terminates the for loop.

After all the rows in the result have been displayed, the database is closed (line 60), and the table's closing tag is written (line 63). The number of rows contained in $counter is printed in line 66. Alternatively, calling function mysql_num_rows($result) would return a count of the number of rows in the result.

26.8 Cookies

A **cookie** is a text file that a Web site stores on a client's computer to maintain information about the client during and between browsing sessions. A Web site can store a cookie on a client's computer to record user preferences and other information that the Web site can retrieve during the client's subsequent visits. For example, many Web sites use cookies to store clients' zip codes. The Web site can retrieve the zip code from the cookie and provide weather reports and news updates tailored to the user's region. Web sites also can use cookies to track information about client activity. Analysis of information collected via cookies can reveal the popularity of Web sites or products. In addition, marketers can use cookies to determine the effects of advertising campaigns.

Web sites store cookies on users' hard drives, which raises issues regarding security and privacy. Web sites should not store critical information, such as credit-card numbers or passwords, in cookies, because cookies are text files that any program can read. Several cookie features address security and privacy concerns. A server can access only the cookies that it has placed on the client. For example, a Web application running on www.deitel.com

cannot access cookies that the Web site www.prenhall.com has placed on the client's computer. A cookie also has an expiration date, after which the Web browser deletes it. Users who are concerned about the privacy and security implications of cookies can disable cookies in their Web browsers. However, the disabling of cookies can make it impossible for the user to interact with Web sites that rely on cookies to function properly.

Microsoft Internet Explorer stores cookies as small text files on the client's hard drive. The information stored in the cookie is sent back to the Web server from which it originated whenever the user requests a Web page from that particular server. The Web server can send the client XHTML output that reflects the preferences or information that is stored in the cookie.

Writing Cookies

Figure 26.20 uses a script to write a cookie to the client's machine. The cookies.html file is used to display an XHTML form that allows a user to enter a name, height and favorite color. When the user clicks the **Write Cookie** button, the cookies.php script (Fig. 26.21) executes.

```
1    <!DOCTYPE html PUBLIC "-//W3C//DTD XHTML 1.0 Transitional//EN"
2       "http://www.w3.org/TR/xhtml1/DTD/xhtml1-transitional.dtd">
3
4    <!-- Fig. 26.20: cookies.html -->
5    <!-- Writing a Cookie          -->
6
7    <html xmlns = "http://www.w3.org/1999/xhtml">
8       <head>
9          <title>Writing a cookie to the client computer</title>
10      </head>
11
12      <body style = "font-family: arial, sans-serif;
13         background-color: #99CCFF">
14
15         <h2>Click Write Cookie to save your cookie data.</h2>
16
17         <form method = "post" action = "cookies.php"
18             style = "font-size: 10pt">
19            <strong>Name:</strong><br />
20            <input type = "text" name = "NAME" /><br />
21
22            <strong>Height:</strong><br />
23            <input type = "text" name = "HEIGHT" /><br />
24
25            <strong>Favorite Color:</strong><br />
26            <input type = "text" name = "COLOR" /><br />
27
28            <input type = "submit" value = "Write Cookie"
29                style = "background-color: #F0E86C; color: navy;
30                font-weight: bold" /></p>
31         </form>
32      </body>
33   </html>
```

Fig. 26.20 Gathering data to be written as a cookie. (Part 1 of 2.)

Fig. 26.20   Gathering data to be written as a cookie. (Part 2 of 2.)

```php
1   <?php
2      // Fig. 26.21: cookies.php
3      // Program to write a cookie to a client's machine
4
5      extract( $_POST );
6      // write each form field's value to a cookie and set the
7      // cookie's expiration date
8      setcookie( "Name", $NAME, time() + 60 * 60 * 24 * 5 );
9      setcookie( "Height", $HEIGHT, time() + 60 * 60 * 24 * 5 );
10     setcookie( "Color", $COLOR, time() + 60 * 60 * 24 * 5 );
11  ?>
12
13  <!DOCTYPE html PUBLIC "-//W3C//DTD XHTML 1.0 Transitional//EN"
14     "http://www.w3.org/TR/xhtml1/DTD/xhtml1-transitional.dtd">
15
16  <html xmlns = "http://www.w3.org/1999/xhtml">
17     <head>
18        <title>Cookie Saved</title>
19     </head>
20
21     <body style = "font-family: arial, sans-serif">
22        <p>The cookie has been set with the following data:</p>
23
24        <!-- print each form field's value -->
25        <br /><span style = "color: blue">Name:</span>
26           <?php print( $NAME ) ?><br />
27
28        <span style = "color: blue">Height:</span>
29           <?php print( $HEIGHT ) ?><br />
30
31        <span style = "color: blue">Favorite Color:</span>
```

Fig. 26.21   Writing a cookie to the client. (Part 1 of 2.)

```
32
33          <span style = "color: <?php print( "$COLOR\">$COLOR" ) ?>
34          </span><br />
35          <p>Click <a href = "readCookies.php">here</a>
36             to read the saved cookie.</p>
37       </body>
38    </html>
```

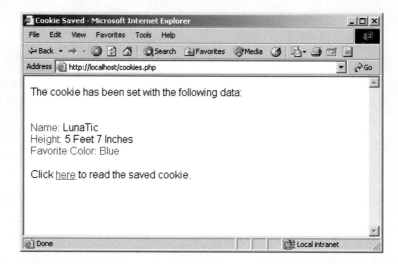

Fig. 26.21 Writing a cookie to the client. (Part 2 of 2.)

Software Engineering Observation 26.3

Some clients do not accept cookies. When a client declines a cookie, the browser application normally informs the client that the site may not function correctly without cookies enabled.

Software Engineering Observation 26.4

Cookies cannot be used to retrieve e-mail addresses or data from the hard drive of a client's computer.

Script `cookies.php` (Fig. 26.21) calls function **setcookie** (lines 8–10) to set the cookies to the values passed from `cookies.html`. Function `setcookie` prints XHTML header information; therefore, it needs to be called before any other XHTML (including comments) is printed.

Function `setcookie` takes the name of the cookie to be set as the first argument, followed by the value to be stored in the cookie. For example, line 8 sets the name of the cookie to `"Name"` and the value to variable `$NAME`, which is passed to the script from `cookies.html`. The optional third argument indicates the expiration date of the cookie. In this example, we set the cookies to expire in five days by taking the current time, which is returned by function **time**, and adding the number of seconds after which the cookie is to expire (60 seconds/minute * 60 minutes/hour * 24 hours/day * 5 = 5 days). If no expiration date is specified, the cookie only lasts until the end of the current session, which is the total time until the user closes the browser. If only the `name` argument is passed to function `set-cookie`, the cookie is deleted from the client's computer. Lines 13–38 send a Web page to the client indicating that the cookie has been written and listing the values that are stored in the cookie.

When using Internet Explorer, cookies are stored in the **Cookies** directory on the client's machine. Figure 26.22 shows the contents of this directory (for a Windows 2000 user luna tic) prior to the execution of cookies.php. After the cookie is written, a text file is added to the directory. In Fig. 26.23, the file luna tic@localhost[1].txt appears in the **Cookies** directory. [*Note*: The name of the file created will vary from user to user.]

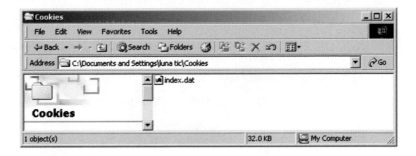

Fig. 26.22 Cookies directory before a cookie is written.

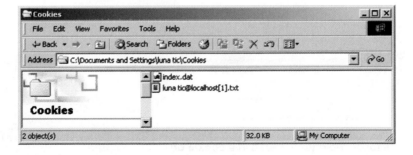

Fig. 26.23 Cookies directory after a cookie is written.

Reading an Existing Cookie
Figure 26.24 (readCookies.php) reads the cookie that is written in Fig. 26.21 and displays the cookie's information in a table. PHP creates the superglobal array $_COOKIE, which contains all the cookie values indexed by their names, similar to the values stored in array $_POST when an XHTML form is posted (see Section 26.5).

```
1   <!DOCTYPE html PUBLIC "-//W3C//DTD XHTML 1.0 Transitional//EN"
2      "http://www.w3.org/TR/xhtml1/DTD/xhtml1-transitional.dtd">
3
4   <!-- Fig. 26.24: readCookies.php                          -->
5   <!-- Program to read cookies from the client's computer -->
6
7   <html xmlns = "http://www.w3.org/1999/xhtml">
```

Fig. 26.24 Displaying the cookie's contents. (Part 1 of 2.)

```
8      <head><title>Read Cookies</title></head>
9
10     <body style = "font-family: arial, sans-serif">
11
12        <p>
13           <strong>
14              The following data is saved in a cookie on your
15              computer.
16           </strong>
17        </p>
18
19        <table border = "5" cellspacing = "0" cellpadding = "10">
20           <?php
21
22              // iterate through array $_COOKIE and print
23              // name and value of each cookie
24              foreach ( $_COOKIE as $key => $value )
25                 print( "<tr>
26                    <td bgcolor=\"#F0E68C\">$key</td>
27                    <td bgcolor=\"#FFA500\">$value</td>
28                    </tr>" );
29           ?>
30
31        </table>
32     </body>
33  </html>
```

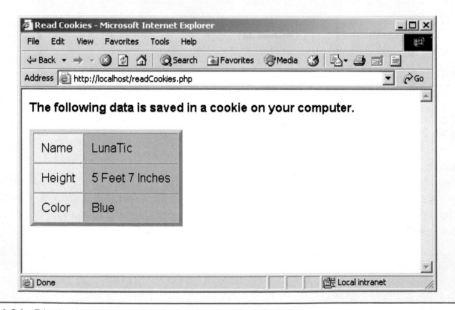

Fig. 26.24 Displaying the cookie's contents. (Part 2 of 2.)

Lines 24–28 iterate through the $_COOKIE array using a foreach loop, printing out the name and value of each cookie in an XHTML table. The foreach loop takes the name of the array ($_COOKIE) and iterates through each index value of the array ($key). In this case, the index values are the names of the cookies. Each element is then stored in variable $value, and these values become the individual cells of the table.

We could have also used the function extract to create individual variables out of the key-value pairs in $_COOKIE, just as we did with $_POST. For example, after the function extract($_COOKIE) is called, the value of a cookie set with the name "Color" is assigned to variable $Color.

26.9 Dynamic Content in PHP

Of PHP's many strengths as a server-side scripting language, perhaps the greatest lies in its ability to dynamically change XHTML output based on user input. In this section, we build on the example presented in Section 26.5, combining the XHTML form of Fig. 26.13 and the PHP script of Fig. 26.14 into one dynamic PHP document. The form in Fig. 26.25 is created using a series of loops, arrays and conditionals. We add error checking to each of the text input fields and inform the user of invalid entries on the form itself, rather than on an error page. If an error exists, the script maintains the previously submitted values in each form element. Finally, after the form has been successfully completed, we store the input from the user in a MySQL database. We recommend reading Sections 26.5 and 26.7 before reading this section, as coverage of much of the functionality introduced in Sections 26.5 and 26.7 is not repeated in this example. Before running the following example, make sure MySQL is installed, then copy the MailingList directory from the Chapter 26 examples directory to the MySQL data directory (e.g., C:\MySQL\data).

```
1   <!DOCTYPE html PUBLIC "-//W3C//DTD XHTML 1.0 Transitional//EN"
2      "http://www.w3.org/TR/xhtml1/DTD/xhtml1-transitional.dtd">
3
4   <!-- Fig. 26.25: dynamicForm.php              -->
5   <!-- Form for use with the form.php program -->
6
7   <html xmlns = "http://www.w3.org/1999/xhtml">
8      <head>
9         <title>Sample form to take user input in XHTML</title>
10   </head>
11
12   <body>
13      <?php
14         extract ( $_POST );
15         $iserror = false;
16
17         // array of book titles
18         $booklist = array( "Internet and WWW How to Program 3e",
19            "C++ How to Program 4e",
20            "Java How to Program 5e",
21            "XML How to Program 1e" );
22
23         // array of possible operating systems
24         $systemlist = array( "Windows XP",
25            "Windows 2000",
26            "Windows 98",
```

Fig. 26.25 Dynamic form using PHP. (Part 1 of 6.)

```
27              "Linux",
28              "Other");
29
30          // array of name and alt values for the text input fields
31          $inputlist = array( "fname" => "First Name",
32              "lname" => "Last Name",
33              "email" => "Email",
34              "phone" => "Phone" );
35
36          if ( isset ( $submit ) ) {
37              if ( $fname == "" ) {
38                  $formerrors[ "fnameerror" ] = true;
39                  $iserror = true;
40              }
41
42              if ( $lname == "" ) {
43                  $formerrors[ "lnameerror" ] = true;
44                  $iserror = true;
45              }
46
47              if ( $email == "" ) {
48                  $formerrors[ "emailerror" ] = true;
49                  $iserror = true;
50              }
51
52              if ( !ereg( "^\([0-9]{3}\)[0-9]{3}-[0-9]{4}$", $phone ) ) {
53                  $formerrors[ "phoneerror" ] = true;
54                  $iserror = true;
55              }
56
57              if ( !$iserror ) {
58
59                  // build INSERT query
60                  $query = "INSERT INTO contacts " .
61                      "( LastName, FirstName, Email, Phone, Book, OS ) " .
62                      "VALUES ( '$lname', '$fname', '$email', " .
63                      "'" . quotemeta( $phone ) . "', '$book', '$os' )";
64
65                  // Connect to MySQL
66                  if ( !( $database = mysql_connect( "localhost",
67                      "httpd", "" ) ) )
68                      die( "Could not connect to database" );
69
70                  // open MailingList database
71                  if ( !mysql_select_db( "MailingList", $database ) )
72                      die( "Could not open MailingList database" );
73
74                  // execute query in MailingList database
75                  if ( !( $result = mysql_query( $query, $database ) ) ) {
76                      print( "Could not execute query! <br />" );
77                      die( mysql_error() );
78                  }
79
```

Fig. 26.25 Dynamic form using PHP. (Part 2 of 6.)

```
80              print( "<p>Hi
81                  <span style = 'color: blue'>
82                  <strong>$fname</strong></span>.
83                  Thank you for completing the survey.<br />
84
85                  You have been added to the
86                  <span style = 'color: blue'>
87                  <strong>$book</strong></span>
88                  mailing list.
89                  </p>
90                  <strong>The following information has been saved
91                  in our database:</strong><br />
92
93                  <table border = '0' cellpadding = '0' cellspacing = '10'>
94                  <tr>
95                  <td bgcolor = '#ffffaa'>Name</td>
96                  <td bgcolor = '#ffffbb'>Email</td>
97                  <td bgcolor = '#ffffcc'>Phone</td>
98                  <td bgcolor = '#ffffdd'>OS</td>
99                  </tr>
100                 <tr>
101
102                 <!-- print each form field's value -->
103                 <td>$fname $lname</td>
104                 <td>$email</td>
105                 <td>$phone</td>
106                 <td>$os</td>
107                 </tr></table>
108
109                 <br /><br /><br />
110                 <div style = 'font-size: 10pt; text-align: center'>
111                 <div style = 'font-size : 18pt'>
112                 <a href = 'formDatabase.php'>
113                 Click here to view entire database.</a></div>
114                 This is only a sample form.
115                 You have not been added to a mailing list.
116                 </div></body></html>" );
117             die();
118         }
119     }
120
121     print( "<h1>This is a sample registration form.</h1>
122         Please fill in all fields and click Register." );
123
124     if ( $iserror ) {
125         print( "<br /><span style = 'color : red'>
126             Fields with * need to be filled in properly.</span>" );
127     }
128
129     print( "<!-- post form data to form.php -->
130         <form method = 'post' action = 'dynamicform.php'>
131         <img src = 'images/user.gif' alt = 'User' /><br />
132         <span style = 'color: blue'>
```

Fig. 26.25   Dynamic form using PHP. (Part 3 of 6.)

```
133            Please fill out the fields below.<br />
134            </span>
135
136            <!-- create four text boxes for user input -->" );
137        foreach ( $inputlist as $inputname => $inputalt ) {
138           $inputtext = $inputvalues[ $inputname ];
139
140           print( "<img src = 'images/$inputname.gif'
141              alt = '$inputalt' /><input type = 'text'
142              name = '$inputname' value = '" . $$inputname . "' />" );
143
144           if ( $formerrors[ ( $inputname )."error" ] == true )
145              print( "<span style = 'color : red'>*</span>" );
146
147           print( "<br />" );
148        }
149
150        print( "<span style = 'font-size : 10pt" );
151
152        if ( $formerrors[ "phoneerror" ] )
153           print( "; color : red" );
154
155        print( "'>Must be in the form (555)555-5555
156           </span><br /><br />
157
158           <img src = 'images/downloads.gif'
159           alt = 'Publications' /><br />
160
161           <span style = 'color: blue'>
162           Which book would you like information about?
163           </span><br />
164
165           <!-- create drop-down list containing book names -->
166           <select name = 'book'>" );
167
168        foreach ( $booklist as $currbook ) {
169           print( "<option" );
170
171           if ( ( $currbook == $book ) )
172              print( " selected = 'true'" );
173
174           print( ">$currbook</option>" );
175        }
176
177        print( "</select><br /><br />
178           <img src = 'images/os.gif' alt = 'Operating System' />
179           <br /><span style = 'color: blue'>
180           Which operating system are you currently using?
181           <br /></span>
182
183           <!-- create five radio buttons -->" );
184
185        $counter = 0;
```

Fig. 26.25 Dynamic form using PHP. (Part 4 of 6.)

```
186
187     foreach ( $systemlist as $currsystem ) {
188        print( "<input type = 'radio' name = 'os'
189           value = '$currsystem'" );
190
191        if ( $currsystem == $os ) print( "checked = 'checked'" );
192        if ( $iserror && $counter == 0 ) print( "checked = 'checked'" );
193
194        print( " />$currsystem" );
195
196        if ( $counter == 2 ) print( "<br />" );
197        $counter++;
198     }
199
200     print( "<!-- create a submit button -->
201        <br />
202        <input type = 'submit' name = 'submit' value = 'Register' />
203        </form></body></html>" );
204  ?>
```

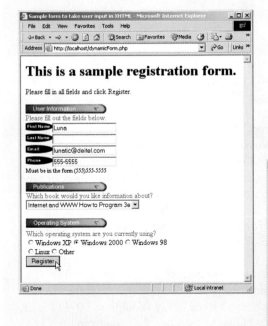

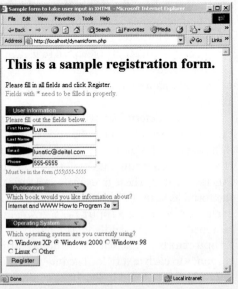

Fig. 26.25 Dynamic form using PHP. (Part 5 of 6.)

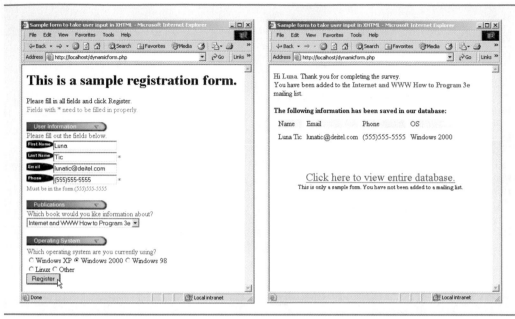

Fig. 26.25 Dynamic form using PHP. (Part 6 of 6.)

Lines 18–34 create three arrays, `$booklist`, `$systemlist` and `$inputlist`, that are used to dynamically create the form's input fields. We specify that the form created in this document is self-submitting (i.e., it posts to itself) by setting the `action` to `'dynamicform.php'` in line 130. [*Note:* We enclose XHTML attribute values within the string argument of a `print` statement in single quotes so that they do not interfere with the double quotes that delimit the string. We could alternatively have used the escape sequence `\"` to print double quotes instead of single quotes.] Line 36 uses function `isset` to determine whether the **Register** button has been pressed. If it has, each of the text input fields' values is validated. If an error is detected (e.g., a text field is blank, or the phone number is improperly formatted), an entry is added to array `$formerrors` containing a key corresponding to the field name with the error and a value of `true`. Also, variable `$iserror` is set to `true`.

Line 57 determines whether any errors were detected. If `$iserror` is `false` (i.e., there were no input errors), the code that displays the page indicating that the form was submitted successfully executes (lines 60–117). We will more to say about lines 60–117 later. If `$iserror` is `true`, the script from lines 60–117 is skipped, and the code from lines 121–203 is executed. These lines include a series of `print` statements and conditionals to output the form, as seen in Fig. 26.25. Lines 137–148 use a `foreach` statement to iterate through each element in the `$inputlist` array. In line 138 the value of variable `$inputtext` is assigned to the text field's `value` attribute. If the form has not yet been submitted, variable `$inputtext`'s value will be the empty string `""`. Lines 140–141 output the image that corresponds to each text field. The image `src` is set to `'images/$inputname.gif'` because the images are stored in the `images` directory, and each image shares the name of its corresponding text field with the addition of a `.gif` extension. Lines 141–142 initialize the input text field. The text field's `name` attribute is set to variable `$inputname`.

In line 142 we encounter the **$$*variable*** notation for specifying **variable variables**. PHP permits the use of variable variables to allow developers to reference variables dynamically. The expression $$*variable* could also be written as ${$*variable*} for added clarity. Developers can use this expression to obtain the value of the variable whose name is equal to the value of $*variable*. PHP first determines the value of $*variable*, then appends this value to the leading $ to form the identifier of the variable the developer wishes to reference dynamically. For example, in the foreach loop in lines 137–148, we write $$inputname to reference the value of each form field variable. During the third execution of the body of the foreach loop, $inputname contains the value "email". Therefore, PHP replaces $inputname in the expression $$inputname (which could be written as ${$input-name}) with the string "email", essentially forming the expression ${"email"}. The entire expression then evaluates to the value of the variable $email. Thus, the variable $email, which stores the value of the e-mail text field after the form has been submitted, is dynamically referenced. This dynamic variable reference is added to the string as the value of the input field (using the concatenation operator) to maintain any possible previous input over multiple submissions of the form.

Lines 144–145 add a red asterisk next to the text input fields that have been filled out incorrectly (assuming the user has already submitted the form). Lines 152–153 color the phone instructions red if the user entered an invalid phone number by adding color: red to the surrounding div element's style attribute.

Lines 168–175 and 187–198 both use a foreach loop to generate options for the book drop-down list and operating-system radio buttons, respectively. Lines 171–172 and 191 ensure that the previously selected or checked element (if one exists) remains selected or checked over multiple attempts to correctly fill out the form. These pieces of code achieve this by comparing the currently stored value for each form element to the form element that is currently being output. If these two values are equal, the script inserts the appropriate attribute to select or check that element. If no previous selections exist, the conditions in lines 171 and 191 will always be false, and the default selections will appear in the Web page.

If the form has been filled out correctly, lines 60–78 enter the form information into the MySQL database MailingList using an INSERT statement. Please refer to Chapter 22 for information on writing this and other SQL statements. Line 63 uses the **quotemeta** function to insert a backslash (\) before any special characters in the passed string. We must use this function so that MySQL does not interpret the parentheses in the phone number as having a special meaning aside from being part of a value to insert into the database. Lines 80–116 generate the Web page indicating a successful form submission, which also provides a link to formDatabase.php (Fig. 26.26). formDatabase.php displays the contents of the MailingList database (similar to Fig. 26.20).

```
1   <!DOCTYPE html PUBLIC "-//W3C//DTD XHTML 1.0 Transitional//EN"
2      "http://www.w3.org/TR/xhtml1/DTD/xhtml1-transitional.dtd">
3
4   <!-- Fig. 26.26: formDatabase.php          -->
5   <!-- Program to query a database and -->
6   <!-- send results to the client.       -->
7
```

Fig. 26.26 Displaying the MailingList database. (Part 1 of 3.)

```
8    <html xmlns = "http://www.w3.org/1999/xhtml">
9       <head>
10         <title>Search Results</title>
11      </head>
12
13      <body style = "font-family: arial, sans-serif"
14         style = "background-color: #F0E68C">
15         <?php
16
17            extract( $_POST );
18
19            // build SELECT query
20            $query = "SELECT * FROM contacts";
21
22            // Connect to MySQL
23            if ( !( $database = mysql_connect( "localhost",
24               "httpd", "" ) ) )
25               die( "Could not connect to database" );
26
27            // open MailingList database
28            if ( !mysql_select_db( "MailingList", $database ) )
29               die( "Could not open MailingList database" );
30
31            // query MailingList database
32            if ( !( $result = mysql_query( $query, $database ) ) ) {
33               print( "Could not execute query! <br />" );
34               die( mysql_error() );
35            }
36         ?>
37
38         <h3 style = "color: blue">
39         Mailing List Contacts</h3>
40
41         <table border = "1" cellpadding = "3" cellspacing = "2"
42            style = "background-color: #ADD8E6">
43
44            <tr>
45               <td>ID</td>
46               <td>Last Name</td>
47               <td>First Name</td>
48               <td>E-mail Address</td>
49               <td>Phone Number</td>
50               <td>Book</td>
51               <td>Operating System</td>
52            </tr>
53            <?php
54
55               // fetch each record in result set
56               for ( $counter = 0;
57                  $row = mysql_fetch_row( $result );
58                  $counter++ ){
59
60                  // build table to display results
```

Fig. 26.26 Displaying the MailingList database. (Part 2 of 3.)

```
61                         print( "<tr>" );
62
63                         foreach ( $row as $key => $value )
64                             print( "<td>$value</td>" );
65
66                         print( "</tr>" );
67                     }
68
69                     mysql_close( $database );
70                 ?>
71
72             </table>
73
74         </body>
75     </html>
```

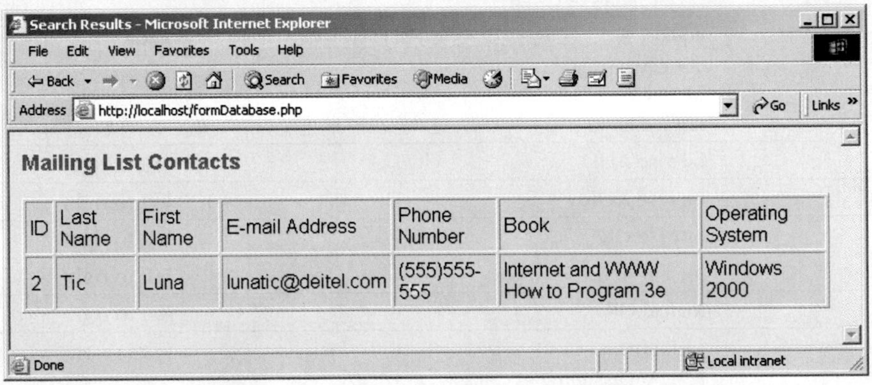

Fig. 26.26 Displaying the `MailingList` database. (Part 3 of 3.)

26.10 Operator Precedence Chart

This section contains the operator precedence chart for PHP. In Fig. 26.27, the operators are shown from top to bottom in decreasing order of precedence.

Operator	Type	Associativity
new	constructor	none
[]	subscript	right to left
~ ! ++ -- - @	bitwise not not increment decrement unary negative error control	right to left

Fig. 26.27 PHP operator precedence and associativity. (Part 1 of 2.)

Operator	Type	Associativity
* / %	multiplication division modulus	left to right
+ - .	addition subtraction concatenation	left to right
<< >>	bitwise shift left bitwise shift right	left to right
< > <= >=	less than greater than less than or equal greater than or equal	none
== != === !==	equal not equal identical not identical	none
&	bitwise AND	left to right
∧	bitwise XOR	left to right
|	bitwise OR	left to right
&&	logical AND	left to right
||	logical OR	left to right
= += -= *= /= &= |= ∧= .= <<= >>=	assignment addition assignment subtraction assignment multiplication assignment division assignment bitwise AND assignment bitwise OR assignment bitwise exclusive OR assignment concatenation assignment bitwise shift left assignment bitwise shift right assignment	left to right
and	logical AND	left to right
xor	exclusive OR	left to right
or	logical OR	left to right
,	list	left to right

Fig. 26.27 PHP operator precedence and associativity. (Part 2 of 2.)

26.11 Web Resources

www.php.net
This official PHP site contains the latest versions of PHP, as well as documentation, a list of FAQs, support and links to many other PHP resources.

www.zend.com
The home of *Zend Technologies*, the developers of the Zend scripting engine. The site also provides code, tips and applications for PHP developers.

www.phpbuilder.com
Contains resources for PHP developers. It also includes a search feature and provides links to articles, code and forums.

www.phpworld.com
Provides PHP-related resources, including articles, documentation, links and a help board.

php.resourceindex.com
Provides access to the PHP community, helping visitors find jobs, chats, developer sites and more. The code section of the site contains scripts, functions and classes. In addition, visitors can sign up to receive e-mail updates regarding new resources.

www.phpwizard.net
Contains resources for PHP development. It provides tutorials, links and many other resources.

SUMMARY

- PHP is an open-source technology that is supported by a large community of users and developers. PHP is platform independent; implementations exist for all major UNIX, Linux and Windows operating systems.

- PHP code is embedded directly into XHTML documents and provides support for a wide variety of different databases. PHP scripts typically have the file extension .php.

- In PHP, code is inserted in special scripting delimiters that begin with <?php and end with ?>.

- Variables are preceded by a $. A variable is created automatically when it is first encountered by the PHP interpreter.

- PHP statements are terminated with a semicolon (;). Comments begin with two forward slashes (//). Text to the right of the slashes is ignored by the interpreter.

- When a variable is encountered inside a double-quoted ("") string, PHP uses interpolation to replace the variable with its associated data.

- PHP variables are multitype, meaning that they can contain different types of data—integers, floating-point numbers or strings.

- Casting converts between data types without changing the value of the variable itself. Function settype converts between data types by changing the value of the variable, which may result in data loss.

- The concatenation operator (.) appends the string on the right of the operator to the string on the left.

- Uninitialized variables have the value undef, which evaluates to different values, depending on the context. When undef is used in a numeric context, it evaluates to 0. When undef is interpreted in a string context, it evaluates to an empty string ("").

- Strings are automatically converted to integers when they are used in arithmetic operations.

- PHP provides the capability to store data in arrays. Arrays are divided into elements that behave like individual variables. Array names also are preceded by a $.

- Individual array elements are accessed by following the array-variable name with the index number in braces ([]). If a value is assigned to an array that does not exist, the array is created.

- In addition to integer indices, arrays can also have nonnumeric indices. Arrays with string indices are called associative arrays.

- Function count returns the number of elements in the array. Function array takes a list of arguments and returns an array. Function array may also be used to initialize arrays with string indices.

- Function `reset` sets the iterator to the first element of the array. Function `key` returns the index of the current element. Function `next` moves the iterator to the next element.
- The `foreach` loop is designed specifically for iterating through arrays.
- Text manipulation in PHP is usually done with regular expressions—a series of characters that serve as pattern-matching templates (or search criteria) in strings, text files and databases. This feature allows complex searching and string processing to be performed using relatively simple expressions.
- Function `strcmp` compares two strings. If the first string alphabetically precedes the second string, -1 is returned. If the strings are equal, 0 is returned. If the first string alphabetically follows the second string, 1 is returned.
- Relational operators (==, !=, <, <=, > and >=) can be used to compare strings. These operators can also be used for numerical comparison of integers and doubles.
- For more powerful string comparisons, PHP provides functions `ereg` and `preg_match`, which use regular expressions to search a string for a specified pattern.
- Function `ereg` uses POSIX extended regular expressions, whereas function `preg_match` provides Perl-compatible regular expressions.
- The caret (^) matches the beginning of a string. A dollar sign ($) searches for the specified pattern at the end of the string. The period (.) is a special character that is used to match any single character. The \ character is an escape character in regular expressions.
- Bracket expressions are lists of characters enclosed in square brackets ([ ]) that match a single character from the list. Ranges can be specified by supplying the beginning and the end of the range separated by a dash (-).
- The special bracket expressions [[:<:]] and [[:>:]] match the beginning and end of a word.
- Character class [[:alpha:]] matches any alphabetic character.
- The quantifier + matches one or more instances of the preceding expression.
- Function `ereg_replace` takes three arguments—the pattern to search, a string to replace the matched string and the string to search.
- PHP stores environment variables and their values in the $_ENV array. Individual array variables can be accessed directly by using an element's key from the $_ENV array as a variable.
- Values sent from an XHTML form to a PHP script appear in the superglobal arrays $_POST or $_GET.
- Function `extract( associativeArray )` creates a variable-value pair corresponding to each key-value pair in *associativeArray*.
- Function `die` terminates script execution.
- Passing a string argument to the `die` function prints that string a message before stopping program execution.
- Function `isset` tests whether a variable has been set.
- Function `fopen` opens a text file.
- A filehandle is a number that the server assigns to the file and is used when the server accesses the file.
- Function `fopen` takes two arguments—the name of the file and the mode in which to open the file. The possible modes include `read`, `write` and `append`.
- Function `feof` returns `true` when the end of a file is reached.
- A line from a text file is read using function `fgets`. This function takes two arguments—the file handle to read and the maximum number of characters to read.

- Function `chop` removes newline characters from the end of a line. Function `split` divides a string into substrings at the specified separator or delimiter. Function `fclose` closes a file.

- Function `mysql_connect` connects to a MySQL database. This function returns a database handle—a reference to the object that is used to represent PHP's connection to the database. Function `mysql_query` returns an object that contains the result set of the query. Function `mysql_error` returns any error strings from the database if the query fails. Function `mysql_fetch_row` returns an array that contains the elements of each row in the result set of a query.

- Cookies maintain state information for each client who uses a Web browser. Cookies are often used to record user preferences or other information that will be retrieved during the client's subsequent visits to a Web site. On the server side, cookies can be used to track information about client activity.

- The data stored in the cookie is sent back to the Web server where it originated whenever the user requests a Web page from that server.

- Function `setcookie` sets a cookie. Function `setcookie` takes as the first argument the name of the cookie to be set, followed by the value to be stored in the cookie.

- PHP creates variables containing contents of a cookie, similar to when values are posted via forms.

- PHP creates array `$_COOKIE`, which contains all the cookie values indexed by their names.

- Of PHP's many strengths as a server-side scripting language, perhaps the greatest lies in its ability to dynamically change its XHTML output in reaction to user input.

- The $$*variable* notation allows developers to refer to variables dynamically.

- The `quotemeta` function inserts a backslash before any special characters in the string passed as a parameter.

TERMINOLOGY

$ metacharacter
∧ metacharacter
* metacharacter
$$*variable* notation for variable variables
`append`
`array` function
`as`
assignment operator (=)
associative array
backslash
bracket expression
caret metacharacter (∧) in PHP
character class
`chop` function
comparison operator
concatenation operator
`$_COOKIE`
`count` function
`current` function
database connectivity
database handle
delimiter
`die` function
environment variable

equality operator
`ereg` function
`ereg_replace` function
`eregi` function
`extract`
`fclose` function
`feof` function
`fgets` function
filehandle
`fopen` function
`foreach` loop
`fputs` function
`$_GET`
`$GLOBALS` array
HTTP connection
HTTP host
Hypertext Preprocessor
index value
interpolation
`isset` function
`key` function
literal character
logical AND operator (&&)
logical OR operator (||)

logical negation operator (!)
metacharacter
MySQL
mysql_connect function
mysql_error function
mysql_fetch_row function
mysql_query function
mysql_selectdb function
newline character
next function
parenthetical memory in PHP
Perl-compatible regular expression
PHP (PHP: Hypertext Preprocessor)
PHP comment
PHP keyword
pos function
POSIX extended regular expression
$_POST
preg_match function
print function

printf function
quantifier
quotemeta
read
regular expression
reset
result set
setcookie function
settype function
split function
SQL query string
strcmp function
string context
superglobal array
typecasting operator
undef
validation
Web server
while loop
write

SELF-REVIEW EXERCISES

26.1 State whether each of the following is *true* or *false*. If *false*, explain why.
   a) PHP code is embedded directly into XHTML.
   b) PHP function names are case sensitive.
   c) The settype function only temporarily changes the type of a variable.
   d) Conversion between data types happens automatically when a variable is used in a context that requires a different data type.
   e) The foreach loop is designed specifically for iterating over arrays.
   f) Relational operators can be used for alphabetic and numeric comparison.
   g) The quantifier +, when used in a regular expression, matches any number of the preceding pattern.
   h) Opening a file in append mode causes the file to be overwritten.
   i) Cookies are stored on the server computer.
   j) The * arithmetic operator has higher precedence than the + operator.

26.2 Fill in the blanks in each of the following statements:
   a) PHP scripts typically have the file extension _____.
   b) The two numeric data types that PHP variables can store are _____ and _____.
   c) In PHP, uninitialized variables have the value _____.
   d) _____ are divided into individual elements, each of which acts like an individual variable.
   e) Function _____ returns the total number of elements in an array.
   f) To use Perl-compatible regular expressions, use the _____ function.
   g) A(n) _____ in a regular expression matches a predefined set of characters.
   h) PHP stores all environment variables in array _____.
   i) Function _____ terminates script execution.
   j) _____ can be used to maintain state information on a client's computer.

ANSWERS TO SELF-REVIEW EXERCISES

26.1 a) True. b) False. Function names are not case sensitive. c) False. Function `settype` permanently changes the type of a variable. d) True. e) True. f) True. g) False. The quantifier + matches one or more of the preceding patterns. h) False. Opening a file in `write` mode causes the file to be overwritten. i) False. Cookies are stored on the client's computer. j) True.

26.2 a) `.php`. b) integers, double. c) `undef`. d) Arrays. e) `count`. f) `preg_match`. g) character class. h) `$_ENV`. i) `die`. j) Cookies.

EXERCISES

26.3 Identify and correct the error in each of the following PHP code examples:

a)

```php
<?php print( "Hello World" ); // printing text ?>
```

b)

```php
<?php
    $name = "Paul";
    print( "$Name" );
?>
```

26.4 How can a PHP program determine the type of browser that a Web client is using?

26.5 Describe how input from an XHTML `form` is retrieved in a PHP program.

26.6 Describe how a text file can be opened and the different modes used to read/write to/from the file.

26.7 Describe how cookies can be used to store information on a computer and how the information can be retrieved by a PHP program. Assume that cookies are not disabled on the client.

26.8 Write a PHP program named `states.php` that creates a variable `$states` with the value `"Mississippi Alabama Texas Massachusetts Kansas"`. Write a program that does the following:
   a) Search for a word in `$states` that ends in `xas`. Store this word in element 0 of an array named `$statesArray`.
   b) Search for a word in `$states` that begins with `k` and ends in `s`. Perform a case-insensitive comparison. Store this word in element 1 of `$statesArray`.
   c) Search for a word in `$states` that begins with `M` and ends in `s`. Store this element in element 2 of the array.
   d) Search for a word in `$states` that ends in `a`. Store this word in element 3 of the array.
   e) Search for a word in `$states` at the beginning of the string that starts with `M`. Store this word in element 4 of the array.
   f) Output the array `$statesArray` to the screen.

26.9 In the text, we presented environment variables. Develop a program that determines whether the client is using Internet Explorer. If so, determine the version number and send this information back to the client.

26.10 Modify the program in Fig. 26.14 to save information sent to the server into a text file. Each time a user submits a form, open the text file and print the file's contents.

26.11 Write a PHP program that tests whether an e-mail address is input correctly. Verify that the input begins with series of characters, followed by the @ character, another series of characters, a period (.) and a final series of characters. Test your program, using both valid and invalid e-mail addresses.

26.12 Using environment variables, write a program that logs the address (obtained with the REMOTE_ADDR key in the $_SERVER array) requesting information from the Web server.

26.13 Write a PHP program that obtains a URL and its description from a user and stores the information into a database using MySQL. The database should be named URLs, and the table should be named Urltable. The first field of the database, which is named URL, should contain an actual URL, and the second, which is named Description, should contain a description of the URL. Use www.deitel.com as the first URL, and input Cool site! as its description. The second URL should be www.php.net, and the description should be The official PHP site. After each new URL is submitted, print the complete results of the database in a table.

27

Macromedia ColdFusion® MX

Objectives

- To create basic ColdFusion templates.
- To use ColdFusion Markup Language tags and functions to add dynamic functionality to Web pages.
- To use information collected from Web forms.
- To create a database-driven bookstore application.
- To create a shopping cart for the bookstore that follows a user through the site.

We should be careful to get out of an experience only the wisdom that is in it—and stop there, lest we be like the cat that sits down on a hot stove lid. She will never sit down on a hot stove lid again…
Mark Twain

I do not ask you much:
I beg cold comfort.
William Shakespeare

There is a basic principle that distinguishes a hot medium like radio from a cool one like the telephone, or a hot medium like the movie from a cool one like TV…Hot media are…low in participation, and cool media are high in participation or completion by the audience.
Marshall Herbert McLuhan

Outline

27.1 Introduction

Welcome to **ColdFusion**! ColdFusion is a popular Web application server that uses a simple tag-based format to enable quick and easy dynamic Web-site development. ColdFusion was originally developed by Allaire, a software engineering firm later acquired by Macromedia. The popularity of ColdFusion lies in its server-side, tag-based **ColdFusion Markup Language** (CFML). CFML is based around a set of tags that work like XHTML tags, making it easy to learn for most Web-site developers. In addition, CFML's support for XML, **ColdFusion Components** (CFCs) and Web services makes CFML as rich as a full-scale programming language. A file created using CFML is saved with a `.cfm` extension, and is referred to as a **ColdFusion template**.

ColdFusion MX 6.1 is a software package available from Macromedia providing a **CFML interpreter** and the **ColdFusion Administrator** that can be installed on most Web servers. Macromedia's ColdFusion MX 6.1 is available for Windows, Mac OS X, Linux and several other UNIX-based operating systems. A 30-day trial version, which turns into a developer edition upon expiration, is included on the CD that accompanies the book. [*Note*: The developer edition of ColdFusion MX 6.1 is a fully functional, free version of the software, intended for educational and development use only. Web applications created using this version can be accessed only from one IP address.]

ColdFusion MX must be installed for a Web server to handle requests for CFML templates, including the examples in this chapter. ColdFusion MX includes a simplified Web server for developing ColdFusion templates. We will use this server for the chapter examples. The default install directory for the server is `C:\CFusionMX` on Windows or `/opt/coldfusionmx` on UNIX platforms. All source and image files should be copied to `C:\CFusionMX\wwwroot` on Windows or `/opt/coldfusionmx/wwwroot` on UNIX platforms. [*Note*: The source code and images for all the examples in this chapter can be found on the CD that accompanies this book and on `www.deitel.com`.]

27.2 Simple ColdFusion Example: Clock

We introduce ColdFusion with a simple example (Fig. 27.1) that displays the current date and time using CFML and XHTML. Notice that we access this CFML template located in the ColdFusion `wwwroot` directory through the URL `http://localhost:8500/clock.cfm`. The `:8500` specifies the port at which the ColdFusion Web server receives requests. Omitting this port number would cause the default Web server (e.g., IIS or Apache) to attempt unsuccessfully to locate `clock.cfm`.

```
1   <?xml version = "1.0"?>
2   <!DOCTYPE html PUBLIC "-//W3C//DTD XHTML 1.1//EN"
3      "http://www.w3.org/TR/xhtml11/DTD/xhtml11.dtd">
4
5   <!--- Fig. 27.1 : clock.cfm          --->
6   <!--- A simple ColdFusion example --->
7
8   <!--- CFML comment tag --->
9   <!-- XHTML comment tag  -->
10
11  <html xmlns = "http://www.w3.org/1999/xhtml">
12     <head>
13        <title>A Simple ColdFusion Example</title>
14
15        <style type = "text/css">
16           p  { font-size: 14pt; color: blue }
17           td { background-color: black; color: yellow }
18        </style>
19     </head>
20
21     <body>
22
23        <p>A Simple ColdFusion Example</p>
24
25        <table border = "1">
26           <tr>
27              <td>
28
29                 <!--- #'s between cfoutput tags are processed --->
30                 <!--- Display the current date --->
31                 <cfoutput>#dateFormat( now(), "mmmm dd, yyyy" )#</cfoutput>
32              </td>
33
34              <td>
35
36                 <!--- Display the current time --->
37                 <cfoutput>#timeFormat( now(), "hh:mm:ss tt" )#</cfoutput>
38              </td>
39           </tr>
40
41           <tr>
42              <td colspan = "2">
43
```

Fig. 27.1　Simple ColdFusion example. (Part 1 of 2.)

```
44                    <!--- Display the output of now() --->
45                    <cfoutput>Date/Time: #now()#</cfoutput>
46            </td>
47          </tr>
48        </table>
49      </body>
50    </html>
```

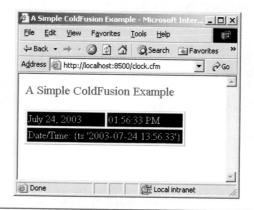

Fig. 27.1   Simple ColdFusion example. (Part 2 of 2.)

Most of the code in `clock.cfm` is XHTML markup. Lines 5–6 contain **CFML comments**. Like XHTML comments, CFML comments help a programmer annotate the template; however, CFML comments are not passed to the client with the template. Therefore, a programmer may comment on the server side without clients being able to gain insight on how the page was created. Additionally, CFML comments have three dashes whereas XHTML comments only have two. Lines 8–9 show both types of comments.

The next piece of CFML markup in the template is the **cfoutput** tag (line 31). Just as with XHTML tags, CFML tags are usually composed of start and end tags. The CFML interpreter processes all CFML between the start and end `cfoutput` tags and replaces it with the appropriate text. A ColdFusion developer also can place plain text and XHTML markup between `cfoutput` start and end tags. The CFML interpreter sends this content to the client unmodified when it processes the `cfoutput` tag.

Line 31 introduces CFML's pound sign (#) notation. The CFML interpreter replaces variables and functions that are enclosed in #'s with their values. The CFML interpreter only processes #'s appearing inside CFML tags. Lines 31, 37 and 45 contain CFML functions (placed between #'s) that handle date and time formatting. The CFML interpreter replaces each function call with the function's return value. The functions **dateFormat** (line 31) and **timeFormat** (line 37) each have two parameters. The first parameter of each function is the date/time to format. The function calls in this example both obtain this date/ time by calling the function **now**, which returns the current date and time at the time of execution. The second parameter of the functions `dateFormat` and `timeFormat` is a string describing how to format the output. The format string "mmmm dd, yyyy" (line 31) specifies a date formatted to show the full name of the month as a string, a two-digit date, a comma and a four-digit year. The format string "hh:mm:ss tt" specifies a time formatted to show a two-digit hour, a colon, a two-digit number of minutes, another colon, a two-digit number of seconds, a space and either AM or PM. Figure 27.1 displays sample values returned by the functions `dateFormat` and `timeFormat` (i.e., the date and time at the moment of each function's execution, formatted according to the format string given as a parameter). The sample screen capture in Fig. 27.1 also reveals the raw date/time information (i.e., a timestamp) returned by the function now (line 45).

The following are two mistakes that commonly occur in CFML code:

```
<cfoutput>Date/Time: now()</cfoutput>
Date/Time: #now()#
```

The first line attempts to display the time without placing the function call between #'s, so the output produced simply is: `Date/Time: now()`. Recall that the CFML interpreter does not modify content placed between `cfoutput` tags unless it is enclosed in #'s. The second example also tries to display the time, but the #'s do not appear inside CFML tags, so the interpreter ignores the #'s and outputs `Date/Time: #now()#`. The following are two ways to correctly display the current date and time:

```
<cfoutput>Date/Time: #now()#</cfoutput>
Date/Time: <cfoutput>#now()#</cfoutput>
```

Both lines in this case would display `Date/Time: {ts '2003-07-21 10:02:07'}`. The position of `"Date/Time:"` in regard to the `cfoutput` tag is not important; this XHTML text can be placed inside or outside the `cfoutput` tag.

Error-Prevention Tip 27.1

The `cfoutput` tag displays the value of a variable or function at a particular point in the template. This is often helpful in debugging a template.

When a request comes in to a Web server for a CFML template, the CFML interpreter first processes all the CFML tags, variables and functions. It then generates and sends output to the client's Web browser. Figure 27.2 shows the XHTML code that is sent to the client's Web browser for the template in Fig. 27.1. Note that this code contains no `cfoutput` tags, and the content that had been inside them—the `dateFormat`, `time-Format` and now functions—has been replaced by the appropriate return values.

```
1   <?xml version = "1.0"?>
2   <!DOCTYPE html PUBLIC "-//W3C//DTD XHTML 1.1//EN"
3      "http://www.w3.org/TR/xhtml11/DTD/xhtml11.dtd">
4
5   <!-- XHTML comment tag  -->
6
7   <html xmlns = "http://www.w3.org/1999/xhtml">
8      <head>
9         <title>A Simple ColdFusion Example</title>
10
11        <style type = "text/css">
12           p { font-size: 14pt; color: blue }
13           td { background-color: black; color: yellow }
14        </style>
15     </head>
```

Fig. 27.2   Generated XHTML from Fig. 27.1. (Part 1 of 2.)

```
16
17      <body>
18
19        <p><strong>A Simple ColdFusion Example</strong></p>
20
21        <table border = "1">
22          <tr>
23            <td>
24                July 24, 2003
25            </td>
26
27            <td>
28                01:56:33 PM
29            </td>
30          </tr>
31
32          <tr>
33            <td colspan = "2">
34                Date/Time: {ts '2003-07-24 13:56:33'}
35            </td>
36          </tr>
37        </table>
38      </body>
39    </html>
```

Fig. 27.2 Generated XHTML from Fig. 27.1. (Part 2 of 2.)

27.3 Using Variables and Expressions

In addition to providing predefined functions, CFML also supports creating and manipulating variables. Figure 27.3 presents a CFML template that creates variables of different data types, manipulates the variables with operators to form expressions and displays the results obtained when the CFML interpreter evaluates these expressions.

```
1   <?xml version = "1.0"?>
2   <!DOCTYPE html PUBLIC "-//W3C//DTD XHTML 1.1//EN"
3       "http://www.w3.org/TR/xhtml11/DTD/xhtml11.dtd">
4
5   <!--- Fig. 27.3 : variables.cfm                   --->
6   <!--- Expressions using Variables and Operators. --->
7
8   <html xmlns = "http://www.w3.org/1999/xhtml">
9     <head>
10        <title>Expressions using Variables and Operators</title>
11
12        <style type = "text/css">
13          p { font-family: arial, sans-serif;
14              font-size: 12pt; color: blue }
15        </style>
16    </head>
17
```

Fig. 27.3 CFML expressions using variables and operators. (Part 1 of 2.)

```
18      <body>
19
20          <!--- Define variables using cfset --->
21          <cfset firstString = "One">
22          <cfset secondString = "Four">
23          <cfset firstNumber = 1>
24          <cfset secondNumber = 4>
25
26          <!--- Concatenate two strings --->
27          <cfset combinedStrings = firstString & secondString>
28
29          <!--- Add two numbers --->
30          <cfset addedNumbers = firstNumber + secondNumber>
31
32          <p><strong>Expressions using Variables and Operators</strong></p>
33
34          <p>
35              <cfoutput>
36                  Concatenation Example: #combinedStrings#
37                  <br />
38                  Addition Example: #addedNumbers#
39              </cfoutput>
40          </p>
41
42      </body>
43  </html>
```

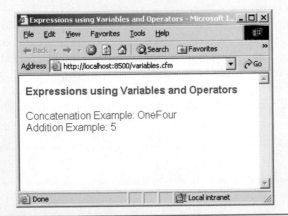

Fig. 27.3   CFML expressions using variables and operators. (Part 2 of 2.)

Variables and Data Types

Variables in CFML behave much like variables in most other programming languages. Line 21 (Fig. 27.3) introduces CFML tag **cfset**. Unlike cfoutput, cfset does not produce any output. Nor does cfset have a close tag, but since CFML markup is removed before sending the processed template to the user, the resulting document still validates as XHTML 1.1. The cfset tag assigns an expression to a variable name for later use. The simplest expression is a single constant (e.g., a string or a number). Line 21 assigns the string "one" to the variable firstString. Line 23 assigns the number 1 to the variable firstNumber. The variable `firstString` is a string data type, and `firstNumber` is a number data type. Figure 27.4 lists the common ColdFusion data types.[1]

Data type	Description
Array	Indexed group of elements (one to three dimensions).
Boolean	True or false.
Date/Time	Any date or time.
List	A string with text values and delimiters.
Number	Any integer or real number.
Query	Format similar to a database table with named columns and numbered rows.
String	Text enclosed in either single (' ') or double ("") quotes.
Structure	Group of associated data using key-value pairs.

Fig. 27.4   ColdFusion data types.

Software Engineering Observation 27.1

Data types are not declared when creating or manipulating variables in ColdFusion. The CFML interpreter infers all data types and performs appropriate conversions based on the operators that are used with the variables.

Expressions and Operators

Figure 27.3 also demonstrates the use of more complex CFML expressions. Line 27 assigns the variable `combinedString` a value formed by evaluating an expression containing two variables and an operator. The & operator in this expression concatenates (i.e., combines) the two string variables `firstString` and `secondString` to form a single string value. Similarly, the + operator (line 30) adds two numbers to produce a sum. Figure 27.5[2] shows the complete list of supported CFML operators. These operators are shown in decreasing order of precedence.

Operator	Type
+	unary positive
−	unary negative
∧	exponent

Fig. 27.5   ColdFusion operator precedence. (Part 1 of 2.)

---

1. Data types from Macromedia's ColdFusion MX manuals. S. Gilson, et al., "Developing ColdFusion MX Applications with CFML," May 2002 <download.macromedia.com/pub/coldfusion/documentation/cfmx_dev_cf_apps.pdf>.
2. Operator precedence from Macromedia's ColdFusion MX manuals. S. Gilson, et al., "Developing ColdFusion MX Applications with CFML," May 2002 <download.macromedia.com/pub/coldfusion/documentation/cfmx_dev_cf_apps.pdf>.

Operator	Type
*	multiplication
/	division
\	integer division
MOD	modulus
+	addition
-	subtraction
&	concatenation
EQ	equal
NEQ	not equal
LT	less than
LTE	less than or equal
GT	greater than
GTE	greater than or equal
CONTAINS	contains
DOES NOT CONTAIN	does not contain
NOT	not
AND	and
OR	or
XOR	exclusive or
EQV	equivalence
IMP	implication

Fig. 27.5   ColdFusion operator precedence. (Part 2 of 2.)

Operators in an expression are processed in the order of precedence (Fig. 27.5). To force the order of evaluation, a programmer must use **(** and **)** to group expressions. These subexpressions can be nested infinitely deep. The CFML interpreter evaluates each subexpression beginning with the one that is most deeply nested.

27.4 Variable Scoping

In ColdFusion, all variables are part of a **scope**. A variable's scope defines from where the variable can be accessed and refers to the named space where the variable is stored. For example, the CFML interpreter creates variables of scope **url** whenever a developer or user passes variables to a CFML template through the URL, as illustrated by the following:

```
http://localhost:8500/name.cfm?name=GalAnt
```

Variables in the URL appear after the **?** in the form *variablename=value*. Multiple variables in the URL are separated by ampersands (**&**). The proper syntax for accessing a **url**-scoped variable in the template receiving the variable is **url**.*variablename*. All the CFML variables in the examples seen thus far are local variables and are part of the **variables** scope. ColdFusion developers often omit the prefix "**variables.**" when accessing variables of the local scope. Figure 27.6 lists several supported CFML variable scopes and whether each requires a prefix.

Scope prefix	Prefix required	References
variables	No	Local variable
form	No	Form
url	No	URL
request	Yes	HTTP request
cgi	No	CGI variable
cookie	No	Cookie
client	No	Application
session	Yes	Application
application	Yes	Application
server	Yes	Server
flash	Yes	Macromedia Flash
queryname	No	Query

Fig. 27.6   ColdFusion variable scopes.

Good Programming Practice 27.1

Although not required, it is good to use scope prefixes for all variable scopes with the exception of local variables.

In Fig. 27.7, we use a `url`-scoped variable, `url.name`, to output the user's name on the template (line 28). Hyperlinks, forms using the HTTP *get* method and users typing directly into the address box of their browsers can all lead to the creation of `url`-scoped variables.

```
1   <?xml version = "1.0"?>
2   <!DOCTYPE html PUBLIC "-//W3C//DTD XHTML 1.1//EN"
3      "http://www.w3.org/TR/xhtml11/DTD/xhtml11.dtd">
4
5   <!--- Fig. 27.7 : name.cfm        --->
6   <!--- Using url scope variables --->
7
8   <html xmlns = "http://www.w3.org/1999/xhtml">
9      <head>
10        <title>Hello</title>
11
12        <style type = "text/css">
13           p { font-family: arial, sans-serif;
```

Fig. 27.7   `url`-scoped variables. (Part 1 of 2.)

```
14                  font-size: 14pt; color: navy }
15          </style>
16      </head>
17
18      <body>
19
20          <!--- IF Control Statement --->
21          <cfif NOT isDefined( "url.name" )>
22
23              <!--- Create default if name variable is not in the URL --->
24              <cfset url.name = "Guest">
25          </cfif>
26
27          <!--- Display URL Variable --->
28          <p>Hello <cfoutput>#url.name#</cfoutput></p>
29      </body>
30  </html>
```

Fig. 27.7   url-scoped variables. (Part 2 of 2.)

Lines 21–25 introduce the **cfif** tag, which behaves like the if statements seen in previous chapters. The CFML interpreter runs the code between the start and end cfif tags only if the boolean expression in the start tag is true. The expression in this case is NOT isDefined("url.name"). The function **isDefined** returns true or false depending upon whether its parameter exists as a variable at the current point in the template. The **NOT** operator reverses the truth or falsity of the entire expression. So this expression is true when the url.name variable does not exist. [*Note:* The variable name passed to the function isDefined is enclosed in quotes because the function determines whether a variable called url.name exists, not whether url.name's value exists.] The cfif tag is often used with **cfelseif** and **cfelse** tags, which behave like elseif and else statements in other languages.

27.5 Form Processing

Form processing in ColdFusion uses the **form** variable scope to gather information from the user. An XHTML form must *post* data to a CFML template to create variables of this scope. Figure 27.8 contains a simple form for submitting an auction bid price. The form tag in the page must specify the "post" method in order for the variables to be form-scoped variables in the template that processes the form data. Omitting method = "post" results in the form variables being submitted by the default HTTP *get* method and the variables becoming url-scoped.

```
1   <?xml version = "1.0"?>
2   <!DOCTYPE html PUBLIC "-//W3C//DTD XHTML 1.1//EN"
3      "http://www.w3.org/TR/xhtml11/DTD/xhtml11.dtd">
4
5   <!-- Fig. 27.8 : form.html      -->
6   <!-- A simple auction bid form -->
7
8   <html xmlns = "http://www.w3.org/1999/xhtml">
9      <head>
10        <title>Simple Auction</title>
11
12        <style type = "text/css">
13           p { font-family: arial, sans-serif;
14              font-size: 14pt; color: navy }
15        </style>
16     </head>
17
18     <body>
19
20        <!-- Form variables created using post method -->
21        <form action = "form_process.cfm" method = "post">
22           <p>Enter your bid:</p>
23
24           <p>
25
26              <!--- name attribute becomes variable name --->
27              $<input name = "bidPrice" type = "text" size = "20" />
28              <input type = "submit" value = "Enter" />
29           </p>
30        </form>
31     </body>
32  </html>
```

Fig. 27.8   Auction bid form.

Submitting the form in Fig. 27.8 passes `form_process.cfm` all the form fields and values as `form`–scoped variables. The `form_process.cfm` template (Fig. 27.9) contains the code to process the auction bid and display the results. For this example, the bid must be a dollar amount greater than or equal to zero.

```
1   <?xml version = "1.0"?>
2   <!DOCTYPE html PUBLIC "-//W3C//DTD XHTML 1.1//EN"
3      "http://www.w3.org/TR/xhtml11/DTD/xhtml11.dtd">
4
5   <!--- Fig. 27.9 : form_process.cfm          --->
6   <!--- A simple auction bid processing form --->
7
8   <html xmlns = "http://www.w3.org/1999/xhtml">
9      <head>
10        <title>Simple Auction</title>
11
12        <style type = "text/css">
13           p { font-family: arial, sans-serif;
14              font-size: 14pt; color: navy }
15        </style>
16     </head>
17
18     <body>
19
20        <!--- Determine if bidPrice exists --->
21        <cfif isDefined( "form.bidPrice" )>
22
23           <!--- Determine if bidPrice is a number --->
24           <cfif isNumeric( form.bidPrice )>
25
26              <!--- Determine is bidPrice is GTE 0 --->
27              <cfif form.bidPrice GTE 0>
28
29                 <!--- Display bid from form field --->
30                 <p>
31                    Your bid is:
32                    <cfoutput>$#form.bidPrice#</cfoutput>
33                 </p>
34              <cfelse>
35                 <p>Your bid must be greater then or equal to $0.00!</p>
36              </cfif>
37
38           <cfelse>
39              <p>Your bid must be a valid numeric dollar amount!</p>
40           </cfif>
41
42        <cfelse>
43           <p>Error, no bid found.</p>
44        </cfif>
45
46     </body>
47  </html>
```

Fig. 27.9　Auction bid processing form. (Part 1 of 2.)

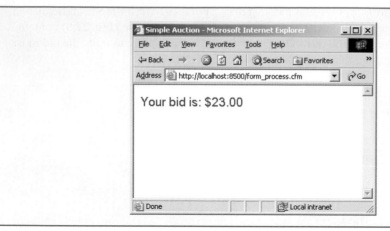

Fig. 27.9   Auction bid processing form. (Part 2 of 2.)

Lines 21–44 of `form_process.cfm` (Fig. 27.9) contain the necessary `if...else` statements to check the bid for the given requirements. Note that the proper syntax to access `form` variables is `form.`*fieldname*, where *fieldname* refers to the `name` of any of the form elements on the XHTML form page (Fig. 27.8).

Line 24 introduces the function **isNumeric**. The `isNumeric` function returns true if the variable passed as a parameter is a number, and false if it is not. Unlike `isDefined`, the parameter for `isNumeric` is not enclosed in quotes since we do not want to know whether the string `"form.bidPrice"` is a number; rather, we want to know whether the value of `form.bidPrice` is a number.

This example illustrates the concept of nested `if` statements seen in previous chapters of the book. A ColdFusion developer can place `cfif` tags inside other `cfif` tags to consider multiple test cases. Figure 27.9 contains two nested `cfif` tags. The code within each executes only if the conditional expression in the enclosing tag is true. For example, we determine whether the variable `form.bidPrice` is a number (line 24) only if we have established that a variable by this name exists (line 21). Furthermore, we determine whether the value of `form.bidPrice` is greater than or equal to 0 (line 27) only if we know already that this variable is in fact a number.

As noted in the preceding section, `cfelse` tags (lines 34–36, 38–40 and 42–44) behave like `else` in other programming languages. For example, the CFML interpreter executes the content of the `cfelse` tag in line 34 only when the corresponding `cfif` start tag's conditional expression (i.e., `form.bidPrice GTE 0` in line 27) is false. We use `cfelse` tags in this example to display error messages when the user's bid fails to satisfy any of the bid requirements.

27.6 Creating a Data Source Name

This section presents the steps necessary to configure database connectivity in ColdFusion MX 6.1. These setup steps are required to allow the bookstore Web application created in the following section to obtain information from a database.

To interact with a database using ColdFusion, we must first connect the database to the ColdFusion server. We configure database access through the ColdFusion Administrator, which is located at `http://localhost:8500/cfide/administrator/` by default. The initial page asks for the password entered when installing ColdFusion. Simply enter the password and click the **Login** button to be taken to the ColdFusion Administrator's home page. From the home page, click **Data Sources**, listed under **Data & Services**, from the menu in the left frame. This will open the **Data Sources** page in the main frame. In the **Add New Data Source** table, enter **books** for the **Data Source Name**, and select Microsoft Access from the drop-down menu for **Driver**. Click the **Add** button to go to the next page (Fig. 27.10), which contains several form fields used to obtain information about the data source. The **CF Data Source Name** field is prepopulated with the name **books**. The **Database File** field is the only additional required field. The example database should be located at `C:\CFusionMX\wwwroot\Books.mdb` if the chapter files were copied as described in Section 27.1. Finally, click **Submit** to create the connection from ColdFusion to the database. If the database was added successfully the message **datasource updated successfully** will appear at the top of the next page. Once a data source exists, CFML templates can interact with the database simply by referring to the data source's name. ColdFusion handles the actual database connection behind the scenes. This is unlike other server-side scripting languages, which often require the developer to write code that creates a database connection for every script.

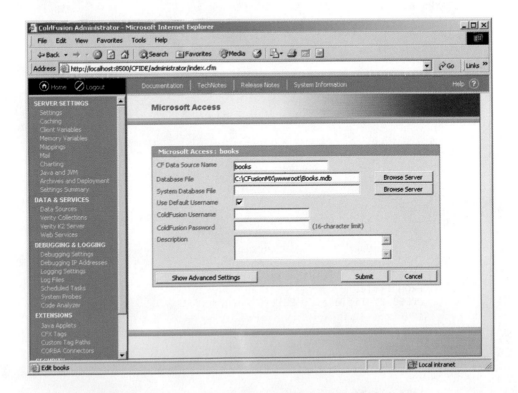

Fig. 27.10 Data source registration in the ColdFusion Administrator.

27.7 Bookstore Case Study: Interface and Database

In this section, we build a simple interface for an online bookstore. The bookstore consists of a page that lists all the available book titles and a page that provides detailed information about a single book. The sample database `Books.mdb`, configured in Section 27.6, stores the information about all the books. Detailed information about the database contents can be found in Chapter 22. We use SQL to retrieve the desired information for each page in our bookstore.

To start, we create a CFML template that queries the database for a list of all the book titles. This template displays all the book titles and allows a customer to select one of them for more information. The first part of this template connects to the database, executes an SQL query and returns the result to ColdFusion.

Figure 27.11 introduces the **cfquery** tag (lines 21–25), which allows developers to run queries against a data source. The **datasource** attribute specifies against which database to execute the query. The **name** attribute specifies the name of a CFML variable scope that should be created to store the result of the query. Finally, SQL is placed between the start and end **cfquery** tags. Please refer to Chapter 22 for help in understanding the SQL used throughout this case study.

```
1    <?xml version = "1.0"?>
2    <!DOCTYPE html PUBLIC "-//W3C//DTD XHTML 1.1//EN"
3       "http://www.w3.org/TR/xhtml11/DTD/xhtml11.dtd">
4
5    <!--- Fig. 27.11 : booklist.cfm --->
6    <!--- Bookstore - List of Books --->
7
8    <html xmlns = "http://www.w3.org/1999/xhtml">
9       <head>
10          <title>Book List</title>
11
12          <style type = "text/css">
13             p  { text-align: center }
14             h1 { text-align: center }
15          </style>
16       </head>
17
18       <body>
19
20          <!--- CFML Query using SQL on 'books' Data Source Name --->
21          <cfquery name = "bookList" datasource = "books">
22             SELECT ISBN, Title, EditionNumber
23             FROM Titles
24             ORDER BY Title ASC, EditionNumber DESC
25          </cfquery>
26
27          <h1>Available Books</h1>
28
29          <hr />
30
31          <p>Select a book from this list and click the button to
```

Fig. 27.11   Bookstore case study: Book list. (Part 1 of 2.)

```
32                view the selected book's information.</p>
33
34          <form action = "bookinfo.cfm" method = "post">
35             <p>
36
37                <!--- Dynamically build select box from database --->
38                <select name = "ISBN" size = "5">
39
40                   <!--- Looping results of query using cfoutput --->
41                   <cfoutput query = "bookList">
42                      <option value = "#bookList.ISBN#">#bookList.Title#
43                      (Edition #bookList.EditionNumber#)</option>
44                   </cfoutput>
45                </select>
46             </p>
47
48             <p><input type = "submit" value = "View Information" /></p>
49          </form>
50       </body>
51    </html>
```

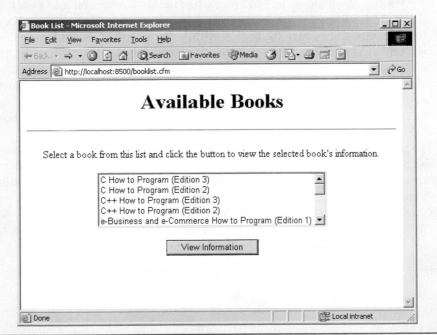

Fig. 27.11   Bookstore case study: Book list. (Part 2 of 2.)

ColdFusion represents database results as variables whose scope is equal to the name attribute in the cfquery tag (i.e., the *queryname*). Thus if the cfquery contains an attribute name = "bookList", a bookList scope exists after the cfquery tag in that same template (Fig. 27.11). The variables in a *queryname* scope correspond to the column names in the result set returned by the cfquery tag of the same name. The scope bookList contains the variables ISBN, Title and EditionNumber. These variables are accessed using their scope name in the same fashion as accessing a url-scoped variable. For example, we specify bookList.ISBN to access an ISBN in the result set from the bookList query.

Software Engineering Observation 27.2

Multiple queries can exist on the same CFML template, and thus multiple queryname scopes can exist at the same time.

Using the cfoutput tag with a query attribute enables developers to access and output the result set of a query. Line 41 shows the proper use of the query attribute:

```
<cfoutput query = "bookList">
```

A cfoutput tag containing a query attribute outputs the content between its start and end tags once for each row in the specified query's result set. For example, if a query has 14 rows in the result set, then the cfoutput tag outputs its content once for each of the 14 rows.

Lines 34–49 define an XHTML form that posts data to the CFML template bookinfo.cfm (Fig. 27.12) for processing. The form consists of one selection box (i.e., select element) containing an option for each of the books in the bookList result set. The cfoutput tag (lines 41–44) dynamically generates the option elements. For each book in the result set, we assign the book's ISBN to the value of an option and output the book's title and edition to be displayed in the selection box. A user selects a title and edition from the list, but only the ISBN gets sent to the form-processing script when the user clicks **View Information**. Recall that because the form uses the HTTP *post* method, and the select element specifies name = "ISBN", ColdFusion creates a form-scoped variable named ISBN in the processing script that contains one of the values held by bookList.ISBN.

The next file, bookinfo.cfm (Fig. 27.12), retrieves detailed information about the selected book using many of the same CFML features as booklist.cfm. The dynamic form created in booklist.cfm determines which book's detailed information to retrieve. Recall that the form effectively sets form.ISBN equal to bookList.ISBN to send the ISBN of the selected book to bookinfo.cfm. The form-processing script, bookinfo.cfm (Fig. 27.12), then uses form.ISBN to create a more complex SQL query to retrieve detailed information about that book.

```
1   <?xml version = "1.0"?>
2   <!DOCTYPE html PUBLIC "-//W3C//DTD XHTML 1.1//EN"
3       "http://www.w3.org/TR/xhtml11/DTD/xhtml11.dtd">
4
5   <!--- Fig. 27.12 : bookinfo.cfm              --->
6   <!--- Bookstore - Detailed Book Information --->
7
8   <html xmlns = "http://www.w3.org/1999/xhtml">
9      <head>
10        <title>Book Info</title>
11
12        <style type = "text/css">
```

Fig. 27.12 Bookstore case study: Book information. (Part 1 of 4.)

```
13              table { border-collapse: collapse }
14              td    { border: 2px solid lightgray;
15                      padding: 5px }
16          </style>
17      </head>
18
19      <body>
20
21          <!--- Make sure that an ISBN was submitted to this page --->
22          <cfif NOT isDefined( "form.ISBN" )>
23
24              <!--- CFML URL Forwarder --->
25              <cflocation url = "booklist.cfm" addtoken = "no">
26              <cfabort>
27          </cfif>
28
29          <!--- CFML Query using SQL on 'books' DSN --->
30          <!--- Dynamically insert form.ISBN variable --->
31          <cfquery name = "bookInfo" datasource = "books">
32              SELECT ISBN, Title, EditionNumber, Copyright, Description,
33                      ImageFile, PublisherName
34              FROM Titles, Publishers
35              WHERE Titles.ISBN = '#form.ISBN#'
36              AND Titles.PublisherID = Publishers.PublisherID
37          </cfquery>
38
39          <!--- Using cfoutput with a query to loop result set --->
40          <cfoutput query = "bookInfo">
41
42              <!--- Based on ISBN, use SQL to retrieve authors --->
43              <cfquery name = "authorInfo" datasource = "books">
44                  SELECT FirstName, LastName
45                  FROM AuthorISBN, Authors
46                  WHERE AuthorISBN.isbn = '#bookInfo.ISBN#'
47                  AND AuthorISBN.AuthorID = Authors.AuthorID
48              </cfquery>
49
50              <h1>#bookInfo.Title#</h1>
51
52              <hr />
53
54              <p>
55
56                  <!--- Display authors by using a CFML Loop --->
57                  <cfloop query = "authorInfo">
58                      #authorInfo.FirstName# #authorInfo.LastName# <br />
59                  </cfloop>
60              </p>
61
62              <!---Output information from database about book --->
63              <table>
64                  <tr>
65                      <td>ISBN:</td>
```

Fig. 27.12   Bookstore case study: Book information. (Part 2 of 4.)

```
66                    <td>#bookInfo.ISBN#</td>
67                    <td rowspan ="4">
68
69                        <!--- Dynamically insert the filename into the tag --->
70                        <img src = "images/#bookInfo.ImageFile#"
71                            alt = "Image File" />
72                    </td>
73                </tr>
74
75                <tr>
76                    <td>Edition:</td>
77                    <td>#bookInfo.EditionNumber#</td>
78                </tr>
79
80                <tr>
81                    <td>Copyright:</td>
82                    <td>#bookInfo.Copyright#</td>
83                </tr>
84
85                <tr>
86                    <td>Publisher:</td>
87                    <td>#bookInfo.PublisherName#</td>
88                </tr>
89            </table>
90            <p>#bookInfo.Description#</p>
91
92            <!--- Used in Section 27.8 --->
93            <!--- Button to add book to shopping cart --->
94            <form action = "shoppingcart.cfm" method = "post">
95                <p>
96                    <input type = "hidden" name = "ISBN"
97                        value = "#bookInfo.ISBN#" />
98
99                    <input type = "hidden" name = "title"
100                        value = "#bookInfo.Title#" />
101
102                    <input type = "hidden" name = "edition"
103                        value = "#bookInfo.EditionNumber#" />
104
105                    <input type = "submit" value = "Add To Cart"
106                        disabled = "disabled" />
107                </p>
108            </form>
109        </cfoutput>
110
111        <!--- Button to go back to the book list --->
112        <form action = "booklist.cfm" method = "post">
113            <p>
114                <input type = "submit" value = "Book List" />
115            </p>
116        </form>
117    </body>
118 </html>
```

Fig. 27.12 Bookstore case study: Book information. (Part 3 of 4.)

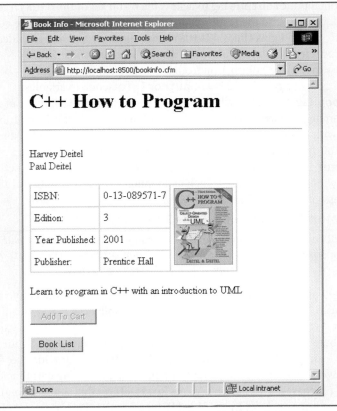

Fig. 27.12 Bookstore case study: Book information. (Part 4 of 4.)

Figure 27.12 introduces three new CFML tags: `cflocation`, `cfabort` and `cfloop`. The tag **cflocation** (line 25) redirects the user to another CFML template. This tag can send a user to any page or template on the Internet that can be reached by a URL. For this example, if the variable `form.ISBN` does not exist (i.e., the user either did not select a book or navigated directly to this template), then we redirect the user to the `booklist.cfm` template. This is important, since the variable `form.ISBN` must exist for the remainder of the template to know what book's information to retrieve. If we skip this check, processing the `cfquery` tag (lines 31–37) would produce an error because we expect `form.ISBN` to be defined. The **cfabort** tag (line 26) instructs the CFML interpreter immediately to stop processing the page. Only the content generated before the `cfabort` tag is sent to the user. This provides a nice way to ensure that the page stops processing under certain conditions to avoid errors. We discuss the third new tag, `cfloop`, momentarily.

Lines 31–37 of Fig. 27.12 contain SQL inside a `cfquery` tag to retrieve detailed information about the book specified by `form.ISBN`. Note that this SQL statement contains the CFML code `#form.ISBN#`. The CFML interpreter processes the CFML code inside a `cfquery` tag before sending the enclosed SQL to the database, making it possible to generate SQL statements dynamically. In this case, the ISBN for the book that was selected on the `booklist.cfm` template replaces `#form.ISBN#` in the SQL statement. ColdFusion stores the result of this query in a scope named `bookInfo`.

Line 40 contains a `cfoutput` tag to access the result set of the `bookInfo` query. Each book has a unique ISBN, so the result set contains only one row. Thus the code inside the `cfoutput` start and end tags (lines 43–108) executes once, and any included `bookInfo`-scoped variables refer to column values for the one selected book. Lines 43–48 execute an additional query to retrieve information from the `books` database about this book's authors. The result of this query goes into a set of `authorInfo`-scoped variables.

The **`cfloop`** tag (line 57), when used with the `query` attribute, outputs the code between its start and end tags once for each record in the query result set. Lines 57–59 use this construct with `query` set to `"authorInfo"` to output the first and last names of each of the authors of the current book. Remember always to use a `cfloop` tag in conjunction with a `cfoutput` tag so the CFML interpreter processes variables or other CFML code. The `cfloop` tag also has other uses, such as looping a specific number of times, looping while an expression is true and iterating over a list.

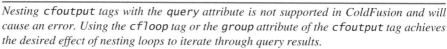

Common Programming Error 27.1

Nesting `cfoutput` tags with the `query` attribute is not supported in ColdFusion and will cause an error. Using the `cfloop` tag or the `group` attribute of the `cfoutput` tag achieves the desired effect of nesting loops to iterate through query results.

Lines 63–90 display a table containing the book's ISBN, edition, copyright, publisher and cover. Line 70 contains the XHTML `img` tag to display the book cover. Note that the interpreter outputs the value of variable `bookInfo.ImageFile` inside the value of the `img` tag's `src` attribute. Remember that CFML variables can go anywhere inside a `cfoutput` tag, including inside XHTML attribute values. Lines 94–108 provide the **Add to Cart** button, which we will use in Section 27.8 to implement a shopping cart that keeps track of users' planned purchases. This button appears inside a form that sends several hidden input values to `shoppingcart.cfm`. Lines 112–116 create an XHTML form containing a single button (i.e., **Book List**) that sends the user back to the `booklist.cfm` template.

27.8 Bookstore Case Study: Shopping Cart

Before adding the functionality of a shopping cart to the bookstore example, we must introduce the ColdFusion application framework. A ColdFusion application consists of several related templates and provides extended functionality for interaction between them. Using a **`cfapplication`** tag in a template named **`Application.cfm`** creates an application and provides access to the variable scopes related to applications. These scopes include **`client`**, **`session`** and **`application`** variables. The shopping cart makes use of the `session` variable scope to store the contents of a user's shopping cart as the user makes selections. A unique set of `session` variables exists for each individual user and follows that user through the site. Variables of scope `session` can be accessed from any template in an application and do not need to be passed between templates by forms or through a URL. This creates a more secure way to remember information about the user. Users potentially can alter variable values in a URL or in data submitted by a form, but they cannot modify `session` variables stored on the server. These variables are deleted either after a specified amount of inactive time or programmatically by CFML code.

Figure 27.13 uses the `cfapplication` tag to create a new application called `bookStore`. In this case we activate `client` and `session` variables through the attributes `clientmanagement` (line 6) and `sessionmanagement` (line 7). The `sessiontimeout` and `applicationtimeout` attributes determine how long ColdFusion should wait before deleting `session` and `application` variables, respectively. We specify that `session` variables expire after 20 minutes (line 8) and that `application` variables (e.g., application-wide settings) get deleted after 2 days (line 9). We use the function **createTimeSpan** to set `sessiontimeout` and `applicationtimeout` appropriately. This function takes four parameters: *days*, *hours*, *minutes* and *seconds*. Developers have the option of storing `client` variables in the server's registry, in a data source or as `cookies` on the user's computer. We specify that they are to be stored as `cookies` for the bookstore case study (line 10). To access a `client` variable, use the form `client.`*variablename*.

```
1   <!--- Fig. 27.13 : Application.cfm      --->
2   <!--- Bookstore - Application Framework --->
3
4   <!--- Initialize the application framework --->
5   <cfapplication name = "bookStore"
6                  clientmanagement = "Yes"
7                  sessionmanagement = "Yes"
8                  sessiontimeout = "#createTimeSpan( 0,0,20,0 )#"
9                  applicationtimeout = "#createTimeSpan( 2,0,0,0 )#"
10                 clientstorage = "cookie">
11
12  <!--- Make sure the shopping cart exists or create one --->
13  <cfif NOT isDefined( "session.shoppingCart" )>
14     <cfset session.shoppingCart = arrayNew( 2 )>
15  </cfif>
```

Fig. 27.13 Bookstore case study: Application framework .

The filename `Application.cfm` is required for the application to be correctly initialized and is case sensitive on UNIX-based platforms. When the CFML interpreter processes a template, the interpreter first looks for an `Application.cfm` template in two places. First, the interpreter looks for this file in the same directory as the requested template. Second, the interpreter checks all parent directories through the Web server's root directory looking for the `Application.cfm` template. If it finds an `Application.cfm` template in one of these locations, the CFML interpreter first processes `Appliction.cfm`, followed by the requested template. For example, if the user requests the template `booklist.cfm`, the server will process `Application.cfm` then `booklist.cfm`. If the interpreter cannot find an `Application.cfm` template in either location, then it does not consider the requested template to be part of an application.

Figure 27.13 initializes the application framework using the `cfapplication` tag. The `Application.cfm` template contains additional code to be executed each time the CFML interpreter processes this file (i.e., each time a user requests a template in the application). Line 13 determines whether the `shoppingCart` variable exists in the `session` scope (i.e., the user has an existing shopping cart). If one does not exist, we create the variable `session.shoppingCart` and set it equal to an empty two-dimensional array to store the products in the user's shopping cart. The **arrayNew** function (line 14) creates an empty array. Arrays in CFML are dynamically sized (i.e., they can increase or decrease in length as needed) but have a set number of dimensions, as indicated by the parameter passed to `arrayNew`. Also, CFML arrays begin with an index value of 1 (i.e., one-based indexing), whereas arrays in most other programming languages start at index 0 (i.e., zero-based indexing). Finally, remember that each visitor to the site gets a private set of session variables. If 50 users access the bookstore simultaneously, then 50 distinct shopping cart arrays exist. The ColdFusion server ensures that each user accesses the correct shopping cart.

Figure 27.14 presents the CFML template that adds a book to the shopping cart and displays the shopping cart's current contents. Lines 11–13 use the function **arrayAppend** to add a book's ISBN, title and edition to the session.shoppingCart array. This template receives values for these form-scoped variables when a user clicks the **Add To Cart** button on bookinfo.cfm (Fig. 27.12). [*Note*: We return to Fig. 27.12 to enable this button later in the section.] Lines 11–13 place the values of form.ISBN, form.title and form.edition in the first, second and third positions, respectively, of a new row in the two-dimensional shopping cart array. Line 17 uses the function **arrayClear** to empty the shopping cart when requested. The **arrayLen** function determines how many items are in the array (line 35). We store the length in a variable arraySize.

```
1   <?xml version = "1.0"?>
2   <!DOCTYPE html PUBLIC "-//W3C//DTD XHTML 1.1//EN"
3      "http://www.w3.org/TR/xhtml11/DTD/xhtml11.dtd">
4
5   <!--- Fig. 27.14 : shoppingcart.cfm    --->
6   <!--- Bookstore - Simple Shopping Cart --->
7
8   <cfif isDefined( "form.ISBN" )>
9
10     <!--- Add a new book to the shopping cart. --->
11     <cfif arrayAppend( session.shoppingCart[ 1 ], form.ISBN )></cfif>
12     <cfif arrayAppend( session.shoppingCart[ 2 ], form.title )></cfif>
13     <cfif arrayAppend( session.shoppingCart[ 3 ], form.edition )></cfif>
14  <cfelseif isDefined( "form.clearCart" )>
15
16     <!--- Empty the shopping cart. --->
17     <cfif arrayClear( session.shoppingCart )></cfif>
18  </cfif>
19
20  <html xmlns = "http://www.w3.org/1999/xhtml">
21     <head>
22        <title>Bookstore Shopping Cart</title>
23
24        <style type = "text/css">
25           table { border-collapse: collapse }
26           td    { border: 2px solid lightgray;
27                   padding: 5px }
28        </style>
29     </head>
30
31     <body>
32        <h1>Shopping Cart</h1>
33
34        <!--- Check the size of the shopping cart --->
35        <cfset arraySize = arrayLen( session.shoppingCart[ 1 ] )>
```

Fig. 27.14   Bookstore case study: Shopping cart. (Part 1 of 2.)

```
36
37        <cfif arraySize GTE 1>
38          <table>
39
40            <!--- Display the items in the shopping cart --->
41            <cfloop index="i" from="1" to="#arraySize#" step="1">
42              <cfoutput>
43                <tr>
44                  <td>#session.shoppingCart[ 1 ][ i ]#</td>
45                  <td>#session.shoppingCart[ 2 ][ i ]#</td>
46                  <td>Edition #session.shoppingCart[ 3 ][ i ]#</td>
47                </tr>
48              </cfoutput>
49            </cfloop>
50          </table>
51        <cfelse>
52          <p>Empty Shopping Cart.</p>
53        </cfif>
54
55        <!--- Button back to the book list --->
56        <form action = "booklist.cfm" method = "post">
57          <p><input type = "submit" value = "Book List" /></p>
58        </form>
59
60        <!--- Button to clear the shopping cart --->
61        <form action = "shoppingcart.cfm" method = "post">
62          <p>
63            <input name = "clearCart" type = "submit"
64                   value = "Empty Cart" />
65          </p>
66        </form>
67      </body>
68   </html>
```

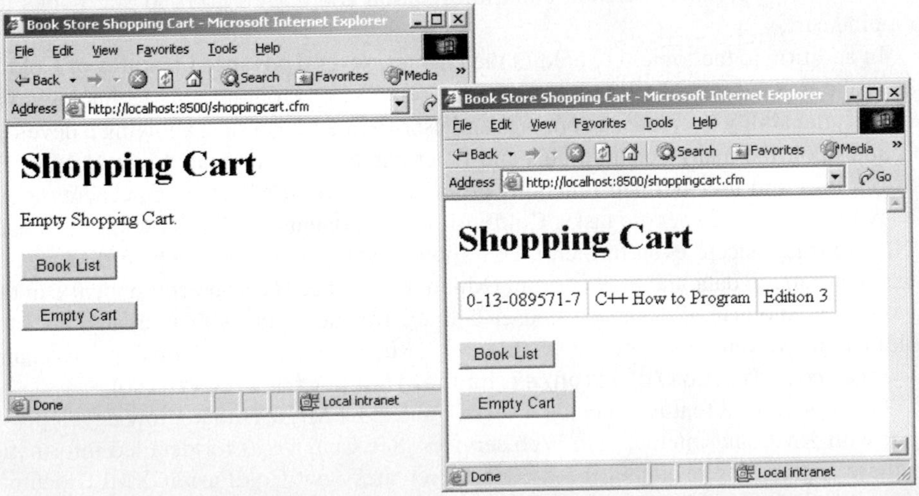

Fig. 27.14 Bookstore case study: Shopping cart. (Part 2 of 2.)

A `cfloop` tag (lines 41–49) repeats the code between its start and end tags once for each item in the shopping cart by incrementing variable i from 1 to `arraySize` by 1. Lines 44–46 output the ISBN, title and edition number of the ith book in the `session.shoppingCart` array. The first index in the array specifies the type of information to display (i.e., ISBN, title or edition number) for the book indicated by the second index. For example, we display the ISBN of the second book when i is 2, and line 44 evaluates to `session.shoppingCart[1][2]`.

Users' shopping carts are empty when they first arrive at the site. Before we can add products to a shopping cart, we need to return to `bookinfo.cfm` (Fig. 27.12) and modify two lines of code to enable the **Add to Cart** button that was previously disabled. Recall that clicking this button submits to `shoppingcart.cfm` three hidden input values pertaining to the currently displayed book. The `input` tag (lines 105–106 of Fig. 27.12) currently is:

```
<input type = "submit" value = "Add To Cart"
       disabled = "disabled" />
```

To enable this button, the `disabled` attribute must be removed from the tag. Thus, the tag must be replaced with:

```
<input type = "submit" value = "Add To Cart" />
```

Now we can select an item from `booklist.cfm`, add the book to the shopping cart from `bookinfo.cfm` and either view or empty the shopping cart on `shoppingcart.cfm`.

27.9 Advanced Topics for ColdFusion Developers

In this chapter we have looked at the basic functionality of the ColdFusion Markup Language (CFML) as supported by Macromedia's ColdFusion MX. We started off by creating and manipulating variables. Then we moved on to accepting and using user input through a URL and via XHTML forms. Finally, we created a database-driven bookstore application that lists books, provides detailed book information and allows users to add books to a shopping cart.

In addition to the topics covered in the chapter, several advanced features of ColdFusion make it stand out as a strong choice for a server-side programming technology. One feature is the ability to create custom tags and user-defined functions, allowing a developer to build upon the many standard tags and functions that are integrated into ColdFusion. Custom tags and user-defined functions promote code reusability and can increase efficiency in performing specific tasks. ColdFusion Components (CFCs), new in ColdFusion MX, take this concept even further. CFCs allow developers to create object-like components that contain data and methods and exhibit inheritance (i.e., one component can take on traits of another). Custom tags, user-defined functions and CFCs created by other ColdFusion developers are available at Macromedia's ColdFusion Exchange (www.macromedia.com/cfusion/exchange/index.cfm?view=sn130).

Other advanced features include a set of built-in CFML tags that allow developers to work with XML and interact with Web services. See Chapter 20 for detailed information on these topics. For example, the `cfxml` tag creates new ColdFusion XML document objects for accessing XML documents through ColdFusion, and the `cfinvoke` tag makes requests from Web services.

Much of ColdFusion's strength lies in these advanced topics. For more information on working with these and other features beyond the scope of this introductory chapter, please visit the Web sites listed in the following section.

27.10 Web Resources

`www.macromedia.com/software/coldfusion`
The official Macromedia ColdFusion Web site contains links to many CFML resources.

`www.macromedia.com/support/coldfusion/documentation.html`
The official ColdFusion documentation page with ColdFusion MX installation instructions, CFML reference guide to building applications and other documents.

`www.macromedia.com/cfusion/exchange/index.cfm?view=sn130`
The Macromedia ColdFusion Exchange is an online forum for ColdFusion developers to share their custom tags, user-defined functions and CFCs.

`www.forta.com`
Ben Forta's official Web site provides ColdFusion tips, resources and articles from one of the most experienced ColdFusion developers.

`www.sys-con.com/coldfusion`
The Web site of the *ColdFusion Developer's Journal*, a widely read technical magazine about Cold-Fusion.

`www.cfhub.com`
CFHub.com contains a comprehensive reference to ColdFusion tags and advanced features, in addition to several helpful articles and tutorials.

SUMMARY

- ColdFusion is a widely used server-side markup language and application server that uses a simple tag-based format to enable quick and easy dynamic Web-site development.
- ColdFusion templates are written in ColdFusion Markup Language (CFML) and saved with `.cfm` extensions.
- CFML comments use `<!---` and `--->`; the text inside these comments is not sent to the Web browser.
- `#` is a special character in CFML. Variables and function calls used for output are enclosed in #'s.
- The `cfoutput` tag converts CFML variables and functions into plain text.
- The `dateFormat` and `timeFormat` functions provide a convenient way to format dates and times.
- The `now` function returns the current date and time.
- The CFML interpreter processes all CFML code and removes it before the template is sent to the Web browser.
- The `cfset` tag assigns a value to a variable and does not have a close tag.
- Variables in CFML are dynamically set to number, string and other data types.
- The `&` operator concatenates strings.
- Expressions are grouped using (and) to form subexpressions.
- All variables in CFML belong to a scope and are accessed in the format *scopetype.variablename*.
- By default, variables created on a template belong to the `variables` scope.
- The `cfif` tag evaluates a boolean expression and is similar to the `if` statement of other languages.
- The `cfelse` and `cfelseif` tags behave like `else` and `elseif` in other languages.

- Variables submitted from a form with the post method become form-scoped variables.
- Data source names created in the ColdFusion Administrator allow ColdFusion to interact with databases.
- The cfquery tag creates a connection with a database and executes an SQL statement.
- The cfquery tag's name attribute becomes the scope for the result set generated by the cfquery tag's SQL statement.
- When the query attribute is specified, the cfoutput tag outputs the content between its start and end tags once for each record in the specified query.
- The cflocation tag redirects a user to another page or template.
- The cfabort tag stops the processing of a CFML template.
- The cfloop tag prints its content once for every iteration of the loop.
- The Application.cfm file builds the foundation of the ColdFusion application framework.
- The cfapplication tag enables the use of client, session and application variables.
- Unique session variables exist on the server for each visitor and are available from all the templates within an application.
- Arrays in CFML are dynamically sized, and only the number of dimensions needs to be specified when they are declared.
- Functions such as arrayAppend, arrayClear and arrayLen are used to interact with arrays.
- Custom tags and user-defined functions allow a developer to build upon the many tags and functions that are integrated into ColdFusion.
- ColdFusion Components (CFCs) allow developers to create object-like components that have constructors, methods and inheritance.
- Advanced features of ColdFusion include a set of built-in CFML tags that allow developers to work with XML and interact with Web services.

TERMINOLOGY

#
.cfm
addition operator (+)
and operator (AND)
application scope
Application.cfm template
array data type
arrayAppend function
arrayClear function
arrayLen function
arrayNew function
boolean data type
cfabort tag
cfapplication tag
cfelse tag
cfelseif tag
cfif tag
cfinvoke tag
cflocation tag
cfloop tag

CFML (ColdFusion Markup Language)
CFML interpreter
cfoutput tag
cfquery tag
cfset tag
cfxml tag
cgi scope
client scope
clientmanagement attribute
ColdFusion Administrator
ColdFusion Component (CFC)
comment tag (<!--- and --->)
concatenation operator (&)
contains operator (CONTAINS)
cookie scope
custom tag
Data Source Name
datasource attribute
date/time data type
dateFormat function

division operator (/)
does not contain operator (DOES NOT CONTAIN)
equal operator (EQ)
equivalence operator (EQV)
exclusive or operator (XOR)
exponent operator (^)
flash scope
form scope
greater than operator (GT)
greater than or equal operator (GTE)
group attribute
implication operator (IMP)
integer division operator (\)
isDefined function
isNumeric function
less than operator (LT)
less than or equal operator (LTE)
list data type
modulus operator (MOD)
multiplication operator (*)
name attribute
not equal operator (NEQ)

not operator (NOT)
now function
number data type
or operator (OR)
query attribute
query data type
queryname scope
request scope
server scope
session scope
sessionmanagement attribute
string data type
structure data type
sub expressions with (and)
subtraction operator (-)
template
timeFormat function
unary negative operator (-)
unary positive operator (+)
url scope
user-defined function
variables scope

SELF-REVIEW EXERCISES

27.1 State whether each of the following is *true* or *false*. If *false*, explain why.
  a) <!-- and --> are CFML comment tags.
  b) Users can see CFML tags when viewing the source code in their browsers.
  c) The cfoutput tag converts variables and functions to text and XHTML.
  d) #'s enclose variables and functions for output.
  e) form-scoped variables are created by submitting forms that use the get method.
  f) (and) can be used to create subexpressions.

27.2 Fill in the blanks in each of the following statements:
  a) ColdFusion templates have the file extension _____.
  b) The _____ attribute of the cfquery tag specifies the database to use.
  c) The cfapplication tag can usually be found in the _____ template.
  d) The _____ scope is the only scope often omitted.
  e) EQ has a(n) _____ operator precedence rank than AND.
  f) 23 and 3.14 are examples of the _____ data type.

ANSWERS TO SELF-REVIEW EXERCISES

27.1 a) False. CFML comment tags are <!--- and --->. b) False. The CFML interpreter removes all CFML before sending the template to the user. c) True. d) True. e) False. form-scoped variables are created by forms submitted using the post method. f) True.

27.2 a) .cfm. b) datasource. c) Application.cfm. d) variables. e) higher. f) number.

EXERCISES

27.3   Order the following CFML operators from highest to lowest order of precedence:
   a) NOT
   b) ∧
   c) GTE
   d) XOR
   e) &
   f) MOD

27.4   Identify and correct the error in the following ColdFusion code example.

```
<cfset aNumber = 23.5>
<cfif aNumber = 20>
   The number is equal to 20.
<cfelse>
   The number does not equal 20.
</cfif>
```

27.5   Describe what the following ColdFusion code displays.

```
<cfset anExpression = ( ( 5 + 2 * 7 ) + 8 / 2 )>
<cfoutput>
   The number is #anExpression#.
</cfoutput>
```

27.6   Describe what the following ColdFusion code displays.

```
<cfset a = true>
<cfset b = false>
<cfif NOT ( a EQV b ) XOR a OR b>
   First expression is true.
<cfelseif NOT a AND b XOR a OR NOT b>
   Second expression is true.
<cfelse>
   Neither expression is true.
</cfif>
```

27.7   Modify the auction bidding program in Fig. 27.9 so that the highest bid is stored in a `cookie`-scoped variable called `highestBid`. Compare all the submitted bids with `highestBid` and determine whether or not the new bid is higher. Remember to update the `highestBid` cookie if necessary.

27.8   Modify the shopping cart in Fig. 27.14 to store quantity information along with the currently stored information. Also, ensure that adding a duplicate book to the cart results in incrementing the quantity of that book instead of adding a duplicate entry to the array.

28

Multimedia: Audio, Video, Speech Synthesis and Recognition

Objectives

- To enhance Web pages with sound and video.
- To use the bgsound element to add background sounds.
- To use the img element's dynsrc property to incorporate video into Web pages.
- To use the embed element to add sound or video.
- To use the Windows Media Player ActiveX control to play a variety of media formats in Web pages.
- To use the Microsoft Agent ActiveX control to create animated characters that speak to users and respond to spoken commands from users.
- To embed RealOne Player™ to include streaming audio and video in a Web page.
- To embed video and create graphics in a Web page using SMIL and SVG.

We'll use a signal I have tried and found far-reaching and easy to yell. Waa-hoo!
Zane Grey

TV gives everyone an image, but radio gives birth to a million images in a million brains.
Peggy Noonan

Noise proves nothing. Often a hen who has merely laid an egg cackles as if she had laid an asteroid.
Mark Twain

Outline

28.1 Introduction

Welcome to what may be the largest revolution in the history of the computer industry. Those of us who entered the field decades ago were interested in using computers primarily to perform arithmetic calculations at high speed. As the computer field evolves, we are beginning to realize that the data-manipulation capabilities of computers are now equally important. The "sizzle" of the Web is **multimedia**—the use of **sound**, **images**, **graphics** and **video** to make Web pages "come alive." Although most multimedia on the Web is two-dimensional, we expect all kinds of exciting new three-dimensional Web capabilities in the near future.

Multimedia programming offers many new challenges. The field is already enormous and continues to grow rapidly. People are rushing to equip their computers for multimedia. Most new computers sold today are "multimedia ready," with CD-RW and DVD drives, audio boards and special video capabilities. Economical desktop and laptop computers are so powerful that they can store and play DVD-quality sound and video, and we expect to see further advances in the kinds of programmable multimedia capabilities available through programming languages. One thing that we have learned—having been in this industry for nearly four decades now—is to plan for the impossible. In the computer and communications fields, the impossible has repeatedly become reality.

In this chapter, we discuss how to add sound, video and animated characters to Web-based applications. Your first reaction may be a sense of caution because you realize that these are complex technologies and most readers have had little if any education in these areas. This is one of the beauties of today's programming languages. They give the programmer easy access to complex technologies and hide most of the complexity.

Multimedia files can be quite large. Some multimedia technologies require that the complete multimedia file be downloaded to the client before the audio or video begins playing. With streaming technologies, audio and video can begin playing while the files are downloading, to reduce delays. Streaming technologies are becoming increasingly popular.

> **Performance Tip 28.1**
>
> *Multimedia is performance intensive. Although processor speed has become less of a concern over the last few years, Internet bandwidth is still a precious resource. Multimedia-based Web applications must be carefully designed to use resources wisely. If not, they may perform poorly.*

Creating audio and video to incorporate into Web pages often requires complex and powerful software, such as Adobe™ After Effects® or Macromedia™ Director®. Rather than discuss how to create media clips, this chapter focuses on using existing audio and video clips to enhance Web pages. The chapter also includes an extensive set of Web resources. Some of these Web sites display examples of interesting multimedia enhancements, others provide instructional information for developers planning to enhance their own sites with multimedia.

28.2 Audio and Video

Audio and video can be used in Web pages in a variety of ways. Audio and video files can be embedded in a Web page or placed on a Web server so that they can be downloaded "on-demand." A variety of audio and video file formats are available for different uses.

Common video file formats include **MPEG (Moving Pictures Experts Group)**, **QuickTime**, **RealOne Player**, **AVI (Audio Video Interleave)** and **MJPEG (Motion JPEG)**. Audio formats include **MP3 (MPEG Layer 3)**, **MIDI (Musical Instrument Digital Interface)**, **WAV (Windows Waveform)** and **AIFF (Audio Interchange File Format**—Macintosh only).

Encoding and **compression** determine a file's format. An **encoding algorithm** or **codec (compressor/decompressor)** transforms raw audio or video into a format that Web browsers (or programs accompanying a Web browser) can interpret and display. Different encoding levels and formats produce file sizes and quality that are ideal for different applications.

Some codecs are available to the public in the form of **encoding applications**. Most encoding applications compress audio and video files. Some serve as **format converters**, converting one file format into another.

28.3 Adding Background Sounds with the bgsound Element

Some Web sites provide background audio to create a particular "atmosphere." There are various methods of adding sound to a Web page, the simplest being the **bgsound** element.

> **Portability Tip 28.1**
>
> *The bgsound element is a Microsoft-specific extension to XHTML. It is considered deprecated in XHTML 1.1, although it still functions in Internet Explorer 6.*

The bgsound element has four key properties—**src**, **loop**, **balance** and **volume**. To change the property values via a script, assign a scripting name to the bgsound element's **id** property.

The src property specifies the URL of the audio clip to be played. Internet Explorer supports a wide variety of audio formats.

Software Engineering Observation 28.1

The audio clip specified with bgsound's src property can be any type supported by Internet Explorer.

The **loop** property specifies the number of times the audio clip will play. The default value **-1** specifies that the audio clip should loop until the user browses to a different Web page or clicks the browser's **Stop** button. A positive integer indicates the exact number of times the audio clip should loop. Negative values (except **-1**) and zero values for this property cause the audio clip to play once.

The **balance** property specifies the balance between the left and right speakers. The value for this property is between **-10000** (sound only from the left speaker) and **10000** (sound only from the right speaker). The default value, **0**, indicates that the sound should be balanced between the two speakers.

Software Engineering Observation 28.2

Scripting cannot set bgsound's property balance.

The **volume** property determines the volume of the audio clip. The value for this property is between **-10000** (minimum volume) and **0** (maximum volume). The default value is **0**.

Software Engineering Observation 28.3

The volume specified with bgsound property volume is relative to the current volume setting on the client computer. If the client computer has sound turned off, the volume property has no effect.

Portability Tip 28.2

On most computers, the minimum audible volume for bgsound property volume is a value much greater than -10000. This value depends on the machine.

The XHTML document in Fig. 28.1 demonstrates the **bgsound** element and scripting the element's properties. This example's audio clip comes from the Microsoft Developer Network's downloads site,

msdn.microsoft.com/downloads/default.asp

This site contains many free images and sounds. [*Note*: Many of the examples in this chapter require an Internet connection to access certain audio or video files.]

```
1   <?xml version = "1.0"?>
2   <!DOCTYPE html PUBLIC "-//W3C//DTD XHTML 1.0 Transitional//EN"
3      "http://www.w3.org/TR/xhtml1/DTD/xhtml1-transitional.dtd">
4
5   <!-- Fig. 28.1: BackgroundAudio.html  -->
6   <!-- Demonstrating the bgsound element -->
7
8   <html xmlns = "http://www.w3.org/1999/xhtml">
9      <head><title>The bgsound Element</title>
10        <bgsound id = "audio" src =
```

Fig. 28.1 Demonstrating background audio with **bgsound**. (Part 1 of 3.)

```
11              "http://msdn.microsoft.com/downloads/sounds/jazzgos.mid"
12              loop = "1"></bgsound>
13
14          <script type = "text/javascript">
15              <!--
16              function changeProperties()
17              {
18                  var loop = parseInt( audioForm.loopit.value );
19                  if ( ( loop >= -1 ) ) {
20                      audio.loop = ( isNaN( loop ) ? 1 : loop );
21                  } else {
22                      alert( "Please enter a integer\n" +
23                          "greater than or equal to -1." );
24                  }
25
26                  var vol = parseInt( audioForm.vol.value );
27                  if ( ( vol >= -10000 ) && ( vol <= 0 ) ) {
28                      audio.volume = ( isNaN( vol ) ? 0 : vol );
29                  } else {
30                      alert( "Please enter an integer\n" +
31                          "between -10000 and 0." );
32                  }
33              }
34
35              function stopSound()
36              {
37                  if ( audioForm.stopButton.value == "Stop Sound" )
38                  {
39                      audio.src = "";
40                      audioForm.stopButton.value =
41                          "Start Sound";
42                  } else {
43                      audio.src =
44                          "http://msdn.microsoft.com/downloads/sounds/jazzgos.mid";
45                      audioForm.stopButton.value =
46                          "Stop Sound";
47                  }
48              }
49              // -->
50          </script>
51      </head>
52
53  <body>
54      <h1>Background Music via the bgsound Element</h1>
55      <h2>Jazz Gospel</h2>
56
57      This sound is from the free sound downloads at the
58      <a href =
59          "http://msdn.microsoft.com/downloads/default.asp">
60          Microsoft Developer Network</a> downloads site.
61      <hr />
62      Use the fields below to change the number of iterations
63      and the volume for the audio clip<br />
```

Fig. 28.1   Demonstrating background audio with **bgsound**. (Part 2 of 3.)

```
64          Press <strong>Stop</strong> to stop playing the sound.
65          <br />Press <strong>Refresh</strong> to begin playing
66          the sound again.
67
68          <form name = "audioForm" action = "">
69          <p>Loop [-1 = loop forever]</p>
70             <input name = "loopit" type = "text" value = "1" />
71             <br />Volume [-10000 (low) to 0 (high)]
72             <input name = "vol" type = "text" value = "0" /><br />
73             <input type = "button" value = "Set Properties"
74                onclick = "changeProperties()" />
75
76             <input type = "button" value = "Stop Sound"
77                id = "stopButton" onClick = "stopSound()" />
78          </form>
79       </body>
80    </html>
```

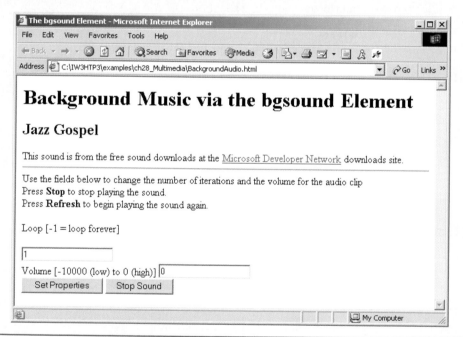

Fig. 28.1   Demonstrating background audio with `bgsound`. (Part 3 of 3.)

The code in lines 10–12 specifies the media source. The `loop` property specifies that the audio clip plays only once. The `balance` and `volume` attributes are omitted, so they default to 0. [*Note*: The `bgsound` element should be placed in the `head` section of the XHTML document.]

Function `changeProperties` (lines 16–33) is called in line 74 when the **Set Properties** button is clicked. Lines 18–24 read the new value for property `loop` from the form's `loopit` text field, convert the value to an integer and set the new property value by assigning a value to `audio.loop` (where `audio` is the `id` of the `bgsound` element and `loop` is a property).

Lines 26–32 read the new value for the `volume` property from the form's `vol` text field, convert the value to an integer and set the new property value by assigning a value to `audio.volume` (where `volume` is the scripting name of the property).

Function `stopSound` (lines 35–48) stops the audio clip from playing when the user clicks the **Stop Sound** button (lines 76–77). Line 39 changes the `audio` element's `src` attribute to an empty string `""`. Clicking the button again changes the `src` attribute back to its original value (lines 43–44).

Look-and-Feel Observation 28.1

When creating a Web page with background sound, always include a way for the user to turn the sound off. Web users often prefer to browse silently.

Look-and-Feel Observation 28.2

Avoid embedding loud or intrusive background sounds into a Web page. These types of audio can deter viewers.

28.4 Adding Video with the `img` Element's `dynsrc` Property

Web designers can enhance their multimedia presentations by incorporating a variety of video formats. The `img` element (introduced in Chapter 4) incorporates both images and videos in a Web page. Using the `src` property indicates that the desired source is an image. Using the **dynsrc** (i.e., dynamic source) property indicates that the source is a video clip. The `dynsrc` property may be followed by properties such as `loop`, which is similar to the `bgsound`'s `loop` property. The XHTML document in Fig. 28.2 demonstrates the `img` element and its `dynsrc` property.

```
1   <?xml version = "1.0"?>
2   <!DOCTYPE html PUBLIC "-//W3C//DTD XHTML 1.0 Transitional//EN"
3      "http://www.w3.org/TR/xhtml1/DTD/xhtml1-transitional.dtd">
4
5   <!-- Fig. 28.2: Dynamicimg.html                        -->
6   <!-- Demonstrating the img element's dynsrc property -->
7
8   <html xmlns = "http://www.w3.org/1999/xhtml">
9      <head>
10        <title>An Embedded Video Using the dynsrc Property</title>
11        <bgsound src =
12           "http://msdn.microsoft.com/downloads/sounds/carib.MID"
13           loop = "-1"></bgsound>
14     </head>
15
16     <body>
17        <h1>An Embedded Video Using the img element's
18           dynsrc Property</h1>
19        <h2>Car and Carribean Music</h2>
20        <table>
21           <tr><td><img dynsrc = "car_hi.wmv"
22                    start = "mouseover" width = "180"
23                    height = "135" loop = "-1"
```

Fig. 28.2   Playing a video with the `img` element's `dynsrc` property. (Part 1 of 2.)

```
24                                    alt = "Car driving in circles" /></td>
25                  <td>This page will play the audio clip and video
26                  in a loop.<br />The video will not begin
27                  playing until you move the mouse over the
28                  video.<br />Press the browser's<strong>Stop</strong>
29                  button to stop playing the sound and the video.</td>
30              </tr>
31          </table>
32      </body>
33  </html>
```

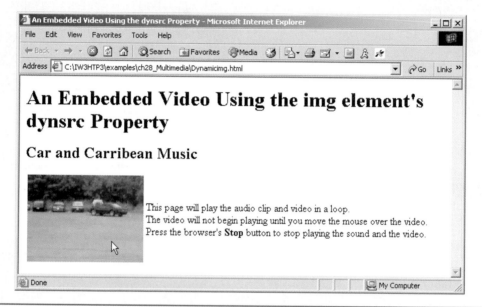

Fig. 28.2   Playing a video with the `img` element's `dynsrc` property. (Part 2 of 2.)

Portability Tip 28.3

The `dynsrc` property of the `img` element is specific to Internet Explorer.

The `img` element in lines 21–24 uses the `dynsrc` property to load and display the video `car_hi.wmv`. Property **start** specifies when the video should start playing. There are two possible start events—**fileopen** indicates that the video should play as soon as it loads into the browser, and **mouseover** indicates that the video should play when the user positions the mouse over the video. Clicking the Web browser's **Stop** button stops the video from playing.

28.5 Adding Audio or Video with the embed Element

So far, we have used elements `bgsound` and `img` to embed audio and video in a Web page. In both cases, viewers of the page have little control over the media clip. In this section, we introduce the **embed** element, which embeds a media clip (audio or video) into a Web page. The `embed` element displays a graphical user interface (GUI) within the browser window that gives the user direct control over the media clip. A browser encountering a media clip in an embed element launches an application that can play it. For each media type, users can set a preferred player. For example, if the media clip is a .wav file (i.e., a Windows Wave file), Internet Explorer typically uses the Windows Media Player ActiveX control to play the clip. The Windows Media Player has a GUI that enables users to play, pause and stop the media clip. Users can also control the volume of audio and move forward and backward through the clip using the GUI.

The embed element is supported by both Microsoft Internet Explorer and Netscape, but it is not part of the XHTML 1.1 recommendation. Documents written in XHTML using the embed element should render properly in either browser, though errors may occur when one tries to validate the document using the World Wide Web Consortium's XHTML 1.1 Validation Service.

The XHTML document in Fig. 28.3 modifies the wave filter example from Chapter 15. This example uses an embed element to add audio to the Web page.

```
1   <?xml version = "1.0"?>
2   <!DOCTYPE html PUBLIC "-//W3C//DTD XHTML 1.0 Transitional//EN"
3      "http://www.w3.org/TR/xhtml1/DTD/xhtml1-transitional.dtd">
4
5   <!-- Fig. 28.3: EmbeddedAudio.html            -->
6   <!-- Background Audio via the embed Element -->
7
8   <html xmlns = "http://www.w3.org/1999/xhtml">
9      <head>
10        <title>Background Audio via the embed Element</title>
11        <style type = "text/css">
12          span    { width: 600 }
13          .big    { color: blue;
14                    font-family: sans-serif;
15                    font-size: 50pt;
16                    font-weight: bold }
17        </style>
18
19        <script type = "text/javascript">
20           <!--
21           var TimerID;
22           var updown = true;
23           var str = 1;
24
25           function start()
26           {
27              TimerID = window.setInterval( "wave()", 100 );
28           }
29
30           function wave()
31           {
32              if ( str > 23 || str < 1 )
33                 updown = !updown;
34
35              if ( updown )
36                 str++;
```

Fig. 28.3   Embedding audio with the embed element. (Part 1 of 2.)

```
37              else
38                 str--;
39
40              wft.filters( "wave" ).phase = str * 20;
41              wft.filters( "wave" ).strength = str;
42          }
43          // -->
44       </script>
45    </head>
46
47    <body onload = "start()">
48       <h1>Background Audio via the embed Element</h1>
49       <p>Click the text to stop the script.</p>
50
51       <p class = "big" align = "center">
52       <span onclick = "window.clearInterval( TimerID )"
53          id = "wft" style = "filter:wave(
54          add = 0, freq = 3, light = 0, phase = 0, strength = 5)">
55          WAVE FILTER EFFECT</p></span>
56
57       <p>These controls can be used to control the audio.</p>
58       <embed src = "humming.wav" loop = "true"></embed>
59    </body>
60 </html>
```

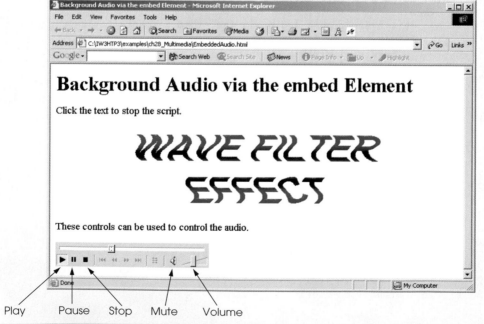

Fig. 28.3   Embedding audio with the embed element. (Part 2 of 2.)

Line 58 uses the embed element to specify that the audio file humming.wav should be embedded in the Web page. The **loop** property indicates that the media clip should loop indefinitely. The width and height properties define the size of the controls for the sound clip. By default, the GUI for the media player is displayed. To prevent the GUI from appearing in the Web page, add hidden = "true" to the embed element. To manipulate the element, specify a scripting name by adding the id property to the embed element.

The embed element can specify video clips as well as audio clips. Figure 28.4 demonstrates an embedded video. The embed element that loads and plays the video is located in line 18.

```
1   <?xml version = "1.0"?>
2   <!DOCTYPE html PUBLIC "-//W3C//DTD XHTML 1.0 Transitional//EN"
3       "http://www.w3.org/TR/xhtml1/DTD/xhtml1-transitional.dtd">
4
5   <!-- Fig. 28.4: EmbeddedVideo.html -->
6   <!-- Video via the embed Element    -->
7
8   <html xmlns = "http://www.w3.org/1999/xhtml">
9       <head>
10          <title>Video via the embed Element</title>
11      </head>
12
13      <body>
14          <h1>Displaying a Video using the embed Element</h1>
15          <h2>Car Driving in Circles</h2>
16
17          <table>
18              <tr><td><embed src = "car_hi.wmv" loop = "false"
19                      width = "240" height = "176">
20                  </embed></td>
21              </tr></table>
22          <hr />
23          This page plays the video once.<br />
24          Use the controls on the embedded video player to play the
25          video again.
26      </body>
27  </html>
```

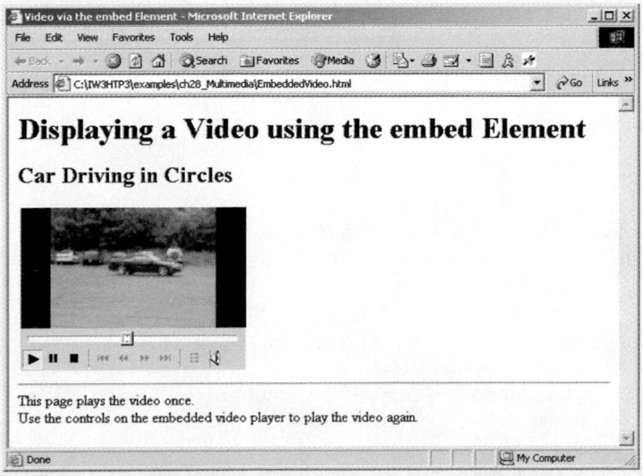

Fig. 28.4   Embedding video with the embed element.

28.6 Using the Windows Media Player ActiveX Control

ActiveX controls enhance the functionality of Web pages with interactivity. In this section, we embed the **Windows Media Player ActiveX control** in a Web page, so that we can access a wide range of media formats supported by the Windows Media Player. The Windows Media Player and other ActiveX controls are embedded into Web pages with the **object** element.

The XHTML document in Fig. 28.5 demonstrates how to use the `object` element to embed two Windows Media Player ActiveX controls in the Web page. One of the controls plays a video. The other control plays an audio clip.

```
1    <?xml version = "1.0"?>
2    <!DOCTYPE html PUBLIC "-//W3C//DTD XHTML 1.0 Transitional//EN"
3       "http://www.w3.org/TR/xhtml1/DTD/xhtml1-transitional.dtd">
4
5    <!-- Fig. 28.5: MediaPlayer.html    -->
6    <!-- Embedded Media Player Objects -->
7
8    <html xmlns = "http://www.w3.org/1999/xhtml">
9       <head><title>Embedded Media Player Objects</title>
10         <script type = "text/javascript">
11            <!--
12            var videoPlaying = true;
13
14            function toggleVideo( b )
15            {
16               videoPlaying = !videoPlaying;
17               b.value = videoPlaying ?
18                  "Pause Video" : "Play Video";
19               videoPlaying ?
20                  VideoPlayer.Play() : VideoPlayer.Pause();
21            }
22            // -->
23         </script>
24      </head>
25
26      <body>
27         <h1>
28            Audio and video through embedded Media Player objects
29         </h1>
30         <hr />
31         <table>
32            <tr><td valign = "top" align = "center">
33            <object id = "VideoPlayer" width = "200" height = "225"
34               classid =
35                  "CLSID:22d6f312-b0f6-11d0-94ab-0080c74c7e95">
36               <param name = "FileName" value =
37                  "car_hi.wmv" />
38               <param name = "AutoStart" value = "true" />
39               <param name = "ShowControls" value = "false" />
```

Fig. 28.5   Using the `object` element to embed the Windows Media Player ActiveX control in a Web page. (Part 1 of 2.)

```
40                  <param name = "Loop" value = "true" />
41              </object></td>
42              <td valign = "bottom" align = "center">
43              <p>Use the controls below to control the audio clip.</p>
44              <object id = "AudioPlayer"
45                  classid =
46                      "CLSID:22d6f312-b0f6-11d0-94ab-0080c74c7e95">
47                  <param name = "FileName" value =
48                      "http://msdn.microsoft.com/downloads/sounds/carib.mid" />
49                  <param name = "AutoStart" value = "true" />
50                  <param name = "Loop" value = "true" />
51              </object></td></tr>
52
53              <tr><td valign = "top" align = "center">
54                  <input name = "video" type = "button" value =
55                      "Pause Video" onclick = "toggleVideo( this )" />
56              </td></tr>
57          </table>
58      </body>
59  </html>
```

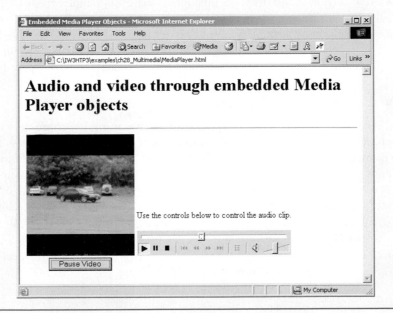

Fig. 28.5   Using the `object` element to embed the Windows Media Player ActiveX control in a Web page. (Part 2 of 2.)

When the body of this document loads, two instances of the Windows Media Player ActiveX control are created. The `object` element in lines 33–41 creates a Media Player object for the file `car_hi.wmv` (the source is specified in line 37). Line 33 indicates the start of the embedded `object` definition. The **id** property specifies the scripting name of the element (i.e., `VideoPlayer`). The **width** and **height** properties specify the width and height, in pixels, that the controls occupy in a Web page. In lines 34–35, property **classid** specifies the ActiveX control ID for the Windows Media Player. ActiveX controls have unique `classid`s that identify them. For more information about ActiveX controls, visit `www.active-x.com`.

Lines 36–40 specify **parameters** that are passed to the control when it is created in the Web page. Each parameter is specified with a **param** element that has **name** and **value** properties. The **FileName** parameter specifies the file containing the media clip. The **AutoStart** parameter is a boolean value indicating whether or not the media clip plays when it is loaded. The **ShowControls** parameter is a boolean value indicating whether the Media Player controls should be displayed. The **Loop** parameter is a boolean value indicating whether the Media Player should play the media clip indefinitely.

The **object** element in lines 44–51 embeds another Media Player object in the Web page. This Media Player plays the MIDI file `carib.mid` (specified with the `FileName` parameter). A **MIDI** (**Musical Instrument Digital Interface**) file is a sound file that conforms to the MIDI standard for digital music playback. The Media Player starts playing the clip when it is loaded (specified by setting the `AutoStart` parameter to `true`) and loops the audio clip indefinitely (specified by setting the `Loop` parameter to `true`).

The script in lines 10–23 controls the media player. Clicking **Pause Video** calls function `toggleVideo` (line 14). The button is defined in the XHTML form in lines 54–55. The `onclick` event sets the `toggleVideo` function as the event handler passes `this` as an argument for the function. `this` serves as a pointer to the element from which it is passed—in this case, the `input` element. This event changes the button text in lines 17–18. Lines 19–20 use the boolean variable `videoPlaying` to determine whether to call `Video-Player`'s `Play` method or `Pause` method, which play or pause the video clip, respectively.

28.7 Microsoft Agent Control

Microsoft Agent is an exciting technology for **interactive animated characters** in a Windows application or a Web page. The **Microsoft Agent control** provides access to **Agent characters** such as **Peedy** (a parrot), **Genie**, **Merlin** (a wizard) and **Robby** (a robot)—as well as those created by third-party developers. These Agent characters allow users to interact with the application using more natural human communication techniques. The control accepts mouse and keyboard interactions, speaks (if a compatible text-to-speech engine is installed) and also supports speech recognition (if a compatible speech-recognition engine is installed). Using Microsoft Agent allows Web pages to speak with users. In this section, we introduce the Microsoft Agent control. The software for Microsoft Agent is on the CD-ROM that accompanies this book.

Software Engineering Observation 28.4

While Microsoft Agents can add fun and informative elements to a Web page, they are rarely used by professional Web designers. They are more commonly added to Windows-specific applications.

Users can create new characters with the help of the *Microsoft Agent Character Editor* and the *Microsoft Linguistic Sound Editing Tool* (both downloadable from the Microsoft Agent Web site: `www.microsoft.com/msagent/default.asp`). This page also provides links to download the *Lernout and Hauspie TruVoice text-to-speech (TTS) engine* and the *Microsoft Speech Recognition engine*, ActiveX controls that power voice integration with Microsoft Agent. [*Note*: The Lernout and Hauspie TruVoice text-to-speech (TTS) engine is a 6 MB download. The download process may take some time from the Microsoft

Web site. It is advisable to install this component directly from the CD-ROM included with this book.] Windows XP users must also download **SAPI** for the TTS engine to work properly. A version of SAPI can be found by clicking the download link provided at www.microsoft.com/msagent/downloads/user.asp#sapi.

Figure 28.6 demonstrates the Microsoft Agent ActiveX control and the Lernout and Hauspie TruVoice text-to-speech engine (also an ActiveX control). This XHTML document embeds these ActiveX controls into a Web page that acts as a tutorial for the various types of programming tips presented in this text. Peedy the Parrot appears and speaks the text that describes each of the programming tips. When the user clicks the icon for a programming tip, Peedy jumps to the tip and recites the appropriate text.

```
1    <?xml version = "1.0"?>
2    <!DOCTYPE html PUBLIC "-//W3C//DTD XHTML 1.0 Transitional//EN"
3       "http://www.w3.org/TR/xhtml1/DTD/xhtml1-transitional.dtd">
4
5    <!-- Fig. 28.6: tutorial.html -->
6    <!-- Microsoft Agent Control   -->
7
8    <html xmlns = "http://www.w3.org/1999/xhtml">
9       <head>
10          <title>Speech Recognition</title>
11
12          <!-- Microsoft Agent ActiveX Control -->
13          <object id = "agent" width = "0" height = "0"
14             classid = "CLSID:D45FD31B-5C6E-11D1-9EC1-00C04FD7081F"
15             codebase = "#VERSION = 2, 0, 0, 0">
16          </object>
17
18          <!-- Lernout & Hauspie TruVoice text to speech engine -->
19          <object width = "0" height = "0"
20             classid = "CLSID:B8F2846E-CE36-11D0-AC83-00C04FD97575"
21             codebase = "#VERSION = 6, 0, 0, 0">
22          </object>
23
24          <!-- Microsoft Speech Recognition Engine -->
25          <object width = "0" height = "0"
26             classid = "CLSID:161FA781-A52C-11d0-8D7C-00A0C9034A7E"
27             codebase = "#VERSION = 4, 0, 0, 0">
28          </object>
29
30          <script type = "text/javascript">
31             <!--
32
33             var currentImage = null;
34             var tips =
35                [ "gpp", "seo", "perf", "port",
36                  "gui", "ept", "cpe" ];
37             var tipNames = [
38                "Good Programming Practice",
39                "Software Engineering Observation",
```

Fig. 28.6   Microsoft Agent and the Lernout and Hauspie TruVoice text-to-speech (TTS) engine. (Part 1 of 7.)

```
40            "Performance Tip", "Portability Tip",
41            "Look-and-Feel Observation",
42            "Error-Prevention Tip",
43            "Common Programming Error" ];
44         var voiceTips = [
45            "Good [Programming Practice]",
46            "Software [Engineering Observation]",
47            "Performance [Tip]",
48            "Portability [Tip]",
49            "Look-and-Feel [Observation]",
50            "Error-Prevention [Tip]",
51            "Common [Programming Error]" ];
52         var explanations = [
53            // Good Programming Practice text
54            "Good Programming Practices highlight " +
55            "techniques for writing programs that are " +
56            "clearer, more understandable, more " +
57            "debuggable, and more maintainable.",
58
59            // Software Engineering Observation text
60            "Software Engineering Observations highlight " +
61            "architectural and design issues that affect " +
62            "the construction of complex software systems.",
63
64            // Performance Tip text
65            "Performance Tips highlight opportunities for " +
66            "improving program performance.",
67
68            // Portability Tip text
69            "Portability Tips help students write portable " +
70            "code that can execute in different Web browsers.",
71
72            // Look-and-Feel Observation text
73            "Look-and-Feel Observations highlight graphical " +
74            "user interface conventions. These observations " +
75            "help students design their own graphical user " +
76            "interfaces in conformance with industry " +
77            "standards.",
78
79            // Error-Prevention Tip text
80            "Error-Prevention Tips tell people how to " +
81            "test and debug their programs. Many of the " +
82            "tips also describe aspects of creating Web " +
83            "pages and scripts that reduce the likelihood " +
84            "of 'bugs' and thus simplify the testing and " +
85            "debugging process.",
86
87            // Common Programming Error text
88            "Common Programming Errors focus the students' " +
89            "attention on errors commonly made by beginning " +
90            "programmers. This helps students avoid making " +
91            "the same errors. It also helps reduce the long " +
```

Fig. 28.6   Microsoft Agent and the Lernout and Hauspie TruVoice text-to-speech (TTS) engine. (Part 2 of 7.)

```
 92                "lines outside instructors' offices during " +
 93                "office hours!" ];
 94
 95        function loadAgent()
 96        {
 97            agent.Connected = true;
 98            agent.Characters.Load( "Peedy",
 99                "C:\\WINNT\\msagent\\chars\\Peedy.acs" );
100            actor = agent.Characters.Character( "Peedy" );
101            actor.LanguageID = 0x0409; // sometimes needed
102
103            // get states from server
104            actor.Get( "state", "Showing" );
105            actor.Get( "state", "Speaking" );
106            actor.Get( "state", "Hiding" );
107
108            // get Greet animation and do Peedy introduction
109            actor.Get( "animation", "Greet" );
110            actor.MoveTo( screenLeft, screenTop - 90);
111            actor.Show();
112            actor.Play( "Greet" );
113            actor.Speak( "Hello. " +
114                "If you would like me to tell you about a " +
115                "programming tip, click its icon, or, press " +
116                "the 'Scroll Lock' key, and speak the name " +
117                "of the tip, into your microphone." );
118
119            // get other animations
120            actor.Get( "animation", "Idling" );
121            actor.Get( "animation", "MoveDown" );
122            actor.Get( "animation", "MoveUp" );
123            actor.Get( "animation", "MoveLeft" );
124            actor.Get( "animation", "MoveRight" );
125            actor.Get( "animation", "GetAttention" );
126            actor.Get( "animation", "GetAttentionReturn" );
127
128            // set up voice commands
129            for ( var i = 0; i < tips.length; ++i )
130                actor.Commands.Add( tips[ i ],
131                    tipNames[ i ], voiceTips[ i ], true, true );
132
133            actor.Commands.Caption = "Programming Tips";
134            actor.Commands.Voice = "Programming Tips";
135            actor.Commands.Visible = true;
136        }
137
138        function imageSelectTip( tip )
139        {
140            actor.Stop();
141            for ( i = 0; i < document.images.length; i++) {
142                document.images[ i ].style.background = "lemonchiffon";
```

Fig. 28.6   Microsoft Agent and the Lernout and Hauspie TruVoice text-to-speech (TTS) engine. (Part 3 of 7.)

```
143                    currentImage = null;
144                }
145            for ( var i = 0; i < document.images.length; ++i )
146                if ( document.images( i ) == tip )
147                    tellMeAboutIt( i );
148        }
149
150        function voiceSelectTip( cmd )
151        {
152            var found = false;
153
154            for ( var i = 0; i < tips.length; ++i )
155                if ( cmd.Name == tips[ i ] ) {
156                    found = true;
157                    break;
158                }
159
160            if ( found )
161                tellMeAboutIt( i );
162        }
163
164        function tellMeAboutIt( element )
165        {
166            currentImage = document.images( element );
167            currentImage.style.background = "red";
168            spanId = document.images( element ).id + "Span";
169            spanObject = document.getElementById( spanId );
170            actor.MoveTo(
171                screenLeft + parseInt( spanObject.style.left ) - 18,
172                screenTop + parseInt( spanObject.style.top )- 103 );
173            actor.Speak( explanations[ element ] );
174        }
175        // -->
176    </script>
177
178    <script type = "text/javascript" for = "agent"
179            event = "Command( cmd )">
180        <!--
181        voiceSelectTip( cmd );
182        // -->
183    </script>
184
185    <script type = "text/javascript" for = "agent"
186            event = "BalloonShow">
187        <!--
188        if ( currentImage != null ) {
189            currentImage.style.background = "lemonchiffon";
190            currentImage = null;
191        }
192        // -->
193    </script>
194
```

Fig. 28.6   Microsoft Agent and the Lernout and Hauspie TruVoice text-to-speech (TTS) engine. (Part 4 of 7.)

```
195       <script type = "text/javascript" for = "agent"
196          event = "Click">
197          <!--
198          actor.Play( "GetAttention" );
199          actor.Speak( "Stop poking me with that pointer!" );
200          actor.Play( "GetAttentionReturn" );
201          // -->
202       </script>
203    </head>
204
205    <body style = "background-color: lemonchiffon"
206          onload = "loadAgent()">
207       <table border = "0">
208          <tr>
209             <th colspan = "4">
210                <h1 style = "color: blue">
211                   Deitel Programming Tips
212                 </h1>
213             </th>
214          </tr>
215          <tr>
216             <td align = "center" valign = "top" width = "120">
217                <span id = "gppSpan" style = "position : absolute;
218                   left : 30; top : 80; width : 130;">
219                   <img id = "gpp" src = "GPP_100h.gif"
220                      alt = "Good Programming Practice" border =
221                      "0" onclick = "imageSelectTip( this )" />
222                Good Programming Practices</span></td>
223             <td align = "center" valign = "top" width = "120">
224                <span id = "seoSpan" style = "position : absolute;
225                   left : 180; top : 80; width : 130;">
226                   <img id = "seo" src = "SEO_100h.gif"
227                      alt = "Software Engineering Observation"
228                      border = "0"
229                      onclick = "imageSelectTip( this )" />
230                Software Engineering Observations</span></td>
231             <td align = "center" valign = "top" width = "120">
232                <span id = "perfSpan" style = "position : absolute;
233                   left : 330; top : 80; width : 130;">
234                   <img id = "perf" src = "PERF_100h.gif"
235                      alt = "Performance Tip" border = "0"
236                      onclick = "imageSelectTip( this )" />
237                Performance Tips</span></td>
238             <td align = "center" valign = "top" width = "120">
239                <span id = "portSpan" style = "position : absolute;
240                   left : 480; top : 80; width : 130;">
241                   <img id = "port" src = "PORT_100h.gif"
242                      alt = "Portability Tip" border = "0"
243                      onclick = "imageSelectTip( this )" />
244                Portability Tips</span></td>
245          </tr>
```

Fig. 28.6   Microsoft Agent and the Lernout and Hauspie TruVoice text-to-speech (TTS) engine. (Part 5 of 7.)

```
246              <tr>
247                  <td align = "center" valign = "top" width = "120">
248                      <span id = "guiSpan" style = "position : absolute;
249                          left : 30; top : 260; width : 130;">
250                          <img id = "gui" src = "GUI_100h.gif"
251                              alt = "Look-and-Feel Observation" border =
252                              "0" onclick = "imageSelectTip( this )" />
253                          Look-and-Feel Observations</span></td>
254                  <td align = "center" valign = "top" width = "120">
255                      <span id = "eptSpan" style = "position : absolute;
256                          left : 180; top : 260; width : 130;">
257                          <img id = "ept" src = "EPT_100h.gif"
258                              alt = "Error-Prevention Tip" border =
259                              "0" onclick = "imageSelectTip( this )" />
260                          Error-Prevention Tips</span></td>
261                  <td align = "center" valign = "top" width = "12">
262                      <span id = "cpeSpan" style = "position : absolute;
263                          left : 330; top : 260; width : 130;">
264                          <img id = "cpe" src = "CPE_100h.gif"
265                              alt = "Common Programming Error" border =
266                              "0" onclick = "imageSelectTip( this )" />
267                          Common Programming Errors</span></td>
268              </tr>
269          </table>
270          <img src = "agent_button.gif" style = "position: absolute;
271              bottom: 10px; right: 10px" />
272      </body>
273  </html>
```

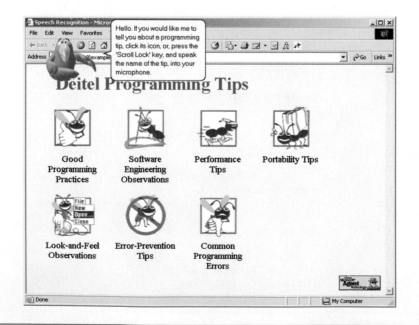

Fig. 28.6   Microsoft Agent and the Lernout and Hauspie TruVoice text-to-speech (TTS) engine. (Part 6 of 7.)

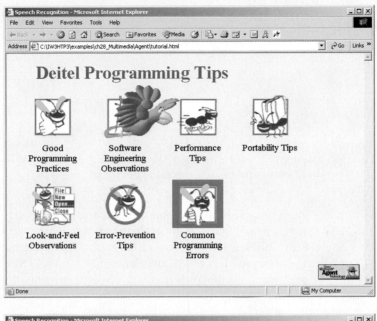

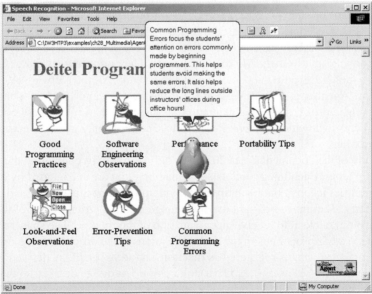

Fig. 28.6   Microsoft Agent and the Lernout and Hauspie TruVoice text-to-speech (TTS) engine. (Part 7 of 7.)

To run this example, install the Microsoft Agent character Peedy from the accompanying CD. Locate the `Peedy.acs` file on your computer, and change

```
"C:\\WINNT\\msagent\\chars\\Peedy.acs"
```

in line 99 to reflect the physical path to the file on your computer. [*Note*: Make sure each backslash character is preceded by a second backslash.] If you would like to run this example from the Internet, change

```
"C:\\WINNT\\msagent\\chars\\Peedy.acs"
```

to

```
"http://agent.microsoft.com/agent2/chars/peedy.acf"
```

 Performance Tip 28.2

The Microsoft Agent control and the Lernout and Hauspie TruVoice TTS engine will be downloaded automatically from the Microsoft Agent Web site if they are not already installed on your computer. Downloading these controls in advance allows the Web page to use Microsoft Agent and the TTS engine as soon as the Web page is loaded.

The first screen capture shows Peedy finishing his introduction. The second screen capture shows Peedy jumping toward the **Common Programming Errors** icon. The last screen capture shows Peedy finishing his discussion of **Common Programming Errors**.

Before using Microsoft Agent or the Lernout and Hauspie TruVoice TTS engine in the Web page, both must be loaded into the Web page via `object` elements. Lines 13–16 embed an instance of the Microsoft Agent ActiveX control into the Web page and give it the scripting name `agent` via the `id` property. Similarly, lines 19–22 embed an instance of the Lernout and Hauspie TruVoice TTS engine into the Web page. The Microsoft Agent uses the TTS engine control to speak the text that Microsoft Agent displays. If either of these controls is not already installed on the computer browsing the Web page, the browser attempts to download it from the Microsoft Web site. The **codebase** attribute (lines 15 and 21) specifies the URL from which to download this version of the software (Version 2 for the Microsoft Agent control and Version 6 for the Lernout and Hauspie TruVoice TTS engine). The Microsoft Agent documentation discusses how to place these controls on a server for clients to download. [*Note*: Placing these controls on your own server requires a license from Microsoft.]

The `body` of the document (lines 205–272) defines a `table` containing the seven programming tip icons. Each image and its accompanying text are surrounded by a `span` element that modifies its position. Each tip image and `span` element is given a scripting id via the `id` property. The image `id`'s are used to change the background color of the `img` element when a user clicks it to receive an explanation of the tip type. The span `id`'s are used to determine Peedy's proper positioning when he jumps to the different tip types. Each `img` element's `onclick` event is registered as function `imageSelectTip`, defined in line 138. Each `img` element passes itself (i.e., `this`) to function `imageSelectTip` so that the function can determine the particular user-selected image.

The XHTML document contains four separate `script` elements. The `script` element in lines 30–176 defines global variables used in all the `script` elements and defines functions `loadAgent` (called in response to the `body` element's `onload` event), `imageSelectTip` (called when users click an `img` element) and `tellMeAboutIt` (called by `imageSelectTip` to speak a few sentences about a tip).

Function `loadAgent` is particularly important because it loads the Microsoft Agent character that is used in this example. Lines 97–99 use the Microsoft Agent control's **Characters** collection to load the character information for Peedy. Method **Load** of the

Characters collection takes two arguments. The first argument specifies a name for the character that can be used later to interact with it, and the second argument specifies the location of the character's data file (Peedy.acs in this example).

Line 100 assigns a reference to the Peedy **Character** object to global variable actor. Object Character of the Characters collection receives as its argument the name that was used to download the character data in lines 98–99. Line 101 sets the Character's **LanguageID** property to 0x0409 (English). Microsoft Agent can actually be used with several different languages (see the documentation for more information).

Lines 104–106 use the Character object's **Get** method to download the **Showing**, **Speaking** and **Hiding** states for the character. The method takes two arguments—the *type* of information to download (in this case, state information) and the *name* of the corresponding element (e.g., Showing). Each state has animations associated with it. When the character is displayed (i.e., the Showing state), its associated animation plays (Peedy flies onto the screen). Downloading the Speaking state provides a default animation that makes the character appear to be speaking. When the character hides (i.e., goes into the Hiding state), the animations that make the character disappear are played (Peedy flies away).

Line 109 calls Character method Get to load an animation (Greet, in this example). Lines 110–117 use a variety of Character methods to interact with Peedy. Line 110 invokes the **MoveTo** method to specify Peedy's position on the screen. Line 111 calls method **Show** to display the character. When this occurs, the character plays the animation assigned to the Showing state (Peedy flies onto the screen). Line 112 calls method Play to play the Greet animation (see the first screen capture). Lines 113–117 invoke method **Speak** to make the character speak its string argument. If there is a compatible TTS engine installed, the character displays a bubble containing the text and speaks the text as well. The Microsoft Agent Web site contains complete lists of the animations available for each character (some are standard to all the characters, others are specific to only one).

Lines 120–126 load several other animations. Line 120 loads the set of **Idling** animations that Microsoft Agent uses when users are not interacting with the character. When running this example, be sure to leave Peedy alone for a while to see some of these idling animations. Lines 121–124 load the animations for moving the character up, down, left and right (**MoveUp**, **MoveDown**, **MoveLeft** and **MoveRight**, respectively).

Clicking an image calls function imageSelectTip (lines 138–148). The method first uses Character method **Stop** to terminate the current animation. Next, the for statement in lines 141–144 sets all the background image colors to lemonchiffon, which is the same as the background color. The next for statement (lines 145–147) determines which image the user clicked. The condition in line 146 calls the document object's **images** collection, which is determined by the index of the clicked img element. If the tip number is equal to the image number (i), then function tellMeAboutIt (lines 164–174) is called, where i is passed as the argument.

Line 166 of function tellMeAboutIt assigns global variable currentImage a reference to the clicked img element. This function then changes the background color of the img element that the user clicked by highlighting that image on the screen. Line 167 changes the background color of the image to red. Line 168 initializes variable spanId, which equals the id value of the span element corresponding to the clicked image. Line 170 invokes Character method MoveTo to position Peedy above the clicked image. When this statement executes, Peedy flies to the image and appears to perch directly on top of it.

We use the span element's `left` and `top` values in combination with the `screenLeft` and `screenTop` properties to position Peedy at the proper coordinates. The `Character` object's `Speak` method (line 173) speaks the text in for the selected tip. The text is stored as strings in array `explanations`.

Lines 185–193 define script that resets the background color of the selected image when Peedy starts speaking. The event listener `event = "BallonShow"` responds to the `agent` control `BalloonShow`, which calls the contained script every time Peedy's speaking balloon appears. If the `currentImage` is not `null`, the background color of the image is changed to `lemonchiffon` (the document's background color) and variable `currentImage` is reset to `null`.

The script for the `agent` control in lines 195–202 is invoked in response to the user's clicking the character. When this occurs, line 198 plays the `GetAttention` animation, line 199 causes Peedy to say "`Stop poking me with that pointer!`" and line 200 plays the last frame of the `GetAttention` animation by specifying `GetAttentionReturn`.

Voice recognition is also included in this example to enable the Agent character to receive voice commands. The first screen capture illustrates Peedy finishing his introduction (Fig. 28.7). The second screen capture shows Peedy after the user presses the *Scroll Lock* key to start issuing voice commands, which initializes the voice-recognition engine (Fig. 28.8). The third screen capture (Fig. 28.9) shows Peedy after receiving a voice command (i.e., "Good Programming Practice," which causes a **Command** event for the `agent` control). The last screen capture shows Peedy discussing Good Programming Practices (Fig. 28.10).

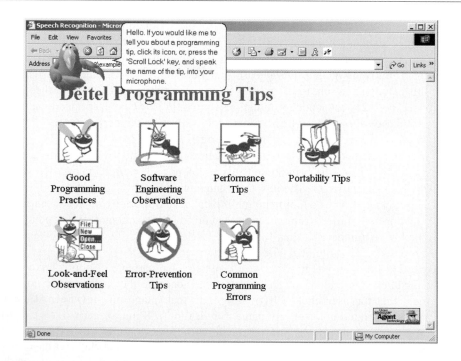

Fig. 28.7   Peedy finishing introduction.

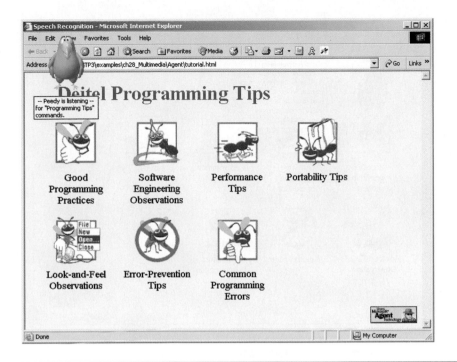

Fig. 28.8   Peedy ready to receive voice commands.

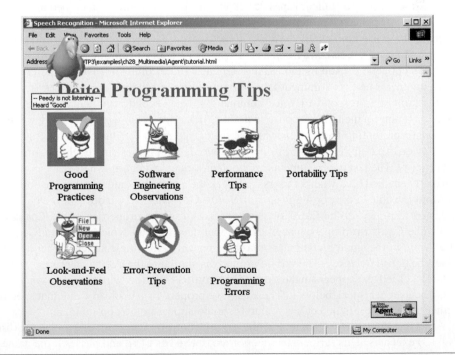

Fig. 28.9   Peedy receiving voice command.

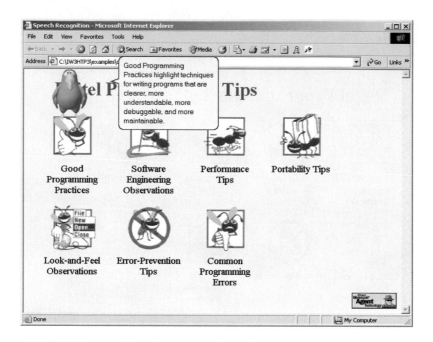

Fig. 28.10 Peedy discussing Good Programming Practices.

To enable Microsoft Agent to recognize voice commands, a compatible voice-recognition engine must be installed. Lines 25–28 use an `object` element to embed an instance of the Microsoft Speech Recognition engine control in the Web page.

Next, the voice commands used to interact with the Peedy must be registered in the `Character` object's **Commands** collection. The `for` statement in lines 129–131 uses the `Commands` collection's **Add** method to register each voice command. The method receives five arguments. The first argument is a string representing the command `name` (typically used in scripts that respond to voice commands). The second argument is a string that appears in a pop-up menu in response to a right click on the character. The third argument is a string representing the words or phrase users can speak for this command (stored in array `voiceTips` in lines 44–51). Optional words or phrases are enclosed in square brackets (`[]`). The last two arguments are boolean values indicating whether the command is currently enabled (i.e., whether users can speak the command) and whether the command is currently visible in the pop-up menu and **Voice Commands** window for the character.

Lines 133–135 set the **Caption**, **Voice** and **Visible** properties of the `Commands` object. The `Caption` property specifies text that describes the voice command set. This text appears in the small rectangular area that appears below the character when the user presses the *Scroll Lock* key. The `Voice` property is similar to the `Caption` property except that the specified text appears in the **Voice Commands** window with the set of voice commands the user can speak below it. The `Visible` property is a boolean value that specifies whether this `Commands` object's commands should appear in the pop-up menu.

After receiving a voice command, the `agent` control's `Command` event handler (lines 178–183) executes. This script calls function `voiceSelectTip` and passes it the name of the received command. Function `voiceSelectTip` (lines 150–162) uses the name of the command in the `for` statement (lines 154–158) to determine the index of the command in the `Commands` object. This value is then passed to function `tellMeAboutIt` (lines 164–174), which causes Peedy to move to the specified tip and discuss it.

This example has covered only the basic features and functionality of Microsoft Agent. Many more features are available. Figure 28.11 lists several other Microsoft Agent events.

Event	Description
BalloonHide	Called when the text balloon for a character is hidden.
BalloonShow	Called when the text balloon for a character is shown.
Hide	Called when a character is hidden.
Move	Called when a character is moved on the screen.
Show	Called when a character is displayed on the screen.
Size	Called when a character's size is changed.

Fig. 28.11 Other events for the Microsoft Agent control.

Figure 28.12 shows some other properties and methods of the `Character` object. Recall that the `Character` object represents the character that is displayed on the screen and enables interaction with it. For a complete listing of properties and methods, see the Microsoft Agent Web site.

Property or method	Description
Properties	
Height	The height of the character in pixels.
Left	The left edge of the character in pixels from the left of the screen.
Name	The default name for the character.
Speed	The speed of the character's speech.
Top	The top edge of the character in pixels from the top of the screen.
Width	The width of the character in pixels.
Methods	
Activate	Sets the currently active character when multiple characters appear on the screen.
GestureAt	Specifies that the character should gesture toward a location on the screen that is specified in pixel coordinates from the upper-left corner of the screen.
Interrupt	Interrupts the current animation. The next animation in the queue of animations for this character is then displayed.
StopAll	Stops all animations of a specified type for the character.

Fig. 28.12 Other properties and methods for the `Character` object.

Figure 28.13 shows some speech-output tags that can customize speech-output properties. The animated character will speak the string inserted into the tag. Speech-output tags generally remain in effect from the time they are encountered until the end of the current Speak method call.

Tag	Description
\Chr = *string*\	Specifies the tone of the voice. Possible values for *string* are Normal (the default) for a normal tone of voice, Monotone for a monotone voice or Whisper for a whispered voice.
\Emp\	Emphasizes the next spoken word.
\Lst\	Repeats the last statement spoken by the character. This tag must be the only content of the string in the Speak method call.
\Pau = *number*\	Pauses speech for *number* milliseconds.
\Pit = *number*\	Changes the pitch of the character's voice. This value must be within the range 50 to 400 hertz for the Microsoft Agent speech engine.
\Spd = *number*\	Changes the speech speed to a value in the range 50 to 250.
\Vol = *number*\	Changes the volume to a value in the range 0 (silent) to 65,535 (maximum volume).

Fig. 28.13 Speech output tags.

28.8 RealOne Player™ Plug-in

A RealOne Player object may be embedded into a Web page to enhance the page with streaming audio and video. RealOne Player can also be delivered as a browser plug-in on multiple platforms. Figure 28.14 demonstrates streaming audio and video in a Web page by embedding two RealOne Player objects in the page using embed elements. Users can select from two different sources; this selection then calls a JavaScript function which invokes RealOne Player methods to play the selected video stream. Viewing the following example requires that RealOne Player be installed. This software is available as a free download from RealNetworks at www.real.com/player.

The embed elements in lines 39–43 and lines 45–49 embed the RealOne Player plug-ins for video and audio, respectively, into the page. The **type** attribute specifies the MIME type of the embedded file, which in this case is the MIME type for streaming video or audio. (Remember that MIME is a standard for specifying the format of content so the browser can determine how to handle the content.) The **width** and **height** attributes specify the dimensions of the space the control occupies on the page. The **autostart** attribute determines whether the media starts playing when the page loads (for this example, we set it to false for both elements). The **controls** attribute specifies which controls users can access (e.g., **Play** button, **Pause** button and **Volume Control**). Setting attribute controls to ImageWindow in line 41 produces a video window. Setting controls to Default in line 47 creates a control bar featuring the standard control buttons. A list of available controls can be found at:

www.audiovideoweb.com/emded_real_html.htm

We do not set the **src** attribute of the embed element. Normally, the src is set to the location of the streaming media, but in this example, we use JavaScript to change the source dynamically based on user selections.

```
1   <?xml version = "1.0"?>
2   <!DOCTYPE html PUBLIC "-//W3C//DTD XHTML 1.0 Transitional//EN"
3      "http://www.w3.org/TR/xhtml1/DTD/xhtml1-transitional.dtd">
4
5   <!-- Fig. 28.14: StreamingMedia.html              -->
6   <!-- Embedding RealOne Player into an XHTML page -->
7
8   <html xmlns = "http://www.w3.org/1999/xhtml">
9      <head>
10         <title>Live Media!</title>
11
12         <script type = "text/javascript">
13            <!--
14            var locations =
15               [ "http://www.noaanews.noaa.gov/video/naturalworld.ram",
16                 "http://www.nasa.gov/ram/35037main_.ram"]
17
18            function change( loc )
19            {
20               videoControl.SetSource( locations[ loc ] );
21               videoControl.DoPlayPause();
22            }
23            // -->
24         </script>
25      </head>
26
27      <body>
28
29         <p>Pick from my favorite video streams:
30
31         <select id = "streamSelect" onchange =
32            "change( this.value )">
33            <option value = "">Select a station</option>
34            <option value = "0">NOAA</option>
35            <option value = "1">NASA</option>
36         </select></p>
37
38         <br />
39         <embed id = "videoControl" src = ""
40            type = "audio/x-pn-realaudio-plugin" width = "275"
41            height = "200" controls = "ImageWindow"
42            console = "streamingAudio"
43            autostart = "false" />
44         <br />
45         <embed id = "audioControl" src = ""
46            type = "audio/x-pn-realaudio-plugin" width = "275"
47            height = "40" controls = "ControlPanel"
```

Fig. 28.14 Embedding RealOne Player in a Web page. (Courtesy of RealNetworks, Inc.) (Part 1 of 2.)

```
48              console = "streamingAudio"
49              autostart = "false" />
50
51      </body>
52   </html>
```

Fig. 28.14 Embedding RealOne Player in a Web page. (Courtesy of RealNetworks, Inc.) (Part 2 of 2.)

Now that the player is embedded in the Web page, we use scripting to activate the streaming media. The `select` menu (line 31) lists two live media streams, corresponding to the two entries in the array `locations` (defined in line 14), which contain the actual URLs for the live video feeds. When the selection changes, function `change` (line 18) is called by the `onchange` event. This function calls methods **SetSource** and **DoPlayPause** of the RealOne Player object. Method `SetSource` sets the source URL of the audio stream to be played. Then, method `DoPlayPause` toggles between pausing and playing the stream. [*Note*: In this example, the stream is initially paused because no source was specified in the `embed` element. Thus, the stream begins playing in response to the call to `DoPlayPause`.]

To view more streaming media, visit the following sites:

```
www.noaa.gov
www.nasa.gov
www.streamingmedia.com/radio/
```

To learn more about programming with RealOne Player, visit the RealPlayer DevZone at

```
service.real.com/help/library/guides/extend/embed.htm
```

A few years ago, broadcasting personal streaming audio or video required a dedicated server and expensive software. Today, open-source software, such as *Darwin Streaming*

Server and *RealNetwork's Helix Universal Server G2*, provide "home-made" servers, such as Linux or Apache running on a PC, with streaming capability. These applications are available for download from www.shareware.com. With limited server-processor power and Internet bandwidth, however, this type of setup cannot support the same number of streams and bit rates as a dedicated streaming server.

28.9 Synchronized Multimedia Integration Language (SMIL)

The **Synchronized Multimedia Integration Language** (SMIL, pronounced "smile") enables Web document authors to coordinate the presentation of a wide range of multimedia elements. SMIL is an XML-based description language that organizes static and dynamic text, audio and video to occur simultaneously or sequentially. Like Flash, SMIL provides a time reference for all instances of text and media. A SMIL document specifies the source (i.e., the URL) and presentation of multimedia elements. In XHTML, multimedia elements are autonomous entities that cannot interact without complicated scripts. In SMIL, multimedia elements can work together, enabling document authors to specify when and how multimedia elements appear in a document. RealOne Player is one application capable of rendering SMIL documents. Apple's Quicktime plug-in also plays SMIL in both Windows and Mac OS environments.

Portability Tip 28.4

SMIL is the W3C-recommended method of embedding audio and video in a Web page.

The example in Fig. 28.15 is a SMIL document that displays jpg images for a variety of *Java How to Program* book covers. The images are displayed sequentially, and sound accompanies each image.

```
1   <smil xmlns="http://www.w3.org/2000/SMIL20/CR/Language">
2
3       <!-- Fig. 20.15 : exampleSMIL.smil -->
4       <!-- Example SMIL Document            -->
5
6       <head>
7           <layout>
8               <root-layout height = "300" width = "280"
9                   background-color = "#bbbbee" title = "Example" />
10
11              <region id = "image1" width = "177" height = "230"
12                  top = "35" left = "50" background-color = "#bbbbee" />
13          </layout>
14
15          <transition id = "wipeForward" dur = "2s" type = "barWipe" />
16          <transition id = "wipeBackward" dur = "2s" type = "barWipe"
17              subtype = "topToBottom" />
18
19          <transition id = "fadeIn" dur = "2s" type = "fade"
20              subtype = "fadeFromColor" fadeColor = "#bbbbee" />
21
```

Fig. 28.15 SMIL document with images and sound. (Part 1 of 2.)

```
22      <transition id = "fadeOut" dur = "2s" type = "fade"
23         subtype = "fadeToColor" fadeColor = "#bbbbee" />
24
25      <transition id = "crossFade" type = "fade" subtype = "crossfade"
26         dur = "2s" />
27
28   </head>
29   <body>
30      <seq>
31         <par>
32            <img src = "book1.jpg" region = "image1"
33               transIn = "wipeForward" transOut = "wipeForward"
34               alt = "book1" dur = "6s" fill = "transition"
35               fit = "fill" />
36            <audio src = "bounce.au" dur = ".5s" />
37         </par>
38         <par>
39            <img src = "book2.jpg" region = "image1" transIn = "fadeIn"
40                transOut = "fadeOut" alt = "book2" dur = "6s"
41                fit = "fill" fill = "transition" />
42            <audio src = "bounce.au" dur = ".5s" />
43         </par>
44         <par>
45            <img src = "book3.jpg" region = "image1"
46                transIn = "wipeBackward" transOut = "fadeOut"
47                alt = "book3" dur = "6s" fit = "fill"
48                fill = "transition" />
49            <audio src = "bounce.au" dur = ".5s" />
50         </par>
51         <par>
52            <img src = "book4.jpg" region = "image1" transIn = "crossFade"
53                transOut = "fadeOut" alt = "book4" dur = "6s"
54                fit = "fill" fill = "transition" />
55            <audio src = "bounce.au" dur = ".5s" />
56         </par>
57         <par>
58            <img src = "book5.jpg" region = "image1"
59               transIn = "wipeForward" transOut = "wipeBackward"
60               alt = "book5" dur = "6s" fit = "fill"
61               fill = "transition" />
62            <audio src = "bounce.au" dur = ".5s" />
63         </par>
64         <par>
65            <img src = "book6.jpg" region = "image1"
66                transIn = "crossFade" alt = "book6" dur = "6s"
67                fit = "fill" fill = "transition" />
68            <audio src = "bounce.au" dur = ".5s" />
69         </par>
70      </seq>
71
72   </body>
73 </smil>
```

Fig. 28.15 SMIL document with images and sound. (Part 2 of 2.)

Element head (lines 6–28) contains all the layout information (lines 7–13) and defines transitions for the document.

Lines 8–9 set the document size, color and title using element **root-layout**. Lines 11–12 set a region for displaying objects (e.g., images) using element **region**. Attribute id is a unique identifier for each region. Attributes width and height specify the size of the region, and attributes top and left provide its relative position. Attribute **background-color** sets the color of the region's background.

Lines 15–26 initialize various transitions that will be used when changing the image. The type and dur attributes of each transition element specify its transition type and duration, respectively. The id attribute assigns a unique id to each transition.

Line 29 begins the body, which encloses the content of the document. Line 30 starts element **seq** (short for sequential), which sets its child elements to execute sequentially (i.e., in the order that they appear in the document). A **par** (short for parallel) element (starting in line 31) sets its child elements to execute simultaneously.

Lines 32–35 show element **img**, which references an image. Attribute **src** contains the location of the image, and attribute **alt** provides a description of the image. Attribute **region** specifies the region in which an image displays; a fit value of fill sets the image to fill the entire region. Attribute **dur** describes how long the image appears on the screen (e.g., one second). Attribute **transIn** and **transOut** each reference the id assigned to a specific transition. transIn determines the transition leading into the image, and transOut specifies the transition as the image changes. RealNetworks provides a list of SMIL transitions at www.realnetworks.com/resources/samples/transitions.html. Line 36 contains element audio, which references audio file bounce.au. The remaining elements in the document (lines 38–69) display different images and play the same audio file.

We can embed a SMIL document in a Web page using the method described in Section 28.7. Visitors to a Web site need the RealOne Player plug-in to view SMIL content. The plug-in is installed with RealOne Player, which, as previously mentioned, is available as a free download from RealNetworks at www.real.com/player.

Figure 28.16 uses an embedded RealOne Player image window to view our example SMIL document. In lines 14–18 we use the embed element to add the SMIL document to the Web page. The many attributes of this tag determine how our SMIL document is displayed. First, set the src attribute in line 14 by giving it the location of the SMIL file. The file is located in the same folder as the XHTML document, so the path is simply the name of the file: exampleSmil.smil. The controls attribute in line 15 is set to ImageWindow, hiding the controls from users. The type attribute in line 16 allows the specification of the MIME type for the embedded object. In this case, we set type to audio/x-pn-realaudio-plugin to inform the browser that the RealOne Player plug-in should display the SMIL file. Users are not provided GUI controls, so the autostart attribute is set to true in line 17 to start the movie as soon as the page loads.

```
1   <?xml version = "1.0"?>
2   <!DOCTYPE html PUBLIC "-//W3C//DTD XHTML 1.0 Transitional//EN"
3      "http://www.w3.org/TR/xhtml1/DTD/xhtml1-transitional.dtd">
4
```

Fig. 28.16 Using RealOne Player plug-in to display a SMIL document. (Part 1 of 2.)

```
5    <!-- Fig. 28.16: SMILexample.html        -->
6    <!-- embedding SMIL with RealOne Player -->
7
8    <html xmlns = "http://www.w3.org/1999/xhtml">
9       <head>
10          <title>Embedding SMIL with RealOne Player</title>
11       </head>
12       <body>
13          <div style = "text-align: center">
14          <embed src = "exampleSMIL.smil"
15             controls = "ImageWindow"
16             type = "audio/x-pn-realaudio-plugin"
17             width = "280" height = "300" autostart = "true">
18          </embed>
19          </div>
20       </body>
21    </html>
```

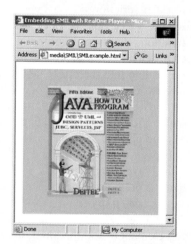

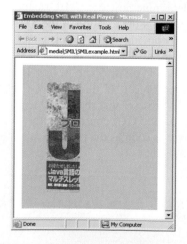

Fig. 28.16   Using RealOne Player plug-in to display a SMIL document. (Part 2 of 2.)

The screen captures in Fig. 28.16 show transitions between images. Here, we see two examples of the wideForward transition.

28.10 Scalable Vector Graphics (SVG)

Scalable Vector Graphics (SVG) markup language describes vector graphic data for JPEG, GIF and PNG formats so that they may be distributed over the Web efficiently. The GIF, JPEG and PNG file formats store images as bitmaps. Bitmaps describe the color of every pixel in an image and can take a long time to download. Because of the method in which bitmap information is stored, images of these file types cannot be enlarged or reduced without a loss of image quality.

Vector graphics are produced by mathematical equations that describe graphical information in terms of lines, curves, and so on. Not only do images rendered by vectors require less bandwidth, but they can be easily scaled and printed without loss of image clarity. Animations created with vector graphics have significantly smaller file sizes than those created by sequencing of bitmap images. Different graphic formats are discussed in detail in Chapter 3.

SVG is an XML vocabulary, comparable to the other XML vocabularies (e.g., MathML and MusicXML) presented in Chapter 20. Thus, SVG documents can be scripted, searched and dynamically created.

Both Internet Explorer and Netscape intend to provide native support for SVG in the near future. Currently, Adobe provides a plug-in for Internet Explorer (IE Version 4.0 or higher for Windows and Version 5.0 or higher for Mac) and for Netscape (Version 4.0 or higher for both Windows and Mac) that enables SVG documents to be rendered directly in those browsers. The SVG plug-in is available free of charge from Adobe at www.adobe.com/svg.

Figure 28.17 presents an SVG document that displays animated shapes in a browser. We use the Adobe plug-in to view the document in Internet Explorer 6.

```
1   <?xml version = "1.0"?>
2
3   <!-- Fig. 28.17 : shapes.svg -->
4   <!-- Simple example of SVG    -->
5
6   <svg viewBox = "0 0 300 300" width = "300" height = "300">
7
8      <!-- Generate a background -->
9      <g>
10        <path style = "fill: #eebb99" d = "M0,0 h300 v300 h-300 z"/>
11     </g>
12
13     <!-- Circle shape and attributes -->
14     <g>
15
16        <circle style = "fill:green;" cx = "150" cy = "150" r = "50">
17           <animate attributeName = "opacity" attributeType = "CSS"
18              from = "0" to = "1" dur = "6s" />
19        </circle>
20
```

Fig. 28.17 SVG document example. (Part 1 of 2.)

```
21        <!-- Rectangle shape and attributes -->
22
23        <rect style = "fill: blue; stroke: white"
24           x = "50" y = "0" width = "100" height = "100">
25           <animate attributeName = "y" begin = "mouseover" dur = "2s"
26              values = "0; -50; 0; 20; 0; -10; 0; 5; 0; -3; 0; 1; 0" />
27        </rect>
28
29        <!-- Text value and attributes -->
30
31        <text style = "fill: red; font-size: 24pt"
32           x = "25" y = "250"> Welcome to SVG!
33           <animateColor attributeName = "fill"
34              attributeType = "CSS" values = "red;blue;yellow;green;red"
35              dur = "10s" repeatCount = "indefinite"/>
36        </text>
37     </g>
38  </svg>
```

Fig. 28.17 SVG document example. (Part 2 of 2.)

Line 6 contains the root element **svg** for the SVG document. Attribute viewBox sets the viewing area for the document. The first two numbers in the string are the *x*- and *y*-coordinates of the upper-left corner of the viewing area, and the last two numbers are the width and height of the viewing area. Attribute width specifies the width of the image, and attribute height specifies the height of the image.

Element g groups elements of an SVG document. Line 10 uses element path to create the outline of the box that serves as the background of the image. Attribute style uses CSS property fill to fill the inside of the box with the color #eebb99. Attribute d defines the points of the box. Property M specifies the starting coordinates (0, 0) of the path. Property h specifies that the next point is horizontally aligned with the current point and spaced 300 pixels to the right of the current point (300, 0). Property v specifies that the next point is vertically aligned with the current point and is spaced 300 pixels below it (300, 300). Property h then places a point 300 pixels to the left of the current point. Property z sets the path to connect the first and last points, thus closing the box.

Lines 14–37 group three elements: a circle, a rectangle and a text element. Lines 16–19 create a circle with element circle. The circle has a center at (150, 150) and a radius (attribute r) of 50 pixels. The circle is filled green, with 50% opacity. The animate element contained within the circle element specifies an opacity transformation from 0 (completely transparent) to 1 (completely opaque) over a period of two seconds, determined by the dur attribute. The attribute attributeName of the animate element specifies the attribute to be altered, such as opacity, and the attributeType determines the type of attribute being altered. We set attributeType to CSS because we are altering a CSS property.

Lines 23–27 use element rect to create a rectangle. The rectangle's upper-left point is determined using attributes x and y. Attribute width sets the width of the rectangle, and attribute height sets the height of the rectangle. Element animate (lines 25–26) adjusts the rectangle's y value over a two-second period (specified by the dur attribute) each time the user rolls over the rectangle with the mouse (specified by attribute begin = "mouseover"). Attribute values specifies the y values between which the rectangle oscillates.

Lines 31–36 create text in the SVG image with element text. The format of the text is defined using attribute style. In this case, the text is initially colored red, with a font size of 24 point. The associated animateColor element (lines 33–35) creates a color-changing effect in the text. The text's fill attribute varies between the colors specified by attribute values over ten seconds.

Figure 28.18 contains a more complex SVG image that simulates the Earth and Moon rotating around the Sun. This example also uses SVG's animation feature.

```
1   <?xml version = "1.0"?>
2
3   <!-- Fig. 28.18: planet.svg   -->
4   <!-- Planetary motion with SVG -->
5
6   <svg viewBox = "-500 -500 1000 1000">
7      <g id = "background">
8         <path style = "fill: black"
9            d = "M -2000,-2000 H 2000 V 2000 H -2000 Z" />
10     </g>
11
12     <circle id = "sun" style = "fill: yellow"
13        cx = "0" cy = "0" r = "100" />
14
15     <g>
16        <animateTransform attributeName = "transform"
17           type = "rotate" dur = "80s" from = "0" to = "360"
18           repeatCount = "indefinite" />
19
20        <circle id = "earth" style = "fill: blue"
21           cx = "400" cy = "0" r = "40" />
```

Fig. 28.18 SVG document with animated elements. (Part 1 of 2.)

```
22
23          <g transform = "translate( 400 0 )">
24             <circle id = "moon" style = "fill: white"
25                cx = "70" cy = "0" r = "10">
26                <animateTransform attributeName = "transform"
27                   type = "rotate" dur = "20s" from = "360"
28                   to = "0" repeatCount = "indefinite" />
29             </circle>
30          </g>
31       </g>
32    </svg>
```

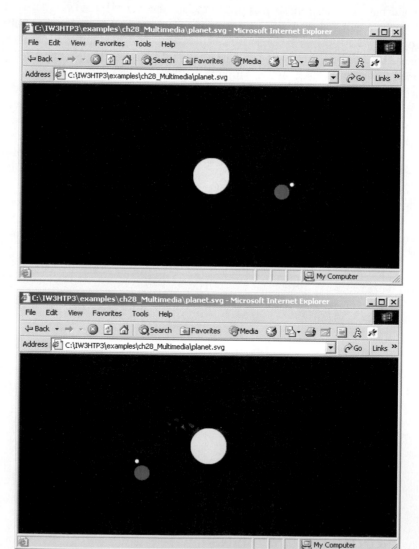

Fig. 28.18 SVG document with animated elements. (Part 2 of 2.)

Lines 8–9 create a box for the background that is much larger than the viewable size. Attribute d has properties H and V that specify absolute coordinates for the path. Thus, the coordinates of the box are (-2000, -2000), (2000, -2000), (2000, 2000) and (-2000, 2000).

Lines 12–13 create a yellow circle with a radius of 100 pixels at coordinate (0, 0) to represent the Sun. Line 15 defines element g, which groups together the circles representing the Earth and Moon. Lines 16–18 use element animateTransform, which changes the attribute of the parent element (i.e., element g) specified in attribute attributeName (i.e., attribute transform). Attribute type defines the property of the attribute that changes (i.e., rotate). The initial and final values of the transformation are set by attributes from and to. Attribute dur sets the time (i.e., 80 seconds) within which the change from the initial to the final values should occur, and attribute repeatCount sets the number of times to perform this transformation. In our example, we rotate the group element, which contains the circle elements earth and moon, from 0 degrees to 360 degrees in 80 seconds, repeating the rotation indefinitely (i.e., continuously).

Lines 20–21 create a blue circle with a radius of 40 pixels at coordinates (400, 0). When the group rotates, this circle's center stays at a distance of 400 pixels from the origin (0, 0).

Line 23 uses element g to group the circle element that represents the Moon. This element has attribute transform, which translates (shifts) the group element 400 pixels to the right, thus centering the group on the blue circle. Please refer to the SVG specification, available at www.w3.org/TR/2003/REC-SVG11-20030114/ for information on other transformations. The white circle (the Moon) in lines 24–25 has a child animateTransform element in lines 26–28 that rotates the Moon 360 degrees counterclockwise around the Earth every 20 seconds.

28.11 Web Resources

There are many multimedia-related resources on the Web. This section lists a variety of resources that can help you learn about multimedia programming and provides a brief description of each.

www.microsoft.com/windows/windowsmedia
The *Windows Media* Web site contains information on Microsoft's streaming media technologies.

www.streamingmedia.com
Offers information regarding creating and viewing streaming media.

www.microsoft.com/msagent/downloads/default.asp
The *Microsoft Agent* downloads area contains all the software downloads you need to build applications and Web pages that use Microsoft Agent.

msdn.microsoft.com/downloads/default.asp
The *Microsoft Developer Network Downloads* home page contains images, audio clips and other free downloads.

www.real.com
The *RealNetworks* site is the home of RealOne Player—one of the most popular software products for receiving streaming media over the Web.

www.adobe.com/svg
Provides the latest SVG information for both programmers and designers. It also provides links to SVG-enabled sites and SVG-relevant downloads.

`www.service.real.com/help/library/guides/extend/embed.htm`
Provides the details of embedding RealOne Player in a Web page and a detailed listing of RealOne Player's methods and events.

`www.nasa.gov/gallery/index.html`
Visit *NASA's Multimedia Gallery* site to view audio, video and images from NASA's exploration of space and Earth.

`www.speech.cs.cmu.edu/comp.speech/SpeechLinks.html`
The *Speech Technology Hyperlinks Page* has over 600 links to sites related to computer-based speech and speech recognition.

`www.mp3.com`
An excellent resource for the MP3 audio format. It offers files, information on the format, hardware information and software information.

`www.mpeg.org`
The primary reference site for information on the MPEG video format.

`www.winamp.com`
Winamp is a popular MP3 player. It can play streaming MP3s over the Internet.

`www.shoutcast.com`
SHOUTcast is a streaming audio system. If you have Winamp and a fast Internet connection, you can broadcast your own net radio.

`www.windowsmedia.com`
Visit this site to learn all about Windows Media capabilities, such as streaming audio and video over the net.

`www.research.att.com/~rws/Sable.v1_0.htm`
The Sable Markup Language is designed to mark up text for input into speech synthesizers.

`www.w3.org/AudioVideo`
This is the W3C Synchronized Multimedia Integration Language (SMIL) home page.

`smw.internet.com/smil/smilhome.html`
Dedicated to SMIL and includes links, resources and definitions.

SUMMARY

- `bgsound` is an Internet Explorer–specific element that adds background audio to a Web site. The `src` property specifies the URL of the audio clip to be played. The `loop` property specifies the number of times the audio clip should play. The `balance` property specifies the balance between the left and right speakers. The `volume` property determines the volume of the audio clip. To change the property values via a script, assign a scripting name to the `id` property.

- Any Web page using the `bgsound` element should include a **Stop Sound** button.

- The `img` element enables both images and videos to be included in a Web page. The `src` property indicates that the source is an image. The `dynsrc` (i.e., dynamic source) property indicates that the source is a video clip. Property `start` indicates when the video should start playing (specify `fileopen` to play when the clip is loaded or `mouseover` to play when the user first positions the mouse over the video).

- The `embed` element embeds a media clip in a Web page. A graphical user interface can be displayed to give the user control over the media clip. The GUI typically enables the user to play, pause and stop the media clip, to specify the volume and to move forward and backward quickly through the clip. The `loop` property indicates that the media clip should loop forever. To prevent the GUI from appearing in the Web page, add the `hidden` property to the `embed` element. To manipulate the element, specify a scripting name by adding the `id` property to the `embed` element.

- Microsoft's ActiveX controls enhance the functionality of Web pages.

- The `object` element is used to embed ActiveX controls in Web pages. The `width` and `height` properties specify the width and height in pixels that the control occupies in the Web page. Property `classid` specifies the unique ActiveX control ID for the ActiveX control.

- Parameters can be passed to an ActiveX control by placing `param` elements between the `object` element's `<object>` and `</object>` tags. Each parameter is specified with a `param` element that contains a `name` property and a `value` property.

- The Windows Media Player ActiveX control's `FileName` parameter specifies the file containing the media clip. Parameter `AutoStart` is assigned a boolean value indicating whether the media clip plays automatically when it is loaded (`true` if so; `false` if not). The `ShowControls` parameter is assigned a boolean value indicating whether the Media Player controls should be displayed (`true` if so; `false` if not). The `Loop` parameter is assigned a boolean value indicating whether the Media Player should play the media clip in an infinite loop (`true` if so; `false` if not).

- The Windows Media Player ActiveX control's `Play` and `Pause` methods can be called to play or pause a media clip, respectively.

- Microsoft Agent is a technology for interactive animated characters in a Windows application or World Wide Web page. These characters allow users of your application to interact with the application by using more natural human communication techniques. The control accepts both mouse and keyboard interactions, speaks (if a compatible text-to-speech engine is installed) and also supports speech recognition (if a compatible speech-recognition engine is installed). With these capabilities, your Web pages can speak to users and can respond to their voice commands.

- The Microsoft Agent control provides four preprogrammed characters—Peedy the Parrot, Genie, Merlin and Robby the Robot.

- The Lernout and Hauspie TruVoice Text to Speech (TTS) engine is used by the Microsoft Agent ActiveX control to speak the text that Microsoft Agent displays.

- The Microsoft Agent control's Characters collection stores information about the characters that are currently available for use in a program. Method `Load` of the `Characters` collection loads character data. The method takes two arguments—a name for the character that can be used later to interact with that character and the URL of the character's data file.

- A Character object is used to interact with the character. Method Character of the `Characters` collection receives as its argument the name that was used to download the character data and returns the corresponding `Character` object.

- The `Character` object's `Get` method downloads character animations and states.

- Each state has animation effects associated with it. When the character enters a state (e.g., the `Showing` state), the state's associated animation plays.

- `Character` method `MoveTo` moves the character to a new position on the screen. Method `Show` displays the character. Method `Play` plays the specified animation. Method `Speak` speaks its string argument. If there is a compatible TTS engine installed, the character displays a bubble containing the text and audibly speaks the text as well.

- Many animations have a "`Return`" animation that smooths the transition between animations.

- The `Idling` animations are displayed by Microsoft Agent when the user is not interacting with the character.

- `Character` method `Stop` terminates the current animation.

- To enable Microsoft Agent to recognize voice commands, a compatible voice-recognition engine, such as the Microsoft Speech-Recognition engine, must be installed.

- The voice commands that the user can use when interacting with a character must be registered in the Character object's Commands collection.

- The Commands collection's Add method registers each voice command.

- The Commands object's Caption property specifies text that describes the voice-command set. This text appears in the small rectangular area that appears below the character when the user presses the *Scroll Lock* key. The Voice property is similar to the Caption property, except that the specified text appears in the command window with the set of voice commands the user can say shown below it. The Visible property is a boolean value that specifies whether the commands of this Commands object should appear in the pop-up menu.

- When a voice command is received, the agent control's Command event handler executes.

- A RealOne Player object can be embedded (with the embed element) in a Web page to add streaming media to a Web page. The type attribute specifies the MIME type of the embedded file. The width and height attributes specify the dimensions the control will occupy on the page. The autostart attribute determines whether the audio should start playing when the page loads. The controls attribute specifies which controls are available to the user. Setting controls to Default places all the control buttons on screen. The src attribute specifies the location of the streaming audio.

- RealOne Player method SetSource sets the source URL of the audio stream to be played. Method DoPlayPause toggles between pausing and playing the stream.

- The Synchronized Multimedia Integration Language (SMIL) enables Web document authors to coordinate the presentation of a wide range of multimedia elements.

- SMIL is an XML-based description language that organizes static and dynamic text, audio and video to occur simultaneously or sequentially.

- A SMIL document specifies the source (i.e., the URL) and presentation of multimedia elements.

- RealOne Player is one application capable of rendering SMIL documents. Apple's Quicktime plug-in also plays SMIL in both Windows and Mac OS environments.

- SMIL is the W3C-recommended method of embedding audio and video in a Web page.

- Various transitions can be used when changing images in a SMIL document using the transition element. The type and dur attributes of each transition element specify its transition type and duration, respectively. The id attribute assigns a unique id to each transition.

- We can embed a SMIL document in a Web page using the embed element.

- Visitors to a Web site need the RealOne Player plug-in to view SMIL content.

- Scalable Vector Graphics (SVG) markup language describes vector graphic data for JPEG, GIF and PNG formats so that they may be distributed over the Web efficiently.

- GIF, JPEG and PNG file formats store images as bitmaps. Bitmaps describe the color of every pixel in an image and can take a long time to download. Because of the method in which bitmap information is stored, images of these file types cannot be enlarged or reduced without a loss of image quality.

- Vector graphics are produced by mathematical equations that describe graphical information in terms of lines, curves, and so on. Not only do images rendered by vectors require less bandwidth, they can be easily scaled and printed without loss of image clarity. Animations created with vector graphics have significantly smaller file sizes than those created by sequencing of bitmap images.

- SVG is an XML vocabulary comparable to the other XML vocabularies presented in Chapter 20, XML (e.g., MathML and MusicXML). Thus, SVG documents can be scripted, searched and dynamically created.

- Adobe provides a plug-in for Internet Explorer and Netscape that enables SVG documents to be directly rendered.

- The root element for an SVG document is svg.
- Attribute viewBox sets the viewing area for the document. The first two numbers in the string are the *x*- and *y*-coordinates of the upper-left corner of the viewing area, and the last two numbers are the width and height of the viewing area.
- Element g groups elements of an SVG document.
- The element path is used to create the outline of a shape in SVG. Attribute style can alter the attributes of the shape.
- The animate element allows us to animate single or grouped SVG elements. The attribute attributeName of the animate element specifies the attribute to be altered, and the attributeType determines the type of attribute being altered.
- SVG element animateTransform changes the attribute of the parent element specified in attribute attributeName. Attribute type defines the property of the attribute that changes. The initial and final values of the transformation are set by attributes from and to. Attribute dur sets the time within which the change from the initial to the final value should occur, and attribute repeatCount sets the number of times to perform this transformation.

TERMINOLOGY

ActiveX control
Add method of Commands
Adobe SVG plug-in
animate element
animated character
animateTransform element
attributeName attribute (animate)
attributeType attribute (animate)
audio
audio format
AutoStart parameter of Media Player
AVI
background sound
balance property of the bgsound element
bgsound element
bitmap
Caption property of Commands
CD-ROM
Character method Characters
Character object (Microsoft Agent)
Characters collection (Microsoft Agent)
classid property of object
codebase property of object
Command event (Microsoft Agent)
Commands collection of Character
Commands Window
DoPlayPause method of RealOne Player
DVD
dynsrc property of img
embed a media clip
embed element

FileName parameter of Media Player
g element
Genie
Get method of Character
GIF
graphical user interface (GUI)
height property of object
hidden property of embed
Hiding state of a character
id property of bgsound
id property of embed
id property of object
Idling animations
interactive animated character
Internet bandwidth
JPEG
Lernout and Hauspie TruVoice TTS engine
load an animation
Load method of Characters
Loop parameter of Media Player
loop property of bgsound
loop property of embed
media clip
Merlin
Microsoft Agent
Microsoft Speech Recognition engine
MoveTo method Character
multimedia
multimedia-based Web application
name property of param
natural human communication technique

`object` element	`start` property of `img`
`par` element	`start` property value `fileopen`
`param` element	`start` property value `mouseover`
`Pause` method of Media Player	streaming audio
`Play` method of `Character`	streaming technology
`Play` method of Media Player	streaming video
PNG	`svg` element
Quicktime	Synchronized Multimedia Integration
RealOne Player	Language (SMIL)
`region` element	text-to-speech (TTS) engine
"`Return`" animation	`transition` element
`rout-layout` element	transitions
Scalable Vector Graphics (SVG)	`value` property of `param`
`seq` element	vector graphic
`SetSource` method of RealOne Player	video clip
`Show` method `Character`	video format
`ShowControls` parameter	`Visible` property of `Commands`
`Showing` state of a character	voice command
sound card	`Voice` property of `Commands`
`Speak` method `Character`	`volume` property of `bgsound`
`Speaking` state of a character	`width` property of `object`
speech recognition	Windows Media Player
`src` property of `bgsound`	Windows Media Player ActiveX control

SELF-REVIEW EXERCISES

28.1   Fill in the blanks in each of the following statements:

a)   _____ is a technology for interactive animated characters.

b)   The _____ element plays a background audio in Internet Explorer.

c)   The _____ property of the `img` element specifies a video clip that should appear in the `img` element's location in the Web page.

d)   The _____ element embeds an ActiveX control on a Web page.

e)   The _____ element places an audio or video clip on a Web page.

f)   The `img` element's _____ property has the values `mouseover` and `fileopen`.

g)   The _____ property of the `embed` element prevents a GUI containing media clip controls from being displayed with the media clip.

h)   Microsoft Agent's _____ animations enable smooth transitions between animations.

i)   When set to `true`, the _____ parameter to the Windows Media Player specifies that a GUI should be displayed so that the user can control a media clip.

j)   When a compatible _____ engine is available to Microsoft Agent, characters can speak text.

k)   The Microsoft Agent control _____ collection keeps track of the information about each loaded character.

28.2   State whether each of the following is *true* or *false*. If *false*, explain why.

a)   The `bgsound` element can be used with any browser.

b)   The `img` element enables both images and videos to be included in a Web page.

c)   `bgsound` property `balance` cannot be set via scripting.

d)   The `name` property of the `object` element specifies a scripting name for the element.

e)   The Microsoft Agent `Character` object's `StopAnimation` method terminates the current animation for the character.

ANSWERS TO SELF-REVIEW EXERCISES

28.1   a) Microsoft Agent. b) `bgsound`. c) `dynsrc`. d) `object`. e) `embed`. f) `start`. g) `hidden`.
h) "Return." i) `ShowControls`. j) text-to-speech. k) `Characters`.

28.2   a) False. The `bgsound` element is specific to Internet Explorer. b) True. c) True. d) False.
The `id` property of the `object` element specifies a scripting name. e) False. The `Stop` method terminates the current animation for the character.

EXERCISES

28.3   *(Story Teller)* Store a large number of nouns, verbs, articles, prepositions, and other parts of
speech. in arrays of strings. Then use random number generation to form sentences and have your
script speak the sentences with Microsoft Agent and the Lernout and Hauspie text-to-speech engine.

28.4   *(Limericks)* Modify the limerick-writing script you wrote in Exercise 12.8 to use a Microsoft
Agent character and the Lernout and Hauspie text-to-speech engine to speak the limericks your program creates. Use the speech output tags in Fig. 28.10 to control the characteristics of the speech (e.g.,
emphasis on certain syllables, volume of the voice, pitch of the voice,).

28.5   Modify the script in Exercise 28.4 to play character animations during pauses in the limerick.

28.6   *(Background Audio)* Write an XHTML document and script that allow users to choose from
a list of the audio downloads available from the Microsoft Developer Network Downloads site

    msdn.microsoft.com/downloads/default.asp

and listen to the chosen audio clip as background music with the `bgsound` element.

28.7   Modify Exercise 28.6 to use the `embed` element to play the audio clips.

28.8   Modify Exercise 28.6 to use the Windows Media Player ActiveX control to play the audio clips.

28.9   *(Video Browser)* Write an XHTML document and script that allow users to choose from a
list of the videos available from the NASA Multimedia Gallery site

    www.nasa.gov/gallery

and view the video using the `embed` element.

28.10   Modify Exercise 28.9 to use the Windows Media Player ActiveX control to play the video
clips.

28.11   Modify the program in Fig. 28.4 to view videos from the SeaWiFs site

    seawifs.gsfc.nasa.gov:80/OCEAN_PLANET/HTML/oceanography_flyby.html

Allow users to select which video to play.

28.12   *(Image Flasher)* Create a script that repeatedly flashes an image on the screen. Do this by
changing the visibility of the image. Allow users to control the "blink speed."

28.13   *(Digital Clock)* Using features of the Dynamic HTML chapters, implement an application
that displays a digital clock in a Web page. You might add options to scale the clock, to display day,
month and year, to issue an alarm, to play certain audios at designated times, and so on.

28.14   *(Analog Clock)* Create a script that displays an analog clock with hour, minute and second
hands that move as the time changes. Use the Structured Graphics Control to create the graphics and
play a tick sound every second. Play other sounds to mark every half-hour and hour.

28.15   *(Karaoke)* Create a karaoke system that plays the music for a song and displays the words for
users to sing.

28.16 *(Calling Attention to an Image)* To emphasize an image, try placing a row of simulated light bulbs around it. You can let the light bulbs flash in unison, or you can let them fire on and off in sequence, one after the other.

28.17 *(Online Product Catalog)* Companies are rapidly realizing the potential for doing business on the Web. Develop an online multimedia catalog from which your customers may select products to be shipped. Use the data-binding features in Chapter 16 to load data into tables. Use a Microsoft Agent to announce descriptions of selected products.

28.18 Modify Exercise 28.17 to support voice commands that allow users to speak a product name to receive a description of the product.

28.19 *(Reaction Time/Reaction Precision Tester)* Create a Web page that moves an image around the screen. The user moves the mouse to catch and click the shape. The shape's speed and size can be varied. Keep statistics on how much time the user typically takes to catch a shape of a given size. The user will probably have more difficulty catching faster-moving, smaller shapes.

28.20 *(Animation)* Create an animation by displaying a series of images that represent the frames in the animation. Allow the user to specify the speed at which the images are displayed.

28.21 *(Tortoise and the Hare)* Develop a multimedia version of the Tortoise and Hare simulation of Exercise 11.20. Record an announcer's voice calling the race: "The contenders are at the starting line." "And they're off!" "The Hare pulls out in front." "The Tortoise is coming on strong."—and so forth. As the race proceeds, play the appropriate recorded audios. Play sounds to simulate the animals' running (and the crowd cheering!). Do an animation of the animals racing up the side of the slippery mountain.

28.22 *(Arithmetic Tutor)* Develop a multimedia version of the Computer-Assisted Instruction (CAI) systems you developed in Exercises 10.27, 10.28 and 10.29.

28.23 *(15 Puzzle)* Write a multimedia-based version of the game of 15. There is a 4-by-4 board for a total of 16 slots. One of the slots is empty. The other slots are occupied by 15 tiles, numbered 1 through 15. Any tile next to the currently empty slot can be moved into the currently empty slot by clicking the tile. Your program should create the board with the tiles out of order. The goal is to arrange the tiles in sequential order row by row. Play sounds with the movement of the tiles.

28.24 *(Morse Code)* Modify your solution to Exercise 12.26 to output the Morse code using audio clips. Use two different audio clips for the dot and dash characters in Morse code.

28.25 *(Calendar File)* Create a general-purpose calendar file. The application should sing "Happy Birthday to You" when you use it on your birthday. Have the application display images and play audios associated with important events and remind you in advance of important events. For example, have the application give you a week's warning so you can pick up an appropriate greeting card for that special person. Store the calendar information in a file for use with the data-binding techniques of Chapter 16 to load the calendar information into a table in the Web page.

28.26 *Wartnose* is a character that was developed by e-Clips (www.e-clips.com.au)—an Australian company that develops Microsoft Agent characters. Download Wartnose and modify Fig. 28.6 to use Wartnose (as shown in Fig. 28.19). Instructions for installing this character are available at www.deitel.com/books/iw3HTP3/index.html. [*Note*: Wartnose is a free download. Before using Wartnose, please read the licensing agreement provided at the e-Clips Web site.]

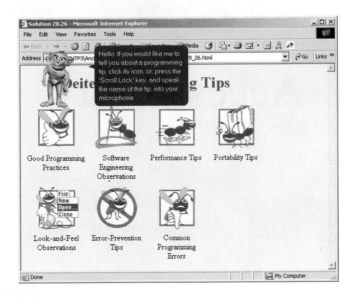

Fig. 28.19   Figure 28.6 modified to use Wartnose. (Courtesy of e-Clips® (Inchain Pty Ltd).)

Accessibility

Objectives

- To introduce the World Wide Web Consortium's Web Content Accessibility Guidelines 1.0 (WCAG 1.0).
- To understand how to use the `alt` attribute of the `img` element to describe images to people with visual impairments, mobile-Web-device users, search engines, etc.
- To understand how to make XHTML tables more accessible to screen reader applications.
- To understand how to verify that XHTML tags are used properly and to ensure that Web pages are viewable on any type of display or reader.
- To understand how VoiceXML and CallXML are changing the way people with disabilities access information on the Web.
- To introduce the various accessibility aids offered in Windows 2000, Windows XP, Macromedia Dreamweaver and Macromedia Flash.

'Tis the good reader that makes the good book. . .
Ralph Waldo Emerson

Outline

29.1 Introduction

Enabling a Web site to meet the needs of individuals with disabilities is a concern for all businesses. People with disabilities are a significant portion of the population, and legal ramifications exist for Web sites that discriminate by not providing adequate and universal access to their resources. In this chapter, we explore the **Web Accessibility Initiative**, its guidelines, various laws regarding businesses and their availability to people with disabilities and how some companies have developed systems, products and services to meet the needs of this demographic.

29.2 Web Accessibility

The Internet enables individuals with disabilities to work in a vast array of new fields. Technologies such as voice activation, visual enhancers and auditory aids afford more employment opportunities. People with visual impairments must use computer monitors with enlarged text, whereas people with physical impairments must use head pointers with on-screen keyboards.

Since 1995, lawsuits have been filed against entities maintaining Web sites that cannot be accessed equally by all people regardless of ability. Many such lawsuits have ended in large settlements. For example, in 1999, the National Federation for the Blind (NFB) filed a lawsuit against AOL for not supplying access to its services for people with visual disabilities. The **Americans with Disabilities Act (ADA)** and many other government efforts address Web accessibility (Fig. 29.1).

Federal regulations similar to the disability ramp mandate have been applied to the Internet to accommodate the needs of people with hearing, vision and speech impairments. Section 508 of the Rehabilitation Act of 1973 was amended by the Workforce Investment Act of 1998 to include a set of Electronic and Information Technology Accessibility Standards. Section 508 § 1194.22 establishes 16 accessibility standards for Web-based intranet and Internet applications to which federal agencies must adhere when designing Web sites. Many U.S. states also have already made provisions to assure Section 508 compliance. The

Act	Purpose
Americans with Disabilities Act of 1990	The ADA prohibits discrimination on the basis of disability in employment, state and local government, public accommodations, commercial facilities, transportation and telecommunications.
Telecommunications Act of 1996	The Telecommunications Act of 1996 contains two amendments to Section 255 and Section 251(a)(2) of the Communications Act of 1934. These amendments require that communication devices, such as cell phones, telephones and pagers, be accessible to individuals with disabilities.
Individuals with Disabilities Education Act of 1997	Educational materials in schools must be made accessible to children with disabilities.
Rehabilitation Act of 1973	Section 504 of the Rehabilitation Act states that college-sponsored activities receiving federal funding cannot discriminate against individuals with disabilities. Section 508 was strengthened in 1998 to require the federal procurement of accessible electronic and information technology. The Electronic and Information Technology Accessibility Standards provide the federal technical standards for accessible Web design. Section 508 mandates that all government institutions receiving federal funding and all businesses that sell services to the government must design their Web sites in accordance with these stipulations.

Fig. 29.1   Acts used to protect access to the Internet for people with disabilities.

16 standards presented in § 1194.22 range in complexity from requiring text equivalents for non-text elements on a Web page to requiring that all script-generated content be identified by descriptive text that users of assistive technologies can access. Please see the Web site `www.access-board.gov/sec508/guide/1194.22.htm` for a complete list of the federal regulations for Web-based applications.

The following sections explore many products and services that make the Internet accessible to people with disabilities. The techniques described in this chapter only begin to provide universal access to Web content. Please refer to the URLs in Section 29.17 for more information about building Web sites that are fully compliant with all accessibility guidelines.

29.3 Web Accessibility Initiative

On April 7, 1997, the World Wide Web Consortium (W3C) launched the **Web Accessibility Initiative** (WAI™). **Accessibility** refers to the usability of an application or Web site by people with disabilities. The majority of Web sites are considered either partially or totally inaccessible to people with visual, learning or mobility impairments. Total accessibility is difficult to achieve because people have varying types of disabilities, language barriers and hardware and software inconsistencies. However, a high level of accessibility is attainable. As more people with disabilities use the Internet, it is imperative that Website designers increase the accessibility of their sites. The WAI aims for such accessibility, as discussed in its mission statement described at `www.w3.org/WAI`.

The WAI published the **Web Content Accessibility Guidelines** (WCAG) **1.0** to help businesses determine whether their Web sites are accessible to everyone. The WCAG 1.0 (`www.w3.org/TR/WCAG10`) uses checkpoints to indicate specific accessibility requirements. Each checkpoint has an associated priority indicating its importance. **Priority-one checkpoints** are goals that must be met to ensure accessibility; we focus on these points in this chapter. **Priority-two checkpoints**, though not essential, are highly recommended. If these checkpoints are not satisfied, people with certain disabilities will experience difficulty accessing Web sites. **Priority-three checkpoints** slightly improve accessibility. These guidelines closely resemble those created by the federal government in Section 508 § 1194.22 but are intended to apply to a considerably larger number of Web sites. For a side-by-side comparison of the two sets of guidelines, see `www.jimthatcher.com/sidebyside.htm`.

At the time of this writing, the WAI is working on a **WCAG 2.0** draft. A single checkpoint in the WCAG 2.0 Working Draft may encompass several checkpoints from WCAG 1.0. WCAG 2.0 checkpoints will supersede those in WCAG 1.0. The new version can be applied to a wider range of markup languages (e.g., XML, Wireless Markup Language) and content types than its predecessor. To obtain more information about the WCAG 2.0 Working Draft, visit `www.w3.org/TR/WCAG20`.

The WAI also presents a supplemental checklist of **quick tips** that reinforce ten important points for accessible Web-site design. More information on the WAI Quick Tips can be found at `www.w3.org/WAI/References/Quicktips`.

29.4 Providing Alternatives for Images

One important WAI requirement is to ensure that every image used on a Web page is accompanied by a textual description that clearly defines the purpose of the image. To accomplish this task, include a text equivalent of each item by using the `alt` attribute of the `img` and `input` elements. Visual elements created in an `object` element can be assigned a description by placing text between the start and end `<object>` tags.

Web developers who do not use the `alt` attribute to provide text equivalents increase the difficulty people with visual impairments experience in navigating the Web. Specialized **user agent**s, such as **screen readers** (programs that allow users to hear all text and text descriptions displayed on their screen) and **braille displays** (devices that receive data from screen-reading software and output it as braille), allow people with visual impairments to access text-based information that is normally displayed on the screen. A user agent visually interprets Web-page source code and translates it into formatted text and images. Web browsers, such as Microsoft Internet Explorer and Netscape, and the screen readers mentioned throughout this chapter are examples of user agents.

Web pages that do not provide text equivalents for video and audio clips are difficult for people with visual and hearing impairments to access. Screen readers cannot read images, movies and most other non-XHTML objects from these Web pages. Providing multimedia-based information in a variety of ways (i.e., using the `alt` attribute or providing in-line descriptions of images) helps maximize the content's accessibility.

Web designers should provide *useful* text equivalents in the `alt` attribute for use in nonvisual user agents. For example, if the `alt` attribute describes a sales growth chart, it should provide a brief summary of the data rather than describe the data in the chart. A complete description of the chart's data should be included in the **`longdesc` attribute**, which is intended to augment the `alt` attribute's description. The `longdesc` attribute contains the URL that links to a Web page describing the image or multimedia content. Though the `longdesc` attribute is part of the W3C's XHTML 1.1 Recommendation, most Web browsers do not currently have a way to make proper use of the `longdesc` attribute. An alternative for the `longdesc` attribute is **D-link**, which provides descriptive text about graphs and charts. More information on D-links can be obtained at the CORDA Technologies Web site (`www.corda.com`).

Using a screen reader for Web-site navigation can be time-consuming and frustrating, as screen readers cannot interpret pictures and other graphical content. A link at the top of each Web page that provides direct access to the page's content could allow users to bypass a long list of navigation links or other inaccessible elements. This jump can save time and eliminate frustration for individuals with visual impairments.

Emacspeak is a screen interface that allows greater Internet access to individuals with visual disabilities by translating text to voice data. The open-source product also implements auditory icons that play various sounds. Emacspeak can be customized for use with Linux operating systems and provides support for the IBM *ViaVoice* speech engine. The Emacspeak Web site is located at `www.cs.cornell.edu/home/raman/emacspeak/emacspeak.html`.

IBM *Home Page Reader (HPR)* is another browser that "reads" text selected by the user. The HPR uses IBM ViaVoice technology to synthesize a voice. A trial version of HPR is available at `www-3.ibm.com/able/solution_offerings/hpr.html`.

29.5 Maximizing Readability by Focusing on Structure

Many Web sites use XHTML elements for aesthetic purposes rather than for the appropriate structural purpose. For example, the `h1` header element is often used erroneously to make text large and bold rather than as a major section head for content. The desired visual effect may be achieved, but it creates a problem for screen readers. When the screen-reader software encounters the h1 element, it may verbally inform the user that a new section has been reached when this is not the case, which may confuse users. Only use the h1 in accordance with its XHTML specifications (e.g., as a heading to introduce an important section of a document). Instead of using h1 to make text large and bold, use CSS (discussed in Chapter 6) or XSL (discussed in Chapter 20) to format and style the text. The strong XHTML element also may be used to make text appear in bold face. Screen readers emphasize bold text by changing the inflection of the voice used to read the text. For further examples, refer to the WCAG 1.0 Web site at www.w3.org/TR/WCAG10.

Another accessibility issue is **readability**. When creating a Web page intended for the general public, it is important to consider the reading level (i.e., the comprehension and level of understanding) at which it is written. Web-site designers can make their sites easier to read by using shorter words. Designers should also limit slang terms and other nontraditional language that may be problematic for users from other countries.

WCAG 1.0 suggests using a paragraph's first sentence to convey its subject. Stating the point of the paragraph in its first sentence makes it easier to find crucial information and allows readers to bypass unwanted material.

The **Gunning Fog Index**, a formula that produces a readability grade when applied to a text sample, evaluates a Web site's readability. More information about the Gunning Fog Index can be obtained from www.trainingpost.org/3-2-inst.htm.

29.6 Accessibility in XHTML Tables

Complex Web pages often contain tables for formatting content and presenting data. Many screen readers are incapable of translating tables correctly unless the tables are properly designed. For example, the CAST *eReader*, a screen reader developed by the Center for Applied Special Technology (www.cast.org), starts at the top-left-hand cell and reads columns from top to bottom, left to right. This procedure is known as reading a table in a **linearized** manner. The CAST eReader reads the table in Fig. 29.2 as follows:

```
Price of Fruit Fruit Price Apple $0.25 Orange $0.50 Banana $1.00
Pineapple $2.00
```

```
1   <?xml version = "1.0"?>
2   <!DOCTYPE html PUBLIC "-//W3C//DTD XHTML 1.1//EN"
3      "http://www.w3.org/TR/xhtml11/DTD/xhtml11.dtd">
4
5   <!-- Fig. 29.2: withoutheaders.html -->
6   <!-- Table without headers              -->
7
8   <html>
9      <head>
10        <title>XHTML Table Without Headers</title>
11
12        <style type = "text/css">
13           body { background-color: #ccffaa;
14                  text-align: center }
```

Fig. 29.2   Table without accessibility modifications. (Part 1 of 2.)

```
15          </style>
16       </head>
17
18       <body>
19
20          <p>Price of Fruit</p>
21
22          <table border = "1" width = "50%">
23
24             <tr>
25                <td>Fruit</td>
26                <td>Price</td>
27             </tr>
28
29             <tr>
30                <td>Apple</td>
31                <td>$0.25</td>
32             </tr>
33
34             <tr>
35                <td>Orange</td>
36                <td>$0.50</td>
37             </tr>
38
39             <tr>
40                <td>Banana</td>
41                <td>$1.00</td>
42             </tr>
43
44             <tr>
45                <td>Pineapple</td>
46                <td>$2.00</td>
47             </tr>
48
49          </table>
50
51       </body>
52    </html>
```

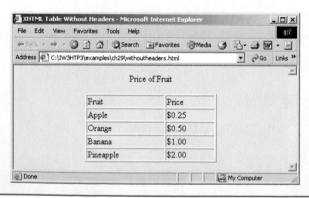

Fig. 29.2   Table without accessibility modifications. (Part 2 of 2.)

This reading does not present the content of the table adequately. WCAG 1.0 recommends using CSS instead of tables, unless the tables' content linearizes in an understandable manner.

If the table in Fig. 29.2 were large, the screen reader's linearized reading would be even more confusing to users. By modifying the td element with the headers attribute and modifying **header cells** (cells specified by the th element) with the id attribute, a table will be read as intended. Figure 29.3 demonstrates how these modifications change the way a table is interpreted.

```
1   <?xml version = "1.0"?>
2   <!DOCTYPE html PUBLIC "-//W3C//DTD XHTML 1.1//EN"
3      "http://www.w3.org/TR/xhtml11/DTD/xhtml11.dtd">
4
5   <!-- Fig. 29.3: withheaders.html -->
6   <!-- Table with headers            -->
7
8   <html>
9      <head>
10        <title>XHTML Table With Headers</title>
11
12        <style type = "text/css">
13           body { background-color: #ccffaa;
14                  text-align: center }
15        </style>
16     </head>
17
18     <body>
19
20     <!-- this table uses the id and headers attributes to   -->
21     <!-- ensure readability by text-based browsers. It also -->
22     <!-- uses a summary attribute, used by screen readers    -->
23     <!-- to describe the content of the table                -->
24
25        <table width = "50%" border = "1"
26           summary = "This table contains information about
27           the price of fruit. The table lists the price of
28           apples, oranges, bananas and pineapples.">
29
30           <caption><strong>Price of Fruit</strong></caption>
31
32           <tr>
33              <th id = "fruit">Fruit</th>
34              <th id = "price">Price</th>
35           </tr>
36
37           <tr>
38              <td headers = "fruit">Apple</td>
39              <td headers = "price">$0.25</td>
40           </tr>
41
42           <tr>
```

Fig. 29.3 Table optimized for screen reading using attribute headers. (Part 1 of 2.)

```
43              <td headers = "fruit">Orange</td>
44              <td headers = "price">$0.50</td>
45          </tr>
46
47          <tr>
48              <td headers = "fruit">Banana</td>
49              <td headers = "price">$1.00</td>
50          </tr>
51
52          <tr>
53              <td headers = "fruit">Pineapple</td>
54              <td headers = "price">$2.00</td>
55          </tr>
56
57      </table>
58
59  </body>
60 </html>
```

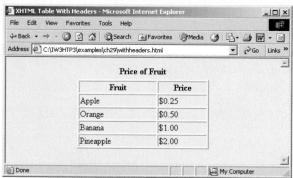

Fig. 29.3   Table optimized for screen reading using attribute `headers`. (Part 2 of 2.)

This table does not appear to be different from a standard XHTML table. However, it is read in a more intelligent manner when using a screen reader. A screen reader vocalizes the data from the table in Fig. 29.3 as follows:

```
Caption: Price of Fruit
Summary: This table uses th and the id and headers attributes to
make the table readable by screen readers.
Fruit: Apple, Price: $0.25
Fruit: Orange, Price: $0.50
Fruit: Banana, Price: $1.00
Fruit: Pineapple, Price: $2.00
```

Every cell in the table is preceded by its corresponding header when read by the screen reader. This format helps the listener understand the table. The **headers** attribute is intended specifically for tables that hold large amounts of data. Most small tables linearize well as long as the th element is used properly. The **summary** attribute and **caption** element are also suggested to provide additional information about the content of the table. For more examples demonstrating how to make tables accessible, visit www.w3.org/TR/ WCAG.

29.7 Accessibility in XHTML Frames

Web designers often use frames to display more than one XHTML file in a single browser window. Frames are a convenient way to ensure that certain content always displays on the screen. Unfortunately, frames often lack proper descriptions, which prevents users with text-based browsers, or users listening with speech synthesizers, from navigating the Web site. [*Note:* Frames are deprecated in XHTML 1.1.]

A site with frames must have meaningful descriptions in the `title` element for each frame. Examples of good titles include "Navigation Frame" and "Main Content Frame." Users with text-based browsers, such as Lynx, must choose which frame they want to open; descriptive titles make this choice simpler. However, assigning titles to frames does not solve all the navigation problems associated with frames. The `noframes` element allows Web designers to offer alternative content for browsers that do not support frames.

Good Programming Practice 29.1

Include a title for each frame's contents with the `frame` element, and, if possible, provide links to the individual pages within the frameset so that users still can navigate through the Web pages. To provide access to browsers that do not support frames, use the `noframes` element. It also provides better access to browsers that have limited support.

WCAG 1.0 suggests using Cascading Style Sheets (CSS) as an alternative to frames, because CSS can provide similar functionality and are highly customizable. The ability to display multiple XHTML documents in a single browser window requires the complete support of HTML 4. However, the second generation of Cascading Style Sheets (CSS2) can display a single document as if it were several documents.

29.8 Accessibility in XML

XML allows developers to create new markup languages that may not necessarily incorporate accessibility features. To prevent the proliferation of inaccessible languages, the WAI is developing guidelines—the **XML Guidelines (XML GL)**—for creating accessible XML documents. The XML GL recommend including a text description, similar to XHTML's `alt` attribute, for each nontext object on a page. To further facilitate accessibility, element types should allow grouping and classification and should identify important content. Without an accessible user interface, other efforts to implement accessibility are less effective, so it is essential to create XSLT (see Chapter 20) or CSS style sheets that can produce multiple outputs, including document outlines.

Many XML languages, including Synchronized Multimedia Integration Language (SMIL) and Scalable Vector Graphics (SVG) (discussed in Chapter 28), have implemented several of the WAI guidelines. The WAI XML Accessibility Guidelines can be found at `www.w3.org/WAI/PF/xmlgl.htm`.

29.9 Accessibility in Cascading Style Sheets (CSS)

The World Wide Web Consortium Cascading Style Sheets Level 2 (CSS2) specification includes a large section on **aural style sheets**. Aural style sheets are style sheets that specify stylistic properties that are important for screen readers, and similar accessibility tools. Aural style sheets can be used to specify properties of the voice used to speak parts of a Web page. These properties include the volume and pitch of the reader's voice. Aural style sheets can also specify moments when the voice should pause or place stress on a word. Aural style sheets aid screen readers, improve accessibility and open new markets for Web-page screen readers. If Web pages incorporate aural style sheets, people will be able to access the World Wide Web from cars, living rooms, industrial settings, medical settings and other places without access to a monitor or a keyboard. For more information on aural style sheets see the World Wide Web Consortium's CSS2 Specification, www.w3.org/TR/REC-CSS2.

29.10 Testing the Accessibility of an XHTML Document

Watchfire Corporation has created a tool called Bobby that is similar to the World Wide Web Consortium's XHTML Validation Service. Bobby tests XHTML documents for accessibility against the federal Section 508 Accessibility standard or against the World Wide Web Consortium's WCAG standard. Like the XHTML Validation Service from the World Wide Web Consortium, Bobby specifies exactly what parts of a document do not comply with accessibility standards and suggests improvements. If a page does comply with the standards, Bobby offers a "Bobby Approved" logo to place in the XHTML document.

Watchfire offers multiple versions of Bobby. The full version of Bobby is a Windows-based application that Watchfire sells on its Web site. The online version of Bobby (Fig. 29.4) is found at: bobby.watchfire.com.

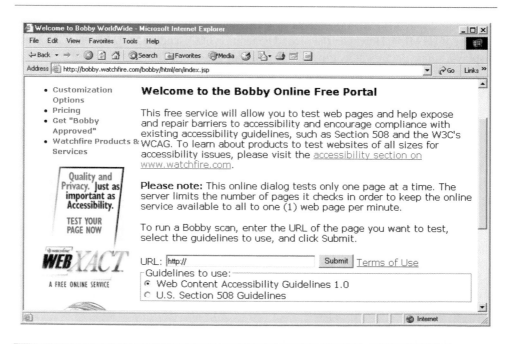

Fig. 29.4   Watchfire Bobby Online.

To test a Web page, enter the URL in the text area, select a set of guidelines (either **Web Content Accessibility Guidelines 1.0** or **U.S. Section 508 Guidelines**) using the radio buttons, then click **Submit**. Bobby processes the document at the given URL and outputs a list of changes to make the document more accessible. Bobby outputs the recommendations in three different priority groupings, showing the most important changes first. Several other Web sites provide similar functionality to test the accessibility of an XHTML document. Please refer to the URLs at the end of the chapter for further information on these additional tools.

29.11 Using Voice Synthesis and Recognition with VoiceXML

A joint effort by AT&T®, IBM®, Lucent™ and Motorola® has created an XML vocabulary that marks up information for **speech synthesizers**. This technology, called **VoiceXML (Voice Extensible Markup Language)**, enables computers to speak to users. It has tremendous implications for people with visual impairments and for people with learning impairments. VoiceXML-enabled applications read Web pages to the user, and understand users' spoken responses through **speech recognition** technology. An example of a speech recognition tool is IBM's *ViaVoice* (www-3.ibm.com/software/speech).

A VoiceXML interpreter and VoiceXML browser process VoiceXML, a platform-independent XML-based technology. Web browsers may incorporate these interpreters in the future. When a VoiceXML document is loaded, a **voice server** sends a message to the VoiceXML browser and begins a conversation between the user and the computer. The W3C has standardized VoiceXML to promote portability among the various VoiceXML platforms (e.g., Motorola, Nuance Communications), though not all VoiceXML browsers comply to the W3C's specification. The W3C's VoiceXML Version 2.0 specification, a Candidate Recommendation at the time of this writing, can be found at www.w3.org/TR/voicexml20.

Figures 29.5 and 29.6 show examples of VoiceXML that would be appropriate for a Web site. The document's text is spoken to the user, and the text embedded in the VoiceXML tags allows for interactivity between the user and the browser. The output included in Fig. 29.5 demonstrates a conversation that might take place between a user and a computer after loading this document.

```
 1   <?xml version = "1.0" encoding = "UTF-8"?>
 2   <vxml version = "2.0">
 3
 4   <!-- Fig. 29.5: main.xml   -->
 5   <!-- Voice page           -->
 6
 7   <link next = "#home">
 8      <grammar type = "text/gsl">home</grammar>
 9   </link>
10
11   <link next = "#end">
12      <grammar type = "text/gsl">exit</grammar>
13   </link>
14
15   <var name = "currentOption" expr = "'home'"/>
16
17   <form>
18      <block>
19         Welcome to the voice page of Deitel and
20         Associates. To exit any time say exit.
```

Fig. 29.5   VoiceXML home page. (Part 1 of 3.)

```
21            To go to the home page any time say home.
22         </block>
23         <subdialog src = "#home"/>
24      </form>
25
26      <menu id = "home">
27         <prompt count = "1" timeout = "10s">
28            You have just entered the Deitel home page.
29            Please make a selection by speaking one of the
30            following options:
31            <enumerate />
32         </prompt>
33
34         <prompt count = "2">
35            Please say one of the following.
36            <enumerate />
37         </prompt>
38
39         <choice next = "#about">About us</choice>
40         <choice next = "#directions">Driving directions</choice>
41         <choice next = "publications.xml">Publications</choice>
42      </menu>
43
44      <form id = "about">
45         <block>
46            About Deitel and Associates, Inc.
47            Deitel and Associates, Inc. is an internationally
48            recognized corporate training and publishing organization,
49            specializing in programming languages, Internet and World
50            Wide Web technology and object technology education.
51            The company provides courses on Java, C++,
52            Visual Basic, C, Internet and World Wide Web programming and
53            and Object Technology.
54            <assign name = "currentOption" expr = "'about'"/>
55            <goto next = "#repeat"/>
56         </block>
57      </form>
58
59      <form id = "directions">
60         <block>
61            Directions to Deitel and Associates, Inc. We are located at
62            Clock Tower Place in Maynard, Massachusetts. Our offices are
63            located just inside the main entrance on Main Street.
64            <assign name = "currentOption" expr = "'directions'"/>
65            <goto next = "#repeat"/>
66         </block>
67      </form>
68
69      <form id = "repeat">
70         <field name = "confirm" type = "boolean">
71            <prompt>
72               To repeat, say yes. To go back to home, say no.
73            </prompt>
```

Fig. 29.5   VoiceXML home page. (Part 2 of 3.)

```
74
75        <filled>
76            <if cond = "confirm == true">
77                <goto expr = "'#' + currentOption"/>
78            <else/>
79                <goto next = "#home"/>
80            </if>
81        </filled>
82
83    </field>
84  </form>
85
86  <form id = "end">
87    <block>
88        Thank you for visiting Deitel and Associates voice page.
89        Have a nice day.
90        <exit/>
91    </block>
92  </form>
93
94  </vxml>
```

Computer:
Welcome to the voice page of Deitel and Associates. To exit any time say
exit. To go to the home page any time say home.

User:
Home

Computer:
You have just entered the Deitel home page. Please make a selection by
speaking one of the following options: About us, Driving directions,
Publications.

User:
Driving directions

Computer:
Directions to Deitel and Associates, Inc. We are located at Clock Tower
Place in Maynard, Massachusetts. Our offices are located just inside the
main entrance on Main Street.

To repeat, say yes. To go back to home, say no.

Fig. 29.5   VoiceXML home page. (Part 3 of 3.)

A VoiceXML document contains a series of dialogs and subdialogs which result in
spoken interaction between the user and the computer. The form and menu elements implement the dialogs. A **form** element presents information and gathers data from the user. A
menu element provides users with options and transfers control to other dialogs, based on
users' selections.

Line 2 contains the vxml element, which encapsulates all the other VoiceXML elements and indicates that this file contains markup written according to the VoiceXML Version 2.0 specification.

Lines 7–9 use element link to create an active link to the home page. Attribute **next** specifies the URI navigated to when the link is selected. Element **grammar** marks up the text that the user must speak to select the link. The type attribute "text/gsl" indicates that the text to be spoken is specified using GSL (Grammar Specification Language), a format for defining valid user input. The speech recognition engine uses the information in a grammar element to react to spoken text. In the link element (lines 7–9), we navigate to the element with id home when the user speaks the word home. Lines 11–13 use element link to create a link to id end when the user speaks the word exit.

Line 15 declares a variable named currentOption to keep track of the user's current location within the document. We initialize this variable to the string 'home', since the user always begins at the home dialog. This variable is updated as the user navigates to other dialogs.

Lines 17–24 create a dialog using element form, that collects information from the user. Lines 18–22 present introductory text. Element block, which can exist only within a form element, groups elements that perform an action or an event.

The menu element (lines 26–42) enables users to select the page to which they would like to link. Lines 27–32 use element **prompt** to instruct the user to make a selection. Attribute **count** maintains the number of times a prompt is spoken (i.e., each time a prompt is read, count increments by one). The count attribute transfers control to another prompt once a certain limit has been reached. Attribute timeout specifies how long the program should wait after outputting the prompt for the user to respond. In the event that the user does not respond before the timeout period expires, lines 34–37 provide a second, shorter prompt to remind the user to make a selection. The choice element, which is always part of either a menu or a form, presents a selection option to the user. The next attribute indicates the page to be loaded when a user makes a selection. The user selects a choice element by speaking the text marked up between the tags into a microphone. In this example, the first and second choice elements in lines 39–40 transfer control to a **local dialog** (i.e., a location within the same document) when they are selected. The third choice element (line 41) transfers the user to the document publications.xml (Fig. 29.6).

Control transfers to the form elements about (lines 44–57) and directions (lines 59–67) when the user speaks the appropriate text. The text in the block element of each of these form elements is spoken by the browser, then the variable currentOption is updated to record the user's current location. Finally, the goto block in each form transfers control to the form named repeat (lines 69–84), which determines whether the browser should repeat the most recently spoken text. A field element (lines 70–83) behaves like an XHTML form field to obtain input from the user (the value of a boolean variable confirm in this case). Lines 90–93 prompt the user to say "yes" or "no." The filled element (lines 75–81) contains elements to be executed when the browser receives user input. If the user says "yes" to repeat the previous content, the variable confirm will be true (line 76), and line 77 executes, sending the user to the local dialog whose id is formed by concatenating # and currentOption. If the user says "no," line 79 sends the user back to the home local dialog.

When the user chooses the publications option, the publications.xml (Fig. 29.6) loads into the browser. Lines 7–12 define link elements that provide links to

main.xml. Lines 13–15 provide a link to the menu element (lines 19–37) named publication, which asks the user to select one of the publications: Java, C or C++. The form
elements in lines 39–86 describe each of the books on these topics. Once the browser
speaks the description, control transfers to the form element with an id attribute that has a
value equal to repeat (lines 88–103).

```
1   <?xml version = "1.0" encoding = "UTF-8"?>
2   <vxml version = "2.0">
3
4   <!-- Fig. 29.6: publications.xml            -->
5   <!-- Voice page for various publications -->
6
7   <link next = "main.xml#home">
8      <grammar type = "text/gsl">home</grammar>
9   </link>
10  <link next = "main.xml#end">
11     <grammar type = "text/gsl">exit</grammar>
12  </link>
13  <link next = "#publication">
14     <grammar type = "text/gsl">menu</grammar>
15  </link>
16
17  <var name = "currentOption" expr = "'home'"/>
18
19  <menu id = "publication">
20
21     <prompt count = "1" timeout = "12s">
22        Following are some of our publications. For more information visit
23        our Web page at www.deitel.com.
24        To repeat the following menu, say menu at any time.
25        Please select by saying one of the following books:
26        <enumerate />
27     </prompt>
28
29     <prompt count = "2">
30        Please select from the following books.
31        <enumerate />
32     </prompt>
33
34     <choice next = "#java">Java.</choice>
35     <choice next = "#c">C.</choice>
36     <choice next = "#cplus">C plus plus.</choice>
37  </menu>
38
39  <form id = "java">
40     <block>
41        Java How to Program, Fifth Edition.
42        The complete, authoritative introduction to Java.
43        Java has revolutionized software development with
44        multimedia-intensive, platform-independent,
45        object-oriented code for conventional, Internet,
46        intranet and extranet-based applets and applications.
```

Fig. 29.6   Publication page of Deitel's VoiceXML page. (Part 1 of 3.)

```
47            This Fifth Edition of the world's most widely used
48            university-level Java textbook carefully explains
49            Java's extraordinary capabilities.
50            <assign name = "currentOption" expr = "'java'"/>
51            <goto next = "#repeat"/>
52         </block>
53      </form>
54
55      <form id = "c">
56         <block>
57            C How to Program, Fourth Edition.
58            World-renowned corporate trainers and best-selling authors
59            Harvey and Paul Deitel offer the most comprehensive, practical
60            introduction to C ever published with hundreds of hands-on
61            exercises, more than 250 complete programs written
62            and documented for easy learning, and exceptional insight into good
63            programming practices, maximizing performance, avoiding errors,
64            debugging, and testing. For anyone who wants to learn C, improve
65            their existing C skills, and understand how C serves as the
66            foundation for C++, Java, and object-oriented development.
67            <assign name = "currentOption" expr = "'c'"/>
68            <goto next = "#repeat"/>
69         </block>
70      </form>
71
72      <form id = "cplus">
73         <block>
74            The C++ How to Program, Fourth Edition.
75            With nearly 250,000 sold, Harvey and Paul Deitel's C++
76            How to Program is the world's best-selling introduction
77            to C++ programming. The Deitels' C++ How to Program
78            is the most comprehensive, practical introduction to C++ ever
79            published with hundreds of hands-on exercises, roughly 250
80            complete programs written and documented for easy learning,
81            and exceptional insight into good programming practices, maximizing
82            performance, avoiding errors, debugging, and testing.
83            <assign name = "currentOption" expr = "'cplus'"/>
84            <goto next = "#repeat"/>
85         </block>
86      </form>
87
88      <form id = "repeat">
89         <field name = "confirm" type = "boolean">
90
91            <prompt>
92               To repeat, say yes. Say no, to go back to home.
93            </prompt>
94
95            <filled>
96               <if cond = "confirm == true">
97                  <goto expr = "'#' + currentOption"/>
98               <else/>
99                  <goto next = "#publication"/>
```

Fig. 29.6   Publication page of Deitel's VoiceXML page. (Part 2 of 3.)

```
100            </if>
101          </filled>
102       </field>
103    </form>
104  </vxml>
```

Fig. 29.6 Publication page of Deitel's VoiceXML page. (Part 3 of 3.)

Figure 29.7 provides a brief description of several commonly used VoiceXML elements.

VoiceXML element	Description
assign	Assigns a value to a variable.
block	A simple form-item container element.
break	Instructs the computer to pause its speech output for a specified period of time.
choice	Specifies an option in a menu element.
enumerate	Lists all the available options to the user.
exit	Exits the program.
filled	Contains elements to be executed when the computer receives user input for a form element.
form	Gathers information from the user for a set of variables.
goto	Transfers control from one dialog to another.
grammar	Specifies grammar for the expected input from the user.
if, else, elseif	Control statements used for making logic decisions.
link	A transfer of control similar to the goto statement, but a link can be executed at any time during the program's execution.
menu	Provides user options and transfers control to other dialogs, based on the selected option.
prompt	Specifies text to be read to the user when a selection is needed.
subdialog	Calls another dialog. After executing the subdialog, the calling dialog resumes control.
var	Declares a variable.
vxml	Top-level tag specifying that the document should be processed by a VoiceXML interpreter.

Fig. 29.7 VoiceXML elements.

To test and deploy a VoiceXML application, register with the Voxeo Community (community.voxeo.com), a Web resource for creating, debugging and deploying voice applications. For the most part, Voxeo is a free Web resource. However, the company charges fees when VoiceXML applications are deployed commercially. Voxeo's voice servers interpret and process VoiceXML applications posted on the Web, and users "browse" to such applications using a telephone. The Voxeo Community assigns a unique telephone number to each VoiceXML application so that external users may access and interact with the application. A phone call to this number simulates the interaction between a user and a VoiceXML browser and eliminates the need for users to run a voice server of their own. Several VoiceXML tutorials are available at `community.voxeo.com/vxml/tutorials/home.jsp` to help get started developing and testing VoiceXML applications on the Voxeo Community site. [*Note*: Voxeo assigns telephone numbers to applications that reside on the Internet. If you have access to a Web server that is accessible from the Internet, use it to post your VoiceXML application. Otherwise, Voxeo allows developers to upload applications to its site using the **Voxeo File Manager** for testing purposes.]

29.12 CallXML

Another advance in voice technology for people with visual impairments is **CallXML**, a technology created and supported by Voxeo (`www.voxeo.com`). CallXML creates phone-to-Web applications that control incoming and outgoing telephone calls. Some examples of CallXML applications include voice mail, interactive voice response systems and Internet call waiting. Whereas VoiceXML assists individuals with visual impairments by reading Web pages, CallXML provides telephone access to Web-based content for individuals with visual impairments.

When users access CallXML applications, a **text-to-speech (TTS)** engine reads information contained within CallXML elements. A TTS engine converts text to an automated voice. Web applications respond to the caller's input. [*Note*: A touch-tone phone is required to access CallXML applications.]

Typically, CallXML applications play prerecorded audio clips or text as output, requesting a response as input. An audio clip may contain a greeting that introduces the caller to the application or to a menu of options that requires the caller to make touch-tone entries. Certain applications, such as voice mail, may require verbal and touch-tone input. Once the input is received, the application responds by invoking CallXML elements such as `text`, which contain the information a TTS engine reads to the user. If the application does not receive input within a designated time frame, it prompts the user to enter valid input.

When a user accesses a CallXML application, the incoming telephone call is referred to as a **session**. A CallXML application can support multiple sessions, enabling the application to receive multiple telephone calls at once. Each session is independent of the others and is assigned a unique **sessionID** for identification. A session terminates either when the user hangs up the telephone or when the CallXML application invokes the `hangup` element. Our first CallXML example shows the classic Hello World example (Fig. 29.8).

Line 1 contains the optional XML declaration. Value `version` indicates the XML version to which the document conforms. The current XML recommendation is version `1.0`. Value `encoding` indicates the type of Unicode encoding to use. For this example we use UTF-8, which requires eight bits to transfer and receive data. More information on Unicode may be found in Appendix F, Unicode. The `callxml` element in lines 6–8 contains the contents of a CallXML document. Line 7 is a `text` element containing `Hello World`. All the text that is to be spoken by a text-to-speech (TTS) engine needs to be placed within `text` elements.

```
1   <?xml version = "1.0" encoding = "UTF-8"?>
2
3   <!-- Fig. 29.8: hello.xml                -->
4   <!-- The classic Hello World example -->
5
6   <callxml>
7      <text>Hello World.</text>
8   </callxml>
```

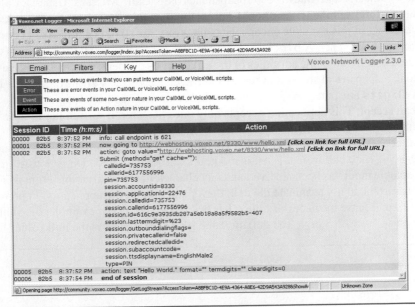

Fig. 29.8   Hello World CallXML example. (Courtesy of Voxeo Corporation.)

CallXML applications may be tested and deployed much like VoiceXML applications at the Voxeo Community (`community.voxeo.com`). To test the applications in this section, register with the Voxeo Community and upload the CallXML examples to a Web server accessible via the Web. The Voxeo Community will assign a unique phone number to each application, enabling users to access and interact with the application from any telephone. Please refer to Voxeo's CallXML tutorials at `community.voxeo.com/cxml/tutorials/home.jsp` for more information on setting up and testing CallXML applications.

Figure 29.8 demonstrates the **Voxeo.net Logger** feature of the Voxeo Community, which is accessible to registered members by clicking **Real-Time Logs** from any page of the site. This **logging** feature records and displays the "conversation" between the user and the application. The third row of the **Voxeo.net Logger** displays the URL of the CallXML application and the **global variables** associated with each session. The application (program) creates and assigns values to global variables at the start of each session that the entire application can access and modify. The subsequent row(s) display(s) the "conversation." This example shows a one-way conversation (because the application does not accept any input from the user) in which the TTS says **Hello World**. The last row shows the **end of session** message, which states that the phone call has terminated. The logging feature assists developers in debugging their applications. By observing the "conversation," a developer can determine at which point the application terminates. If the application terminates abruptly ("crashes"), the logging feature states the type and location of the error, so that the developer knows which section of the application to focus on.

The next example (Fig. 29.9) shows a CallXML application that reads the ISBN values of three Deitel textbooks—*Internet and World Wide Web How to Program: Third Edition*, *XML How to Program* and *Java How to Program: Fifth Edition*—based on the user's touch-tone input.

The **block** element (lines 7–69) encapsulates other CallXML tags. Usually, CallXML tags that perform similar tasks should be enclosed within <block>...</block>. The block element in this example encapsulates the **text**, **getDigits**, **onMaxSilence** and **onTermDigit** elements. A block element can also contain nested block elements.

Lines 20–23 show some attributes of the getDigits element, which obtains the user's touch-tone response and stores it in the variable declared by the **var** attribute (i.e., ISBN). The **maxDigits** attribute (line 21) indicates the maximum number of digits that the application can accept. This application accepts only one character. If no number is stated, then the application uses the default value—**nolimit**.

The **termDigits** attribute (line 22) contains the list of characters that terminate user input. When a character from this list is input, the CallXML application is notified that the last acceptable input has been received and any character entered after this point is invalid. These characters do not terminate the call; they simply notify the application to proceed to the next step because the necessary input has been received. In our example, the values for termDigits are 1, 2, 3 or 4. The default value for termDigits is the null value ("").

```
1   <?xml version = "1.0" encoding = "UTF-8"?>
2
3   <!-- Fig. 29.9: isbn.xml                            -->
4   <!-- Reads the ISBN value of three Deitel books -->
5
6   <callxml>
7     <block>
8       <text>
9         Welcome. To obtain the ISBN of Internet and World
10        Wide Web How to Program: Third Edition, please enter 1.
11        To obtain the ISBN of XML How to Program,
12        please enter 2. To obtain the ISBN of Java How
13        to Program: Fifth Edition, please enter 3. To exit the
14        application, please enter 4.
15      </text>
16
17      <!-- obtains the numeric value entered by the user and -->
18      <!-- stores it in the variable ISBN. The user has 60   -->
19      <!-- seconds to enter one numeric value                -->
20      <getDigits var = "ISBN"
21        maxDigits = "1"
22        termDigits = "1234"
23        maxTime = "60s" />
```

Fig. 29.9   CallXML example that reads three ISBN values. (Courtesy of Voxeo Corporation.) (Part 1 of 3.)

```
24
25        <!-- requests that the user enter a valid numeric -->
26        <!-- value after the elapsed time of 60 seconds   -->
27        <onMaxSilence>
28           <text>
29              Please enter either 1, 2, 3 or 4.
30           </text>
31
32           <getDigits var = "ISBN"
33              termDigits = "1234"
34              maxDigits = "1"
35              maxTime = "60s" />
36
37        </onMaxSilence>
38
39        <onTermDigit value = "1">
40           <text>
41              The ISBN for the Internet book is 0 1 3 1 4 5 0 9 1 3.
42              Thank you for calling our CallXML application.
43              Good-bye.
44           </text>
45        </onTermDigit>
46
47        <onTermDigit value = "2">
48           <text>
49              The ISBN for the XML book is 0 1 3 0 2 8 4 1 7 3.
50              Thank you for calling our CallXML application.
51              Good-bye.
52           </text>
53        </onTermDigit>
54
55        <onTermDigit value = "3">
56           <text>
57              The ISBN for the Java book is 0 1 3 1 0 1 6 2 1 0.
58              Thank you for calling our CallXML application.
59              Good-bye.
60           </text>
61        </onTermDigit>
62
63        <onTermDigit value = "4">
64           <text>
65              Thank you for calling our CallXML application.
66              Good-bye.
67           </text>
68        </onTermDigit>
69     </block>
70
71     <!-- event handler that terminates the call -->
72     <onHangup />
73  </callxml>
```

Fig. 29.9   CallXML example that reads three ISBN values. (Courtesy of Voxeo Corporation.) (Part 2 of 3.)

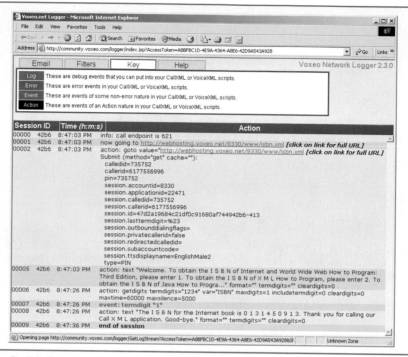

Fig. 29.9   CallXML example that reads three ISBN values. (Courtesy of Voxeo Corporation.) (Part 3 of 3.)

The **maxTime** attribute (line 23) indicates the maximum amount of time to wait for a user response (e.g., 60 seconds). If no input is received within the given time frame, then the CallXML application may terminate—a drastic measure. The default value for this attribute is 30 seconds.

The **onMaxSilence** element (lines 27–37) is an **event handler** that is invoked when the maxTime (or maxSilence) expires. An event handler notifies the application of the appropriate action to perform. In this case, the application asks the user to enter a value because the maxTime has expired. After receiving input, getDigits (line 32) stores the value in the **ISBN** variable.

The **onTermDigit** element (lines 39–68) is an event handler that notifies the application of the appropriate action to perform when the user selects one of the termDigits characters. At least one onTermDigit element tag must be associated with the get-Digits element, even if the default value ("") is used. We provide four actions that the application can perform depending on the user-entered value. For example, if the user enters **1**, the application reads the ISBN value of the *Internet and World Wide Web How to Program: Third Edition* textbook.

Line 72 contains the **onHangup** event handler that terminates the telephone call when the user hangs up the telephone. Our onHangup event handler is an empty element (i.e., there is no action to perform when this element is invoked).

The **Voxeo.net Logger** in Fig. 29.9 displays the "conversation" between the application and the user. The third row displays the URL of the application and the global variables of the session. The subsequent rows display the "conversation"—the application asks the caller which ISBN value to read, the caller enters **1** (*Internet and World Wide Web How to Program: Third Edition*) and the application reads the corresponding ISBN. The **end of session** message states that the application has terminated.

Brief descriptions of several logic and action CallXML elements are provided in Fig. 29.10. **Logic elements** assign values to, and clear values from, the session variables, and **action elements** perform specified tasks, such as answering and terminating a telephone call during the current session. A complete list of CallXML elements is available at:

www.oasis-open.org/cover/callxmlv2.html

Element	Description
assign	Assigns a value to a variable (var).
clear	Clears the contents of the var attribute.
clearDigits	Clears all digits that the user has entered.
goto	Navigates to another section of the current CallXML application or to a different CallXML application. The value attribute specifies the application URL. The submit attribute lists the variables that are passed to the invoked application. The method attribute states whether to use the HTTP *get* or *post* request types when sending and retrieving information. A *get* request retrieves data from a Web server without modifying the contents, while the *post* request sends modified data.
run	Starts a new CallXML session for each call. The value attribute specifies which CallXML application to retrieve. The submit attribute lists the variables that are passed to the invoked application. The method attribute states whether to use the HTTP *get* or *post* request type. The var attribute stores the identification number of the session.
sendEvent	Allows multiple sessions to exchange messages. The value attribute stores the message, and the session attribute specifies the identification number of the session that receives the message.
answer	Answers an incoming telephone call.
call	Calls the URL specified by the value attribute. The callerID attribute contains the phone number that is displayed on a CallerID device. The maxTime attribute specifies the length of time to wait for the call to be answered before disconnecting.
conference	Connects multiple sessions so that people can participate in a conference call. The targetSessions attribute specifies the identification numbers of the sessions, and the termDigits attribute indicates the touch-tone keys that terminate the call.
wait	Waits for user input. The value attribute specifies how long to wait. The termDigits attribute indicates the touch-tone keys that terminate the wait element.

Fig. 29.10 CallXML elements. (Part 1 of 2.)

Element	Description
play	Plays an audio file or a value that is stored as a number, date or amount of money and is indicated by the format attribute. The value attribute contains the information (location of the audio file, number, date or amount of money) that corresponds to the format attribute. The clearDigits attribute specifies whether or not to delete the previously entered input. The termDigits attribute indicates the touch-tone keys that terminate the audio file, etc.
recordAudio	Records an audio file and stores it at the URL specified by value. The format attribute indicates the file extension of the audio clip. Other attributes include termDigits, clearDigits, maxTime and maxSilence.

Fig. 29.10 CallXML elements. (Part 2 of 2.)

29.13 JAWS® for Windows

JAWS (Job Access with Sound) is one of the leading screen readers on the market today. Henter-Joyce, a division of Freedom Scientific,™ created this application to help people with visual impairments use technology.

To download a demonstration version of JAWS, visit

    www.freedomscientific.com/fs_products/software_jaws.asp

and select the **Downloads** link. The demo expires after 40 minutes. The computer must be rebooted before another 40-minute session can be started.

The JAWS demo is fully functional and includes an extensive, highly customized help system. Users can select which voice to use and the rate at which text is spoken. Users also can create keyboard shortcuts. Although the demo is in English, the full version of JAWS 5.0 (the most recent version at the time of this writing) allows the user to choose one of several supported languages.

JAWS also includes special key commands for popular programs such as Microsoft Internet Explorer and Microsoft Word. For example, when browsing in Internet Explorer, The capabilities of JAWS extend beyond reading the content on the screen. If JAWS is enabled, pressing *Insert + F7* in Internet Explorer opens a **Links List** dialog, which displays all the links available on a Web page. For more information about JAWS and the other products offered by Henter-Joyce, visit www.hj.com.

29.14 Other Accessibility Tools

Many additional accessibility products are available to assist people with disabilities. This section describes a variety of accessibility products, including hardware items and advanced technologies.

A **braille keyboard**, in addition to having each key labeled with the letter it represents, has the equivalent braille symbol printed on the key. Braille keyboards are combined most often with a speech synthesizer or a braille display, so users can interact with the computer to verify that their typing is correct.

Despite the existence of adaptive software and hardware for people with visual impairments, the accessibility of computers and the Internet is still hampered by the high costs, rapid obsolescence and unnecessary complexity of current technology. Moreover, almost all the software currently available requires installation by a person who can see. **Ocularis** is a project launched in the open-source community to help address these problems. Open-source software for people with visual impairments already exists, and although it is often superior to its proprietary, closed-source counterparts, it has not yet reached its full potential. Ocularis provides an Audio User Interface (AUI) that enables the blind to use the Linux operating system fully. Products that integrate with Ocularis include a word processor, calculator, basic finance application, Internet browser and e-mail client. A screen reader will also be included with programs that have a command-line interface. The official Ocularis Web site is located at `sourceforge.net/projects/ocularis`. Another Linux-based program that is very similar to Ocularis is Oralux. The official Oralux Web site is located at `www.oralux.org`.

People with visual impairments are not the only beneficiaries of the effort being made to improve markup languages. People with hearing impairments also have a number of tools to help them interpret auditory information delivered over the Web, such as Synchronized Multimedia Integration Language (SMIL™), discussed in Chapter 28. This markup language is designed to add extra **tracks**—layers of content found within a single audio or video file—to multimedia content. The additional tracks can contain closed captioning.

Technologies also are being designed to help people with severe disabilities, such as **quadriplegia**, a form of paralysis that affects the body from the neck down. One such technology, *EagleEyes*, developed by researchers at Boston College (`www.bc.edu/eagleeyes`), is a system that translates eye movements into mouse movements. Users move their mouse cursor by moving their eyes or heads and thereby can control their computer. For more information on regulations governing the design of Web sites to accommodate people with disabilities, visit `www.access-board.gov`.

An alliance of Microsoft, GW Micro, Henter-Joyce and Adobe Systems, Inc. is working on software to aid people with disabilities. JetForm Corp. is also accommodating the needs of people with disabilities by developing server-based XML software. The new software allows users to download a format that best meets their needs.

There are many services on the Web that assist e-business owners in designing their Web sites to be accessible to individuals with disabilities. For additional information, the U.S. Department of Justice (`www.usdoj.gov`) provides extensive resources detailing legal issues and current technologies related to people with disabilities.

These examples are just a few of the accessibility projects and technologies that currently exist. For more information on Web and general computer accessibility, see the resources provided in Section 29.17.

29.15 Accessibility in Microsoft Windows 2000 and XP

Beginning with Microsoft *Windows 95*, Microsoft has included accessibility features in its operating systems and many of its applications, including *Office 2000*, *Office XP* and *Windows Messenger*. In Microsoft *Windows 2000*, the accessibility features have been significantly enhanced. Microsoft *Windows XP* contains the same accessibility features as *Windows 2000*. All the accessibility options provided by Windows 2000 and Windows XP are available through the **Accessibility Wizard**, which guides users through all the Windows 2000 and Windows XP accessibility features and configures their computers according to the chosen specifications. This section guides users through the configuration of their Windows 2000 or Windows XP accessibility options using the **Accessibility Wizard**.[1]

To access the **Accessibility Wizard**, you must have Microsoft Windows 2000 or Microsoft Windows XP. In Windows 2000, click the **Start** button and select **Programs**, followed by **Accessories**, **Accessibility** and **Accessibility Wizard**. In Windows XP, click the **Start** button and select **All Programs**, followed by **Accessories**, **Accessibility** and **Accessibility Wizard**. When the wizard starts, the **Welcome** screen is displayed. Click **Next** to display a dialog (Fig. 29.11) that asks you to select a text size. Click **Next**.

Figure 29.12 shows the next dialog displayed. This dialog allows the user to activate the font-size settings chosen in the previous window, change the screen resolution, enable the *Microsoft Magnifier* (a program that displays an enlarged section of the screen in a separate window) and disable personalized menus (a feature that hides rarely used programs from the start menu, which can be a hindrance to users with disabilities). Make selections and click **Next**.

The next dialog (Fig. 29.13) displayed asks questions about the user's disabilities, which allows the **Accessibility Wizard** to customize Windows to better suit the user's needs. We selected everything for demonstration purposes. Click **Next** to continue.

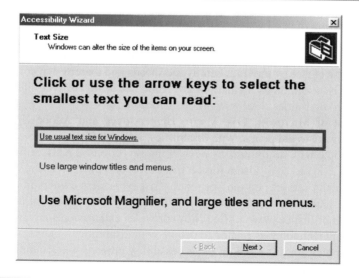

Fig. 29.11 Text Size dialog.

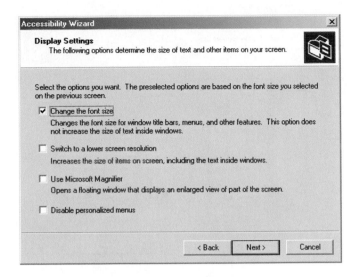

Fig. 29.12 Display Settings dialog.

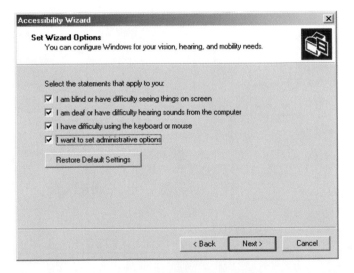

Fig. 29.13 Accessibility Wizard initialization options.

29.15.1 Tools for People with Visual Impairments

When we checked all the options in Fig. 29.13, the wizard began configuring Windows for people with visual impairments. As shown in Fig. 29.14, this dialog box allows the user to resize the scroll bars and window borders to increase their visibility. Click **Next** to proceed to the next dialog.

The dialog in Fig. 29.15 allows the user to resize icons. Users with poor vision, as well as users who have trouble reading, benefit from large icons.

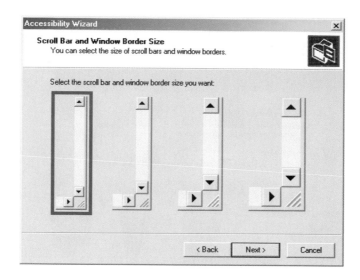

Fig. 29.14   Scroll Bar and Window Border Size dialog.

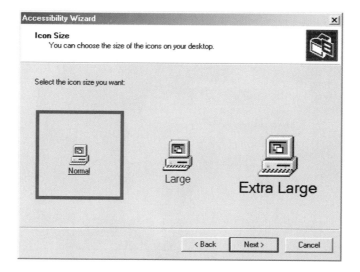

Fig. 29.15   Setting up window element sizes.

Clicking **Next** displays the **Display Color Settings** dialog (Fig. 29.16). These settings allow users to change the Windows color scheme and resize various screen elements. Click **Next** to view the dialog (Fig. 29.17) for customizing the mouse cursor.

Anyone who has ever used a laptop computer knows how difficult it is to see the mouse cursor. This is also a problem for people with visual impairments. To help solve this problem, the wizard offers larger cursors, black cursors and cursors that invert the colors of objects underneath them. Click **Next**.

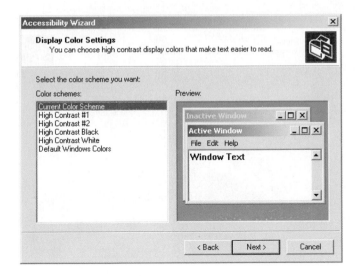

Fig. 29.16 Display Color Settings options.

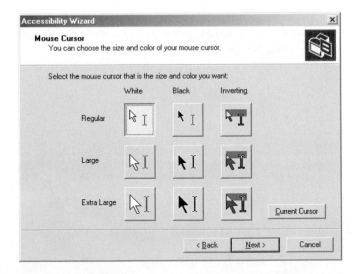

Fig. 29.17 Mouse Cursor adjustment tool.

29.15.2 Tools for People with Hearing Impairments

This section, which focuses on accessibility for people with hearing impairments, begins with the **SoundSentry** window (Fig. 29.18). **SoundSentry** is a tool that creates visual signals when system events occur. For example, people with hearing impairments are unable to hear the beeps that normally warn users, so **SoundSentry** flashes the screen when a beep occurs. To continue to the next dialog, click **Next**.

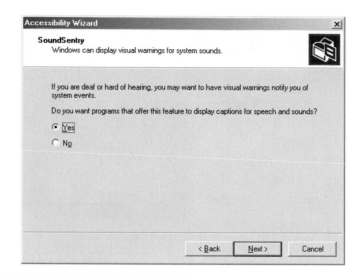

Fig. 29.18   SoundSentry dialog.

The next window is the **ShowSounds** window (Fig. 29.19). **ShowSounds** adds captions to spoken text and other sounds produced by today's multimedia-rich software. For **ShowSounds** to work, the developer of the software being used must have provided the captions and spoken text specifically within the software. Make selections and click **Next**.

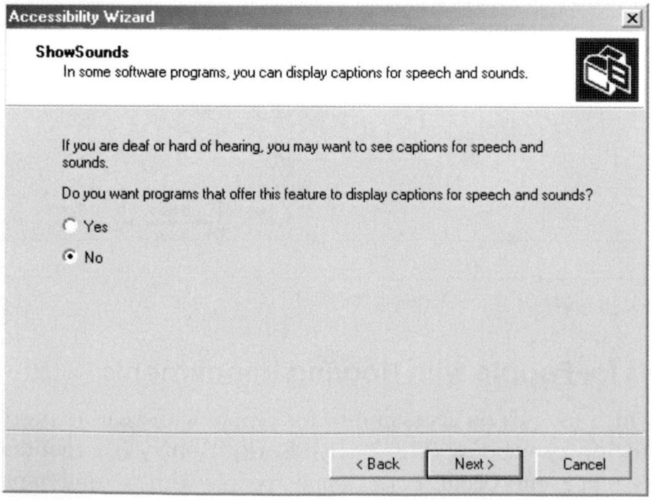

Fig. 29.19   ShowSounds dialog.

29.15.3 Tools for Users Who Have Difficulty Using the Keyboard

The next dialog is **StickyKeys** (Fig. 29.20). **StickyKeys** is a program that helps users who have difficulty pressing multiple keys at the same time. Many important computer commands can be invoked only by pressing specific key combinations. For example, the reboot command requires pressing *Ctrl+Alt+Delete* simultaneously. **StickyKeys** allows the user to press key combinations in sequence rather than at the same time. Click **Next** to continue to the **BounceKeys** dialog (Fig. 29.21).

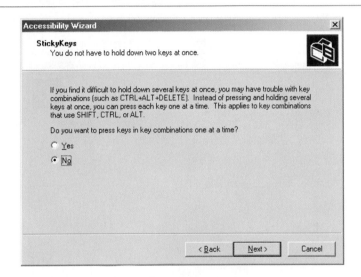

Fig. 29.20   StickyKeys window.

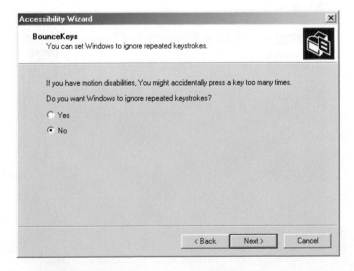

Fig. 29.21   BounceKeys dialog.

Another common problem for users with certain disabilities is accidentally pressing the same key more than once. This problem typically is caused by holding a key down too long. **BounceKeys** forces the computer to ignore repeated keystrokes. Click **Next**.

ToggleKeys (Fig. 29.22) alerts users that they have pressed one of the lock keys (i.e., *Caps Lock*, *Num Lock* and *Scroll Lock*) by sounding an audible beep. Make selections and click **Next**.

Next, the **Extra Keyboard Help** dialog (Fig. 29.23) is displayed. This section activates a tool that displays information such as keyboard shortcuts and tool tips when they are available. Like ShowSounds, this tool requires that the software developer provide the content to be displayed. Clicking **Next** will load the **MouseKeys** (Fig. 29.24) customization window.

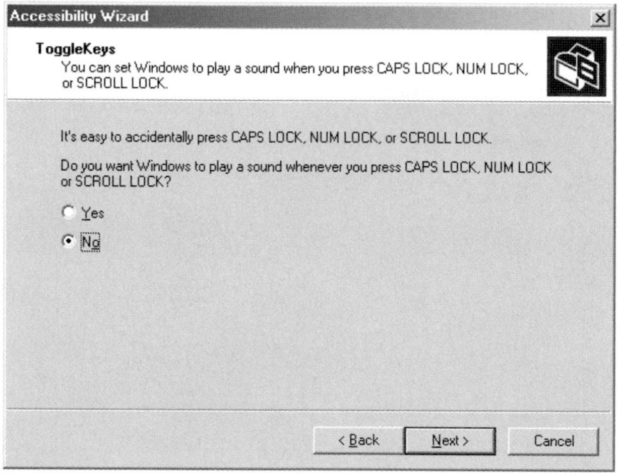

Fig. 29.22 **ToggleKeys** window.

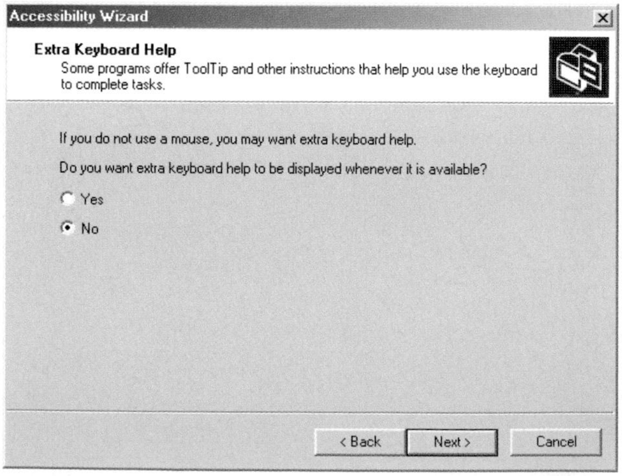

Fig. 29.23 **Extra Keyboard Help** dialog.

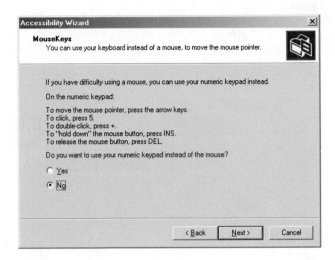

Fig. 29.24 MouseKeys window.

MouseKeys is a tool that uses the keyboard to emulate mouse movements. The arrow keys direct the mouse, while the *5* key sends a single click. To double click, the user must press the + key; to simulate holding down the mouse button, the user must press the *Ins* (Insert) key, and to release the mouse button, the user must press the *Del* (Delete) key. To continue to the next screen in the **Accessibility Wizard**, click **Next**.

Today's computer tools are made almost exclusively for right-handed users, including most computer mice. Microsoft recognizes this problem and provides the **Mouse Button Settings** window (Fig. 29.25) during the **Accessibility Wizard**. This tool allows the user to create a virtual left-handed mouse by swapping the button functions. Click **Next**.

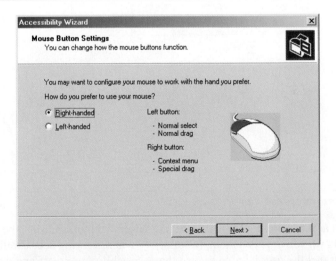

Fig. 29.25 Mouse Button Settings window.

Mouse speed is adjusted by using the **MouseSpeed** (Fig. 29.26) section of the **Accessibility Wizard**. Dragging the scroll bar changes the speed. Clicking the **Next** button sets the speed and displays the wizard's **Set Automatic Timeouts** window (Fig. 29.27).

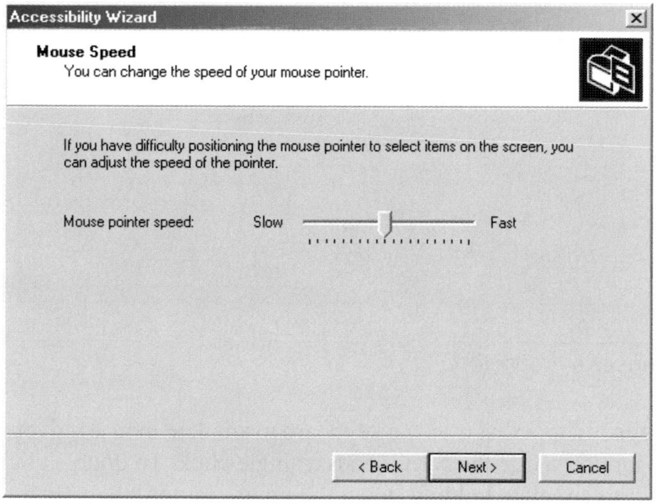

Fig. 29.26 Mouse Speed dialog.

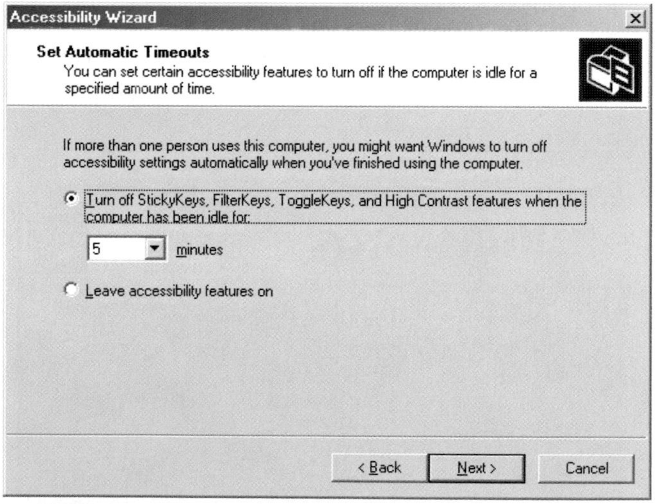

Fig. 29.27 Set Automatic Timeouts dialog.

Although accessibility tools are important to users with disabilities, they can be a hindrance to users who do not need them. In situations where varying accessibility needs exist, it is important that the user be able to turn the accessibility tools off and on as necessary. The **Set Automatic Timeouts** window specifies a **timeout** period for the tools. A timeout either enables or disables a certain action after the computer has idled for a specified amount of time. A screen saver is a common example of a program with a timeout period. Here, a timeout is set to toggle the accessibility tools.

After clicking **Next**, the **Save Settings to File** dialog appears (Fig. 29.28). This dialog determines whether the accessibility settings should be used as the **default settings**, which are loaded when the computer is rebooted or after a timeout. Set the accessibility settings as the default if the majority of users need them. Users can also save the accessibility settings by creating an `.acw` file, which, when clicked, activates the saved accessibility settings on any Windows 2000 or Windows XP computer.

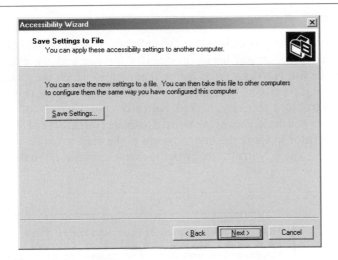

Fig. 29.28 Saving new accessibility settings.

29.15.4 Microsoft Narrator

Microsoft **Narrator** is a text-to-speech program for people with visual impairments. It reads text, describes the current desktop environment and alerts the user when certain Windows events occur. **Narrator** is intended to aid in configuring Microsoft Windows. It is a screen reader that works with Internet Explorer, Wordpad, Notepad and most programs in the **Control Panel**. Although it is limited outside these applications, **Narrator** is excellent at navigating the Windows environment.

To get an idea of what **Narrator** does, we will explain how to use it with various Windows applications. In Windows 2000, click the **Start** button and select **Programs**, followed by **Accessories, Accessibility** and **Narrator**. In Windows XP, click the **Start** button and select **All Programs**, followed by **Accessories, Accessibility** and **Narrator**. Once **Narrator** is open, it describes the current foreground window. It then reads the text inside the window aloud to the user. Clicking **OK** displays Fig. 29.29's dialog.

Checking the first option instructs **Narrator** to describe menus and new windows when they are opened. The second option instructs **Narrator** to speak the characters you are typing as you type them. The third option moves the mouse cursor to the region being read by **Narrator**. Clicking the **Voice...** button enables the user to change the pitch, volume and speed of the narrator voice.

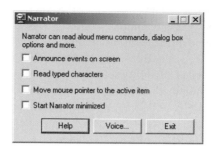

Fig. 29.29 Narrator window.

With **Narrator** running, open **Notepad** and click the **File** menu. **Narrator** announces the opening of the program and begins to describe the items in the **File** menu. When scrolling down the list, **Narrator** reads the current item to which the mouse is pointing. Type some text and press *Ctrl-Shift-Enter* to hear **Narrator** read it (Fig. 29.30). If the **Read typed characters** option is checked, **Narrator** reads each character as it is typed. The direction arrows on the keyboard can be used to make **Narrator** read. The up and down arrows cause **Narrator** to speak the lines adjacent to the current mouse position, and the left and right arrows cause **Narrator** to speak the characters adjacent to the current mouse position.

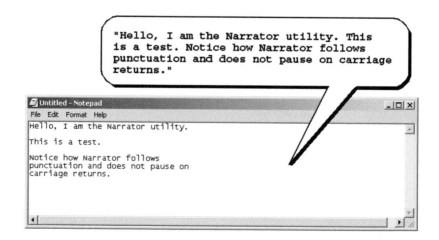

Fig. 29.30 Narrator reading Notepad text.

29.15.5 Microsoft On-Screen Keyboard

Some computer users lack the ability to use a keyboard but can use a pointing device such as a mouse. For these users, the **On-Screen Keyboard** is helpful. To access the On-Screen Keyboard, click the **Start** button and select **Programs**, followed by **Accessories**, **Accessibility** and **On-Screen Keyboard**. Figure 29.31 shows the layout of the Microsoft On-Screen Keyboard.

Fig. 29.31 Microsoft **On-Screen Keyboard**.

Users who still have difficulty using the On-Screen Keyboard should purchase more sophisticated products, such as Clicker 4™ by Inclusive Technology. Clicker 4 is an aid for people who cannot effectively use a keyboard. Its best feature is its ability to be customized. Keys can have letters, numbers, entire words or even pictures on them. For more information regarding Clicker 4, visit `www.inclusive.co.uk/catalog/clicker.shtml`.

29.15.6 Accessibility Features in Microsoft Internet Explorer

Internet Explorer offers many options to improve usability. To access IE's accessibility features, launch the program, click the **Tools** menu and select **Internet Options...**. From the **Internet Options** menu, press the button labeled **Accessibility...** to open the accessibility options (Fig. 29.32).

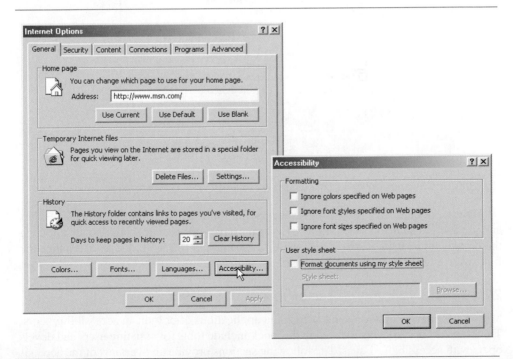

Fig. 29.32 Microsoft Internet Explorer's accessibility options.

The accessibility options in IE augment users' Web browsing. Users can ignore Web colors, Web fonts and font-size tags. This eliminates problems that arise from poor Web-page design and allows users to customize their Web browsing. Users can even specify a style sheet that formats every Web site visited according to their personal preferences.

These are not the only accessibility options offered in IE. In the **Internet Options** dialog, click the **Advanced** tab. This opens the dialog shown in Fig. 29.33. The first option that can be set is labeled **Always expand ALT text for images**. By default, IE hides some of the `alt` text if it exceeds the size of the image it describes. This option forces all the text to be shown. The second option reads: **Move system caret with focus/selection changes**. This option is intended to make screen reading more effective. Some screen readers use the **system caret** (the blinking vertical bar associated with editing text) to decide what is read. If this option is not activated, screen readers may not read Web pages correctly.

Fig. 29.33   Advanced accessibility settings in Microsoft Internet Explorer.

Web designers often forget to take accessibility into account when creating Web sites and use fonts that are too small. Many user agents have addressed this problem by allowing the user to adjust the text size. Click the **View** menu and select **Text Size** to change the font size using IE. By default, the text size is set to **Medium**.

29.16 Accessibility in Macromedia Products

Most modern Web authoring and Web client applications offer built-in accessibility tools. The Macromedia products covered in this book include tools for assisting users and developers with accessibility issues. The following sections provide an overview of the accessibility features in Macromedia Dreamweaver and Macromedia Flash.

29.16.1 Dreamweaver

Macromedia Dreamweaver is an easy-to-use XHTML editor with a WYSIWYG (What You See Is What You Get) interface. Since Dreamweaver creates XHTML code for the user, it must take accessibility requirements into account. By default, Dreamweaver does not create the necessary XHTML code for accessible Web pages. To enable accessibility options, click **Preferences** in the **Edit** menu of the Dreamweaver environment. In the **Category** menu select **Accessibility**. This will open the **Preferences** window and show the Dreamweaver accessibility options (Fig. 29.34).

The options in this window enable Dreamweaver's accessibility features. Checking any of the boxes next to XHTML element types on the right side of this window forces Dreamweaver to prompt the user to enter accessibility attributes when inserting elements of that type. For example, if **Images** is checked, Dreamweaver will prompt the user to enter an `alt` tag and a `longdesc` tag when inserting new images in a Web page. (Fig. 29.35).

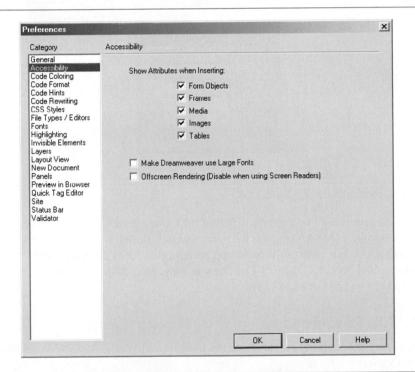

Fig. 29.34 **Accessibility Preferences** window in Macromedia Dreamweaver.

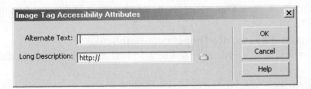

Fig. 29.35 **Image Tag Accessibility Attributes** dialog in Dreamweaver.

Dreamweaver also includes advanced accessibility features, such as accessibility validation. For more information on these features, go to the Dreamweaver Accessibility Overview at www.macromedia.com/macromedia/accessibility/mx/dw/overview.html.

29.16.2 Flash

Macromedia Flash includes features for making Flash movies more accessible. Flash authors can specify text alternatives for elements in Flash movies that serve the same purpose as alt attributes in XHTML documents. Every element in a Flash movie can be given a brief name and a longer description to help screen readers and other accessibility tools interpret the Flash movie. To open the **Accessibility** window (Fig. 29.36) in Flash MX, click **Accessibility** in the **View** menu. To specify a name or a description for an element, select the element on the editing stage and fill in the corresponding **Accessibility** window.

Fig. 29.36   **Accessibility** dialog in Flash

When an accessible Flash movie is played on a client computer, Flash uses Microsoft Active Accessibility (MSAA) to pass the name and description to screen readers and other accessibility tools. For more information on accessibility tools in Macromedia Flash, see the Macromedia Flash Accessibility Overview at www.macromedia.com/macromedia/accessibility/features/flash.

29.17 Web Resources

There are many accessibility resources on the Internet and World Wide Web, and this section lists a variety of them.

www.w3.org/WAI
The World Wide Web Consortium's Web Accessibility Initiative (WAI) site promotes the design of universally accessible Web sites. This site contains the current guidelines and forthcoming standards for Web accessibility.

deafness.about.com/health/deafness/msubmenu6.htm
The About Guide to Deafness is a resource to find information pertaining to deafness.

www.cast.org
CAST (Center for Applied Special Technology) offers software, including a valuable accessibility checker, that helps individuals with disabilities use a computer. The accessibility checker is a Web-based program that validates the accessibility of Web sites.

`www.trainingpost.org/3-2-inst.htm`
A tutorial on the Gunning Fog Index. The Gunning Fog Index is a method of grading text on its readability.

`www.w3.org/TR/REC-CSS2/aural.html`
Discusses aural style sheets, outlining the purpose and uses of this new technology.

`java.sun.com/products/java-media/speech/forDevelopers/JSML`
Outlines the specifications for JSML, Sun Microsystem's Java Speech Markup Language. This language, like VoiceXML, can drastically improve accessibility for people with visual impairments.

`www.wgbh.org/wgbh/pages/ncam/accesslinks.html`
Links to many accessibility pages across the Web.

`www.w3.org/TR/voice-tts-reqs`
Explains the speech synthesis markup requirements for voice markup languages.

`www.voicexmlcentral.com`
Contains information about VoiceXML, such as the specification and the document type definition (DTD).

`deafness.about.com/msubvib.htm?once=true&`
Provides information on vibrotactile devices that allow individuals with hearing impairments to experience audio in the form of vibrations.

`www.abledata.com/text2/icg_hear.htm`
Contains a consumer guide that discusses technologies for people with hearing impairments.

`www.washington.edu/doit`
The University of Washington's DO-IT (Disabilities, Opportunities, Internetworking and Technology) site provides information and Web development resources for creating universally accessible Web sites.

`www.webaim.org`
The *WebAIM* site provides a number of tutorials, articles, simulations and other useful resources that demonstrate how to design accessible Web sites. The site provides a screen reader simulation.

`www.speech.cs.cmu.edu/comp.speech/SpeechLinks.html`
The *Speech Technology Hyperlinks* page has over 500 links to sites related to computer-based speech and speech-recognition tools.

`www.chantinc.com/technology`
The *Chant* Web site discusses speech technology and how it works. Chant also provides speech-synthesis and speech-recognition software.

`www.oasis-open.org/cover/callxmlv2.html`
Provides a comprehensive list of the CallXML tags, complete with descriptions of each tag and short examples on how to apply the tags in various applications.

`www.macromedia.com/macromedia/accessibility/mx/dw/overview.html`
Contains the Macromedia *Dreamweaver Accessibility Overview*, which outlines the accessibility features of Macromedia Dreamweaver and provides more specific instructions on how to use them.

`www.macromedia.com/macromedia/accessibility/features/flash`
The Macromedia *Flash Accessibility Overview* outlines the accessibility features of Macromedia Flash and provides more specific instructions on how to use them.

`bobby.watchfire.com`
Watchfire's *Bobby* is an accessibility tool that tests XHTML documents for compliance with accessibility standards.

`www.icdri.org`
The International Center for Disability Resources on the Internet has global resources including information on laws and policies on accessible Web design.

`www.cynthiasays.com`
The *Cynthia Says*™ *Portal* provides several tools for aid in the development of accessible Web pages. Contains a tool to test any Web site against either federal or W3C accessibility standards.

`www.jimthatcher.com/site_resources.htm`
Provides resources on the Web accessibility guidelines of Section 508 and several tutorials on designing accessible Web sites.

`www.section508.gov`
Presents detailed information about Section 508 of the Rehabilitation Act.

SUMMARY

- Enabling a Web site to meet the needs of individuals with disabilities is an issue relevant to all business owners.

- Legal ramifications exist for Web sites that discriminate against people with disabilities (i.e., by not providing them with adequate access to the site's resources).

- Section 508 of the Rehabilitation Act of 1973 was amended by the Workforce Investment Act of 1998 to include a set of Electronic and Information Technology Accessibility Standards. Section 508 § 1194.22 establishes 16 accessibility standards for Web-based intranet and Internet applications to which federal agencies must adhere when designing Web sites.

- Technologies such as voice activation, visual enhancers and auditory aids enable individuals with disabilities to work at many kinds of jobs that would otherwise be unavailable to them.

- On April 7, 1997, the World Wide Web Consortium (W3C) launched the Web Accessibility Initiative (WAI). The WAI is an attempt to make the Web more accessible; its mission is described at `www.w3.org/WAI`.

- Accessibility refers to the level of usability of an application or a Web site for people with disabilities. Total accessibility is difficult to achieve because there are many different disabilities, language barriers, and hardware and software inconsistencies.

- The majority of Web sites are considered either partially or totally inaccessible to people with visual, learning or mobility impairments.

- The WAI publishes the Web Content Accessibility Guidelines 1.0, which assigns priorities to a three-tier structure of checkpoints. The WAI currently is working on a draft of the Web Content Accessibility Guidelines 2.0.

- One important WAI requirement is to ensure that every image, movie and sound on a Web site is accompanied by a description that clearly defines the object's purpose; this is called an `<alt>` tag.

- Specialized user agents, such as screen readers (programs that allow users to hear what is being displayed on their screen) and braille displays (devices that receive data from screen-reading software and output it as braille), allow people with visual impairments to access text-based information that is normally displayed on the screen.

- Using a screen reader to navigate a Web site can be time-consuming and frustrating, because screen readers are unable to interpret pictures and other graphical content that do not have alternative text.

- Including links at the top of each Web page provides easy access to the page's main content.

- Web pages with large amounts of multimedia content are difficult for user agents to interpret unless they are designed properly. Images, movies and most non-XHTML objects cannot be read by screen readers.

- Web designers should avoid misuse of the `alt` attribute; it is intended to provide a short description of an XHTML object that may not load properly on all user agents.

- The value of the `longdesc` attribute is a text-based URL, linked to a Web page, that describes the image associated with the attribute.

- When creating a Web page intended for the general public, it is important to consider the reading level at which it is written. Web site designers can make their sites more readable through the use of shorter words, because some users may have difficulty reading long words. In addition, users from other countries may have difficulty understanding slang and other nontraditional language.

- Web designers may use frames to display more than one XHTML file at a time. This is a convenient way to ensure that certain content is always on screen. Unfortunately, frames often lack proper descriptions, which prevents users with text-based browsers, or users who lack sight, from navigating the Web site.

- The `noframes` and `noscript` elements allow the designer to offer alternative content to users whose browsers do not support frames or scripting, respectively.

- VoiceXML has tremendous implications for people with visual impairments and for the illiterate. VoiceXML, a speech-recognition and speech-synthesis technology, reads Web pages to users and understands words spoken into a microphone.

- A VoiceXML document is made up of a series of dialogs and subdialogs that result in spoken interaction between the user and the computer. VoiceXML is a voice-recognition technology.

- CallXML, a language created and supported by Voxeo, creates phone-to-Web applications.

- When a user accesses a CallXML application, the incoming telephone call is referred to as a session. A CallXML application can support multiple sessions that enable the application to receive multiple telephone calls at any given time.

- A session terminates either when the user hangs up the telephone or when the CallXML application invokes the `hangup` element.

- The contents of a CallXML application are inserted within the `<callxml>` tag.

- CallXML tags that perform similar tasks should be enclosed in a `block` element.

- To deploy a CallXML application, register with the Voxeo Community, which assigns a telephone number to the application so that other users may access it.

- Voxeo's logging feature enables developers to debug their telephone application by observing the "conversation" between the user and the application.

- Braille keyboards are similar to standard keyboards, except that in addition to having each key labeled with the letter it represents, they have the equivalent braille symbol printed on the key. Most often, braille keyboards are combined with a speech synthesizer or a braille display, so users can interact with the computer to verify that their typing is correct.

- People with visual impairments are not the only beneficiaries of the effort to improve markup languages. Individuals with hearing impairments also have a great number of tools to help them interpret auditory information delivered over the Web.

- Speech synthesis is another research area that will help people with disabilities.

- Open-source software for people with visual impairments already exists and is often superior to most of its proprietary, closed-source counterparts.

- People with hearing impairments will soon benefit from what is called Synchronized Multimedia Integration Language (SMIL). This markup language is designed to add extra tracks—layers of content found within a single audio or video file. The additional tracks can contain data such as captioning.

- EagleEyes, developed by researchers at Boston College (www.bc.edu/eagleeyes), is a system that translates eye movements into mouse movements. Users move the mouse cursor by moving their eyes or heads and are thereby able to control computers.

- All of the accessibility options provided by Windows 2000 and Windows XP are available through the **Accessibility Wizard**. The **Accessibility Wizard** takes the user step by step through all of the Windows accessibility features and configures his or her computer according to the chosen specifications.

- Microsoft Magnifier enlarges the section of your screen surrounding the mouse cursor.

- To solve problems seeing the mouse cursor, Microsoft offers the ability to use larger cursors, black cursors and cursors that invert objects underneath them.

- **SoundSentry** is a tool that creates visual signals when system events occur.

- **ShowSounds** adds captions to spoken text and other sounds produced by today's multimedia-rich software.

- **StickyKeys** is a program that helps users who have difficulty pressing multiple keys at the same time.

- **BounceKeys** forces the computer to ignore repeated keystrokes, solving the problem of accidentally pressing the same key more than once.

- **ToggleKeys** causes an audible beep to alert users that they have pressed one of the lock keys (i.e., *Caps Lock*, *Num Lock*, or *Scroll Lock*).

- **MouseKeys** is a tool that uses the keyboard to emulate mouse movements.

- The **Mouse Button Settings** tool allows you to create a virtual left-handed mouse by swapping the button functions.

- A timeout either enables or disables a certain action after the computer has idled for a specified amount of time. A common example of a timeout is a screen saver.

- You can create an .acw file, that, when clicked, will automatically activate the saved accessibility settings on any Windows 2000 or Windows XP computer.

- Microsoft **Narrator** is a text-to-speech program for people with visual impairments. It reads text, describes the current desktop environment and alerts the user when certain Windows events occur.

- Macromedia Dreamweaver has tools for creating Web pages with XHTML-accessibility features.

- Macromedia Flash has the ability to include text alternatives for movie elements, making them more accessible.

TERMINOLOGY

accessibility
Accessibility Wizard
Accessibility Wizard: Display Color Settings
Accessibility Wizard: Icon Size
Accessibility Wizard: Mouse Cursor
Accessibility Wizard: Scroll Bar and Window Border Size
action element
`alt` attribute
Americans with Disabilities Act (ADA)
`assign` element in VoiceXML
AuralCSS
`block` element in VoiceXML
BounceKeys
braille display

braille keyboard
b element (bold)
CallXML
`callxml` element in CallXML
`caption`
Cascading Style Sheets (CSS)
`count` attribute in VoiceXML
`choice` element in VoiceXML
CSS2
D-link
default setting
EagleEyes
`encoding`
`enumerate` element in VoiceXML
event handler
`exit` element in VoiceXML

SELF-REVIEW EXERCISES

29.1   Spell out the following acronyms:
    a) W3C.
    b) WAI.
    c) JAWS.

    d) SMIL.

    e) CSS.

29.2   Fill in the blanks in each of the following statements.

    a) One WCAG rule is to ensure that each _____, _____ and _____ is accompanied by a description that clearly defines its purpose.

    b) Technologies such as _____, _____ and _____ enable individuals with disabilities to work in a large number of positions.

    c) Although they may be a great layout tool, _____ are difficult for screen readers to interpret and convey clearly to a user.

    d) To make your frame accessible to individuals with disabilities, it is important to include _____ elements on your page.

    e) Blind people using computers are often assisted by _____ and _____ .

    f) CallXML is used to create _____ applications that allow businesses to receive and send telephone calls.

    g) A(n) _____ element must be associated with the `getDigits` element.

29.3   State whether each of the following is *true* or *false*. If *false*, explain why.

    a) Screen readers have no problem reading and translating images.

    b) When writing pages for the general public, it is important to consider the reading difficulty level of the text you are writing.

    c) The `alt` attribute helps screen readers describe images in a Web page.

    d) Left-handed people have been helped by the improvements made in speech-recognition technology more than any other group of people.

    e) VoiceXML lets some users interact with Web content using speech-recognition and speech-synthesis technologies.

    f) Elements such as `onMaxSilence`, `onTermDigit` and `onMaxTime` are event handlers because they perform a specified task when invoked.

ANSWERS TO SELF-REVIEW EXERCISES

29.1   a) World Wide Web Consortium. b) Web Accessibility Initiative. c) Job Access with Sound. d) Synchronized Multimedia Integration Language. e) Cascading Style Sheets.

29.2   a) image, movie, sound. b) voice activation, visual enhancers and auditory aids. c) tables. d) `noframes`. e) braille displays, braille keyboards. f) phone-to-Web. g) `onTermDigit`.

29.3   a) False. Screen readers have no way of telling a user what is shown in an image. If the programmer includes an `alt` attribute inside the `img` element, the screen reader reads this description to the user. b) True. c) True. d) False. Although left-handed people can use speech-recognition technology just as everyone else can, speech-recognition technology has had the largest impact on the blind and on people who have trouble typing. e) True. f) True.

EXERCISES

29.4   Insert XHTML markup into each segment to make the segment accessible to someone with disabilities. The contents of images and frames should be apparent from the context and filenames.

    a)
```
<img src = "dogs.jpg" width = "300" height = "250" />
```

    b)
```
<table width = "75%">
     <tr><th>Language</th><th>Version</th></tr>
     <tr><td>XHTML</td><td>1.1</td></tr>
     <tr><td>Perl</td><td>5.8.0</td></tr>
     <tr><td>Java</td><td>1.4</td></tr>
</table>
```

29.5   Define the following terms:
   a)   Action element.
   b)   Gunning Fog Index.
   c)   Screen reader.
   d)   Session.
   e)   Web Accessibility Initiative (WAI).

29.6   Describe the three-tier structure of checkpoints (priority-one, priority-two and priority-three) set forth by the WAI.

29.7   Why do misused h1 heading tags create problems for screen readers?

29.8   Use CallXML to create a voice mail system that plays a voice mail greeting and records the message. Have friends and classmates call your application and leave a message.

30

Dynamic HTML: Structured Graphics Control (On CD)

Objectives

- To be able to use the Structured Graphics Control to create various shapes.
- To understand the Structured Graphics Control methods for modifying lines and borders.
- To understand the Structured Graphics Control methods for modifying colors and fill styles.
- To be able to enable event capturing for the Structured Graphics Control.
- To be able to import external lists of methods into the Structured Graphics Control.
- To be able to scale, rotate and translate shapes in the Structured Graphics Control.

[*Note:* This chapter is located on the CD that accompanies this book in printable Adobe® Acrobat® PDF format. The chapter includes pages 1080–1097.]

31

Dynamic HTML: Path, Sequencer and Sprite Controls (On CD)

Objectives

- To be able to use the DirectAnimation multimedia ActiveX controls, including the Path, Sequencer and Sprite controls.
- To be able to add animation to Web pages with the DirectAnimation ActiveX controls.
- To use the Path Control to specify the path along which an animated Web page element moves.
- To use the Sequencer Control to control the timing and synchronization of actions on a Web page.
- To use the Sprite Control to create animated images for a Web page.

[Note: This chapter is located on the CD that accompanies this book in printable Adobe® Acrobat® PDF format. The chapter includes pages 1098–1117.]

32

VBScript
(On CD)

Objectives

- To become familiar with the VBScript language.
- To use VBScript keywords, operators and functions to write client-side scripts.
- To be able to write Sub and Function procedures.
- To use VBScript arrays and regular expressions.
- To be able to write VBScript abstract data types called Classes.
- To be able to create objects from Classes.
- To be able to write Property Let, Property Get and Property Set procedures.

[Note: This chapter is located on the CD that accompanies this book in printable Adobe® Acrobat® PDF format. The chapter includes pages 1118–1164.]

33

Active Server Pages (ASP) (On CD)

Objectives

- To program Active Server Pages using VBScript.
- To understand how Active Server Pages work.
- To understand the differences between client-side scripting and server-side scripting.
- To be able to pass data between Web pages.
- To be able to use server-side include statements.
- To be able to use server-side ActiveX components.
- To be able to create sessions.
- To be able to use cookies.
- To be able to use ActiveX Data Objects (ADO) to access a database.

[Note: This chapter is located on the CD that accompanies this book in printable Adobe® Acrobat® PDF format. The chapter includes pages 1165–1217.]

34

Case Study: Active Server Pages and XML (On CD)

Objectives

- To create a Web-based message forum using Active Server Pages.
- To use XML with Active Server Pages.
- To be able to add new forums.
- To be able to post messages to the message forum.
- To use Microsoft's DOM to manipulate an XML document.
- To use XSLT to transform XML documents.

[Note: This chapter is located on the CD that accompanies this book in printable Adobe® Acrobat® PDF format. The chapter includes pages 1218–1241.]

35

Python
(On CD)

Objectives

- To understand basic Python data types.
- To understand string processing and regular expressions in Python.
- To use exception handling.
- To perform basic CGI tasks in Python.
- To construct programs that interact with MySQL databases using the Python Database Application Programming Interface (DB-API).

[Note: This chapter is located on the CD that accompanies this book in printable Adobe® Acrobat® PDF format. The chapter includes pages 1242–1287.]

36

Servlets: Bonus for Java™ Developers (On CD)

Objectives

- To execute servlets with the Apache Tomcat server.
- To be able to respond to HTTP requests from an `HttpServlet`.
- To be able to redirect requests to static and dynamic Web resources.

[Note: This chapter is located on the CD that accompanies this book in printable Adobe® Acrobat® PDF format. The chapter includes pages 1288–1327.]

37

JavaServer Pages (JSP): Bonus for Java Developers (On CD)

Objectives

- To be able to create and deploy JavaServer Pages.
- To use JSP's implicit objects and scriptlets to create dynamic Web pages.
- To specify global JSP information with directives.
- To use actions to manipulate JavaBeans in a JSP, to include resources dynamically and to forward requests to other JSPs.

[Note: This chapter is located on the CD that accompanies this book in printable Adobe® Acrobat® PDF format. The chapter includes pages 1328–1373.]

38

e-Business & e-Commerce (On CD)

Objectives

- To understand how the Internet and World Wide Web are revolutionizing business processes.
- To introduce various business models used on the Web.
- To explore the advantages and disadvantages of creating an online business.
- To examine marketing, payment, security and legal issues that affect e-businesses.

[Note: This chapter is located on the CD that accompanies this book in printable Adobe® Acrobat® PDF format. The chapter includes pages 1374–1428.]

XHTML Special Characters

The table of Fig. A.1 shows many commonly used XHTML special characters—called **character entity references** by the World Wide Web Consortium. For a complete list of character entity references, see the site www.w3.org/TR/REC-html40/sgml/entities.html.

Character	XHTML encoding	Character	XHTML encoding
non-breaking space		ê	&#234;
§	&#167;	ì	&#236;
©	&#169;	í	&#237;
®	&#174;	î	&#238;
π	&#188;	ñ	&#241;
∫	&#189;	ò	&#242;
Ω	&#190;	ó	&#243;
à	&#224;	ô	&#244;
á	&#225;	õ	&#245;
â	&#226;	÷	&#247;
ã	&#227;	ù	&#249;
å	&#229;	ú	&#250;
ç	&#231;	û	&#251;
è	&#232;	•	&#8226;
é	&#233;	™	&#8482;

Fig. A.1   XHTML special characters.

XHTML Colors

Colors may be specified by using a standard name (such as aqua) or a hexadecimal RGB value (such as #00FFFF for aqua). Of the six hexadecimal digits in an RGB value, the first two represent the amount of red in the color, the middle two represent the amount of green in the color, and the last two represent the amount of blue in the color. For example, black is the absence of color and is defined by #000000, whereas white is the maximum amount of red, green and blue and is defined by #FFFFFF. Pure red is #FF0000, pure green (which the standard calls lime) is #00FF00 and pure blue is #00FFFF. Note that green in the standard is defined as #008000. Figure B.1 contains the XHTML standard color set. Figure B.2 contains the XHTML extended color set.

Color name	Value	Color name	Value
aqua	#00FFFF	navy	#000080
black	#000000	olive	#808000
blue	#0000FF	purple	#800080
fuchsia	#FF00FF	red	#FF0000
gray	#808080	silver	#C0C0C0
green	#008000	teal	#008080
lime	#00FF00	yellow	#FFFF00
maroon	#800000	white	#FFFFFF

Fig. B.1   XHTML standard colors and hexadecimal RGB values.

Color name	Value	Color name	Value
aliceblue	#F0F8FF	dodgerblue	#1E90FF
antiquewhite	#FAEBD7	firebrick	#B22222
aquamarine	#7FFFD4	floralwhite	#FFFAF0
azure	#F0FFFF	forestgreen	#228B22
beige	#F5F5DC	gainsboro	#DCDCDC
bisque	#FFE4C4	ghostwhite	#F8F8FF
blanchedalmond	#FFEBCD	gold	#FFD700
blueviolet	#8A2BE2	goldenrod	#DAA520
brown	#A52A2A	greenyellow	#ADFF2F
burlywood	#DEB887	honeydew	#F0FFF0
cadetblue	#5F9EA0	hotpink	#FF69B4
chartreuse	#7FFF00	indianred	#CD5C5C
chocolate	#D2691E	indigo	#4B0082
coral	#FF7F50	ivory	#FFFFF0
cornflowerblue	#6495ED	khaki	#F0E68C
cornsilk	#FFF8DC	lavender	#E6E6FA
crimson	#DC1436	lavenderblush	#FFF0F5
cyan	#00FFFF	lawngreen	#7CFC00
darkblue	#00008B	lemonchiffon	#FFFACD
darkcyan	#008B8B	lightblue	#ADD8E6
darkgoldenrod	#B8860B	lightcoral	#F08080
darkgray	#A9A9A9	lightcyan	#E0FFFF
darkgreen	#006400	lightgoldenrodyellow	#FAFAD2
darkkhaki	#BDB76B	lightgreen	#90EE90
darkmagenta	#8B008B	lightgrey	#D3D3D3
darkolivegreen	#556B2F	lightpink	#FFB6C1
darkorange	#FF8C00	lightsalmon	#FFA07A
darkorchid	#9932CC	lightseagreen	#20B2AA
darkred	#8B0000	lightskyblue	#87CEFA
darksalmon	#E9967A	lightslategray	#778899
darkseagreen	#8FBC8F	lightsteelblue	#B0C4DE
darkslateblue	#483D8B	lightyellow	#FFFFE0
darkslategray	#2F4F4F	limegreen	#32CD32
darkturquoise	#00CED1	linen	#FAF0E6
darkviolet	#9400D3	magenta	#FF00FF
deeppink	#FF1493	mediumaquamarine	#66CDAA
deepskyblue	#00BFFF	mediumblue	#0000CD
dimgray	#696969	mediumorchid	#BA55D3

Fig. B.2   XHTML extended colors and hexadecimal RGB values. (Part 1 of 2.)

Color name	Value	Color name	Value
mediumpurple	#9370DB	plum	#DDA0DD
mediumseagreen	#3CB371	powderblue	#B0E0E6
mediumslateblue	#7B68EE	rosybrown	#BC8F8F
mediumspringgreen	#00FA9A	royalblue	#4169E1
mediumturquoise	#48D1CC	saddlebrown	#8B4513
mediumvioletred	#C71585	salmon	#FA8072
midnightblue	#191970	sandybrown	#F4A460
mintcream	#F5FFFA	seagreen	#2E8B57
mistyrose	#FFE4E1	seashell	#FFF5EE
moccasin	#FFE4B5	sienna	#A0522D
navajowhite	#FFDEAD	skyblue	#87CEEB
oldlace	#FDF5E6	slateblue	#6A5ACD
olivedrab	#6B8E23	slategray	#708090
orange	#FFA500	snow	#FFFAFA
orangered	#FF4500	springgreen	#00FF7F
orchid	#DA70D6	steelblue	#4682B4
palegoldenrod	#EEE8AA	tan	#D2B48C
palegreen	#98FB98	thistle	#D8BFD8
paleturquoise	#AFEEEE	tomato	#FF6347
palevioletred	#DB7093	turquoise	#40E0D0
papayawhip	#FFEFD5	violet	#EE82EE
peachpuff	#FFDAB9	wheat	#F5DEB3
peru	#CD853F	whitesmoke	#F5F5F5
pink	#FFC0CB	yellowgreen	#9ACD32

Fig. B.2   XHTML extended colors and hexadecimal RGB values. (Part 2 of 2.)

JavaScript Operator Precedence Chart

This appendix contains the operator precedence chart for JavaScript/JScript/ECMAScript (Fig. C.1). The operators are shown in decreasing order of precedence from top to bottom.

Operator	Type	Associativity
.	member acccss	left to right
[]	array indexing	
()	function calls	
++	increment	right to left
--	decrement	
-	unary minus	
~	bitwise complement	
!	logical NOT	
delete	delete an array element or object property	
new	create a new object	
typeof	returns the data type of its argument	
void	prevents an expression from returning a value	
*	multiplication	left to right
/	division	
%	modulus	
+	addition	left to right
-	subtraction	
+	string concatenation	

Fig. C.1 JavaScript/JScript/ECMAScript operator precedence and associativity. (Part 1 of 2.)

Operator	Type	Associativity
`<<`	left shift	left to right
`>>`	right shift with sign extension	
`>>>`	right shift with zero extension	
`<`	less than	left to right
`<=`	less than or equal	
`>`	greater than	
`>=`	greater than or equal	
`instanceof`	type comparison	
`==`	equality	left to right
`!=`	inequality	
`===`	identity	
`!==`	nonidentity	
`&`	bitwise AND	left to right
`^`	bitwise XOR	left to right
`|`	bitwise OR	left to right
`&&`	logical AND	left to right
`||`	logical OR	left to right
`?:`	conditional	left to right
`=`	assignment	right to left
`+=`	addition assignment	
`-=`	subtraction assignment	
`*=`	multiplication assignment	
`/=`	division assignment	
`%=`	modulus assignment	
`&=`	bitwise AND assignment	
`^=`	bitwise exclusive OR assignment	
`|=`	bitwise inclusive OR assignment	
`<<=`	bitwise left shift assignment	
`>>=`	bitwise right shift with sign extension assignment	
`>>>=`	bitwise right shift with zero extension assignment	

Fig. C.1   JavaScript/JScript/ECMAScript operator precedence and associativity. (Part 2 of 2.)

ASCII Character Set

	0	1	2	3	4	5	6	7	8	9
0	nul	soh	stx	etx	eot	enq	ack	bel	bs	ht
1	nl	vt	ff	cr	so	si	dle	dc1	dc2	dc3
2	dc4	nak	syn	etb	can	em	sub	esc	fs	gs
3	rs	us	sp	!	"	#	$	%	&	'
4	(	)	*	+	,	-	.	/	0	1
5	2	3	4	5	6	7	8	9	:	;
6	<	=	>	?	@	A	B	C	D	E
7	F	G	H	I	J	K	L	M	N	O
8	P	Q	R	S	T	U	V	W	X	Y
9	Z	[	\	]	^	_	'	a	b	c
10	d	e	f	g	h	i	j	k	l	m
11	n	o	p	q	r	s	t	u	v	w
12	x	y	z	{	|	}	~	del		

Fig. D.1   ASCII character set.

The digits at the left of the table are the left digits of the decimal equivalent (0–127) of the character code, and the digits at the top of the table are the right digits of the character code. For example, the character code for "F" is 70, and the character code for "&" is 38.

Most users of this book are interested in the ASCII character set used to represent English characters on many computers. The ASCII character set is a subset of the Unicode character set used by scripting languages to represent characters from most of the world's languages. For more information on the Unicode character set, see Appendix F.

Number Systems

Objectives

- To understand basic number systems concepts such as base, positional value and symbol value.
- To understand how to work with numbers represented in the binary, octal and hexadecimal number systems
- To be able to abbreviate binary numbers as octal numbers or hexadecimal numbers.
- To be able to convert octal numbers and hexadecimal numbers to binary numbers.
- To be able to covert back and forth between decimal numbers and their binary, octal and hexadecimal equivalents.
- To understand binary arithmetic, and how negative binary numbers are represented using two's complement notation.

Here are only numbers ratified.
William Shakespeare

Nature has some sort of arithmetic-geometrical coordinate system, because nature has all kinds of models. What we experience of nature is in models, and all of nature's models are so beautiful.

It struck me that nature's system must be a real beauty, because in chemistry we find that the associations are always in beautiful whole numbers—there are no fractions.
Richard Buckminster Fuller

E.1 Introduction

In this appendix, we introduce the key number systems that JavaScript programmers use, especially when they are working on software projects that require close interaction with "machine-level" hardware. Projects like this include operating systems, computer networking software, compilers, database systems, and applications requiring high performance.

When we write an integer such as 227 or –63 in a JavaScript program, the number is assumed to be in the decimal (base 10) number system. The digits in the decimal number system are 0, 1, 2, 3, 4, 5, 6, 7, 8, and 9. The lowest digit is 0 and the highest digit is 9—one less than the base of 10. Internally, computers use the binary (base 2) number system. The binary number system has only two digits, namely 0 and 1. Its lowest digit is 0 and its highest digit is 1—one less than the base of 2.

As we will see, binary numbers tend to be much longer than their decimal equivalents. Programmers who work in assembly languages and in high-level languages like JavaScript that enable programmers to reach down to the "machine level," find it cumbersome to work with binary numbers. So two other number systems the octal number system (base 8) and the hexadecimal number system (base 16)—are popular primarily because they make it convenient to abbreviate binary numbers.

In the octal number system, the digits range from 0 to 7. Because both the binary number system and the octal number system have fewer digits than the decimal number system, their digits are the same as the corresponding digits in decimal.

The hexadecimal number system poses a problem because it requires sixteen digits—a lowest digit of 0 and a highest digit with a value equivalent to decimal 15 (one less than the base of 16). By convention, we use the letters A through F to represent the hexadecimal digits corresponding to decimal values 10 through 15. Thus in hexadecimal we can have numbers like 876 consisting solely of decimal-like digits, numbers like 8A55F consisting of digits and letters, and numbers like FFE consisting solely of letters. Occasionally, a hexadecimal number spells a common word such as FACE or FEED—this can appear strange to programmers accustomed to working with numbers.

Each of these number systems uses positional notation—each position in which a digit is written has a different positional value. For example, in the decimal number 937 (the 9, the 3, and the 7 are referred to as symbol values), we say that the 7 is written in the ones position, the 3 is written in the tens position, and the 9 is written in the hundreds position. Notice that each of these positions is a power of the base (base 10), and that these powers begin at 0 and increase by 1 as we move left in the number (Fig. E.3).

Binary digit	Octal digit	Decimal digit	Hexadecimal digit
0	0	0	0
1	1	1	1
	2	2	2
	3	3	3
	4	4	4
	5	5	5
	6	6	6
	7	7	7
		8	8
		9	9
			A (decimal value of 10)
			B (decimal value of 11)
			C (decimal value of 12)
			D (decimal value of 13)
			E (decimal value of 14)
			F (decimal value of 15)

Fig. E.1   Digits of the binary, octal, decimal and hexadecimal number systems.

Attribute	Binary	Octal	Decimal	Hexadecimal
Base	2	8	10	16
Lowest digit	0	0	0	0
Highest digit	1	7	9	F

Fig. E.2   Comparing the binary, octal, decimal and hexadecimal number systems.

Positional values in the decimal number system			
Decimal digit	9	3	7
Position name	Hundreds	Tens	Ones
Positional value	100	10	1
Positional value as a power of the base (10)	10^2	10^1	10^0

Fig. E.3   Positional values in the decimal number system.

For longer decimal numbers, the next positions to the left would be the thousands position (10 to the 3rd power), the ten-thousands position (10 to the 4th power), the hundred-thousands position (10 to the 5th power), the millions position (10 to the 6th power), the ten-millions position (10 to the 7th power) and so on.

In the binary number 101, we say that the rightmost 1 is written in the ones position, the 0 is written in the twos position and the leftmost 1 is written in the fours position. Notice that each of these positions is a power of the base (base 2), and that these powers begin at 0 and increase by 1 as we move left in the number (Fig. E.4).

Positional values in the binary number system			
Binary digit	1	0	1
Position name	Fours	Twos	Ones
Positional value	4	2	1
Positional value as a power of the base (2)	2^2	2^1	2^0

Fig. E.4　Positional values in the binary number system.

For longer binary numbers, the next positions to the left would be the eights position (2 to the 3rd power), the sixteens position (2 to the 4th power), the thirty-twos position (2 to the 5th power), the sixty-fours position (2 to the 6th power) and so on.

In the octal number 425, we say that the 5 is written in the ones position, the 2 is written in the eights position, and the 4 is written in the sixty-fours position. Notice that each of these positions is a power of the base (base 8), and that these powers begin at 0 and increase by 1 as we move left in the number (Fig. E.5).

Positional values in the octal number system			
Decimal digit	4	2	5
Position name	Sixty-fours	Eights	Ones
Positional value	64	8	1
Positional value as a power of the base (8)	8^2	8^1	8^0

Fig. E.5　Positional values in the octal number system.

For longer octal numbers, the next positions to the left would be the five-hundred-and-twelves position (8 to the 3rd power), the four-thousand-and-ninety-sixes position (8 to the 4th power), the thirty-two-thousand-seven-hundred-and-sixty eights position (8 to the 5th power) and so on.

In the hexadecimal number 3DA, we say that the A is written in the ones position, the D is written in the sixteens position and the 3 is written in the two-hundred-and-fifty-sixes position. Notice that each of these positions is a power of the base (base 16), and that these powers begin at 0 and increase by 1 as we move left in the number (Fig. E.6).

Positional values in the hexadecimal number system			
Decimal digit	3	D	A
Position name	Two-hundred-and-fifty-sixes	Sixteens	Ones
Positional value	256	16	1
Positional value as a power of the base (16)	16^2	16^1	16^0

Fig. E.6   Positional values in the hexadecimal number system.

For longer hexadecimal numbers, the next positions to the left would be the four-thousand-and-ninety-sixes position (16 to the 3rd power), the sixty-five-thousand-five-hundred-and-thirty-six position (16 to the 4th power) and so on.

E.2 Abbreviating Binary Numbers as Octal and Hexadecimal Numbers

The main use for octal and hexadecimal numbers in computing is for abbreviating lengthy binary representations. Figure E.7 highlights the fact that lengthy binary numbers can be expressed concisely in number systems with higher bases than the binary number system.

Decimal number	Binary representation	Octal representation	Hexadecimal representation
0	0	0	0
1	1	1	1
2	10	2	2
3	11	3	3
4	100	4	4
5	101	5	5
6	110	6	6
7	111	7	7
8	1000	10	8
9	1001	11	9
10	1010	12	A
11	1011	13	B
12	1100	14	C
13	1101	15	D
14	1110	16	E
15	1111	17	F
16	10000	20	10

Fig. E.7   Decimal, binary, octal and hexadecimal equivalents.

A particularly important relationship that both the octal number system and the hexadecimal number system have to the binary system is that the bases of octal and hexadecimal (8 and 16 respectively) are powers of the base of the binary number system (base 2). Consider the following 12-digit binary number and its octal and hexadecimal equivalents. See if you can determine how this relationship makes it convenient to abbreviate binary numbers in octal or hexadecimal. The answer follows the numbers.

Binary number	Octal equivalent	Hexadecimal equivalent
100011010001	4321	8D1

To see how the binary number converts easily to octal, simply break the 12-digit binary number into groups of three consecutive bits each, and write those groups over the corresponding digits of the octal number as follows

100	011	010	001
4	3	2	1

Notice that the octal digit you have written under each group of thee bits corresponds precisely to the octal equivalent of that 3-digit binary number as shown in Fig. E.7.

The same kind of relationship may be observed in converting numbers from binary to hexadecimal. In particular, break the 12-digit binary number into groups of four consecutive bits each and write those groups over the corresponding digits of the hexadecimal number as follows

1000	1101	0001
8	D	1

Notice that the hexadecimal digit you wrote under each group of four bits corresponds precisely to the hexadecimal equivalent of that 4-digit binary number as shown in Fig. E.7.

E.3 Converting Octal and Hexadecimal Numbers to Binary Numbers

In the previous section, we saw how to convert binary numbers to their octal and hexadecimal equivalents by forming groups of binary digits and simply rewriting these groups as their equivalent octal digit values or hexadecimal digit values. This process may be used in reverse to produce the binary equivalent of a given octal or hexadecimal number.

For example, the octal number 653 is converted to binary simply by writing the 6 as its 3-digit binary equivalent 110, the 5 as its 3-digit binary equivalent 101 and the 3 as its 3-digit binary equivalent 011 to form the 9-digit binary number 110101011.

The hexadecimal number FAD5 is converted to binary simply by writing the F as its 4-digit binary equivalent 1111, the A as its 4-digit binary equivalent 1010, the D as its 4-digit binary equivalent 1101 and the 5 as its 4-digit binary equivalent 0101 to form the 16-digit 1111101011010101.

E.4 Converting from Binary, Octal or Hexadecimal to Decimal

Because we are accustomed to working in decimal, it is often convenient to convert a binary, octal or hexadecimal number to decimal to get a sense of what the number is "really" worth. Our diagrams in Section E.1 express the positional values in decimal. To convert a number to decimal from another base, multiply the decimal equivalent of each digit by its positional value, and sum these products. For example, the binary number 110101 is converted to decimal 53 as shown in Fig. E.8.

Converting a binary number to decimal					
Positional values:	32	16	8	4	2	1
Symbol values:	1	1	0	1	0	1
Products:	1*32=32	1*16=16	0*8=0	1*4=4	0*2=0	1*1=1
Sum:	= 32 + 16 + 0 + 4 + 0 + 1 = 53					

Fig. E.8   Converting a binary number to decimal.

To convert octal 7614 to decimal 3980, we use the same technique, this time using appropriate octal positional values as shown in Fig. E.9.

Converting an octal number to decimal			
Positional values:	512	64	8	1
Symbol values:	7	6	1	4
Products	7*512=3584	6*64=384	1*8=8	4*1=4
Sum:	= 3584 + 384 + 8 + 4 = 3980			

Fig. E.9   Converting an octal number to decimal.

To convert hexadecimal AD3B to decimal 44347, we use the same technique, this time using appropriate hexadecimal positional values as shown in Fig. E.10.

Converting a hexadecimal number to decimal			
Positional values:	4096	256	16	1
Symbol values:	A	D	3	B
Products	A*4096=40960	D*256=3328	3*16=48	B*1=11
Sum:	= 40960 + 3328 + 48 + 11 = 44347			

Fig. E.10   Converting a hexadecimal number to decimal.

E.5 Converting from Decimal to Binary, Octal or Hexadecimal

The conversions of the previous section follow naturally from the positional notation conventions. Converting from decimal to binary, octal or hexadecimal also follows these conventions.

Suppose we wish to convert decimal 57 to binary. We begin by writing the positional values of the columns right to left until we reach a column whose positional value is greater than the decimal number. We do not need that column, so we discard it. Thus, we first write:

Positional values: 64 32 16 8   4   2   1

Then we discard the column with positional value 64 leaving:

Positional values: 32 16 8   4   2   1

Next we work from the leftmost column to the right. We divide 32 into 57 and observe that there is one 32 in 57 with a remainder of 25, so we write 1 in the 32 column. We divide 16 into 25 and observe that there is one 16 in 25 with a remainder of 9 and write 1 in the 16 column. We divide 8 into 9 and observe that there is one 8 in 9 with a remainder of 1. The next two columns each produce quotients of zero when their positional values are divided into 1 so we write 0s in the 4 and 2 columns. Finally, 1 into 1 is 1 so we write 1 in the 1 column. This yields:

Positional values: 32 16 8   4   2   1
Symbol values: 1   1   1   0   0   1

and thus decimal 57 is equivalent to binary 111001.

To convert decimal 103 to octal, we begin by writing the positional values of the columns until we reach a column whose positional value is greater than the decimal number. We do not need that column, so we discard it. Thus, we first write:

Positional values: 512 64 8   1

Then we discard the column with positional value 512, yielding:

Positional values: 64 8   1

Next we work from the leftmost column to the right. We divide 64 into 103 and observe that there is one 64 in 103 with a remainder of 39, so we write 1 in the 64 column. We divide 8 into 39 and observe that there are four 8s in 39 with a remainder of 7 and write 4 in the 8 column. Finally, we divide 1 into 7 and observe that there are seven 1s in 7 with no remainder so we write 7 in the 1 column. This yields:

Positional values: 64 8   1
Symbol values: 1   4   7

and thus decimal 103 is equivalent to octal 147.

To convert decimal 375 to hexadecimal, we begin by writing the positional values of the columns until we reach a column whose positional value is greater than the decimal number. We do not need that column, so we discard it. Thus, we first write

Positional values: 4096 256   16 1

Then we discard the column with positional value 4096, yielding:

Positional values: 256   16 1

Next we work from the leftmost column to the right. We divide 256 into 375 and observe that there is one 256 in 375 with a remainder of 119, so we write 1 in the 256 column. We divide 16 into 119 and observe that there are seven 16s in 119 with a remainder of 7 and write 7 in the 16 column. Finally, we divide 1 into 7 and observe that there are seven 1s in 7 with no remainder so we write 7 in the 1 column. This yields:

Positional values: 256   16   1
Symbol values: 1   7   7

and thus decimal 375 is equivalent to hexadecimal 177.

E.6 Negative Binary Numbers: Two's Complement Notation

The discussion in this appendix has been focussed on positive numbers. In this section, we explain how computers represent negative numbers using **two's complement notation**. First we explain how the two's complement of a binary number is formed, and then we show why it represents the negative value of the given binary number.

Consider a machine with 32-bit integers. Suppose

```
var value = 13;
```

The 32-bit representation of `value` is

```
00000000 00000000 00000000 00001101
```

To form the negative of `value` we first form its **one's complement** by applying JavaScript's bitwise complement operator (~):

```
onesComplementOfValue = ~value;
```

Internally, `~value` is now `value` with each of its bits reversed—ones become zeros and zeros become ones as follows:

```
value:
00000000 00000000 00000000 00001101

~value (i.e., value's ones complement):
11111111 11111111 11111111 11110010
```

To form the two's complement of `value` we simply add one to `value`'s one's complement. Thus

```
Two's complement of value:
11111111 11111111 11111111 11110011
```

Now if this is in fact equal to –13, we should be able to add it to binary 13 and obtain a result of 0. Let us try this:

```
  00000000 00000000 00000000 00001101
+11111111 11111111 11111111 11110011
-----------------------------------
  00000000 00000000 00000000 00000000
```

The carry bit coming out of the leftmost column is discarded and we indeed get zero as a result. If we add the one's complement of a number to the number, the result would be all 1s. The key to getting a result of all zeros is that the twos complement is 1 more than the one's complement. The addition of 1 causes each column to add to 0 with a carry of 1. The carry keeps moving leftward until it is discarded from the leftmost bit, and hence the resulting number is all zeros.

Computers actually perform a subtraction such as

```
x = a - value;
```

by adding the two's complement of `value` to `a` as follows:

```
x = a + (~value + 1);
```

Suppose `a` is 27 and `value` is 13 as before. If the two's complement of `value` is actually the negative of `value`, then adding the two's complement of value to a should produce the result 14. Let us try this:

```
a (i.e., 27)           00000000 00000000 00000000 00011011
+(~value + 1)         +11111111 11111111 11111111 11110011
                      ------------------------------------
                       00000000 00000000 00000000 00001110
```

which is indeed equal to 14.

SUMMARY

- When we write an integer such as 19 or 227 or –63 in a JavaScript program, the number is automatically assumed to be in the decimal (base 10) number system. The digits in the decimal number system are 0, 1, 2, 3, 4, 5, 6, 7, 8, and 9. The lowest digit is 0 and the highest digit is 9—one less than the base of 10.

- Internally, computers use the binary (base 2) number system. The binary number system has only two digits, namely 0 and 1. Its lowest digit is 0 and its highest digit is 1—one less than the base of 2.

- The octal number system (base 8) and the hexadecimal number system (base 16) are popular primarily because they make it convenient to abbreviate binary numbers.

- The digits of the octal number system range from 0 to 7.

- The hexadecimal number system poses a problem because it requires sixteen digits—a lowest digit of 0 and a highest digit with a value equivalent to decimal 15 (one less than the base of 16). By convention, we use the letters A through F to represent the hexadecimal digits corresponding to decimal values 10 through 15.

- Each number system uses positional notation—each position in which a digit is written has a different positional value.

- A particularly important relationship that both the octal number system and the hexadecimal number system have to the binary system is that the bases of octal and hexadecimal (8 and 16 respectively) are powers of the base of the binary number system (base 2).

- To convert an octal number to a binary number, simply replace each octal digit with its three-digit binary equivalent.

- To convert a hexadecimal number to a binary number, simply replace each hexadecimal digit with its four-digit binary equivalent.

- Because we are accustomed to working in decimal, it is convenient to convert a binary, octal or hexadecimal number to decimal to get a sense of the number's "real" worth.

- To convert a number to decimal from another base, multiply the decimal equivalent of each digit by its positional value, and sum these products.

- Computers represent negative numbers using two's complement notation.

- To form the negative of a value in binary, first form its one's complement by applying JavaScript's bitwise complement operator (~). This reverses the bits of the value. To form the two's complement of a value, simply add one to the value's one's complement.

TERMINOLOGY

base	digit
base 2 number system	hexadecimal number system
base 8 number system	negative value
base 10 number system	octal number system
base 16 number system	one's complement notation
binary number system	positional notation
bitwise complement operator (~)	positional value
conversions	symbol value
decimal number system	two's complement notation

SELF-REVIEW EXERCISES

E.1 The bases of the decimal, binary, octal, and hexadecimal number systems are _____, _____, _____ and _____ respectively.

E.2 In general, the decimal, octal and hexadecimal representations of a given binary number contain (more/fewer) digits than the binary number contains.

E.3 (True/False) A popular reason for using the decimal number system is that it forms a convenient notation for abbreviating binary numbers simply by substituting one decimal digit per group of four binary bits.

E.4 The (octal / hexadecimal / decimal) representation of a large binary value is the most concise (of the given alternatives).

E.5 (True/False) The highest digit in any base is one more than the base.

E.6 (True/False) The lowest digit in any base is one less than the base.

E.7 The positional value of the rightmost digit of any number in either binary, octal, decimal or hexadecimal is always _____.

E.8 The positional value of the digit to the left of the rightmost digit of any number in binary, octal, decimal or hexadecimal is always equal to _____.

E.9 Fill in the missing values in this chart of positional values for the rightmost four positions in each of the indicated number systems:

decimal	1000	100	10	1
hexadecimal	. . .	256	. . .	. . .
binary	. . .	. . .	. . .	. . .
octal	512	. . .	8	. . .

E.10 Convert binary 110101011000 to octal and to hexadecimal.

E.11 Convert hexadecimal FACE to binary.

E.12 Convert octal 7316 to binary.

E.13 Convert hexadecimal 4FEC to octal. [*Hint:* First convert 4FEC to binary then convert that binary number to octal.]

E.14 Convert binary 1101110 to decimal.

E.15 Convert octal 317 to decimal.

E.16 Convert hexadecimal EFD4 to decimal.

E.17 Convert decimal 177 to binary, to octal and to hexadecimal.

E.18 Show the binary representation of decimal 417. Then show the one's complement of 417 and the two's complement of 417.

E.19   What is the result when a number and its two's complement are added to each other?

ANSWERS TO SELF-REVIEW EXERCISES

E.1   10, 2, 8, 16.

E.2   Fewer.

E.3   False.

E.4   Hexadecimal.

E.5   False. The highest digit in any base is one less than the base.

E.6   False. The lowest digit in any base is zero.

E.7   1 (the base raised to the zero power).

E.8   The base of the number system.

E.9   Fill in the missing values in this chart of positional values for the rightmost four positions in each of the indicated number systems:

decimal	1000	100	10	1
hexadecimal	4096	256	16	1
binary	8	4	2	1
octal	512	64	8	1

E.10   Octal 6530; Hexadecimal D58.

E.11   Binary 1111 1010 1100 1110.

E.12   Binary 111 011 001 110.

E.13   Binary 0 100 111 111 101 100; Octal 47754.

E.14   Decimal 2+4+8+32+64=110.

E.15   Decimal 7+1*8+3*64=7+8+192=207.

E.16   Decimal 4+13*16+15*256+14*4096=61396.

E.17   Decimal 177
      to binary:

```
256 128 64 32 16 8 4 2 1
128 64 32 16 8 4 2 1
(1*128)+(0*64)+(1*32)+(1*16)+(0*8)+(0*4)+(0*2)+(1*1)
10110001
```

      to octal:

```
512 64 8 1
64 8 1
(2*64)+(6*8)+(1*1)
261
```

      to hexadecimal:

```
256 16 1
16 1
(11*16)+(1*1)
(B*16)+(1*1)
B1
```

E.18   Binary:

```
512 256 128 64 32 16 8 4 2 1
256 128 64 32 16 8 4 2 1
(1*256)+(1*128)+(0*64)+(1*32)+(0*16)+(0*8)+(0*4)+(0*2)+
(1*1)
110100001
```

One's complement: 001011110
Two's complement: 001011111
Check: Original binary number + its two's complement

```
 110100001
+001011111
----------
 000000000
```

E.19   Zero.

EXERCISES

E.20   Some people argue that many of our calculations would be easier in the base 12 number system because 12 is divisible by so many more numbers than 10 (for base 10). What is the lowest digit in base 12? What might the highest symbol for the digit in base 12 be? What are the positional values of the rightmost four positions of any number in the base 12 number system?

E.21   How is the highest symbol value in the number systems we discussed related to the positional value of the first digit to the left of the rightmost digit of any number in these number systems?

E.22   Complete the following chart of positional values for the rightmost four positions in each of the indicated number systems:

decimal	1000	100	10	1
base 6	...	...	6	...
base 13	...	169	...	...
base 3	27	...	...	...

E.23   Convert binary 100101111010 to octal and to hexadecimal.

E.24   Convert hexadecimal 3A7D to binary.

E.25   Convert hexadecimal 765F to octal. [*Hint:* First convert 765F to binary, then convert that binary number to octal.]

E.26   Convert binary 1011110 to decimal.

E.27   Convert octal 426 to decimal.

E.28   Convert hexadecimal FFFF to decimal.

E.29   Convert decimal 299 to binary, to octal, and to hexadecimal.

E.30   Show the binary representation of decimal 779. Then show the one's complement of 779, and the two's complement of 779.

E.31   What is the result when the two's complement of a number is added to itself?

E.32   Show the two's complement of integer value –1 on a machine with 32-bit integers.

7

Unicode®

Objectives

- To become familiar with Unicode.
- To discuss the mission of the Unicode Consortium.
- To discuss the design basis of Unicode.
- To understand the three Unicode encoding forms: UTF-8, UTF-16 and UTF-32.
- To introduce characters and glyphs.
- To discuss the advantages and disadvantages of using Unicode.
- To provide a brief tour of the Unicode Consortium's Web site.

Outline

F.1 Introduction

The use of inconsistent character **encodings** (i.e., numeric values associated with characters) when developing global software products causes serious problems because computers process information using numbers. For instance, the character "a" is converted to a numeric value so that a computer can manipulate that piece of data. Many countries and corporations have developed their own encoding systems that are incompatible with the encoding systems of other countries and corporations. For example, the Microsoft Windows operating system assigns the value 0xC0 to the character "A with a grave accent" while the Apple Macintosh operating system assigns that same value to an upside-down question mark. This results in the misrepresentation and possible corruption of data because data is not processed as intended.

In the absence of a widely-implemented universal character encoding standard, global software developers had to **localize** their products extensively before distribution. Localization includes the language translation and cultural adaptation of content. The process of localization usually includes significant modifications to the source code (such as the conversion of numeric values and the underlying assumptions made by programmers), which results in increased costs and delays releasing the software. For example, some English-speaking programmers might design global software products assuming that a single character can be represented by one byte. However, when those products are localized for Asian markets, the programmer's assumptions are no longer valid, thus the majority, if not the entirety, of the code needs to be rewritten. Localization is necessary with each release of a version. By the time a software product is localized for a particular market, a newer version, which needs to be localized as well, may be ready for distribution. As a result, it is cumbersome and costly to produce and distribute global software products in a market where there is no universal character encoding standard.

In response to this situation, the **Unicode Standard**, an encoding standard that facilitates the production and distribution of software, was created. The Unicode Standard outlines a specification to produce consistent encoding of the world's characters and **symbols**. Software products which handle text encoded in the Unicode Standard need to be localized, but the localization process is simpler and more efficient because the numeric values need not be converted and the assumptions made by programmers about the character encoding are universal. The Unicode Standard is maintained by a non-profit organization called the

Unicode Consortium, whose members include Apple, IBM, Microsoft, Oracle, Sun Microsystems, Sybase and many others.

When the Consortium envisioned and developed the Unicode Standard, they wanted an encoding system that was **universal**, **efficient**, **uniform** and **unambiguous**. A universal encoding system encompasses all commonly used characters. An efficient encoding system allows text files to be parsed easily. A uniform encoding system assigns fixed values to all characters. An unambiguous encoding system represents a given character in a consistent manner. These four terms are referred to as the Unicode Standard **design basis**.

F.2 Unicode Transformation Formats

Although Unicode incorporates the limited ASCII **character set** (i.e., a collection of characters), it encompasses a more comprehensive character set. In ASCII each character is represented by a byte containing 0s and 1s. One byte is capable of storing the binary numbers from 0 to 255. Each character is assigned a number between 0 and 255, thus ASCII-based systems can support only 256 characters, a tiny fraction of the world's characters. Unicode extends the ASCII character set by encoding the vast majority of the world's characters. The Unicode Standard encodes all of those characters in a uniform numerical space from 0 to 10FFFF hexadecimal. An implementation will express these numbers in one of several transformation formats, choosing the one that best fits the particular application at hand.

Three such formats are in use, called **UTF-8**, **UTF-16** and **UTF-32**, depending on the size of the units—in **bits**—being used. UTF-8, a variable width encoding form, requires one to four bytes to express each Unicode character. UTF-8 data consists of 8-bit bytes (sequences of one, two, three or four bytes depending on the character being encoded) and is well suited for ASCII-based systems when there is a predominance of one-byte characters (ASCII represents characters as one-byte). Currently, UTF-8 is widely implemented in UNIX systems and in databases. [*Note*: Currently, Internet Explorer 6 and Netscape 7.1 only support UTF-8, so document authors should use UTF-8 for encoding XML and XHTML documents.]

The variable width UTF-16 encoding form expresses Unicode characters in units of 16 bits (i.e., as two adjacent bytes, or a short integer in many machines). Most characters of Unicode are expressed in a single 16-bit unit. However, characters with values above FFFF hexadecimal are expressed with an ordered pair of 16-bit units called **surrogates**. Surrogates are 16-bit integers in the range D800 through DFFF, which are used solely for the purpose of "escaping" into higher numbered characters. Approximately one million characters can be expressed in this manner. Although a surrogate pair requires 32 bits to represent characters, it is space-efficient to use these 16-bit units. Surrogates are rare characters in current implementations. Many string-handling implementations are written in terms of UTF-16. [*Note*: Details and sample-code for UTF-16 handling are available on the Unicode Consortium Web site at www.unicode.org.]

Implementations that require significant use of rare characters or entire scripts encoded above FFFF hexadecimal, should use UTF-32, a 32-bit, fixed-width encoding form that usually requires twice as much memory as UTF-16 encoded characters. The major advantage of the fixed-width UTF-32 encoding form is that it uniformly expresses all characters, so it is easy to handle in arrays.

There are few guidelines that state when to use a particular encoding form. The best encoding form to use depends on computer systems and business protocols, not on the data itself. Typically, the UTF-8 encoding form should be used where computer systems and business protocols require data to be handled in 8-bit units, particularly in legacy systems being upgraded because it often simplifies changes to existing programs. For this reason, UTF-8 has become the encoding form of choice on the Internet. Likewise, UTF-16 is the encoding form of choice on Microsoft Windows applications. UTF-32 is likely to become more widely used in the future as more characters are encoded with values above FFFF hexadecimal. Also, UTF-32 requires less sophisticated handling than UTF-16 in the presence of surrogate pairs. Figure F.1 shows the different ways in which the three encoding forms handle character encoding.

F.3 Characters and Glyphs

The Unicode Standard consists of **characters**, written components (i.e., alphabetic letters, numerals, punctuation marks, accent marks, etc.) that can be represented by numeric values. Examples of characters include: U+0041 LATIN CAPITAL LETTER A. In the first character representation, U+*yyyy* is a **code value**, in which U+ refers to Unicode code values, as opposed to other hexadecimal values. The *yyyy* represents a four-digit hexadecimal number of an encoded character. Code values are bit combinations that represent encoded characters. Characters are represented using **glyphs**, various shapes, fonts and sizes for displaying characters. There are no code values for glyphs in the Unicode Standard. Examples of glyphs are shown in Fig. F.2.

The Unicode Standard encompasses the alphabets, ideographs, syllabaries, punctuation marks, **diacritics**, mathematical operators, etc. that comprise the written languages and scripts of the world. A diacritic is a special mark added to a character to distinguish it from another letter or to indicate an accent (e.g., in Spanish, the tilde "~" above the character "n"). Currently, Unicode provides code values for 94,140 character representations, with more than 880,000 code values reserved for future expansion.

F.4 Advantages/Disadvantages of Unicode

The Unicode Standard has several significant advantages that promote its use. One is the impact it has on the performance of the international economy. Unicode standardizes the characters for the world's writing systems to a uniform model that promotes transferring and sharing data. Programs developed using such a schema maintain their accuracy because each character has a single definition (i.e., *a* is always U+0061, % is always U+0025). This enables corporations to manage the high demands of international markets by processing different writing systems at the same time. Also, all characters can be managed in an identical manner, thus avoiding any confusion caused by different character code architectures. Moreover, managing data in a consistent manner eliminates data corruption, because data can be sorted, searched and manipulated using a consistent process.

Another advantage of the Unicode Standard is **portability** (i.e., the ability to execute software on disparate computers or with disparate operating systems). Most operating systems, databases, programming languages and Web browsers currently support, or are planning to support, Unicode.

Character	UTF-8	UTF-16	UTF-32
LATIN CAPITAL LETTER A	0x41	0x0041	0x00000041
GREEK CAPITAL LETTER ALPHA	0xCD 0x91	0x0391	0x00000391
CJK UNIFIED IDEOGRAPH-4E95	0xE4 0xBA 0x95	0x4E95	0x00004E95
OLD ITALIC LETTER A	0xF0 0x80 0x83 0x80	0xDC00 0xDF00	0x00010300

Fig. F.1   Correlation between the three encoding forms.

Fig. F.2   Various glyphs of the character A.

A disadvantage of the Unicode Standard is the amount of memory required by UTF-16 and UTF-32. ASCII character sets are 8 bits in length, so they require less storage than the default 16-bit Unicode character set. However, the **double-byte character set (DBCS)** and the **multi-byte character set (MBCS)** that encode Asian characters (ideographs) require two to four bytes, respectively. In such instances, the UTF-16 or the UTF-32 encoding forms may be used with little hindrance on memory and performance.

Another disadvantage of Unicode is that although it includes more characters than any other character set in common use, it does not yet encode all of the world's written characters. One additional disadvantage of the Unicode Standard is that UTF-8 and UTF-16 are variable width encoding forms, so characters occupy different amounts of memory.

F.5 Unicode Consortium's Web Site

If you would like to learn more about the Unicode Standard, visit www.unicode.org. This site provides a wealth of information about the Unicode Standard. Currently, the home page is organized into various sections: **New to Unicode?**, **General Information**, **The Consortium**, **The Unicode Standard**, **Work in Progress** and **For Members**.

The **New to Unicode?** section consists of two subsections: **What is Unicode?** and **How to Use this Site**. The first subsection provides a technical introduction to Unicode by describing design principles, character interpretations and assignments, text processing and Unicode conformance. This subsection is recommended reading for anyone new to Unicode. Also, this subsection provides a list of related links that provide the reader with additional information about Unicode. The **How to Use this Site** subsection contains information about using and navigating the site as well hyperlinks to additional resources.

The **General Information** section contains six subsections: **Where is my Character?**, **Display Problems?**, **Useful Resources**, **Enabled Products**, **Mail Lists** and **Conferences**. The main areas covered in this section include a link to the Unicode code charts (a complete listing of code values) assembled by the Unicode Consortium as well as a detailed outline on how to locate an encoded character in the code chart. Also, the section contains advice on how to configure different operating systems and Web browsers so that the Unicode characters can be viewed properly. Moreover, from this section, the user can navigate to other sites that provide information on various topics such as, fonts, linguistics and other standards such as the *Armenian Standards Page* and the *Chinese GB 18030 Encoding Standard*.

The **Consortium** section consists of five subsections: **Who we are**, **Our Members**, **How to Join**, **Press Info** and **Contact Us**. This section provides a list of the current Unicode Consortium members as well as information on how to become a member. Privileges for each member type—*full*, *associate*, *specialist* and *individual*—and the fees assessed to each member are listed here.

The **Unicode Standard** section consists of nine subsections: **Start Here**, **Latest Version**, **Technical Reports**, **Code Charts**, **Unicode Data**, **Updates & Errata**, **Unicode Policies**, **Glossary** and **Technical FAQ**. This section describes the updates applied to the latest version of the Unicode Standard as well as categorizing all defined encoding. The user can learn how the latest version has been modified to encompass more features and capabilities. For instance, one enhancement of Version 4.0 is that it contains additional encoded characters. Also, if users are unfamiliar with vocabulary terms used by the Unicode Consortium, then they can navigate to the **Glossary** subsection.

The **Work in Progress** section consists of three subsections: **Calendar of Meetings**, **Proposed Characters** and **Submitting Proposals**. This section presents the user with a catalog of the recent characters included into the Unicode Standard scheme as well as those characters being considered for inclusion. If users determine that a character has been overlooked, then they can submit a written proposal for the inclusion of that character. The **Submitting Proposals** subsection contains strict guidelines that must be adhered to when submitting written proposals.

The **For Members** section consists of two subsections: **Member Resources** and **Working Documents**. These subsections are password protected; only consortium members can access these links.

F.6 Using Unicode

The primary use of the Unicode Standard is the Internet; it has become the default encoding system for XML and any language derived from XML such as XHTML. Figure F.3 marks up (as XML) the text "Welcome to Unicode!" in ten different languages: English, French, German, Japanese, Kannada (India), Portuguese, Russian, Spanish, Telugu (India) and Traditional Chinese. [*Note*: The Unicode Consortium's Web site contains a link to code charts that lists the 16-bit Unicode code values.]

Line 1 of the document specifies the XML declaration that contains the Unicode `encoding` used. A UTF-8 `encoding` indicates that the document conforms to the form of Unicode that uses sequences of one to four bytes. [*Note*: This document uses XML **entity references** to represent characters. Also, UTF-16 and UTF-32 have yet to be supported by Internet Explorer 5.5 and Netscape Communicator 6.] Line 6 defines the root element, `UnicodeEncodings`, which contains all other elements (e.g., `WelcomeNote`) in the document. The first `WelcomeNote` element (lines 9–15) contains the entity references for the English text. The **Code Charts** page on the Unicode Consortium Web site contains the code values for the **Basic Latin block** (or category), which includes the English alphabet. The entity reference on line 10 equates to "Welcome" in basic text. When marking up Unicode characters in XML (or XHTML), the entity reference &#x*yyyy*; is used, where *yyyy* represents the hexadecimal Unicode encoding. For example, the letter "W" (in "Welcome") is denoted by W. Lines 11 and 13 contain the entity reference for the *space* character. The entity reference for the word "to" is on line 12 and the word "Unicode" is on line 14. "Unicode" is not encoded because it is a registered trademark and has no equivalent translation in most languages. Line 14 also contains the ! notation for the exclamation mark (!).

```
1   <?xml version = "1.0" encoding = "UTF-8"?>
2
3   <!-- Fig. F.3: Unicode.xml                             -->
4   <!-- Unicode encoding for ten different languages -->
5
6   <UnicodeEncodings>
7
8      <!-- English -->
9      <WelcomeNote>
10        &#x0057;&#x0065;&#x006C;&#x0063;&#x006F;&#x006D;&#x0065;
11        &#x0020;
12        &#x0074;&#x006F;
13        &#x0020;
14        Unicode&#x0021;
15     </WelcomeNote>
16
17     <!-- French -->
18     <WelcomeNote>
19  &#x0042;&#x0069;&#x0065;&#x006E;&#x0076;&#x0065;&#x006E;&#x0075;&#x0065;
20        &#x0020;
21        &#x0061;&#x0075;
22        &#x0020;
23        Unicode&#x0021;
24     </WelcomeNote>
25
26     <!-- German -->
27     <WelcomeNote>
28  &#x0057;&#x0069;&#x006C;&#x006B;&#x006F;&#x006D;&#x006D;&#x0065;&#x006E;
29        &#x0020;
30        &#x007A;&#x0075;
31        &#x0020;
32        Unicode&#x0021;
33     </WelcomeNote>
34
35     <!-- Japanese -->
36     <WelcomeNote>
37        Unicode
38        &#x3078;&#x3087;&#x3045;&#x3053;&#x305D;&#x0021;
39     </WelcomeNote>
40
41     <!-- Kannada -->
```

Fig. F.3 XML document using Unicode encoding (Part 1 of 3.).

```
42    <WelcomeNote>
43        &#x0CB8;&#x0CC1;&#x0CB8;&#x0CCD;&#x0CB5;&#x0C97;&#x0CA4;
44        &#x0020;
45        Unicode&#x0021;
46    </WelcomeNote>
47
48    <!-- Portuguese -->
49    <WelcomeNote>
50        &#x0053;&#x00E9;&#x006A;&#x0061;
51        &#x0020;
52        &#x0042;&#x0065;&#x006D;&#x0076;&#x0069;&#x006E;&#x0064;&#x006F;
53        &#x0020;
54        Unicode&#x0021;
55    </WelcomeNote>
56
57    <!-- Russian -->
58    <WelcomeNote>
59        &#x0414;&#x043E;&#x0431;&#x0440;&#x043E;
60        &#x0020;
61 &#x043F;&#x043E;&#x0436;&#x0430;&#x043B;&#x043E;&#x0432;&#x0430;&#x0442;&#x044A;
44A;
62        &#x0020;
63        &#x0432;
64        &#x0020;
65        Unicode&#x0021;
66    </WelcomeNote>
67
68    <!-- Spanish -->
69    <WelcomeNote>
70 &#x0042;&#x0069;&#x0065;&#x006E;&#x0076;&#x0065;&#x006E;&#x0069;&#x0064;&#x0061;
061;
71        &#x0020;
72        &#x0061;
73        &#x0020;
74        Unicode&#x0021;
75    </WelcomeNote>
76
77    <!-- Telugu -->
78    <WelcomeNote>
79        &#x0C38;&#x0C41;&#x0C38;&#x0C3E;&#x0C35;&#x0C17;&#x0C24;&#x0C02;
80        &#x0020;
81        Unicode&#x0021;
82    </WelcomeNote>
83
84    <!-- Traditional Chinese -->
85    <WelcomeNote>
86        &#x6B22;&#x8FCE;
87        &#x4F7F;&#x7528;
88        &#x0020;
89        Unicode&#x0021;
90    </WelcomeNote>
91
92 </UnicodeEncodings>
```

Fig. F.3   XML document using Unicode encoding (Part 2 of 3.).

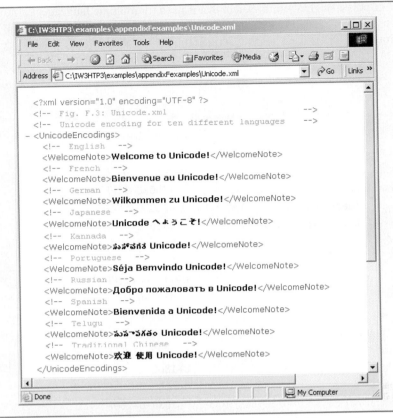

Fig. F.3   XML document using Unicode encoding (Part 3 of 3.).

The remaining `WelcomeNote` elements (lines 18–90) contain the entity references for the other nine languages. The code values used for the French, German, Portuguese and Spanish text are located in the **Basic Latin** block, the code values used for the Traditional Chinese text are located in the **CJK Unified Ideographs** block, the code values used for the Russian text are located in the **Cyrillic** block, the code values used for the Japanese text are located in the **Hiragana** block, and the code values used for the Kannada and Telugu texts are located in their respective blocks.

[*Note*: To render the Asian characters on a Web browser, the proper language files must be installed on your computer. For Windows XP/2000, the language files can be obtained from the Microsoft Web site at www.microsoft.com. For additional assistance, visit www.unicode.org/help/display_problems.html.]

F.7 Character Ranges

The Unicode Standard assigns code values, which range from 0000 (**Basic Latin**) to E007F (**Tags**), to the written characters of the world. Currently, there are code values for 94,140 characters. To simplify the search for a character and its associated code value, the Unicode Standard generally groups code values by **script** and function (i.e., Latin characters are grouped in a block, mathematical operators are grouped in another block, etc.). As a rule, a script is a single writing system that is used for multiple languages (e.g., the Latin script is used for English, French, Spanish, etc.). The **Code Charts** page on the Unicode Consortium Web site lists all the defined blocks and their respective code values. Figure F.4 lists some blocks (scripts) from the Web site and their range of code values.

Script	Range of Code Values
Arabic	U+0600–U+06FF
Basic Latin	U+0000–U+007F
Bengali (India)	U+0980–U+09FF
Cherokee (Native America)	U+13A0–U+13FF
CJK Unified Ideographs (East Asia)	U+4E00–U+9FAF
Cyrillic (Russia and Eastern Europe)	U+0400–U+04FF
Ethiopic	U+1200–U+137F
Greek	U+0370–U+03FF
Hangul Jamo (Korea)	U+1100–U+11FF
Hebrew	U+0590–U+05FF
Hiragana (Japan)	U+3040–U+309F
Khmer (Cambodia)	U+1780–U+17FF
Lao (Laos)	U+0E80–U+0EFF
Mongolian	U+1800–U+18AF
Myanmar	U+1000–U+109F
Ogham (Ireland)	U+1680–U+169F
Runic (Germany and Scandinavia)	U+16A0–U+16FF
Sinhala (Sri Lanka)	U+0D80–U+0DFF
Telugu (India)	U+0C00–U+0C7F
Thai	U+0E00–U+0E7F

Fig. F.4   Some character ranges.

SUMMARY

- Before Unicode, software developers were plagued by the use of inconsistent character encoding (i.e., numeric values for characters). Most countries and organizations had their own encoding systems, which were incompatible. A good example is the individual encoding systems on the Windows and Macintosh platforms.

- Computers process data by converting characters to numeric values. For instance, the character "a" is converted to a numeric value so that a computer can manipulate that piece of data.

- Without Unicode, localization of global software requires significant modifications to the source code, which results in increased cost and in delays releasing the product.

- Localization is necessary with each release of a version. By the time a software product is localized for a particular market, a newer version, which needs to be localized as well, is ready for distribution. As a result, it is cumbersome and costly to produce and distribute global software products in a market where there is no universal character encoding standard.

- The Unicode Consortium developed the Unicode Standard in response to the serious problems created by multiple character encodings and the use of those encodings.

- The Unicode Standard facilitates the production and distribution of localized software. It outlines a specification for the consistent encoding of the world's characters and symbols.

- Software products which handle text encoded in the Unicode Standard need to be localized, but the localization process is simpler and more efficient because the numeric values need not be converted.

- The Unicode Standard is designed to be universal, efficient, uniform and unambiguous.

- A universal encoding system encompasses all commonly used characters; an efficient encoding system parses text files easily; a uniform encoding system assigns fixed values to all characters; and an unambiguous encoding system represents the same character for any given value.

- Unicode extends the limited ASCII character set to include all the major characters of the world.

- Unicode makes use of three Unicode Transformation Formats (UTF): UTF-8, UTF-16 and UTF-32, each of which may be appropriate for use in different contexts.

- UTF-8 data consists of 8-bit bytes (sequences of one, two, three or four bytes depending on the character being encoded) and is well suited for ASCII-based systems when there is a predominance of one-byte characters (ASCII represents characters as one-byte).

- UTF-8 is a variable width encoding form that is more compact for text involving mostly Latin characters and ASCII punctuation.

- UTF-16 is the default encoding form of the Unicode Standard. It is a variable width encoding form that uses 16-bit code units instead of bytes. Most characters are represented by a single unit, but some characters require surrogate pairs.

- Surrogates are 16-bit integers in the range D800 through DFFF, which are used solely for the purpose of "escaping" into higher numbered characters.

- Without surrogate pairs, the UTF-16 encoding form can only encompass 65,000 characters, but with the surrogate pairs, this is expanded to include over a million characters.

- UTF-32 is a 32-bit encoding form. The major advantage of the fixed-width encoding form is that it uniformly expresses all characters, so that they are easy to handle in arrays and so forth.

- The Unicode Standard consists of characters. A character is any written component that can be represented by a numeric value.

- Characters are represented using glyphs, various shapes, fonts and sizes for displaying characters.

- Code values are bit combinations that represent encoded characters. The Unicode notation for a code value is U+$yyyy$ in which U+ refers to the Unicode code values, as opposed to other hexadecimal values. The $yyyy$ represents a four-digit hexadecimal number.

- Currently, the Unicode Standard provides code values for 94,140 character representations.

- An advantage of the Unicode Standard is its impact on the overall performance of the international economy. Applications that conform to an encoding standard can be processed easily by computers anywhere.

- Another advantage of the Unicode Standard is its portability. Applications written in Unicode can be easily transferred to different operating systems, databases, Web browsers, etc. Most companies currently support, or are planning to support, Unicode.

- To obtain more information about the Unicode Standard and the Unicode Consortium, visit www.unicode.org. It contains a link to the code charts, which contain the 16-bit code values for the currently encoded characters.

- The Unicode Standard has become the default encoding system for XML and any language derived from XML, such as XHTML.

- When marking up XML-derived documents, the entity reference &#x*yyyy*; is used, where *yyyy* represents the hexadecimal code value.

TERMINOLOGY

&#x*yyyy*; notation
ASCII
block
character
character set
code value
diacritic
double-byte character set (DBCS)
efficient (Unicode design basis)
encode
entity reference
glyph
hexadecimal notation
localization
multi-byte character set (MBCS)

portability
script
surrogate
symbol
unambiguous (Unicode design basis)
Unicode Consortium
Unicode design basis
Unicode Standard
Unicode Transformation Format (UTF)
uniform (Unicode design basis)
universal (Unicode design basis)
UTF-8
UTF-16
UTF-32

SELF-REVIEW EXERCISES

F.1   Fill in the blanks in each of the following.
   a) Global software developers had to _____ their products to a specific market before distribution.
   b) The Unicode Standard is a(n) _____ standard that facilitates the uniform production and distribution of software products.
   c) The four design basis that constitute the Unicode Standard are: _____, _____, _____ and _____.
   d) A(n) _____ is the smallest written component the can be represented with a numeric value.
   e) Software that can execute on different operating systems is said to be _____.
   f) Of the three encoding forms, _____ is currently supported by Internet Explorer 6 and Netscape 7.1.

F.2   State whether each of the following is *true* or *false*. If *false*, explain why.
   a) The Unicode Standard encompasses all the world's characters.
   b) A Unicode code value is represented as U+*yyyy*, where *yyyy* represents a number in binary notation.
   c) A diacritic is a character with a special mark that emphasizes an accent.
   d) Unicode is portable.
   e) When designing XHTML and XML documents, the entity reference is denoted by #U+*yyyy*.

ANSWERS TO SELF-REVIEW EXERCISES

F.1   a) localize. b) encoding. c) universal, efficient, uniform, unambiguous. d) character. e) portable. f) UTF-8.

F.2   a) False. It encompasses the majority of the world's characters. b) False. The *yyyy* represents a hexadecimal number. c) False. A diacritic is a special mark added to a character to distinguish it from another letter or to indicate an accent. d) True. e) False. The entity reference is denoted by &#x*yyyy*.

EXERCISES

F.3   Navigate to the Unicode Consortium Web site (`www.unicode.org`) and write the hexadecimal code values for the following characters. In which block are they located?
  a) Latin letter "Z."
  b) Latin letter "n" with the "tilde (~)."
  c) Greek letter "delta."
  d) Mathematical operator "less than or equal to."
  e) Punctuation symbol "open quote (")."

F.4   Describe the Unicode Standard design basis.

F.5   Define the following terms:
  a) code value.
  b) surrogates.
  c) Unicode Standard.
  d) UTF-8.
  e) UTF-16.
  f) UTF-32.

F.6   Describe a scenario where it is optimal to store your data in UTF-16 format.

F.7   Using the Unicode Standard code values, create an XML document that prints your first and last name. The documents should contain the tags `<Uppercase>` and `<Lowercase>` that encode your name in uppercase and lowercase letters, respectively. If you know other writing systems, print your first and last name in those as well. Use a Web browser to render the document.

F.8   Write a JavaScript program that prints "Welcome to Unicode!" in English, French, German, Japanese, Kannada, Portuguese, Russian, Spanish, Telugu and Traditional Chinese. Use the code values provided in Fig. F.3. In JavaScript, a code value is represented through an escape sequence \u*yyyy*, where *yyyy* is a four-digit hexadecimal number. Call `document.write` to render the text in a Web browser.

Career Opportunities
(On CD)

Objectives

- To explore various online career services.
- To examine the advantages and disadvantages of posting and finding jobs online.
- To review the major online career services Web sites available to job seekers.
- To explore online services available to employers seeking to build their workforces.

[*Note:* This appendix is located on the CD that accompanies this book in printable Adobe® Acrobat® PDF format. The appendix includes pages 1462–1478.]

Bibliography

Abualsamid, A. "XML: The Big Picture." *Network Computing* 16 April 2001: 85-93.

Alsop, S. "Adios, Netscape! Bye-Bye, Fun." *Fortune* 2 April 2001: 48.

Anderson, R. "The Long and Winding Road to Web-Based Apps." *Network Computing* 19 March 2001: 79-84.

Beazley, D., *Python Essential Reference, Second Edition.* Indianapolis, IN: New Riders Publishing, 2001.

Bleyle, J., et. al., *Macromedia Flash MX 2004 ActionScript Reference Guide.* <http://download.macromedia.com/pub/documentation/en/flash/mx2004/fl_actionscript_reference.pdf>, San Francisco, CA: Macromedia, Inc., 2003.

Boumphrey, F., et. al., *Beginning XHTML.* U.S.: Wrox Press Ltd, 2000.

Choi, W., et. al., *Beginning PHP 4.* US: Wrox Press Ltd, 2000.

Chun, Russell. *Macromedia Flash Advanced.* U.S.: Peachpit Press, 2001.

Chun, W., *Core Python Programming.* Upper Saddle River, NJ: Prentice Hall PTR, 2001.

Cohen, D. "Construct Your E-Commerce Business Tier the Easy Way With XML, ASP, and Scripting." *Microsoft Systems Journal* February 2000: 35-55.

Converse, T. and J. Park, *PHP4 Bible, Second Edition.* Foster City, CA: IDG Books Worldwide, Inc., 2002.

Curtis, H. *Flash Web Design: The Art of Motion Graphics.* U.S.: New Riders Publishing, 2000.

Danesh, A., R. Camden, S. Bainum and G. Rish. *Mastering ColdFusion MX.* San Francisco, CA: Sybex, 2002.

Deitel, H., et. al., *Advanced Java™ 2 Platform How to Program.* Upper Saddle River, NJ: Prentice Hall, 2002.

Deitel, H., et. al., *e-Business & e-Commerce How to Program.* Upper Saddle River, NJ: Prentice Hall, 2001.

Deitel, H., et. al., *e-Business & e-Commerce for Managers.* Upper Saddle River, NJ: Prentice Hall, 2001.

Deitel, H. and P. Deitel, *Java How to Program, Fifth Edition.* Upper Saddle River, NJ: Prentice Hall, 2003.

Deitel, H., et. al., *Perl How to Program.* Upper Saddle River, NJ: Prentice Hall, 2001.

Deitel, H., et. al., *XML How to Program.* Upper Saddle River, NJ: Prentice Hall, 2001.

Dick, K. *XML A Manager's Guide.* Reading, MA: Addison Wesley Longman, Inc., 2000.

Dyck, T. "Translating XML Schema." *eWeek* 28 May 2001: 1, 28.

Feiler, J. *Perl 5 Programming Notebook.* Upper Saddle River, NJ: Prentice Hall, 2001.

Floyd, M. *Building Web Sites With XML.* Upper Saddle River, NJ: Prentice Hall, 2000.

Floyd, M. "Generating Style Sheets Dynamically." *Webtechniques* January 2001: 62.

Gibbs, M. "XML Worth A Thousand Pics." *Network World* 11 June 2001: 46.

Goldfarb, C. F., et. al., *The XML Handbook, 3rd Edition.* Upper Saddle River, NJ: Prentice Hall, 2001.

Harms, D. and K. McDonald, *The Quick Python Book,* Greenwich: Manning, 2000.

Hoenisch, S. "Structuring Documents with XML." *XML Journal* 31 August 2001: 40-43.

Holzschlag, M.E. "XMHTML Basic: Modularization in Action." *Webtechniques* February 2001: 36-39.

Lamont, J. "Even-handed XML Brings Commonality to Diverse Applications." *KMWorld* June 2000: 10-12.

Lewis, J. "Vendors' Support For XML Is All In The Semantics." *Internet Week* 13 November 2000: 44.

Luh, J. C. "Style and Substance." *Internet Technology* 1 April 2001: 48-51.

Lutz, M., *Programming Python, Second Edition.* Sebastopol, CA: O'Reilly, 2002.

Marchal, B. *XML By Example, Second Edition.* U.S.: Que Publishing, 2001.

Mohler, J. L. *Flash 5 Graphics, Animation & Interactivity.* Canada: OnWord Press, 2001.

Nairn, G. "Online Collaborations Aim to Speak Same Language." *Financial Times* 18 April 2001: 10.

O'Brien, L. "XSL Plays Important Role In Transformation of XML." *Software Development Times* 1 February 2001: 7.

Orenstein, D. "Time to Talk the Talk." *Business 2.0* 14 November 2000: 108-113.

Patton, T. "XML Schemas In Action." *XML Journal* 31 August 2001: 34-35.

Peschko, E., et. al., *Perl Developers Guide.* U.S.: McGraw-Hill, 2000.

Sebesta, R. W. *A Little Book on Perl.* Upper Saddle River, *NJ: Prentice Hall, 2001.*

Skonnard, A. "Understanding XML Namespaces." *MSDN Magazine* July 2001: 33-43.

"The X-Factor." *Global Technology Business* August 2000: 48-49.

Thomas, O. "Form and Function, Together at Last." *eCompany* July 2001: 92-93.

Wall, L., et. al., *Programming Perl, Third Edition.* U.S.: O'Reilly & Associates, Inc., 2001.

Webster, J. "Transaction Spec Is Proposed." *InternetWeek* 13 November 2000: 24.

Zellen, B. "Apache 2.0 Released In Beta." *Application Development Trends* May 2001: 12.

Index

[*Note:* Page number references that appear in red indicate pages from chapters that are on the CD as Adobe Acrobat PDF documents.]

End User License Agreements

5. TRANSFER RESTRICTIONS: The enclosed SOFTWARE is licensed only to you and may not be transferred to any one else without the prior written consent of the Company. Any unauthorized transfer of the SOFTWARE shall result in the immediate termination of this Agreement.

6. TERMINATION: This license is effective until terminated. This license will terminate automatically without notice from the Company and become null and void if you fail to comply with any provisions or limitations of this license. Upon termination, you shall destroy the Documentation and all copies of the SOFTWARE. All provisions of this Agreement as to warranties, limitation of liability, remedies or damages, and our ownership rights shall survive termination.

7. MISCELLANEOUS: This Agreement shall be construed in accordance with the laws of the United States of America and the State of New York and shall benefit the Company, its affiliates, and assignees.

8.LIMITED WARRANTY AND DISCLAIMER OF WARRANTY: The Company warrants that the SOFTWARE, when properly used in accordance with the Documentation, will operate in substantial conformity with the description of the SOFTWARE set forth in the Documentation. The Company does not warrant that the SOFTWARE will meet your requirements or that the operation of the SOFTWARE will be uninterrupted or error-free. The Company warrants that the media on which the SOFTWARE is delivered shall be free from defects in materials and workmanship under normal use for a period of thirty (30) days from the date of your purchase. Your only remedy and the Company's only obligation under these limited warranties is, at the Company's option, return of the warranted item for a refund of any amounts paid by you or replacement of the item. Any replacement of SOFTWARE or media under the warranties shall not extend the original warranty period. The limited warranty set forth above shall not apply to any SOFTWARE which the Company determines in good faith has been subject to misuse, neglect, improper installation, repair, alteration, or damage by you. EXCEPT FOR THE EXPRESSED WARRANTIES SET FORTH ABOVE, THE COMPANY DISCLAIMS ALL WARRANTIES, EXPRESS OR IMPLIED, INCLUDING WITHOUT LIMITATION, THE IMPLIED WARRANTIES OF MERCHANTABILITY AND FITNESS FOR A PARTICULAR PURPOSE. EXCEPT FOR THE EXPRESS WARRANTY SET FORTH ABOVE, THE COMPANY DOES NOT WARRANT, GUARANTEE, OR MAKE ANY REPRESENTATION REGARDING THE USE OR THE RESULTS OF THE USE OF THE SOFTWARE IN TERMS OF ITS CORRECTNESS, ACCURACY, RELIABILITY, CURRENTNESS, OR OTHERWISE.

IN NO EVENT, SHALL THE COMPANY OR ITS EMPLOYEES, AGENTS, SUPPLIERS, OR CONTRACTORS BE LIABLE FOR ANY INCIDENTAL, INDIRECT, SPECIAL, OR CONSEQUENTIAL DAMAGES ARISING OUT OF OR IN CONNECTION WITH THE LICENSE GRANTED UNDER THIS AGREEMENT, OR FOR LOSS OF USE, LOSS OF DATA, LOSS OF INCOME OR PROFIT, OR OTHER LOSSES, SUSTAINED AS A RESULT OF INJURY TO ANY PERSON, OR LOSS OF OR DAMAGE TO PROPERTY, OR CLAIMS OF THIRD PARTIES, EVEN IF THE COMPANY OR AN AUTHORIZED REPRESENTATIVE OF THE COMPANY HAS BEEN ADVISED OF THE POSSIBILITY OF SUCH DAMAGES. IN NO EVENT SHALL LIABILITY OF THE COMPANY FOR DAMAGES WITH RESPECT TO THE SOFTWARE EXCEED THE AMOUNTS ACTUALLY PAID BY YOU, IF ANY, FOR THE SOFTWARE.

SOME JURISDICTIONS DO NOT ALLOW THE LIMITATION OF IMPLIED WARRANTIES OR LIABILITY FOR INCIDENTAL, INDIRECT, SPECIAL, OR CONSEQUENTIAL DAMAGES, SO THE ABOVE LIMITATIONS MAY NOT ALWAYS APPLY. THE WARRANTIES IN THIS AGREEMENT GIVE YOU SPECIFIC LEGAL RIGHTS AND YOU MAY ALSO HAVE OTHER RIGHTS WHICH VARY IN ACCORDANCE WITH LOCAL LAW.

ACKNOWLEDGMENT

YOU ACKNOWLEDGE THAT YOU HAVE READ THIS AGREEMENT, UNDERSTAND IT, AND AGREE TO BE BOUND BY ITS TERMS AND CONDITIONS. YOU ALSO AGREE THAT THIS AGREEMENT IS THE COMPLETE AND EXCLUSIVE STATEMENT OF THE AGREEMENT BETWEEN YOU AND THE COMPANY AND SUPERSEDES ALL PROPOSALS OR PRIOR AGREEMENTS, ORAL, OR WRITTEN, AND ANY OTHER COMMUNICATIONS BETWEEN YOU AND THE COMPANY OR ANY REPRESENTATIVE OF THE COMPANY RELATING TO THE SUBJECT MATTER OF THIS AGREEMENT.

Should you have any questions concerning this Agreement or if you wish to contact the Company for any reason, please contact in writing at the address below.

Robin Short

Prentice Hall PTR

One Lake Street

Upper Saddle River, New Jersey 07458

ADOBE SYSTEMS INCORPORATED END USER LICENSE AGREEMENT FOR ADOBE READER

NOTICE TO USER: PLEASE READ THIS CONTRACT CAREFULLY. BY USING ALL OR ANY PORTION OF THE ADOBE READER SOFTWARE ("SOFTWARE") YOU ACCEPT ALL THE TERMS AND CONDITIONS OF THIS AGREEMENT, INCLUDING, IN PARTICULAR THE LIMITATIONS ON: USE CONTAINED IN SECTION 2; TRANSFERABILITY IN SECTION 4; WARRANTY IN SECTION 6; AND LIABILITY IN SECTION 7. YOU AGREE THAT THIS AGREEMENT IS ENFORCEABLE LIKE ANY WRITTEN NEGOTIATED AGREEMENT SIGNED BY YOU. IF YOU DO NOT AGREE, DO NOT USE THIS SOFTWARE. IF YOU ACQUIRED THE SOFTWARE ON TANGIBLE MEDIA (e.g. CD) WITHOUT AN OPPORTUNITY TO REVIEW THIS LICENSE AND YOU DO NOT ACCEPT THIS AGREEMENT, YOU MAY OBTAIN A REFUND OF ANY AMOUNT YOU ORIGINALLY PAID IF YOU: (A) DO NOT USE THE SOFTWARE AND (B) RETURN IT, WITH PROOF OF PAYMENT, TO THE LOCATION FROM WHICH IT WAS OBTAINED WITHIN THIRTY (30) DAYS OF THE PURCHASE DATE.

Adobe and its suppliers own all intellectual property in the Software. Adobe permits you to Use the Software only in accordance with the terms of this Agreement. Use of some third party materials included in the Software may be subject to other terms and conditions typically found in a separate license agreement or "Read Me" file located near such materials.

1. Definitions. "Software" means (a) all of the contents of the files, disk(s), CD-ROM(s) or other media with which this Agreement is provided, including but not limited to (i) Adobe or third party computer information or software; (ii) related explanatory written materials or files ("Documentation"); and (iii) fonts; and (b) upgrades, modified versions, updates, additions, and copies of the Software, if any, licensed to you by Adobe (collectively, "Updates"). "Use" or "Using" means to access, install, download, copy or otherwise benefit from using the functionality of the Software in accordance with the Documentation. "Permitted Number" means one (1) unless otherwise indicated under a valid license (e.g. volume license) granted by Adobe. "Computer" means an electronic device that accepts information in digital or similar form and manipulates it for a specific result based on a sequence of instructions. "Adobe" means Adobe Systems Incorporated, a Delaware corporation, 345 Park Avenue, San Jose, California 95110, if subsection 10(a) of this Agreement applies; otherwise it means Adobe Systems Software Ireland Limited, Unit 3100, Lake Drive, City West Campus, Saggart D24, Republic of Ireland, a company organized under the laws of Ireland and an affiliate and licensee of Adobe Systems Incorporated.

2. Software License. As long as you comply with the terms of this Software License Agreement (this "Agreement"), Adobe grants to you a non-exclusive license to Use the Software for the purposes described in the Documentation.

2.1 General Use. You may install and Use a copy of the Software on your compatible computer, up to the Permitted Number of computers.

2.2 Server Use and Distribution.

2.2.1 Subject to the terms of this Agreement, you may install one copy of the Software on a computer file server within your internal network for the sole and exclusive purpose of using the Software (from an unlimited number of client computers on your internal network) via (a) the Network File System (NFS) for UNIX versions of the Software or (b) Windows Terminal Services. Unless otherwise expressly permitted hereunder, no other server or network use of the Software is permitted, including but not limited to use of the Software (i) either directly or through commands, data or instructions from or to another computer or (ii) for internal network, internet or web hosting services.

2.2.2 For information on how to distribute the Software on tangible media or through an internal network please refer to the sections entitled "How to Distribute Adobe Reader" at http://www.adobe.com.

2.3 Backup Copy. You may make one backup copy of the Software, provided your backup copy is not installed or used on any computer. You may not transfer the rights to a backup copy unless you transfer all rights in the Software as provided under Section 4.

2.4 Portable or Home Computer Use. In addition to the single copy permitted under Sections 2.2.1 and 2.3, the primary user of the computer on which the Software is installed may make a second copy of the Software for his or her exclusive use on either a portable Computer or a Computer located at his or her home, provided the Software on the portable or home Computer is not used at the same time as the Software on the primary computer.

2.5 No Modification. You may customize or extend the functionality of the installer for the Software as specifically allowed by instructions found at http://www.adobe.com or http://partners.adobe.com (e.g., installation of additional plug-in and help files). You may not otherwise alter or modify the Software or create a new installer for the Software. The Software is licensed and distributed by Adobe for viewing, distributing and sharing PDF files. You are not authorized to integrate or use the Software with any other software, plug-in or enhancement which uses or relies upon the Software when converting or transforming PDF files into other file formats (e.g., a PDF file into a TIFF, JPEG, or SVG file). You are not authorized to integrate or use the Software with any (a) plug-in software not developed in accordance with the Adobe Integration Key License Agreement or (b) other software or enhancement that uses Inter Application Communication (IAC) to programmatically interface with the Software for the purpose of (i) creating a file that contains data (e.g., an XML or comments file), (ii) saving modifications to a PDF file or (iii) rendering a PDF file in such other software's application window.

2.6 Third Party Website Access. The Software allows you to access third party websites ("Third Party Sites"). Your access to and use of any Third Party Sites, including any goods, services or information made available from such sites, is governed by the terms and conditions found at each Third Party Site, if any. Third Party Sites are not owned or operated by Adobe. YOUR USE OF THIRD PARTY SITES IS AT YOUR OWN RISK. ADOBE MAKES NO WARRANTIES, CONDITIONS, INDEMNITIES, REPRESENTATIONS OR TERMS, EXPRESS OR IMPLIED, WHETHER BY STATUTE, COMMON LAW, CUSTOM, USAGE OR OTHERWISE AS TO ANY OTHER MATTERS, INCLUDING BUT NOT LIMITED TO NON-INFRINGEMENT OF THIRD PARTY RIGHTS, TITLE, INTEGRATION, ACCURACY, SECURITY, AVAILABILITY, SATISFACTORY QUALITY, MERCHANTABILITY OR FITNESS FOR ANY PARTICULAR PURPOSE WITH RESPECT TO THE THIRD PARTY SITES.

2.7 Certified Documents.

2.7.1 Certified Documents and CD Services. The Software allows you to validate Certified Documents. A "Certified Document" or "CD" is a PDF file that has been digitally signed using (a) the Software CD feature set, (b) a certificate, and (c) a "private" encryption key that corresponds to the "public" key in the certificate. Validation of a CD requires CD Services from the CD Service Provider that issued the certificate. "CD Service Provider" is an independent third party service vendor listed at http://www.adobe.com/security/partners_cds.html. "CD Services" are services provided by CD Service Providers, including without limitation (a) certificates issued by such CD Service Provider for use with the Software's CD feature set, (b) services related to issuance of certificates, and (c) other services related to certificates, including without limitation verification services.

2.7.2 CD Service Providers. Although the Software provides validation features, Adobe does not supply the necessary CD Services required to use these features. Purchasing, availability and responsibility for the CD Services are between you and the CD Service Provider. Before you rely upon any CD, any digital signature applied thereto, and/or any related CD Services, you must first review and agree to the applicable Issuer Statement and this Agreement. "Issuer Statement" means the terms and conditions under which each CD Service Provider offers CD Services (see the links on http://www.adobe.com/security/partners_cds.html), including for example any subscriber agreements, relying party agreements, certificate policies and practice statements, and Section 2.7 of this Agreement. By validating a CD using CD Services, you acknowledge and agree that (i) the certificate used to digitally sign a CD may be revoked at the time of verification, making the digital signature on the CD appear valid when in fact it is not, (ii) the security or integrity of a CD may be compromised due to an act or omission by the signer of the CD, the applicable CD Service Provider, or any other third party; and (iii) you must read, understand, and be bound by the applicable Issuer Statement.

2.7.3 Warranty Disclaimer. CD Service Providers offer CD Services solely in accordance with the applicable Issuer Statement. ACCESS TO THE CD SERVICES THROUGH THE USE OF THE SOFTWARE IS MADE AVAILABLE ON AN "AS IS" BASIS ONLY AND WITHOUT ANY WARRANTY OR INDEMNITY OF ANY KIND (EXCEPT AS SUPPLIED BY A CD SERVICES PROVIDER IN ITS ISSUER STATEMENT). ADOBE AND EACH CD SERVICE PROVIDER (EXCEPT AS EXPRESSLY PROVIDED IN ITS ISSUER STATEMENT) MAKE NO WARRANTIES, CONDITIONS, INDEMNITIES, REPRESENTATIONS OR TERMS, EXPRESS OR IMPLIED, WHETHER BY STATUTE, COMMON LAW, CUSTOM, USAGE OR OTHERWISE AS TO ANY OTHER MATTERS, INCLUDING BUT NOT LIMITED TO NON-INFRINGEMENT OF THIRD PARTY RIGHTS, TITLE, INTEGRATION, ACCU-

RACY, SECURITY, AVAILABILITY, SATISFACTORY QUALITY, MERCHANTABILITY OR FIT-
NESS FOR ANY PARTICULAR PURPOSE WITH RESPECT TO THE CD SERVICES.

2.7.4 Indemnity. You agree to hold Adobe and any applicable CD Service Provider (except as expressly
provided in its Issuer Statement) harmless from any and all liabilities, losses, actions, damages, or claims
(including all reasonable expenses, costs, and attorneys fees) arising out of or relating to any use of, or reliance on, any CD Service, including, without limitation (a) reliance on an expired or revoked certificate; (b)
improper verification of a certificate; (c) use of a certificate other than as permitted by any applicable Issuer
Statement, this Agreement or applicable law; (d) failure to exercise reasonable judgment under the circumstances in relying on the CD Services; or (e) failure to perform any of the obligations as required in an applicable Issuer Statement.

2.7.5 Limit of Liability. UNDER NO CIRCUMSTANCES WILL ADOBE OR ANY CD SERVICE
PROVIDER (EXCEPT AS EXPRESSLY SET FORTH IN ITS ISSUER STATEMENT) BE LIABLE TO
YOU, OR ANY OTHER PERSON OR ENTITY, FOR ANY LOSS OF USE, REVENUE OR PROFIT, LOST
OR DAMAGED DATA, OR OTHER COMMERCIAL OR ECONOMIC LOSS OR FOR ANY DIRECT,
INDIRECT, INCIDENTAL, SPECIAL, STATUTORY, PUNITIVE, EXEMPLARY OR CONSEQUEN-
TIAL DAMAGES WHATSOEVER RELATED TO YOUR USE OR RELIANCE UPON CD SERVICES,
EVEN IF ADVISED OF THE POSSIBILITY OF SUCH DAMAGES OR IF SUCH DAMAGES ARE FORE-
SEEABLE. THIS LIMITATION SHALL APPLY EVEN IN THE EVENT OF A FUNDAMENTAL OR
MATERIAL BREACH OR A BREACH OF THE FUNDAMENTAL OR MATERIALTERMS OF THIS
AGREEMENT.

2.7.6 Third Party Beneficiaries. You agree that any CD Service Provider you utilize shall be a third
party beneficiary with respect to this Section 2.7 of this Agreement, and that such CD Service Provider shall
have the right to enforce such provisions in its own name as if the CD Service Provider were Adobe.

3. Intellectual Property Ownership, Copyright Protection. The Software and any authorized copies that
you make are the intellectual property of and are owned by Adobe Systems Incorporated and its suppliers.
The structure, organization and code of the Software are the valuable trade secrets and confidential information of Adobe Systems Incorporated and its suppliers. The Software is protected by law, including without
limitation the copyright laws of the United States and other countries, and by international treaty provisions.
Except as expressly stated herein, this Agreement docs not grant you any intellectual property rights in the
Software and all rights not expressly granted are reserved by Adobe and its suppliers.

4. Restrictions.

4.1 Notices. You shall not copy the Software except as set forth in Section 2. Any copy of the Software
that you make must contain the same copyright and other proprietary notices that appear on or in the Software.

4.2 No Modifications. You shall not modify, adapt or translate the Software. You shall not reverse engineer, decompile, disassemble or otherwise attempt to discover the source code of the Software except to the
extent you may be expressly permitted to decompile under applicable law, it is essential to do so in order to
achieve operability of the Software with another software program, and you have first requested Adobe to
provide the information necessary to achieve such operability and Adobe has not made such information
available. Adobe has the right to impose reasonable conditions and to request a reasonable fee before providing such information. Any such information supplied by Adobe and any information obtained by you by
such permitted decompilation may only be used by you for the purpose described herein and may not be disclosed to any third party or used to create any software which is substantially similar to the expression of the
Software. Requests for information should be directed to the Adobe Customer Support Department.

4.3 Document Features. The Software may contain features and functionality that appear disabled or
"grayed out" (the "Document Features"). The Document Features will only activate when opening certain
PDF documents that have been created using corresponding enabling technology available from Adobe. You
agree not to access, or attempt to access, disabled Document Features or otherwise circumvent the permissions that control activation of such Document Features.

4.4 Transfer. You may not, rent, lease, sublicense, assign or transfer your rights in the Software, or
authorize all or any portion of the Software to be copied onto another user's computer except as may be
expressly permitted herein. You may, however, transfer all your rights to Use the Software to another person
or legal entity provided that: (a) you also transfer (i) this Agreement, and (ii) the Software and all other software or hardware bundled or pre-installed with the Software, including all copies, Updates and prior versions, to such person or entity; (b) you retain no copies, including backups and copies stored on a computer;
and (c) the receiving party accepts the terms and conditions of this Agreement and any other terms and con-

ditions upon which you legally purchased a license to the Software. Notwithstanding the foregoing, you may not transfer education, pre-release, or not for resale copies of the Software.

5. Updates. If the Software is an Update to a previous version of the Software, you must possess a valid license to such previous version in order to Use such Update. All Updates are provided to you on a license exchange basis. You agree that by Using an Update you voluntarily terminate your right to use any previous version of the Software. As an exception, you may continue to Use previous versions of the Software on your Computer after you Use the Update buy only to assist you in the transition to the Update, provided that: (a) the Update and the previous versions are installed on the same computer; (b) the previous versions or copies thereof are not transferred to another party or Computer unless all copies of the Update are also transferred to such party or Computer; and (c) you acknowledge that any obligation Adobe may have to support the previous versions of the Software may be ended upon availability of the Update.

6. NO WARRANTY. The Software is being delivered to you "AS IS" and Adobe makes no warranty as to its use or performance. ADOBE AND ITS SUPPLIERS DO NOT AND CANNOT WARRANT THE PERFORMANCE OR RESULTS YOU MAY OBTAIN BY USING THE SOFTWARE. EXCEPT FOR ANY WARRANTY, CONDITION, REPRESENTATION OR TERM TO THE EXTENT TO WHICH THE SAME CANNOT OR MAY NOT BE EXCLUDED OR LIMITED BY LAW APPLICABLE TO YOU IN YOUR JURISDICTION, ADOBE AND ITS SUPPLIERS MAKE NO WARRANTIES CONDITIONS, REPRE- SENTATIONS, OR TERMS (EXPRESS OR IMPLIED WHETHER BY STATUTE, COMMON LAW, CUSTOM, USAGE OR OTHERWISE) AS TO ANY MATTER INCLUDING WITHOUT LIMITATION NONINFRINGEMENT OF THIRD PARTY RIGHTS, MERCHANTABILITY, INTEGRATION, SATIS- FACTORY QUALITY, OR FITNESS FOR ANY PARTICULAR PURPOSE. The provisions of Section 6 and Section 7 shall survive the termination of this Agreement, howsoever caused, but this shall not imply or create any continued right to Use the Software after termination of this Agreement.

7. LIMITATION OF LIABILITY. IN NO EVENT WILL ADOBE OR ITS SUPPLIERS BE LIABLE TO YOU FOR ANY DAMAGES, CLAIMS OR COSTS WHATSOEVER OR ANY CONSEQUENTIAL, INDIRECT, INCIDENTAL DAMAGES, OR ANY LOST PROFITS OR LOST SAVINGS, EVEN IF AN ADOBE REPRESENTATIVE HAS BEEN ADVISED OF THE POSSIBILITY OF SUCH LOSS, DAM- AGES, CLAIMS OR COSTS OR FOR ANY CLAIM BY ANY THIRD PARTY. THE FOREGOING LIM- ITATIONS AND EXCLUSIONS APPLY TO THE EXTENT PERMITTED BY APPLICABLE LAW IN YOUR JURISDICTION. ADOBE'S AGGREGATE LIABILITY AND THAT OF ITS SUPPLIERS UNDER OR IN CONNECTION WITH THIS AGREEMENT SHALL BE LIMITED TO THE AMOUNT PAID FOR THE SOFTWARE, IF ANY. Nothing contained in this Agreement limits Adobe's liability to you in the event of death or personal injury resulting from Adobe's negligence or for the tort of deceit (fraud). Adobe is acting on behalf of its suppliers for the purpose of disclaiming, excluding and/or limiting obligations, warranties and liability as provided in this Agreement, but in no other respects and for no other purpose. For further information, please see the jurisdiction specific information at the end of this Agreement, if any, or contact Adobe's Customer Support Department.

8. Export Rules. You agree that the Software will not be shipped, transferred or exported into any country or used in any manner prohibited by the United States Export Administration Act or any other export laws, restrictions or regulations (collectively the "Export Laws"). In addition, if the Software is identified as export controlled items under the Export Laws, you represent and warrant that you are not a citizen, or oth- erwise located within, an embargoed nation (including without limitation Iran, Iraq, Syria, Sudan, Libya, Cuba, North Korea, and Serbia) and that you are not otherwise prohibited under the Export Laws from receiving the Software. All rights to Use the Software are granted on condition that such rights are forfeited if you fail to comply with the terms of this Agreement.

9. Governing Law. This Agreement will be governed by and construed in accordance with the substan- tive laws in force: (a) in the State of California, if a license to the Software is obtained when you are in the United States, Canada, or Mexico; or (b) in Japan, if a license to the Software is obtained when you are in Japan, China, Korea, or other Southeast Asian country where all official languages are written in either an ideographic script (e.g., hanzi, kanji, or hanja), and/or other script based upon or similar in structure to an ideographic script, such as hangul or kana; or (c) Ireland, if a license to the Software is purchased when you are in any other jurisdiction not described above. The respective courts of Santa Clara County, California when California law applies, Tokyo District Court in Japan, when Japanese law applies, and the competent courts of Ireland, when the law of Ireland applies, shall each have non-exclusive jurisdiction over all disputes relating to this Agreement. This Agreement will not be governed by the conflict of law rules of any jurisdic-

tion or the United Nations Convention on Contracts for the International Sale of Goods, the application of which is expressly excluded.

10. General Provisions. If any part of this Agreement is found void and unenforceable, it will not affect the validity of the balance of this Agreement, which shall remain valid and enforceable according to its terms. This Agreement shall not prejudice the statutory rights of any party dealing as a consumer. This Agreement may only be modified by a writing signed by an authorized officer of Adobe. Updates may be licensed to you by Adobe with additional or different terms. This is the entire agreement between Adobe and you relating to the Software and it supersedes any prior representations, discussions, undertakings, communications or advertising relating to the Software.

11. Notice to U.S. Government End Users. The Software and Documentation are "Commercial Items," as that term is defined at 48 C.F.R. §2.101, consisting of "Commercial Computer Software" and "Commercial Computer Software Documentation," as such terms are used in 48 C.F.R. §12.212 or 48 C.F.R. §227.7202, as applicable. Consistent with 48 C.F.R. §12.212 or 48 C.F.R. §§227.7202-1 through 227.7202-4, as applicable, the Commercial Computer Software and Commercial Computer Software Documentation are being licensed to U.S. Government end users (a) only as Commercial Items and (b) with only those rights as are granted to all other end users pursuant to the terms and conditions herein. Unpublished-rights reserved under the copyright laws of the United States. Adobe Systems Incorporated, 345 Park Avenue, San Jose, CA 95110-2704, USA. For U.S. Government End Users, Adobe agrees to comply with all applicable equal opportunity laws including, if appropriate, the provisions of Executive Order 11246, as amended, Section 402 of the Vietnam Era Veterans Readjustment Assistance Act of 1974 (38 USC 4212), and Section 503 of the Rehabilitation Act of 1973, as amended, and the regulations at 41 CFR Parts 60-1 through 60-60, 60-250, and 60-741. The affirmative action clause and regulations contained in the preceding sentence shall be incorporated by reference in this Agreement.

12. Compliance with Licenses. If you are a business or organization, you agree that upon request from Adobe or Adobe's authorized representative, you will within thirty (30) days fully document and certify that use of any and all Software at the time of the request is in conformity with your valid licenses from Adobe.

13. Specific Exceptions.

13.1 Limited Warranty for Users Residing in Germany or Austria. If you obtained the Software in Germany or Austria, and you usually reside in such country, then Section 6 does not apply, instead, Adobe warrants that the Software provides the functionalities set forth in the Documentation (the "agreed upon functionalities") for the limited warranty period following receipt of the Software when used on the recommended hardware configuration. As used in this Section, "limited warranty period" means one (1) year if you are a business user and two (2) years if you are not a business user. Non-substantial variation from the agreed upon functionalities shall not be considered and does not establish any warranty rights. THIS LIMITED WARRANTY DOES NOT APPLY TO SOFTWARE PROVIDED TO YOU FREE OF CHARGE, FOR EXAMPLE, UPDATES, PRE-RELEASE, TRYOUT, PRODUCT SAMPLER, NOT FOR RESALE (NFR) COPIES OF SOFTWARE, OR SOFTWARE THAT HAS BEEN ALTERED BY YOU, TO THE EXTENT SUCH ALTERATIONS CAUSED A DEFECT. To make a warranty claim, during the limited warranty period you must return, at our expense, the Software and proof of purchase to the location where you obtained it. If the functionalities of the Software vary substantially from the agreed upon functionalities, Adobe is entitled -- by way of re-performance and at its own discretion -- to repair or replace the Software. If this fails, you are entitled to a reduction of the purchase price (reduction) or to cancel the purchase agreement (rescission). For further warranty information, please contact Adobe's Customer Support Department

13.2 Limitation of Liability for Users Residing in Germany and Austria.

13.2.1 If you obtained the Software in Germany or Austria, and you usually reside in such country, then Section 7 does not apply, Instead, subject to the provisions in Section 13.2.2, Adobe's statutory liability for damages shall be limited as follows: (i) Adobe shall be liable only up to the amount of damages as typically foreseeable at the time of entering into the purchase agreement in respect of damages caused by a slightly negligent breach of a material contractual obligation and (ii) Adobe shall not be liable for damages caused by a slightly negligent breach of a non-material contractual obligation.

13.2.2 The aforesaid limitation of liability shall not apply to any mandatory statutory liability, in particular, to liability under the German Product Liability Act, liability for assuming a specific guarantee or liability for culpably caused personal injuries.

13.2.3 You are required to take all reasonable measures to avoid and reduce damages, in particular to make back-up copies of the Software and your computer data subject to the provisions of this Agreement.

13.3 Pre-release Product Additional Terms. If the product you have received with this license is pre-commercial release or beta Software ("Pre-release Software"), then the following Section applies. To the extent that any provision in this Section is in conflict with any other term or condition in this Agreement, this Section shall supercede such other term(s) and condition(s) with respect to the Pre-release Software, but only to the extent necessary to resolve the conflict. You acknowledge that the Software is a pre-release version, does not represent final product from Adobe, and may contain bugs, errors and other problems that could cause system or other failures and data loss. Consequently, the Pre-release Software is provided to you "AS-IS", and Adobe disclaims any warranty or liability obligations to you of any kind. WHERE LIABILITY CANNOT BE EXCLUDED FOR PRE-RELEASE SOFTWARE, BUT IT MAY BE LIMITED, ADOBE'S LIABILITY AND THAT OF ITS SUPPLIERS SHALL BE LIMITED TO THE SUM OF FIFTY DOLLARS (U.S. $50) IN TOTAL. You acknowledge that Adobe has not promised or guaranteed to you that Pre-release Software will be announced or made available to anyone in the future, Adobe has no express or implied obligation to you to announce or introduce the Pre-release Software and that Adobe may not introduce a product similar to or compatible with the Pre-release Software. Accordingly, you acknowledge that any research or development that you perform regarding the Pre-release Software or any product associated with the Pre-release Software is done entirely at your own risk. During the term of this Agreement, if requested by Adobe, you will provide feedback to Adobe regarding testing and use of the Pre-release Software, including error or bug reports. If you have been provided the Pre-release Software pursuant to a separate written agreement, such as the Adobe Systems Incorporated Serial Agreement for Unreleased Products, your use of the Software is also governed by such agreement. You agree that you may not and certify that you will not sublicense, lease, loan, rent, assign or transfer the Pre-release Software. Upon receipt of a later unreleased version of the Pre-release Software or release by Adobe of a publicly released commercial version of the Software, whether as a stand-alone product or as part of a larger product, you agree to return or destroy all earlier Pre-release Software received from Adobe and to abide by the terms of the license agreement for any such later versions of the Pre-release Software. Notwithstanding anything in this Section to the contrary, if you are located outside the United States of America, you agree that you will return or destroy all unreleased versions of the Pre-release Software within thirty (30) days of the completion of your testing of the Software when such date is earlier than the date for Adobe's first commercial shipment of the publicly released (commercial) Software.

If you have any questions regarding this Agreement or if you wish to request any information from Adobe please use the address and contact information included with this product to contact the Adobe office serving your jurisdiction.

Adobe and Reader are either registered trademarks or trademarks of Adobe Systems Incorporated in the United States and/or other countries.

THE APACHE SOFTWARE LICENSE, VERSION 1.1

Copyright (c) 2000-2003 The Apache Software Foundation. All rights reserved.

Redistribution and use in source and binary forms, with or without modification, are permitted provided that the following conditions are met:

1.Redistributions of source code must retain the above copyright notice, this list of conditions and the following disclaimer.

2.Redistributions in binary form must reproduce the above copyright notice, this list of conditions and the following disclaimer in the documentation and/or other materials provided with the distribution.

3.The end-user documentation included with the redistribution, if any, must include the following acknowledgment:

"This product includes software developed by the Apache Software Foundation (http://www.apache.org/)."

Alternately, this acknowledgment may appear in the software itself, if and wherever such third-party acknowledgments normally appear.

4.The names "Apache" and "Apache Software Foundation" must not be used to endorse or promote products derived from this software without prior written permission. For written permission, please contact apache@apache.org.

5.Products derived from this software may not be called "Apache", nor may "Apache" appear in their name, without prior written permission of the Apache Software Foundation.

THIS SOFTWARE IS PROVIDED ``AS IS'' AND ANY EXPRESSED OR IMPLIED WARRANTIES, IN-CLUDING, BUT NOT LIMITED TO, THE IMPLIED WARRANTIES OF MERCHANTABILITY AND

FITNESS FOR A PARTICULAR PURPOSE ARE DISCLAIMED. IN NO EVENT SHALL THE APACHE SOFTWARE FOUNDATION OR ITS CONTRIBUTORS BE LIABLE FOR ANY DIRECT, INDIRECT, INCIDENTAL, SPECIAL, EXEMPLARY, OR CONSEQUENTIAL DAMAGES (INCLUDING, BUT NOT LIMITED TO, PROCUREMENT OF SUBSTITUTE GOODS OR SERVICES; LOSS OF USE, DATA, OR PROFITS; OR BUSINESS INTERRUPTION) HOWEVER CAUSED AND ON ANY THEORY OF LIABILITY, WHETHER IN CONTRACT, STRICT LIABILITY, OR TORT (INCLUDING NEGLIGENCE OR OTHERWISE) ARISING IN ANY WAY OUT OF THE USE OF THIS SOFTWARE, EVEN IF ADVISED OF THE POSSIBILITY OF SUCH DAMAGE.

This software consists of voluntary contributions made by many individuals on behalf of the Apache Software Foundation. For more information on the Apache Software Foundation, please see <http://www.apache.org/>.

Portions of this software are based upon public domain software originally written at the National Center for Supercomputing Applications, University of Illinois, Urbana-Champaign.

END-USER LICENSE AGREEMENT FOR MACROMEDIA® COLDFUSION® MX 6.1

IMPORTANT: THIS SOFTWARE END USER LICENSE AGREEMENT ("EULA") IS A LEGAL AGREEMENT BETWEEN YOU AND MACROMEDIA. READ IT CAREFULLY BEFORE COMPLETING THE INSTALLATION PROCESS AND USING THE SOFTWARE. IT PROVIDES A LICENSE TO USE THE SOFTWARE AND CONTAINS WARRANTY INFORMATION AND LIABILITY DISCLAIMERS. BY INSTALLING AND USING THE SOFTWARE, YOU ARE CONFIRMING YOUR ACCEPTANCE OF THE SOFTWARE AND AGREEING TO BECOME BOUND BY THE TERMS OF THIS AGREEMENT. IF YOU DO NOT AGREE TO BE BOUND BY THESE TERMS, THEN DO NOT INSTALL THE SOFTWARE AND RETURN THE SOFTWARE TO YOUR PLACE OF PURCHASE FOR A FULL REFUND.

THIS EULA SHALL APPLY ONLY TO THE SOFTWARE SUPPLIED BY MACROMEDIA HEREWITH REGARDLESS OF WHETHER OTHER SOFTWARE IS REFERRED TO OR DESCRIBED HEREIN.

1. Definitions

(a) "Bundle" means the Software, together with such other Macromedia software product, if any, distributed with the Software that may be operated on the same type of computer on which the Software is operated.

(b) "CFMX 6.1 Enterprise Update" means version 6.1 of the Enterprise Edition of Macromedia ColdFusion software that is provided as an upgrade from version 6.0 of the Enterprise Edition of Macromedia ColdFusion MX Server software.

(c) "Commercial Version" means a version of the Software that is neither a Developer Version, an Education Version, a Not For Resale Version, nor a Trial Version.

(d) "CPU-Based Software" means, if applicable, a Software (including, but not limited to, Macromedia Flash Remoting software, Macromedia JRun, and the Enterprise Edition of Macromedia ColdFusion software that is not CFMX 6.1 Enterprise Update) that is not a Server-Based Software.

(e) "Developer Version" means a version of the Software, so identified, to be used internally only and solely for the purposes of design, development and evaluation.

(f) "Education Version" means a version of the Software, so identified, for use by qualified educational institutions, including the students and faculty thereof, only.

(g) "Not For Resale (NFR) Version" means a version, so identified, of the Software to be used to review and evaluate the Software, only.

(h) "Macromedia" means Macromedia, Inc. and its licensors, if any.

(i) "Sample Application Code" shall have the meaning ascribed to it in Section 2(c) of this Agreement.

(j) "Server-Based Software" means, if applicable, Macromedia Flash Communication Server software, CFMX 6.1 Enterprise Update, or the Standard Edition of Macromedia ColdFusion software.

(k) "Software" means only the Macromedia software program(s) and third party software programs, in each case, supplied by Macromedia herewith, and corresponding documentation, associated media, printed materials, and online or electronic documentation.

(l) "Trial Version" means a version of the Software, so identified, to be used only to review, demonstrate and evaluate the Software for a limited time period. The Trial Version may have limited features, may lack the ability for the end-user to save the end product, and will cease operating after a predetermined amount of time due to an internal mechanism within the Trial Version.

2. License Grants

The licenses granted in this Section 2 are subject to the terms and conditions set forth in this EULA:

(a) If the Software is (i) a Developer Version, (ii) a Trial Version, or (iii) any version of a Server-Based Software, this Section 2(a), and not Section 2(b), shall apply: Subject to the terms and conditions of this Agreement, Macromedia hereby grants, and you accept, the right and license to install and use the Software on a single computer. A license for the Software may not be shared, installed nor used concurrently on different computers.

(b) If the Software is a (i) Commercial Version, (ii) Education Version or (iii) Not For Resale Version, in each case, of a CPU-Based Software, this Section 2(b), and not Section 2(a), shall apply: Subject to the terms and conditions of this Agreement, Macromedia hereby grants, and you accept, the right and license to install and use the Software on one or more computers, provided, however, that the total number of CPUs from all of the computers in which the Software is installed does not exceed the total number of CPU licenses purchased for such installation and use.

(c) For Sample Application Code, if any, only: You may modify the HTML, CFML, ActionScript, Flash Files (FLA), or similar sample application code form of those portions of the Software that are identified, if any, as sample application code in the documentation (the "Sample Application Code") solely for the purposes of designing, developing and testing your own software applications. However, you are permitted to use, copy and redistribute your modified sample code only if all of the following conditions are met: (A) you include Macromedia's copyright notice (if any) with your application, including every location in which any other copyright notice appears in your application; (B) you do not otherwise use Macromedia's name, logos or other Macromedia trademarks to market your application; (C) there is installed and running on each server in conjunction with which your application is running one or more duly licensed copies, as required, of the Commercial Version or, if applicable and subject to Section 3(f) hereof, Education Version; and (D) such modified sample code is designed to operate only in connection with the Software. You agree to indemnify, hold harmless and defend Macromedia from and against any loss, damage, claims or lawsuits, including attorney's fees, that arise or result from the use or distribution of your application.

(d) You may make one copy of the Software in machine-readable form solely for backup purposes. You must reproduce on any such copy all copyright notices and any other proprietary legends on the original copy of the Software.

(e) You agree that Macromedia may audit your use of the Software for compliance with these terms at any time, upon reasonable notice. In the event that such audit reveals any use of the Software by you other than in full compliance with the terms of this Agreement, you shall reimburse Macromedia for all reasonable expenses related to such audit in addition to any other liabilities you may incur as a result of such non-compliance.

(f) Your license rights under this EULA are non-exclusive.

3. License Restrictions

Except to the extent contrary to applicable law:

(a) Other than as expressly set forth in Section 2, you may not make or distribute copies of the Software, or electronically transfer the Software from one computer to another or over a network.

(b) You may not alter, merge, adapt or translate the Software, or decompile, reverse engineer, disassemble, or otherwise reduce the Software to a human-perceivable form.

(c) Unless otherwise provided herein, you may not rent, lease, or sublicense the Software.

(d) Other than with respect to a Trial Version, Developer Version or a Not For Resale Version of the Software, you may permanently transfer all of your rights under this EULA only as part of a sale or transfer, provided you retain no copies, you transfer all of the Software (including all component parts, the media and printed materials, any upgrades, this EULA, the serial numbers, and, if applicable, all other software products provided together with the Software), and the recipient agrees to the terms of this EULA. If the Software is an upgrade, any transfer must include all prior versions of the Software from which you are upgrading. If the copy of the Software is licensed as part of the Bundle, the Software shall be transferred only with and as part of the sale or transfer of the whole Bundle and not separately. You may retain no copies of the Software. You may not sell or transfer any Software purchased under a volume discount. You may not sell or transfer any Trial Version, Developer Version or Not For Resale Version of the Software.

(e) Other than as expressly set forth in Section 2(c) hereof, you may not modify the Software or create derivative works based upon the Software.

(f) Education Versions may not be used for, or distributed to any party for, any commercial purpose.

(g) Unless otherwise provided herein, you shall not (A) in the aggregate, install or use more than one copy of the Trial Version of the Software, (B) download the Trial Version of the Software under more than one username, (C) alter the contents of a hard drive or computer system to enable the use of the Trial Version of the Software for an aggregate period in excess of the trial period for one license to such Trial Version, (D) disclose the results of software performance benchmarks obtained using the Trial Version to any third party without Macromedia's prior written consent, (E) use the Trial Version for any application deployment or ultimate production purpose, or (F) use the Trial Version of the Software for a purpose other than the sole purpose of determining whether to purchase a license to a commercial or education version of the software; provided, however, notwithstanding the foregoing, you are strictly prohibited from installing or using the Trial Version of the Software for any commercial training purpose.

(h) You shall not (A) use the Developer Version for any application deployment in a live or stand-by production environment or staging environment, in each case, including, without limitation, in any environment accessed by application end-users including but not limited to servers, workstations, kiosks, and mobile computers, (B) use or deploy the Developer Version other than internally for the sole purpose of designing, developing, and evaluating applications pursuant to the terms and conditions set forth in this EULA, (C) access the Developer Version from more than a single IP address at any given time, (D) access the Developer Version from a computer other than the computer on which such Developer Version was installed, or (E) use the Developer Version to deploy applications that are accessed by multiple browsers or users.

(i) You shall not use the Software to develop any application having the same primary function as the Software.

(j) You may only use the Not for Resale Version of the Software to review and evaluate the Software.

(k) You may not export the Software into any country prohibited by the United States Export Administration Act and the regulations thereunder.

(l) You may receive the Software in more than one medium but you shall only install or use one medium. Regardless of the number of media you receive, you may use only the medium that is appropriate for the computer on which the Software is to be installed.

(m) The license of the Bundle is licensed as a single product and none of the products in the Bundle, including the Software, may be separated for installation or use on more than one computer.

(n) You shall not use the Software to develop any application having the same primary function as the Software.

(o) If and only if the Software is a CFMX 6.1 Enterprise Update or a Standard Edition of the Macromedia ColdFusion software : You may not install the Software on a computer with more than eight (8) CPUs unless you purchase additional licenses to the Software such that the aggregate number of such licenses you have purchased for such installation is equal to, or greater than, the quotient (rounded up to the nearest whole number) obtained by dividing by eight (8) the number of CPUs for such server in which the Software is installed.

(p) If and only if the Software is Macromedia ColdFusion software of any version and of any edition: You are prohibited from using Macromedia JRun application server included within the Software other than solely in connection with your use of the Software and solely in conformance with the documentations provided therewith.

(q) If and only if the Software is Macromedia Flash Communication Server software: You may use the Software to serve only such capacity corresponding to the license for the Software you have purchased.

(r) In the event that you fail to comply with this EULA, Macromedia may terminate the license and you must destroy all copies of the Software (with all other rights of both parties and all other provisions of this EULA surviving any such termination).

4. Upgrades and Bundles

If this copy of the Software is an upgrade from an earlier version of the Software, it is provided to you on a license exchange basis. You agree by your installation and use of such copy of the Software to voluntarily terminate your earlier EULA and that you will not continue to use the earlier version of the Software or transfer it to another person or entity unless such transfer is pursuant to Section 3(d). If this copy of the Software is licensed as part of the Bundle, and you have a prior license to the same version of the Software, and the Bundle was licensed to you with a discount based, in whole or in part, on your prior license to the same version of the Software, the Software is provided to you on a license exchange basis. You agree by your installation and use of this copy of the Software to voluntarily terminate your EULA with respect to such prior license to the Software and that you will not continue to install or use such prior license of the Software or transfer it to another person or entity.

5. Ownership

The foregoing grants of rights give you limited license to use the Software. Except as expressly provided in this Agreement, Macromedia and its suppliers retain all right, title and interest, including all copyright and intellectual property rights, in and to, the Software (as an independent work and as an underlying work serving as a basis for any improvements, modifications, derivative works, and applications you may develop), and all copies thereof. All rights not specifically granted in this EULA, including Federal and International Copyrights, are reserved by Macromedia and its suppliers.

6. LIMITED WARRANTY AND DISCLAIMER

(a) Except with respect to the Sample Application Code and the Trial Version, the Developer Version and Not For Resale Version of the Software, Macromedia warrants that, for a period of ninety (90) days from the date of delivery (as evidenced by a copy of your receipt): (i) when used with a recommended hardware configuration, the Software will perform in substantial conformance with the documentation supplied with the Software; and (ii) the physical media on which the Software is furnished will be free from defects in materials and workmanship under normal use.

(b) MACROMEDIA PROVIDES NO REMEDIES OR WARRANTIES, WHETHER EXPRESS OR IMPLIED, FOR THE SAMPLE APPLICATION CODE OR THE TRIAL VERSION, THE DEVELOPER VERSION AND THE NOT FOR RESALE VERSION OF THE SOFTWARE. THE SAMPLE APPLICATION CODE AND THE TRIAL VERSION, THE DEVELOPER VERSION AND THE NOT FOR RESALE VERSION OF THE SOFTWARE ARE PROVIDED "AS IS".

(c) EXCEPT AS SET FORTH IN THE FOREGOING LIMITED WARRANTY WITH RESPECT TO SOFTWARE OTHER THAN THE SAMPLE APPLICATION CODE AND THE TRIAL VERSION, THE DEVELOPER VERSION AND NOT FOR RESALE VERSION, MACROMEDIA AND ITS SUPPLIERS DISCLAIM ALL OTHER WARRANTIES AND REPRESENTATIONS, WHETHER EXPRESS, IMPLIED, OR OTHERWISE, INCLUDING THE WARRANTIES OF MERCHANTABILITY OR FITNESS FOR A PARTICULAR PURPOSE. ALSO, THERE IS NO WARRANTY OF NON-INFRINGEMENT AND TITLE OR QUIET ENJOYMENT. MACROMEDIA DOES NOT WARRANT THAT THE SOFTWARE IS ERROR-FREE OR WILL OPERATE WITHOUT INTERRUPTION. NO RIGHTS OR REMEDIES REFERRED TO IN ARTICLE 2A OF THE UCC WILL BE CONFERRED ON YOU UNLESS EXPRESSLY GRANTED HEREIN. THE SOFTWARE IS NOT DESIGNED, INTENDED OR LICENSED FOR USE IN HAZARDOUS ENVIRONMENTS REQUIRING FAIL-SAFE CONTROLS, INCLUDING WITHOUT LIMITATION, THE DESIGN, CONSTRUCTION, MAINTENANCE OR OPERATION OF NUCLEAR FACILITIES, AIRCRAFT NAVIGATION OR COMMUNICATION SYSTEMS, AIR TRAFFIC CONTROL, AND LIFE SUPPORT OR WEAPONS SYSTEMS. MACROMEDIA SPECIFICALLY DISCLAIMS ANY EXPRESS OR IMPLIED WARRANTY OF FITNESS FOR SUCH PURPOSES.

(d) IF APPLICABLE LAW REQUIRES ANY WARRANTIES WITH RESPECT TO THE SOFTWARE, ALL SUCH WARRANTIES ARE LIMITED IN DURATION TO NINETY (90) DAYS FROM THE DATE OF DELIVERY.

(e) NO ORAL OR WRITTEN INFORMATION OR ADVICE GIVEN BY MACROMEDIA, ITS DEALERS, DISTRIBUTORS, AGENTS OR EMPLOYEES SHALL CREATE A WARRANTY OR IN ANY WAY INCREASE THE SCOPE OF ANY WARRANTY PROVIDED HEREIN.

(f) SOME JURISDICTIONS DO NOT ALLOW THE EXCLUSION OF IMPLIED WARRANTIES, SO THE ABOVE EXCLUSION MAY NOT APPLY TO YOU. THIS WARRANTY GIVES YOU SPECIFIC LEGAL RIGHTS AND YOU MAY ALSO HAVE OTHER LEGAL RIGHTS THAT VARY FROM STATE TO STATE.

7. Exclusive Remedy

Your exclusive remedy under the preceding is to return the Software to the place you acquired it, with a copy of your receipt and a description of the problem. Provided that any non-compliance with the above warranty is reported in writing to Macromedia no more than ninety (90) days following delivery to you, Macromedia will use reasonable commercial efforts to supply you with a replacement copy of the Software that substantially conforms to the documentation, provide a replacement for defective media, or refund to you your purchase price for the Software, at its option. Macromedia shall have no responsibility if the Software has been altered in any way, if the media has been damaged by misuse, accident, abuse, modification or misapplication, or if the failure arises out of use of the Software with other than a recommended hardware configuration. Any such misuse, accident, abuse, modification or misapplication of the Software will void the warranty above. THIS REMEDY IS THE SOLE AND EXCLUSIVE REMEDY AVAILABLE TO YOU FOR BREACH OF EXPRESS OR IMPLIED WARRANTIES WITH RESPECT TO THE SOFTWARE AND RELATED DOCUMENTATION.

8. LIMITATION OF LIABILITY

(a) NEITHER MACROMEDIA NOR ITS SUPPLIERS SHALL BE LIABLE TO YOU OR ANY THIRD PARTY FOR ANY INDIRECT, SPECIAL, INCIDENTAL, PUNITIVE, COVER OR CONSEQUENTIAL DAMAGES (INCLUDING, BUT NOT LIMITED TO, DAMAGES FOR THE INABILITY TO USE EQUIPMENT OR ACCESS DATA, LOSS OF BUSINESS, LOSS OF PROFITS, BUSINESS INTERRUPTION OR THE LIKE), ARISING OUT OF THE USE OF, OR INABILITY TO USE, THE SOFTWARE AND BASED ON ANY THEORY OF LIABILITY INCLUDING BREACH OF CONTRACT, BREACH OF WARRANTY, TORT (INCLUDING NEGLIGENCE), PRODUCT LIABILITY OR OTHERWISE, EVEN IF MACROMEDIA OR ITS REPRESENTATIVES HAVE BEEN ADVISED OF THE POSSIBILITY OF SUCH DAMAGES AND EVEN IF A REMEDY SET FORTH HEREIN IS FOUND TO HAVE FAILED OF ITS ESSENTIAL PURPOSE.

(b) MACROMEDIA'S TOTAL LIABILITY TO YOU FOR ACTUAL DAMAGES FOR ANY CAUSE WHATSOEVER WILL BE LIMITED TO THE GREATER OF $500 OR THE AMOUNT PAID BY YOU FOR THE SOFTWARE THAT CAUSED SUCH DAMAGE.

(c) SOME JURISDICTIONS DO NOT ALLOW THE LIMITATION OR EXCLUSION OF LIABILITY FOR INCIDENTAL OR CONSEQUENTIAL DAMAGES, SO THE ABOVE LIMITATION OR EXCLUSION MAY NOT APPLY TO YOU AND YOU MAY ALSO HAVE OTHER LEGAL RIGHTS THAT VARY FROM STATE TO STATE.

(d) THE FOREGOING LIMITATIONS ON LIABILITY ARE INTENDED TO APPLY TO THE WARRANTIES AND DISCLAIMERS ABOVE AND ALL OTHER ASPECTS OF THIS EULA.

9. Basis of Bargain

The Limited Warranty and Disclaimer, Exclusive Remedies and Limitation of Liability set forth above are fundamental elements of the basis of the agreement between Macromedia and you. Macromedia would not be able to provide the Software on an economic basis without such limitations. Such Limited Warranty and Disclaimer, Exclusive Remedies and Limitation of Liability inure to the benefit of Macromedia's licensors.

10. U.S. GOVERNMENT RESTRICTED RIGHTS LEGEND

This Software and the documentation are provided with "RESTRICTED RIGHTS" applicable to private and public licenses alike. Without limiting the foregoing, use, duplication, or disclosure by the U.S. Government is subject to restrictions as set forth in this EULA and as provided in DFARS 227.7202-1(a) and 227.7202-3(a) (1995), DFARS 252.227-7013 (c)(1)(ii)(OCT 1988), FAR 12.212(a)(1995), FAR 52.227-19, or FAR 52.227-14, as applicable. Manufacturer: Macromedia, Inc., 600 Townsend, San Francisco, CA 94103.

11. (Outside of the USA) Consumer End Users Only

The limitations or exclusions of warranties and liability contained in this EULA do not affect or prejudice the statutory rights of a consumer, i.e., a person acquiring goods otherwise than in the course of a business.

The limitations or exclusions of warranties, remedies or liability contained in this EULA shall apply to you only to the extent such limitations or exclusions are permitted under the laws of the jurisdiction where you are located.

12. Third Party Software

The Software may contain third party software which requires notices and/or additional terms and conditions. Such required third party software notices and/or additional terms and conditions are located at http://www.macromedia.com/go/thirdparty/ and are made a part of and incorporated by reference into this EULA. By accepting this EULA, you are also accepting the additional terms and conditions, if any, set forth therein.

13. General

This EULA shall be governed by the internal laws of the State of California, without giving effect to principles of conflict of laws. You hereby consent to the exclusive jurisdiction and venue of the state courts sitting in San Francisco County, California or the federal courts in the Northern District of California to resolve any disputes arising under this EULA. In each case this EULA shall be construed and enforced without regard to the United Nations Convention on the International Sale of Goods.

This EULA contains the complete agreement between the parties with respect to the subject matter hereof, and supersedes all prior or contemporaneous agreements or understandings, whether oral or written. You agree that any varying or additional terms contained in any purchase order or other written notification or document issued by you in relation to the Software licensed hereunder shall be of no effect. The failure or delay of Macromedia to exercise any of its rights under this EULA or upon any breach of this EULA shall not be deemed a waiver of those rights or of the breach.

No Macromedia dealer, agent or employee is authorized to make any amendment to this EULA.

If any provision of this Agreement shall be held by a court of competent jurisdiction to be contrary to law, that provision will be enforced to the maximum extent permissible, and the remaining provisions of this Agreement will remain in full force and effect.

All questions concerning this EULA shall be directed to: Macromedia, Inc., 600 Townsend, San Francisco, CA 94103, Attention: General Counsel.

Macromedia and other trademarks contained in the Software are trademarks or registered trademarks of Macromedia, Inc. in the United States and/or other countries. Third party trademarks, trade names, product names and logos may be the trademarks or registered trademarks of their respective owners. You may not remove or alter any trademark, trade names, product names, logo, copyright or other proprietary notices, legends, symbols or labels in the Software. This EULA does not authorize you to use Macromedia's or its licensors' names or any of their respective trademarks.

END-USER LICENSE AGREEMENT FOR MACROMEDIA® DREAMWEAVER® MX 2004

IMPORTANT: THIS SOFTWARE END USER LICENSE AGREEMENT ("EULA") IS A LEGAL AGREEMENT BETWEEN YOU (EITHER AN INDIVIDUAL OR, IF PURCHASED OR OTHERWISE ACQUIRED BY OR FOR AN ENTITY, AN ENTITY) AND MACROMEDIA. READ IT CAREFULLY BEFORE COMPLETING THE INSTALLATION PROCESS AND USING THE SOFTWARE. IT PROVIDES A LICENSE TO USE THE SOFTWARE AND CONTAINS WARRANTY INFORMATION AND LIABILITY DISCLAIMERS. BY INSTALLING AND USING THE SOFTWARE, YOU ARE CONFIRMING YOUR ACCEPTANCE OF THE SOFTWARE AND AGREEING TO BECOME BOUND BY THE TERMS OF THIS AGREEMENT. IF YOU DO NOT AGREE TO BE BOUND BY THESE TERMS, THEN DO NOT INSTALL THE SOFTWARE AND RETURN THE SOFTWARE TO YOUR PLACE OF PURCHASE FOR A FULL REFUND. THIS EULA SHALL APPLY ONLY TO THE SOFTWARE SUPPLIED BY MACROMEDIA HEREWITH REGARDLESS OF WHETHER OTHER SOFTWARE IS REFERRED TO OR DESCRIBED HEREIN.

1. Definitions

(a) "Education Version" means a version of the Software, so identified, for use by students and faculty of educational institutions, only.

(b) "Not For Resale (NFR) Version" means a version, so identified, of the Software to be used to review and evaluate the Software, only.

(c) "Macromedia" means Macromedia, Inc. and its licensors, if any.

(d) "Software" means only the Macromedia software program(s) and third party software programs, in each case, supplied by Macromedia herewith, and corresponding documentation, associated media, printed materials, and online or electronic documentation.

(e) "Trial Version" means a version of the Software, so identified, to be used only to review, demonstrate and evaluate the Software for a limited time period. The Trial Version may have limited features, may lack the ability for the end-user to save the end product, and will cease operating after a predetermined amount of time due to an internal mechanism within the Trial Version.

2. License Grants

The licenses granted in this Section 2 are subject to the terms and conditions set forth in this EULA:

(a) Subject to Section 2(b), you may install and use the Software on a single computer; OR install and store the Software on a storage device, such as a network server, used only to install the Software on your other computers over an internal network, provided you have a license for each separate computer on which the Software is installed and run. Except as otherwise provided in Section 2(b), a license for the Software may not be shared, installed or used concurrently on different computers.

(b) Portable or Home Computer Use for Software Requiring Mandatory Product Activation. For Software requiring Mandatory Production Activation, in addition to the single copy of the Software permitted in Section 2(a), the primary user of the computer on which the Software is installed may make a second copy of the Software and install it on either a portable computer or a computer located at his or her home for his or her exclusive use, provided that:

(A) the second copy of the Software on the portable or home computer (i) is not used at the same time as the copy of the Software on the primary computer and (ii) is used by the primary user solely as allowed for such version or edition (such as for educational use only), (B) the second copy of the Software is not installed or used after the time such user is no longer the primary user of the primary computer on which the Software is installed, and (C) the Software was not licensed under a volume discount.

(c) In the event the Software is distributed along with other Macromedia software products as part of a suite of products (collectively, the "Studio"), the license of the Studio is licensed as a single product and none of the products in the Studio, including the Software, may be separated for installation or use on more than one computer.

(d) You may make one copy of the Software in machine-readable form solely for backup purposes. You must reproduce on any such copy all copyright notices and any other proprietary legends on the original copy of the Software. You may not sell or transfer any copy of the Software made for backup purposes.

(e) You agree that Macromedia may audit your use of the Software for compliance with these terms at any time, upon reasonable notice. In the event that such audit reveals any use of the Software by you other than in full compliance with the terms of this Agreement, you shall reimburse Macromedia for all reasonable expenses related to such audit in addition to any other liabilities you may incur as a result of such non-compliance.

(f) Unless otherwise set forth in the documentation relating to such code and/or the Software or in a separate agreement between you and Macromedia, you may modify the source code form of those portions of such software programs that are identified as sample code, sample application code, or components (each, "Sample Application Code") in the accompanying documentation solely for the purposes of designing, developing and testing websites and website applications developed using Macromedia software programs; provided, however, you are permitted to copy and distribute the Sample Application Code (modified or unmodified) only if all of the following conditions are met: (1) you distribute the compiled object Sample Application Code with your application; (2) you do not include the Sample Application Code in any product or application designed for website development; and (3) you do not use Macromedia's name, logos or other Macromedia trademarks to market your application. You agree to indemnify, hold harmless and defend Macromedia from and against any loss, damage, claims or lawsuits, including attorney's fees, that arise or result from the use or distribution of your application.

(g) You may not use the Macromedia® Breeze™ plug-in for Microsoft® PowerPoint® software to create media content for conversion by any means other than with the use of other Macromedia Breeze products without the express written consent of Macromedia.

(h) Your license rights under this EULA are non-exclusive.

(i) Mandatory Product Activation. The license rights granted under this Agreement may be limited to the first thirty (30) days after you first install the Software unless you supply information required to activate your licensed copy in the manner described during the setup sequence of the Software. You may need to activate the Software through the use of the Internet or telephone; toll charges may apply. There are technological measures in this Software that are designed to prevent unlicensed or illegal use of the Software. You agree that Macromedia may use those measures and you agree to follow any requirements regarding such technological measures. You may also need to reactivate the Software if you modify your computer hardware or alter the Software. Product activation is based on the exchange of information between your computer and Macromedia. None of this information contains personally identifiable information nor can they be used to identify any personal information about you or any characteristics of your computer configuration.

3. License Restrictions

(a) Other than as set forth in Section 2, you may not make or distribute copies of the Software, or electronically transfer the Software from one computer to another or over a network.

(b) You may not alter, merge, modify, adapt or translate the Software, or decompile, reverse engineer, disassemble, or otherwise reduce the Software to a human-perceivable form.

(c) Unless otherwise provided herein, you may not rent, lease, or sublicense the Software.

(d) Other than with respect to a Trial Version or a Not For Resale Version of the Software, you may permanently transfer all of your rights under this EULA only as part of a sale or transfer, provided you retain no copies, you transfer all of the Software (including all component parts, the media and printed materials, any upgrades, this EULA, the serial numbers, and, if applicable, all other software products provided together with the Software), and the recipient agrees to the terms of this EULA. If the Software is an upgrade, any transfer must include all prior versions of the Software from which you are upgrading. If the copy of the Software is licensed as part of the whole Studio (as defined above), the Software shall be transferred only with and as part of the sale or transfer of the whole Studio, and not separately. You may retain no copies of the Software. You may not sell or transfer any Software purchased under a volume discount. You may not sell or transfer any Trial Version or Not For Resale Version of the Software.

(e) Unless otherwise provided herein, you may not modify the Software or create derivative works based upon the Software.

(f) Education Versions may not be used for, or distributed to any party for, any commercial purpose.

(g) Unless otherwise provided herein, you shall not (A) in the aggregate, install or use more than one copy of the Trial Version of the Software, (B) download the Trial Version of the Software under more than one username, (C) alter the contents of a hard drive or computer system to enable the use of the Trial Version of the Software for an aggregate period in excess of the trial period for one license to such Trial Version, (D) disclose the results of software performance benchmarks obtained using the Trial Version to any third party without Macromedia's prior written consent, or (E) use the Trial Version of the Software for a purpose other than the sole purpose of determining whether to purchase a license to a commercial or education version of the software; provided, however, notwithstanding the foregoing, you are strictly prohibited from installing or using the Trial Version of the Software for any commercial training purpose.

(h) You may only use the Not for Resale Version of the Software to review and evaluate the Software.

(i) You may not export the Software into any country prohibited by the United States Export Administration Act and the regulations thereunder.

(j) You may receive the Software in more than one medium but you shall only install or use one medium. Regardless of the number of media you receive, you may use only the medium that is appropriate for the server or computer on which the Software is to be installed.

(k) You may receive the Software in more than one platform but you shall only install or use one platform.

(l) You shall not use the Software to develop any application having the same primary function as the Software.

(m) In the event that you fail to comply with this EULA, Macromedia may terminate the license and you must destroy all copies of the Software (with all other rights of both parties and all other provisions of this EULA surviving any such termination).

(n) Notwithstanding anything herein to the contrary, you may not (A) install FlashPaper Printer on a server for multiple user access or use, or (B) modify or replace the FlashPaper Printer viewer user interface that displays FlashPaper documents.

(o) Your rights to use any Macromedia Flash player, projector, standalone player, plug-in, or ActiveX control, provided to you as part of or with the Software, shall be solely as set forth in the following link, http://www.macromedia.com/go/flashprojectorusage_en. Unless and except as provided therein, you shall have no rights to use or distribute such software.

4. Upgrades

If this copy of the Software is an upgrade from an earlier version of the Software, it is provided to you on a license exchange basis. You agree by your installation and use of such copy of the Software to voluntarily terminate your earlier EULA and that you will not continue to use the earlier version of the Software or transfer it to another person or entity unless such transfer is pursuant to Section 3.

5. Prior Same Version License

If this copy of the Software is licensed as part of the Studio (as defined above), and you have a prior license to the same version of the Software, and the Studio was licensed to you with a discount based, in whole or in part, on your prior license to the same version, the Software is provided to you on a license exchange basis. You agree by your installation and use of this copy of the Software to voluntarily terminate your EULA with respect to such prior license and that you will not continue to install or use such prior license of the Software or transfer it to another person or entity.

6. Ownership

The foregoing license gives you limited license to use the Software. Macromedia and its suppliers retain all right, title and interest, including all copyright and intellectual property rights, in and to, the Software (as an independent work and as an underlying work serving as a basis for any application you may develop), and all copies thereof. All rights not specifically granted in this EULA, including Federal and International Copyrights, are reserved by Macromedia and its suppliers.

7. LIMITED WARRANTY AND DISCLAIMER

(a) Except with respect to any Sample Application Code, Trial Version and Not For Resale Version of the Software, Macromedia warrants that, for a period of ninety (90) days from the date of delivery (as evidenced by a copy of your receipt): (i) when used with a recommended hardware configuration, the Software will perform in substantial conformance with the documentation supplied with the Software; and (ii) the physical media on which the Software is furnished will be free from defects in materials and workmanship under normal use.

(b) MACROMEDIA PROVIDES NO REMEDIES OR WARRANTIES, WHETHER EXPRESS OR IMPLIED, FOR ANY SAMPLE APPLICATION CODE, TRIAL VERSION AND THE NOT FOR RESALE VERSION OF THE SOFTWARE. ANY SAMPLE APPLICATION CODE, TRIAL VERSION AND THE NOT FOR RESALE VERSION OF THE SOFTWARE ARE PROVIDED "AS IS".

(c) EXCEPT AS SET FORTH IN THE FOREGOING LIMITED WARRANTY WITH RESPECT TO SOFT-WARE OTHER THAN ANY SAMPLE APPLICATION CODE, TRIAL VERSION AND NOT FOR RESALE VERSION, MACROMEDIA AND ITS SUPPLIERS DISCLAIM ALL OTHER WARRANTIES AND REPRE-SENTATIONS, WHETHER EXPRESS, IMPLIED, OR OTHERWISE, INCLUDING THE WARRANTIES OF MERCHANTABILITY OR FITNESS FOR A PARTICULAR PURPOSE. ALSO, THERE IS NO WARRANTY OF NON-INFRINGEMENT AND TITLE OR QUIET ENJOYMENT. Macromedia does not warrant that the Software is error-free or will operate without interruption. NO RIGHTS OR REMEDIES REFERRED TO IN AR-TICLE 2A OF THE UCC WILL BE CONFERRED ON YOU UNLESS EXPRESSLY GRANTED HEREIN. The Software is not designed, intended or licensed for use in hazardous environments requiring fail-safe controls, in-cluding without limitation, the design, construction, maintenance or operation of nuclear facilities, aircraft navi-gation or communication systems, air traffic control, and life support or weapons systems. Macromedia specifically disclaims any express or implied warranty of fitness for such purposes.

(d) IF APPLICABLE LAW REQUIRES ANY WARRANTIES WITH RESPECT TO THE SOFTWARE, ALL SUCH WARRANTIES ARE LIMITED IN DURATION TO NINETY (90) DAYS FROM THE DATE OF DE-LIVERY.

(e) No oral or written information or advice given by Macromedia, its dealers, distributors, agents or employees shall create a warranty or in any way increase the scope of ANY warranty PROVIDED HEREIN.

(f) (USA only) SOME STATES DO NOT ALLOW THE EXCLUSION OF IMPLIED WARRANTIES, SO THE ABOVE EXCLUSION MAY NOT APPLY TO YOU. THIS WARRANTY GIVES YOU SPECIFIC LEGAL RIGHTS AND YOU MAY ALSO HAVE OTHER LEGAL RIGHTS THAT VARY FROM STATE TO STATE.

8. Exclusive Remedy

Your exclusive remedy under the preceding is to return the Software to the place you acquired it, with a copy of your receipt and a description of the problem. Provided that any non-compliance with the above warranty is re-ported in writing to Macromedia no more than ninety (90) days following delivery to you, Macromedia will use reasonable commercial efforts to supply you with a replacement copy of the Software that substantially conforms to the documentation, provide a replacement for defective media, or refund to you your purchase price for the Soft-ware, at its option. Macromedia shall have no responsibility if the Software has been altered in any way, if the media has been damaged by misuse, accident, abuse, modification or misapplication, or if the failure arises out of use of the Software with other than a recommended hardware configuration. Any such misuse, accident, abuse, modification or misapplication of the Software will void the warranty above. THIS REMEDY IS THE SOLE AND EXCLUSIVE REMEDY AVAILABLE TO YOU FOR BREACH OF EXPRESS OR IMPLIED WAR-RANTIES WITH RESPECT TO THE SOFTWARE AND RELATED DOCUMENTATION.

9. LIMITATION OF LIABILITY

(a) NEITHER MACROMEDIA NOR ITS SUPPLIERS SHALL BE LIABLE TO YOU OR ANY THIRD PAR-TY FOR ANY INDIRECT, SPECIAL, INCIDENTAL, PUNITIVE, COVER OR CONSEQUENTIAL DAMAG-ES (INCLUDING, BUT NOT LIMITED TO, DAMAGES FOR THE INABILITY TO USE EQUIPMENT OR ACCESS DATA, LOSS OF BUSINESS, LOSS OF PROFITS, BUSINESS INTERRUPTION OR THE LIKE), ARISING OUT OF THE USE OF, OR INABILITY TO USE, THE SOFTWARE AND BASED ON ANY THE-ORY OF LIABILITY INCLUDING BREACH OF CONTRACT, BREACH OF WARRANTY, TORT (IN-CLUDING NEGLIGENCE), PRODUCT LIABILITY OR OTHERWISE, EVEN IF MACROMEDIA OR ITS REPRESENTATIVES HAVE BEEN ADVISED OF THE POSSIBILITY OF SUCH DAMAGES AND EVEN IF A REMEDY SET FORTH HEREIN IS FOUND TO HAVE FAILED OF ITS ESSENTIAL PURPOSE.

(b) MACROMEDIA'S TOTAL LIABILITY TO YOU FOR ACTUAL DAMAGES FOR ANY CAUSE WHAT-SOEVER WILL BE LIMITED TO THE GREATER OF $500 OR THE AMOUNT PAID BY YOU FOR THE SOFTWARE THAT CAUSED SUCH DAMAGE.

(c) (USA only) SOME STATES DO NOT ALLOW THE LIMITATION OR EXCLUSION OF LIABILITY FOR INCIDENTAL OR CONSEQUENTIAL DAMAGES, SO THE ABOVE LIMITATION OR EXCLUSION MAY NOT APPLY TO YOU AND YOU MAY ALSO HAVE OTHER LEGAL RIGHTS THAT VARY FROM STATE TO STATE.

(d) THE FOREGOING LIMITATIONS ON LIABILITY ARE INTENDED TO APPLY TO THE WARRAN-
TIES AND DISCLAIMERS ABOVE AND ALL OTHER ASPECTS OF THIS EULA.

10. Basis of Bargain

The Limited Warranty and Disclaimer, Exclusive Remedies and Limited Liability set forth above are fundamental
elements of the basis of the agreement between Macromedia and you. Macromedia would not be able to provide
the Software on an economic basis without such limitations. Such Limited Warranty and Disclaimer, Exclusive
Remedies and Limited Liability inure to the benefit of Macromedia's licensors.

11. U.S. GOVERNMENT RESTRICTED RIGHTS LEGEND

This Software and the documentation are provided with "RESTRICTED RIGHTS" applicable to private and public licenses alike. Without limiting the foregoing, use, duplication, or disclosure by the U.S. Government is subject
to restrictions as set forth in this EULA and as provided in DFARS 227.7202-1(a) and 227.7202-3(a) (1995),
DFARS 252.227-7013 (c)(1)(ii)(OCT 1988), FAR 12.212(a)(1995), FAR 52.227-19, or FAR 52.227-14, as applicable. Manufacturer: Macromedia, Inc., 600 Townsend, San Francisco, CA 94103.

12. (Outside of the USA) Consumer End Users Only

The limitations or exclusions of warranties and liability contained in this EULA do not affect or prejudice the statutory rights of a consumer, i.e., a person acquiring goods otherwise than in the course of a business.

The limitations or exclusions of warranties, remedies or liability contained in this EULA shall apply to you only
to the extent such limitations or exclusions are permitted under the laws of the jurisdiction where you are located.

13. Third Party Software

The Software may contain third party software which requires notices and/or additional terms and conditions.
Such required third party software notices and/or additional terms and conditions are located at http://www.mac-
romedia.com/go/thirdparty/ and are made a part of and incorporated by reference into this EULA. By accepting
this EULA, you are also accepting the additional terms and conditions, if any, set forth therein.

14. General

This EULA shall be governed by the internal laws of the State of California, without giving effect to principles of
conflict of laws. You hereby consent to the exclusive jurisdiction and venue of the state courts sitting in San Francisco County, California or the federal courts in the Northern District of California to resolve any disputes arising
under this EULA. In each case this EULA shall be construed and enforced without regard to the United Nations
Convention on the International Sale of Goods.

This EULA contains the complete agreement between the parties with respect to the subject matter hereof, and
supersedes all prior or contemporaneous agreements or understandings, whether oral or written. You agree that
any varying or additional terms contained in any purchase order or other written notification or document issued
by you in relation to the Software licensed hereunder shall be of no effect. The failure or delay of Macromedia to
exercise any of its rights under this EULA or upon any breach of this EULA shall not be deemed a waiver of those
rights or of the breach.

No Macromedia dealer, agent or employee is authorized to make any amendment to this EULA.

If any provision of this EULA shall be held by a court of competent jurisdiction to be contrary to law, that provision will be enforced to the maximum extent permissible, and the remaining provisions of this EULA will remain
in full force and effect.

All questions concerning this EULA shall be directed to: Macromedia, Inc., 600 Townsend, San Francisco, CA
94103, Attention: General Counsel.

Macromedia and other trademarks contained in the Software are trademarks or registered trademarks of Macromedia, Inc. in the United States and/or other countries. Third party trademarks, trade names, product names and
logos may be the trademarks or registered trademarks of their respective owners. You may not remove or alter any
trademark, trade names, product names, logo, copyright or other proprietary notices, legends, symbols or labels
in the Software. This EULA does not authorize you to use Macromedia's or its licensors' names or any of their
respective trademarks.

OPERA BROWSER SOFTWARE END USER LICENSE AGREEMENT

IN THE EVENT OPERA BROWSER SOFTWARE IS PROVIDED IN OR ALONG WITH THE SOFTWARE
DESCRIBED ABOVE, WITH RESPECT TO THE USE OF SUCH OPERA BROWSER SOFTWARE ONLY,
THE FOLLOWING END USER LICENSE AGREEMENT SHALL GOVERN:

Opera Browser Information: LICENSE.TXT

Copyright (C) Opera Software 1995-2003

IMPORTANT NOTE

The Software, as defined below, is protected by copyright, which are vested in Opera Software ASA/its suppliers.

Registration codes, as defined below, are protected by copyright, which is vested in Opera Software ASA.

The Software and Registration Codes may only be used in accordance with the terms and conditions set out in this document.

If you do not read and agree to be bound by the terms and conditions defined in this document, you are not permitted to keep or use the Software or Registration Codes in any way whatsoever and must destroy or return all copies of these items which are in your possession.

To make personalized advertising possible, users of the ad-sponsored software may provide ad-related profile information on strictly a voluntary basis. The Opera Software ASA privacy policy, found at http://www.opera.com/privacy/ governs the use of such profile information.

END USER LICENSE AGREEMENT

DEFINITIONS

The following definitions apply to the terms and conditions included in this Agreement.

Opera

means a Browser, developed by Opera Software ASA, for reading and writing files to and from a network and/or file system.

Software

means Opera, all program and information files and other documentation which are part of the Opera Software package, with the exception of the Registration Codes.

Registration Code

registers a paid version of the software. This disables the advertising banner in the Browser's top right hand corner, and removes advertising content which has been cached.

Individualmeans a particular person.

TERMS OF AGREEMENT

This is a legal agreement between you, the users, and Opera Software ASA. By installing or using this Software, you agree to be bound by the terms of this agreement. If you do not agree to those terms, you may not use or install the Software.

You are entitled to use your copy of the Software on one computer. "Use" means loaded in temporary memory or permanent storage on the computer. Installation on a network server for distribution to other computers is not allowed, unless you have a separate license for each computer to which the Software is distributed. You are obligated to have a reasonable process to assure that the number of persons using the Software concurrently does not exceed the number of licenses.

The Software is protected by Norwegian and United States copyright laws and international treaties. You may make one copy of the Software solely for backup or archival purposes or transfer it to a single hard disk provided you keep the original disk solely for backup or archival purposes. You may not rent or lease the Software or copy any written materials accompanying the Software. You may transfer the Software and all accompanying materials to another individual on a permanent basis, if you retain no copies and the recipient agrees to the terms of this Agreement. Any transfer must include the most recent update and all prior versions.

All intellectual property rights such as but not limited to patents, trademarks, copyrights or trade secret rights related to the Software are the property of and remains vested in Opera Software ASA/its suppliers.

You shall not modify, translate, reverse engineer, decompile or disassemble the Software or any part thereof or otherwise attempt to derive source code or create derivative works therefrom.

You are not allowed to remove, alter or destroy any proprietary, trademark or copyright markings or notices placed upon or contained with the Software.

Registration Codes may be used, stored or copied only by the person or organization, which has licensed the Software, and solely for the purpose of using the Software within the terms and conditions of this Agreement. No person or organization is permitted to store or copy a Registration Code for any other purpose without written agreement from Opera Software ASA.

The cpyright of all Registration Codes remains vested in Opera Software ASA which reserves the right to withhold or withdraw authorization of use of all Registration Codes issued to a person or organization if there is reasonable evidence to indicate that the person or organization is involved in a breach of the terms of this document.

YOU EXPRESSLY ACKNOWLEDGE AND AGREE THAT USE OF THE SOFTWARE IS AT YOUR OWN RISK AND THAT THE SOFTWARE IS PROVIDED "AS IS" WITHOUT ANY WARRANTIES OR CONDITIONS WHATSOEVER. OPERA SOFTWARE ASA OR ITS SUPPLIERS DOES NOT WARRANT THAT THE FUNCTIONS OF THE SOFTWARE WILL MEET YOUR REQUIREMENTS OR THAT THE OPERATION OF THE SOFTWARE WILL BE UNINTERRUPTED OR ERROR FREE. YOU ASSUME RESPONSI-

BILITY FOR SELECTING THE SOFTWARE TO ACHIEVE YOUR INTENDED RESULTS, AND FOR THE USE AND THE RESULTS OBTAINED FROM THE SOFTWARE.

YOU ACKNOWLEDGE THAT THE SOFTWARE IS NOT INTENDED FOR USE IN (I) ON-LINE CONTROL OF AIRCRAFT, AIR TRAFFIC, AIRCRAFT NAVIGATION OR AIRCRAFT COMMUNICATIONS; OR (II) IN THE DESIGN, CONSTRUCTION, OPERATION OR MAINTENANCE OF ANY NUCLEAR FACILITY.

OPERA SOFTWARE ASA AND ITS SUPPLIERS DISCLAIM ALL WARRANTIES, EXPRESS OR IMPLIED, INCLUDING BUT NOT LIMITED TO WARRANTIES RELATED TO: NON-INFRINGEMENT, LACK OF VIRUSES, ACCURACY OR COMPLETENESS OF RESPONSES OR RESULTS, IMPLIED WARRANTIES OF MERCHANTABILITY AND FITNESS FOR A PARTICULAR PURPOSE .

IN NO EVENT SHALL OPERA SOFTWARE ASA OR ITS SUPPLIERS BE LIABLE FOR ANY INDIRECT, INCIDENTAL, SPECIAL OR CONSEQUENTIAL DAMAGES OR FOR ANY DAMAGES WHATSOEVER (INCLUDING BUT NOT LIMITED TO DAMAGES FOR LOSS OF BUSINESS PROFITS, BUSINESS INTERRUPTION, LOSS OF BUSINESS INFORMATION, PERSONAL INJURY, LOSS OF PRIVACY OR OTHER PECUNIARY OR OTHER LOSS WHATSOEVER) ARISING OUT OF USE OR INABILITY TO USE THE SOFTWARE, EVEN IF ADVISED OF THE POSSIBILITY OF SUCH DAMAGES. OPERA SOFTWARE ASA ALSO DISCLAIMS ALL LIABILITY FOR ACTS OR MATERIAL PRESENTED BY THE ADVERTISER, AD-SERVING PARTNERS OR OTHERS (INCLUDING UNAUTHORIZED USERS, OR "CRACKERS"). REGARDLESS OF THE FORM OF ACTION, OPERA SOFTWARE ASA AND ITS SUPPLIERS AGGREGATE LIABILITY ARISING OUT OF OR RELATED TO THIS AGREEMENT SHALL NOT EXCEED THE TOTAL AMOUNT PAYABLE BY YOU UNDER THIS AGREEMENT. THE FOREGOING LIMITATIONS, EXCLUSIONS AND DISCLAIMERS SHALL APPLY TO THE MAXIMUM EXTENT ALLOWED BY APPLICABLE LAW.

The Software may be subject to export or import regulations, and the user agrees to comply strictly with all such laws and regulations. The user agrees not to export or re-export the Software or any part thereof or information pertaining thereto to any country for which a U.S. government agency requires an export license or other governmental approval without first obtaining such license or approval.

Notice to U.S. Government Users: The Software and any associated documentation are "Commercial Items," as that term is defined at 48 C.F.R. 2.101, consisting of "Commercial Computer Software" and "Commercial Computer Software Documentation," as such terms are used in 48 C.F.R. 12.212 or 48 C.F.R. 227.7202, as applicable. Consistent with 48 C.F.R. 12.212 or 48 C.F.R. 227.7202-1 through 227.7202-4, as applicable, the Commercial Computer Software and Commercial Computer Software Documentation are licensed to U.S. Government end users (a) only as Commercial Items and (b) with only those rights as are granted to all other end users pursuant to the terms and conditions herein.

Privacy statement: Opera Software ASA strives to protect the security and privacy of the users of its products, and will strictly protect the security of the users personal information, within the confines of the Opera domain. The Opera Software ASA privacy statement found at http://www.opera.com/privacy/, is incorporated in this Agreement by reference.

Any variation to the terms of this Agreement shall only be valid if made in writing by Opera Software ASA.

Any and all disputes arising out of the rights and obligations in this Agreement shall be submitted to ordinary court proceedings. You accept the Oslo City Court as legal venue under this Agreement.

This Agreement shall be governed by Norwegian law, and the stipulations set forth herein to be construed in accordance with same.

Postal enquiries:

Opera Software ASA

Postboks 2648 St. Hanshaugen

NO-0131 OSLO

NORWAY

Office Hours: 9:00am - 4:00pm (+1 GMT) Monday - Friday

Phone: +47 24 16 40 00

Fax: +47 24 16 40 01

Please visit our Web site before you send us e-mail. We provide many services to our users that will help us respond to you faster than if we receive e-mail.

Web site:

http://www.opera.com/

Contact us:

http://www.opera.com/contact/

END-USER LICENSE AGREEMENT FOR MACROMEDIA® FLASH™ MX 2004

ATTENTION: YOU MAY NEED TO SCROLL DOWN TO THE END OF THIS EULA BEFORE YOU CAN AGREE TO THE EULA AND CONTINUE WITH THE SOFTWARE INSTALLATION. IMPORTANT: THIS SOFTWARE END USER LICENSE AGREEMENT ("EULA") IS A LEGAL AGREEMENT BETWEEN YOU (EITHER AN INDIVIDUAL OR, IF PURCHASED OR OTHERWISE ACQUIRED BY OR FOR AN ENTITY, AN ENTITY) AND MACROMEDIA. READ IT CAREFULLY BEFORE COMPLETING THE INSTALLATION PROCESS AND USING THE SOFTWARE. IT PROVIDES A LICENSE TO USE THE SOFTWARE AND CONTAINS WARRANTY INFORMATION AND LIABILITY DISCLAIMERS. BY INSTALLING AND USING THE SOFTWARE, YOU ARE CONFIRMING YOUR ACCEPTANCE OF THE SOFTWARE AND AGREEING TO BECOME BOUND BY THE TERMS OF THIS AGREEMENT. IF YOU DO NOT AGREE TO BE BOUND BY THESE TERMS, THEN DO NOT INSTALL THE SOFTWARE AND RETURN THE SOFTWARE TO YOUR PLACE OF PURCHASE FOR A FULL REFUND. THIS EULA SHALL APPLY ONLY TO THE SOFTWARE SUPPLIED BY MACROMEDIA HEREWITH REGARDLESS OF WHETHER OTHER SOFTWARE IS REFERRED TO OR DESCRIBED HEREIN.

1. Definitions

(a) "Education Version" means a version of the Software, so identified, for use by students and faculty of educational institutions, only.

(b) "Not For Resale (NFR) Version" means a version, so identified, of the Software to be used to review and evaluate the Software, only.

(c) "Macromedia" means Macromedia, Inc. and its licensors, if any.

(d) "Software" means only the Macromedia software program(s) and third party software programs, in each case, supplied by Macromedia herewith, and corresponding documentation, associated media, printed materials, and online or electronic documentation.

(e) "Trial Version" means a version of the Software, so identified, to be used only to review, demonstrate and evaluate the Software for a limited time period. The Trial Version may have limited features, may lack the ability for the end-user to save the end product, and will cease operating after a predetermined amount of time due to an internal mechanism within the Trial Version.

2. License Grants

The licenses granted in this Section 2 are subject to the terms and conditions set forth in this EULA:

(a) Subject to Section 2(b), you may install and use the Software on a single computer; OR install and store the Software on a storage device, such as a network server, used only to install the Software on your other computers over an internal network, provided you have a license for each separate computer on which the Software is installed and run. Except as otherwise provided in Section 2(b), a license for the Software may not be shared, installed or used concurrently on different computers.

(b) Portable or Home Computer Use for Software Requiring Mandatory Product Activation. For Software requiring Mandatory Production Activation, in addition to the single copy of the Software permitted in Section 2(a), the primary user of the computer on which the Software is installed may make a second copy of the Software and install it on either a portable computer or a computer located at his or her home for his or her exclusive use, provided that: (A) the second copy of the Software on the portable or home computer (i) is not used at the same time as the copy of the Software on the primary computer and (ii) is used by the primary user solely as allowed for such version or edition (such as for educational use only), (B) the second copy of the Software is not installed or used after the time such user is no longer the primary user of the primary computer on which the Software is installed, and (C) the Software was not licensed under a volume discount.

(c) In the event the Software is distributed along with other Macromedia software products as part of a suite of products (collectively, the "Studio"), the license of the Studio is licensed as a single product and none of the products in the Studio, including the Software, may be separated for installation or use on more than one computer.

(d) You may make one copy of the Software in machine-readable form solely for backup purposes. You must reproduce on any such copy all copyright notices and any other proprietary legends on the original copy of the Software. You may not sell or transfer any copy of the Software made for backup purposes.

(e) You agree that Macromedia may audit your use of the Software for compliance with these terms at any time, upon reasonable notice. In the event that such audit reveals any use of the Software by you other than in full compliance with the terms of this Agreement, you shall reimburse Macromedia for all reasonable expenses related to such audit in addition to any other liabilities you may incur as a result of such non-compliance.

(f) Unless otherwise set forth in the documentation relating to such code and/or the Software or in a separate agreement between you and Macromedia, you may modify the source code form of those portions of such software programs that are identified as sample code, sample application code, or components (each, "Sample Application Code") in the accompanying documentation solely for the purposes of designing, developing and testing websites and website applications developed using Macromedia software programs; provided, however, you are permitted to copy and distribute the Sample Application Code (modified or unmodified) only if all of the following conditions are met: (1) you distribute the compiled object Sample Application Code with your application; (2) you do not include the Sample Application Code in any product or application designed for website development; and (3) you do not use Macromedia's name, logos or other Macromedia trademarks to market your application. You agree to indemnify, hold harmless nd defend Macromedia from and against any loss, damage, claims or lawsuits, including attorney's fees, that arise or result from the use or distribution of your application.

(g) You may not use the MACROMEDIA® Breeze™ plug-in for Microsoft® PowerPoint® software to create media content for conversion by any means other than with the use of other Macromedia Breeze products without the express written consent of Macromedia.

(h) Your license rights under this EULA are non-exclusive.

(i) Mandatory Product Activation. The license rights granted under this Agreement may be limited to the first thirty (30) days after you first install the Software unless you supply information required to activate your licensed copy in the manner described during the setup sequence of the Software. You may need to activate the Software through the use of the Internet or telephone; toll charges may apply. There are technological measures in this Software that are designed to prevent unlicensed or illegal use of the Software. You agree that Macromedia may use those measures and you agree to follow any requirements regarding such technological measures. You may also need to reactivate the Software if you modify your computer hardware or alter the Software. Product activation is based on the exchange of information between your computer and Macromedia. None of this information contains personally identifiable information nor can they be used to identify any personal information about you or any characteristics of your computer configuration. 3. License Restrictions

(a) Other than as set forth in Section 2, you may not make or distribute copies of the Software, or electronically transfer the Software from one computer to another or over a network.

(b) You may not alter, merge, modify, adapt or translate the Software, or decompile, reverse engineer, disassemble, or otherwise reduce the Software to a human-perceivable form.

(c) Unless otherwise provided herein, you may not rent, lease, or sublicense the Software.

(d) Other than with respect to a Trial Version or a Not For Resale Version of the Software, you may permanently transfer all of your rights under this EULA only as part of a sale or transfer, provided you retain no copies, you transfer all of the Software (including all component parts, the media and printed materials, any upgrades, this EULA, the serial numbers, and, if applicable, all other software products provided together with the Software), and the recipient agrees to the terms of this EULA. If the Software is an upgrade, any transfer must include all prior versions of the Software from which you are upgrading. If the copy of the Software is licensed as part of the whole Studio (as defined above), the Software shall be transferred only with and as part of the sale or transfer of the whole Studio, and not separately. You may retain no copies of the Software. You may not sell or transfer any Software purchased under a volume discount. You may not sell or transfer any Trial Version or Not For Resale Version of the Software.

(e) Unless otherwise provided herein, you may not modify the Software or create derivative works based upon the Software.

(f) Education Versions may not be used for, or distributed to any party for, any commercial purpose.

(g) Unless otherwise provided herein, you shall not (A) in the aggregate, install or use more than one copy of the Trial Version of the Software, (B) download the Trial Version of the Software under more than one username, (C) alter the contents of a hard drive or computer system to enable the use of the Trial Version of the Software for an aggregate period in excess of the trial period for one license to such Trial Version, (D) disclose the results of software performance benchmarks obtained using the Trial Version to any third party without MACROMEDIA®s prior written consent, or (E) use the Trial Version of the Software for a purpose other than the sole purpose of determining whether to purchase a license to a commercial or education version of the software; provided, however, notwithstanding the foregoing, you are strictly prohibited from installing or using the Trial Version of the Software for any commercial training purpose.

(h) You may only use the Not for Resale Version of the Software to review and evaluate the Software.

(i) You may not export the Software into any country prohibited by the United States Export Administration Act and the regulations thereunder.

(j) You may receive the Software in more than one medium but you shall only install or use one medium. Regardless of the number of media you receive, you may use only the medium that is appropriate for the server or computer on which the Software is to be installed.

(k) You may receive the Software in more than one platform but you shall only install or use one platform.

(l) You shall not use the Software to develop any application having the same primary function as the Software.

(m) In the event that you fail to comply with this EULA, Macromedia may terminate the license and you must destroy all copies of the Software (with all other rights of both parties and all other provisions of this EULA surviving any such termination).

(n) Notwithstanding anything herein to the contrary, you may not (A) install FlashPaper Printer on a server for multiple user access or use, or (B) modify or replace the FlashPaper Printer viewer user interface that displays FlashPaper documents.

(o) Your rights to use any Macromedia Flash player, projector, standalone player, plug-in, or ActiveX control, provided to you as part of or with the Software, shall be solely as set forth in the following link, . Unless and except as provided therein, you shall have no rights to use or distribute such software.

4. Upgrades

If this copy of the Software is an upgrade from an earlier version of the Software, it is provided to you on a license exchange basis. You agree by your installation and use of such copy of the Software to voluntarily terminate your earlier EULA and that you will not continue to use the earlier version of the Software or transfer it to another person or entity unless such transfer is pursuant to Section 3.

5. Prior Same Version License

If this copy of the Software is licensed as part of the Studio (as defined above), and you have a prior license to the same version of the Software, and the Studio was licensed to you with a discount based, in whole or in part, on your prior license to the same version, the Software is provided to you on a license exchange basis. You agree by your installation and use of this copy of the Software to voluntarily terminate your EULA with respect to such prior license and that you will not continue to install or use such prior license of the Software or transfer it to another person or entity.

6. Ownership

The foregoing license gives you limited license to use the Software. Macromedia and its suppliers retain all right, title and interest, including all copyright and intellectual property rights, in and to, the Software (as an independent work and as an underlying work serving as a basis for any application you may develop), and all copies thereof. All rights not specifically granted in this EULA, including Federal and International Copyrights, are reserved by Macromedia and its suppliers.

7. LIMITED WARRANTY AND DISCLAIMER

(a) Except with respect to any Sample Application Code, Trial Version and Not For Resale Version of the Software, Macromedia warrants that, for a period of ninety (90) days from the date of delivery (as evidenced by a copy of your receipt): (i) when used with a recommended hardware configuration, the Software will perform in substantial conformance with the documentation supplied with the Software; and (ii) the physical media on which the Software is furnished will be free from defects in materials and workmanship under normal use.

(b) MACROMEDIA PROVIDES NO REMEDIES OR WARRANTIES, WHETHER EXPRESS OR IMPLIED, FOR ANY SAMPLE APPLICATION CODE, TRIAL VERSION AND THE NOT FOR RESALE VERSION OF THE SOFTWARE. ANY SAMPLE APPLICATION CODE, TRIAL VERSION AND THE NOT FOR RESALE VERSION OF THE SOFTWARE ARE PROVIDED "AS IS".

(c) EXCEPT AS SET FORTH IN THE FOREGOING LIMITED WARRANTY WITH RESPECT TO SOFTWARE OTHER THAN ANY SAMPLE APPLICATION CODE, TRIAL VERSION AND NOT FOR RESALE VERSION, MACROMEDIA AND ITS SUPPLIERS DISCLAIM ALL OTHER WARRANTIES AND REPRESENTATIONS, WHETHER EXPRESS, IMPLIED, OR OTHERWISE, INCLUDING THE WARRANTIES OF MERCHANTABILITY OR FITNESS FOR A PARTICULAR PURPOSE. ALSO, THERE IS NO WARRANTY OF NON-INFRINGEMENT AND TITLE OR QUIET ENJOYMENT. MACROMEDIA DOES NOT WARRANT THAT THE SOFTWARE IS ERROR-FREE OR WILL OPERATE WITHOUT INTERRUPTION. NO RIGHTS OR REMEDIES REFERRED TO IN ARTICLE 2A OF THE UCC WILL BE CONFERRED ON YOU UNLESS EXPRESSLY GRANTED HEREIN. THE SOFTWARE IS NOT DESIGNED, INTENDED OR LICENSED FOR USE IN HAZARDOUS ENVIRONMENTS REQUIRING FAIL-SAFE CONTROLS, INCLUDING WITHOUT LIMITATION, THE DESIGN, CONSTRUCTION, MAINTENANCE OR OPERA-

TION OF NUCLEAR FACILITIES, AIRCRAFT NAVIGATION OR COMMUNICATION SYSTEMS, AIR TRAFFIC CONTROL, AND LIFE SUPPORT OR WEAPONS SYSTEMS. MACROMEDIA SPECIFICALLY DISCLAIMS ANY EXPRESS OR IMPLIED WARRANTY OF FITNESS FOR SUCH PURPOSES.

(d) IF APPLICABLE LAW REQUIRES ANY WARRANTIES WITH RESPECT TO THE SOFTWARE, ALL SUCH WARRANTIES ARE LIMITED IN DURATION TO NINETY (90) DAYS FROM THE DATE OF DELIVERY.

(e) NO ORAL OR WRITTEN INFORMATION OR ADVICE GIVEN BY MACROMEDIA, ITS DEALERS, DISTRIBUTORS, AGENTS OR EMPLOYEES SHALL CREATE A WARRANTY OR IN ANY WAY INCREASE THE SCOPE OF ANY WARRANTY PROVIDED HEREIN.

(f) (USA only) SOME STATES DO NOT ALLOW THE EXCLUSION OF IMPLIED WARRANTIES, SO THE ABOVE EXCLUSION MAY NOT APPLY TO YOU. THIS WARRANTY GIVES YOU SPECIFIC LEGAL RIGHTS AND YOU MAY ALSO HAVE OTHER LEGAL RIGHTS THAT VARY FROM STATE TO STATE.

8. Exclusive Remedy

Your exclusive remedy under the preceding is to return the Software to the place you acquired it, with a copy of your receipt and a description of the problem. Provided that any non-compliance with the above warranty is reported in writing to Macromedia no more than ninety (90) days following delivery to you, Macromedia will use reasonable commercial efforts to supply you with a replacement copy of the Software that substantially conforms to the documentation, provide a replacement for defective media, or refund to you your purchase price for the Software, at its option. Macromedia shall have no responsibility if the Software has been altered in any way, if the media has been damaged by misuse, accident, abuse, modification or misapplication, or if the failure arises out of use of the Software with other than a recommended hardware configuration. Any such misuse, accident, abuse, modification or misapplication of the Software will void the warranty above. THIS REMEDY IS THE SOLE AND EXCLUSIVE REMEDY AVAILABLE TO YOU FOR BREACH OF EXPRESS OR IMPLIED WARRANTIES WITH RESPECT TO THE SOFTWARE AND RELATED DOCUMENTATION.

9. LIMITATION OF LIABILITY

(a) NEITHER MACROMEDIA NOR ITS SUPPLIERS SHALL BE LIABLE TO YOU OR ANY THIRD PARTY FOR ANY INDIRECT, SPECIAL, INCIDENTAL, PUNITIVE, COVER OR CONSEQUENTIAL DAMAGES (INCLUDING, BUT NOT LIMITED TO, DAMAGES FOR THE INABILITY TO USE EQUIPMENT OR ACCESS DATA, LOSS OF BUSINESS, LOSS OF PROFITS, BUSINESS INTERRUPTION OR THE LIKE), ARISING OUT OF THE USE OF, OR INABILITY TO USE, THE SOFTWARE AND BASED ON ANY THEORY OF LIABILITY INCLUDING BREACH OF CONTRACT, BREACH OF WARRANTY, TORT (INCLUDING NEGLIGENCE), PRODUCT LIABILITY OR OTHERWISE, EVEN IF MACROMEDIA OR ITS REPRESENTATIVES HAVE BEEN ADVISED OF THE POSSIBILITY OF SUCH DAMAGES AND EVEN IF A REMEDY SET FORTH HEREIN IS FOUND TO HAVE FAILED OF ITS ESSENTIAL PURPOSE.

(b) MACROMEDIA'S TOTAL LIABILITY TO YOU FOR ACTUAL DAMAGES FOR ANY CAUSE WHATSOEVER WILL BE LIMITED TO THE GREATER OF $500 OR THE AMOUNT PAID BY YOU FOR THE SOFTWARE THAT CAUSED SUCH DAMAGE.

(c) (USA only) SOME STATES DO NOT ALLOW THE LIMITATION OR EXCLUSION OF LIABILITY FOR INCIDENTAL OR CONSEQUENTIAL DAMAGES, SO THE ABOVE LIMITATION OR EXCLUSION MAY NOT APPLY TO YOU AND YOU MAY ALSO HAVE OTHER LEGAL RIGHTS THAT VARY FROM STATE TO STATE.

(d) THE FOREGOING LIMITATIONS ON LIABILITY ARE INTENDED TO APPLY TO THE WARRANTIES AND DISCLAIMERS ABOVE AND ALL OTHER ASPECTS OF THIS EULA.

10. Basis of Bargain

The Limited Warranty and Disclaimer, Exclusive Remedies and Limited Liability set forth above are fundamental elements of the basis of the agreement between Macromedia and you. Macromedia would not be able to provide the Software on an economic basis without such limitations. Such Limited Warranty and Disclaimer, Exclusive Remedies and Limited Liability inure to the benefit of MACROMEDIA®s licensors.

11. U.S. GOVERNMENT RESTRICTED RIGHTS LEGEND

This Software and the documentation are provided with "RESTRICTED RIGHTS" applicable to private and public licenses alike. Without limiting the foregoing, use, duplication, or disclosure by the U.S. Government is subject to restrictions as set forth in this EULA and as provided in DFARS 227.7202-1(a) and 227.7202-3(a) (1995), DFARS 252.227-7013 (c)(1)(ii)(OCT 1988), FAR 12.212(a)(1995), FAR 52.227-19, or FAR 52.227-14, as applicable. Manufacturer: Macromedia, Inc., 600 Townsend, San Francisco, CA 94103.

12. (Outside of the USA) Consumer End Users Only

The limitations or exclusions of warranties and liability contained in this EULA do not affect or prejudice the statutory rights of a consumer, i.e., a person acquiring goods otherwise than in the course of a business.

The limitations or exclusions of warranties, remedies or liability contained in this EULA shall apply to you only to the extent such limitations or exclusions are permitted under the laws of the jurisdiction where you are located. 13. Third Party Software

The Software may contain third party software which requires notices and/or additional terms and conditions. Such required third party software notices and/or additional terms and conditions are located at http://www.macromedia.com/go/thirdparty/ and are made a part of and incorporated by reference into this EULA. By accepting this EULA, you are also accepting the additional terms and conditions, if any, set forth therein.

14. General

This EULA shall be governed by the internal laws of the State of California, without giving effect to principles of conflict of laws. You hereby consent to the exclusive jurisdiction and venue of the state courts sitting in San Francisco County, California or the federal courts in the Northern District of California to resolve any disputes arising under this EULA. In each case this EULA shall be construed and enforced without regard to the United Nations Convention on the International Sale of Goods. This EULA contains the complete agreement between the parties with respect to the subject matter hereof, and supersedes all prior or contemporaneous agreements or understandings, whether oral or written. You agree that any varying or additional terms contained in any purchase order or other written notification or document issued by you in relation to the Software licensed hereunder shall be of no effect. The failure or delay of Macromedia to exercise any of its rights under this EULA or upon any breach of this EULA shall not be deemed a waiver of those rights or of the breach.

No Macromedia dealer, agent or employee is authorized to make any amendment to this EULA.

If any provision of this EULA shall be held by a court of competent jurisdiction to be contrary to law, that provision will be enforced to the maximum extent permissible, and the remaining provisions of this EULA will remain in full force and effect.

All questions concerning this EULA shall be directed to: Macromedia, Inc., 600 Townsend, San Francisco, CA 94103, Attention: General Counsel.

Macromedia and other trademarks contained in the Software are trademarks or registered trademarks of Macromedia, Inc. in the United States and/or other countries. Third party trademarks, trade names, product names and logos may be the trademarks or registered trademarks of their respective owners. You may not remove or alter any trademark, trade names, product names, logo, copyright or other proprietary notices, legends, symbols or labels in the Software. This EULA does not authorize you to use MACROMEDIA®s or its licensors' names or any of their respective trademarks.

OPERA BROWSER SOFTWARE END USER LICENSE AGREEMENT

IN THE EVENT OPERA BROWSER SOFTWARE IS PROVIDED IN OR ALONG WITH THE SOFTWARE DESCRIBED ABOVE, WITH RESPECT TO THE USE OF SUCH OPERA BROWSER SOFTWARE ONLY, THE FOLLOWING END USER LICENSE AGREEMENT SHALL GOVERN:

Opera Browser Information: LICENSE.TXT

Copyright (C) Opera Software 1995-2003

IMPORTANT NOTE

The Software, as defined below, is protected by copyright, which are vested in Opera Software ASA/its suppliers.

Registration codes, as defined below, are protected by copyright, which is vested in Opera Software ASA.

The Software and Registration Codes may only be used in accordance with the terms and conditions set out in this document.

If you do not read and agree to be bound by the terms and conditions defined in this document, you are not permitted to keep or use the Software or Registration Codes in any way whatsoever and must destroy or return all copies of these items which are in your possession.

To make personalized advertising possible, users of the ad-sponsored software may provide ad-related profile information on strictly a voluntary basis. The Opera Software ASA privacy policy, found at governs the use of such profile information.

END USER LICENSE AGREEMENT

DEFINITIONS

The following definitions apply to the terms and conditions included in this Agreement.

Opera

means a Browser, developed by Opera Software ASA, for reading and writing files to and from a network and/or file system.

Software

means Opera, all program and information files and other documentation which are part of the Opera Software package, with the exception of the Registration Codes.

Registration Code registers a paid version of the software. This disables the advertising banner in the Browser's top right hand corner, and removes advertising content which has been cached.

Individual means a particular person.

TERMS OF AGREEMENT

This is a legal agreement between you, the users, and Opera Software ASA. By installing or using this Software, you agree to be bound by the terms of this agreement. If you do not agree to those terms, you may not use or install the Software.

You are entitled to use your copy of the Software on one computer. "Use" means loaded in temporary memory or permanent storage on the computer. Installation on a network server for distribution to other computers is not allowed, unless you have a separate license for each computer to which the Software is distributed. You are obligated to have a reasonable process to assure that the number of persons using the Software concurrently does not exceed the number of licenses.

The Software is protected by Norwegian and United States copyright laws and international treaties. You may make one copy of the Software solely for backup or archival purposes or transfer it to a single hard disk provided you keep the original disk solely for backup or archival purposes. You may not rent or lease the Software or copy any written materials accompanying the Software. You may transfer the Software and all accompanying materials to another individual on a permanent basis, if you retain no copies and the recipient agrees to the terms of this Agreement. Any transfer must include the most recent update and all prior versions.

All intellectual property rights such as but not limited to patents, trademarks, copyrights or trade secret rights related to the Software are the property of and remains vested in Opera Software ASA/its suppliers.

You shall not modify, translate, reverse engineer, decompile or disassemble the Software or any part thereof or otherwise attempt to derive source code or create derivative works therefrom.

You are not allowed to remove, alter or destroy any proprietary, trademark or copyright markings or notices placed upon or contained with the Software.

Registration Codes may be used, stored or copied only by the person or organization, which has licensed the Software, and solely for the purpose of using the Software within the terms and conditions of this Agreement. No person or organization is permitted to store or copy a Registration Code for any other purpose without written agreement from Opera Software ASA.

The copyright of all Registration Codes remains vested in Opera Software ASA which reserves the right to withhold or withdraw authorization of use of all Registration Codes issued to a person or organization if there is reasonable evidence to indicate that the person or organization is involved in a breach of the terms of this document.

YOU EXPRESSLY ACKNOWLEDGE AND AGREE THAT USE OF THE SOFTWARE IS AT YOUR OWN RISK AND THAT THE SOFTWARE IS PROVIDED "AS IS" WITHOUT ANY WARRANTIES OR CONDITIONS WHATSOEVER. OPERA SOFTWARE ASA OR ITS SUPPLIERS DOES NOT WARRANT THAT THE FUNCTIONS OF THE SOFTWARE WILL MEET YOUR REQUIREMENTS OR THAT THE OPERATION OF THE SOFTWARE WILL BE UNINTERRUPTED OR ERROR FREE. YOU ASSUME RESPONSIBILITY FOR SELECTING THE SOFTWARE TO ACHIEVE YOUR INTENDED RESULTS, AND FOR THE USE AND THE RESULTS OBTAINED FROM THE SOFTWARE.

YOU ACKNOWLEDGE THAT THE SOFTWARE IS NOT INTENDED FOR USE IN (I) ON-LINE CONTROL OF AIRCRAFT, AIR TRAFFIC, AIRCRAFT NAVIGATION OR AIRCRAFT COMMUNICATIONS; OR (II) IN THE DESIGN, CONSTRUCTION, OPERATION OR MAINTENANCE OF ANY NUCLEAR FACILITY.

OPERA SOFTWARE ASA AND ITS SUPPLIERS DISCLAIM ALL WARRANTIES, EXPRESS OR IMPLIED, INCLUDING BUT NOT LIMITED TO WARRANTIES RELATED TO: NON-INFRINGEMENT, LACK OF VIRUSES, ACCURACY OR COMPLETENESS OF RESPONSES OR RESULTS, IMPLIED WARRANTIES OF MERCHANTABILITY AND FITNESS FOR A PARTICULAR PURPOSE .

IN NO EVENT SHALL OPERA SOFTWARE ASA OR ITS SUPPLIERS BE LIABLE FOR ANY INDIRECT, INCIDENTAL, SPECIAL OR CONSEQUENTIAL DAMAGES OR FOR ANY DAMAGES WHATSOEVER (INCLUDING BUT NOT LIMITED TO DAMAGES FOR LOSS OF BUSINESS PROFITS, BUSINESS INTERRUPTION, LOSS OF BUSINESS INFORMATION, PERSONAL INJURY, LOSS OF PRIVACY OR OTHER PECUNIARY OR OTHER LOSS WHATSOEVER) ARISING OUT OF USE OR INABILITY TO USE THE SOFTWARE, EVEN IF ADVISED OF THE POSSIBILITY OF SUCH DAMAGES. OPERA SOFTWARE

ASA ALSO DISCLAIMS ALL LIABILITY FOR ACTS OR MATERIAL PRESENTED BY THE ADVER-TISER, AD-SERVING PARTNERS OR OTHERS (INCLUDING UNAUTHORIZED USERS, OR "CRACKERS").

REGARDLESS OF THE FORM OF ACTION, OPERA SOFTWARE ASA AND ITS SUPPLIERS AGGREGATE LIABILITY ARISING OUT OF OR RELATED TO THIS AGREEMENT SHALL NOT EXCEED THE TOTAL AMOUNT PAYABLE BY YOU UNDER THIS AGREEMENT. THE FOREGOING LIMITATIONS, EXCLUSIONS AND DISCLAIMERS SHALL APPLY TO THE MAXIMUM EXTENT ALLOWED BY APPLICABLE LAW.

The Software may be subject to export or import regulations, and the user agrees to comply strictly with all such laws and regulations. The user agrees not to export or re-export the Software or any part thereof or information pertaining thereto to any country for which a U.S. government agency requires an export license or other governmental approval without first obtaining such license or approval.

Notice to U.S. Government Users: The Software and any associated documentation are "Commercial Items," as that term is defined at 48 C.F.R. 2.101, consisting of "Commercial Computer Software" and "Commercial Computer Software Documentation," as such terms are used in 48 C.F.R. 12.212 or 48 C.F.R. 227.7202, as applicable. Consistent with 48 C.F.R. 12.212 or 48 C.F.R. 227.7202-1 through 227.7202-4, as applicable, the Commercial Computer Software and Commercial Computer Software Documentation are licensed to U.S. Government end users (a) only as Commercial Items and (b) with only those rights as are granted to all other end users pursuant to the terms and conditions herein.

Privacy statement: Opera Software ASA strives to protect the security and privacy of the users of its products, and will strictly protect the security of the users personal information, within the confines of the Opera domain. The Opera Software ASA privacy statement found at , is incorporated in this Agreement by reference.

Any variation to the terms of this Agreement shall only be valid if made in writing by Opera Software ASA.

Any and all disputes arising out of the rights and obligations in this Agreement shall be submitted to ordinary court proceedings. You accept the Oslo City Court as legal venue under this Agreement.This Agreement shall be governed by Norwegian law, and the stipulations set forth herein to be construed in accordance with same.

Postal enquiries:
Opera Software ASA
Postboks 2648 St. Hanshaugen
NO-0131 OSLO
NORWAY
Office Hours: 9:00am - 4:00pm (+1 GMT) Monday - Friday
Phone:+47 24 16 40 00
Fax:+47 24 16 40 01
Please visit our Web site before you send us e-mail. We provide many services to our users that will help us respond to you faster than if we receive e-mail.

Web site:
http://www.opera.com/
Contact us:
http://www.opera.com/contact/
MACROMEDIA® Software End User License Agreement (07/25/03)

END-USER LICENSE AGREEMENT FOR MICROSOFT® AGENT

IMPORTANT-READ CAREFULLY: This Microsoft End-User License Agreement ("EULA") is a legal agreement between you (either an individual or a single entity) and Microsoft Corporation ("Microsoft") for the Microsoft software product identified above, which includes computer software and may include associated media, printed materials, and "online" or electronic documentation (collectively, "SOFTWARE PRODUCT"). By installing, copying, or otherwise using the SOFTWARE PRODUCT, you agree to be bound by the terms of this EULA. If you do not agree to the terms of this EULA, you may not use the SOFTWARE PRODUCT.

SOFTWARE PRODUCT LICENSE

The SOFTWARE PRODUCT is protected by copyright laws and international copyright treaties, as well as other intellectual property laws and treaties. The SOFTWARE PRODUCT is licensed, not sold.

INTRODUCTION. The SOFTWARE PRODUCT is comprised of the following components: (i) the core cabinet file components which include Microsoft Agent Server, Microsoft Agent Control and Microsoft

Agent Provider; (ii) Microsoft Character Animation Data and Image Files; and (iii) Foreign Language .DLL files. The Foreign Language .DLL files provided by Microsoft for use with Microsoft Agent are subject to this EULA, which EULA will only be provided in English. English shall be deemed the language that controls the terms of this EULA.

This EULA describes your rights with respect to the SOFTWARE PRODUCT and its components.

1. GRANT OF LICENSE. This EULA grants you the following rights:

* Standard Use. You may install and use one (1) copy of the SOFTWARE PRODUCT on a single computer.

* Development Use. Microsoft grants you a non-exclusive, limited license, subject to the development use requirements below, to: (i) use the Character Animation Data and Image Files and Foreign Language .DLL files Microsoft has designated at the Microsoft Site (as defined below) for development use with Microsoft Agent, and (ii) create Web pages, scripts or programs that call the Microsoft Agent API to animate the character and display the static or animated images that are provided by Microsoft to enable the end-user selection of an animated image.

* Development Use Requirements.

Software Product. If you exercise the Development Use rights described above, you agree to: (a) only exercise the development rights described above for your Web site or application that uses the SOFTWARE PRODUCT; (b) only allow access to the SOFTWARE PRODUCT by your end-users by (i) providing instructions or a hyperlink URL so that your end-user customers can download the components from Microsoft's Web site located at http://msdn.microsoft.com/msagent/ (the "Microsoft Site") or (ii) including the SOFT-WARE PRODUCT's CLSID in an HTML Object tag on your Web site that will automatically download the SOFTWARE PRODUCT for your end-user customers from the Microsoft Site; (c) place one of the following notices on your Web site or application that includes or uses the SOFTWARE PRODUCT: (i) place the notice "Uses Microsoft Agent technology" on your Web site on the introductory page where the SOFT-WARE PRODUCT is used or (ii) place the notice "Includes Microsoft Agent technology" in your application's copyright information or packaging; (d) not use Microsoft's name, logo, or trademarks to market your Web site or application; (e) include a valid copyright notice on your Web site or application; and (e) indemnify, hold harmless, and defend Microsoft from and against any claims or lawsuits, including attorney's fees, that arise or result from the use or distribution of your Web site or application.

Microsoft Character Animation Data and Image Files. If you use any of the Character Animation Data and Image Files, you agree to: (a) only use the Character Animation Data and Image Files on your Web site or application that uses the SOFTWARE PRODUCT; (b) display the character's name with the following copyright notice "(c) 1996-1998 Microsoft Corporation. All rights reserved." with the Web site's or application's copyright information or adjacent to the character's image; (c) not use the Character Animation Data and Image Files to disparage Microsoft, its products or services or for promotional goods or for products which, in Microsoft's sole judgment, may diminish or otherwise damage Microsoft's goodwill in the SOFT-WARE PRODUCT including but not limited to uses which could be deemed under applicable law to be obscene or pornographic, uses which are excessively violent, unlawful, or which purpose is to encourage unlawful activities; (d) not use the Character Animation Data and Image files to imply Microsoft's sponsorship, endorsement or approval of your software application, service or content provided on your Internet site; (e) not alter the Character Animation Dataand Image Files in any way; and (f) not combine the Animated Character(s) or Animation data files with any other object, including, but not limited to, other logos, words, graphics, photos, slogans, numbers, design features or symbols.

2. DESCRIPTION OF OTHER RIGHTS AND LIMITATIONS.

* Support Services. Microsoft may provide you with support services related to the SOFTWARE PRODUCT ("Support Services"). Use of Support Services is governed by the Microsoft policies and programs described in the user manual, in "on line" documentation and/or other Microsoft-provided materials. Any supplemental software code provided to you as part of the Support Services shall be considered part of the SOFTWARE PRODUCT and subject to the terms and conditions of this EULA. With respect to technical information you provide to Microsoft as part of the Support Services, Microsoft may use such information for its business purposes, including for product support and development. Microsoft will not utilize such technical information in a form that personally identifies you.

* Limitations on Reverse Engineering, Decompilation, and Disassembly. You may not reverse engineer, decompile, or disassemble the SOFTWARE PRODUCT, except and only to the extent that such activity is expressly permitted by applicable law notwithstanding this limitation.

* Rental. You may not rent, lease or lend the SOFTWARE PRODUCT.

* Software Transfer. You may permanently transfer all of your rights under this EULA, provided you retain no copies, you transfer all of the SOFTWARE PRODUCT (including all component parts, the media and printed materials, any upgrades, this EULA, and, if applicable, the Certificate of Authenticity), and the recipient agrees to the terms of this EULA.

3. ALL RIGHTS NOT EXPRESSLY GRANTED HEREIN ARE RESERVED BY MICROSOFT.

4. TERMINATION. Without prejudice to any other rights, Microsoft may terminate this EULA if you fail to comply with the terms and conditions of this EULA. In such event, you must destroy all copies of the SOFTWARE PRODUCT and all of its component parts.

5. COPYRIGHT. All title and copyrights in and to the SOFTWARE PRODUCT (including but not limited to any images, photographs, animations, video, audio, music, text, and "applets" incorporated into the SOFTWARE PRODUCT), the accompanying printed materials, and any copies of the SOFTWARE PRODUCT are owned by Microsoft or its suppliers. The SOFTWARE PRODUCT is protected by copyright laws and international treaty provisions. Therefore, you must treat the SOFTWARE PRODUCT like any other copyrighted material. You may not copy the printed materials accompanying the SOFTWARE PRODUCT.

6. U.S. GOVERNMENT RESTRICTED RIGHTS. All SOFTWARE PRODUCT and documentation provided to the U.S. Government pursuant to solicitations issued on or after December 1, 1995 is provided with the commercial rights and restrictions described elsewhere herein. All SOFTWARE PRODUCT provided to the U.S. Government pursuant to solicitations issued prior to December 1, 1995 is provided with RESTRICTED RIGHTS as provided for in FAR, 48 CFR 52.227-14 (JUNE 1987) or FAR, 48 CFR 252.227-7013 (OCT 1988), as applicable.

7. EXPORT RESTRICTIONS. You acknowledge that the SOFTWARE PRODUCT licensed hereunder is subject to the export control laws and regulations of the U.S.A., and any amendments thereof. You confirm that with respect to the SOFTWARE PRODUCT, you will not export or re-export it, directly or indirectly, to any countries that are subject to U.S.A. export restrictions. You further acknowledge that the SOFTWARE PRODUCT may include technical data subject to export and re-export restrictions imposed by U.S.A. law.

MISCELLANEOUS

If you acquired this product in the United States, this EULA is governed by the laws of the State of Washington.

If you acquired this product in Canada, this EULA is governed by the laws of the Province of Ontario, Canada. Each of the parties hereto irrevocably attorns to the jurisdiction of the courts of the Province of Ontario and further agrees to commence any litigation which may arise hereunder in the courts located in the Judicial District of York, Province of Ontario.

If this product was acquired outside the United States, then local law may apply.

If you are interested in additional information on licensing or use of Microsoft Agent, please visit the Microsoft Agent Web site at http://www.microsoft.com/msagent. Should you have any questions concerning this EULA, or if you desire to contact Microsoft for any reason, please contact the Microsoft subsidiary serving your country, or write: Microsoft Sales Information Center/One Microsoft Way/Redmond, WA 98052-6399.

LIMITED WARRANTY

NO WARRANTIES. TO THE MAXIMUM EXTENT PERMITTED BY APPLICABLE LAW, MICROSOFT AND ITS SUPPLIERS DISCLAIM ALL WARRANTIES AND CONDITIONS, EITHER EXPRESS OR IMPLIED, INCLUDING, BUT NOT LIMITED TO, IMPLIED WARRANTIES OF MERCHANTABILITY, FITNESS FOR A PARTICULAR PURPOSE, TITLE AND NON-INFRINGEMENT, WITH REGARD TO THE SOFTWARE PRODUCT, AND THE PROVISION OF OR FAILURE TO PROVIDE SUPPORT SERVICES. THIS LIMITED WARRANTY GIVES YOU SPECIFIC LEGAL RIGHTS. YOU MAY HAVE OTHERS, WHICH VARY FROM STATE/JURISDICTION TO STATE/JURISDICTION.

LIMITATION OF LIABILITY. TO THE MAXIMUM EXTENT PERMITTED BY APPLICABLE LAW, IN NO EVENT SHALL MICROSOFT OR ITS SUPPLIERS BE LIABLE FOR ANY SPECIAL, INCIDENTAL, INDIRECT, OR CONSEQUENTIAL DAMAGES WHATSOEVER (INCLUDING, WITHOUT LIMITATION, DAMAGES FOR LOSS OF BUSINESS PROFITS, BUSINESS INTERRUPTION, LOSS OF BUSINESS INFORMATION, OR ANY OTHER PECUNIARY LOSS) ARISING OUT OF THE USE OF OR INABILITY TO USE THE SOFTWARE PRODUCT OR THE PROVISION OF OR FAILURE TO PROVIDE SUPPORT SERVICES, EVEN IF MICROSOFT HAS BEEN ADVISED OF THE

POSSIBILITY OF SUCH DAMAGES. IN ANY CASE, MICROSOFT'S ENTIRE LIABILITY UNDER ANY PROVISION OF THIS EULA SHALL BE LIMITED TO THE GREATER OF THE AMOUNT ACTU-ALLY PAID BY YOU FOR THE SOFTWARE PRODUCT OR US$5.00; PROVIDED HOWEVER, IF YOU HAVE ENTERED INTO A MICROSOFT SUPPORT SERVICES AGREEMENT, MICROSOFT'S ENTIRE LIABILITY REGARDING SUPPORT SERVICES SHALL BE GOVERNED BY THE TERMS OF THAT AGREEMENT. BECAUSE SOME STATES AND JURISDICTIONS DO NOT ALLOW THE EXCLUSION OR LIMITATION OF LIABILITY, THE ABOVE LIMITATION MAY NOT APPLY TO YOU.

Si vous avez acquis votre produit Microsoft au CANADA, la garantie limitée suivante vous concerne :
GARANTIE LIMITÉE

AUCUNE AUTRE GARANTIE - DANS LA MESURE PRÉVUE PAR LA LOI, MICROSOFT ET SES FOURNISSEURS EXCLUENT TOUTE AUTRE GARANTIE OU CONDITION, EXPRESSE OU IMPLICITE, Y COMPRIS MAIS NE SE LIMITANT PAS AUX GARANTIES OU CONDITIONS IMPLIC-ITES DU CARACTÈRE ADÉQUAT POUR LA COMMERCIALISATION OU UN USAGE PARTICU-LIER EN CE QUI CONCERNE LE LOGICIEL OU CONCERNANT LE TITRE , L'ABSENCE DE CONTREFAÇON DUDIT LOGICIEL, ET TOUTE DOCUMENTATION ÉCRITE QUI L'ACCOMPAGNE, AINSI QUE POUR TOUTE DISPOSITION CONCERNANT LE SUPORT TECHNIQUE OU LA FAÇON DONT CELUI-CI A ÉTÉ RENDU. CETTE GARANTIE LIMITÉE VOUS ACCORDE DES DROITS JURIDIQUES SPÉCIFIQUES.

PAS DE RESPONSABILITÉ POUR LES DOMMAGES INDIRECTS - MICROSOFT OU SES FOURNISSEURS NE SERONT PAS RESPONSABLES EN AUCUNE CIRCONSTANCE POUR TOUT DOMMAGE SPÉCIAL, INCIDENT, INDIRECT, OU CONSÉQUENT QUEL QU'IL SOIT (Y COMPRIS, SANS LIMITATION, LES DOMMAGES ENTRAINÉS PAR LA PERTE DE BÉNÉFICES, L'INTERRUP-TION DES ACTIVITÉS, LA PERTE D'INFORMATION OU TOUTE AUTRE PERTE PÉCUNIAIRE) DÉCOULANT DE L'UTILISATION OU DE L'IMPOSSIBILITÉ D'UTILISATION DE CE LOGICIEL AINSI QUE POUR TOUTE DISPOSITION CONCERNANT LE SUPORT TECHNIQUE OU LA FAÇON DONT CELUI-CI A ÉTÉ RENDU ET CE, MÊME SI MICROSOFT A ÉTÉ AVISÉE DE LA POSSIBILITÉ DE TELS DOMMAGES. LA RESPONSABILITÉ DE MICROSOFT EN VERTU DE TOUTE DISPOSI-TION DE

CETTE CONVENTION NE POURRA EN AUCUN TEMPS EXCÉDER LE PLUS ÉLEVÉ ENTRE i) LE MONTANT EFFECTIVEMENT PAYÉ PAR VOUS POUR LE LOGICIEL OU ii) US$5.00. ADVE-NANT QUE VOUS AYEZ CONTRACTÉ PAR ENTENTE DISTINCTE AVEC MICROSOFT POUR UN SUPPORT TECHNIQUE ÉTENDU, VOUS SEREZ LIÉ PAR LES TERMES D' UNE TELLE ENTENTE.

La présente Convention est régie par les lois de la province d'Ontario, Canada. Chacune des parties à la présente reconnaît irrévocablement la compétence des tribunaux de la province d'Ontario et consent à instituer tout litige qui pourrait découler de la présente auprès des tribunaux situés dans le district judiciaire de York, province d'Ontario.

Au cas où vous auriez des questions concernant cette licence ou que vous désiriez vous mettre en rap-port avec Microsoft pour quelque raison que ce soit, veuillez contacter la succursale Microsoft desservant votre pays, dont l'adresse est fournie dans ce produit, ou écrivez à : Microsoft Sales Information Center, One Microsoft Way, Redmond, Washington 98052-6399.

END-USER LICENSE AGREEMENT FOR MICROSOFT® .NET FRAMEWORK 1.1

IMPORTANT: READ CAREFULLY - These Microsoft Corporation ("Microsoft") operating system components, including any "online" or electronic documentation ("OS Components") are subject to the terms and conditions of the agreement under which you have licensed the applicable Microsoft operating system product described below (each an "End User License Agreement" or "EULA") and the terms and conditions of this Supplemental EULA. BY INSTALLING, COPYING OR OTHERWISE USING THE OS COMPO-NENTS, YOU AGREE TO BE BOUND BY THE TERMS AND CONDITIONS OF THE APPLICABLE OPERATING SYSTEM PRODUCT EULA AND THIS SUPPLEMENTAL EULA. IF YOU DO NOT AGREE TO THESE TERMS AND CONDITIONS, DO NOT INSTALL, COPY OR USE THE OS COM-PONENTS.

NOTE: IF YOU DO NOT HAVE A VALIDLY LICENSED COPY OF ANY VERSION OR EDITION OF MICROSOFT WINDOWS 95, WINDOWS 98, WINDOWS NT 4.0 WINDOWS 2000 OPERATING

SYSTEM OR ANY MICROSOFT OPERATING SYSTEM THAT IS A SUCCESSOR TO ANY OF THOSE OPERATING SYSTEMS (each an "OS Product"), YOU ARE NOT AUTHORIZED TO INSTALL, COPY OR OTHERWISE USE THE OS COMPONENTS AND YOU HAVE NO RIGHTS UNDER THIS SUPPLEMENTAL EULA.

Capitalized terms used in this Supplemental EULA and not otherwise defined herein shall have the meanings assigned to them in the applicable OS Product EULA.

General. Each of the OS Components available from this site is identified as being applicable to one or more of the OS Products. The applicable OS Components are provided to you by Microsoft to update, supplement, or replace existing functionality of the applicable OS Product. Microsoft grants you a license to use the applicable OS Components under the terms and conditions of the EULA for the applicable OS Product (which are hereby incorporated by reference except as set forth below), the terms and conditions set forth in this Supplemental EULA, and the terms and conditions of any additional end user license agreement that may accompany the individual OS Components (each an "Individual EULA"), provided that you comply with all such terms and conditions. To the extent that there is a conflict among any of these terms and conditions applicable to the OS Components, the following hierarchy shall apply: 1) the terms and conditions of the Individual EULA; 2) the terms and conditions in this Supplemental EULA; and 3) the terms and conditions of the applicable OS Product EULA.

Additional Rights and Limitations.

*If you have multiple validly licensed copies of any OS Product, you may reproduce, install and use one copy of the applicable OS Components as part of the applicable OS Product on all of your computers running validly licensed copies of the applicable OS Product, provided that you use such additional copies of such OS Components in accordance with the terms and conditions above. For each validly licensed copy of the applicable OS Product, you also may reproduce one additional copy of the applicable OS Components solely for archival purposes or reinstallation of the OS Components on the same computer as the OS Components were previously installed. Microsoft retains all right, title and interest in and to the OS Components. All rights not expressly granted are reserved by Microsoft.

*If you are installing the OS Components on behalf of an organization other than your own, prior to installing any of the OS Components, you must confirm that the end-user (whether an individual or a single entity) has received, read and accepted these terms and conditions.

*The OS Components may contain technology that enables applications to be shared between two or more computers, even if an application is installed on only one of the computers. You may use this technology with all Microsoft application products for multi-party conferences. For non-Microsoft applications, you should consult the accompanying license agreement or contact the licensor to determine whether application sharing is permitted by the licensor.

*You may not disclose the results of any benchmark test of the .NET Framework component of the OS Components to any third party without Microsoft's prior written approval.

IF THE APPLICABLE OS PRODUCT WAS LICENSED TO YOU BY MICROSOFT OR ANY OF ITS WHOLLY OWNED SUBSIDIARIES, THE LIMITED WARRANTY (IF ANY) INCLUDED IN THE APPLICABLE OS PRODUCT EULA APPLIES TO THE APPLICABLE OS COMPONENTS PROVIDED THE APPLICABLE OS COMPONENTS HAVE BEEN LICENSED BY YOU WITHIN THE TERM OF THE LIMITED WARRANTY IN THE APPLICABLE OS PRODUCT EULA. HOWEVER, THIS SUPPLEMENTAL EULA DOES NOT EXTEND THE TIME PERIOD FOR WHICH THE LIMITED WARRANTY IS PROVIDED.

IF THE APPLICABLE OS PRODUCT WAS LICENSED TO YOU BY AN ENTITY OTHER THAN MICROSOFT OR ANY OF ITS WHOLLY OWNED SUBSIDIARIES, MICROSOFT DISCLAIMS ALL WARRANTIES WITH RESPECT TO THE APPLICABLE OS COMPONENTS AS FOLLOWS:

DISCLAIMER OF WARRANTIES. TO THE MAXIMUM EXTENT PERMITTED BY APPLICABLE LAW, MICROSOFT AND ITS SUPPLIERS PROVIDE TO YOU THE OS COMPONENTS, AND ANY (IF ANY) SUPPORT SERVICES RELATED TO THE OS COMPONENTS ("SUPPORT SERVICES") AS IS AND WITH ALL FAULTS; AND MICROSOFT AND ITS SUPPLIERS HEREBY DISCLAIM WITH RESPECT TO THE OS COMPONENTS AND SUPPORT SERVICES ALL WARRANTIES AND CONDITIONS, WHETHER EXPRESS, IMPLIED OR STATUTORY, INCLUDING, BUT NOT LIMITED TO, ANY (IF ANY) WARRANTIES, DUTIES OR CONDITIONS OF OR RELATED TO: MERCHANTABILITY, FITNESS FOR A PARTICULAR PURPOSE, LACK OF VIRUSES, ACCURACY OR COMPLETENESS OF RESPONSES, RESULTS, WORKMANLIKE EFFORT AND LACK OF NEGLIGENCE. ALSO THERE IS NO WARRANTY, DUTY OR CONDITION OF TITLE, QUIET ENJOYMENT, QUIET

POSSESSION, CORRESPONDENCE TO DESCRIPTION OR NON-INFRINGEMENT. THE ENTIRE RISK ARISING OUT OF USE OR PERFORMANCE OF THE OS COMPONENTS AND ANY SUPPORT SERVICES REMAINS WITH YOU.

EXCLUSION OF INCIDENTAL, CONSEQUENTIAL AND CERTAIN OTHER DAMAGES. TO THE MAXIMUM EXTENT PERMITTED BY APPLICABLE LAW, IN NO EVENT SHALL MICROSOFT OR ITS SUPPLIERS BE LIABLE FOR ANY SPECIAL, INCIDENTAL, INDIRECT, PUNITIVE OR CONSEQUENTIAL DAMAGES WHATSOEVER (INCLUDING, BUT NOT LIMITED TO, DAMAGES FOR: LOSS OF PROFITS, LOSS OF CONFIDENTIAL OR OTHER INFORMATION, BUSINESS INTERRUPTION, PERSONAL INJURY, LOSS OF PRIVACY, FAILURE TO MEET ANY DUTY (INCLUDING OF GOOD FAITH OR OF REASONABLE CARE), NEGLIGENCE, AND ANY OTHER PECUNIARY OR OTHER LOSS WHATSOEVER) ARISING OUT OF OR IN ANY WAY RELATED TO THE USE OF OR INABILITY TO USE THE OS COMPONENTS OR THE SUPPORT SERVICES, OR THE PROVISION OF OR FAILURE TO PROVIDE SUPPORT SERVICES, OR OTHERWISE UNDER OR IN CONNECTION WITH ANY PROVISION OF THIS SUPPLEMENTAL EULA, EVEN IF MICROSOFT OR ANY SUPPLIER HAS BEEN ADVISED OF THE POSSIBILITY OF SUCH DAMAGES.

LIMITATION OF LIABILITY AND REMEDIES. NOTWITHSTANDING ANY DAMAGES THAT YOU MIGHT INCUR FOR ANY REASON WHATSOEVER (INCLUDING, WITHOUT LIMITATION, ALL DAMAGES REFERENCED ABOVE AND ALL DIRECT OR GENERAL DAMAGES), THE ENTIRE LIABILITY OF MICROSOFT AND ANY OF ITS SUPPLIERS UNDER ANY PROVISION OF THIS SUPPLEMENTAL EULA AND YOUR EXCLUSIVE REMEDY FOR ALL OF THE FOREGOING SHALL BE LIMITED TO ACTUAL DAMAGES INCURRED BY YOU BASED ON REASONABLE RELIANCE UP TO THE GREATER OF THE AMOUNT ACTUALLY PAID BY YOU FOR THE OS COMPONENTS OR U.S.$5.00. THE FOREGOING LIMITATIONS, EXCLUSIONS AND DISCLAIMERS SHALL APPLY TO THE MAXIMUM EXTENT PERMITTED BY APPLICABLE LAW, EVEN IF ANY REMEDY FAILS ITS ESSENTIAL PURPOSE.

END-USER LICENSE AGREEMENT FOR MICROSOFT® .NET FRAMEWORK 1.1

IMPORTANT-READ CAREFULLY: This End-User License Agreement ("EULA") is a legal agreement between you (either an individual or a single entity) and Microsoft Corporation ("Microsoft") for the Microsoft software that accompanies this EULA, which includes computer software and may include associated media, printed materials, "online" or electronic documentation, and Internet-based services ("Software"). An amendment or addendum to this EULA may accompany the Software. YOU AGREE TO BE BOUND BY THE TERMS OF THIS EULA BY INSTALLING, COPYING, OR OTHERWISE USING THE SOFTWARE. IF YOU DO NOT AGREE, DO NOT INSTALL, COPY, OR USE THE SOFTWARE; YOU MAY RETURN IT TO YOUR PLACE OF PURCHASE (IF APPLICABLE) FOR A FULL REFUND.

MICROSOFT Software LICENSE

1.GRANTS OF LICENSE. Microsoft grants you the rights described in this EULA provided that you comply with all terms and conditions of this EULA.

1.1General License Grant. Microsoft grants to you as an individual, a personal, nonexclusive license to use the Software, and to make and use copies of the Software for the purposes of designing, developing, testing, and demonstrating your software product(s), provided that you are the only individual using the Software.

If you are an entity, Microsoft grants to you a personal, nonexclusive license to use the Software, and to make and use copies of the Software, provided that for each individual using the Software within your organization, you have acquired a separate and valid license for each such individual.

1.2Documentation. You may make and use an unlimited number of copies of any documentation, provided that such copies shall be used only for personal purposes and are not to be republished or distributed (either in hard copy or electronic form) beyond your premises.

1.3Storage/Network Use. You may also store or install a copy of the Software on a storage device, such as a network server, used only to install or run the Software on computers used by licensed end users in accordance with Section 1.1. A single license for the Software may not be shared or used concurrently by multiple end users.

1.4Effect of EULA. The Software may contain development tools, utilities and other Microsoft software programs (each such tool or software program, a "Component"); such Components may include a separate end-user license agreement (each, a "Component EULA"). Except as provided in Section 4 ("Prerelease Code"), in the event of inconsistencies between this EULA and any Component EULA, the terms of this EULA shall control. The Software may also contain third-party software programs. Any such software is provided for your use as a convenience and your use is subject to the terms and conditions of any license agreement contained in that software.

2.ADDITIONAL LICENSE RIGHTS -- REDISTRIBUTABLE CODE. In addition to the rights granted in Section 1, certain portions of the Software, as described in this Section 2, are provided to you with additional license rights. These additional license rights are conditioned upon your compliance with the distribution requirements and license limitations described in Section 3.

2.1Sample Code. Microsoft grants you a limited, nonexclusive, royalty-free license to: (a) use and modify the source code version of those portions of the Software identified as "Samples" in REDIST.TXT or elsewhere in the Software ("Sample Code") for the sole purposes of designing, developing, and testing your software product(s), and (b) reproduce and distribute the Sample Code, along with any modifications thereof, in object and/or source code form. For applicable redistribution requirements for Sample Code, see Section 3.1 below.

2.2Redistributable Code-General. Microsoft grants you a limited, nonexclusive, royalty-free license to reproduce and distribute the object code form of any portion of the Software listed in REDIST.TXT ("Redistributable Code"). For general redistribution requirements for Redistributable Code, see Section 3.1 below.

2.3Simple Managed C Compiler ("SMC"). Microsoft grants you a limited, nonexclusive, royalty-free license to: (a) use and modify of the software code and documentation associated with SMC in both source and object code form, and (b) reproduce and distribute SMC, along with any modifications thereof, in object code form. For redistribution requirements for SMC, see Sections 3.1 and 3.2 below.

3.DISTRIBUTION REQUIREMENTS AND OTHER LICENSE RIGHTS AND LIMITATIONS. If you choose to exercise your rights under Section 2, any redistribution by you is subject to your compliance with Section 3.1; some of the Redistributable Code has additional limited use rights described in Section 3.2.

3.1General Distribution Requirements.

(a)If you choose to redistribute Sample Code, Redistributable Code, or SMC (collectively, the "Redistributables") as described in Section 2, you agree: (i) except as otherwise noted in Section 2.1 (Sample Code), to distribute the Redistributables only in object code form and in conjunction with and as a part of a software application product developed by you that adds significant and primary functionality to the Redistributables ("Licensee Software"); (ii) that the Redistributables only operate in conjunction with Microsoft Windows platforms; (iii) that if the Licensee Software is distributed beyond Licenseeís premises or externally from Licenseeís organization, to distribute the Licensee Software containing the Redistributables pursuant to an end user license agreement (which may be "break-the-seal", "click-wrap" or signed), with terms no less protective than those contained in this EULA; (iv) not to use Microsoftís name, logo, or trademarks to market the Licensee Software; (v) to display your own valid copyright notice which shall be sufficient to protect Microsoftís copyright in the Software; (vi) not to remove or obscure any copyright, trademark or patent notices that appear on the Software as delivered to you; (vii) to indemnify, hold harmless, and defend Microsoft from and against any claims or lawsuits, including attorneyís fees, that arise or result from the use or distribution of the Licensee Software; (viii) to otherwise comply with the terms of this EULA; and (ix) agree that Microsoft reserves all rights not expressly granted.

You also agree not to permit further distribution of the Redistributables by your end users except you may permit further redistribution of the Redistributables by your distributors to your end-user customers if your distributors only distribute the Redistributables in conjunction with, and as part of, the Licensee Software, you comply with all other terms of this EULA, and your distributors comply with all restrictions of this EULA that are applicable to you.

(b)If you use the Redistributables, then in addition to your compliance with the applicable distribution requirements described for the Redistributables, the following also applies. Your license rights to the Redistributables are conditioned upon your not (i) creating derivative works of the Redistributables in any manner that would cause the Redistributables in whole or in part to become subject to any of the terms of an Excluded License; or (ii) distributing the Redistributables (or derivative works thereof) in any manner that would cause the Redistributables to become subject to any of the terms of an Excluded License. An "Excluded License" is any license that requires as a condition of use, modification and/or distribution of software subject to the Excluded License, that such software or other software combined and/or distributed with such software be

(x) disclosed or distributed in source code form; (y) licensed for the purpose of making derivative works; or (z) redistributable at no charge.

3.2Additional Distribution Requirements for Certain Redistributable Code. If you choose to redistribute the files discussed in this Section, then in addition to the terms of Section 3.1, you must ALSO comply with the following:

(a)SMC. ll versions of SMC, including any modifications made by you, that you distribute in Licensee Software must faithfully generate the Microsoft Intermediate Language.

(b)Microsoft SQL Server Desktop Engine ("MSDE"). If you redistribute MSDE you agree to comply with the following additional requirements: (a) you also agree to redistribute such file in object code only in conjunction with and as a part of a Licensee Software developed by you with the Software; (b) Licensee Software shall not substantially duplicate the capabilities of Microsoft Access or, in the reasonable opinion of Microsoft, compete with same; and (c) unless Licensee Software requires your customers to license Microsoft Access in order to operate, you shall not reproduce or use MSDE for commercial distribution in conjunction with a general purpose word processing, spreadsheet or database management software product, or an integrated work or product suite whose components include a general purpose word processing, spreadsheet, or database management software product except for the exclusive use of importing data to the various formats supported by Microsoft Access. A product that includes limited word processing, spreadsheet or database components along with other components which provide significant and primary value, such as an accounting product with limited spreadsheet capability, is not considered to be a "general purpose" product.

3.3Separation of Components. The Software is licensed as a single product. Its component parts may not be separated for use by more than one user.

3.4Benchmark Testing. You may not disclose the results of any benchmark test of the .NET Framework component of the Software to any third party without Microsoftís prior written approval.

4.PRERELEASE CODE. Portions of the Software may be identified as prerelease code ("Prerelease Code"). Such Prerelease Code is not at the level of performance and compatibility of the final, generally available product offering. The Prerelease Code may not operate correctly and may be substantially modified prior to first commercial shipment. Microsoft is not obligated to make this or any later version of the Prerelease Code commercially available. The grant of license to use Prerelease Code expires upon availability of a commercial release of the Prerelease Code from Microsoft. NOTE: In the event that Prerelease Code contains a separate end-user license agreement, the terms and conditions of such end-user license agreement shall govern your use of the corresponding Prerelease Code.

5.RESERVATION OF RIGHTS AND OWNERSHIP. Microsoft reserves all rights not expressly granted to you in this EULA. The Software is protected by copyright and other intellectual property laws and treaties. Microsoft or its suppliers own the title, copyright, and other intellectual property rights in the Software. The Software is licensed, not sold.

6.LIMITATIONS ON REVERSE ENGINEERING, DECOMPILATION, AND DISASSEMBLY. You may not reverse engineer, decompile, or disassemble the Software, except and only to the extent that such activity is expressly permitted by applicable law notwithstanding this limitation.

7.NO RENTAL/COMMERCIAL HOSTING. You may not rent, lease, lend or provide commercial hosting services with the Software.

8.CONSENT TO USE OF DATA. You agree that Microsoft and its affiliates may collect and use technical information gathered as part of the product support services provided to you, if any, related to the Software. Microsoft may use this information solely to improve our products or to provide customized services or technologies to you and will not disclose this information in a form that personally identifies you.

9.LINKS TO THIRD PARTY SITES. You may link to third party sites through the use of the Software. The third party sites are not under the control of Microsoft, and Microsoft is not responsible for the contents of any third party sites, any links contained in third party sites, or any changes or updates to third party sites. Microsoft is not responsible for webcasting or any other form of transmission received from any third party sites. Microsoft is providing these links to third party sites to you only as a convenience, and the inclusion of any link does not imply an endorsement by Microsoft of the third party site.

10.ADDITIONAL SOFTWARE/SERVICES. This EULA applies to updates, supplements, add-on components, or Internet-based services components, of the Software that Microsoft may provide to you or make available to you after the date you obtain your initial copy of the Software, unless we provide other terms along with the update, supplement, add-on component, or Internet-based services component. Microsoft reserves the right to discontinue any Internet-based services provided to you or made available to you through the use of the Software.

11.NOT FOR RESALE SOFTWARE. Software identified as "Not For Resale" or "NFR," may not be sold or otherwise transferred for value, or used for any purpose other than demonstration, test or evaluation.

12.EXPORT RESTRICTIONS. You acknowledge that the Software is subject to U.S. export jurisdiction. You agree to comply with all applicable international and national laws that apply to the Software, including the U.S. Export Administration Regulations, as well as end-user, end-use, and destination restrictions issued by U.S. and other governments. For additional information see <http://www.microsoft.com/exporting/>

13.SOFTWARE TRANSFER. The initial user of the Software may make a one-time permanent transfer of this EULA and Software to another end user, provided the initial user retains no copies of the Software. This transfer must include all of the Software (including all component parts, the media and printed materials, any upgrades this EULA, and, if applicable, the Certificate of Authenticity). The transfer may not be an indirect transfer, such as a consignment. Prior to the transfer, the end user receiving the Software must agree to all the EULA terms.

14.TERMINATION. Without prejudice to any other rights, Microsoft may terminate this EULA if you fail to comply with the terms and conditions of this EULA. In such event, you must destroy all copies of the Software and all of its component parts.

15.DISCLAIMER OF WARRANTIES. TO THE MAXIMUM EXTENT PERMITTED BY APPLICABLE LAW, MICROSOFT AND ITS SUPPLIERS PROVIDE THE SOFTWARE AND SUPPORT SERVICES (IF ANY) AS IS AND WITH ALL FAULTS, AND HEREBY DISCLAIM ALL OTHER WARRANTIES AND CONDITIONS, WHETHER EXPRESS, IMPLIED OR STATUTORY, INCLUDING, BUT NOT LIMITED TO, ANY (IF ANY) IMPLIED WARRANTIES, DUTIES OR CONDITIONS OF MERCHANTABILITY, OF FITNESS FOR A PARTICULAR PURPOSE, OF RELIABILITY OR AVAILABILITY, OF ACCURACY OR COMPLETENESS OF RESPONSES, OF RESULTS, OF WORKMANLIKE EFFORT, OF LACK OF VIRUSES, AND OF LACK OF NEGLIGENCE, ALL WITH REGARD TO THE SOFTWARE, AND THE PROVISION OF OR FAILURE TO PROVIDE SUPPORT OR OTHER SERVICES, INFORMATION, SOFTWARE, AND RELATED CONTENT THROUGH THE SOFTWARE OR OTHERWISE ARISING OUT OF THE USE OF THE SOFTWARE. ALSO, THERE IS NO WARRANTY OR CONDITION OF TITLE, QUIET ENJOYMENT, QUIET POSSESSION, CORRESPONDENCE TO DESCRIPTION OR NON-INFRINGEMENT WITH REGARD TO THE SOFTWARE.

16.EXCLUSION OF INCIDENTAL, CONSEQUENTIAL AND CERTAIN OTHER DAMAGES. To the maximum extent permitted by applicable law, in no event shall Microsoft or its suppliers be liable for any special, incidental, punitive, indirect, or consequential damages whatsoever (including, but not limited to, damages for loss of profits or confidential or other information, for business interruption, for personal injury, for loss of privacy, for failure to meet any duty including of good faith or of reasonable care, for negligence, and for any other pecuniary or other loss whatsoever) arising out of or in any way related to the use of or inability to use the SOFTWARE, the provision of or failure to provide Support OR OTHER Services, information, software, and related CONTENT through the software or otherwise arising out of the use of the software, or otherwise under or in connection with any provision of this EULA, even in the event of the fault, tort (including negligence), misrepresentation, strict liability, breach of contract or breach of warranty of Microsoft or any supplier, and even if Microsoft or any supplier has been advised of the possibility of such damages.

17.LIMITATION OF LIABILITY AND REMEDIES. NOTWITHSTANDING ANY DAMAGES THAT YOU MIGHT INCUR FOR ANY REASON WHATSOEVER (INCLUDING, WITHOUT LIMITATION, ALL DAMAGES REFERENCED HEREIN AND ALL DIRECT OR GENERAL DAMAGES IN CONTRACT OR ANYTHING ELSE), THE ENTIRE LIABILITY OF MICROSOFT AND ANY OF ITS SUPPLIERS UNDER ANY PROVISION OF THIS EULA AND YOUR EXCLUSIVE REMEDY HEREUNDER SHALL BE LIMITED TO THE GREATER OF THE ACTUAL DAMAGES YOU INCUR IN REASONABLE RELIANCE ON THE SOFTWARE UP TO THE AMOUNT ACTUALLY PAID BY YOU FOR THE SOFTWARE OR US$5.00. THE FOREGOING LIMITATIONS, EXCLUSIONS AND DISCLAIMERS SHALL APPLY TO THE MAXIMUM EXTENT PERMITTED BY APPLICABLE LAW, EVEN IF ANY REMEDY FAILS ITS ESSENTIAL PURPOSE.

END-USER LICENSE AGREEMENT FOR MySQL

MySQL software is licensed under the GPL license. The formal terms of the GPL license can be found below.

Version 2, June 1991

Copyright © 1989, 1991 Free Software Foundation, Inc.

59 Temple Place - Suite 330, Boston, MA 02111-1307, USA

Everyone is permitted to copy and distribute verbatim copies of this license document, but changing it is not allowed.

12.4 Preamble

The licenses for most software are designed to take away your freedom to share and change it. By contrast, the GNU General Public License is intended to guarantee your freedom to share and change free software--to make sure the software is free for all its users. This General Public License applies to most of the Free Software Foundation's software and to any other program whose authors commit to using it. (Some other Free Software Foundation software is covered by the GNU Library General Public License instead.) You can apply it to your programs, too.

When we speak of free software, we are referring to freedom, not price. Our General Public Licenses are designed to make sure that you have the freedom to distribute copies of free software (and charge for this service if you wish), that you receive source code or can get it if you want it, that you can change the software or use pieces of it in new free programs; and that you know you can do these things.

To protect your rights, we need to make restrictions that forbid anyone to deny you these rights or to ask you to surrender the rights. These restrictions translate to certain responsibilities for you if you distribute copies of the software, or if you modify it.

For example, if you distribute copies of such a program, whether gratis or for a fee, you must give the recipients all the rights that you have. You must make sure that they, too, receive or can get the source code. And you must show them these terms so they know their rights.

We protect your rights with two steps: (1) copyright the software, and (2) offer you this license which gives you legal permission to copy, distribute and/or modify the software.

Also, for each author's protection and ours, we want to make certain that everyone understands that there is no warranty for this free software. If the software is modified by someone else and passed on, we want its recipients to know that what they have is not the original, so that any problems introduced by others will not reflect on the original authors' reputations.

Finally, any free program is threatened constantly by software patents. We wish to avoid the danger that redistributors of a free program will individually obtain patent licenses, in effect making the program proprietary. To prevent this, we have made it clear that any patent must be licensed for everyone's free use or not licensed at all.

The precise terms and conditions for copying, distribution and modification follow.

12.5 TERMS AND CONDITIONS FOR COPYING, DISTRIBUTION AND MODIFICATION

1.This License applies to any program or other work which contains a notice placed by the copyright holder saying it may be distributed under the terms of this General Public License. The ``Program'', below, refers to any such program or work, and a ``work based on the Program'' means either the Program or any derivative work under copyright law: that is to say, a work containing the Program or a portion of it, either verbatim or with modifications and/or translated into another language. (Hereinafter, translation is included without limitation in the term ``modification''.) Each licensee is addressed as ``you''. Activities other than copying, distribution and modification are not covered by this License; they are outside its scope. The act of running the Program is not restricted, and the output from the Program is covered only if its contents constitute a work based on the Program (independent of having been made by running the Program). Whether that is true depends on what the Program does.

2.You may copy and distribute verbatim copies of the Program's source code as you receive it, in any medium, provided that you conspicuously and appropriately publish on each copy an appropriate copyright notice and disclaimer of warranty; keep intact all the notices that refer to this License and to the absence of any warranty; and give any other recipients of the Program a copy of this License along with the Program. You may charge a fee for the physical act of transferring a copy, and you may at your option offer warranty protection in exchange for a fee.

3.You may modify your copy or copies of the Program or any portion of it, thus forming a work based on the Program, and copy and distribute such modifications or work under the terms of Section 1 above, provided that you also meet all of these conditions:

1.You must cause the modified files to carry prominent notices stating that you changed the files and the date of any change.

2. You must cause any work that you distribute or publish, that in whole or in part contains or is derived from the Program or any part thereof, to be licensed as a whole at no charge to all third parties under the terms of this License.

3. If the modified program normally reads commands interactively when run, you must cause it, when started running for such interactive use in the most ordinary way, to print or display an announcement including an appropriate copyright notice and a notice that there is no warranty (or else, saying that you provide a warranty) and that users may redistribute the program under these conditions, and telling the user how to view a copy of this License. (Exception: if the Program itself is interactive but does not normally print such an announcement, your work based on the Program is not required to print an announcement.)

These requirements apply to the modified work as a whole. If identifiable sections of that work are not derived from the Program, and can be reasonably considered independent and separate works in themselves, then this License, and its terms, do not apply to those sections when you distribute them as separate works. But when you distribute the same sections as part of a whole which is a work based on the Program, the distribution of the whole must be on the terms of this License, whose permissions for other licensees extend to the entire whole, and thus to each and every part regardless of who wrote it. Thus, it is not the intent of this section to claim rights or contest your rights to work written entirely by you; rather, the intent is to exercise the right to control the distribution of derivative or collective works based on the Program. In addition, mere aggregation of another work not based on the Program with the Program (or with a work based on the Program) on a volume of a storage or distribution medium does not bring the other work under the scope of this License.

4. You may copy and distribute the Program (or a work based on it, under Section 2) in object code or executable form under the terms of Sections 1 and 2 above provided that you also do one of the following:

1. Accompany it with the complete corresponding machine-readable source code, which must be distributed under the terms of Sections 1 and 2 above on a medium customarily used for software interchange; or,

2. Accompany it with a written offer, valid for at least three years, to give any third-party, for a charge no more than your cost of physically performing source distribution, a complete machine-readable copy of the corresponding source code, to be distributed under the terms of Sections 1 and 2 above on a medium customarily used for software interchange; or,

3. Accompany it with the information you received as to the offer to distribute corresponding source code. (This alternative is allowed only for noncommercial distribution and only if you received the program in object code or executable form with such an offer, in accord with Subsection b above.)

The source code for a work means the preferred form of the work for making modifications to it. For an executable work, complete source code means all the source code for all modules it contains, plus any associated interface definition files, plus the scripts used to control compilation and installation of the executable. However, as a special exception, the source code distributed need not include anything that is normally distributed (in either source or binary form) with the major components (compiler, kernel, and so on) of the operating system on which the executable runs, unless that component itself accompanies the executable. If distribution of executable or object code is made by offering access to copy from a designated place, then offering equivalent access to copy the source code from the same place counts as distribution of the source code, even though third parties are not compelled to copy the source along with the object code.

5. You may not copy, modify, sublicense, or distribute the Program except as expressly provided under this License. Any attempt otherwise to copy, modify, sublicense or distribute the Program is void, and will automatically terminate your rights under this License. However, parties who have received copies, or rights, from you under this License will not have their licenses terminated so long as such parties remain in full compliance.

6. You are not required to accept this License, since you have not signed it. However, nothing else grants you permission to modify or distribute the Program or its derivative works. These actions are prohibited by law if you do not accept this License. Therefore, by modifying or distributing the Program (or any work based on the Program), you indicate your acceptance of this License to do so, and all its terms and conditions for copying, distributing or modifying the Program or works based on it.

7. Each time you redistribute the Program (or any work based on the Program), the recipient automatically receives a license from the original licensor to copy, distribute or modify the Program subject to these terms and conditions. You may not impose any further restrictions on the recipients' exercise of the rights granted herein. You are not responsible for enforcing compliance by third parties to this License.

8.If, as a consequence of a court judgment or allegation of patent infringement or for any other reason (not limited to patent issues), conditions are imposed on you (whether by court order, agreement or otherwise) that contradict the conditions of this License, they do not excuse you from the conditions of this License. If you cannot distribute so as to satisfy simultaneously your obligations under this License and any other pertinent obligations, then as a consequence you may not distribute the Program at all. For example, if a patent license would not permit royalty-free redistribution of the Program by all those who receive copies directly or indirectly through you, then the only way you could satisfy both it and this License would be to refrain entirely from distribution of the Program. If any portion of this section is held invalid or unenforceable under any particular circumstance, the balance of the section is intended to apply and the section as a whole is intended to apply in other circumstances. It is not the purpose of this section to induce you to infringe any patents or other property right claims or to contest validity of any such claims; this section has the sole purpose of protecting the integrity of the free software distribution system, which is implemented by public license practices. Many people have made generous contributions to the wide range of software distributed through that system in reliance on consistent application of that system; it is up to the author/donor to decide if he or she is willing to distribute software through any other system and a licensee cannot impose that choice. This section is intended to make thoroughly clear what is believed to be a consequence of the rest of this License.

9.If the distribution and/or use of the Program is restricted in certain countries either by patents or by copyrighted interfaces, the original copyright holder who places the Program under this License may add an explicit geographical distribution limitation excluding those countries, so that distribution is permitted only in or among countries not thus excluded. In such case, this License incorporates the limitation as if written in the body of this License.

10.The Free Software Foundation may publish revised and/or new versions of the General Public License from time to time. Such new versions will be similar in spirit to the present version, but may differ in detail to address new problems or concerns. Each version is given a distinguishing version number. If the Program specifies a version number of this License which applies to it and ``any later version'', you have the option of following the terms and conditions either of that version or of any later version published by the Free Software Foundation. If the Program does not specify a version number of this License, you may choose any version ever published by the Free Software Foundation.

11.If you wish to incorporate parts of the Program into other free programs whose distribution conditions are different, write to the author to ask for permission. For software which is copyrighted by the Free Software Foundation, write to the Free Software Foundation; we sometimes make exceptions for this. Our decision will be guided by the two goals of preserving the free status of all derivatives of our free software and of promoting the sharing and reuse of software generally.

12.6 NO WARRANTY

12.BECAUSE THE PROGRAM IS LICENSED FREE OF CHARGE, THERE IS NO WARRANTY FOR THE PROGRAM, TO THE EXTENT PERMITTED BY APPLICABLE LAW. EXCEPT WHEN OTHERWISE STATED IN WRITING THE COPYRIGHT HOLDERS AND/OR OTHER PARTIES PROVIDE THE PROGRAM ``AS IS'' WITHOUT WARRANTY OF ANY KIND, EITHER EXPRESSED OR IMPLIED, INCLUDING, BUT NOT LIMITED TO, THE IMPLIED WARRANTIES OF MERCHANTABILITY AND FITNESS FOR A PARTICULAR PURPOSE. THE ENTIRE RISK AS TO THE QUALITY AND PERFORMANCE OF THE PROGRAM IS WITH YOU. SHOULD THE PROGRAM PROVE DEFECTIVE, YOU ASSUME THE COST OF ALL NECESSARY SERVICING, REPAIR OR CORRECTION.

13.IN NO EVENT UNLESS REQUIRED BY APPLICABLE LAW OR AGREED TO IN WRITING WILL ANY COPYRIGHT HOLDER, OR ANY OTHER PARTY WHO MAY MODIFY AND/OR REDISTRIBUTE THE PROGRAM AS PERMITTED ABOVE, BE LIABLE TO YOU FOR DAMAGES, INCLUDING ANY GENERAL, SPECIAL, INCIDENTAL OR CONSEQUENTIAL DAMAGES ARISING OUT OF THE USE OR INABILITY TO USE THE PROGRAM (INCLUDING BUT NOT LIMITED TO LOSS OF DATA OR DATA BEING RENDERED INACCURATE OR LOSSES SUSTAINED BY YOU OR THIRD PARTIES OR A FAILURE OF THE PROGRAM TO OPERATE WITH ANY OTHER PROGRAMS), EVEN IF SUCH HOLDER OR OTHER PARTY HAS BEEN ADVISED OF THE POSSIBILITY OF SUCH DAMAGES.

12.7 END OF TERMS AND CONDITIONS

12.8 How to Apply These Terms to Your New Programs

If you develop a new program, and you want it to be of the greatest possible use to the public, the best way to achieve this is to make it free software which everyone can redistribute and change under these terms.

To do so, attach the following notices to the program. It is safest to attach them to the start of each source file to most effectively convey the exclusion of warranty; and each file should have at least the ``copyright'' line and a pointer to where the full notice is found.

one line to give the program's name and a brief idea of what it does.

Copyright (C) yyyy name of author

This program is free software; you can redistribute it and/or modify

it under the terms of the GNU General Public License as published by

the Free Software Foundation; either version 2 of the License, or

(at your option) any later version.

This program is distributed in the hope that it will be useful,

but WITHOUT ANY WARRANTY; without even the implied warranty of

MERCHANTABILITY or FITNESS FOR A PARTICULAR PURPOSE. See the

GNU General Public License for more details.

You should have received a copy of the GNU General Public License along with this program; if not, write to the Free Software Foundation, Inc., 59 Temple Place - Suite 330, Boston, MA 02111-1307, USA.

Also add information on how to contact you by electronic and paper mail.

If the program is interactive, make it output a short notice like this when it starts in an interactive mode:

Gnomovision version 69, Copyright (C) 19yy name of author

Gnomovision comes with ABSOLUTELY NO WARRANTY; for details type `show w'.

This is free software, and you are welcome to redistribute it under certain conditions; type `show c' for details.

The hypothetical commands `show w' and `show c' should show the appropriate parts of the General Public License. Of course, the commands you use may be called something other than `show w' and `show c'; they could even be mouse-clicks or menu items--whatever suits your program.

You should also get your employer (if you work as a programmer) or your school, if any, to sign a ``copyright disclaimer'' for the program, if necessary. Here is a sample; alter the names:

Yoyodyne, Inc., hereby disclaims all copyright interest in the program

`Gnomovision' (which makes passes at compilers) written by James Hacker.

signature of Ty Coon, 1 April 1989

Ty Coon, President of Vice

This General Public License does not permit incorporating your program into proprietary programs. If your program is a subroutine library, you may consider it more useful to permit linking proprietary applications with the library. If this is what you want to do, use the GNU Library General Public License instead of this License.

END-USER LICENSE AGREEMENT FOR MySQL

Copyright (c) 1999 - 2003 The PHP Group. All rights reserved. Redistribution and use in source and binary forms, with or without modification, is permitted provided that the following conditions are met:

1. Redistributions of source code must retain the above copyright notice, this list of conditions and the following disclaimer.

2. Redistributions in binary form must reproduce the above copyright notice, this list of conditions and the following disclaimer in the documentation and/or other materials provided with the distribution.

3. The name "PHP" must not be used to endorse or promote products derived from this software without prior written permission. For written permission, please contact group@php.net.

4. Products derived from this software may not be called "PHP", nor may "PHP" appear in their name, without prior written permission from group@php.net. You may indicate that your software works in conjunction with PHP by saying "Foo for PHP" instead of calling it "PHP Foo" or "phpfoo"

5. The PHP Group may publish revised and/or new versions of the license from time to time. Each version will be given a distinguishing version number. Once covered code has been published under a particular version of the license, you may always continue to use it under the terms of that version. You may also choose to use such covered code under the terms of any subsequent version of the license published by the PHP Group. No one other than the PHP Group has the right to modify the terms applicable to covered code created under this License.

6. Redistributions of any form whatsoever must retain the following acknowledgment: "This product includes PHP, freely available from http://www.php.net/".

THIS SOFTWARE IS PROVIDED BY THE PHP DEVELOPMENT TEAM ``AS IS" AND ANY EXPRESSED OR IMPLIED WARRANTIES, INCLUDING, BUT NOT LIMITED TO, THE IMPLIED WARRANTIES OF MERCHANTABILITY AND FITNESS FOR A PARTICULAR PURPOSE ARE DISCLAIMED. IN NO EVENT SHALL THE PHP DEVELOPMENT TEAM OR ITS CONTRIBUTORS BE LIABLE FOR ANY DIRECT, INDIRECT, INCIDENTAL, SPECIAL, EXEMPLARY, OR CONSEQUENTIAL DAMAGES (INCLUDING, BUT NOT LIMITED TO, PROCUREMENT OF SUBSTITUTE GOODS OR SERVICES; LOSS OF USE, DATA, OR PROFITS; OR BUSINESS INTERRUPTION) HOWEVER CAUSED AND ON ANY THEORY OF LIABILITY, WHETHER IN CONTRACT, STRICT LIABILITY, OR TORT (INCLUDING NEGLIGENCE OR OTHERWISE) ARISING IN ANY WAY OUT OF THE USE OF THIS SOFTWARE, EVEN IF ADVISED OF THE POSSIBILITY OF SUCH DAMAGE.

This software consists of voluntary contributions made by many individuals on behalf of the PHP Group.

The PHP Group can be contacted via Email at group@php.net.

For more information on the PHP Group and the PHP project, please see http://www.php.net.

This product includes the Zend Engine, freely available at http://www.zend.com.

The DEITEL® Suite of Products...

Getting Started with Microsoft® Visual C++™ 6 with an Introduction to MFC

BOOK / CD-ROM

©2000, 163 pp., paper
(0-13-016147-0)

Visual C++ .NET® How To Program

BOOK / CD-ROM

©2004, 1400 pp., paper
(0-13-437377-4)

Written by the authors of the world's best-selling introductory/intermediate C and C++ textbooks, this comprehensive book thoroughly examines Visual C++® .NET. *Visual C++® .NET How to Program* begins with a strong foundation in the introductory and intermediate programming principles students will need in industry, including fundamental topics such as arrays, functions and control structures. Readers learn the concepts of object-oriented programming, including how to create reusable software components with classes and assemblies. The text then explores such essential topics as networking, databases, XML and multimedia. Graphical user interfaces are also extensively covered, giving students the tools to build compelling and fully interactive programs using the "drag-and-drop" techniques provided by the latest version of Visual Studio .NET, Visual Studio .NET 2003.

Advanced Java™ 2 Platform How to Program

BOOK / CD-ROM

©2002, 1811 pp., paper
(0-13-089560-1)

Expanding on the world's best-selling Java textbook—*Java™ How to Program*—*Advanced Java™ 2 Platform How To Program* presents advanced Java topics for developing sophisticated, user-friendly GUIs; significant, scalable enterprise applications; wireless applications and distributed systems. Primarily based on Java 2 Enterprise Edition (J2EE), this textbook integrates technologies such as XML, JavaBeans, security, JDBC™, JavaServer Pages (JSP™), servlets, Remote Method Invocation (RMI), Enterprise JavaBeans™ (EJB) and design patterns into a production-quality system that allows developers to benefit from the leverage and platform independence Java 2 Enterprise Edition provides. The book also features the development of a complete, end-to-end e-business solution using advanced Java technologies. Additional topics include Swing, Java 2D and 3D, XML, design patterns,

CORBA, Jini™, JavaSpaces™, Jiro™, Java Management Extensions (JMX) and Peer-to-Peer networking with an introduction to JXTA. This textbook also introduces the Java 2 Micro Edition (J2ME™) for building applications for handheld and wireless devices using MIDP and MIDlets. Wireless technologies covered include WAP, WML and i-mode.

C# How to Program

BOOK / CD-ROM

©2002, 1568 pp., paper
(0-13-062221-4)

An exciting addition to the *How to Program Series*, *C# How to Program* provides a comprehensive introduction to Microsoft's new object-oriented language. C# builds on the skills already mastered by countless C++ and Java programmers, enabling them to create powerful Web applications and components—ranging from XML-based Web services on Microsoft's .NET platform to middle-tier business objects and system-level applications. *C# How to Program* begins with a strong foundation in the introductory- and intermediate-programming principles students will need in industry. It then explores such essential topics as object-oriented programming and exception handling. Graphical user interfaces are extensively covered, giving readers the tools to build compelling and fully interactive programs. Internet technologies such as XML, ADO .NET and Web services are covered as well as topics including regular expressions, multithreading, networking, databases, files and data structures.

Visual Basic® .NET How to Program Second Edition

BOOK / CD-ROM

©2002, 1400 pp., paper
(0-13-029363-6)

Learn Visual Basic .NET programming from the ground up! The introduction of Microsoft's .NET Framework marks the beginning of major revisions to all of Microsoft's programming languages. This book provides a comprehensive introduction to the next version of Visual Basic—Visual Basic .NET—featuring extensive updates and increased functionality. *Visual Basic .NET How to Program, Second Edition* covers introductory programming techniques as well as more advanced topics, featuring enhanced treatment of developing Web-based applications. Other topics discussed include an extensive treatment of XML and wireless applications, databases, SQL and ADO .NET, Web forms, Web services and ASP .NET.

Internet & World Wide Web How to Program, Third Edition

BOOK / CD-ROM

©2004, 1250 pp., paper
(0-13-145091-3)

This book introduces students with little or no programming experience to the exciting world of Web-based applications. A comprehensive book that teaches the fundamentals needed to program on the Internet, this text provides in-depth coverage of introductory programming principles, various markup languages (XHTML, Dynamic HTML and XML), several scripting languages (JavaScript, JScript .NET, ColdFusion, Flash ActionScript, Perl, PHP, VBScript and Python), Web servers (IIS and Apache) and relational databases (MySQL)-all the skills and tools needed to create dynamic Web-based applications. The text contains a comprehensive introduction to ASP .NET and the Microsoft .NET Framework. A case study illustrating how to build an online message board using ASP .NET and XML is also included. New in this edition are chapters on Macromedia ColdFusion, Macromedia Dreamweaver and a much enhanced treatment of Flash, including a case study on building a video game in Flash. Hundreds of *LIVE-CODE* examples of real applications throughout the book and on the accompanying CD allow readers to run the applications and see and hear the outputs. After mastering the material in this book, students will be well prepared to build real-world, industrial-strength, Web-based applications.

Wireless Internet & Mobile Business How to Program

©2002, 1292 pp., paper
(0-13-062226-5)

This book offers a thorough treatment of both the management and technical aspects of this growing area, including coverage of current practices and future trends. The first half explores the business issues surrounding wireless technology and mobile business, including an overview of existing and developing communication technologies and the application of business principles to wireless devices. It also discusses location-based services and location-identifying technologies, a topic that is revisited throughout the book. Wireless payment, security, legal and social issues, international communications and more are also discussed. The book then turns to programming for the wireless Internet, exploring topics such as WAP (including 2.0), WML, WMLScript, XML, XHTML™, wireless Java programming (J2ME™), Web Clipping and more. Other topics covered include career resources, wireless marketing, accessibility, Palm™, PocketPC, Windows CE, i-mode, Bluetooth, MIDP, MIDlets, ASP, Microsoft .NET Mobile Framework, BREW™, multimedia, Flash™ and VBScript.

Python How to Program

BOOK / CD-ROM

©2002, 1376 pp., paper
(0-13-092361-3)

This exciting new textbook provides a comprehensive introduction to Python—a powerful object-oriented programming language with clear syntax and the ability to bring together various technologies quickly and easily. This book covers introductory-programming techniques and more advanced topics such as graphical user interfaces, databases, wireless Internet programming, networking, security, process management, multithreading, XHTML, CSS, PSP and multimedia. Readers will learn principles that are applicable to both systems development and Web programming. The book features the consistent and applied pedagogy that the *How to Program Series* is known for, including the Deitels' signature *LIVE-CODE* Approach, with thousands of lines of code in hundreds of working programs; hundreds of valuable programming tips identified with icons throughout the text; an extensive set of exercises, projects and case studies; two-color four-way syntax coloring and much more.

e-Business & e-Commerce for Managers

©2001, 794 pp., cloth
(0-13-032364-0)

This comprehensive overview of building and managing e-businesses explores topics such as the decision to bring a business online, choosing a business model, accepting payments, marketing strategies and security, as well as many other important issues (such as career resources). The book features Web resources and online demonstrations that supplement the text and direct readers to additional materials. The book also includes an appendix that develops a complete Web-based shopping-cart application using HTML, JavaScript, VBScript, Active Server Pages, ADO, SQL, HTTP, XML and XSL. Plus, company-specific sections provide "real-world" examples of the concepts presented in the book.

XML How to Program

BOOK / CD-ROM

©2001, 934 pp., paper
(0-13-028417-3)

This book is a comprehensive guide to programming in XML. It teaches how to use XML to create customized tags and includes chapters that address markup languages for science and technology, multimedia, commerce and many other fields. Concise introductions to Java, JavaServer Pages, VBScript, Active Server Pages and Perl/CGI provide readers with the essentials of these programming languages and server-side development technologies to enable them to work effectively with XML. The book also covers cutting-edge topics such as XSL, DOM™ and SAX, plus a real-world e-commerce case study and a complete chapter on Web accessibility that addresses Voice XML. It includes tips such as Common Programming Errors, Software Engineering Observations, Portability Tips and Debugging Hints. Other topics covered include XHTML, CSS, DTD, schema, parsers, XPath, XLink, namespaces, XBase, XInclude, XPointer, XSLT, XSL Formatting Objects, JavaServer Pages, XForms, topic maps, X3D, MathML, OpenMath, CML, BML, CDF, RDF, SVG, Cocoon, WML, XBRL and BizTalk™ and SOAP™ Web resources.

Perl How to Program

BOOK / CD-ROM

©2001, 1057 pp., paper (0-13-028418-1)

This comprehensive guide to Perl programming emphasizes the use of the Common Gateway Interface (CGI) with Perl to create powerful, dynamic multi-tier Web-based client/server applications. The book begins with a clear and careful introduction to programming concepts at a level suitable for beginners, and proceeds through advanced topics such as references and complex data structures. Key Perl topics such as regular expressions and string manipulation are covered in detail. The authors address important and topical issues such as object-oriented programming, the Perl database interface (DBI), graphics and security. Also included is a treatment of XML, a bonus chapter introducing the Python programming language, supplemental material on career resources and a complete chapter on Web accessibility. The text includes tips such as Common Programming Errors, Software Engineering Observations, Portability Tips and Debugging Hints.

e-Business & e-Commerce How to Program

BOOK / CD-ROM

©2001, 1254 pp., paper (0-13-028419-X)

This innovative book explores programming technologies for developing Web-based e-business and e-commerce solutions, and covers e-business and e-commerce models and business issues. Readers learn a full range of options, from "build-your-own" to turnkey solutions. The book examines scores of the top e-businesses (examples include Amazon, eBay, Priceline, Travelocity, etc.), explaining the technical details of building successful e-business and e-commerce sites and their underlying business premises. Learn how to implement the dominant e-commerce models—shopping carts, auctions, name-your-own-price, comparison shopping and bots/ intelligent agents—by using markup languages (HTML, Dynamic HTML and XML), scripting languages (JavaScript, VBScript and Perl), server-side technologies (Active Server Pages and Perl/CGI) and database (SQL and ADO), security and online payment technologies. Updates are regularly posted to www.deitel.com and the book includes a CD-ROM with software tools, source code and live links.

Visual Basic® 6 How to Program

BOOK / CD-ROM

©1999, 1015 pp., paper (0-13-456955-5)

Visual Basic® 6 How to Program was developed in cooperation with Microsoft to cover important topics such as graphical user interfaces (GUIs), multimedia, object-oriented programming, networking, database programming, VBScript®, COM/DCOM and ActiveX®.

Introducing the _new_ SIMPLY SERIES!

The Deitels are pleased to announce the new _Simply Series_. These books take an engaging new approach to teaching programming languages from the ground up. The pedagogy of this series combines the DEITEL® signature _LIVE-CODE Approach_ with an _APPLICATION-DRIVEN Tutorial Approach_ to teaching programming with outstanding pedagogical features that help students learn. We have merged the notion of a lab manual with that of a conventional textbook, creating a book in which readers build and execute complete applications from start to finish, while learning the basics of programming from the ground up!

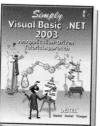

Simply Visual Basic®.NET An APPLICATION-DRIVEN Tutorial Approach

Visual Studio .NET 2002 Version:
©2003, 830 pp., paper
(0-13-140553-5)

Visual Studio .NET 2003 Version:
©2004, 960 pp., paper
(0-13-142640-0)

Simply Visual Basic® .NET An APPLICATION-DRIVEN Tutorial Approach guides readers through building real-world applications that incorporate Visual Basic .NET programming fundamentals. Learn GUI design, controls, methods, functions, data types, control statements, procedures, arrays, object-oriented programming, strings and characters, sequential files and more in this comprehensive introduction to Visual Basic .NET. We also include higher-end topics such as database programming, multimedia and graphics and Web applications development. If you're using Visual Studio® .NET 2002, choose _Simply Visual Basic .NET_; or, if you're moving to Visual Studio .NET 2003, you can use _Simply Visual Basic .NET 2003_, which includes updated screen captures and line numbers consistent with Visual Studio .NET 2003.

Simply Java™ Programming An APPLICATION-DRIVEN Tutorial Approach

©2004, 950 pp., paper
(0-13-142648-6)

Simply Java™ Programming An APPLICATION-DRIVEN Tutorial Approach guides readers through building real-world applications that incorporate Java programming fundamentals. Learn GUI design, components, methods, event-handling, types, control statements, arrays, object-oriented programming, exception-handling, strings and characters, sequential files and more in this comprehensive introduction to Java. We also include higher-end topics such as database programming, multimedia, graphics and Web applications development.

Simply C# An APPLICATION-DRIVEN Tutorial Approach

©2004, 850 pp., paper
(0-13-142641-9)

Simply C# An APPLICATION-DRIVEN Tutorial Approach guides readers through building real-world applications that incorporate C# programming fundamentals. Learn GUI design, controls, methods, functions, data types, control statements, procedures, arrays, object-oriented programming, strings and characters, sequential files and more in this comprehensive introduction to C#. We also include higher-end topics such as database programming, multimedia and graphics and Web applications development.

Simply C++ An APPLICATION-DRIVEN Tutorial Approach

©2005, 800 pp., paper
(0-13-142660-5)

For information about _Simply C++ An APPLICATION-DRIVEN Tutorial Approach_ and other _Simply Series_ books under development, visit **www.deitel.com**. You may also sign up for the DEITEL® Buzz Online at **www.deitel.com/newsletter/subscribe.html** for monthly updates on the entire DEITEL® publishing program.

BOOK/MULTIMEDIA PACKAGES

Complete Training Courses

Each complete package includes the corresponding *How to Program Series* textbook and interactive multimedia Windows-based CD-ROM Cyber Classroom. *Complete Training Courses* are perfect for anyone interested in Web and e-commerce programming. They are affordable resources for college students and professionals learning programming for the first time or reinforcing their knowledge.

Intuitive Browser-Based Interface

You'll love the *Complete Training Courses'* new browser-based interface, designed to be easy and accessible to anyone who's ever used a Web browser. Every *Complete Training Course* features the full text, illustrations and program listings of its corresponding *How to Program* book—all in full color—with full-text searching and hyperlinking.

Further Enhancements to the Deitels' Signature LIVE-CODE Approach

Every code sample from the main text can be found in the interactive, multimedia, CD-ROM-based *Cyber Classrooms* included in the *Complete Training Courses*. Syntax coloring of code is included for the *How to Program* books that are published in full color. Even the recent two-color and one-color books use effective syntax shading. The *Cyber Classroom* products are always in full color.

Audio Annotations

Hours of detailed, expert audio descriptions of thousands of lines of code help reinforce concepts.

Easily Executable Code

With one click of the mouse, you can execute the code or save it to your hard drive to manipulate using the programming environment of your choice. With selected *Complete Training Courses*, you can also load all of the code into a development environment such as Microsoft® Visual Studio®.NET, enabling you to modify and execute the programs with ease.

Abundant Self-Assessment Material

Practice exams test your understanding of key concepts with hundreds of test questions and answers in addition to those found in the main text. The textbook includes hundreds of programming exercises, while the *Cyber Classrooms* include answers to about half the exercises.

www.phptr.com/phptrinteractive

BOOK/MULTIMEDIA PACKAGES

The Complete C++ Training
Course, Fourth Edition

(0-13-100252-X)

The Complete e-Business &
e-Commerce Programming
Training Course

(0-13-089549-0)

The Complete Java™
Training Course, Fifth Edition

(0-13-101766-7)

The Complete Perl
Training Course

(0-13-089552-0)

The Complete Visual Basic® .NET
Training Course, Second Edition

(0-13-042530-3)

The Complete Visual Basic® 6
Training Course

(0-13-082929-3)

The Complete C# Training Course

(0-13-064584-2)

The Complete Python
Training Course

(0-13-067374-9)

The Complete XML
Programming Training Course

(0-13-089557-1)

The Complete Wireless
Internet & Mobile Business
Programming Training Course

(0-13-062335-0)

All of these ISBNs are retail ISBNs. College and university instructors should contact your local Prentice Hall representative or write to cs@prenhall.com *for the corresponding student edition ISBNs.*

If you would like to purchase the Cyber Classrooms separately...

Prentice Hall offers Multimedia Cyber Classroom CD-ROMs to accompany the *How to Program Series* texts for the topics listed at right. If you have already purchased one of these books and would like to purchase a stand-alone copy of the corresponding *Multimedia Cyber Classroom,* you can make your purchase at the following Web site:

www.informit.com/cyberclassrooms

C++ Multimedia Cyber Classroom, 4/E, ISBN # 0-13-100253-8

C# Multimedia Cyber Classroom, ask for product number 0-13-064587-7

e-Business & e-Commerce Cyber Classroom, ISBN # 0-13-089540-7

Java Multimedia Cyber Classroom, 5/E, ISBN # 0-13-101769-1

Perl Multimedia Cyber Classroom, ISBN # 0-13-089553-9

Python Multimedia Cyber Classroom, ISBN # 0-13-067375-7

Visual Basic 6 Multimedia Cyber Classroom, ISBN # 0-13-083116-6

Visual Basic .NET Multimedia Cyber Classroom, 2/E, ISBN # 0-13-065193-1

XML Multimedia Cyber Classroom, ISBN # 0-13-089555-5

Wireless Internet & Mobile Business Programming Multimedia Cyber Classroom, ISBN # 0-13-062337-7

Our official e-mail newsletter, the *DEITEL® BUZZ ONLINE*, is a free publication designed to keep you updated on our publishing program, instructor-led corporate training courses, hottest industry trends and topics and more.

Issues of our newsletter include:

- **Technology Spotlights** that feature articles and information on the hottest industry topics drawn directly from our publications or written during the research and development process.

- **Anecdotes** and/or **challenges** that allow our readers to interact with our newsletter and with us. We always welcome and appreciate your comments, answers and feedback. We will summarize all responses we receive in future issues.

- **Highlights** and **Announcements** on current and upcoming products that are of interest to professionals, students and instructors.

- Information on our **instructor-led corporate training courses delivered at organizations worldwide**. Complete course listings and special course highlights provide readers with additional details on DEITEL® training offerings.

- Our newsletter is available in both **full-color HTML** or **plain-text** formats depending on your viewing preferences and e-mail client capabilities.

- Learn about the history of Deitel & Associates, our brands, the bugs and more in the **Lore and Legends** section of the newsletter.

- **Hyperlinked Table of Contents** allows readers to navigate quickly through the newsletter by jumping directly to specific topics of interest.

To sign up for the *DEITEL® BUZZ ONLINE* newsletter, visit `www.deitel.com/newsletter/subscribe.html`.

Turn the page to find out more about Deitel & Associates!

> The Deitels are the authors of best-selling Java™, C++, C#, C, Visual Basic® and Internet and World Wide Web books and multimedia packages.

Corporate Training Delivered Worldwide

Deitel & Associates, Inc. provides intensive, lecture-and-laboratory courses to organizations worldwide. The programming courses use our signature *LIVE-CODE Approach*, presenting complete working programs.

Deitel & Associates, Inc. has trained over one million students and professionals worldwide through corporate training courses, public seminars, university teaching, *How to Program Series* textbooks, *DEITEL® Developer Series* books, *Simply Series* textbooks, *Cyber Classroom Series* multimedia packages, *Complete Training Course Series* textbook and multimedia packages, broadcast-satellite courses and Web-based training.

Educational Consulting

Deitel & Associates, Inc. offers complete educational consulting services for corporate training programs and professional schools including:

- Curriculum design and development
- Preparation of Instructor Guides
- Customized courses and course materials
- Design and implementation of professional training certificate programs
- Instructor certification
- Train-the-trainers programs
- Delivery of software-related corporate training programs

> **Visit our Web site for more information on our corporate training curriculum and to purchase our training products.**
>
> www.deitel.com/training

Would you like to review upcoming publications?

If you are a professor or senior industry professional interested in being a reviewer of our forthcoming publications, please contact us by email at **deitel@deitel.com**. Insert "Content Reviewer" in the subject heading.

Are you interested in a career in computer education, publishing and training?

We offer a limited number of full-time positions available for college graduates in computer science, information systems, information technology, management information systems, English and communications, marketing, multimedia technology and other areas. Please check our Web site for the latest job postings or contact us by email at **deitel@deitel.com**. Insert "Full-time Job" in the subject heading.

Are you a Boston-area college student looking for an internship?

We have a limited number of competitive summer positions and 20-hr./week school-year opportunities for computer science, English and business majors. Students work at our worldwide headquarters west of Boston. We also offer full-time internships for students taking a semester off from school. This is an excellent opportunity for students looking to gain industry experience and earn money to pay for school. Please contact us by email at **deitel@deitel.com**. Insert "Internship" in the subject heading.

Would you like to explore contract training opportunities with us?

Deitel & Associates, Inc. is looking for contract instructors to teach software-related topics at our clients' sites in the United States and worldwide. Applicants should be experienced professional trainers or college professors. For more information, please visit **www.deitel.com** and send your resume to Abbey Deitel at **abbey.deitel@deitel.com**.

Are you a training company in need of quality course materials?

Corporate training companies worldwide use our *Complete Training Course Series* book and multimedia packages, our *Web-Based Training Series* courses and our *DEITEL® Developer Series* books in their classes. We have extensive ancillary instructor materials for each of our products. For more details, please visit **www.deitel.com** or contact us by email at **deitel@deitel.com**.

License Agreement and Limited Warranty

Using the CD-ROM

The contents of this CD are designed to be accessed through the interface provided in the file **AUTORUN.EXE**. If a startup screen does not pop up automatically when you insert the CD into your computer, double click on the icon for **AUTORUN.EXE** to launch the program or refer to the file **readme.txt** on the CD.

Contents of the CD-ROM

- Adobe® Reader® 6.0
- Macromedia® Flash™ MX 2004 (30-Day Trial)
- Macromedia® Dreamweaver® MX 2004 (30-Day Trial)
- Apache HTTP Server 2.0.47
- MySQL™ 4.0
- Microsoft® .NET Framework (And SDK) 1.1
- PHP 4.3.3
- Macromedia® ColdFusion MX 6.1 (30-Day Trial)
- Microsoft® Agent 2.0

Software and Hardware System Requirements

- 600 MHz Pentium III processor
- Microsoft Windows® XP or Windows 2000 Professional
- 256 MB of RAM
- CD-ROM drive
- Internet connection and Web browser